# Tax Formula for Corporate Taxpayers

| | |
|---|---|
| **Income** (*from whatever source*) | $xxx,xxx |
| Less: Exclusions from gross income | − xx,xxx |
| **Gross Income** | $xxx,xxx |
| Less: Deductions | − xx,xxx |
| **Taxable Income** | $xxx,xxx |
| Applicable tax rates | × xx% |
| **Gross Tax** | $ xx,xxx |
| Less: Tax credits and prepayments | − x,xxx |
| **Tax Due** (*or refund*) | $ xx,xxx |

# Study Guide Available

For more practice problems that help you to expand your understanding of corporations, partnerships, estates, and trusts, we recommend the *Study Guide* that accompanies *West Federal Taxation: Corporations, Partnerships, Estates, and Trusts*. The *Study Guide* uses a workbook approach and includes chapter outlines and summaries highlighting major points in the text, self-evaluation tests, problems, and drills using furnished tax forms.

If you cannot locate copies of the *Study Guide* in your bookstore, ask your bookstore manager to order a copy for you.

# 3 simple ways Checkpoint® helps you make sense of all those taxes.

1 — Intuitive Web-based design makes it fast and simple to find what you need.

2 — A comprehensive collection of primary tax law, cases and rulings along with analytical insight you simply can't find anywhere else.

3 — Because more tax pros use Checkpoint® than any other resource today!

## Checkpoint®

**Look no further**

For technical support call: 800.423.0563

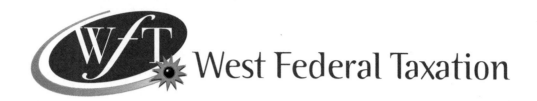

West Federal Taxation

# Corporations, Partnerships, Estates & Trusts

## 2004 EDITION

### General Editors

**William H. Hoffman, Jr.**
*J.D., Ph.D., C.P.A.*

**William A. Raabe**
*Ph.D., C.P.A.*

**James E. Smith**
*Ph.D., C.P.A.*

**David M. Maloney**
*Ph.D., C.P.A.*

### Contributing Authors

**James H. Boyd**
*Ph.D., C.P.A.*
*Arizona State University*

**D. Larry Crumbley**
*Ph.D., C.P.A.*
*Louisiana State University*

**Jon S. Davis**
*Ph.D., C.P.A.*
*University of Wisconsin-Madison*

**Steven C. Dilley**
*J.D., Ph.D., C.P.A.*
*Michigan State University*

**William H. Hoffman, Jr.**
*J.D., Ph.D., C.P.A.*
*University of Houston*

**David M. Maloney**
*Ph.D., C.P.A.*
*University of Virginia*

**Gary A. McGill**
*Ph.D., C.P.A.*
*University of Florida*

**Mark B. Persellin**
*Ph.D., C.P.A., C.F.P.*
*St. Mary's University*

**William A. Raabe**
*Ph.D., C.P.A.*
*Ohio State University*

**Boyd C. Randall**
*J.D., Ph.D.*
*Brigham Young University*

**Debra L. Sanders**
*Ph.D., C.P.A.*
*Washington State University*

**W. Eugene Seago**
*J.D., Ph.D., C.P.A.*
*Virginia Polytechnic
Institute and State University*

**James E. Smith**
*Ph.D., C.P.A.*
*College of William and Mary*

**Eugene Willis**
*Ph.D., C.P.A.*
*University of Illinois at Urbana*

**THOMSON**

**SOUTH-WESTERN**

Australia · Canada · Mexico · Singapore · Spain · United Kingdom · United States

THOMSON

SOUTH-WESTERN

*West Federal Taxation: Corporations, Partnerships, Estates & Trusts, 2004e*

William H. Hoffman, Jr., William A. Raabe, James E. Smith, David M. Maloney

**Vice President/Editorial Director:**
Jack W. Calhoun

**Vice President/Editor-in-Chief:**
George Werthman

**Acquisitions Editor:**
Jennifer L. Codner

**Senior Developmental Editor:**
Craig Avery

**Marketing Manager:**
Heather MacMaster

**Production Editors:**
Marci Combs, Lora Arduser

**Media Technology Editor:**
Jim Rice

**Media Developmental Editor:**
Christine A. Wittmer

**Media Production Editor:**
Amy Wilson

**Manufacturing Coordinator:**
Doug Wilke

**Compositor:**
Texterity, Inc.

**Production House:**
Litten Editing and Production, Inc.

**Printer:**
Quebecor World
Versailles, KY

**Senior Design Project Manager:**
Michelle Kunkler

**Cover and Internal Designer:**
Ann Small/a small design studio

**Cover Image:**
© William J. Hebert/Getty Images, Inc.

For more information contact
South-Western
5191 Natorp Boulevard
Mason, Ohio 45040.
Or you can visit our Internet site at:
http://www.swlearning.com

For permission to use material from
this text or product, contact us by:
Tel (800) 730-2214
Fax (800) 730-2215
http://www.thomsonrights.com

# West Federal Taxation

# Preface

## 2004 EDITION

YOU have in your hands a volume from the most successful taxation series in publishing. Our fresh new design, new logo, and this colorful new preface filled with examples of our many features for 2004, all symbolize our commitment to bringing you the best, most up-to-date, and most comprehensive Federal taxation series available. For over twenty-six years, the market-leading *West Federal Taxation (WFT)* Series has helped more than one million users master the ever-changing nature of Federal taxation. The 2004 Editions are no exception. Each continues to offer unparalleled comprehensive coverage—while presenting information in a manner users find accessible yet authoritative.

◆

Often emulated but never duplicated, *WFT* began as a single textbook on Corporations, Partnerships, Estates and Trusts, followed a year later by Individual taxation. Today, this unrivaled package includes five major textbooks and a selection of more than 50 outstanding ancillaries. With the 2004 Editions, *WFT* continues to build on the quality of these materials—adding timely innovations that enhance instruction and make learning even more engaging. As always, *WFT* strives to show its users the importance and relevance of taxation to individual taxpayers as well as all areas of business.

# The 2004 Edition of
# *WFT: Corporations, Partnerships, Estates & Trusts*

## The Leadership You Trust

*WFT* is a flexible series that seeks to match and exceed instructors' course needs. *WFT: Corporations, Partnerships, Estates & Trusts* has served as an ideal basis for a second course in Federal taxation — perfect for both undergraduate and graduate accounting, business, and law students. With simple modification in coverage, this proven text can also be used in a survey course for Federal taxation. In addition, because of its numerous straightforward examples and real-world problems, many users find it to be a valuable tool for self-study as well.

With its comprehensive and accessible coverage, no other text is as effective at helping students master the ever-changing individual tax code. Because of its adherence to the recommendations of the Accounting Education Change Commission (AECC) and the American Institute of Certified Public Accountants (AICPA)—and because its authors and editors stay on top of trends in both tax law and tax education—the 2004 Edition is thoroughly up-to-date, current in its thinking, and pedagogically advanced.

It is essential to provide users with the latest information reflecting statutory, judicial, and administrative changes in Federal tax law. The dynamic nature of tax law requires that materials be continually updated. The *WFT* Web site, **http://wft.swlearning.com**, offers instant access to all relevant updates. In addition, *WFT* sends hard copies of major tax law changes and updates to all adopters — ensuring that important changes in Federal tax law will not be overlooked.

**Format and Content.** The text is divided into parts to facilitate compartmentalization of the subjects covered. Part 2, which includes Chapters 2 through 9, largely deals with C corporations. Part 3, designated Flow-Through Entities, contains the material on partnerships (Chapters 10 and 11) and S corporations (Chapter 12). Further groupings are made to help the user work through the text.

The material on C corporations is arranged to flow logically so as to parallel the life cycle of the entity. Advanced corporate structuring is addressed in Chapter 7 on the tax effects of mergers and acquisitions, and Chapter 8 on the taxation of conglomerates operating as consolidated groups. Increased foreign trade has generated new interest in the tax aspects of international transactions, and Chapter 9 introduces these issues in a very accessible manner.

Part 4 (Advanced Tax Practice Considerations) contains material of critical interest to the serious tax practitioner. Chapter 13 presents a detailed analysis of the various considerations that enter into the decision-making process in choosing the form of doing business. As such, the material is the capstone of what has been previously discussed and furnishes the foundation for choosing the appropriate business form. Chapter 14 deals with tax-exempt organizations, a controversial area that is receiving considerable media attention and Congressional inquiry, and one that is now covered in the CPA exam. Chapter 15 explores the problems

"In my opinion, this book is the best on the market for the second tax course...[T]he topics are thoroughly covered, well organized, and in a logical sequence with detailed exhibits, examples, and footnoted passages."

— *Scott Yetmar, Cleveland State University**

*From Scott Yetmar, review of* WFT: Corporations, Partnerships, Estates & Trusts, *in* Journal of the American Taxation Association *(Fall 2002), pp. 110-112. Courtesy of the American Accounting Association and Scott Yetmar. Reprinted by permission.*

"The West series that I use does an excellent job of dividing up the material I teach in ACCTG 306 [individual taxation] versus what I teach in ACCTG 406 [corporations and partnerships]."

— *Charles R. Enis, Pennsylvania State University*

encountered when business is (or could be) conducted in more than one state. Many of the multistate taxation issues are of vital interest in today's climate of competitive economic development.

The purpose of Part 4 is to illustrate some of the specialized areas that tax practice involves. Furthermore, the subjects are arranged so as to maximize selectivity. For example, the user may wish to omit tax-exempt organizations (Chapter 14) and emphasize the material on multistate taxation (Chapter 15). Since these modules are not interdependent, selective omission does not detract from the effectiveness of what the user chooses to cover.

# The Innovation You Expect

## TECHNOLOGY FOR LEARNING

With today's mobile *WFT* users and tomorrow's electronic CPA exam in mind, it's imperative that a course in Federal taxation includes the latest tax research capabilities and technology options. *WFT*'s 2004 edition of *Corporations, Partnerships, Estates & Trusts* offers a wealth of cutting-edge learning tools that provide unparalleled opportunities for skill-building, CPA exam preparation, assessment, and course-building.

## SKILL-BUILDING: TECHNOLOGY TOOLS AND RESOURCES

♦ **Computerized Tax Return Problems.** The 2004 Editions offer numerous tax return problems that lend themselves to computerized solutions. These problems can be solved using CrossLink or any commercially available tax software.

♦ **The Exclusive RIA Checkpoint®, Student Edition.** Integrating tax research is easier than ever—because each new copy of *WFT: Corporations, Partnerships, Estates & Trusts* includes six months of access to RIA's Checkpoint Student Edition online tax research database. This abbreviated form of the database used by tax professionals everywhere allows users to answer tax research questions found throughout the text—a core skill for a future tax professional.

THOMSON
RIA

♦ **CCH's U.S. Master Tax Guide Plus™.** In partnership with CCH (Commerce Clearing House), South-Western offers the opportunity to use one of the most comprehensive Federal tax research libraries online. The U.S. Master Tax Guide Plus provides access to thousands of primary source documents with unprecedented ease and speed.

♦ **Internet Exercises.** *WFT*'s online tax research capability provides ample opportunity for research. To be both flexible and comprehensive in scope, a number of *WFT*'s Research Problems are designed for the exploration of tax resources on the Internet. As the basis for their answers, users are asked to review newsgroups, practitioner sites and resources, chat rooms, discussion groups, and other resources.

## CPA EXAM PREPARATION

**NEW!** ◆ **Becker CPA Tax Review Included.** The Becker Conviser CPA Review Course is the number one program used to prepare professionals for the CPA Exam. This CD-ROM, bundled with every new text, contains four interactive hours of the Becker CPA review. Lectures focus on both the content and the skills needed to study for the tax portion of the CPA exam. Self-paced, flexible, focused, visually stimulating, and easy to use, this CD is another way we make *WFT: Corporations, Partnerships, Estates & Trusts* an incomparable value to CPA examinees.

## ASSESSMENT AND COURSE MANAGEMENT

◆ **Enhanced WebTutor™ in WebCT™ or Blackboard®.** This rich course management product is a specially designed extension of the classroom experience that enlivens the course by leveraging the power of the Internet with comprehensive educational content. This powerful, turnkey solution provides not only the trademark communication tools for each platform but also the following content customized for this edition:

**NEW!** ✦ **Quiz Bowl Game.** This multimedia Jeopardy!®-type game quizzes users on their understanding of glossary terms.

✦ **Interactive Quizzes.** Multiple choice, true/false, and sentence completion questions, which test the knowledge of the chapter content, provide immediate feedback on the accuracy of the response. These quizzes help students assess areas needing more study.

✦ **Threaded Discussion.** Threaded discussion questions, now tied to Tax in the News and Ethical Consideration boxes, directly link each chapter's topics to open-ended discussion prompts. Students can now engage in guided discussion to further enrich course content.

✦ **Flashcards.** A terminology quiz so that students have a complete understanding of the language that makes up the chapter content.

✦ **Chapter Summaries.** Tied to each learning objective, these chapter summaries reinforce important concepts from each chapter.

✦ **PowerPoint® Presentation Slides.** Students can use these slides to review chapter concepts.

✦ **Crossword Puzzles.** Understanding of the chapters' key terms are tested using this fun and interactive media.

✦ **Test Bank.** Instructors can upload the ExamView® computerized test bank files in order to test students online. See your sales representative for details.

◆ **Text Web Site.** The Web site for this edition, **http://wft.swlearning.com**, continues to offer users even more resources for teaching and learning than the previous edition. Among the many elements available are:

**NEW!** ✦ **More Extensive Online Tutorials.** WFT's Interactive Study Center has a full range of tutorial and interactive quizzing among its student resources—multiple choice and true-false quizzes for each chapter.

**NEW!** ✦ **Deloitte & Touche Tax Case Study Competition.** These cases, available online for download, focus on business entities rather than on individual taxation. They are the same cases used in national and regional competition hosted by Deloitte & Touche. They may be used as team projects emphasizing issue identification, problem solving, communication, tax planning, and research. Solutions are available to instructors via download.

**NEW!**

+ **Tax Ticker from AccountingWEB.** The IRS's Tax Tips for Individual Taxpayers has been formatted into a scrolling Tax Ticker by AccountingWEB that displays these tips during the tax season. **To see this ticker, go to http://www.swlearning.com/tax/tax.html.**

   + **Links to many resources on the Web,** including all of the Web sites listed in the text; this provides a quick connection to key information.

   + **PowerPoint® presentation slides** for review of chapter coverage.

   + **Crossword puzzles** provide fun testing of vocabulary knowledge for each chapter.

   + **Learning objectives** from the chapter are repeated as a study aid to keep clear focus on the core goals.

   + **Tax legislation articles and updates** are posted twice each month to our Web site and can be viewed by users. Take advantage of these articles and updates to stay current in tax, or use them to generate discussion in the classroom.

   + **Instructor's Resource Center.** Password protected and for instructors only, this site provides access to downloadable electronic versions of the instructor's guide, solutions manual, tax legislation updates, and PowerPoint slides. Instructors can obtain a secure password by emailing **password@kdc.com.**

## PROVEN PEDAGOGY: OPPORTUNITIES FOR LEARNING

*WFT: Corporations, Partnerships, Estates & Trusts* offers proven pedagogy that not only supports AECC and AICPA recommendations — but also fosters comprehension of presented topics. The result: users are better able to see beyond textbook examples to the real application of tax concepts and tax law.

♦ **Learning Objectives.** Every chapter begins with helpful learning objectives that guide users in mastering key tax concepts and principles.

> **L.O.1**
> Identify the tax consequences of incorporating a business.

Learning objectives also appear in the margins where the related material is introduced.

> | L.O.1 Identify the tax consequences of incorporating a business. | **Organization of and Transfers to Controlled Corporations** |
> |---|---|
> | | **IN GENERAL** |

♦ **Chapter Outline.** Material in each chapter is highlighted by a topical outline at the beginning of the chapter, complete with page references that provide ready access to each topic.

♦ **Chapter Introductions.** In the introductions, material in the current chapter is often linked to content in those chapters preceding it—frequently citing real-world examples that convey the relevance of chapter content.

♦ **Numerous Examples.** Each chapter contains many numbered examples that enliven the concepts with realistic tax situations.

> **EXAMPLE 21**  Arts Corporation owns a chain of retail stores located in several states. To enable each store to file and report the income earned only in that state, each store was organized as a separate subsidiary in the state in which it did business. In this manner, each store is separately subject to tax only in the state in which it is located. ■

◆ **Concept Summaries.** Concept Summary charts and tables, located throughout each chapter, make reviewing material for exams and class quizzes less time-consuming.

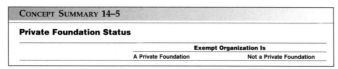

| CONCEPT SUMMARY 14–5 | | |
|---|---|---|
| **Private Foundation Status** | | |
| | **Exempt Organization Is** | |
| | A Private Foundation | Not a Private Foundation |

◆ **Key Terms.** Whenever a key term is introduced in a chapter, it's presented in bold print and is later defined in the Glossary (Appendix C). Also, a list of key terms with page references appears before the Problem Materials in each chapter so students may easily review for further reinforcement.

A profits (loss) interest is simply the partner's percentage allocation of current partnership operating results. **Profit and loss sharing ratios** are usually specified in the partnership agreement and are used to determine each partner's allocation of partnership ordinary taxable income and separately stated items.[8] The partnership can change its profit and loss allocations at any time simply by amending the partnership agreement.

*Key Term in text.*

*Key Term in Glossary appendix.*

**Profit and loss sharing ratios.** Specified in the partnership agreement and used to determine each partner's allocation of ordinary taxable income and separately stated items. Profits and losses can be shared in different ratios. The ratios can be changed by amending the partnership agreement. § 704(a).

◆ **Tax Planning Considerations.** Since the early 1980s, *WFT* has recognized and emphasized the importance of careful tax planning. As a result, most chapters include a separate section calling attention to this ever-growing area. Additionally, tax planning applications and suggestions appear throughout each chapter.

**Tax Planning Considerations** The inconsistencies in the tax laws and rates among the states not only complicate state tax planning, but also provide the nucleus of pertinent planning opportunities. Although several tax planning devices are available to a corporation that does business in only one state, most planning techniques are directed toward corporations that do business or maintain property in more than one state. All suggested tax planning strategies should be reviewed in light of practical business considerations and the additional administrative and other costs that may be incurred, because

◆ **Global Tax Issues.** Given today's increasing global concerns, it's critical for users to understand just how international implications influence Federal taxation. *WFT*'s Global Tax Issues feature gives insight into the ways taxation is affected by international concerns, as well as the impact of tax law across the globe.

**GLOBAL TAX ISSUES**

**DEEMED DIVIDENDS FROM CONTROLLED FOREIGN CORPORATIONS**

It is not uncommon for U.S. multinational companies to conduct business overseas through the use of foreign corporations. Most often, these foreign corporations are controlled by the U.S. parent. Called controlled foreign corporations (CFCs), such entities would be ideal for income avoidance if incorporated in a low-tax jurisdiction (i.e., a tax haven country). Further, U.S. income tax on their profits would be deferred if no dividends are distributed to the U.S. parent.

◆ **Tax in the News.** Drawn from today's business and popular press, this boxed feature enlivens class discussions by presenting current issues that highlight chapter material. Tax in the News boxes can also serve as the basis for open-ended, online discussions in WebTutor.

**TAX IN THE NEWS**

**HOW LONG SHOULD PROBATE TAKE?**

Although Marilyn Monroe died on August 5, 1962, her estate is still in probate. Surely, a probate that has already continued for over 40 years must establish some kind of record!

The trouble stems from the wording of Marilyn's will. According to its terms, equal shares of the estate went to her psychoanalyst and her manager. The psychoanalyst then left his half to a mental health care center, while the manager's portion went to his children. The manager's children dispute the transfer to the medical institution. They contend that Marilyn's intent was to benefit persons, not organizations.

"Concept summaries provide students with quick reference for important concepts."

— *Patricia Mounce, Mississippi College*

◆

"I am completely sold on this textbook. The resources available to the professor and student are abundant. The tax topics are covered with depth, the examples are plentiful and very useful, and the different features (ethical considerations, tax in the news, tax planning considerations, and international implications) within a chapter add a lot of color and insight into relevant and current tax issues. Overall, I feel the students get their money's worth."

— *Scott Yetmar, Cleveland State University\**

*From Scott Yetmar, review of *WFT: Corporations, Partnerships, Estates & Trusts, in* Journal of the American Taxation Association *(Fall 2002), pp. 110-112. Courtesy of the American Accounting Association and Scott Yetmar. Reprinted by permission.*

♦ **Ethical Considerations.** Most issues don't have just one correct answer —
a big reason why *WFT*'s Ethical Considerations sections present thought-
provoking situations related to chapter topics. These questions are designed
to spark classroom and online discussion and invite oral debate, leading to an
examination of various value systems.

♦ **Decision Making Problems.** Whether in their future tax practice, in individual
tax planning situations, within a firm's tax department, or in business
contexts throughout their careers, users of *WFT: Corporations, Partnerships,
Estates & Trusts* can model their decision making on problems at the end of
every chapter that hone their analytical and decision-making skills.

♦ **Communications Assignments.** These end-of-chapter exercises, written in
compliance with the AICPA task force, help develop essential analytical and
writing skills users will need throughout their business career.

♦ **Issue Identification.** A large part of understanding taxation is the ability to
discern a tax issue within an individual or business situation or case. The
end-of-chapter problem material includes **"Issue ID"** questions designed to
help identify important tax issues. The questions are multifaceted and
generally have no single right answer.

♦ **End-of-Chapter Problems.** Instructors have come to expect that 20 to 30
percent of the problem materials in every edition are new and match
all changes in the latest tax legislation. *WFT* delivers on this promise again
for 2004.

♦ **Study Guide.** Prepared by James C. Young (Northern Illinois University),
the Study Guide encourages learners to review the chapter's main focus, key
concepts, and key terms and brush up on homework and test-taking skills.
Using the available answers and solutions to its quizzes and problems, users
can prepare for tests and quizzes in their course or use the Study Guide as a
self-paced quiz when preparing to take the CPA exam.

♦ **Practice Sets for *Corporations, Partnerships, Estates & Trusts.*** These
practice sets, by Donald R. Trippeer (University of Southern Colorado), are
comprehensive and designed to be completed after the related materials have
been covered. Complete with tax forms and instructions, they will provide
students with a realistic and challenging experience to accompany the text.

"Well-written
problem
material."

— *Danny A. Pannese,
Sacred Heart
University*

## A FULL RANGE OF INDISPENSABLE REFERENCES

*WFT: Corporations, Partnerships, Estates & Trusts* contains appendices that make teaching, learning, and researching taxation easier, more flexible, and more thorough. Among the appendices are handy tax rate schedules and tables, a glossary, as well as research aids, indexes, and code tables. The appendices include these valuable references:

◆ **Basic Tax Forms (Appendix B).** Although *WFT: Corporations, Partnerships, Estates & Trusts* is not oriented toward the preparation of tax returns, some familiarity with tax forms is helpful. The text includes tax return problems in chapters where appropriate. (Tax return problems can be solved manually or by using any commercially available corporate tax preparation software.) For convenience, Appendix B reprints some of the basic tax forms encountered in actual practice.

◆ **Comprehensive Tax Return Problems (Appendix F).** This valuable appendix challenges students' comprehensive knowledge and application of tax concepts and tax form preparation. These problems are ideal for use as term projects, as they reflect many of the issues encountered in everyday situations. **All problems are revised to include new factual information every year.** In past years, six comprehensive tax return problems have been included in Appendix F. For 2004, a **NEW seventh problem**, on Estate Taxes, using **Form 706**, has been added. **Solutions to the comprehensive problems in Appendix F are in the *Instructor's Guide with Lecture Notes* as well as on our Web site in the instructor's resource section.**

# The Service You Deserve

*WFT: Corporations, Partnerships, Estates & Trusts* offers the most comprehensive and easy-to-use supplements package available on the market.

### Supplements for the Instructor:

◆ **Instructor's Resource CD-ROM with ExamView®.** Key instructor ancillaries (*Solutions Manual, Instructor's Manual, Test Bank,* and *PowerPoint® Presentation Slides*) are provided on CD-ROM—giving instructors the ultimate tool for customizing lectures and presentations. The test bank files on the CD are provided in ExamView® format. This program is an easy-to-use test creation software compatible with Microsoft® Windows. Instructors can add or edit questions, instructions, and answers, and select questions (randomly or numerically) by previewing them on the screen. Instructors can also create and administer quizzes online, whether over the Internet, a local area network (LAN), or a wide area network (WAN).

◆ The **Instructor's Guide with Lecture Notes** contains lecture notes for each chapter, comments on the text's Ethical Considerations, and solutions to Research Problems and Comprehensive Tax Return Problems. Offering various teaching aids as well as material not covered in the text, the lecture notes are presented as an outline the professor can use in classroom presentation. These notes are also available on disk and on the *WFT* Web site.

> "If I need anything or have any questions, the South-Western/ Thomson Learning sales representatives are always extremely helpful."
>
> — *Patricia Mounce, Mississippi College*

"It is well written and has good supplemental materials."

— *Richard Alltizer, Wichita State University*

- ◆ *WFT* **Online** (http://wft.swlearning.com) offers immediate access to current information as soon as it's available. Qualified adopters can log on and learn about the most recent tax information—including the Code and Regulations, case citations, new court rulings, and other newsworthy items. This information can then be transferred to word processing programs for editing, printout, and classroom use. Instructors can also access the *Instructor's Guide with Lecture Notes, Solutions Manual, PowerPoint Presentation Slides,* and extra test questions.

- ◆ The **Solutions Manual** features solutions arranged in accordance with the sequence of chapter material. A matrix labels the problems by topical coverage and also denotes which problems are new, modified, or unchanged from the prior edition. This matrix also references the prior edition's problem number for the unchanged and modified problems. The solutions are referenced to the relevant pages in the text. The solutions manual is available on the *Instructor's Resource CD* and on the Web site as well.

- ◆ The **Test Bank** contains questions and solutions arranged in accordance with the sequence of chapter material. To help create an exam, a matrix labels the questions by topical coverage—reflecting which are new or modified—from the prior edition. Approximately 20 percent of the questions in the 2004 Edition are new or modified. In addition, ten more multiple-choice questions per chapter are available on the *WFT* Web site. **NEW!** For the convenience of our adopters, the 2004 Test Bank items are numbered in the same format as in ExamView.

- ◆ **PowerPoint Presentation Slides** allow qualified adopters to create interactive lectures and manipulate graphs, charts, and figures in the classroom. The package contains more than 30 slides per chapter—consisting of alternate figures, outlines, and key points.

- ◆ **Teaching Transparency Acetates.** For instructors who wish to use traditional overheads, these teaching transparencies contain the key charts and tables from the PowerPoint package.

- ◆ **Loose Leaf Edition.** As a service to adopting instructors, we provide copies of the text in loose-leaf format, drilled for use in three-ring binders. To order a copy, call your South-Western sales representative.

- ◆ **Tax Subscription Service.** Adopters of the *WFT* Series may participate in this convenient service. As a subscription service member, you receive the new edition of your adopted text, plus the key print supplements you need to teach your course. The *WFT* Series Subscription Service is another way we ensure that our customers have what they need, when they need it, every time. Contact your local sales representative for details.

- ◆ **Custom Solutions to Fit Your Course.** Thomson Custom Publishing gives you the opportunity to add your own personal touch to your favorite text. Custom publishing also allows you to build a text or supplement suited to your curriculum. You have the freedom to select and arrange content from Thomson's vast library of printed material and our online digital database. You can add your own notes, supplements, articles, study guide . . . you name it. You determine the length, sequence of materials, and even the cover design. In the end, you'll have a custom text of exceptional quality that is exactly what you want. Ask your sales representative, custom publisher, or customer representative for details.

# Acknowledgments

Special thanks to James C. Young (Northern Illinois University) for continuing to provide us with his inflation adjustments, which are available prior to the release of the official amounts by the IRS.

We are most appreciative of the many suggestions that we have received for revising the textbook, many of which have been incorporated in past editions and in the 2004 Edition. The *WFT* philosophy is not only to encourage user input, but also to actively seek the advice of users as the basis for improving the textbook. We would like to thank the following reviewers of the *WFT* volumes for this year; their thoughts have contributed much to this textbook for 2004:

**Richard Alltizer** (Wichita State University), **Donna Bobeck** (University of Central Florida), **Rebekah Sheely** (Emporia State University), **Dan Pannese** (Sacred Heart University), **John Kohler** (Washington University), **Ken Milani** (University of Notre Dame), **Priscilla O'Clock** (Xavier University), **Charles Enis** (Pennsylvania State University), **Lee Parker** (Nash Community College), **Ron Stunda** (Birmingham-Southern College), **Roger Lirely** (Western Carolina University), **Patricia Mounce** (Mississippi College), **Sharon Walters** (Morehead State University), **Janet Trewin** (Drexel University), **Lucretia Mattson** (University of Wisconsin–Eau Claire), **Bill Whitley** (Athens State University).

We are grateful to **Jon Davis** (University of Wisconsin—Madison), **Tom Omer** (University of Illinois, Chicago), and **Mark B. Persellin** (St. Mary's University) for their perceptive comments on tax planning issues.

We would also like to thank the people who have painstakingly worked through all the problems and test questions and generally acted as problem checkers to ensure the accuracy of the book and ancillary package. They are **Sara Linton** (University of Scranton), **Dorothea Malloy** (University of Maryland University College), **Frank M. Messina** (University of Alabama at Birmingham), **Shawn Novak** (Boise State University), **Mark B. Persellin** (St. Mary's University), **Randall K. Serrett** (University of Houston–Downtown), **Julie Shapland** (University of Illinois–Urbana/Champaign), **Donald R. Trippeer** (University of Southern Colorado), and **Raymond F. Wacker** (Southern Illinois University at Carbondale).

Finally, this 2004 Edition would not have been possible without the technical assistance of and manuscript review by **Bonnie Hoffman**, CPA; **Freda Mulhall**, CPA; and **Nora Smith**, M.Ed. We are indebted to them for their efforts.

*William H. Hoffman, Jr.*
*William A. Raabe*
*James E. Smith*
*David M. Maloney*

April 1, 2003

# Additional Offerings from the West Federal Taxation Series

*To find out more about these books, go to* **http://wft.swlearning.com.**

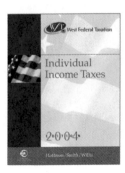

***West Federal Taxation: Individual Income Taxes*, 2004 Edition (Hoffman, Smith, Willis, editors)** continues to set the standard in introductory tax. Because it adheres to the recommendations of the Accounting Education Change Commission (AECC) and the American Institute of Certified Public Accountants (AICPA) and because its authors and editors stay on top of trends in both tax law and tax education, the 2004 Edition is thoroughly up-to-date, current in its thinking, and pedagogically advanced. No other text is as effective at helping users master the ever-changing Individual Tax Code. It provides accessible, comprehensive, and authoritative coverage of the relevant tax Code and regulations as they pertain to the individual taxpayer, as well as coverage of all major developments in Federal taxation.

> "The textbook does a great job of explaining concepts, provisions, and exceptions to provisions."
>
> — *Patricia Mounce,*
> *Mississippi College*

***West Federal Taxation: Comprehensive Volume*, 2004 Edition (Willis, Hoffman, Maloney, Raabe, editors).** Combining the number one Individual tax text with the number one Corporations text, *WFT: Comprehensive Volume*, 2004 Edition is a true winner. An edited version of the first two *WFT* textbooks, this book offers a thorough and balanced treatment of relevant tax Code and regulations as applied to individuals and corporations. Ideal for undergraduate or graduate levels, this text works for either a one-semester course in which an instructor wants to integrate coverage of individual and corporate taxation or for a two-semester sequence in which the use of only one book is desired.

> "Good examples in the text, good homework exercises ...good coverage of the most important issues."
>
> — *William Whitley,*
> *Athens State University*

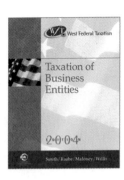

***West Federal Taxation: Taxation of Business Entities*, 2004 Edition (Smith, Raabe, Maloney, Willis, editors).** The 2004 Edition of *WFT: Taxation of Business Entities* provides thorough coverage of all relevant tax Code sections and regulations, emphasizing the high-interest and multidisciplinary aspects of taxation. Designed with the AICPA model tax curriculum in mind, this text presents the introductory Federal taxation course from a business entity perspective. Its **NEW Tax Planning Framework** helps users fit tax planning strategies into an innovative pedagogical framework. *WFT: Taxation of Business Entities* is an ideal fit for the program that offers only one course in taxation where users need to be exposed to corporate taxation as well as individual taxation. This text assumes no prior course in taxation has been taken.

> "It seems to be the best textbook for the entities approach."
>
> — *John F. Kohler,*
> *Washington University (St. Louis)*

**NEW TO WFT FOR 2004!** *West Federal Taxation: Advanced Business Entity Taxation,* **2004 Edition (Raabe, Willis, Maloney, Smith, editors).** Edited by members of the market-leading West Federal Taxation Series, the **NEW** 2004 Edition of *WFT: Advanced Business Entity Taxation* provides thorough coverage of all relevant Code and regulations, emphasizing the high-interest and multidisciplinary aspects of taxation for the second tax course. Designed with the AICPA model tax curriculum in mind, this text presents the second Federal taxation course from a business entity perspective. Its **NEW Tax Planning Framework** helps users fit tax planning strategies into an innovative pedagogical framework. It is an ideal follow-up to *Taxation of Business Entities* or any first course in taxation that uses the business entities approach. This course is intended for accounting or finance majors who take it to fulfill curriculum requirements and for students likely to sit for the CPA or CFA Exams.

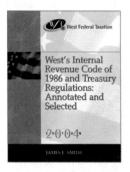

*West's Internal Revenue Code of 1986 and Treasury Regulations: Annotated and Selected,* **2004 Edition (James E. Smith, College of William and Mary).** An ideal alternative to the traditional, bulky, and expensive multivolume set of Code and Regulations, this single-volume reference book provides a useful selection of Code and Regulations sections and clear annotations in the form of editorial summaries. These concise annotations explain, analyze, and cross-reference topics to help students fully understand the intricacies of the tax Code. Smith's *Internal Revenue Code* is a perfect supplement for any West Federal Taxation text as well as an excellent primary text for a Federal taxation course that stresses a Code and Regulations approach.

> "Its many innovative features and ease of use make it superior, for educational purposes, to the complete codes and regulations."
>
> — *James E. Smith,*
> *"Preface"*

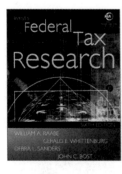

*West's Federal Tax Research,* **6e (William A. Raabe, Ohio State University; Gerald E. Whittenburg, San Diego State University; Debra Sanders, Washington State University; John Bost, San Diego State University).** *West's Federal Tax Research* is the most thorough and up-to-date text available on the market. No other text can better prepare the user on tax research procedures and their multiple applications. From its tax planning orientation to the real-life cases, this is one book that conveys a true understanding of the most important elements of the Federal tax law.

> "A hands-on, case-based approach to becoming a high-level tax practitioner, incorporating the latest technology and expert learning methods, supplemented with a tax planning orientation and a focus on spoken and written communication skills."
>
> — *William A. Raabe,*
> *Co-author*

# About the Editors

*William H. Hoffman, Jr.*, earned B.A. and J.D. degrees from the University of Michigan and M.B.A. and Ph.D. degrees from The University of Texas. He is a licensed CPA and attorney in Texas. His teaching experience includes: The University of Texas (1957-1961), Louisiana State University (1961-1967), and the University of Houston (1967-1999). Professor Hoffman has addressed many tax institutes and conferences and has published extensively in academic and professional journals. His articles appear in *The Journal of Taxation, The Tax Adviser, Taxes—The Tax Magazine, The Journal of Accountancy, The Accounting Review,* and *Taxation for Accountants.*

*William A. Raabe* teaches tax courses in the Fisher College of Business at the Ohio State University. A graduate of Carroll College (WI) and the University of Illinois, Dr. Raabe's teaching and research interests include international and multistate taxation, technology in tax education, personal financial planning, and the economic impact of sports teams and fine arts groups. Dr. Raabe also is the author of *Federal Tax Research* and the *Multistate Corporate Tax Guide*. He coordinates the material on the West Federal Taxation Internet page, and he has written estate planning software used widely by tax professionals. Dr. Raabe has been a visiting tax faculty member for a number of public accounting firms, bar associations, and CPA societies. He has received numerous teaching awards, including the Accounting Educator of the Year award from the Wisconsin Institute of CPAs.

*James E. Smith* is the John S. Quinn Professor of Accounting at the College of William and Mary. He has been a member of the Accounting Faculty for thirty years. He received his Ph.D. degree from the University of Arizona.

Professor Smith has served as a discussion leader for Continuing Professional Education programs for the AICPA, Federal Tax Workshops, and various state CPA societies. He has conducted programs in over 40 states for approximately 25,000 CPAs. He has been the recipient of the AICPAs' Outstanding Discussion Leader Award and the American Taxation Association/Arthur Andersen Teaching Innovation Award.

Other awards received by him include the Virginia Society of CPAs' Outstanding Accounting Educator Award and the James Madison University's Outstanding Accounting Educator Award. He was the President of the Administrators of Accounting Programs Group (AAPG) in 1991-1992. He was the faculty adviser for the William and Mary teams that received first place in the Andersen Tax Challenge in 1994, 1995, 1997, 2000, and 2001 and in the Deloitte & Touche Tax Case Study Competition in 2002.

*David M. Maloney*, Ph.D., CPA, completed his undergraduate work at the University of Richmond and his graduate work at the University of Illinois at Urbana-Champaign. He teaches courses in Federal taxation in the graduate and undergraduate programs at the University of Virginia's McIntire School of Commerce. Since joining the Virginia faculty in January 1984, Professor Maloney has been a recipient of major research grants from the Ernst & Young and KPMG Foundation. In addition, his work has been published in numerous professional journals, including *The Journal of Taxation, The Tax Adviser, Tax Notes, The Journal of Corporate Taxation, Accounting Horizons,* and *The Journal of Accountancy.* He is a member of several professional organizations, including the American Accounting Association and the American Taxation Association.

# Contents in Brief

**PART FIVE**          FAMILY TAX PLANNING

# Contents

**PART THREE    FLOW-THROUGH ENTITIES**

---

**PART FOUR** ADVANCED TAX PRACTICE CONSIDERATIONS

## PART FIVE    FAMILY TAX PLANNING

# APPENDIXES

# Introduction

The Federal law is an unbelievably complex set of rules. In working with these rules, however, it is helpful to understand *why* they came about. Also necessary is the ability to locate the sources of these rules. Part I, therefore, is devoted to the "whys" of the tax law and the applications of the tax research process.

### CHAPTER 1

Understanding and Working with the Federal Tax Law

# Understanding and Working with the Federal Tax Law

## LEARNING OBJECTIVES

*After completing Chapter 1, you should be able to:*

**LO.1**
Realize the importance of revenue needs as an objective of Federal tax law.

**LO.2**
Appreciate the influence of economic, social, equity, and political considerations on the development of the tax law.

**LO.3**
Understand how the IRS, as the protector of the revenue, has affected tax law.

**LO.4**
Recognize the role of the courts in interpreting and shaping tax law.

**LO.5**
Identify tax law sources—statutory, administrative, and judicial.

**LO.6**
Locate tax law sources.

**LO.7**
Assess the validity and weight of tax law sources.

**LO.8**
Make use of various tax planning procedures.

**LO.9**
Have an awareness of computer-assisted tax research.

http://wft.swlearning.com

## OUTLINE

# The Whys of the Tax Law

The Federal tax law is a mixture of statutory provisions, administrative pronouncements, and court decisions. Anyone who has attempted to work with this body of knowledge is familiar with its complexity. Commenting on his 48-page tax return, the author James Michener said, "It is unimaginable in that I graduated from one of America's better colleges, yet I am totally incapable of understanding tax returns." For the person who has to wade through rule upon rule to find the solution to a tax problem, it may be of some consolation to know that the law's complexity can be explained. There is a reason for the formulation of every rule. Knowing these reasons, therefore, is a considerable step toward understanding the Federal tax law.

The major objective of the Federal tax law is the raising of revenue. Despite the importance of the fiscal needs of the government, however, other considerations explain certain portions of the law. In particular, economic, social, equity, and political factors play a significant role. Added to these factors is the marked impact the Internal Revenue Service (IRS) and the courts have had and will continue to have on the evolution of Federal tax law. These matters are treated in the first part of this chapter. Wherever appropriate, the discussion is related to subjects covered later in the text.

## LO.1

Realize the importance of revenue needs as an objective of Federal tax law.

### REVENUE NEEDS

The foundation of any tax system has to be the raising of revenue to absorb the cost of government operations. Ideally, annual outlays should not exceed anticipated revenues. This situation leads to a balanced budget with no deficit. Many states have achieved this objective by passing laws or constitutional amendments precluding deficit spending. Unfortunately, the Federal government has no such prohibition, and the national debt has grown, reaching $6.25 trillion in late 2002. Concern about the rising debt has caused Congress to become more deficit-conscious when enacting tax legislation.

When enacting tax legislation, Congress often is guided by the concept of **revenue neutrality** so that any changes neither increase nor decrease the net revenues raised under the prior rules. Revenue neutrality does not mean that any one taxpayer's tax liability remains the same. Since this liability depends upon the circumstances involved, one taxpayer's increased tax liability could be another's tax saving. Revenue-neutral tax reform does not reduce deficits, but at least it does not aggravate the problem.

**LO.2**

Appreciate the influence of economic, social, equity, and political considerations on the development of the tax law.

## ECONOMIC CONSIDERATIONS

Using the tax system to attempt to accomplish economic objectives has become increasingly popular in recent years. Generally, this process involves amending the Internal Revenue Code[1] through tax legislation and emphasizes measures designed to help control the economy or encourage certain activities and businesses.

**Control of the Economy.** Congress has made use of depreciation write-offs as a means of controlling the economy. Theoretically, shorter asset lives and accelerated methods should encourage additional investment in depreciable property acquired for business use. Conversely, longer class lives and the required use of the straight-line method of depreciation dampen the tax incentive for capital outlays.

Another approach that utilizes depreciation as a means of controlling capital investment is the amount of write-off allowed upon the acquisition of assets. This approach is followed by the § 179 election to expense assets. It also was the approach used by Congress in a provision contained in the Job Creation and Worker Assistance Act of 2002 that permits 30 percent additional first-year depreciation.

A change in the tax rate structure has a more immediate impact on the economy. When tax rates are lowered, taxpayers are able to obtain additional spendable funds. In the interest of revenue neutrality, however, rate decreases may be accompanied by a reduction or elimination of deductions or credits. Thus, lower rates do not always mean lower taxes.

**Encouragement of Certain Activities.** Without passing judgment on the wisdom of any such choices, it is quite clear that the tax law does encourage certain types of economic activity or segments of the economy. For example, the desire to foster technological progress helps explain the favorable treatment accorded to research and development expenditures. Under the tax law, such expenditures can be deducted in the year incurred or, alternatively, capitalized and amortized over a period of 60 months or more. In terms of timing the tax saving, such options usually are preferable to a capitalization of the cost with a write-off over the estimated useful life of the asset created.[2]

The encouragement of technological progress can also explain why the tax law places the inventor in a special position. Not only can patents qualify as capital assets, but under certain conditions their disposition automatically carries long-term capital gain treatment.[3]

---

[1]The Internal Revenue Code is a compilation of Federal tax legislation that appears in Title 26 of the U.S. Code.

[2]If the asset developed has no estimated useful life, no write-off would be available without the two options allowed by the tax law.

[3]A long-term capital gain has a favorable tax advantage for individuals.

Are ecological considerations a desirable objective? If they are, it explains why the tax law permits a 60-month amortization period for costs incurred in the installation of pollution control facilities.

Does stimulating the development and rehabilitation of low-income rental housing benefit the economy? The tax law definitely favors these activities by allowing generous tax credits to taxpayers incurring such costs.

Is saving desirable for the economy? Saving leads to capital formation and thus makes funds available to finance home construction and industrial expansion. The tax law provides incentives to encourage saving by giving private retirement plans preferential treatment. Not only are contributions to Keogh (H.R. 10) plans and certain Individual Retirement Accounts (IRAs) deductible, but income from such contributions accumulates on a tax-free basis. As noted in a following section, the encouragement of private-sector pension plans can be justified under social considerations as well.

**Encouragement of Certain Industries.**   Who can question the proposition that a sound agricultural base is necessary for a well-balanced national economy? Undoubtedly, this belief can explain why farmers are accorded special treatment under the Federal tax system. Among the benefits are the election to expense rather than capitalize certain expenditures for soil and water conservation and fertilizers and the election to defer the recognition of gain on the receipt of crop insurance proceeds.

The tax law also favors the development of natural resources by permitting the use of percentage depletion on the extraction and sale of oil and gas and specified mineral deposits and a write-off (rather than a capitalization) of certain exploration costs. The railroad and banking industries also receive special tax treatment. All of these provisions can be explained, in whole or in part, by economic considerations.

**Encouragement of Small Business.**   At least in the United States, a consensus exists that what is good for small business is good for the economy as a whole. This assumption has led to a definite bias in the tax law favoring small business.

In the corporate tax area, several provisions can be explained by the desire to benefit small business. One provision enables a shareholder in a small business corporation to obtain an ordinary deduction for any loss recognized on a stock investment. Normally, such a loss would receive the less attractive capital loss treatment. The point of this favoritism is to encourage additional equity investments in small business corporations.[4] Another provision permits the shareholders of a small business corporation to make a special election that generally will avoid the imposition of the corporate income tax.[5] Furthermore, such an election enables the corporation to pass through to its shareholders any of its operating losses.[6]

The tax rates applicable to corporations tend to favor small business in that size is relative to the amount of taxable income generated in any one year. Since a corporate tax rate of 34 percent applies only to taxable income in excess of $75,000, corporations that stay within this limit are subject to lower average tax rates.

---

[4]Known as Section 1244 stock, this subject is covered in Chapter 3.
[5]Known as the S corporation election, the subject is discussed extensively in Chapter 12. The rules applicable to S corporations were made more tenable by the enactment of the Small Business Job Protection Act of 1996.

[6]In general, an operating loss can benefit only the corporation incurring the loss through a carryback or carryover to profitable years. Consequently, the shareholders of the corporation usually cannot take advantage of any such loss.

**EXAMPLE 1**

For calendar year 2003, Brown Corporation has taxable income of $75,000, and Red Corporation has taxable income of $100,000. Based on this information, the corporate income tax is $13,750 for Brown Corporation and $22,250 for Red Corporation (see Chapter 2). Brown Corporation is subject to an average tax rate of 18.33% ($13,750/$75,000), while Red Corporation is subject to an average rate of 22.25% ($22,250/$100,000). ■

If a corporation has taxable income in excess of $100,000, the benefits of the lower brackets are phased out until all income is taxed at the maximum rate of 34 percent. Once taxable income reaches $10 million, the rate becomes 35 percent.

One of the justifications for the enactment of the tax law governing corporate reorganizations (see Chapter 7) was the economic benefit it would provide for small businesses. By allowing corporations to combine without adverse tax consequences, small corporations would be in a position to compete more effectively with larger concerns.

## SOCIAL CONSIDERATIONS

Some of the tax laws, especially those related to the Federal income tax of individuals, can be explained by social considerations. Rather than using loans, grants, and other programs to reach desired goals, Congress often uses the Tax Code to provide incentives and benefits (e.g., the new higher education incentives). The following are some notable examples:

- The refundable earned income tax credit. As Congress has deemed it socially desirable to reduce the number of people on the welfare rolls and to cut funding for welfare programs, this credit has come to replace some welfare programs.
- The nontaxability of certain benefits provided to employees through accident and health plans financed by employers. It is socially desirable to encourage such plans, since they provide medical benefits in the event of an employee's illness or injury.
- The nontaxability to the employee of some of the premiums paid by an employer for group term insurance covering the life of the employee. These arrangements can be justified in that they provide funds to help the family unit adjust to the loss of wages caused by the employee's death.
- The tax treatment to the employee of contributions made by an employer to qualified pension or profit sharing plans. The contribution and any income it earns are not taxed to the employee until the funds are distributed. Private retirement plans are encouraged because they supplement the subsistence income level the employee would otherwise have under the Social Security system.[7]
- The deduction allowed for contributions to qualified charitable organizations. The deduction attempts to shift some of the financial and administrative burden of socially desirable programs from the public (the government) to the private (the citizens) sector.
- Various tax credits, deductions, and exclusions that are designed to encourage taxpayers to obtain additional education (e.g., HOPE scholarship credit, lifetime learning credit, and the Coverdell Education Savings Account).[8]

---

[7]The same rationale explains the availability of similar arrangements for self-employed persons (the H.R. 10 or Keogh plan).

[8]These provisions can also be justified under the category of economic considerations. No one can take issue with the conclusion that a better educated workforce carries a positive economic impact.

- The credit allowed for amounts spent to furnish care for certain minor or disabled dependents to enable the taxpayer to seek or maintain gainful employment. Who could deny the social desirability of encouraging taxpayers to provide care for their children while they work?
- The disallowance of a tax deduction for certain expenditures that are deemed to be contrary to public policy. This disallowance extends to such items as fines, penalties, illegal kickbacks, and bribes to government officials. Public policy considerations also have been used to disallow gambling losses in excess of gambling gains and political campaign expenditures in excess of campaign contributions. Social considerations dictate that the tax law should not encourage these activities by permitting a deduction.
- The adoption tax credit of up to $10,000 to cover expenses incurred by individuals who adopt or attempt to adopt a child.

Many other examples could be included, but the conclusion would be unchanged: social considerations do explain a significant part of the Federal tax law.

## EQUITY CONSIDERATIONS

The concept of equity is relative. Reasonable persons can, and often do, disagree about what is fair or unfair. In the tax area, moreover, equity is generally tied to a particular taxpayer's personal situation. To illustrate, Ms. Jones may have difficulty understanding why none of the rent she pays on her apartment is deductible, while her brother, Mr. Jones, is able to deduct a large portion of the monthly payments he makes on his personal residence in the form of interest and taxes.[9]

In the same vein, compare the tax treatment of a corporation with that of a partnership. Two businesses may be of equal size, similarly situated, and competitors in the production of goods or services, but they are not comparably treated under the tax law. The corporation is subject to a separate Federal income tax; the partnership is not. Whether the differences in tax treatment can be logically justified in terms of equity is beside the point. The tax law can and does make a distinction between these business forms.

Equity, then, is not what appears fair or unfair to any one taxpayer or group of taxpayers. It is, instead, what the tax law recognizes. Some recognition of equity does exist, however, and explains part of the law. The concept of equity appears in tax provisions that alleviate the effect of multiple taxation and postpone the recognition of gain when the taxpayer lacks the ability or wherewithal to pay the tax. Equity also helps mitigate the effect of the application of the annual accounting period concept and helps taxpayers cope with the eroding result of inflation.

**Alleviating the Effect of Multiple Taxation.**    The same income earned by a taxpayer may be subject to taxes imposed by different taxing authorities. If, for example, the taxpayer is a resident of New York City, income might generate Federal, State of New York, and City of New York income taxes. To compensate for this inequity, the Federal tax law allows a taxpayer to claim a deduction for state and local income taxes. The deduction, however, does not neutralize the effect of multiple taxation since the benefit derived depends on the taxpayer's Federal income tax rate.[10]

---

[9]The encouragement of home ownership can be justified on both economic and social grounds. In this regard, it is interesting to note that some state income tax laws allow a form of relief (e.g., tax credit) to the taxpayer who rents his or her personal residence.

[10]A tax credit, rather than a deduction, would eliminate the effects of multiple taxation on the same income.

Equity considerations can explain the Federal tax treatment of certain income from foreign sources. Since double taxation results when the same income is subject to both foreign and U.S. income taxes, the tax law permits the taxpayer to choose either a credit or a deduction for the foreign taxes paid.

The imposition of a separate income tax on corporations leads to multiple taxation of the same income.

**EXAMPLE 2**

During the current year, Gray Corporation has net income of $100,000, of which $5,000 was received as dividends from stock it owns in IBM Corporation. Assume Gray Corporation distributes the after-tax income to its shareholders (all individuals). At a minimum, the distribution received by the shareholders will be subject to two income taxes: the corporate income tax when the income is earned by Gray Corporation and the individual income tax when the balance is distributed to the shareholders as a dividend. The $5,000 Gray receives from IBM Corporation fares even worse. Because it is paid from income earned by IBM, it has been subjected to a third income tax (the corporate income tax imposed on IBM).[11] ■

For corporate shareholders, for whom triple taxation is possible, the law provides a deduction for dividends received from certain domestic corporations. The deduction, usually 70 percent of the dividends, would be allowed to Gray Corporation for the $5,000 it received from IBM Corporation. (See the discussion in Chapter 2.)

In the area of the Federal estate tax, several provisions reflect attempts to mitigate the effect of multiple taxation. Some degree of equity is achieved, for example, by allowing a limited credit against the estate tax for foreign death taxes imposed on the same transfer. Other estate tax credits are available and can be explained on the same grounds.[12]

**The Wherewithal to Pay Concept.**   The **wherewithal to pay** concept recognizes the inequity of taxing a transaction when the taxpayer lacks the means with which to pay the tax. It is particularly suited to situations when the taxpayer's economic position has not changed significantly as a result of a transaction.

**EXAMPLE 3**

White Corporation holds unimproved land as an investment. The land has a basis to White of $60,000 and a fair market value of $100,000. The land is exchanged for a building (worth $100,000) that White will use in its business.[13] ■

**EXAMPLE 4**

White Corporation owns a warehouse that it uses in its business. At a time when the warehouse has an adjusted basis of $60,000, it is destroyed by fire. White collects the insurance proceeds of $100,000 and, within two years of the end of the year in which the fire occurred, uses all of the proceeds to purchase a new warehouse.[14] ■

**EXAMPLE 5**

Tom, a sole proprietor, decides to incorporate his business. In exchange for the business's assets (adjusted basis of $60,000 and a fair market value of $100,000), Tom receives all of the stock of Azure Corporation, a newly created corporation.[15] The Azure stock is worth $100,000. ■

---

[11]This result materializes because under the tax law a corporation is not allowed a deduction for the dividend distributions it makes.
[12]See Chapter 17.
[13]The nontaxability of like-kind exchanges applies to the exchange of property held for investment or used in a trade or business for property to be similarly held or used.
[14]The nontaxability of gains realized from involuntary conversions applies when the proceeds received by the taxpayer are reinvested

within a prescribed period of time in property similar or related in service or use to that converted. Involuntary conversions take place as a result of casualty losses, theft losses, and condemnations by a public authority.
[15]Transfers of property to controlled corporations are discussed in Chapter 3.

**EXAMPLE 6**

Rose, Sam, and Tom want to develop unimproved land owned by Tom. The land has a basis to Tom of $60,000 and a fair market value of $100,000. The RST Partnership is formed with the following investment: land worth $100,000 transferred by Tom, $100,000 cash by Rose, and $100,000 cash by Sam. Each party receives a one-third interest in the RST Partnership.[16] ■

**EXAMPLE 7**

Amber Corporation and Crimson Corporation decide to consolidate to form Aqua Corporation.[17] Pursuant to the plan of reorganization, Tera exchanges her stock in Amber Corporation (basis of $60,000 and fair market value of $100,000) for stock in Aqua Corporation worth $100,000. ■

In all of the preceding examples, White Corporation, Tom, or Tera had a realized gain of $40,000 [$100,000 (fair market value of the property received) − $60,000 (basis of the property given up)].[18] It seems inequitable to force the taxpayer to recognize any of this gain for two reasons. First, without disposing of the property or interest acquired, the taxpayer would be hard-pressed to pay the tax.[19] Second, the taxpayer's economic situation has not changed significantly. To illustrate by referring to Example 5, can it be said that Tom's position as sole shareholder of Azure Corporation is much different from his prior status as owner of a sole proprietorship?

Several warnings are in order concerning the application of the wherewithal to pay concept. Recognized gain is merely postponed and not necessarily avoided. Because of the basis carryover to the new property or interest acquired in these nontaxable transactions, the gain element is still present and might be recognized upon a subsequent taxable disposition. Referring to Example 5, suppose Tom later sold the stock in Azure Corporation for $100,000. Tom's basis in the stock is $60,000 (the same basis as in the assets transferred), and the sale results in a recognized gain of $40,000. Also, many of the provisions previously illustrated prevent the recognition of realized losses. Since such provisions are automatic in application (not elective with the taxpayer), they could operate to the detriment of a taxpayer who wishes to obtain a deduction for a loss. The notable exception involves involuntary conversions (Example 4). Here, nonrecognition treatment is elective with the taxpayer and will not apply to a realized loss if it is otherwise deductible.

The wherewithal to pay concept has definitely served as a guideline in shaping part of the tax law. Nevertheless, it is not a hard and fast principle that is followed in every case. Only when the tax law specifically provides for no tax consequences will this result materialize.

**EXAMPLE 8**

Mary Jo exchanges stock in Green Corporation (basis of $60,000 and fair market value of $100,000) for stock in Purple Corporation (fair market value of $100,000). The exchange is not pursuant to a reorganization. Under these circumstances, Mary Jo's realized gain of $40,000 is recognized for Federal income tax purposes.[20] ■

The result reached in Example 8 seems harsh in that the exchange does not place Mary Jo in a position to pay the tax on the $40,000 gain. How can this result

---

[16]The formation of a partnership is discussed in Chapter 10.

[17]Corporate reorganizations are discussed in Chapter 7.

[18]Realized gain can be likened to economic gain. However, the Federal income tax is imposed only on that portion of realized gain considered to be recognized under the law. Generally, recognized (or taxable) gain can never exceed realized gain.

[19]If the taxpayer ends up with other property (boot) as part of the transfer, gain may be recognized to this extent. The presence of

boot, however, helps solve the wherewithal to pay problem, since it provides property (other than the property or interest central to the transaction) with which to pay the tax.

[20]The exchange of stock does not qualify for nontaxable treatment as a like-kind exchange (refer to Example 3).

be reconciled with that reached in Example 7 when the exchange was nontaxable? In other words, why does the tax law apply the wherewithal to pay concept to the exchange of stock pursuant to a corporate reorganization (Example 7) but not to certain other stock exchanges (Example 8)?

Recall that the wherewithal to pay concept is particularly suited to situations in which the taxpayer's economic position has not changed significantly as a result of a transaction. In Example 7, Tera's stock investment in Amber Corporation really continues in the form of the Aqua Corporation stock since Aqua was formed through a consolidation of Amber and Crimson Corporations.[21] In Example 8, however, the investment has not continued. Here Mary Jo's ownership in Green Corporation has ceased, and an investment in an entirely different corporation has been substituted.

**Mitigating the Effect of the Annual Accounting Period Concept.** For purposes of effective administration of the tax law, all taxpayers must report to and settle with the Federal government at periodic intervals. Otherwise, taxpayers would remain uncertain as to their tax liabilities, and the government would have difficulty judging revenues and budgeting expenditures. The period selected for final settlement of most tax liabilities is one year. At the close of each year, a taxpayer's position becomes complete for that particular year. Referred to as the annual accounting period concept, the effect is to divide each taxpayer's life into equal annual intervals for tax purposes.

The finality of the annual accounting period concept can lead to dissimilar tax treatment for taxpayers who are, from a long-range standpoint, in the same economic position.

**EXAMPLE 9**

Rena and Samuel are both sole proprietors and have experienced the following results during the past three years:

| | Profit (or Loss) | |
|---|---|---|
| Year | Rena | Samuel |
| 2001 | $50,000 | $150,000 |
| 2002 | 60,000 | 60,000 |
| 2003 | 60,000 | (40,000) |

Although Rena and Samuel have the same profit of $170,000 over the period 2001–2003, the finality of the annual accounting period concept places Samuel at a definite disadvantage for tax purposes. The net operating loss procedure offers Samuel some relief by allowing him to apply some or all of his 2003 loss to the earliest profitable years (in this case 2001). Thus, Samuel, with a net operating loss carryback, is placed in a position to obtain a refund for some of the taxes he paid on the $150,000 profit reported for 2001. ∎

The same reasoning used to support the deduction of net operating losses can be applied to explain the special treatment excess capital losses and excess charitable contributions receive. Carryback and carryover procedures help mitigate the effect of limiting a loss or a deduction to the accounting period in which it is realized. With such procedures, a taxpayer may be able to salvage a loss or a deduction that might otherwise be wasted.

---

[21]This continuation is known as the continuity of interest concept, which forms the foundation for all nontaxable corporate reorganizations. The concept is discussed at length in Chapter 7.

The installment method of recognizing gain on the sale of property allows a taxpayer to spread tax consequences over the payout period.[22] The harsh effect of taxing all the gain in the year of sale is avoided. The installment method can also be explained by the wherewithal to pay concept since recognition of gain is tied to the collection of the installment notes received from the sale of the property. Tax consequences tend to correspond to the seller's ability to pay the tax.

**EXAMPLE 10**

In 2001, Tim sold unimproved real estate (cost of $40,000) for $100,000. Under the terms of the sale, Tim receives two notes from the purchaser, each for $50,000 (plus interest). One note is payable in 2002 and the other note in 2003. Without the installment method, Tim would have to recognize and pay a tax on the gain of $60,000 for the year of the sale (2001). This result is harsh, since none of the sale proceeds will be received until 2002 and 2003. With the installment method, and presuming the notes are paid when each comes due, Tim recognizes half of the gain ($30,000) in 2002 and the remaining half in 2003. ■

The annual accounting period concept has been modified to apply to situations in which taxpayers may have difficulty accurately assessing their tax positions by year-end. In many such cases, the law permits taxpayers to treat transactions taking place in the next year as having occurred in the prior year.

**EXAMPLE 11**

Monica, a calendar year taxpayer, is a participant in an H.R. 10 (Keogh) retirement plan. (See Appendix C for a definition of a Keogh plan.) Under the plan, Monica contributes 20% of her net self-employment income, such amount being deductible for Federal income tax purposes. On April 10, 2003, Monica determines that her net self-employment income for calendar year 2002 was $80,000. Consequently, she contributes $16,000 (20% × $80,000) to the plan. Even though the $16,000 contribution was made in 2003, the law permits Monica to claim it as a deduction for tax year 2002. Requiring Monica to make the contribution by December 31, 2002, in order to obtain the deduction for that year would force her to arrive at an accurate determination of net self-employment income long before her income tax return must be prepared and filed. ■

Similar exceptions to the annual accounting period concept cover certain charitable contributions by accrual basis corporations (Chapter 2), dividend distributions by S corporations (Chapter 12), and the dividend deduction allowed in applying the tax on unreasonable accumulation of corporate earnings and the tax on personal holding companies (Chapter 6).

**Coping with Inflation.**   During periods of inflation, bracket creep has plagued the working person. Because of the progressive nature of the income tax, any wage adjustment to compensate for inflation can increase the income tax bracket of the recipient. The overall impact is an erosion of purchasing power. Congress recognized this problem and began to adjust various income tax components (the **indexation** procedure) in 1985, based upon the rise in the consumer price index over the prior year. For example, due to the inflation factor, the amount of a personal and dependency exemption has been increased over the years. Indexation also applies to dollar amounts of other components, including the tax brackets and the standard deduction.

---

[22]Under the installment method, each payment received by the seller represents a return of basis (the nontaxable portion) and profit from the sale (the taxable portion).

## POLITICAL CONSIDERATIONS

A large segment of the Federal tax law is made up of statutory provisions. Since these statutes are enacted by Congress, is it any surprise that political considerations influence tax law? For purposes of discussion, the effect of political considerations on the tax law is divided into the following topics: special interest legislation, political expediency, and state and local influences.

**Special Interest Legislation.**   Unquestionably, certain provisions of the tax law can be explained largely by looking to the political influence some pressure groups have exerted on Congress. For example, is there any other reason why prepaid subscription and dues income is not taxed until earned while prepaid rents are taxed to the landlord in the year received? These exceptions came about because certain organizations (e.g., the American Automobile Association) convinced Congress that special tax treatment was needed to cover income received from multiyear dues and subscriptions.

Special interest legislation is not necessarily to be condemned if it can be justified on economic or social grounds. At any rate, it is an inevitable product of our political system.

**Political Expediency.**   Various tax reform proposals rise and fall in favor, depending upon the shifting moods of the American public. That Congress is sensitive to popular feeling is an accepted fact. Therefore, certain provisions of the tax law can be explained on the basis of the political climate at the time of enactment. Once the general public became aware that certain large and profitable corporations were able to avoid the corporate income tax, Congress responded with an alternative minimum tax. Since a portion of a corporation's adjusted current earnings has been made a tax preference item, many large corporations no longer escape taxation (see Chapter 6).

Measures that deter more affluent taxpayers from obtaining so-called preferential tax treatment have always had popular appeal and, consequently, the support of Congress. Provisions such as the alternative minimum tax, the imputed interest rules, and the limitation on the deductibility of interest on investment indebtedness can be explained on this basis. In the same vein are the provisions imposing penalty taxes on corporations that unreasonably accumulate earnings or are classified as personal holding companies (see Chapter 6).

The provisions raising income tax rates on more affluent taxpayers and increasing the amount of the earned income credit are also at least partially attributable to political expediency.

**State and Local Influences.**   Political considerations have played a major role in the exclusion from gross income of interest received on state and local obligations. In view of the furor that has been raised by state and local political figures every time repeal of this tax provision has been proposed, one might well regard it as sacred.

Somewhat less apparent has been the influence state law has had in shaping our present Federal tax law. Of prime importance in this regard has been the effect of the community property system employed in some states.[23] At one time, the tax

---

[23]The states with community property systems are Louisiana, Texas, New Mexico, Arizona, California, Washington, Idaho, Nevada, Wisconsin, and (if elected by the spouses) Alaska. The rest of the states are classified as common law jurisdictions. The difference between common law and community property systems centers around the property rights possessed by married persons. In a common law system, each spouse owns whatever he or she earns. Under a community property system, one-half of the earnings of

position of the residents of these states was so advantageous that many common law states actually adopted community property systems.[24] The political pressure placed on Congress to correct the disparity in tax treatment was considerable. To a large extent, this was accomplished in the Revenue Act of 1948, which extended many of the community property tax advantages to residents of common law jurisdictions.[25] Thus, common law states avoided the trauma of discarding the time-honored legal system familiar to everyone. The impact of community property law on the Federal estate and gift taxes is further explored in Chapters 17 and 18.

## INFLUENCE OF THE INTERNAL REVENUE SERVICE

**LO.3**

Understand how the IRS, as the protector of the revenue, has affected tax law.

The IRS has been influential in many areas beyond its role in issuing administrative pronouncements. In its capacity as the protector of the national revenue, the IRS has been instrumental in securing the passage of much legislation designed to curtail the most flagrant tax avoidance practices (closing tax loopholes). In its capacity as the administrator of the tax laws, the IRS has sought and obtained legislation to make its job easier (administrative feasibility).

**The IRS as Protector of the Revenue.**   Innumerable examples can be given of provisions in the tax law that have stemmed from the direct efforts of the IRS to prevent taxpayers from exploiting a loophole. Working within the letter of existing law, ingenious taxpayers and their advisers devise techniques that accomplish indirectly what cannot be accomplished directly. As a consequence, legislation is enacted to close the loophole that taxpayers have located and exploited. The following examples can be explained in this fashion and are discussed in more detail in the chapters to follow:

- The use of a fiscal year by personal service corporations, partnerships, S corporations, and trusts to defer income recognition to the owners (see Chapters 2, 10, 12, and 19).
- The use of the cash basis method of accounting by certain large corporations (see Chapter 2).
- The deduction of passive investment losses and expenses against other income (see Chapter 11).
- The shifting of income to lower-bracket taxpayers through the use of reversionary trusts (see Chapter 19).

In addition, the IRS has secured from Congress legislation of a more general nature that enables it to make adjustments based upon the substance, rather than the formal construction, of what a taxpayer has done. One provision, for example, authorizes the IRS to establish guidelines on the thin capitalization issue. This question involves when corporate debt will be recognized as debt for tax purposes and when it will be reclassified as equity or stock (see the discussion of thin capitalization in Chapter 3). Another provision permits the IRS to make adjustments to a taxpayer's method of accounting when the method used by the taxpayer does not clearly reflect income. The IRS has also been granted the authority to allocate

---

each spouse is considered owned by the other spouse. Assume, for example, Harold and Ruth are husband and wife, and their only income is the $40,000 annual salary Harold receives. If they live in New York (a common law state), the $40,000 salary belongs to Harold. If, however, they live in Texas (a community property state), the $40,000 salary is divided equally, in terms of ownership, between Harold and Ruth.
[24]Such states included Michigan, Oklahoma, and Pennsylvania.

[25]The major advantage extended was the provision allowing married taxpayers to file joint returns and compute the tax liability as if the income had been earned one-half by each spouse. This result is automatic in a community property state since half of the income earned by one spouse belongs to the other spouse. The income-splitting benefits of a joint return are now incorporated as part of the tax rates applicable to married taxpayers.

income and deductions among businesses owned or controlled by the same interests when the allocation is necessary to prevent the evasion of taxes or to reflect the income of each business clearly.

**EXAMPLE 12**

Gold Corporation and Silver Corporation are brother-sister corporations (the stock of each is owned by the same shareholders), and both use the calendar year for tax purposes. For the current tax year, each has taxable income as follows: $335,000 for Gold Corporation and $50,000 for Silver Corporation. Not included in Gold Corporation's taxable income, however, is $10,000 of rent income usually charged Silver Corporation for the use of some property owned by Gold. Since the parties have not clearly reflected the taxable income of each business, the IRS can allocate $10,000 of rent income to Gold Corporation. After the allocation, Gold Corporation has taxable income of $345,000, and Silver Corporation has taxable income of $40,000.[26] ■

Also of a general nature is the authority Congress has given the IRS to prevent taxpayers from acquiring corporations to obtain a tax advantage when the principal purpose of the acquisition is the evasion or avoidance of the Federal income tax. The provision of the tax law that provides this authority is discussed briefly in Chapter 7.

**Administrative Feasibility.** Some of the tax law is justified on the grounds that it simplifies the task of the IRS in collecting the revenue and administering the law. With regard to collecting the revenue, the IRS long ago realized the importance of placing taxpayers on a pay-as-you-go basis. Elaborate withholding procedures apply to wages, while the tax on other types of income may have to be paid at periodic intervals throughout the year. The IRS has been instrumental in convincing the courts that accrual basis taxpayers should pay taxes on prepaid income in the year received and not when earned. This approach may be contrary to generally accepted accounting principles, but it is consistent with the wherewithal to pay concept.

Of considerable aid to the IRS in collecting revenue are the numerous provisions that impose interest and penalties on taxpayers for noncompliance with the tax law. These provisions include penalties for failure to pay a tax or to file a return that is due and the negligence penalty for intentional disregard of rules and regulations. Various penalties for civil and criminal fraud also serve as deterrents to taxpayer noncompliance. This aspect of the tax law is discussed in Chapter 16.

One of the keys to the effective administration of our tax system is the audit process conducted by the IRS. To carry out this function, the IRS is aided by provisions that reduce the chance of taxpayer error or manipulation and therefore simplify the audit effort that is necessary. An increase in the amount of the standard deduction reduces the number of individual taxpayers who will be in a position to claim itemized deductions. With fewer deductions to check, the audit function is simplified.[27] The same objective can be used to explain the $345,800 unified estate and gift tax credit in 2003 and the $11,000 annual gift tax exclusion (see Chapter 17). These provisions decrease the number of tax returns that must be filed (as well as reduce the taxes paid) and thereby save audit effort.[28]

---

[26]By shifting $10,000 of income to Gold Corporation (which is in the 34% bracket), the IRS gains $3,400 in taxes. Allowing the $10,000 deduction to Silver Corporation (which is in the 15% bracket) costs the IRS only $1,500. See Chapter 2 for a further discussion of the income tax rates applicable to corporations.

[27]The IRS gave the same justification when it proposed to Congress the $100 per event limitation on personal casualty and theft losses. Imposition of the limitation eliminated many casualty and theft

loss deductions and, as a consequence, saved the IRS considerable audit time. Also, an additional limitation equal to 10% of adjusted gross income applies to the total of nonbusiness losses after reduction by the floor of $100 for each loss.

[28]Particularly in the case of nominal gifts among family members, taxpayer compliance in reporting and paying a tax on such transfers would be questionable. The absence of the $11,000 gift tax exclusion would create a serious enforcement problem for the IRS.

LO.4

Recognize the role of the courts in interpreting and shaping tax law.

## INFLUENCE OF THE COURTS

In addition to interpreting statutory provisions and the administrative pronouncements issued by the IRS, the Federal courts have influenced tax law in two other respects.[29] First, the courts have formulated certain judicial concepts that serve as guides in the application of various tax provisions. Second, certain key decisions have led to changes in the Internal Revenue Code. Understanding this influence helps explain some of our tax laws.

**Judicial Concepts Relating to Tax Law.**   Although ranking the tax concepts developed by the courts in order of importance is difficult, the concept of substance over form would almost certainly be near the top of any list. Variously described as the "telescoping" or "collapsing" process or the "step transaction approach," it involves determining the true substance of what occurred. In a transaction involving many steps, any one step may be collapsed (or disregarded) to arrive directly at the result reached.

**EXAMPLE 13**

In 2003, Mrs. Greer, a widow, wants to give $22,000 to Jean without incurring any gift tax liability.[30] She knows that the law permits her to give up to $11,000 each year per person without any tax consequences (the annual exclusion). With this in mind, the following steps are taken: a gift by Mrs. Greer to Jean of $11,000 (nontaxable because of the $11,000 annual exclusion), a gift by Mrs. Greer to Ben of $11,000 (also nontaxable), and a gift by Ben to Jean of $11,000 (nontaxable because of Ben's annual exclusion). Considering only the form of what Mrs. Greer and Ben have done, all appears well from a tax standpoint. In substance, however, what has happened? By collapsing the steps involving Ben, it is apparent that Mrs. Greer has made a gift of $22,000 to Jean and therefore has not avoided the Federal gift tax. ■

The substance over form concept plays an important role in transactions involving corporations.

Another leading tax concept developed by the courts deals with the interpretation of statutory tax provisions that operate to benefit taxpayers. The courts have established the rule that these relief provisions are to be narrowly construed against taxpayers if there is any doubt about their application. Suppose, for example, Beige Corporation wants to be treated as an S corporation (see Chapter 12) but has not satisfied the statutory requirements for making the required election. Because S corporation status is a relief provision favoring taxpayers, chances are the courts will deny Beige Corporation this treatment.

Important in the area of corporate-shareholder dealings (see the discussion of constructive dividends in Chapter 4) and in the resolution of valuation problems for estate and gift tax purposes (see Chapters 17 and 18) is the **arm's length concept.** Particularly in dealings between related parties, transactions can be tested by questioning whether the taxpayers acted in an "arm's length" manner. The question to be asked is: Would unrelated parties have handled the transaction in the same way?

**EXAMPLE 14**

The sole shareholder of a corporation leases property to the corporation for a monthly rental of $50,000. To test whether the corporation should be allowed a rent deduction for this amount, the IRS and the courts will apply the arm's length concept. Would the corporation have paid $50,000 a month in rent if the same property had been leased from an unrelated party (rather than from the sole shareholder)? ■

---

[29]A great deal of case law is devoted to ascertaining congressional intent. The courts, in effect, ask: What did Congress have in mind when it enacted a particular tax provision?

[30]The example assumes that Mrs. Greer has exhausted her unified tax credit. See Chapter 17.

The **continuity of interest concept** originated with the courts but has, in many situations, been incorporated into statutory provisions of the tax law. Primarily concerned with business readjustments, the concept permits tax-free treatment only if the taxpayer retains a substantial continuing interest in the property transferred to the new business. Due to the continuing interest retained, the transfer should not have tax consequences because the position of the taxpayer has not changed. This concept applies to transfers to controlled corporations (Chapter 3), corporate reorganizations (Chapter 7), and transfers to partnerships (Chapter 10). The continuity of interest concept helps explain the results reached in Examples 5 through 7 of this chapter. This concept is further discussed in Chapter 7.

Also developed by the courts, the **business purpose concept** principally applies to transactions involving corporations. Under this concept, some sound business reason that motivates the transaction must be present in order for the prescribed tax treatment to result. The avoidance of taxation is not considered to be a sound business purpose.

**EXAMPLE 15**

Beth and Charles are equal shareholders in Brown Corporation. They have recently disagreed about the company's operations and are at an impasse about the future of Brown Corporation. This shareholder disagreement on corporate policy constitutes a sound business purpose and would justify a division of Brown Corporation that will permit Beth and Charles to go their separate ways. Whether the division of Brown would be nontaxable to the parties depends on their compliance with the statutory provisions dealing with corporate reorganizations. The point is, however, that compliance with statutory provisions would not be enough to ensure nontaxability without a business purpose for the transaction. ■

The business purpose concept is discussed further in Chapter 7.

**Judicial Influence on Statutory Provisions.**    Some court decisions have been of such consequence that Congress has incorporated them into statutory tax law. An illustration of this influence appears in Example 16.

**EXAMPLE 16**

In 1983, Brad claimed a capital loss of $100,000 for Tan Corporation stock that had become worthless during the year. In the absence of any offsetting gains, the capital loss deduction produced no income tax savings for Brad either in 1983 or in future years. In 1986, Brad institutes a lawsuit against the former officers of Tan Corporation for their misconduct that resulted in the corporation's failure and thereby led to Brad's $100,000 loss. In settlement of the suit, the officers pay $50,000 to Brad. The IRS argued that the full $50,000 should be taxed as gain to Brad. The Tan stock was written off in 1983 and had a zero basis for tax purposes. The $50,000 recovery Brad received on the stock was, therefore, all gain. The IRS's position was logical, but not equitable. The court stated that Brad should not be taxed on the recovery of an amount previously deducted unless the deduction produced a tax savings. Since the $100,000 capital loss deduction in 1983 produced no tax benefit, none of the $50,000 received in 1986 results in gain. ■

The decision reached by the courts in Example 16, known as the **tax benefit rule,** is part of the statutory tax law.

Court decisions sometimes create uncertainty about the tax law. Such decisions may reach the right result but do not produce the guidelines necessary to enable taxpayers to comply. In many situations, Congress may be compelled to add certainty to the law by enacting statutory provisions specifying when a particular tax consequence will or will not materialize. The following are examples of this type of judicial "cause" and the statutory "effect":

- When a stock redemption will be treated as an exchange or as a dividend (see Chapter 5).
- What basis a parent corporation will have in the assets received from a subsidiary that is liquidated shortly after its acquisition (see Chapter 5).

Some of the statutory provisions can be explained by a negative reaction by Congress to a particular court decision. One decision, for example, held that the transfer of a liability to a controlled corporation should be treated as boot received by the transferor (see Chapter 3). Congress apparently disagreed with this treatment and promptly enacted legislation to change the result.

### SUMMARY

In addition to its revenue-raising objective, the Federal tax law has developed in response to several other factors:

- *Economic considerations.* Here, the emphasis is on tax provisions that help regulate the economy and encourage certain activities and types of businesses.
- *Social considerations.* Some tax provisions are designed to encourage or discourage certain socially desirable or undesirable practices.
- *Equity considerations.* Of principal concern in this area are tax provisions that alleviate the effect of multiple taxation, recognize the wherewithal to pay concept, mitigate the effect of the annual accounting period concept, and recognize the eroding effect of inflation.
- *Political considerations.* Of significance in this regard are tax provisions that represent special interest legislation, reflect political expediency, and illustrate the effect of state law.
- *Influence of the IRS.* Many tax provisions are intended to aid the IRS in collecting revenue and administering the tax law.
- *Influence of the courts.* Court decisions have established a body of judicial concepts relating to tax law and have, on occasion, led Congress to enact statutory provisions that either clarify or negate their effect.

These factors explain various tax provisions and thereby help in understanding why the tax law developed to its present state. The next step involves learning to work with the tax law.

# Working with the Tax Law—Tax Sources

Understanding taxation requires a mastery of the sources of tax law. These sources include not only the legislative provisions in the Internal Revenue Code, but also congressional Committee Reports, Regulations, Treasury Department pronouncements, and court decisions. Thus, the primary sources of tax information are the pronouncements of the three branches of government: legislative, executive, and judicial.

The law is of little significance, however, until it is applied to a set of facts and circumstances. A tax researcher must not only be able to read and interpret the sources of the law but must also understand the relative weight of authority within the rules of law. Learning to work with the tax law involves three basic steps:

1. Familiarity with the sources of the law.
2. Application of research techniques.
3. Effective use of planning procedures.

The remainder of this chapter introduces the sources of tax law and explains how the law is applied to problems and conditions of individual and business transactions. Statutory, administrative, and judicial sources of the tax law are considered first.

## STATUTORY SOURCES OF THE TAX LAW

**Origin of the Internal Revenue Code.**   Before 1939, the statutory provisions relating to taxation were contained in the individual revenue acts enacted by Congress. The inconvenience and confusion that resulted from dealing with many separate acts led Congress to codify all of the Federal tax laws. Known as the Internal Revenue Code of 1939, the codification arranged all Federal tax provisions in a logical sequence and placed them in a separate part of the Federal statutes. A further rearrangement took place in 1954 and resulted in the Internal Revenue Code of 1954.

Perhaps to emphasize the magnitude of the changes made by the Tax Reform Act (TRA) of 1986, Congress redesignated the Internal Revenue Code of 1954 as the Internal Revenue Code of 1986. This change is somewhat deceiving since the tax law was not recodified in 1986, as it had been in 1954. TRA of 1986 merely amended, deleted, or added provisions to the Internal Revenue Code of 1954. For example, before TRA of 1986, § 336 provided the general rule that no gain or loss would be recognized by a corporation when it distributed assets in kind to its shareholders in complete liquidation (see Chapter 5). After the effective date of TRA of 1986, § 336 provides that gain or loss will be recognized upon the same distributions.

The following observations will help clarify the significance of the three Codes:

- Neither the 1939, the 1954, nor the 1986 Code changed all of the tax law existing on the date of enactment. Much of the 1939 Code, for example, was incorporated into the 1954 Code. The same can be said for the transition from the 1954 to the 1986 Code. This point is important in assessing judicial and administrative decisions interpreting provisions under prior Codes. For example, a decision interpreting § 61 of the Internal Revenue Code of 1954 will have continuing validity since this provision carried over unchanged to the Internal Revenue Code of 1986.
- Statutory amendments to the tax law are integrated into the existing Code. Thus, the Tax Relief Reconciliation Act of 2001 and the Job Creation and Worker Assistance Act of 2002 became part of the Internal Revenue Code of 1986.

Do not conclude, however, that the codification and recodification process has made the Internal Revenue Code a simplistic body of laws. To a large extent, the complexity of our current Code can be attributed to its growth.

**The Legislative Process.**   Federal tax legislation generally originates in the House of Representatives, where it is first considered by the House Ways and Means Committee. Tax bills originate in the Senate when they are attached as riders to other legislative proposals.[31] If acceptable to the House Ways and Means Committee, the proposed bill is referred to the entire House of Representatives for approval or disapproval. Approved bills are sent to the Senate, where they are referred to the Senate Finance Committee for further consideration.

---

[31]The Tax Equity and Fiscal Responsibility Act of 1982 originated in the Senate; its constitutionality was unsuccessfully challenged in the courts. The Senate version of the Deficit Reduction Act of 1984 was attached as an amendment to the Federal Boat Safety Act.

In the next step, the bill is referred from the Senate Finance Committee to the whole Senate. Assuming no disagreement between the House and the Senate, a bill passed by the Senate is referred to the President for approval or veto. If the bill is approved or if the President's veto is overridden, the bill becomes law and part of the Internal Revenue Code.

When the Senate version of the bill differs from that passed by the House, the Joint Conference Committee resolves these differences. The Joint Conference Committee includes members of the House Ways and Means Committee and the Senate Finance Committee.

Referrals from the House Ways and Means Committee, the Senate Finance Committee, and the Joint Conference Committee are usually accompanied by Committee Reports. These Committee Reports often explain the provisions of the proposed legislation and are therefore a valuable source in ascertaining the *intent* of Congress. What Congress has in mind when it considers and enacts tax legislation is, of course, the key to interpreting that legislation. Since Regulations normally are not issued immediately after a statute is enacted, taxpayers often look to Committee Reports to ascertain congressional intent.

The typical legislative process dealing with tax bills can be summarized as follows:

## NAMING TAX BENEFITS

Education IRAs have been renamed Coverdell Education Savings Accounts after the late Senator Paul Coverdell (a Republican from Georgia). They join other named benefits including Roth IRAs, Archer Medical Savings Accounts, and Keogh Plans.

A former IRS Commissioner, Donald Alexander, has suggested that "since we can't keep politicians' names out of the Internal Revenue Code and our surplus is disappearing, how about getting needed revenue by auctioning naming rights to Code provisions? Naming rights might be marketed for five-year terms (or until repeal), and bidding should be brisk for the most desirable provisions."

The role of the Joint Conference Committee indicates the importance of compromise in the legislative process. The practical effect of the compromise process can be illustrated by reviewing what happened in the Revenue Reconciliation Act (RRA) of 1993 (H.R. 2264) with respect to the amortization of acquired goodwill:

Some tax provisions are commonly referred to by the number the bill received in the House when first proposed or by the name of the member of Congress sponsoring the legislation. For example, the Self-Employed Individuals Tax Retirement Act of 1962 is popularly known as H.R. 10 (the House of Representatives Bill No. 10) or as the Keogh Act (Keogh being one of the members of Congress sponsoring the bill).

**Arrangement of the Code.**   In working with the Code, it helps to understand the format. Note the following partial table of contents:

Subtitle A. Income Taxes
  Chapter 1. Normal Taxes and Surtaxes
    Subchapter A. Determination of Tax Liability
      Part I. Tax on Individuals
        Sections 1–5
      Part II. Tax on Corporations
        Sections 11–12
          * * *

In referring to a provision of the Code, the *key* is usually the Section number. In citing Section 2(a) (dealing with the status of a surviving spouse), for example, it is unnecessary to include Subtitle A, Chapter 1, Subchapter A, Part I. Merely mentioning Section 2(a) will suffice since the Section numbers run consecutively and do not begin again with each new Subtitle, Chapter, Subchapter, or Part. Not all Code Section numbers are used, however. Note that Part I ends with Section 5 and Part II starts with Section 11 (at present there are no Sections 6, 7, 8, 9, and 10).[32]

Tax practitioners commonly refer to a specific area of income taxation by Subchapter designation. Some of the more common Subchapter designations include Subchapter C (Corporate Distributions and Adjustments), Subchapter K (Partners and Partnerships), and Subchapter S (Tax Treatment of S Corporations and Their Shareholders). Particularly in the last situation, it is much more convenient to describe the subject of the applicable Code provisions (Sections 1361 through 1379) as S corporation status rather than as the "Tax Treatment of S Corporations and Their Shareholders."

**Citing the Code.**   Code Sections often are broken down into subparts.[33] Section 2(a)(1)(A) serves as an example.

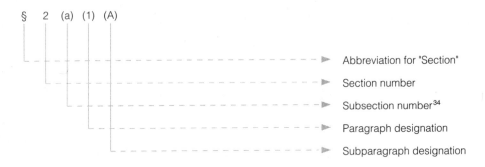

Broken down as to content, § 2(a)(1)(A) becomes:

Throughout this text, references to Code Sections are in the form just given. The symbols "§" and "§§" are used in place of "Section" and "Sections." Unless otherwise stated, all Code references are to the Internal Revenue Code of 1986. The format followed in the remainder of the text is summarized as follows:

---

[32]When the 1954 Code was drafted, Section numbers were intentionally omitted. This omission provided flexibility to incorporate later changes into the Code without disrupting its organization. When Congress does not leave enough space, subsequent Code Sections are given A, B, C, etc., designations. A good example is the treatment of §§ 280A through 280H.

[33]Some Code Sections do not have subparts. See, for example, § 482.
[34]Some Code Sections omit the subsection designation and use, instead, the paragraph designation as the first subpart. See, for example, §§ 212(1) and 1221(1).

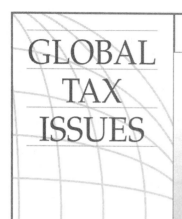

### PROTECTION AGAINST DOUBLE TAXATION

In order to eliminate the double taxation that a taxpayer might incur if subject to tax in two countries, the United States has entered into treaties with most of the major countries of the world. Often there are multiple treaties with a country covering various tax issues. Treasury Publication 901 entitled "U.S. Tax Treaties" states that treaty provisions are generally reciprocal (apply to both treaty countries). Thus, a U.S. citizen or resident who receives income from a treaty country may refer to tables in this publication to see if a tax treaty might affect the tax to be paid to that foreign country. As part of the proof of entitlement to the treaty benefits, foreign countries sometimes require certification from the U.S. Government that an applicant files an income tax return as a U.S. citizen or resident.

| Complete Reference | Text Reference |
|---|---|
| Section 2(a)(1)(A) of the Internal Revenue Code of 1986 | § 2(a)(1)(A) |
| Sections 1 and 2 of the Internal Revenue Code of 1986 | §§ 1 and 2 |
| Section 2 of the Internal Revenue Code of 1954 | § 2 of the Internal Revenue Code of 1954 |
| Section 12(d) of the Internal Revenue Code of 1939[35] | § 12(d) of the Internal Revenue Code of 1939 |

**Effect of Treaties.**   The United States signs certain tax treaties (sometimes called tax conventions) with foreign countries to render mutual assistance in tax enforcement and to avoid double taxation. The Technical and Miscellaneous Revenue Act of 1988 provided that neither a tax law nor a tax treaty takes general precedence. Thus, when there is a direct conflict, the most recent item will take precedence. More than 34 Sections of the Code contain direct references to treaties [e.g., § 245(a)(10)].

## ADMINISTRATIVE SOURCES OF THE TAX LAW

The administrative sources of the Federal tax law can be grouped as follows: Treasury Department Regulations, Revenue Rulings and Procedures, and various other administrative pronouncements. All are issued either by the U.S. Treasury Department or the IRS. The role played by the IRS in this process is considered in greater depth in Chapter 16.

**Treasury Department Regulations.**   Regulations are issued by the U.S. Treasury Department under authority granted by Congress. Interpretative by nature, they provide taxpayers with considerable guidance on the meaning and application of the Code. Although not issued by Congress, Regulations do carry considerable weight. They are an important factor to consider in complying with the tax law.

---

[35]Section 12(d) of the Internal Revenue Code of 1939 is the predecessor to § 2 of the Internal Revenue Code of 1954. Keep in mind that the 1954 Code superseded the 1939 Code.

Anyone taking a position contrary to a finalized Regulation must disclose that fact on Form 8275 or Form 8275–R in order to avoid costly penalties.

Since Regulations interpret the Code, they are arranged in the same sequence. Regulations are, however, prefixed by a number that indicates the type of tax or administrative, procedural, or definitional matter to which they relate. For example, the prefix 1 designates the Regulations under the income tax law. Thus, the Regulations under Code § 2 would be cited as Reg. § 1.2, with subparts added for further identification. The numbering of these subparts often has no correlation with the Code subsections. The prefix 20 designates estate tax Regulations; 25 covers gift tax Regulations; 31 relates to employment taxes; and 301 refers to Regulations dealing with procedure and administration. This listing is not all-inclusive.

New Regulations and changes in existing Regulations usually are issued in proposed form before they are finalized. The time interval between the proposal of a Regulation and its finalization permits taxpayers and other interested parties to comment on the propriety of the proposal. **Proposed Regulations** under Code § 2, for example, would be cited as Prop.Reg. § 1.2.

Sometimes the Treasury Department issues **Temporary Regulations** relating to elections and other matters where immediate guidance is critical. Temporary Regulations often are needed for recent legislation that takes effect immediately. Temporary Regulations have the same authoritative value as final Regulations and may be cited as precedent for three years. Temporary Regulations also are issued as Proposed Regulations and automatically expire within three years after the date of issuance. Temporary Regulations and the simultaneously issued Proposed Regulations carry more weight than traditional Proposed Regulations. An example of a Temporary Regulation is Temp.Reg. § 1.861–9T(g)(3)(i), which clarifies single-category assets.

Proposed, final, and Temporary Regulations are published in the *Federal Register* and are reproduced in major tax services. Final Regulations are issued as Treasury Decisions (TDs).

### Revenue Rulings and Revenue Procedures.

**Revenue Rulings** are official pronouncements of the National Office of the IRS. Like Regulations, Revenue Rulings are designed to provide interpretation of the tax law. However, they do not carry the same legal force and effect as Regulations and usually deal with more restricted problems.

A Revenue Ruling often results from a specific taxpayer's request for a letter ruling. If the IRS believes that a taxpayer's request for a letter ruling deserves official publication due to its widespread impact, the holding will be converted into a Revenue Ruling. In making this conversion, names, identifying facts, and money amounts are changed to disguise the identity of the requesting taxpayer. The IRS then issues what would have been a letter ruling as a Revenue Ruling.

**Revenue Procedures** are issued in the same manner as Revenue Rulings, but deal with the internal management practices and procedures of the IRS. Familiarity with these procedures increases taxpayer compliance and helps make the administration of the tax laws more efficient. Revenue Procedures often involve mechanical rules, but sometimes substantive positions are embedded in them as well. Revenue Rulings and Revenue Procedures serve an important function in that they provide guidance to both IRS personnel and taxpayers in handling routine tax matters.

Both Revenue Rulings and Revenue Procedures are published weekly by the U.S. Government in the *Internal Revenue Bulletin* (I.R.B.). Semiannually, the bulletins for a six-month period are gathered together and published in a bound volume called the *Cumulative Bulletin* (C.B.).[36] The proper form for citing Rulings and Procedures depends on whether the item has been published in the *Cumulative Bulletin* or is available in I.R.B. form. Consider, for example, the following transition:

Temporary Citation
{ Rev.Rul. 2002–4, I.R.B. No. 4, 389.
*Explanation:* Revenue Ruling Number 4, appearing on page 389 of the 4th weekly issue of the *Internal Revenue Bulletin* for 2002.

Permanent Citation
{ Rev.Rul. 2002–4, 2002–1 C.B. 389.
*Explanation:* Revenue Ruling Number 4, appearing on page 389 of volume 1 of the *Cumulative Bulletin* for 2002.

Note that the page reference of 389 is the same for both the I.R.B. (temporary) and the C.B. (permanent) versions of the Ruling. The IRS numbers the pages of the I.R.B.s consecutively for each six-month period to facilitate their conversion to C.B. form.

Revenue Procedures are cited in the same manner, except that "Rev.Proc." is substituted for "Rev.Rul." Procedures, like Rulings, are published in the *Internal Revenue Bulletin* (the temporary source) and later transferred to the *Cumulative Bulletin* (the permanent source).

**Other Administrative Pronouncements.**　Treasury Decisions (TDs) are issued by the Treasury Department to promulgate new Regulations, to amend or otherwise change existing Regulations, or to announce the position of the Government on selected court decisions. Like Revenue Rulings and Revenue Procedures, TDs are published in the *Internal Revenue Bulletin* and subsequently transferred to the *Cumulative Bulletin*.

Technical Information Releases (TIRs) are usually issued to announce the publication of various IRS pronouncements (e.g., Revenue Rulings, Revenue Procedures).

**Letter rulings** are issued for a fee by the National Office of the IRS upon a taxpayer's request and describe how the IRS will treat a proposed transaction for tax purposes. In general, they apply only to the taxpayer who asks for and obtains the ruling, but post-1984 rulings may be substantial authority for purposes of avoiding the accuracy-related penalties.[37] This procedure may sound like the only real way to carry out effective tax planning. However, the IRS limits the issuance of letter rulings to restricted, preannounced areas of taxation. Thus, a ruling may not be obtained on many of the problems that are particularly troublesome for taxpayers.[38] For example, the IRS will not issue a ruling as to whether compensation paid to shareholder-employees is reasonable (see Chapter 4) or whether § 269 applies (the acquisition of a corporation to evade or avoid income tax [see Chapter 7]). The main reason the IRS will not rule on such matters is that they involve fact-oriented situations.

The IRS must make letter rulings available for public inspection after identifying details are deleted. Published digests of private letter rulings can be found in *Private Letter Rulings* (published by Research Institute of America), BNA *Daily Tax Reports*, and Tax Analysts & Advocates *Tax Notes*. IRS Letter Rulings Reports (published by

---

[36]Usually, only two volumes of the *Cumulative Bulletin* are published each year. However, when major tax legislation has been enacted by Congress, other volumes may be published containing the congressional Committee Reports supporting the Revenue Act. See, for example, the two extra volumes for 1984 dealing with the Deficit Reduction Act of 1984. The 1984–3 *Cumulative Bulletin*, Volume 1, contains the text of the law itself; 1984–3, Volume 2, contains the Committee Reports. There are a total of four volumes of the *Cumula-*

*tive Bulletin* for 1984: 1984–1; 1984–2; 1984–3, Volume 1; and 1984–3, Volume 2.

[37]Notice 90–20, 1990–1 C.B. 328, part V (A).

[38]Rev.Proc. 2003–3, I.R.B. No. 1, 113, contains a listing of areas in which the IRS will not issue advance rulings. From time to time, subsequent Revenue Procedures are issued that modify or amplify Rev.Proc. 2003–3.

Commerce Clearing House) contains both digests and full texts of all letter rulings. *Letter Ruling Review* (Tax Analysts), a monthly publication, selects and discusses the more important of the approximately 200 letter rulings per month.

The National Office of the IRS releases technical advice memoranda (TAMs) weekly. TAMs resemble letter rulings in that they give the IRS's determination of an issue. Letter rulings, however, are responses to requests by taxpayers, whereas TAMs are issued by the National Office of the IRS in response to questions raised by taxpayers or IRS field personnel during audits. TAMs deal with completed rather than proposed transactions and are often requested for questions relating to exempt organizations and employee plans. Although TAMs are not officially published and may not be cited or used as precedent, post-1984 TAMs may be substantial authority for purposes of the accuracy-related penalties. See Chapter 16 for a discussion of these penalties.

*Both* letter rulings and TAMs are issued with multidigit file numbers. Consider, for example, Ltr.Rul. 200231006, which states that an S corporation may split off one of its businesses to a shareholder in a tax-free divisive reorganization. Broken down by digits, the file number reveals the following information:

| Ltr.Rul. | 2002 | 31 | 006 |
|---|---|---|---|
| | 2002 was year of issuance | Was issued in the 31st week | Was the 6th ruling issued during the 31st week |

Letter rulings and TAMs issued before 2000 are often cited with only two-digit years (e.g., Ltr.Rul. 9933108).

Like letter rulings, **determination letters** are issued at the request of taxpayers and provide guidance concerning the application of the tax law. They differ from individual rulings in that the issuing source is the Area Director rather than the National Office of the IRS. Also, determination letters usually involve completed (as opposed to proposed) transactions. Determination letters are not published but are made known only to the party making the request.

The following examples illustrate the distinction between individual rulings and determination letters:

**EXAMPLE 17**

The shareholders of Black Corporation and White Corporation want assurance that the consolidation of the corporations into Gray Corporation will be a nontaxable reorganization (see Chapter 7). The proper approach is to request from the National Office of the IRS an individual ruling concerning the income tax effect of the proposed transaction. ∎

**EXAMPLE 18**

Gilbert operates a barber shop in which he employs eight barbers. To comply with the rules governing income tax and payroll tax withholdings, Gilbert wants to know whether the barbers working for him are employees or independent contractors. The proper procedure is to request a determination letter on the status of the barbers from the Area Director in Austin, Texas, or Newport, Vermont, depending on the location of the requesting firm. ∎

Field service advice (FSA) memoranda are prepared by the Office of Chief Counsel to help IRS employees. They are issued in response to requests for advice, guidance, and analysis on difficult or significant tax issues. FSAs are not binding on either the taxpayer to whom they pertain or the IRS. For example, FSA 200233016 states that § 269 may be used to disallow foreign tax credits and deductions that

**■ FIGURE 1–1**

Federal Judicial Tax Process

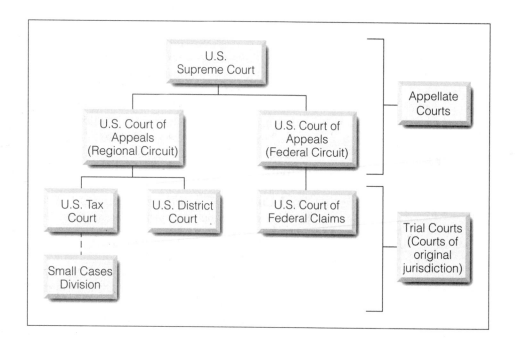

arise from a series of reorganizations if the underlying transaction's principal purpose is to secure tax benefits.

The FSAs are being replaced by a new form of field guidance called the technical expedited advice memorandum (TEAM). The purpose of TEAMs is to expedite legal guidance to field agents as disputes are developing. FSAs revert to their original purpose of case-specific development of facts.

## JUDICIAL SOURCES OF THE TAX LAW

**The Judicial Process in General.**   After a taxpayer has exhausted some or all of the remedies available within the IRS (no satisfactory settlement has been reached at the agent or at the conference level discussed in Chapter 16), the dispute can be taken to the Federal courts. The dispute is first considered by a court of original jurisdiction (known as a trial court) with any appeal (either by the taxpayer or the IRS) taken to the appropriate appellate court. In most situations, the taxpayer has a choice of any of four trial courts: a Federal District Court, the U.S. Court of Federal Claims, the Tax Court, or the Small Cases Division of the Tax Court. The trial and appellate court system for Federal tax litigation is illustrated in Figure 1–1.

The broken line between the Tax Court and the Small Cases Division indicates that there is no appeal from the Small Cases Division. Currently, the jurisdiction of the Small Cases Division of the Tax Court is limited to $50,000 or less. The proceedings of the Small Cases Division are informal, and its decisions are not precedents for any other court decision and are not reviewable by any higher court. Proceedings can be more timely and less expensive in the Small Cases Division. Some of these cases can now be found on the U.S. Tax Court Internet site.

American law, following English law, is frequently *made* by judicial decisions. Under the doctrine of *stare decisis*, each case (except in the Small Cases Division) has precedential value for future cases with the same controlling set of facts.

Judges are not required to follow judicial precedent beyond their own jurisdiction. For example, the decisions of an appellate court are binding only on the trial courts within its jurisdiction and not on other trial courts. Different appellate courts may reach different opinions about the same issue. Further, the doctrine of precedential authority requires a court to follow prior cases only where the issues and material facts of the current case are essentially the same as those involved in the prior decisions.

Most Federal and state appellate court decisions and some decisions of trial courts are published. More than 4 million judicial opinions have been published in the United States; over 130,000 cases are published each year.[39] Published court decisions are organized by jurisdiction (Federal or state) and level of court (appellate or trial).

**Trial Courts.**    The differences between the various trial courts (courts of original jurisdiction) can be summarized as follows:

- There is only one Court of Federal Claims and only one Tax Court, but there are many Federal District Courts. The taxpayer does not select the District Court that will hear the dispute but must sue in the one that has jurisdiction.
- The U.S. Court of Federal Claims has jurisdiction over any claim against the United States that is based on the Constitution, any Act of Congress, or any regulation of an executive department.
- Each District Court has only one judge, the Court of Federal Claims has 16 judges, and the Tax Court has 19 regular judges. In the case of the Tax Court, the whole court will review a case (the case is sent to court conference) only when more important or novel tax issues are involved. Many cases will be heard and decided by one of the 19 regular judges. If a case is reviewed by the full Tax Court, such an *en banc* decision has compelling authority.
- The Court of Federal Claims meets most often in Washington, D.C., while a District Court meets at a prescribed seat for the particular district. Since each state has at least one District Court and many of the populous states have more, the inconvenience and expense of traveling for the taxpayer and counsel (present with many suits in the Court of Federal Claims) are largely eliminated. The Tax Court is officially based in Washington, D.C., but the various judges travel to different parts of the country and hear cases at predetermined locations and dates. This procedure eases the distance problem for the taxpayer, but it can mean a delay before the case comes to trial and is decided.
- The Tax Court hears only tax cases; the Court of Federal Claims and District Courts hear nontax litigation as well. This difference, as well as the fact that many Tax Court justices have been appointed from IRS or Treasury Department positions, has led some to conclude that the Tax Court has more expertise in tax matters.
- The only court in which a taxpayer can obtain a jury trial is a District Court. Juries can decide only questions of fact and not questions of law, however. Therefore, taxpayers who choose the District Court route often do not request a jury trial. In this event, the judge will decide all issues. Note that a District Court decision is controlling only in the district in which the court has jurisdiction.
- Before the Court of Federal Claims or a District Court can have jurisdiction, the taxpayer must pay the tax deficiency assessed by the IRS and then sue

---

[39]Jacobstein, Mersky, and Dunn, *Fundamentals of Legal Research*, 6th edition (Westbury, N.Y.: The Foundation Press, 1994).

## CONCEPT SUMMARY 1–1

### Federal Judicial System

| Issue | U.S. Tax Court | U.S. District Court | U.S. Court of Federal Claims |
|---|---|---|---|
| Number of judges per court | 19* | 1 | 16 |
| Payment of deficiency before trial | No | Yes | Yes |
| Jury trial available | No | Yes | No |
| Types of disputes | Tax cases only | Most criminal/civil cases | Claims against the United States |
| Jurisdiction | Nationwide | Location of taxpayer | Nationwide |
| Appeal route | U.S. Court of Appeals | U.S. Court of Appeals | U.S. Court of Appeals for the Federal Circuit |

*There are also 14 special trial judges and 9 senior judges.

for a refund. If the taxpayer wins (assuming no successful appeal by the IRS), the tax paid plus appropriate interest will be recovered. Jurisdiction in the Tax Court, however, is usually obtained without first paying the assessed tax deficiency. In the event the taxpayer loses in the Tax Court (and no appeal is taken or any appeal is unsuccessful), the deficiency must be paid with accrued interest.

• Appeals from a District Court or a Tax Court decision are to the appropriate U.S. Court of Appeals. Appeals from the Court of Federal Claims go to the Court of Appeals for the Federal Circuit.

• Special trial judges hear small tax cases and write summary opinions. The IRS's deficiency recovery rate is higher here than in regular Tax Court decisions. Beginning in 2001, these summary opinions are now posted on the U.S. Tax Court's Internet site along with regular decisions.

Some of the characteristics of the judicial system described above are summarized in Concept Summary 1–1.

**Appellate Courts.** An appeal from a trial court goes to the U.S. Court of Appeals of appropriate jurisdiction. Generally, a three-judge panel hears a Court of Appeals case, but occasionally the *full* court will decide more controversial conflicts. A jury trial is not available.

Figure 1–2 shows the geographic area within the jurisdiction of each Federal Court of Appeals.

If the IRS loses at the trial court level (District Court, Tax Court, or Court of Federal Claims), it need not (and frequently does not) appeal. The fact that an appeal is not made, however, does not indicate that the IRS agrees with the result and will not litigate similar issues in the future.

The IRS may decide not to appeal for a number of reasons. First, the current litigation load may be heavy. As a consequence, the IRS may decide that available personnel should be assigned to other, more important cases. Second, the IRS may determine that this is not a good case to appeal. For example, the taxpayer may be in a sympathetic position, or the facts may be particularly strong in his or her

**■ FIGURE 1–2**
The Federal Courts of Appeals

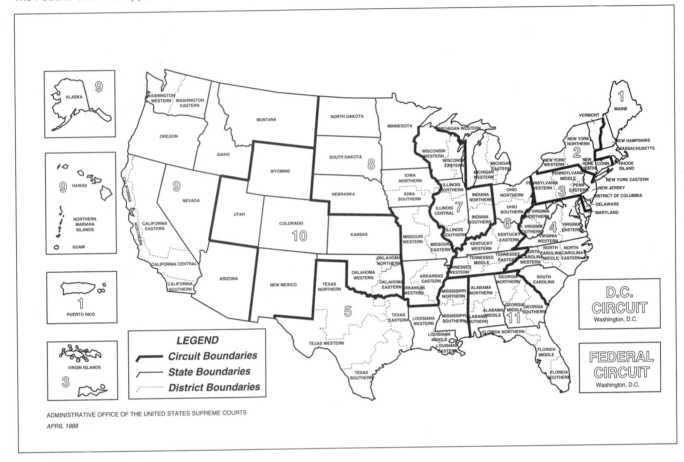

ADMINISTRATIVE OFFICE OF THE UNITED STATES SUPREME COURTS
*APRIL 1988*

favor. In such event, the IRS may wait to test the legal issues involved with a taxpayer who has a much weaker case. Third, if the appeal is from a District Court or the Tax Court, the Court of Appeals of jurisdiction could have some bearing on whether the IRS decides to pursue an appeal. Based on past experience and precedent, the IRS may conclude that the chance for success on a particular issue might be more promising in another Court of Appeals. The IRS will wait for a similar case to arise in a different jurisdiction.

**ETHICAL CONSIDERATIONS**          **Choosing Cases for Appeal**

The IRS loses a tax case against a prominent citizen in the U.S. District Court of Iowa. The taxpayer, a minister, had set up three separate trusts for each of his three children (i.e., a total of nine trusts). The IRS argued that under Reg. § 1.641(a)–0(c) these trusts should be consolidated and treated as three trusts to stop the taxpayer from mitigating the progressive tax structure (e.g., the 38.6 percent top tax bracket).

The IRS has decided to appeal a case in the multiple trust area. As one of the IRS's attorneys, you must choose between the Iowa case and a similar multiple trust conflict in the U.S. District Court of Virginia. Here the taxpayer is a CPA who has established four different trusts for her two children (i.e., a total of eight trusts). [See *Estelle Morris Trusts*, 51 T.C. 20 (1968).] In making your decision, you note that potentially more sympathy may be associated with the minister's profession than with the CPA's. Other considerations are the facts indicating that the attempt at tax avoidance is more egregious in the Iowa case and a colleague's opinion that the Virginia case is winnable. Which case will you select? Comment on whether it is fair for the IRS to select a case to appeal in this fashion.

District Courts, the Tax Court, and the Court of Federal Claims must abide by the precedents set by the Court of Appeals of jurisdiction. A particular Court of Appeals need not follow the decisions of another Court of Appeals. All courts, however, must follow the decisions of the U.S. Supreme Court.

The Tax Court is a national court, meaning that it hears and decides cases from all parts of the country. For many years, the Tax Court followed a policy of deciding cases based on what it thought the result should be, even when its decision might be appealed to a Court of Appeals that had previously decided a similar case differently.

Some years ago, this policy was changed. Now the Tax Court will still decide a case as it feels the law should be applied *only* if the Court of Appeals of appropriate jurisdiction has not yet passed on the issue or has previously decided a similar case in accordance with the Tax Court's decision. If the Court of Appeals of appropriate jurisdiction has previously held squarely in point otherwise, the Tax Court will conform even though it disagrees with the holding.[40] This policy is known as the *Golsen* rule.

**EXAMPLE 19**    Gene lives in Texas and sues in the Tax Court on Issue A. The Fifth Circuit Court of Appeals, the appellate court of appropriate jurisdiction, has already decided, in a case involving similar facts but a different taxpayer, that Issue A should be resolved against the IRS. Although the Tax Court feels that the Fifth Circuit Court of Appeals is wrong, under the *Golsen* rule, it will render judgment for Gene. Shortly thereafter, Beth, a resident of New York, in a comparable case, sues in the Tax Court on Issue A. Assume that the Second Circuit Court of Appeals, the appellate court of appropriate jurisdiction, has never expressed itself on Issue A. Presuming the Tax Court has not reconsidered its position on Issue A, it will decide against Beth. Thus, it is entirely possible for two taxpayers suing in the same court to end up with opposite results merely because they live in different parts of the country. ■

Appeal to the U.S. Supreme Court is by Writ of **Certiorari.** If the Court agrees to hear the case, it will grant the Writ (*cert. granted*). Most often, it will deny jurisdiction (*cert. denied*). For whatever reason or reasons, the Supreme Court rarely hears tax cases. The Court usually grants certiorari to resolve a conflict among the Courts of Appeals (e.g., two or more appellate courts have assumed opposing positions on a particular issue) or when the tax issue is extremely important. The granting of a Writ of Certiorari indicates that at least four members of the Supreme Court believe that the issue is of sufficient importance to be heard by the full Court.

The role of appellate courts is limited to a review of the trial record compiled by the trial courts. Thus, the appellate process usually involves a determination of

---

[40]*Jack E. Golsen*, 54 T.C. 742 (1970); see also *John A. Lardas*, 99 T.C. 490 (1992).

whether the trial court applied the proper law in arriving at its decision. Usually, an appellate court will not dispute a lower court's fact-finding determination.

An appeal can have any of a number of possible outcomes. The appellate court may approve (affirm) or disapprove (reverse) the lower court's finding, and it may also send the case back for further consideration (remand). When many issues are involved, it is not unusual to encounter a mixed result. Thus, the lower court may be affirmed (*aff'd*) on Issue A and reversed (*rev'd*) on Issue B, while Issue C is remanded (*rem'd*) for additional fact finding.

When more than one judge is involved in the decision-making process, disagreement is not uncommon. In addition to the majority view, one or more judges may concur (agree with the result reached but not with some or all of the reasoning) or dissent (disagree with the result). In any one case, the majority view controls. But concurring and dissenting views can have influence on other courts or, at some subsequent date when the composition of the court has changed, even on the same court.

### Judicial Citations—General.

Having briefly described the judicial process, it is appropriate to consider the more practical problem of the relationship of case law to tax research. As previously noted, court decisions are an important source of tax law. The ability to cite a case and to locate it is therefore a must in working with the tax law. The usual pattern for a judicial citation is as follows: case name, volume number, reporter series, page or paragraph number, and court (where necessary).

### Judicial Citations—The U.S. Tax Court.

A good starting point is the U.S. Tax Court. The Tax Court issues three types of decisions: Regular decisions, Memorandum decisions, and summary opinions. They differ in both substance and form. In terms of substance, Memorandum decisions deal with situations necessitating only the application of already established principles of law. Regular decisions involve novel issues not previously resolved by the Tax Court. In actual practice, this distinction is not always preserved. Not infrequently, Memorandum decisions will be encountered that appear to warrant Regular status and vice versa. At any rate, do not conclude that Memorandum decisions possess no value as precedents. Both Memorandum and Regular decisions represent the position of the Tax Court and, as such, can be relied upon. Summary opinions, on the other hand, are issued in small tax cases and may not be used as precedent in any other case.

Regular decisions are published by the U.S. Government in a series called *Tax Court of the United States Reports* (T.C.). Each volume of these reports covers a six-month period (January 1 through June 30 and July 1 through December 31) and is given a succeeding volume number. But, as was true of the *Cumulative Bulletin*, there is usually a time lag between the date a decision is rendered and the date it appears in bound form. A temporary citation may be necessary to help the researcher locate a recent Regular decision. Consider, for example, the temporary and permanent citations for *Charles H. Addis*, a decision filed on June 10, 2002:

Temporary Citation { *Charles H. Addis*, 118 T.C. \_\_\_\_, No. 32 (2002).
*Explanation:* Page number left blank because not yet known.

Permanent Citation { *Charles H. Addis*, 118 T.C. 528 (2002).
*Explanation:* Page number now available.

Both citations tell us that the case ultimately will appear in Volume 118 of the *Tax Court of the United States Reports*. But until this volume is bound and made available to the general public, the page number must be left blank. Instead, the temporary citation identifies the case as being the 32d Regular decision issued by the Tax Court since Volume 117 ended. With this information, the decision can be easily located in either of the special Tax Court services published by Commerce Clearing House (CCH) and by Research Institute of America (RIA—formerly by Prentice-Hall [P-H]). Once Volume 118 is released, the permanent citation can be substituted and the number of the case dropped. Starting in 1999, both Regular and Memorandum decisions are issued on the U.S. Tax Court Web site (**http://www.ustaxcourt.gov/**).

Before 1943, the Tax Court was called the Board of Tax Appeals, and its decisions were published as the *United States Board of Tax Appeals Reports* (B.T.A.). These 47 volumes cover the period from 1924 to 1942. For example, the citation *Karl Pauli* 11 B.T.A. 784 (1928) refers to the 11th volume of the *Board of Tax Appeals Reports*, page 784, issued in 1928.

Memorandum decisions are published by CCH and by RIA (formerly by P-H). Consider, for example, the three different ways that *Walter H. Johnson* can be cited:

> *Walter H. Johnson*, T.C.Memo. 1975–245
> The 245th Memorandum decision issued by the Tax Court in 1975.
>
> *Walter H. Johnson*, 34 TCM 1056
> Page 1056 of Vol. 34 of the CCH *Tax Court Memorandum Decisions*.
>
> *Walter H. Johnson*, P-H T.C.Mem.Dec. ¶75,245
> Paragraph 75,245 of the P-H *T.C. Memorandum Decisions*.

Note that the third citation contains the same information as the first. Thus, ¶75,245 indicates the following information about the case: year 1975, 245th T.C.Memo. decision.[41]

Starting in 2001, summary opinions are issued on the U.S Tax Court Web site. For example, *Jared R. Nield*, filed on August 27, 2002, is cited as follows:

> *Jared R. Nield*, T.C. Summ.Op. 2002–110.

### Judicial Citations—The U.S. District Courts, Claims Court, and Courts of Appeals.

District Court, Claims Court (now Court of Federal Claims), Court of Appeals, and Supreme Court decisions dealing with Federal tax matters are reported in both the CCH *U.S. Tax Cases* (USTC) and the RIA (formerly P-H) *American Federal Tax Reports* (AFTR) series.

Federal District Court decisions, dealing with *both* tax and nontax issues, are also published by West Publishing Company in its *Federal Supplement 2d* (F.Supp.2d) series. This series follows the *Federal Supplement* (F.Supp.) series, which concluded in 1998 with Volume 999. The following examples illustrate how a District Court case can be cited in three different forms:

> *Simons-Eastern Co. v. U.S.*, 73–1 USTC ¶9279 (D.Ct.Ga., 1972).
> *Explanation:* Reported in the first volume of the *U.S. Tax Cases* (USTC) published by Commerce Clearing House for calendar year 1973 (73–1) and located at paragraph 9279 (¶9279).

---

[41]In this text, the Research Institute of America (RIA) citation for Memorandum decisions of the U.S. Tax Court is omitted. Thus, *Walter H. Johnson* would be cited as: 34 TCM 1056, T.C.Memo. 1975–245. Prentice-Hall is now owned by RIA. This edition continues to use the Prentice-Hall name in some instances of older volumes.

*Simons-Eastern Co. v. U.S.*, 31 AFTR2d 73–640 (D.Ct.Ga., 1972).

*Explanation:* Reported in the 31st volume of the second series of the *American Federal Tax Reports* (AFTR2d) published by Prentice-Hall (now RIA) and beginning on page 640. The "73" preceding the page number indicates the year the case was published but is a designation used only in recent decisions.

*Simons-Eastern Co. v. U.S.*, 354 F.Supp. 1003 (D.Ct.Ga., 1972).

*Explanation:* Reported in the 354th volume of the *Federal Supplement Series* (F.Supp.) published by West Publishing Company and beginning on page 1003.

In all of the preceding citations, note that the name of the case is the same (Simons-Eastern Co. being the taxpayer), as is the reference to the Federal District Court of Georgia (D.Ct.Ga.,) and the year the decision was rendered (1972).[42]

Beginning in October of 1982, decisions of the Claims Court are reported by West Publishing Company in a series designated *Federal Claims Reporter*. Thus, the Claims Court decision in *Recchie v. U.S.* appears as follows:

*Recchie v. U.S.,*　　　　　　　　　　　　　　　　　(Cl.Ct., 1983)

83–1 USTC ¶9312 (CCH citation)
51 AFTR2d 83–1010 (P-H citation)
1 Cl.Ct. 726 (West citation)

Beginning October 30, 1992, the Claims Court underwent a further name change. The new designation, U.S. Court of Federal Claims, began with Volume 27 of the former Cl.Ct. (West citation), now abbreviated as Fed.Cl.

Decisions of the Courts of Appeals are published in a West Publishing Company reporter designated as the *Federal Third* (F.3d) series, which began in October 1993, at the conclusion of the *Federal Second* (F.2d) series. Illustrations of the different forms follow:

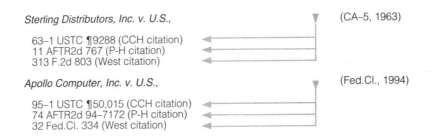

*Sterling Distributors, Inc. v. U.S.,*　　　　　　　　　(CA–5, 1963)

63–1 USTC ¶9288 (CCH citation)
11 AFTR2d 767 (P-H citation)
313 F.2d 803 (West citation)

*Apollo Computer, Inc. v. U.S.,*　　　　　　　　　　(Fed.Cl., 1994)

95–1 USTC ¶50,015 (CCH citation)
74 AFTR2d 94–7172 (P-H citation)
32 Fed.Cl. 334 (West citation)

Note that *Sterling Distributors, Inc. v. U.S.* is a decision rendered by the Fifth Circuit Court of Appeals in 1963 (CA–5, 1963) while *Apollo Computer, Inc. v. U.S.* was rendered in 1994 by the U.S. Court of Federal Claims.

If the IRS loses in a decision, it may indicate whether it agrees or disagrees with the results reached by the court by publishing an **acquiescence** ("A" or "*Acq.*") or **nonacquiescence** ("NA" or "*Nonacq.*"), respectively. The acquiescence or nonacquiescence is published in the *Internal Revenue Bulletin* and the *Cumulative Bulletin* as an *Action on Decision*. The IRS can retroactively revoke an acquiescence or nonacquiescence. Originally, acquiescences and nonacquiescences were published

---

[42]In this text, the case will be cited in the following form: *Simons-Eastern Co. v. U.S.*, 73–1 USTC ¶9279, 31 AFTR2d 73–640, 354 F.Supp. 1003 (D.Ct.Ga., 1972).

only for Regular U.S. Tax Court decisions, but since 1991 the IRS has expanded its acquiescence program to include other civil tax cases where guidance is helpful.

**Judicial Citations—The U.S. Supreme Court.**   Like all other Federal tax cases (except those rendered by the U.S. Tax Court), Supreme Court decisions are published by Commerce Clearing House in the USTCs and by Research Institute of America (formerly P-H) in the AFTRs. The U.S. Government Printing Office also publishes these decisions in the *United States Supreme Court Reports* (U.S.) as does West Publishing Company in its *Supreme Court Reporter* (S.Ct.) and the Lawyer's Co-operative Publishing Company in its *United States Reports, Lawyer's Edition* (L.Ed.). The following illustrates the different ways the same decision can be cited:

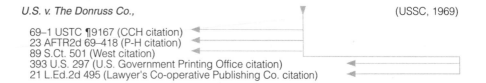

*U.S. v. The Donruss Co.,*                                                                (USSC, 1969)

    69–1 USTC ¶9167 (CCH citation)
    23 AFTR2d 69–418 (P-H citation)
    89 S.Ct. 501 (West citation)
    393 U.S. 297 (U.S. Government Printing Office citation)
    21 L.Ed.2d 495 (Lawyer's Co-operative Publishing Co. citation)

The parenthetical reference (USSC, 1969) identifies the decision as having been rendered by the U.S. Supreme Court in 1969. The citations given in this text for Supreme Court decisions will be limited to the CCH (USTC), the RIA or P-H for older volumes (AFTR), and the West (S.Ct.) versions.

# Working with the Tax Law—Tax Research

Tax research is the method used to determine the best available solution to a situation that possesses tax consequences. In other words, it is the process of finding a competent and professional conclusion to a tax problem. The problem may originate from either completed or proposed transactions. In the case of a completed transaction, the objective of the research is to determine the tax result of what has already taken place. For example, is the expenditure incurred by the taxpayer deductible or not deductible for tax purposes? When dealing with proposed transactions, the tax research process is concerned with the determination of possible alternative tax consequences. To the extent that tax research leads to a choice of alternatives or otherwise influences the future actions of the taxpayer, it becomes the key to effective tax planning.

Tax research involves the following procedures:

- Identifying and refining the problem.
- Locating the appropriate tax law sources.
- Assessing the validity of the tax law sources.
- Arriving at the solution or at alternative solutions while giving due consideration to nontax factors.
- Effectively communicating the solution to the taxpayer or the taxpayer's representative.
- Following up on the solution (where appropriate) in light of new developments.

This process is depicted schematically in Figure 1–3. The broken lines indicate steps of particular interest when tax research is directed toward proposed, rather than completed, transactions.

■ **FIGURE 1–3**
Tax Research Process

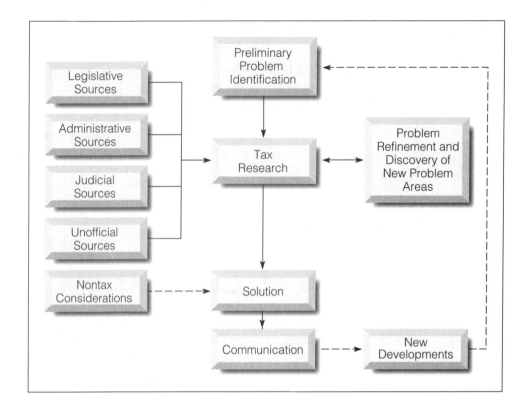

### IDENTIFYING THE PROBLEM

Problem identification starts with a compilation of the relevant facts involved. In this regard, *all* of the facts that might have a bearing on the problem must be gathered as any omission could modify the solution reached. To illustrate, consider what appears to be a very simple problem.

**EXAMPLE 20**

Dana Pehrson advances $52,000 to her nephew in 1996 to enable him to attend a private college. Seven years later, she claims a bad debt deduction for $42,000 that the nephew has not repaid. The problem: Is Dana entitled to a bad debt deduction? ■

**Refining the Problem.**   Before a bad debt deduction can arise, it must be established that a debt really existed. In a related-party setting (e.g., aunt and nephew), the IRS may contend that the original advance was not a loan but, in reality, a gift. Of key significance in this regard would be whether the lender (the aunt) had an honest and real expectation of payment by the borrower (the nephew).[43] Indicative of this repayment expectation is whether the parties preserved the formalities of a loan, including the following:

- The borrower issued a written instrument evidencing the obligation.
- Interest was provided for as part of the loan arrangement.
- The note specified a set due date.
- Collateral was available to the lender in the event of default by the borrower.[44]

---

[43]*William F. Mercil*, 24 T.C. 1150 (1955), and *Evans Clark*, 18 T.C. 780 (1952), *aff'd* 53–2 USTC ¶9452, 44 AFTR 70, 205 F.2d 353 (CA–2, 1953).

[44]*Arthur T. Davidson*, 37 TCM 725, T.C.Memo. 1978–167.

The presence of some or all of these formalities does not, however, guarantee that a bona fide loan will be found. By the same token, the absence of some or all of the formalities does not make the advance a gift. Applying the formalities criteria to Example 20 is not possible since key facts (e.g., the presence or absence of a written note) are not given. Nevertheless, several inferences might be made that lead to a loan interpretation:

- It appears that the nephew has repaid at least $10,000 of the $52,000 that he borrowed. If the parties intended a gift of the full amount of the loan, why was partial repayment made?
- Although one would not expect a nephew on his way to college to have assets to serve as collateral for a loan, the fact that he was obtaining additional education could reinforce any expectation of repayment. In most situations, a person with a college education will possess a higher earning potential than one without such education. This education would improve the nephew's financial ability to repay the loan.

**Further Refinement of the Problem.** It may be impossible to determine whether the advance constitutes a loan or a gift with any degree of certainty. In either event, however, the tax consequences of each possibility must be ascertained.

If the advance is determined to be a gift, it is subject to the Federal gift tax.[45] Whether or not a gift tax results depends upon how much of the unified tax credit the aunt has available to absorb the gift tax on $42,000 [$52,000 (total gift) – $10,000 (annual exclusion in 1996)].[46] Whether the transfer results in a gift tax or not, it must be reported on Form 709 (United States Gift Tax Return) since the amount of the gift exceeds the annual exclusion.

Even if it is assumed that Dana made a gift to her nephew in 1996, does not the intervention of seven years preclude the IRS from assessing any gift tax that might be due as a result of the transfer?[47] Further research indicates that the statute of limitations on assessments does not begin to run when a tax return is not filed.[48]

To complete the picture, what are the tax consequences if the advance is treated as a loan? Aside from the bad debt deduction aspects (covered later in the chapter), the tax law provides more immediate tax ramifications:[49]

- If interest is not provided for, it is imputed with the following effect:
    a. The lender (the aunt) must recognize interest income as to the imputed value.
    b. Since the lender has not received the interest, she is deemed to have made a gift of the interest to the borrower.
    c. The borrower (nephew) may be entitled to deduct (as an itemized expense) in some tax years a portion of the amount of interest deemed paid to the lender (aunt).
- If interest is provided for but the rate is lower than market (as determined by the yield on certain U.S. government securities), the differential is treated as noted above.

---

[45]The transfer does not come within the unlimited gift tax exclusion of § 2503(e)(2)(A) since the aunt did not pay the amount directly to an educational institution. Besides, the exclusion covers only tuition payments and not other costs attendant on going to college (e.g., room and board).

[46]The tax, in turn, depends upon the amount of taxable gifts the aunt has made in the past. For a discussion of the mechanics of the Federal gift tax, see Chapter 17.

[47]Throughout the discussion of Example 20, the assumption has been made that if a gift occurred, it took place in 1996. That assumption need not be the case. Depending upon the aunt's intent, she could have decided to make a gift of the unpaid balance anytime after the loan was made (e.g., 1997, 1998, etc.).

[48]See § 6501(c)(3) and the discussion of the statute of limitations in Chapter 16.

[49]§ 7872.

- For gift loans of $100,000 or less, the imputed element cannot exceed the net investment income of the borrower.

## LOCATING THE APPROPRIATE TAX LAW SOURCES

**LO.6**

Locate tax law sources.

Once the problem is clearly defined, what is the next step? Although the next step is a matter of individual judgment, most tax research begins with the index volume of the tax service or a key word search on an online tax service (see the subsequent discussion of Electronic Tax Research). If the problem is not complex, the researcher may bypass the tax service and turn directly to the Internal Revenue Code and the Treasury Regulations. For the beginner, this latter procedure saves time and will solve many of the more basic problems. If the researcher does not have a personal copy of the Code or Regulations, resorting to the appropriate volume(s) of a tax service or a CD-ROM may be necessary. Several of the major tax services publish paperback editions of the Code and Treasury Regulations that can be purchased at modest prices. These editions are usually revised twice each year.

Tax services are either annotated or topical. The two major annotated services are organized by Internal Revenue Code Sections, whereas most of the services are organized by major topics. The following major services are available:

> *Standard Federal Tax Reporter*, Commerce Clearing House. (annotated)
>
> *United States Tax Reporter*, Research Institute of America (entitled *Federal Taxes* prior to July 1992). (annotated)
>
> *Mertens Law of Federal Income Taxation*, Callaghan and Co. (topical)
>
> *Federal Tax Coordinator 2d*, Research Institute of America. (topical)
>
> *Tax Management Portfolios*, Bureau of National Affairs. (topical)
>
> CCH's *Federal Tax Service*, Commerce Clearing House. (topical)
>
> *Analysis of Federal Taxes: Income*, Research Institute of America. (topical)
>
> *Federal Taxation of Income, Estates and Gifts*, Warren, Gorham and Lamont. (topical)

**Working with the Tax Services.**   In this text, it is not feasible to teach the use of any particular tax service because this knowledge can be obtained only by practice. The representatives of the various tax services provide users with printed booklets and individual instruction on the use of the services. However, several important observations about the use of tax services cannot be overemphasized. First, always check for current developments. The main text of any service is revised too infrequently to permit reliance on that portion as the *latest* word on any subject. Where such current developments can be found depends on which service is being used. The CCH service contains a special volume devoted to current matters. Second, when dealing with a tax service synopsis of a Treasury Department pronouncement or a judicial decision, remember there is no substitute for the original source.

To illustrate, do not base a conclusion solely on a tax service's commentary on *Simons-Eastern Co. v. U.S.*[50] If the case is vital to the research, look it up. The facts of the decision may be distinguishable from those in the problem being researched. This is not to say that the case synopsis contained in the tax service is wrong; it might just be misleading or incomplete.

---

[50]Cited in Footnote 42.

Citators help researchers learn the history of tax decisions and Revenue Rulings and evaluate the strengths of their holdings. The three major multivolume citators are the RIA Citator 2nd Series, the CCH Citator, and Shepard's Federal Tax Citations. Computerized citators can be found in WESTLAW (KeyCite, RIA Citator 2nd Series) and LEXIS (Auto-Cite and Shepard's). The RIA and CCH Citators are available through their computerized tax services. The last section of this chapter describes the use of the RIA Citator.

**Tax Periodicals.** Additional sources of tax information are the various tax periodicals. The easiest way to locate a journal article on a particular tax problem is through *Federal Tax Articles* (CCH) or *Index to Federal Tax Articles* (Warren, Gorham and Lamont). CCH's six-volume service includes a subject index, a Code Section number index, and an author's index. In addition, the RIA tax service has a topical "Index to Tax Articles" section that is organized using that service's paragraph index system. Also, beginning in 1992, *The Accounting & Tax Index* is available in three quarterly issues plus a cumulative year-end volume covering all four quarters. The original *Accountant's Index* started in 1921 and ended in 1991.

The following are some of the more useful tax periodicals:

*The Journal of Taxation*
*Tax Law Review*
*Taxation for Accountants*
*Journal of Corporate Taxation*
*Estate Planning*
*Journal of Partnership Taxation*
Warren, Gorham and Lamont
31 St. James Avenue
Boston, MA 02116–4112

*The Tax Executive*
1200 G Street NW
Suite 300
Washington, DC 20005

*The Practical Accountant*
395 Hudson Street
New York, NY 10014

*Trusts and Estates*
6151 Powers Ferry Rd. NW
Atlanta, GA 30339–2941

*TAXES—The Tax Magazine*
CCH, Inc.
2700 Lake Cook Road
Riverwood, IL 60015

*National Tax Journal*
725 15th Street NW
Suite 600
Washington, DC 20005

*The Tax Adviser*
AICPA
1211 Avenue of the Americas
New York, NY 10036

*The Tax Lawyer*
American Bar Association
750 N. Lake Shore Drive
Chicago, IL 60611

*Journal of the American Taxation Association*
American Accounting Association
5717 Bessie Drive
Sarasota, FL 33583

*Oil, Gas & Energy Quarterly*
Matthew Bender & Co.
Albany, NY 12201

*The International Tax Journal*
Aspen Publishing, Inc.
1185 Avenue of the Americas
New York, NY 10036

*Tax Notes*
Tax Analysts
6830 Fairfax Drive
Arlington, VA 22213

**LO.7**

Assess the validity and weight of tax law sources.

## ASSESSING THE VALIDITY OF TAX LAW SOURCES

After a source has been located, the next step is to assess the source in light of the problem at hand. Proper assessment involves careful interpretation of the tax law and consideration of the law's relevance and validity.

**Interpreting the Internal Revenue Code.**   The language of the Code often is extremely difficult to comprehend. For example, a subsection [§ 341(e)] relating to collapsible corporations contains *one* sentence of more than 450 words (twice as many as in the Gettysburg Address). Within this same subsection is another sentence of 300 words.

The Code must be read carefully for restrictive language such as "*at least* 80 percent" and "*more* than 80 percent" or "*less* than 50 percent" and "*exceeds* 50 percent." It also makes a great deal of difference, for example, whether two or more clauses are connected by "*or*" or by "*and*."

If an answer is not in the Code, it may be necessary to resort to the Regulations and judicial decisions. In 1969, Congress directed the Treasury Department to promulgate Regulations under § 385 to distinguish corporate debt from corporate equity. As of yet, there are no Regulations under § 385. The researcher, therefore, must resort to past judicial decisions for a definition of debt.

Sometimes the Code directs the researcher elsewhere for the answer. For example, § 162(c) refers to the Foreign Corrupt Practices Act for purposes of determining when payments to foreign officials are deductible.

Cross-referencing between Code Sections is often poor or nonexistent. Code Sections are enacted at different times by Congresses that are operating under stringent deadlines. Consequently, a certain lack of integration within the Code is frequently apparent.

Definitions vary from one Code Section to another. For example, § 267 disallows losses between related parties and includes brothers and sisters in the definition of related parties. Not so with § 318, which deals with the definition of related parties as to certain stock redemptions.

**Assessing the Validity of a Treasury Regulation.**   Treasury Regulations are often said to have the force and effect of law. This statement is certainly true for most Regulations, but some judicial decisions have held a Regulation or a portion thereof invalid. Usually, this is done on the grounds that the Regulation is contrary to the intent of Congress.

Keep the following observations in mind when assessing the validity of a Regulation:

- In a challenge, the burden of proof is on the taxpayer to show that the Regulation is wrong. However, a court may invalidate a Regulation that varies from the language of the statute and has no support in the Committee Reports.
- If the taxpayer loses the challenge, the negligence penalty may be imposed. This accuracy-related provision deals with the "intentional disregard of rules and regulations" on the part of the taxpayer and is explained further in Chapter 16.
- Some Regulations merely reprint or rephrase what Congress has stated in its Committee Reports issued in connection with the enactment of tax legislation. Such Regulations are "hard and solid" and almost impossible to overturn because they clearly reflect the intent of Congress.
- In some Code Sections, Congress has given to the "Secretary or his delegate" the authority to prescribe Regulations to carry out the details of administration or to otherwise complete the operating rules. Under such circumstances, it could almost be said that Congress is delegating its legislative powers to the Treasury Department. The Congressional Research Service found that Congress delegated regulatory authority to the Treasury on more than 240 occasions from 1992 through 2000, an average of more than 26 delegations per year. Regulations issued pursuant to this type of authority truly possess

the force and effect of law and are often called "legislative" Regulations. They are to be distinguished from "interpretative" Regulations, which purport to explain the meaning of a particular Code Section. Examples of legislative Regulations are those dealing with consolidated returns issued under §§ 1501 through 1505. As a further example, note the authority granted to the Treasury Department by § 385 to issue Regulations setting forth guidelines on when corporate debt can be reclassified as equity (see Chapter 3).

**Assessing the Validity of Other Administrative Sources of the Tax Law.** Revenue Rulings issued by the IRS carry less weight than Treasury Department Regulations. Rulings are important, however, in that they reflect the position of the IRS on tax matters. In any dispute with the IRS on the interpretation of tax law, taxpayers should expect agents to follow the results reached in any applicable rulings.

*Actions on Decisions* further tell the taxpayer the IRS's reaction to certain court decisions. Recall that the IRS follows a practice of either acquiescing (agreeing) or nonacquiescing (not agreeing) with court decisions where guidance may be helpful. This practice does not mean that a particular decision has no value if the IRS has nonacquiesced in the result. It does, however, indicate that the IRS will continue to litigate the issue involved.

The validity of individual letter rulings issued by the IRS is discussed in Chapter 16.

**Assessing the Validity of Judicial Sources of the Tax Law.** The judicial process as it relates to the formulation of tax law has been described. How much reliance can be placed on a particular decision depends upon the following variables:

- The level of the court. A decision rendered by a trial court (e.g., a Federal District Court) carries less weight than one issued by an appellate court (e.g., the Fifth Circuit Court of Appeals). Unless Congress changes the Code, decisions by the U.S. Supreme Court represent the last word on any tax issue.
- The legal residence of the taxpayer. If, for example, a taxpayer lives in Texas, a decision of the Fifth Circuit Court of Appeals means more than one rendered by the Second Circuit Court of Appeals. This is true because any appeal from a U.S. District Court or the U.S. Tax Court would be to the Fifth Circuit Court of Appeals and not to the Second Circuit Court of Appeals.
- Whether the decision represents the weight of authority on the issue. In other words, is it supported by the results reached by other courts?
- The outcome or status of the decision on appeal. For example, was the decision appealed and, if so, with what result?

In connection with the last two variables, the use of a manual citator or a computer search is invaluable to tax research.[51] The use of a manual citator is described in the last section of this chapter.

**Assessing the Validity of Other Sources.** Primary sources of tax law include the Constitution, legislative history materials, statutes, treaties, Treasury Regulations, IRS pronouncements, and judicial decisions. The IRS regards only primary sources as substantial authority. However, reference to secondary materials such

---

[51]The major manual citators are published by Commerce Clearing House, RIA, and Shepard's Citations, Inc. See the prior comments under Working with the Tax Services.

as legal periodicals, treatises, legal opinions, general counsel memoranda, technical advice memoranda, and written determinations can be useful. In general, secondary sources are not authority.

Although the statement that the IRS regards only primary sources as substantial authority is generally true, there is one exception. For purposes of the accuracy-related penalty in § 6662, the IRS has expanded the list of substantial authority to include a number of secondary materials (e.g., letter rulings, general counsel and technical advice memoranda, and the "Blue Book").[52] The "Blue Book" is the general explanation of tax legislation prepared by the Joint Committee on Taxation of the U.S. Congress.

As under former § 6661, "authority" does not include conclusions reached in treatises, legal periodicals, and opinions rendered by tax professionals.

## ARRIVING AT THE SOLUTION OR AT ALTERNATIVE SOLUTIONS

Returning to Example 20, assume the parties decide that the loan approach can be justified from the factual situation involved. Does this assumption lead to a bad debt deduction for the aunt? Before this question can be resolved, the loan needs to be classified as either a business or a nonbusiness debt. One of the reasons the classification is important is that a nonbusiness bad debt cannot be deducted until it becomes entirely worthless. Unlike a business debt, no deduction for partial worthlessness is allowed.[53]

It is very likely that the loan the aunt made in 1996 falls into the nonbusiness category. Unless exceptional circumstances exist (e.g., the lender was in the trade or business of lending money), loans in a related-party setting are treated as nonbusiness. The probability is high that the aunt would be relegated to nonbusiness bad debt status.

The aunt has the burden of proving that the remaining unpaid balance of $42,000 is *entirely* worthless.[54] In this connection, what collection effort, if any, has the aunt made? But would any such collection effort be fruitless? Perhaps the nephew is insolvent, ill, unemployed, or has departed for parts unknown.

Even if the debt is entirely worthless, one further issue remains to be resolved. In what year did the worthlessness occur? It could be, for example, that worthlessness took place in a year before it was claimed.[55]

A clear-cut answer may not be possible as to a bad debt deduction for the aunt in year 2003 (seven years after the advance was made). This uncertainty does not detract from the value of the research. Often a guarded judgment is the best possible solution to a tax problem.

## COMMUNICATING TAX RESEARCH

Once the problem has been researched adequately, a memo, letter, or spoken presentation setting forth the result may be required. The form such a communication takes could depend on a number of considerations. For example, is any particular procedure or format for communicating tax research recommended by either an employer or an instructor? Are the research results to be given directly to the client, or will they first pass to the preparer's employer? If an oral presentation is

---

[52]Notice 90–20, 1990–1 C.B. 328, part V (A).

[53]See § 166 and the discussion of Investor Losses in Chapter 3.

[54]Compare *John K. Sexton*, 48 TCM 512, T.C.Memo. 1984–360, with *Stewart T. Oatman*, 45 TCM 214, T.C.Memo. 1982–684.

[55]*Ruth Wertheim Smith*, 34 TCM 1474, T.C.Memo. 1975–339.

**■ FIGURE 1–4**
Client Letter

---

Hoffman, Raabe, Smith, & Maloney, CPAs
5191 Natorp Boulevard
Mason, OH 45040

August 29, 2003

Homer Lynch
111 Avenue G
Lakeway, OH 45232

Dear Mr. Lynch:

This letter is in response to your request that we review the tax result of a gift made in 1976 and determine the unified tax credit available upon Sonya's death in 2003. Our conclusions are based upon the facts as outlined in your letter of August 14.

    The gift of $66,000 made to your son on October 1, 1976, did not result in any Federal gift tax for several reasons. First, your wife, Sonya, elected to split the gift with you. Second, both of you chose to use the $30,000 specific exemption that was in effect at that time. As a consequence, the transfer was treated as follows:

|  | Homer | Sonya |
|---|---|---|
| Amount of gift made | $ 33,000 | $ 33,000 |
| Annual exclusion available in 1976 | (3,000) | (3,000) |
| Specific exemption used | (30,000) | (30,000) |
| Taxable gift | $ –0– | $ –0– |

    When the specific exemption is used after September 8, 1976, an adjustment must be made to the unified transfer tax credit. The adjustment requires that the credit be reduced by 20 percent of the exemption used.

    When Sonya died in 2003, the credit available to her estate was not the standard $345,800 for 2003. Because of the adjustment required, the credit must be reduced by $6,000 (20% × $30,000 specific exemption previously used). Her credit, then, is $339,800 ($345,800 – $6,000).

    Should you desire more information or a further clarification of our conclusions, do not hesitate to contact me.

Sincerely,

James Randolph, CPA
Partner

---

required, who will be the audience? How long should you talk?[56] Whatever form it takes, a good tax research communication should contain the following elements:

- A clear statement of the issue.
- In more complex situations, a short review of the factual pattern that raises the issue.
- A review of the pertinent tax law sources (e.g., Code, Regulations, rulings, judicial authority).
- Any assumptions made in arriving at the solution.
- The solution recommended and the logic or reasoning in its support.
- The references consulted in the research process.

Figures 1–4, 1–5, and 1–6 present a sample client letter and memoranda for the tax files.

---

[56]For more on crafting oral presentations, see W. A. Raabe and G. E. Whittenburg, "Talking Tax: How to Make a Tax Presentation," *Tax Adviser*, March 1997, pp. 179–182.

■ **FIGURE 1–5**

Tax File Memorandum

August 15, 2003

TAX FILE MEMORANDUM

FROM: James Randolph

SUBJECT: Homer Lynch
             Engagement Issues

Today, I talked to Homer Lynch with regard to his letter of August 14, 2003.
     On October 1, 1976, Homer made a gift of $66,000 to his son. Homer's wife, Sonya, elected to split the gift, and each elected to use the full $30,000 specific exemption. Sonya died this year, and Homer is the executor of her estate.

ISSUE: Was any gift tax due on the 1976 transfer? How much unified transfer tax credit can Homer claim when he files a Form 706 for Sonya's estate? I told Homer that we would have the answers to these questions within a month.

■ **FIGURE 1–6**

Tax File Memorandum

August 29, 2003

TAX FILE MEMORANDUM

FROM: James Randolph

SUBJECT: Homer Lynch
             Engagement Conclusions

Homer made a gift of $66,000 to his son on October 1, 1976. No gift tax resulted because Homer's wife, Sonya, elected (under § 2513) to split the gift. This election made two annual exclusions available ($3,000 each) and allowed the use of the specific exemptions ($30,000 each). As neither spouse had a taxable gift ($33,000 − $3,000 − $30,000 = $0), no gift tax resulted.
     What is the unified tax credit available to Sonya's estate when she dies in 2003? Section 2010(b) requires that the credit be reduced by 20 percent of the specific exemption used after September 8, 1976. Does this adjustment apply to a nonowner donor spouse such as Sonya? *Estate of James O. Gawne,* 80 T.C. 478 (1983), makes clear that it does.

## LO.8

Make use of various tax planning procedures.

# Working with the Tax Law—Tax Planning

Tax research and tax planning are inseparable. The *primary* purpose of effective tax planning is to reduce the taxpayer's total tax bill. This reduction does not mean that the course of action selected must produce the lowest possible tax under the circumstances. The minimization of tax payments must be considered in the context of the legitimate business goals of the taxpayer.

A *secondary* objective of effective tax planning is to reduce, defer, or eliminate the tax. Specifically, this objective aims to accomplish one or more results. Some possibilities are eradicating the tax entirely, eliminating the tax in the current year, deferring the receipt of income, and proliferating taxpayers (i.e., forming partnerships and corporations or making lifetime gifts to family members). Further examples include eluding double taxation, avoiding ordinary income, or creating, increasing, or accelerating deductions. However, this second objective should be pursued with considerable reservation. Although the maxim "A bird in the hand is worth two in the bush" has general validity, the rule frequently breaks down. For example, a tax election in one year may accomplish a current reduction in taxes, but it could saddle future years with a disadvantageous tax position.

## NONTAX CONSIDERATIONS

There is a danger that tax motivations may take on a significance that does not conform to the true values involved. In other words, tax considerations can operate to impair the exercise of sound business judgment. Thus, the tax planning process can lead to ends that are socially and economically objectionable. Unfortunately, a tendency exists for planning to move toward the opposing extremes of either not enough or too much emphasis on tax considerations. The happy medium is a balance that recognizes the significance of taxes, but not beyond the point at which planning detracts from the exercise of good business judgment.

The remark is often made that a good rule to follow is to refrain from pursuing any course of action that would not be followed were it not for certain tax considerations. This statement is not entirely correct, but it does illustrate the desirability of preventing business logic from being "sacrificed at the altar of tax planning."

## TAX AVOIDANCE AND TAX EVASION

A fine line exists between legal tax planning and illegal tax planning—tax avoidance versus tax evasion. Tax avoidance is merely tax minimization through legal techniques. In this sense, tax avoidance becomes the proper objective of all tax planning. Though eliminating or reducing taxes is also a goal of tax evasion, the term implies the use of subterfuge and fraud as a means to this end. Perhaps because common goals are involved, popular usage has blurred the distinction between the two concepts. Consequently, the association of tax avoidance with tax evasion has kept some taxpayers from properly taking advantage of planning possibilities. The now-classic words of Judge Learned Hand in *Commissioner v. Newman* reflect the true values a taxpayer should have:

> Over and over again courts have said that there is nothing sinister in so arranging one's affairs as to keep taxes as low as possible. Everybody does so, rich or poor; and all do right, for nobody owes any public duty to pay more than the law demands: taxes are enforced extractions, not voluntary contributions. To demand more in the name of morals is mere cant.[57]

## FOLLOW-UP PROCEDURES

Tax planning usually involves a proposed (as opposed to a completed) transaction and is based upon the continuing validity of the advice resulting from tax research. A change in the tax law (either legislative, administrative, or judicial) could alter the original conclusion. Additional research may be necessary to test the solution in light of current developments.

Under what circumstances does a tax practitioner have an obligation to inform a client as to changes in the tax law? The legal and ethical aspects of this question are discussed in Chapter 16.

## TAX PLANNING—A PRACTICAL APPLICATION

Returning to the facts in Example 20, what should be done to help protect the aunt's bad debt deduction?

* All formalities of a loan should be present (e.g., written instrument, definite and realistic due date).

---

[57]47–1 USTC ¶9175, 35 AFTR 857, 159 F.2d 848 (CA–2, 1947).

- Upon default, the lender (aunt) should make a reasonable effort to collect from the borrower (nephew). If not, the aunt should be in a position to explain why any such effort would be to no avail.
- If interest is provided for, it should be paid.
- Any interest paid (or imputed under § 7872) should be recognized as income by the aunt.
- Because of the annual exclusion of $10,000 in 1996 (now $11,000), it appears doubtful that actual (or imputed) interest would necessitate the filing of a Federal gift tax return by the aunt. But should one be due, it should be filed.
- If § 7872 applies (not enough or no interest is provided for), the nephew should keep track of his net investment income. This record keeping is important since the income the aunt must recognize may be limited by this amount.

Throughout this text, each chapter concludes with observations on Tax Planning Considerations. Such observations are not all-inclusive but are intended to illustrate some of the ways in which the material in the chapter can be effectively used to minimize taxes.

## LO.9

Have an awareness of computer-assisted tax research.

## ELECTRONIC TAX RESEARCH

The computer is being used more frequently in the day-to-day practice of tax professionals, students, and educators. Many software vendors offer tax return software programs for individual, corporate, partnership, and fiduciary returns. The use of computers, however, is not limited to batch-processed tax returns. Computer materials for quantitative tax and problem-solving planning and calculations have added a new dimension to tax research.

Computer-based tax research tools hold a prominent position in the tax practice. Electronic tax resources allow the tax library to reflect the tax law with its dynamic and daily changes. Using electronic means to locate tax law sources is not a substitute, however, for developing and maintaining a thorough knowledge of the tax law and applying logical and analytical review in addressing open tax research issues.

Accessing tax documents through electronic sources offers several important advantages over a strictly paper-based approach to the task:

- Materials are available to the practitioner more quickly through an electronic system, which eliminates delays by streamlining the composition and proof-reading, production, and distribution of the new materials.
- Some tax documents, such as so-called slip opinions of trial-level courts and interviews with policymakers, are available only through electronic sources.
- Commercial subscriptions to electronic tax services are likely to provide, at little or no cost, additional tax law sources to which the researcher would not have access through stand-alone purchases of traditional material. For example, the full texts of private letter rulings are quite costly to acquire in a paper-based format, but electronic publishers may bundle the rulings with other materials for a reasonable cost.

Comparing the cost of paper and electronic tax research materials is difficult, especially when the practitioner uses hardware, including workstations and communications equipment, that is already in place and employed elsewhere in the practice. Over time, though, the convenience, cost, and reliability of electronic research tools clearly make them the dominant means of finding and analyzing tax law.

## HELP FOR HARASSED TAXPAYERS

The Internal Revenue Code has grown from 500 pages in 1939 to more than 7,600 pages today. When IRS Regulations, rulings, court cases, and other interpretative materials are added, the total is in excess of 47,000 pages. For comparison purposes, *Webster's Unabridged Dictionary* (which lists and defines every word in the English language) contains only 2,783 pages. Dealing with all this verbiage can be extremely time-consuming. For the unfortunate taxpayer who still attempts to prepare and file his or her own tax return, the average time expended is approximately 28 hours.

Fortunately, the complexity of the Internal Revenue Code is being overtaken by the intelligence of emerging technology. As Congress and the states construct an income tax system utterly beyond the comprehension of humans, computers are mastering this unthinkable code and the exploding number of Federal Regulations.

Record-keeping software like *Quicken* simplifies the compiling of records. Likewise, tax preparation software like *TurboTax* drains some of the complexity from tax compliance.

**Using Electronic Services.** Tax researchers often use electronic sources to find the tax law. Usually, the law is found using one of the following approaches:

- *Search* various databases using key words that are likely to be found in the underlying documents, as written by Congress, the judiciary, or administrative sources.
- *Link* to tax documents for which all or part of the proper citation is known.
- *Browse* the tax databases, examining various tables of contents and indexes in a traditional manner, or using cross-references in the documents to jump from one tax law source to another.

Virtually all of the major commercial tax publishers, and most of the primary sources of the law itself (e.g., the Supreme Court and some of the Courts of Appeals), now provide tax materials in electronic formats. Competitive pressures are forcing tax practitioners to become computer literate. Thus, the user-friendliness of the best of the tax search software is of great benefit to both the daily and the occasional user.

**CD-ROM Services.** The CD has been a major source of electronic tax data for about a decade. Every year data compression techniques allow more tax materials to fit on a single disc. CCH, RIA, WESTLAW, and others offer vast tax libraries to the practitioner. Often these resources are available in conjunction with a subscription to traditional paper-based resources and are accompanied by newsletters, training seminars, and ongoing technical support.

At its best, a CD-based tax library forms the archival data that make up the permanent, core library of tax documents. For about $300 a year, the tax CDs are updated quarterly and provide more comprehensive tax resources than the researcher is ever likely to need. In contrast, a paper-based library of a decade ago cost perhaps $20,000 to establish and $5,000 per year in perpetuity to maintain. If the library is contained on a small number of discs, portability (through use on notebook computers) becomes an additional feature of the service. Exhibit 1–1 summarizes the most popular electronic tax services on the market today.

**Online Systems.** An online research system allows a practitioner to access the computer of the service provider, giving virtually instantaneous use of tax law

| Service | Description |
|---------|-------------|
| CCH | Includes the CCH tax service, primary sources including treatises, and other subscription materials. 10–20 discs and online. |
| RIA | Includes the RIA topical *Coordinator* and the annotated tax service formerly provided by Prentice-Hall. The citator has elaborate document-linking features, and major tax treatises also are provided. 1–10 discs and online. |
| WESTLAW | Code, Regulations, *Cumulative Bulletins*, cases, citators, and editorial material. About 12 discs and online. |
| Kleinrock's | A single disc with tax statutory, administrative, and judicial law. Another disc provides tax forms and instructions for Federal and state jurisdictions. |

| Service | Description |
|---------|-------------|
| LEXIS/NEXIS | Federal and state statutory, administrative, and judicial material. Extensive libraries of newspapers, magazines, patent records, and medical and economic databases, both U.S.- and foreign-based. |
| RIA | Includes the RIA and P-H tax services, major tax treatises, Federal and state statutes, administrative documents, and court opinions. Extensive citator access, editorial material, and practitioner aids. |
| CCH | Includes the CCH tax service, primary sources including treatises, and other subscription materials. Tax and economic news sources, extensive editorial material, and practitioner support tools. |
| WESTLAW | Federal and state statutes, administrative documents, and court opinions. Extensive citator access, editorial material, and gateways to third-party publications. Extensive government document databases. |

sources. Online services employ price-per-search cost structures that average close to $200 per hour, making them significantly more expensive than paper or CD-ROM materials. Thus, unless a practitioner can pass along related costs to clients or others, online searching is limited to the most important issues and to the researchers with the most experience and training in search techniques.

Perhaps the best combination of electronic tax resources is to use a CD system for day-to-day work where the budget is known in advance and augment the CD with online access where it is deemed to be critical. Exhibit 1–2 lists the most commonly used commercial online tax services.

**The Internet.**    The Internet provides a wealth of tax information in several popular forms, sometimes at no direct cost to the researcher. Using so-called browser software, which is often distributed with new computer systems and their communication devices, a tax professional can access worldwide information in several popular forms that can aid the research process.

**■ EXHIBIT 1–3**
The IRS's *Digital Daily*

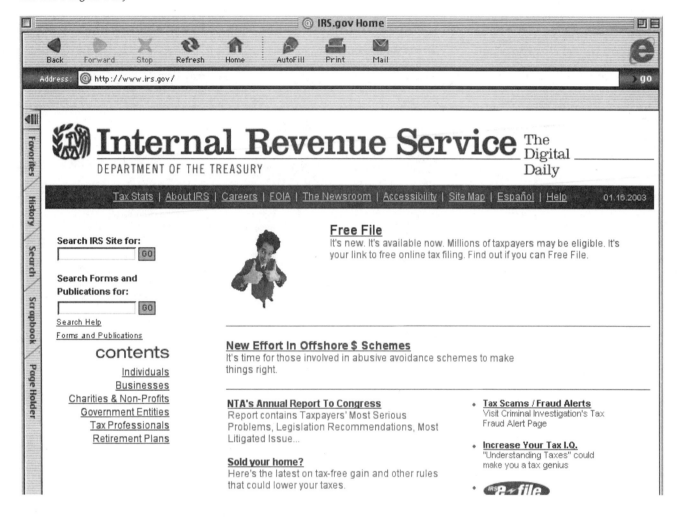

- *Home pages on the World Wide Web (WWW)* are provided by accounting firms, consulting firms, publishers, tax academics, libraries, and governmental bodies as a means of making information widely available or soliciting subscriptions or consulting engagements. Links to other sites and direct contact to the site providers are found in the best pages. One of the most useful sites available to the tax practitioner is the IRS's *Digital Daily*, illustrated in Exhibit 1–3. This site offers downloadable forms and instructions, "plain English" versions of Regulations, and news updates. Exhibit 1–4 lists some other Web sites that may be most useful to tax researchers along with their Internet addresses as of press date.
- *Newsgroups* provide a means by which information related to the tax law can be exchanged among taxpayers, tax professionals, and others who subscribe to the group's services. Newsgroup members can read the exchanges among other members and offer replies and suggestions to inquiries as desired. Discussions address the interpretation and application of existing law, analysis of proposals and new pronouncements, and reviews of tax software.
- *E-mail capabilities* are available to most tax professionals through an employer's equipment or by a subscription providing Internet access at a low and

■ **EXHIBIT 1–4**
Web Sites for the Tax
Practitioner

| Web Site | WWW Address at Press Date (Usually preceded by http://www.) | Description |
|---|---|---|
| Internal Revenue Service | **irs.gov/** | News releases, downloadable forms and instructions, tables, and e-mail |
| Court opinions | The site at **law.emory.edu/FEDCTS** allows the researcher to link to the site of the jurisdiction (other than the Tax Court) that is the subject of the query (see Exhibit 1–5). | |
| Discussion groups moderated by Tax Analysts | **tax.org/discuss/discussion.htm** | Policy-oriented discussions of the tax law and proposals to change it, excerpts from the *Tax Notes* newsletter, and a tax calendar |
| *Tax Sites Directory* | **taxsites.com** | References and links to tax sites on the Internet, including state and Federal tax sites, academic and professional pages, tax forms, and software |
| Tax laws online | Regulations are at **www4.law.cornell.edu/cfr/26cfrI.htm** and the Code is at **uscode.house.gov/usc.htm** | |
| *Tax World* | **taxworld.org** | References and links to tax sites on the Internet, including property tax and international tax links |
| Commercial tax publishers | For instance, **tax.com** and **cch.com** | Information about products and services available for subscription, newsletter excerpts |
| Large accounting firms and professional organizations | For instance, the AICPA's page is at **aicpa.org**, Ernst and Young is at **ey.com/home.asp**, and KPMG is at **kpmg.com** | Tax planning newsletters, descriptions of services offered and career opportunities, exchange of data with clients and subscribers |
| South-Western/Thomson Learning | **wft.swlearning.com** | Informational updates, newsletters, support materials for students and adopters, and continuing education |
| U.S. Tax Court decisions | **ustaxcourt.gov** | Recent U.S. Tax Court decisions |

NOTE: Caution, addresses change frequently.

usually fixed cost for the period. E-mail allows virtually instantaneous sending and receiving of messages, letters, tax returns and supporting data, spreadsheets, and other documents necessary to solve tax problems.

In many situations, solutions to research problems benefit from, or require, the use of various electronic tax research tools. The competent tax professional must become familiar and proficient with the various means of using electronic tax resources to meet the expectations of clients and the necessities of work in the modern world.[58]

---

[58]For more detail, see Raabe, Whittenburg, Sanders, and Bost, *West's Federal Tax Research*, 6th ed. (Cincinnati: South-Western/Thomson Learning, 2003).

■ **EXHIBIT 1–5**
The Emory *Federal Courts Finder*

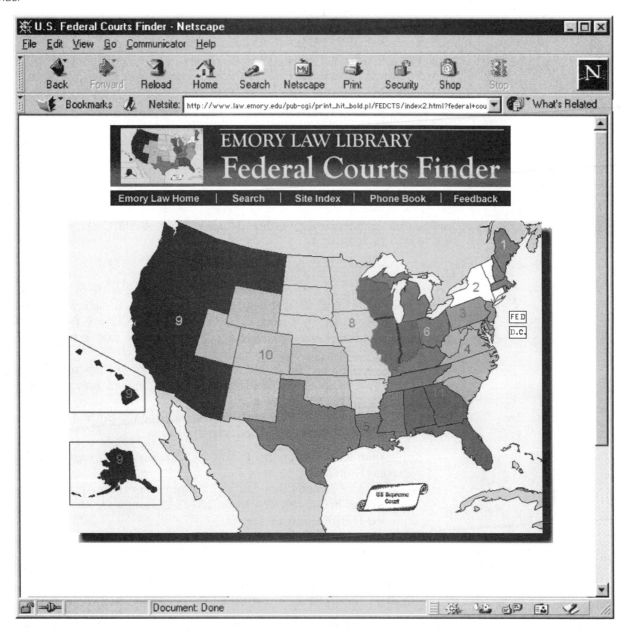

## Use of the RIA Citator

The *Federal Tax Citator* is a separate multivolume service with monthly supplements that may be used to determine the status of tax decisions, Revenue Rulings, and Revenue Procedures. A similar citation process is available with the online research system. Cases that are reported by the *Citator* are divided into the various issues involved. Since the researcher may be interested in only one or two issues, only cases involving the particular issue need to be checked.

The volumes of the *Federal Tax Citator* and the period of time covered by each are as follows:

- Volume 1 (1863–1941).
- Volume 2 (1942–1948).
- Volume 3 (1948–1954).
- Volume 1, Second Series (1954–1977).
- Volume 2, Second Series (1978–1989).
- Volume 3, Second Series (1990–1996).
- Volume 4, Second Series (1997–2002).
- Monthly cumulative paperback supplements.

Through the use of symbols, the *Citator* indicates whether a decision is followed, explained, criticized, questioned, or overruled by a later court decision. These symbols are reproduced in Figure 1–7.

**EXAMPLE 21**

Determine the background and validity of *Adda v. Comm.*, 49 USTC ¶9109, 37 AFTR 654, 171 F.2d 457 (CA–4, 1948). ■

Turning directly to the case itself (reproduced as Figure 1–8), note the two issues involved ("1" and "2"). For purposes of emphasis, these issues have been bracketed and identified by a marginal notation added to Figure 1–8. The reason for the division of the issues becomes apparent when the case is traced through the *Citator*.

Refer to Volume 3 for the AFTR Series (covering the period from October 7, 1948, through July 29, 1954) of the *Federal Tax Citator*. Information about the case is located on page 5505 (reproduced in Figure 1–9).

Correlating the symbols in Figure 1–7 with the shaded portion of Figure 1–9 reveals the following information about *Adda v. Comm.*:

- Application for certiorari (appeal to the U.S. Supreme Court) filed by the taxpayer (T) on March 1, 1949.
- Certiorari was denied (x) by the U.S. Supreme Court on April 18, 1949.
- The trial court decision is reported in 10 T.C. 273 and was affirmed on appeal (sa) to the Fourth Court of Appeals.
- During the time frame of Volume 3 of the *Citator* (October 7, 1948, through July 29, 1954), one decision (*Milner Hotels, Inc.*) has agreed "on all fours with the cited case" (iv). One decision (*Comm. v. Nubar*) has limited the cited case to its facts (l), and two decisions (*The Scottish American Investment Co., Ltd.* and *Zareh Nubar*) have distinguished the cited case on issue 1 (g–1).

Reference to Volume 1 of the *Citator* Second Series (covering the period from 1954 through 1977) shows the *Adda v. Comm.* case on page 25. This page is reproduced in Figure 1–10.

Correlating the symbols in Figure 1–7 with the shaded portion of Figure 1–10 reveals the following additional information about *Adda v. Comm.*:

- The case was cited without comment in two rulings and two decisions: Rev.Rul. 56–145 and Rev.Rul. 56–392, *Balanovski* and *Liang*.
- It was followed in *Asthmanefrin Co.* (f–1).
- It was distinguished in *de Vegvar* and *Purvis* (g–1).
- It was reconciled in *deKrause* (k–1).

■ **FIGURE 1–7**
RIA Citator Symbols

Citator Symbols*
COURT DECISIONS
Judicial History of the Case

| | |
|---|---|
| a | affirmed (by decision of a higher court) |
| d | dismissed (appeal to a higher court dismissed) |
| m | modified (decision modified by a higher court, or on rehearing) |
| r | reversed (by a decision of a higher court) |
| s | same case (e.g., on rehearing) |
| rc | related case (companion cases and other cases arising out of the same subject matter are so designated) |
| x | certiorari denied (by the Supreme Court of the United States) |
| (C or G) | The Commissioner or Solicitor General has made the appeal |
| (T) | Taxpayer has made the appeal |
| (A) | Tax Court's decision acquiesced in by Commissioner |
| (NA) | Tax Court's decision nonacquiesced in by Commissioner |
| sa | same case affirmed (by the cited case) |
| sd | same case dismissed (by the cited case) |
| sm | same case modified (by the cited case) |
| sr | same case reversed (by the cited case) |
| sx | same case—certiorari denied |

Syllabus of the Cited Case

| | |
|---|---|
| iv | four (on all fours with the cited case) |
| f | followed (the cited case followed) |
| e | explained (comment generally favorable, but not to a degree that indicates the cited case is followed) |
| k | reconciled (the cited case reconciled) |
| n | dissenting opinion (cited in a dissenting opinion) |
| g | distinguished (the cited case distinguished either in law or on the facts) |
| l | limited (the cited case limited to its facts. Used when an appellate court so limits a prior decision, or a lower court states that in its opinion the cited case should be so limited) |
| c | criticized (adverse comment on the cited case) |
| q | questioned (the cited case not only criticized, but its correctness questioned) |
| o | overruled |

*Reproduced from the *Citator 2nd Series* with the permission of the publisher, Research Institute of America, New York, NY 10011.

Reference to the "Court Decisions" section of Volume 2, Second Series of the *Citator* covering the period from 1978 through 1989 shows that *Adda v. Comm.* was cited in *Robert E. Cleveland* and *Judith C. Connelly*, each case limited to its facts (l).

The *Citator* includes a cumulative supplement, and each month there is a cumulative paperback supplement. Be sure to refer to these monthly supplements, or very recent citations might be overlooked.

Except as otherwise noted, it would appear that *Adda v. Comm.* has withstood the test of time.

■ **FIGURE 1–8**
Actual Court Case

**ADDA v. COMMISSIONER OF INTERNAL REVENUE.**

No. 5796.

United States Court of Appeals
Fourth Circuit.

Dec. 3, 1948.

**1. Internal revenue** ⊜⇒792

ISSUE 1 { Where nonresident alien's brother residing in United States traded for alien's benefit on commodity exchanges in United States at authorization of alien, who vested full discretion in brother with regard thereto, and many transactions were effected through different brokers, several accounts were maintained, and substantial gains and losses realized, transactions constituted a "trade or business," profits of which were "capital gains" taxable as income to the alien. 26 U.S.C.A. § 211(b).

See Words and Phrases, Permanent Edition, for other judicial constructions and definitions of "Capital Gains" and "Trade or Business".

**2. Internal revenue** ⊜⇒792

ISSUE 2 { The exemption of a nonresident alien's commodity transactions in the United States provided for by the Internal Revenue Code does not apply where alien has agent in United States using his own discretion in effecting transactions for alien's account. 26 U.S.C.A. § 211(b).

On Petition to Review the Decision of The Tax Court of the United States.

Petition by Fernand C. A. Adda to review a decision of the Tax Court redetermining a deficiency in income tax imposed by the Commissioner of Internal Revenue.

Decision affirmed.

Rollin Browne and Mitchell B. Carroll, both of New York City, for petitioner.

Irving I. Axelrad, Sp. Asst. to Atty. Gen. (Theron Lamar Caudle, Asst. Atty. Gen., and Ellis N. Slack and A. F. Prescott, Sp. Assts. to Atty. Gen., on the brief), for respondent.

Before PARKER, Chief Judge, and SOPER and DOBIE, Circuit Judges.

PER CURIAM.

[1, 2] This is a petition by a non-resident alien to review a decision of the Tax Court. Petitioner is a national of Egypt, who in the year 1941 was residing in France. He had a brother who at that time was residing in the United States and who traded for petitioner's benefit on commodity exchanges in the United States in cotton, wool, grains, silk, hides and copper. This trading was authorized by petitioner who vested full discretion in his brother with regard thereto, and it resulted in profits in the sum of $193,857.14. The Tax Court said: "While the number of transactions or the total amount of money involved in them has not been stated, it is apparent that many transactions were effected through different brokers, several accounts were maintained, and gains and losses in substantial amounts were realized. This evidence shows that the trading was extensive enough to amount to a trade or business, and the petitioner does not contend, nor has he shown, that the transactions were so infrequent or inconsequential as not to amount to a trade or business." We agree with the Tax Court that, for reasons adequately set forth in its opinion, this income was subject to taxation, and that the exemption of a non-resident alien's commodity transactions in the United States, provided by section 211(b) of the Internal Revenue Code, 26 U.S.C.A. § 211(b), does not apply to a case where the alien has an agent in the United States using his own discretion in effecting the transactions for the alien's account. As said by the Tax Court, "Through such transactions the alien is engaging in trade or business within the United States, and the profits on these transactions are capital gains taxable to him." Nothing need be added to the reasoning of the Tax Court in this connection, and the decision will be affirmed on its opinion.

Affirmed.

**■ FIGURE 1–9**
From Volume 3, First Series

» Adamson — Adler «                                               5505

ADAMSON, JAMES H. & MARION C. v
U. S., — F Supp —, 36 AFTR 1529, 1946
P.-H. ¶ 72,418 (DC Calif) (See Adamson
v U. S.)
ADAMSON, R. R., MRS., — BTA —, 1934 (P.-
H.) BTA Memo. Dec. ¶ 34,370
ADAMSON v U. S., 26 AFTR 1188 (DC Calif,
Sept 8, 1939)
    iv—Coggan, Linus C., 1939 (P.-H.) BTA
    Memo. Dec. page 39—806
ADAMSON; U. S. v, 161 F(2d) 942, 35 AFTR
1404 (CCA 9)
    1—Lazier v U. S., 170 F(2d) 524, 37 AFTR
    545, 1948 P.-H. page 73,174 (CCA 9)
    1—Grace Bros., Inc. v Comm., 173 F(2d)
    178, 37 AFTR 1014, 1949 P.-H. page 72,433
    (CCA 9)
    1—Briggs; Hofferbert v, 178 F(2d) 744, 38
    AFTR 1219, 1950 P.-H. page 72,267 (CCA
    4)
    1—Rogers v Comm., 180 F(2d) 722, 39 AFTR
    115, 1950 P.-H. page 72,531 (CCA 4)
    1—Lamar v Granger, 99 F Supp 41, 40
    AFTR 270, 1951 P.-H. page 72,945 (DC Pa)
    1—Herbert v Riddell, 103 F Supp 383, 41
    AFTR 975, 1952 P.-H. page 72,383 (DC
    Calif)
    1—Hudson, Galvin, 20 TC 737, 20-1953
    P.-H. TC 418
ADAMSON v U. S., — F Supp —, 36 AFTR
1529, 1946 P.-H. ¶ 72,418 (DC Calif, Jan
28, 1946)
ADAMS-ROTH BAKING CO., 8 BTA 458
    1—Gunderson Bros. Engineering Corp., 16
    TC 129, 16-1951 P.-H. TC 72
ADAMSTON FLAT GLASS CO. v COMM.,
162 F(2d) 875, 35 AFTR 1579 (CCA 6)
    4—Forrest Hotel Corp. v. Fly, 112 F Supp
    789, 43 AFTR 1080, 1953 P.-H. page 72,856
    (DC Miss)
ADDA v COMM., 171 F(2d) 457, 37 AFTR 654,
1948 P.-H. ¶ 72,655 (CCA 4, Dec 3, 1948)
Cert. filed, March 1, 1949 (T)
No cert. (G) 1949 P-H ¶ 71,050
    x—Adda v Comm., 336 US 952, 69 S Ct 883,
    93 L Ed 1107, April 18, 1949 (T)
    sa—Adda, Fernand C. A., 10 TC 273 (No.
    33), ¶ 10.33 P.-H. TC 1948
    iv—Milner Hotels, Inc., N. Y., 173 F (2d)
    567, 37 AFTR 1170, 1949 P.-H. page 72,528
    (CCA 6)
    1—Nubar; Comm. v, 185 F(2d) 588, 39 AFTR
    1315, 1950 P.-H. page 73,423 (CCA 4)
    g-1—Scottish Amer. Invest. Co., Ltd.,
    The, 12 TC 59, 12-1949 P.-H. TC 32
    g-1—Nubar, Zareh, 13 TC 579, 13-1949
    P.-H. TC 318
ADDA, FERNAND C. A., 10 TC 273 (No.
33), ¶ 10.33 P.-H. TC 1948 (A) 1948-2 CB 1
    a—Adda v Comm., 171 F(2d) 457, 37 AFTR
    654, 1948 P.-H. ¶ 72,655 (CCA 4)
    1—Nubar; Comm. v, 185 F(2d) 588, 39 AFTR
    1315, 1950 P.-H. page 73,423 (CCA 4)
    g-1—Scottish Amer. Invest. Co., Ltd.,
    The, 12 TC 59, 12-1949 P.-H. TC 32
    g-1—Nubar, Zareh, 13 TC 579, 13-1949
    P.-H. TC 318
ADDA, FERNAND C. A., 10 TC 1291 (No.
168), ¶ 10.168 P.-H. TC 1948 (A) 1953-1
CB 3, 1953 P.-H. ¶ 76,453 (NA) 1948-2
CB 5, 1948 P.-H. ¶ 76,434 withdrawn
    1—Scottish Amer. Invest. Co., Ltd., The,
    12 TC 59, 12-1949 P.-H. TC 32
ADDA INC., 9 TC 199 (A) 1949-1 CB 1, 1949
P.-H. ¶ 76,260 (NA) 1947-2 CB 6 with-
drawn
    a—Adda, Inc.; Comm. v, 171 F(2d) 367, 37
    AFTR 641, 1948 P.-H. ¶ 72,654 (CCA 2)
    a—Adda, Inc.; Comm. v, 171 F(2d) 367, 37
    AFTR 641, 1949 P.-H. ¶ 72,303 (CCA 2)
    e-1—G.C.M. 26069, 1949-2 CB 38, 1949 P.-H.
    page 76,226
    3—Koshland, Execx.; U.S. v, 208 F(2d)
    640, — AFTR —, 1953 P.-H. page 73,597
    (CCA 9)
    4—Kent, Otis Beall, 1954 (P. H.) TC
    Memo. Dec. page 54—47

ADDA, INC.; COMM. v, 171 F(2d) 367, 37
AFTR 641, 1948 P.-H. ¶ 72,654 (CCA 2, Dec
6, 1948)
    sa—Adda, Inc., 9 TC 199
    s—Adda, Inc.; Comm. v, 171 F(2d) 367, 37
    AFTR 641, 1949 P.-H. ¶ 72,303 (CCA 2) reh.
    den.
    e-1—G.C.M. 26069, 1949-2 CB 39, 1949 P.-H.
    page 76,227
    e-2—G.C.M. 26069, 1949-2 CB 39, 1949 P.-H.
    page 76,227
ADDA, INC.; COMM. v, 171 F(2d) 367, 37
AFTR 641, 1949 P.-H. ¶ 72,303 (CCA 2, Dec
6, 1948) reh. den.
    sa—Adda, Inc., 9 TC 199
    s—Adda, Inc.; Comm. v, 171 F(2d) 367, 37
    AFTR 641, 1949 P.-H. ¶ 72,654 (CCA 2)
ADDISON-CHEVROLET SALES, INC. v
CHAMBERLAIN, L. A. & NAT. BANK
OF WASH., THE, — F Supp —, — AFTR
—, 1954 P.-H. ¶ 72,550 (DC DC) (See
Campbell v Chamberlain)
ADDISON v COMM., 177 F(2d) 521, 38 AFTR
821, 1949 P.-H. ¶ 72,637 (CCA 8, Nov 3,
1949)
    sa—Addison, Irene D., — TC —, 1948
    (P.-H.) TC Memo. Dec. ¶ 48,177
    1—Roberts, Supt. v U. S., 115 Ct Cl 439,
    87 F Supp 937, 38 AFTR 1314, 1950 P.-H.
    page 72,292
    1—Cold Metal Process Co., The, 17 TC
    934, 17-1951 P.-H. TC 512
    1—Berger, Samuel & Lillian, 1954 (P.-H.)
    TC Memo. Dec. page 54—232
    2—Urquhart, George Gordon & Mary F.,
    20 TC 948, 20-1953 P.-H. TC 536
ADDISON, IRENE D., — TC —, 1948 (P.-
H.) TC Memo. Dec. ¶ 48,177
    App (T) Jan 14, 1949 (CCA 8)
    a—Addison v Comm., 177 F(2d) 521, 38
    AFTR 821, 1949 P.-H. ¶ 72,637 (CCA 8)
    1—Urquhart, George Gordon & Mary F.,
    20 TC 948, 20-1953 P.-H. TC 536
ADDITON, HARRY L. & ANNIE S., 3
TC 427
    1—Lum, Ralph E., 12 TC 379, 12-1949 P.-H.
    TC 204
    1—Christie, John A. & Elizabeth H., —
    TC —, 1949 (P.-H.) TC Memo. Dec.
    page 49—795
ADDRESSOGRAPH - MULTIGRAPH
CORP., 1945 (P.-H.) TC Memo. Dec.
¶ 45,058
    f-10—Rev. Rul. 54-71, 1954 P.-H. page
    76,453
ADDRESSOGRAPH-MULTIGRAPH CORP.
v U. S., 112 Ct Cl 201, 78 F Supp 111, 37
AFTR 53, 1948 P.-H. ¶ 72,504 (June 1, 1948)
No cert (G) 1949 P.-H. ¶ 71,041
    1—New Oakmont Corp., The v U. S., 114
    Ct Cl 686, 86 F Supp 901, 38 AFTR 924, 1949
    P.-H. page 73,181
ADELAIDE PARK LAND, 25 BTA 211
    g—Amer. Security & Fidelity Corp., — BTA
    —, 1940 (P.-H.) BTA Memo. Dec. page
    40—571
ADELPHI PAINT & COLOR WORKS,
INC., 18 BTA 436
    1—Neracher, William A., — BTA —, 1939
    (P.-H.) BTA Memo. Dec. page 39—69
    1—Lyman-Hawkins Lumber Co., — BTA —,
    1939 (P.-H.) BTA Memo. Dec. page 39—350
ADEMAN v U. S., 174 F(2d) 283, 37 AFTR
1406 (CCA 9, April 25, 1949)
ADICONIS, NOELLA L. (PATNAUDE),
1953 (P.-H.) TC Memo. Dec. ¶ 53,305
ADJUSTMENT BUREAU OF ST. LOUIS
ASSN., OF CREDIT MEN, 21 BTA 232
    1—Cook County Loss Adjustment Bureau,
    — BTA —, 1940 (P.-H.) BTA Memo. Dec.
    page 40—331
ADKINS, CHARLES I., — BTA —, 1933
(P.-H.) BTA Memo. Dec. ¶ 33,457
ADLER v COMM., 77 F(2d) 733, 16 AFTR 162
(CCA 5)
    g-2—McEuen v Comm., 196 F(2d) 130, 41
    AFTR 1172, 1952 P.-H. page 72,604 (CCA 5)

Copyright 1955 by Prentice-Hall, Inc.—Federal Tax Citator

Reproduced from the *Citator 1st Series* with permission of the publisher, Research Institute of America, New York, NY 10011.

■ **FIGURE 1–10**

From Volume 1, Second Series

## ADASKAVICH—ADELSON 25

ADASKAVICH, STEPHEN A. v U.S., 39 AFTR2d 77-517, 422 F Supp 276 (DC Mont) (See Wiegand, Charles J., Jr. v U.S.)

AD. AURIEMA, INC., 1943 P-H TC Memo ¶ 43,422
  e-1—Miller v U.S., 13 AFTR2d 1515, 166 Ct Cl 257, 331 F2d 859

ADAY v SUPERIOR CT. OF ALAMEDA COUNTY, 8 AFTR2d 5367, 13 Cal Reptr 415, 362 P2d 47 (Calif, 5-11-61)

ADCO SERVICE, INC., ASSIGNEE v CYBERMATICS, INC., 36 AFTR2d 75-6342 (NJ) (See Adco Service, Inc., Assignee v Graphic Color Plate)

ADCO SERVICE, INC., ASSIGNEE v GRAPHIC COLOR PLATE, 36 AFTR2d 75-6342 (NJ, Supr Ct, 11-10-75)

ADCO SERVICE, INC., ASSIGNEE v GRAPHIC COLOR PLATE, INC., 36 AFTR2d 75-6342 (NJ) (See Adco Service, Inc., Assignee v Graphic Color Plate)

ADDA v COMM., 171 F2d 457, 37 AFTR 654 (USCA 4)
  Rev. Rul. 56-145, 1956-1 CB 613
  1—Balanovski; U.S. v, 236 F2d 304, 49 AFTR 2013 (USCA 2)
  1—Liang, Chang Hsiao, 23 TC 1045, 23-1955 P-H TC 624
  f-1—Asthmanefrin Co., Inc., 25 TC 1141, 25-1956 P-H TC 639
  g-1—de Vegvar, Edward A. Neuman, 28 TC 1061, 28-1957 P-H TC 599
  g-1—Purvis, Ralph E. & Patricia Lee, 1974 P-H TC Memo 74-669
  k-1—deKrause, Piedad Alvarado, 1974 P-H TC Memo 74-1291
  1—Rev. Rul. 56-392, 1956-2 CB 971

ADDA, FERNAND C.A., 10 TC 273, ¶ 10,133 P-H TC 1948
  1—Balanovski; U.S. v, 236 F2d 303, 49 AFTR 2012 (USCA 2)
  1—Liang, Chang Hsiao, 23 TC 1045, 23-1955 P-H TC 624
  g-1—de Vegvar, Edward A. Neuman, 28 TC 1061, 28-1957 P-H TC 599
  g-1—Purvis, Ralph E. & Patricia Lee, 1974 P-H TC Memo 74-669
  k-1—deKrause, Piedad Alvarado, 1974 P-H TC Memo 74-1291

ADDA, INC., 9 TC 199
  Pardee, Marvin L., Est. of, 49 TC 152, 49 P-H TC 107 [See 9 TC 206-208]
  f-1—Asthmanefrin Co., Inc., 25 TC 1141, 25-1956 P-H TC 639
  1—Keil Properties, Inc. (Dela), 24 TC 1117, 24-1955 P-H TC 615
  1—Saffan, Samuel, 1957 P-H TC Memo 57—701
  1—Rev. Rul. 56-145, 1956-1 CB 613
  1—Rev. Rul. 56-392, 1956-2 CB 971
  4— Midler Court Realty, Inc., 61 TC 597, 61 P-H TC 368

ADDA, INC.; COMM. v, 171 F2d 367, 37 AFTR 641 (USCA 2)
  1—Pardee, Marvin L., Est. of, 49 TC 152, 49 P-H TC 107
  1—Saffan, Samuel, 1957 P-H TC Memo 57-701
  2—Midler Court Realty, Inc., 61 TC 597, 61 P-H TC 368

ADDELSTON, ALBERT A. & SARAH M., 1965 P-H TC Memo ¶ 65,215

ADDISON v COMM., 177 F2d 521, 38 AFTR 821 (USCA 8)
  g-1—Industrial Aggregate Co. v U.S., 6 AFTR2d 5963, 284 F2d 645 (USCA 8)
  1—Sturgeon v McMahon, 155 F Supp 630, 52 AFTR 789 (DC NY)
  1—Gilmore v U.S., 16 AFTR2d 5211, 5213, 245 F Supp 384, 386 (DC Calif)
  1—Waldheim & Co., Inc., 25 TC 599, 25-1955 P-H TC 332
  g-1—Galewitz, Samuel & Marian, 50 TC 113, 50 P-H TC 79
  1—Buder, G. A., Est. of, 1963 P-H TC Memo 63-345
  e-1—Rhodes, Lynn E. & Martha E., 1963 P-H TC Memo 63-1374
  2—Shipp v Comm., 217 F2d 402, 46 AFTR 1170 (USCA 9)

ADDISON—Contd.
  g-2—Industrial Aggregate Co. v U.S., 6 AFTR2d 5964, 284 F2d 645 (USCA 8)
  e-2—Buder, Est. of v Comm., 13 AFTR2d 1238, 330 F2d 443 (USCA 8)
  2—Iowa Southern Utilities Co. v Comm., 14 AFTR2d 5063, 333 F2d 385 (USCA 8)
  2—Kelly, Daniel, S.W., 23 TC 687, 23-1955 P-H TC 422
  f-2—Morgan, Joseph P., Est. of, 37 TC 36, 37, 37-1961 P-H TC 26, 27
  n-2—Woodward, Fred W. & Elsie M., 49 TC 385, 49 P-H TC 270

ADDISON, IRENE D., 1948 P-H TC Memo ¶ 48,177
  1—Waldheim & Co., Inc., 25 TC 599, 25-1955 P-H TC 332
  f-1—Morgan, Joseph P., Est. of, 37 TC 36, 37, 37-1961 P-H TC 26, 27
  1—Buder, G. A., Est. of, 1963 P-H TC Memo 63-345
  e-1—Rhodes, Lynn E. & Martha E., 1963 P-H TC Memo 63-1374

ADDISON, JOHN MILTON, BKPT; U.S. v, 20 AFTR2d 5630, 384 F2d 748 (USCA 5) (See Rochelle Jr., Trtee; U.S. v)

ADDRESSOGRAPH - MULTIGRAPH CORP., 1945 P-H TC Memo ¶ 45,058
  Conn. L. & P. Co., The v U.S., 9 AFTR2d 679, 156 Ct Cl 312, 314, 299 F2d 264
  Copperhead Coal Co., Inc., 1958 P-H TC Memo 58-33
  1—Seas Shipping Co., Inc. v Comm., 19 AFTR2d 596, 371 F2d 529 (USCA 2)
  e-1—Hitchcock, E. R., Co., The v U.S., 35 AFTR2d 75-1207, 514 F2d 487 (USCA 2)
  f-2—Vulcan Materials Co. v U.S., 25 AFTR2d 70-446, 308 F Supp 57 (DC Ala)
  f-3—Marlo Coil Co. v U.S., 1969 P-H 58,133 (Ct Cl Comr Rep)
  4—United Gas Improvement Co. v Comm., 240 F2d 318, 50 AFTR 1354 (USCA 3)
  10—St. Louis Co. (Del) (in Dissolution) v U.S., 237 F2d 156, 50 AFTR 257 (USCA 3)

ADDRESSOGRAPH - MULTIGRAPH CORP. v U.S., 112 Ct Cl 201, 78 F Supp 111, 37 AFTR 53
  f-1—St. Joseph Lead Co v U.S., 9 AFTR2d 712, 299 F2d 350 (USCA 2)
  e-1—Central & South West Corp. v U.S., 1968 P-H 58,175 (Ct Cl Comr Rep)
  1—Smale & Robinson, Inc. v U.S., 123 F Supp 469, 46 AFTR 375 (DC Calif)
  1—St. Joseph Lead Co. v U.S., 7 AFTR2d 401, 190 F Supp 640 (DC NY)
  1—Eisenstadt Mfg. Co., 28 TC 230, 28-1957 P-H TC 132
  f-2—St. Joseph Lead Co. v U.S., 9 AFTR2d 712, 299 F2d 350 (USCA 2)
  f-3—Consol, Coppermines Corp. v U.S., 8 AFTR2d 5873, 155 Ct Cl 736, 296 F2d 745

ADELAIDE PARK LAND, 25 BTA 211
  g—Custom Component Switches, Inc. v U.S., 19 AFTR2d 560 (DC Calif) [See 25 BTA 215]
  O'Connor, John C., 1957 P-H TC Memo 57-190

ADELBERG, MARVIN & HELEN, 1971 P-H TC Memo ¶ 71,015

ADELMAN v U.S., 27 AFTR2d 71-1464, 440 F2d 991 (USCA 9, 5-3-71)
  sa—Adelman v U.S., 24 AFTR2d 69-5769, 304 F Supp 599 (DC Calif)

ADELMAN v U.S., 24 AFTR2d 69-5769, 304 F Supp 599 (DC Calif, 9-30-69)
  a—Adelman v U.S., 27 AFTR2d 71-1464, 440 F2d 991 (USCA 9)

ADELSON, SAMUEL; U.S. v, 52 AFTR 1798 (DC RI) (See Sullivan Co., Inc.: U.S. v)

ADELSON v U.S., 15 AFTR2d 246, 342 F2d 332 (USCA 9, 1-13-65)
  sa—Adelson v U.S., 12 AFTR2d 5010, 221 F Supp 31 (DC Calif)
  g-1—Greenlee, L. C. & Gladys M., 1966 P-H TC Memo 66-985
  f-1—Cochran, Carol J., 1973 P-H TC Memo 73-459
  f-1—Marchionni, Siro L., 1976 P-H TC Memo 76-1321
  f-2—Krist, Edwin F. v Comm., 32 AFTR2d 73-5663, 483 F2d 1351 (USCA 2)
  f-2—Fugate v U.S., 18 AFTR2d 5607, 259 F Supp 401 (DC Tex) [See 15 AFTR2d 249, 342 F2d 335]

## KEY TERMS

| | | |
|---|---|---|
| Acquiescence, 1–32 | Determination letters, 1–24 | Revenue Procedures, 1–22 |
| Arm's length concept, 1–14 | Indexation, 1–10 | Revenue Rulings, 1–22 |
| Business purpose concept, 1–15 | Letter rulings, 1–23 | Tax benefit rule, 1–15 |
| Certiorari, 1–29 | Nonacquiescence, 1–32 | Temporary Regulations, 1–22 |
| Continuity of interest concept, 1–15 | Proposed Regulations, 1–22 | Wherewithal to pay, 1–7 |
| | Revenue neutrality, 1–3 | |

## PROBLEM MATERIALS

### Discussion Questions

1. Have nonrevenue factors had any impact upon the development of our taxation system?

2. How does the tax law encourage technological progress?

3. Do the tax laws provide any stimulus for farmers and developers of natural resources? Explain.

4. Why is personal saving desirable for the U.S. economy?

5. Explain how the following tax provisions encourage small business:
   a. The nature of a shareholder's loss on a stock investment.
   b. The tax rates applicable to corporations.
   c. Nontaxable corporate divisive reorganizations.

6. What purpose is served by allowing a refundable earned income credit?

7. What purpose is served by permitting the HOPE scholarship credit?

8. What purpose is served by the credit allowed for certain child or disabled dependent care expenses?

9. Why should the deductibility of excess political campaign expenditures be contrary to public policy?

10. In the past, Congress has considered proposals that would allow a taxpayer to claim a tax credit for tuition paid to send a dependent to a private school. Is there any justification for such a proposal?

11. Why has Congress moved toward credits rather than deductions in recent years?

12. Some states that impose a state income tax allow the taxpayer a deduction for any Federal income taxes paid. What is the justification for such an approach?

**Issue ID**

13. A provision of the Code allows a taxpayer a deduction for Federal income tax purposes for state and local income taxes paid. Does this provision eliminate the effect of multiple taxation of the same income? Why or why not? In this connection, consider the following:
    a. Taxpayer, an individual, has itemized deductions that are less than the standard deduction.
    b. Taxpayer is in the 10% tax bracket for Federal income tax purposes. The 30% tax bracket.

14. Yvonne operates a profitable sole proprietorship. Because the business is expanding, she would like to transfer it to a newly created corporation. Yvonne is concerned, however, over the possible tax consequences that would result from incorporating. Please comment.

15. Assume the same facts as in Question 14. Yvonne is also worried that once she incorporates, the business will be subject to the Federal corporate income tax. Any suggestions?

16. In regard to situations in which the tax law recognizes the wherewithal to pay concept, discuss the effect of the following:
    a. The basis to the transferor of property received in a nontaxable exchange.
    b. The recognition by the transferor of any realized loss on the transfer.
    c. The receipt of boot or other property by the transferor.

17. Does the wherewithal to pay concept enable a transferor to permanently avoid the recognition of any gain or loss? Give an example of the law permanently forgiving the recognition of gain or loss.

18. Brenda exchanges 600 shares of Veritex Corporation stock for a one-fourth interest in the Blue Partnership. Since this exchange is not pursuant to a nontaxable reorganization, does the wherewithal to pay concept shield Brenda from the recognition of gain or loss? Why?

19. What is the purpose of the installment method?

20. Mel, a calendar year cash basis taxpayer, is a participant in an H.R. 10 (Keogh) retirement plan for self-employed persons. To get the deduction for 2003, Mel makes his contribution on December 30, 2003.
    a. Why was there an element of urgency in Mel's action?
    b. Was Mel misinformed about the tax law? Explain.

21. Explain why prepaid subscription and dues income is not taxed until earned, while prepaid rents are taxed to the landlord in the year received.

22. Lucy operates a service business as a sole proprietor. For tax purposes, she recognizes income using the cash method but deducts expenses as they accrue.
    a. What is Lucy trying to accomplish?
    b. Is this procedure proper?
    c. Does the IRS have any recourse?

23. In what way does the wherewithal to pay concept aid the IRS in the collection of tax revenue?

24. Describe how the IRS achieves administrative feasibility through each of the following tax provisions:
    a. The standard deduction allowed to individual taxpayers.
    b. The $345,800 unified tax credit allowed for estate tax purposes in 2003.
    c. The $11,000 annual exclusion allowed for gift tax purposes.

25. What is meant by the concept of substance over form? Why is it variously described as the "telescoping," "collapsing," or "step transaction" approach?

26. What is meant by the concept that statutory relief provisions of the tax law are to be narrowly construed? Where did the concept originate?

27. When does the tax benefit rule apply? With what effect?

28. White Corporation lends $404,000 to Red Corporation with no provision for interest. White Corporation and Red Corporation are owned by the same shareholders. How might the IRS restructure this transaction with adverse tax consequences?

29. Under what circumstances can court decisions lead to changes in the Code?

30. In 1986, Congress codified the then-existing Federal tax provisions, and this compilation became the Internal Revenue Code of 1986. Discuss the validity of this statement.

31. How may a tax bill originate in the Senate?

32. Of what value are House and Senate Committee Reports?

33. Determine the subparts of § 4977(b)(2)(A).

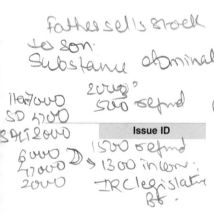

34. Is § 1221(1) a proper Code Section?

35. Why are certain Code Section numbers missing from the Internal Revenue Code (e.g., §§ 6, 7, 8, 9, 10)?

36. Do Temporary Regulations carry more weight than traditional Proposed Regulations?

37. Interpret each of the following citations:
    a. FSA 200005006.
    b. Rev.Proc. 89–50, 1989–2 C.B. 631.
    c. Rev.Rul. 80–265, 1980–2 C.B. 378.

**Communications**

38. Cy Young calls you requesting an explanation of the fact-finding determination of a Federal Court of Appeals. Prepare a letter dated October 15, 2003, to be sent to Cy answering this query. His address is 1072 Richmond Lane, Keene, NH 01720.

**Communications**

39. Milt Pappas calls you with respect to a tax issue. He has found a tax case in the U.S. District Court of South Carolina that is in favor of his position. The IRS lost and did not appeal the case. Over the phone, you explain to Milt the significance of the failure to appeal. Prepare a tax file memorandum dated September 13, 2003, outlining your remarks to Milt.

40. In assessing the validity of a court decision, discuss the significance of the following:
    a. The decision was rendered by the U.S. District Court of Wyoming. Taxpayer lives in Wyoming.
    b. The decision was rendered by the U.S. Court of Federal Claims. Taxpayer lives in Wyoming.
    c. The decision was rendered by the Second Circuit Court of Appeals. Taxpayer lives in California.
    d. The decision was rendered by the U.S. Supreme Court.
    e. The decision was rendered by the U.S. Tax Court. The IRS has acquiesced in the result.
    f. Same as (e) except that the IRS has issued a nonacquiescence as to the result.

41. Answer the following questions based upon this citation: *American Bantam Car Co.*, 11 T.C. 397 (1948), *aff'd per curiam* 177 F.2d 513 (CA–3, 1949), *cert. den.* 339 U.S. 920, 70 S.Ct. 622 (USSC, 1950).
    a. In which court did this decision first appear?
    b. Who was the plaintiff?
    c. Who was the respondent?
    d. Did the appellate court agree or disagree with the trial court?
    e. Did the Supreme Court hear the decision?

42. Refer to Figures 1–7 and 1–9 illustrating the use of the RIA *Federal Tax Citator*. Explain the following abbreviations:
    a. sx        f. e
    b. NA        g. k
    c. r         h. c
    d. a         i. q
    e. f         j. o

**Decision Making**

43. Kenny Rogers needs to learn quickly about a personal holding company. How should Kenny approach his research?

44. What is tax avoidance? Give an example.

45. Compare the cost of paper and electronic tax research materials.

## Problems

46. Thelma owns some real estate (basis of $120,000 and fair market value of $65,000) that she would like to sell to her son, Sandy, for $65,000. Thelma is aware, however, that losses on sales between certain related parties are disallowed for Federal income tax purposes [§ 267(a)(1)]. Thelma therefore sells the property to Paul (an unrelated party)

for $65,000. On the next day, Paul sells the property to Sandy for the same amount. Is Thelma's realized loss of $55,000 deductible? Explain.

47. Bart exchanges some real estate (basis of $800,000 and fair market value of $1 million) for other real estate owned by Roland (basis of $1.2 million and fair market value of $900,000) and $100,000 in cash. The real estate involved is unimproved and is held by Bart and Roland, before and after the exchange, as investment property.
   a. What is Bart's realized gain on the exchange? Recognized gain?
   b. What is Roland's realized loss? Recognized loss?
   c. Support your results to (a) and (b) under the wherewithal to pay concept as applied to like-kind exchanges (§ 1031).

48. Using the legend provided, classify the overall objective of the particular tax provision:

| Legend | |
|---|---|
| CE = Control of the economy | W   = Wherewithal to pay concept |
| EA = Encouragement of certain activities | AF   = Administrative feasibility |
| EI  = Encouragement of certain industries | ESB = Encouragement of small business |
| SC = Social considerations | |

   a. Involuntary conversion of a business building.   W
   b. An increase in the individual tax rate.   CE
   c. The S corporation election.   ESB
   d. Adoption expense credit.   SC
   e. Percentage depletion.   EI
   f. $11,000 gift tax exclusion.   AF
   g. Charitable contribution deduction.   SC

49. Determine whether the following states are community property or common law states:
   a. Louisiana.
   b. Virginia.
   c. Washington.
   d. New York.
   e. Alaska.
   f. California.

50. Troy sells property (basis of $30,000) to Beige Corporation for $45,000. Based on the following conditions, how could the IRS challenge this transaction?
   a. Troy is the sole shareholder of Beige Corporation.
   b. Troy is the son of the sole shareholder of Beige Corporation.
   c. Troy is neither a shareholder in Beige Corporation nor related to any of Beige's shareholders.

51. Identify the governmental unit that produces the following tax sources:
   a. Temporary Regulations.
   b. Revenue Procedures.
   c. Letter rulings.
   d. Determination letters.
   e. Technical advice memoranda.
   f. Field service advice.

52. Explain what is meant by this citation: Rev.Rul. 93–61, 1993–2 C.B. 118.

53. Using the legend provided, classify each of the following citations as to the location. There may be more than one answer for a citation.

| Legend | |
| --- | --- |
| IRC = Internal Revenue Code | FR = *Federal Register* |
| IRB = *Internal Revenue Bulletin* | NA = Not applicable |
| CB = *Cumulative Bulletin* | |

a. § 1503(a).
b. Rev.Rul. 66–365, 1966–2 C.B. 116.
c. Prop.Reg. § 1.631–2(a).
d. Ltr.Rul. 9314022.
e. Temp.Reg. § 1.382–2T(e).
f. Rev.Proc. 86–42, 1986–2 C.B. 722.
g. H. Rep. No. 105–220, 105th Cong. 1st Sess. (1997), p. 34.

54. Identify the U.S. Court of Appeals that has authority over each of the following states:
    a. Texas.
    b. New Mexico.
    c. Nebraska.
    d. Idaho.
    e. North Carolina.

55. Using the legend provided, classify each of the following citations as to the court:

| Legend | |
| --- | --- |
| T = U.S. Tax Court | D = U.S. District Court |
| C = U.S. Court of Federal Claims | A = U.S. Court of Appeals |
| U = U.S. Supreme Court | N = None of the above |

a. 388 F.2d 420 (CA–7, 1968).
b. 79 T.C. 7 (1982).
c. 54 S.Ct. 8 (USSC, 1933).
d. 3 B.T.A. 1042 (1926).
e. T.C.Memo. 1954–141.
f. 597 F.2d 760 (Ct.Cl., 1979).
g. Ltr.Rul. 9414051.
h. 465 F.Supp. 341 (D.Ct.Okla., 1978).

56. What group or company publishes the following tax periodicals?
    a. *Journal of Taxation*.
    b. *Journal of the American Taxation Association*.
    c. *The Tax Lawyer*.
    d. *The Tax Adviser*.
    e. *Oil, Gas & Energy Quarterly*.

57. Locate the following tax services in your library and indicate the name of the publisher and whether the service is organized by topic or by Code Section:
    a. *United States Tax Reporter*.
    b. *Standard Federal Tax Reporter*.
    c. *Federal Tax Coordinator 2d*.
    d. *Mertens Law of Federal Income Taxation*.
    e. *Tax Management Portfolios*.
    f. *Federal Taxation of Income, Estates and Gifts*.
    g. CCH's *Federal Tax Service*.

58. Using the legend provided, classify each of the following tax sources:

| **Legend** | |
| --- | --- |
| P = Primary tax source | B = Both |
| S = Secondary tax source | N = Neither |

   a. Sixteenth Amendment to the Constitution.
   b. Tax treaty between the United States and China.
   c. Proposed Regulations.
   d. Revenue Procedure.
   e. General Counsel Memoranda (1988).
   f. Tax Court Memorandum decision.
   g. *Harvard Law Review* article.
   h. Legislative Regulations.
   i. Letter ruling (before 1985).
   j. District Court decision.
   k. Small Cases Division of U.S. Tax Court decision.
   l. Senate Finance Committee Report.
   m. Technical advice memorandum (1991).

59. Using the legend provided, classify each of the following decisions or statements in regard to the RIA *Federal Tax Citator:*

| **Legend** | |
| --- | --- |
| a = affirmed | q = questioned |
| d = dismissed | c = criticized |
| r = reversed | f = followed |
| o = overruled | x = certiorari denied |

   a. *Leroy Frantz, Jr.,* 83 T.C. 162 (1984), *aff'd* 784 F.2d 119 (CA–2, 1986), *cert. den.*
   b. *Ronald D. Anderson,* 67 T.C. 522 (1977), *aff'd* 583 F.2d 953 (CA–7, 1978).
   c. *Henry C. Tilford, Jr.,* 75 T.C. 134 (1980), *rev'd* 705 F.2d 828 (CA–6, 1983), *cert. den.*
   d. q-2 *McEuen v. Comm.,* 196 F.2d 127 (CA–5, 1952).
   e. f-2 *Joseph P. Morgan,* 37 T.C. 31 (1961).

## Research Problems

A THOMSON COMPANY

*Note: Solutions to Research Problems can be prepared by using the* **RIA Checkpoint® Student Edition** *online research product, or the* **CCH U.S. Master Tax Guide Plus™** *online Federal tax research database, which is available to accompany this text. It is also possible to prepare solutions to the Research Problems by using tax research materials found in a standard tax library.*

**Research Problem 1.**   Locate the following cited items and give a brief description of the topic or opinion in the item:
   a. § 59A(a).
   b. Reg. § 1.6166(a)(8)(D)(i).
   c. Ltr.Rul. 200134022.
   d. FSA 200005006.

**Research Problem 2.**   Determine the validity of the following items:
   a. Rev.Rul. 67–225, 1967–2 C.B. 238.
   b. *Walter F. O'Brien,* 38 T.C. 707 (1962).
   c. Rev.Proc. 99–77, 1999–1 C.B. 1186.

**Research Problem 3.** Determine the disposition of the following decisions at the appellate level:
  a. *Gary A. Sargent*, 93 T.C. 572 (1989).
  b. *Charles Johnson*, 78 T.C. 882 (1982).
  c. *Smith & Wiggins Gin, Inc.*, 37 T.C. 861 (1962).
  d. *George W. Wiebusch*, 59 T.C. 777 (1973).
  e. *Zanesville Inv. Co.*, 38 T.C. 406 (1962).

**Research Problem 4.** Determine the disposition of the following decisions at the Supreme Court level or on rehearing:
  a. *Union Pacific R.R. Co. v. U.S.*, 524 F.2d 1343 (Ct.Cl., 1975).
  b. *Gordon v. Comm.*, 424 F.2d 378 (CA–2, 1970).
  c. *Rafferty v. Comm.*, 452 F.2d 767 (CA–1, 1971).
  d. *Davant v. Comm.*, 366 F.2d 874 (CA–5, 1966).

**Research Problem 5.** Is *Tate & Tate*, 103 T.C. 656 (1994) a valid decision? Why? What was the issue?

**Communications**

**Research Problem 6.** You have a client who collected and truthfully accounted for a tax, but failed to pay it over to the IRS. Section 7202 states:

> Any person required under this article to collect, account for, and pay over any tax imposed by this title who willfully fails to collect or truthfully account for and pay over such tax shall . . . be guilty of a felony.

Is your client guilty of a felony? Show support for your answer in a tax memorandum dated February 12, 2003.

*Partial list of research aids:*
*U.S. v. Evangelista*, 97–2 USTC ¶50,608, 80 AFTR2d 97–6085, 122 F.3d 112 (CA–2, 1997).
*U.S. v. Poll*, 75–2 USTC ¶9625, 36 AFTR2d 75–5470, 521 F.2d 329 (CA–9, 1975).
*Wilson v. U.S.*, 57–2 USTC ¶10,040, 52 AFTR 1048, 250 F.2d 312 (CA–9, 1957).

**Research Problem 7.** Complete the following citations to the extent that the research materials are available to you:
  a. Rev.Rul. 69–292, 1969–1 C.B. \_\_\_\_.
  b. *Soliman v. Comm.*, 935 F.2d 52 (CA–4, \_\_\_\_).
  c. Notice 93–12, 1993–\_\_\_\_ C.B. 298.
  d. *James A. Henry*, T.C.Memo. 1982–\_\_\_\_.
  e. *Korn Industries, Inc. v. U.S.*, 532 F.2d 1352 (\_\_\_\_, 1976).
  f. *Henslee v. Union Planters National Bank & Trust Co.*, 69 S.Ct. 290 (USSC, \_\_\_\_).

**Research Problem 8.** Find *Estate of Shelfer*, 103 T.C. 10 (1994) and answer these questions:
  a. Who is the petitioner (plaintiff)?
  b. Who is the respondent (defendant)?
  c. What is the holding of the court?
  d. What is Rule 122(a)?
  e. Was this a reviewed decision?
  f. How many judges agreed with the majority opinion?
  g. Was this decision entered under Rule 155?

**Internet Activity**

*Use the tax resources of the Internet to address the following questions. Do not restrict your search to the World Wide Web, but include a review of newsgroups and general reference materials, practitioner sites and resources, primary sources of the tax law, chat rooms and discussion groups, and other opportunities.*

**Research Problem 9.** Go to each of the following Internet locations:
  a. Several primary sources of the tax law, including the U.S. Supreme Court, a Court of Appeals, the Internal Revenue Service, the U.S. Tax Court, and final Regulations.
  b. Sources of proposed Federal tax legislation.
  c. A collection of tax rules for your state.

**Research Problem 10.** Go to each of the following Internet locations to find some tax information:

    a. Several newspapers and magazines, such as *Tax Notes*, *USA Today*, the *New York Times*, the *Washington Post*, *Newsweek* magazine, your local newspaper, and a local television station.

    b. Other news sources such as *CNN Interactive*, Newspapers OnLine, and a collection of online versions of magazines.

**Research Problem 11.** Try to find the definition of "per curiam" on the Internet. What does it mean? When does a court tend to use this phrase?

# Corporations

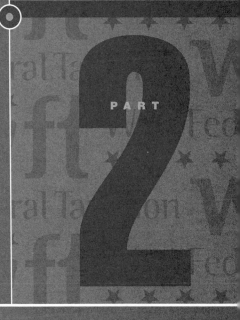

**PART 2**

Corporations are separate entities for Federal income tax purposes. Subchapter C of the Code is devoted to the tax treatment of regular corporations. Part II deals mainly with the operating rules contained in Subchapter C that apply to regular corporations and with the effects of various capital transactions on the C corporation and its shareholders.

http://wft.swlearning.com

# Corporations: Introduction, Operating Rules, and Related Corporations

## LEARNING OBJECTIVES

*After completing Chapter 2, you should be able to:*

**L O . 1**
Summarize the various forms of conducting a business.

**L O . 2**
Compare the taxation of individuals and corporations.

**L O . 3**
Discuss the tax rules unique to corporations.

**L O . 4**
Compute the corporate income tax.

**L O . 5**
Explain the tax rules unique to multiple corporations.

**L O . 6**
Describe the reporting process for corporations.

**L O . 7**
Evaluate corporations for conducting a business.

http://wft.swlearning.com

## OUTLINE

---

**L O . 1**

Summarize the various forms of conducting a business.

# Tax Treatment of Various Business Forms

Business operations can be conducted in a number of different forms. Among the various possibilities are the following:

- Sole proprietorships.
- Partnerships.
- Trusts and estates.
- S corporations (also known as Subchapter S corporations).
- Regular corporations (also called Subchapter C or C corporations).

For Federal income tax purposes, the distinctions between these forms of business organization are very important. The following discussion of the tax treatment of sole proprietorships, partnerships, and regular corporations highlights these distinctions. Trusts and estates are covered in Chapter 19, and S corporations are discussed in Chapter 12.

### SOLE PROPRIETORSHIPS

A sole proprietorship is not a taxable entity separate from the individual who owns the proprietorship. The owner of a sole proprietorship reports all business transactions of the proprietorship on Schedule C of Form 1040. The net profit or loss from the proprietorship is then transferred from Schedule C to Form 1040, which is used by the taxpayer to report taxable income. The proprietor reports all of the net profit from the business, regardless of the amount actually withdrawn during the year.

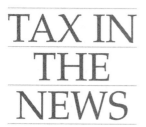

## CORPORATE TAX WELFARE?

Critics of "corporate tax welfare" argue that corporations are taking undue advantage of provisions in the tax law to minimize their tax payments. One way to measure the corporate tax burden is to calculate corporate taxes as a percentage of gross domestic product (GDP). Without making value judgments as to what the appropriate percentage might be, it is interesting to note that in 2001 corporate taxes were only 1.3 percent of GDP—the lowest percentage since 1983, when the rate was 1.1 percent. The highest rate since 1942 was 7.2 percent (in 1945). From 1994 through 2000, the rate was 2 percent or higher. It last exceeded 4 percent in 1967 and 3 percent in 1972. The following are examples of the tax rates paid by some major corporations:

| Corporation | Tax Period | Reported Profits | Tax Rate |
|---|---|---|---|
| Microsoft | 1999 | $12.3 billion | 0% |
| General Electric | 1996–2000 | 50.8 billion | 11.5% |
| Ford | 1999–2000 | 18.6 billion | 5.7% |
| IBM | 2000 | 5.7 billion | 3.4% |
| General Motors | 1996–2000 | 12.5 billion | 0% |

SOURCES: Information from "Corporate Tax Payments Near Record Low This Year" (March 15, 2002), and "Surge in Corporate Tax Welfare Drives Corporate Tax Payments to Near Record Low" (April 17, 2002), Citizens for Tax Justice, **http://www.ctj.org**. Citizens for Tax Justice data are based on information from the Congressional Budget Office, Joint Committee on Taxation, corporate annual reports, and Forms 10–K.

Income and expenses of the proprietorship retain their character when reported by the proprietor. For example, ordinary income of the proprietorship is treated as ordinary income when reported by the proprietor, and capital gain is treated as capital gain.

**EXAMPLE 1**

George is the sole proprietor of George's Record Shop. Gross income of the business for the year is $200,000, and operating expenses are $110,000. George also sells a capital asset held by the business for a $10,000 long-term capital gain. During the year, he withdraws $60,000 from the business for living expenses. George reports the income and expenses of the business on Schedule C, resulting in net profit (ordinary income) of $90,000. Even though he withdrew only $60,000, George reports all of the $90,000 net profit from the business on Form 1040, where he computes taxable income for the year. He also reports a $10,000 long-term capital gain on Schedule D. ∎

## PARTNERSHIPS

Partnerships are not subject to the income tax. However, a partnership is required to file Form 1065, which reports the results of the partnership's business activities. Most income and expense items are aggregated in computing the net profit of the partnership on Form 1065. Any income and expense items that are not aggregated in computing the partnership's net income are reported separately to the partners.

Some examples of separately reported income items are interest income, dividend income, and long-term capital gain. Examples of separately reported expenses include charitable contributions and expenses related to interest and dividend income. Partnership reporting is discussed in detail in Chapter 10.

The partnership net profit (loss) and the separately reported items are allocated to each partner according to the partnership's profit sharing agreement, and the partners receive separate K–1 schedules from the partnership. Schedule K–1 reports each partner's share of the partnership net profit and separately reported income and expense items. Each partner reports these items on his or her own tax return.

**EXAMPLE 2**

Jim and Bob are equal partners in Canary Enterprises, a calendar year partnership. During the year, Canary Enterprises had $500,000 gross income and $350,000 operating expenses. In addition, the partnership sold land that had been held for investment purposes for a long-term capital gain of $60,000. During the year, Jim withdrew $40,000 from the partnership, and Bob withdrew $45,000. The partnership's Form 1065 reports net profit of $150,000 ($500,000 income − $350,000 expenses). The partnership also reports the $60,000 long-term capital gain as a separately stated item on Form 1065. Jim and Bob both receive a Schedule K–1 reporting net profit of $75,000 and separately stated long-term capital gain of $30,000. Each partner reports net profit of $75,000 and long-term capital gain of $30,000 on his own return. ■

## REGULAR CORPORATIONS

Corporations are governed by Subchapter C or Subchapter S of the Internal Revenue Code. Those governed by Subchapter C are referred to as **C corporations** or **regular corporations.** Corporations governed by Subchapter S are referred to as **S corporations.**

S corporations, which do not pay Federal income tax, are similar to partnerships in that net profit or loss flows through to the shareholders to be reported on their separate returns. Also like partnerships, S corporations do not aggregate all income and expense items in computing net profit or loss. Certain items flow through to the shareholders and retain their separate character when reported on the shareholders' returns. See Chapter 12 for detailed coverage of S corporations.

Unlike proprietorships, partnerships, and S corporations, C corporations are taxpaying entities. This results in what is known as a *double tax* effect. A C corporation reports its income and expenses on Form 1120 (or Form 1120–A, the corporate short form). The corporation computes tax on the net income reported on the corporate tax return using the rate schedule applicable to corporations (refer to the rate schedule inside the front cover of this text). When a corporation distributes its income, the corporation's shareholders report dividend income on their own tax returns. Thus, income that has already been taxed at the corporate level is also taxed at the shareholder level.

**EXAMPLE 3**

Tan Corporation files Form 1120, which reports net profit of $100,000. The corporation pays tax of $22,250. This leaves $77,750, all of which is distributed as a dividend to Carla, the sole shareholder of the corporation. Carla, who has income from other sources and is in the 38.6% tax bracket, pays income tax of $30,012 on the distribution. The combined tax on the corporation's net profit is $52,262. ■

**EXAMPLE 4**

Assume the same facts as in Example 3, except that the business is organized as a sole proprietorship. Carla reports the $100,000 net profit from the business on her tax return and pays tax of $38,600 ($100,000 net profit × 38.6% marginal rate). Therefore, operating the business as a sole proprietorship results in a tax saving of $13,662 ($52,262 tax from Example 3 – $38,600). ■

Shareholders in closely held corporations frequently attempt to avoid double taxation by paying out all the profit of the corporation as salary to themselves.

**EXAMPLE 5**

Orange Corporation has net income of $180,000 during the year ($300,000 revenue – $120,000 operating expenses). Emilio is the sole shareholder of Orange Corporation. In an effort to avoid tax at the corporate level, Emilio has Orange pay him a salary of $180,000, which results in zero taxable income for the corporation. ■

Will the strategy described in Example 5 effectively avoid double taxation? The answer depends on whether the compensation paid to the shareholder is *reasonable*. Section 162 provides that compensation is deductible only to the extent that it is reasonable in amount. The IRS is aware that many taxpayers use this strategy to bail out corporate profits and, in an audit, looks closely at compensation expense. If the IRS believes that compensation is too high based on the amount and quality of services performed by the shareholder, the compensation deduction of the corporation is reduced to a reasonable amount. Compensation that is determined to be unreasonable is usually treated as a constructive dividend to the shareholder and is not deductible by the corporation.

**EXAMPLE 6**

Assume the same facts as in Example 5, and that the IRS determines that $80,000 of the amount paid to Emilio is unreasonable compensation. As a result, $80,000 of the corporation's compensation deduction is disallowed and treated as a constructive dividend to Emilio. Orange has taxable income of $80,000. Emilio would report salary of $100,000 and a taxable dividend of $80,000. The net effect is that $80,000 is subject to double taxation. ■

The unreasonable compensation issue is discussed in more detail in Chapter 4.

## Comparison of Corporations and Other Forms of Doing Business.

Comparison of the tax results in Examples 3 and 4 might lead to the conclusion that incorporation is not a wise tax strategy. In some cases, that would be a correct conclusion, but in others it would not. In many situations, tax and nontax factors combine to make the corporate form of doing business the only reasonable choice.

Chapter 13 presents a detailed comparison of sole proprietorships, partnerships, S corporations, and C corporations as forms of doing business. However, it is appropriate at this point to consider some of the tax and nontax factors that favor corporations over proprietorships.

Consideration of tax factors requires an examination of the corporate rate structure. The income tax rate schedule applicable to corporations is reproduced below.[1]

---

[1]Corporate tax rates are specified in § 11(b).

| Taxable Income | | Tax Is: | Of the Amount Over— |
|---|---|---|---|
| Over— | But Not Over— | | |
| $          0 | $      50,000 | 15% | $              0 |
| 50,000 | 75,000 | $      7,500 + 25% | 50,000 |
| 75,000 | 100,000 | 13,750 + 34% | 75,000 |
| 100,000 | 335,000 | 22,250 + 39% | 100,000 |
| 335,000 | 10,000,000 | 113,900 + 34% | 335,000 |
| 10,000,000 | 15,000,000 | 3,400,000 + 35% | 10,000,000 |
| 15,000,000 | 18,333,333 | 5,150,000 + 38% | 15,000,000 |
| 18,333,333 | — | 35% | 0 |

As this schedule shows, corporate rates on taxable income up to $75,000 are lower than individual rates for persons in the 27 percent and higher brackets. Therefore, corporate tax will be lower than individual tax. Furthermore, there is no corporate marginal rate that is higher than the 38.6 percent top bracket for individuals. When dividends are paid, however, the double taxation problem occurs. This leads to an important question: Will incorporation ever result in Federal income tax savings? The following example illustrates a situation where this occurs.

**EXAMPLE 7**

Ned, an individual in the 38.6% tax bracket, owns a business that produces net profit of $50,000 each year. Ned has significant income from other sources, so he does not withdraw any of the profit from the business. If the business is operated as a proprietorship, Ned's Federal income tax on the net profit of the business is $19,300 ($50,000 × 38.6%). However, if the business is operated as a corporation and pays no dividends, the tax will be $7,500 ($50,000 × 15%). Operating as a corporation saves $11,800 of Federal income tax each year. If Ned invests his $11,800 tax saving each year for several years, it is possible that a positive cash flow will result, even though Ned will be required to pay tax on dividends distributed by the corporation some time in the future. ■

The preceding example deals with a specific set of facts. The conclusions reached in this situation cannot be extended to all decisions about a form of business organization. Each specific set of facts and circumstances requires a thorough analysis of the tax factors.

Another tax consideration involves the nature of dividend income. All income and expense items of a proprietorship retain their character when reported on the proprietor's tax return. In the case of a partnership, several separately reported items (e.g., charitable contributions and long-term capital gains) retain their character when passed through to the partners. However, the tax attributes of income and expense items of a corporation are lost as they pass through the corporate entity to the shareholders.

Losses of a C corporation are treated differently than losses of a proprietorship, partnership, or S corporation. A loss incurred by a proprietorship may be deductible by the owner, because all income and expense items are reported by the proprietor. Partnership losses are passed through the partnership entity and may be deductible by the partners, and S corporation losses are passed through to the shareholders. C corporation losses, however, have no effect on the taxable income of the shareholders. Income from a C corporation is reported when the shareholders receive dividends. C corporation losses are not reported by the shareholders.

| **EXAMPLE 8** | Franco plans to start a business this year. He expects the business will incur operating losses for the first three years and then become highly profitable. Franco decides to operate as an S corporation during the loss period, because the losses will flow through and be deductible on his personal return. When the business becomes profitable, he intends to switch to C corporation status. ∎ |

**Nontax Considerations.**   Nontax considerations will sometimes override tax considerations and lead to the conclusion that a business should be operated as a corporation. The following are some of the more important nontax considerations:

- Sole proprietors and *general* partners in partnerships face the danger of *unlimited liability*. That is, creditors of the business may file claims not only against the assets of the business but also against the personal assets of proprietors or general partners. Shareholders are protected from claims against their personal assets by state corporate law.
- The corporate form of business organization can provide a vehicle for raising large amounts of capital through widespread stock ownership. Most major businesses in the United States are operated as corporations.
- Shares of stock in a corporation are freely transferable, whereas a partner's sale of his or her partnership interest is subject to approval by the other partners.
- Shareholders may come and go, but a corporation can continue to exist. Death or withdrawal of a partner, on the other hand, may terminate the existing partnership and cause financial difficulties that result in dissolution of the entity. This *continuity of life* is a distinct advantage of the corporate form of doing business.
- Corporations have *centralized management*. All management responsibility is assigned to a board of directors, who appoint officers to carry out the corporation's business. Partnerships, by contrast, may have decentralized management, in which every owner has a right to participate in the organization's business decisions; limited partnerships, though, may have centralized management. Centralized management is essential for the smooth operation of a widely held business.

## LIMITED LIABILITY COMPANIES

The **limited liability company (LLC)** has proliferated greatly in recent years, particularly since 1988 when the IRS first ruled that it would treat qualifying LLCs as partnerships for tax purposes. All 50 states and the District of Columbia have passed laws that allow LLCs, and thousands of companies have chosen LLC status. As with a corporation, operating as an LLC allows an entity to avoid unlimited liability, which is a primary *nontax* consideration in choosing the form of business organization. The tax advantage of LLCs is that qualifying businesses may be treated as partnerships for tax purposes, thereby avoiding the problem of double taxation associated with regular corporations.

Some states allow an LLC to have centralized management, but not continuity of life or free transferability of interests. Other states allow LLCs to adopt any or all of the corporate characteristics of centralized management, continuity of life, and free transferability of interests. Chapter 13's comparison of business entities includes a discussion of LLCs.

GLOBAL TAX ISSUES

### ENTITY CHOICE: S CORPORATION VERSUS C CORPORATION

S corporations (see Chapter 12) are subject to some restrictions that do not apply to C corporations. Among these is a requirement that the corporation be a domestic corporation, incorporated and organized in the United States. Also, an S corporation cannot have a shareholder who is a nonresident alien. Thus, the C corporation, rather than the S corporation, would be the appropriate choice for businesses that are organized outside the United States and for corporations that plan to have shareholders who are nonresident aliens.

## ENTITY CLASSIFICATION PRIOR TO 1997

Can an organization not qualifying as a corporation under state law still be treated as such for Federal income tax purposes? Unfortunately, the tax law defines a corporation as including "associations, joint stock companies, and insurance companies."[2] As the Code contains no definition of what constitutes an "association," the issue became the subject of frequent litigation.

It was finally determined that an entity would be treated as a corporation if it had a majority of characteristics common to corporations. For this purpose, relevant characteristics are:

- Continuity of life.
- Centralized management.
- Limited liability.
- Free transferability of interests.

These criteria did not resolve all of the problems that continued to arise over corporate classification. When a new type of business entity—the limited liability company—was developed, the IRS was deluged with inquiries regarding its tax status. As LLCs became increasingly popular with professional groups, all states enacted statutes allowing some form of this entity. Invariably, the statutes permitted the corporate characteristic of limited liability and, often, that of centralized management. Because continuity of life and free transferability of interests are absent, partnership classification was hoped for. This treatment avoided the double tax result inherent in the corporate form.

## ENTITY CLASSIFICATION AFTER 1996

In late 1996, the IRS issued its so-called **check-the-box Regulations**.[3] Effective beginning in 1997, the Regulations enable taxpayers to choose the tax status of a business entity without regard to its corporate (or noncorporate) characteristics. These rules have simplified tax administration considerably and should eliminate the type of litigation that arose with regard to the association (i.e., corporation) status.

Under the rules, entities with more than one owner can elect to be classified as either a partnership or a corporation. An entity with only one owner can elect to be classified as a corporation or as a sole proprietorship. In the event of default (i.e., no election is made), multi-owned entities are classified as partnerships and single-person businesses as sole proprietorships.

---

[2]§ 7701(a)(3).

[3]Reg. §§ 301.7701–1 through –4, and –7.

The election is not available to entities that are actually incorporated under state law or to entities that are required to be corporations under Federal law (e.g., certain publicly traded partnerships). Otherwise, LLCs are not treated as being incorporated under state law. Consequently, they can elect either corporation or partnership status.

Eligible entities make the election as to tax status by filing Form 8832 (Entity Classification Election).

L0.2

Compare the taxation of individuals and corporations.

# An Introduction to the Income Taxation of Corporations

## AN OVERVIEW OF CORPORATE VERSUS INDIVIDUAL INCOME TAX TREATMENT

In a discussion of how corporations are treated under the Federal income tax, a useful approach is to compare their treatment with that applicable to individual taxpayers.

**Similarities.** Gross income of a corporation is determined in much the same manner as it is for individuals. Thus, gross income includes compensation for services rendered, income derived from a business, gains from dealings in property, interest, rents, royalties, dividends—to name only a few items. Both individuals and corporations are entitled to exclusions from gross income. However, corporate taxpayers are allowed fewer exclusions. Interest on municipal bonds is excluded from gross income whether the bondholder is an individual or a corporate taxpayer.

Gains and losses from property transactions are handled similarly. For example, whether a gain or loss is capital or ordinary depends upon the nature of the asset in the hands of the taxpayer making the taxable disposition. In defining what is not a capital asset, § 1221 makes no distinction between corporate and noncorporate taxpayers.

In the area of nontaxable exchanges, corporations are like individuals in that they do not recognize gain or loss on a like-kind exchange and may defer recognized gain on an involuntary conversion of property. The exclusion of gain provisions dealing with the sale of a personal residence do not apply to corporations. Both corporations and individuals are vulnerable to the disallowance of losses on sales of property to related parties or on wash sales of securities. The wash sales rules do not apply to individuals who are traders or dealers in securities or to corporations that are dealers if the securities are sold in the ordinary course of the corporation's business. Upon the sale or other taxable disposition of depreciable property, the recapture rules generally make no distinction between corporate and noncorporate taxpayers.[4]

The business deductions of corporations also parallel those available to individuals. Deductions are allowed for all ordinary and necessary expenses paid or incurred in carrying on a trade or business. Specific provision is made for the deductibility of interest, certain taxes, losses, bad debts, accelerated cost recovery, charitable contributions, net operating losses, research and experimental expenditures, and other less common deductions. A corporation does not distinguish between business and nonbusiness interest or business and nonbusiness bad debts.

[4]§§ 1245 and 1250, but see § 291(a).

Thus, these amounts are deductible in full as ordinary deductions by corporations. No deduction is permitted for interest paid or incurred on amounts borrowed to purchase or carry tax-exempt securities. The same holds true for expenses contrary to public policy and certain unpaid expenses and interest between related parties.

Some of the tax credits available to individuals can also be claimed by corporations. This is the case with the foreign tax credit. Not available to corporations are certain credits that are personal in nature, such as the child care credit, the credit for elderly or disabled taxpayers, and the earned income credit.

**Dissimilarities.**   The income taxation of corporations and individuals also differs significantly. As noted earlier, different tax rates apply to corporations and to individuals. Corporate tax rates are discussed in more detail later in the chapter (see Examples 25 and 26).

All allowable corporate deductions are treated as business deductions. Thus, the determination of adjusted gross income (AGI), so essential for individual taxpayers, has no relevance to corporations. Taxable income is computed simply by subtracting from gross income all allowable deductions and losses. Corporations need not be concerned with itemized deductions or the standard deduction. The deduction for personal and dependency exemptions is not available to corporations.

The $100 floor on the deductible portion of personal casualty and theft losses applicable to individuals does not apply to corporations. Also inapplicable is the provision limiting the deductibility of nonbusiness casualty losses to the amount in excess of 10 percent of AGI.

## SPECIFIC PROVISIONS COMPARED

In comparing the tax treatment of individuals and corporations, the following areas warrant special discussion:

- Accounting periods and methods.
- Capital gains and losses.
- Passive losses.
- Charitable contributions.
- Net operating losses.
- Special deductions available only to corporations.

## ACCOUNTING PERIODS AND METHODS

**Accounting Periods.**   Corporations generally have the same choices of accounting periods as do individual taxpayers. Like an individual, a corporation may choose a calendar year or a fiscal year for reporting purposes. Corporations, however, enjoy greater flexibility in the selection of a tax year. For example, corporations usually can have different tax years from those of their shareholders. Also, newly formed corporations (as new taxpayers) usually have a choice of any approved accounting period without having to obtain the consent of the IRS. **Personal service corporations (PSCs)** and S corporations, however, are subject to severe restrictions in the use of a fiscal year. The rules applicable to S corporations are discussed in Chapter 12.

A PSC has as its principal activity the performance of personal services. Such services are substantially performed by owner-employees. The performance of services must be in the fields of health, law, engineering, architecture, accounting, actuarial science, performing arts, or consulting.[5] Because placing a PSC on a fiscal

---

[5]§ 448(d)(2)(A).

year and retaining a calendar year for the employee-owner can result in a significant deferral of income, a PSC must generally use a calendar year.[6] However, a PSC can *elect* a fiscal year under any of the following conditions:

- A business purpose for the year can be demonstrated.
- The PSC year results in a deferral of not more than three months' income. The corporation must pay the shareholder-employee's salary during the portion of the calendar year after the close of the fiscal year. Furthermore, the salary for that period must be at least proportionate to the employee's salary received for the fiscal year.
- The PSC retains the same year that was used for its fiscal year ending 1987, provided the latter two requirements applicable to the preceding condition are satisfied.

**EXAMPLE 9**

Valdez & Vance is a professional association of public accountants. Because it receives over 40% of its gross receipts in March and April of each year from the preparation of tax returns, Valdez & Vance has a May 1 to April 30 fiscal year. Under these circumstances, the IRS might permit Valdez & Vance to continue to use the fiscal year chosen since it reflects a natural business cycle (the end of the tax season). Valdez & Vance has a business purpose for using a fiscal year. ■

**EXAMPLE 10**

Beige Corporation, a PSC, paid Burke $120,000 in salary during its fiscal year ending September 30, 2003. The corporation cannot satisfy the business purpose test for a fiscal year. However, the corporation can continue to use its fiscal year without any negative tax effects, provided Burke receives at least $30,000 [(3 months/12 months) × $120,000] as salary during the period October 1 through December 31, 2003. ■

**Accounting Methods.** As a general rule, the cash method of accounting is unavailable to *regular* corporations.[7] Exceptions apply to the following types of corporations:

- S corporations. *Cash method is available.*
- Corporations engaged in the trade or business of farming and timber.
- Qualified PSCs.
- Corporations with average annual gross receipts of $5 million or less. (In applying the $5 million-or-less test, the corporation uses the average of the three prior taxable years.)

Both individuals and corporations that maintain inventory for sale to customers are required to use the accrual method of accounting for determining sales and cost of goods sold. However, as a matter of administrative convenience, the IRS issued Notice 2001–76 (2001–2 C.B. 613), which permits qualified service providers with average annual gross receipts of not more than $10 million for the most recent three-year period to use the cash method. This applies even if the taxpayer is buying and selling inventory.

A corporation that uses the accrual method of accounting must observe a special rule in dealing with related parties. If the corporation has an accrual outstanding at the end of any taxable year, it cannot claim a deduction until the recipient reports the amount as income.[8] This rule is most often encountered when a corporation deals with a person who owns more than 50 percent of the corporation's stock.

*[handwritten margin note: Qualified service providers with annual gross receipts of not more than 10 million for most recent three year period to use cash method]*

---

[6] § 441(i).
[7] § 448.

[8] § 267(a)(2).

E X A M P L E   1 1

Teal, an accrual method corporation, uses the calendar year for tax purposes. Bob, a cash method taxpayer, owns more than 50% of the corporation's stock at the end of 2003. On December 31, 2003, Teal has accrued $25,000 of salary to Bob. Bob receives the salary in 2004 and reports it on his 2004 tax return. Teal cannot claim a deduction for the $25,000 until 2004. ■

## CAPITAL GAINS AND LOSSES

Capital gains and losses result from the taxable sales or exchanges of capital assets.[9] Whether these gains and losses are long term or short term depends upon the holding period of the assets sold or exchanged. Each year, a taxpayer's long-term capital gains and losses are combined, and the result is either a *net* long-term capital gain or a *net* long-term capital loss. A similar aggregation is made with short-term capital gains and losses, the result being a *net* short-term capital gain or a *net* short-term capital loss. The following combinations and results are possible:

1. A net long-term capital gain and a net short-term capital loss. These are combined, and the result is either a net capital gain or a net capital loss.
2. A net long-term capital gain and a net short-term capital gain. No further combination is made.
3. A net long-term capital loss and a net short-term capital gain. These are combined, and the result is either a net capital gain or a net capital loss.
4. A net long-term capital loss and a net short-term capital loss. No further combination is made.

**Capital Gains.**   Individuals generally pay tax on net (long-term) capital gains at a maximum rate of 20 percent.[10] Corporations, by contrast, receive no favorable rate on capital gains and must include the net capital gain, in full, as part of taxable income.

**Capital Losses.**   Net capital losses (refer to combinations 3 and 4 and, possibly, to combination 1) of corporate and noncorporate taxpayers receive different income tax treatment. Generally, noncorporate taxpayers can deduct up to $3,000 of such net losses against other income. Any remaining capital losses can be carried forward to future years until absorbed by capital gains or by the $3,000 deduction.[11] Carryovers do not lose their identity but remain either long term or short term.

E X A M P L E   1 2

Robin, an individual, incurs a net long-term capital loss of $7,500 for calendar year 2003. Assuming adequate taxable income, Robin may deduct $3,000 of this loss on his 2003 return. The remaining $4,500 ($7,500 − $3,000) of the loss is carried to 2004 and years thereafter until completely deducted. The $4,500 will be carried forward as a long-term capital loss. ■

Unlike individuals, corporate taxpayers are not permitted to claim any net capital losses as a deduction against ordinary income. Capital losses, therefore, can be used only as an offset against capital gains. Corporations may, however, carry back net capital losses to three preceding years, applying them first to the earliest year in point of time. Carryforwards are allowed for a period of five years from

---

[9]See Chapter 16 of *West Federal Taxation: Individual Income Taxes (2004 Edition)* for a detailed discussion of capital gains and losses.
[10]A maximum rate of 10% (in some cases, 8%) applies to taxpayers in the 15% bracket.

[11]§ 1212.

the year of the loss. When carried back or forward, a long-term capital loss is
treated as a short-term capital loss.

**EXAMPLE 13**

Assume the same facts as in Example 12, except that Robin is a corporation. None of the
$7,500 long-term capital loss incurred in 2003 can be deducted in that year. Robin Corporation
may, however, carry back the loss to years 2000, 2001, and 2002 (in this order) and offset
it against any capital gains recognized in these years. If the carryback does not exhaust the
loss, it may be carried forward to calendar years 2004, 2005, 2006, 2007, and 2008 (in this
order). Either a carryback or a carryforward of the long-term capital loss converts the loss
to a short-term capital loss. ∎

## PASSIVE LOSSES

The **passive loss** rules apply to noncorporate taxpayers and to closely held C
corporations and personal service corporations (PSCs).[12] For S corporations and
partnerships, passive income or loss flows through to the owners, and the passive
loss rules are applied at the owner level. The passive loss rules are applied to
closely held corporations and to PSCs to prevent taxpayers from incorporating to
avoid the passive loss limitation.

A corporation is closely held if, at any time during the taxable year, more than
50 percent of the value of the corporation's outstanding stock is owned, directly
or indirectly, by or for not more than five individuals. The definition used for a
closely held corporation is the same as that used in determining the ownership
requirement for personal holding companies (see Chapter 6). A corporation is
classified as a PSC if it meets the following requirements:

* The principal activity of the corporation is the performance of personal
  services.
* Such services are substantially performed by owner-employees.
* More than 10 percent of the stock (in value) is held by owner-employees.
  *Any* stock held by an employee on *any* one day causes the employee to be
  an owner-employee.

The general passive activity loss rules apply to PSCs. Passive activity losses
cannot be offset against either active income or portfolio income. The application
of the passive activity rules is not as harsh for closely held corporations. They may
offset passive losses against active income, but not against portfolio income.

**EXAMPLE 14**

Brown, a closely held C corporation that is not a PSC, has $300,000 of passive losses from
a rental activity, $200,000 of active business income, and $100,000 of portfolio income. The
corporation may offset $200,000 of the $300,000 passive loss against the $200,000 active
business income, but may not offset the remainder against the $100,000 of portfolio income. ∎

Subject to certain exceptions, individual taxpayers are not allowed to offset
passive losses against *either* active or portfolio income.

## CHARITABLE CONTRIBUTIONS

Both corporate and noncorporate taxpayers may deduct charitable contributions
if the recipient is a qualified charitable organization. Generally, a deduction will
be allowed only for the year in which the payment is made. However, an important

---

[12]§ 469(a).

exception is made for *accrual basis corporations.* They may claim the deduction in the year preceding payment if two requirements are met. First, the contribution must be authorized by the board of directors by the end of that year. Second, it must be paid on or before the fifteenth day of the third month of the next year.

**EXAMPLE 15**

On December 28, 2003, Blue Company, a calendar year, accrual basis taxpayer, authorizes a $5,000 donation to the Atlanta Symphony Association (a qualified charitable organization). The donation is made on March 14, 2004. If Blue Company is a partnership, the contribution can be deducted only in 2004.[13] However, if Blue Company is a corporation and the December 28, 2003 authorization was made by its board of directors, Blue may claim the $5,000 donation as a deduction for calendar year 2003. ■

**Property Contributions.**    The amount that can be deducted for a noncash charitable contribution depends on the type of property contributed. Property must be identified as long-term capital gain property or ordinary income property. *Long-term capital gain property* is property that, if sold, would result in long-term capital gain for the taxpayer. Such property generally must be a capital asset and must be held for the long-term holding period (more than 12 months). *Ordinary income property* is property that, if sold, would result in ordinary income for the taxpayer.

The deduction for a charitable contribution of long-term capital gain property is generally measured by fair market value.

**EXAMPLE 16**

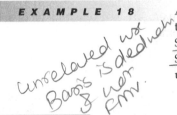

In 2003, Mallard Corporation donates a parcel of land (a capital asset) to Oakland Community College. Mallard acquired the land in 1988 for $60,000, and the fair market value on the date of the contribution is $100,000. The corporation's charitable contribution deduction (subject to a percentage limitation discussed later) is measured by the asset's fair market value of $100,000, even though the $40,000 appreciation on the land has never been included in income. ■

In two situations, a charitable contribution of long-term capital gain property is measured by the basis of the property, rather than fair market value. If the corporation contributes *tangible personal property* and the charitable organization puts the property to an unrelated use, the appreciation on the property is not deductible. Unrelated use is defined as use that is not related to the purpose or function that qualifies the organization for exempt status.

**EXAMPLE 17**

White Corporation donates a painting worth $200,000 to Western States Art Museum (a qualified organization), which exhibits the painting. White had acquired the painting in 1980 for $90,000. Because the museum put the painting to a related use, White is allowed to deduct $200,000, the fair market value of the painting. ■

**EXAMPLE 18**

Assume the same facts as in the previous example, except that White Corporation donates the painting to the American Cancer Society, which sells the painting and deposits the $200,000 proceeds in the organization's general fund. White's deduction is limited to the $90,000 basis because it contributed tangible personal property that was put to an unrelated use by the charitable organization. ■

---

[13]Each calendar year partner will report an allocable portion of the charitable contribution deduction as of December 31, 2004 (the end of the partnership's tax year). See Chapter 10.

| ETHICAL CONSIDERATIONS | **Is It Better Not to Know?** |
|---|---|

Puffin Corporation, your client, donated a painting to Tri-City Art Museum. The painting, which had been displayed in the corporate offices for several years, had a basis of $20,000 and a fair market value of $100,000. Puffin deducted a charitable contribution of $100,000 on its tax return.

You have learned that Tri-City Art Museum, also a client of yours, did not display the painting because it did not fit well with the museum's collection. Instead, Tri-City sold the painting for $100,000 and placed the funds in its operating budget. What action, if any, should you take?

2. The deduction for charitable contributions of long-term capital gain property to certain private nonoperating foundations is also limited to the basis of the property. Ordinary income property is property that, if sold, would result in ordinary income. Examples of ordinary income property include inventory and capital assets that have not been held long term. In addition, § 1231 property (depreciable property used in a trade or business) is treated as ordinary income property to the extent of any ordinary income recaptured under § 1245 or § 1250. As a general rule, the deduction for a contribution of ordinary income property is limited to the basis of the property. On certain contributions, however, corporations enjoy two special exceptions that allow a deduction for 50 percent of the appreciation (but not to exceed twice the basis) on property. The first exception concerns inventory if the property is used in a manner related to the exempt purpose of the charity. Also, the charity must use the property solely for the care of the ill, the needy, or infants.

**EXAMPLE 19**

Lark Corporation, a grocery chain, donates canned goods to the Salvation Army to be used to feed the needy. Lark's basis in the canned goods was $2,000, and the fair market value was $3,000. Lark's deduction is $2,500 [$2,000 basis + 50%($3,000 − $2,000)]. ▪

The second exception involves gifts of scientific property to colleges and certain scientific research organizations for use in research, provided certain conditions are met.[14] As was true of the inventory exception, 50 percent of the appreciation on such property is allowed as an additional deduction.

**Limitations Imposed on Charitable Contribution Deductions.** Like individuals, corporations are subject to percentage limits on the charitable contribution deduction.[15] For any one year, a corporate taxpayer's contribution deduction is limited to 10 percent of taxable income. For this purpose, taxable income is computed without regard to the charitable contribution deduction, any net operating loss carryback or capital loss carryback, and the dividends received deduction. Any contributions in excess of the 10 percent limitation may be carried forward to the five succeeding tax years. Any carryforward must be added to subsequent contributions and will be subject to the 10 percent limitation. In applying this limitation, the current year's contributions must be deducted first, with excess deductions from previous years deducted in order of time.[16]

[14]These conditions are set forth in § 170(e)(4). For the inventory exception, see § 170(e)(3).

[15]The percentage limitations applicable to individuals and corporations are set forth in § 170(b).

[16]The carryover rules relating to all taxpayers are in § 170(d).

**EXAMPLE 20**

During 2003, Orange Corporation (a calendar year taxpayer) had the following income and expenses:

| | |
|---|---|
| Income from operations | $140,000 |
| Expenses from operations | 110,000 |
| Dividends received | 10,000 |
| Charitable contributions made in May 2003 | 5,000 |

For purposes of the 10% limitation *only*, Orange Corporation's taxable income is $40,000 ($140,000 − $110,000 + $10,000). Consequently, the allowable charitable deduction for 2003 is $4,000 (10% × $40,000). The $1,000 unused portion of the contribution can be carried forward to 2004, 2005, 2006, 2007, and 2008 (in that order) until exhausted. ■

**EXAMPLE 21**

Assume the same facts as in Example 20. In 2004, Orange Corporation has taxable income (for purposes of the 10% limitation) of $50,000 and makes a charitable contribution of $4,500. The maximum deduction allowed for 2004 would be $5,000 (10% × $50,000). The first $4,500 of the allowed deduction must be allocated to the contribution made in 2004, and $500 of the balance is carried over from 2003. The remaining $500 of the 2003 contribution may be carried over to 2005, etc. ■

## NET OPERATING LOSSES

Like the net operating loss (NOL) of an individual, the NOL of a corporation may be carried back 2 years and forward 20 to offset taxable income for those years. A corporation does not adjust its tax loss for the year for capital losses as do individual taxpayers, because a corporation is not permitted a deduction for net capital losses. Nor does a corporation make adjustments for any nonbusiness deductions as do individual taxpayers. Further, a corporation is allowed to include the dividends received deduction (discussed below) in computing its NOL.[17]

**EXAMPLE 22**

In 2003, Green Corporation has gross income (including dividends) of $200,000 and deductions of $300,000 excluding the dividends received deduction. Green Corporation had received taxable dividends of $100,000 from ExxonMobil stock. Green has an NOL computed as follows:

| | | |
|---|---|---|
| Gross income (including dividends) | | $ 200,000 |
| Less: | | |
| Business deductions | $300,000 | |
| Dividends received deduction (70% of $100,000) | 70,000 | (370,000) |
| Taxable income (or loss) | | ($ 170,000) |

The NOL is carried back two years to 2001. (Green Corporation may forgo the carryback option and elect instead to carry forward the loss.) Assume Green had taxable income of $40,000 in 2001. The carryover to 2002 is computed as follows:

| | |
|---|---|
| Taxable income for 2001 | $ 40,000 |
| Less NOL carryback | (170,000) |
| Taxable income for 2001 after NOL carryback (carryover to 2002) | ($ 130,000) |

■

---

[17]The modifications required to arrive at the amount of NOL that can be carried back or forward are in § 172(d).

## LO.3

Discuss the tax rules unique to corporations.

*DRD is available only to corp* (handwritten)

# DEDUCTIONS AVAILABLE ONLY TO CORPORATIONS

**Dividends Received Deduction.** The purpose of the **dividends received deduction** is to mitigate triple taxation. Without the deduction, income paid to a corporation in the form of a dividend would be taxed to the recipient corporation with no corresponding deduction to the distributing corporation. Later, when the recipient corporation paid the income to its individual shareholders, the income would again be subject to taxation with no corresponding deduction to the corporation. The dividends received deduction alleviates this inequity by causing only some or none of the dividend income to be taxable to the recipient corporation.

As the following table illustrates, the amount of the dividends received deduction depends upon the percentage of ownership the recipient corporate shareholder holds in a domestic corporation making the dividend distribution.[18]

| Percentage of Ownership by Corporate Shareholder | Deduction Percentage |
| --- | --- |
| Less than 20% | 70% |
| 20% or more (but less than 80%) | 80% |
| 80% or more* | 100% |

*The payor corporation must be a member of an affiliated group with the recipient corporation.

The dividends received deduction is limited to a percentage of the taxable income of a corporation. For this purpose, taxable income is computed without regard to the NOL, the dividends received deduction, and any capital loss carryback to the current tax year. The percentage of taxable income limitation corresponds to the deduction percentage. Thus, if a corporate shareholder owns less than 20 percent of the stock in the distributing corporation, the dividends received deduction is limited to 70 percent of taxable income. However, the taxable income limitation does not apply if the corporation has an NOL for the current taxable year.[19]

In working with this myriad of rules, the following steps are useful:

1. Multiply the dividends received by the deduction percentage.
2. Multiply the taxable income by the deduction percentage.
3. The deduction is limited to the lesser of Step 1 or Step 2, unless subtracting the amount derived in Step 1 from 100 percent of taxable income *generates* an NOL. If so, the amount derived in Step 1 should be used. This is referred to as the NOL rule.

**EXAMPLE 23**

Red, White, and Blue Corporations, three unrelated calendar year corporations, have the following transactions for the year:

| | Red Corporation | White Corporation | Blue Corporation |
| --- | --- | --- | --- |
| Gross income from operations | $ 400,000 | $ 320,000 | $ 260,000 |
| Expenses from operations | (340,000) | (340,000) | (340,000) |
| Dividends received from domestic corporations (less than 20% ownership) | 200,000 | 200,000 | 200,000 |
| Taxable income before the dividends received deduction | $ 260,000 | $ 180,000 | $ 120,000 |

---

[18]§ 243(a).

[19]§ 246(b).

In determining the dividends received deduction, use the three-step procedure described above:

| | | | |
|---|---|---|---|
| Step 1 (70% × $200,000) | $140,000 | $140,000 | $140,000 |
| Step 2 | | | |
| 70% × $260,000 (taxable income) | $182,000 | | |
| 70% × $180,000 (taxable income) | | $126,000 | |
| 70% × $120,000 (taxable income) | | | $ 84,000 |
| Step 3 | | | |
| Lesser of Step 1 or Step 2 | $140,000 | $126,000 | |
| Deduction generates an NOL | | | $140,000 |

White Corporation is subject to the 70 percent of taxable income limitation. It does not qualify for NOL rule treatment since subtracting $140,000 (Step 1) from $180,000 (100 percent of taxable income) does not yield a negative figure. Blue Corporation does qualify for NOL rule treatment because subtracting $140,000 (Step 1) from $120,000 (100 percent of taxable income) yields a negative figure. In summary, each corporation has a dividends received deduction for the year as follows: $140,000 for Red Corporation, $126,000 for White Corporation, and $140,000 for Blue Corporation.

**Deduction of Organizational Expenditures.**   Expenses incurred in connection with the organization of a corporation normally are chargeable to a capital account. That they benefit the corporation during its existence seems clear. But how can they be amortized when most corporations possess unlimited life? The lack of a determinable and limited estimated useful life would therefore preclude any tax write-off. Section 248 was enacted to solve this problem.

Under § 248, a corporation may elect to amortize **organizational expenditures** over a period of 60 months or more. The period begins with the month in which the corporation begins business.[20] Organizational expenditures *subject to the election* include the following:

- Legal services incident to organization (e.g., drafting the corporate charter, bylaws, minutes of organizational meetings, terms of original stock certificates).
- Necessary accounting services.
- Expenses of temporary directors and of organizational meetings of directors or shareholders.
- Fees paid to the state of incorporation.

Expenditures that *do not qualify* include those connected with issuing or selling shares of stock or other securities (e.g., commissions, professional fees, and printing costs) or with the transfer of assets to a corporation. Such expenditures reduce the amount of capital raised and are not deductible at all.

To qualify for the election, the expenditure must be *incurred* before the end of the taxable year in which the corporation begins business. In this regard, the corporation's method of accounting is of no consequence. Thus, an expense incurred by a cash basis corporation in its first tax year qualifies even though not paid until a subsequent year.

[20]The month in which a corporation begins business may not be immediately apparent. See Reg. § 1.248–1(a)(3). For a similar problem in the Subchapter S area, see Chapter 12.

The election is made in a statement attached to the corporation's return for its first taxable year. The return and statement must be filed no later than the due date of the return (including any extensions).

If the election is not made on a timely basis, organizational expenditures cannot be deducted until the corporation ceases to do business and liquidates. These expenditures will be deductible if the corporate charter limits the life of the corporation.

**EXAMPLE 24**

Black Corporation, an accrual basis taxpayer, was formed and began operations on May 1, 2003. The following expenses were incurred during its first year of operations (May 1– December 31, 2003):

| | |
|---|---|
| Expenses of temporary directors and of organizational meetings | $500 |
| Fee paid to the state of incorporation | 100 |
| Accounting services incident to organization | 200 |
| Legal services for drafting the corporate charter and bylaws | 400 |
| Expenses incident to the printing and sale of stock certificates | 300 |

Assume Black Corporation makes a timely election under § 248 to amortize qualifying organizational expenses over a period of 60 months. The monthly amortization is $20 [($500 + $100 + $200 + $400) ÷ 60 months], and $160 ($20 × 8 months) is deductible for tax year 2003. Note that the $300 of expenses incident to the printing and sale of stock certificates does not qualify for the election. These expenses cannot be deducted at all but reduce the amount of the capital realized from the sale of stock. ∎

Organizational expenditures are distinguished from start-up expenditures covered by § 195. Start-up expenditures include various investigation expenses involved in entering a new business, whether incurred by a corporate or a noncorporate taxpayer. Start-up expenses also include operating expenses, such as rent and payroll, that are incurred by a corporation before it actually begins to produce any gross income. At the election of the taxpayer, such expenditures (e.g., travel, market surveys, financial audits, legal fees) can be amortized over a period of 60 months or longer rather than capitalized as part of the cost of the business.

**LO.4**

Compute the corporate income tax.

# Determining the Corporate Income Tax Liability

## CORPORATE INCOME TAX RATES

Corporate income tax rates have fluctuated widely over past years. Refer to the inside front cover of the text for a schedule of current corporate income tax rates.

**EXAMPLE 25**

Gold Corporation, a calendar year taxpayer, has taxable income of $90,000 for 2003. Its income tax liability is $18,850, determined as follows:

| | |
|---|---|
| Tax on $75,000 | $13,750 |
| Tax on $15,000 × 34% | 5,100 |
| Tax liability | $18,850 |

∎

For a corporation that has taxable income in excess of $100,000 for any tax year, the amount of the tax is increased by the lesser of (1) 5 percent of the excess or (2) $11,750. In effect, the additional tax means a 39 percent rate for every dollar of taxable income from $100,000 to $335,000.[21]

**EXAMPLE 2.6**

Silver Corporation, a calendar year taxpayer, has taxable income of $335,000 for 2003. Its income tax liability is $113,900, determined as follows:

| | |
|---|---|
| Tax on $100,000 | $ 22,250 |
| Tax on $235,000 × 39% | 91,650 |
| Tax liability | $113,900 |

Note that the tax liability of $113,900 is 34% of $335,000. Thus, due to the 39% rate (34% normal rate + 5% additional tax on taxable income between $100,000 and $335,000), the benefit of the lower rates on the first $75,000 of taxable income completely phases out at $335,000. Note that the normal rate drops back to 34% on taxable income between $335,000 and $10 million. ■

Personal service corporations (defined on page 2–10) are taxed at a flat 35 percent rate on all taxable income. Thus, PSCs do not enjoy the tax savings of being in the 15 percent to 34 percent brackets applicable to other corporations. For this purpose, a PSC is a corporation that is substantially employee owned. Also, it must engage in one of the following activities: health, law, engineering, architecture, accounting, actuarial science, performing arts, or consulting.

## ALTERNATIVE MINIMUM TAX

Corporations are subject to an alternative minimum tax (AMT) that is similar to the AMT applicable to individuals.[22] The AMT for corporations, as for individuals, involves a broader tax base than does the regular tax. Like an individual, a corporation is required to apply a minimum tax rate to the expanded base and pay the difference between the AMT tax liability and the regular tax. Many of the adjustments and tax preference items necessary to arrive at alternative minimum taxable income (AMTI) are the same for individuals and corporations.

Although the objective of the AMT is the same for individual and corporate taxpayers, the rate and exemptions are different. Computation of the AMT for corporations is discussed in Chapter 6.

**LO.5**

Explain the tax rules unique to multiple corporations.

## TAX LIABILITY OF RELATED CORPORATIONS

**Related corporations** are subject to special rules for computing the income tax, the accumulated earnings credit, and the AMT exemption.[23] If these restrictions did not exist, the shareholders of a corporation could gain significant tax advantages by splitting a single corporation into *multiple* corporations. The next two examples illustrate the potential *income tax* advantage of multiple corporations.

**EXAMPLE 27**

Gray Corporation annually yields taxable income of $300,000. The corporate tax on $300,000 is $100,250, computed as follows:

---

[21]§ 11(b).

[22]Small corporations are not subject to the alternative minimum tax for tax years beginning after 1997. See Chapter 6 for details.

[23]§ 1561(a).

| | |
|---|---|
| Tax on $100,000 | $ 22,250 |
| Tax on $200,000 × 39% | 78,000 |
| Tax liability | $100,250 |

**EXAMPLE 28**

Assume that Gray Corporation in the previous example is divided equally into four corporations. Each corporation would have taxable income of $75,000, and the tax for each (absent the special provisions for related corporations) would be computed as follows:

| | |
|---|---|
| Tax on $50,000 | $ 7,500 |
| Tax on $25,000 × 25% | 6,250 |
| Tax liability | $13,750 |

The total liability for the four corporations would be $55,000 ($13,750 × 4). The savings would be $45,250 ($100,250 − $55,000). ■

To preclude the advantages that could be gained by using multiple corporations, the tax law requires special treatment for *controlled groups* of corporations. A comparison of Examples 27 and 28 reveals that the income tax savings that could be achieved by using multiple corporations result from having more of the total income taxed at lower rates. To close this potential loophole, the law limits a controlled group's taxable income in the tax brackets below 35 percent to the amount the corporations in the group would have if they were one corporation. Thus, in Example 28, under the controlled corporation rules, only $12,500 (one-fourth of the first $50,000 of taxable income) for each of the four related corporations would be taxed at the 15 percent rate. The 25 percent rate would apply to the next $6,250 (one-fourth of the next $25,000) of taxable income of each corporation. This equal allocation of the $50,000 and $25,000 amounts is required unless all members of the controlled group consent to an apportionment plan providing for an unequal allocation.

Similar limitations apply to the $250,000 accumulated earnings credit for controlled groups and to the $40,000 exemption amount for purposes of computing the AMT. Both the accumulated earnings tax and the AMT are discussed in Chapter 6.

## CONTROLLED GROUPS

A **controlled group** of corporations includes parent-subsidiary groups, brother-sister groups, combined groups, and certain insurance companies. Groups of the first three types are discussed in the following sections. Insurance groups are not discussed in this text.

**Parent-Subsidiary Controlled Group.** A **parent-subsidiary controlled group** consists of one or more *chains* of corporations connected through stock ownership with a common parent corporation. The ownership connection can be established through either a *voting power test* or a *value test*. The voting power test requires ownership of stock possessing at least 80 percent of the total voting power of all classes of stock entitled to vote.[24]

**EXAMPLE 29**

Aqua Corporation owns 80% of White Corporation. Aqua and White Corporations are members of a parent-subsidiary controlled group. Aqua is the parent corporation, and White is the subsidiary. ■

---

[24]§ 1563(a)(1).

■ **FIGURE 2–1**
Controlled Groups—
Parent-Subsidiary Corporations

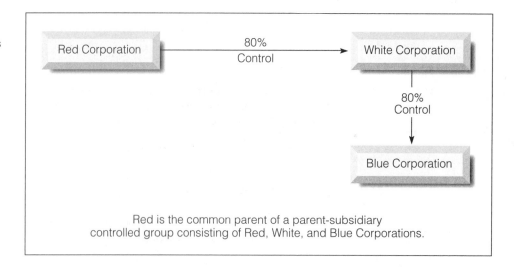

Red is the common parent of a parent-subsidiary
controlled group consisting of Red, White, and Blue Corporations.

The parent-subsidiary relationship described in Example 29 is easy to recognize because Aqua Corporation is the direct owner of White Corporation. Real-world business organizations are often much more complex, sometimes including numerous corporations with chains of ownership connecting them. In these complex corporate structures, determining whether the controlled group classification is appropriate becomes more difficult. The ownership requirements can be met through direct ownership (refer to Example 29) or through indirect ownership, as illustrated in the two following examples.

**EXAMPLE 30**

Red Corporation owns 80% of the voting stock of White Corporation, and White Corporation owns 80% of the voting stock of Blue Corporation. Red, White, and Blue Corporations constitute a controlled group in which Red is the common parent and White and Blue are subsidiaries. The same result would occur if Red Corporation, rather than White Corporation, owned the Blue Corporation stock. This parent-subsidiary relationship is diagrammed in Figure 2–1. ■

**EXAMPLE 31**

Brown Corporation owns 80% of the stock of Green Corporation, which owns 30% of Blue Corporation. Brown also owns 80% of White Corporation, which owns 50% of Blue Corporation. Brown, Green, Blue, and White Corporations constitute a parent-subsidiary controlled group in which Brown is the common parent and Green, Blue, and White are subsidiaries. This parent-subsidiary relationship is diagrammed in Figure 2–2. ■

The value test requires ownership of at least 80 percent of the total value of all shares of all classes of stock of each of the corporations, except the parent corporation, by one or more of the other corporations.

**Brother-Sister Corporations.**   A **brother-sister controlled group** *may* exist if two or more corporations are owned by five or fewer *persons* (individuals, estates, or trusts). Brother-sister status will apply if such a shareholder group meets an 80 percent total ownership test *and* a 50 percent common ownership test.[25]

---

[25]§ 1563(a)(2).

■ **FIGURE 2–2**
Controlled Groups—
Parent-Subsidiary Corporations

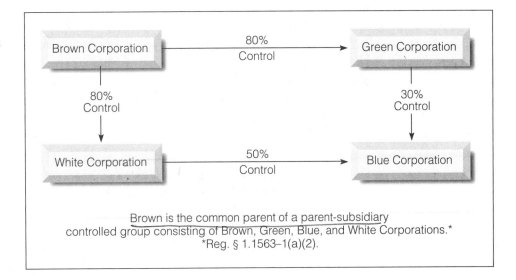

Brown is the common parent of a parent-subsidiary controlled group consisting of Brown, Green, Blue, and White Corporations.*
*Reg. § 1.1563–1(a)(2).

- The *total* ownership test is met if the shareholder group possesses stock representing at least 80 percent of the total combined voting power of all classes of stock entitled to vote, *or* at least 80 percent of the total value of shares of all classes of stock of each corporation.
- The *common* ownership test is met if the shareholder group owns more than 50 percent of the total combined voting power of all classes of stock entitled to vote, *or* more than 50 percent of the total value of shares of all classes of stock of each corporation.

In applying the common ownership test, the stock held by each person is considered only to the extent that the stock ownership is *identical* for each corporation. That is, if a shareholder owns 30 percent of Silver Corporation and 20 percent of Gold Corporation, such shareholder has identical ownership of 20 percent of each corporation.

**EXAMPLE 32**

The outstanding stock of Hawk, Eagle, Crane, and Dove Corporations, each of which has only one class of stock outstanding, is owned by the following unrelated individuals:

| | Corporations | | | | Identical |
|---|---|---|---|---|---|
| **Individuals** | **Hawk** | **Eagle** | **Crane** | **Dove** | **Ownership** |
| Allen | 40% | 30% | 60% | 60% | 30% |
| Barton | 50% | 20% | 30% | 20% | 20% |
| Carter | 10% | 30% | 10% | 10% | 10% |
| Dixon | | 20% | | 10% | |
| Total | 100% | 100% | 100% | 100% | 60% |

Five or fewer individuals (Allen, Barton, and Carter) with more than a 50% common ownership own at least 80% of all classes of stock in Hawk, Eagle, Crane, and Dove. They own 100% of Hawk, 80% of Eagle, 100% of Crane, and 90% of Dove. Consequently, Hawk, Eagle, Crane, and Dove are regarded as members of a brother-sister controlled group. ■

**EXAMPLE 33**

Changing the facts in Example 32, assume the ownership is as follows:

| Individuals | Corporations | | | | Identical Ownership |
|---|---|---|---|---|---|
| | **Hawk** | **Eagle** | **Crane** | **Dove** | |
| Allen | 20% | 10% | 5% | 60% | 5% |
| Barton | 10% | 20% | 60% | 5% | 5% |
| Carter | 10% | 70% | 35% | 25% | 10% |
| Dixon | 60% | | | 10% | |
| Total | 100% | 100% | 100% | 100% | 20% |

In this situation, the identical ownership is only 20%. Consequently, the four corporations are not members of a brother-sister controlled group. However, Eagle and Crane would be brother-sister corporations because both the total ownership and the common ownership tests are met. Allen, Barton, and Carter own 100% of each corporation, and common ownership exceeds 50% (5% by Allen, 20% by Barton, and 35% by Carter). ■

**EXAMPLE 34**

The outstanding stock of Black Corporation and Brown Corporation, each of which has only one class of stock outstanding, is owned as follows:

| Individuals | Corporations | | Identical Ownership |
|---|---|---|---|
| | **Black** | **Brown** | |
| Rossi | 55% | 100% | 55% |
| Smith | 45% | | |
| Total | 100% | 100% | 55% |

Although the 50% common ownership test is met, the 80% test is not since there is no common ownership in Brown Corporation. Are Black and Brown brother-sister corporations? No, according to the U.S. Supreme Court.[26] ■

---

## ETHICAL CONSIDERATIONS    A Bookkeeper's Mistake

You recently agreed to prepare a tax return for Fox Corporation. Fox's bookkeeper, who has little tax experience, has filed a tax return for Fox each year during the corporation's existence. In your discussions with Maria Fox, president and majority shareholder of Fox Corporation, you find that she also owns substantial interests in Wolf Corporation and Coyote Corporation. You also find that two other individuals own stock in each of the three corporations, and that, along with Maria, the group owns 100 percent of all three corporations. Both Wolf and Coyote Corporations have always filed separate returns. What are the tax issues, and what action, if any, should you take?

---

**Combined Groups.**    A combined controlled group exists if all of the following conditions are met:

- Each corporation is a member of either a parent-subsidiary controlled group or a brother-sister controlled group.

---

[26]*U.S. v. Vogel Fertilizer Co.*, 82–1 USTC ¶9134, 49 AFTR2d 82–491, 102 S.Ct. 821 (USSC, 1982). See also Reg. § 1.1563–1(a)(3).

- At least one of the corporations is a parent of a parent-subsidiary controlled group.
- The parent corporation is also a member of a brother-sister controlled group.

**EXAMPLE 35**

Robert owns 80% of all classes of stock of Red and Orange Corporations. Red Corporation, in turn, owns 80% of all classes of stock of Blue Corporation. Orange owns all the stock of Green Corporation. Red, Blue, Orange, and Green are members of the same combined group. As a result, Red, Blue, Orange, and Green are limited to taxable income in the tax brackets below 35% and the $250,000 accumulated earnings credit as though they were one corporation. This is also the case for the election to expense certain depreciable business assets under § 179 and the $40,000 exemption for purposes of computing the AMT. ∎

**Application of § 482.**   Congress has recognized that a parent corporation has the power to shift income among its subsidiaries. Likewise, shareholders who control brother-sister groups can shift income and deductions among the related corporations.

When the true taxable income of a subsidiary or other related corporation has been understated or overstated, the IRS can reallocate the income and deductions of the related corporations under § 482. Section 482 permits the IRS to allocate gross income, deductions, and credits between any two or more organizations, trades, or businesses that are owned or controlled by the same interests. This is appropriate when the allocation is necessary to prevent avoidance of taxes or to reflect income correctly. Controlled groups of corporations are particularly vulnerable to § 482.

**LO.6**

Describe the reporting process for corporations.

# Procedural Matters

## FILING REQUIREMENTS FOR CORPORATIONS

A corporation must file a Federal income tax return whether or not it has taxable income.[27] A corporation that was not in existence throughout an entire annual accounting period is required to file a return for the fraction of the year during which it was in existence. In addition, a corporation must file a return even though it has ceased to do business if it has valuable claims for which it will bring suit. A corporation is relieved of filing income tax returns only when it ceases to do business and retains no assets.

The corporate return is filed on Form 1120 unless the corporation is a small corporation entitled to file the shorter Form 1120–A. A corporation may file Form 1120–A if it meets *all* the following requirements:

- Gross receipts or sales are under $500,000.
- Total income (gross profit plus other income including gains on sales of property) is under $500,000.
- Total assets are under $500,000.
- The corporation is not involved in a dissolution or liquidation.
- The corporation is not a member of a controlled group under §§ 1561 and 1563.
- The corporation does not file a consolidated return.

---

[27]§ 6012(a)(2).

## TAX IN THE NEWS

### SHOULD CEOS BE REQUIRED TO ATTEST TO CORPORATE TAX RETURNS?

The Sarbanes-Oxley Act, enacted in response to recent corporate financial reporting scandals, requires chief executive officers to attest to the accuracy of financial statements filed with the Securities and Exchange Commission. S. 1971, a bill being considered by the Senate, would extend the CEO's responsibility to the corporate tax return. Section 6062 currently requires that an officer of a corporation must sign the corporate tax return, but it allows wide latitude as to who may sign: "The return of a corporation with respect to income shall be signed by the president, vice-president, treasurer, assistant treasurer, chief accounting officer or any other officer duly authorized so to act."

S. 1971 proposes that § 6062 be amended to read as follows: "The return of a corporation with respect to income shall be signed by the chief executive officer of such corporation (or other such officer of the corporation as the Secretary may designate if the corporation does not have a chief executive officer)."

The Committee on Taxation of the Financial Executives Institute (FEI) agrees that the Sarbanes-Oxley requirements may be reasonable in that CEOs are expected to have at least a general understanding of GAAP. However, the FEI argues, CEOs are not expected to have general knowledge of the complexities of the Internal Revenue Code and how it differs from GAAP. Therefore, the FEI recommends that the corporate tax return be signed by the chief tax officer of the corporation.

SOURCES: Section 6062 of the Internal Revenue Code and § 511 of the National Employee Savings and Trust Equity Act (S. 1971).

- The corporation does not have ownership in a foreign corporation.
- The corporation does not have foreign shareholders who directly or indirectly own 50 percent or more of its stock.

Corporations electing under Subchapter S (see Chapter 12) file on Form 1120S. Forms 1120, 1120–A, and 1120S are reproduced in Appendix B.

The return must be filed on or before the fifteenth day of the third month following the close of a corporation's tax year. As noted previously, a regular corporation, other than a PSC, can use either a calendar or a fiscal year to report its taxable income. The tax year of the shareholders has no effect on the corporation's tax year.

Corporations can receive an automatic extension of six months for filing the corporate return by filing Form 7004 by the due date for the return.[28] However, the IRS may terminate the extension by mailing a 10-day notice to the taxpayer corporation. A Form 7004 must be accompanied by the corporation's estimated tax liability.

### ESTIMATED TAX PAYMENTS

A corporation must make payments of estimated tax unless its tax liability can reasonably be expected to be less than $500. The required annual payment (which includes any estimated AMT liability) is the lesser of (1) 100 percent of the corporation's final tax or (2) 100 percent of the tax for the preceding year (if that was a 12-month tax year and the return filed showed a tax liability).[29] Estimated payments

---

[28]§ 6081.                    [29]§§ 6655(d) and (e).

can be made in four installments due on or before the fifteenth day of the fourth month, the sixth month, the ninth month, and the twelfth month of the corporate taxable year. The full amount of the unpaid tax is due on the due date of the return. For a calendar year corporation, the payment dates are as follows:

April 15

June 15

September 15

December 15

A corporation failing to pay its required estimated tax payments will be subjected to a nondeductible penalty on the amount by which the installments are less than the tax due. However, the underpayment penalty will not be imposed if the estimated payments are timely and are equal to the tax liability of the corporation for the prior year or equal to the tax due computed on an annualized basis. If the annualized method is used for one installment and the corporation does not use this method for a subsequent installment, any shortfall from using the annualized method for a prior payment(s) must be made up in the subsequent installment payment. The penalty is imposed on each installment; that is, a corporation must pay one-fourth of its required annual payment by the due date of each installment.

A *large* corporation cannot base its installment payments on its previous year's tax liability except for its first installment payment. A corporation is considered large if it had taxable income in excess of $1 million in any of its three preceding years.

## RECONCILIATION OF TAXABLE INCOME AND FINANCIAL NET INCOME

**Schedule M–1** on the last page of Form 1120 is used to reconcile net income as computed for financial accounting purposes with taxable income reported on the corporation's income tax return. The starting point on Schedule M–1 is net income per books (financial accounting net income). Additions and subtractions are entered for items that affect net income per books and taxable income differently. The following items are entered as additions (see lines 2 through 5 of Schedule M–1):

- Federal income tax liability (deducted in computing net income per books but not deductible in computing taxable income).
- The excess of capital losses over capital gains (deducted for financial accounting purposes but not deductible by corporations for income tax purposes).
- Income that is reported in the current year for tax purposes that is not reported in computing net income per books (e.g., prepaid income).
- Various expenses that are deducted in computing net income per books but are not allowed in computing taxable income (e.g., charitable contributions in excess of the 10 percent ceiling applicable to corporations).

The following subtractions are entered on lines 7 and 8 of Schedule M–1:

- Income reported for financial accounting purposes but not included in taxable income (e.g., tax-exempt interest).
- Expenses deducted on the tax return but not deducted in computing net income per books (e.g., a charitable contributions carryover deducted in a prior year for financial accounting purposes but deductible in the current year for tax purposes).

The result is taxable income (before the NOL deduction and the dividends received deduction).

**EXAMPLE 36**

During the current year, Tern Corporation had the following transactions:

| | |
|---|---|
| Net income per books (after tax) | $92,400 |
| Taxable income | 50,000 |
| Federal income tax liability (15% × $50,000) | 7,500 |
| Interest income from tax-exempt bonds | 5,000 |
| Interest paid on loan, the proceeds of which were used to purchase the tax-exempt bonds | 500 |
| Life insurance proceeds received as a result of the death of a key employee | 50,000 |
| Premiums paid on key employee life insurance policy | 2,600 |
| Excess of capital losses over capital gains | 2,000 |

For book and tax purposes, Tern Corporation determines depreciation under the straight-line method. Tern's Schedule M–1 for the current year is as follows:

| Schedule M-1 | Reconciliation of Income (Loss) per Books With Income per Return | | | | |
|---|---|---|---|---|---|
| 1 | Net income (loss) per books | 92,400 | 7 | Income recorded on books this year not included on this return (itemize): | |
| 2 | Federal income tax per books | 7,500 | | Tax-exempt interest $ 5,000 | |
| 3 | Excess of capital losses over capital gains | 2,000 | | *Life insurance proceeds on key* | |
| 4 | Income subject to tax not recorded on books this year (itemize): | | | *employee $50,000* | 55,000 |
| | | | 8 | Deductions on this return not charged against book income this year (itemize): | |
| 5 | Expenses recorded on books this year not deducted on this return (itemize): | | | a Depreciation $ | |
| a | Depreciation $ | | | b Charitable contributions $ | |
| b | Charitable contributions $ | | | | |
| c | Travel and entertainment $ | | | | |
| | *Prem.–life ins. $2,600; Int.–exempt bonds $500* | 3,100 | 9 | Add lines 7 and 8 | 55,000 |
| 6 | Add lines 1 through 5 | 105,000 | 10 | Income (line 28, page 1)—line 6 less line 9 | 50,000 |

Schedule M–2 reconciles unappropriated retained earnings at the beginning of the year with unappropriated retained earnings at year-end. Beginning balance plus net income per books, as entered on line 1 of Schedule M–1, less dividend distributions during the year equals ending retained earnings. Other sources of increases or decreases in retained earnings are also listed on Schedule M–2.

**EXAMPLE 37**

Assume the same facts as in Example 36. Tern Corporation's beginning balance in unappropriated retained earnings is $125,000. During the year, Tern distributed a cash dividend of $30,000 to its shareholders. Based on these further assumptions, Tern's Schedule M–2 for the current year is as follows:

| Schedule M-2 | Analysis of Unappropriated Retained Earnings per Books (Line 25, Schedule L) | | | | |
|---|---|---|---|---|---|
| 1 | Balance at beginning of year | 125,000 | 5 Distributions: a Cash | 30,000 |
| 2 | Net income (loss) per books | 92,400 | | b Stock | |
| 3 | Other increases (itemize): | | | c Property | |
| | | | 6 Other decreases (itemize): | |
| | | | 7 Add lines 5 and 6 | 30,000 |
| 4 | Add lines 1, 2, and 3 | 217,400 | 8 Balance at end of year (line 4 less line 7) | 187,400 |

Starting with the 2002 tax year, corporations with less than $250,000 of gross receipts and less than $250,000 in assets will no longer have to complete Schedule L (balance sheet) and Schedules M–1 and M–2 of Form 1120. Similar omissions are allowed for Forms 1120–A and 1120S. This change is intended to ease the compliance burden on small business.

## FORM 1120 ILLUSTRATED

Swift Corporation was formed on January 10, 1985, by James Brown and Martha Swift to sell men's clothing. Pertinent information regarding Swift is summarized as follows:

- The business address is 6210 Norman Street, Buffalo, TX 79330.
- The employer identification number is 75–3284680; the principal business activity code is 448110.
- James Brown and Martha Swift each own one-half of the outstanding common stock; no other class of stock is authorized. James Brown is president of the company, and Martha Swift is secretary-treasurer. Both are full-time employees of the corporation, and each receives a salary of $70,000. James's Social Security number is 299-50-2594; Martha's Social Security number is 400-40-6680.
- The corporation uses the accrual method of accounting and reports on a calendar basis. The specific chargeoff method is used in handling bad debt losses, and inventories are determined using the lower of cost or market method. For book and tax purposes, the straight-line method of depreciation is used.
- During 2002, the corporation distributed a cash dividend of $35,000. Selected portions of Swift's profit and loss statement reflect the following debits and credits:

| Account | Debit | Credit |
|---|---|---|
| Gross sales | | $1,040,000 |
| Sales returns and allowances | $ 50,000 | |
| Purchases | 506,000 | |
| Dividends received from stock investments in less-than-20%-owned U.S. corporations | | 60,000 |
| Interest income | | |
| State bonds | $ 9,000 | |
| Certificates of deposit | 11,000 | 20,000 |
| Premiums on term life insurance policies on the lives of James Brown and Martha Swift; Swift Corporation is the designated beneficiary | 8,000 | |
| Salaries—officers | 140,000 | |
| Salaries—clerical and sales | 100,000 | |
| Taxes (state, local, and payroll) | 35,000 | |
| Repairs | 20,000 | |
| Interest expense | | |
| Loan to purchase state bonds | $ 4,000 | |
| Other business loans | 10,000 | 14,000 |
| Advertising | 8,000 | |
| Rental expense | 24,000 | |
| Depreciation | 16,000 | |
| Other deductions | 21,000 | |

A comparative balance sheet for Swift Corporation reveals the following information:

| Assets | January 1, 2002 | December 31, 2002 |
|---|---|---|
| Cash | $ 240,000 | $ 163,850 |
| Trade notes and accounts receivable | 104,200 | 142,300 |
| Inventories | 300,000 | 356,000 |
| Federal bonds | 50,000 | 50,000 |
| State bonds | 100,000 | 100,000 |
| Prepaid Federal tax | — | 1,700 |
| Stock investment | 300,000 | 400,000 |
| Buildings and other depreciable assets | 120,000 | 120,000 |
| Accumulated depreciation | (44,400) | (60,400) |
| Land | 10,000 | 10,000 |
| Other assets | 1,800 | 1,000 |
| Total assets | $1,181,600 | $1,284,450 |

| Liabilities and Equity | January 1, 2002 | December 31, 2002 |
|---|---|---|
| Accounts payable | $ 150,000 | $ 125,000 |
| Other current liabilities | 40,150 | 33,300 |
| Mortgages | 105,000 | 100,000 |
| Capital stock | 250,000 | 250,000 |
| Retained earnings | 636,450 | 776,150 |
| Total liabilities and equity | $1,181,600 | $1,284,450 |

Net income per books (before any income tax accrual) is $234,000. During 2002, Swift Corporation made estimated tax payments to the IRS of $61,000. Swift Corporation's Form 1120 for 2002 is reproduced on the following pages.

Although most of the entries on Form 1120 for Swift Corporation are self-explanatory, the following comments may be helpful:

- In order to arrive at the cost of goods sold amount (line 2 on page 1), Schedule A (page 2) must be completed.
- Reporting of dividends requires the completion of Schedule C (page 2). Gross dividends are shown on line 4 (page 1), and the dividends received deduction appears on line 29b (page 1). Separating the dividend from the deduction facilitates the application of the 80 percent and 70 percent of taxable income exception (which did not apply in Swift's case).
- Income tax liability is $59,300, computed as follows:

| | |
|---|---|
| Tax on $100,000 | $22,250 |
| Tax on $95,000 at 39% | 37,050 |
| | $59,300 |

The result is transferred to line 3 of Schedule J and ultimately is listed on line 31 (page 1). Because the estimated tax payment of $61,000 is more than the tax liability of $59,300, Swift will receive a tax refund of $1,700.
- In completing Schedule M–1 (page 4), the net income per books (line 1) is net of the Federal income tax ($234,000 − $59,300). The left side of Schedule M–1 (lines 2–5) represents positive adjustments to net income per books. After the negative adjustments are made (line 9), the result is taxable income before NOLs and special deductions (line 28, page 1).

- In completing Schedule M–2 (page 4), the beginning retained earnings figure of $636,450 is added to the net income per books as entered on Schedule M–1 (line 1). The dividends distributed in the amount of $35,000 are entered on line 5 and subtracted to arrive at the ending balance in unappropriated retained earnings of $776,150.
- Because this example lacks certain details, supporting schedules that would be attached to Form 1120 have not been included. For example, a Form 4562 would be included to verify the depreciation deduction (line 20, page 1), and other deductions (line 26, page 1) would be supported by a schedule.

## CONSOLIDATED RETURNS

Corporations that are members of a parent-subsidiary affiliated group may be able to file a consolidated income tax return for a taxable year. Consolidated returns are discussed in Chapter 8.

**LO.7**

Evaluate corporations for conducting a business.

**Tax Planning Considerations**

## CORPORATE VERSUS NONCORPORATE FORMS OF BUSINESS ORGANIZATION

The decision to use the corporate form in conducting a trade or business must be weighed carefully. Besides the nontax considerations attendant on the corporate form (limited liability, continuity of life, free transferability of interests, and centralized management), tax ramifications will play an important role in any such decision. Close attention should be paid to the following:

1. Operating as a regular corporate entity (C corporation) results in the imposition of the corporate income tax. Corporate taxable income will be taxed twice—once as earned by the corporation and again when distributed to the shareholders. Since dividends are not deductible, a closely held corporation has a strong incentive to structure corporate distributions in a deductible form. Thus, profits can be bailed out by the shareholders in the form of salaries, interest, or rents. Such procedures lead to a multitude of problems, one of which, the reclassification of debt as equity, is discussed in Chapter 3. The problems of unreasonable salaries and rents are covered in Chapter 4 in the discussion of constructive dividends.
2. The current tax rates appear to favor corporations over individuals, since corporations have a maximum tax rate of 35 percent and individuals may be subject to a 38.6 percent top rate. Relatively few individuals or corporations are in the top rate brackets, however. For moderate-income taxpayers, the differences in Federal tax brackets between an individual and a corporation may not be substantial. Several state and local governments impose higher taxes on corporations than on individuals. In these jurisdictions, the combined Federal, state, and local tax rates on the two types of taxpayers are practically identical. If a corporation's taxable income does not exceed $100,000, a substantial tax savings may be achieved by accumulating income inside the corporation. Refer to Example 7.
3. Corporate-source income loses its identity as it passes through the corporation to the shareholders. Thus, items that normally receive preferential tax treatment (e.g., interest on municipal bonds) are not taxed as such to the shareholders.

| | | |
|---|---|---|
| Form **1120** | **U.S. Corporation Income Tax Return** | OMB No. 1545-0123 |
| Department of the Treasury Internal Revenue Service | For calendar year 2002 or tax year beginning .............. , 2002, ending .............. , 20 .... ▶ **Instructions are separate. See page 20 for Paperwork Reduction Act Notice.** | 2002 |

**A** Check if a:
1 Consolidated return (attach Form 851) ☐
2 Personal holding co. (attach Sch. PH) ☐
3 Personal service corp. (as defined in Regulations sec. 1.441-3(c) — see instructions) ☐

**Use IRS label. Otherwise, print or type.**

Name
*Swift Corporation*

Number, street, and room or suite no. (If a P.O. box, see page 7 of instructions.)
*6210 Norman Street*

City or town, state, and ZIP code
*Buffalo, TX 79330*

**B** Employer identification number
75 : 3284680

**C** Date incorporated
*1-10-85*

**D** Total assets (see page 8 of instructions)
$ 1,284,450 | 00

**E** Check applicable boxes: (1) ☐ Initial return  (2) ☐ Final return  (3) ☐ Name change  (4) ☐ Address change

| Income | | | | | |
|---|---|---|---|---|---|
| | 1a | Gross receipts or sales  1,040,000 00  **b** Less returns and allowances  50,000 00  **c** Bal ▶ | 1c | 990,000 | 00 |
| | 2 | Cost of goods sold (Schedule A, line 8) | 2 | 450,000 | 00 |
| | 3 | Gross profit. Subtract line 2 from line 1c | 3 | 540,000 | 00 |
| | 4 | Dividends (Schedule C, line 19) | 4 | 60,000 | 00 |
| | 5 | Interest | 5 | 11,000 | 00 |
| | 6 | Gross rents | 6 | | |
| | 7 | Gross royalties | 7 | | |
| | 8 | Capital gain net income (attach Schedule D (Form 1120)) | 8 | | |
| | 9 | Net gain or (loss) from Form 4797, Part II, line 18 (attach Form 4797) | 9 | | |
| | 10 | Other income (see page 9 of instructions—attach schedule) | 10 | | |
| | 11 | **Total income.** Add lines 3 through 10 ▶ | 11 | 611,000 | 00 |

| Deductions (See instructions for limitations on deductions.) | | | | | |
|---|---|---|---|---|---|
| | 12 | Compensation of officers (Schedule E, line 4) | 12 | 140,000 | 00 |
| | 13 | Salaries and wages (less employment credits) | 13 | 100,000 | 00 |
| | 14 | Repairs and maintenance | 14 | 20,000 | 00 |
| | 15 | Bad debts | 15 | | |
| | 16 | Rents | 16 | 24,000 | 00 |
| | 17 | Taxes and licenses | 17 | 35,000 | 00 |
| | 18 | Interest | 18 | 10,000 | 00 |
| | 19 | Charitable contributions (see page 11 of instructions for 10% limitation) | 19 | | |
| | 20 | Depreciation (attach Form 4562)   20  16,000 00 | | | |
| | 21 | Less depreciation claimed on Schedule A and elsewhere on return   21a | 21b | 16,000 | 00 |
| | 22 | Depletion | 22 | | |
| | 23 | Advertising | 23 | 8,000 | 00 |
| | 24 | Pension, profit-sharing, etc., plans | 24 | | |
| | 25 | Employee benefit programs | 25 | | |
| | 26 | Other deductions (attach schedule) | 26 | 21,000 | 00 |
| | 27 | **Total deductions.** Add lines 12 through 26 ▶ | 27 | 374,000 | 00 |
| | 28 | Taxable income before net operating loss deduction and special deductions. Subtract line 27 from line 11 | 28 | 237,000 | 00 |
| | 29 | **Less:** **a** Net operating loss (NOL) deduction (see page 13 of instructions)  29a | | | |
| | | **b** Special deductions (Schedule C, line 20)  29b  42,000 00 | 29c | 42,000 | 00 |

| Tax and Payments | | | | | |
|---|---|---|---|---|---|
| | 30 | **Taxable income.** Subtract line 29c from line 28 | 30 | 195,000 | 00 |
| | 31 | **Total tax** (Schedule J, line 11) | 31 | 59,300 | 00 |
| | 32 | **Payments: a** 2001 overpayment credited to 2002  32a | | | |
| | **b** | 2002 estimated tax payments  32b  61,000 00 | | | |
| | **c** | Less 2002 refund applied for on Form 4466  32c (          )  **d** Bal ▶  32d  61,000 00 | | | |
| | **e** | Tax deposited with Form 7004  32e | | | |
| | **f** | Credit for tax paid on undistributed capital gains (attach Form 2439)  32f | | | |
| | **g** | Credit for Federal tax on fuels (attach Form 4136). See instructions  32g | 32h | 61,000 | 00 |
| | 33 | Estimated tax penalty (see page 14 of instructions). Check if Form 2220 is attached ▶ ☐ | 33 | | |
| | 34 | **Tax due.** If line 32h is smaller than the total of lines 31 and 33, enter amount owed | 34 | | |
| | 35 | **Overpayment.** If line 32h is larger than the total of lines 31 and 33, enter amount overpaid | 35 | 1,700 | 00 |
| | 36 | Enter amount of line 35 you want: **Credited to 2003 estimated tax** ▶        **Refunded** ▶ | 36 | 1,700 | 00 |

**Sign Here**
Under penalties of perjury, I declare that I have examined this return, including accompanying schedules and statements, and to the best of my knowledge and belief, it is true, correct, and complete. Declaration of preparer (other than taxpayer) is based on all information of which preparer has any knowledge.

▶ _____   ▶ _____   ▶ _____
Signature of officer             Date                  Title

May the IRS discuss this return with the preparer shown below (see instructions)? ☐ **Yes** ☐ **No**

**Paid Preparer's Use Only**

| | | | | |
|---|---|---|---|---|
| Preparer's signature ▶ | | Date | Check if self-employed ☐ | Preparer's SSN or PTIN |
| Firm's name (or yours if self-employed), address, and ZIP code ▶ | | | EIN | |
| | | | Phone no. (    ) | |

Cat. No. 11450Q                                         Form **1120** (2002)

Form 1120 (2002)                                                                 Page **2**

### Schedule A    Cost of Goods Sold (see page 14 of instructions)

| | | |
|---|---|---:|
| 1 | Inventory at beginning of year | 300,000 |
| 2 | Purchases | 506,000 |
| 3 | Cost of labor | |
| 4 | Additional section 263A costs (attach schedule) | |
| 5 | Other costs (attach schedule) | |
| 6 | **Total.** Add lines 1 through 5 | 806,000 |
| 7 | Inventory at end of year | 356,000 |
| 8 | **Cost of goods sold.** Subtract line 7 from line 6. Enter here and on line 2, page 1 | 450,000 |

9a  Check all methods used for valuing closing inventory:

(i) ☐ Cost as described in Regulations section 1.471-3

(ii) ☒ Lower of cost or market as described in Regulations section 1.471-4

(iii) ☐ Other (Specify method used and attach explanation.) ▶ --------------------

b  Check if there was a writedown of subnormal goods as described in Regulations section 1.471-2(c) . . . . . . . ▶ ☐

c  Check if the LIFO inventory method was adopted this tax year for any goods (if checked, attach Form 970) . . . . . ▶ ☐

d  If the LIFO inventory method was used for this tax year, enter percentage (or amounts) of closing inventory computed under LIFO . . .  **9d**

e  If property is produced or acquired for resale, do the rules of section 263A apply to the corporation? . . . . . ☐ Yes ☒ No

f  Was there any change in determining quantities, cost, or valuations between opening and closing inventory? If "Yes," attach explanation . . . . . ☐ Yes ☒ No

### Schedule C    Dividends and Special Deductions (see instructions beginning on page 15)

| | | (a) Dividends received | (b) % | (c) Special deductions (a) × (b) |
|---|---|---:|---:|---:|
| 1 | Dividends from less-than-20%-owned domestic corporations that are subject to the 70% deduction (other than debt-financed stock) | 60,000 | 70 | 42,000 |
| 2 | Dividends from 20%-or-more-owned domestic corporations that are subject to the 80% deduction (other than debt-financed stock) | | 80 see instructions | |
| 3 | Dividends on debt-financed stock of domestic and foreign corporations (section 246A) | | | |
| 4 | Dividends on certain preferred stock of less-than-20%-owned public utilities | | 42 | |
| 5 | Dividends on certain preferred stock of 20%-or-more-owned public utilities | | 48 | |
| 6 | Dividends from less-than-20%-owned foreign corporations and certain FSCs that are subject to the 70% deduction | | 70 | |
| 7 | Dividends from 20%-or-more-owned foreign corporations and certain FSCs that are subject to the 80% deduction | | 80 | |
| 8 | Dividends from wholly owned foreign subsidiaries subject to the 100% deduction (section 245(b)) | | 100 | |
| 9 | **Total.** Add lines 1 through 8. See page 16 of instructions for limitation | | | 42,000 |
| 10 | Dividends from domestic corporations received by a small business investment company operating under the Small Business Investment Act of 1958 | | 100 | |
| 11 | Dividends from certain FSCs that are subject to the 100% deduction (section 245(c)(1)) | | 100 | |
| 12 | Dividends from affiliated group members subject to the 100% deduction (section 243(a)(3)) | | 100 | |
| 13 | Other dividends from foreign corporations not included on lines 3, 6, 7, 8, or 11 | | | |
| 14 | Income from controlled foreign corporations under subpart F (attach Form(s) 5471) | | | |
| 15 | Foreign dividend gross-up (section 78) | | | |
| 16 | IC-DISC and former DISC dividends not included on lines 1, 2, or 3 (section 246(d)) | | | |
| 17 | Other dividends | | | |
| 18 | Deduction for dividends paid on certain preferred stock of public utilities | | | |
| 19 | **Total dividends.** Add lines 1 through 17. Enter here and on line 4, page 1 ▶ | 60,000 | | |
| 20 | **Total special deductions.** Add lines 9, 10, 11, 12, and 18. Enter here and on line 29b, page 1 ▶ | | | 42,000 |

### Schedule E    Compensation of Officers (see instructions for line 12, page 1, on page 10 of instructions)

Note: Complete Schedule E only if total receipts (line 1a plus lines 4 through 10 on page 1) are $500,000 or more.

| (a) Name of officer | (b) Social security number | (c) Percent of time devoted to business | (d) Common | (e) Preferred | (f) Amount of compensation |
|---|---|---|---|---|---:|
| 1 James Brown | 299-50-2594 | 100 % | 50 % | % | 70,000 |
| Martha Swift | 400-40-6680 | 100 % | 50 % | % | 70,000 |
| | | % | % | % | |
| | | % | % | % | |
| | | % | % | % | |

| | | |
|---|---|---:|
| 2 | Total compensation of officers | 140,000 |
| 3 | Compensation of officers claimed on Schedule A and elsewhere on return | |
| 4 | Subtract line 3 from line 2. Enter the result here and on line 12, page 1 | 140,000 |

Form **1120** (2002)

Form 1120 (2002)                                                                                                     Page **3**

## Schedule J    Tax Computation (see page 17 of instructions)

**1**  Check if the corporation is a member of a controlled group (see sections 1561 and 1563) . . . . . ▶ ☐

**Important:** Members of a controlled group, see instructions on page 17.

**2a**  If the box on line 1 is checked, enter the corporation's share of the $50,000, $25,000, and $9,925,000 taxable income brackets (in that order):

**(1)** $_____      **(2)** $_____      **(3)** $_____

**b**  Enter the corporation's share of: **(1)** Additional 5% tax (not more than $11,750)   $_____

   **(2)** Additional 3% tax (not more than $100,000)   $_____

| | | | |
|---|---|---|---|
| **3** | Income tax. Check if a qualified personal service corporation under section 448(d)(2) (see page 17) . ▶ ☐ | **3** | 59,300 \| 00 |
| **4** | Alternative minimum tax (attach Form 4626) . . . . . . . . . . | **4** | |
| **5** | Add lines 3 and 4 . . . . . . . . . . . . . . . . . | **5** | 59,300 \| 00 |

**6a**  Foreign tax credit (attach Form 1118) . . . . . .   **6a** |

**b**  Possessions tax credit (attach Form 5735) . . . . .   **6b** |

**c**  Check: ☐ Nonconventional source fuel credit ☐ QEV credit (attach Form 8834)   **6c** |

**d**  General business credit. Check box(es) and indicate which forms are attached.

   ☐ Form 3800   ☐ Form(s) (specify) ▶ ...............................   **6d** |

**e**  Credit for prior year minimum tax (attach Form 8827) . . . . .   **6e** |

**f**  Qualified zone academy bond credit (attach Form 8860) . . . . .   **6f** |

| | | | |
|---|---|---|---|
| **7** | **Total credits.** Add lines 6a through 6f . . . . . . . . | **7** | |
| **8** | Subtract line 7 from line 5 . . . . . . . . . . . . | **8** | |
| **9** | Personal holding company tax (attach Schedule PH (Form 1120)) . . . . . . . | **9** | 59,300 \| 00 |

**10**  Other taxes. Check if from: ☐ Form 4255   ☐ Form 8611   ☐ Form 8697

   ☐ Form 8866   ☐ Other (attach schedule) . . . .   **10** |

| | | | |
|---|---|---|---|
| **11** | **Total tax.** Add lines 8 through 10. Enter here and on line 31, page 1 . . . . . . . . | **11** | 59,300 \| 00 |

## Schedule K    Other Information (see page 19 of instructions)

| | | Yes | No |
|---|---|---|---|
| **1** | Check method of accounting: **a** ☐ Cash **b** ☒ Accrual   **c** ☐ Other (specify) ▶ ................ | | |

**2**  See page 21 of the instructions and enter the:

**a**  Business activity code no. ▶ *448110* ....................

**b**  Business activity ▶ *Retail sales* ..............................

**c**  Product or service ▶ *Men's clothing* ........................

**3**  At the end of the tax year, did the corporation own, directly or indirectly, 50% or more of the voting stock of a domestic corporation? (For rules of attribution, see section 267(c).) . . . . . . . . . . [No: *X*]

   If "Yes," attach a schedule showing: **(a)** name and employer identification number (EIN), **(b)** percentage owned, and **(c)** taxable income or (loss) before NOL and special deductions of such corporation for the tax year ending with or within your tax year.

**4**  Is the corporation a subsidiary in an affiliated group or a parent-subsidiary controlled group? . . . . . [No: *X*]

   If "Yes," enter name and EIN of the parent corporation ▶ ..................................

**5**  At the end of the tax year, did any individual, partnership, corporation, estate, or trust own, directly or indirectly, 50% or more of the corporation's voting stock? (For rules of attribution, see section 267(c).) . . . . . . . [Yes: *X*]
   If "Yes," attach a schedule showing name and identifying number. (Do not include any information already entered in **4** above.) Enter percentage owned ▶ *100%*

**6**  During this tax year, did the corporation pay dividends (other than stock dividends and distributions in exchange for stock) in excess of the corporation's current and accumulated earnings and profits? (See sections 301 and 316.) . . . [No: *X*]

   If "Yes," file **Form 5452,** Corporate Report of Nondividend Distributions.

   If this is a consolidated return, answer here for the parent corporation and on **Form 851,** Affiliations Schedule, for each subsidiary.

| | | Yes | No |
|---|---|---|---|
| **7** | At any time during the tax year, did one foreign person own, directly or indirectly, at least 25% of **(a)** the total voting power of all classes of stock of the corporation entitled to vote or **(b)** the total value of all classes of stock of the corporation? . . . . . . . . | | *X* |

   If "Yes," enter: **(a)** Percentage owned ▶ ....................

   and **(b)** Owner's country ▶ ....................

**c**  The corporation may have to file **Form 5472,** Information Return of a 25% Foreign-Owned U.S. Corporation or a Foreign Corporation Engaged in a U.S. Trade or Business. Enter number of Forms 5472 attached ▶ ............

**8**  Check this box if the corporation issued publicly offered debt instruments with original issue discount . . ▶ ☐

   If checked, the corporation may have to file **Form 8281,** Information Return for Publicly Offered Original Issue Discount Instruments.

**9**  Enter the amount of tax-exempt interest received or accrued during the tax year ▶ $ *9,000* ............

**10**  Enter the number of shareholders at the end of the tax year (if 75 or fewer) ▶ *2* ............................

**11**  If the corporation has an NOL for the tax year and is electing to forego the carryback period, check here ▶ ☐

   If the corporation is filing a consolidated return, the statement required by Regulations section 1.1502-21(b)(3)(i) or (ii) must be attached or the election will not be valid.

**12**  Enter the available NOL carryover from prior tax years (Do not reduce it by any deduction on line 29a.) ▶ $ ............................

**13**  Are the corporation's total receipts (line 1a plus lines 4 through 10 on page 1) for the tax year **and** its total assets at the end of the tax year less than $250,000?. . . . .

   If "Yes," the corporation is not required to complete Schedules L, M-1, and M-2 on page 4. Instead, enter the total amount of cash distributions and the book value of property distributions (other than cash) made during the tax year. ▶ $ ............

**Note:** *If the corporation, at any time during the tax year, had assets or operated a business in a foreign country or U.S. possession, it may be required to attach **Schedule N (Form 1120)**, Foreign Operations of U.S. Corporations, to this return. See Schedule N for details.*

Form **1120** (2002)

Form 1120 (2002)                                                  Page **4**

**Note:** *The corporation is not required to complete Schedules L, M-1, and M-2 if Question 13 on Schedule K is answered "Yes."*

### Schedule L   Balance Sheets per Books

| Assets | (a) Beginning of tax year | (b) | (c) End of tax year | (d) |
|---|---|---|---|---|
| **1** Cash | | 240,000 | | 163,850 |
| **2a** Trade notes and accounts receivable | 104,200 | | 142,300 | |
| **b** Less allowance for bad debts | ( ) | 104,200 | ( ) | 142,300 |
| **3** Inventories | | 300,000 | | 356,000 |
| **4** U.S. government obligations | | 50,000 | | 50,000 |
| **5** Tax-exempt securities (see instructions) | | 100,000 | | 100,000 |
| **6** Other current assets (attach schedule) | | | | 1,700 |
| **7** Loans to shareholders | | | | |
| **8** Mortgage and real estate loans | | | | |
| **9** Other investments (attach schedule) | | 300,000 | | 400,000 |
| **10a** Buildings and other depreciable assets | 120,000 | | 120,000 | |
| **b** Less accumulated depreciation | ( 44,400 ) | 75,600 | ( 60,400 ) | 59,600 |
| **11a** Depletable assets | | | | |
| **b** Less accumulated depletion | ( ) | | ( ) | |
| **12** Land (net of any amortization) | | 10,000 | | 10,000 |
| **13a** Intangible assets (amortizable only) | | | | |
| **b** Less accumulated amortization | ( ) | | ( ) | |
| **14** Other assets (attach schedule) | | 1,800 | | 1,000 |
| **15** Total assets | | 1,181,600 | | 1,284,450 |
| **Liabilities and Shareholders' Equity** | | | | |
| **16** Accounts payable | | 150,000 | | 125,000 |
| **17** Mortgages, notes, bonds payable in less than 1 year | | | | |
| **18** Other current liabilities (attach schedule) | | 40,150 | | 33,300 |
| **19** Loans from shareholders | | | | |
| **20** Mortgages, notes, bonds payable in 1 year or more | | 105,000 | | 100,000 |
| **21** Other liabilities (attach schedule) | | | | |
| **22** Capital stock: **a** Preferred stock | | | | |
| **b** Common stock | 250,000 | 250,000 | 250,000 | 250,000 |
| **23** Additional paid-in capital | | | | |
| **24** Retained earnings—Appropriated (attach schedule) | | | | |
| **25** Retained earnings—Unappropriated | | 636,450 | | 776,150 |
| **26** Adjustments to shareholders' equity (attach schedule) | | | | |
| **27** Less cost of treasury stock | | ( ) | | ( ) |
| **28** Total liabilities and shareholders' equity | | 1,181,600 | | 1,284,450 |

### Schedule M-1   Reconciliation of Income (Loss) per Books With Income per Return (see page 20 of instructions)

| | | | |
|---|---|---|---|
| **1** Net income (loss) per books | 174,700 | **7** Income recorded on books this year not included on this return (itemize): Tax-exempt interest $ 9,000 | |
| **2** Federal income tax per books | 59,300 | | |
| **3** Excess of capital losses over capital gains | | | |
| **4** Income subject to tax not recorded on books this year (itemize): _____ | | | 9,000 |
| | | **8** Deductions on this return not charged against book income this year (itemize): | |
| **5** Expenses recorded on books this year not deducted on this return (itemize): | | **a** Depreciation . . . . $_____ | |
| **a** Depreciation . . . $_____ | | **b** Charitable contributions $_____ | |
| **b** Charitable contributions $_____ | | | |
| **c** Travel and entertainment $_____ Prem.—life ins. $8,000; Int.— state bonds $4,000 | 12,000 | **9** Add lines 7 and 8 | 9,000 |
| **6** Add lines 1 through 5 | 246,000 | **10** Income (line 28, page 1)—line 6 less line 9 | 237,000 |

### Schedule M-2   Analysis of Unappropriated Retained Earnings per Books (Line 25, Schedule L)

| | | | |
|---|---|---|---|
| **1** Balance at beginning of year | 636,450 | **5** Distributions: **a** Cash | 35,000 |
| **2** Net income (loss) per books | 174,700 | **b** Stock | |
| **3** Other increases (itemize): _____ | | **c** Property | |
| | | **6** Other decreases (itemize): _____ | |
| | | **7** Add lines 5 and 6 | 35,000 |
| **4** Add lines 1, 2, and 3 | 811,150 | **8** Balance at end of year (line 4 less line 7) | 776,150 |

Form **1120** (2002)

4. As noted in Chapter 4, it may be difficult for shareholders to recover some or all of their investment in the corporation without an ordinary income result. Most corporate distributions are treated as dividends to the extent of the corporation's earnings and profits.

5. Corporate losses cannot be passed through to the shareholders.[30]

6. The liquidation of a corporation will normally generate tax consequences to both the corporation and its shareholders (see Chapter 5).

7. The corporate form provides shareholders with the opportunity to be treated as employees for tax purposes if the shareholders render services to the corporation. Such status makes a number of attractive tax-sheltered fringe benefits available. They include, but are not limited to, group term life insurance and excludible meals and lodging. One of the most attractive benefits of incorporation is the ability of the business to provide accident and health insurance to its employees, including shareholders. Such benefits are not included in the employee's gross income. Similar rules apply to other medical costs paid by the employer. These benefits are not available to partners and sole proprietors.

## OPERATING THE CORPORATION

Tax planning to reduce corporate income taxes should occur before the end of the tax year. Effective planning can cause income to be shifted to the next tax year and can produce large deductions by incurring expenses before year-end. Particular attention should be focused on the following.

**Charitable Contributions.** Recall that accrual basis corporations may claim a deduction for charitable contributions in the year preceding payment. The contribution must be authorized by the board of directors by the end of the tax year and paid on or before the fifteenth day of the third month of the following year. Even though the contribution may not ultimately be made, it might well be authorized. A deduction cannot be thrown back to the previous year (even if paid within the two and one-half months) if it has not been authorized.

**Timing of Capital Gains and Losses.** A corporation should consider offsetting profits on the sale of capital assets by selling some of the depreciated securities in the corporate portfolio. In addition, any already realized capital losses should be carefully monitored. Recall that corporate taxpayers are not permitted to claim any net capital losses as deductions against ordinary income. Capital losses can be used only as an offset against capital gains. Further, net capital losses can only be carried back three years and forward five. Gains from the sales of capital assets should be timed to offset any capital losses. The expiration of the carryover period for any net capital losses should be watched carefully so that sales of appreciated capital assets occur before that date.

**Net Operating Losses.** In some situations, electing to forgo an NOL carryback and utilizing the carryforward option may generate greater tax savings.

---

[30]Points 1, 2, and 5 could be resolved through a Subchapter S election (see Chapter 12), assuming the corporation qualifies for such an election. In part, the same can be said for point 3.

**EXAMPLE 38**

Ruby Corporation incurred a $50,000 NOL in 2003. Ruby, which was in the 15% bracket in 2001 and 2002, has developed a new product that management predicts will push the corporation into the 34% bracket in 2004. If Ruby carries the NOL back, the tax savings will be $7,500 ($50,000 × 15%). However, if Ruby elects to carry the NOL forward, assuming management's prediction is accurate, the tax savings will be $17,000 ($50,000 × 34%). ■

When deciding whether to forgo the carryback option, take into account three considerations. First, the time value of the tax refund that is lost by not using the carryback procedure should be calculated. Second, the election to forgo an NOL carryback is irrevocable. Thus, one cannot later choose to change if the predicted high profits do not materialize. Third, consider the future increases (or decreases) in corporate income tax rates that can reasonably be anticipated. This last consideration is the most difficult to work with. Although corporate tax rates have remained relatively stable in recent years, taxpayers have little assurance that future rates will remain constant.

**Dividends Received Deduction.** The dividends received deduction normally is limited to the lesser of 70 percent of the qualifying dividends or 70 percent of taxable income. The deduction limits are raised to 80 percent for a dividend received from a corporation in which the recipient owns 20 percent or more of the stock. An exception is made when the full deduction yields an NOL. In close situations, therefore, the proper timing of income or deductions to generate an NOL may yield a larger dividends received deduction.

**Organizational Expenditures.** To qualify for the 60-month amortization procedure of § 248, only organizational expenditures incurred in the first taxable year of the corporation can be considered. This rule could prove to be an unfortunate trap for corporations formed late in the year.

**EXAMPLE 39**

Thrush Corporation is formed in December 2003. Qualified organizational expenditures are incurred as follows: $2,000 in December 2003 and $3,000 in January 2004. If Thrush uses the calendar year for tax purposes, only $2,000 of the organizational expenditures can be written off over a period of 60 months. ■

The solution to the problem posed by Example 39 is for Thrush Corporation to adopt a fiscal year that ends on or beyond January 31. All organizational expenditures will then have been incurred before the close of the first taxable year.

**Shareholder-Employee Payment of Corporate Expenses.** In a closely held corporate setting, shareholder-employees often pay corporate expenses (e.g., travel and entertainment) for which they are not reimbursed by the corporation. The IRS often disallows the deduction of these expenses by the shareholder-employee, since the payments are voluntary on his or her part. If the deduction is more beneficial at the shareholder-employee level, a corporate policy against reimbursement of such expenses should be established. Proper planning in this regard would be to decide before the beginning of each tax year where the deduction would do the most good. Corporate policy on reimbursement of such expenses could be modified on a year-to-year basis depending upon the circumstances.

In deciding whether corporate expenses should be kept at the corporate level or shifted to the shareholder-employee, the treatment of unreimbursed employee expenses must be considered. First, since employee expenses are itemized deductions, they will be of no benefit to the taxpayer who chooses the standard deduction

## CONCEPT SUMMARY 2–1

### Income Taxation of Individuals and Corporations Compared

| | Individuals | Corporations |
|---|---|---|
| Computation of gross income | § 61. | § 61. |
| Computation of taxable income | §§ 62, 63(b) through (h). | § 63(a). Concept of AGI has no relevance. |
| Deductions | Trade or business (§ 162); nonbusiness (§ 212); some personal and employee expenses (generally deductible as itemized deductions). | Trade or business (§ 162). |
| Charitable contributions | Limited in any tax year to 50% of AGI; 30% for long-term capital gain property unless election is made to reduce fair market value of gift. | Limited in any tax year to 10% of taxable income computed without regard to the charitable contribution deduction, net operating loss, and dividends received deduction. |
| | Excess charitable contributions carried over for five years. | Same as for individuals. |
| | Amount of contribution is the fair market value of long-term capital gain property; ordinary income property is limited to adjusted basis; capital gain property is treated as ordinary income property if certain tangible personalty is donated to a nonuse charity or a private nonoperating foundation is the donee. | Same as individuals, but exceptions allowed for certain inventory and for scientific property where one-half of the appreciation is allowed as a deduction. |
| | Time of deduction—year in which payment is made. | Time of deduction—year in which payment is made unless accrual basis taxpayer. Accrual basis corporation can take deduction in year preceding payment if contribution was authorized by board of directors by end of year and contribution is paid by fifteenth day of third month of following year. |
| Casualty losses | $100 floor on personal casualty and theft losses; personal casualty losses deductible only to extent losses exceed 10% of AGI. | Deductible in full. |
| Net operating loss | Adjusted for several items, including nonbusiness deductions over nonbusiness income and personal exemptions. | Generally no adjustments. |
| | Carryback period is 2 years while carryforward period is 20 years. | Same as for individuals. |
| Dividends received deduction | None. | 70%, 80%, or 100% of dividends received depending on percentage of ownership by corporate shareholder. |

|  | **Individuals** | **Corporations** |
|---|---|---|
| Net capital gains | Taxed in full. Tax rate generally cannot exceed 20% on net long-term capital gains. | Taxed in full. |
| Capital losses | Only $3,000 of capital loss per year can offset ordinary income; loss is carried forward indefinitely to offset capital gains or ordinary income up to $3,000; short-term and long-term carryovers retain their character. | Can offset only capital gains; carried back three years and forward five; carryovers and carrybacks are short-term losses. |
| Passive losses | In general, passive activity losses cannot offset either active income or portfolio income. | Passive loss rules apply to closely held C corporations and personal service corporations. For personal service corporations, passive losses cannot offset either active income or portfolio income. For closely held C corporations, passive losses may offset active income but not portfolio income. |
| Tax rates | Progressive with six rates (10%, 15%, 27%, 30%, 35%, 38.6%). | Progressive with four rates (15%, 25%, 34%, 35%). Two lowest brackets phased out between $100,000 and $335,000 of taxable income, and additional tax imposed between $15,000,000 and $18,333,333 of taxable income. |
| Alternative minimum tax | Applied at a graduated rate schedule of 26% and 28%. Exemption allowed depending on filing status (e.g., $49,000 for married filing jointly); phaseout begins when AMTI reaches a certain amount (e.g., $150,000 for married filing jointly). | Applied at a 20% rate on AMTI less exemption; $40,000 exemption allowed but phaseout begins when AMTI reaches $150,000; adjustments and tax preference items are similar to those applicable to individuals but also include 75% adjusted current earnings. Small corporations (gross receipts of $5 million or less) are not subject to AMT. |

option. Second, these expenses will be subject to the 2 percent-of-AGI floor. No such limitation will be imposed if the corporation claims the expenses.

## RELATED CORPORATIONS

**Controlled Groups.**    Recall that § 1561 was designed to prevent shareholders from operating a business as multiple corporations to obtain lower tax brackets and multiple accumulated earnings tax credits or AMT exemptions. Corporations in which substantially all the stock is held by five or fewer persons are subject to the provisions of § 1561. Dividing ownership so that control of each corporation does not lie with individuals having common control of all corporations avoids the prohibitions of § 1561.

| | | |
|---|---|---|
| **EXAMPLE 40** | Arthur, Baker, and Collins have voting stock in Red, White, and Blue Corporations as follows: | |

| Shareholder | Red | White | Blue | Common Ownership |
|---|---|---|---|---|
| Arthur | 40% | 30% | 30% | 30% |
| Baker | 40% | 20% | 30% | 20% |
| Collins | 20% | 50% | 40% | 20% |
| Total | 100% | 100% | 100% | 70% |

Because the total combined ownership is more than 50% and the three individuals own at least 80% of the combined voting power, Red, White, and Blue are treated as a controlled group and are subject to § 1561. Thus, Red, White, and Blue are limited to taxable income in the first two tax brackets and to the $250,000 accumulated earnings tax credit as though they were one corporation. ∎

Assume, however, that the voting stock is divided differently so that each of the individuals—Arthur, Baker, and Collins—controls one of the corporations rather than having common control of all the corporations.

| | | |
|---|---|---|
| **EXAMPLE 41** | Arthur, Baker, and Collins hold voting stock in Red, White, and Blue Corporations in the following percentages: | |

| Shareholder | Red | White | Blue | Common Ownership |
|---|---|---|---|---|
| Arthur | 80% | 10% | 10% | 10% |
| Baker | 10% | 80% | 10% | 10% |
| Collins | 10% | 10% | 80% | 10% |
| Total | 100% | 100% | 100% | 30% |

Now the total combined ownership is less than 50%. Consequently, the corporations are not treated as a controlled group; the prohibitions of § 1561 are not applicable. ∎

The differences in ownership in the corporations can be alleviated somewhat by issuing nonvoting preferred stock to the shareholders with the 10 percent ownership. (Nonvoting stock is not considered to be stock for purposes of § 1563.)

## KEY TERMS

| | | |
|---|---|---|
| Brother-sister controlled group, 2–22 | Limited liability company (LLC), 2–7 | Personal service corporation (PSC), 2–10 |
| C corporation, 2–4 | Limited partnership, 2–7 | Regular corporation, 2–4 |
| Check-the-box Regulations, 2–8 | Organizational expenditures, 2–18 | Related corporations, 2–20 |
| Controlled group, 2–21 | Parent-subsidiary controlled group, 2–21 | S corporation, 2–4 |
| Dividends received deduction, 2–17 | Passive loss, 2–13 | Schedule M–1, 2–27 |

## PROBLEM MATERIALS

### Discussion Questions

1. Zachary is the sole proprietor of Zach's Golf World, which had gross income of $180,000 and operating expenses of $125,000 during the year. In addition, Zachary sold a capital asset that had been used in the business for 14 months for a $4,500 capital loss. He withdrew $40,000 from the business for living expenses during the year. What is Zachary's net income from the proprietorship for the year?

2. George owns a sole proprietorship, and Mike is the sole shareholder of a corporation. Both businesses make a profit of $75,000 in 2003. Neither owner withdraws any funds from his business during 2003. How much income must George and Mike report on their individual tax returns for 2003?

**Decision Making**

3. Art, an executive with Azure Corporation, plans to start a part-time business selling products on the Internet. He will devote about 15 hours each week to running the business. Art's salary from Azure places him in the 38.6% tax bracket. He projects substantial losses from the new business in each of the first three years and expects sizable profits thereafter. Art plans to leave the profits in the business for several years, sell the business, and retire. Would you advise Art to incorporate the business or operate it as a sole proprietorship?

4. Lucille owns a sole proprietorship, and Mabel is the sole shareholder of a C (regular) corporation. Each business sustained a $20,000 operating loss and a $7,000 capital loss for the year. How will these losses affect the taxable income of the two owners?

5. Harry is the sole shareholder of Purple Corporation, which is an S corporation. Purple earned net operating income of $60,000 during the year and had a long-term capital loss of $8,000. Harry withdrew $30,000 of the profit from the corporation. How much income must Harry report on his individual tax return for 2003?

**Issue ID**

6. Tanesha is the sole shareholder of Egret Corporation. Egret's sales have doubled in the last four years, and Tanesha has determined that the business needs a new warehouse. Tanesha has asked your advice as to whether she should (1) have the corporation acquire the warehouse or (2) acquire the warehouse herself and rent it to the corporation. What are the relevant tax issues that you will discuss with Tanesha?

7. Shareholders in closely held corporations frequently pay themselves large salaries in order to avoid double taxation on corporate income. Explain how this strategy avoids double taxation, but also entails possible pitfalls.

8. Trace Corporation has net income of $400,000 during the year ($750,000 revenue – $350,000 operating expenses). Juan and Rosita are equal shareholders of Trace and work in similar jobs as employees of the corporation. They have Trace pay each a salary of $200,000, which results in zero taxable income for the corporation. On audit, an IRS agent determines that $150,000 of the amount paid to the shareholders is unreasonable compensation. The shareholders' tax adviser has told them that the IRS agent is probably correct in his determination. What effect will the IRS agent's finding have on the taxable income of Juan, Rosita, and Trace Corporation?

9. Ed and Barbara have formed a new business entity as a limited liability company (LLC). They plan to elect partnership treatment for the LLC. How is the election made?

10. Your friend George informs you that he is choosing to operate his new business as an LLC because that form provides the "best of both worlds." What does George mean by this statement?

11. C corporations can elect fiscal years that are different from those of their shareholders, but personal service corporations (PSCs) are subject to substantial restrictions in the choice of a fiscal year. Why are the fiscal year choices of PSCs limited?

12. Paul, the sole shareholder of a calendar year, accrual basis C corporation, loaned the corporation a substantial amount of money on January 1, 2003. The corporation accrued $45,000 of interest expense on the loan on December 31, 2003. It plans to pay the interest to Paul, a cash basis taxpayer, on April 1, 2004. In which year will the corporation be allowed to deduct the interest? In which year will Paul be required to report the interest income?

13. Rose Corporation sells and installs heating and air conditioning units. Violet Corporation provides repair, inspection, and maintenance services for heating and air conditioning units. Which corporation is more likely to be required to use the accrual basis of accounting? Why?

14. Kathy owns all of the stock in Eagle Corporation. During 2003, Kathy incurs a $25,000 long-term capital loss, and Eagle Corporation also incurs a $25,000 long-term capital loss. Compare the treatment of these transactions on the tax returns of Kathy and Eagle.

15. Judy, a sole proprietor, sold one of her business assets for a $20,000 long-term capital gain. Judy's marginal tax rate is 35%. Link Corporation sold one of its assets for a $20,000 long-term capital gain. Link's marginal tax rate is 35%. What tax rates are applicable to these capital gains?

16. John, a sole proprietor, incurs a $7,000 capital loss from the sale of an asset held by his business. Fox Corporation incurs a $7,000 capital loss on the sale of an asset held by the corporation. How do John and Fox Corporation treat these losses in computing taxable income?

17. Falcon Corporation, a closely held corporation that is a personal service corporation, has $60,000 of active income, $36,000 of portfolio income, and a $90,000 loss from a passive activity. How much of the passive loss can Falcon deduct?

18. Hummingbird Corporation, a closely held corporation that is not a personal service corporation, has $30,000 of active income, $18,000 of portfolio income, and a $60,000 loss from a passive activity. How much of the passive loss can Hummingbird deduct?

19. On December 20, 2003, the directors of Partridge Corporation (a cash basis, calendar year taxpayer) authorized a cash donation of $10,000 to the American Heart Association, a qualified charity. The payment is made on April 15, 2004. Can Partridge claim the $10,000 contribution as a deduction for tax year 2003?

20. Taupe Corporation owns 90% of the stock of Mocha Corporation, which pays Taupe a substantial dividend each year. Taupe Corporation plans to sell half of its stock in Mocha Corporation. How will this stock disposition affect the amount of dividend income that Taupe Corporation will report for the year?

21. Amber Corporation owns 75% of the stock of Mauve Corporation and has net operating income of $500,000 for the year. Mauve Corporation pays Amber a dividend of $100,000. What amount of dividends received deduction may Amber claim? What amount of dividends received deduction may Amber claim if it acquires an additional 10% of the stock of Mauve Corporation, receives a dividend of $110,000, and files a consolidated return with Mauve?

22. In connection with organizational expenditures, comment on the following:
    a. Those that qualify for amortization.
    b. Those that do not qualify for amortization.
    c. The period over which amortization can take place.
    d. Expenses incurred but not paid by a cash basis corporation.
    e. Expenses incurred by a corporation in its second year of operation.
    f. The alternative if the election to amortize is not made.
    g. The timing of the election to amortize.

23. George is the sole shareholder of Palmetto Corporation, which has annual taxable income of approximately $75,000. He decides to form two new corporations and transfer one-third of the Palmetto assets to Poplar Corporation and one-third to Spruce Corporation. This will result in each of the three corporations having approximately $25,000

taxable income each year. George believes this plan will reduce overall corporate income taxes. Will George's plan work? Discuss.

24. Ted, an individual, owns 80% of all classes of stock of Brown Corporation and Green Corporation. Brown Corporation, in turn, owns all the stock of White Corporation, and Green Corporation owns 80% of the stock of Orange Corporation. Are Brown, Green, Orange, and White Corporations members of a combined group? Explain.

25. Taxable income and financial accounting income for a corporation are seldom the same amount. Discuss some common reasons for differences and how these differences affect the reconciliation of taxable income and financial accounting income on Schedule M–1 of Form 1120.

26. Martin Corporation was organized in 2002 and had profits in 2002 and 2003. The corporation had an NOL in 2004. Under what circumstances should the corporation elect to forgo carrying the NOL back to the two prior years?

27. Teal, Inc., a calendar year corporation, incorporated in January 2004 and incurred $5,000 of rent and payroll expense before it opened its store for business in March. How much, if any, of the $5,000 is deductible in 2004?

## Problems

28. Emu Company, which was formed in 2003, had operating income of $100,000 and operating expenses of $80,000 in 2003. In addition, Emu had a long-term capital loss of $5,000. How does Andrew, the owner of Emu Company, report this information on his individual tax return under the following assumptions?
    a. Emu Company is a proprietorship, and Andrew does not withdraw any funds from Emu during the year.
    b. Emu Company is a corporation and pays no dividends during the year.

29. Bunting Company, a computer retailer, had a net loss of $50,000 from merchandising operations in 2003. Lena, who owns Bunting, works 20 hours a week in the business. She has a large amount of income from other sources and is in the 38.6% marginal tax bracket. What is Lena's tax situation if Bunting Company is a proprietorship? A C corporation?

30. Cardinal Company has approximately $400,000 in net income in 2003 before deducting any compensation or other payment to its sole owner, Carla. Carla is single. Her income aside from the company's profits is low and would be offset by her personal exemption and standard deduction. Discuss the tax aspects of each of the following arrangements:
    a. Carla operates Cardinal Company as a proprietorship.
    b. Carla incorporates Cardinal Company and pays herself a salary of $50,000 and no dividend.
    c. Carla incorporates the company and pays herself a $50,000 salary and a dividend of $231,000 ($350,000 – $119,000 corporate income tax).
    d. Carla incorporates the company and pays herself a salary of $400,000.

31. Teal Company has approximately $200,000 in net income in 2003 before deducting any compensation or other payment to its sole owner, Joan (who is single). Assume that her income aside from the company's profits is low and would be offset by her personal exemption and standard deduction. Discuss the tax aspects of each of the following arrangements:
    a. Joan operates Teal Company as a proprietorship.
    b. Joan incorporates Teal Company and pays herself a salary of $50,000 and no dividend.
    c. Joan incorporates the company and pays herself a $50,000 salary and a dividend of $108,250 ($150,000 – $41,750 corporate income tax).
    d. Joan incorporates the company and pays herself a salary of $200,000.

32. Chris owns 100% of Orange Company, which had an NOL of $150,000 ($400,000 operating income − $550,000 operating expenses) in 2003. Chris was a material participant in the activities of the business during the year. Orange Company also had a long-term capital loss of $20,000. Chris has sufficient income from other activities to be in the 38.6% marginal tax bracket before considering results from Orange Company. Explain the tax treatment if Orange Company is:
    a. A corporation.
    b. A proprietorship.

33. Jones Company had revenue of $100,000 and incurred business expenses of $20,000 in 2003. Ken Jones, owner of the company, is single, has no dependents, and uses the $4,750 standard deduction in computing taxable income for 2003. The personal exemption amount for 2003 is $3,050. Jones Company is Ken's only source of income. Compute Ken's after-tax income if:
    a. Jones Company is a sole proprietorship, and Ken withdrew $60,000 for living expenses during the year.
    b. Jones Company is a corporation, Ken is the sole shareholder, and the corporation pays out all of its after-tax income as a dividend to Ken.
    c. Jones Company is a corporation, Ken is the sole shareholder, and the corporation pays Ken a salary of $80,000. This will increase the corporation's business expenses to $100,000.

34. Dakota Enterprises, a calendar year taxpayer, suffers a casualty loss of $75,000. How much of the casualty loss will be a tax deduction to Dakota under the following circumstances?
    a. Dakota is an individual and has AGI of $110,000. The casualty loss was a personal loss, and the insurance recovered is $30,000.
    b. Dakota is a corporation, and the insurance recovered is $30,000.

**Decision Making**
**Communications**

35. Benton Company has one owner, who is in the 38.6% Federal income tax bracket. Benton's gross income is $200,000, and its ordinary trade or business deductions are $90,000. It also pays accident and health insurance premiums for the benefit of its owner, in the amount of $7,000 for the current year. Compute the tax liability on Benton's income for 2003 under the following assumptions:
    a. Benton Company is operated as a proprietorship, and the owner withdraws $70,000 for personal use.
    b. Benton is operated as a corporation, pays out $70,000 as salary, and pays no dividends to its shareholder.
    c. Benton is operated as a corporation and pays out no salary or dividends to its shareholder.
    d. Benton is operated as a corporation, pays out $70,000 as salary, and pays out the remainder of its earnings as dividends.
    e. Assume Robert Benton of 1121 Monroe Street, Ironton, OH 45638 is the owner of Benton Company, which was operated as a proprietorship in 2003. Robert is thinking about incorporating the business in 2004 and asks your advice. He expects about the same amounts of income and expenses in 2004 and plans to take $70,000 per year out of the company whether he incorporates or not. Write a letter to Robert [based on your analysis in (a) and (b) above] containing your recommendations.

36. Janine, an architect, is the sole shareholder of Magenta Corporation. Magenta is a PSC with a fiscal year ending October 31. The corporation paid Janine a salary of $240,000 during its fiscal year ending October 31, 2003. How much salary must Magenta pay Janine during the period November 1 through December 31, 2003, if the corporation is to continue to use its fiscal year without negative tax effects?

37. Mallard Corporation had $400,000 operating income and $350,000 operating expenses during the year. In addition, Mallard had a $30,000 long-term capital gain and a $52,000 short-term capital loss.
    a. Compute Mallard's taxable income for the year.
    b. Assume the same facts as above except that Mallard's long-term capital gain was $64,000. Compute Mallard's taxable income for the year.

38. Egret has two shareholders who are unrelated to each other. Sam owns 51% of the stock, and Hugh owns the remaining 49%. During the current year, Egret pays a salary of $60,000 to each shareholder. At the beginning of the year, Egret had accrued $20,000 salary to each shareholder, and at the end of the year, it had accrued $25,000 to each shareholder. Compute Egret's deduction for the above amounts if it uses the accrual method of accounting.

39. In 2003, a business sells a capital asset, which it had held for two years, at a loss of $15,000. How much of the capital loss may be deducted in 2003, and how much is carried back or forward under the following circumstances?
    a. The business was a sole proprietorship owned by Joe. Joe had a short-term capital gain of $3,000 in 2003 and a long-term capital gain of $2,000. Joe had ordinary net income from the proprietorship of $60,000.
    b. The business is incorporated. The corporation had a short-term capital gain of $3,000 and a long-term capital gain of $2,000. Its ordinary net income from the business was $60,000.

40. Pelican Corporation has net short-term capital gains of $30,000 and net long-term capital losses of $190,000 during 2003. Pelican Corporation had taxable income from other sources of $500,000.

    Prior years' transactions included the following:

    | | | |
    |---|---|---|
    | 1999 | Net short-term capital gains | $100,000 |
    | 2000 | Net long-term capital gains | 40,000 |
    | 2001 | Net short-term capital gains | 30,000 |
    | 2002 | Net long-term capital gains | 70,000 |

    a. How are the capital gains and losses treated on Pelican's 2003 tax return?
    b. Determine the amount of the 2003 capital loss that is carried back to each of the previous years.
    c. Compute the amount of capital loss carryover, if any, and indicate the years to which the loss may be carried.
    d. If Pelican were a proprietorship, how would Sylvia, the owner, report these transactions on her 2003 tax return?

41. Condor Corporation, a closely held corporation, has $45,000 of active business income, $35,000 of portfolio income, and an $80,000 passive loss from a rental activity. Can Condor deduct the passive loss? Would your answer differ if Condor were a PSC?

42. Eagle Corporation is a wholesale grocery store. During 2003, it donated canned goods (held as inventory) worth $28,000 to a local food bank. The basis of the canned goods was $20,000. Eagle Corporation has taxable income, before the deduction for charitable contributions, of $250,000.
    a. What amount qualifies as a charitable deduction?
    b. If the donation were a stock investment instead of canned goods, how would your answer change?

**Decision Making**
**Communications**

43. Joseph Thompson is president and sole shareholder of Jay Corporation. In December 2003, Joe asks your advice regarding a charitable contribution he plans to have the corporation make to the University of Maine, a qualified public charity. Joe is considering the following alternatives as charitable contributions in December 2003:

| | **Fair Market Value** |
|---|---|
| (1) Cash donation | $120,000 |
| (2) Unimproved land held for six years ($20,000 basis) | 120,000 |
| (3) Maize Corporation stock held for eight months ($20,000 basis) | 120,000 |
| (4) Brown Corporation stock held for two years ($170,000 basis) | 120,000 |

Joe has asked you to help him decide which of these potential contributions will be most advantageous taxwise. Jay's taxable income is $3.5 million before considering the contribution. Rank the four alternatives and write a letter to Joe communicating your advice. The corporation's address is 1442 Main Street, Freeport, ME 04032.

44. Bobwhite, Inc. (a calendar year C corporation) had the following income and expenses in 2004:

| | |
|---|---|
| Income from operations | $250,000 |
| Expenses from operations | 100,000 |
| Dividends received (less than 20% ownership) | 20,000 |
| Charitable contribution | 20,000 |

a. How much is Bobwhite, Inc.'s charitable contribution deduction for 2004?
b. What happens to the portion of the contribution not deductible in 2004?

*Decision Making*
*Communications*

45. Dan Simms is the president and sole shareholder of Simms Corporation, 1121 Madison Street, Seattle, WA 98121. Dan plans for the corporation to make a charitable contribution to the University of Washington, a qualified public charity. He will have the corporation donate Jaybird Corporation stock, held for five years, with a basis of $8,000 and a fair market value of $20,000. Dan projects a $200,000 net profit for Simms Corporation in 2003 and a $100,000 net profit in 2004. Dan calls you on December 5, 2003, and asks whether he should make the contribution in 2003 or 2004. Write a letter advising Dan about the timing of the contribution.

46. During the year, Roadrunner Corporation (a calendar year taxpayer) has the following transactions:

| | |
|---|---|
| Income from operations | $330,000 |
| Expenses from operations | 360,000 |
| Dividends received from Crow Corporation | 120,000 |

a. Roadrunner owns 18% of Crow Corporation's stock. How much is Roadrunner Corporation's taxable income or NOL for the year?
b. Would your answer change if Roadrunner owned 30% of Crow Corporation's stock?

47. In each of the following independent situations, determine the dividends received deduction. Assume that none of the corporate shareholders owns 20% or more of the stock in the corporations paying the dividends.

| | Red Corporation | White Corporation | Blue Corporation |
|---|---|---|---|
| Income from operations | $ 700,000 | $ 800,000 | $ 700,000 |
| Expenses from operations | (600,000) | (900,000) | (740,000) |
| Qualifying dividends | 100,000 | 200,000 | 200,000 |

48. Owl Corporation was formed on December 1, 2003. Qualifying organizational expenses were incurred and paid as follows:

| | |
|---|---|
| Incurred and paid in December 2003 | $12,000 |
| Incurred in December 2003 but paid in January 2004 | 6,000 |
| Incurred and paid in February 2004 | 3,600 |

Assume Owl Corporation makes a timely election under § 248 to amortize organizational expenditures over a period of 60 months. What amount may be amortized in the corporation's first tax year under each of the following assumptions?

*[handwritten margin notes:]*
*18000/60 = 300*
*p.m.*
*21600/60 = 360 x 12*
*18000/60 = 300*
*21600/60 = 360 x 12*

a. Owl Corporation adopts a calendar year and the cash basis of accounting for tax purposes.
b. Same as (a), except that Owl Corporation chooses a fiscal year of December 1–November 30.
c. Owl Corporation adopts a calendar year and the accrual basis of accounting for tax purposes.
d. Same as (c), except that Owl Corporation chooses a fiscal year of December 1–November 30.

49. Topaz Corporation, an accrual basis taxpayer, was formed and began operations on July 1, 2003. The following expenses were incurred during the first tax year (July 1 to December 31, 2003) of operations:

| | |
|---|---|
| Expenses of temporary directors and of organizational meetings | $3,500 |
| Fee paid to the state of incorporation | 1,000 |
| Accounting services incident to organization | 1,500 |
| Legal services for drafting the corporate charter and bylaws | 2,300 |
| Expenses incident to the printing and sale of stock certificates | 1,000 |
| | $9,300 |

Assume Topaz Corporation makes an appropriate and timely election under § 248(c) and the related Regulations. What is the maximum organizational expense Topaz may write off for tax year 2003?

50. In each of the following independent situations, determine the corporation's income tax liability. Assume that all corporations use a calendar year for tax purposes and that the tax year involved is 2003.

*[handwritten margin notes and diagram]*

| | Taxable Income |
|---|---|
| Violet Corporation | $ 46,000 |
| Indigo Corporation | 260,000 |
| Blue Corporation | 1,620,000 |
| Green Corporation | 24,000,000 |

*[handwritten: Calculate as per corporate tax rate]*

51. The outstanding stock in Black and White Corporations, each of which has only one class of stock, is owned by the following unrelated individuals:

| | Shares | |
|---|---|---|
| **Shareholders** | **Black** | **White** |
| Ahmad | 20 | 16 |
| Luis | 5 | 54 |
| Sara | 75 | 30 |
| Total | 100 | 100 |

a. Determine if a brother-sister controlled group exists.
b. Assume that Luis owns no stock in Black Corporation and Sara owns 80 shares. Would a brother-sister controlled group exist? Why or why not?

52. The outstanding stock of Wren, Robin, Finch, and Jay Corporations is owned by the following unrelated individual and corporate shareholders as follows:

*Parent sub* (handwritten)

| Shareholders | Corporations | | | |
|---|---|---|---|---|
| | **Wren** | **Robin** | **Finch** | **Jay** |
| Ann | 30% | 20% | 30% | 10% |
| Bob | 50% | | 50% | 5% |
| Carl | 20% | | 20% | |
| Wren Corporation | | 80% | | |

*(handwritten totals: 100, —, 100, 15)*

Which corporations, if any, are members of a controlled group?

*(handwritten left margin notes: "WFR are combined grp 30 50 20 100", "W & F are brother sister combined and robin and Jay combined are sub combined WRF are...")*

*(handwritten right margin: "① 5 or more own ≥ 80%", "② common ownership is > 50%")*

**Decision Making**
**Communications**

53. Eagle and Cardinal Corporations both have 100 shares of stock outstanding. Each shareholder paid $500 for his stock in each corporation, and the fair market value of the stock of each corporation is $800 per share. The stock is owned by the following unrelated individuals:

| Shareholders | Eagle Shares | Cardinal Shares |
|---|---|---|
| George | 30 | 15 |
| Sam | 5 | 50 |
| Tom | 65 | 35 |
| Total | 100 | 100 |

*(handwritten left: "Brother sister common 15 5 35 55 more than 50")*

*(handwritten right: "No parent sub")*

a. Does a brother-sister controlled group exist?
b. Will a brother-sister controlled group exist if Tom sells 10 of his shares in Cardinal Corporation to Sam? *NO*
c. Discuss any tax advantages that will result if Tom sells 10 of his Cardinal shares to Sam.
d. Sam has suggested to Tom that they complete the transaction in (c). Tom asks your advice and says that he is in the 30% marginal bracket. Write a letter to Tom Roland at 3435 Grand Avenue, South Point, OH 45680, explaining the tax advantages that will result if he sells 10 of his Cardinal shares to Sam. Also, identify any problems, both tax and nontax, that the sale could cause for Tom. *LTS cap gain*

*(handwritten left: "For brother sister — ② Conditions — ① & ② 5 or fewer persons own ≥ 80% of corp ② common ownership more than 50% Sub can never be part of brother sister group he/r sal")*

54. The outstanding stock in corporations Amber, Sand, Tan, Beige, and Purple, which have only one class of stock outstanding, is owned by the following unrelated individuals:

| Individuals | Corporations | | | | |
|---|---|---|---|---|---|
| | **Amber** | **Sand** | **Tan** | **Beige** | **Purple** |
| Anna | 55% | 51% | 55% | 55% | 55% |
| Bill | 45% | 49% | –0– | –0– | –0– |
| Carol | –0– | –0– | 45% | –0– | –0– |
| Don | –0– | –0– | –0– | 45% | –0– |
| Eve | –0– | –0– | –0– | –0– | 45% |
| Total | 100% | 100% | 100% | 100% | 100% |

Determine if a brother-sister controlled group exists.

55. Indicate in each of the following independent situations whether the corporation may file Form 1120–A:

| | Jay Corporation | Shrike Corporation | Martin Corporation |
|---|---|---|---|
| Sales of merchandise | $600,000 | $400,000 | $300,000 |
| Total assets | 200,000 | 360,000 | 400,000 |
| Total income (gross profit plus other income, including gains) | 480,000 | 490,000 | 380,000 |
| Member of controlled group | no | yes | no |
| Ownership in foreign corporation | no | no | no |
| Entitled to file Form 1120–A (Circle Y for yes or N for no) | Y N | Y N | Y N |

56. The following information for 2003 relates to Martin Corporation, a calendar year, accrual method taxpayer. You are to determine the amount of Martin's taxable income for the year using this information. You may use Schedule M–1 if provided by your instructor.

| | |
|---|---|
| Net income per books (after-tax) | $209,710 |
| Federal income tax liability | 30,050 |
| Interest income from tax-exempt bonds | 12,000 |
| Interest paid on loan incurred to purchase tax-exempt bonds | 1,200 |
| Life insurance proceeds received as a result of death of corporation president | 120,000 |
| Premiums paid on policy on the life of corporation president | 6,240 |
| Excess of capital losses over capital gains | 4,800 |

57. Albatross Corporation, a calendar year, accrual basis taxpayer, provides the following information for 2003 and asks you to prepare Schedule M–1:

| | |
|---|---|
| Net income per books (after-tax) | $257,950 |
| Taxable income | 150,000 |
| Federal income tax liability | 41,750 |
| Interest income from tax-exempt bonds | 15,000 |
| Interest paid on loan incurred to purchase tax-exempt bonds | 1,500 |
| Life insurance proceeds received as a result of death of Albatross's president | 150,000 |
| Premiums paid on policy on life of Albatross's president | 7,800 |
| Excess of capital losses over capital gains | 6,000 |
| Retained earnings at beginning of year | 375,000 |
| Cash dividends paid | 90,000 |

58. In January, Don and Steve each invested $100,000 cash to form a corporation to conduct business as a retail golf equipment store. On January 5, they paid Bill, an attorney, to draft the corporate charter, file the necessary forms with the state, and write the bylaws. They leased a store building and began to acquire inventory, furniture, display equipment, and office equipment in February. They hired a sales staff and clerical personnel in March and conducted training sessions during the month. They had a successful opening on April 1, and sales increased steadily throughout the summer. The weather turned cold in October, and all local golf courses closed by October 15, which resulted in a drastic decline in sales. Don and Steve expect business to be very good during the Christmas season and then to taper off significantly from January 1 through February 28. The corporation accrued bonuses to Don and Steve on December 31, payable on April 15 of the following year. The corporation made timely estimated tax payments throughout the year. The corporation hired a bookkeeper in February, but he does not know much about taxation. Don and Steve have hired you as a tax consultant and have asked you to identify the tax issues that they should consider.

**Issue ID**

> See Appendix F for Comprehensive Tax Return Problem—Form 1120

## Research Problems

*Note: Solutions to Research Problems can be prepared by using the **RIA Checkpoint® Student Edition** online research product, or the **CCH U.S. Master Tax Guide Plus™** online Federal tax research database, which is available to accompany this text. It is also possible to prepare solutions to the Research Problems by using tax research materials found in a standard tax library.*

**Communications**

**Research Problem 1.**   Joe and Tom Moore are brothers and equal shareholders in Orange Corporation, a calendar year taxpayer. In 2003, they incurred certain travel and entertainment expenditures, as employees, on behalf of Orange Corporation. Because Orange was in a precarious financial condition, Joe and Tom decided not to seek reimbursement for these expenditures. Instead, each brother deducted what he spent on his own individual return (Form 1040). Upon audit of the returns filed by Joe and Tom for 2003, the IRS disallowed these expenditures. Write a letter to Joe at 568 Wood Avenue, Waynesburg, PA 15370 and indicate whether he should challenge the IRS action. Explain your conclusion to Joe using nontechnical language.

**Communications**

**Research Problem 2.**   Bill Miller and Tom Tracey, who are each 50% shareholders in BT Graphics Corporation, received a letter following an IRS audit. The letter stated that BT's deduction for compensation to Bill and Tom would be reduced by over $1 million. Bill, who had been assured by his tax attorney that the payments would qualify as reasonable, contacted the IRS auditor and asked for a meeting to discuss the disallowance. The auditor replied that the disallowance was not based on the reasonableness criterion, but rather on a conclusion that the disallowed amounts were not intended to be compensation. Therefore, the amounts would not be deductible. Bill has asked you to determine whether the IRS can disallow a deduction for compensation without a determination that the compensation is unreasonable. Write a letter to Bill Miller, 4502 Main Street, Monticello, IL 61856 and explain the basis for the IRS auditor's position.

*Partial list of research aids:*
§ 162(a)(1).
*Elliotts, Inc. v. Comm.*, 83–2 USTC ¶9610, 52 AFTR2d 83–5976, 716 F.2d 1241 (CA–9, 1983).

**Communications**

**Research Problem 3.**   John Hunter, the president and sole shareholder of Hunter, Inc., has asked you to assist him in obtaining the maximum charitable contribution deduction for his corporation. The corporation has 36 desktop computers that are almost two years old. Due to recent advances in technology, Hunter has decided to replace all of these computers with new, more powerful models. Each computer cost $5,000 and has a market value of $3,400 and a basis of $2,600. Hunter plans to donate the computers to a qualified charitable organization, but has not decided which charity will be the beneficiary of the corporation's generosity. Draft a letter to John Hunter at Hunter Inc., 1200 West Madison, Bellwood, IL 60104 and advise him on the issue he has raised.

**Internet Activity**

*Use the tax resources of the Internet to address the following questions. Do not restrict your search to the World Wide Web, but include a review of newsgroups and general reference materials, practitioner sites and resources, primary sources of the tax law, chat rooms and discussion groups, and other opportunities.*

**Research Problem 4.**   Find the IRS Web site and print a copy of Form 1120. If the 2003 Form 1120 is available, compare it with the 2002 Form 1120 in the text and discuss any changes.

**Research Problem 5.**   Download the forms used to compute a corporation's estimated tax payments and to transmit the payment to an approved bank. Complete the forms for a corporation that must make quarterly estimated payments of $11,000 this year.

# Corporations: Organization and Capital Structure

## LEARNING OBJECTIVES

*After completing Chapter 3, you should be able to:*

### LO.1
Identify the tax consequences of incorporating a business.

### LO.2
Understand the special rules that apply when liabilities are assumed by a corporation.

### LO.3
Recognize the basis issues relevant to the shareholder and the corporation.

### LO.4
Appreciate the tax aspects of the capital structure of a corporation.

### LO.5
Recognize the tax differences between debt and equity investments.

### LO.6
Handle the tax treatment of shareholder debt and stock losses.

### LO.7
Identify tax planning opportunities associated with organizing and financing a corporation.

## O U T L I N E

Chapter 2 dealt with three principal areas fundamental to working with corporations: (1) determination of whether an entity is a corporation for Federal income tax purposes, (2) tax rules applicable to the day-to-day operation of a corporation, and (3) filing and reporting procedures governing corporations.

Chapter 3 addresses more sophisticated issues involving corporations:

- The tax consequences to the shareholders and the corporation upon the organization of and original transfer of property to the corporation.
- The tax result that ensues when shareholders make transfers of property to a corporation after organization.
- The capital structure of a corporation, including equity and debt financing.
- The tax treatment of investor losses.

### LO.1

Identify the tax consequences of incorporating a business.

# Organization of and Transfers to Controlled Corporations

## IN GENERAL

Property transactions normally produce tax consequences if a gain or loss is realized. As a result, unless an exception in the Code applies, a transfer of property to a corporation in exchange for stock constitutes a taxable sale or exchange of property. The amount of gain or loss is measured by the difference between the value of the stock received and the tax basis of the property transferred.

When a taxpayer's economic status has not changed and the wherewithal to pay is lacking, however, the Code does provide special exceptions to the requirement that gain or loss be recognized. One such exception is a like-kind exchange. When a taxpayer exchanges property for other property of a like kind, § 1031 provides that gain (or loss) on the exchange is postponed because there has not been a substantive change in the taxpayer's investment. Section 1031 is merely a deferral mechanism and does not authorize the permanent nonrecognition of gain or loss. The deferral mechanism is accomplished by calculating a substituted basis

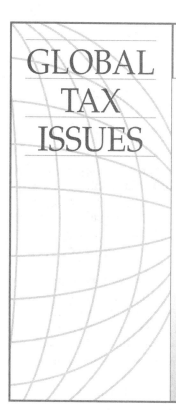

GLOBAL TAX ISSUES

## CHOICE OF ORGANIZATIONAL FORM WHEN OPERATING OVERSEAS

When the management of a corporation decides to expand its business by establishing a presence in a foreign market, the new business venture may take one of several organizational forms. As each form comes with its respective advantages and disadvantages, making the best choice can be difficult.

One common approach is to conduct the foreign activity as a *branch* operation of the U.S. corporation. The foreign branch is not a separate legal entity, but a division of the U.S. corporation established overseas. As a result, any gains and losses produced by the foreign unit are included in the corporation's overall financial results.

Another possibility is to organize the foreign operations as a *subsidiary* of the U.S. parent corporation. If this route is chosen, the subsidiary may be either a *domestic* subsidiary (i.e., organized in the United States) or a *foreign* subsidiary (organized under the laws of a foreign country).

One fundamental tax difference between these two approaches is that the gains and losses of a domestic subsidiary may be consolidated with the operations of the U.S. parent, while the operations of a foreign subsidiary may not. Thus, the use of a domestic subsidiary to conduct foreign operations will generally yield the same final result as the use of a branch. With both approaches, the financial statements of the U.S. parent reflect the results of its worldwide operations.

for the like-kind property received. With this substituted basis, the potential gain or loss on the property given up is recognized when the property received in the exchange is sold.

Another exception to the general rule deals with transfers to controlled corporations. Section 351 provides for the nonrecognition of gain or loss upon the transfer of property to a corporation when certain conditions are met. This provision reflects the principle that gain should not be recognized when a taxpayer's investment has not substantively changed. When a business is incorporated, the owner's economic status remains the same; only the *form* of the investment has changed. The investment in the business assets carries over to the investment in corporate stock. Further, if only stock in the corporation is received, the taxpayer is hardly in a position to pay a tax on any realized gain. Thus, this approach also is justified under the wherewithal to pay concept discussed in Chapter 1. As noted later, however, if the taxpayer receives property other than stock (i.e., boot) from the corporation, realized gain may be recognized.

Finally, § 351 exists because Congress believes that tax rules should not impede the exercise of sound business judgment (e.g., choice of corporate form of doing business). For example, a taxpayer would think twice about forming a corporation if gain recognition (and the payment of a tax) would always be a consequence.

Therefore, the same principles govern the nonrecognition of gain or loss under § 1031 and § 351. With both provisions, gain or loss is postponed until a substantive change in the taxpayer's investment occurs (e.g., a sale to outsiders).

**EXAMPLE 1**

Ron is considering incorporating his donut shop in order to obtain the limited liability of the corporate form. Ron realizes that if he incorporates the shop, he will be personally liable only for the debts of the business that he has guaranteed. If Ron incorporates, the following assets will be transferred to the corporation:

|  | Tax Basis | Fair Market Value |
|---|---|---|
| Cash | $10,000 | $ 10,000 |
| Furniture and fixtures | 20,000 | 60,000 |
| Land and building | 40,000 | 100,000 |
|  | $70,000 | $170,000 |

In this change of business form, Ron will receive the corporation's stock worth $170,000 in exchange for the assets he transfers. Without the nonrecognition provisions of § 351, Ron would recognize a taxable gain of $100,000 on the transfer ($170,000 value of the stock received – $70,000 basis of the assets transferred). Under § 351, however, Ron does not recognize any gain because his economic status has not really changed. Ron's investment in the assets of his unincorporated donut shop is now represented by his ownership of stock in the incorporated donut shop. Thus, § 351 provides for tax neutrality on the incorporation decision. ■

In a like-kind exchange, the recognition of gain is avoided only to the extent that the taxpayer receives like-kind property. However, the taxpayer must recognize any realized gain when receiving "boot" (i.e., property of an unlike kind, such as cash). For example, if a taxpayer exchanges a truck used in a business for another truck to be used in the business and also receives cash, the taxpayer has the wherewithal to pay an income tax on the cash involved. Further, the taxpayer's economic status has changed to the extent that cash is received. Thus, any realized gain on the exchange is recognized to the extent of the cash received. In like manner, if a taxpayer transfers property to a corporation and receives cash or property other than stock, gain (but not loss) is recognized to the extent of the lesser of the gain realized or the boot received (i.e., the amount of cash and the fair market value of other property received). Any gain recognized is classified (e.g., ordinary, capital) according to the type of assets transferred.[1] As discussed later, the nonrecognition of gain or loss is accompanied by a substituted basis in the shareholder's stock.[2]

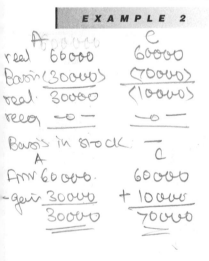

**EXAMPLE 2**

Amanda and Calvin form Quail Corporation. Amanda transfers property with an adjusted basis of $30,000, fair market value of $60,000, for 50% of the stock, worth $60,000. Calvin transfers property with an adjusted basis of $70,000, fair market value of $60,000, for the remaining 50% of the stock. The transfer qualifies under § 351. Amanda has an unrecognized gain of $30,000, and Calvin has an unrecognized loss of $10,000. Both have a substituted basis in the stock in Quail Corporation. Amanda has a basis of $30,000 in her stock, and Calvin has a basis of $70,000 in his stock. Therefore, if either Amanda or Calvin later disposes of the Quail stock in a taxable transaction (e.g., a sale), this deferred gain/loss will then be fully recognized—a $30,000 gain to Amanda and a $10,000 loss to Calvin. ■

Section 351 is mandatory if a transaction satisfies the provision's requirements. The three requirements for nonrecognition of gain or loss under § 351 are that (1) *property* is transferred (2) in exchange for *stock* and (3) the property transferors are in *control* of the corporation after the exchange. Therefore, if recognition of gain or loss is *desired*, the taxpayer must plan to fail to meet at least one of these requirements.

## PROPERTY DEFINED

Questions have arisen concerning what constitutes **property** for purposes of § 351. In general, the definition of property is comprehensive. For example, along with

---

[1]§ 351(b) and Rev.Rul. 68–55, 1968–1 C.B. 140.      [2]§ 358(a). See the discussion preceding Example 19.

plant and equipment, unrealized receivables of a cash basis taxpayer and installment obligations are considered property.[3] Although the disposition of an installment note receivable normally triggers deferred gain, its transfer under § 351 is not treated as a disposition. Thus, gain is not recognized to the transferor. Secret processes and formulas, as well as secret information in the general nature of a patentable invention, also qualify as property under § 351.[4]

However, the Code specifically excludes services rendered from the definition of property. Services are not considered to be property under § 351 for a critical reason. A taxpayer must report as income the fair market value of any consideration received as compensation for services rendered.[5] Consequently, when a taxpayer receives stock in a corporation as consideration for rendering services to the corporation, taxable income results. In this case, the amount of income recognized by the taxpayer is equal to the fair market value of the stock received. The taxpayer's basis in the stock received is its fair market value.

| EXAMPLE 3 |
|---|

Ann and Bob form Olive Corporation with the transfer of the following consideration:

| | Consideration Transferred | | |
|---|---|---|---|
| | Basis to Transferor | Fair Market Value | Number of Shares Issued |
| From Ann: | | | |
| Personal services rendered to Olive Corporation | $ –0– | $20,000 | 200 |
| From Bob: | | | |
| Installment obligation | 5,000 | 40,000 | 800 |
| Inventory | 10,000 | 30,000 | |
| Secret process | –0– | 10,000 | |

The value of each share in Olive Corporation is $100.[6] Ann has income of $20,000 on the transfer because services do not qualify as "property." She has a basis of $20,000 in her 200 shares of Olive. Bob has no recognized gain on the receipt of stock because all of the consideration he transfers to Olive qualifies as "property" and he has "control" of Olive after the transfer; see the discussion concerning control that follows. Bob has a substituted basis of $15,000 in the Olive stock. ∎

## STOCK TRANSFERRED

Nonrecognition of gain occurs only when the shareholder receives stock. Stock includes both common and most preferred. It does not include "nonqualified preferred stock," which possesses many of the attributes of debt. The Regulations state that the term "stock" does not include stock rights and stock warrants. Otherwise, however, the term "stock" generally needs no clarification.[7]

Thus, under current law, any corporate debt or **securities** (e.g., long-term debt such as bonds) received are treated as boot because they are not an equity interest

---

[3]*Hempt Brothers, Inc. v. U.S.*, 74–1 USTC ¶9188, 33 AFTR2d 74–570, 490 F.2d 1172 (CA–3, 1974), and Reg. § 1.453–9(c)(2).
[4]Rev.Rul. 64–56, 1964–1 C.B. 133; Rev.Rul. 71–564, 1971–2 C.B. 179.
[5]§§ 61 and 83.
[6]The value of closely held stock normally is presumed to be equal to the value of the property transferred.
[7]§ 351(g). Examples of nonqualified preferred stock include preferred stock that is redeemable within 20 years of issuance and whose

dividend rate is based on factors other than corporate performance. Therefore, gain is recognized up to the fair market value of the nonqualified preferred stock received. Loss may be recognized when the transferor receives *only* nonqualified preferred stock (or nonqualified preferred stock and other boot) in exchange for property. See also Reg. § 1.351–1(a)(1)(ii).

or stock. Therefore, the receipt of debt in exchange for the transfer of appreciated property to a controlled corporation causes recognition of gain.

## CONTROL OF THE CORPORATION

For the transaction to qualify as nontaxable under § 351, the property transferors must be in **control** of the corporation immediately after the exchange. Control means that the person or persons transferring the property must have at least an 80 percent stock ownership in the transferee corporation. More specifically, the transferor shareholders must own stock possessing at least 80 percent of the total combined *voting power* of all classes of stock entitled to vote *and* at least 80 percent of the total *number of shares* of all other classes of stock.[8]

**Control Immediately after the Transfer.**   Immediately after the exchange, the property transferors must control the corporation. Control can apply to a single person or to several taxpayers if they are all parties to an integrated transaction. When more than one person is involved, the exchange does not necessarily require simultaneous exchanges by those persons. However, the rights of those transferring property to the corporation must be previously set out and determined. Also, the agreement to transfer property should be executed "with an expedition consistent with orderly procedure."[9] Therefore, if two or more persons transfer property to a corporation for stock and want to defer gain, it is helpful if the transfers occur close together in time and are made in accordance with an agreement among the parties.

| | |
|---|---|
| **EXAMPLE 4** | Jack exchanges property, basis of $60,000 and fair market value of $100,000, for 70% of the stock of Gray Corporation. The other 30% of the stock is owned by Jane, who acquired it several years ago. The fair market value of Jack's stock is $100,000. Jack recognizes a taxable gain of $40,000 on the transfer because he does not have control of the corporation after his transfer and his transaction cannot be integrated with Jane's for purposes of the control requirement. ■ |

| | |
|---|---|
| **EXAMPLE 5** | Rebecca, Daryl, and Paige incorporate their businesses by forming Green Corporation. Rebecca exchanges her property for 300 shares in Green on January 6, 2003. Daryl exchanges his property for 400 shares of Green Corporation stock on January 10, 2003, and Paige exchanges her property for 300 shares in Green on March 5, 2003. Because the three exchanges are part of a prearranged plan and the control test is met, the nonrecognition provisions of § 351 apply to all of the exchanges. ■ |

Stock need not be issued to the property transferors in the same proportion as the relative value of the property transferred by each. However, when stock received is not proportionate to the value of the property transferred, the actual effect of the transactions must be properly characterized. For example, in such situations one transferor may actually be making a gift of valuable consideration to another transferor.

| | |
|---|---|
| **EXAMPLE 6** | Ron and Shelia, father and daughter, form Oak Corporation. Ron transfers property worth $50,000 in exchange for 100 shares of stock, while Shelia transfers property worth $50,000 for 400 shares of stock. The transfers qualify under § 351 because Ron and Shelia have control of the Oak stock immediately after the transfers of property. However, the implicit |

---

[8]§ 368(c). Nonqualified preferred stock is treated as stock, and not boot, for purposes of this control test.

[9]Reg. § 1.351–1(a)(1).

gift by Ron to Shelia must be recognized and appropriately characterized. As such, the value of the gift might be subject to the gift tax (see Chapter 17). ■

Once control has been achieved, it is not necessarily lost if stock received by shareholders is sold or given to persons who are not parties to the exchange shortly after the transaction. However, a different result might materialize if a *plan* for the ultimate disposition of the stock existed *before* the exchange.[10]

**EXAMPLE 7**

Naomi and Eric form Eagle Corporation. They transfer appreciated property to the corporation with each receiving 50 shares of the stock. Shortly after the formation, Naomi gives 25 shares to her son. Because Naomi was not committed to make the gift, she is considered to own her original shares of Eagle Corporation stock and, along with Eric, to control Eagle "immediately after the exchange." Therefore, the requirements of § 351 are met, and neither Naomi nor Eric is taxed on the exchange. Alternatively, had Naomi immediately given 25 shares to a business associate pursuant to a plan to satisfy an outstanding obligation, the formation of Eagle would be taxable to Naomi and Eric because of their lack of control. ■

**Transfers for Property and Services.**   Nonrecognition treatment for the property transferors may be lost if "too much" stock is transferred to persons who did not contribute property.

**EXAMPLE 8**

Kate transfers property with a value of $60,000 and a basis of $5,000 for 60% of the stock in newly formed Wren Corporation. Rodney receives 40% of the stock in Wren for services worth $40,000 rendered to the corporation. Both Kate and Rodney have taxable gain on the transaction. Rodney has taxable income of $40,000 because he does not transfer property in exchange for stock. Kate has a taxable gain of $55,000 [$60,000 (fair market value of the stock in Wren Corporation) – $5,000 (basis in the transferred property)] because she, as the sole property transferor, receives only 60% of the stock in Wren Corporation. ■

A person who receives stock both in exchange for services and for property transferred may be treated as a member of the transferring group for purposes of the control test. When this is the case, the person is taxed on the value of the stock issued for services but not on the stock issued for property, assuming the property transferors control the corporation. In this case, all the stock received by the person transferring both property and services is counted in determining whether the transferors acquired control of the corporation.[11]

**EXAMPLE 9**

Assume the same facts as in Example 8 except that Rodney transfers property worth $30,000 (basis of $3,000) in addition to services rendered to the corporation (valued at $10,000). Now Rodney becomes a part of the control group. Kate and Rodney, as property transferors, together receive 100% of the stock in Wren Corporation. Consequently, § 351 is applicable to the exchanges. As a result, Kate has no recognized gain. Rodney does not recognize gain on the transfer of the property, but he has taxable income to the extent of the value of the shares issued for services rendered. Rodney has current taxable income of $10,000. ■

**Transfers for Services and Nominal Property.**   To be a member of the group and aid in qualifying all transferors under the 80 percent control test, the person contributing services must transfer property having more than a "relatively small value" compared to the services performed. The Regulations provide that stock

---

[10]*Wilgard Realty Co. v. Comm.*, 42–1 USTC ¶9452, 29 AFTR 325, 127 F.2d 514 (CA–2, 1942).

[11]Reg. § 1.351–1(a)(2), Ex. 3.

issued for property whose value is relatively small compared to the value of the stock already owned (or to be received for services rendered) will not be treated as issued in return for property. This will be the result when the primary purpose of the transfer is to qualify the transaction under § 351 for concurrent transferors.[12]

**EXAMPLE 10**

Rosalyn and Mark transfer property to Redbird Corporation, each in exchange for one-third of the stock. Reed receives the other one-third of the stock for services rendered. The transaction does not qualify under § 351 because Reed is not a member of the group transferring property and Rosalyn and Mark, as the sole property transferors, together receive only 66⅔% of the stock. As a result, the post-transfer control requirement is not met.

Assume instead that Reed also transfers a substantial amount of property. Then he is a member of the group, and the transaction qualifies under § 351. Reed is taxed on the value of the stock issued for services, but the remainder of the transaction does not trigger gain or loss recognition. However, if the property transferred by Reed is of a relatively small value in comparison to the stock he receives for his services, and the primary purpose for transferring the property is to cause the transaction to be tax-free for Rosalyn and Mark, the exchange does not qualify under § 351 for any of the taxpayers. ■

Exactly when a taxpayer who renders services and transfers property is included in the control group is often subject to question. However, the IRS has stated that such a transferor can be included in the control group if the value of the property transferred is at least 10 percent of the value of the services provided.[13] If the value of the property transferred is less than this amount, the IRS will not issue an advance ruling that the exchange meets the requirements of § 351.

**EXAMPLE 11**

Sara and Rick form Grouse Corporation. Sara transfers land (worth $100,000, basis of $20,000) for 50% of the stock in Grouse. Rick transfers equipment (worth $50,000, adjusted basis of $10,000) and provides services worth $50,000 for 50% of the stock. Because the relative amount of property Rick transfers is not small compared to the value of the services he renders, his stock in Grouse Corporation is counted in determining control for purposes of § 351; thus, the transferors own 100% of the stock in Grouse. In addition, all of Rick's stock, not just the shares received for the equipment, is counted in determining control. As a result, Sara does not recognize gain on the transfer of the land. Rick, however, must recognize income of $50,000 on the transfer of services. Even though the transfer of the equipment qualifies under § 351, his transfer of services for stock does not.

Alternatively, had the value of Rick's property been small relative to the value of his services, the transaction would be fully taxable to both Sara and Rick. In that situation, Sara, the sole property transferor, would not have at least 80% control of Grouse Corporation following the transfer. As a result, she would fully recognize her realized gain. Further, because Rick would not be treated as having transferred property, the § 351 deferral would not be available to him either. ■

**Transfers to Existing Corporations.** Once a corporation is in operation, § 351 also applies to any later transfers of property for stock by either new or existing shareholders.

**EXAMPLE 12**

Tyrone and Seth formed Blue Corporation three years ago. Both Tyrone and Seth transferred appreciated property to Blue in exchange for 50 shares each in the corporation. The original transfers qualified under § 351, and neither Tyrone nor Seth was taxed on the exchange. In the current year, Tyrone transfers property (worth $90,000, adjusted basis of $5,000) for 50

---

[12]Reg. § 1.351–1(a)(1)(ii).

[13]Rev.Proc. 77–37, 1977–2 C.B. 568.

additional Blue shares. Tyrone has a taxable gain of $85,000 on the transfer. The exchange does not qualify under § 351 because Tyrone does not have 80% control of Blue Corporation immediately after the transfer—he owns 100 shares of the 150 shares outstanding, or a 66⅔% interest. ■

See the Tax Planning Considerations portion of this chapter for additional discussion of this issue.

<table>
<tr><td>

**LO.2**

Understand the special rules that apply when liabilities are assumed by a corporation.

</td><td>

## ASSUMPTION OF LIABILITIES—§ 357

</td></tr>
</table>

Without special provision, the transfer of mortgaged property to a controlled corporation could trigger gain to the property tranferor if the corporation assumed the mortgage. This would be consistent with the rule dealing with like-kind exchanges under § 1031. Generally, when liabilities are assumed by another party, the party no longer responsible for the debt is treated as having received cash or boot. Section 357(a) provides, however, that when the acquiring corporation **assumes a liability** in a § 351 transaction, the transfer does *not* result in boot to the transferor-shareholder for gain recognition purposes. Nevertheless, liabilities assumed by the transferee corporation are treated as boot in determining the basis of the stock received by the shareholder. As a result, the basis of the stock received is reduced by the amount of the liabilities assumed by the corporation. See the more complete discussion of basis computations later.

**EXAMPLE 13**

Vera transfers property with an adjusted basis of $60,000, fair market value of $100,000, to Oriole Corporation for 100% of the stock in Oriole. The property is subject to a liability of $25,000 that Oriole Corporation assumes. The exchange is tax-free under §§ 351 and 357. However, the basis to Vera of the Oriole stock is $35,000 [$60,000 (basis of property transferred) − $25,000 (amount of the liability assumed by Oriole)]. ■

The general rule of § 357(a) has two exceptions: (1) § 357(b) provides that if the principal purpose of the assumption of the liabilities is to avoid tax *or* if there is no bona fide business purpose behind the exchange, the liabilities are treated as boot; and (2) § 357(c) provides that if the sum of the liabilities exceeds the adjusted basis of the properties transferred, the excess is taxable gain.

**Exception (1): Tax Avoidance or No Bona Fide Business Purpose.**   Unless liabilities are incurred shortly before incorporation, § 357(b) generally poses few problems. A tax avoidance purpose for transferring liabilities to a controlled corporation normally is not a concern in view of the basis adjustment as noted above. Since the liabilities transferred reduce the basis of the stock received, any realized gain merely is deferred and not completely eliminated. Any postponed gain is recognized when and if the stock is disposed of in a taxable sale or exchange.

Satisfying the bona fide business purpose requirement is not difficult if the liabilities were incurred in connection with the transferor's normal course of conducting a trade or business. But this requirement can cause difficulty if the liability is taken out shortly before the property is transferred and the proceeds are utilized for personal purposes.[14] This type of situation is analogous to a cash distribution by the corporation to the shareholder, which is taxed as boot.

---

[14]See, for example, *Campbell, Jr. v. Wheeler*, 65–1 USTC ¶9294, 15 AFTR2d 578, 342 F.2d 837 (CA-5, 1965).

**EXAMPLE 14**

Dan transfers real estate (basis of $40,000 and fair market value of $90,000) to a controlled corporation in return for stock in the corporation. However, shortly before the transfer, Dan mortgages the real estate and uses the $20,000 proceeds to meet personal obligations. Thus, along with the real estate, the mortgage is transferred to the corporation. In this case, the assumption of the mortgage lacks a bona fide business purpose. Consequently, the release of the liability is treated as boot received, and Dan has a taxable gain on the transfer of $20,000.[15]

| Amount realized: | |
|---|---|
| Stock | $ 70,000 |
| Release of liability—treated as boot | 20,000 |
| Total amount realized | $ 90,000 |
| Less: Basis of real estate | (40,000) |
| Realized gain | $ 50,000 |
| Recognized gain | $ 20,000 → treated as boot |

The effect of the application of § 357(b) is to taint *all* liabilities transferred even if some are supported by a bona fide business purpose.

**EXAMPLE 15**

Tim, an accrual basis taxpayer, incorporates his sole proprietorship. Among the liabilities transferred to the new corporation are trade accounts payable of $100,000 and a MasterCard bill of $5,000. Tim had used the MasterCard to purchase a wedding anniversary gift for his wife. Under these circumstances, *all* of the $105,000 liabilities are treated as boot and trigger the recognition of gain to the extent gain is realized. ■

---

**ETHICAL CONSIDERATIONS**

### Rectifying a Mistake?

Jean decides to incorporate her sole proprietorship. Consequently, all assets and liabilities of the business are transferred to a newly formed corporation. Part of the liabilities include a credit card charge for a family reunion Jean had hosted. After the corporation has paid the charge and upon the advice of her tax adviser, Jean issues a note to the corporation. The note is a promise by Jean to reimburse the corporation for the charge it paid. What problem are the parties worried about? Has the problem been satisfactorily resolved?

---

**Exception (2): Liabilities in Excess of Basis.** The second exception, § 357(c), provides that if the amount of the **liabilities** assumed **exceeds** the total of the adjusted **bases** of the properties transferred, the excess is taxable gain. Without this provision, when liabilities exceed the basis in property exchanged, a taxpayer would have a negative basis in the stock received in the controlled corporation.[16] Section 357(c) precludes the negative basis possibility by treating the excess over basis as gain to the transferor.

---

[15]§ 351(b).
[16]*Jack L. Easson,* 33 T.C. 963 (1960), *rev'd* in 61–2 USTC ¶9654, 8 AFTR2d 5448, 294 F.2d 653 (CA–9, 1961).

**EXAMPLE 16**

Andre transfers land and equipment with adjusted bases of $35,000 and $5,000, respectively, to a newly formed corporation in exchange for 100% of the stock. The corporation assumes the liability on the transferred properties in the amount of $50,000. Without § 357(c), Andre's basis in the stock of the new corporation would be a negative $10,000 [$40,000 (bases of properties transferred) + $0 (gain recognized) – $0 (boot received) – $50,000 (liability assumed)]. Section 357(c), however, requires Andre to recognize a gain of $10,000 ($50,000 liability assumed – $40,000 bases of assets transferred). As a result, the stock has a zero basis in Andre's hands, determined as follows:

| | |
|---|---:|
| Bases in the properties transferred ($35,000 + $5,000) | $ 40,000 |
| Plus: Gain recognized | 10,000 |
| Less: Boot received | –0– |
| Less: Liability assumed | (50,000) |
| Basis in the stock received | $    –0– |

Thus, Andre recognizes $10,000 of gain, and a negative stock basis is avoided. ■

The definition of liabilities under § 357(c) excludes obligations that would have been deductible to the transferor had those obligations been paid before the transfer. Therefore, accounts payable of a cash basis taxpayer are not considered to be liabilities for purposes of § 357(c). In addition, they are not considered in the computation of stock basis.

**EXAMPLE 17**

Tina, a cash basis taxpayer, incorporates her sole proprietorship. In return for all of the stock of the new corporation, she transfers the following items:

| | Adjusted Basis | Fair Market Value |
|---|---:|---:|
| Cash | $10,000 | $10,000 |
| Unrealized accounts receivable (amounts due to Tina but not yet paid to her) | –0– | 40,000 |
| Trade accounts payable | –0– | 30,000 |
| Note payable | 5,000 | 5,000 |

Because the unrealized accounts receivable and trade accounts payable have a zero basis under the cash method of accounting, no income is recognized until the receivables are collected, and no deduction materializes until the payables are satisfied. The note payable has a basis because it was issued for consideration received.

In this situation, the trade accounts payable are disregarded for gain recognition purposes and in determining Tina's stock basis. Thus, for purposes of § 357(c), because the balance of the note payable does not exceed the basis of the assets transferred, Tina does not have a problem of liabilities in excess of basis (i.e., the note payable of $5,000 does not exceed the aggregate basis in the cash and accounts receivable of $10,000). ■

Conceivably, a situation could arise where both §§ 357(b) and (c) apply in the same transfer. In such a situation, § 357(b) predominates.[17] This could be significant because § 357(b) does not create gain on the transfer, as does § 357(c), but merely

---

[17]§ 357(c)(2)(A).

converts the liability to boot. Thus, the realized gain limitation continues to apply to § 357(b) transactions.

**EXAMPLE 18**

Chris forms Robin Corporation by transferring land with a basis of $100,000, fair market value of $1,000,000. The land is subject to a mortgage of $300,000. One month prior to incorporating Robin, Chris borrows $200,000 for personal purposes and gives the lender a second mortgage on the land. Therefore, on the incorporation, Robin issues stock worth $500,000 to Chris and assumes the two mortgages on the land. Section 357(c) seems to apply to the transfer, given that the mortgages on the property ($500,000) exceed the basis of the property ($100,000). Thus, Chris would have a gain of $400,000 under § 357(c). Section 357(b), however, also applies to the transfer because Chris borrowed $200,000 just prior to the transfer and used the loan proceeds for personal purposes. Thus, under § 357(b), Chris has boot of $500,000 in the amount of the liabilities. Note that *all* of the liabilities are treated as boot, not just the tainted $200,000 liability. Consequently, he has realized gain of $900,000 [$1,000,000 (stock of $500,000 and assumption of liabilities of $500,000) − $100,000 (basis in the land)], and gain is recognized to the extent of the boot of $500,000. Unfortunately for Chris, the relatively more onerous rule of § 357(b) predominates over § 357(c). ■

**LO.3**

Recognize the basis issues relevant to the shareholder and the corporation.

## BASIS DETERMINATION AND RELATED ISSUES

Recall that § 351(a) postpones gain or loss until the shareholder-transferor disposes of the stock in a taxable transaction. The postponement of shareholder gain or loss has a corollary effect on the basis of the stock received by the shareholder and the basis of the property received by the corporation. This procedure ensures that any gain or loss postponed under § 351 ultimately will be recognized when the affected asset is disposed of in a taxable transaction.

**Basis of Stock to Shareholder.**  For a taxpayer transferring property to a corporation in a § 351 transaction, the *stock* received in the transaction is given a substituted basis. Essentially, the stock's basis is the same as the basis the taxpayer had in the property transferred, increased by any gain recognized on the exchange and decreased by boot received. Recall that for basis purposes, boot received includes any liabilities transferred by the shareholder to the corporation. Also note that if the shareholder receives any *other property* (i.e., boot) along with the stock, it takes a basis equal to its fair market value.[18]

**Basis of Property to Corporation.**  The basis of *property* received by the corporation is determined under a carryover basis rule. This rule provides that the basis to the corporation is equal to the basis in the hands of the transferor increased by the amount of any gain recognized to the transferor-shareholder.[19]

The basis rules are summarized in Figures 3–1 and 3–2 and illustrated in Examples 19 and 20.

**EXAMPLE 19**

Kesha and Ned form Brown Corporation. Kesha transfers land (basis of $30,000 and fair market value of $70,000); Ned invests cash ($60,000). They each receive 50 shares in Brown Corporation, worth $60,000, but Kesha also receives $10,000 in cash from Brown. The transfers

---

[18]§ 358(a).                                [19]§ 362(a).

■ **FIGURE 3–1**

Shareholder's Basis in Stock Received

| | |
|---|---|
| Adjusted basis of property transferred | $xx,xxx |
| Plus: Gain recognized | x,xxx |
| Minus: Boot received (including any liabilities transferred) | (x,xxx) |
| Equals: Basis of stock received | $xx,xxx |

■ **FIGURE 3–2**

Corporation's Basis in Property Received

| | |
|---|---|
| Adjusted basis of property transferred | $xx,xxx |
| Plus: Gain recognized by transferor-shareholder | xxx |
| Equals: Basis of property to corporation | $xx,xxx |

of property, the realized and recognized gain on the transfers, and the basis of the stock in Brown Corporation to Kesha and Ned are as follows:

| | A | B | C | D | E | F |
|---|---|---|---|---|---|---|
| | Basis of Property Transferred | FMV of Stock Received | Boot Received | Realized Gain (B + C − A) | Recognized Gain (Lesser of C or D) | Basis of Stock in Brown (A − C + E) |
| From Kesha: | | | | | | |
| Land | $30,000 | $60,000 | $10,000 | $40,000 | $10,000 | $30,000 |
| From Ned: | | | | | | |
| Cash | 60,000 | 60,000 | –0– | –0– | –0– | 60,000 |

Brown Corporation has a basis of $40,000 in the land: Kesha's basis of $30,000 plus her recognized gain of $10,000. ■

**EXAMPLE 20**

Assume the same facts as in Example 19 except that Kesha's basis in the land is $68,000 (instead of $30,000). Because recognized gain cannot exceed realized gain, the transfer generates only $2,000 of gain to Kesha. The realized and recognized gain and the basis of the stock in Brown Corporation to Kesha are as follows:

| | A | B | C | D | E | F |
|---|---|---|---|---|---|---|
| | Basis of Property Transferred | FMV of Stock Received | Boot Received | Realized Gain (B + C − A) | Recognized Gain (Lesser of C or D) | Basis of Stock in Brown (A − C + E) |
| Land | $68,000 | $60,000 | $10,000 | $2,000 | $2,000 | $60,000 |

Brown's basis in the land is $70,000 ($68,000 basis to Kesha + $2,000 gain recognized by Kesha). ■

*[handwritten margin notes: "Service rev & Basis in stock"; "Service rev 100000 / Corp basis 90000 / Carl's basis 190000"]*

### Stock Issued for Services Rendered.

A transfer of shares for services is not a taxable transaction to a corporation.[20] But another issue arises: Can a corporation deduct the fair market value of the stock it issues in consideration of services as a business expense? Yes, unless the services are such that the payment is characterized as a capital expenditure.[21]

**EXAMPLE 21**

Esther and Carl form White Corporation. Esther transfers cash of $500,000 for 100 shares of White Corporation stock. Carl transfers property worth $400,000 (basis of $90,000) and agrees to serve as manager of the corporation for one year; in return, Carl receives 100 shares of stock in White. The value of Carl's services to White Corporation is $100,000. Esther's and Carl's transfers qualify under § 351. Neither Esther nor Carl is taxed on the transfer of their property. However, Carl has income of $100,000, the value of the stock received for the services he will render to White Corporation. White has a basis of $90,000 in the property it acquired from Carl, and it may claim a compensation expense deduction under § 162 for $100,000. Carl's stock basis is $190,000 ($90,000 + $100,000). ■

**EXAMPLE 22**

Assume the same facts as in Example 21 except that Carl provides legal services (instead of management services) in organizing the corporation. The value of Carl's legal services is $100,000. Carl has no gain on the transfer of the property but has income of $100,000 for the value of the stock received for the services rendered. White Corporation has a basis of $90,000 in the property it acquired from Carl and must capitalize the $100,000 as an organizational expense. Carl's stock basis is $190,000 ($90,000 + $100,000). ■

### Holding Period for Shareholder and Transferee Corporation.

In a § 351 transfer, the shareholder's holding period for stock received in exchange for a capital asset or § 1231 property includes the holding period of the property transferred to the corporation. That is, the holding period of the property is "tacked on" to the holding period of the stock. The holding period for stock received for any other property (e.g., inventory) begins on the day after the exchange. The corporation's holding period for property acquired in a § 351 transfer is the holding period of the transferor-shareholder, regardless of the character of the property in the transferor's hands.[22]

### Recapture Considerations.

In a pure § 351(a) transfer where no gain is recognized, the recapture of accelerated cost recovery rules do not apply.[23] However, any recapture potential associated with the property carries over to the corporation as it steps into the shoes of the transferor-shareholder for purposes of basis determination.

**EXAMPLE 23**

Paul transfers equipment (adjusted basis of $30,000, original cost of $120,000, and fair market value of $100,000) to a controlled corporation in return for stock. If Paul had sold the equipment, it would have yielded a gain of $70,000, all of which would be recaptured as ordinary income under § 1245. Because the transfer comes within § 351(a), Paul has no recognized gain and no accelerated cost recovery to recapture. However, if the corporation later disposes of the equipment in a taxable transaction, it must take into account the § 1245 recapture potential originating with Paul. ■

---

[20]Reg. § 1.1032–1(a).
[21]Rev.Rul. 62–217, 1962–2 C.B. 59, modified by Rev.Rul. 74–503, 1974–2 C.B. 117.

[22]§§ 1223(1) and (2).
[23]§§ 1245(b)(3) and 1250(d)(3).

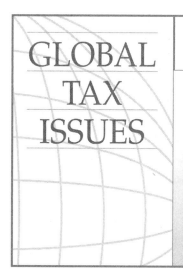

### DOES § 351 COVER THE INCORPORATION OF A FOREIGN BUSINESS?

When a taxpayer wishes to incorporate a business overseas by moving assets across U.S. borders, the deferral mechanism of § 351 applies in certain situations, but not in others. In general, § 351 is available to defer gain recognition when starting up a new corporation outside the United States unless so-called tainted assets are involved. Under § 367, tainted assets, which include assets such as inventory and accounts receivable, are treated as having been sold by the taxpayer prior to the corporate formation; therefore, their transfer results in the current recognition of gain. The presence of tainted assets triggers gain because Congress does not want taxpayers to be able to shift the gain outside the U.S. jurisdiction. The gain recognized is ordinary or capital, depending on the nature of the asset involved.

---

**LO.4**

Appreciate the tax aspects of the capital structure of a corporation.

# Capital Structure of a Corporation

## CAPITAL CONTRIBUTIONS

When a corporation receives money or property in exchange for capital stock (including treasury stock), neither gain nor loss is recognized by the corporation.[24] Nor does a corporation's gross income include shareholders' contributions of money or property to the capital of the corporation. Moreover, additional money or property received from shareholders through voluntary pro rata transfers also is not income to the corporation. This is the case even though there is no increase in the outstanding shares of stock of the corporation. The contributions represent an additional price paid for the shares held by the shareholders and are treated as additions to the operating capital of the corporation.[25]

Contributions by nonshareholders, such as land contributed to a corporation by a civic group or a governmental group to induce the corporation to locate in a particular community, are also excluded from the gross income of a corporation.[26] However, if the property is transferred to a corporation by a nonshareholder in exchange for goods or services, then the corporation must recognize income.[27]

**EXAMPLE 24**

A cable television company charges its customers an initial fee to hook up to a new cable system installed in the area. These payments are used to finance the total cost of constructing the cable facilities. In addition, the customers will make monthly payments for the cable service. The initial payments are used for capital expenditures, but they represent payments for services to be rendered by the cable company. As such, they are taxable income to the cable company and not contributions to capital by nonshareholders. ■

The basis of property received by a corporation from a shareholder as a **capital contribution** is equal to the basis of the property in the hands of the shareholder

---

[24]§ 1032.
[25]§ 118 and Reg. § 1.118–1.
[26]See *Edwards v. Cuba Railroad Co.*, 1 USTC ¶139, 5 AFTR 5398, 45 S.Ct. 614 (USSC, 1925).

[27]Reg. § 1.118–1. See also *Teleservice Co. of Wyoming Valley*, 27 T.C. 722 (1957), *aff'd* in 58–1 USTC ¶9383, 1 AFTR2d 1249, 254 F.2d 105 (CA–3, 1958), *cert. den.* 78 S.Ct. 1360 (USSC, 1958).

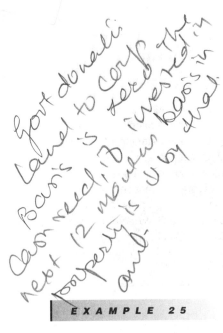

increased by any gain recognized to the shareholder on the transfer. The basis of property transferred to a corporation by a nonshareholder as a contribution to capital is zero.

If a corporation receives *money* as a contribution to capital from a nonshareholder, a special rule applies. The basis of any property acquired with the money during a 12-month period beginning on the day the contribution was received is reduced by the amount of the contribution. The excess of money received over the cost of new property reduces the basis of other property held by the corporation and is applied in the following order:

- Depreciable property.
- Property subject to amortization.
- Property subject to depletion.
- All other remaining properties.

The basis of property within each category is reduced in proportion to the relative bases of the properties.[28]

**EXAMPLE 25**

A city donates land to Teal Corporation as an inducement for Teal to locate in the city. The receipt of the land produces no taxable income to Teal, and the land's basis to the corporation is zero. If, in addition, the city gives the corporation $10,000 in cash, the money is not taxable income to the corporation. However, if the corporation purchases property with the $10,000 within the next 12 months, the basis of the acquired property is reduced by $10,000. Any excess cash not used is handled according to the ordering rules noted above. ■

## LO.5

Recognize the tax differences between debt and equity investments.

## DEBT IN THE CAPITAL STRUCTURE

**Advantages of Debt.**    Significant tax differences exist between debt and equity in the capital structure. The advantages of issuing long-term debt instead of stock are numerous. Interest on debt is deductible by the corporation, while dividend payments are not. Further, loan repayments are not taxable to investors unless the repayments exceed basis. A shareholder's receipt of property from a corporation, however, cannot be tax-free as long as the corporation has earnings and profits (see Chapter 4). Such distributions will be deemed to be taxable dividends to the extent of earnings and profits of the distributing corporation.

**EXAMPLE 26**

Wade transfers cash of $100,000 to a newly formed corporation for 100% of the stock. In its initial year, the corporation has net income of $40,000. The income is credited to the earnings and profits account of the corporation. If the corporation distributes $9,500 to Wade, the distribution is a taxable dividend to Wade with no corresponding deduction to the corporation. Assume, instead, that Wade transfers to the corporation cash of $50,000 for stock and cash of $50,000 for a note of the same amount. The note is payable in equal annual installments of $5,000 and bears interest at the rate of 9%. At the end of the year, the corporation pays Wade interest of $4,500 ($50,000 × 9%) and a note repayment of $5,000. The interest payment is deductible to the corporation and taxable to Wade. The $5,000 principal repayment on the note is neither deducted by the corporation nor taxed to Wade. ■

**Reclassification of Debt as Equity (Thin Capitalization Problem).**    In situations where the corporation is said to be thinly capitalized, the IRS contends that debt is really an equity interest and denies shareholders the tax advantages of debt financing. If the debt instrument has too many features of stock, it may be

---

[28]§ 362(a) and Reg. § 1.362–2(b).

## SOME CORPORATIONS PASS ON THE ADVANTAGES OF DEBT

The tax advantages of financing a corporation with some debt are clear and beyond question. In fact, debt is so advantageous from a tax perspective that some corporations "overdo it." Nonetheless, some well-known, successful corporations choose to operate without long-term debt. Microsoft, Walgreen, and Cisco Systems apparently have decided that the nontax advantages of avoiding debt (e.g., not having to contend with debt service costs) outweigh the tax advantages of using debt. Such debt-free companies may be the envy of corporations that have relied on debt, perhaps excessively, as a means of financing growth (e.g., US Airways and WorldCom). In some cases, corporate debt does little to enhance a shareholder's investment and may even destroy it.

treated for tax purposes as stock. In that case, the principal and interest payments are considered dividends.

Section 385 lists several factors that *may* be used to determine whether a debtor-creditor relationship or a shareholder-corporation relationship exists. The section authorizes the Treasury to prescribe Regulations that provide more definitive guidelines. To date, the Treasury has not drafted acceptable Regulations. Consequently, taxpayers must rely on judicial decisions to determine whether a true debtor-creditor relationship exists.

For the most part, the principles used to classify debt as equity developed in connection with closely held corporations. Here, the holders of the debt are also shareholders. Consequently, the rules have often proved inadequate for dealing with such problems in large, publicly traded corporations.

Together, Congress, through § 385, and the courts have identified the following factors to be considered in resolving the **thin capitalization** issue:

- Whether the debt instrument is in proper form. An open account advance is more easily characterized as a contribution to capital than a loan evidenced by a properly written note.[29]
- Whether the debt instrument bears a reasonable rate of interest and has a definite maturity date. When a shareholder advance does not provide for interest, the return expected may appear to be a share of the profits or an increase in the value of the shares.[30] Likewise, a lender unrelated to the corporation will usually be unwilling to commit funds to the corporation without a definite due date.
- Whether the debt is paid on a timely basis. A lender's failure to insist upon timely repayment or satisfactory renegotiation indicates that the return sought does not depend upon interest income and the repayment of principal.
- Whether payment is contingent upon earnings. A lender ordinarily will not advance funds that are likely to be repaid only if the venture is successful.
- Whether the debt is subordinated to other liabilities. Subordination tends to eliminate a significant characteristic of the creditor-debtor relationship. Creditors should have the right to share with other general creditors in the event of the corporation's dissolution or liquidation. Subordination also

---

[29]*Estate of Mixon, Jr. v. U.S.*, 72–2 USTC ¶9537, 30 AFTR2d 72–5094, 464 F.2d 394 (CA–5, 1972).

[30]*Slappey Drive Industrial Park v. U.S.*, 77–2 USTC ¶9696, 40 AFTR2d 77–5940, 561 F.2d 572 (CA–5, 1977).

destroys another basic attribute of creditor status—the power to demand payment at a fixed maturity date.[31]

- Whether holdings of debt and stock are proportionate (e.g., each shareholder owns the same percentage of debt as stock). When debt and equity obligations are held in the same proportion, shareholders are, apart from tax considerations, indifferent as to whether corporate distributions are in the form of interest or dividends.
- Whether funds loaned to the corporation are used to finance initial operations or capital asset acquisitions. Funds used to finance initial operations or to acquire capital assets the corporation needs are generally obtained through equity investments.
- Whether the corporation has a high ratio of shareholder debt to shareholder equity. Thin capitalization occurs when shareholder debt is high relative to shareholder equity. This indicates the corporation lacks reserves to pay interest and principal on debt when corporate income is insufficient to meet current needs.[32] In determining a corporation's debt-equity ratio, courts look at the relation of the debt both to the book value of the corporation's assets and to their actual fair market value.[33]

Under § 385, the IRS also has the authority to classify an instrument either as *wholly* debt or equity or as *part* debt and *part* equity. This flexible approach is important because some instruments cannot readily be classified either wholly as stock or wholly as debt. It may also provide an avenue for the IRS to address problems in publicly traded corporations.

## Investor Losses

LO.6

Handle the tax treatment of shareholder debt and stock losses.

The difference between equity and debt financing involves a consideration of the tax treatment of worthless stock and securities versus that applicable to bad debts.

### STOCK AND SECURITY LOSSES

If stocks and bonds are capital assets in their owner's hands, losses from their worthlessness are governed by § 165(g)(1). Under this provision, a capital loss materializes as of the last day of the taxable year in which the stocks or bonds become worthless. No deduction is allowed for a mere decline in value. The burden of proving complete worthlessness is on the taxpayer claiming the loss. One way to recognize partial worthlessness is to dispose of the stocks or bonds in a taxable sale or exchange.[34] But even then, the **investor loss** is disallowed if the sale or exchange is to a related party.

When the stocks or bonds are not capital assets, worthlessness yields an ordinary loss.[35] For example, if the stocks or bonds are held by a broker for resale to customers in the normal course of business, they are not capital assets. Usually, however, stocks and bonds are held as investments and, as a result, are capital assets.

---

[31]*Fin Hay Realty Co. v. U.S.*, 68–2 USTC ¶9438, 22 AFTR2d 5004, 398 F.2d 694 (CA–3, 1968).

[32]A court held that a debt-equity ratio of approximately 14.6:1 was not excessive. See *Tomlinson v. 1661 Corp.*, 67–1 USTC ¶9438, 19 AFTR2d 1413, 377 F.2d 291 (CA–5, 1967).

[33]In *Bauer v. Comm.*, 84–2 USTC ¶9996, 55 AFTR2d 85–433, 748 F.2d 1365 (CA–9, 1984), a debt-equity ratio of 92:1 resulted when book

value was used. But the ratio ranged from 2:1 to 8:1 when equity included both paid-in capital and accumulated earnings.

[34]Reg. § 1.165–4(a).

[35]§ 165(a) and Reg. § 1.165–5(b).

Under certain circumstances involving stocks and bonds of affiliated corporations, an ordinary loss is allowed upon worthlessness.[36] A corporation is an affiliate of another corporation if the corporate shareholder owns at least 80 percent of the voting power of all classes of stock entitled to vote and 80 percent of each class of nonvoting stock. Further, to be considered affiliated, the corporation must have derived more than 90 percent of its aggregate gross receipts for all taxable years from sources other than passive income. Passive income for this purpose includes such items as rents, royalties, dividends, and interest.

## BUSINESS VERSUS NONBUSINESS BAD DEBTS

In addition to worthlessness of stocks and bonds, the financial demise of a corporation can result in bad debt deductions to those who have extended credit to the corporation. These deductions can be either business bad debts or **nonbusiness bad debts.** The distinction between the two types of deductions is important for tax purposes in the following respects:

- Business bad debts are deducted as ordinary losses while nonbusiness bad debts are treated as short-term capital losses.[37] A business bad debt can generate a net operating loss while a nonbusiness bad debt cannot.[38]
- A deduction is allowed for the partial worthlessness of a business debt while nonbusiness debts can be written off only when they become entirely worthless.[39]
- Nonbusiness bad debt treatment is limited to noncorporate taxpayers. However, all of the bad debts of a corporation qualify as business bad debts.[40]

When is a debt business or nonbusiness? Unfortunately, since the Code sheds little light on the matter, the distinction has been left to the courts.[41] In a leading decision, the Supreme Court somewhat clarified the picture when it held that if individual shareholders lend money to a corporation in their capacity as investors, any resulting bad debt is classified as nonbusiness.[42] Nevertheless, the Court did not preclude the possibility of a shareholder-creditor incurring a business bad debt.

If a loan is made in some capacity that qualifies as a trade or business, nonbusiness bad debt treatment is avoided. For example, if an employee, who is also a shareholder, makes a loan to preserve employment status, the loan qualifies for business bad debt treatment.[43] Shareholders also receive business bad debt treatment if they are in the trade or business of lending money or of buying, promoting, and selling corporations. If the shareholder has multiple motives for making the loan, according to the Supreme Court, the "dominant" or "primary" motive for making the loan controls the classification of the loss.[44]

**EXAMPLE 27**

Norman owns 48% of the stock of Lark Corporation, which he acquired several years ago at a cost of $200,000. Norman is also employed by the corporation at an annual salary of $80,000. At a time when Lark Corporation is experiencing financial problems, Norman lends it $100,000. Subsequently, the corporation becomes bankrupt, and both Norman's stock investment and his loan become worthless. ■

---

[36]§ 165(g)(3).

[37]Compare § 166(a) with § 166(d)(1)(B).

[38]Note the modification required by § 172(d)(2).

[39]Compare § 166(a)(2) with § 166(d)(1)(A).

[40]§ 166(d)(1).

[41]For definitional purposes, § 166(d)(2) is almost as worthless as the debt it purports to describe.

[42]*Whipple v. Comm.*, 63–1 USTC ¶9466, 11 AFTR2d 1454, 83 S.Ct. 1168 (USSC, 1963).

[43]*Trent v. Comm.*, 61–2 USTC ¶9506, 7 AFTR2d 1599, 291 F.2d 669 (CA–2, 1961).

[44]*U.S. v. Generes*, 72–1 USTC ¶9259, 29 AFTR2d 72–609, 92 S.Ct. 827 (USSC, 1972).

Norman's stock investment is treated as a long-term capital loss (assuming § 1244 does not apply, as discussed below). But how is the bad debt classified? If Norman can prove that his dominant or primary reason for making the loan was to protect his salary, a business bad debt deduction results. If not, it is assumed that Norman was trying to protect his stock investment, and nonbusiness bad debt treatment results. Factors to be considered in resolving this matter include the following:

- A comparison of the amount of the stock investment with the trade or business benefit derived. In Example 27, the stock investment of $200,000 is compared with the annual salary of $80,000. In this regard, the salary should be considered as a recurring item and not viewed in isolation. A salary of $80,000 each year means a great deal to a person who has no other means of support and may have difficulty obtaining similar employment elsewhere.
- A comparison of the amount of the loan with the stock investment and the trade or business benefit derived.
- The percentage of ownership held by the shareholder. A minority shareholder, for example, is under more compulsion to lend the corporation money to protect a job than one who is in control of corporate policy.

In summary, it is impossible to conclude whether Norman in Example 27 suffered a business or nonbusiness bad debt without additional facts. Even with such facts, the guidelines are vague. Recall that a taxpayer's intent or motivation is at issue. For this reason, the problem is the subject of frequent litigation.[45]

## SECTION 1244 STOCK

In an exception to the capital treatment that generally results, § 1244 permits ordinary loss treatment for losses on the sale or worthlessness of stock of so-called small business corporations. By placing shareholders on a more nearly equal basis with proprietors and partners in terms of the tax treatment of losses, the provision encourages investment of capital in small corporations. Gain on the sale of § 1244 stock remains capital. Consequently, the shareholder has nothing to lose and everything to gain by complying with § 1244.

**Qualification for § 1244.** Only a *small business corporation* can issue qualifying § 1244 stock. To be a small business corporation, the total amount of stock that can be offered under the plan to issue § 1244 stock cannot exceed $1 million. For these purposes, property received in exchange for stock is valued at its adjusted basis, reduced by any liabilities assumed by the corporation or to which the property is subject. The fair market value of the property is not considered. The $1 million limitation is determined on the date the stock is issued. Consequently, even though a corporation fails to meet these requirements when the stock later is disposed of by the shareholder, the stock can still qualify as § 1244 stock if the requirements were met on the date the stock was issued.

**Mechanics of the Loss Deduction.** The amount of ordinary loss deductible in any one year from the disposition of § 1244 stock is limited to $50,000 (or $100,000 for spouses filing a joint return). If the amount of the loss sustained in the taxable year exceeds these amounts, the remainder is considered a capital loss.

---

[45]See, for example, *Kelson v. U.S.*, 74–2 USTC ¶9714, 34 AFTR2d 74–6007, 503 F.2d 1291 (CA–10, 1974).

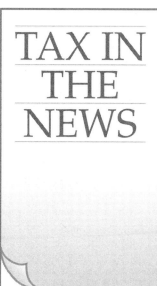

## TAX IN THE NEWS

### LOSS TREATMENT FOR STOCK INVESTORS: TIME FOR A CHANGE?

Under the tax rules applicable to individual investors, a loss incurred on the sale or worthlessness of a stock investment results in capital loss treatment. For these taxpayers, the deduction for *net* capital losses is limited to a $3,000 per year offset to ordinary income. In contrast, qualifying investors who meet the requirements of § 1244 may deduct a loss of as much as $100,000 per year. Further, a loss from the sale or disposition of § 1244 stock is accorded ordinary rather than capital treatment.

A recent proposal would increase the $3,000 loss limitation to provide greater tax incentives for small investors. Given that the proposal comes at a time when many investors have sustained significant stock market losses, it could prove highly popular among voters. In addition, it could be justified on the ground that it would bring the tax treatment of ordinary investors' losses more in line with that of § 1244. Furthermore, is it not time to change the $3,000 limitation after all these years? After all, this threshold has not changed since the 1970s!

**EXAMPLE 28**

Harvey acquires § 1244 stock at a cost of $100,000. He sells the stock for $10,000 in the current year. He has an ordinary loss of $50,000 and a capital loss of $40,000. Alternatively, on a joint return, the entire $90,000 loss is ordinary. ■

Only the original holder of § 1244 stock, whether an individual or a partnership, qualifies for ordinary loss treatment. If the stock is sold or donated, it loses its § 1244 status.

Special treatment applies if § 1244 stock is issued by a corporation in exchange for property that has an adjusted basis above its fair market value immediately before the exchange. For purposes of determining ordinary loss upon a subsequent sale, the stock basis is reduced to the fair market value of the property on the date of the exchange.

**EXAMPLE 29**

Dana transfers property with a basis of $10,000 and a fair market value of $5,000 to a corporation in exchange for shares of § 1244 stock. Assuming the transfer qualifies under § 351, the basis of the stock is $10,000, the same as Dana's basis in the property. However, for purposes of § 1244 and measuring the amount of ordinary loss, the stock basis is only $5,000. If the stock is later sold for $3,000, the total loss sustained is $7,000 ($3,000 − $10,000); however, only $2,000 of the loss is ordinary ($3,000 − $5,000). The remaining portion of the loss, $5,000, is a capital loss. ■

Recall the advantages of issuing some debt to shareholders in exchange for cash contributions to a corporation. A disadvantage of issuing debt is that it does not qualify under § 1244. Should the debt become worthless, the taxpayer generally has a short-term capital loss rather than the ordinary loss for § 1244 stock.

## Gain from Qualified Small Business Stock

Shareholders are given special tax relief for gains recognized on the sale or exchange of stock acquired in a **qualified small business corporation.** The holder of **qualified small business stock** may exclude 50 percent of any gain from the sale or exchange of such stock.[46] To qualify for the exclusion, the taxpayer must have held the stock for more than five years and must have acquired the stock as part of an original issue.[47] Only noncorporate shareholders qualify for the exclusion.

A qualified small business corporation is a C corporation whose aggregate gross assets did not exceed $50 million on the date the stock was issued.[48] The corporation must be actively involved in a trade or business. This means that at least 80 percent of the corporation's assets must be used in the active conduct of one or more qualified trades or businesses.

A shareholder can apply the 50 percent exclusion to the greater of (1) $10 million or (2) 10 times the shareholder's aggregate adjusted basis in the qualified stock disposed of during a taxable year.[49]

---

**ETHICAL CONSIDERATIONS**

## A Professional-Free Incorporation

Allen and Beth agree to form Jay Corporation. Allen, who has a reputation for being extremely frugal, decides to follow instructions for incorporating a business that he has found on a free Internet site. Based on his plan, Allen transfers appreciated property to Jay Corporation in exchange for 75 percent of its stock. Beth agrees to provide services to the business for 25 percent of the stock.

Several months later, Allen learns that he has made a terrible blunder. To avoid paying tax on the transfer of his appreciated property, he should have received 80 percent, not 75 percent, of the stock. To correct the problem, Allen convinces Beth to transfer to him 5 percent of the corporation's stock. In return, Allen will give Beth some antiques he has collected. Allen tells Beth that this is a better deal for her because now she will have to report the value of only 20 percent of the corporation's stock as income (instead of 25 percent). Further, she receives the antiques as a tax-free gift.

How do you react to Allen's actions?

---

**LO.7**

Identify tax planning opportunities associated with organizing and financing a corporation.

## WORKING WITH § 351

Effective tax planning with transfers of property to corporations requires a clear understanding of § 351 and its related Code provisions. The most important question in planning is simply: Does the desired tax result come from complying with § 351 or from avoiding it?

**Tax Planning Considerations**

**Utilizing § 351.** If the tax-free treatment of § 351 is desired, ensure that the parties transferring property (which includes cash) receive control of the corporation. Simultaneous transfers are not necessary, but a long period of time between transfers could be disastrous if the transfers are not properly documented as part of a single plan. The parties should document and preserve evidence of their intentions. Also, it is helpful to have some reasonable explanation for any delay in the transfers.

To meet the requirements of § 351, mere momentary control on the part of the transferor may not suffice if loss of control is compelled by a prearranged agreement.[50]

---

[46]§ 1202. The 10% and 20% capital gains rates do not apply. Thus, the maximum effective tax rate on the sale of qualified small business stock is 14% (28% × 50%).

[47]The stock must have been issued after August 10, 1993, which is the effective date of § 1202.

[48]§ 1202(d). Its aggregate assets may not exceed this amount at any time between August 10, 1993, and the date the stock was issued.

[49]§ 1202(b). The amount is $5 million for married taxpayers filing separately.

[50]Rev.Rul. 54–96, 1954–1 C.B. 111.

**EXAMPLE 30**

For many years, Paula operated a business as a sole proprietor employing Brooke as manager. To dissuade Brooke from quitting and going out on her own, Paula promised her a 30% interest in the business. To fulfill this promise, Paula transfers the business to newly formed Green Corporation in return for all its stock. Immediately thereafter, Paula transfers 30% of the stock to Brooke. Section 351 probably does not apply to Paula's transfer to Green Corporation because it appears that Paula was under an obligation to relinquish control. However, if this is not the case and the loss of control was voluntary on Paula's part, momentary control would suffice.[51] ■

Be sure that later transfers of property to an existing corporation satisfy the control requirement if recognition of gain is to be avoided. In this connection, another transferor's interest cannot be counted if the value of stock received is relatively small compared with the value of stock already owned and the primary purpose of the transfer is to qualify other transferors for § 351 treatment.[52]

**Avoiding § 351.** Because § 351 provides for the nonrecognition of gain on transfers to controlled corporations, it is often regarded as a favorable relief provision. In some situations, however, avoiding § 351 may produce a more advantageous tax result. The transferors might prefer to recognize gain on the transfer of property if they cannot be particularly harmed by the gain. For example, they may be in low tax brackets, or the gain may be a capital gain from which substantial capital losses can be offset. The corporation will then have a stepped-up basis in the transferred property.

A transferor might also prefer to avoid § 351 to allow for immediate recognition of a loss. Recall that § 351 provides for the nonrecognition of both gains and losses. A transferor who wishes to recognize loss has several alternatives:

- Sell the property to the corporation for its stock. The IRS could attempt to collapse the "sale," however, by taking the approach that the transfer really falls under § 351.[53] If the sale is disregarded, the transferor ends up with a realized, but unrecognized, loss.
- Sell the property to the corporation for other property or boot. Because the transferor receives no stock, § 351 is inapplicable.
- Transfer the property to the corporation in return for securities or nonqualified preferred stock. Recall that § 351 does not apply to a transferor who receives securities or nonqualified preferred stock. In both this and the previous alternatives, watch for the possible disallowance of the loss under the related-party rules.

Suppose the loss property is to be transferred to the corporation and no loss is recognized by the transferor due to § 351. This could present an interesting problem in terms of assessing the economic realities involved.

**EXAMPLE 31**

Iris and Lamont form Wren Corporation with the following investments: property by Iris (basis of $40,000 and fair market value of $50,000) and property by Lamont (basis of $60,000 and fair market value of $50,000). Each receives 50% of the Wren stock. Has Lamont acted wisely in settling for only 50% of the stock? At first, it would appear so, since Iris and Lamont each invested property of the same value ($50,000). But what about tax considerations? Due to the carryover basis rules, the corporation now has a basis of $40,000 in Iris's property

---

[51]Compare *Fahs v. Florida Machine and Foundry Co.*, 48–2 USTC ¶9329, 36 AFTR 1161, 168 F.2d 957 (CA–5, 1948), with *John C. O'Connor*, 16 TCM 213, T.C.Memo. 1957–50, *aff'd* in 58–2 USTC ¶9913, 2 AFTR2d 6011, 260 F.2d 358 (CA–6, 1958).

[52]Reg. § 1.351–1(a)(1)(ii).
[53]*U.S. v. Hertwig*, 68–2 USTC ¶9495, 22 AFTR2d 5249, 398 F.2d 452 (CA–5, 1968).

and $60,000 in Lamont's property. In essence, Iris has shifted a possible $10,000 gain to the corporation while Lamont has transferred a $10,000 potential loss. With this in mind, an equitable allocation of the Wren stock would call for Lamont to receive a greater percentage interest than Iris. ∎

## SELECTING ASSETS TO TRANSFER

When a business is incorporated, the organizers must determine which assets and liabilities should be transferred to the corporation. A transfer of assets that produce passive income (rents, royalties, dividends, and interest) can cause the corporation to be a personal holding company in a tax year when operating income is low. Thus, the corporation could be subject to the personal holding company penalty tax (see the discussion in Chapter 6) in addition to the regular income tax.

Leasing property to the corporation may be a more attractive alternative than transferring ownership. Leasing provides the taxpayer with the opportunity to withdraw money from the corporation without the payment being characterized as a dividend. If the property is given to a family member in a lower tax bracket, the lease income can be shifted as well. If the depreciation and other deductions available in connection with the property are larger than the lease income, the taxpayer would retain the property until the income exceeds the deductions.

When an existing cash basis business is incorporated, an important issue to consider is whether the business's accounts receivable and accounts payable will be transferred to the new corporation or be retained by the owner of the unincorporated business. Depending on the approach taken, either the new corporation or the owner of the old unincorporated business will recognize the income associated with the cash basis receivables when they are collected. The cash basis accounts payable raise the corresponding issue of who will claim the deduction.

Another way to shift income to other taxpayers is by the use of corporate debt. Shareholder debt in a corporation can be given to family members in a lower tax bracket. This technique also causes income to be shifted without a loss of control of the corporation.

## DEBT IN THE CAPITAL STRUCTURE

The advantages of debt as opposed to equity have previously been noted. To increase debt without incurring the thin capitalization problem, consider the following:

* Preserve the formalities of the debt. This includes providing for written instruments, realistic interest rates, and specified due dates.
* If possible, have the corporation repay the debt when it becomes due. If this is not possible, have the parties renegotiate the arrangement. Try to proceed as a nonshareholder creditor would. It is not unusual, for example, for bondholders of publicly held corporations to extend due dates when default occurs. The alternative is to foreclose and perhaps seriously impair the amount the creditors will recover.
* Avoid provisions in the debt instrument that make the debt convertible to equity in the event of default. These provisions are standard practice when nonshareholder creditors are involved. They serve no purpose if the shareholders are also the creditors and hold debt in proportion to ownership shares.

**EXAMPLE 32**

Gail, Gary, and Grace are equal shareholders in Magenta Corporation. Each transfers cash of $100,000 to Magenta in return for its bonds. The bond agreement provides that the holders will receive additional voting rights in the event Magenta Corporation defaults on its bonds. The voting rights provision is worthless and merely raises the issue of thin capitalization. Gail, Gary, and Grace already control Magenta Corporation, so what purpose is served by increasing their voting rights? The parties probably used a "boilerplate" bond agreement that was designed for third-party lenders (e.g., banks and other financial institutions). ■

- Pro rata holding of debt is difficult to avoid. For example, if each of the shareholders owns one-third of the stock, then each will want one-third of the debt. Nevertheless, some variation is possible.

**EXAMPLE 33**

Assume the same facts as Example 32 except that only Gail and Gary acquire the bonds. Grace leases property to Magenta Corporation at an annual rent that approximates the yield on the bonds. Presuming the rent passes the arm's length test (i.e., what unrelated parties would charge), all parties reach the desired result. Gail and Gary withdraw corporate profits in the form of interest income, and Grace is provided for with rent income. Magenta Corporation can deduct both the interest and the rent payments. ■

- Try to keep the debt-equity ratio within reasonable proportions. A problem frequently arises when the parties form the corporation. Often the amount invested in capital stock is the minimum required by state law. For example, if the state of incorporation permits a minimum of $1,000, limiting the investment to this amount does not provide much safety for later debt financing by the shareholders.
- Stressing the fair market value of the assets rather than their tax basis to the corporation can be helpful in preparing to defend debt-equity ratios.

**EXAMPLE 34**

Emily, Josh, and Miles form Black Corporation with the following capital investments: cash of $200,000 from Emily; land worth $200,000 (basis of $20,000) from Josh; and a patent worth $200,000 (basis of $0) from Miles. To state that the equity of Black Corporation is $220,000 (the tax basis to the corporation) does not reflect reality. The equity account is more properly stated at $600,000 ($200,000 + $200,000 + $200,000). ■

- The nature of the business can have an effect on what is an acceptable debt-equity ratio. Capital-intensive industries (e.g., manufacturing, transportation) characteristically rely heavily on debt financing. Consequently, larger debt should be tolerated.

## INVESTOR LOSSES

Be aware of the danger of losing § 1244 attributes. Only the original holder of § 1244 stock is entitled to ordinary loss treatment. If, after a corporation is formed, the owner transfers shares of stock to family members to shift income within the family group, the benefits of § 1244 are lost.

**EXAMPLE 35**

Norm incorporates his business by transferring property with a basis of $100,000 for 100 shares of stock. The stock qualifies as § 1244 stock. Norm later gives 50 shares each to his children, Susan and Paul. Eventually, the business fails, and the shares of stock become worthless. If Norm had retained the stock, he would have had an ordinary loss deduction of $100,000 (assuming he filed a joint return). Susan and Paul, however, have a capital loss of $50,000 each because the § 1244 attributes are lost as a result of the gift (i.e., neither Susan nor Paul was an original holder of the stock). ■

## KEY TERMS

| | | |
|---|---|---|
| Assumption of liabilities, 3–9 | Nonbusiness bad debt, 3–19 | Section 1244 stock, 3–20 |
| Capital contribution, 3–15 | Property, 3–4 | Securities, 3–5 |
| Control, 3–6 | Qualified small business corporation, 3–21 | Thin capitalization, 3–17 |
| Investor losses, 3–18 | | |
| Liabilities in excess of basis, 3–10 | Qualified small business stock, 3–21 | |

## PROBLEM MATERIALS

### Discussion Questions

1. In terms of justification and effect, § 351 (transfer to a controlled corporation) and § 1031 (like-kind exchange) are much alike. Explain.

2. Under what circumstances will gain and/or loss be recognized on a § 351 transfer?

3. What does the term "property" include for purposes of § 351?

4. Can boot ever be taxable in a § 351 transfer in the absence of realized gain? Explain.

5. Does the receipt of securities in exchange for the transfer of appreciated property to a controlled corporation cause recognition of gain?

6. What is the control requirement of § 351? Describe the effect of the following in satisfying this requirement:
   a. A shareholder renders only services to the corporation for stock.
   b. A shareholder both renders services and transfers property to the corporation for stock.
   c. A shareholder has only momentary control after the transfer.
   d. A long period of time elapses between the transfers of property by different shareholders.

**Issue ID**

**Decision Making**

7. Several entrepreneurs plan to form a corporation for purposes of constructing a housing project. Travis, the party who will be contributing the land for the project, wants more security than shareholder status provides. He is contemplating two possibilities: receive corporate bonds for his land, or take out a mortgage on the land before transferring it to the corporation for stock. Comment on the choices Travis is considering. What alternatives can you suggest?

8. Marvin and June form Warbler Corporation. They transfer appreciated property to the corporation with each receiving 50 shares of the Warbler stock. If Marvin gives his shares to his favorite charity immediately after the exchange, are the exchanges taxable?

9. Paul and Mary transfer property to Falcon Corporation, each in exchange for one-third of Falcon's stock. Matt receives the other one-third of Falcon's stock for services rendered. Will the exchanges be taxable?

10. May a transferor who receives stock for both property and services be included in the control group in determining whether an exchange meets the requirements of § 351? Explain.

**Issue ID**

11. At a point when Robin Corporation has been in existence for six years, shareholder Ted transfers real estate (adjusted basis of $20,000 and fair market value of $100,000) to the corporation for additional stock. At the same time, Peggy, the other shareholder, acquires one share of stock for cash. After the two transfers, the percentages of stock ownership are as follows: 79% by Ted and 21% by Peggy.

    a. What were the parties trying to accomplish?

    b. Will it work? Explain.

12. How does the transfer of mortgaged property to a controlled corporation affect the transferor-shareholder's basis in stock received in the corporation? Assume no gain is recognized on the transfer.

13. Does the transfer of mortgaged property to a controlled corporation trigger gain to the extent of the mortgage? Explain.

14. Before incorporating her apartment rental business, Beth takes out second mortgages on several of the units. She uses the mortgage proceeds to make capital improvements to the rental units. Along with all of the rental units, Beth transfers the mortgages to the newly formed corporation in return for all of its stock. Discuss the tax consequences of these procedures to Beth.

15. Why does the application of § 357(c) cause gain to be recognized? Why is this not the case with § 357(b)?

16. In arriving at the basis of stock received by a shareholder in a § 351 transfer, discuss how each of the following affects the calculation:

    a. The receipt of "other property" (i.e., boot) by the shareholder in addition to stock.

    b. The shareholder transferring a liability to the corporation along with property.

    c. The shareholder's basis in the property transferred to the corporation.

17. Identify a situation when a corporation can deduct the value of the stock it issues for the rendition of services. Identify a situation when a deduction is not available.

18. Pursuant to a § 351 transfer, Mallard Corporation receives property in exchange for stock. Will Mallard's holding period for the property be the same as the shareholder's holding period for the stock? Explain.

19. A corporation acquires property as a contribution to capital from a shareholder and from a nonshareholder. Are the rules pertaining to the property's basis the same? Explain.

20. In structuring the capitalization of a corporation, what are the advantages of utilizing debt rather than equity?

21. Assuming § 1244 does not apply, what is the tax treatment of stock that has become worthless?

22. Under what circumstances, if any, may a shareholder deduct a business bad debt on a loan made to the corporation?

**Decision Making**
23. Several years ago, Mark purchased stock in Brown Corporation for $40,000. The stock has a current value of $5,000. Mark needs to decide which of the following alternatives to pursue. Determine the tax effect of each.

    a. Without selling the stock, Mark deducts $35,000 for the partial worthlessness of the Brown Corporation investment.

    b. Mark sells the stock to his son for $5,000 and deducts a $35,000 long-term capital loss.

    c. Mark sells the stock to a third party and deducts a $35,000 long-term capital loss.

    d. Mark sells the stock to a third party and deducts an ordinary loss.

**Issue ID**
24. Keith's sole proprietorship holds assets that, if sold, would yield a gain of $100,000. It also owns assets that would yield a loss of $30,000. Keith incorporates his business using only the gain assets. Two days later, Keith sells the loss assets to the newly formed corporation. What is Keith trying to accomplish? Will he be successful?

**Issue ID**
25. Emily incorporates her sole proprietorship, but does not transfer the building the business uses to the corporation. Subsequently, the building is leased to the corporation for an annual rent. What tax reasons might Emily have for not transferring the building to the corporation when the business was incorporated?

*[Handwritten notes in left margin:]*

a) Sam – a & b
Amt real 96000   30
 – AB  (30000)  × 3000
        66000      90000
 – recog   6000

Basis in stock  90000 FMV
  – (60000) postphmd
        30000 gain

c) Lark's basis in Inventory
30000 AB + gain 6000 = 36000
d) & e) Seth –
Amt realised  99000
 less ad Basis  (45000)
              54000
 recognized      9000
Basis FMV.      90000
 – postphmd gain (45000)
                45000
f) Lark's basis in equip
45000 + 9000 = 54000
g) & h) PAM –
Amt realised  90000
 – Basis  (15000)
          75000
 recognized  – 0 –
Basis in stock  15000
i) Lark's basis in process
  15000
j) & k) Kelly –
No income.
Basis  30000

## Problems

26. Sam, Seth, Pam, and Kelly form Lark Corporation with the following consideration:

| | Consideration Transferred | | |
| --- | --- | --- | --- |
| | Basis to Transferor | Fair Market Value | Number of Shares Issued |
| From Sam— | | | |
| Inventory | $30,000 | $96,000 | 30* |
| From Seth— | | | |
| Equipment ($30,000 of depreciation taken by Seth in prior years) | 45,000 | 99,000 | 30** |
| From Pam— | | | |
| Secret process | 15,000 | 90,000 | 30 |
| From Kelly— | | | |
| Cash | 30,000 | 30,000 | 10 |

 *Sam receives $6,000 in cash in addition to the 30 shares.
**Seth receives $9,000 in cash in addition to the 30 shares.

Assume the value of each share of Lark Corporation stock is $3,000.
a. What, if any, is Sam's recognized gain or loss? How is any such gain or loss treated?
b. What is Sam's basis in the Lark Corporation stock?
c. What is Lark Corporation's basis in the inventory?
d. How much gain or loss must Seth recognize? How is the gain or loss treated?
e. What is Seth's basis in the Lark Corporation stock?
f. What is Lark Corporation's basis in the equipment?
g. What, if any, is Pam's recognized gain or loss?
h. What is Pam's basis in the Lark Corporation stock?
i. What is Lark Corporation's basis in the secret process?
j. How much income, if any, must Kelly recognize?
k. What is Kelly's basis in the Lark Corporation stock?

27. Mark and Gail form Maple Corporation with the following consideration:

| | Consideration Transferred | | |
| --- | --- | --- | --- |
| | Basis to Transferor | Fair Market Value | Number of Shares Issued |
| From Mark— | | | |
| Cash | $ 40,000 | $ 40,000 | |
| Installment obligation | 140,000 | 360,000 | 40 |
| From Gail— | | | |
| Cash | 140,000 | 140,000 | |
| Equipment | 120,000 | 180,000 | |
| Patent | 4,000 | 280,000 | 60 |

The installment obligation has a face amount of $360,000 and was acquired last year from the sale of land held for investment purposes (adjusted basis of $140,000).
a. How much gain, if any, must Mark recognize?
b. What is Mark's basis in the Maple Corporation stock?
c. What is Maple Corporation's basis in the installment obligation?
d. How much gain, if any, must Gail recognize?
e. What is Gail's basis in the Maple Corporation stock?

f. What is Maple Corporation's basis in the equipment and the patent?

g. How would your answers to the preceding questions change if Mark received common stock and Gail received preferred stock?

h. How would your answers change if Gail were a partnership?

**Decision Making**

28. Jane, Jon, and Clyde incorporate their respective businesses and form Starling Corporation. On March 1 of the current year, Jane exchanges her property (basis of $50,000 and value of $200,000) for 200 shares in Starling Corporation. On April 15, Jon exchanges his property (basis of $70,000 and value of $300,000) for 300 shares in Starling. On May 10, Clyde transfers his property (basis of $90,000 and value of $500,000) for 500 shares in Starling.

a. If the three exchanges are part of a prearranged plan, what gain will each of the parties recognize on the exchanges?

b. Assume Jane and Jon exchanged their property for stock four years ago while Clyde transfers his property for 500 shares in the current year. Clyde's transfer is not part of a prearranged plan with Jane and Jon to incorporate their businesses. What gain will Clyde recognize on the transfer?

c. If the property that Clyde contributes has a basis of $590,000 instead of $90,000, how might the parties otherwise structure the transaction?

**Communications**

29. Andrew Boninti (1635 Maple Street, Syracuse, NY 13201) exchanges property, basis of $30,000 and fair market value of $600,000, for 60% of the stock of Gray Corporation. The other 40% is owned by Kendall Smith, who acquired her stock several years ago. You represent Andrew, who asks whether he must report gain on the transfer. Prepare a letter to Andrew and a memorandum for the tax files where you document your response.

**Issue ID**

30. Kate transfers property worth $400,000 (basis of $50,000) to Crow Corporation in exchange for 50% of Crow's stock. Kevin transfers a secret process worth $300,000 (zero basis) and services for 50% of Crow's stock. Kevin's services relate to his acquiring the secret process and securing a letter of credit from a local bank. The letter of credit states that the newly formed Crow Corporation can obtain a loan of up to $150,000 to further develop the process. What are the tax issues?

31. Dan and Vera form Crane Corporation. Dan transfers land (worth $200,000, basis of $60,000) for 50% of the stock in Crane. Vera transfers machinery (worth $150,000, adjusted basis of $30,000) and provides services worth $50,000 for 50% of the stock.

a. Will the transfers qualify under § 351?

b. What are the tax consequences to Dan and Vera?

c. What is Crane Corporation's basis in the land and the machinery?

32. On January 2 three years ago, Irene and Julie formed Hummingbird Corporation. Each transferred property to Hummingbird in exchange for 50 shares of its stock. On July 1 of the current year, Jaime transfers property worth $600,000 (basis of $90,000) for 50 shares (or a one-third interest) in Hummingbird Corporation. What are the tax consequences to Jaime and to Hummingbird on the transfer of property for stock in the current year?

33. Ann and Bob form Robin Corporation. Ann transfers property worth $420,000 (basis of $150,000) for 70 shares in Robin Corporation. Bob receives 30 shares for property worth $165,000 (basis of $30,000) and for legal services in organizing the corporation; the services are worth $15,000.

a. What gain, if any, will the parties recognize on the transfer?

b. What basis do Ann and Bob have in the stock in Robin Corporation?

c. What is Robin Corporation's basis in the property and services it received from Ann and Bob?

34. Assume in Problem 33 that the property Bob transfers to Robin Corporation is worth $15,000 (basis of $3,000) and his services in organizing the corporation are worth $165,000. What are the tax consequences to Ann, Bob, and Robin Corporation?

35. Kim is an employee of Azure Corporation. In the current year, she receives a salary of $30,000 and is also given 10 shares of Azure stock for services she renders to the corporation. The shares in Azure Corporation are worth $1,000 each. How will the transfer of the 10 shares to Kim be handled for tax purposes by Kim and by Azure Corporation?

36. Paul transfers property with an adjusted basis of $85,000, fair market value of $250,000, to Swift Corporation for 90% of the stock. The property is subject to a liability of $105,000, which Swift assumes. What is the basis of the Swift stock to Paul? What is the basis of the property to Swift Corporation?

**Issue ID**

37. Three years ago, Chris exchanged an apartment worth $1,500,000 (basis of $300,000), which was subject to a mortgage of $200,000, for land worth $1,150,000, subject to a mortgage of $150,000, and cash of $300,000. In the current year, Chris transfers the land that he received in the exchange to newly formed Amber Corporation for all of the stock in Amber. Amber Corporation assumes the original mortgage on the land, currently in the amount of $100,000, and another mortgage in the amount of $20,000 that Chris later placed on the land to secure his purchase of some equipment that he uses in this business. What are the tax issues?

38. Lori, a sole proprietor, was engaged in a service business and reported her income on the cash basis. On February 1, 2003, she incorporated her business and transferred the assets of the business to the corporation in return for all the stock plus the corporation's assumption of her proprietorship's liabilities. All the receivables and the unpaid trade payables were transferred to the newly formed corporation. The balance sheet of the corporation immediately following its formation was as follows:

### GREEN CORPORATION
### BALANCE SHEET
### FEBRUARY 1, 2003

#### Assets

|  | Basis to Green | Fair Market Value |
|---|---|---|
| Cash | $ 80,000 | $ 80,000 |
| Accounts receivable | –0– | 240,000 |
| Equipment (cost $180,000; depreciation claimed $60,000) | 120,000 | 320,000 |
| Building (straight-line depreciation) | 160,000 | 400,000 |
| Land | 40,000 | 160,000 |
| Total | $400,000 | $1,200,000 |

#### Liabilities and Stockholder's Equity

| Liabilities: |  |
|---|---|
| Accounts payable—trade | $ 120,000 |
| Notes payable—bank | 360,000 |
| Stockholder's equity: |  |
| Common stock | 720,000 |
| Total | $1,200,000 |

Discuss the tax consequences of the incorporation of the business to Lori and to Green Corporation.

39. David organizes White Corporation with a transfer of land (basis of $200,000, fair market value of $600,000) that is subject to a mortgage of $150,000. A month before incorporation, David borrowed $100,000 for personal purposes and gave the bank a lien on the land.

Amt realized 600 000

— AB     200 000

Real gain   400 000

r recog    250 000

    150 000

100% liability gets
tainted if not valid
purpose.

FMV   350 000 | Basis in stock

— post gain <150 000>

    200 000.

Corp bain 450000.

White Corporation issues stock worth $350,000 to David and assumes the mortgage of $150,000 and the personal loan of $100,000. What are the tax consequences of the incorporation to David and to White Corporation?

40. Sara and Jane form Wren Corporation. Sara transfers property, basis of $25,000 and value of $200,000, for 50 shares in Wren Corporation. Jane transfers property, basis of $10,000 and value of $185,000, and agrees to serve as manager of Wren for one year; in return Jane receives 50 shares in Wren. The value of Jane's services to Wren is $15,000.
a. What gain do Sara and Jane recognize on the exchange?
b. What is Wren Corporation's basis in the property transferred by Sara and Jane? How does Wren treat the value of the services Jane renders?

41. Assume in Problem 40 that Jane receives the 50 shares of Wren Corporation stock in consideration for the appreciated property and for providing legal services in organizing the corporation. The value of Jane's services is $15,000.
a. What gain does Jane recognize?
b. What is Wren Corporation's basis in the property transferred by Jane? How does Wren treat the value of the services Jane renders?

42. On January 10, 2003, Carol transferred machinery worth $100,000 (basis of $20,000) to a controlled corporation, Lark, in a transfer that qualified under § 351. Carol had deducted depreciation on the machinery in the amount of $85,000 when she held the machinery for use in her proprietorship. On November 15, 2003, Lark Corporation sells the machinery for $95,000. What are the tax consequences to Carol and to Lark Corporation on the sale of the machinery?

If co does not
spend within 12
months then ↓ basis
in other asset NO income
→ 0 →
gain when sell → 0 —

25000

43. The city of Hampton donates land (worth $100,000) to Rose Corporation as an inducement for Rose to locate there. The city also donates $50,000 in cash to Rose.
a. What income, if any, must Rose recognize as a result of these transfers?
b. What is Rose's basis in the land?
c. If Rose purchases property six months later with the $50,000 of cash, what basis will it have in the property?
d. Assume Rose uses $25,000 of its funds along with the $50,000 provided by the city to purchase property costing $75,000. What basis will it have in the property?

**Communications**

44. Emily Patrick (36 Paradise Road, Northampton, MA 01060) formed Teal Corporation a number of years ago with an investment of $200,000 cash, for which she received $20,000 in stock and $180,000 in bonds bearing interest of 8% and maturing in nine years. Several years later, Emily lent the corporation an additional $50,000 on open account. In the current year, Teal Corporation becomes insolvent and is declared bankrupt. During the corporation's existence, Emily was paid an annual salary of $60,000. Write a letter to Emily in which you explain how she would treat her losses for tax purposes.

**Communications**

45. Stock in Jaybird Corporation (555 Industry Lane, Pueblo, CO 81001) is held equally by Vera, Wade, and Wes. Jaybird seeks additional capital in the amount of $900,000 to construct a building. Vera, Wade, and Wes each propose to lend Jaybird Corporation $300,000, taking from Jaybird a $300,000 four-year note with interest payable annually at two points below the prime rate. Jaybird Corporation has current taxable income of $2 million. You represent Jaybird Corporation. It asks you how the payments on the notes might be treated for tax purposes. Prepare a letter to the president of Jaybird, Steve Ferguson, and a memo to your tax files where you document your conclusions.

46. Sam, a single taxpayer, acquired stock in a corporation that qualified as a small business corporation under § 1244, at a cost of $100,000 three years ago. He sells the stock for $10,000 in the current tax year. How will the loss be treated for tax purposes?

47. Assume that Sam in Problem 46 gave the stock to his sister, Kara, a few months after he acquired it. The stock was worth $100,000 on the date of the gift. Kara sells the stock for $10,000 in the current tax year. How will Kara treat the loss for tax purposes?

*handwritten notes:*
sold for only 20000

20000
< 50000 >
30000 loss

50000 ord
loss

25000
Capital
loss

only 5000 is
related to _____
in nalve so that is
ord loss

Single — Cap — $50000
MFJ — cap 100000
rest becomes cap loss

48. Paul Sanders, a married taxpayer who files a joint return with his wife, acquired stock in a corporation that qualified as a small business corporation under § 1244. The stock cost $30,000 and was acquired three years ago. A few months after he acquired the stock he gave it to his brother, Mike Sanders. The stock was worth $30,000 on the date of the gift. Mike, who is married and files a joint return with his wife, sells the stock for $10,000 in the current tax year. You represent Mike who asks you whether he can take a loss deduction on the sale of the stock. If so, how will the loss be treated for tax purposes? Prepare a letter to your client and a memo to the file. Mike's address is 2600 Riverview Drive, Plank, MO 63701.

49. Susan transfers property with a basis of $50,000 and a fair market value of $25,000 to Thrush Corporation in exchange for shares of § 1244 stock. (Assume the transfer qualifies under § 351.)
    a. What is the basis of the stock to Susan?
    b. What is the basis of the stock to Susan for purposes of § 1244?
    c. If Susan sells the stock for $20,000 two years later, how will the loss be treated for tax purposes?

50. Frank, Cora, and Mitch are equal shareholders in Blue Corporation. The corporation's assets have a tax basis of $50,000 and a fair market value of $600,000. In the current year, Frank and Cora each loan Blue Corporation $150,000. The notes to Frank and Cora bear interest of 8% per annum. Mitch leases equipment to Blue Corporation for an annual rental of $12,000. Discuss whether the shareholder loans from Frank and Cora might be reclassified as equity. Consider in your discussion whether Blue Corporation has an acceptable debt-equity ratio.

## Research Problems

*Note: Solutions to Research Problems can be prepared by using the **RIA Checkpoint® Student Edition** online research product, or the **CCH U.S. Master Tax Guide Plus™** online Federal tax research database, which is available to accompany this text. It is also possible to prepare solutions to the Research Problems by using tax research materials found in a standard tax library.*

**Research Problem 1.** Skeeter has owned and operated an accrual basis golf driving range for a number of years. The sole proprietorship has been successful and has grown to the point where it now also offers golf lessons and sponsors tournaments and other activities. Skeeter has been advised that incorporating his proprietorship would give him an opportunity to restructure the business debt and to acquire additional working capital at more favorable rates.

Based on this advice, Skeeter transfers the business assets (fair market value $1 million, adjusted basis $200,000) along with the associated debt ($325,000) to the newly formed corporation. As far as he is concerned, nothing has really changed in his relationship with the creditor bank; he still feels personally obligated to pay off the debt. In fact, before the debt is assigned to the newly formed corporation, the bank insists that Skeeter remain secondarily responsible for its payment. Even though the proprietorship's liabilities transferred exceed the basis of the assets transferred, Skeeter regards the transaction as tax-free because:

• nothing has changed with his business other than its form of operation,

• a business justification exists for changing its form to that of a corporation, and

• he has enjoyed no personal gain from the transaction.

Determine if Skeeter's belief is justified. If you believe that the transaction as currently planned would be taxable, identify strategies that could be employed to eliminate or minimize any recognition of gain.

*Partial list of research aids:*
§ 357(c).

**Research Problem 2.** Lynn Jones, Shawn, Walt, and Donna are trying to decide whether they should organize a corporation and transfer their shares of stock in several corporations to this new corporation. All their shares are listed on the New York Stock Exchange and are readily marketable. Lynn would transfer shares in Brown Corporation; Shawn would transfer stock in Rust Corporation; Walt would transfer stock in White Corporation; and Donna would transfer stock in several corporations. The stock would be held by the newly formed corporation for investment purposes. Lynn asks you, her tax adviser, if she would have gain on the transfer of her substantially appreciated shares in Brown Corporation if she transfers the shares to a newly formed corporation. She also asks whether there will be tax consequences if she, Shawn, Walt, and Donna form a partnership, rather than a corporation, to which they would transfer their readily marketable stock. Your input will be critical as they make their decision. Prepare a memo to the client, Lynn Jones, and a memo for the firm's files. Lynn's address is 1540 Maxwell Avenue, Highland, KY 41099.

**Research Problem 3.** A cash basis partnership is incorporated. The newly formed corporation elects the cash method of accounting. The partnership transfers $30,000 of accounts receivable along with equipment, land, and cash to the corporation. The corporation also agrees to pay accounts payable of the partnership in the amount of $40,000. When the corporation files its tax return for its first year of operation, it does not report the $30,000 received on the partnership's accounts receivable as income. It does deduct the $40,000 it paid on the partnership's accounts payable. The IRS disallows the deductions totaling $40,000 and increases the corporation's taxable income by $30,000, which represents the collection of the partnership's accounts receivable. What is the result?

**Research Problem 4.** Your client, Gail Smithson, owns 100% of the stock of the following four corporations:

- Smithson Management Company (SMC), which provides consulting services to a number of convenience stores in the region.

- Inventory Suppliers, Inc. (ISI), a wholesaling operation that provides inventory to many of the convenience stores that SMC services.

- Gas Operations Corporation (GOC), which offers gasoline and gasoline storage tanks to the convenience stores for their gasoline sales operations.

- Smithson Administrative Services (SAS), which provides administrative support services to SMC, ISI, and GOC.

Over several years, SMC has lent over $2 million to the other related entities on open account to help them meet working capital requirements. The interest due on the loans has been paid sporadically by ISI, GOC, and SAS. In the absence of an actual payment when due, an interest expense was accrued, and this increased the outstanding loan balance. When any payments were received, SMC recognized interest income (to the extent that the payments did not constitute repayments of principal).

More recently, and because of competitive pressures and consolidation in the convenience store industry, many of Smithson's clients have either gone out of business or have been purchased by large national firms. These changes have had a drastic effect on Smithson's operations and have forced her to suspend the businesses conducted by ISI, GOC, and SAS. Of the amounts lent to these entities by SMC, $1.5 million remains unpaid. Also, it has become clear that the amount will never be paid. Therefore, SMC has claimed a business bad debt deduction of $1.5 million.

During the course of a tax audit of SMC, the IRS disallows the deduction. It contends that the unpaid $1.5 million should instead be treated as a long-term capital loss. This conclusion is based on the notion that the amounts transferred by SMC were actually equity contributions rather than loans.

How do you advise Gail Smithson in her dealings with the IRS?

**Internet Activity**

*Use the tax resources of the Internet to address the following questions. Do not restrict your search to the World Wide Web, but include a review of newsgroups and general reference materials, practitioner sites and resources, primary sources of the tax law, chat rooms and discussion groups, and other opportunities.*

**Research Problem 5.**   Do the provisions of § 1202 relating to qualified small business stock seem to have become popular since they became effective in 1993? What leads you to your conclusion?

**Research Problem 6.**   Limited liability company (LLC) status has become a very popular form of operating a business over the past several years. Investigate how the growth of LLC status has affected the relative number of new businesses that have chosen to operate as a corporation.

**Research Problem 7.**    Identify two publicly traded corporations that have issued more than one class of stock to their shareholders. Determine the rationale for their actions.

# Corporations: Earnings & Profits and Dividend Distributions

## LEARNING OBJECTIVES

*After completing Chapter 4, you should be able to:*

### L O . 1
Understand the role that earnings and profits play in determining the tax treatment of distributions.

### L O . 2
Compute a corporation's earnings and profits.

### L O . 3
Apply the rules for allocating earnings and profits to distributions.

### L O . 4
Understand the tax impact of property dividends on the recipient shareholder and the corporation making the distribution.

### L O . 5
Understand the nature and treatment of constructive dividends.

### L O . 6
Distinguish between taxable and nontaxable stock dividends and stock rights.

http://wft.swlearning.com

## OUTLINE

Chapter 3 examined the tax consequences of corporate formation. In this chapter and Chapter 5, the focus shifts to the tax treatment of corporate distributions, a topic that plays a leading role in tax planning. The importance of corporate distributions derives from the variety of tax treatments that may apply. From the shareholder's perspective, distributions received from the corporation may be treated as ordinary income, capital gain, or a nontaxable recovery of capital. From the corporation's perspective, distributions made to shareholders are generally not deductible. However, a corporation may recognize losses in liquidating distributions (see Chapter 5), and gains may be recognized at the corporate level on distributions of appreciated property. In the most common scenario, a distribution triggers ordinary income to the shareholder and provides no deduction to the paying corporation, resulting in a double tax (at both the corporate and the shareholder level). This double tax may be mitigated by a variety of factors including the corporate dividends received deduction.

As will become apparent in the subsequent discussion, the tax treatment of corporate distributions can be affected by a number of considerations, including:

- The availability of earnings to be distributed.
- The basis of the stock in the hands of the shareholder.
- The character of the property being distributed.
- Whether the shareholder gives up ownership in return for the distribution.
- Whether the distribution is liquidating or nonliquidating.

This chapter discusses the tax rules related to nonliquidating distributions (in the form of cash and property). Distributions of stock and stock rights are also addressed. Chapter 5 extends the discussion by addressing the tax treatment of stock redemptions and corporate liquidations.

## LO.1

Understand the role that earnings and profits play in determining the tax treatment of distributions.

## Taxable Dividends—In General

To the extent that a distribution is made from corporate earnings and profits (E & P), the shareholder is deemed to receive a dividend, taxed as ordinary income.[1] Generally, corporate distributions are presumed to be paid out of E & P (defined

---

[1]§§ 301(c)(1) and 316.

later in this chapter) and are treated as dividends, *unless* the parties to the transaction can show otherwise. Distributions that are not treated as dividends (because of insufficient E & P) are nontaxable to the extent of the shareholder's basis in the stock. The stock basis is reduced accordingly. The excess of the distribution over the shareholder's basis is treated as a capital gain if the stock is a capital asset.[2]

**EXAMPLE 1**

At the beginning of the year, Amber Corporation (a calendar year taxpayer) has E & P of $15,000. The corporation generates no additional E & P during the year. On July 1, the corporation distributes $20,000 to its sole shareholder, Bonnie. Assume Bonnie's stock basis is $4,000. In this situation, Bonnie recognizes dividend income of $15,000 (the amount of E & P distributed). In addition, she reduces her stock basis from $4,000 to zero, and she recognizes a capital gain of $1,000 (the excess of the distribution over the stock basis). ■

**LO.2**

Compute a corporation's earnings and profits.

# Earnings and Profits (E & P)—§ 312

The notion of **earnings and profits** is similar in many respects to the accounting concept of retained earnings. Both are measures of the firm's capital accumulation (E & P includes both the accumulated E & P of the corporation since February 28, 1913, and the current year's E & P). However, while these two concepts are similar, they differ in one fundamental way. The computation of retained earnings is based on financial accounting rules while E & P is determined using rules specified in the tax law.

E & P fixes the upper limit on the amount of dividend income that shareholders must recognize as a result of a distribution by the corporation. In this sense, E & P represents the corporation's economic ability to pay a dividend without impairing its capital. Thus, the effect of a specific transaction on the E & P account often can be determined by considering whether the transaction increases or decreases the corporation's capacity to pay a dividend.

## COMPUTATION OF E & P

The Code does not explicitly define the term *earnings and profits*. Instead, a series of adjustments to taxable income are identified to provide a measure of the corporation's economic income. Both cash basis and accrual basis corporations use the same approach when determining E & P.[3]

**Additions to Taxable Income.**  It is necessary to add all previously excluded income items back to taxable income to determine current E & P. Included among these positive adjustments are interest on municipal bonds, excluded life insurance proceeds (in excess of cash surrender value), Federal income tax refunds from tax paid in prior years, and the dividends received deduction.

**EXAMPLE 2**

A corporation collects $100,000 on a key employee life insurance policy (the corporation is the owner and beneficiary of the policy). At the time the policy matured on the death of the insured employee, it possessed a cash surrender value of $30,000. None of the $100,000 is included in the corporation's taxable income, but $70,000 is added to taxable income when computing current E & P. ■

---

[2]§§ 301(c)(2) and (3).
[3]Section 312 describes most of the adjustments to taxable income necessary to determine E & P. Regulations relating to E & P begin at Reg. § 1.312–6.

**Subtractions from Taxable Income.**    Some of the corporation's nondeductible expenditures are subtracted from taxable income to arrive at E & P. These negative adjustments include related-party losses, excess capital losses, expenses incurred to produce tax-exempt income, Federal income taxes paid, nondeductible key employee life insurance premiums (net of increases in cash surrender value), and nondeductible fines and penalties.

**EXAMPLE 3**

A corporation sells property (basis of $10,000) to its sole shareholder for $8,000. Because of § 267 (disallowance of losses on sales between related parties), the $2,000 loss cannot be deducted in arriving at the corporation's taxable income. But since the overall economic effect of the transaction is a decrease in the corporation's assets by $2,000, the loss reduces the current E & P for the year of sale. ■

**EXAMPLE 4**

A corporation pays a $10,000 premium on a key employee life insurance policy covering the life of its president. As a result of the payment, the cash surrender value of the policy is increased by $7,000. Although none of the $10,000 premium is deductible for tax purposes, current E & P is reduced by $3,000. ■

**Timing Adjustments.**    Some E & P adjustments shift the effect of a transaction from the year of its inclusion in taxable income to the year in which it has an economic effect on the corporation. Charitable contribution carryovers, net operating loss carryovers, and capital loss carryovers all give rise to this kind of adjustment.

**EXAMPLE 5**

During 2003, a corporation makes charitable contributions, $12,000 of which cannot be deducted in arriving at the taxable income for the year because of the 10% taxable income limitation. Consequently, the $12,000 is carried forward to 2004 and fully deducted in that year. The excess charitable contribution reduces the corporation's current E & P for 2003 by $12,000 and increases its current E & P for 2004, when the deduction is allowed, by a like amount. The increase in E & P in 2004 is necessary because the charitable contribution carryover reduces the taxable income for that year (the starting point for computing E & P) and already has been taken into account in determining the E & P for 2003. ■

Gains and losses from property transactions generally affect the determination of E & P only to the extent that they are recognized for tax purposes. Thus, gains and losses deferred under the like-kind exchange provision and deferred involuntary conversion gains do not affect E & P until recognized. Accordingly, no adjustment is required for these items.

**Accounting Method Adjustments.**    In addition to the above adjustments, accounting methods used for determining E & P are generally more conservative than those allowed under the income tax. For example, the installment method is not permitted for E & P purposes. Thus, an adjustment is required for the deferred gain attributable to sales of property made during the year under the installment method. All principal payments are treated as having been received in the year of sale.[4]

**EXAMPLE 6**

In 2003, Cardinal Corporation, a calendar year taxpayer, sells unimproved real estate (basis of $20,000) for $100,000. Under the terms of the sale, beginning in 2004, Cardinal will receive two annual payments of $50,000 each with interest of 9%. Cardinal Corporation

---

[4]§ 312(n)(5).

does not elect out of the installment method. Since Cardinal's taxable income for 2003 will not reflect any of the gain from the sale, the corporation must make an $80,000 positive adjustment for 2003 (the deferred gain from the sale). Similarly, negative adjustments will be required in 2004 and 2005 (when the deferred gain is recognized under the installment method). ■

The alternative depreciation system (ADS) must be used for purposes of computing E & P.[5] This method requires straight-line depreciation over a recovery period equal to the Asset Depreciation Range (ADR) midpoint life.[6] Also, no 30 percent additional first-year depreciation is allowed under ADS.[7] If MACRS cost recovery is used for income tax purposes, a positive or negative adjustment equal to the difference between MACRS and ADS must be made each year. Likewise, when assets are disposed of, an additional adjustment to taxable income is required to allow for the difference in gain or loss resulting from the difference in income tax basis and E & P basis.[8] The adjustments arising from depreciation are illustrated in the following example.

**EXAMPLE 7**

On January 2, 2001, White Corporation paid $30,000 to purchase equipment with an ADR midpoint life of 10 years and a MACRS class life of 7 years. The equipment was depreciated under MACRS. The asset was sold on July 2, 2003, for $27,000. For purposes of determining taxable income and E & P, cost recovery claimed on the equipment is summarized below.

| Year | Cost Recovery Computation | MACRS | ADS | Adjustment Amount |
|------|---------------------------|-------|-----|-------------------|
| 2001 | $30,000 × 14.29% | $ 4,287 | | |
| | $30,000 ÷ 10-year ADR recovery period × ½ (half-year for first year of service) | | $1,500 | $2,787 |
| 2002 | $30,000 × 24.49% | 7,347 | | |
| | $30,000 ÷ 10-year ADR recovery period | | 3,000 | 4,347 |
| 2003 | $30,000 × 17.49% × ½ (half-year for year of disposal) | 2,624 | | |
| | $30,000 ÷ 10-year ADR recovery period × ½ (half-year for year of disposal) | | 1,500 | 1,124 |
| Total cost recovery | | $14,258 | $6,000 | $8,258 |

Each year White Corporation will increase taxable income by the adjustment amount indicated above to determine E & P. In addition, when computing E & P for 2003, White will reduce taxable income by $8,258 to account for the excess gain recognized for income tax purposes, as shown below.

---

[5]§ 312(k)(3)(A).
[6]See § 168(g)(2). The ADR midpoint life for most assets is set out in Rev.Proc. 87–56, 1987–2 C.B. 674. The recovery period is 5 years for automobiles and light-duty trucks and 40 years for real property. For assets with no class life, the recovery period is 12 years.

[7]§ 168(k)(2)(C).
[8]§ 312(f)(1).

|  | Income Tax | E & P |
|---|---|---|
| Amount realized | $ 27,000 | $ 27,000 |
| Adjusted basis for income tax ($30,000 cost − $14,258 MACRS) | (15,742) | |
| Adjusted basis for E & P ($30,000 cost − $6,000 ADS) | | (24,000) |
| Gain on sale | $ 11,258 | $ 3,000 |
| Adjustment amount ($3,000 − $11,258) | ($ 8,258) | |

In addition to more conservative depreciation methods, the E & P rules impose limitations on the deductibility of § 179 expense. In particular, this expense must be deducted over a period of five years for E & P purposes.[9] Thus, in any year that § 179 is elected, 80 percent of the resulting expense must be added back to taxable income to determine current E & P. In each of the following four years, a negative adjustment equal to 20 percent of the § 179 expense must be made.

A variety of other accounting method adjustments are also required to determine current E & P. For example, cost depletion is required for E & P purposes, so an adjustment must be made to taxable income in cases where percentage depletion is used. Similarly, the percentage of completion method is required for E & P purposes when accounting for long-term contracts, so an adjustment is required when the completed contract method is employed.[10] Intangible drilling costs and mine exploration and development costs may be deducted currently for income tax purposes, but must be capitalized for E & P. Once capitalized, these expenditures can be amortized under the E & P rules over 60 months for intangible drilling costs and over 120 months for mine exploration and development costs.[11]

## SUMMARY OF E & P ADJUSTMENTS

E & P serves as a measure of the earnings of the corporation that are available for distribution as taxable dividends to the shareholders. Current E & P is determined by making a series of adjustments to the corporation's taxable income. These adjustments are reviewed in Concept Summary 4–1. Other items that affect E & P, such as property dividends, are covered later in the chapter and are not incorporated in the concept summary. The effect of stock redemptions on E & P is covered in Chapter 5.

## CURRENT VERSUS ACCUMULATED E & P

Accumulated E & P is the total of all previous years' current E & P (since February 28, 1913) as computed on the first day of each tax year, reduced by distributions made from E & P. It is important to distinguish between **current E & P** and **accumulated E & P**, since the taxability of corporate distributions depends on how these two accounts are allocated to each distribution made during the year. A complex set of rules governs the allocation process.[12] These rules are described in the following section and summarized in Concept Summary 4–2.

---

[9]§ 312(k)(3)(B).
[10]§ 312(n)(6).
[11]§ 312(n)(2).

[12]Regulations relating to the source of a distribution are at Reg. § 1.316–2.

## CONCEPT SUMMARY 4–1

### E & P Adjustments

| Nature of the Transaction | Adjustment to Taxable Income to Determine Current E & P | |
|---|---|---|
| | Addition | Subtraction |
| Tax-exempt income *↑ ability to pay dividend* | X | |
| Dividends received deduction | X | |
| Collection of proceeds from insurance policy on life of corporate officer (in excess of cash surrender value) | X | |
| Deferred gain on installment sale (all gain is added to E & P in year of sale) | X | |
| Future recognition of installment sale gross profit | | X |
| Excess capital loss and excess charitable contribution (over 10% limitation) in year incurred | | X |
| Deduction of charitable contribution, NOL, or capital loss carryovers in succeeding taxable year (increase E & P because deduction reduces taxable income while E & P was reduced in a prior year) | X | |
| Federal income taxes paid *↓ ability to pay div.* | | X |
| Federal income tax refund | X | |
| Loss on sale between related parties | | X |
| Nondeductible fines and penalties | | X |
| Payment of premiums on insurance policy on life of corporate officer (in excess of increase in cash surrender value of policy) | | X |
| Realized gain (not recognized) on an involuntary conversion | No effect | |
| Realized gain or loss (not recognized) on a like-kind exchange | No effect | |
| Percentage depletion (only cost depletion can reduce E & P) | X | |
| Accelerated depreciation (E & P is reduced only by straight-line, units-of-production, or machine hours depreciation) | X | X |
| Additional 30% first-year depreciation | X | |
| Section 179 expense in year elected (80%) | X | |
| Section 179 expense in four years following election (20% each year) | | X |
| Intangible drilling costs deducted currently (reduce E & P in future years by amortizing costs over 60 months) | X | |
| Mine exploration and development costs (reduce E & P in future years by amortizing costs over 120 months) | X | |

**LO.3**

Apply the rules for allocating earnings and profits to distributions.

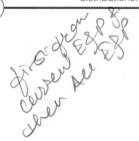

### ALLOCATING E & P TO DISTRIBUTIONS

When a positive balance exists in both the current and the accumulated E & P accounts, corporate distributions are deemed to be made first from current E & P and then from accumulated E & P. When distributions exceed the amount of current E & P, it becomes necessary to allocate current and accumulated E & P to each distribution made during the year. Current E & P is allocated on a pro rata basis to each distribution made during the year. Accumulated E & P is applied in chronological order, beginning with the earliest distribution. As can be seen in the following example, this allocation is important if any shareholder sells stock during the year.

## CONCEPT SUMMARY 4-2

### Allocating E & P to Distributions

1. Current E & P is allocated first to distributions on a pro rata basis; then, accumulated E & P is applied (to the extent necessary) in chronological order beginning with the earliest distribution. See Example 8.
2. Unless and until the parties can show otherwise, it is presumed that current E & P covers all distributions. See Example 9.
3. When a deficit exists in accumulated E & P and a positive balance exists in current E & P, distributions are regarded as dividends to the extent of current E & P. See Example 10.
4. When a deficit exists in current E & P and a positive balance exists in accumulated E & P, the two accounts are netted at the date of distribution. If the resulting balance is zero or a deficit, the distribution is treated as a return of capital, first reducing the basis of the stock to zero, then generating capital gain. If a positive balance results, the distribution is a dividend to the extent of the balance. Any loss in current E & P is allocated ratably during the year unless the parties can show otherwise. See Example 11.

**EXAMPLE 8**

As of January 1 of the current year, Black Corporation has accumulated E & P of $10,000. Current E & P for the year amounts to $30,000. Megan and Matt are sole *equal* shareholders of Black from January 1 to July 31. On August 1, Megan sells all of her stock to Helen. Black makes two distributions to shareholders during the year: $40,000 to Megan and Matt ($20,000 to each) on July 1, and $40,000 to Matt and Helen ($20,000 to each) on December 1. Current and accumulated E & P are allocated to the two distributions as follows:

|  | Source of Distribution | | |
|---|---|---|---|
|  | **Current E & P** | **Accumulated E & P** | **Return of Capital** |
| July 1 distribution ($40,000) | $15,000 | $10,000 | $15,000 |
| December 1 distribution ($40,000) | 15,000 | — | 25,000 |

Thus, since 50% of the total distributions are made on July 1 and December 1, respectively, one-half of current E & P is allocated to each of the two distributions. Accumulated E & P is applied in chronological order, so the entire amount is attributed to the July 1 distribution. The tax consequences to the shareholders are presented below.

|  | Shareholder | | |
|---|---|---|---|
|  | **Megan** | **Matt** | **Helen** |
| July distribution ($40,000) | | | |
| Dividend income— | | | |
| From current E & P ($15,000) | $ 7,500 | $ 7,500 | $ –0– |
| From accumulated E & P ($10,000) | 5,000 | 5,000 | –0– |
| Return of capital ($15,000) | 7,500 | 7,500 | –0– |
| December distribution ($40,000) | | | |
| Dividend income— | | | |
| From current E & P ($15,000) | –0– | 7,500 | 7,500 |
| From accumulated E & P ($0) | –0– | –0– | –0– |
| Return of capital ($25,000) | –0– | 12,500 | 12,500 |
| Total dividend income | $12,500 | $20,000 | $ 7,500 |
| Nontaxable return of capital (presuming sufficient basis in the stock investment) | $ 7,500 | $20,000 | $12,500 |

*(handwritten in margin:)*
Dism    E&P    Return of Cap
40000 - 25000 = 15000
40000 - 15000 = 25000

Because the balance in the accumulated E & P account is exhausted when it is applied to the July 1 distribution, Megan has more dividend income than Helen, even though both receive equal distributions during the year. In addition, each shareholder's basis is reduced by the nontaxable return of capital; any excess over basis results in capital gain. ■

When the tax years of the corporation and its shareholders are not the same, it may be impossible to determine the amount of current E & P on a timely basis. For example, if shareholders use a calendar year and the corporation uses a fiscal year, then current E & P may not be ascertainable until after the shareholders' returns have been filed. To address this timing problem, the allocation rules presume that current E & P is sufficient to cover every distribution made during the year unless or until the parties can show otherwise.

**EXAMPLE 9**

Green Corporation uses the fiscal year of July 1 through June 30 for tax purposes. Carol, Green's only shareholder, uses a calendar year. As of July 1, 2003, Green Corporation has a zero balance in its accumulated E & P account. For fiscal year 2003–2004, the corporation suffers a $5,000 deficit in current E & P. On August 1, 2003, Green distributed $10,000 to Carol. The distribution is dividend income to Carol and is reported when she files her income tax return for the 2003 calendar year, on or before April 15, 2004. Because Carol cannot prove until June 30, 2004, that the corporation has a deficit for the 2003–2004 fiscal year, she must assume the $10,000 distribution is fully covered by current E & P. When Carol learns of the deficit, she can file an amended return for 2003 showing the $10,000 as a return of capital. ■

Additional difficulties arise when either the current or the accumulated E & P account has a deficit balance. In particular, when current E & P is positive and accumulated E & P has a deficit balance, accumulated E & P is *not* netted against current E & P. Instead, the distribution is deemed to be a taxable dividend to the extent of the positive current E & P balance.

**EXAMPLE 10**

At the beginning of the current year, Brown Corporation has a deficit of $30,000 in accumulated E & P. For the year, it has current E & P of $10,000 and distributes $5,000 to its shareholders. The $5,000 distribution is treated as a taxable dividend since it is deemed to have been made from current E & P. This is the case even though Brown Corporation still has a deficit in accumulated E & P at the end of the year. ■

---

**ETHICAL CONSIDERATIONS** | **Shifting E & P**

Ten years ago, Joe began a new business venture with his best friend and college roommate, Frankie. Joe owns 60 percent of the outstanding stock, and Frankie owns 40 percent. The business has had some difficult times, but things are starting to look up.

Yesterday, on December 1, Frankie told Joe that he wants a change of career and is planning to sell all of his stock to Joe's sister, Cindy, at the beginning of the following year. He would sell immediately, but he wants to wait until after the company pays out the current-year shareholder distribution (which is expected to be about $100,000). Cindy has been

a long-time employee of the business and has often expressed an interest in becoming more involved. Joe is looking forward to working with his sister, but he now faces a terrible dilemma.

The corporation has a $350,000 deficit in accumulated E & P and only a small amount of current E & P to date (about $20,000). Within the next six weeks, however, Joe expects to sign a major deal with a very large client. If Joe signs the contract this month, the corporation will experience a $300,000 increase in current E & P for the year, causing the forthcoming dividend to be fully taxable to Frankie. As a result, most of next year's distribution would be treated as a tax-free return of capital for Cindy. Alternatively, if Joe waits until January, both he and Frankie will receive a nontaxable distribution this year, but next year's annual distribution will be taxable as a dividend to his sister. What should Joe do?

---

In contrast to the above rule, when a deficit exists in current E & P and a positive balance exists in accumulated E & P, the accounts are netted at the date of distribution. If the resulting balance is zero or negative, the distribution is a return of capital. If a positive balance results, the distribution is a dividend to the extent of the balance. Any current E & P is allocated ratably during the year unless the parties can show otherwise.

**EXAMPLE 11**

At the beginning of the current year, Gray Corporation (a calendar year taxpayer) has accumulated E & P of $10,000. During the year, the corporation incurs a $15,000 deficit in current E & P that accrues ratably. On July 1, Gray Corporation distributes $6,000 in cash to Hal, its sole shareholder. To determine how much of the $6,000 cash distribution represents dividend income to Hal, the balances of both accumulated and current E & P as of July 1 are determined and netted. This is necessary because of the deficit in current E & P.

|  | Source of Distribution | |
|---|---|---|
|  | Current E & P | Accumulated E & P |
| January 1 |  | $10,000 |
| July 1 (½ of $15,000 net loss) | ($7,500) | 2,500 |
| July 1 distribution—($6,000): |  |  |
| Dividend income: ($2,500) |  |  |
| Return of capital: ($3,500) |  |  |

The balance in E & P on July 1 is $2,500. Thus, of the $6,000 distribution, $2,500 is taxed as a dividend, and $3,500 represents a return of capital. ■

**LO.4**

Understand the tax impact of property dividends on the recipient shareholder and the corporation making the distribution.

# Property Dividends—In General

The previous discussion assumed that all distributions by a corporation to its shareholders are in the form of cash. Although most corporate distributions are cash, a corporation may distribute a **property dividend** for various reasons. The shareholders could want a particular property that is held by the corporation. Or a corporation that is strapped for cash may want to distribute a dividend to its shareholders.

Property distributions have the same impact as distributions of cash except for effects attributable to any difference between the basis and the fair market value of the distributed property. In most situations, distributed property is appreciated, so its sale would result in a gain to the corporation. Distributions of property with a basis that differs from fair market value raise several tax questions.

- For the shareholder:
  - What is the amount of the distribution?
  - What is the basis of the property in the shareholder's hands?

*Property dividend*

*FMV of property*

For the corporation:

- Is a gain or loss recognized as a result of the distribution?
- What is the effect of the distribution on E & P?

## PROPERTY DIVIDENDS—EFFECT ON THE SHAREHOLDER

When a corporation distributes property rather than cash to a shareholder, the amount distributed is measured by the fair market value of the property on the date of distribution.[13] As with a cash distribution, the portion of a property distribution covered by existing E & P is a dividend, and any excess is treated as a return of capital. If the fair market value of the property distributed exceeds the corporation's E & P and the shareholder's basis in the stock investment, a capital gain usually results.

The amount distributed is reduced by any liabilities to which the distributed property is subject immediately before and immediately after the distribution and by any liabilities of the corporation assumed by the shareholder. The basis in the distributed property to the shareholder is the fair market value of the property on the date of the distribution.

**EXAMPLE 12**

*Basis is FMV taxable Div is (FMV − liability)*

Robin Corporation has E & P of $60,000. It distributes land with a fair market value of $50,000 (adjusted basis of $30,000) to its sole shareholder, Charles. The land is subject to a liability of $10,000, which Charles assumes. Charles has a taxable dividend of $40,000 [$50,000 (fair market value) − $10,000 (liability)]. The basis of the land to Charles is $50,000. ■

**EXAMPLE 13**

*FMV becomes basis FMV = Taxable dividend*

Red Corporation owns 10% of Tan Corporation. Tan has ample E & P to cover any distributions made during the year. One distribution made to Red Corporation consists of a vacant lot with adjusted basis of $5,000 and a fair market value of $3,000. Red has a taxable dividend of $3,000, and its basis in the lot becomes $3,000. ■

Distributing property that has depreciated in value as a property dividend may reflect poor planning. Note what happens in Example 13. Basis of $2,000 disappears due to the loss (adjusted basis $5,000, fair market value $3,000). As an alternative, if Tan Corporation sells the lot, it could use the loss to reduce its taxes. Then Tan could distribute the $3,000 of proceeds to shareholders.

## PROPERTY DIVIDENDS—EFFECT ON THE CORPORATION

All distributions of appreciated property generate gain to the distributing corporation.[14] In effect, a corporation that distributes gain property is treated as if it had sold the property to the shareholder for its fair market value. However, the distributing corporation does *not* recognize loss on distributions of property.

**EXAMPLE 14**

*Recognize gain on appreciated property*

A corporation distributes land (basis of $10,000 and fair market value of $30,000) to a shareholder. The corporation recognizes a gain of $20,000. ■

**EXAMPLE 15**

*does not recognize loss on depreciated property*

Assume the property in Example 14 has a basis of $30,000 and a fair market value of $10,000. The corporation does not recognize a loss on the distribution. ■

If the distributed property is subject to a liability in excess of basis or the shareholder assumes such a liability, a special rule applies. The fair market value

[13]Section 301 describes the tax treatment of corporate distributions to shareholders.

[14]Section 311 describes how corporations are taxed on distributions.

of the property for purposes of determining gain on the distribution is treated as not being less than the amount of the liability.[15]

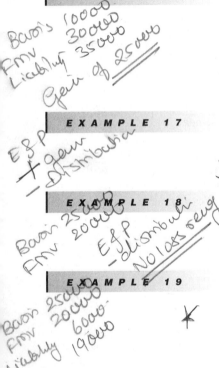

**EXAMPLE 16**

Assume the land in Example 14 is subject to a liability of $35,000. The corporation recognizes gain of $25,000 on the distribution. ■

Corporate distributions reduce E & P by the amount of money distributed or by the greater of the fair market value or the adjusted basis of property distributed, less the amount of any liability on the property.[16] E & P is increased by gain recognized on appreciated property distributed as a property dividend.

**EXAMPLE 17**

Crimson Corporation distributes property (basis of $10,000 and fair market value of $20,000) to Brenda, its shareholder. Crimson Corporation recognizes a gain of $10,000. Crimson's E & P is increased by the $10,000 gain and decreased by the $20,000 fair market value of the distribution. Brenda has dividend income of $20,000 (presuming sufficient E & P). ■

**EXAMPLE 18**

Assume the same facts as in Example 17, except that the adjusted basis of the property in the hands of Crimson Corporation is $25,000. Because loss is not recognized and the adjusted basis is greater than fair market value, E & P is reduced by $25,000. Brenda reports dividend income of $20,000. ■

**EXAMPLE 19**

Assume the same facts as in Example 18, except that the property is subject to a liability of $6,000. E & P is now reduced by $19,000 [$25,000 (adjusted basis) – $6,000 (liability)]. Brenda has a dividend of $14,000 [$20,000 (amount of the distribution) – $6,000 (liability)], and her basis in the property is $20,000. ■

Under no circumstances can a distribution, whether cash or property, either generate a deficit in E & P or add to a deficit in E & P. Deficits can arise only through corporate losses.

**EXAMPLE 20**

Teal Corporation has accumulated E & P of $10,000 at the beginning of the current tax year. During the year, it has current E & P of $15,000. At the end of the year, it distributes cash of $30,000 to its sole shareholder, Walter. Teal's E & P at the end of the year is zero. The accumulated E & P of $10,000 is increased by current E & P of $15,000 and reduced $25,000 by the dividend distribution. The remaining $5,000 of the distribution to Walter does not reduce E & P because a distribution cannot generate a deficit in E & P. ■

**LO.5**

Understand the nature and treatment of constructive dividends.

# Constructive Dividends

Any measurable economic benefit conveyed by a corporation to its shareholders can be treated as a dividend for Federal income tax purposes even though it is not formally declared or designated as a dividend. Also, it need not be issued pro rata to all shareholders.[17] Nor must the distribution satisfy the legal requirements of a dividend as set forth by applicable state law. This benefit, often described as a **constructive dividend,** is distinguishable from actual corporate distributions of cash and property in form only.

---

[15]§ 311(b)(2).
[16]§§ 312(a), (b), and (c).

[17]See *Lengsfield v. Comm.*, 57–1 USTC ¶9437, 50 AFTR 1683, 241 F.2d 508 (CA–5, 1957).

Constructive dividend situations usually arise in closely held corporations. Here, the dealings between the parties are less structured, and frequently, formalities are not preserved. The constructive dividend serves as a substitute for actual distributions. Usually, it is intended to accomplish some tax objective not available through the use of direct dividends. The shareholders may be attempting to distribute corporate profits in a form deductible to the corporation.[18] Alternatively, the shareholders may be seeking benefits for themselves while avoiding the recognition of income. Some constructive dividends are, in reality, disguised dividends. But not all constructive dividends are deliberate attempts to avoid actual and formal dividends; many are inadvertent. Thus, an awareness of the various constructive dividend situations is essential to protect the parties from unanticipated, undesirable tax consequences.

## TYPES OF CONSTRUCTIVE DIVIDENDS

The most frequently encountered types of constructive dividends are summarized below.

**Shareholder Use of Corporate-Owned Property.** A constructive dividend can occur when a shareholder uses corporation property for personal purposes at no cost. Personal use of corporate-owned automobiles, airplanes, yachts, fishing camps, hunting lodges, and other entertainment facilities is commonplace in some closely held corporations. The shareholder has dividend income to the extent of the fair rental value of the property for the period of its personal use.

**Bargain Sale of Corporate Property to a Shareholder.** Shareholders often purchase property from a corporation at a cost below the fair market value of the property. These bargain sales produce dividend income to the extent that the property's fair market value on the date of sale differs from the amount the shareholder paid for the property.[19] These situations might be avoided by appraising the property on or about the date of the sale. The appraised value should become the price to be paid by the shareholder.

**Bargain Rental of Corporate Property.** A bargain rental of corporate property by a shareholder also produces dividend income. Here the measure of the constructive dividend is the excess of the property's fair rental value over the rent actually paid. Again, appraisal data should be used to avoid any questionable situations.

**Payments for the Benefit of a Shareholder.** If a corporation pays an obligation of a shareholder, the payment is treated as a constructive dividend. The obligation involved need not be legally binding on the shareholder; it may, in fact, be a moral obligation.[20] Forgiveness of shareholder indebtedness by the corporation creates an identical problem.[21] Excessive rentals paid by a corporation for the use of shareholder property also are treated as constructive dividends.

**Unreasonable Compensation.** A salary payment to a shareholder-employee that is deemed to be **unreasonable compensation** is frequently treated as a constructive dividend. As a consequence, it is not deductible by the corporation. In determining the reasonableness of salary payments, the following factors are considered:

---

[18]Recall that dividend distributions do not provide the distributing corporation with an income tax deduction, although they do reduce E & P.

[19]Reg. § 1.301–1(j).

[20]*Montgomery Engineering Co. v. U.S.*, 64–2 USTC ¶9618, 13 AFTR2d 1747, 230 F.Supp. 838 (D.Ct. N.J., 1964), *aff'd* in 65–1 USTC ¶9368, 15 AFTR2d 746, 344 F.2d 996 (CA–3, 1965).

[21]Reg. § 1.301–1(m).

# TAX IN THE NEWS

## THE $6,000 SHOWER CURTAIN: COMPENSATION OR CONSTRUCTIVE DIVIDEND?

Recently, there have been several well-publicized accounts of compensation abuse (to some) and illegal looting of corporate coffers (to others) by corporate executives. At the forefront of these scandals are the payments to L. Dennis Kozlowski by Tyco International (a large multinational conglomerate) and to members of the Rigas family by Adelphia Communications Corporation (a cable television company founded by the family).

Kozlowski, during a four-year stint as CEO of Tyco, received about $400 million from the company in salary and stock-related compensation. In addition, Kozlowski received fringe benefits valued at $135 million. Most of the benefits were authorized by the Tyco board and included:

- A new 15,000-square-foot home in Boca Raton, Florida, complete with pool, tennis court, and fountain. Tyco initially loaned the money interest-free to Kozlowski and then later forgave the entire loan. It paid him an extra $13 million to help him handle the income taxes on the income that resulted from forgiveness of the debt.
- More than $11 million in corporate funds used to decorate an $18 million Fifth Avenue apartment that Kozlowski stayed in when visiting New York. The funds were used to purchase antiques, art, and a $6,000 gold-and-burgundy floral-patterned shower curtain.
- Half the cost of a $2.1 million birthday party for Kozlowski's wife, on the island of Sardinia. The weeklong party included a performance by singer Jimmy Buffett.

Though Kozlowski is under investigation for state sales tax evasion in New York and Tyco is being investigated by the Securities and Exchange Commission for failure to disclose Kozlowski's true compensation, the payments made by Tyco to Kozlowski otherwise appear legal.

In contrast to Kozlowski's board-authorized compensation, John J. Rigas and his sons were arrested and charged with illegally extracting hundreds of millions of dollars from Adelphia. While chairman of Adelphia, the elder Rigas ran up $66 million in personal debt and then withdrew so much money from the corporation that one of his sons, then Adelphia's chief financial officer, had to limit him to $1 million per month. In public filings, Rigas's compensation was listed at only $1.9 million. Other unauthorized benefits received by the family purportedly included personal use of corporate jets and two Manhattan apartments. The Rigas father and sons are charged with securities fraud, wire fraud, and bank fraud and are currently under investigation for criminal tax fraud for failure to report the alleged payments as income on their tax returns. Adelphia, which filed for bankruptcy in June 2002, supports the arrests because the payments to the family were apparently unauthorized.

How should the payments to the executives be treated in these two cases? Kozlowski and the Rigas family owned stock in their employers. Should the corporations involved treat the payments to the executives as compensation, a constructive dividend, or a theft loss? Avoidance of the double tax does not seem to have been a motive for the payments in either case (recall that compensation in excess of $1 million is not deductible unless it is contingent on performance), and neither corporation is closely held. Consequently, it would be difficult for the IRS to argue for constructive dividend treatment. In Tyco's case, the payments to Kozlowski are probably compensation because they were authorized. The payments to the Rigas family were not authorized, however, so they may be treated as a theft of Adelphia's assets.

- The employee's qualifications.
- A comparison of salaries with dividend distributions.
- The prevailing rates of compensation for comparable positions in comparable business concerns.
- The nature and scope of the employee's work.
- The size and complexity of the business.
- A comparison of salaries paid with both gross and net income.
- The taxpayer's salary policy toward all employees.
- For small corporations with a limited number of officers, the amount of compensation paid the employee in question in previous years.
- Whether a reasonable shareholder would have agreed to the level of compensation paid.[22]

**Loans to Shareholders.** Advances to shareholders that are not bona fide loans are constructive dividends. Whether an advance qualifies as a bona fide loan is a question of fact to be determined in light of the particular circumstances. Factors considered in determining whether the advance is a bona fide loan include the following:[23]

- Whether the advance is on open account or is evidenced by a written instrument.
- Whether the shareholder furnished collateral or other security for the advance.
- How long the advance has been outstanding.
- Whether any repayments have been made.
- The shareholder's ability to repay the advance.
- The shareholder's use of the funds (e.g., payment of routine bills versus nonrecurring, extraordinary expenses).
- The regularity of the advances.
- The dividend-paying history of the corporation.

Even when a corporation makes a bona fide loan to a shareholder, a constructive dividend may be triggered, equal to the amount of imputed (forgone) interest on the loan.[24] Imputed interest equals the amount by which interest the Federal government pays on new borrowings, compounded semiannually, exceeds the interest charged on the loan. When the imputed interest provision applies, the shareholder is deemed to have made an interest payment to the corporation equal to the amount of imputed interest, and the corporation is deemed to have repaid the imputed interest to the shareholder through a constructive dividend. As a result, the corporation receives interest income and makes a nondeductible dividend payment, and the shareholder has taxable dividend income that may be offset with an interest deduction.

**EXAMPLE 21**

Mallard Corporation lends its principal shareholder, Henry, $100,000 on January 2 of the current year. The loan is interest-free and payable on demand. On December 31, the imputed interest rules are applied. Assuming the Federal rate is 6%, compounded semiannually, the amount of imputed interest is $6,090. This amount is deemed paid by Henry to Mallard in the form of interest. Mallard is then deemed to return the amount to Henry as a constructive

---

[22]All but the final factor in this list are identified in *Mayson Manufacturing Co. v. Comm.*, 49–2 USTC ¶9467, 38 AFTR 1028, 178 F.2d 115 (CA–6, 1949). The final factor, the "reasonable shareholder" test, is more recent. For example, see *Alpha Medical, Inc. v. Comm.*, 99–1 USTC ¶50,461, 83 AFTR2d 99–697, 172 F.3d 942 (CA–6, 1999).

[23]*Fin Hay Realty Co. v. U.S.*, 68–2 USTC ¶9438, 22 AFTR2d 5004, 398 F.2d 694 (CA–3, 1968).

[24]See § 7872.

dividend. Thus, Henry has dividend income of $6,090, which may be offset with a deduction for the interest paid to Mallard. Mallard has interest income of $6,090 for the interest received, with no offsetting deduction for the dividend payment. ■

**Loans to a Corporation by Shareholders.**   Shareholder loans to a corporation may be reclassified as equity because the debt has too many features of stock. Any interest and principal payments made by the corporation to the shareholder are then treated as constructive dividends. This topic was covered more thoroughly in the discussion of "thin capitalization" in Chapter 3.

## TAX TREATMENT OF CONSTRUCTIVE DIVIDENDS

For tax purposes, constructive distributions are treated the same as actual distributions.[25] Thus, a corporate shareholder is entitled to the dividends received deduction (see Chapter 2). The constructive distribution is taxable as a dividend only to the extent of the corporation's current and accumulated E & P. The burden of proving that the distribution constitutes a return of capital because of inadequate E & P rests with the taxpayer.[26]

<table>
<tr><td>LO.6</td></tr>
<tr><td>Distinguish between taxable and nontaxable stock dividends and stock rights.</td></tr>
</table>

# Stock Dividends and Stock Rights

## STOCK DIVIDENDS—§ 305

Historically, **stock dividends** were excluded from income on the theory that the ownership interest of the shareholder was unchanged as a result of the distribution.[27] Recognizing that some distributions of stock could affect ownership interests, the 1954 Code included a provision (§ 305) taxing stock dividends where (1) the stockholder could elect to receive either stock or property or (2) the stock dividends were in discharge of preference dividends. However, because this provision applied to only a narrow range of transactions, corporations were able to develop an assortment of alternative methods that circumvented taxation and still affected shareholders' proportionate interests in the corporation.[28] In response, the scope of § 305 was expanded.

In its current state, the provisions of § 305 are based on the proportionate interest concept. As a general rule, stock dividends are excluded from income if they are pro rata distributions of stock or stock rights, paid on common stock. Five exceptions to this general rule exist. For each of these exceptions, listed below, stock distributions may be taxed.

1. Distributions payable in either stock or property, at the election of the shareholder.
2. Distributions of property to some shareholders, with a corresponding increase in the proportionate interest of other shareholders in either assets or E & P of the distributing corporation.
3. Distributions of preferred stock to some common shareholders and of common stock to other common shareholders.

[25]*Simon v. Comm.*, 57–2 USTC ¶9989, 52 AFTR 698, 248 F.2d 869 (CA–8, 1957).

[26]*DiZenzo v. Comm.*, 65–2 USTC ¶9518, 16 AFTR2d 5107, 348 F.2d 122 (CA–2, 1965).

[27]See *Eisner v. Macomber*, 1 USTC ¶32, 3 AFTR 3020, 40 S.Ct. 189 (USSC, 1920).

[28]See "Stock Dividends," Senate Report 91–552, 1969–3 C.B. 519.

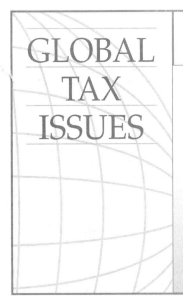

GLOBAL TAX ISSUES

**DEEMED DIVIDENDS FROM CONTROLLED FOREIGN CORPORATIONS**

It is not uncommon for U.S. multinational companies to conduct business overseas through the use of foreign corporations. Most often, these foreign corporations are controlled by the U.S. parent. Called controlled foreign corporations (CFCs), such entities would be ideal for income avoidance if incorporated in a low-tax jurisdiction (i.e., a tax haven country). Further, U.S. income tax on their profits would be deferred if no dividends are distributed to the U.S. parent.

Well aware of the latter possibility, the tax law compels a U.S. shareholder to recognize as income the profits of a CFC that are not distributed. In contrast to constructive dividends, the "deemed dividend" distribution increases the basis the U.S. company has in the foreign corporation's stock. Furthermore, when the deemed dividend is ultimately distributed to the parent (i.e., repatriated), no income results. Thus, the CFC rules prevent deferral but are not intended to lead to double taxation.

4. Distributions of stock to preferred shareholders. However, changes in the conversion ratio of convertible preferred stock to account for a stock dividend or stock split are not taxable in some circumstances.
5. Distributions of convertible preferred stock, unless it can be shown that the distribution will not result in a disproportionate distribution.

These exceptions to nontaxability of stock dividends deal with various disproportionate distribution situations.

Holders of convertible securities are considered shareholders. Thus, under the second exception above, when interest is paid on convertible debentures and stock dividends are paid on common stock, the stock dividends are taxable. This result is avoided if the conversion ratio or conversion price is adjusted to reflect the price of the stock dividend.[29]

If stock dividends are not taxable, the corporation's E & P is not reduced.[30] If the stock dividends are taxable, the distributing corporation treats the distribution in the same manner as any other taxable property dividend.

If a stock dividend is taxable, the shareholder's basis in the newly received shares is fair market value, and the holding period starts on the date of receipt. If a stock dividend is not taxable, the basis of the stock on which the dividend is distributed is reallocated.[31] If the dividend shares are identical to these formerly held shares, basis in the old stock is reallocated by dividing the taxpayer's cost in the old stock by the total number of shares. If the dividend stock is not identical to the underlying shares (e.g., a stock dividend of preferred on common), basis is determined by allocating the basis of the formerly held shares between the old and new stock according to the fair market value of each. The holding period includes the holding period of the formerly held stock.[32]

EXAMPLE 22

Gail bought 1,000 shares of common stock two years ago for $10,000. In the current tax year, Gail receives 10 shares of common stock as a nontaxable stock dividend. Gail's basis of

---

[29]See Reg. § 1.305–3(d) for illustrations on how to compute required adjustments on conversion ratios or prices.
[30]§ 312(d)(1).

[31]§ 307(a).
[32]§ 1223(5).

## THE REIT KIND OF DIVIDENDS

Public Storage, a real estate investment trust or REIT, is the largest owner and operator of self-storage space in the United States. REITs are tax-exempt corporations (and sometimes trusts) that receive most of their earnings from real estate activities. To qualify, the entity must pay out at least 95 percent of its taxable income as dividends each year. As a result of this requirement, REITs typically have a difficult time retaining cash to expand and acquire new properties.

Recently, in a bid to overcome the tax-based growth restriction, Public Storage offered a creative dividend plan to its owners. In this plan, each shareholder could choose between two types of dividends: either $0.65 cash per share of common stock or an equivalent value in depositary shares, representing an interest in the company's newly created class of common stock. Ordinarily, stock distributions are not considered taxable dividends and do not meet the 95 percent distribution requirement imposed on REITs. However, because shareholders were given a choice between stock and cash, the stock was considered a property distribution and, to the extent of E & P, was taxed to shareholders at its fair market value. This new technique enabled Public Storage to meet the requirements imposed on REITs while permitting the company to accumulate the cash needed to grow.

SOURCE: Adapted from Shirley A. Lazo, "Speaking of Dividends: A Firm Tries Doing the REIT Thing," *Barron's*, November 29, 1999, p. 48.

$10,000 is divided by 1,010. Each share of stock has a basis of $9.90 instead of the pre-dividend $10 basis. ■

**EXAMPLE 23**

Assume Gail received, instead, a nontaxable preferred stock dividend of 100 shares. The preferred stock has a fair market value of $1,000, and the common stock, on which the preferred is distributed, has a fair market value of $19,000. After the receipt of the stock dividend, the basis of the common stock is $9,500, and the basis of the preferred is $500, computed as follows:

| | |
|---|---|
| Fair market value of common | $19,000 |
| Fair market value of preferred | 1,000 |
| | $20,000 |
| Basis of common: $19/20 \times \$10,000$ | $ 9,500 |
| Basis of preferred: $1/20 \times \$10,000$ | $ 500 |

■

## STOCK RIGHTS

The rules for determining taxability of **stock rights** are identical to those for determining taxability of stock dividends. If the rights are taxable, the recipient has income to the extent of the fair market value of the rights. The fair market value then becomes the shareholder-distributee's basis in the rights.[33] If the rights are exercised, the holding period for the new stock begins on the date the rights (whether taxable or nontaxable) are exercised. The basis of the new stock is the basis of the rights plus the amount of any other consideration given.

---

[33]Reg. § 1.305–1(b).

## STOCK RIGHT DISTRIBUTION PROVIDES INSURANCE AGAINST CORPORATE TAKEOVER

Hemagen Diagnostics, Inc., develops, manufactures, and markets medical test kits used in the diagnosis of diseases and for blood analysis. Anticipating the possibility of a corporate takeover, on February 10, 1999, Hemagen distributed nontaxable stock rights permitting the purchase of one common share for each outstanding share of common stock owned. According to Dr. Carl Franzblau, Hemagen's chief executive officer, the distribution was designed to ensure that all Hemagen stockholders are treated fairly in any unsolicited merger or other acquisition. The purchase rights can be exercised only if a person or group acquires 15 percent or more of Hemagen's common stock, or if someone announces a tender offer that would result in ownership of 15 percent or more of the company's common stock.

Each right permits its holder (other than the 15 percent person or group) to purchase one newly issued share of Hemagen common stock (or of any company that acquires Hemagen) at half the market price. Alternatively, Hemagen's board of directors can choose to redeem the rights for $0.001 each up until 10 days after a public announcement that any group or person has acquired 15 percent or more of the company. If the rights are not redeemed or exercised, they will expire on January 27, 2009.

If stock rights are not taxable and the value of the rights is less than 15 percent of the value of the old stock, the basis of the rights is zero. However, the shareholder may elect to have some of the basis in the formerly held stock allocated to the rights.[34] The election is made by attaching a statement to the shareholder's return for the year in which the rights are received.[35] If the fair market value of the rights is 15 percent or more of the value of the old stock and the rights are exercised or sold, the shareholder *must* allocate some of the basis in the formerly held stock to the rights.

**EXAMPLE 24**

A corporation with common stock outstanding declares a nontaxable dividend payable in rights to subscribe to common stock. Each right entitles the holder to purchase one share of stock for $90. One right is issued for every two shares of stock owned. Fred owns 400 shares of stock purchased two years ago for $15,000. At the time of the distribution of the rights, the market value of the common stock is $100 per share, and the market value of the rights is $8 per right. Fred receives 200 rights. He exercises 100 rights and sells the remaining 100 rights three months later for $9 per right.

Fred need not allocate the cost of the original stock to the rights because the value of the rights is less than 15% of the value of the stock ($1,600 ÷ $40,000 = 4%). If Fred does not allocate his original stock basis to the rights, the tax consequences are as follows:

* Basis in the new stock is $9,000 ($90 × 100). The holding period of the new stock begins on the date the stock was purchased.
* Sale of the rights produces long-term capital gain of $900 ($9 × 100). The holding period of the rights starts with the date the original 400 shares of stock were acquired.

---

[34]§ 307(b)(1).                                     [35]Reg. § 1.307–2.

If Fred elects to allocate basis to the rights, the tax consequences are as follows:

* Basis in the stock is $14,423 [$40,000 ÷ $41,600 (value of rights and stock) × $15,000 (cost of stock)].
* Basis in the rights is $577 [$1,600 (value of rights) ÷ $41,600 (value of rights and stock) × $15,000 (cost of stock)].
* When Fred exercises the rights, his basis in the new stock will be $9,288.50 [$9,000 (cost) + $288.50 (basis in 100 rights)].
* Sale of the rights would produce a long-term capital gain of $611.50 [$900 (selling price) − $288.50 (basis in the remaining 100 rights)]. ■

**Tax Planning Considerations**

## CORPORATE DISTRIBUTIONS

In connection with the discussion of corporate distributions, the following points need reinforcement:

* Because E & P is the measure of dividend income, its periodic determination is essential to corporate planning. Thus, an E & P account should be established and maintained, particularly if the possibility exists that a corporate distribution might be a return of capital.
* Accumulated E & P is the sum of all past years' current E & P. There is no statute of limitations on the computation of E & P. The IRS can, for example, redetermine a corporation's current E & P for a tax year long since passed. Such a change affects accumulated E & P and has a direct impact on the taxability of current distributions to shareholders.
* Distributions can be planned to avoid or minimize dividend exposure.

**EXAMPLE 25**

Flicker Corporation has accumulated E & P of $100,000 as of January 1 of the current year. During the year, it expects to have earnings from operations of $80,000 and to sell an asset for a loss of $100,000. Thus, it anticipates a current E & P deficit of $20,000. Flicker Corporation also expects to make a cash distribution of $60,000. The best approach is to recognize the loss as soon as possible and immediately thereafter make the cash distribution to the shareholders. Suppose these two steps take place on January 1. Because the current E & P has a deficit, the accumulated E & P account must be brought up to date (refer to Example 11 in this chapter). Thus, at the time of the distribution, the combined E & P balance is zero [$100,000 (beginning balance in accumulated E & P) − $100,000 (existing deficit in current E & P)], and the $60,000 distribution to the shareholders constitutes a return of capital. Current deficits are allocated pro rata throughout the year unless the parties can prove otherwise. Here they can. ■

**EXAMPLE 26**

After several unprofitable years, Darter Corporation has a deficit in accumulated E & P of $100,000 as of January 1, 2003. Starting in 2003, Darter expects to generate annual E & P of $50,000 for the next four years and would like to distribute this amount to its shareholders. The corporation's cash position (for dividend purposes) will correspond to the current E & P generated. Compare the following possibilities:

1. On December 31 of 2003, 2004, 2005, and 2006, Darter Corporation distributes a cash dividend of $50,000.
2. On December 31 of 2004 and 2006, Darter Corporation distributes a cash dividend of $100,000.

The two alternatives are illustrated below.

| Year | Accumulated E & P (First of Year) | Current E & P | Distribution | Amount of Dividend |
|------|-----------------------------------|---------------|--------------|--------------------|
| | | *Alternative 1* | | |
| 2003 | ($ 100,000) | $50,000 | $ 50,000 | $50,000 |
| 2004 | (100,000) | 50,000 | 50,000 | 50,000 |
| 2005 | (100,000) | 50,000 | 50,000 | 50,000 |
| 2006 | (100,000) | 50,000 | 50,000 | 50,000 |
| | | *Alternative 2* | | |
| 2003 | ($ 100,000) | $50,000 | $ –0– | $ –0– |
| 2004 | (50,000) | 50,000 | 100,000 | 50,000 |
| 2005 | (50,000) | 50,000 | –0– | –0– |
| 2006 | –0– | 50,000 | 100,000 | 50,000 |

Alternative 1 produces $200,000 of dividend income, because each $50,000 distribution is fully covered by current E & P. Alternative 2, however, produces only $100,000 of dividend income to the shareholders. The remaining $100,000 is a return of capital. Why? At the time Darter Corporation made its first distribution of $100,000 on December 31, 2004, it had a deficit of $50,000 in accumulated E & P (the original deficit of $100,000 is reduced by the $50,000 of current E & P from 2003). Consequently, the $100,000 distribution yields a $50,000 dividend (the current E & P for 2004) and $50,000 is treated as a return of capital. As of January 1, 2005, Darter's accumulated E & P now has a deficit balance of $50,000, since a distribution cannot increase a deficit in E & P. Adding the remaining $50,000 of current E & P from 2005, the balance as of January 1, 2006, is zero. Thus, the second distribution of $100,000 made on December 31, 2006, also yields $50,000 of dividends (the current E & P for 2006) and a $50,000 return of capital. ■

---

## ETHICAL CONSIDERATIONS

### Playing Games with the Statute of Limitations

In 1996, Beige Corporation made a cash distribution to its shareholders, one of whom was Steve Jordan. At that time, the parties involved believed that the distribution was a return of capital because Beige had no E & P. Accordingly, none of the shareholders reported dividend income. In Steve's case, he reduced the $200,000 original basis of his stock investment by $40,000, his share of the distribution. In 2003, it is discovered that E & P had been incorrectly computed. The 1996 distribution was fully covered by E & P and *should not have been treated as a return of capital.*

In 2004, Steve sells his stock in Beige Corporation for $350,000. He plans to report a gain of $150,000 [$350,000 (selling price) – $200,000 (original basis)] on the sale. Although Steve realizes that he should have recognized dividend income of $40,000 for 1996, the statute of limitations has made this a closed year.

Comment on Steve's situation.

---

## CONSTRUCTIVE DIVIDENDS

Tax planning can be particularly effective in avoiding constructive dividend situations. Shareholders should try to structure their dealings with the corporation on an arm's length basis. For example, reasonable rent should be paid for the use of corporate property, and a fair price should be paid for its purchase. The parties should make every effort to support the amount involved with appraisal data or market information obtained from reliable sources at or near the time of the transaction. Dealings between shareholders and a closely held corporation should be as formal as possible. In the case of loans to shareholders, for example, the parties should provide for an adequate rate of interest and written evidence of the debt. Shareholders also should establish and follow a realistic repayment schedule.

If shareholders wish to bail out corporate profits in a form deductible to the corporation, a balanced mix of the possible alternatives lessens the risk of constructive dividend treatment. Rent for the use of shareholder property, interest on amounts borrowed from shareholders, or salaries for services rendered by shareholders are all feasible substitutes for dividend distributions. But overdoing any one approach may attract the attention of the IRS. Too much interest, for example, may mean the corporation is thinly capitalized, and some of the debt may be reclassified as equity investment.

Much can be done to protect against the disallowance of unreasonable compensation. Example 27 is an illustration, all too common in a family corporation, of what *not* to do.

**EXAMPLE 27**

Bob Cole wholly owns Eagle Corporation. Corporate employees and annual salaries include Mrs. Cole ($30,000), Cole, Jr. ($20,000), Bob Cole ($160,000), and Ed ($80,000). The operation of Eagle Corporation is shared about equally between Bob Cole and Ed, who is an unrelated party. Mrs. Cole performed significant services for Eagle during its formative years but now merely attends the annual meeting of the board of directors. Cole, Jr., Bob Cole's son, is a full-time student and occasionally signs papers for the corporation in his capacity as treasurer. Eagle Corporation has not distributed a dividend for 10 years, although it has accumulated substantial E & P. Mrs. Cole, Cole, Jr., and Bob Cole run the risk of a finding of unreasonable compensation, based on the following factors:

- Mrs. Cole's salary is vulnerable unless proof is available that some or all of her $30,000 annual salary is payment for services rendered to the corporation in prior years, if she was underpaid for those years.[36]
- Cole, Jr.'s salary is also vulnerable; he does not appear to earn the $20,000 paid to him by the corporation. True, neither Cole, Jr., nor Mrs. Cole is a shareholder, but each one's relationship to Bob Cole is enough of a tie-in to raise the unreasonable compensation issue.
- Bob Cole's salary appears susceptible to challenge. Why is he receiving $80,000 more than Ed when it appears that they share equally in the operation of the corporation?
- The fact that Eagle Corporation has not distributed dividends over the past 10 years, even though it is capable of doing so, increases the likelihood of a constructive dividend. ■

What could have been done to improve the tax position of the parties in Example 27? Mrs. Cole and Cole, Jr., are not entitled to a salary as neither seems to be performing any services for the corporation. Paying them a salary simply aggravates the problem. The IRS is more apt to consider *all* the salaries to members of the family as being excessive under the circumstances. Bob Cole should probably reduce his compensation to correspond to that paid Ed. He can then attempt to distribute corporate earnings to himself in some other form.

Paying some dividends to Bob Cole would also help alleviate the problem raised in Example 27. The IRS has been successful in denying a deduction for salary

---

[36]See, for example, *R.J. Nicoll Co.*, 59 T.C. 37 (1972).

paid to a shareholder-employee, even when the payment was reasonable, in a situation where the corporation had not distributed any dividends.[37] Most courts, however, have not denied deductions for compensation solely because a dividend was not paid. A better approach is to compare an employee's compensation with the level of compensation prevalent in the particular industry.

The corporation can substitute *indirect* compensation for Bob Cole by paying expenses that benefit him personally but are nevertheless deductible to the corporation. For example, premiums paid by the corporation for sickness, accident, and hospitalization insurance for Bob Cole are deductible to the corporation and nontaxable to him.[38] Any payments under the policy are not taxable to Bob Cole unless they exceed his medical expenses.[39] The corporation can also pay for travel and entertainment expenses incurred by Cole on behalf of the corporation. If these expenses are primarily for the benefit of the corporation, Bob Cole will not recognize any taxable income, and the corporation will receive a deduction.[40]

When testing for reasonableness, the IRS looks at the total compensation package, including indirect compensation payments to a shareholder-employee. Thus, indirect payments must not be overlooked.

**EXAMPLE 28**

Cora, the president and sole shareholder of Willet Corporation, is paid an annual salary of $100,000 by the corporation. Cora would like to draw funds from the corporation but is concerned that additional salary payments might cause the IRS to contend her salary is unreasonable. Cora does not want Willet to pay any dividends. She also wishes to donate $50,000 to her alma mater to establish scholarships for needy students. Willet Corporation could make the contribution on Cora's behalf. The payment clearly benefits Cora, but the amount of the contribution will not be taxed to her.[41] Willet can take a charitable contribution deduction for the payment. ∎

**EXAMPLE 29**

Assume in Example 28 that Cora has made an individual pledge to the university to provide $50,000 for scholarships for needy students. Willet Corporation satisfies Cora's pledge by paying the $50,000 to the university. The $50,000 will be taxed to Cora.[42] In this context, the $50,000 payment to the university may be treated as *indirect* compensation to Cora. In determining whether Cora's salary is unreasonable, both the *direct* payment of $100,000 and the *indirect* $50,000 payment will be considered. Cora's total compensation package is $150,000. ∎

## KEY TERMS

| | | |
|---|---|---|
| Accumulated earnings and profits, 4–6 | Current earnings and profits, 4–6 | Stock dividend, 4–16 |
| | Earnings and profits (E & P), 4–3 | Stock rights, 4–18 |
| Constructive dividend, 4–12 | Property dividend, 4–10 | Unreasonable compensation, 4–13 |

---

[37]*McCandless Tile Service v. U.S.*, 70–1 USTC ¶9284, 25 AFTR2d 70–870, 422 F.2d 1336 (Ct.Cls., 1970). The court in *McCandless* concluded that a return on equity of 15% of net profits was reasonable.

[38]Reg. § 1.162–10.

[39]The medical reimbursement plan must meet certain nondiscrimination requirements of § 105(h)(2).

[40]Reg. § 1.62–2(c)(4).

[41]*Henry J. Knott*, 67 T.C. 681 (1977).

[42]*Schalk Chemical Co. v. Comm.*, 62–1 USTC ¶9496, 9 AFTR2d 1579, 304 F.2d 48 (CA–9, 1962).

## PROBLEM MATERIALS

### Discussion Questions

1. What factors affect the tax treatment of corporate distributions?

2. What is meant by the term *earnings and profits?*

3. In determining Plover Corporation's current E & P for 2003, how should taxable income be adjusted by the following transactions?
   a. Sale of inventory on installment in 2003, with the first payment due in 2004.
   b. A net operating loss carryover from 2002, fully used in 2003.
   c. Excess capital losses incurred in 2003 that are carried forward to 2004.
   d. Gain deferred in a qualifying like-kind exchange that occurred in 2003.
   e. A Federal income tax refund received in 2003.
   f. Section 179 expenses elected and deducted in 2001.

4. In what ways does the computation of E & P require more conservative accounting than the computation of taxable income?

5. Describe the effect of a distribution in a year when the distributing corporation has:
   a. A deficit in accumulated E & P and a positive amount in current E & P.
   b. A positive amount in accumulated E & P and a deficit in current E & P.
   c. A deficit in both current and accumulated E & P.
   d. A positive amount in both current and accumulated E & P.

6. How do gains and losses from property transactions affect the determination of E & P?

7. A calendar year corporation has no accumulated E & P but expects to earn current E & P for the year. A cash distribution to its shareholders on January 1 should result in a return of capital. Comment on the validity of this statement.

8. Why would a corporation distribute a property dividend?

**Decision Making**

9. Crimson Corporation owns three automobiles that it uses in its business. It no longer needs two of these cars and is considering the possibility of distributing them to its two shareholders as a property dividend. All three automobiles have a fair market value of $15,000. Automobile A has a basis of $8,000; automobile B has a basis of $15,000; and automobile C has a basis of $20,000. The corporation has asked you for advice. What actions do you recommend?

**Issue ID**

10. A corporation is contemplating a possible property distribution to its shareholders. If appreciated property is to be used, does it matter to the distributing corporation whether the property distributed is a long-term capital asset or depreciable property subject to recapture?

11. Discuss the effects of the following in generating or adding to a deficit in E & P:
    a. A dividend distribution by the corporation.
    b. An operating loss of the corporation.

12. How do liabilities affect the tax treatment of a property distribution?

**Issue ID**

13. Willet Corporation distributes $125,000 to each of its three shareholders, Tom, Michelle, and Hawk Corporation. What factors must be considered when determining how the distribution is treated for tax purposes both to the shareholders and to Willet Corporation?

14. To be treated as a dividend for tax purposes, must a corporation's distribution to its shareholders meet the legal requirements of a dividend as set forth by applicable state law, be formally declared, or be issued pro rata to all shareholders? Discuss.

**Issue ID**

15. Becky is the president and sole shareholder of Tan Corporation. She is paid a salary of $400,000 in the current year. Her daughter, Jill, is the company's chief financial officer

and is paid a salary of $40,000. Jill works for Tan on a part-time basis while she completes her accounting degree at a local university. Tan Corporation also advances $30,000 to Becky this year as an interest-free loan. What are the tax issues?

16. Whether compensation paid to a corporate employee is reasonable is a question of fact to be determined from the surrounding circumstances. How would the resolution of this problem be affected by each of the following factors?
    a. The employee is not a shareholder but is related to the sole owner of the corporate employer.
    b. The shareholder-employee never completed high school.
    c. The shareholder-employee is a full-time college student.
    d. The shareholder-employee was underpaid for her services during the formative period of the corporate employer.
    e. The corporate employer pays only a nominal dividend each year.
    f. Year-end bonuses are paid to all shareholder-employees, but not to nonshareholder-employees.

**Decision Making** 17. Condor Corporation is considering a joint venture with Seagull Corporation. The officers of Condor have requested your advice on the choice of entity for the joint venture. Representatives from Seagull prefer the partnership form because double taxation can be avoided. Are their concerns regarding the double tax justified? How would your answer change if Condor and Seagull were individuals instead of corporations?

18. Peregrine Corporation has several employees. Their names and salaries are:

| | |
|---|---|
| Walter | $400,000 |
| Sam (Walter's son) | 60,000 |
| Jennifer (Walter's daughter) | 60,000 |
| Richard (an unrelated party) | 50,000 |

Sam and Jennifer are the only shareholders of Peregrine Corporation. Walter and Richard share the company's operation equally. Sam and Jennifer are both full-time college students at a university about 600 miles away. Peregrine has substantial E & P and has distributed only one small dividend in the past 10 years. Discuss problems related to Peregrine's salary arrangement.

19. Chartreuse Corporation pays its president and sole shareholder, Brianna, an annual salary of $250,000. Brianna wishes to avoid dividends because of the double tax. She is concerned that if she were to receive any more salary, the IRS might treat it as a constructive dividend. Each year, Brianna gives her favorite charity $65,000. This year, if she makes a pledge for the usual amount, would she have a problem if Chartreuse paid the pledge on her behalf? Explain.

**Communications** 20. Your client, Cormorant Corporation, declares a dividend permitting its common stockholders to elect to receive 8 shares of cumulative preferred stock or 2 additional shares of Cormorant common stock for every 10 shares of common stock currently held. Cormorant currently has only common stock outstanding. Cormorant's common stock has a fair market value of $50 per share. Two shareholders elect to receive preferred stock, and all the remaining shareholders elect to receive common stock. Cormorant asks you whether the shareholders have any taxable income on the receipt of the stock. Prepare a letter to Cormorant and a memo to the file. Cormorant's address is 6730 Pima Drive, Madison, WI 53708.

21. Describe the rationale underlying the tax treatment of stock distributions.

22. How are nontaxable and taxable stock rights handled for tax purposes?

Online quizzing @ WFT Interactive Study Center

*Handwritten marginal notes (left):*

Kelly    Laura
100 000   100000
CEP (25000)  (25000)
75000    75000
ACEPP (55000)  (55000)
200000    20000
Tax
Pree (13000)  (20 000)
Basis
↓   7000   —0—
capgn 7000

Stock basis
13000   30000
Basis (13000)  (20000)
red.   —0—   10000

## Problems

23. At the start of the current year, Mallard Corporation (a calendar year taxpayer) has accumulated E & P of $110,000. Mallard's current E & P is $50,000, and during the year, it distributes $200,000 ($100,000 each) to its equal shareholders, Kelly and Laura. Kelly has a basis of $13,000 in her stock, and Laura has a basis of $30,000 in her stock. How will the distribution be treated for tax purposes?

24. Cardinal Corporation, a calendar year taxpayer, received dividend income of $400,000 from a corporation in which it holds a 15% interest. Cardinal also received interest income of $60,000 from municipal bonds during the year. The municipality used the proceeds from the bond sale to construct a new public library. Cardinal borrowed funds to purchase the municipal bonds and paid $30,000 in interest on the loan this year. Cardinal's taxable income exclusive of the items noted above was $250,000.
    a. What is Cardinal Corporation's taxable income after considering the dividend income, the interest from the municipal bonds, and the interest paid on the indebtedness to purchase the municipals?
    b. What is Cardinal Corporation's accumulated E & P at the end of the year if its accumulated E & P account balance was $90,000 as of January 1?

25. On November 15, 2003, Red Corporation sold a parcel of land. The land had a basis of $350,000, and Red received a $900,000 note as consideration in the sale. The note is to be paid in five installments, the first of which is due on December 15, 2004. Because Red did not elect out of the installment method, none of the $550,000 gain is included in taxable income for 2003.
    Red Corporation had a deficit in accumulated E & P of $280,000 on January 1, 2003. For 2003, before considering the effect of the land sale, Red had a deficit in current E & P of $120,000.
    Buck, the sole shareholder in Red, has a basis of $100,000 in his stock. If Red distributes $300,000 to Buck on December 31, 2003, how much must Buck report on the distribution for tax purposes?

26. Rose Corporation is a calendar year taxpayer. At the beginning of the current year, Rose has accumulated E & P of $250,000. The corporation incurs a current E & P deficit of $300,000 that accrues ratably throughout the year. On June 30, Rose distributes $300,000 to its sole shareholder, Dean. If Dean has a basis in his stock of $20,000, how is the distribution taxed to him?

27. Complete the following schedule for each case. Assume the shareholders have ample basis in the stock investment.

| | Accumulated E & P Beginning of Year | Current E & P | Cash Distributions (All on Last Day of Year) | Amount Taxable | Return of Capital |
|---|---|---|---|---|---|
| a. | ($150,000) | $ 70,000 | $130,000 | $70000 | $60000 |
| b. | 200,000 | (60,000) | 210,000 | 140000 | 70000 |
| c. | 130,000 | 50,000 | 150,000 | 150000 | —0— |
| d. | 120,000 | (40,000) | 130,000 | 80000 | 50000 |
| e. | Same as (d), except the distribution of $130,000 is made on June 30 and the corporation uses the calendar year for tax purposes. | | | 100000 | 30000 |

*Handwritten marginal note (lower left):* No cap gain as anyone bases of div Maximization of interest is aim

28. Complete the following schedule. For each case, assume that there is one shareholder whose basis in the corporate stock is $20,000. Also assume that current losses accrue ratably throughout the year.

*Handwritten below:* 120000  (20000)  130000  150000  30000

| | Accumulated E & P Beginning of Year | Current E & P | Cash Distributions (All on Last Day of Year) | Amount Taxable | Capital Gain |
|---|---|---|---|---|---|
| a. | ($ 100,000) | $ 120,000 | $150,000 | $ 120000 | $ 10000 |
| b. | 70,000 | 30,000 | 110,000 | 100000 | 0 |
| c. | (100,000) | 80,000 | 70,000 | 70000 | 0 |
| d. | 210,000 | (160,000) | 90,000 | 50000 | 20000 |
| e. | Same as (d), except the distribution of $90,000 is made on June 30 and the corporation uses the calendar year for tax purposes. | | | 90000 | 0 |

*(handwritten: Complete before deduction)*

29. Marie, the sole shareholder of Purple Corporation, had a basis of $40,000 in Purple stock that she sold to Juan on July 30 for $150,000. Purple had accumulated E & P of $100,000 on January 1 and current E & P of $90,000. During the year, Purple made the following distributions: $160,000 cash to Marie on July 1, and $160,000 cash to Juan on December 30. How will the distributions be taxed to Marie and Juan? What gain will Marie recognize on the sale of her stock to Juan?

30. In each of the following *independent* situations, indicate the effect on taxable income and E & P, stating the amount of any increase (or decrease) as a result of the transaction. Assume E & P has already been increased by the taxable amount.

| Transaction | Taxable Income Increase (Decrease) | E & P Increase (Decrease) |
|---|---|---|
| a. Recognition of $20,000 gain from payment received on installment note from sale in prior year. | 20000 | (20000) |
| b. Payment of $27,000 in Federal income taxes. | 0 | (27000) |
| c. $8,000 in premiums paid for life insurance on corporate officer's life. As a result of premium payment, cash surrender value of policy increased $500. | 0 | (7500) |
| d. Capital loss, $43,000. No capital gains were recognized in the current year. | 0 | (43000) |
| e. Disallowed portion (50%) of meals and entertainment expenses, $8,500. | 0 | (8500) |
| f. Realized gain on involuntary conversion of $175,000 ($25,000 of gain is recognized). | 25000 | 0 |

31. In each of the following *independent* situations, indicate the effect on taxable income and E & P, stating the amount of any increase (or decrease) as a result of the transaction. Assume E & P has already been increased by taxable income.

*(Handwritten marginal note, upper left):* Related party — if you own directly or indirectly more than 50% related party so no loss — can immediate appears then for appeal for pup! 100000 = 25% gain 40000 to be recognized

| Transaction | Taxable Income Increase (Decrease) | E & P Increase (Decrease) |
|---|---|---|
| a. Sale of unimproved real estate to the sole shareholder of the corporation at a realized loss of $40,000. | —0— | <40000> |
| b. Intangible drilling costs incurred on May 1 of the current year; $30,000 is deductible from current-year taxable income. *(handwritten: amortized over 60 months for E&P — 9 months)* | <30000> | 26000 *(handwritten: for E&P have to capitalize & amortize over 60 months E&P <4000> current E&P <4000>)* |
| c. Sale of unimproved real estate to unrelated third party; basis is $200,000, fair market value is $400,000 (no election out of installment method; payments in year of sale total $100,000). | 50000 | 150000 |
| d. Dividends of $10,000 received from 10%-owned corporation, together with dividends received deduction (assume taxable income limit does not apply). | 3000 | 7000 |
| e. Realized gain of $150,000 from qualifying like-kind exchange ($30,000 of gain is recognized). | 30000 | —0— |
| f. Section 179 expense deduction of $12,000 in current year. | (12000) | 9600 |
| g. Impact of current-year § 179 expense deduction in succeeding year. | —0— | (2400) |
| h. MACRS depreciation of $80,000. ADS depreciation would have been $50,000. | (80000) | 30000 |
| i. A $60,000 refund of Federal income taxes paid in previous year. | —0— | 60000 |

32. Pelican Corporation distributes property ($150,000 basis and $175,000 fair market value) to its sole shareholder, Ginger. The property is subject to a liability of $225,000, which Ginger assumes. Pelican has E & P of $300,000 prior to the distribution.
   a. What gain, if any, does Pelican recognize on the distribution?
   b. What is the amount of Ginger's dividend income on the distribution?

33. Pearl Corporation, with E & P of $600,000, distributes land worth $175,000, adjusted basis of $220,000, to Azure, a corporate shareholder. The land is subject to a liability of $50,000, which Azure assumes.
   a. What is the amount of dividend income to Azure?
   b. What is Azure's basis in the land it received?
   c. How does the distribution affect Pearl Corporation's E & P account?

34. At the beginning of the current year, Dove Corporation (a calendar year taxpayer) has accumulated E & P of $40,000. During the year, Dove incurs a $30,000 loss from operations that accrued ratably. On July 1, Dove distributes $35,000 in cash to Marv, its sole shareholder. How will the $35,000 be taxed to Marv?

35. Pintail Corporation has E & P of $150,000. It distributes equipment with a fair market value of $130,000 (adjusted basis of $45,000) to its sole shareholder, Niro. The equipment

*(Handwritten marginal notes, lower left):*
Property dividend
FMV 175000
−lia 50000
125000 distribution
Enough E & P →
S/H · Div income 125000    Baon 175000
Corp No gain    Basis
liab is not    adj to
in excess of bas    E & P
→ +gain—0—
→ greater of
FMV−liability or
AB−liability

liability 50000
E&P 170000
land 220000

is subject to a liability of $20,000, which Niro assumes. What are the tax consequences to Pintail Corporation and to Niro?

36. Petrel Corporation distributes land with an adjusted basis of $200,000 and a fair market value of $120,000 to its shareholder, Tyler. What are the tax consequences to Petrel Corporation and to Tyler?

Issue ID

37. Copper Corporation has two equal shareholders, Cybil and Sally. Cybil acquired her Copper stock three years ago by transferring property worth $600,000, basis of $200,000, for 60 shares of the stock. Sally acquired 60 shares in Copper Corporation two years ago by transferring property worth $620,000, basis of $70,000. Copper Corporation's accumulated E & P as of January 1 of the current year is $300,000. On March 1 of the current year, the corporation distributed to Cybil property worth $100,000, basis to Copper of $30,000. It distributed cash of $200,000 to Sally. On July 1 of the current year, Sally sold her stock to Dana for $800,000. On December 1 of the current year, Copper distributed cash of $80,000 each to Dana and to Cybil. What are the tax issues?

38. Redwing Corporation is a closely held company with accumulated E & P of $500,000 and current E & P of $55,000. Mike and Royce are brothers, and each owns a 50% share in Redwing. On a day-to-day basis, Mike and Royce share management responsibilities equally. What are the tax consequences of the following transactions between Redwing, Mike, and Royce? How does each transaction affect Redwing's E & P? Assume each transaction is independent.

a. Redwing sells a parking lot (adjusted basis of $33,000, fair market value of $18,000) to Mike for $5,000.

b. Redwing lends Royce $200,000 on July 1 of this year. The loan, evidenced by a note, is due on demand. No interest is charged on the loan. The current applicable Federal interest rate is 9%.

c. Redwing owns a yacht in Miami, Florida. It rents the yacht to vacationers throughout the year. During the current year, Mike and Royce each use the yacht for one month and pay no rent to Redwing. The rental value of the yacht is $7,500 per week. Mike has indicated that the average maintenance cost per week for the rental is $500.

d. Mike leases equipment to Redwing for $20,000 per year. If the corporation were to lease the same equipment from another company, the cost of the lease would be $13,000.

Decision Making

39. Plover Corporation has beginning E & P of $51,000. Its current-year taxable income is $320,000. On December 31, Plover distributed business property worth $100,000, adjusted basis of $300,000, to Lea, its sole shareholder. Lea assumes an $80,000 liability on the property. Included in the determination of Plover's current taxable income is $10,000 of income recognized from an installment sale in a previous year. In addition, the corporation incurred a Federal income tax liability of $108,050, paid life insurance premiums of $2,000, and received term life insurance proceeds of $46,400 on the death of an officer in the current year.

a. What is the amount of taxable income to Lea?

b. What is the E & P of Plover Corporation after the property distribution?

c. What is Lea's tax basis in the property received?

d. How would your answers to (a) and (b) change if Plover had sold the property at its fair market value, used $80,000 of the proceeds to pay off the liability, and then distributed the remaining cash and any tax savings to Lea?

40. Verdigris Corporation owns 25% of the stock of Rust Corporation. Rust Corporation, with E & P of $150,000 on December 20, distributes land with a fair market value of $60,000 and a basis of $90,000 to Verdigris. The land is subject to a liability of $50,000, which Verdigris assumes.

a. How is Verdigris Corporation taxed on the distribution?

b. What is Rust Corporation's E & P after the distribution?

41. Bluebird Corporation, a cash basis, calendar year taxpayer, had the following income and expenses in the current year: income from services rendered, $300,000; salaries paid to employees, $80,000; tax-exempt interest income, $25,000; dividends from a corporation

*Calculation of E&P — indirect method* (handwritten top)

$$\text{MACRS}\quad 7yr = \frac{1}{7}\times 2 = \frac{2}{7}\times\frac{1}{2} = \frac{1}{7} \to 80000$$

$$\frac{\text{ADS}}{80000}{10} = \frac{8000}{2} = 4000$$

Handwritten left column:

```
Tax In        300000
Salaries      (80000)
Div rec'd      80000
Dep MACRS    (11432)
IT befor DRD  258568
DRD          (35000)
TI            223568

+DRD          35000
+TEint        25000
–STCL        (20000)
– Fed tax    (15400)
+ ADS          7432
             ─────────
             255600
```

in which Bluebird holds a 5% interest, $50,000; short-term capital loss on the sale of stock, $20,000; estimated Federal income taxes paid, $15,400. Bluebird Corporation purchased seven-year MACRS property in the current year for $80,000. No § 179 election was made, and Bluebird elected *not* to deduct additional 30% first-year depreciation. The property has a 10-year ADR midpoint life. Determine taxable income and E & P for Bluebird Corporation.

42. At the beginning of its taxable year, Bunting Corporation had E & P of $175,000. Bunting Corporation sold an asset at a loss of $175,000 on June 30. Bunting incurred a deficit in current E & P of $195,000, which includes the $175,000 loss on the sale of the asset, for the calendar year. Assume Bunting made a distribution of $40,000 to its sole individual shareholder on July 1. How will the shareholder be taxed on the $40,000?

43. Teal Corporation is a calendar year taxpayer. At the beginning of the current year, Teal had a deficit in accumulated E & P of $130,000. Its net profit for the period January 1 through September 30 was $160,000, but its E & P for the entire taxable year was only $20,000. Teal made a distribution of $50,000 to its sole individual shareholder on December 31. How will the shareholder be taxed on this distribution?

44. Indigo Corporation and Lucy each own 50% of Tanager Corporation's common stock. On January 1, Tanager had a deficit in accumulated E & P of $250,000. Its current E & P was $180,000. During the year, Tanager made cash distributions of $70,000 each to Indigo and Lucy. How will the two shareholders be taxed on the distribution? What is the accumulated E & P of Tanager Corporation at the end of the year?

45. Wren Corporation lends its principal shareholder, James, $200,000 on January 3 of the current year. The loan is interest-free. Assume the Federal rate is 10%. What are the tax consequences to Wren Corporation and to James with respect to the interest-free loan?

Handwritten (Below market loans):

```
James
200000 × 10% ½        10500
= 200000/2           +10000
Compound              ─────
Semiannual            20500
210000 × 10% ½        int
= 10500               income
= 20500 int to corp   to corp
```

46. Stan purchased 6,000 shares of Robin Corporation common stock five years ago for $30,000. In the current year, Stan receives a nontaxable preferred stock dividend of 300 shares. The preferred stock has a fair market value of $10,000. Stan's common stock in Robin has a fair market value of $50,000. What is Stan's basis in the preferred stock and common stock after the dividend is received?

**Communications**

Handwritten:

```
10000   = 2.50 basis
30000+1000
Amt real    8000
– Basis    (2500)
gain        5500
```

47. Sarah Beckert bought 3,000 shares of Grebe Corporation stock two years ago for $10,000. Last year, Sarah received a nontaxable stock dividend of 1,000 shares in Grebe Corporation. In the current tax year, Sarah sold all of the stock received as a dividend for $8,000. Prepare a letter to Sarah and a memo to the file describing the tax consequences of the stock sale. Sarah's address is 1822 N. Sarnoff Road, Tucson, AZ 85710.

Handwritten:

```
1 right + $50 = 1 share
200 sh = 6000 cost
FMV 100 < 70 exercise
          30 sell
FMV right    Allocate
Basis if     original
nontaxed     basis
       No allocat

De minimus rule →
FMV right  > 15% Allow
FMV stock  > 15%
 45500   > 15% 40
200000(200×100)
```

48. Stork Corporation declares a nontaxable dividend payable in rights to subscribe to common stock. One right and $50 entitle the holder to subscribe to one share of stock. One right is issued for every two shares of stock owned. At the date of distribution of the rights, the market value of the stock was $100 per share, and the market value of the rights was $45 per right. Cindy, a shareholder, owns 200 shares of stock that she purchased two years ago for $6,000. Cindy received 100 rights, of which she exercises 70 to purchase 70 additional shares. She sells the remaining 30 rights for $1,650. What are the tax consequences of these transactions to Cindy?

**Decision Making**

49. Partridge Corporation has accumulated E & P of $300,000 as of January 1 of the current year. It expects to have earnings from operations of $240,000 and to make a cash distribution of $180,000 during the year. Partridge Corporation also expects to sell an asset for a loss of $300,000. Thus, it anticipates incurring a current E & P deficit of $60,000 for the year. What can Partridge do to cause its shareholders to have the least amount of dividend income?

**Communications**

50. Diver Corporation has a deficit in accumulated E & P of $200,000 as of January 1. Diver Corporation expects to generate annual E & P of $100,000 for the next four years, starting this year, and would like to distribute this amount to its shareholders. How should Diver Corporation distribute the $400,000 over the four-year period to provide the least amount of dividend income to its shareholders (all individuals)? Prepare a letter to

Handwritten bottom:

```
Allocate relative to FMV
FMV rights   × Original cost
─────────────
FMV rights + stock

= 45500 / 45500 + 200000 × 6000 = 1102
```

your client, Diver Corporation, and a memo for the file. Diver Corporation's address is 1010 Oak Street, Oldtown, MD 20742.

## Research Problems

*Note: Solutions to Research Problems can be prepared by using the* **RIA Checkpoint® Student Edition** *online research product, or the* **CCH U.S. Master Tax Guide Plus™** *online Federal tax research database, which is available to accompany this text. It is also possible to prepare solutions to the Research Problems by using tax research materials found in a standard tax library.*

**Research Problem 1.** Walter and Shirley Black are married taxpayers. Their address is 6102 Regal Street, Spring Water, MN 55964. Walter owns 25% of Tulip Corporation and 90% of Rose Corporation. Shirley owns 75% of Tulip Corporation and 10% of Rose Corporation. Tulip Corporation has been operating successfully over the last decade. Rose Corporation was formed three years ago, with initial capitalization of $1,000. Walter and Shirley are active in the management of both corporations. During Rose's first year, Tulip Corporation provided it with an $85,000 advance so that Rose could purchase capital assets. Near the end of that year, to account for the advance, Rose issued an unsecured demand note to Tulip. The note was subordinated to all other debt owed by Rose. No payments have ever been made on the loan.

In November of this year, Rose Corporation filed for dissolution, and it is clear that Tulip's loan will not be repaid. The Blacks propose that Rose include the $85,000 loan in income as a result of forgiveness of the debt and that Tulip deduct the $85,000 on its tax return for the year as a bad debt. They have asked you for advice on whether this tax treatment will be allowed by the IRS. Prepare a letter to Walter and Shirley describing the results of your research and a memo for your firm's client files.

*Partial list of research aids:*
*Sammons v. Comm.,* 73–1 USTC ¶9138, 31 AFTR2d 73–497, 472 F.2d 449 (CA–5, 1972).

**Research Problem 2.** Your client, Preston Legal Sevices, Inc. (PLS), was formed in 1991 by Julie Preston with a capital contribution of $1,000. PLS is a law firm specializing in product liability litigation. Since its formation, the company has been principally involved in one class action lawsuit. In 2001, a $40 million settlement was finally reached in the suit. As part of the settlement, the court awarded $6 million of legal fees to PLS, to be paid between 2001 and 2003. Julie is the only attorney employed by PLS and its sole shareholder. In addition, the corporation employs a secretary. A summary of the company's financial situation for 2001 and 2002 is provided below.

|  | 2001 | 2002 |
|---|---|---|
| Legal fees received | $ 4,000,000 | $ 1,500,000 |
| Compensation to Preston | (1,900,000) | (1,450,000) |
| Other expenses | (100,000) | (50,000) |
| Taxable income | $ 2,000,000 | $ –0– |
| Approximate Federal tax paid | (700,000) | –0– |
| Cash for future expenses | $ 1,300,000 | $ –0– |

Every year since the corporation's formation, the board of directors has held an annual meeting to establish the level of compensation to be paid to Julie. The typical formula used by the board sets compensation equal to the legal fees she earned on behalf of PLS, less expenses and funds needed for future operations.

In 2003, PLS expects to receive the remaining $500,000 in legal fees from the class action lawsuit. No other revenues will be received during the year. At the 2003 board meeting, Julie proposes that her salary be set at $2.5 million. She suggests that the salary payment be funded by (1) the legal fees to be received in 2003, (2) the $1.3 million cash balance remaining in the corporation (there is no longer any anticipated need for the

**Communications**

**Communications**

cash), and (3) the $700,000 tax refund that PLS will receive as a result of the $2 million net operating loss [$500,000 (legal fees) – $2,500,000 (compensation expense)] generated in 2003 and carried back to 2001. To help the corporation's cash flow, Julie further proposes that she loan the corporation $700,000 until the tax refund is received. As the company's tax adviser, you have been asked to ascertain the tax consequences of the plan. Prepare a letter to Julie reporting on the results of your research. Her address is 1803 E. Monroe Street, Madison, WI 53706. When drafting your letter, remember that Julie is an attorney and she prefers that you provide her with legal authority supporting your conclusions.

*Partial list of research aids:*
*Richard Ashare, P.C., 78 TCM 348, T.C.Memo. 1999–282.*

**Communications**

**Research Problem 3.**  Aqua Corporation wholly owns Egret Corporation. Aqua formed Egret four years ago with the transfer of several assets to the corporation, together with a substantial amount of cash. Aqua's basis in Egret stock is $5.5 million. Since it was formed, Egret has been a very profitable software company and currently has accumulated E & P of $4 million. The company's principal assets are software patents currently worth $5 million and cash and marketable securities of approximately $4.5 million (a total fair market value of $9.5 million).

Aqua and Egret are members of an affiliated group and have made the election under § 243(b) so that Aqua is entitled to a 100% dividends received deduction. From a strategic perspective, Aqua is no longer interested in the software industry and so is considering a sale of Egret. In anticipation of a sale in the next year or two, the management of Aqua has contacted you for advice. If Egret is sold outright, then Aqua Corporation will have a capital gain of $4 million ($9.5 million fair market value less a basis of $5.5 million). As an alternative, it has been suggested that taxes on a future sale would be minimized if Egret pays Aqua a dividend (using existing cash and securities) equal to its E & P. With the 100% dividends received deduction, this payment would be a tax-free transfer from Egret to Aqua. Subsequent to the dividend payment, Egret could be sold for its remaining value of $5.5 million ($5 million in software patents plus $500,000 in cash), generating no additional loss or gain to Aqua.

a. Prepare a letter to the president of Aqua Corporation describing the results of your research on the proposed plan. The president's name and address is Bill Gateson, 601 Pittsfield Dr., Champaign, IL 61821.
b. Prepare a memo for your firm's client files.

*Partial list of research aids:*
*Waterman Steamship Corp. v. Comm., 70–2 USTC ¶9514, 26 AFTR2d 70–5185, 430 F.2d 1185 (CA–5, 1970).*

**Research Problem 4.**  Your client, Green Corporation, has done well over the last decade and has grown significantly. Earlier this year, it recognized a $40 million capital gain from the sale of a subsidiary. Bart Bremmer, Green's CEO, suggests the following as a way to reduce the tax on the capital gain. Green will begin by purchasing all of the common stock in Blue Corporation for $100 million. Blue is a profitable corporation that has $43 million in cash and marketable securities, $57 million in operating assets, and approximately $80 million in E & P. After acquisition, Blue will distribute $40 million in cash and marketable securities as a dividend to Green. Green will then resell Blue for $60 million. Since Green owned all of Blue's stock, it will qualify for a 100% dividends received deduction. Thus, no taxable income results from the dividend. The subsequent sale of Blue for $60 million will generate a $40 million capital loss (Green's stock basis is $100 million). The loss from the stock sale can then be used to offset the preexisting $40 million capital gain. Will the plan work?

**Internet Activity**

*Use the tax resources of the Internet to address the following questions. Do not restrict your search to the World Wide Web, but include a review of newsgroups and general reference materials, practitioner sites and resources, primary sources of the tax law, chat rooms and discussion groups, and other opportunities.*

**Research Problem 5.**  Just how common are dividend distributions? Are dividends concentrated in the companies traded on the New York Stock Exchange, or do closely held corporations pay dividends with the same frequency and at the same rates? Financial institutions and observers are acutely interested in these issues. Search for comments on such questions at various commercial Web sites as well as one or two academic journals or newsgroups.

**Research Problem 6.**   The last few years have seen the rise of a new security, called "trust preferred stock." Search for Web sites dealing with trust preferred stock. Briefly describe the security and identify its key tax and financial reporting characteristics.

**Research Problem 7.**   Which techniques have become popular in the last few years as a means of working around the § 162(m) limitation on deductions for executive compensation?

# Corporations: Redemptions and Liquidations

## LEARNING OBJECTIVES

*After completing Chapter 5, you should be able to:*

### LO.1
Identify the stock redemptions that qualify for sale or exchange treatment.

### LO.2
Understand the tax impact of stock redemptions on the distributing corporation.

### LO.3
Recognize the restrictions on sale or exchange treatment for certain redemption-like transactions.

### LO.4
Understand the tax consequences of complete liquidations for both the corporation and its shareholders.

### LO.5
Understand the tax consequences of a subsidiary liquidation for both the parent and the subsidiary corporations.

### LO.6
Identify tax planning opportunities available to minimize the tax impact in stock redemptions and complete liquidations.

http://wft.swlearning.com

## OUTLINE

**S**andra is the sole shareholder of Mockingbird Corporation. She acquired 100 shares in the corporation 10 years ago at a cost of $40,000; currently, the shares are worth $300,000. Mockingbird has been profitable for most of those years and currently has earnings and profits (E & P) of $200,000.

Sandra needs to raise $150,000 for an investment opportunity. To obtain the necessary funds, she has considered several possible alternatives involving her ownership interest in Mockingbird:

- Mockingbird could declare a dividend, but Sandra wants to avoid the associated ordinary income treatment, if possible (see Chapter 4).
- Sandra could sell one-half of her stock to an unrelated third party, but she does not want to give up control of the corporation.
- Sandra could sell one-half of her stock directly to Mockingbird in a stock redemption.

Sandra prefers the stock redemption as she believes it would provide her with the following favorable tax consequences while allowing her to retain sole control of Mockingbird:

- Return of capital treatment to the extent of her basis in the stock sold ($20,000).
- Long-term capital gain treatment on the excess of the amount realized over the basis ($130,000).

These favorable tax outcomes typically apply to sales or exchanges of stock held for the required long-term holding period. For example, Sandra would be taxed in this manner on a sale of the stock to an unrelated third party. In the sale to Mockingbird, however, a key characteristic inherent in typical stock sales—a reduction in ownership interest—is missing. Because Sandra would still own 100 percent of Mockingbird after the proposed stock redemption, the Code treats the transaction as a nonliquidating distribution resulting in $150,000 of ordinary dividend income (i.e., a return *from* her investment), not as a sale or exchange. However, current tax law does allow *certain* kinds of stock redemptions to qualify for sale or exchange treatment (i.e., a return *of* the owner's investment). In these transactions, as a general rule, the shareholder's ownership interest must be diminished as a result of the redemption. Additionally, a disposition of stock in a complete liquidation of a corporation will generally produce sale or exchange treatment. This chapter examines the tax implications of corporate distributions that are not dividend distributions.

| | |
|---|---|
| **LO.1**<br><br>Identify the stock redemptions that qualify for sale or exchange treatment. | |

# Stock Redemptions—In General

In a **stock redemption,** a corporation distributes cash or other property in exchange for a shareholder's stock in the corporation. Except for the fact that the shareholder is selling the stock back to the issuing corporation, a stock redemption resembles a sale of stock to an unrelated third party. While a sale of stock to an outsider invariably results in sale or exchange treatment, only a *qualifying* stock redemption is treated as a sale for tax purposes.

Nonqualified stock redemptions are denied sale or exchange treatment because they may have the same effect as dividend distributions. For example, if a shareholder owns all the stock of a corporation and sells a portion of that stock to the corporation, the shareholder's ownership interest in the corporation does not change. After the redemption, the shareholder still owns all the outstanding stock of the corporation. In this situation, the stock redemption resembles a dividend distribution and is taxed as such.

Stock redemptions occur for a variety of reasons. For instance, a redemption can be used to acquire the stock of a retiring shareholder or the stock of a deceased shareholder's estate. In both cases, having the corporation provide the funds to purchase the stock relieves the remaining shareholders of the need to use their own money to acquire the stock. Further, stock redemptions also occur as a result of property settlements in divorce actions. For example, in a divorce action involving joint ownership of corporate shares, often only one spouse winds up owning any of the shares. By having the corporation redeem the other spouse's shares, the spouse who remains as a shareholder is relieved of the need to obtain funds for the buyout.

# Stock Redemptions—Sale or Exchange Treatment

Noncorporate taxpayers will, in most cases, prefer to have a stock redemption treated as a *sale or exchange*. For high-income individual taxpayers, the 20 percent maximum tax rate on long-term capital gains is preferable to the rate on ordinary dividend income. Further, only the amount received in excess of the adjusted basis

*[handwritten margin note: High income individuals Prefer to get dividend otherwise most cases prefer stock redemption]*

of the stock is taxed, not the total redemption proceeds. Capital gain treatment can also benefit a shareholder with substantial capital losses.

**EXAMPLE 1**

*If treated as redemption LTCG @ 15/5*
*If treated as dividend @ 15% Max.*

Abby, an individual in the 38.6% tax bracket, acquired stock in Quail Corporation four years ago for $100,000. In the current year, Quail Corporation redeems her shares for $200,000. If the redemption qualifies for sale or exchange treatment, Abby will have a long-term capital gain of $100,000 [$200,000 (redemption amount) – $100,000 (cost of the shares)]. Her income tax liability on the $100,000 gain will be $20,000 ($100,000 × 20%). If the stock redemption does not qualify as a sale or exchange, it will be treated as a dividend distribution, and Abby's tax liability will be $77,200 ($200,000 × 38.6%). Thus, Abby will save $57,200 ($77,200 – $20,000) in income taxes if the transaction is a qualifying stock redemption. ∎

**EXAMPLE 2**

*Can offset the LTCG against Carryover (Cap loss)*

Assume in Example 1 that Abby has a capital loss carryover of $80,000 in the current tax year. If the transaction is a qualifying stock redemption, Abby can offset the entire $80,000 capital loss carryover against her $100,000 long-term capital gain. As a result, only $20,000 of the gain will be taxed, and her tax liability will be only $4,000 ($20,000 × 20%). On the other hand, if the transaction does not qualify for sale or exchange treatment, the entire $200,000 will be taxed at 38.6%. In addition, assuming she has no capital gains in the current year, Abby will be able to deduct only $3,000 of the $80,000 capital loss carryover to offset her other (ordinary) income. ∎

Corporate shareholders, however, normally receive *more* favorable tax treatment from a dividend distribution than would result from a qualifying stock redemption. Because of the dividends received deduction (see Chapter 2), corporate shareholders would report only a small portion of a dividend distribution as taxable income. Consequently, tax planning for stock redemptions must consider the varying preferences of corporate and noncorporate shareholders.

**EXAMPLE 3**

*If noncash property is recd. adjt. basis is FMV of the property*

Assume in Example 1 that Abby is a corporation, that the stock represents a 40% ownership interest in Quail Corporation, and that Abby has corporate taxable income of $350,000 before the redemption transaction. If the transaction is a qualifying stock redemption, Abby will have a long-term capital gain of $100,000 that will be subject to tax at 34%, or $34,000. On the other hand, if the $200,000 distribution is a dividend, Abby will have a dividends received deduction of $160,000 ($200,000 × 80%) so that only $40,000 of the payment will be taxed. Consequently, Abby's tax liability on the transaction would be only $13,600 ($40,000 × 34%). ∎

If a qualifying stock redemption results in a loss to the shareholder rather than a gain, § 267 disallows loss recognition when the shareholder owns directly or indirectly more than 50 percent of the corporation's stock. If noncash property is received in a qualifying stock redemption, a shareholder's basis in such property generally will be its fair market value, determined as of the date of the redemption. Further, the holding period of the property begins on that date.

The Code establishes the criteria for determining whether a transaction is a qualifying stock redemption for tax purposes and thus receives sale or exchange treatment. The terminology in an agreement between the parties is not controlling, nor is state law. Under § 302(a), a redemption satisfying one of four special rules will receive sale or exchange treatment. Additionally, certain distributions of property to an estate in exchange for a decedent shareholder's stock are treated as qualifying stock redemptions under § 303.

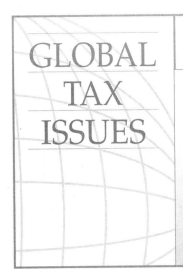

**FOREIGN SHAREHOLDERS PREFER SALE OR EXCHANGE TREATMENT IN STOCK REDEMPTIONS**

As a general rule, foreign shareholders of U.S. corporations are subject to U.S. tax on dividend income but not on capital gains. In some situations, a nonresident alien is taxed on a capital gain from the disposition of stock in a U.S. corporation, but only if the stock was effectively connected with the conduct of a U.S. trade or business of the individual. Foreign corporations are similarly taxed on gains from the sale of U.S. stock investments. Whether a stock redemption qualifies for sale or exchange treatment therefore takes on added significance for foreign shareholders. If one of the qualifying stock redemption rules can be satisfied, the foreign shareholder typically will avoid U.S. tax on the transaction. If, instead, dividend income is the result, a 30 percent withholding tax typically applies. For further details, see Chapter 9.

## HISTORICAL BACKGROUND AND OVERVIEW

Under prior law, stock redemptions that constituted dividend distributions were distinguished from those qualifying for sale or exchange treatment by the so-called *dividend equivalency rule.* When a redemption was essentially equivalent to a dividend, it did not qualify for sale or exchange treatment. The entire amount received by the shareholder was subject to taxation as ordinary income to the extent of the corporation's E & P.

To eliminate the uncertainty and subjectivity surrounding the dividend equivalency rule, Congress enacted several objective tests for determining the status of a redemption. Currently, the following five types of stock redemptions qualify for sale or exchange treatment:

- Distributions not essentially equivalent to a dividend (subsequently referred to as not essentially equivalent redemptions).
- Distributions substantially disproportionate in terms of shareholder effect (subsequently referred to as disproportionate redemptions).
- Distributions in complete termination of a shareholder's interest (subsequently referred to as complete termination redemptions).
- Distributions to noncorporate shareholders in partial liquidation of a corporation (subsequently referred to as partial liquidations).
- Distributions to pay a shareholder's death taxes (subsequently referred to as redemptions to pay death taxes).

Concept Summary 5–1 at the end of this section summarizes the requirements for each of the qualifying stock redemptions.

## STOCK ATTRIBUTION RULES

To qualify for sale or exchange treatment, a stock redemption generally must result in a substantial reduction in a shareholder's ownership in the corporation. In the absence of this reduction in ownership interest, the redemption proceeds are taxed as ordinary dividend income. In determining whether a stock redemption has sufficiently reduced a shareholder's interest, the stock owned by certain related parties is attributed to the redeeming shareholder.[1] Thus, the stock **attribution**

---

[1]§ 318.

■ **EXHIBIT 5–1**
Stock Attribution Rules

| Deemed or Constructive Ownership | |
| --- | --- |
| • Family | Stock owned by the spouse, children, grandchildren, and parents (not siblings or grandparents) is deemed to be owned by the individual. |
| • Partnership | A partner is deemed to be the owner of shares owned by a partnership to the extent of the partner's proportionate interest in the partnership. |
| | Stock owned by a partner is deemed to be owned in full by a partnership. |
| • Estate or trust | A beneficiary or heir is deemed to be the owner of shares owned by an estate or trust to the extent of the beneficiary or heir's proportionate interest in the estate or trust. |
| | Stock owned by a beneficiary or heir is deemed to be owned in full by an estate or trust. |
| • Corporation | Stock owned by a corporation is deemed to be owned proportionately by any shareholder owning 50% or more of the corporation's stock. |
| | Stock owned by a shareholder who owns 50% or more of a corporation is deemed to be owned in full by the corporation. |

rules must be considered along with the stock redemption provisions. Under these rules, related parties are defined to include the following family members: spouses, children, grandchildren, and parents. Attribution also takes place *from* and *to* partnerships, estates, trusts, and corporations (50 percent or more ownership required in the case of regular corporations). Exhibit 5–1 summarizes the stock attribution rules.

**EXAMPLE 4**

Larry owns 30% of the stock in Blue Corporation, with the other 70% being held by his children. For purposes of the stock attribution rules, Larry is treated as owning 100% of the stock in Blue Corporation. He owns 30% directly and, because of the family attribution rules, 70% indirectly. ■

**EXAMPLE 5**

Chris owns 40% of the stock in Gray Corporation. The other 60% is owned by a partnership in which Chris has a 20% interest. Chris is deemed to own 52% of Gray Corporation: 40% directly and, because of the partnership interest, 12% indirectly (20% × 60%). ■

As discussed later, the *family* attribution rules (refer to Example 4) can be waived in the case of some complete termination redemptions. In addition, the stock attribution rules do not apply to partial liquidations or redemptions to pay death taxes.

## NOT ESSENTIALLY EQUIVALENT REDEMPTIONS

Under § 302(b)(1), a redemption qualifies for sale or exchange treatment if it is "not essentially equivalent to a dividend." This provision represents a continuation of the dividend equivalency rule applicable under prior law. The earlier redemption language was retained specifically for redemptions of preferred stock because shareholders often have no control over when corporations call in such stock.[2] Like its

[2]See S.Rept. No. 1622, 83d Cong., 2d Sess. 44 (1954).

predecessor, the not essentially equivalent to a dividend redemption lacks an objective test. Instead, each case must be resolved on a facts and circumstances basis.[3]

Based upon the Supreme Court's decision in *U.S. v. Davis*,[4] a redemption will qualify as a **not essentially equivalent redemption** only when the shareholder's interest in the redeeming corporation has been meaningfully reduced. In determining whether the **meaningful reduction test** has been met, the stock attribution rules apply. A decrease in the redeeming shareholder's voting control appears to be the most significant indicator of a meaningful reduction,[5] but reductions in the rights of redeeming shareholders to share in corporate earnings or to receive corporate assets upon liquidation are also considered.[6] The meaningful reduction test is applied whether common stock or preferred stock is being redeemed.

| | |
|---|---|
| **EXAMPLE 6** | Pat owns 58% of the common stock of Falcon Corporation. After a redemption of part of Pat's stock, he owns 51% of the stock of Falcon. Pat continues to have dominant voting rights in Falcon; thus, the redemption is treated as essentially equivalent to a dividend, and Pat has dividend income on the entire amount of the distribution, assuming adequate E & P. ■ |

*[Handwritten note: 58% → 51% essentially equivalent to a dividend]*

| | |
|---|---|
| **EXAMPLE 7** | Maroon Corporation redeems 2% of its stock from Maria. Before the redemption, Maria owned 10% of Maroon Corporation. In this case, the redemption may qualify as not essentially equivalent to a dividend. Maria experiences a reduction in her voting rights, her right to participate in current earnings and accumulated surplus, and her right to share in net assets upon liquidation. ■ |

*[Handwritten note: 10% → 8% Not essentially equivalent to a dividend]*

If a redemption is treated as an ordinary dividend, the basis in the stock redeemed attaches to the shareholder's remaining stock (or to stock the shareholder owns constructively).[7] This is the case in any redemption that does not satisfy the requirements of any of the qualifying stock redemption provisions.

| | |
|---|---|
| **EXAMPLE 8** | Floyd and Fran, husband and wife, each own 50 shares in Grouse Corporation, representing 100% of the corporation's stock. All the stock was purchased for $50,000. Both Floyd and Fran serve as directors of the corporation. The corporation redeems Floyd's 50 shares. Floyd continues to serve as a director of the corporation. The redemption is treated as a taxable dividend (assuming adequate E & P) because he constructively owns Fran's stock. Floyd's basis in the 50 shares redeemed, $25,000, attaches to Fran's stock. She then has a basis of $50,000 in the 50 shares she owns in Grouse. ■ |

## DISPROPORTIONATE REDEMPTIONS

*[Handwritten note: Second Rule]*

A stock redemption qualifies for sale or exchange treatment under § 302(b)(2) as a **disproportionate redemption** if two conditions are met:

*[Handwritten note: Two conditions are required to be met to qualify for sale or exchange. Redemption less than (80% of 60%) 48. Own over 60%]*

- The distribution is substantially disproportionate. To be substantially disproportionate, the shareholder must own, after the distribution, *less than* 80 percent of the interest owned in the corporation before the redemption. For example, if a shareholder owns a 60 percent interest in a corporation that redeems part of the stock, the redemption is substantially disproportionate only if the shareholder's ownership interest after the redemption is less than 48 percent (80 percent of 60 percent).
- The shareholder owns, after the distribution, *less than* 50 percent of the total combined voting power of all classes of stock entitled to vote.

---

[3]Reg. § 1.302–2(b).
[4]70–1 USTC ¶9289, 25 AFTR2d 70–827, 90 S.Ct. 1041 (USSC, 1970).
[5]See, for example, *Jack Paparo*, 71 T.C. 692 (1979).

[6]See, for example, *Grabowski Trust*, 58 T.C. 650 (1972).
[7]Reg. § 1.302–2(c).

In determining a shareholder's ownership interest before and after a redemption, the attribution rules apply.

**EXAMPLE 9**

Bob, Carl, and Dan, unrelated individuals, own 30 shares, 30 shares, and 40 shares, respectively, in Wren Corporation. Wren has E & P of $200,000. The corporation redeems 20 shares of Dan's stock for $30,000. Dan paid $200 a share for the stock two years ago. Dan's ownership in Wren Corporation before and after the redemption is as follows:

|  | Total Shares | Dan's Ownership | Ownership Percentage | 80% of Original Ownership |
|---|---|---|---|---|
| Before redemption | 100 | 40 | 40% (40 ÷ 100) | 32% (80% × 40%) |
| After redemption | 80 | 20 | 25% (20 ÷ 80)* | |

*Note that the denominator of the fraction is reduced after the redemption (from 100 to 80).

Dan's 25% ownership after the redemption meets both tests of § 302(b)(2). It is less than 80% of his original ownership and less than 50% of the total voting power. The distribution therefore qualifies as a stock redemption that receives sale or exchange treatment. As a result, Dan has a long-term capital gain of $26,000 [$30,000 − $4,000 (20 shares × $200)]. ■

**EXAMPLE 10**

Assume that Carl and Dan are father and son. The redemption described above would not qualify for sale or exchange treatment because of the effect of the attribution rules. Dan is deemed to own Carl's stock before and after the redemption. Dan's ownership in Wren Corporation before and after the redemption is as follows:

|  | Total Shares | Dan's Direct Ownership | Carl's Ownership | Dan's Direct and Indirect Ownership | Ownership Percentage | 80% of Original Ownership |
|---|---|---|---|---|---|---|
| Before redemption | 100 | 40 | 30 | 70 | 70% (70 ÷ 100) | 56% (80% × 70%) |
| After redemption | 80 | 20 | 30 | 50 | 62.5% (50 ÷ 80) | |

Dan's direct and indirect ownership of 62.5% fails to meet either of the tests of § 302(b)(2). After the redemption, Dan owns more than 80% of his original ownership and more than 50% of the voting stock. Thus, the redemption does not qualify for sale or exchange treatment and results in a dividend distribution of $30,000 to Dan. The basis in the 20 shares redeemed is added to Dan's basis in his remaining 20 shares. ■

Even if a redemption is not substantially disproportionate, it may still qualify as a not essentially equivalent redemption if it meets the meaningful reduction test (see Example 7). A reduction in voting control when the shareholder does not have a majority controlling interest may qualify as a not essentially equivalent redemption. However, the stock attribution rules apply in determining whether there has been a reduction in voting control.

## COMPLETE TERMINATION REDEMPTIONS

A stock redemption that terminates a shareholder's *entire* stock ownership in a corporation will qualify for sale or exchange treatment under § 302(b)(3). The attribution rules generally apply in determining whether the shareholder's stock ownership has been completely terminated. However, the *family* attribution rules do not apply to a **complete termination redemption** if the following conditions are met:

## FRINGE BENEFITS NOT A PROHIBITED INTEREST

The IRS has ruled (FSA 200203021) that fringe benefits provided to a redeemed share-holder do not constitute a prohibited interest for purposes of the family attribution waiver. The former shareholder received several fringe benefits as a result of his spouse's contin-ued employment with the corporation. Those benefits included medical insurance cover-age, corporate preparation of the couple's joint tax return, and primary use of a corporate truck provided to his spouse.

In the same ruling, however, the IRS also held that installment notes received by the former shareholder in the redemption constituted a prohibited interest, not a creditor interest. The IRS reached this conclusion after examining the redemption agreement, which provided that the installment notes would be payable in full if the corporation breached an employment contract it had entered into with the former shareholder's spouse. This acceleration clause was deemed to be broader in scope than necessary to protect the former shareholder's claim and thus failed a test under Regulation § 1.302–4(d) for creditor status.

- The former shareholder has no interest, other than that of a creditor, in the corporation for at least 10 years after the redemption (including an interest as an officer, director, or employee).
- The former shareholder files an agreement to notify the IRS of any prohibited interest acquired within the 10-year period and to retain all necessary records pertaining to the redemption during this time period.

Acquisition of stock in the corporation by bequest or inheritance will not constitute a prohibited interest. The required agreement should be in the form of a separate statement signed by the former shareholder and attached to the return for the year in which the redemption occurs. The agreement should state that the former shareholder agrees to notify the IRS within 30 days of acquiring a prohibited interest in the corporation within the 10-year period following the redemption.[8]

**EXAMPLE 11**

Kevin owns 50% of the stock in Green Corporation while the remaining interest in Green is held as follows: 40% by Wilma (Kevin's wife) and 10% by Carmen (a key employee). Green redeems all of Kevin's stock for its fair market value. As a result, Wilma and Carmen are the only remaining shareholders, now owning 80% and 20%, respectively. If the require-ments for the family attribution waiver are met, the transaction will qualify as a complete termination redemption and result in sale or exchange treatment. If the waiver is not allowed, Kevin will be deemed to own Wilma's (his wife's) stock, and the entire distribution will be a dividend, assuming adequate E & P. ■

**EXAMPLE 12**

Assume in Example 11 that Kevin qualifies for the family attribution waiver for the redemp-tion. In the year of the redemption, Kevin treats the transaction as a sale or exchange. However, if he purchases Carmen's stock seven years after the redemption, he has acquired a prohibited interest, and the redemption is reclassified as a dividend. Kevin owes additional taxes due to this revised treatment. ■

---

[8]Reg. § 1.302–4(a)(1).

## ETHICAL CONSIDERATIONS    Good Friend or Good CPA?

Eight years ago, Blue Corporation redeemed all of Elton's shares in the corporation. Elton reported the transaction as a complete termination redemption resulting in sale or exchange treatment. At the time of the redemption, Elton's children owned the remaining shares in Blue. To obtain the family attribution waiver, Elton resigned as an officer and filed the requisite agreement with the IRS. Elton's CPA at the time of the redemption was his good friend John.

John has recently learned that Elton is struggling financially with retirement and, as a result, has taken a management position with Blue Corporation. Elton has indicated that he is unlikely to inform the IRS of this prohibited interest, as he does not have the wherewithal to pay the related additional tax liability. How should John proceed with respect to Elton's predicament?

*Fourth Rule*

## PARTIAL LIQUIDATIONS

Under § 302(b)(4), a *noncorporate* shareholder is allowed sale or exchange treatment for a distribution that qualifies as a **partial liquidation**. A partial liquidation is a distribution that (1) is *not essentially equivalent to a dividend* and (2) is both pursuant to a plan and made within the plan year or within the succeeding taxable year. There is no requirement for stock to be redeemed in a partial liquidation. If there is a redemption pursuant to a partial liquidation, the redemption may be pro rata with respect to the shareholders.

In determining whether a distribution is not essentially equivalent to a dividend, the effect of the distribution on the *corporation* is examined.[9] As a result, to qualify as a partial liquidation, the distribution must result in a *genuine contraction* of the business of the corporation.

**EXAMPLE 13**

Dove Corporation owned a building with seven floors. Part of the building was rented, and part was used directly in Dove's business. A fire destroyed the two top floors, and Dove received insurance proceeds in reimbursement for the damage sustained. For business reasons, Dove did not rebuild the two floors, but chose to operate on a smaller scale than before the fire. Pursuant to a plan adopted in the current year, Dove uses unreinvested insurance proceeds to redeem some stock from its shareholders. The distribution is not essentially equivalent to a dividend and qualifies as a partial liquidation.[10] ∎

Applying the genuine contraction of a corporate business concept has proved difficult due to the lack of objective tests. The IRS has ruled that using proceeds from the sale of investments or excess inventory to redeem part of the shareholders' stock will not qualify.[11] To minimize uncertainty, the genuine contraction test should be relied upon only after obtaining a favorable ruling from the IRS.

**EXAMPLE 14**

Pink Corporation has been selling a single product for eight years. It loses its major customer, and a severe drop in sales results. The corporation reduces its inventory investment and has substantial cash on hand. It distributes the excess cash to its shareholders in a pro rata stock redemption. Lynn, one of Pink's shareholders, receives $10,000 for stock that cost her $5,000 two years ago. Since Lynn's ownership interest in Pink remains unchanged, the redemption does not qualify as a not essentially equivalent redemption, a substantially

---

[9]§ 302(e).
[10]See *Joseph W. Imler*, 11 T.C. 836 (1948) and Reg. § 1.346–1(a)(2).

[11]Rev.Rul. 60–322, 1960–2 C.B. 118.

disproportionate redemption, or a complete termination redemption. Further, the reduction in inventory does not qualify as a general contraction of Pink Corporation's business; thus, the distribution is not a partial liquidation. Therefore, the $10,000 is an ordinary dividend to Lynn, assuming adequate E & P. The $5,000 basis in the stock redeemed attaches to the basis of Lynn's remaining shares of Pink. ■

A safe-harbor rule, the *termination of an active business* test, will satisfy the not essentially equivalent to a dividend requirement. In contrast to the genuine contraction test, the termination of an active business test does follow objective requirements. A distribution will qualify under the termination of an active business test if the following conditions are met:

- The corporation has two or more trades or businesses that (1) have been in existence for the five-year period ending on the date of the redemption and (2) were not acquired in taxable transactions during that period ("qualified trades or businesses").
- The corporation terminates one qualified trade or business while continuing another qualified trade or business.

The distribution can be in the form of the assets of the terminated business or the proceeds from the sale of such assets.

**EXAMPLE 15**

Loon Corporation, the owner and operator of a wholesale grocery business with a substantial amount of excess cash, purchased a freight-hauling concern. Six years later, Loon distributes the freight-hauling assets in kind on a pro rata basis to all its noncorporate shareholders. The distribution satisfies the requirements of the termination of an active business test. Loon had conducted the freight-hauling business for at least five years and continues to conduct the wholesale grocery business. Thus, the distribution qualifies as a partial liquidation and is treated as a sale or exchange to the shareholders. ■

## REDEMPTIONS TO PAY DEATH TAXES

Section 303 provides sale or exchange treatment to a redemption of stock included in, and representing a substantial amount of, a decedent's gross estate. The purpose of this provision is to provide an estate with liquidity to pay death-related expenses when a significant part of the estate consists of stock in a closely held corporation. Often such stock is not easily marketable, and a stock redemption represents the only viable option for its disposition. The redemption might not qualify for sale or exchange treatment under the other redemption rules because of the stock attribution rules (e.g., attribution to estate from beneficiaries). A **redemption to pay death taxes** provides sale or exchange treatment without regard to the attribution rules, but the provision limits this treatment to the sum of the death taxes and funeral and administration expenses. A redemption in excess of these expenses may qualify for sale or exchange treatment under one of the § 302 provisions.

The income tax basis of property owned by a decedent's estate is the property's fair market value on the date of death (or alternate valuation date if available and if elected).[12] Therefore, in a redemption to pay death taxes, the redemption price generally equals (or approximates) the basis of the stock. When the redemption price equals the estate's basis that results from the step-up to date of death value (see Chapter 18), the exchange is free of any income tax consequences to the estate.

Section 303 applies only to a distribution made with respect to stock of a corporation when the value of that one corporation's stock in the gross estate of a

---

[12]§ 1014(a).

decedent *exceeds* 35 percent of the value of the adjusted gross estate. (For a definition of "gross estate" and "adjusted gross estate," see the Glossary of Tax Terms in Appendix C.)

**EXAMPLE 16**

Juan's adjusted gross estate is $900,000. The death taxes and funeral and administration expenses of the estate total $200,000. Included in the gross estate is stock of Yellow Corporation valued at $340,000. Juan had acquired the stock years ago at a cost of $60,000. Yellow redeems $200,000 of the stock from Juan's estate. Because the value of the Yellow stock in Juan's estate exceeds the 35% threshold ($340,000 ÷ $900,000 = 37.8%), the redemption qualifies under § 303 as a sale or exchange to Juan's estate. Assuming the value of the stock has remained unchanged since the date of Juan's death, there is no recognized gain (or loss) on the redemption [$200,000 (amount realized) − $200,000 (stock basis)]. ■

In determining whether the value of stock of one corporation exceeds 35 percent of the value of the adjusted gross estate of a decedent, the stock of two or more corporations may be treated as the stock of a single corporation. Stock of corporations in which the decedent held a 20 percent or more interest is treated as stock of a single corporation for this purpose.[13] When this exception is used, the stock redeemed can be that of any of the 20 percent or more shareholder interests.

**EXAMPLE 17**

The adjusted gross estate of a decedent is $300,000. The gross estate includes stock of Owl and Robin Corporations valued at $100,000 and $80,000, respectively. Unless the two corporations are treated as a single corporation, § 303 does not apply to a redemption of the stock of either corporation. Assuming the decedent owned all the stock of Owl Corporation and 80% of the stock of Robin, § 303 applies because the decedent's estate includes a 20% or more interest in the stock of each corporation. The 35% test is met when the stock of Owl and Robin is treated as that of a single corporation [($100,000 + $80,000) ÷ $300,000 = 60%]. The stock of Owl or Robin (or both) can be redeemed under § 303. ■

## LO.2

Understand the tax impact of stock redemptions on the distributing corporation.

# Effect on the Corporation Redeeming Its Stock

Thus far, the discussion has focused on the effect of stock redemptions to the *shareholder*. If sale or exchange treatment is allowed for the shareholder, what is the tax effect on the *corporation* redeeming its stock? Does the corporation recognize gain or loss on the distribution of property other than cash to carry out the redemption? Also, what effect does the redemption have on the corporation's E & P? Furthermore, can the corporation deduct expenditures incurred in the redemption of its stock? These matters are discussed in the following paragraphs.

## RECOGNITION OF GAIN OR LOSS

Section 311 provides that corporations are taxed on all nonliquidating distributions of appreciated property as if the property had been sold for its fair market value. This is the case for all stock redemptions, qualifying or not. Losses, however, are not recognized on nonliquidating distributions. When distributed property is subject to a corporate liability, the fair market value of that property is treated as not being less than the amount of the liability.

---

[13]§ 303(b)(2)(B).

## TAX IN THE NEWS

### BASEBALL TEAM OWNER STRIKES OUT ON DEDUCTION OF REDEMPTION COSTS

Ewing Kauffman owned 100 percent of the stock of the Kansas City Royals Baseball Corporation, an S corporation holding the franchise rights to the Kansas City Royals baseball team. In 1983, Kauffman sold a 49 percent interest in the Royals to Avron Fogelman for $10 million. Fogelman later acquired an additional 1 percent interest and an option to purchase Kauffman's remaining interest in the Royals. By 1990, Fogelman was experiencing severe financial problems, and the Royals stock and option represented his only unencumbered assets.

Fearful that Fogelman's creditors would end up owning the team, an agreement was reached that would provide Fogelman with cash from his Royals ownership interest. Pursuant to that agreement, Kauffman "loaned" $34 million to the Royals, which then "loaned" the $34 million to Fogelman. The purported loan to Fogelman was secured only by his Royals stock and option. Also pursuant to the agreement, the Royals were granted an option to purchase that stock and option for a price equal to the amount of the outstanding "loan." Fogelman subsequently "defaulted" on the purported loan, and the Royals retained his Royals stock and option.

The Royals claimed a bad debt deduction for the unpaid "loan" (and interest) and, as an S corporation, passed the deduction through to the sole shareholder, Kauffman. The IRS disallowed the deduction, arguing that the substance of the transaction was a redemption of Fogelman's Royals stock and that redemption-related expenditures are not deductible. A district court and a circuit court of appeals agreed with the IRS's position.

---

**EXAMPLE 18**

To carry out a stock redemption, Blackbird Corporation transfers land (basis of $80,000, fair market value of $300,000) to a shareholder. Blackbird has a recognized gain of $220,000 ($300,000 − $80,000). If the value of the property distributed was less than its adjusted basis, the realized loss would not be recognized. ■

Because of the loss disallowance, a corporation should not use property that has depreciated in value as consideration in the redemption of a shareholder's stock. However, the corporation could sell the property in a taxable transaction in which it can recognize a loss and then distribute the proceeds.

## EFFECT ON EARNINGS AND PROFITS

The E & P account of a corporation is reduced by a qualifying stock redemption in an amount not in excess of the ratable share of the E & P of the distributing corporation attributable to the stock redeemed.[14]

**EXAMPLE 19**

Navy Corporation has 100 shares of stock outstanding. It redeems 30 shares for $100,000 at a time when it has paid-in capital of $120,000 and E & P of $150,000. The charge to E & P is 30% of the amount in the E & P account ($45,000), and the remainder of the redemption price ($55,000) is a reduction of the capital account. If, instead, the 30 shares were redeemed for $40,000, the charge to E & P would be limited to $40,000, the amount paid by the corporation for the stock. ■

---

[14]§ 312(n)(7).

## CONCEPT SUMMARY 5–1

### Summary of the Qualifying Stock Redemption Rules

| Type of Redemption | Requirements to Qualify |
|---|---|
| Not essentially equivalent to a dividend [§ 302(b)(1)] | Meaningful reduction in shareholder's voting interest. If less than a majority interest, reduction in interest in assets and E & P also considered. |
| | Stock attribution rules apply. |
| Substantially disproportionate [§ 302(b)(2)] | Shareholder's interest in the corporation, after the redemption, must be less than 80% of interest before the redemption and less than 50% of total combined voting power of all classes of stock entitled to vote. |
| | Stock attribution rules apply. |
| Complete termination [§ 302(b)(3)] | Entire stock ownership terminated. |
| | In general, stock attribution rules apply. However, *family* stock attribution rules may be waived. Former shareholder must have no interest, other than as a creditor, in the corporation for at least 10 years and must file an agreement to notify IRS of any prohibited interest acquired during 10-year period. Shareholder must retain all necessary records during 10-year period. |
| Partial liquidation [§ 302(b)(4)] | Not essentially equivalent to a dividend. |
| | • Genuine contraction of corporation's business. |
| | • Termination of an active business. |
| |    • Corporation has two or more qualified trades or businesses. |
| |      • Corporation terminates one qualified trade or business while continuing another qualified trade or business. |
| | Distribution may be in form of cash or property. |
| | Redemption may be pro rata. |
| | Attribution rules do not apply. |
| Redemption to pay death taxes [§ 303] | Value of stock of one corporation in gross estate exceeds 35% of value of adjusted gross estate. |
| | • Stock of two or more corporations treated as stock of a single corporation in applying the 35% test if decedent held a 20% or more interest in the stock of the corporations. |
| | Redemption limited to amount of death taxes and funeral and administration expenses. |
| | Generally tax-free because tax basis of stock is FMV on date of decedent's death and value is unchanged at redemption. |

### REDEMPTION EXPENDITURES

In redeeming its shares, a corporation may incur certain expenditures such as accounting, brokerage, legal, and loan fees. Section 162(k) specifically denies a deduction for expenditures incurred in a stock redemption.

**LO.3**

*Recognize the restrictions on sale or exchange treatment for certain redemption-like transactions.*

## Stock Redemptions—Additional Limitations

Stock redemptions that do not fall under any of the qualifying stock redemption provisions are treated as dividend distributions to the extent of E & P. Resourceful taxpayers, however, devised ways to circumvent the redemption provisions. Two

*Not responsible*

types of these transactions involved structuring what was, in effect, a stock redemption or a dividend distribution as a sale of the stock. The widespread use of these approaches to obtain capital gain treatment led to the enactment of § 306, dealing with preferred stock bailouts, and § 304, dealing with sales of stock to related corporations. These two loophole-closing provisions are explained next. Some corporate divisions resemble stock redemptions, and those distributions are also briefly discussed.

## PREFERRED STOCK BAILOUTS

When a corporation's stock is owned entirely (or predominantly) by one or more family members, the attribution rules severely limit the opportunities for effecting a qualifying stock redemption. A complete termination redemption, in conjunction with the family attribution waiver, is one possibility, but the former shareholder must sever all ties (other than that as a creditor) with the corporation. Another possibility, the redemption to pay death taxes, is limited for obvious reasons (i.e., death of the shareholder is required). Further, a redemption qualifying as a partial liquidation is generally limited to unique situations involving a genuine contraction of the corporate business. Sale or exchange treatment could be attained by completely liquidating the corporation, but the liquidation of a going concern with good present and future profit potential may not be wise. Another possibility, a sale of the stock to a third party, would provide sale or exchange treatment but have the effect of diluting family ownership interests.

Clever taxpayers devised a scheme called the **preferred stock bailout** in an attempt to obtain the benefits of a qualifying stock redemption without the attendant limitations.[15] Under this scheme, a corporation would issue a nontaxable (nonvoting) preferred stock dividend on common stock.[16] The shareholder would assign a portion of his or her basis in the common stock to the preferred stock. The shareholder then would sell the preferred stock to a third party. Unlike a sale of common shares, the sale of preferred stock would not reduce the shareholder's percentage ownership in the corporation. Since the transaction would not take the form of a stock redemption, the related limitations on sale or exchange treatment would not apply. The difference between the selling price and the shareholder's basis would be a capital gain. The result would be a bailout of corporate profits as a capital gain. No diminution in control of the corporation would occur because the voting common stock would remain intact.

**Tax Treatment of Preferred Stock Bailouts.** The tax avoidance possibilities of the preferred stock bailout led to the enactment of § 306. In the case of a sale of § 306 stock to a third party, the tax consequences are as follows:

- The shareholder has ordinary income on the sale equal to the fair market value of the preferred stock on the date of the distribution. However, the ordinary income amount is limited to the amount that would have been a dividend had the corporation distributed cash in lieu of stock (the "§ 306 taint").[17] If the selling price of the preferred stock exceeds the § 306 taint, the excess is an untaxed return of capital that reduces the shareholder's basis in the preferred stock. Any excess received over the § 306 taint and the preferred stock's basis is capital gain.

---

[15]See, e.g., *Chamberlin v. Comm.*, 53–2 USTC ¶9576, 44 AFTR 494, 207 F.2d 462 (CA–6, 1953), *cert. den.* 74 S.Ct. 516 (USSC, 1954).

[16]§ 305(a).

[17]§ 306(a)(1).

- The ordinary income to the shareholder is *not a dividend* and has no effect on the issuing corporation's E & P. In this respect, the statutory solution leads to a harsher result than does a taxable dividend distribution.
- No loss is recognized on any sale of the preferred stock by the shareholder.[18] Instead, any unrecovered basis in the preferred stock sold is added to the basis of the shareholder's common stock.[19]
- Section 306 does not apply to stock sales that terminate the shareholder's entire stock interest (§ 318 attribution rules apply) or result from the complete liquidation of the corporation.[20]

**EXAMPLE 20**

As of January 1 of the current year, Tern Corporation has E & P of $150,000. Naomi owns all of Tern's common stock (100 shares) with a basis of $60,000. On that date, Tern declares and pays a nontaxable preferred stock dividend of 100 shares. After the dividend, the fair market value of one share of common is $2,000, and the fair market value of one share of preferred is $1,000. Two days later, Naomi sells the 100 shares of preferred to Emily for $100,000. Section 306 produces the following results:

- After the distribution and before the sale, the preferred stock has a basis to Naomi of $20,000 [($100,000 value of preferred ÷ $300,000 value of preferred and common) × $60,000 (the original basis of the common stock)]. At this time, the common stock has a new basis of $40,000.
- The sale of the preferred stock generates $100,000 of ordinary income to Naomi. This is the amount of dividend income Naomi would have recognized had cash been distributed instead of preferred stock.
- The $20,000 basis allocated to the preferred stock is added to the basis of the common stock; thus, the common stock basis is increased back to $60,000.
- Tern Corporation's E & P account is unaffected by either the stock distribution or its subsequent sale. ■

**EXAMPLE 21**

Assume in Example 20 that Tern Corporation's E & P is only $50,000 on the date the preferred stock is distributed. Under these circumstances, the $100,000 sale proceeds are accounted for as follows: $50,000 ordinary income (limited to the § 306 taint), $20,000 applied against the basis of the preferred stock, and $30,000 capital gain. Whether the capital gain is long term or short term depends upon the holding period of the underlying common stock. ■

If the preferred stock is not sold to a third party but instead is redeemed by the issuing corporation, § 306 produces the following tax consequences:

- The redemption proceeds constitute dividend income to the extent of the corporation's E & P on the date of the *redemption*.[21]
- Because the transaction is treated as a § 301 distribution, the corporation's E & P is reduced the same as in the case of an ordinary dividend.
- The basis of the preferred stock redeemed is added to the basis of the shareholder's common stock.
- If the redemption results in a complete termination redemption or a partial liquidation, § 306 does not apply to the transaction.[22]

**EXAMPLE 22**

Assume in Example 20 that Tern Corporation (not Emily) acquires Naomi's 100 shares of preferred stock for $100,000 and that Tern's E & P at the time of the redemption is $150,000. Since sufficient E & P exists at the time of redemption, the entire $100,000 is dividend income

---

[18]§ 306(a)(1)(C).
[19]Reg. § 1.306–1(b)(2) (Example 2).
[20]§ 306(b).

[21]§ 306(a)(2).
[22]§ 306(b)(1)(B).

to Naomi. The $20,000 basis allocated to the preferred stock is added back to the basis of the common stock (i.e., common stock basis is increased back to $60,000). Tern's E & P is reduced by the $100,000 distribution. ■

**Definition of § 306 Stock.**    Section 306 stock is stock other than common that either (1) is received as a nontaxable stock dividend, (2) is received tax-free in a corporate reorganization or separation to the extent that either the effect of the transaction was substantially the same as the receipt of a stock dividend or the stock was received in exchange for § 306 stock, or (3) has a basis determined by reference to the basis of § 306 stock (e.g., such as a gift of § 306 stock). (Corporate reorganizations are discussed in Chapter 7.) If a corporation has no E & P on the date of distribution of a nontaxable preferred stock dividend, the stock will not be § 306 stock.[23]

## REDEMPTIONS THROUGH THE USE OF RELATED CORPORATIONS

A shareholder possessing a controlling interest (i.e., direct or indirect ownership of at least 50 percent)[24] in two or more corporations could, in the absence of any statutory limitation, obtain sale or exchange treatment by having one corporation purchase some of the shareholder's stock in a second related corporation. This result could occur even if the shareholder's ownership interest in the corporation whose stock is sold has not been substantively reduced. Section 304 closes this loophole by treating the sale of stock of one corporation to a related corporation as a stock redemption subject to the rules discussed earlier in this chapter. This provision applies to a transfer involving brother-sister corporations as well as to parent-subsidiary situations (see Chapter 2).

In general, § 304 requires a redemption through the use of related corporations to result in a reduction of ownership interest that would satisfy one of the qualifying stock redemptions of § 302 (e.g., disproportionate redemption) or § 303.[25] If the redemption does not qualify under those rules, the transaction is characterized as a dividend distribution.[26] When brother-sister corporations are involved, the shareholder increases the basis in the stock of the acquiring corporation by the basis of the stock surrendered in the transaction. Likewise, the acquiring corporation's basis in the stock acquired is equal to the basis the shareholder had in such shares.[27] Transfers involving the application of § 304 to brother-sister corporations are summarized in Figure 5–1.

## DISTRIBUTION OF STOCK AND SECURITIES OF A CONTROLLED CORPORATION

If one corporation controls another corporation, stock in the subsidiary corporation can be distributed to the shareholders of the parent corporation tax-free under § 355. When a subsidiary is newly formed to perfect a corporate division, this provision applies through the divisive corporate reorganization rules discussed in Chapter 7. When a subsidiary already exists, § 355 alone applies, and the transaction can resemble either a dividend, a stock redemption, or a complete liquidation. The rules surrounding these transactions are covered in detail in Chapter 7.

---

[23]§ 306(c).
[24]§ 304(c).
[25]See § 304(a)(1).

[26]The distribution is dividend income to the extent of the sum of E & P of the two related corporations. § 304(b)(2).
[27]Reg. § 1.304–2(a) and § 362(a).

■ **FIGURE 5–1**
Redemptions Involving
Brother-Sister Corporations

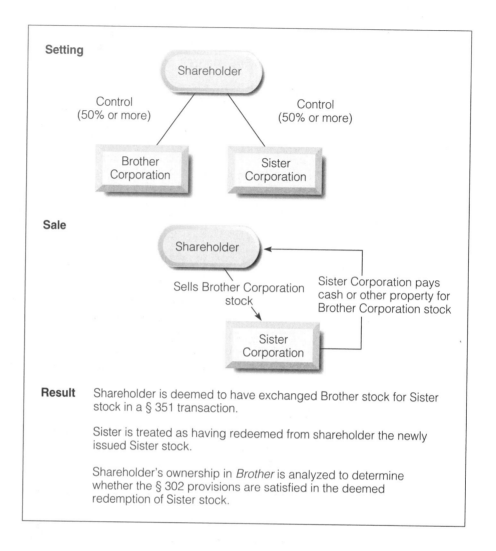

Setting

Shareholder

Control                                    Control
(50% or more)                          (50% or more)

Brother                                    Sister
Corporation                            Corporation

Sale

Shareholder

Sells Brother Corporation          Sister Corporation pays
stock                                    cash or other property for
                                           Brother Corporation stock

Sister
Corporation

**Result**  Shareholder is deemed to have exchanged Brother stock for Sister
stock in a § 351 transaction.

Sister is treated as having redeemed from shareholder the newly
issued Sister stock.

Shareholder's ownership in *Brother* is analyzed to determine
whether the § 302 provisions are satisfied in the deemed
redemption of Sister stock.

## LO.4

Understand the tax
consequences of complete
liquidations for both the
corporation and its
shareholders.

# Liquidations—In General

When a corporation makes a nonliquidating distribution (e.g., stock redemption),
the entity typically will continue as a going concern. With a complete liquidation,
however, corporate existence terminates, as does the shareholder's ownership interest. A complete liquidation, like a qualifying stock redemption, produces sale or
exchange treatment to the *shareholder*. However, the tax effects of a liquidation to the
*corporation* vary somewhat from those of a redemption. Sale or exchange treatment is
the general rule for the liquidating corporation, although some losses are
disallowed.

## THE LIQUIDATION PROCESS

A **corporate liquidation** exists when a corporation ceases to be a going concern.
The corporation continues solely to wind up affairs, pay debts, and distribute any
remaining assets to its shareholders. Legal dissolution under state law is not required for the liquidation to be complete for tax purposes. A transaction is treated

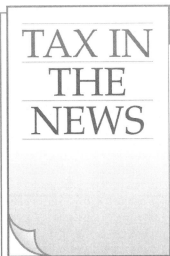

## TAX IN THE NEWS

### DECISION TO LIQUIDATE PROMPTS SHAREHOLDER LAWSUI

When considering the liquidation or sale of a corporation's assets, corporate management must keep shareholder value in mind. Failure to choose the option that maximizes shareholder value may result in management feeling the legal wrath of unhappy shareholders. Such was the case with Federated Department Stores, whose shareholders filed a lawsuit against the corporation's management for deciding to liquidate a subsidiary, Fingerhut, without first attempting to sell the business as a going concern. The lawsuit alleged that the failure to seek a purchaser for Fingerhut amounted to gross mismanagement by Federated's executives and board of directors. Arguing a loss of shareholder value, the lawsuit asserted that management had breached its fiduciary responsibility to the shareholders. The lawsuit also claimed that a liquidation of Fingerhut would allow management to hide losses.

as a liquidation even if the corporation retains a nominal amount of assets to pay remaining debts and preserve legal status.[28]

Shareholders may decide to liquidate a corporation for one or more reasons, including the following:

- The corporate business has been unsuccessful.
- The shareholders wish to acquire the corporation's assets.
- Another person or corporation wants to purchase the corporation's assets. The purchaser may buy the shareholders' stock and then liquidate the corporation to acquire the assets. Alternatively, the purchaser may buy the assets directly from the corporation. After the assets are sold, the corporation distributes the sales proceeds to its shareholders and liquidates.

As one might expect, the different means used to liquidate a corporation produce varying tax results.

### LIQUIDATIONS AND OTHER DISTRIBUTIONS COMPARED

As noted previously, a *nonliquidating* property distribution, whether in the form of a dividend or a stock redemption, produces gain (but not loss) to the distributing corporation. For the shareholder, the receipt of cash or property produces dividend income to the extent of the corporation's E & P or, in the case of a qualifying stock redemption, results in sale or exchange treatment.

Like a qualifying stock redemption, a complete liquidation produces sale or exchange treatment for the shareholders. Similarly, E & P has no impact on the gain or loss to be recognized by the shareholder in either type of distribution.[29] However, a complete liquidation produces different tax consequences to the liquidating corporation. With certain exceptions, a liquidating corporation recognizes gain *and* loss upon the distribution of its assets.

**EXAMPLE 23**

Goose Corporation, with E & P of $40,000, makes a cash distribution of $50,000 to its sole shareholder. The shareholder's basis in the Goose stock is $20,000. If the distribution is not a qualifying stock redemption or in complete liquidation, the shareholder recognizes dividend

---

[28]Reg. § 1.332–2(c).

[29]§ 331.

*Complete liqui*
*No Conseq on E & P*

income of $40,000 (the amount of Goose's E & P) and treats the remaining $10,000 of the distribution as a return of capital. If the distribution is a qualifying stock redemption or is pursuant to a complete liquidation, the shareholder has a capital gain of $30,000 ($50,000 distribution – $20,000 stock basis). In the latter case, Goose's E & P is of no consequence to the tax result to the shareholder. ■

In the event a corporate distribution results in a *loss* to the shareholder, an important distinction exists between qualifying stock redemptions and liquidations. Section 267 disallows recognition of losses between related parties in redemption transactions but not losses arising out of complete liquidations.

**EXAMPLE 24**

The stock of Orange Corporation is owned equally by three brothers, Rex, Sam, and Ted. When Ted's basis in his stock is $40,000, the corporation distributes $30,000 to him in cancellation of all his shares. If the distribution is a qualifying stock redemption, the $10,000 realized loss is not recognized because Ted and Orange Corporation are related parties. Under § 267, Ted is deemed to own more than 50% in value of the corporation's outstanding stock. Ted's direct ownership is limited to 33⅓%, but through his brothers he owns indirectly another 66⅔% for a total of 100%. On the other hand, if the distribution qualifies as a complete liquidation, Ted's $10,000 realized loss is recognized. ■

The rules governing the basis of property received from the corporation are identical for both liquidations and stock redemptions. Section 334(a) specifies that the basis of property distributed in a complete liquidation is its fair market value on the date of distribution.

In the following pages, the tax consequences of a complete liquidation are examined, first from the view of the distributing corporation and then in terms of the shareholder. Because the tax rules differ when a subsidiary corporation is liquidated, the rules relating to the liquidation of a subsidiary corporation receive separate treatment.

# Liquidations—Effect on the Distributing Corporation

## THE GENERAL RULE

Section 336(a) provides, as a general rule, that a liquidating corporation recognizes gain or loss on the distribution of property in a complete liquidation. The property is treated as if it were sold at its fair market value. This requirement is consistent with the notion of double taxation that is inherent in operating a business as a C corporation—once at the corporate level and again at the shareholder level.

As in the case of a nonliquidating distribution, when property distributed in a complete liquidation is subject to a liability of the liquidating corporation, the fair market value used to calculate gain or loss may not be less than the amount of the liability.

**EXAMPLE 25**

Pursuant to a complete liquidation, Warbler Corporation distributes to its shareholders land held as an investment (basis of $200,000, fair market value of $300,000). If no liability is involved, Warbler has a gain of $100,000 on the distribution ($300,000 – $200,000). Likewise, if the land is subject to a liability of $250,000, Warbler Corporation has a gain of $100,000. If, instead, the liability were $350,000, Warbler's gain on the distribution would be $150,000 ($350,000 – $200,000). ■

There are four exceptions to the general rule of gain and loss recognition upon liquidation of a corporation:

- Losses are not recognized on certain liquidating distributions to related-party shareholders.
- Losses are not recognized on certain sales and liquidating distributions of property that was contributed to the corporation with a built-in loss shortly before the adoption of a plan of liquidation.
- A subsidiary corporation does not recognize gains and losses on liquidating distributions to its parent corporation.
- A subsidiary corporation does not recognize losses on liquidating distributions to its minority shareholders.

The first two exceptions, referred to as the "antistuffing rules," are discussed in detail in the next section and are summarized in Figure 5–2 at the end of the section. The last two exceptions, dealing with the liquidation of a subsidiary corporation, are discussed later in this chapter.

## ANTISTUFFING RULES

A transfer of property to a corporation under § 351 or as a contribution of capital results in no gain or loss recognition to either the shareholder or the corporation (see Chapter 3). The shareholder's basis in the transferred property becomes the basis in the stock received (or, in the case of a capital contribution, is added to the shareholder's existing stock basis). Additionally, the corporation's basis in the transferred property is typically the shareholder's basis in such property. Concerned that these carryover basis rules would allow taxpayers to create artificial losses in liquidation transactions, Congress enacted two loss limitation provisions.[30]

**EXAMPLE 26**

Nora, a shareholder in Canary Corporation, transfers property (basis of $10,000, fair market value of $3,000) to the corporation in a transaction that qualifies under § 351. Nora's basis in the additional stock acquired in Canary Corporation, in exchange for the property, is $10,000. Canary Corporation's basis in the property is also $10,000. A few months after the transfer, Canary Corporation adopts a plan of complete liquidation. Upon liquidation, Canary distributes the property to Nora. If Canary were permitted a loss deduction of $7,000, there would be a double loss because Nora would also recognize a loss of $7,000 upon receipt of the property [$3,000 (fair market value of the property) – $10,000 (basis in Nora's stock)]. To prevent the doubling of losses, the law disallows Canary Corporation's loss on the distribution. ■

**Related-Party Loss Limitation.**   Losses are disallowed on distributions to *related parties* in either of the following cases:

- The distribution is *not* pro rata, or
- The property distributed is disqualified property.

A corporation and a shareholder are considered related if the shareholder owns (directly or indirectly) more than 50 percent in value of the corporation's outstanding stock.[31]

A *pro rata distribution* is one where each shareholder receives his or her share of *each* corporate asset. *Disqualified property* is property that is acquired by the liquidating corporation in a § 351 transaction or as a contribution to capital during

---

[30]§ 336(d).

[31]Section 267 provides the definition of related party for purposes of this provision. The rules are similar to the stock attribution rules

discussed earlier in this chapter; one exception, however, is that stock owned by a sibling is treated as owned by the taxpayer under § 267.

the five-year period ending on the date of the distribution. The related-party loss limitation can apply even if the property was appreciated (fair market value greater than basis) when it was transferred to the corporation.

**EXAMPLE 27**

Bluebird Corporation stock is owned by Ana and Sanjay, who are unrelated. Ana owns 80% and Sanjay owns 20% of the stock in the corporation. Bluebird has the following assets (none of which were acquired in a § 351 transaction or as a contribution to capital) that are distributed in complete liquidation of the corporation:

| | Adjusted Basis | Fair Market Value |
| --- | --- | --- |
| Cash | $600,000 | $600,000 |
| Equipment | 150,000 | 200,000 |
| Building | 400,000 | 200,000 |

Assume Bluebird Corporation distributes the equipment to Sanjay and the cash and the building to Ana. Bluebird recognizes a gain of $50,000 on the distribution of the equipment. The loss of $200,000 on the building will be disallowed because the property is distributed to a related party and the distribution is not pro rata. ■

**EXAMPLE 28**

Assume in Example 27 that Bluebird Corporation distributes the cash and equipment to Ana and the building to Sanjay. Again, Bluebird recognizes the $50,000 gain on the equipment. However, it can now recognize the $200,000 loss on the building because the property is not distributed to a related party (i.e., Sanjay does not own more than 50% of the stock in Bluebird Corporation). ■

**EXAMPLE 29**

Wren Corporation's stock is held equally by three brothers. One year before Wren's liquidation, the shareholders transfer jointly owned property (basis of $150,000, fair market value of $100,000) to the corporation in return for stock in a § 351 transaction. In liquidation, Wren transfers the property (still worth $100,000) back to the brothers. Because each brother owns directly and indirectly more than 50% (i.e., 100% in this situation) of the stock and disqualified property is involved, none of the $50,000 realized loss is recognized by Wren Corporation. ■

**Built-in Loss Limitation.**   The loss limitation provisions are extended to sales, exchanges, or distributions to *unrelated parties* when built-in loss property (fair market value less than basis) is transferred to a corporation shortly before the corporation is liquidated. This second exception to the general rule likewise is imposed to prevent the doubling of losses. (See Example 26.)

The built-in loss limitation applies when the following two conditions are met:

- The property was acquired by the corporation in a § 351 transaction or as a contribution to capital.
- Such acquisition was part of a plan whose principal purpose was to recognize a loss on that property by the liquidating corporation. A tax avoidance purpose is presumed in the case of transfers occurring within two years of the adoption of a plan of liquidation.

The loss disallowed under the provision is limited to the amount by which the property's basis exceeded its fair market value at the time it was acquired by the corporation. Any loss attributable to a decline in value that occurs subsequent to the property's contribution to the corporation is recognized (subject to the related-party loss limitation).[32]

---

[32]§ 336(d)(2).

The built-in loss limitation applies to a broader range of transactions than the related-party exception, which disallows losses only on certain distributions to related parties. This limitation can apply to distributions of property to any shareholder, including an unrelated party. Further, the built-in loss limitation is not limited to distributions, as it can also apply to a sale or exchange of property by a liquidating corporation. However, the limitation is narrower than the related-party exception in that it applies only to property that had a built-in loss upon its acquisition by the corporation and only as to the amount of the built-in loss.

**EXAMPLE 30**

On January 2, 2003, Brown Corporation acquires property (basis of $10,000, fair market value of $3,000) in a transaction that qualifies under § 351. Brown adopts a plan of liquidation on July 1, 2003, and distributes the property to Rick, an unrelated party, on November 10, 2003, when the property is worth $1,000. Brown Corporation can recognize a loss of $2,000, the difference between the value of the property on the date of acquisition and the value of the property on the date of distribution. Only the built-in loss of $7,000 [$3,000 (fair market value on date of acquisition) – $10,000 (basis)] is disallowed. ■

**EXAMPLE 31**

Assume in Example 30 that the property was worth $12,000 on the date Brown Corporation acquired the property. If the distribution is to an unrelated shareholder, Brown Corporation will recognize the entire $9,000 loss [$1,000 (fair market value on date of distribution) – $10,000 (basis)]. However, if the distribution is to a related party, Brown cannot recognize any of the loss under the related-party loss limitation because the property is disqualified property. When the distribution is to a related party, the loss is disallowed even though the entire decline in value occurred during the period the corporation held the property. ■

The built-in loss limitation can apply regardless of how long the corporation has held the property prior to liquidation. The presumption of a tax avoidance purpose for property transferred to a corporation in the two years preceding the liquidation can be rebutted if there is a clear and substantial relationship between the contributed property and the business of the corporation. When there was a business reason for transferring the property to the liquidating corporation, the built-in loss limitation will not apply to a distribution or sale of the property.

**EXAMPLE 32**

Cardinal Corporation's stock is held 60% by Manuel and 40% by Jack. One year before Cardinal's liquidation, property (basis of $150,000, fair market value of $100,000) is transferred to the corporation as a contribution to capital. There is no business reason for the transfer. In liquidation, Cardinal distributes the property (now worth $90,000) to Jack. Even though the distribution is to an unrelated party, the built-in loss of $50,000 is not recognized. However, Cardinal can recognize the loss of $10,000 ($90,000 – $100,000) that occurred while it held the property. If, instead, the property is distributed to Manuel, a related party, the entire $60,000 loss is disallowed under the related-party loss limitation. ■

**EXAMPLE 33**

Assume in Example 32 that the property is transferred to Cardinal Corporation because a bank required the additional capital investment as a condition to making a loan to the corporation. Because there is a business purpose for the transfer, all of the $60,000 loss is recognized if the property is distributed to Jack in liquidation. If, instead, the property is distributed to Manuel, a related party, the entire loss is disallowed. ■

**Tax Paid on Net Gain.** To the extent that a corporation pays tax on the net amount of gain recognized at the corporate level, the proceeds available to be distributed to the shareholder are likewise reduced. This reduction for the payment of taxes will reduce the amount realized by the shareholder, which will then reduce the shareholder's gain or increase the loss recognized.

■ **FIGURE 5–2**
Distributions of Loss Property by
a Liquidating Corporation

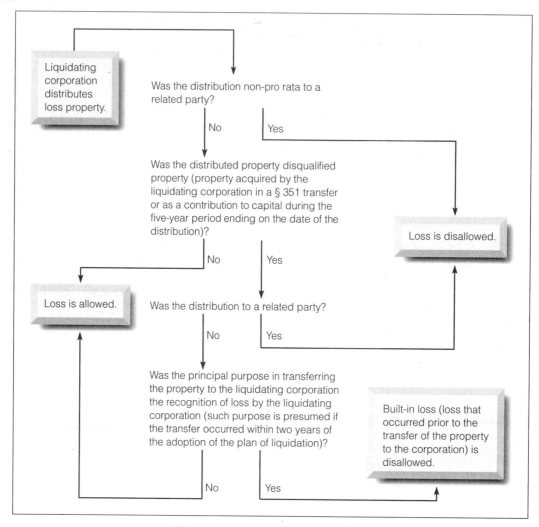

Purple Corporation's assets are valued at $2,000,000 after payment of all corporate debts except for $300,000 of taxes payable on net gains it recognized on the liquidation. Therefore, the amount realized by the shareholders is $1,700,000 ($2,000,000 – $300,000). As described below, in determining the gain or loss recognized by a shareholder, the amount realized is offset by the stock's adjusted basis. ■

# Liquidations—Effect on the Shareholder

The tax consequences to the shareholders of a corporation in the process of liquidation are governed either by the general rule of § 331 or by the exception of § 332 relating to the liquidation of a subsidiary.

## THE GENERAL RULE

In the case of a complete liquidation, the general rule of § 331 provides for sale or exchange treatment.[33] The shareholders are treated as having sold their stock to the liquidating corporation. The difference between the fair market value of the assets received from the corporation and the adjusted basis of the stock surrendered is the gain or loss recognized by the shareholder. Typically, the stock is a capital asset in the hands of the shareholder, and capital gain or loss results. The burden of proof is on the taxpayer to furnish evidence as to the adjusted basis of the stock. In the absence of such evidence, the stock is deemed to have a zero basis, and the full amount of the liquidation proceeds equals the amount of the gain recognized.[34] The basis for property received in a liquidation is the property's fair market value on the date of distribution.[35]

---

| ETHICAL CONSIDERATIONS | Shareholder Liability for Tax Deficiency of Liquidated Corporation |
| --- | --- |

In 2001, Duckbill Corporation distributed all of its remaining assets to its two equal shareholders in a complete liquidation. The two shareholders, Dena Hall and Rosa Garcia, each received a distribution of $50,000 for their stock in Duckbill. In 2003, the IRS audited Duckbill Corporation and assessed additional tax of $45,000 (plus penalties and interest) against the corporation. Since Duckbill was defunct (and without assets), the IRS then assessed the entire $45,000 deficiency against Dena Hall, based on transferee liability. The IRS did not attempt to collect any of the deficiency from Rosa Garcia. Is this an equitable solution to the collection of Duckbill's tax deficiency?

---

## SPECIAL RULE FOR CERTAIN INSTALLMENT OBLIGATIONS

Corporations often sell assets pursuant to a plan of liquidation, and sometimes these sales are made on the installment basis. If the installment notes are then distributed in liquidation, the *shareholders* can use the installment method to defer gain to the point of collection. This treatment requires the shareholders to allocate their stock basis between the installment notes and the other assets received from the corporation.[36] The liquidating *corporation*, however, must recognize the gain on the distribution of the installment notes.[37]

**EXAMPLE 35**

After a plan of complete liquidation has been adopted, Beige Corporation sells its only asset, unimproved land held as an investment. The land has appreciated in value and is sold to Jane (an unrelated party) for $100,000. Under the terms of the sale, Beige Corporation receives cash of $25,000 and Jane's notes for the balance of $75,000. The notes are payable over 10 years ($7,500 per year) and carry an appropriate rate of interest. Immediately after the sale, Beige Corporation distributes the cash and notes to Earl, the sole shareholder. Earl has an adjusted basis of $20,000 in the Beige stock, and the installment notes have a value equal to their face amount ($75,000). These transactions have the following tax results:

---

[33]§ 331(a).

[34]*John Calderazzo*, 34 TCM 1, T.C.Memo. 1975–1.

[35]§ 334(a).

[36]§ 453(h). Installment notes attributable to the sale of inventory qualify only if the inventory was sold in a bulk sale to one person.

[37]§ 453B(a). Gain is not recognized in the distribution of installment notes by a subsidiary liquidating pursuant to § 332. See the discussion below and §§ 337(a) and 453B(d).

- Beige Corporation recognizes gain on the distribution of the installment notes, measured by the difference between the $75,000 fair market value and the basis Beige had in the notes.
- Earl may defer the gain on the receipt of the notes to the point of collection.
- Earl must allocate the adjusted basis in his stock ($20,000) between the cash and the installment notes as follows:

$$\frac{\text{Cash}}{\text{Total receipts}} = \frac{\$25,000}{\$100,000} \times \$20,000 = \$5,000 \text{ basis allocated to the cash}$$

$$\frac{\text{Notes}}{\text{Total receipts}} = \frac{\$75,000}{\$100,000} \times \$20,000 = \$15,000 \text{ basis allocated to the notes}$$

- On the cash portion of the transaction, Earl must recognize $20,000 of gain [$25,000 (cash received) − $5,000 (basis allocated to the cash)] in the year of liquidation.
- Over the next 10 years, Earl must recognize a total gain of $60,000 on the notes, computed as follows:

$$\$75,000 \text{ (fair market value)} - \$15,000 \text{ (basis allocated to the notes)}$$

$$= \$60,000 \text{ (gross profit)}$$

- The gross profit percentage on the notes is 80%, computed as follows:

$$\frac{\$60,000 \text{ (gross profit)}}{\$75,000 \text{ (contract price)}} = 80\%$$

Thus, Earl must report a gain of $6,000 [$7,500 (amount of note) × 80% (gross profit percentage)] on the collection of each note over the next 10 years.

- The interest element is accounted for separately. ■

## LO.5

Understand the tax consequences of a subsidiary liquidation for both the parent and the subsidiary corporations.

# Liquidations—Parent-Subsidiary Situations

Section 332, an exception to the general rule of § 331, provides that a parent corporation does *not* recognize gain or loss on a liquidation of its subsidiary. In addition, the subsidiary corporation recognizes *neither gain nor loss* on distributions of property to its parent.[38]

The requirements for applying § 332 are as follows:

- The parent must own at least 80 percent of the voting stock of the subsidiary and at least 80 percent of the value of the subsidiary's stock.
- The subsidiary must distribute all its property in complete cancellation of all its stock within the taxable year or within three years from the close of the tax year in which the first distribution occurred.
- The subsidiary must be solvent.[39]

If these requirements are met, nonrecognition of gains and losses becomes mandatory. However, if the subsidiary is insolvent, the parent corporation will have an ordinary loss deduction under § 165(g).

When a series of distributions occurs in the liquidation of a subsidiary corporation, the parent corporation must own the required amount of stock (80 percent) on the date the plan of liquidation is adopted. Such ownership must continue at

---

[38] § 337(a). This is an exception to the general rule of § 336.

[39] § 332(b) and Reg. §§ 1.332–2(a) and (b).

all times until all property has been distributed.[40] If the parent fails the control requirement at any time, the provisions for nonrecognition of gain or loss do not apply to any distribution.[41]

## MINORITY SHAREHOLDER INTERESTS

A distribution of property to a minority shareholder in a liquidation otherwise governed by § 332 is treated in the same manner as a *nonliquidating* distribution. That is, the distributing corporation recognizes gain (but not loss) on the property distributed to the minority shareholder.[42]

**EXAMPLE 36**

The stock of Tan Corporation is held as follows: 80% by Mustard Corporation and 20% by Arethia. Tan Corporation is liquidated on December 10, 2003, pursuant to a plan adopted on January 10, 2003. At the time of its liquidation, Tan Corporation has assets with a basis of $100,000 and fair market value of $500,000. Tan Corporation distributes the property pro rata to Mustard Corporation and to Arethia. Tan must recognize gain of $80,000 [($500,000 fair market value − $100,000 basis) × 20% minority interest]. Since the corporate tax due in this liquidation relates entirely to the minority shareholder distribution, that amount will most likely be deducted from the $100,000 distribution ($500,000 × 20%) going to Arethia. The remaining gain of $320,000 is not recognized because it is attributable to property being distributed to Mustard, the parent corporation. ∎

A minority shareholder is subject to the general rule requiring the recognition of gain or loss in a liquidation. Accordingly, the difference between the fair market value of the assets received and the basis of the minority shareholder's stock is the amount of gain or loss recognized. Further, the basis of property received by the minority shareholder is the property's fair market value on the date of distribution.[43]

## INDEBTEDNESS OF THE SUBSIDIARY TO THE PARENT

If a subsidiary transfers appreciated property to its parent to satisfy a debt, it must recognize gain on the transaction unless the subsidiary is liquidating and the conditions of § 332 (discussed above) apply. When § 332 applies, the subsidiary does not recognize gain or loss upon the transfer of properties to the parent in satisfaction of indebtedness.[44]

**EXAMPLE 37**

Eagle Corporation owes its parent, Finch Corporation, $20,000. It satisfies the obligation by transferring land (basis of $8,000, fair market value of $20,000). Normally, Eagle would recognize a gain of $12,000 on the transaction. However, if the transfer is made pursuant to a liquidation under § 332, Eagle does not recognize a gain. ∎

The special provision noted above will not apply to the parent corporation. The parent corporation recognizes gain or loss on the receipt of property in satisfaction of indebtedness, even if the property is received during liquidation of the subsidiary.

**EXAMPLE 38**

Pelican Corporation owns bonds (basis of $95,000) of its subsidiary, Crow Corporation, that were acquired at a discount. Upon liquidation of Crow pursuant to § 332, Pelican receives a distribution of $100,000, the face amount of the bonds. The transaction has no tax effect

---

[40]Establishing the date of the adoption of a plan of complete liquidation could be crucial in determining whether § 332 applies. See, for example, *George L. Riggs, Inc.*, 64 T.C. 474 (1975).

[41]§ 332(b)(3) and Reg. § 1.332–2(a).

[42]§§ 336(a) and (d)(3).

[43]§ 334(a).

[44]§ 337(b)(1).

on Crow. However, Pelican Corporation recognizes gain of $5,000—the difference between its basis in the bonds and the amount received in payment. ■

## BASIS OF PROPERTY RECEIVED BY THE PARENT CORPORATION—THE GENERAL RULE

*[handwritten: Gen rule — carryover basis]*

Property received in the complete liquidation of a subsidiary has the same basis it had in the hands of the subsidiary.[45] Unless the parent corporation makes a § 338 election (discussed below), this carryover basis in the assets generally will differ significantly from the parent's basis in the stock of the subsidiary. Since the liquidation is a nontaxable exchange, the parent's gain or loss on the difference in basis is not recognized. Further, the parent's basis in the stock of the liquidated subsidiary disappears.

| EXAMPLE 39 | Lark, the parent corporation, has a basis of $20,000 in the stock of Heron Corporation, a subsidiary in which it owns 85% of all classes of stock. Lark purchased the Heron stock 10 years ago. In the current year, Lark liquidates Heron Corporation and acquires assets that are worth $50,000 and have a tax basis to Heron of $40,000. Lark Corporation takes a basis of $40,000 in the assets, with a potential gain upon their sale of $10,000. Lark's $20,000 basis in Heron's stock disappears. ■ |

| EXAMPLE 40 | Indigo Corporation has a basis of $60,000 in the stock of Kackie Corporation, a wholly owned subsidiary acquired 10 years ago. It liquidates Kackie Corporation and receives assets that are worth $50,000 and have a tax basis to Kackie of $40,000. Indigo Corporation takes a basis of $40,000 in the assets it acquires from Kackie. If Indigo sells the assets, it has a gain of $10,000 even though its basis in the Kackie stock was $60,000. Indigo's loss on its stock investment in Kackie will never be recognized. ■ |

In addition to the parent corporation taking the subsidiary's basis in its assets, the carryover rules of § 381 apply (see Chapter 7). Under that provision, the parent acquires various tax attributes of the subsidiary, including the subsidiary's net operating loss, business credit carryover, capital loss carryover, and E & P.

## BASIS OF PROPERTY RECEIVED BY THE PARENT CORPORATION—§ 338 ELECTION

**Background.** As discussed above, the liquidation of a subsidiary generally is a nontaxable transaction, resulting in the nonrecognition of gain or loss for both the parent and the subsidiary corporation and the carryover of the subsidiary's asset bases (and other tax attributes). This treatment reflects the fact that such a liquidation often is merely a change in corporate structure and not a change in substance. This is particularly the case when the parent has owned the stock of the subsidiary since the subsidiary's inception. In such cases, the carried-over bases are comparable to what the parent would have in the subsidiary's assets if the parent, and not the subsidiary, had originally acquired the assets. However, inequities can develop when a subsidiary is liquidated shortly after its acquisition by the parent.

When a corporation acquires a controlling interest (80 percent) in another corporation over a short time period, the acquisition cost of the stock will reflect

---

[45]§ 334(b)(1) and Reg. § 1.334–1(b).

the fair market value of the subsidiary's assets (including goodwill). In all but a few unusual situations, the parent's basis in the stock of the subsidiary will vary greatly from the subsidiary's basis in its assets. Under the general rule of nonrecognition, the difference between the parent's basis in the stock and the carried-over basis in the assets is a nonrecognized gain (if the stock basis is less than the carried-over basis) or loss (if the stock basis is greater than the carried-over basis). This is the case even if the parent acquired the subsidiary stock solely to obtain the subsidiary's assets. If a parent corporation could treat the stock purchase as a purchase of the assets, it could take a basis in the assets equal to the acquisition cost of the stock. In most cases, this would mean a higher asset basis and, as a result, larger depreciation deductions for the parent corporation.

To obtain the stock-basis-for-asset-basis result, taxpayers successfully devised stock purchase/subsidiary liquidation transactions that fell outside the general rule.[46] Congress codified this treatment by enacting § 338, which permits the purchase of a controlling interest of stock to be treated as a purchase of the subsidiary's assets.

**Requirements for Application.** A corporation (the "parent") may *elect* the provisions of § 338 if it acquires stock representing at least 80 percent of the voting power and at least 80 percent of the value of another corporation (the "subsidiary") within a 12-month period ("*qualified stock purchase*"). The stock must be acquired in a taxable transaction (i.e., § 351 and other nonrecognition provisions do not apply). An acquisition of stock by any member of an affiliated group that includes the parent corporation is considered to be an acquisition by the parent. The **§ 338 election** must be made by the fifteenth day of the ninth month beginning after the month in which a qualified stock purchase occurs. If made, the election is irrevocable.

**Tax Consequences.** Upon a qualified § 338 election, the subsidiary is treated as having sold its assets on the qualified stock purchase date for a value that is determined with reference to the parent's basis in the subsidiary stock plus any liabilities of the subsidiary.[47] The subsidiary is then treated as a new corporation that purchased those assets for a similarly computed amount on the day following the qualified stock purchase date.[48] The deemed sale results in gain (or loss) recognition to the subsidiary, and the deemed purchase results in a stepped-up (or -down) basis for the subsidiary's assets.[49] The subsidiary may, but need not, be liquidated. If the subsidiary is liquidated, the parent will obtain a carryover of the stepped-up (or -down) basis of the subsidiary's assets.

**A Comparison of the General Rule and the § 338 Election.** Under the general rule of nonrecognition, the liquidation of a subsidiary is tax-free to both the subsidiary (except for any minority interest) and the parent corporation. Under § 338, the subsidiary recognizes gain (loss) on the deemed disposition of its assets. A liquidation of the subsidiary remains tax-free to the parent. While a carryover basis rule applies in both cases, the subsidiary's assets generally will have a

---

[46]See, e.g., *U.S. v. M.O.J. Corp.*, 60–1 USTC ¶9209, 5 AFTR2d 535, 274 F.2d 713 (CA–5, 1960). See also *Kimbell-Diamond Milling Co.*, 14 T.C. 74 (1950), *aff'd* 51–1 USTC ¶9201, 40 AFTR 328, 187 F.2d 718 (CA–5, 1951), *cert. den.* 72 S.Ct. 50 (USSC, 1951) (IRS argued stock-for-asset basis).

[47]See §§ 338(a)(1) and (b) and Reg. § 1.338–4.

[48]See §§ 338(a)(2) and (b) and Reg. § 1.338–5.

[49]For the rules governing the allocation of the purchase price to the assets, see § 338(b)(5) and Reg. § 1.338–6.

## Concept Summary 5–2

### Summary of Liquidation Rules

| Effect on the Shareholder | Basis of Property Received | Effect on the Corporation |
| --- | --- | --- |
| § 331—The general rule provides for capital gain treatment on the difference between the FMV of property received and the basis of the stock in the corporation. | § 334(a)—Basis of assets received by the shareholder will be the FMV on the date of distribution (except for installment obligations on which gain is deferred to the point of collection). | § 336—Gain or loss is recognized for distributions in kind and for sales by the liquidating corporation. Losses are not recognized for distributions to related parties if the distribution is not pro rata or if disqualified property is distributed. Losses may be disallowed on sales and distributions of built-in loss property even if made to unrelated parties. |
| § 332—In liquidation of a subsidiary, no gain or loss is recognized to the parent. Subsidiary must distribute all of its property within the taxable year or within three years from the close of the taxable year in which the first distribution occurs. | § 334(b)(1)—Property has the same basis as it had in the hands of the subsidiary. Parent's basis in the stock disappears. Carryover rules of § 381 apply. | § 337—No gain or loss is recognized to the subsidiary on distributions to the parent. Gain (but not loss) is recognized on distributions to minority shareholders. |
| | § 338—Subsidiary need not be liquidated. If subsidiary is liquidated, parent's basis is new stepped-up (or -down) basis. Parent's basis in the stock disappears. Carryover rules of § 381 apply, but such amounts are likely to be nominal. | § 338—Gain or loss is recognized to the subsidiary. Subsidiary is treated as a new corporation, and its basis in assets is stepped up (or down) to reflect parent's basis in subsidiary stock plus subsidiary's liabilities. New basis is allocated among various asset classes. |

stepped-up basis as a result of the § 338 election, and a liquidation of the subsidiary will result in a carryover of the stepped-up basis to the parent. Further, a liquidation of the subsidiary results in a carryover of its other tax attributes (e.g., E & P) to the parent whether or not a § 338 election is made. However, when the election is made, the subsidiary is treated as a new corporation as of the day following the qualified stock purchase date; as a result, any tax attributes acquired by the parent are likely to be nominal (or zero) in amount.

The holding period of the subsidiary's assets is determined with reference to the substance of the transaction. When the subsidiary is liquidated and there is no § 338 election, the subsidiary's historical holding period in its assets carries over to the parent. This is the typical carryover rule found in other nonrecognition provisions. A § 338 election, however, assumes a sale and repurchase of the subsidiary's assets. As a result of these deemed transactions, the holding period starts anew. If there is a § 338 election and the subsidiary is liquidated, the holding period of the property received by the parent begins on the date of the qualified stock purchase. On the other hand, if there is a § 338 election and the subsidiary is not liquidated, the holding period of the assets begins on the day after the qualified stock acquisition date. The parent-subsidiary liquidation rules are set out in Concept Summary 5–2.

_holding period_

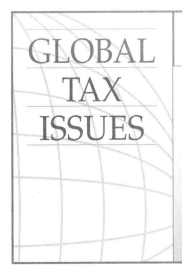

## GLOBAL TAX ISSUES

### EXCEPTION TO § 332 FOR LIQUIDATIONS OF U.S. SUBSIDIARIES OF FOREIGN CORPORATIONS

When a U.S. subsidiary is liquidated into a U.S. parent, gains (or losses) are not recognized immediately, but rather are deferred as a result of the carryover basis rule. Gains inherent in the transferred assets will be recognized upon their disposition by the parent. Foreign corporations generally are not subject to U.S. taxation, so the liquidation of a U.S. subsidiary into a foreign parent could avoid gain recognition entirely if § 332 were to apply unabated. Section 367(b) overrides § 332 when a U.S. subsidiary is liquidated into a foreign parent, however. Under § 367(b), the subsidiary will recognize gain on the transfer of certain "tainted" assets. Tainted assets include inventory, installment obligations, accounts receivable, and depreciable property (to the extent of depreciation recapture). For further details, see Chapter 9.

---

**LO.6**

Identify tax planning opportunities available to minimize the tax impact in stock redemptions and complete liquidations.

**Tax Planning Considerations**

## STOCK REDEMPTIONS

Stock redemptions offer several possibilities for tax planning:

- The alternative to a qualifying stock redemption is dividend treatment. However, a dividend is not always undesirable from a tax standpoint. A nonqualified redemption may be preferable if the distributing corporation has little or no E & P or the distributee-shareholder is another corporation. In the latter situation, dividend treatment may be preferred due to the availability of the dividends received deduction.
- Stock redemptions are particularly well suited for purchasing the interest of a retiring or deceased shareholder. Rather than the remaining shareholders buying the stock of the retiring or deceased shareholder, the corporation uses its funds to redeem the stock from the retiring shareholder or from the decedent shareholder's estate. The ability to use the corporation's funds to buy out a shareholder's interest is also advantageous in property settlements between divorcing taxpayers.
- A third party who wishes to purchase all the stock of a corporation can use a stock redemption to obtain the needed purchase money. This technique is referred to as a "bootstrap acquisition." The third party first purchases a small amount of stock from the shareholders. The corporation then redeems all the stock except that of the third party. The third party becomes the sole shareholder of the corporation, but the corporation furnished most of the purchase money.
- A not essentially equivalent redemption provides minimal utility and generally should be relied upon only as a last resort. Instead, the redemption should be structured to satisfy the objective tests required of one of the other qualifying redemptions. These include disproportionate redemptions, complete termination redemptions, or redemptions to pay death taxes.
- The timing and sequence of a redemption should be handled carefully, as illustrated in the following example.

**EXAMPLE 41**

Sparrow Corporation's stock is held as follows: Alma (60 shares), Antonio (20 shares), and Ali (20 shares). Alma, Antonio, and Ali are not related to each other. The corporation redeems 24 of Alma's shares. Shortly thereafter, it redeems 5 of Antonio's shares. Does Alma's redemption qualify as a disproportionate redemption? Taken in isolation, it would appear to meet the 80% and 50% tests. Yet, if the IRS takes into account the later redemption of Antonio's shares, Alma has not satisfied the 50% test; she still owns ³⁶⁄₇₁ of the corporation after the two redemptions. A greater time lag between the redemptions places Alma in a better position to argue against collapsing the two redemptions as parts of one integrated plan. ■

- For a family corporation in which all of the shareholders are related to each other, the only hope of achieving sale or exchange treatment may lie in the use of a redemption that completely terminates a shareholder's interest or one that follows a shareholder's death. In a complete termination redemption, it is important that the family stock attribution rules be avoided. Here, strict compliance with the requirements for the family attribution waiver (e.g., the withdrawing shareholder does not continue as an employee of the corporation and does not acquire a prohibited interest in the corporation within 10 years) is crucial.
- In a redemption to pay death taxes, the amount to be sheltered from dividend treatment is limited to the sum of death taxes and funeral and administration expenses. However, a redemption in excess of the limitation does not destroy the applicability of § 303. Instead, any such excess (if properly structured) may qualify as a sale or exchange under one of the other redemption rules.

## DISPOSING OF § 306 STOCK

Avoiding ordinary income on the disposition of § 306 stock is a difficult feat. Unless the corporation's E & P was nominal at the time of the stock dividend (in the case of a § 306 stock sale) or at the time of the redemption (in the case of a § 306 stock redemption), the disposition of § 306 stock typically produces only ordinary income. The gifting of § 306 stock does not defeat the ordinary income taint as the taint remains with the stock. Further, under § 170(e), the deduction for a charitable contribution of § 306 stock must be reduced by the ordinary income taint.

The sale of § 306 stock in a transaction that terminates the shareholder's entire stock interest in the corporation will avoid ordinary income treatment, as will a disposition in liquidation of the corporation. Similarly, a redemption of § 306 stock in a complete termination redemption or a partial liquidation avoids the ordinary income result. However, these exceptions are of limited use in the typical disposition of § 306 stock.

## CORPORATE LIQUIDATIONS

With the exception of parent-subsidiary liquidations, distributions in liquidation are taxed at both the corporate level and the shareholder level. When a corporation liquidates, it can, as a general rule, claim losses on assets that have depreciated in value. These assets should not be distributed in the form of a property dividend or stock redemption because losses are not deductible on nonliquidating distributions.

Shareholders faced with large prospective gains in a liquidation may consider shifting part or all of that gain to other taxpayers. One approach is to donate stock to charity. A charitable contribution of the stock produces a deduction equal to the stock's fair market value (see Chapter 2). Alternatively, the stock may be given to family members. Whether these procedures will be successful in shifting the liquidation-related gain from the taxpayer depends on the timing of the transfer. If the donee of the stock is not in a position to prevent the liquidation of the corporation, the donor may be deemed to have made an anticipatory assignment of income. In such a case, the gain is still taxed to the donor. In addition, the gift tax must be considered (see Chapter 17). Hence, advance planning of stock transfers is crucial in arriving at the desired tax result.

The installment sale provisions provide some relief from the general corporate liquidation rule that the shareholder recognizes all gain upon receiving the liquidation proceeds. If the assets of the liquidating corporation are not to be distributed in kind, a sale of the assets in exchange for installment notes should be considered. Shareholders receiving the notes in a liquidation can then report their gain on the installment method as the notes are collected.

## PARENT-SUBSIDIARY LIQUIDATIONS

The nonrecognition provision applicable to the liquidation of a subsidiary, § 332, is not elective. Nevertheless, some flexibility may be available:

- Whether § 332 applies depends on the 80 percent stock ownership test. A parent corporation may be able to avoid § 332 by reducing its stock ownership in the subsidiary below this percentage to allow for recognition of a loss. On the other hand, the opposite approach may be desirable to avoid gain recognition. A corporate shareholder possessing less than the required 80 percent ownership may want to acquire additional stock to qualify for § 332 treatment.
- Once § 332 becomes effective, less latitude is allowed in determining the parent's basis in the subsidiary's assets. Generally, the subsidiary's existing basis in its assets carries over to the parent. If a timely § 338 election is made, the subsidiary's basis in its assets is stepped up to reflect, in part, the parent's basis in the subsidiary stock. If the subsidiary also is liquidated, the parent obtains assets with the stepped-up basis.
- An election to have the § 338 rules apply should be carefully weighed as the election can be detrimental. The subsidiary's recognized gain that results from the deemed sale of its assets is the cost under § 338 for obtaining the stepped-up basis. As a result, a § 338 election may be a viable option only when the subsidiary possesses loss and/or credit carryovers that can be used to offset the associated tax.

## ASSET PURCHASE VERSUS STOCK PURCHASE

The acquisition of a corporation's assets generally takes one of two forms. In one form, the acquiring corporation purchases the stock of the target corporation, and then the target (subsidiary) is liquidated. In the other form, the acquiring corporation purchases the assets of the target corporation, and then the target distributes the proceeds in liquidation. Nontax considerations may affect the form of acquisition, with each form having both favorable and unfavorable aspects.

An asset purchase requires that title be transferred and that creditors be notified. Further, an asset purchase may not be feasible if valuable nontransferable trademarks, contracts, or licenses are involved. Alternatively, an asset purchase may be preferable to a stock purchase if the target's shareholders refuse to sell their stock. Additionally, an asset purchase avoids the transfer of liabilities (including unknown liabilities) generally inherent in stock acquisitions. An asset purchase also has the advantage of allowing the purchaser to avoid the acquisition of unwanted assets, whereas a stock purchase would involve all of a target's assets.

## KEY TERMS

| | | |
|---|---|---|
| Attribution, 5–5 | Meaningful reduction test, 5–7 | Preferred stock bailout, 5–15 |
| Complete termination redemption, 5–8 | Not essentially equivalent redemption, 5–7 | Redemption to pay death taxes, 5–11 |
| Corporate liquidation, 5–18 | Partial liquidation, 5–10 | Section 338 election, 5–29 |
| Disproportionate redemption, 5–7 | | Stock redemption, 5–3 |

## PROBLEM MATERIALS

### Discussion Questions

1. Compare the tax treatment of nonliquidating distributions that are treated as a return *from* a shareholder's investment with the tax treatment of distributions that are treated as a return *of* a shareholder's investment.

2. Shareholders always prefer qualifying stock redemption treatment to dividend income treatment. Assess the validity of this statement.

3. Why are there limitations on sale or exchange treatment for stock redemptions?

**Issue ID**

4. Leona wants to retire and sell her shares in Brown Corporation either to Brown's remaining shareholders, Jacob and Ivan, or to a third party. What issues may support a preference for Brown Corporation to redeem Leona's shares rather than for Jacob and Ivan or a third party to purchase them?

5. During the current year, Flicker, Inc., distributed $20,000 each to Kanisha and Susan in redemption of some of their Flicker stock. The two shareholders are in the 38.6% tax bracket, and each had a $5,000 basis in her redeemed stock. Kanisha incurred $7,720 of tax on her redemption, but Susan incurred only $3,000 on her redemption. Discuss the likely reason for the difference in their tax liabilities.

6. What basis does a shareholder take in property received in a qualifying stock redemption?

7. Does the treatment of a corporate distribution under state law control the tax consequences of a stock redemption?

8. For purposes of the stock attribution rules, what family members are included as "related parties"?

9. Under the attribution rules, a shareholder is deemed to own the stock of certain "related parties." When is stock attributed *from* and *to* an entity?

10. If a redemption is treated as an ordinary dividend ("nonqualifying stock redemption"), what happens to the basis of the stock redeemed?

11. Under what circumstances will a stock redemption qualify as a not essentially equivalent redemption?

12. Discuss the requirements for a disproportionate redemption.

**Issue ID**

13. Two years ago, Jorge transferred property he had used in his sole proprietorship to Flycatcher Corporation, a newly formed corporation, for 50 shares of stock in Flycatcher. The property had an adjusted basis of $300,000 and a fair market value of $800,000. Six months later, Jorge's friend, Polly, transferred property she had used in her sole proprietorship to Flycatcher Corporation for 50 shares of the stock in Flycatcher and cash of $100,000. Her property had an adjusted basis of $150,000 and a value of $900,000. Both Jorge and Polly serve on the board of directors of Flycatcher Corporation. In addition, Polly has a contract with Flycatcher to perform consulting services for the

corporation. In the current year, Flycatcher Corporation redeems all of Polly's shares in Flycatcher for property with a value of $1.4 million. What are the tax issues for Polly and Flycatcher?

14. To qualify as a partial liquidation, a distribution must not be essentially equivalent to a dividend. Discuss how this requirement is met.

15. Do the stock attribution rules apply to a redemption to pay death taxes?

16. At the time of her death, Yolanda owned 40% of the outstanding stock of Violet Corporation (basis of $100,000, fair market value of $500,000). Yolanda's adjusted gross estate is $1.8 million, and the death taxes and funeral and administration expenses total $250,000. Can Yolanda's estate qualify for a redemption to pay death taxes under § 303?

**Issue ID**

17. Angie and her daughter, Ann, who are the only shareholders of Bluebird Corporation, each paid $100,000 four years ago for their shares in Bluebird. Angie also owns 20% of the stock in Redbird Corporation. The Redbird stock is worth $500,000, and Angie's basis in the stock is $50,000. Angie died in the current year leaving all her property to her husband, Gary, but Ann wants to be the sole shareholder of Bluebird Corporation. Bluebird has assets worth $2 million (basis of $700,000) and E & P of $1 million. Angie's estate is worth approximately $4 million. Angie has made gifts during her lifetime to Ann. What are the tax issues for Angie's estate, Ann, and Bluebird?

**Decision Making**

18. Indigo Corporation desires to transfer cash of $30,000 or property worth $30,000 to its sole shareholder, Linda, in a redemption transaction that will be treated as a dividend to Linda. If Indigo distributes property, the corporation will choose between two assets that are each worth $30,000 and are no longer needed in its business: Property A (basis of $12,000) and Property B (basis of $36,000). Indigo is indifferent as to the form of the distribution, but Linda prefers a cash distribution. Considering the tax consequences to Indigo on the distribution to redeem Linda's shares, what should Indigo distribute?

**Issue ID**

19. Kackie Corporation (E & P of $1 million) is currently in negotiations to redeem stock from one or more of its shareholders. The form (i.e., cash and/or property) and amount of the distribution(s) to the shareholder(s) are key points of the negotiations. What are the tax issues for Kackie Corporation?

20. Pete, a 30% shareholder in Black Corporation, sells for a gain one-half of his preferred stock and one-half of his common stock to a third party.
    a. Is there any danger that the § 306 prohibition on preferred stock bailouts could apply to the sale of the preferred stock?
    b. If § 306 does apply, what would be the treatment of Pete's gain on the sale of the preferred stock?
    c. How would your answers to (a) and (b) change if, instead of a sale, the stock had been redeemed by Black Corporation?

21. A taxpayer owning a controlling interest in two or more corporations easily could obtain sale or exchange treatment by selling the stock of one controlled corporation to another controlled corporation. Since the transaction is not a redemption of stock by the issuing corporation, it avoids the scrutiny of the qualifying stock redemption rules. Assess the validity of this position.

22. When does a corporate liquidation exist for tax purposes?

23. One difference in the tax treatment of a liquidation and a qualifying stock redemption involves the applicability of § 267. Explain.

24. For purposes of the related-party loss limitation within the context of a complete liquidation, what is the definition of "disqualified property"?

25. Explain the tax consequences to a shareholder of a corporation in the process of liquidation under the general rule of § 331. May a shareholder use the installment method to report gain on a complete liquidation?

26. In terms of the rules applying to parent-subsidiary liquidations, describe the effect of each of the following:
    a. The date of the adoption of a plan of complete liquidation.
    b. The period of time in which the corporation must liquidate.
    c. The solvency of the subsidiary being liquidated.

27. In a liquidation otherwise subject to § 332, does a subsidiary corporation recognize gain and loss on the distribution of property to a minority shareholder?

28. In the context of a § 332 liquidation, does the nonrecognition rule apply to a transfer of property by a subsidiary to a parent in satisfaction of indebtedness? Explain.

29. Condor Corporation pays $1.3 million for 100% of the stock in Dove Corporation. Dove has a basis of $900,000 in its assets. If Condor liquidates Dove and makes no special election, what are the tax consequences to Condor and to Dove?

30. What are the requirements for the application of § 338?

31. What are the tax consequences of a § 338 election to the parent and subsidiary corporations?

## Problems

**Decision Making**

32. Teal Corporation, with E & P of $2.5 million, distributes property with a basis of $200,000 and a fair market value of $450,000 to Grace, one of its three shareholders. Each shareholder has a one-third interest in the corporation.
    a. What are the tax consequences to Teal Corporation and to Grace if the distribution is a property dividend?
    b. What are the tax consequences in (a) if Grace is a corporation?
    c. What are the tax consequences to Teal Corporation and to Grace if the distribution is a qualifying stock redemption? Assume that half of Grace's stock (basis of $120,000) is redeemed in the transaction.
    d. What are the tax consequences in (c) if Grace is a corporation?
    e. If the parties involved could choose from among the preceding options, which would they choose and why?

33. Julio is in the 35% tax bracket. He acquired 500 shares of stock in Gray Corporation three years ago at a cost of $80 per share. In the current year, Julio received a payment of $90,000 from Gray Corporation in exchange for 100 of his shares in Gray. Gray has E & P of $800,000. What tax liability would Julio incur on the $90,000 payment in each of the following situations? Assume that Julio has no capital losses.
    a. The payment qualifies for stock redemption (i.e., sale or exchange) treatment.
    b. The payment does not qualify for stock redemption (i.e., sale or exchange treatment is not applicable) treatment.

34. How would your answer to Problem 33 differ if Julio were a corporate shareholder (in the 34% tax bracket) rather than an individual shareholder and the stock ownership in Gray Corporation represented a 15% interest?

**Decision Making**

35. Assume in Problem 33 that Julio has a capital loss carryover of $40,000 in the current tax year. Julio has no other capital gain transactions during the year. What amount of the capital loss may Julio deduct in the current year in the following situations?
    a. The $90,000 payment from Gray Corporation is a qualifying stock redemption for tax purposes (i.e., receives sale or exchange treatment).
    b. The $90,000 payment from Gray Corporation does not qualify as a stock redemption for tax purposes (i.e., does not receive sale or exchange treatment).
    c. If Julio had the flexibility to structure the transaction as described in either (a) or (b), which form would he choose?

36. How would your answer to parts (a) and (b) of Problem 35 differ if Julio were a corporate shareholder (in the 34% tax bracket) rather than an individual shareholder and the stock ownership in Gray Corporation represented a 15% interest?

37. Silver Corporation has 800 shares of common stock outstanding. Beatrice owns 300 shares, Beatrice's husband owns 120 shares, Beatrice's daughter owns 80 shares, and Beatrice's grandson owns 50 shares. In addition, Maroon Corporation owns 150 shares. Beatrice owns 70% of the stock in Maroon Corporation.
    a. Applying the § 318 stock attribution rules, how many shares does Beatrice own in Silver Corporation?
    b. Assume Beatrice owns only 30% of Maroon Corporation. How many shares does Beatrice own directly or indirectly in Silver Corporation?
    c. Assume the same facts as in (a) above, but in addition, Beatrice owns 20% of Yellow Partnership. The partnership owns 100 shares in Silver Corporation. How many shares does Beatrice own in Silver Corporation?

38. Shonda owns 20 shares of the 200 shares of Hawk Corporation. Shonda paid $1,000 per share for the stock five years ago. The remaining stock in Hawk Corporation is owned as follows: 95 shares by Vulcan Corporation and 85 shares by several unrelated individuals. Shonda owns 100% of the stock of Vulcan Corporation. In the current year, Hawk redeems Shonda's 20 shares for $60,000 ($3,000 per share). Hawk has E & P of $200,000.
    a. How must Shonda report the $60,000?
    b. What happens to Shonda's basis in the redeemed shares?
    c. What is Hawk's E & P after the redemption?

39. **Communications** Stork Corporation has 1,000 shares of common stock outstanding. The shares are owned by the following unrelated shareholders: Leo Jones, 300 shares; Lori Johnson, 400 shares; and Lana Pierce, 300 shares. The corporation redeems 200 shares of Lana's stock for $80,000. Lana paid $50 per share for her stock two years ago. Stork's E & P was $350,000 on the date of redemption. What is the tax effect to Lana of the redemption? Prepare a letter to Lana (1000 Main Street, Oldtown, MN 55166) and a memo for the file in which you explain your conclusions.

40. Thrush Corporation has 2,000 shares of common stock outstanding. The shares are owned as follows: Jacque Jones, 800 shares; Monique Jones (Jacque's daughter), 800 shares; and Enrique Jones (Jacque's brother) 400 shares. In the current year, Thrush redeems all of Jacque's shares. Determine whether the redemption can qualify for sale or exchange treatment under the complete termination redemption rules in the following independent circumstances.
    a. Jacque remains as a director of Thrush Corporation.
    b. Jacque resigns as director of Thrush Corporation; Monique becomes a director of Thrush to replace Jacque.
    c. Two years after the redemption, Jacque acquires 25 shares in Thrush Corporation as a gift from Enrique.

41. Roberta and Lori, unrelated individuals, own all the stock in Swan Corporation (E & P of $700,000). Each has a basis of $25,000 in her 100 shares. Roberta wishes to retire in the current year and wants to sell her stock for $400,000, the fair market value. Lori would like to purchase Roberta's shares and, thus, become the sole shareholder in Swan, but Lori is short of funds. What are the tax consequences to Roberta, Lori, and Swan Corporation under the following circumstances?
    a. Swan Corporation distributes cash of $400,000 to Lori, and she uses the cash to purchase Roberta's shares.
    b. Swan Corporation redeems all of Roberta's shares for $400,000.

42. Sean owns all 100 shares of the outstanding stock of Crane Corporation (E & P of $800,000). Sean acquired the stock 10 years ago for $60,000. Crane has several trades or businesses that it has developed and operated for more than five years. In the current year, Crane Corporation sells one of those trades or businesses and, in a transaction qualifying as a partial liquidation [under § 302(b)(4)], redeems 20 shares of Sean's stock for $300,000. What are the tax consequences of the redemption to Sean and to Crane Corporation?

Complete redemption
Amt red. 1,400,000
AB        1,400,000
           —0—     or
gain / on
~~redemption~~ to pay estate tax
If stock > 35% of adj gr estate
Gr. Estate 2 mill so this is
more than 35% meets term
Amt real      900,000
AB            900,000
               —0—
Rest as complete redemp
Amt realized  500,000
Ad Basis     <500,000>
               —0—

15% redeemed.
Redeemed with cash.
E&P 135,000
PI Cap  65,000
Cash     200,000
Do not always take
out of PIC.

$$\frac{600-x}{1000-x} < .48$$

$600 - x < 480 - .48x$

$120 < .52x$

$$\frac{120}{.5x} < x$$

$x = 231$

If redeemed 135 or other
E&P  135,000
Cash      135,000

43. Raul's adjusted gross estate is $2 million. The estate will incur death taxes and funeral and administration expenses of $900,000. Raul's gross estate includes stock of Orange Corporation (fair market value of $1.4 million; original cost to Raul of $300,000). Raul owned 70% of the stock of Orange Corporation at the time of his death. In the current year, Orange Corporation (E & P of $3 million) redeems all of the estate's stock for $1.4 million. Raul named his daughter, Rachel, who has no interest in Orange Corporation, as his sole heir. What are the tax consequences of the redemption to Raul's estate and to Orange Corporation?

44. In the current year, Red Corporation (E & P of $7 million) transfers land to a shareholder's estate to carry out a §303 redemption (redemption to pay death taxes). The shares redeemed represent 20% of the total Red Corporation shares outstanding. The deceased shareholder had a basis of $600,000 in the redeemed Red Corporation stock; the stock was worth $1 million on her date of death. The land is worth $1 million and has a tax basis to Red Corporation of $700,000. The estate sells the land nine months later for $900,000. What are the tax results to Red Corporation and to the estate as a result of the transfer? The death taxes and funeral and administration costs for the estate total $2 million.

45. On January 1, 2003, Warbler Corporation has paid-in capital of $500,000 and accumulated E & P of $900,000. Warbler has no current E & P for 2003. Warbler's 450 shares outstanding are held equally by three unrelated shareholders: Tia, Jorge, and Gabriel. Each of the shareholders acquired their Warbler stock four years ago for $110,000. On September 3, 2003, Warbler Corporation redeems all of Jorge's stock for $700,000 in a transaction that qualifies as a complete termination redemption. On December 10, 2003, Warbler distributes $400,000 to Tia and $400,000 to Gabriel. What are the tax consequences of the redemption to Jorge and the distributions to Tia and Gabriel?

46. Crane Corporation has 1,000 shares of stock outstanding. It redeems 150 shares for $200,000 when it has paid-in capital of $500,000 and E & P of $900,000. The redemption qualifies for sale or exchange treatment for the shareholder. Crane incurred $30,000 of accounting and legal fees in the redemption transaction. What is the effect of the distribution on Crane Corporation's E & P? Also, what is the proper tax treatment of the redemption expenditures? Prepare a letter to the president of Crane Corporation (506 Wall Street, Winona, MN 55987) and a memo for the file in which you explain your conclusions.

**Communications**

47. Ahmad and Cora are the sole shareholders of Blue Corporation. Ahmad and Cora each have a basis of $20,000 in their 200 shares of Blue common stock. When its E & P was $900,000, Blue Corporation issued a preferred stock dividend on the common shares of Ahmad and Cora, giving each 100 shares of preferred stock with a par value of $50 per share. Fair market value of one share of common was $200, and fair market value of one share of preferred was $100.
   a. What are the tax consequences of the distribution to Ahmad and Cora?
   b. What are the tax consequences to Ahmad if he later sells his preferred stock to Adam for $25,000? Adam is not related to Ahmad.
   c. What are the tax consequences to Ahmad if Blue Corporation later redeems his preferred stock for $25,000 at a time when its E & P balance is $950,000?

48. Bob owns 1,000 shares of stock in Goose Corporation and 500 shares of stock in Heron Corporation, representing a 100% interest in each corporation. Bob sells 200 shares of Goose stock to Heron Corporation for $30,000. The Goose stock was acquired 10 years ago; the tax basis to Bob of these 200 shares is $5,000. On the date of sale, Goose Corporation and Heron Corporation have E & P of $100,000 and $150,000, respectively. What are the tax consequences of this transaction?

49. The stock of Hawk Corporation is owned equally by three sisters, Michele, Melanie, and Miranda. Hawk owns land (basis of $200,000, fair market value of $180,000) that it has held for investment for eight years. When Michele's basis in her stock is $220,000, Hawk distributes the land to her in exchange for all of her shares. What are the tax consequences for both Hawk and Michele:

*Basis – liability is gain*

*900 000 FMV*
*<300 000> AB*
*————————*
*600 000 gain*

*b) 1 million - AB*
*700 000 gain*

a. If the distribution is a qualifying stock redemption?

b. If the distribution is a liquidating distribution?

50. Pursuant to a complete liquidation, Oriole Corporation distributes to its shareholders land held for three years as an investment (adjusted basis of $300,000, fair market value of $900,000). The land is subject to a liability of $500,000.

a. What are the tax consequences to Oriole Corporation on the distribution of the land?

b. If the land is, instead, subject to a liability of $1 million, what are the tax consequences to Oriole on the distribution?

51. Gray Corporation acquired land in a § 351 tax-free exchange in 2002. At that time, the land had a basis of $300,000 and a fair market value of $400,000. Gray has two equal shareholders, Arnold and Beatrice, who are father and daughter. Gray adopts a plan of liquidation in 2003. During that year and pursuant to the liquidation, the corporation sells the land to an unrelated buyer for its current market value of $280,000 and distributes the proceeds to Arnold and Beatrice. What amount of loss may Gray Corporation recognize on the sale of the land?

52. Assume in Problem 51 that the land had a fair market value of $295,000 when it was acquired in the § 351 exchange. What amount of loss may Gray Corporation recognize on the 2003 sale of the land for $280,000?

53. Assume in Problem 51 that, instead of selling the land, Gray Corporation distributed it proportionately to Arnold and Beatrice in a liquidating distribution. The fair market value of the land at the time of distribution is $280,000. What amount of loss may Gray Corporation recognize on the 2003 distribution of the land?

Decision Making

54. Pink Corporation acquired land in a § 351 tax-free exchange in 2002. The land had a basis of $1,800,000 and a fair market value of $1,950,000 on the date of the transfer. Pink Corporation has two shareholders, Maria and Paul, unrelated individuals. Maria owns 80% of the stock in Pink Corporation and Paul owns 20%. The corporation adopts a plan of liquidation in 2003. On this date the value of the land has decreased to $600,000. What is the effect of each of the following on Pink Corporation? Which option should be selected?

a. Distribute all the land to Maria.

b. Distribute all the land to Paul.

c. Distribute 80% of the land to Maria and 20% to Paul.

d. Distribute 50% of the land to Maria and 50% to Paul.

e. Sell the land and distribute the proceeds of $600,000 proportionately to Maria and to Paul.

Decision Making

55. Assume in Problem 54 that the land had a fair market value of $1.5 million on the date of its transfer to Pink Corporation. On the date of the liquidation, the land's fair market value has decreased to $600,000. How would your answer to Problem 54 change if:

a. All the land is distributed to Maria?

b. All the land is distributed to Paul?

c. The land is distributed 80% to Maria and 20% to Paul?

d. The land is distributed 50% to Maria and 50% to Paul?

e. The land is sold and the proceeds of $600,000 are distributed proportionately to Maria and to Paul?

56. After a plan of complete liquidation has been adopted, Purple Corporation sells its only asset, land, to Rex (an unrelated party) for $400,000. Under the terms of the sale, Purple receives cash of $100,000 and Rex's note in the amount of $300,000. The note is payable over five years ($60,000 per year) and carries an appropriate rate of interest. Immediately after the sale, Purple distributes the cash and notes to Helen, the sole shareholder of Purple Corporation. Helen has a basis of $100,000 in the Purple stock. What are the tax results to Helen if she wishes to defer as much gain as possible on the transaction? Assume the installment notes possess a value equal to their face amount.

*Handwritten margin notes:*

Parent    Sub

Income   —0—    —0—

Basis Carryover   NA

Sub     Minority

Income Antred 50000   50000

+TB ⟨75000⟩   ⟨30000⟩

loss    20000

Basis   NIt   cap gain

FMV 50000

Sub liquidation

a) No gain or loss

b) None too free

c) 900 000 carryover

Basis in stock 600 000 disappears

d) They carryover to parent

See additional class problem

**57.** The stock of Magenta Corporation is owned by Fuchsia Corporation (95%) and Marta (5%). Magenta is liquidated on September 5, 2003, pursuant to a plan of liquidation adopted earlier in the same year. In the liquidation, Magenta distributes various assets worth $950,000 (basis of $620,000) to Fuchsia (basis of $700,000 in Magenta stock) and a parcel of land worth $50,000 (basis of $75,000) to Marta (basis of $30,000 in Magenta stock). Assuming the § 338 election is not made, what are the tax consequences of the liquidation to Magenta, Fuchsia, and Marta?

**58.** Orange Corporation purchased bonds (basis of $570,000) of its wholly owned subsidiary, Green Corporation, at a discount. Upon liquidation of Green pursuant to § 332, Orange receives payment in the form of land worth $600,000, the face amount of the bonds. Green had a basis of $620,000 in the land. What are the tax consequences of this land transfer to Green Corporation and to Orange Corporation?

**59.** Three years ago, Cardinal Corporation acquired 100% of all classes of stock of Wren Corporation for $600,000. In the current year, Cardinal liquidates Wren Corporation and acquires assets worth $1.3 million with an adjusted basis to Wren of $900,000. At the time of its liquidation, Wren had E & P of $500,000 and a net operating loss carryover of $120,000.

a. How much gain (or loss) will Wren Corporation recognize as a result of its liquidation?
b. How much gain (or loss) will Cardinal Corporation recognize as a result of Wren Corporation's liquidation?
c. What basis does Cardinal Corporation take in the assets acquired in the liquidation?
d. What happens to Wren Corporation's E & P and net operating loss carryover?

**60.** Quail Corporation paid $5.4 million for all the stock of Sparrow Corporation 10 years ago. Sparrow Corporation's balance sheet currently reflects the following fair market values:

| Assets | | Liabilities and Shareholders' Equity | |
|---|---|---|---|
| Cash | $ 135,000 | Accounts payable | $ 5,400,000 |
| Inventory | 405,000 | Common stock | 5,400,000 |
| Machinery | 270,000 | Deficit | (7,560,000) |
| Equipment | 1,080,000 | | |
| Land | 1,350,000 | | |
| | $3,240,000 | | $ 3,240,000 |

*Handwritten: is larger than the equity.*

What are the tax consequences to Quail Corporation if it liquidates Sparrow Corporation? Prepare a letter to your client Quail Corporation (1010 Cypress Lane, Community, MN 55166) and a memo for the file in which you explain your conclusions.

**61.** Falcon Corporation is owned 90% by Canary Corporation. The parent is contemplating a liquidation of Falcon Corporation and the acquisition of its assets. Canary Corporation purchased the Falcon stock from Falcon's two individual shareholders a month ago on January 1, 2003, for $400,000. The financial statements of Falcon Corporation as of January 1, 2003, reflect the following:

| Assets | Basis to Falcon Corporation | Fair Market Value |
|---|---|---|
| Cash | $ 40,000 | $ 40,000 |
| Inventory | 80,000 | 60,000 |
| Accounts receivable | 160,000 | 100,000 |
| Equipment | 400,000 | 320,000 |
| Land | 520,000 | 280,000 |
| | $1,200,000 | $800,000 |

*Yes Can make*
*$338 electr*
*Carryover basis*
*1,200000 go 20*
*108 00000*
*Not feasible .*

| | Liabilities and Shareholders' Equity | |
|---|---|---|
| Accounts payable | $ 120,000 | $120,000 |
| Mortgages payable | 200,000 | 200,000 |
| Common stock | 1,000,000 | 480,000 |
| Retained earnings | (120,000) | |
| | $1,200,000 | $800,000 |

The management of Canary Corporation asks your advice on the feasibility of an election under § 338.

a.  Can Canary Corporation make a § 338 election?

b.  Assuming Canary can make a § 338 election, is such an election feasible?

## Research Problems

A THOMSON COMPANY

*Note: Solutions to Research Problems can be prepared by using the **RIA Checkpoint**® **Student Edition** online research product, or the **CCH U.S. Master Tax Guide Plus**™ online Federal tax research database, which is available to accompany this text. It is also possible to prepare solutions to the Research Problems by using tax research materials found in a standard tax library.*

**Research Problem 1.**   Delissa and Mauricio Ramirez were divorced three years ago. Prior to their divorce, Delissa and Mauricio jointly owned 100% of the stock of Roadrunner Corporation (E & P of $1.7 million). Under the terms of their divorce decree, Delissa or, at Delissa's option, Roadrunner was required to purchase Mauricio's 50% shareholder interest (basis of $600,000, fair market value of $1 million). Further, if Delissa opted for Roadrunner to purchase Mauricio's shares, the divorce decree required her to personally guarantee payment of any note issued by Roadrunner in that stock redemption. Delissa opted for Roadrunner to acquire Mauricio's shares, and she personally guaranteed the 10-year $1 million (interest-bearing) installment note issued by Roadrunner in the transaction. The IRS asserts that, by reason of the terms of the divorce decree, the transaction is a deemed redemption of Roadrunner Corporation stock from Delissa, not Mauricio, and that Delissa must recognize $1 million of dividend income as a result. Comment on the IRS's position and provide support for your position.

**Communications**

**Research Problem 2.**   Twenty years ago, Galvin Alexander (6870 Broadway, San Antonio, TX 78209) formed Beige Corporation and became its sole shareholder (1,000 shares). Since that time, Galvin's son, Joseph, has been substantially involved in the management and operation of the corporation's businesses. Galvin has made several gifts of Beige stock to Joseph in an effort to increase his son's vested interest in the success of the corporation. By 2000, when Galvin owned 600 shares of Beige and Joseph owned the remaining 400 shares, the working and personal relationship between father and son had soured to the point that they refused to speak to each other. Recognizing that Beige's success was at risk, the parties agreed that the corporation (E & P of $3 million) would redeem all of Galvin's stock for $1 million (basis of $200,000). The redemption occurred in 2001, and Galvin reported the transaction as a sale or exchange, resulting in a long-term capital gain of $800,000. Under the agreement between the father and son, Galvin continued to serve as a director on the board of Beige until 2005. He was compensated $20,000 annually for serving as a director. In the current year, the IRS audited Galvin's return for 2001 and assessed additional taxes (plus penalties and interest) based on the recharacterization of the redemption as a $1 million dividend distribution. Galvin has contacted you regarding whether he should contest the proposed deficiency. Prepare a letter to Galvin and a memo for the file documenting your conclusions.

**Research Problem 3.**   Beth Thorson has owned 80% of the common stock of Green Corporation (basis of $10,000) since the corporation's formation. In 2001, when Green had E & P of $300,000, the corporation issued to Beth a nontaxable dividend of 100 shares of preferred stock (value of $80,000 on date of distribution) on her common stock interest (value of $320,000 on date of distribution). In 2002, Beth donated the 100 shares of preferred stock to her favorite charity, State University. Beth deducted $80,000, the fair market value of the stock on the date of the gift, as a charitable contribution on her 2002 income tax return. Beth's adjusted gross income for 2002 was $500,000. Two months after the contribution, Green Corporation redeemed the preferred stock from State University for $80,000. Upon an audit of Beth's 2002 tax return, the IRS disallowed the entire deduction, asserting that the preferred stock was § 306 stock and that § 170(e)(1)(A) precluded a deduction for contributions of such stock. What is the proper tax treatment for Beth's charitable contribution of the Green Corporation preferred stock?

*Partial list of research aids:*
Reg. § 1.170(A)–4(b)(1).
§ 306(b)(4).

**Communications**

**Research Problem 4.**   Scott Davison (255 N. Bayshore Boulevard, Clearwater, FL 34619) is the president and sole shareholder of Bluebird Corporation (stock basis of $270,000). Since 1989, Bluebird has imported fine Mexican pottery and sold it to large nurseries and hardware stores across the United States. On July 1, 2001, Bluebird transferred its entire pottery inventory to Davison in a transaction described by the parties as a sale. According to Davison and collaborated by the minutes of the corporation's board of directors, the inventory was "sold" to him for the sum of $1 million, the fair market value of the inventory (Bluebird's basis, $350,000). The terms of the sale provided that Davison would pay Bluebird the $1 million at some future date. This debt obligation was not evidenced by a promissory note, and, to date, Davison has made no payments (principal or interest) on the obligation. The inventory transfer was not reported on Bluebird's 2001 tax return, either as a sale or as a distribution. After the transfer of inventory to Davison, Bluebird had no remaining assets and ceased to conduct any business. Upon an audit of Bluebird's 2001 tax return, the IRS asserted that the transfer of inventory constituted a liquidation of Bluebird and, as such, that the corporation recognized a gain on the liquidating distribution in the amount of $650,000 ($1 million value – $350,000 basis). Further, the IRS assessed a tax due from Davison for his gain recognized in the purported liquidating distribution. Davison has contacted you regarding the IRS's determination. Prepare a letter to Scott Davison and a memo for the file documenting your research.

*Partial list of research aids:*
Reg. § 1.332–2(c).
*Kennemer v. Comm.*, 38–1 USTC ¶9297, 21 AFTR 103, 96 F.2d 177 (CA–5, 1938).

**Internet Activity**

*Use the tax resources of the Internet to address the following questions. Do not restrict your search to the World Wide Web, but include a review of newsgroups and general reference materials, practitioner sites and resources, primary sources of the tax law, chat rooms and discussion groups, and other opportunities.*

**Communications**

**Research Problem 5.**   Shareholders of closely held corporations frequently use buy-sell agreements to address the disposition of stock by a retiring or deceased shareholder. Using the Internet as your sole research source, prepare an outline discussing the planning opportunities (and pitfalls) of using a buy-sell agreement in conjunction with the qualifying stock redemption provisions.

**Communications**

**Research Problem 6.**   Review the Internet sites of several public accounting firms and find discussions regarding the § 338 election. Based on your findings, prepare an outline discussing the advantages and disadvantages of the § 338 election.

# Alternative Minimum Tax and Certain Penalty Taxes Imposed on Corporations

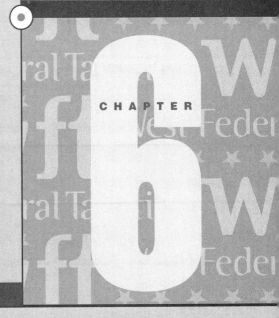

CHAPTER

6

## LEARNING OBJECTIVES

*After completing Chapter 6, you should be able to:*

### L O . 1
Explain the reason for the alternative minimum tax.

### L O . 2
Calculate the alternative minimum tax applicable to corporations.

### L O . 3
Understand the function of adjusted current earnings (ACE).

### L O . 4
Appreciate the purpose of the accumulated earnings tax.

### L O . 5
Determine the reasonable needs of the business.

### L O . 6
Compute the accumulated earnings tax.

### L O . 7
Discuss the reason for the personal holding company tax.

### L O . 8
Recognize the requirements for personal holding company status.

### L O . 9
Compute the personal holding company tax.

### L O . 1 0
Compare the accumulated earnings and personal holding company taxes.

In the eyes of the public, corporations do not always bear their fair share of taxation through the regular corporate income tax. This chapter deals with three taxes imposed by Congress in an attempt to tax these corporations at a more equitable rate:

- The alternative minimum tax (AMT), paid by corporations that appear to be earning substantial economic income but are paying little regular tax.
- The penalty tax on unreasonable accumulations, imposed when a corporation seems to be holding an unreasonable amount of income within the corporation instead of distributing it to shareholders as dividends.
- Personal holding company (PHC) status and the resulting increase in tax rates, also designed to discourage use of the corporate form to shelter shareholder income from the individual income tax.

The accumulated earnings penalty and PHC status most often apply to small, closely held corporations that are attempting to minimize the total of the corporate tax and the individual tax paid by the shareholders. In contrast, after 1998, the AMT applies only to large corporations. Neither the accumulated earnings tax nor the PHC tax applies to a business organized as a limited liability company.

This chapter both describes these three taxes and explains some ways tax planning can be used to avoid them.

**LO.1**
Explain the reason for the alternative minimum tax.

# Alternative Minimum Tax

The perception that many large corporations were not paying their fair share of Federal income tax was especially widespread in the early 1980s. A study released in 1986 reported that 130 of the 250 largest corporations in the United States paid zero or less in Federal taxes in at least one year between 1981 and 1985 (e.g., Reynolds Metals, General Dynamics, Georgia Pacific, and Texas Commerce Bankshares).

Political pressure subsequently led to the adoption of an alternative minimum tax to ensure that corporations with substantial economic income pay a minimum amount of Federal taxes. Corporations are now less able to use exclusions, deductions, and credits available under the law to pay no taxes. A separate tax system with a quasi-flat tax rate is applied each year to a corporation's economic income. If the tentative alternative minimum tax is greater than the regular corporate income tax under § 11, then the corporation must pay the regular tax plus this excess, the **alternative minimum tax (AMT).**

Despite the AMT, a number of corporations continue to pay taxes at relatively low rates. According to the 2000 tax report of the Institute on Taxation and Economic Policy (ITEP) for the tax years 1996, 1997, and 1998, 133 of the 250 largest U.S. corporations paid tax at rates less than half of the 35 percent corporate tax rate. In 1998, 41 companies paid less than zero in Federal taxes while reporting $25 billion in pretax profits. Wide discrepancies exist between industries and among companies in the same industry. For example, Maytag paid 35 percent of its income in taxes, whereas General Electric paid only 8.1 percent. The ITEP report asserts that accelerated depreciation, tax credits, and stock options allow corporations to escape the full statutory tax rate.

Meanwhile, receipts from the corporate AMT continue to decline, dropping to $3.1 billion in 1999 from $3.4 billion in 1998. Only 14,901 companies paid the tax in 1999, whereas 30,226 companies filed in 1998. Receipts from the corporate AMT amounted to less than 1.8 percent of corporate tax liabilities in 1998, down from 8 percent in 1991.

In general, a corporation is likely to pay an AMT for one or more of three reasons:

* A high level of investment in assets such as equipment and structures.
* Low taxable income due to a cyclical downturn, strong international competition, a low-margin industry, or other factors.
* Investment at low real interest rates, which increases the company's deductions for depreciation relative to those for interest payments.

The 20 percent AMT applicable to many regular corporations is similar to the AMT applicable to individuals.[1] Many of the adjustments and tax preference items necessary to arrive at **alternative minimum taxable income (AMTI)** are the same. The rates and exemptions are different, but the objective is identical—to force taxpayers who are more profitable than their taxable income reflects to pay additional income taxes.

The AMT is in addition to the regular corporate tax, but is computed somewhat differently. Separate and independent calculations of the amount and character of all items affecting the computation of the AMT are required. The Code itself mandates the treatment of many items affecting the computation of the AMT. Regulations provide broad rules governing the treatment of other items for AMT purposes. However, the Code and Regulations do not provide guidance for many items.

The formula for determining the AMT liability of corporate taxpayers appears in Figure 6–1 and follows the format of Form 4626 (Alternative Minimum Tax—Corporations).

## SMALL CORPORATION EXEMPTION

For tax years beginning after December 31, 1997, many smaller corporations are not subject to the AMT. Certain corporations that meet several gross receipts tests are exempted from the AMT as long as they remain "small corporations." A corporation initially qualifies as a "small corporation" if it had *average* gross receipts of $5

---

[1]The AMT provisions are contained in §§ 55 through 59.

**■ FIGURE 6–1**
AMT Formula for Corporations

| | |
|---|---|
| Regular taxable income before NOL deduction | |
| **Plus/minus:** | AMT adjustments (except ACE adjustment) |
| **Plus:** | Tax preferences |
| **Equals:** | AMTI before AMT NOL deduction and ACE adjustment |
| **Plus/minus:** | ACE adjustment |
| **Equals:** | AMTI before AMT NOL deduction |
| **Minus:** | AMT NOL deduction (limited to 90%) |
| **Equals:** | Alternative minimum taxable income (AMTI) |
| **Minus:** | Exemption |
| **Equals:** | Tentative minimum tax base |
| **Times:** | 20% rate |
| **Equals:** | Tentative minimum tax before AMT foreign tax credit |
| **Minus:** | AMT foreign tax credit (possibly limited to 90%) |
| **Equals:** | Tentative minimum tax |
| **Minus:** | Regular tax liability before credits minus regular foreign tax credit |
| **Equals:** | Alternative minimum tax (AMT) |

million or less in the preceding three-year period. If a corporation is not in existence for the entire three-year period, the $5 million test is applied on the basis of the period during which the corporation is in existence.

**EXAMPLE 1**

Swan Corporation had average gross receipts of $3.7 million, $4.8 million, and $4.6 million, respectively, for tax years 2000, 2001, and 2002. For 2003 AMT purposes, Swan is considered to be a small corporation. ■

A corporation that passes the $5 million average gross receipts test will continue to be treated as a small corporation as long as its *average* gross receipts for the three-year period preceding the taxable year do not exceed $7.5 million. For both the $7.5 million and the $5 million test, certain aggregating rules apply to related taxpayers. Once a corporation loses its small corporation protection, the corporation is then liable for the AMT for that year and future years. However, many of the AMT and adjusted current earnings adjustments are modified so that they pertain only to transactions and investments that were entered into *after* the corporation lost its small corporation status (e.g., property placed into service in or after the change year).

**EXAMPLE 2**

In 2005, Swan Corporation determines that its average gross receipts for the three-year period of 2002, 2003, and 2004 were $8.7 million. Thus, Swan must calculate its AMT liability for 2005, but only on the transactions and investments that it entered into after the start of the year 2005 (e.g., mining exploration and development costs paid or incurred on or after January 1, 2005). ■

**LO.2**

Calculate the alternative minimum tax applicable to corporations.

## AMT ADJUSTMENTS

As Figure 6–1 indicates, the starting point for computing AMTI is the taxable income of the corporation before any net operating loss (NOL) deduction. Certain adjustments must be made to this amount. Unlike tax preference items, which are always additions, the adjustments may either increase or decrease taxable income.

The positive adjustments arise as a result of timing differences and are added back to the taxable income in computing AMTI. Since most preferences only defer taxes, a corporation may recoup AMT paid on tax preferences when the deferral of regular tax created by the preference is reversed and the regular tax is due. Once AMT adjustments reverse themselves, they are deducted from taxable income to arrive at AMTI. This mechanism is called the *netting process*.

Although NOLs are separately stated in Figure 6–1, they are actually negative adjustments. They are separately stated in Figure 6–1 and on Form 4626 because they may not exceed 90 percent of AMTI. Thus, such adjustments cannot be determined until all other adjustments and tax preference items are considered.

Other adjustments to regular taxable income include the following:

- A portion of depreciation on property placed in service after 1986. For realty placed in service before 1999, the adjustment amount is the difference between depreciation for regular tax purposes and ADS depreciation using a 40-year life. For personalty placed in service before 1999, the adjustment is the excess of accelerated depreciation over the amount determined using the 150 percent declining-balance method switching to straight-line. Thus, the depreciation allowances for purposes of the AMT are generally much less favorable than for the regular corporate income tax. For property placed into service after December 31, 1998, this adjustment applies only to MACRS 3-, 5-, 7-, and 10-year property that is depreciated using the 200 percent declining-balance method. Also, the adjustment is only the difference between the depreciation claimed for regular tax purposes and the depreciation using the 150 percent declining-balance method over the property's shorter regular MACRS recovery period.

**EXAMPLE 3**

Purple Corporation placed an asset costing $10,000 in service on March 15, 2002. Based upon a three-year recovery class life, this personalty has the following effect upon AMTI:

| Year | Tax Deduction 200% | AMT Deduction 150% | Increase or (Decrease) AMT Adjustment |
|------|--------------------|--------------------|---------------------------------------|
| 2002 | $3,333 | $2,500 | $ 833 |
| 2003 | 4,445 | 3,750 | 695 |
| 2004 | 1,481 | 2,500 | (1,019) |
| 2005 | 741 | 1,250 | (509) |

- Since different depreciation methods are used for AMT and regular tax purposes especially before 1999, the adjusted bases for these depreciable assets are affected. When the bases are different and the asset is disposed of, a basis adjustment is necessary to reflect the difference in the AMT gain or loss *and* the regular tax gain or loss.

**EXAMPLE 4**

Assume the same facts as in Example 3, except that the asset is sold at the end of the second year for $4,000. For regular tax purposes, the basis is $2,222 ($10,000 – $3,333 – $4,445), and the basis for AMT purposes is $3,750 ($10,000 – $2,500 – $3,750). Thus, the regular tax gain is $1,778 ($4,000 – $2,222), and the AMT gain is $250 ($4,000 – $3,750). Consequently, a $1,528 negative basis adjustment is required when computing AMT ($1,778 – $250). ■

- Passive activity losses of certain closely held corporations and personal service corporations.
- The excess of mining exploration and development costs deducted over what would have resulted if the costs had been capitalized and written off over 10 years.

- The difference between completed contract and percentage of completion reporting on long-term construction contracts, for some contracts reported under the completed contract method. The percentage of completion method must be used for AMTI purposes for contracts entered into after March 1, 1986.
- The difference between installment and total gain, for dealers using the installment method to account for sales. The installment method is not allowed for AMTI purposes.
- A portion of the difference between **adjusted current earnings (ACE)** and unadjusted AMTI (post-1989).

## TAX PREFERENCES

AMTI includes designated **tax preference items.** In many cases, this inclusion has the effect of subjecting nontaxable income to the AMT. Some of the most common tax preferences include the following:

- Amortization claimed on certified pollution control facilities.
- Accelerated depreciation on real property in excess of straight-line (placed in service before 1987).
- Tax-exempt interest on state and local bonds where the generated funds are not used for an essential function of the government.
- Percentage depletion claimed in excess of the adjusted basis of property.
- For integrated oil companies (ExxonMobil, ChevronTexaco), the excess of intangible drilling costs over 10-year amortization if in excess of 65 percent of net oil and gas income. This item is not a tax preference for independent oil and gas producers and royalty owners.

## COMPUTING ALTERNATIVE MINIMUM TAXABLE INCOME

The following example illustrates the effect of tax preferences and adjustments in arriving at AMTI.

**EXAMPLE 5**

For 2003, Tan Corporation (a calendar year, integrated oil company) had the following transactions:

| | |
|---|---|
| Taxable income | $6,000,000 |
| Mining exploration costs | 500,000 |
| Percentage depletion claimed (the property has a zero adjusted basis) | 700,000 |
| Donation of land held since 1980 as an investment (basis of $400,000 and fair market value of $500,000) to a qualified charity | 500,000 |
| Interest on City of Elmira (Michigan) bonds. The proceeds were used for nongovernmental purposes | 300,000 |

Tan Corporation's AMTI for 2003 is determined as follows:

| | | |
|---|---|---|
| Taxable income | | $6,000,000 |
| Adjustments: | | |
| Excess mining exploration costs [$500,000 (amount expensed) – $50,000 (amount allowed over a 10-year amortization period)] | | 450,000 |
| Tax preferences: | | |
| Excess depletion | $700,000 | |
| Interest on bonds | 300,000 | 1,000,000 |
| AMTI | | $7,450,000 |

■ **FIGURE 6–2**
Determining the ACE
Adjustment*

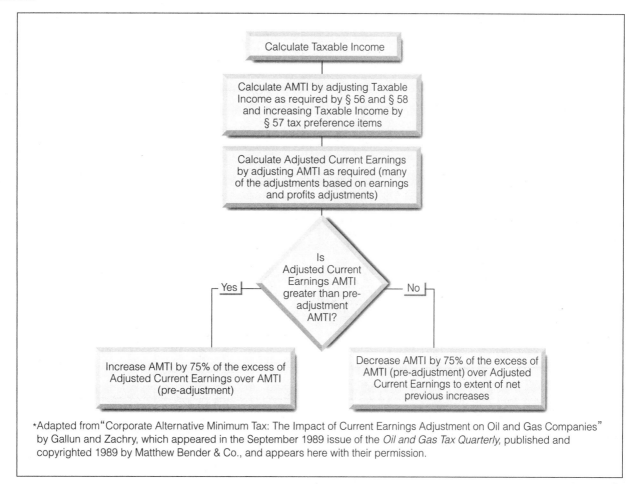

Calculate Taxable Income

Calculate AMTI by adjusting Taxable Income as required by § 56 and § 58 and increasing Taxable Income by § 57 tax preference items

Calculate Adjusted Current Earnings by adjusting AMTI as required (many of the adjustments based on earnings and profits adjustments)

Is Adjusted Current Earnings AMTI greater than pre-adjustment AMTI?

Yes — Increase AMTI by 75% of the excess of Adjusted Current Earnings over AMTI (pre-adjustment)

No — Decrease AMTI by 75% of the excess of AMTI (pre-adjustment) over Adjusted Current Earnings to extent of net previous increases

*Adapted from "Corporate Alternative Minimum Tax: The Impact of Current Earnings Adjustment on Oil and Gas Companies" by Gallun and Zachry, which appeared in the September 1989 issue of the *Oil and Gas Tax Quarterly*, published and copyrighted 1989 by Matthew Bender & Co., and appears here with their permission.

**LO.3**

Understand the function of adjusted current earnings (ACE).

## ADJUSTED CURRENT EARNINGS (ACE)

The purpose of the ACE adjustment is to ensure that the mismatching of earnings and profits (E & P) and taxable income will not produce inequitable results. The calculation of ACE is similar to the calculation of E & P (which is similar to the economic concept of income). S corporations, real estate investment trusts, regulated investment companies, and real estate mortgage investment conduits are not subject to the ACE provisions.

The ACE adjustment is tax-based and can be a negative amount. ACE is calculated as shown in Concept Summary 6–1. AMTI is increased by 75 percent of the excess of ACE over unadjusted AMTI. Or, AMTI is reduced by 75 percent of the excess of unadjusted AMTI over ACE. This negative adjustment is limited to the aggregate of the positive adjustments under ACE for prior years reduced by the previously claimed negative adjustments (see Figure 6–2). Thus, the ordering of the timing differences is crucial because any unused negative adjustment is lost forever. Unadjusted AMTI is AMTI without the ACE adjustment or the AMT NOL.[2]

---

[2]§§ 56(g)(1) and (2).

**CONCEPT SUMMARY 6-1**

## Impact of Various Transactions on ACE and E & P

| | Effect on Unadjusted AMTI in Arriving at ACE | Effect on Taxable Income in Arriving at E & P |
|---|---|---|
| Tax-exempt income (net of expenses) | Add | Add |
| Federal income tax | No effect | Subtract |
| Dividends received deduction (80% and 100% rules) | No effect | Add |
| Dividends received deduction (70% rule) | Add | Add |
| Exemption amount of $40,000 | No effect | No effect |
| Key employee insurance proceeds | Add | Add |
| Excess charitable contribution | No effect | Subtract |
| Excess capital losses | No effect | Subtract |
| Disallowed travel and entertainment expenses | No effect | Subtract |
| Penalties and fines | No effect | Subtract |
| Intangible drilling costs deducted currently | Add | Add |
| Deferred gain on installment sales | Add | Add |
| Realized (not recognized) gain on an involuntary conversion | No effect | No effect |
| Loss on sale between related parties | No effect | Subtract |
| Gift received | No effect | No effect |
| Net buildup on life insurance policy | Add | Add |

NOTE: See also Concept Summary 4–1.

**EXAMPLE 6**

A calendar year corporation has the following data:

| | 2002 | 2003 | 2004 |
|---|---|---|---|
| Unadjusted AMTI | $6,000,000 | $6,000,000 | $6,100,000 |
| Adjusted current earnings | 7,000,000 | 6,000,000 | 5,000,000 |

In 2002, since ACE exceeds unadjusted AMTI by $1 million, $750,000 (75% × $1,000,000) is included as a positive adjustment to AMTI. No adjustment is necessary for 2003. Unadjusted AMTI exceeds ACE by $1.1 million in 2004, so there is a potential negative adjustment to AMTI of $825,000. Since the total increases to AMTI for prior years equal $750,000 (and there are no negative adjustments), only $750,000 of the potential negative adjustment will reduce AMTI for 2004. Further, $75,000 of the negative amount is lost forever ($825,000 – $750,000). Prior book income adjustments are ignored for limitation purposes. ■

ACE should not be confused with current E & P. Many items are treated in the same manner, but certain items that are deductible in computing E & P (but are not deductible in calculating taxable income) generally are not deductible in computing ACE (e.g., Federal income taxes). Concept Summary 6–1 compares the impact various transactions will have on the determination of ACE and E & P.

The starting point for computing ACE is AMTI, which is defined as regular taxable income after AMT adjustments (other than the NOL and ACE adjustments) and after tax preferences.[3] The resulting figure is adjusted for the following items in order to determine ACE:

- *Exclusion items.* These are income items (net of related expenses) that are included in E & P, but will never be included in regular taxable income or AMTI (except on liquidation or disposal of a business). In essence, items that are permanently excluded from unadjusted AMTI but are included in E & P are therefore included in ACE (e.g., life insurance proceeds, interest on tax-exempt bonds, and tax benefit exclusions).
- *Depreciation.* For property placed in service before 1994, the depreciation is calculated using the alternative depreciation system outlined in § 168(g). Thus, depreciation is based on acquisition costs using the straight-line method without regard to salvage value. For property placed in service after 1993, the ACE adjustment is eliminated. This change will speed up the depreciation allowance for capital-intensive industries. But computing the prior ACE depreciation adjustment for pre-1994 assets remains complex.
- *Disallowed items.* A deduction is not allowed in computing ACE if it is never deductible in computing E & P. Thus, the NOL deduction is not allowed. However, since the starting point for ACE is AMTI before the NOL, no adjustment is necessary for the NOL. A deduction *is not allowed* for the dividends received deduction of 70 percent (less than 20 percent ownership). But a deduction *is allowed* for the dividends received deduction of 80 percent (20 percent but less than 80 percent ownership) and 100 percent (80 percent or more ownership).[4]
- *Other adjustments.* The following adjustments, which are required for regular E & P purposes, are necessary: intangible drilling costs, circulation expenditures, organization expense amortization, LIFO inventory adjustments, and installment sales.[5]
- *Both AMTI and ACE.* Deduction items must be deductible for both AMTI and E & P purposes in order to be deductible for ACE. For example, certain deductible items do not reduce ACE: excess charitable contributions, excess capital losses, disallowed travel and entertainment expenses, penalties, fines, bribes, and golden parachute payments.
- *Lessee improvements.* The value of improvements made by a lessee to a lessor's property that is excluded from the lessor's income is excluded from both unadjusted AMTI and ACE.
- *LIFO recapture adjustments.* An increase or decrease in the LIFO recapture amount will result in a corresponding increase or decrease in ACE.

**EXAMPLE 7**

Crimson Corporation makes the ACE adjustment calculation as follows:

| | | |
|---|---:|---:|
| AMTI | | $ 5,780,000 |
| Plus: | | |
| Municipal bond interest | $210,000 | |
| Installment gain | 140,000 | |
| 70% dividends received deduction | 300,000 | |
| Income element in cash surrender life insurance | 60,000 | |
| Organization expense amortization | 70,000 | 780,000 |
| | | $ 6,560,000 |

---

[3]§ 56(g)(3).
[4]§§ 56(g)(4)(C)(i) and (ii).

[5]Reg. § 1.65(g)–1(f).

| | | |
|---|---|---|
| Less: | | |
| ACE depreciation in excess of amount allowed for AMTI (property placed in service before 1994) | $230,000 | |
| Life insurance expense | 10,000 | $    240,000 |
| Adjusted current earnings | | $ 6,320,000 |
| AMTI | | –5,780,000 |
| Base amount | | $    540,000 |
| Times | | .75 |
| ACE adjustment (positive) | | $    405,000 |

## EXEMPTION

The AMT is 20 percent of AMTI that exceeds the exemption amount. The exemption amount for a corporation is $40,000 reduced by 25 percent of the amount by which AMTI exceeds $150,000.

**EXAMPLE 8**

Beige Corporation has lost its small corporation status and has AMTI of $180,000. Since the exemption amount is reduced by $7,500 [25% × ($180,000 – $150,000)], the amount remaining is $32,500 ($40,000 – $7,500). Thus, Beige Corporation's alternative minimum tax base (refer to Figure 6–1) is $147,500 ($180,000 – $32,500). ∎

Note that the exemption phases out entirely when AMTI reaches $310,000. With the $5 million small corporation exception, this exemption is less important to profitable corporations.

## MINIMUM TAX CREDIT

The AMT is a separate tax system that is computed side-by-side with the regular tax. Along with the "netting concept," a **minimum tax credit** is available to eliminate the possibility of double taxation. Essentially, the AMT paid in one tax year may be carried forward indefinitely and used as a credit against the corporation's future *regular* tax liability that exceeds its tentative minimum tax. The minimum tax credit may not be carried back and may not be offset against any future *minimum* tax liability.

Unfortunately, the law does not cover the reverse situation (a preference item generates a regular tax in one year and results in an AMT in a later year). An example could be unearned income that is taxed in the year of receipt but is not recognized for book income purposes until the year earned. Consequently, it is entirely possible that the same income could be taxed twice.

**EXAMPLE 9**

Returning to the facts of Example 5, Tan Corporation's AMTI exceeds $310,000, so there is no exemption amount. The tentative minimum tax is $1,490,000 (20% of $7,450,000). Assuming the regular tax liability in 2003 is $1,400,000, the AMT liability is $90,000 ($1,490,000 – $1,400,000). The amount of the minimum tax credit carryover is $90,000, which is all of the current year's AMT. ∎

Since the tentative minimum tax of a small corporation will be zero, a small corporation with unused minimum tax credits after 1997 may use them up to the amount of the corporation's regular tax liability (after other credits) *less* 25 percent of the excess, if any, of the regular tax liability over $25,000. This will accelerate a small corporation's ability to use any available tax credits.

**EXAMPLE 10**

Purple Corporation, a small company, has a significant amount of minimum tax credits, but no AMT liability in 2003. The corporation's regular tax liability (less other credits) for 2003 is $75,000. Purple's allowable minimum tax credit for 2003 is limited to $62,500 [$75,000 − .25($75,000 − $25,000)]. ■

## OTHER ASPECTS OF THE AMT

In addition to paying their regular tax liability, corporations have to make estimated tax payments of the AMT liability. Even corporations that prepare quarterly financial statements may find this requirement adds to compliance costs. Unfortunately, the estimated tax payment dates will not coincide with the dates of the financial statements. Accordingly, estimating book income accurately for AMT purposes from the information usually available may be difficult.

The AMT can be computed and reported by completing Form 4626.

**LO.4**

Appreciate the purpose of the accumulated earnings tax.

# Penalty Tax on Unreasonable Accumulations

One major advantage to the corporate form is the opportunity to control the income tax burden of the owner(s). One way this control can be accomplished is by accumulating the earnings of the business at the corporate level, deferring the second tax at the shareholder level.

If the board of directors is aware of the shareholders' tax problems, it can then channel the earnings into the shareholders' pockets with a minimum of tax cost by using several mechanisms. The corporation might distribute dividends only in years when the major shareholders are in lower tax brackets. Alternatively, dividend distributions might be curtailed, causing the value of the stock to increase in a manner similar to a savings account. Later, the shareholders can sell their stock in the year of their choice at an amount that reflects the increased retained earnings and receive capital gain treatment. In this manner, the capital gain could be postponed to years when the shareholders have capital losses to offset the gains. At most, long-term capital gains are taxed at 20 percent. Dividend income is ordinary income and can be taxed at a rate as high as 38.6 percent (in 2002 and 2003).

Alternatively, the shareholders can retain their shares. Upon death, the estate or heirs will receive a step-up in basis equal to the fair market value of the stock on the date of death or, if elected, on the alternate valuation date. The increment in value represented by the step-up in basis will be largely attributable to the earnings retained by the corporation and will not be subject to income taxation.

Accumulating corporate earnings always entails problems, however. Congress took steps to stem corporate accumulations as early as the first income tax law enacted under the Sixteenth Amendment. Today, in addition to the usual corporate income tax or AMT, an extra tax is imposed on earnings accumulated beyond the reasonable needs of the business. Another problem is that a personal holding company tax may be levied on certain accumulated passive income. Consider first the 38.6 percent **accumulated earnings tax (AET)** in 2002 and 2003. The tax law is framed to discourage the retention of earnings that are unrelated to the business needs of the company. Earnings retained in the business to avoid the imposition of the tax that would have been imposed on distributions to the shareholders are subject to a 38.6 percent penalty tax.

**EXAMPLE 11**

Janet operated a consulting business as a sole proprietor in 2002. Assume she is in the 38.6% tax bracket in 2003, and she incorporates her business at the beginning of the year. Her business earns $120,000 in 2003, before her salary of $60,000. Since $60,000 of the income is accumulated, $13,160 of taxes are "saved" ($23,160 individual tax versus $10,000 corporate tax on the $60,000 accumulated). This accumulated savings could occur each year with the corporation reinvesting the saved taxes. Thus, without an accumulated earnings tax or personal holding company tax, Janet could use her corporation like a savings account. For example, the corporation could take advantage of the 70% dividends received deduction for dividend-paying stocks. With the top individual tax rate (38.6% for 2003) above the top corporate tax rate (35% for 2003), it is more attractive to hold investment property in a C corporation than in a flow-through entity (partnership, S corporation, or sole proprietor). However, the earnings are still at the corporate level, and Janet might be in a higher individual rate when the accumulated earnings are distributed. ■

## THE ELEMENT OF INTENT

Although the penalty tax is normally applied against closely held corporations, a corporation is not exempt from the tax merely because its stock is widely held.[6] For example, a Second Circuit Court of Appeals decision[7] imposed the tax upon a widely held corporation with over 1,500 shareholders. However, a much smaller group of shareholders actually controlled the corporation. As a practical matter, a widely held corporation that is not under the legal or effective control of a small group is unlikely to be suspected of accumulating earnings for the purpose of tax avoidance.

The key to imposition of the tax is not the number of the shareholders in the corporation but whether a shareholder group controls corporate policy. If such a group does exist and withholds dividends to protect its own tax position, an AET (§ 531) problem might materialize.

When a corporation is formed or used to shield its shareholders from individual taxes by accumulating rather than distributing earnings and profits, the "bad" purpose for accumulating earnings is considered to exist under § 532(a). This subjective test, in effect, asks, Did the corporation and/or shareholder(s) *intend* to retain the earnings in order to avoid the tax on dividends? According to the Supreme Court, the tax avoidance motive need *not* be the dominant or controlling purpose to trigger application of the penalty tax; it need only be a contributing factor to the retention of earnings.[8] If a corporation accumulates funds beyond its reasonable needs, such action is determinative of the existence of a "bad" purpose, unless the contrary can be proved by the preponderance of the evidence. The fact that a business is a mere holding or investment company is *prima facie* evidence of this tax avoidance purpose.[9]

## IMPOSITION OF THE TAX AND THE ACCUMULATED EARNINGS CREDIT

Contrary to its name, the accumulated earnings tax is not levied on the corporate accumulated earnings balance. Instead, the tax is imposed on the current year's addition to this balance not needed for a reasonable business purpose. The penalty tax is not imposed upon S corporations, personal holding companies, foreign personal holding companies, tax-exempt organizations, and passive foreign investment

---

[6]§ 532(c).

[7]*Trico Products v. Comm.*, 43–2 USTC ¶9540, 31 AFTR 394, 137 F.2d 424 (CA–2, 1943).

[8]*U.S. v. The Donruss Co.*, 69–1 USTC ¶9167, 23 AFTR2d 69–418, 89 S.Ct. 501 (USSC, 1969).

[9]§ 533. See, for example, *H. C. Cockrell Warehouse Corp.*, 71 T.C. 1036 (1979).

## TAX IN THE NEWS

### RALPH NADER VERSUS MICROSOFT

Consumer activist Ralph Nader wrote Bill Gates in January 2002, suggesting that the quantitative failure of Microsoft to pay any dividends was an unlawful device to shelter earnings from Federal income tax. Nader pointed out that Microsoft is run by a small number of people who hold a substantial portion of the company's stock. According to the 2001 proxy statement, 17.3 percent of the stock was owned by executive officers and directors.

By having the company follow a policy of not paying dividends, these wealthy Microsoft shareholder-employees avoid paying the top marginal tax rate of 38.6 percent that would apply to dividend income. Instead, by taking earnings entirely from stock sales, these shareholder-employees lowered their tax rate to the minimum 20 percent capital gain rate.

Nader argued that Microsoft should be subject to the accumulated earnings tax because of the $36 billion of cash and short-term securities on its balance sheet (twice the cash of General Motors, with sales seven times greater than Microsoft's).

SOURCE: R. Buckman and J. Wilke, "Microsoft Comes under Fire from Nader for Its Practice of Not Paying Dividends," *Wall Street Journal*, January 7, 2002, p. A16.

companies. The tax is in addition to the regular corporate tax and the 20 percent alternative minimum tax. The tax rate is 38.6 percent in 2002 and 2003.

The **accumulated earnings credit** is the greater of the following:

1. The current E & P for the tax year that are needed to meet the reasonable needs of the business (see the subsequent discussion) *less* the net long-term capital gain for the year (net of any tax). In determining the reasonable needs for any one year, the accumulated E & P of past years must be taken into account.

2. The amount by which the **minimum credit** allowable to the corporation exceeds the accumulated E & P of the corporation at the close of the preceding tax year. Most corporations are allowed a minimum credit of $250,000 against accumulated taxable income, even when earnings are accumulating beyond reasonable business needs. However, certain personal service corporations in health, law, engineering, architecture, accounting, actuarial science, performing arts, and consulting are limited to a $150,000 accumulated earnings credit. Moreover, a nonservice corporation (other than a holding or investment company) may retain more than $250,000 ($150,000 for a service organization) of accumulated earnings if the company can justify the accumulation as necessary to meet the reasonable needs of the business.[10]

**EXAMPLE 12**

Yellow Corporation, a calendar year manufacturing concern, has accumulated E & P of $120,000 as of December 31, 2002. For 2003, it has no capital gains and current E & P of $140,000. A realistic estimate places Yellow Corporation's reasonable needs of the business for 2003 at $200,000.

The allowable credit is the *greater* of (1) or (2).

---

[10]§§ 535(c) and 537 and Reg. § 1.537–1.

|  | **(1)** | **(2)** |
|---|---|---|
| Reasonable needs | $200,000 | |
| Minimum credit | | $250,000 |
| Accumulated E & P | 120,000 | 120,000 |
| Potential credit | $ 80,000 | $130,000 |

Thus, the credit becomes $130,000 (the *greater* of $80,000 or $130,000). ∎

Several observations can be made about the accumulated earnings credit. *First,* the minimum credit of $250,000 is of no consequence as long as the prior year's ending balance in accumulated E & P is $250,000 or more. *Second,* when the credit is based on reasonable needs, the credit is the amount that exceeds accumulated E & P. *Third,* a taxpayer must choose between the reasonable needs credit (item 1) and the minimum credit (item 2). Combining the two in the same year is not permissible. *Fourth,* although the § 531 tax is not imposed on accumulated E & P, the amount of the credit depends upon the balance of this account as of the end of the preceding year.

## LO.5
Determine the reasonable needs of the business.

## REASONABLE NEEDS OF THE BUSINESS

If a corporation's funds are invested in assets essential to the needs of the business, the IRS will have a difficult time imposing the AET. "Thus, the size of the accumulated earnings and profits or surplus is not the crucial factor; rather it is the reasonableness and nature of the surplus."[11] What are the reasonable business needs of a corporation? This question is difficult to answer and creates controversy with the IRS.

**Justifiable Needs—In General.** The **reasonable needs of a business** include the business's reasonably anticipated needs.[12] These anticipated needs must be specific, definite, and feasible. A number of court decisions illustrate that indefinite plans referred to only briefly in corporate minutes merely provide a false feeling of security for the taxpayer.[13]

The Regulations list some legitimate reasons that could indicate that the earnings of a corporation are being accumulated to meet the reasonable needs of the business. Earnings may be allowed to accumulate to provide for bona fide expansion of the business enterprise or replacement of plant and facilities as well as to acquire a business enterprise through the purchase of stock or assets. Provision for the retirement of bona fide indebtedness created in connection with the trade or business (e.g., the establishment of a sinking fund for the retirement of bonds issued by the corporation) is a legitimate reason for accumulating earnings under ordinary circumstances. Providing necessary working capital for the business (e.g., to acquire inventories) and providing for investment or loans to suppliers or customers (if necessary to maintain the business of the corporation) are valid grounds for accumulating earnings.[14] Funds may be retained for self-insurance[15] and realistic business contingencies (e.g., lawsuits, patent infringement).[16] Accumulations to avoid an

---

[11]*Smoot Sand & Gravel Corp. v. Comm.,* 60–1 USTC ¶9241, 5 AFTR2d 626, 274 F.2d 495 (CA–4, 1960).

[12]§ 537(a)(1).

[13]See, for example, *Fine Realty, Inc. v. U.S.,* 62–2 USTC ¶9758, 10 AFTR2d 5751, 209 F.Supp. 286 (D.Ct. Minn., 1962).

[14]Reg. § 1.537–2(b).

[15]*Halby Chemical Co., Inc. v. U.S.,* 67–2 USTC ¶9500, 19 AFTR2d 1589, 180 Ct.Cls. 584 (Ct.Cls., 1967).

[16]*Dielectric Materials Co.,* 57 T.C. 587 (1972).

unfavorable competitive position[17] and to carry key employee life insurance policies[18] are justifiable. Accumulation for the possible loss of a key customer or client is a reasonable need of the business.[19]

The reasonable business needs of a company also include the post-death § 303 redemption requirements of a corporation.[20] Accumulations for such purposes are limited to the amount needed (or reasonably anticipated to be needed) to redeem stock included in the gross estate of the decedent-shareholder.[21] This amount may not exceed the sum of the death taxes and funeral and administration expenses allowable under § 2053 or § 2106.[22]

Section 537(b) provides that reasonable accumulations to pay future product liability losses represent a reasonable anticipated need of the business. Guidelines for the application of this change are prescribed in Proposed Regulations.

### Justifiable Needs—Working Capital Requirements for Inventory Situations.

For many years the penalty tax on accumulated earnings was based upon the concept of retained earnings. The courts generally looked at retained earnings alone to determine whether there was an unreasonable accumulation. However, a corporation may have a large retained earnings balance and yet possess no liquid assets with which to pay dividends. Therefore, the emphasis should more appropriately be placed upon the liquidity of a corporation. Does the business have liquid assets *not* needed that could be used to pay dividends? The courts, however, did not begin to use this liquidity approach until 1960.

Looking for an objective approach to determine a corporation's need for liquid assets, the courts seized upon the operating cycle. The operating cycle of a business is the average time interval between the acquisition of materials (or services) entering the business and the final realization of cash. A normal business has two distinct cycles:

1. Purchase of inventory → the production process → finished goods inventory.
2. Sale of merchandise → accounts receivable → cash collection.

A systematic operating cycle formula was developed in *Bardahl Manufacturing Co.* and *Bardahl International Corp.*[23] The technique became known as the **Bardahl formula.** This formula is not a precise tool and is subject to various interpretations.

The following is the standard formula used to determine the reasonable working capital needs for a corporation:

$$\text{Inventory cycle} = \frac{\text{Average inventory}}{\text{Cost of goods sold}}$$

*Plus*

$$\text{Accounts receivable cycle} = \frac{\text{Average accounts receivable}}{\text{Net sales}}$$

---

[17]*North Valley Metabolic Laboratories*, 34 TCM 400, T.C.Memo. 1975–79.

[18]*Emeloid Co. v. Comm.*, 51–1 USTC ¶66,013, 40 AFTR 674, 189 F.2d 230 (CA–3, 1951). Key employee life insurance is a policy on the life of a key employee that is owned by and made payable to the employer. Such insurance enables the employer to recoup some of the economic loss that could materialize upon the untimely death of the key employee.

[19]*EMI Corp.*, 50 TCM 569, T.C.Memo. 1985–386, and *James H. Rutter*, 52 TCM 326, T.C.Memo. 1986–407.

[20]The § 303 redemption to pay death taxes and administration expenses of a deceased shareholder is discussed in Chapter 5. See § 537(a).

[21]§§ 537(a)(2) and (b)(1).

[22]§ 303(a).

[23]*Bardahl Manufacturing Co.*, 24 TCM 1030, T.C.Memo. 1965–200; *Bardahl International Corp.*, 25 TCM 935, T.C.Memo. 1966–182. See also *Apollo Industries, Inc. v. Comm.*, 66–1 USTC ¶9294, 17 AFTR2d 518, 358 F.2d 867 (CA–1, 1966).

*Minus*

$$\text{Accounts payable cycle} = \frac{\text{Average accounts payable}^{24}}{\text{Purchases + cash operating expenses}}$$

*Equals*

A decimal percentage

This imprecise formula assumes that working capital needs are computed on a yearly basis. However, this may not provide the most favorable result. A business that experiences seasonally based high and low cycles illustrates this point. For example, a construction company can justify a greater working capital need if computations are based on a cycle that includes the winter months only and not on an annual average.[25] In the same vein, an incorporated CPA firm would choose a cycle during the slow season.

The decimal percentage derived above, when multiplied by the cost of goods sold plus general, administrative, and selling expenses (not including unpaid Federal income taxes and depreciation),[26] equals the working capital needs of the business. Working capital is the excess of current assets over current liabilities. This amount is the relatively liquid portion of the total business capital that is a buffer for meeting obligations within the normal operating cycle of the business. Paid estimated Federal income taxes are treated as operating expenses, but profit sharing contributions and charitable contributions are not operating expenses.

If the statistically computed working capital needs plus any extraordinary expenses are more than the current year's net working capital, no penalty tax is imposed. However, if working capital needs plus any extraordinary expenses are less than the current year's net working capital, the possibility of the imposition of a penalty tax does exist.[27]

The IRS normally takes the position that the operating cycle should be reduced by the accounts payable cycle. The IRS maintains that the payment of such expenses may be postponed by various credit arrangements that will reduce the operating capital requirements. However, a number of court decisions have omitted such a reduction. Some courts use all payables, while other courts use only material and trade payables. In any case, a corporate tax planner should not have to rely on creditors to avoid the accumulated earnings penalty tax. The corporation with the most acute working capital problem will probably have a large accounts payable balance. If the formula for determining reasonable working capital needs is used, a large accounts payable balance will result in a sizable reduction in the maximum working capital allowable before the tax is imposed. For tax planning purposes, a corporation should hold accounts payable at a reduced level.

**Justifiable Needs—Working Capital Requirements for Noninventory Situations.** A service business does not purchase inventories, so part of the operating cycle in the *Bardahl* formula is missing. However, a service business incurs certain costs such as salaries and overhead for a period of time before billing customers for services. Some courts have used a rough rule of thumb to determine

---

[24]The accounts payable cycle was developed in *Kingsbury Investments, Inc.*, 28 TCM 1082, T.C.Memo. 1969–205. Some courts have used only purchases and not total operating expenses: *Suwannee Lumber Mfg. Co., Inc.*, 39 TCM 572, T.C.Memo. 1979–477. But see *Snow Manufacturing*, 86 T.C. 260 (1986).

[25]See *Audits of Construction Contracts*, AICPA, 1965, p. 25.

[26]In *W. L. Mead, Inc.*, 34 TCM 924, T.C.Memo. 1975–215, the Tax Court allowed depreciation to be included in the expenses of a

service firm with no inventory. Likewise, in *Doug-Long, Inc.*, 72 T.C. 158 (1979), the Tax Court allowed a truck stop to include quarterly estimated tax payments in operating expenses.

[27]*Electric Regulator Corp. v. Comm.*, 64–2 USTC ¶9705, 14 AFTR2d 5447, 336 F.2d 339 (CA–2, 1964) used "quick assets" (current assets less inventory).

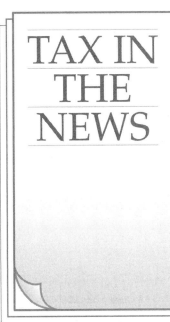

## APPLYING THE *BARDAHL* FORMULA COULD BE MISLEADING

The *Bardahl* formula is a double-edged sword because it measures working capital, not cash. But dividends can only be paid in cash. When the *Bardahl* formula is harmful to a corporation, one must determine how much cash is available for distribution. Court decisions indicate that a corporation should not be forced to incur debt or sell off business assets merely to pay dividends so as to avoid the punitive accumulated earnings tax (AET).

A statement of cash flows may be used to defend against an AET attack because it spotlights fixed assets acquired and other business investments made. Obviously, cash on hand at the end of the year may not be a fair statement of the average cash available during the year. Also, bank covenants, which prevent the payment of dividends or require certain levels of working capital, should be taken into consideration since they show a nonprohibited purpose for accumulated earnings. Loans to shareholders, for example, cause a lack of cash, but will not avoid AET attacks.

However, when the *Bardahl* formula indicates that working capital needs are greater than available working capital, IRS agents may avoid assessing the AET.

an inventory equivalent cycle. Under certain circumstances, a human resource accounting (HRA) approach may be used to determine the working capital needs of a noninventory corporation. The use of an HRA approach is based on the contention that the strength of a service business—and its major asset—is its highly educated, skilled technicians. Such individuals must be available both to attract clients and to execute projects efficiently. In the event of a business downturn, it would be foolish to discharge highly paid specialists, recruited and trained at considerable expense. The business decline might prove to be of brief duration.

One court[28] allowed an engineering firm to add to the IRS's *Bardahl*-calculated operating reserve the reasonable professional and technical payroll for an additional period of 60 days. The court felt that this extra amount would "allow sufficient reserve for one cycle of full operation plus a reasonable period of curtailed operation to recapture business or, in the alternative, to face up to hard decisions on reducing the scope of the entire operation or abandoning it." Further, the court expressed its opinion that a multiple of reasonable professional and technical salaries is a useful method for determining the amount to be included in an operating reserve. However, the court did not indicate why it selected two months as the magic number. Courts will continue to evolve a *Bardahl*-like formula for noninventory corporations.

**No Justifiable Needs.** Certain situations do *not* call for the accumulation of earnings. For example, accumulating earnings to make loans to shareholders[29] or brother-sister corporations is not considered within the reasonable needs of the business.[30] Accumulations to retire stock without curtailment of the business and for unrealistic business hazards (e.g., depression of the U.S. economy) are invalid reasons for accumulating funds.[31] The same holds true for accumulations made to

---

[28]*Simons-Eastern Co. v. U.S.*, 73–1 USTC ¶9279, 31 AFTR2d 73–640, 354 F.Supp. 1003 (D.Ct. Ga., 1972). See also *Delaware Trucking Co., Inc.*, 32 TCM 105, T.C.Memo. 1973–29; *Magic Mart, Inc.*, 51 T.C. 775 (1969); and *Technalysis*, 101 T.C. 397 (1993), for a three-month period.

[29]Reg. §§ 1.537–2(c)(1), (2), and (3).
[30]See *Young's Rubber Corp.*, 21 TCM 1593, T.C.Memo. 1962–300.
[31]*Turnbull, Inc. v. Comm.*, 67–1 USTC ¶9221, 19 AFTR2d 609, 373 F.2d 91 (CA–5, 1967), and Reg. § 1.537–2(c)(5).

## CONCEPT SUMMARY 6–2

### Reasonable Business Needs

| Legitimate Reasons | Invalid Reasons |
| --- | --- |
| Expansion of a business. | Loans to shareholders. |
| Replacement of capital assets. | Loans to brother-sister corporations. |
| Replacement of plant. | Future depression. |
| Acquisition of a business. | Unrealistic contingencies. |
| Working capital needs. | Investment in assets unrelated to the business. |
| Product liability loss. | Retirement of stock without a curtailment of the business.* |
| Loans to suppliers or customers. | |
| Redemption under § 303 to pay death taxes and administration expenses of a shareholder. | |
| Realistic business hazards. | |
| Loss of a major customer or client. | |
| Reserve for actual lawsuit. | |
| Protection of a family business from takeover by outsiders. | |
| Debt retirement. | |
| Self-insurance. | |

*But see *Technalysis*, 101 T.C. 397 (1993).

carry out investments in properties or securities unrelated to the corporation's activity.[32]

Concept Summary 6–2 reviews the previous discussion regarding what does and does not constitute a reasonable need of the business.

**EXAMPLE 13**

For a period of years, Brown, Inc., a trucking company, has considered the purchase of various vehicles and other facilities directly related to its business. During the same time, it has also invested in oil and gas drilling projects (mostly wildcats). Despite substantial accumulated earnings, the corporation made no distributions of dividends during the same period of years. The Claims Court imposed the penalty tax because the plan to acquire vehicles and facilities was not supported by documents in existence or prepared during the taxable years at issue. Furthermore, accumulations to further the oil and gas investments were unjustified. Brown was not in the oil and gas business and was only a minor investor.[33] ■

**Measuring the Accumulation.**   Should the cost or the fair market value of assets be used to determine whether a corporation has accumulated E & P beyond its reasonable needs? This issue remains unclear. The Supreme Court has indicated that fair market value is to be used when dealing with marketable securities.[34] Although the Court admitted that the concept of E & P does not include unrealized appreciation, it asserted that the current asset ratio must be considered in determining if accumulated earnings are reasonable. Thus, the Court looked to the economic realities of the situation and held that fair market value is to be used with respect to readily marketable securities. The Court's opinion did not address the proper

---

[32]Reg. § 1.537–2(c)(4).

[33]*Cataphote Corp. of Miss. v. U.S.*, 75–2 USTC ¶9753, 36 AFTR2d 75–5990 (Ct.Cls., 1975).

[34]*Ivan Allen Co. v. U.S.*, 75–2 USTC ¶9557, 36 AFTR2d 75–5200, 95 S.Ct. 2501 (USSC, 1975).

basis for valuation of assets other than marketable securities. Howev
may assert that this rule should be extended to include other assets. Th.
advisers and corporate personnel should regularly check all security holdings to
guard against accumulations caused by the appreciation of investments.

**EXAMPLE 14**

Two of Robin Company's shareholders, father and son, own 75% of the stock. Robin had
accumulated E & P of approximately $2 million. Five years ago, the company invested
$150,000 in various stocks and bonds. At the end of the current tax year, the fair market
value of these securities approximates $2.5 million. If these securities are valued at cost,
current assets minus current liabilities are deemed to be equal to the reasonable needs of
the business. However, if the marketable securities are valued at their $2.5 million fair
market value, the value of the liquid assets greatly exceeds the corporation's reasonable
needs. Under the Supreme Court's economic reality test, the fair market value is used.
Consequently, the corporation is subject to the § 531 penalty tax. ∎

**LO.6**

Compute the accumulated
earnings tax.

## MECHANICS OF THE PENALTY TAX

The taxable base of the AET is a company's accumulated taxable income (ATI).
Taxable income of the corporation is modified as follows:[35]

The "certain adjustments" include the following items (for a corporation not a mere
holding or investment company):
  As deductions—

1. Corporate income tax for the year.
2. Charitable contributions in excess of 10 percent of adjusted taxable income.
3. Capital loss adjustment.[36]
4. Excess of net long-term capital gain over net short-term capital loss, dimin-
   ished by the capital gain tax and reduced by net capital losses from earlier years.

  And as additions—

5. Capital loss carryovers and carrybacks.
6. Net operating loss deduction.
7. The dividends received deduction.

The purpose of each of these adjustments is to produce an amount that more
closely represents the dividend-paying capacity of the corporation. For example,
the corporate income tax is deducted from taxable income because the corporation
does not have this money to pay dividends. Conversely, the dividends received
deduction is added to taxable income since the deduction has no impact upon the

---

[35]§ 535(a).

[36]This deduction (item 3) and item 4 are either/or deductions, since
a corporation would not have both in the same year. For the capital
loss adjustment, see § 535(b)(5).

ability to pay a dividend. Note that item 4, in effect, allows a corporation to accumulate any capital gains without a penalty tax.

Payment of dividends reduces the amount of ATI subject to the penalty tax. The dividends paid deduction includes those dividends paid during the tax year that the shareholders must report as ordinary income *and* any dividends paid within 2½ months after the close of the tax year.[37] However, a nontaxable stock dividend does not affect the dividends paid deduction.

A shareholder may file a consent statement to treat as a dividend the amount specified in the statement. A consent dividend is taxed to the shareholder even though it is not actually distributed. The consent dividend is treated as a contribution to the capital of the corporation (paid-in capital) by the shareholder.[38]

**EXAMPLE 15**

A nonservice closely held corporation that had no capital gains or losses in prior years has the following financial transactions for calendar year 2003:

| | |
|---|---|
| Taxable income | $300,000 |
| Tax liability | 100,250 |
| Excess charitable contributions | 22,000 |
| Short-term capital loss | (40,000) |
| Dividends received (less than 20% owned) | 100,000 |
| Research and development expenses | 46,000 |
| Dividends paid in 2003 | 40,000 |
| Accumulated earnings (1/1/2003) | 220,000 |

Presuming the corporation is subject to the § 531 tax and has *no* reasonable business needs that justify its accumulations, the ATI is calculated as follows:

| | | |
|---|---|---|
| Taxable income | | $300,000 |
| Plus: 70% dividends received deduction | | 70,000 |
| | | $370,000 |
| Less: Tax liability | $100,250 | |
| Excess charitable contributions | 22,000 | |
| Net short-term capital loss adjustment | 40,000 | |
| Dividends paid | 40,000 | |
| Accumulated earnings minimum credit ($250,000 − $220,000) | 30,000 | 232,250 |
| Accumulated taxable income (ATI) | | $137,750 |

Thus, the accumulated earnings penalty tax for 2003 would be $53,172 ($137,750 × 38.6%). ■

**EXAMPLE 16**

In Example 15, assume that the reasonable needs of the business of § 535(c) amount to $270,000 in 2003. The current year's accumulated earnings are now reduced by $50,000, rather than the $30,000, of accumulated earnings minimum credit. ATI is $117,750, and the penalty tax is $45,452. Note that the $220,000 of beginning accumulated earnings *cannot* be omitted in determining whether taxable income for the current year is reasonably needed by the enterprise. ■

---

[37]§§ 535(a), 561(a), and 563(a).
[38]§§ 565(a) and (c)(2). The consent dividend procedure would be appropriate if the corporation is not in a position to make a cash or property distribution to its shareholders. The dividends paid deduction is discussed more fully later in the chapter.

L0.7

Discuss the reason for the
personal holding company
tax.

# Personal Holding Company Penalty Tax

The personal holding company (PHC) tax, § 541, was enacted to discourage the sheltering of certain types of passive income in corporations owned by high tax bracket individuals. These "incorporated pocketbooks" were frequently found in the entertainment and construction industries. For example, a taxpayer could shelter the income from securities in a corporation, which would pay no dividends, and allow the corporation's stock to increase in value. Like the accumulated earnings tax, the purpose of the 38.6 percent PHC tax (in 2002 and 2003) is to force the distribution of corporate earnings to the shareholders. However, in any one year, the IRS cannot impose both the PHC tax and the accumulated earnings tax.[39]

**EXAMPLE 17**

Considerable tax savings could be achieved by incorporating a "pocketbook" if § 541 did not exist. Assume that investments that yield $50,000 a year are transferred to a corporation by a 38.6% income tax bracket shareholder. A tax savings of $11,800 will occur if no dividends are paid to the shareholder. With no corporation, there would be a total tax liability of $19,300, but with a corporation the tax liability is only $7,500 in 2003 (15% × $50,000). Further, if the yield of $50,000 is in the form of dividends, the corporate tax will be even less because of the dividends received deduction. ■

Whether a corporation will be included within the statutory definition of a PHC for any particular year depends upon the facts and circumstances during that year.[40] Therefore, PHC status may be conferred even in the absence of any avoidance intent on the part of the corporation. In one situation,[41] a manufacturing operation adopted a plan of complete liquidation, sold its business, and invested the proceeds of the sale in U.S. Treasury bills and certificates of deposit. During the liquidating corporation's last tax year, 100 percent of the corporation's adjusted ordinary gross income was interest income. Since the corporation was owned by one shareholder, the corporation was a PHC, even though in the process of liquidation.

Certain types of corporations are expressly excluded from PHC status in § 542(c):

- Tax-exempt organizations under § 501(a).
- Banks and domestic building and loan associations.
- Life insurance companies.
- Surety companies.
- Foreign personal holding companies.
- Lending or finance companies.
- Foreign corporations.
- Small business investment companies.

These exceptions allow the business world to perform necessary activities without a high rate of taxation. For example, a legitimate finance company should not be burdened by the PHC tax because it is performing a valuable business function of lending money. In contrast, in the case of a classic incorporated pocketbook, the major purpose is to shelter the investment income from possible higher individual tax rates.

---

[39]§ 532(b)(1) and Reg. § 1.541–1(a).
[40]*Affiliated Enterprises, Inc. v. Comm.*, 44–1 USTC ¶9178, 32 AFTR 153, 140 F.2d 647 (CA–10, 1944).

[41]*Weiss v. U.S.*, 75–2 USTC ¶9538, 36 AFTR2d 75–5186 (D.Ct. Ohio, 1975). See also *O'Sullivan Rubber Co. v. Comm.*, 41–2 USTC ¶9521, 27 AFTR 529, 120 F.2d 845 (CA–2, 1941).

## LO.8

Recognize the requirements for personal holding company status.

# DEFINITION OF A PERSONAL HOLDING COMPANY

The PHC provisions include two tests:

1. Was more than 50 percent of the *value* of the outstanding stock owned by five or fewer individuals at any time during the *last half* of the taxable year?
2. Is a substantial portion (60 percent or more) of the corporate income (adjusted ordinary gross income) composed of passive types of income such as dividends, interest, rents, royalties, or certain personal service income?

If the answer to *both* of these questions is yes, the corporation is classified as a **personal holding company (PHC).** Once classified as a PHC, the corporation must pay a penalty tax at the highest individual rate (38.6 percent in 2002 and 2003) in addition to the regular corporate income tax.

**Stock Ownership Test.**   To meet the stock ownership test, more than 50 percent *in value* of the outstanding stock must be owned, directly or indirectly, by or for not more than five individuals sometime during the last half of the tax year. Thus, if the corporation has nine or fewer shareholders, it automatically meets this test. If 10 unrelated individuals own an *equal* portion of the value of the outstanding stock, the stock ownership requirement is not met. However, if these 10 individuals do not hold equal value, the test is met.

The ownership test is based on fair market value and not on the number of shares outstanding. Fair market value is determined in light of all the circumstances and is based on the company's net worth, earning and dividend-paying capacity, appreciation of assets, and other relevant factors. If there are two or more classes of stock outstanding, the total value of all the stock is allocated among the various classes according to the relative value of each class.[42]

In determining the stock ownership of an individual, broad constructive ownership rules apply. Under § 544, the following attribution rules determine indirect ownership:

1. Any stock owned by a corporation, partnership, trust, or estate is considered to be owned proportionately by the shareholders, partners, or beneficiaries.
2. The stock owned by the members of an individual's family (brothers, sisters, spouse, ancestors, and lineal descendants) or by the individual's partner is considered to be owned by the individual.
3. If an individual has an option to purchase stock, the stock is regarded as owned by that person.[43]
4. Convertible securities are treated as outstanding stock.

**EXAMPLE 18**

Aaron and Barbara, two individuals, are the equal beneficiaries of a trust that owns the entire capital stock of Wren Corporation. Wren Corporation owns all of the stock of New Corporation. All of the stock of Wren and New is considered to be owned equally by Aaron and Barbara by reason of indirect ownership under § 544(a)(1). ∎

**EXAMPLE 19**

During the last half of the tax year, Azure Corporation has 1,000 shares of outstanding stock, 499 of which are held by various individuals having no relationship to one another and none of whom are partners. The remaining 501 shares are held by seven shareholders as follows:

---

[42]Reg. § 1.542–3(c).

[43]For examples of how these constructive ownership rules operate, see Reg. §§ 1.544–2, –3(a), and –4.

■ **FIGURE 6–3**
Adjusted Ordinary Gross
Income Determination

| | | |
|---|---|---|
| Gross income (defined in § 61) | | |
| **Less:** | a. Capital gains. | |
| | b. Section 1231 gains. | |
| **Equals:** | Ordinary gross income (OGI). | |
| **Less:** | c. Depreciation, property taxes, interest expense, and rental expenses directly related to gross income from rents (not to exceed the income from rents). | |
| | d. Depreciation, property and severance taxes, interest expense, and rental expenses directly related to gross income from mineral, oil, and gas royalties (not to exceed gross income from the royalties). | |
| | e. Interest on a condemnation award, a judgment, a tax refund, and an obligation of the United States held by a dealer. | |
| **Equals:** | Adjusted ordinary gross income (AOGI). | |

| | |
|---|---|
| Dana | 100 |
| Dana's spouse | 50 |
| Dana's brother | 20 |
| Dana's sister | 70 |
| Dana's father | 120 |
| Dana's son | 80 |
| Dana's daughter | 61 |

Under the family attribution rules of § 544(a)(2), Dana owns 501 shares of Azure for purposes of determining stock ownership in a PHC. ■

Basically, the broad constructive ownership rules make it difficult for a closely held corporation to avoid application of the stock ownership test. Attribution rules 2, 3, and 4 are applicable only for the purpose of classifying a corporation as a PHC and cannot be used to avoid the application of the PHC provisions. For example, convertible securities are treated as outstanding stock only if the effect of the inclusion is to make the corporation a PHC (and not to expand the total amount of stock in order to avoid PHC classification).

**Gross Income Test.** The gross income test is met if 60 percent or more of the corporation's **adjusted ordinary gross income (AOGI)** consists of certain passive income items (PHC income). AOGI is calculated by subtracting certain items from gross income (as defined by § 61).[44] The adjustments required to arrive at AOGI appear in Figure 6–3.

In Figure 6–3, the deduction of items (a) and (b) from gross income results in the intermediate concept, **ordinary gross income (OGI)**, the use of which is noted subsequently. The starting point, gross income, is not necessarily synonymous with gross receipts. In fact, for transactions in stocks, securities, and commodities, the term "gross income" includes only the excess of gains over any losses.[45]

PHC income includes income from dividends; interest; royalties; annuities;[46] rents; mineral, oil, and gas royalties; copyright royalties; produced film rents; computer software royalties; and amounts from certain personal service contracts.

[44]§§ 543(b)(1) and (2).
[45]Reg. § 1.542–2.

[46]§ 543(a)(1).

**EXAMPLE 20**

Crow Corporation has four shareholders, and its AOGI is $95,000, consisting of gross income of $40,000 from a merchandising operation, interest income of $15,000, dividend income of $25,000, and adjusted income of $15,000 from rents. Total passive income is $55,000 ($15,000 + $25,000 + $15,000). Since 60% of AOGI ($57,000) is greater than the passive income ($55,000), the corporation is not a PHC. ■

**EXAMPLE 21**

Assume in Example 20 that the corporation received $21,000 in interest income rather than $15,000. Total passive income is now $61,000 ($21,000 + $25,000 + $15,000). Since 60% of AOGI ($60,600) is less than passive income of $61,000, the corporation is a PHC. ■

Most passive types of income such as dividends, interest, royalties, and annuities cause few classification problems. Certain income items, however, may or may not be classified as PHC income. Special rules apply to rent income, mineral, oil, and gas royalties, and personal service contracts.

**Rent Income.**   Although rent income is normally classified as PHC income, such income can be excluded from that category if two tests are met. The *first test* is met if a corporation's adjusted income from rents is 50 percent or more of the corporation's AOGI. The *second test* is satisfied if the total dividends for the tax year are equal to or greater than the amount by which the *nonrent* PHC income *exceeds* 10 percent of OGI.[47] Dividends for this purpose include those actually paid, those considered as paid on the last day of the tax year, and consent dividends (see the later discussion of the dividends paid deduction). The taxpayer must meet both tests for the rent income to be excluded from PHC income (see Figure 6–6 later in the chapter).

With respect to the 50 percent test, "adjusted income from rents" is defined as gross income from rents reduced by certain deductions. The deductions are depreciation, property taxes, interest, and rent. Generally, compensation is not included in the term "rents" and is not an allowable deduction. The final amount included in AOGI as adjusted income from rents cannot be less than zero.

**EXAMPLE 22**

Assume that a corporation has rent income of $10,000 and the following business deductions:

| | |
|---|---|
| Depreciation on rental property | $1,000 |
| Interest on mortgage | 2,500 |
| Real property taxes | 1,500 |
| Salaries and other business expenses (§ 162) | 3,000 |

The adjusted income from rents included in AOGI is $5,000 ($10,000 − $1,000 − $2,500 − $1,500). Salaries and other § 162 expenses do not affect the calculation of AOGI. ■

A company deriving its income primarily from rental activities can avoid PHC status by merely distributing as dividends the amount of nonrental PHC income that exceeds 10 percent of its OGI.

**EXAMPLE 23**

During the tax year, Amber Corporation receives $15,000 in rent income, $4,000 in dividends, and a $1,000 long-term capital gain. Corporate deductions for depreciation, interest, and real estate taxes allocable to the rent income are $10,000. The company pays a total of $2,500 in dividends to its eight shareholders. To determine whether or not rent income is PHC income, OGI, AOGI, and adjusted income from rents must be calculated.

---

[47]§ 543(a)(2).

| | |
|---|---:|
| Rent income | $15,000 |
| Dividends | 4,000 |
| Long-term capital gain | 1,000 |
| Gross income | $20,000 |
| Deduct: Gains from sale or disposition of capital assets | 1,000 |
| OGI | $19,000 |
| Deduct: Depreciation, interest, and real estate taxes | 10,000 |
| AOGI | $ 9,000 |

First, adjusted income from rents must be 50% or more of AOGI.

| | |
|---|---:|
| Rent income | $15,000 |
| Deduct: Depreciation, interest, and real estate taxes | 10,000 |
| Adjusted income from rents | $ 5,000 |
| 50% of AOGI | $ 4,500 |

Amber Corporation has satisfied the first test.

Second, total dividends paid for the year are $2,500. This figure must be *equal to or greater than* the amount by which nonrent PHC income exceeds 10% of OGI.

| | |
|---|---:|
| Nonrent PHC income | $4,000 |
| Less: 10% of OGI | 1,900 |
| Excess | $2,100 |

Amber Corporation meets *both* tests, and the adjusted income from rents is *not* PHC income. ◼

**Mineral, Oil, and Gas Royalties.**   As with rent income, adjusted income from mineral, oil, and gas royalties can be excluded from PHC income if certain tests are met.[48] *First*, adjusted income from the royalties must constitute 50 percent or more of AOGI. *Second*, nonroyalty PHC income may not exceed 10 percent of OGI. Note that this 10 percent test is not accompanied by the dividend escape clause previously described in relation to rent income. Therefore, corporations receiving income from mineral, oil, or gas royalties must be careful to minimize nonroyalty PHC income. Furthermore, adjusted income from rents and copyright royalties are considered to be nonroyalty PHC income whether or not treated as such by §§ 543(a)(2) and (4). *Third*, the company's business expenses under § 162 (other than compensation paid to shareholders) must be at least 15 percent of AOGI.

**EXAMPLE 24**

Lark Corporation has gross income of $4,000, which consists of gross income from oil royalties in the amount of $2,500, $400 of dividends, and $1,100 from the sale of merchandise. The total amount of the deductions for depletion, interest, and property and severance taxes allocable to the gross income from oil royalties equals $1,000. Ordinary and necessary business expenses allowable under § 162 are $450. Lark Corporation's adjusted income from

---

[48]§ 543(a)(3). Special rules also apply to copyright royalties. See § 543(a)(4).

oil royalties will not be PHC income if the three tests are met. Therefore, OGI, AOGI, and adjusted income from oil royalties must be determined:

| | |
|---|---|
| Oil royalties income | $2,500 |
| Dividends | 400 |
| Sale of merchandise | 1,100 |
| Gross income (*and* OGI) | $4,000 |
| Deduct: Depletion, interest, and property and severance taxes | 1,000 |
| AOGI | $3,000 |

Adjusted income from oil royalties must be 50% or more of AOGI.

| | |
|---|---|
| Oil royalties income | $2,500 |
| Deduct: Depletion, interest, and property and severance taxes | 1,000 |
| Adjusted income from oil royalties | $1,500 |
| 50% of AOGI | $1,500 |

The first test is met. Since nonroyalty PHC income is $400 (composed solely of the $400 of dividends) and this amount is not more than 10% of OGI, the second test is also satisfied. The third requirement is satisfied if deductible expenses under § 162 amount to at least 15% of AOGI.

| | |
|---|---|
| § 162 expenses | $450 |
| 15% of $3,000 (AOGI) | $450 |

Lark Corporation's adjusted income from oil royalties is *not* PHC income. ■

**Personal Service Contracts.**   Any amount from personal service contracts is classified as PHC income only if (1) some person other than the corporation has the right to designate, by name or by description, the individual who is to perform the services and (2) the person so designated owns, directly or indirectly, 25 percent or more in value of the outstanding stock of the corporation at some time during the taxable year.[49]

**EXAMPLE 25**

Blair, Cody, and Dana (all attorneys) are equal shareholders in Canary Company, a personal service corporation engaged in the practice of law. Irene, a new client, retains Canary Company to pursue a legal claim. Under the terms of the retainer agreement, Irene designates Blair as the attorney who will perform the legal services. The suit is successful, and 30% of the judgment Irene recovers is paid to Canary Company as a fee. Since the parties have met all of the requirements of § 543(a)(7), the fee received by Canary is PHC income.[50] ■

The result reached in Example 25 could have been avoided had Blair not been specifically named in the retainer agreement as the party to perform the services.

---

[49]§ 543(a)(7). For an application of the "right to designate," see *Thomas P. Byrnes, Inc.*, 73 T.C. 416 (1979).

[50]The example presumes Canary Company will be treated as a corporation for Federal tax purposes.

■ **FIGURE 6–4**
Undistributed PHC Income
Determination

Taxable income

| | | |
|---|---|---|
| **Plus:** | | a. Dividends received deduction. |
| | | b. Net operating loss (NOL), other than the NOL from the preceding year (computed without the dividends received deduction). |
| | | c. Certain business expenses and depreciation attributable to nonbusiness property owned by the corporation that exceed the income derived from such property (unless taxpayer proves that the rent was the highest obtainable and the rental business was a bona fide business activity).* |
| **Less:** | | d. Federal income tax accrual (other than the PHC tax and the accumulated earnings tax). |
| | | e. Excess charitable contributions beyond the 10% corporate limitation (with a maximum of the 20%, 30%, or 50% limitation imposed on individuals).** |
| | | f. Excess of long-term capital gain over short-term capital loss (net of tax). |
| **Equals:** | | Adjusted taxable income. |
| **Less:** | | Dividends paid deduction. |
| **Equals:** | | Undistributed PHC (UPHC) income. |

*§ 545(b).
**Reg. § 1.545–2.

**LO.9**

Compute the personal holding company tax.

## CALCULATION OF THE PHC TAX

To this point, the discussion has focused on the determination of PHC status. Once a corporation is classified as a PHC, the amount upon which the 38.6 percent penalty tax is imposed must be computed. The tax base is called undistributed PHC income (UPHC income). Basically, this amount is taxable income, subject to certain adjustments, minus the dividends paid deduction. After the adjustments, UPHC income more clearly represents the corporation's dividend-paying capacity. Figure 6–4 shows how this amount is determined.

**Dividends Paid Deduction.** Since the purpose of the PHC penalty tax is to force a corporation to pay dividends, *five* types of **dividends paid deductions** reduce the amount subject to the penalty tax (see Table 6–1). First, dividends actually paid during the tax year ordinarily reduce UPHC income.[51] However, such distributions must be pro rata. They must exhibit no preference to any shares of stock over shares of the same class or to any class of stock over other classes outstanding.[52] The prohibition is especially harsh when portions of an employee-shareholder's salary are declared unreasonable and classified as a disguised or constructive dividend.[53] In the case of a property dividend of appreciated property, the dividends paid deduction should be the fair market value of the property (not the adjusted basis). Otherwise, a distribution of appreciated property would increase the PHC tax. However, Regulation § 1.562–1(a) states that the deduction is limited to adjusted basis.

**EXAMPLE 26**

Three individuals are equal shareholders in a PHC. A property dividend is paid to the three shareholders in the following proportion: 25%, 35%, and 40%. This dividend is not a pro rata distribution, and the dividends are not deductible from UPHC income. ■

---

[51]§§ 561(a)(1) and 562.
[52]§ 562(c).

[53]Refer to Chapter 4 and *Henry Schwartz Corp.*, 60 T.C. 728 (1973).

**⌐E 6–1**
⌐ds Paid Deductions

| Type of Dividend | Availability | Timing | Statutory Location | Effect on Shareholders |
|---|---|---|---|---|
| Current year | Both § 531 and § 541 | By end of year. | § 561(a)(1) | Reduction in ATI and UPHC income. |
| 2½-month grace period | Both § 531 and § 541* | On or before the 15th day of the 3rd month after end of year. | §§ 563(a) and (b) | Reduction in ATI and UPHC income. |
| Consent dividend | Both § 531 and § 541 | Not later than due date of the corporate tax return. | § 565(a) | Treated as a dividend as of end of tax year and given back as a contribution to capital. |
| Dividend carryover | § 541 | Not later than due date of the corporate tax return. | § 564 | Reduction in UPHC income. |
| Deficiency dividend | § 541 | Within 90 days after determination of PHC tax deficiency. | § 547 | Treated as if dividend paid in offending year. No impact on interest and penalties. |

*Limited to 20% of current-year dividends paid for a PHC.

A 2½-month grace period exists following the close of the tax year. Dividends paid during this period may be treated as paid during the tax year just closed. However, the amount allowed as a deduction from UPHC income cannot exceed either (1) the UPHC income for the tax year or (2) 20 percent of the total dividends distributed during the tax year.[54] Reasonable cause may not be used to overcome the 20 percent limitation even if the taxpayer relied upon incorrect advice given by an accountant.[55]

The **consent dividend** procedure[56] involves a hypothetical distribution of the corporate income to be taxed to the shareholders. Since the consent dividend is taxable, a dividends paid deduction is allowed. The shareholder's basis in his or her stock is increased by the consent dividend (a contribution to capital). The consent election is filed by the shareholders at any time not later than the due date of the corporate tax return. The consent dividend is considered distributed by the corporation on the last day of the tax year and is included in the gross income of the shareholder in the tax year in which or with which the tax year of the corporation ends. The disadvantage of this special election is that the shareholders must pay taxes on dividends they do not actually receive. However, if cash is not available for dividend distributions, the consent dividend route is a logical alternative.

**EXAMPLE 27**

Snipe Corporation, a calendar year taxpayer solely owned by Tracy, is a PHC. Dividends of $30,000 must be paid to avoid the PHC tax, but the company has a poor cash position. Tracy elects the consent dividend treatment under § 565 and is taxed on $30,000 of dividends. Her basis in Snipe Corporation stock is increased by $30,000 as a result of this special election. Thus, Snipe does not incur the PHC tax, but Tracy is taxed even though she receives no cash from the corporation with which to pay the tax. ■

---

[54]§§ 563(b) and 543(a)(2)(B)(ii).
[55]*Kenneth Farmer Darrow*, 64 T.C. 217 (1975).

[56]Reg. § 1.565–1.

Even after a corporation has been classified as a PHC, a
distribution made in a subsequent tax year can avoid the PH
**deficiency dividend** provision[57] allows a dividend to be paid
the determination of the PHC tax deficiency for a prior tax year. I.
occurs when a decision of a court is final, a closing agreement (see Chap...
signed, or a written agreement is signed between the taxpayer and the IRS. The
dividend distribution *cannot be made* before the determination or after the running
of the 90-day time period. Furthermore, the deficiency dividend procedure does
not relieve the taxpayer of interest, additional amounts, or assessable penalties
computed with respect to the PHC tax.

A dividend carryover from two prior years may be available to reduce the
UPHC income. When the dividends paid by a company in its prior years exceed
the company's UPHC income for those years, the excess may be deducted in the
current year. See § 564(b) for the computation of this dividend carryover.

Table 6–1 summarizes these dividends paid deductions.

**Personal Holding Company Planning Model.** Some of the complex PHC
provisions may be developed into a flow chart format. Figures 6–5 and 6–6 provide
a PHC planning model and the rules for the rent exclusion test.

**Computations Illustrated.** After the appropriate adjustments are made to corporate taxable income and the sum of the dividends paid is subtracted, the resulting
figure is UPHC income. This amount is multiplied by the 38.6 percent penalty tax
rate (in 2002 and 2003) to obtain the PHC tax.

The consequences of this confiscatory tax can be severe. Taxpayers should
monitor their corporations and take the necessary steps to avoid the tax. Because
most corporations use planning procedures to avoid PHC status, revenues from
the tax are small.

**EXAMPLE 28**

Bluebird Corporation had the following items of income and expense in the current year:

| | |
|---|---:|
| Dividend income (less than 20% owned) | $ 40,000  70% |
| Rent income | 150,000 |
| Depreciation expense | 40,000 |
| Mortgage interest | 35,000 |
| Real estate taxes | 25,000 |
| Salaries | 20,000 |
| Dividends paid (three shareholders) | 20,500 |
| Corporate income tax liability (§ 11) | 6,300 |

OGI is $190,000 ($40,000 + $150,000), and AOGI is $90,000 ($190,000 − $40,000 − $35,000 −
$25,000). Taxable income is $42,000, computed as follows:

| | |
|---|---:|
| Rent income | $ 150,000 |
| Dividend income | 40,000 |
| T income | $ 190,000 |

[57]§ 547.

**FIGURE 6–5**
Personal Holding Company
Planning Model

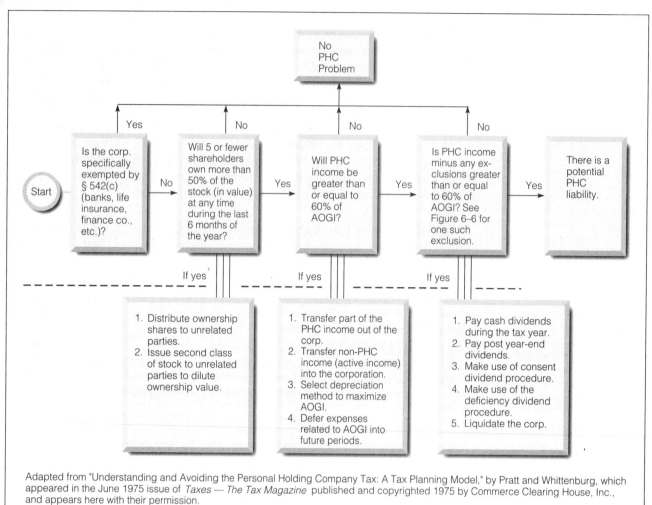

Adapted from "Understanding and Avoiding the Personal Holding Company Tax: A Tax Planning Model," by Pratt and Whittenburg, which appeared in the June 1975 issue of *Taxes — The Tax Magazine* published and copyrighted 1975 by Commerce Clearing House, Inc., and appears here with their permission.

*Computation of PHC tax*

| | | |
|---|---:|---:|
| Less: Depreciation expense | $40,000 | |
| Mortgage interest | 35,000 | |
| Real estate taxes | 25,000 | |
| Salaries | 20,000 | (120,000) |
| | | $ 70,000 |
| Less: Dividends received deduction ($40,000 × 70%) | | (28,000) |
| Taxable income | | $ 42,000 |

The adjusted income from rents is $50,000 ($150,000 − $100,000). Bluebird does meet the 50% rent income test, since $50,000 is greater than 50% of AOGI ($90,000 × 50% = $45,000). But the corporation did not meet the second test for excluding rent income from PHC

■ **FIGURE 6–6**
Rent Exclusion Test

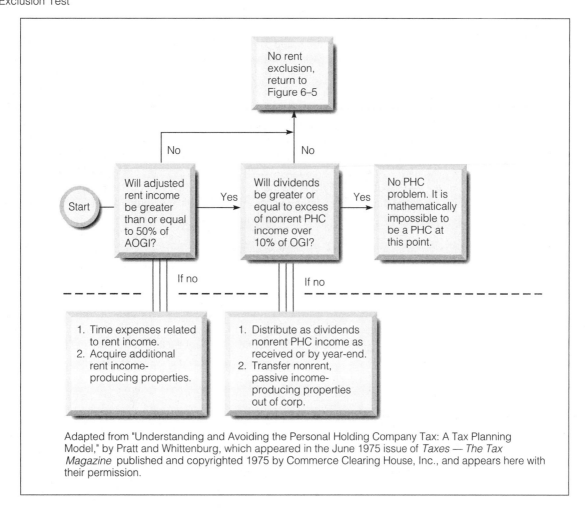

Adapted from "Understanding and Avoiding the Personal Holding Company Tax: A Tax Planning Model," by Pratt and Whittenburg, which appeared in the June 1975 issue of *Taxes — The Tax Magazine* published and copyrighted 1975 by Commerce Clearing House, Inc., and appears here with their permission.

income. It did not pay at least $21,000 of dividends (nonrent PHC income $40,000 – $19,000 = $21,000). Therefore, the 10% test is not met, and the rent income is classified as PHC income. Since all income is passive, Bluebird Corporation is a PHC. The PHC tax of $16,675 is calculated as follows:

| | |
|---|---|
| Taxable income | $ 42,000 |
| Plus: Dividends received deduction ($40,000 × 70%) | 28,000 |
| | $ 70,000 |
| Less: Corporate income tax | (6,300) |
| | $ 63,700 |
| Less: Dividends paid | (20,500) |
| UPHC income | $ 43,200 |
| | × .386 |
| PHC tax liability | $ 16,675 |

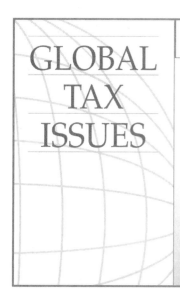

### FOREIGN INVESTMENT VEHICLES CAN TRIGGER U.S. TAX

Some taxpayers have attempted to minimize the tax burden on their investment income by both "incorporating their pocketbook" *and* maintaining the corporation in an offshore tax haven country. Congress has enacted two provisions to limit the deferral benefits associated with earning investment income through a foreign corporation. Both the foreign personal holding company (FPHC) and the passive foreign investment company (PFIC) rules can trigger constructive dividends to U.S. persons.

These penalty taxes resemble the domestic §§ 531 and 541 taxes. An FPHC is a foreign corporation that receives a substantial percentage of its income from investment activities and is closely held by U.S. persons. The primary difference between the FPHC tax and the domestic PHC tax is that the FPHC tax is levied on the FPHC's U.S. shareholders rather than the corporation itself. A PFIC is similar in theory to an FPHC, but the rules are more restrictive. Foreign-based mutual funds are often PFICs to their U.S. owners.

---

**EXAMPLE 29**

Assume in Example 28 that dividends of $22,000 (instead of $20,500) are paid to the shareholders. In this case, the rent income is not PHC income because the 10% test is met ($22,000 is equal to or greater than the nonrent PHC income in excess of 10% of OGI). Thus, an increase of at least $1,500 in the dividends paid in Example 28 avoids the $16,675 PHC tax liability. ■

---

**LO.10**

Compare the accumulated earnings and personal holding company taxes.

# Comparison of the Accumulated Earnings and PHC Taxes

A review of several important distinctions between the penalty tax on the unreasonable accumulation of earnings (§ 531) and the tax on PHCs (§ 541) sets the stage for the presentation of tax planning considerations applicable to these taxes.

- Unlike § 531, no element of intent is necessary for the imposition of the § 541 tax.[58] Consequently, § 541 can be a real trap for the unwary.
- The imposition of the § 541 tax is not affected by the past history of the corporation. Thus, the tax could be just as applicable to a newly formed corporation as to one that has been in existence for many years. This is not the case with the § 531 tax. Past accumulations have a direct bearing on the determination of the accumulated earnings credit. In this sense, younger corporations are less vulnerable to the § 531 tax since complete insulation generally is guaranteed until accumulations exceed $250,000.
- Although both taxes pose threats for closely held corporations, the § 541 tax presents the more explicit threat due to the constructive stock ownership rules. However, publicly held corporations can be subject to the § 531 tax if corporate policy is dominated by certain shareholders who are using the corporate form to avoid income taxes on dividends through the accumulation of corporate profits.

---

[58]In light of the Supreme Court decision in *Donruss* (refer to Footnote 8 and the related text), what role, if any, will intent play in the future in helping taxpayers avoid the § 531 tax? In this connection, see the dissenting opinion issued by Justice Harlan.

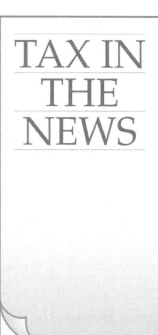

## TAX IN THE NEWS

### "BUNGLED AND WRONGHEADED"?

AMT supporters maintain that the AMT parallel tax system prevents corporations and wealthy individuals from abusing the tax code by taking advantage of credits, deductions, and exemptions in the law. Conversely, the Tax Foundation says that the AMT acts as a brake on the effectiveness of tax incentives: the effect is like driving a car with the emergency brake engaged.

Companies in capital-intensive industries and those with large overseas operations are especially hard hit. In 1999, corporations spent an estimated $40 billion on tax compliance, with $7 billion spent on the AMT. Thus, the AMT compliance cost in 1999 was greater than the $3.1 billion AMT collected. Rob Norton in *Fortune* said that the AMT is bungled and wrongheaded and should have been repealed long ago. The Tax Foundation states that the corporate "AMT raises little revenue, distorts investment incentives, imposes compliance costs that exceed the amount of collections it produces, and does not truly further its purported goal of improving the fairness of the tax system."

SOURCES: Rob Norton, "This Tax Won't Die—But Should," *Fortune*, April 15, 2002, p. 70; J. S. Barry, T. R. Chorvat, and M. S. Knoll, "The Corporate Alternative Minimum Tax," Tax Foundation, November 5, 2001.

- Sufficient dividend distributions can eliminate both taxes. In the case of § 531, however, such dividends must be distributed on a timely basis. Both taxes allow a 2½-month grace period and provide for the consent dividend procedure.[59] Only the § 541 tax allows the deficiency dividend procedure.
- Differences in reporting procedures arise because the § 541 tax is a self-assessed tax and the § 531 tax is not. For example, if a corporation is a PHC, the company must file a Schedule PH along with its Form 1120 (the corporate income tax return) for the year involved. Failure to file the Schedule PH can result in the imposition of interest and penalties and also brings into play a special six-year statute of limitations for the assessment of the § 541 tax.[60] On the other hand, the § 531 tax is assessed by the IRS and consequently requires no reporting procedures on the part of the corporate taxpayer.

**Tax Planning Considerations**

## ALTERNATIVE MINIMUM TAX

Planning for the AMT is complicated by the fact that many of the procedures recommended run counter to what is done to reduce the regular corporate income tax. Further, the AMT has the perverse effect of increasing a company's effective tax rate during economic slowdowns.

### Avoiding Preferences and Adjustments.
Investments in state and local bonds are attractive for income tax purposes because the interest is not included in gross income. Some of these bonds are issued to generate funds that are not used for an

---

[59]Under the § 531 tax, dividends paid within the first 2½ months of the succeeding year *must* be carried back to the preceding year. In the case of the § 541 tax, the carryback is optional—some or all of the dividends can be deducted in the year paid. The 20% limit on carrybacks applicable to § 541 [see § 563(a)] does not cover § 531 situations.

[60]§ 6501(f).

essential function of the government. The interest on such bonds is a tax preference item and could lead to the imposition of the AMT. When the AMT applies, an investment in regular tax-exempt bonds or even fully taxed private-sector bonds might yield a higher after-tax rate of return.

For a corporation anticipating AMT problems, capitalizing rather than expensing certain costs can avoid generating preferences and adjustments. The decision should be based on the present discounted value of after-tax cash flows under the available alternatives. Costs that may be capitalized and amortized, rather than expensed, include circulation expenditures, mining exploration and development costs, and research and experimentation expenditures.

**Controlling the Timing of Preferences and Adjustments.**   In many situations, smaller corporations may be able to avoid the AMT by making use of the exemption. To maximize the exemption, taxpayers should attempt to avoid bunching positive adjustments and tax preferences in any one year. When the expenditure is largely within the control of the taxpayer, timing to avoid bunching is more easily accomplished.

**Optimum Use of the AMT and Regular Corporate Income Tax Rate Difference.**   A corporation that cannot avoid the AMT in a particular year can often save taxes by taking advantage of the difference between the AMT and the regular tax rates. In general, a corporation that expects to be subject to the AMT should accelerate income and defer deductions for the remainder of the year. Since the difference between the regular tax and the AMT may be as much as 14 or 15 percentage points, this strategy results in the income being taxed at less than it would be if reported in the next year. There is always the risk that the regular corporate rates may increase in future years. If the same corporation expects to be subject to the AMT for the next year (or years), this technique must be reversed. The corporation should defer income and accelerate deductions. The strategy delays the date the corporation has to pay the tax.

**EXAMPLE 30**

Falcon Corporation expects to be in the 34% tax bracket in 2004 but is subject to the AMT in 2003. In late 2003, Falcon is contemplating selling a tract of unimproved land (basis of $200,000 and fair market value of $1 million). Under these circumstances, it is preferable to sell the land in 2003. The gain of $800,000 ($1,000,000 − $200,000) generates a tax of $160,000 [$800,000 (recognized gain) × 20% (AMT rate)]. However, if the land is sold in 2004, the resulting tax is $272,000 [$800,000 (recognized gain) × 34% (regular corporate income tax rate)]. A savings of $112,000 ($272,000 − $160,000) materializes by making the sale in 2003. ■

**The S Corporation Option.**   Corporations that make the S election will not be subject to the corporate AMT. As noted in Chapter 12, however, various AMT adjustments and preferences pass through to the individual shareholders. But one troublesome adjustment, the one involving the ACE adjustment, is eliminated since it does not apply to individual taxpayers.

## THE PENALTY TAX ON UNREASONABLE ACCUMULATIONS

The modification of capital gain rates has made most corporate distributions less attractive, and many companies prefer permanent rather than temporary deferral of accumulated earnings. Even when corporate rates are higher than individual rates, a corporation can invest accumulated funds in tax-free securities or purchase high-yield corporate stocks to take advantage of the dividends received deductions. Thus, the threat of the accumulated earnings tax and the PHC tax continues to be a prime concern of many corporations.

**Justifying the Accumulations.** The key defense against imposition of the § 531 tax is to show that the accumulations are necessary to meet the reasonable needs of the business. Several points should be kept in mind:

- To the extent possible, the justification for the accumulation should be documented. If, for example, the corporation plans to acquire additional physical facilities for use in its trade or business, the minutes of the board of directors' meetings should reflect the decision. Furthermore, such documentation should take place during the period of accumulation. This planning may require some foresight on the part of the taxpayer. Meaningful planning to avoid a tax problem should not be based on what happens after the issue has been raised by an agent as the result of an audit. In the case of a profitable closely held corporation that accumulates some or all of its profits, the parties should operate under the assumption that § 531 is always a potential issue. Recognition of a tax problem at an early stage is the first step in a satisfactory resolution.
- Multiple reasons for making an accumulation are not only permissible but invariably advisable. Suppose, for example, a manufacturing corporation plans to expand its plant. It would not be wise to stop with the cost of the expansion as the only justification for all accumulations. What about further justification based on the corporation's working capital requirements as determined under the *Bardahl* formula or some variation? Other reasons for making the accumulation may be present and should be recognized.
- The reasons for the accumulation should be sincere and, once established, pursued to the extent feasible.

**EXAMPLE 31**

In 1998, the directors of Gull Corporation decide to accumulate $1 million to fund the replacement of Gull's plant. Five years pass, and no steps are taken to begin construction. ■

**EXAMPLE 32**

In 1998, the directors of Grouse Corporation decide to accumulate $1 million to fund the replacement of Grouse's plant. In the ensuing five-year period, the following steps are taken: a site selection committee is appointed (1998); a site is chosen (1999); the site (land) is purchased (2000); an architect is retained, and plans are drawn up for the new plant (2002); bids are requested and submitted for the construction of the new plant (2003). ■

Compare Examples 31 and 32. Grouse Corporation is in a much better position to justify the accumulation. Even though the plant has not yet been replaced some five years after the accumulations began, the progress toward its ultimate construction speaks for itself. Gull Corporation may be hard-pressed to prove the sincerity of its objective for the accumulations in light of its failure to follow through on the projected replacement.

- The amount of the accumulation should be realistic under the circumstances.

**EXAMPLE 33**

Bunting Corporation plans to replace certain machinery at an estimated cost of $500,000. The original machinery was purchased for $300,000 and, because $200,000 in depreciation was deducted for tax purposes, has a present book value of $100,000. How much of an accumulation can be justified for the replacement to avoid the § 531 tax? Initially, $500,000 seems to be the appropriate amount since this represents the estimated replacement cost of the machinery. But what about the $200,000 in depreciation that Bunting already deducted? If it is counted again as part of a reasonable accumulation, a double tax benefit results. Only $300,000 [$100,000 (the unrecovered cost of the old machinery) + $200,000 (the additional outlay necessary)] can be justified as the amount for an accumulation.[61] ■

**EXAMPLE 34**

During the current year, a competitor files a $2 million patent infringement suit against Egret Corporation. Competent legal counsel advises Egret that the suit is groundless. Under such conditions, the corporation can hardly justify accumulating $2 million because of the pending lawsuit. ■

• Since the § 531 tax is imposed on an annual basis, justification for accumulations may vary from year to year.[62]

**EXAMPLE 35**

For calendar years 2002 and 2003, Red Corporation was able to justify large accumulations due to a pending additional income tax assessment. In early 2004, the assessment is settled and paid. After the settlement, Red Corporation can no longer consider the assessment as a reasonable anticipated need of the business. ■

**Danger of Loans to Shareholders.** The presence of loans made by a corporation to its shareholders often raises the § 531 issue. If this same corporation has a poor dividend-paying record, the company becomes particularly vulnerable. The avowed goal of the § 531 tax is to force certain corporations to distribute dividends. If a corporation can spare funds for loans to shareholders, the company certainly has the capacity to pay dividends. Unfortunately, the presence of such loans can also cause other tax problems for the parties.

**EXAMPLE 36**

During the year in question, Quail Corporation made advances of $120,000 to its sole shareholder, Tom. Although prosperous and maintaining substantial accumulations, Quail has never paid a dividend. Under these circumstances, the IRS could move in either of two directions. The IRS could assess the § 531 tax against Quail Corporation for its unreasonable accumulation of earnings. Alternatively, the IRS could argue that the advances were not bona fide loans but, instead, taxable dividends.[63] The dual approach places the taxpayers in a difficult position. If, for example, they contend that the advance was a bona fide loan, Tom avoids dividend income, but Quail becomes vulnerable to the imposition of the § 531 tax.[64] On the other hand, a concession that the advance was not a loan hurts Tom but helps Quail avoid the penalty tax. ■

**Role of Dividends.** The relationship between dividend distribution and the § 531 tax can be further clarified. The payment of enough dividends can completely avoid the § 531 tax due to the operation of § 535. This provision defines accumulated taxable income as *taxable income* (adjusted by certain items) *minus the sum of the dividends paid deduction and the accumulated earnings credit*. Since the § 531 tax is

---

[61]*Battelstein Investment Co. v. U.S.,* 71–1 USTC ¶9227, 27 AFTR2d 71–713, 442 F.2d 87 (CA–5, 1971).

[62]Compare *Hardin's Bakeries, Inc. v. Martin, Jr.,* 67–1 USTC ¶9253, 19 AFTR2d 647, 293 F.Supp. 1129 (D.Ct. Miss., 1967), with *Hardin v. U.S.,* 70–2 USTC ¶9676, 26 AFTR2d 70–5852 (D.Ct. Miss., 1970),

*aff'd, rev'd, rem'd* by 72–1 USTC ¶9464, 29 AFTR2d 72–1446, 461 F.2d 865 (CA–5, 1972).

[63]Refer to the discussion of constructive dividends in Chapter 4.

[64]*Ray v. U.S.,* 69–1 USTC ¶9334, 23 AFTR2d 69–1141, 409 F.2d 1322 (CA–6, 1969).

imposed on accumulated taxable income, no tax is due if the taxable dividends paid and the accumulated earnings credit are large enough to offset taxable income.

But can the payment of a smaller dividend completely avoid the § 531 tax? Theoretically, even significant dividend distributions will not insulate a corporation from the tax. From a practical standpoint, however, the payment of dividends indicates that the corporation is not being used exclusively to shield its shareholders from tax consequences. In applying § 531, the IRS will consider such payments to the extent that they reflect the good faith of the parties and the lack of tax avoidance motivation.

**Role of the S Corporation Election.**   An S corporation election circumvents the application of the § 531 tax. However, the protection covers only the period of S corporation status and is not retroactive to years during which the entity was a regular corporation.

**EXAMPLE 37**

Eagle Corporation, a calendar year taxpayer, makes a timely and proper election under Subchapter S effective for tax year 2003. Since its formation in 1985, Eagle has accumulated significant earnings and has never paid a dividend. The election protects the corporation from the imposition of the § 531 tax for year 2003 and for any subsequent years it remains in effect. The S election does not, however, preclude the IRS from assessing the tax on Eagle for those years open under the statute of limitations in which it qualified as a regular corporation. ■

## AVOIDING THE PHC TAX

The classification of a corporation as a personal holding company requires the satisfaction of *both* the stock ownership and the gross income tests. Failure to meet either of these two tests avoids PHC status and the § 541 tax. The following planning suggestions may help in avoiding the PHC tax:

- The stock ownership test can be handled through a dispersion of stock ownership. In this regard, however, watch the application of the stock attribution rules.
- Remember the following relationship when working with the gross income test:

$$\frac{\text{PHC income}}{\text{AOGI}} = 60\% \text{ or more}$$

Decreasing the numerator (PHC income) or increasing the denominator (AOGI) of the fraction reduces the resulting percentage. Keeping the percentage below 60 percent precludes classification as a PHC. To control PHC income, investments in low-yield growth securities are preferable to those that generate heavy interest or dividend income. Capital gains from the sale of such securities will not affect PHC status since they are not included in either the numerator or the denominator of the fraction. Investments in tax-exempt securities are attractive because the interest income, like capital gains, has no effect in applying the gross income test.

- Income from personal service contracts may, under certain conditions, be PHC income. Where a 25 percent or more owner of a PHC is specifically designated in a retainer agreement as the party to perform the services, the personal service contract income will be PHC income. See Example 25 earlier in the chapter.
- Rent income may or may not be PHC income. The relative amount of rent income is the key consideration. If

$$\frac{\text{Adjusted income from rents}}{\text{AOGI}} = 50\% \text{ or more}$$

and nonrent PHC income less 10 percent of OGI is distributed as a dividend, rent income is not PHC income. Maximizing adjusted income from rents clearly improves the situation for taxpayers. Since adjusted income from rents represents gross rents less attributable expenses, a conservative approach in determining such expenses is helpful. The taxpayer should minimize depreciation (e.g., choose straight-line over accelerated cost recovery method). This approach to the handling of expenses attributable to rental property is confusing to many taxpayers because it contradicts what is normally done to reduce income tax consequences.

- In some cases, a company may reduce PHC exposure by readjusting its corporate structure. Business combinations (e.g., mergers and consolidations) or the filing of a consolidated return by an affiliated group of corporations can be used to dilute the PHC income of one corporation with the income from operations of another to avoid meeting the gross income test.

Corporations in the process of liquidation can be particularly susceptible to the PHC tax for two reasons. Operating income may be low because the corporation is in the process of winding up its business. If passive investment income remains at the level maintained during periods of normal operations or perhaps increases, the corporation might satisfy the gross income test. This danger increases if the corporation, pending complete dissolution, invested some or all of the proceeds from the sale of its operating assets. In addition, the parties may never realize that the corporation was a PHC until it has been completely liquidated. At this point, the tax can no longer be neutralized through the issuance of a deficiency dividend.[65] The solution to the problem is to recognize the vulnerability of the corporation and keep it on the safe side of the gross income test. Good control can be obtained over the situation if the earlier corporate distributions in liquidation include those assets that generate PHC income.

PHC status need not carry tragic tax consequences if the parties are aware of the issue and take appropriate steps. Since the tax is imposed on undistributed PHC income, properly timed dividend distributions neutralize the tax and avoid interest and penalties. Also, as long as a corporation holds PHC status, the § 531 tax cannot be imposed.

---

## KEY TERMS

---

[65]*Michael C. Callan*, 54 T.C. 1514 (1970), and *L. C. Bohart Plumbing & Heating Co., Inc.*, 64 T.C. 602 (1975).

## PROBLEM MATERIALS

### Discussion Questions

1. What is the purpose of the alternative minimum tax?

2. If the tentative AMT is greater than the regular corporate income tax under § 11, then a corporation must pay the larger AMT. Discuss.

3. Regular taxable income – AMT adjustments (except ACE) + tax preferences = tentative AMTI – ACE adjustment = AMTI before NOL deduction. Please comment.

4. What is the definition of a small corporation for purposes of the AMT?

5. In arriving at AMTI, why are NOLs stated separately instead of being included with other adjustments?

6. Using the legend provided, classify the impact each of the following items has upon unadjusted AMTI in arriving at ACE:

   **Legend**

   I  =  Increase in AMTI

   D  =  Decrease in AMTI

   E  =  Either an increase or a decrease in AMTI

   N  =  No impact

   a. Loss on sale of a piece of equipment to a related party.
   b. Currently deducted intangible drilling costs.
   c. Purchase of raw materials.
   d. Nondeductible transportation fines.
   e. Proceeds from a key employee insurance policy.
   f. Dividends received deduction for a 15%-owned business.
   g. Tax-exempt interest.
   h. Gift received from grandmother.

7. Using the legend provided, classify the impact each of the following items has upon taxable income or loss for purposes of determining AMTI:

   **Legend**

   I  =  Increase in taxable income

   D  =  Decrease in taxable income

   E  =  Either an increase or a decrease in taxable income

   N  =  No impact

   a. Amortization claimed on certified pollution control facilities.
   b. Adjusted current earnings (ACE) adjustment.
   c. Excess mining exploration and development costs.
   d. AMT net operating loss deduction.
   e. Statutory AMT exemption.
   f. Accelerated depreciation on post-1986 property acquisitions.
   g. Tax-exempt interest on private activity bonds.
   h. LIFO inventory.
   i. Excess percentage depletion of an integrated oil company.

8. Why has the $40,000 exemption become less important for profitable corporations?

9. Robert Barrack calls you to ask whether his company will have to make estimated tax payments of its AMT liability of approximately $102,200. Prepare a tax file memo dated February 12, 2003, indicating what you told Mr. Barrack.

10. A regular corporation is anticipating AMT problems during 2003. Point out some strategies available to help this corporation avoid or minimize the AMT.

11. Charlene creates a corporation in order to obtain limited liability. She would prefer to avoid the second shareholder tax. Suggest some techniques that would help Charlene avoid double taxation.

12. What types of companies are limited to a $150,000 accumulated earnings credit?

13. Omar is considering merging two of his brother-sister corporations. Outline any relevant tax issues facing this merger.

14. Which of the following purposes can be used to justify accumulations to meet the reasonable needs of the business?
    a. A corporation creates a reserve for a depression that might occur in 2005.
    b. A corporation has an extraordinarily high working capital need.
    c. A manufacturing corporation invests in several oil and gas drilling funds.
    d. A hotel corporation is being sued because of a structural accident that injured 27 people.
    e. A corporation is considering establishing a sinking fund to retire some bonds.
    f. A corporation carries seven key employee life insurance policies.
    g. Robin Corporation makes loans to Crane Corporation, an unrelated party that is having financial problems and is a key customer.
    h. A corporation agrees to retire 15% of its outstanding stock without curtailing its business.

15. Cecil McDowell is preparing *Bardahl* calculations for his closely held corporation. Should he include other operating expenses in the calculation of the accounts payable cycle?

16. Determine whether the following factors or events will increase (+), decrease (−), or have no effect (*NE*) on the working capital needs of a corporation when calculating the *Bardahl* formula:
    a. An increase in depreciation deduction.
    b. Use of peak inventory figure rather than average inventory.
    c. A decrease in the annual cost of goods sold.
    d. Purchase of a tract of land for a future parking lot.
    e. Use of average receivables rather than peak receivables.
    f. An increase in annual net sales.
    g. A decrease in accounts payable.
    h. An increase in the annual expenses.
    i. A loss on the sale of treasury stock.

17. What relevance do capital transactions (gains and losses) have for purposes of the accumulated earnings tax?

18. In making the adjustments to taxable income needed to arrive at ATI, which of the following items should be added (+), should be subtracted (−), or will have no effect (*NE*) on taxable income?
    a. A nontaxable stock dividend distributed by the corporation to its shareholders.
    b. Corporate income tax incurred and paid.
    c. Charitable contributions paid in the amount of 10% of taxable income.
    d. Deduction of an NOL carried over from a prior year.
    e. The dividends received deduction.

19. If a corporation has an effective Federal income tax rate of 34% and also incurs an accumulated earnings tax, what is the company's aggregate tax rate in 2003?

20. What tax rate is used to calculate the accumulated earnings tax and the PHC tax in 2003?

21. Which of the following corporations are specifically exempted from the PHC tax?
    a. A foreign personal holding company.
    b. A CPA.
    c. A finance company.
    d. A small business investment company.
    e. A pharmaceutical company.
    f. A foreign corporation.

**Issue ID**

22. The election to capitalize (rather than to depreciate) certain expenses for rental property could make a difference in determining whether or not the corporate lessor is a PHC. Explain.

23. A friend tells you that a commercial building she owns is incorporated as a C corporation. She rents the building to another business and is worried that her corporation may be subject to the PHC tax. If the corporation has a profit and pays no dividends, will it be subject to the PHC tax? Advise your friend.

24. Which of the following income items *could* be PHC income?
    a. Annuities.
    b. Interest.
    c. Rent income.
    d. Sales of stock in trade.
    e. Dividends.
    f. Copper royalties.
    g. Computer software royalties.
    h. Produced film rents.
    i. Gain from sale of a dump truck.
    j. Gas royalties.

25. What two tests must be met in order for rent income not to be considered PHC income?

26. With respect to the PHC tax, what is meant by the consent dividend procedure?

27. Explain the deficiency dividend procedure for purposes of the accumulated earnings tax and the PHC tax.

28. Regular taxable income + NOL − Federal income tax accrual − dividends received deduction = undistributed PHC income. Please comment.

29. Compare the accumulated earnings tax to the PHC tax with respect to the following items:
    a. The element of intent.
    b. Applicability of the tax to a newly created corporation.
    c. Applicability of the tax to a publicly held corporation.
    d. The 2½-month rule with respect to the dividends paid deduction.
    e. The availability of the deficiency dividend procedure.
    f. Procedures for reporting and paying the tax.

**Communications**

30. Explain how each of the following points is related to the avoidance of the PHC tax:
    a. Sale of stock to outsiders.
    b. An increase in AOGI.
    c. A decrease in PHC income.
    d. Section 1231 gains recognized by the corporation.
    e. Corporate investment in tax-exempt bonds.
    f. Income from personal service contracts.
    g. A merger of several corporations.
    h. The liquidation of a corporation.

    Prepare a short discussion paper for your managing partner, Cora Zicko, on item (h).

31. What impact may loans by a corporation to its shareholders have upon a possible application of the accumulated earnings tax?

## Problems

**32.** Avocet, Inc., has the following items related to the AMT:

| | |
|---|---|
| Alternative minimum taxable income | $102,755,000 |
| Regular tax (net of foreign tax credit) | 11,125,000 |
| Foreign tax credit (for AMT purposes) | 2,300,000 |

Calculate Avocet's AMT, if any.

**33.** For 2003, Mallard Corporation (a calendar year integrated oil company) had the following transactions:

| | |
|---|---|
| Taxable income | $5,000,000 |
| Regular tax depreciation on realty in excess of ADS (placed in service in 1989) | 1,700,000 |
| Amortization of certified pollution control facilities | 200,000 |
| Tax-exempt interest on municipal bonds (funds were used for nongovernmental purposes) | 300,000 |
| Percentage depletion in excess of the property's adjusted basis | 700,000 |

a. Determine Mallard Corporation's AMTI for 2003.
b. Determine the tentative minimum tax base (refer to Figure 6–1).
c. Determine the tentative minimum tax.
d. What is the amount of the AMT?

**34.** Grouse Corporation (a calendar year corporation) reports the following information for the years listed:

| | 2002 | 2003 | 2004 |
|---|---|---|---|
| Adjusted current earnings | $7,000,000 | $5,000,000 | $4,000,000 |
| Unadjusted AMTI | 5,000,000 | 5,000,000 | 7,000,000 |

Compute the ACE adjustment for each year.

**35.** Based upon the following facts, calculate adjusted current earnings (ACE):

| | |
|---|---|
| Alternative minimum taxable income (AMTI) | $7,120,000 |
| Municipal bond interest | 630,000 |
| Expenses related to municipal bonds | 50,000 |
| Key employee life insurance proceeds in excess of cash surrender value | 2,000,000 |
| Excess of FIFO over LIFO | 160,000 |
| Organization expense amortization | 100,000 |
| Cost of goods sold | 5,220,000 |
| Advertising expenses | 625,000 |
| Loss between related parties | 260,000 |
| Life insurance expense | 300,000 |

**36.** Purple Corporation, a calendar year taxpayer, has the following preadjusted AMTI and ACE for 2002 through 2005:

|      | Preadjusted AMTI | ACE |
|------|------------------|-----|
| 2002 | $80,000,000 | $70,000,000 |
| 2003 | 60,000,000 | 90,000,000 |
| 2004 | 50,000,000 | 40,000,000 |
| 2005 | 60,000,000 | 20,000,000 |

Calculate Purple's positive and negative adjustments, if any, for ACE.

37. Determine whether each of the following transactions is a preference (*P*), an adjustment (*A*), or not applicable (*NA*) for purposes of the corporate AMT:
   a. Depletion in excess of basis of an integrated oil company.
   b. Accelerated depreciation on property placed in service after 1986.
   c. Mining exploration and development costs.
   d. Adjusted current earnings.
   e. Tax-exempt interest where funds were used for nongovernmental purposes.
   f. Untaxed appreciation on property donated to charity.
   g. Dividends paid deduction.

38. In each of the following independent situations, determine the tentative minimum tax (assume the companies are not in small corporation status):

|                  | AMTI (before the Exemption Amount) |
|------------------|------------------------------------|
| Brant Corporation | $170,000 |
| Tern Corporation  | 190,000 |
| Snipe Corporation | 325,000 |

39. A manufacturing company has accumulated E & P of $220,000 as of December 31, 2002. The company has taxable income of $130,000 for the taxable year 2003 and has a dividends paid deduction of $40,000 (paid during the last half of the tax year). The corporation determines that the earnings for the tax year that may be retained for the reasonable needs of the business are $70,000 over the minimum credit, and that the company is entitled to a $7,000 deduction for net capital gain (after adjustment for attributable tax and prior capital losses). Calculate the accumulated earnings credit for the tax year ending December 31, 2003.

40. In 2003, Willet Corporation, a manufacturing company, retained $70,000 for its reasonable business needs. The company had a long-term capital gain of $20,000 and a short-term capital loss of $15,000, with a resulting capital gain tax of $1,250. The accumulated E & P at the end of 2002 was $170,000. On June 25, 2003, Willet paid a taxable dividend of $90,000. Calculate the accumulated earnings credit for 2003.

**Communications**

41. Garcia Pullig, CEO for a local company, asks you to calculate his company's operating cycle needs without considering accrued Federal income taxes as an operating expense. March is the longest operating cycle for the company, which has reasonable business needs of $40,000 in addition to the working capital required for one operating cycle. Additional information is provided as follows:

| | |
|---|---|
| Accounts receivable—March | $ 120,000 |
| Inventory—March | 160,000 |
| Accounts payable—March | 101,000 |
| Cost of goods sold | 1,000,000 |
| Other expenses (less depreciation) | 100,000 |
| Purchases | 900,000 |

| Depreciation | $   90,000 |
|---|---|
| Sales | 2,000,000 |
| Dividends paid | 7,000 |
| Accumulated earnings (beginning) | 180,000 |
| Accrued Federal income taxes | 220,000 |

Respond to Mr. Pullig in a letter dated June 2, 2003. Mr. Pullig's address is 451 Maple St., Athens, OH 45701.

42. Charlene calculates the following variables for the *Bardahl* formula for her closely held corporation (as a fraction of a year): the inventory cycle, .21; the receivable cycle, .12; and the payable cycle, .13. Operating expenses are $540,000, current assets (fair market value) are $295,000, current liabilities are $200,000, and total liabilities are $425,000. If the corporation has no other reasonable business needs, is it susceptible to the accumulated earnings tax?

43. A wholly owned motor freight corporation has permitted its earnings to accumulate. The company has no inventory but wishes to use the *Bardahl* formula to determine the amount of operating capital required for a business cycle. The following facts are relevant:

| Yearly revenues | $3,300,000 |
|---|---|
| Average accounts receivable | 300,000 |
| Yearly expenses | 3,500,000 |
| Average accounts payable | 213,000 |

   a. Determine the turnover rate of average accounts receivable.
   b. Determine the number of days in the accounts receivable cycle.
   c. Determine the expenses for one accounts receivable cycle.
   d. Determine the number of days in the accounts payable cycle.
   e. Determine the operating capital needed for one business cycle.
   f. Explain why the time allowed a taxpayer for the payment of accounts payable should be taken into consideration in applying the *Bardahl* formula.

44. Maroon Corporation is having accumulated earnings problems so Debbie, the corporate controller, provides you with the following information:

Year-end balances:

| Current assets | | |
|---|---|---|
| Cash | | $  10,000 |
| Accounts receivable (average) | | 15,000 |
| Inventory (average) | | 72,000 |
| | | $  97,000 |
| Current liabilities | | (17,000) |
| Working capital available | | $  80,000 |

Income statement:

| Gross sales | | $ 330,000 |
|---|---|---|
| Less: Sales returns and allowances | | (30,000) |
| Less: Cost of goods sold | $170,000 | |
| Other operating expenses | 50,000 | |
| Depreciation | 15,000 | |
| Income taxes | 9,000 | (244,000) |
| Net income | | $  56,000 |

Calculate the working capital *required* for the corporation if its purchases total $63,334.

*Divpd deduction*

*Curent  pd 1st  Concew*
*yr     1-2½    as it*
*70000  month   div*
*       nextyrs.  has*
*       5000    occured*
*              35000*

*110000*

45. Kingfisher, a calendar year closely held corporation, is not a PHC. If the company reports the following items, calculate accumulated taxable income.

| | |
|---|---|
| Taxable income | $200,000 |
| Long-term capital gain | 30,000 |
| Federal income tax on long-term capital gain | 11,700 |
| Dividends received deduction | 18,000 |
| Accumulated earnings credit | 90,000 |
| Federal income taxes | 65,150 |

46. A manufacturing corporation is accumulating a significant amount of E & P. Although the corporation is closely held, it is not a PHC. The following facts relate to the tax year 2003:

*final test*

*TI    450000*
*IT   <153000>*
*+DRD  28000*
*−Chari <12000>*
*Caploss <6000>*
*−dRD  <70000>*
*−AET cred <10000>*
*        187000*
*        .15*
*AET    28050*

- Taxable income, $450,000.

- Federal income tax, $153,000.

- Dividend income from a qualified domestic corporation (less than 20% owned), $40,000.  *70%*

- Dividends paid in 2003, $70,000.

- Consent dividends, $35,000.

- Dividends paid on February 1, 2004, $5,000.

- Accumulated earnings credit, $10,000.

- Excess charitable contributions of $12,000 (the portion in excess of the amount allowed as a deduction in computing the corporate income tax).

- Net capital loss adjustment, $6,000.

Compute the accumulated earnings tax, if any.

**Decision Making**

47. The following data relate to a closely held manufacturing corporation's 2003 tax year:

| | |
|---|---|
| Net taxable income | $500,000 |
| Federal income taxes | 170,000 |
| Excess charitable contributions | 30,000 |
| Capital loss adjustment | 20,000 |
| Dividends received (17% owned) | 140,000 |
| Dividends paid | 60,000 |
| Accumulated earnings, 1/1/2003 | 130,000 |

a. Assume that the corporation is not a PHC. Calculate any accumulated earnings tax and total tax payable in 2003.

b. Can the deficiency dividend procedure be used to avoid this accumulated earnings tax?

48. In each of the following independent situations, calculate accumulated taxable income, if any. Assume the corporation is not a mere holding or investment company.

| | Gold Corporation | Silver Corporation |
|---|---|---|
| Taxable income | $150,000 | $500,000 |
| Accrued Federal income taxes | 41,750 | 170,000 |
| Capital loss adjustment | 2,000 | |

|  | Gold Corporation | Silver Corporation |
|---|---|---|
| Net LTCG |  | $ 42,000 |
| Tax on LTCG |  | 14,280 |
| Contributions in excess of 10% | $ 15,000 |  |
| NOL deduction | 24,000 |  |
| 70% dividends received deduction |  | 35,000 |
| Dividends paid deduction | 6,000 | 8,000 |
| Accumulated earnings credit | 30,000 | 90,000 |

49. Teal Corporation has gross income of $200,000, which consists of $110,000 of rent income and $90,000 of interest income. The corporation has $30,000 of rent income adjustments and pays $80,000 to its eight shareholders.
    a. Calculate adjusted income from rents.
    b. Calculate AOGI.
    c. Is the 50% test met? Show calculations.
    d. Is the 10% rent income test met? Show calculations.
    e. Is the corporation a PHC?

**Decision Making**

50. Assume the same facts as in Problem 49, except that rent income adjustments decrease from $30,000 to $20,000. Answer the same questions as in Problem 49.

**Communications**

51. Peggy Segal, the president of a local company, asks you to determine if her corporation is a PHC. The company has $20,000 of interest income, $40,000 of gross income from rents, and $20,000 of personal service income (not PHC income). Expenses in the amount of $20,000 relate directly to the rent income. Assume there are eight shareholders and the 10% test is met.

    Communicate your answer to Ms. Segal in a letter dated January 18, 2003. Ms. Segal's address is 152 Patterson Drive, Eugene, OR 97331.

52. Using the legend provided, determine whether each of the following types of companies is statutorily exempted from the accumulated earnings tax, the personal holding company tax, both, or neither.

**Legend**

AET = Exempted from the accumulated earnings tax
PHC = Exempted from the personal holding company tax
B   = Exempted from both the AET and the PHC tax
N   = Exempted from neither tax

    *AET* a. Personal holding company.
    *both* b. S corporation.
    c. Foreign personal holding company.
    d. Foreign corporation.
    e. Tax-exempt organization under § 501(a).
    *N* f. Consulting corporation.
    *PHC* g. Bank.
    h. Finance company.
    *N* i. Law firm.
    *both* j. Limited liability company.

53. Oriole, Inc., is a PHC and has the following receipts for the current year:

| | |
|---|---|
| Operating income | $42,000 |
| Rent income | 19,000 |
| Dividend income | 17,000 |
| Interest income | 18,000 |
| Section 1231 gain | 9,000 |
| Long-term capital gain | 21,000 |
| Short-term capital gain | 7,000 |

Calculate the PHC income.

**Decision Making**

54. Meg is the sole owner of Purple Corporation. The following information is relevant to the corporation's tax year just ended:

| | |
|---|---|
| Capital gain | $ 20,000 |
| Dividend income | 30,000 |
| Rent income | 130,000 |
| Rent expenses | 40,000 |
| Section 162 business expenses | 15,000 |
| Dividends paid | 12,000 |

   a. Calculate OGI.
   b. Calculate AOGI.
   c. Calculate adjusted income from rents.
   d. Calculate nonrent PHC income.
   e. Does this corporation meet the 50% rent income test? Explain.
   f. Does this corporation meet the 10% rent income test? Explain.
   g. Is this company a PHC?
   h. If the 2003 corporate income tax return has not been filed, what would you suggest for Purple Corporation?

55. Using the legend provided, classify each of the following statements accordingly:

**Legend**

A = Relates only to the tax on unreasonable accumulation of
      earnings (the § 531 tax)
P = Relates only to the PHC tax (the § 541 tax)
B = Relates to both the § 531 tax and the § 541 tax
N = Relates to neither the § 531 tax nor the § 541 tax

   a. The tax is applied to taxable income after adjustments are made.
   b. The tax is a self-assessed tax.
   c. Showing that an accumulation of funds is for reasonable business purposes will help *avoid* the tax.
   d. A consent dividend mechanism can be used to *avoid* the tax.
   e. If the stock of the corporation is equally held by 10 unrelated individuals, the tax cannot be imposed.
   f. Any charitable deduction in excess of the 10% limitation is allowed as a deduction before the tax is imposed.
   g. Gains from the sale or disposition of capital assets are *not* subject to the tax.
   h. A sufficient amount of rent income will cause the tax *not* to be imposed.
   i. A life insurance company would *not* be subject to the tax.
   j. A corporation with only dividend income would *avoid* the tax.

56. The PHC tax is computed on an amount called undistributed personal holding company (UPHC) income. To arrive at UPHC income, certain adjustments are made to taxable income. Determine whether the following independent items are positive (+), negative (−), or no adjustment (*NA*):
    a. Federal income taxes on the accrual basis.
    b. Tax-free interest from municipal bonds.
    c. Charitable deductions in excess of 10%.
    d. Net capital gain minus any taxes.
    e. Dividends paid during the taxable year.
    f. Dividends received deduction.
    g. NOL carryforward from three tax years ago.
    h. Consent dividends under § 565.
    i. Deficiency dividend.

57. Indicate in each of the following independent situations whether or not the corporation involved is a PHC (assume the stock ownership test is met):

|  | Robin Corporation | Wren Corporation | Stork Corporation | Swallow Corporation |
|---|---|---|---|---|
| Sales of merchandise | $ 8,000 | $ –0– | $ –0– | $ 2,500 |
| Capital gains | –0– | –0– | –0– | 1,000 |
| Dividend income | 15,000 | 5,000 | 1,000 | 2,500 |
| Gross rent income | 10,000 | 5,000 | 9,000 | 15,000 |
| Expenses related to rents | 8,000 | 2,500 | 8,000 | 10,000 |
| Dividends paid | –0– | –0– | –0– | 500 |
| Personal holding company? (Circle Y for yes or N for no.) | Y  N | Y  N | Y  N | Y  N |

58. Indicate in each of the following independent situations whether or not the corporation involved is a PHC (assume the stock ownership test is met):

|  | White Corporation | Red Corporation | Lavender Corporation | Aqua Corporation |
|---|---|---|---|---|
| Sales of merchandise | $ –0– | $3,000 | $ –0– | $ –0– |
| Capital gains | –0– | –0– | 1,000 | –0– |
| Interest income | 20,000 | 4,800 | 2,000 | 60,000 |
| Gross rent income | 80,000 | 1,200 | 20,000 | 50,000 |
| Expenses related to rents | 60,000 | 1,000 | 10,000 | –0– |
| Dividends paid | 12,000 | –0– | –0– | 20,000 |
| Personal holding company? (Circle Y for yes or N for no.) | Y  N | Y  N | Y  N | Y  N |

59. In each of the following independent situations, calculate the PHC tax liability in 2003:

|  | Peregrine Corporation | Quail Corporation |
|---|---|---|
| Taxable income | $160,000 | $580,000 |
| Dividends received deduction | 37,000 | 70,000 |
| Contributions in excess of 10% | 3,000 | 10,000 |
| Federal income taxes | 47,650 | 197,200 |
| Net capital gain | 70,000 | 40,000 |

|                                 | Peregrine Corporation | Quail Corporation |
| ------------------------------- | :-------------------: | :---------------: |
| Capital gain tax                |       $ 26,800        |     $ 13,600      |
| NOL under § 172                 |                       |      12,000       |
| Current-year dividends paid     |        24,000         |      120,000      |
| Consent dividends               |                       |      30,000       |
| Two and one-half month dividends |         6,000        |                   |

## Research Problems

A THOMSON COMPANY

*Note: Solutions to Research Problems can be prepared by using the **RIA Checkpoint® Student Edition** online research product, or the **CCH U.S. Master Tax Guide Plus**™ online Federal tax research database, which is available to accompany this text. It is also possible to prepare solutions to the Research Problems by using tax research materials found in a standard tax library.*

**Communications**

**Research Problem 1.**  Snap, Inc., was owned entirely by Jeri Belk and Jerry Gore, each owning 620,000 of the 1,240,000 shares of common stock outstanding. On January 1, 2003, Snap established an employee stock ownership plan (ESOP), which later received a favorable determination letter from the IRS.

On February 1, 2003, Belk and Gore each sold 500,000 of their shares to the ESOP, each receiving $2.5 million. To facilitate the transaction, the ESOP borrowed $5 million from a local bank; the loan was guaranteed by Snap, Inc. During the year, Snap paid $1.4 million in cash dividends to the ESOP with respect to its stock. The ESOP transferred the cash to the bank as payment of principal and interest under the note.

Jeri Belk calls you and asks if Snap may claim a deduction under § 404(k) for the $1.4 million cash dividends. Does Snap have to include the dividends in its computation of ACE, thus avoiding any AMT? Write a memo dated March 23 for the tax files in response to Ms. Belk.

**Research Problem 2.**  Night Furniture Company has retained E & P in excess of $6 million in each of three consecutive years. Night Furniture has a history of limited debt, high liquidity, and conservative management. The company argues that it had several justifications for retaining earnings and not paying dividends: a pending class-action lawsuit, business expansion plans, redemption of stock of dissenting shareholders, investments in unrelated businesses, liquidity needs, a dividend history, and a need for repairs and renovations. During the three years, current assets minus current liabilities were $4.9 million, $4.7 million, and $4.8 million. The Night family owns 55% of the stock, and the Perruti family owns the other 45%. Should this company be subject to the accumulated earnings tax?

**Communications**

**Research Problem 3.**  Charlotte Corporation is a real estate company that normally holds properties for rental, but will sell a piece of property if it receives a good offer. Charlotte is not in the regular business of selling real estate, however. When the company sells properties, it takes back purchase money obligations, which guarantee a significant amount of interest income. The company maintains that this interest income falls under the definition of rent in § 542(b)(3). If the income is treated as rent income, Charlotte can pass the 50% rent income hurdle. What do you think? Prepare a research memorandum for your manager, Don Crump, dated August 21, 2003.

**Research Problem 4.**  Kelly Caleb, a motion picture music editor, formed Blair Corporation. Kelly is Blair's sole shareholder, director, and officer. The company contracts with motion picture studios for Kelly's services as a music editor. All of the contracts were memorialized, in part, by a "loan-out agreement" or a "deal memorandum." Each contract with the studios made specific reference to Kelly's music services.

Other than compensation paid to Kelly, the company paid no salary or compensation to other employees. The company reported total income of $222,000 from music editing services and also received $68,000 from rent income. Determine any tax problems.

**Internet Activity**

*Use the tax resources of the Internet to address the following questions. Do not restrict your search to the World Wide Web, but include a review of newsgroups and general reference materials, practitioner sites and resources, primary sources of the tax law, chat rooms and discussion groups, and other opportunities.*

**Research Problem 5.**   Some parties believe that many corporations are not paying any corporate income tax and blame the AMT for being ineffective. Examine both government and press sites on the Internet and summarize these complaints.

**Research Problem 6.**   Owners of closely held businesses and their tax advisers make available substantial in-depth information about the dangers of the AET and the best means of avoiding it. Outline the key techniques promoted by these sources as effective in minimizing § 531 exposure.

**Research Problem 7.**   Locate a current proposal to modify the structure or scope of the AMT on corporations. Describe the proposal, the party making the proposal, and potential motivations for submitting the modification to Congress.

# Corporations: Reorganizations

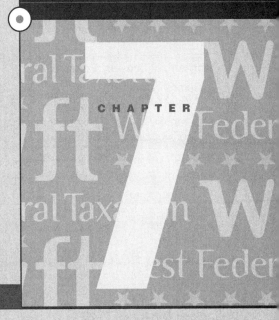

## LEARNING OBJECTIVES

*After completing Chapter 7, you should be able to:*

### LO.1
Understand the general requirements of corporate reorganizations.

### LO.2
Determine the tax consequences of a corporate reorganization.

### LO.3
Explain the statutory requirements for the different types of reorganizations.

### LO.4
Delineate the judicial and administrative conditions for a nontaxable corporate reorganization.

### LO.5
Apply the rules pertaining to the carryover of tax attributes in a corporate reorganization.

### LO.6
Structure corporate reorganizations to obtain the desired tax consequences.

## O U T L I N E

One of the tenets of U.S. tax policy is to encourage business development. To this end, the tax laws allow entities to form without taxation, assuming certain requirements are met. As an extension of this concept, corporate restructurings are also given favored tax treatment. Corporations may engage in a variety of acquisitions, combinations, consolidations, and divisions tax-free, as long as the "reorganization" requirements in the Code are met.

Mergers and acquisitions are a popular method of increasing the economic vitality of corporate businesses. The restructuring frenzy peaked in 1999–2000, when more than 20,000 major deals occurred (values greater than $5 million) amounting to almost $2.7 trillion in value. Unfortunately, the downturn in the global economy and stock market has dramatically slowed merger and acquisition activity. In 2001–2002, the number of major U.S. restructurings fell by more than 25 percent, and the value of these deals was less than 50 percent of the 1999–2000 high. Only one of the 10 largest mergers and acquisitions in the past five years occurred in the 2001–2002 period (see Exhibit 7–1). However, one type of restructuring has seen a dramatic increase over the 2001–2002 period—mega-bankruptcies. This increase has been fueled by the economy and financial statement misstatements. As Exhibit 7–2 indicates, 7 of the top 10 largest U.S. bankruptcies in the last 15 years occurred in 2001 or 2002. Additional details of recent bankruptcies, mergers, and acquisitions are provided below.

- *Bankruptcies.* The number and value of publicly traded companies filing for bankruptcy reached record levels in 2001–2002. The total assets of these failed corporations amounted to more than $525 billion. Most of the large bankruptcies have occurred in the telecommunications industry, but the energy and retail trades also have some notable entries.
  - *WorldCom* became the largest publicly traded corporation in history to file for bankruptcy protection under Chapter 11. The filing was the result of

■ **EXHIBIT 7–1**

The Largest Mergers and Acquisitions in the United States, 1998–2002

| Companies | Year | Total Assets (in Billions) |
|---|---|---|
| Sprint and MCI | 1999 | $116.0 |
| Time Warner and AOL | 2000 | 165.9 |
| Warner-Lambert and Pfizer | 1999 | 82.4 |
| Mobil and Exxon | 1998 | 77.2 |
| Air Touch and Vodafone | 1999 | 62.0 |
| Ameritech and SBC Communications | 1998 | 61.4 |
| Pharmacia and Pfizer | 2002 | 58.3 |
| Amoco and British Petroleum | 1998 | 56.2 |
| Media One and AT&T | 1999 | 55.8 |
| GTE and Bell Atlantic | 1998 | 52.9 |

SOURCE: Data are from Mergerstat.com.

financial statement improprieties that overstated the company's earnings by almost $4 billion. An erosion in its market share may have prompted the attempt to overstate earnings. WorldCom's shareholders have lost almost everything; the bondholders and bankers will now control what was once one of the world's most valuable companies.

• *Enron* filed for bankruptcy in 2001 after Dynegy, Inc., abandoned its plans to acquire the energy trader. Like WorldCom, Enron was plagued with financial statement scandals. The Enron debacle has been costly not only for its shareholders and bondholders, but also for its employees and its auditors. Many lives were ruined by Enron's bankruptcy.

• *Global Crossing*, a leader in undersea international fiber-optic communications, was bought to its knees by a combination of a sinking economy, overwhelming debt, and an inadequate long-term business plan. Accounting irregularities were also a problem for Global Crossing, and former finance officers have told Congress that top executives misled stock analysts about the company's financial condition.

• *Adelphia Communications'* scandals go far beyond improper accounting for its transactions. Although overstatements of cash flows and inflated subscriber numbers led the company down the road to bankruptcy, it was the numerous allegations of self-dealing with the founders and their controlled entities that ruined Adelphia's credibility. The self-dealing loan guarantees alone amounted to more than $3.1 billion. These loans, added to an already high level of debt caused by its acquisition spree during the 1990's boom, caused Adelphia to have one of the highest debt levels in the cable industry.

• *Pacific Gas and Electric Company* became the largest utility company in history to file for bankruptcy protection. Bankruptcies among utility companies are rare; only two other publicly owned utilities have filed for Chapter 11 protection—Public Services of New Hampshire and El Paso Electric Company.

• *Kmart* holds the dubious honor of being the largest retail business to file for bankruptcy ($17 billion). It beat out Federated Department Stores, which filed in 1990 ($9 billion). Although some of Kmart's stores have been closed, most are still open for business as usual, and for this company,

■ **EXHIBIT 7–2**
The Largest Bankruptcies in the
United States, 1985–2002

| Company | Year | Total Assets (in Billions) |
|---|---|---|
| WorldCom, Inc. | 2002 | $103.9 |
| Enron Corp. | 2001 | 63.4 |
| Texaco, Inc. | 1987 | 35.9 |
| Financial Corp. of America | 1988 | 33.8 |
| Global Crossing, Ltd. | 2002 | 25.5 |
| Adelphia Communications | 2002 | 24.4 |
| Pacific Gas and Electric Co. | 2001 | 21.5 |
| Mcorp (financial services) | 1989 | 20.2 |
| Kmart Corp. | 2002 | 17.0 |
| NTL, Inc. (cable company in NY) | 2002 | 16.8 |

SOURCES: Data are from BankruptcyData.com; New Generation
Research, Inc., Boston, Mass.

bankruptcy reorganization may signal survival rather than its imminent
demise.

• *Mergers and acquisitions.* Unlike bankruptcies, the recent year has seen few
mega-mergers or acquisitions. The technology industry still leads in the
number of major mergers and acquisitions, but pharmaceutical restructurings
lead in dollar value, largely as a result of the mega-merger between Pharmacia and Pfizer.

  • In the only 2002 merger to make the list of the top 10 deals, *Pfizer* is
  acquiring *Pharmacia* for nearly $60 billion in stock. Pharmacia will spin off
  its Monsanto division to its current shareholders before the stock-for-stock
  restructuring with Pfizer. Already the largest pharmaceutical company,
  Pfizer expects the addition to increase its revenues by more than $12
  billion. The merger is likely to cause other pharmaceuticals to seek mergers
  just to be able to compete with this powerhouse.

  • *IBM* has reached an agreement with *PricewaterhouseCoopers* (PwC) to acquire its consulting arm (named Monday) for approximately $3.5 billion
  in stock and cash. The deal still faces regulatory hurdles, but IBM appears
  confident that these will not sabotage the acquisition. Slightly more than
  a year earlier, Hewlett-Packard (HP) had been in negotiations with PwC
  for this consulting practice. However, this deal fell apart when IBM showed
  interest in acquiring Monday and suggested that its value was significantly
  less than HP initially offered.

  • *Hewlett-Packard* acquired *Compaq* for approximately $25.7 billion, but not
  without some acrimony. Although Compaq's shareholders overwhelm-
  ingly approved the deal, HP's shareholders were sharply divided. One
  of HP's directors adamantly opposed the restructuring, which he considered to be a huge mistake. A bitter proxy fight ensued, but in the end,
  HP's shareholders narrowly approved the acquisition. Only time will tell
  which shareholders were right about the wisdom of merging with
  Compaq.

Given the magnitude of the dollar amounts involved in most reorganizations,
tax avoidance strategies play an important role in corporate restructurings. Careful
planning can reduce or eliminate taxation for both the corporations involved in

the reorganization and their shareholders. Therefore, tax law often dictates the form of the restructuring. Corporate mergers and divisions generally are tax-free when the target corporation exchanges stock or assets for the stock of the acquiring corporation. If other property or cash is given by the acquiring corporation, the reorganization may be partly or fully taxable. When the reorganization is taxable for the shareholders, the low applicable capital gains rates reduce some of the negative tax implications. Since corporations do not receive the special capital gains treatment, it may be paramount that the transaction be structured to meet the requirements for nontaxable treatment.

Courts originally concluded that even minor changes in a corporation's structure would produce taxable gain to the shareholders involved.[1] Congress, however, determined that businesses should be allowed to make necessary capital adjustments without being subject to taxation.[2] The theory for nonrecognition in certain corporate restructurings or "reorganizations" is similar to that underlying § 351 treatment and like-kind exchanges. As the Regulations state:

> . . . the new property is substantially a continuation of the old investment . . . and, in the case of reorganizations, . . . the new enterprise, the new corporate structure, and the new property are substantially continuations of the old . . .[3]

<table>
<tr><td>

**LO.1**

Understand the general requirements of corporate reorganizations.

</td><td>

# Reorganizations—In General

</td></tr>
</table>

Although the term **reorganization** is commonly associated with a corporation in financial difficulty, for tax purposes the term refers to any corporate restructuring that may be tax-free under § 368. To qualify as a tax-free reorganization, a corporate restructuring transaction must meet not only the specific requirements of § 368 but also several general requirements. These requirements include the following.

1. There must be a *plan of reorganization*.
2. The reorganization must meet the *continuity of interest* and the *continuity of business enterprise* tests set out in the Regulations.
3. The restructuring must meet the judicial doctrine of having a *sound business purpose*.
4. The court-imposed *step transaction* doctrine should not apply to the reorganization.

All of these concepts are discussed in this chapter. The initial and most important consideration, however, is whether the reorganization qualifies for nonrecognition status under § 368.

## SUMMARY OF THE DIFFERENT TYPES OF REORGANIZATIONS

Section 368(a) specifies seven corporate restructurings or *reorganizations* that will qualify as nontaxable exchanges. If the transaction fails to qualify as a reorganization, it will not receive the special tax-free treatment. Therefore, a corporation considering a business reorganization must determine in advance if the proposed transaction specifically falls within one of these seven types. In situations involving substantial tax dollars, the parties should obtain a letter ruling from the IRS verifying that the proposed combination qualifies as a tax-free reorganization under § 368.

---

[1]*U.S. v. Phellis*, 1 USTC ¶54, 3 AFTR 3123, 42 S.Ct. 63 (USSC, 1921).
[2]Reg. § 1.368–1(b). See S.Rept. No. 275, 67th Cong., 1st Sess. (1921), at 1939–1 C.B. 181.

[3]Reg. § 1.1002–1(c).

## CONCEPT SUMMARY 7–1

### Gain and Basis Rules for Nontaxable Exchanges

| (1) Realized Gain/Loss | (2) Recognized Gain (Not Loss) | (3) Postponed Gain/Loss | (4) Basis of New Asset |
|---|---|---|---|
| FMV of asset (stock) received − Adjusted basis of asset surrendered | Lesser of boot received or gain realized | Gain/loss realized (column 1) − Gain recognized (column 2) | FMV of asset (stock) received − Postponed gain (column 3) or + Postponed loss (column 3) |
| Gain/loss realized | Gain recognized | Gain/loss postponed | Adjusted basis in new asset (stock) |

Section 368(a)(1) states that the term *reorganization* applies to any of the following.

A.  A statutory merger or consolidation.
B.  The acquisition by a corporation of another using solely stock of each corporation (voting-stock-for-stock exchange).
C.  The acquisition by a corporation of substantially all of the property of another corporation in exchange for voting stock (stock-for-asset exchange).
D.  The transfer of all or part of a corporation's assets to another corporation when the original corporation's shareholders are in control of the new corporation immediately after the transfer (divisive exchange, also known as a spin-off, split-off, or split-up).
E.  A recapitalization.
F.  A mere change in identity, form, or place of organization.
G.  A transfer by a corporation of all or a part of its assets to another corporation in a bankruptcy or receivership proceeding.

These seven types of tax-free reorganizations typically are designated by their identifying letters: "Type A," "Type B," "Type C," and so on. Each will be described in more detail later in the chapter.

**LO.2**
Determine the tax consequences of a corporate reorganization.

### SUMMARY OF TAX CONSEQUENCES IN A TAX-FREE REORGANIZATION

The tax treatment of the parties involved in a tax-free reorganization almost exactly parallels the treatment under the like-kind exchange provisions of § 1031. In the simplest like-kind exchange, neither gain nor loss is recognized on the exchange of "like-kind" property. When "boot" (defined as non-like-kind property) is involved, gain may be recognized. The four-column template of Concept Summary 7–1 can be used to compute the amount of gain recognized and the adjusted basis in the new asset received in the like-kind exchange.

Unfortunately, the like-kind exchange provisions do not apply to the exchange of stock or securities.[4] Therefore, when an investor exchanges stock in one corporation for stock in another, the exchange is a taxable transaction. If the transaction

[4]§ 1031(a)(2)(B).

## REEVALUATION OF FCC RULES COULD SPUR MERGERS

The Federal Communications Commission (FCC) has decided to undertake a comprehensive review of the ownership regulations for newspapers, television stations, and radio stations with the intent of possibly weakening or eliminating some of the media ownership restrictions. These regulations were originally enacted to ensure that no company or individual could dominate the viewpoints available to the public through the popular media and undermine the free flow of information. Thus, the rules discourage a company from owning television, radio, and newspaper outlets in the same market region. The FCC thinks that the time is right to reexamine these rules in light of the changes that have occurred in this industry since the rules were written.

Relaxing or abolishing the media ownership rules will likely encourage numerous mergers and acquisitions among media companies. More mega-mergers such as the 2000 acquisition of CBS by Viacom, a $34.5 billion deal, could be the wave of the future if the ownership rules are relaxed. As the requirements currently stand, the Viacom/CBS merger is in violation of the dual-network regulation that bars companies from owning more than one of the four major television networks. Viacom owns both CBS and UPN networks. Viacom is hoping the proposed changes in the regulations will sanction its present media ownership. This would end the need for the current temporary waiver it holds from the FCC and its lawsuit challenging these rules.

SOURCE: Adapted from Yochi J. Dreasen, "FCC Is Reviewing Rules Governing Media Ownership," *Wall Street Journal*, September 13, 2002.

---

can qualify as a reorganization under § 368, however, the exchange will be nontaxable. Thus, a § 368 reorganization, in substance, is similar to a nontaxable exchange of like-kind property, and the four-column template of Concept Summary 7–1 is useful for reorganizations as well.

**EXAMPLE 1**

Ram holds 1,000 shares of Lotus stock that he purchased for $10,000 several years ago. In a merger of Lotus into Blossom, Ram exchanges his 1,000 shares of Lotus for 1,000 shares of Blossom. Both investments are valued at $18 per share. Ram's realized gain on the exchange is $8,000 [($18 per share × 1,000 shares) – $10,000 basis]. Assuming this exchange qualifies for tax-free treatment under § 368, Ram's recognized gain is zero. Since his postponed gain is $8,000, Ram's basis in his new stock is $10,000 [$18,000 (FMV of new stock) – $8,000 postponed gain]. The exchange of Ram's stock has no tax consequences for Lotus or Blossom. ■

**Gain or Loss.**   The general rule is that the corporations involved in a § 368 reorganization do not recognize gain or loss on the restructuring. There are exceptions to the nonrecognition rule, however. If the target corporation receives property from the acquiring corporation along with its stock and securities, gain, but not loss, may be recognized. The target may also recognize gain, but not loss, when it fails to distribute the *other property* it receives in the restructuring or distributes its own appreciated property to its shareholders. *Other property* in this case is defined as anything received other than stock or securities.[5]

---

[5]§§ 361(a) and (b).

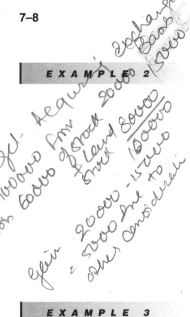

In a restructuring qualifying as a reorganization, Acquiring Corporation exchanges $80,000 of stock and land with a fair market value of $20,000 (basis of $15,000) for all of the assets of Target Corporation. Target's assets have a fair market value of $100,000 and a basis of $60,000. Due to the *other property* (land) Acquiring uses in the transfer, it recognizes a gain of $5,000 ($20,000 − $15,000) on the reorganization. If Target distributes the land to its shareholders, it does not recognize gain. If Target retains the land, however, it recognizes gain to the extent of the *other property* received, $20,000. ■

Generally, the stockholders of the corporations involved in a tax-free reorganization do not recognize gain or loss on the exchange of their stock unless they receive cash or other property in addition to stock. The cash or other property is considered boot, and the gain recognized by the stockholder is the lesser of the boot received or the realized gain. This is analogous to the treatment of boot in a like-kind exchange.

**EXAMPLE 3**

Kalla, the sole shareholder of Target Corporation in Example 2, has a basis in her stock of $70,000. She exchanges her Target stock for the $80,000 of Acquiring stock plus the land ($20,000) transferred by Acquiring to Target. Kalla has a realized gain of $30,000 ($80,000 + $20,000 − $70,000), and the land (boot) causes her to recognize a $20,000 gain. ■

Once the gain is computed, its character must be determined. The following are the possibilities for gain characterization.

- Dividend to the extent of the shareholder's proportionate share of corporate earnings and profits. The remaining gain is generally capital gain.
- If the requirements of § 302(b) can be met, the transaction will qualify for stock redemption treatment (see Chapter 5).
  - Gains from qualifying stock redemptions are treated as capital gains.
  - In computing the shareholder's ownership reduction, shares actually received in the acquiring corporation are compared with the number of shares the shareholder would have received if solely stock of the acquiring corporation had been distributed in the reorganization.[6]

**EXAMPLE 4**

Sam exchanges his 2% stock interest in Target (basis $8,000) for $2,000 cash and stock in Acquiring worth $13,000. At the time of the reorganization, Target's E & P is $25,000. Sam has a realized gain of $7,000 ($15,000 − $8,000) and a $2,000 recognized gain (the boot received). The first $500 ($25,000 × 2%) is taxable as a dividend, and the remaining $1,500 is treated as capital gain.

Suppose Sam received 1% of Acquiring stock with a fair market value of $10,000 and $5,000 cash. If Sam had received solely stock, he would have received 1.5% of Acquiring stock. Since Sam owns less than 80% of what he would have owned (1% ÷ 1.5% is less than 80%) and less than 50% of Acquiring, he meets the qualifications for sale or exchange treatment under § 302(b)(2). Therefore, Sam's $5,000 recognized gain is a capital gain. ■

Debt security (debenture) holders receive treatment similar to shareholders. They recognize gain only when the principal amount of the debentures received is greater than the debt securities given up. If debentures are received and no securities are surrendered, the debenture holders also recognize gain.

---

[6]*Comm. v. Clark*, 89–1 USTC ¶9230, 63 AFTR2d 89–860, 109 S.Ct. 1455
(USSC, 1989), and Rev.Rul. 93–61, 1993–2 C.B. 118.

## CONCEPT SUMMARY 7–2

### Basis Rules for a Tax-Free Reorganization

**Basis to Acquiring Corporation of Property Received**

| | |
|---|---:|
| Target's basis in property transferred | $xx,xxx |
| Plus: Gain recognized by Target on the transaction | x,xxx |
| Equals: Basis of property to Acquiring Corporation | $xx,xxx |

**Basis to Target Shareholders of Stock and Securities Received**

| | |
|---|---:|
| Basis of stock and securities transferred | $xx,xxx |
| Plus: Gain and dividend income recognized | x,xxx |
| Minus: Money and fair market value of other property received | (x,xxx) |
| Equals: Basis of stock and securities received | $xx,xxx |

**EXAMPLE 5**

Alejandra was a debenture holder in Hibiscus. She owned bonds with a principal value of $10,000. As part of the merger of Hibiscus with Carnation, Alejandra surrenders her Hibiscus bonds and receives long-term Carnation debentures with a principal value of $15,000. Alejandra recognizes a $5,000 capital gain on the exchange. ■

**Basis.** The assets transferred from the target corporation to the acquiring corporation retain their basis. This carryover basis is increased by any gain recognized by the target corporation on the reorganization. Concept Summary 7–2 shows this computation.

**EXAMPLE 6**

Target exchanges its assets with a fair market value of $50,000 and a basis of $30,000 for $45,000 of Acquiring stock and $5,000 of land. Target does not distribute the land to its shareholders. Target recognizes a $5,000 gain on the reorganization (due to the other property not being distributed). Acquiring's basis in the assets received from Target is $35,000 [$30,000 (Target's basis) + $5,000 (Target's gain recognized)]. ■

The tax basis of the stock and securities received by a shareholder pursuant to a tax-free reorganization generally is the same as the basis of those surrendered. This basis is decreased by the fair market value of boot received and increased by the gain and/or dividend income recognized on the transaction. Concept Summary 7–2 provides a summary of these calculations. Another way to compute the basis in the stock and securities, using the template of Concept Summary 7–1, is to subtract the gain (or add the loss) postponed from the fair market value of the stock and securities received. This basis computation ensures that the postponed gain or loss will be recognized when the new stock or securities are disposed of in a taxable transaction.

**EXAMPLE 7**

Quinn exchanges all of his stock in Target Corporation for stock in Acquiring Corporation plus $3,000 cash. The exchange is pursuant to a tax-free reorganization. Quinn paid $10,000 for the stock in Target two years ago. The Acquiring stock received has a fair market value of $12,000. Quinn has a realized gain of $5,000 ($12,000 + $3,000 − $10,000), which is recognized to the extent of the boot received, $3,000. Quinn's basis in the Acquiring stock is $10,000. This can be computed using the template in Concept Summary 7–1 [$12,000 (value of Acquiring stock) − $2,000 (postponed gain)] or Concept Summary 7–2 [$10,000 (basis) + $3,000 (gain) − $3,000 (money received)].

## CONCEPT SUMMARY 7–3

### Tax Consequences of Tax-Free Reorganizations

Treatment Similar to Like-Kind Exchanges

- No gain or loss is recognized by the acquiring or target corporation unless other property (i.e., boot) is transferred or received by any parties to the reorganization.
- Basis in the assets received by the acquiring corporation is generally carried over from the target corporation.
- Basis in the stock received by the target corporation's shareholders takes a substituted basis, derived from the basis in their target stock.
- Gain, but not loss, may be recognized when boot is transferred by the acquiring corporation.
- Gain, but not loss, may be recognized when the target corporation receives boot and does not distribute the boot to its shareholders.
- Gain, but not loss, may be recognized when target shareholders receive anything other than stock (i.e., boot) in exchange for their target stock.

**EXAMPLE 8**

Assume the same facts as in Example 7, except that Quinn's basis in the Target stock was $16,000. Quinn realizes a loss of $1,000 on the exchange, none of which is recognized. His basis in the Acquiring stock is $13,000 [Concept Summary 7–1: $12,000 (value of stock received) + $1,000 (loss postponed) or Concept Summary 7–2: $16,000 (basis) − $3,000 (money received)]. ∎

Concept Summary 7–3 furnishes a review of the tax consequences of tax-free reorganizations.

**LO.3**

Explain the statutory requirements for the different types of reorganizations.

# Types of Tax-Free Reorganizations

## TYPE A

Although the terms are not analogous, "Type A" reorganizations include both mergers and consolidations. A **merger** is the union of two or more corporations, in which one of the corporations retains its corporate existence and absorbs the others. The other corporations cease to exist by operation of law. A **consolidation** occurs when a new corporation is created to take the place of two or more corporations. The "Type A" reorganizations are illustrated in Figure 7–1. To qualify as a "Type A" reorganization, mergers and consolidations must comply with the requirements of state law.

■ **FIGURE 7–1**

"Type A" Reorganization

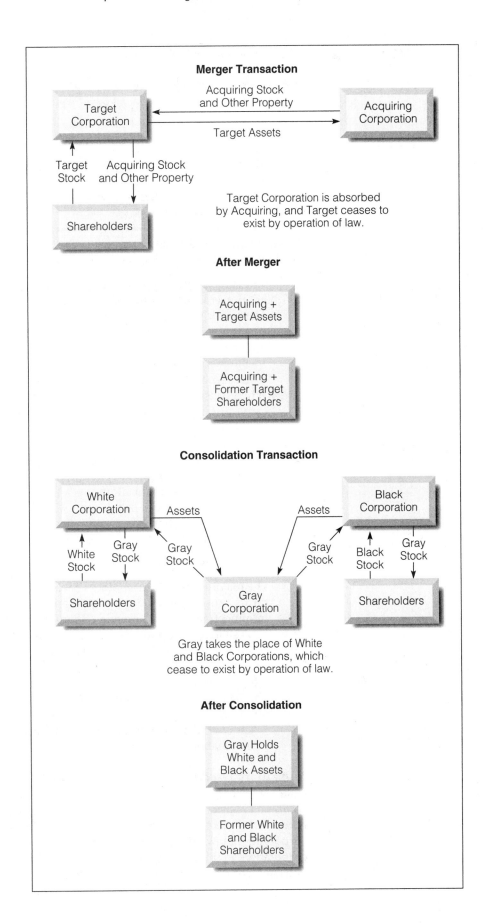

**EXAMPLE 9**

Acquiring Corporation obtains all the assets of Target Corporation in exchange for 5,000 shares of Acquiring stock. Target is liquidated by distributing the Acquiring stock to its shareholders in exchange for their shares in Target. This transaction qualifies as a "Type A" reorganization (assuming that all other requirements of state law are met). It is a statutory merger. ■

**EXAMPLE 10**

White and Black Corporations are united under state law into new Gray Corporation by transferring all of their assets to Gray in exchange for all of Gray Corporation's stock. White and Black Corporations are then liquidated by distributing Gray stock to their shareholders in exchange for the shareholders' stock in White and Black. This is a "Type A" reorganization in the form of a consolidation. ■

**Advantages and Disadvantages.** The "Type A" reorganization allows more flexibility than the other types of reorganizations.

*[handwritten: Any stock is allowed]*

- Unlike both the "Type B" and the "Type C" reorganizations, the consideration need not be voting stock.
- The acquiring corporation can transfer money or other property to the target corporation without destroying the tax-free treatment for the stock also exchanged.
  - The money or other property, however, constitutes boot and may cause the recognition of gain by the target or its shareholders.

*[handwritten: @ least 50% of consideration must be stock]*

- When consideration other than stock is given by the acquiring corporation, care must be taken not to run afoul of the **continuity of interest test**.
  - This test, promulgated by the courts, requires that at least 50 percent of the consideration given by the acquiring corporation must be stock.

*[handwritten: No req of substantially all assets to be tfr]*

- In a "Type A" reorganization, there is no requirement that "substantially all" of the assets of the target be transferred to the acquiring corporation as in a "Type C" reorganization.
  - Thus, the target can sell or otherwise dispose of assets not desired by the acquiring corporation without affecting the tax-free nature of the restructuring.

A "Type A" is not without its disadvantages.

*[handwritten: S/H must approve]*

- The majority of the shareholders of each corporation involved in the restructuring must approve the reorganization.
- In almost all states, dissenting shareholders have the right to require that their shares be appraised and purchased.

*[handwritten: Expensive]*

- Meeting the demands of objecting shareholders can become so cumbersome and expensive that the parties may be forced to abandon the "Type A" reorganization.

*[handwritten: Acquiring Corp have to assume all the liabilities]*

- The acquiring corporation is required to assume *all* liabilities (including unknown and contingent liabilities) of the target corporation.
  - The surviving corporation assumes the liabilities of the target corporation as a matter of state law.

**Subsidiary Used in a "Type A" Reorganization.** Many of the problems with state law in the "Type A" reorganization can be reduced if a third corporation, a controlled subsidiary of the corporation desiring to acquire the target corporation, becomes the actual acquiring corporation. Using a subsidiary as the acquiring corporation allows the parent to protect its assets from the creditors of the target corporation. In this way, the acquirer can avoid any responsibility for the unknown and contingent liabilities of the target corporation. Further, the problem of securing

**■ FIGURE 7–2**

Use of a Subsidiary in a "Type A" Reorganization

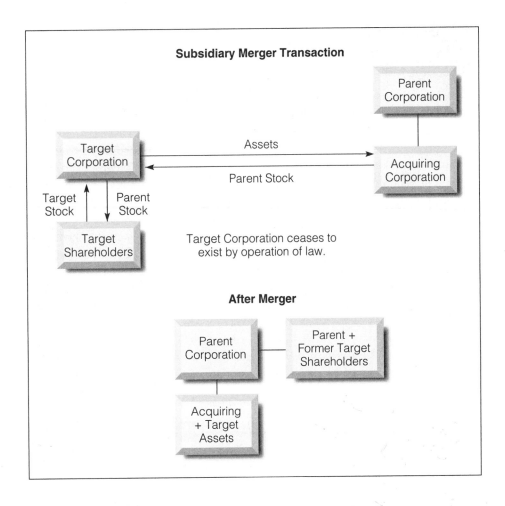

the approval of the majority of shareholders of the acquiring corporation is lessened.[7] Only the approval of the board of directors of the parent corporation need be obtained. For these reasons, the use of a subsidiary corporation to effect the "Type A" reorganization offers advantages.

The parent may want the shareholders of the target corporation to hold its stock rather than the stock of the subsidiary. This enables the parent to retain control over the subsidiary. A typical "Type A" reorganization using a subsidiary is diagrammed in Figure 7–2. The exchange of a parent's stock by a subsidiary in a statutory merger qualifies the reorganization as a tax-free "Type A" reorganization if (1) no subsidiary stock is used and (2) the exchange would have been a "Type A" reorganization had the merger been into the parent.

**EXAMPLE 11**

Acquiring Corporation is a subsidiary of Parent Corporation. One of its assets is stock in Parent. Acquiring transfers the Parent stock it owns to Target Corporation for substantially all the assets of Target. Target is liquidated by distributing Parent stock to its shareholders in exchange for their shares in Target. This is a subsidiary "Type A" reorganization using parent company stock. ■

---

[7]The approval of a majority of the shareholders of the target corporation still is required.

| ETHICAL CONSIDERATIONS | A White Knight Merger Gone Astray |

Retail Corporation is a small regional chain of upscale clothing stores. With the trend toward allowing business casual dress in the workplace, Retail has become very profitable. Consequently, it has substantial liquid assets and very low levels of liabilities. Retail is so encouraged by its profitability that it is considering becoming a national chain.

Retail's success has not gone unnoticed in the marketplace. Mirage Corporation, a privately owned conglomerate, has decided to make an unsolicited tender offer for the stock of Retail. In the past, Mirage has made such offers for other small corporations with substantial liquid assets. Once it owns enough stock to take control of the board of directors, Mirage forces the liquidation of the company to obtain its liquid assets. Therefore, Retail is very concerned about Mirage's interest in obtaining its stock. To avoid being taken over by Mirage, Retail negotiates with Warehouse Corporation, one of its suppliers, for a merger of the two companies.

Warehouse is fully aware of the dangers faced by Retail as it was the target of an unsuccessful takeover by Mirage in the past. It was rescued from the takeover by a similar "white knight" merger with one of its competitors.

Through an informer at Warehouse, Mirage discovers Retail's plan to foil its hostile takeover. To sabotage the merger, Mirage offers Warehouse an exclusive contract for selling its merchandise in Mirage's national chain of discount department stores. The contract requires that Warehouse not own or be affiliated with any corporation in the retail clothing business. Warehouse's board of directors feels this contract could boost its profits by 20 percent. Therefore, the board votes to enter into the contract with Mirage and abandon its merger negotiations with Retail. Retail ultimately is taken over by Mirage and liquidated.

What ethical issues, if any, did Warehouse's directors face in their dealings with Mirage and Retail?

## TYPE B

In a "Type B" reorganization, the acquiring corporation obtains the target corporation in an exchange involving solely stock. Immediately after the acquisition, the acquiring corporation must be in "control" of the target corporation. Thus, both corporations survive, and a parent-subsidiary relationship is created. In simple terms, this transaction is an exchange of stock for voting stock. Voting stock must be the sole consideration given by the acquiring corporation, a requirement that is strictly construed.[8] The target's stock relinquished in the transaction may be common or preferred, voting or nonvoting.

Since the "Type B" reorganization precludes the use of boot, gain is never recognized in this type of reorganization. If the acquiring corporation exchanges nonvoting preferred stock in addition to voting stock, the transaction does not qualify as a "Type B" reorganization. An exception to the requirement that only voting stock be used occurs when the shareholders must receive fractional shares. The shareholders of the target corporation may receive cash rather than fractional shares in the acquiring corporation.[9] The "Type B" reorganization is illustrated in Figure 7–3.

| EXAMPLE 12 | Acquiring Corporation exchanges 20% of its voting stock with the Target Corporation shareholders for 80% of all classes of stock in Target Corporation. The exchange qualifies as a "Type B" reorganization. Acquiring becomes the parent of Target. ∎

---

[8] *A. S. Heverly*, 80–1 USTC ¶9322, 45 AFTR2d 80–1122, 621 F.2d 1227, and *E. S. Chapman*, 80–1 USTC ¶9330, 45 AFTR2d 80–1290, 618 F.2d 856.

[9] Rev.Rul. 66–365, 1966–2 C.B. 116.

■ **FIGURE 7–3**
"Type B" Reorganization

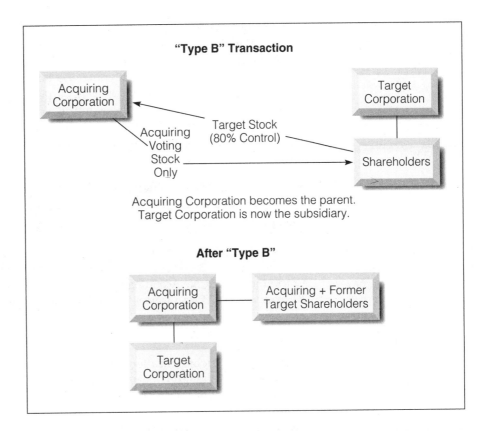

The Voting Stock Requirements.   To meet the requirements of a "Type B" reorganization, the acquiring corporation's *sole* consideration must be voting stock,[10] and the acquiring corporation must be in "control" of the target corporation immediately after the reorganization. **Control** for this purpose requires ownership of at least 80 percent of all classes of the target corporation's stock. The 80 percent-control-after-reorganization requirement does not mean that all 80 percent must be "acquired" in the restructuring transaction. Stock previously purchased in separate transactions can be counted in determining the 80 percent ownership.[11] Further, the stock may be acquired from the shareholders directly or from the target corporation.

**EXAMPLE 13**   Acquiring Corporation purchased 30% of Target for cash six years ago. It acquires another 60% in the current year through the issuance of voting stock. Thus, even though some of the shares of Target were acquired with cash, the requirements of a "Type B" reorganization are satisfied through the current 60% acquisition.

What if Acquiring Corporation purchased 30% of Target's stock for cash three months ago? Now the acquisition of the additional 60% of Target's stock for voting stock seems to be part of a two-step transaction. The acquisition of the remaining stock for voting stock is probably not tax-free. ■

The solely voting stock consideration requirement is a substantial disadvantage of the "Type B" reorganization. Another disadvantage is that if the acquiring

---

[10]The exchange of the acquiring corporation's bonds for the target's bonds may be considered a separate and distinct transaction from a "Type B" reorganization according to Rev.Rul. 98–10, 1998–1

C.B. 643. Consequently, this exchange will not affect an otherwise qualifying "Type B" reorganization.
[11]Reg. § 1.368–2(c).

corporation does not obtain 100 percent control of the target corporation, problems may arise with the minority interest remaining in the target.

Nevertheless, the voting-stock-for-stock acquisition has the advantage of simplicity. Generally, the shareholders of the target corporation act individually in transferring their stock to the acquiring corporation. Thus, the target corporation itself and the shareholders of the acquiring corporation are not directly involved. This assumes the acquiring corporation has sufficient treasury or unissued shares to effect the transaction without formal shareholder action to increase authorized shares.

**Subsidiary Used in a "Type B" Reorganization.**   As in the "Type A" reorganization, voting stock of the acquiring corporation's parent may be used in the "Type B."

**EXAMPLE 14**

Ancestor Corporation is the parent of Acquiring Corporation. Acquiring also owns some stock in Ancestor. It exchanges Ancestor voting stock for a controlling interest in Target Corporation's stock. No Acquiring stock is used in the transaction. This qualifies as a "Type B" reorganization. Target is now the subsidiary of Acquiring. ■

## TYPE C

In the "Type C" reorganization, the acquiring corporation obtains substantially all of the assets of the target corporation in exchange for voting stock and a limited amount of other property. The target corporation must distribute all assets it receives in the reorganization, as well as any of its own property retained. The target corporation then liquidates.[12] Thus, a "Type C" reorganization is essentially an exchange of assets for voting stock followed by liquidation of the target corporation. The exchange is a taxable transaction for the shareholders to the extent that they receive assets other than stock in the acquiring corporation. The "Type C" reorganization is illustrated in Figure 7–4.

**EXAMPLE 15**

Acquiring Corporation transfers voting stock representing a 30% ownership interest to Target Corporation for substantially all of Target's assets. After the exchange, Target's only assets are cash and Acquiring voting stock. Target distributes the Acquiring stock and cash to its shareholders in exchange for their Target stock. The exchange qualifies as a "Type C" reorganization if Target liquidates after the distribution. The exchange is a taxable transaction for the shareholders to the extent that they received cash. ■

The "Type C" reorganization can also be carried out using a subsidiary. The stock exchanged for the target's assets may be that of the acquiring parent. Rather than using parent stock, the acquiring subsidiary's stock could be used. Either parent or subsidiary stock may be exchanged, but not both.[13] If stock of both the acquiring parent and the subsidiary is exchanged, the transaction will not qualify as a "Type C" reorganization.

**EXAMPLE 16**

Parent Corporation is in control of Acquiring Corporation. Acquiring holds stock in Parent. It transfers the Parent (voting) stock to Target Corporation for substantially all of Target's assets. Target is then liquidated. The transaction qualifies as a "Type C" reorganization. ■

---

[12]Distributions may be to creditors as well as to shareholders. § 368(a)(2)(G).

[13]Reg. § 1.368–2(d)(1).

■ **FIGURE 7–4**
"Type C" Reorganization

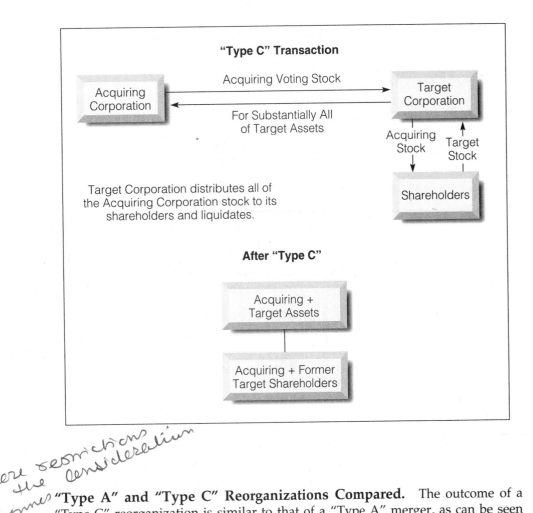

**"Type A" and "Type C" Reorganizations Compared.** The outcome of a "Type C" reorganization is similar to that of a "Type A" merger, as can be seen by comparing the diagrams for these reorganizations (Figure 7–4 versus Figure 7–1). However, their requirements differ. A "Type C" has more restrictions regarding the consideration that may be used by the acquiring corporation. Nevertheless, the "Type C" can be preferable to the "Type A," because in the "Type C" the acquiring corporation assumes only the liabilities of the target that it chooses. It normally is not liable for unknown or contingent liabilities. Further, in some states, only the approval of the shareholders in the target corporation is required in the "Type C" reorganization.

**Consideration in the "Type C" Reorganization.** The acquiring corporation's consideration in the "Type C" reorganization normally consists of voting stock. However, there are exceptions to this rule. Cash and other property do not destroy a "Type C" reorganization if at least 80 percent of the fair market value of the target's property is obtained with voting stock.

Although the acquiring corporation has more freedom in the consideration given in a "Type C" reorganization than in a "Type B," this freedom is not without a cost. When the acquiring corporation gives solely voting stock for the target corporation's assets, the target corporation's liabilities assumed by the acquiring corporation are not considered *other property* (i.e., boot) in the exchange. The transaction is an exchange of assets for voting stock, and the 80 percent-of-property requirement is met. However, liabilities assumed by the acquiring corporation *are* treated as *other property* if the target corporation receives any property other than voting stock in the reorganization. Liabilities assumed by the acquiring corporation are likely to exceed 20 percent of the fair market value of the assets acquired.

**EXAMPLE 17**

Target Corporation transfers assets with a fair market value of $200,000 to Acquiring Corporation for voting stock valued at $150,000 and assumption of $50,000 of liabilities. Target distributes the stock to its shareholders and liquidates. The transaction qualifies as a "Type C" reorganization. The liabilities are not treated as *other property* received. Acquiring obtained 100% of Target's assets for voting stock. The liabilities assumed by Acquiring are disregarded as boot when no consideration other than stock is given.

Suppose Target had transferred assets for Acquiring stock valued at $150,000, cash of $30,000, and the assumption of $20,000 of liabilities. The liabilities would be considered *other property* because Target also received cash. *Other property* amounts to $50,000, which exceeds 20% of the fair market value of Target's assets. The transaction does not qualify as a "Type C" reorganization.

Had Acquiring given Target voting stock worth $170,000 and cash of $30,000, the transaction would qualify as a "Type C" reorganization. No liabilities are assumed, and the *other property* transferred is less than 20% of the fair market value of the assets ($200,000). ■

According to Regulation § 1.368–2(d), the acquiring corporation's prior ownership of the target's stock will not prevent the "solely-for-voting-stock" requirement from being met in "Type C" reorganizations. This pronouncement reverses a long-standing position of the IRS. If the acquiring corporation purchased stock in the target corporation in a previously unrelated transaction, the previously acquired stock will not be considered in determining whether 80 percent of the target's assets were acquired with stock of the acquiring corporation.

**EXAMPLE 18**

Acquiring Corporation purchased 30% of Target Corporation stock five years ago. In the current year, Acquiring transfers voting stock to Target in exchange for all of its assets. This qualifies as a "Type C" reorganization. The previous purchase of Target stock is not considered to be part of the reorganization transaction. ■

**Asset Transfers.**   The "Type C" reorganization requires that substantially all of the assets of the target corporation be transferred to the acquiring corporation. However, there is no statutory definition of "substantially all." To obtain a favorable ruling from the IRS, assets representing at least 90 percent of the fair market value of the net assets and at least 70 percent of the fair market value of the gross assets held by the target corporation must be transferred.[14] Smaller percentages may still qualify. However, the parties must rely on their particular facts and circumstances to obtain a favorable decision.[15]

## TYPE D

The first three types of tax-free corporate reorganizations are designed for corporate combinations. The "Type D" reorganization is different; it is generally used to effect a corporate division, called a "divisive" reorganization. However, the "Type D" reorganization can also be used to carry out a corporate combination, called an "acquisitive" reorganization. "Type D" reorganizations also differ from the other

---

[14]Rev.Rul. 77–37, 1977–2 C.B. 568, amplified by Rev.Proc. 86–42, 1986–2 C.B. 722.

[15]Where 70% of the assets were transferred and 30% retained to discharge the liabilities of the target prior to liquidation, the IRS found that substantially all of the assets were transferred. Rev.Rul. 57–518, 1957–2 C.B. 253.

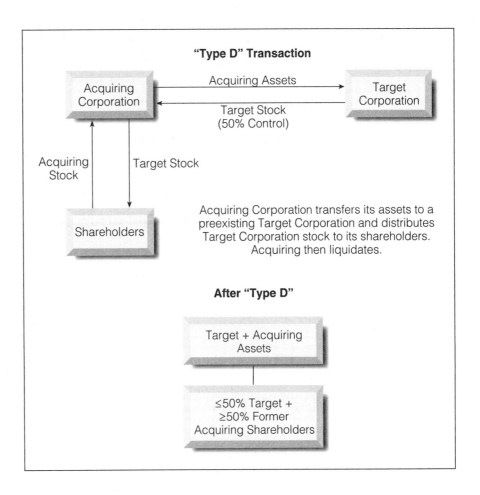

**■ FIGURE 7–5**
Acquisitive "Type D"
Reorganization

reorganizations in that the entity that transfers assets is the acquiring corporation rather than the target corporation.

**Acquisitive "Type D" Reorganization.**   If a combination meets the following requirements, it will be treated as a "Type D" reorganization.

- Substantially all of the property of the acquiring corporation must be transferred to the target corporation.
- The acquiring corporation must obtain control (50 percent) of the target.[16]
- Stock received by the acquiring corporation, as well as any remaining assets of the acquiring corporation, must be distributed to its shareholders.
- The acquiring corporation must liquidate.

This type of transaction may also meet the requirements of a "Type C" reorganization. If the reorganization can be classified as both a "Type C" and a "Type D" reorganization, it is treated as a "Type D" reorganization.[17] The "Type D" acquisitive reorganization is diagrammed in Figure 7–5.

---

[16]No attribution of ownership is allowed in determining whether there is 50% control. §§ 368(a)(2)(H) and 304(c).

[17]Reg. § 1.368–2(d)(3).

**EXAMPLE 19**

Acquiring Corporation wishes to obtain Target Corporation, but Target holds a nontransferable license. Thus, Target must be the surviving corporation. Acquiring transfers all its assets to Target for 70% of Target's stock. Acquiring then distributes all the Target stock to its shareholders and liquidates. The transaction qualifies as a "Type D" reorganization. ■

**Divisive "Type D" Reorganization.** Rather than combining, shareholders may wish to divide corporate assets and split the business of the corporation. This might occur for many reasons including antitrust problems, differences of opinion among the shareholders, product liability concerns, or family tax planning. The more typical divisive "Type D" reorganization allows shareholders to accomplish their goals without incurring tax. In a divisive reorganization, one or more new corporations are formed to receive part or all of the assets of the original corporation. In exchange for its assets, the original corporation must receive stock.

The remaining requirements for a divisive "Type D" reorganization are as follows.

- The stock received by the original corporation must constitute control (80 percent) of the new corporation(s).
- The stock of the new corporation(s) must be distributed to the shareholders of the original corporation.
- Both the assets transferred and those retained by the original corporation must represent active businesses that have been owned and conducted by the original corporation for at least five years before the transfer.
- The distributions of stock and securities to the shareholders cannot be principally a device for distributing the earnings and profits of either the original corporation or the controlled corporation.

**EXAMPLE 20**

Bell, Inc., has been engaged in manufacturing. It also owns investment securities. Bell transfers the investment securities to a newly formed corporation and distributes the stock of the new corporation to its shareholders. The transaction does not qualify as a "Type D" reorganization. Holding investment securities does not constitute a trade or business. The shareholders of Bell, Inc., are taxed on the receipt of the stock. ■

**EXAMPLE 21**

Jane and Ivan are the sole shareholders of WB Corporation. WB was organized 10 years ago and has been actively engaged in manufacturing two products, widgets and bolts. Considerable friction has developed between Jane and Ivan, who now wish to divide the business. Jane wants the assets used in manufacturing widgets, and Ivan wants to continue manufacturing bolts. The separation of the business assets can be accomplished tax-free using one of the divisive "Type D" reorganizations. ■

**EXAMPLE 22**

QVC, Inc., has manufactured a single product at two plants for the past 10 years. It transfers one plant and related activities to a new corporation. QVC then distributes the stock of the new corporation to its shareholders. The activities of each plant constitute a trade or business. The transaction qualifies as a "Type D" reorganization. ■

**Spin-Offs, Split-Offs, and Split-Ups.** There are three different types of divisive "Type D" reorganizations: spin-offs, split-offs, and split-ups.

- In a **spin-off**, a new corporation is formed to receive some of the assets of the original corporation in exchange for the new corporation's stock. The stock of the new corporation is distributed to the shareholders of the original stock. No stock of the original corporation is surrendered. The shareholders' basis in their original stock is allocated between the original and the new stock based on the relative fair market value of each.

- A **split-off** resembles a spin-off except that in a split-off the shareholders surrender stock of the original corporation in exchange for stock in the new corporation. Stock basis is computed in the same manner as for a spin-off.
- In a **split-up**, two or more corporations are formed to receive substantially all of the assets of the original corporation. The stock of the new corporation is distributed to the shareholders of the original corporation in exchange for their original stock. The original corporation is then liquidated. The shareholders' basis in the relinquished original stock carries over as the basis of the new stock.

The spin-off and split-off are illustrated in Figure 7–6, and the split-up is illustrated in Figure 7–7.

**EXAMPLE 23**

Shawnee purchased 10% (500 shares) of OriginalCo eight years ago for $60,000. Before a spin-off reorganization, the total value of OriginalCo stock is $900,000, and Shawnee's stock is valued at $90,000. OriginalCo spins off 30% of its business assets into NewCo (fair market value $270,000) and distributes 10,000 shares of stock to its shareholders. Shawnee's 1,000 shares of NewCo have a $27,000 value. After the spin-off, the value of OriginalCo is reduced to $630,000, and the value of Shawnee's stock in OriginalCo, therefore, is $63,000. Shawnee's $60,000 beginning basis in OriginalCo is allocated to the two companies' stock as follows: $18,000 to NewCo stock [$60,000 × ($27,000/$90,000)] and $42,000 to OriginalCo stock [$60,000 × ($63,000/$90,000)]. ■

**EXAMPLE 24**

Assume the same facts as in Example 23, except that OriginalCo creates NewCo through a split-off. Shawnee is required to surrender 150 shares of OriginalCo to receive the 1,000 shares of NewCo. The fair market value of Shawnee's OriginalCo stock is now $63,000 [($90,000 ÷ 500) × (500 − 150)], and the value of the NewCo stock is $27,000 ($90,000 − $63,000). Shawnee's $60,000 beginning basis in OriginalCo is allocated to the two companies' stock as follows: $42,000 to OriginalCo stock [$60,000 × ($63,000/$90,000)] and $18,000 to NewCo stock [$60,000 × ($27,000/$90,000)]. ■

**EXAMPLE 25**

Gail and Gary are the sole shareholders of Publishers Corporation. Publishers was organized six years ago and has been actively engaged in publishing both books and periodicals. Because of antitrust problems, Publishers wishes to divide its business. Two new corporations are formed, Books and Periodicals. All the assets relating to the book publishing business are transferred to Books. All assets relating to the publishing of periodicals are transferred to Periodicals. Gail exchanges all her stock in Publishers for the stock in Books. Gary exchanges all his stock in Publishers for the stock in Periodicals. Publishers is liquidated. The transaction qualifies as a "Type D" reorganization split-up. Neither Gail nor Gary recognizes gain on the exchange. Gail's basis in her stock in Publishers becomes the basis for her stock in Books. Gary's basis in his stock in Publishers becomes his basis for his stock in Periodicals. ■

## TYPE E

The "Type E" reorganization is a **recapitalization**—a major change in the character and amount of outstanding capital stock, securities, or paid-in capital of a corporation. The transaction is significant only for the stock- or bondholders who exchange their equity or securities. The corporation itself exchanges no property. The "Type E" reorganization has no tax implications for the corporation, because it does not receive property. Further, transactions in a corporation's own stock or bonds are not taxable events.[18]

---

[18]Reg. §§ 1.1032–1(a) and (c).

■ **FIGURE 7–6**
"Type D" Reorganizations:
Spin-Off and Split-Off

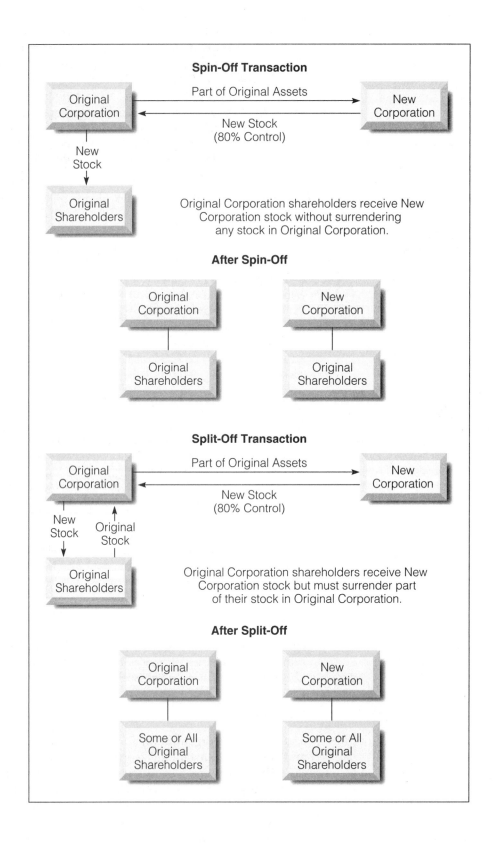

**■ FIGURE 7–7**
"Type D" Reorganization:
Split-Up

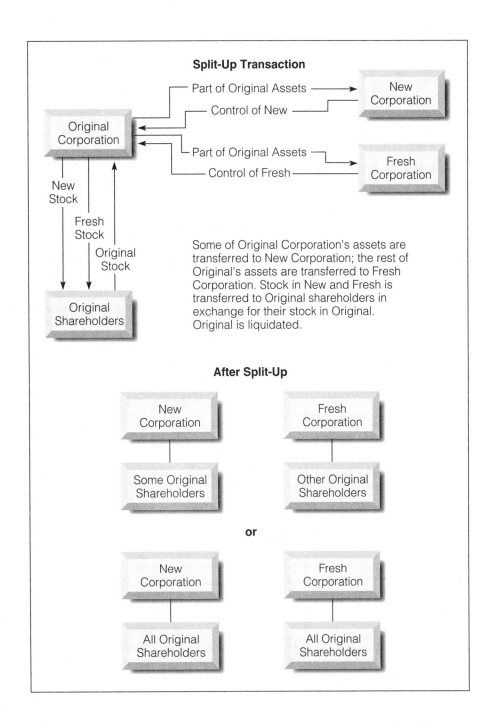

**Split-Up Transaction**

Some of Original Corporation's assets are transferred to New Corporation; the rest of Original's assets are transferred to Fresh Corporation. Stock in New and Fresh is transferred to Original shareholders in exchange for their stock in Original. Original is liquidated.

**After Split-Up**

The following types of exchanges qualify for nonrecognition treatment as a "Type E" reorganization: bonds for stock, stock for stock, and bonds for bonds. A corporation can exchange its common stock for preferred stock or its preferred stock for common stock tax-free. The exchange of bonds for other bonds is tax-free when the principal amount of the debt surrendered is not less than that of the debt received.

**EXAMPLE 26**   Half of the stock in Blue Corporation is owned by Wade and half by his children, Mark and Marcia. Wade wishes to retire and relinquish control of the corporation. He exchanges

## MERGER AND ACQUISITION DOWNTURN HITS THE INVESTMENT BANKERS HARD

The number of mergers and acquisitions (M & A) in the United States has declined significantly from its all-time high in 2000 when more than 11,000 $1 million mergers occurred. The decrease is worldwide. Global M & A activity reached a five-year low in 2002, falling behind the 1997 volume and down by more than 50 percent from the 2001 dollar amounts. Every area of the world is feeling the effects of the slower global economy. For example, in 2002 M & A activity was down by almost 50 percent in Western Europe, by one-third in Australia, by 40 percent in Canada, and by more than 70 percent in Asia.

The decline in M & A business is hitting the investment banking industry hard. Fees for M & A services are down by more than 20 percent on average and by as much as 40 percent in some countries. Competition for merger fees is also heating up with several banks bidding for merger work. During the boom years, these "beauty contests" were uncommon, as bankers relied on their client relationships to secure contracts for merger services. There seemed to be enough M & A work for all the bankers. Now investment bankers are losing their jobs by the thousands, and the corporate clients feel that they are in the driver's seat. Accordingly, clients are being more aggressive in fee negotiations and are pressing their advantage in this excessively competitive market. The M & A industry is hoping for a turnaround to the record deals of 2000. Unfortunately, the return of the "good old days" may be a long time coming.

his common voting stock for nonvoting preferred stock. The exchange qualifies as a "Type E" reorganization. However, any difference in value between stock received and stock surrendered could be treated as compensation or as a gift. ∎

## TYPE F

The "Type F" reorganization is "a mere change in identity, form, or place of organization . . . however effected." Since a "Type F" reorganization is restricted to a single operating corporation, the successor corporation is the same corporation as its predecessor. Consequently, the tax characteristics of the predecessor carry over to the successor. A "Type F" reorganization does not jeopardize the status of § 1244 stock, nor will it terminate a valid S corporation election. The IRS has ruled that if a reorganization could qualify as a "Type A," "Type C," or "Type D" reorganization as well as a "Type F" reorganization, "Type F" reorganization treatment prevails.[19]

**EXAMPLE 27**

Dianithus Corporation changes its name to Rose Corporation. This is a "Type F" reorganization. ∎

**EXAMPLE 28**

Orchard Corporation is organized as a Subchapter S corporation. Its shareholders wish to revoke its S election. Changing from an S corporation to a regular C corporation qualifies as a "Type F" reorganization. ∎

---

[19]Rev.Rul. 57–276, 1957–1 C.B. 126.

**TAX IN THE NEWS**

## "TYPE G" REORGANIZATIONS DEVASTATE EMPLOYEE RETIREMENT PLANS

Over the last two years, more and more companies have filed for protection under the Chapter 11 bankruptcy rules ("Type G" reorganizations). The dollar amounts involved are staggering—the total assets of these companies exceed $525 billion. The largest failure was WorldCom at $103.9 billion with Enron a distant second at $63.4 billion.

Not only do shareholders, bondholders, and creditors lose in a bankruptcy, but so do employees, especially those whose pension plans are heavily invested in the company's stock. Employees of other companies whose pension plans invested in these bankrupt companies are also on the long list of losers. Both Enron and WorldCom had more than 50 percent of their pension assets invested in their own stock. According to the employees, management strongly encouraged them to invest their retirement contributions in the company's stock. Most employees chose to follow management's advice. WorldCom and Enron also matched their employees' contributions using their own stock, thereby exacerbating the concentration problem. Having the majority of a pension plan's assets in company stock is not unusual, however. The plans of General Electric and Coca-Cola, among others, have more than 75 percent of their assets in company stock. WorldCom maintains that it is not liable for its employees' losses. Pointing out that employees had 17 other options for investing their retirement contributions, WorldCom contends that the losses are due to the employees' unwillingness to diversify their retirement holdings, rather than the fault of the company.

SOURCES: Adapted from articles by Julie Earle in *The Financial Times Limited*, July 16, 2002, and July 22, 2002.

### TYPE G

Bankruptcy legislation introduced the "Type G" reorganization. In this type of reorganization, all or a part of the assets of a debtor corporation are transferred to an acquiring corporation in a bankruptcy or similar proceeding of a Federal or state court. The debtor corporation's creditors must receive voting stock of the acquiring corporation in exchange for debt representing 80 percent or more of the total fair market value of the debtor corporation's liabilities. Since a "Type G" reorganization must proceed according to a plan approved under a bankruptcy proceeding, planning for its use is limited.

A summary of the advantages and disadvantages of the various corporate reorganizations described in this chapter is found in Concept Summary 7–4.

**LO.4**

Delineate the judicial and administrative conditions for a nontaxable corporate reorganization.

# Judicial Doctrines

Besides the statutory requirements for reorganizations, several judicially created doctrines have become basic requirements for tax-free reorganizations. These doctrines include the sound business purpose, continuity of interest, and continuity of business enterprise doctrines. The courts have also formulated the step transaction doctrine to determine the tax status of a reorganization occurring through a series

NCEPT SUMMARY 7–4

# Corporate Reorganizations

| Reorganization | Type | Advantages | Disadvantages |
|---|---|---|---|
| A | Merger or consolidation | • No requirement that consideration be voting stock. As much as 50% of consideration can be cash and property without tax consequences for the stock received (cash and other property received *are* taxed). | • All liabilities of target corporation are assumed by acquiring corporation as a matter of law.<br>• Since state law must be followed, acquiring approval of majority shareholders, dealing with dissenters' rights, and holding required shareholder meetings may present problems. |
| | Subsidiary "A" | • As parent is majority stockholder, problem of securing approval of majority shareholders of both corporations is lessened.<br>• Subsidiary, rather than parent, assumes liabilities of target corporation. | |
| B | Stock-for-stock exchange | • Stock may be acquired from shareholders.<br>• Procedures to effect reorganization are not complex. | • *Only* voting stock of acquiring corporation may be used.<br>• Must have 80% control of a target corporation.<br>• May have minority interest remaining in target corporation. |
| C | Assets-for-stock exchange | • Less complex as to state law than "Type A."<br>• Cash or property can be used as consideration for 20% or less of fair market value of property transferred.<br>• Acquiring corporation assumes only the liabilities of the target it chooses. | • *Substantially all* assets of target corporation must be transferred.<br>• Liabilities count as *other property* for 20% rule if any consideration other than stock and liabilities is used.<br>• The target corporation must distribute the stock, securities, and other properties it receives in the reorganization to its shareholders. |
| D | Corporate division: spin-off, split-off, split-up | • Permits corporate division without tax consequences if no *boot* is involved. | |
| | Acquisitive | • Allows smaller target corporation to retain its existence. | |
| E | Recapitalization | • Allows for major change in makeup of shareholders' equity. | |
| F | Change in identity, form, or place of organization | • Survivor is treated as same entity as predecessor; thus, tax attributes of predecessor can be carried back as well as forward. | |
| G | Court-approved reorganization of debtor corporation | • Creditors can exchange notes for stock tax-free.<br>• State merger laws need not be followed. | • Planning for use is limited. |

of related transactions. In addition, a plan of reorganization that is consistent with one of the Code reorganizations is required.[20]

## SOUND BUSINESS PURPOSE

Even if the statutory requirements of a reorganization have been literally followed, a transaction will not be tax-free unless it exhibits a **business purpose.**[21] The business purpose requirement is meant to limit nonrecognition treatment to transactions that are motivated, at least in part, by the valid needs of the corporations. The transaction must have economic consequences germane to the businesses that go beyond the mere avoidance of Federal taxes. Avoidance of taxes is not, by itself, considered a business purpose. However, the absence of a tax avoidance motive does not establish that there was the requisite business purpose.[22]

Given that a business purpose is required for a reorganization, whose business purpose must it be—the corporation's or the shareholders'? The Regulations indicate that the corporation's business purpose should be paramount.[23] However, the courts have considered the purposes of both the corporation and the shareholders, because it is sometimes impossible to distinguish between the corporate and shareholder business purposes.[24]

Cases indicate that the business purpose doctrine does not operate in reverse. It is normally the IRS agent who asserts lack of business purpose to deny tax-free status to a corporate reorganization. Occasionally, however, the taxpayer may want the transaction to be taxable in order to step up the basis in the assets or to recognize a loss. Taxpayers have attempted to employ the business purpose doctrine to prevent the transaction from being considered a reorganization. In those instances, however, the courts have required the taxpayers to abide by the form of the transaction and have agreed with the IRS that a reorganization was involved.[25]

## CONTINUITY OF INTEREST

The *continuity of interest* requirement prevents transactions that appear to be sales from qualifying as nontaxable reorganizations. Thus, the continuity of interest test provides that if a shareholder has substantially the same investment after the restructuring as before, the transaction is not a taxable event. To qualify for tax-favored reorganization status, the target corporation shareholders must receive an equity interest in the acquiring corporation.[26]

The Regulations deem the continuity of interest test to be met when the shareholders of the target corporation receive acquiring corporation stock equal to at least 50 percent of their prior stock ownership in the target.[27] Not all shareholders of the target corporation need to receive stock in the surviving corporation. The

[20]Reg. § 1.368–1(c) and *William Hewitt*, 19 B.T.A. 771 (1930). For a definition of a plan of reorganization, see Reg. § 1.368–2(g).

[21]Reg. §§ 1.368–1(c) and 1.355–2. See also *Gregory v. Helvering*, 35–1 USTC ¶9043, 14 AFTR 1191, 55 S.Ct. 266 (USSC, 1935). The doctrine as developed in the *Gregory* case became a precedent for all transactions that might be shams devised merely for tax avoidance purposes. It brought about the principle of substance over form. All business transactions must have a sound business purpose.

[22]Reg. § 1.355–2(b) and *Marnes Wilson*, 66–1 USTC ¶9103, 16 AFTR2d 6030, 353 F.2d 184 (CA–9, 1966).

[23]Reg. § 1.355–2.

[24]*Lewis Trustee v. Comm.*, 49–2 USTC ¶9377, 38 AFTR 377, 176 F.2d 646 (CA–1, 1949); *Estate of Parshelsky v. Comm.*, 62–1 USTC ¶9460, 9 AFTR2d 1382, 303 F.2d 14 (CA–2, 1962).

[25]*Survaunt v. Comm.*, 47–2 USTC ¶9344, 35 AFTR 1557, 162 F.2d 753 (CA–8, 1947).

[26]*Pinellas Ice & Cold Storage v. Comm.*, 3 USTC ¶1023, 11 AFTR 1112, 53 S.Ct. 257 (USSC, 1933), and *LeTulle v. Scofield*, 40–1 USTC ¶9150, 23 AFTR 789, 60 S.Ct. 313 (USSC, 1940). In *LeTulle*, a corporation transferred all its assets to another corporation for cash and bonds. The Court held that the transaction was not a tax-free reorganization if the transferor's only retained interest was that of a creditor. This concept is now in Reg. §§ 1.368–1(b) and (c).

[27]Reg. § 1.368–1(e)(6).

requirement is applied to the aggregate consideration given by the acquiring corporation.

**EXAMPLE 29**

Target Corporation merges into Acquiring Corporation pursuant to state statutes. Under the merger plan, Target's shareholders can elect to receive either cash or stock in Acquiring. The shareholders who hold 40% of Target's outstanding stock elect to receive cash; the remaining 60% of the shareholders elect to receive Acquiring stock. This plan satisfies the continuity of interest test. The shareholders receiving cash are taxed on the transaction. Those receiving stock are not. ◼

**EXAMPLE 30**

Juanita owns 100% of the stock of Target Corporation. Target merges into Acquiring Corporation. Juanita receives 1% of Acquiring's outstanding stock in exchange for all of her stock in Target. The continuity of interest test is met; Juanita received only stock for her interest. ◼

If the continuity of interest requirement is met at the time of the reorganization, a sale of stock to an unrelated party immediately before or after the restructuring will not destroy the continuity of interest. Unrelated parties include individuals, noncorporate entities, and corporations that are not part of either the acquirer's or the target's affiliated group.[28]

**EXAMPLE 31**

Pursuant to a preexisting contract, Juanita, in Example 30, sells all her stock in Acquiring Corporation to Ying for its fair market value. This sale occurs one week after the reorganization. Since Ying is not considered a party related to Juanita, the sale to Ying does not affect the continuity of interest test. Continuity of interest is determined at the time of the reorganization, and subsequent (or preceding) transactions between unrelated parties are disregarded. ◼

## CONTINUITY OF BUSINESS ENTERPRISE

The **continuity of business enterprise** test ensures that tax-free reorganization treatment is limited to situations where there is a continuing interest in the target's business. Specifically, this test requires the acquiring corporation to either (1) continue the target corporation's historic business or (2) use a significant portion of the target corporation's assets in business. The acquiring corporation's continuation of one of the target corporation's significant lines of business satisfies the continuity of business requirement. The use of a "significant" portion of the assets test is based on the relative importance of the assets to the target's former business or their net fair market value.[29] Whether these requirements are met depends on the facts of each case.

## STEP TRANSACTION

The **step transaction** doctrine ensures that taxpayers cannot engage in a series of transactions for the purpose of obtaining tax benefits that would not be allowed if the transaction was accomplished in a single step. When the steps are so interdependent that the accomplishment of one step would be fruitless without the completion of the series of steps, the transactions are collapsed into a single step.[30]

---

[28]Reg. § 1.368–1(e)(3).
[29]Reg. § 1.368–1(d).
[30]*American Bantam Car Co.,* 11 T.C. 397 (1948), *aff'd* in 49–2 USTC ¶9471, 38 AFTR 820, 177 F.2d 513 (CA–3, 1949), *cert. den.* 70 S.Ct.

622 (USSC, 1950). If the steps have independent economic significance, the doctrine does not apply. See *Esmark, Inc.,* 90 T.C. 171 (1988) and Rev.Rul. 79–250, 1979–2 C.B. 156.

The step transaction doctrine presents problems for reorganizations when the acquiring corporation does not want all of the assets of the target. For "Type C," acquisitive "Type D," and subsidiary "Type A" reorganizations, the target (acquirer for "Type D") is required to transfer substantially all of its assets to the acquiring (target for "Type D") corporation. If the target corporation attempts to dispose of its unwanted assets before a reorganization, the doctrine could ruin the tax-favored status of the reorganization because the acquiring corporation has failed to acquire substantially all of the target corporation's assets. Without direct evidence to the contrary, the IRS generally views any transactions occurring within one year of a reorganization as part of the restructuring.[31]

**LO.5**

Apply the rules pertaining to the carryover of tax attributes in a corporate reorganization.

# Carryover of Corporate Tax Attributes

Some tax features of the target corporation (the carryover of losses, tax credits, and E & P deficits) are welcomed by the successor corporation. Others may prove less desirable (positive E & P and assumption of liabilities). The mandatory carryover rules should be carefully considered in every corporate acquisition; they may, in fact, determine the form of the acquisition.

## ASSUMPTION OF LIABILITIES

Since a corporate reorganization must result in some continuation of the business activities of the previous corporations, existing liabilities seldom are liquidated (a "Type G" reorganization is the exception). The acquiring corporation either assumes the liabilities of the target corporation or takes the target's property subject to its liabilities. These liabilities are not considered boot when determining gain recognition by the corporations that are parties to the restructuring. Generally, liabilities are problematic only in the "Type C" reorganization, when the acquiring corporation transfers other property to the target as well as stock. In this situation, the liabilities can cause a violation of the 80 percent-of-property-for-voting-stock requirement.

## ALLOWANCE OF CARRYOVERS

Section 381 determines which tax benefits of the target corporation can be carried over to the successor in certain tax-free reorganizations. When a corporation acquires the assets of a target corporation, the target's tax attributes are also acquired. This occurs in the "Type A," "Type C," acquisitive "Type D," "Type F," and "Type G" reorganizations. The "Type B," divisive "Type D," and "Type E" reorganizations do not fall under the carryover rules of § 381. In a "Type B" reorganization, the target corporation merely becomes a subsidiary. The corporation remains intact and its tax attributes are retained. With the spin-off and split-off "Type D" divisions, the old distributing corporation retains its tax attributes, and the new corporation starts fresh with regard to its tax attributes (with the exception of E & P). A split-up division, on the other hand, causes the tax attributes of the distributing corporation to disappear when it liquidates. Like a "Type B" reorganization, the "Type E" involves exchanges of stock between the corporation and shareholders, with no

---

[31]Reg. § 1.368–2(c), but in Rev.Rul. 69–48, 1969–1 C.B. 106, the IRS applied the step transaction doctrine to transactions that were 22 months apart.

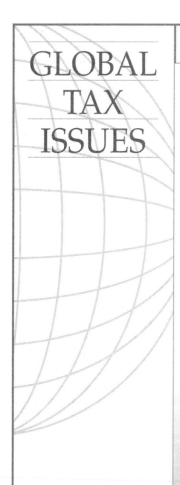

## GLOBAL TAX ISSUES

### EUROPE MOVES TOWARD U.S.-STYLE DISCLOSURES

The European Union (EU) has more than 20 stock exchanges and even more regulating bodies issuing different requirements for financial disclosures. For example, some countries, such as Germany, allow corporations to release earnings information only twice a year. Others, such as the United Kingdom, require quarterly reporting. As another example, if a French company wants to acquire a U.K.-listed corporation, the British rules apply. However, if a U.K. company is merging with a French corporation, the French regulations must be met. Such inconsistencies are difficult to manage and are frustrating the European security markets.

Many of the major European financial players would like to have a single set of rules covering disclosure, trading, and takeovers and a single regulating body overseeing these rules. However, a report issued recently by the so-called Committee of Wise Men—a committee of influential individuals in the securities industry selected by the European finance ministers—indicates that a single regulating agency like the U.S. Securities and Exchange Commission is not in the near future for Europe. Even if all the countries could agree on such a body, the treaty governing the EU would have to be amended to create it—a process that would take a minimum of four years.

Meanwhile, some progress is being made. The EU is considering the use of electronic disclosures, and it has proposed requiring public companies to issue quarterly reports and follow U.S.-style disclosure rules. These changes would consolidate all disclosure requirements and upgrade regular reporting requirements. Current European reporting does not meet U.S. standards, so the dissemination of financial statements in the United States is limited. Ultimately, the market will drive the changes needed for global reporting standards. As the desires to access cross-border capital increase, the private sector will demand a universal system of providing the information needed to assess the value of a firm.

change in the corporation's assets. Since only one corporation is involved in the "Type E" reorganization, it retains its tax attributes.

### NET OPERATING LOSS CARRYOVERS

A net operating loss (NOL) of a target corporation is one of the beneficial tax attributes that may be carried forward to the acquiring corporation. The NOL cannot be carried back to a prior acquiring corporation tax year; it can only be used prospectively. An NOL is a valuable asset of the target because it can offset future income of the combined successor corporation.

**EXAMPLE 32**

Target Corporation has an NOL of $3 million. Acquiring Corporation averages taxable income of $5 million. It expects about the same amount of taxable income in future years. Acquiring undoubtedly will incur a large tax liability in the future years unless it can use Target's NOL. Upon merging, Target's $3 million NOL carries over to offset Acquiring's taxable income of $5 million, reducing it to $2 million. Acquiring will save approximately $1,020,000 in tax liability [$3 million (reduction in taxable income) × 34%)]. ∎

**Ownership Changes.**  Due to the beneficial nature of NOLs, § 382 limits the amount of NOL that can be utilized each year by the successor corporation. The **§ 382 limitation** applies when there has been an ownership change for the target's (loss corporation's) common shareholders of more than 50 percentage points (by value). An **ownership change** occurs on the day (called the *change date*) when there is either an *equity structure shift* or an *owner shift* in the stockholders' holdings.

- An **equity structure shift** occurs when a tax-free reorganization causes an owner shift. The change date for an equity shift is the date the reorganization takes place. The equity shift limitation is not applicable to "Type F," divisive "Type D," or "Type G" reorganizations.
- An **owner shift** is any change in the common stock ownership involving a 5 percent shareholder. Owner shifts can be caused by purchases, issuances of corporate stock, redemptions, recapitalizations, and transfers to controlled corporations. Ownership changes caused by transfers of stock to a spouse or trust, or due to gifts, death, divorce, or separation, are not considered owner shifts.[32]

Whether an ownership change has occurred is determined by examining the common stock ownership during a testing period, generally the prior three years.[33] Shareholders owning less than a 5 percent interest during the testing period are aggregated and treated as one shareholder for determining ownership changes. Thus, transfers between shareholders who own less than 5 percent do not influence the percentage-point ownership change computation.

**EXAMPLE 33**

Target Corporation is merged into Acquiring Corporation in a "Type A" reorganization. At the time of the merger, Target had an NOL of $100,000. Pursuant to the merger, Target's shareholders, none of whom owns a 5% interest, receive 40% of the stock of Acquiring. An equity structure shift has taken place. Since all of Target's shareholders owned less than 5%, they are aggregated in determining the owner shift. Therefore, they owned 100% of the loss corporation prior to the reorganization and only 40% of the successor corporation after the reorganization. More than a 50-percentage-point change in ownership has occurred. ■

When an ownership change has occurred, the yearly amount of NOL available to the successor corporation is limited to the value of the target loss corporation multiplied by the **long-term tax-exempt rate** (the highest adjusted Federal long-term rate for the prior three-month period). The value of the loss corporation is the fair market value of the stock (both common and preferred) immediately before the ownership change occurs.[34] The value of stock received or the price paid for the loss corporation's stock generally indicates the fair market value of the stock. Since the § 382 limitation is based on the value of the loss corporation, there is an incentive to inflate its value prior to the ownership change. This could be accomplished through capital contributions. The so-called anti-stuffing rules prohibit this behavior by disregarding assets contributed within the two years prior to the change date.

**EXAMPLE 34**

Winner Corporation acquires Loser Corporation when Loser has a $250,000 NOL carryforward. Winner exchanges 30% of its stock valued at $600,000 for all of Loser's stock. The applicable long-term tax-exempt rate at the time of the reorganization is 10%. Several months before the acquisition by Winner, the shareholders of Loser contributed investment assets with a fair market value of $100,000, thus increasing the value of Loser from $500,000 to

---

[32]Temp.Reg. § 1.382-2T(a) and (e).
[33]The testing period is the period following the most recent ownership change if that change occurred within the past three years. Further, the testing period cannot begin before the year in which the carryforward being tested occurs. See § 382(i).

[34]The determination of value occurs immediately *after* the ownership change in the case of redemptions or other contractions that are associated with the ownership change.

$600,000. The § 382 limitation computation will not include the recent increase in Loser's fair market value. Consequently, the yearly § 382 limitation is $50,000 ($500,000 × 10%). ∎

Any authorized current-year NOL deduction that is not utilized, because current taxable income is insufficient to offset the loss, may be carried forward and added to the next year's § 382 limitation.

The objective of the *§ 382 limitation* is to restrict the benefit of NOLs to a hypothetical future income stream of the loss corporation. The possible income is measured by the yield that could have been received if the stock had been sold and the proceeds invested in long-term tax-exempt securities. Section 382 does not disallow an NOL. It merely limits the amount of NOL carryover that the surviving corporation can utilize on an annual basis.

A further limitation on the ability to utilize the NOL carryforward arises in the year that the ownership change occurs (change year). The amount of NOL available to the successor corporation in the change year is limited to the percentage of days remaining in the tax year after the change day. The amount of the § 382 yearly NOL limitation is multiplied by this percentage.

Lastly, the NOL carryover is disallowed for future taxable years if the surviving corporation fails to satisfy the continuity of business enterprise requirement for at least two years following any ownership equity shift. The continuity of business enterprise test is the same as for tax-free reorganizations. That is, the significant historical line of the loss corporation's business must be continued, or the successor corporation must use a significant amount of the loss corporation's assets in its business.

**EXAMPLE 35**

On December 1, Minus transfers all of its assets to Plus (a calendar year corporation) in exchange for 40% of Plus's stock. At the time of the merger, Minus is valued at $900,000 and has an NOL carryover of $500,000. The long-term tax-exempt rate is 10%. Since there has been an ownership change of more than 50 percentage points for Minus's shareholders, the amount of NOL available for use in the merger year is $7,397 [$900,000 × 10% = $90,000 × (30/365)]. The NOL available to reduce Plus's taxable income in the next year is $90,000. If Plus fails to continue Minus's historical business or use substantially all of its assets for a two-year period, Plus is not allowed to use any of Minus's NOL. ∎

## EARNINGS AND PROFITS

The E & P of an acquired corporation carries over to a successor corporation.[35] However, the Supreme Court later held that a successor corporation was not permitted to apply a deficit in the acquired corporation's E & P against its own E & P.[36] The result was confusion in applying these general rules. Earnings and profits of a deficit corporation are now deemed to have been received by the acquiring corporation as of the change date. A deficit may be used only to offset E & P accumulated by the successor corporation after the change date.[37]

Consequently, the successor corporation must maintain two separate E & P accounts after the change date: one account contains the prior accumulated E & P as of the change date, and the other contains the deficit transferred and E & P accumulated since the change date. The deficit in the post-transfer account may not be used to reduce accumulated E & P in the pre-transfer account.

---

[35]*Comm. v. Sansome*, 3 USTC ¶978, 11 AFTR 854, 60 F.2d 931 (CA–2, 1931), *cert. den.* 53 S.Ct. 291 (USSC, 1932).

[36]*Comm. v. Phipps*, 49–1 USTC ¶9204, 37 AFTR 827, 69 S.Ct. 616 (USSC, 1949).

[37]§ 381(c)(2) and Reg. § 1.381(c)(2)–1(a)(5).

**EXAMPLE 36**

Target Corporation is merged into Acquiring Corporation on December 31, 2003. On that date, the E & P balance for Target is a negative $75,000, and for Acquiring it is a positive $400,000. In 2004, the current E & P for Acquiring is $50,000. Acquiring now has two E & P balances: pre-2004 $400,000 and post-2003 negative $25,000 ($50,000 − $75,000). ■

## OTHER CARRYOVERS

The benefits to the successor corporation of capital losses and excess tax credits carried over from a target loss corporation are also limited when there has been an ownership change.[38] The capital loss carryovers are characterized as short term when carried to the successor corporation. These losses are taken before the NOL carryovers in applying the § 382 limitation. Computing the amount of excess credits allowable in the current year is more complicated than determining the capital loss or NOL carryover, as the steps below indicate.

- First, the amount of the regular tax liability after allowable losses must be calculated.
- Next, the regular tax liability is computed as if the full § 382 limitation were deducted.
- Lastly, the latter tax liability is subtracted from the former to determine the § 382 limitation remaining for excess credits.

**EXAMPLE 37**

Two years ago, Loss Corporation was acquired by Gain Corporation in a transaction causing an ownership change. The § 382 limitation is calculated as $100,000 for the current year. Gain Corporation's taxable income before considering carryovers is $500,000. The Loss Corporation carryovers to the current year include a capital loss of $20,000, an NOL of 60,000, and excess business credits of $30,000. The capital loss is utilized first to offset taxable income, and then the NOL is used. Taxable income becomes $420,000 ($500,000 − $20,000 − $60,000), and the tax on this amount would be $142,800 ($420,000 × 34%). If the full § 382 limitation were utilized, taxable income would be $400,000 ($500,000 − $100,000), and the tax would be $136,000. Therefore, the amount of excess business credit allowable in the current year is $6,800 ($142,800 − $136,000). ■

The benefit from all loss corporation carryovers taken in the current year cannot, in total, exceed the calculated yearly § 382 limitation. When a corporation has several types of carryovers, the sequence in which the loss corporation carryovers are applied to the § 382 limitation is as follows.

1. Built-in capital losses.
2. Capital loss carryovers.
3. Built-in ordinary losses.
4. NOL carryovers.
5. Foreign tax credits.
6. Business credit carryovers.
7. Minimum tax credit carryovers.[39]

Besides the § 382 limitation, the year-of-transfer limitation applies to all of these carryovers.

Numerous other carryover items also fall under the carryover rules of § 381. For example, the successor corporation determines depreciation on acquired assets

---

[38]§ 383.

[39]Reg. § 1.383–1(d).

## CONCEPT SUMMARY 7–5

### Summary of Carryover Rules

Tax attributes that carry over from a loss corporation to the successor corporation:

1. Loss carryovers—subject to the § 382 limitation.
    A. Annual limitations on use of carryovers are evoked when there is an ownership change—a more than 50-percentage-point owner shift or an equity structure shift.
       • Owner shift is a change in the ownership of shareholders owning 5% or more of the corporate stock.
       • Equity shift occurs in tax-free reorganizations, other than a divisive "Type D," a "Type F," or a "Type G."
    B. Annual carryover usage cannot exceed the value of the old loss corporation on the change date (date of transfer) multiplied by the highest long-term Federal rate for the three calendar months prior to the structure change.
    C. Year of transfer. The loss claimed in the year of transfer is limited to the annual limitation multiplied by a percentage representing the remaining days in the year of transfer.
    D. Loss corporation carryovers are applied to the § 382 limitation in this order: built-in capital losses, capital loss carryovers, built-in ordinary losses, NOL carryovers, foreign tax credits, business credit carryovers, and lastly minimum tax credit carryovers.
2. Earnings and profits.
    A. Positive E & P of an acquired corporation carries over.
    B. If either corporation has a deficit in E & P, the surviving corporation will have two E & P accounts. One account contains the total positive accumulated E & P as of the date of the transfer. The other contains the total deficit as of the date of the transfer. Future positive E & P may offset the deficit E & P account.
3. Other tax attributes.
    A. Depreciation and cost recovery methods carry over.
    B. The installment method of reporting carries over.

in the same manner as did the predecessor corporation. Should installment obligations pass to the acquiring corporation in a reorganization, the acquiring corporation reports the income from the obligations on the installment method.

### DISALLOWANCE OF CARRYOVERS

Irrespective of the carryover rules, the IRS can utilize § 269 to disallow the carryover of tax benefits if a tax avoidance scheme is apparent. Such items are disallowed when a corporation acquires property of another corporation primarily to evade or avoid Federal income tax by securing the benefit of a deduction, credit, or other allowance that the acquiring corporation would not otherwise enjoy. Whether the principal purpose is the evasion or avoidance of taxes becomes a question of fact. If the business of the loss corporation is promptly discontinued after a corporate reorganization, the IRS may use § 269 in an attempt to disallow the loss carryover.

### THE ROLE OF THE LETTER RULING

When feasible, the parties contemplating a corporate reorganization should apply for and obtain from the IRS a letter ruling concerning the income tax effect of the transaction(s). Assuming the parties carry out the transfers as proposed in the ruling request, a favorable ruling provides, in effect, an insurance policy. If the tax implications are significant, as they often are with corporate reorganizations, the advantage of obtaining prior IRS approval is clear.

## LO.6

Structure corporate reorganizations to obtain the desired tax consequences.

**Tax Planning Considerations**

## ASSESSING THE POSSIBLE BENEFITS OF RESTRUCTURING OPTIONS

Corporate reorganizations are valuable tools in the tax-free restructuring of corporations. However, it may not be possible to achieve the desired corporate structure by utilizing a single type of reorganization. For this reason, reorganizations should not be seen as mutually exclusive transactions; they can be combined with other tax-favored transactions into a comprehensive plan. The tax law allows a series of reorganizations to be recognized when the statutory requirements for each are met.

**EXAMPLE 38**

Black Corporation operates two businesses, both of which have been in existence for five years. One business is a manufacturing operation; the other is a wholesale distributorship. White Corporation wishes to acquire only the manufacturing business and refuses to purchase all of Black's assets. ■

What course of action might be advisable to transfer the manufacturing operation from Black to White with the least, if any, tax costs? Compare the following three possibilities.

1. Black Corporation transfers the manufacturing operation to White Corporation in return for some of the latter's stock.
2. Black Corporation forms Orange Corporation and transfers the wholesale distributorship to it in return for all of Orange's stock. The Orange stock is then distributed to Black's shareholders. This portion of the arrangement is a nontaxable spin-off. Black now transfers the manufacturing operation to White Corporation in exchange for some of the latter's stock.
3. After the nontaxable spin-off described in possibility 2, White acquires all of the Black stock in exchange for some of White's voting stock. Black is now a subsidiary of White.

Possibility 1 probably will not fit within the definition of a "Type C" reorganization, because Black does not transfer substantially all of the assets in return for White stock. The manufacturing operation is transferred, but the wholesale distributorship is not.

Possibility 2 suffers from these same shortcomings. If the spin-off is disregarded, the transaction becomes an unsuccessful attempt to carry out a "Type C" reorganization (possibility 1). Disregarding the spin-off is the natural result of following the step transaction doctrine.[40]

Possibility 3 follows a different approach. It starts with the spin-off of the *unwanted* assets and concludes with White obtaining the *wanted* assets by exchanging its stock for the Black stock. Taken by itself, this last step satisfies the stock-for-stock requirement of a "Type B" reorganization. If, however, the step transaction doctrine is applied and the spin-off is disregarded, the Orange stock distributed to Black's shareholders might be considered as property *other than voting stock* in White. The IRS has not chosen to take this position and probably will recognize the nontaxability of a spin-off of *unwanted* assets followed by a "Type B" reorganization.[41] Thus, possibility 3, the "Type B" reorganization, appears to be the best choice, although there is still some risk of current taxation.

**Carryover Considerations.**   Careful consideration of the forms of restructuring can enhance the preservation of desirable tax carryover attributes.

---

[40]*Helvering v. Elkhorn Coal Co.*, 38–1 USTC ¶9238, 20 AFTR 1301, 95 F.2d 732 (CA–4, 1938), *cert. den.* 59 S.Ct. 65 (USSC, 1938).

[41]Rev.Rul. 70–434, 1970–2 C.B. 83.

**EXAMPLE 39**

Acquiring Corporation wants to obtain the assets of Target Corporation. These assets have a basis to Target of $300,000 and a fair market value of $200,000. Target has incurred losses in its operations during the past several years and possesses NOLs of $250,000. Acquiring plans to continue the business conducted by Target, hoping to do so on a profitable basis. ■

To carry out the planned acquisition of Target's assets, Acquiring could consider the following alternatives.

1. Using cash and/or other property, Acquiring purchases the assets directly from Target. Following the purchase, Target liquidates and distributes the cash and/or property to its shareholders.
2. Acquiring purchases for cash and/or other property all of the stock in Target from its shareholders. Shortly thereafter, Acquiring liquidates Target.
3. Utilizing a "Type A" reorganization, Target merges into Acquiring. In exchange for their stock, the shareholders of Target receive stock in Acquiring.
4. Under a "Type C" reorganization, Target transfers all of its assets to Acquiring in return for the latter's voting stock. Target distributes the Acquiring stock to its shareholders.

A satisfactory solution must center around the preservation of Target Corporation's favorable tax attributes—the high basis in the assets and the NOL carryovers. Alternative 1 is highly unsatisfactory. It will not retain Target's favorable tax attributes. The purchase price (probably $200,000) becomes the basis of the assets in the hands of Acquiring Corporation. Further, any unused NOLs disappear upon the liquidation of Target. Target has a realized loss of $100,000 [$300,000 (basis in the assets) – $200,000 (sale proceeds)] from the sale of its assets. Yet the realized loss may generate little, if any, tax savings to Target. In view of Target's history of unabsorbed NOL carryovers, it appears doubtful that the company will generate much income in the year of sale.

Alternative 2 appears to be a better solution but has a major risk. When a subsidiary is liquidated under § 332, the subsidiary's basis in its assets carries over to the acquiring corporation.[42] Therefore, Target's $300,000 basis in its assets becomes Acquiring's basis in the assets. What Acquiring paid (probably $200,000 plus the expected value of the NOL) for the Target stock becomes irrelevant. Target's NOLs also carry over to Acquiring. However, § 269 (disallowing any deduction or credit when the acquisition was made to evade or avoid income tax) could present a problem. Section 269(b) specifically applies to a liquidation within two years after the acquisition date.

Alternatives 3 and 4 should accomplish the same tax result, but with less tax risk. Presuming Acquiring can establish a business purpose for the "Type A" or "Type C" reorganization, § 269 can be avoided. The preservation of favorable tax attributes, such as the NOL carryover and any capital loss or credit carryovers, should be considered in the context of the sale of a small corporation.

The alternatives are illustrated in Figure 7–8.

**EXAMPLE 40**

Cardinal Corporation, worth $200,000, has an NOL of $150,000. The stock in Cardinal is owned by Kevin, 55%, and Fran, 45%. Kevin wants to sell his interest in Cardinal and retire. But what happens to the NOL if Kevin sells his entire interest? There would be a more than 50-percentage-point change in the ownership of Cardinal Corporation. Therefore, the § 382 limitation would be $200,000 times the long-term tax-exempt rate. Assume the rate is 10%. The loss of $150,000 is now limited to $20,000 annually. Can a sale be structured so that the NOL is not so limited?

---

[42]§ 334(b)(1).

■ **FIGURE 7–8**
Four Alternatives for Acquiring
Corporate Assets

**Alternative 1: Purchase of Target Assets**

In a purchase of Target's assets for their fair market value of $200,000, Acquiring Corporation has a $200,000 basis in the assets. Target's higher basis of $300,000 is lost. In addition, its NOL of $250,000 disappears. Although Target recognizes a loss on the liquidation, the loss is not beneficial, as Target does not have taxable income that the loss can offset.

**Alternative 2: Purchase of Target Stock—
Liquidation of Target by Acquiring**

If Acquiring obtains all of Target's stock from the shareholders and liquidates Target, thereby obtaining all of Target's assets, there is a carryover of Target's basis in its assets. Thus, Acquiring has a basis of $300,000 in the assets. Target's NOL of $250,000 carries over to Acquiring, subject to the § 382 limitation. However, § 269 may be applied to disallow the basis carryover and NOL carryover.

**Alternatives 3 and 4: "Type A" or "Type C" Reorganization**

In a "Type A" or a "Type C" reorganization, the $300,000 basis in Target's assets will carry over to Acquiring. In addition, the $250,000 NOL carries over to Acquiring, subject to the § 382 limitation. Section 269 is less of a problem than in a subsidiary liquidation under § 332.

An owner shift is calculated for the three-year testing period. Kevin could sell 35% of Cardinal stock in Year 1, 5% in Year 2, 5% in Year 3, and 10% in Year 4. None of the three-year testing periods has a more than 50-percentage-point change in the ownership of the corporation. Thus, there is no § 382 limitation. Cardinal can deduct the entire $150,000 NOL sooner rather than later. ■

## KEY TERMS

| | | |
|---|---|---|
| Business purpose, 7–27 | Equity structure shift, 7–31 | Reorganization, 7–5 |
| Consolidation, 7–10 | Long-term tax-exempt rate, 7–31 | Section 382 limitation, 7–30 |
| Continuity of business enterprise, 7–28 | Merger, 7–10 | Spin-off, 7–20 |
| | Owner shift, 7–31 | Split-off, 7–21 |
| Continuity of interest test, 7–12 | Ownership change, 7–31 | Split-up, 7–21 |
| Control, 7–15 | Recapitalization, 7–21 | Step transaction, 7–28 |

## PROBLEM MATERIALS

### Discussion Questions

1. Why has the number of mergers and acquisitions declined?

2. Dicsuss two of the major problems that have been cited as contributing to the string of recent mega-bankruptcies.

3. The tax treatment of reorganizations parallels that of what other type of transaction? How are the tax treatments of the two types of transactions similar?

4. Is it possible for the acquiring corporation and the target corporation to recognize gains and/or losses on a reorganization falling under § 368? Is it possible for the corporations involved in the reorganization to permanently avoid the tax on the transaction?

5. How does a "Type A" merger differ from a "Type C" reorganization or an acquisitive "Type D" reorganization?

**Issue ID**

6. Channel purchased 1,000 shares of Fern Corporation five years ago. This represented 20% of Fern's outstanding stock. As part of a merger agreement between Fern and Ivy Corporation, Channel receives Ivy stock with a fair market value of $100,000 and a $30,000 bond, in exchange for all of her stock in Fern. The stock represents 10% of Ivy's outstanding shares after the merger is completed. Fern Corporation is liquidated after the merger. What are the tax issues regarding this transaction?

7. Compare a "Type B" reorganization with a "Type A" consolidation with respect to the entities in existence after the restructuring.

8. How does an acquisitive "Type D" reorganization differ from the other combination-type reorganizations?

9. Evaluate the following statement regarding "Type D" reorganizations: "A spin-off and a split-off are very similar whereas a split-up is more distinctive."

10. Explain why "Type E" and "Type F" reorganizations have no tax implications for the corporation. When will a "Type E" reorganization have tax implications for the corporation's shareholders?

11. What legislation created the "Type G" reorganization? What are the requirements for a "Type G" reorganization?

12. Green Corporation (a steel manufacturer) is interested in acquiring Yellow (a toy manufacturer) because it has a substantial capital loss carryover and below their basis of $450,000. Before the merger takes place, Green would to sell all of its assets that Green is not interested in acquiring. Green will exchange 25% of its stock and $200,000 in cash for all of the stock in Yellow. After the merger, Green will sell most of Yellow's assets to obtain the built-in losses. As Green's tax adviser, what concerns do you have regarding the proposed merger of Green and Yellow?

13. How does the step transaction doctrine affect the tax consequences of corporate combinations?

14. How is the assumption of the target corporation's liabilities by the acquiring corporation treated in a reorganization qualifying under § 368?

15. For § 382 to limit the amount of losses the successor corporation can utilize in successive years, there must be an ownership change. Explain what is meant by an *ownership change*.

16. Does § 382 disallow the deduction of NOLs of a loss corporation by the successor corporation? Explain your answer.

17. A classmate asks you why corporations would want to split up using a "Type D" reorganization rather than liquidate and let the shareholders contribute the assets to new corporations of their choosing. Write a note to your classmate that summarizes the advantages of a reorganization over a liquidation.

18. Evaluate the following statement: "One of the beneficial aspects of acquiring a loss corporation is that the successor corporation can reduce its positive E & P by the loss corporation's E & P."

19. Jaysa Jones, president of Sea Corporation, is negotiating the acquisition of Salt Corporation. Salt is a supplier of raw materials to Sea but has been incurring substantial losses due to poor management. It also holds tax credits that it has not been able to use due to its lack of taxable income. Ms. Jones is aware that there are some limitations on the use of Salt's losses but is unclear as to the particulars. Write a memo to Jaysa Jones explaining the application of § 382 and the order in which losses and credits are allowed each year.

## Problems

20. What type of reorganization is effected in each of the following transactions?

a. Purple Corporation manufactures toys and plastic pots. Due to the possible product liability associated with toys, Purple wants to separate the two divisions. Purple creates two corporations, Blue and Red. It transfers the toy division assets to Blue and the plastic pot division assets to Red in exchange for all of the stock of Blue and Red. Purple then liquidates.

b. Green Corporation originally was organized as a Subchapter S corporation. It violates the S election requirements and becomes a regular C corporation.

c. Yellow Corporation and Red Corporation are interested in merging. To indicate to the public that the transaction is not a takeover, a new entity, Orange Corporation, will be formed. Yellow and Red will transfer all of their assets to Orange in exchange for 100% of Orange's common stock worth $500,000 and $600,000 in long-term bonds. The stock and bonds are distributed to the shareholders of Yellow and Red in exchange for their stock. Yellow and Red then liquidate.

d. Same as (c), except that only Orange stock worth $1.1 million is received and exchanged with the Yellow and Red shareholders.

e. Amber Corporation has been having financial difficulties and is not able to make the interest payments to its bondholders. Under the guidance of a state court, all of its assets are transferred to New Corporation. New Corporation's voting stock is distributed to all of Amber's bondholders.

f. Brown Corporation has a wholly owned subsidiary, Green Corporation. One of the assets that Green owns is Brown stock. Green exchanges its stock in Brown for all of the assets in Red Corporation. Red distributes the Brown stock to its shareholders in exchange for their Red stock. Red then liquidates.

g. Black Corporation exchanges 40% of its voting stock for 90% of White's assets worth $900,000 and all of White's liabilities amounting to $200,000. The remaining White assets are distributed to its shareholders. The Black stock is also distributed to the White shareholders in exchange for their stock. White then terminates.

h. Same as (g), except that Black transfers 40% of its stock and $100,000 in bonds in exchange for all of White's assets.

i. The shareholders of Blue Corporation and Yellow Corporation agree to form Green Corporation. All of the assets of Blue and 60% of the assets of Yellow are transferred to Green in exchange for all of Green's common stock. Some Green stock is distributed to the shareholders of Blue in exchange for all of their Blue stock. Blue then terminates. The Yellow shareholders receive the remaining Green stock and do not have any of their Yellow stock redeemed.

j. Pink Corporation redeems its 20-year, 5% bonds. The bonds have a face value of $1,000. For each bond, Pink issues 10 shares of preferred stock with $100 par value.

k. Gray Corporation offers to acquire White stock by exchanging two shares of its voting stock for each share of White stock issued and outstanding. Ninety percent of the White shareholders enter into the exchange with Gray. After the exchange, the White shareholders own 30% of Gray's common stock.

l. Teal Corporation has been selling and servicing computers for the last 10 years. The shareholders think that it would be wise to separate the company into two corporations for marketing purposes. Aqua Corporation is created. Teal transfers all of the service division to Aqua in exchange for all of the stock of Aqua. The stock of Aqua is distributed to the Teal shareholders.

21. Kamiak paid $70,000 for a 10% interest in Beaver Corporation three years ago. As part of Beaver's merger with Bear Corporation, Kamiak receives a 4% interest in Bear stock worth $120,000 and $30,000 in cash. At the time of the merger, Beaver had accumulated E & P of $200,000, and Bear's E & P was $500,000. How will Kamiak treat this transaction for tax purposes?

22. Quinn purchased 20% of Redbird Corporation for $100,000 and a $50,000 bond five years ago. In a transaction qualifying as a reorganization under § 368, Redbird exchanges all of its assets valued at $1.6 million (basis of $900,000) for 395,000 shares of Bluebird Corporation stock plus a parcel of land. Redbird distributes 700 shares of Bluebird stock (valued at $280,000), a $60,000 Bluebird bond, and the land (valued at $20,000) to Quinn in exchange for his Redbird stock and bond. Redbird's current and accumulated E & P before the reorganization amount to $150,000.

a. How will Quinn treat this transaction for tax purposes? What is Quinn's basis in the stock, bond, and land?

b. How will Redbird treat this transaction for tax purposes? What is Bluebird's basis in the assets it receives from Redbird?

23. Rosa and Arvid are the sole shareholders of Pine Corporation. Rosa paid $60,000 for her stock eight years ago, and Arvid paid $190,000 for his stock two years ago. Pine enters into a tax-free reorganization with Lodgepole, after which the corporations will be consolidated into Lodgepole Pine Corporation. Rosa receives $20,000 cash plus a 20% interest (worth $100,000) in the new corporation in exchange for her stock in Pine. Arvid receives land worth $35,000 plus a 29% interest (worth $145,000) in the new corporation in exchange for his stock in Pine. The land had a basis to Pine of $10,000.

a. What are Rosa's and Arvid's bases in their new Lodgepole Pine stock?

b. What is the amount of gain (loss) recognized by Rosa, Arvid, Pine, and Lodgepole on the reorganization?

24. Target Corporation has assets with a fair market value of $4 million (adjusted basis of $1 million) and liabilities of $500,000. It transfers assets worth $3.7 million to Acquiring Corporation in a "Type C" reorganization in exchange for Acquiring voting stock and the assumption of Target's liabilities. Target retained a building worth $300,000 (adjusted basis of $150,000). Target distributes the voting stock in Acquiring and the building to

Wanda, its sole shareholder. How much gain does Target recognize on the reorganization?

25. Assume in Problem 24 that the consideration Acquiring Corporation gives for all of the assets of Target Corporation is voting stock worth $3.2 million and a building worth $300,000, basis of $150,000. Target distributes the stock and the building to its sole shareholder, Wanda. Will either Target or Acquiring recognize any gain on the reorganization?

**Communications**

26. Vine Corporation is considering the acquisition of Lawn Corporation. Lawn has assets valued at $3 million and known liabilities of $1 million. Lawn has just received a patent on a new chemical fertilizer that should revolutionize the gardening industry. The product has been tested for the past two years and appears to be safe for outdoor plants. However, there is always the possibility that individuals or pets could have an undesirable reaction to the chemical. Further, the EPA has not finished testing the product. Because of the potential for product liabilities, Vine is concerned about going through with the acquisition. Vine's president calls you for guidance in this matter. You discuss the merits of using either a "Type B" reorganization or a "Type A" with a subsidiary as the acquiring corporation. Write a memo to the tax files documenting the advice you gave to the president of Vine Corporation.

**Issue ID**

27. Sitka Corporation has 100,000 shares outstanding valued at $5 million. Canada Corporation would like to acquire Sitka but has had a difficult time negotiating with Sitka's management. Canada makes a tender offer to the Sitka shareholders of two shares of Canada (value of $26 per share) for each share of Sitka or $50 per share. Of the Sitka shareholders, 77% exchange their stock for Canada stock, and 15% take cash. The remaining 8% of the shareholders prefer to retain their Sitka stock. Discuss the tax consequences of this transaction to Sitka, Canada, and the Sitka shareholders. Suggest changes to the transaction that would produce more favorable tax treatment. Assume that Canada is only interested in owning Sitka as a subsidiary.

**Communications**

28. Target Corporation has assets worth $1.5 million and liabilities of $200,000. Acquiring Corporation wants to obtain assets in Target worth $1.4 million. (Acquiring does not want a specific group of assets worth $100,000.) It agrees to assume all of Target's liabilities. Target's shareholders are agreeable to the takeover if they receive some cash, but they want the takeover to qualify as a tax-free reorganization. The chair of the board of directors of Target has requested your advice in this matter. Target's address is 3443 E. Riverbank Road, Walla Walla, WA 99160. Write a letter to the chair indicating how much cash Acquiring may pay Target's shareholders in addition to distributing its voting stock without disqualifying the takeover as a tax-free "Type C" reorganization. Be sure to discuss whether the amount of assets being transferred from Target to Acquiring meets the requirements of a "Type C" reorganization.

**Issue ID**

29. Home Corporation is owned by four shareholders: Alicia, Boyd, Camille, and Devon. Each shareholder contributed $100,000 10 years ago for a 25% interest in Home. Home was initially engaged in the manufacture and installation of prefabricated homes, but in the last three years it has branched into the design and service of these homes. The addition of the new lines of business has caused tension among the owners. Alicia thinks the new lines have potential for rapid growth, whereas Camille feels that Home should focus on what it does best—manufacturing and installation. Devon thinks that design and manufacturing naturally form one business but that installation and service should each be a separate business. Boyd, on the other hand, thinks that installation and service are complementary businesses and should be one company.

After much negotiation, it is decided that Home should become three corporations: Home, Design, and Service. Home will retain the manufacturing and installation businesses, and all four shareholders will retain their interests in it. Design will be owned by Alicia and Devon, and Service will be owned by Boyd. Discuss the tax consequences of the proposed transaction.

Issue ID

30. Assume that Home, in Problem 29, transfers the installation and service lines of business to a new corporation called InstaServ and the design and manufacturing lines to another new corporation called ManuSign. Boyd and Camille will receive the stock in InstaServ, and Alicia and Devon will acquire ManuSign. Home will not retain any assets and will therefore liquidate. Discuss the tax consequences of this proposed transaction.

31. Yong owns all 1,000 shares of Jade Corporation's common stock. His basis is $50,000, and the fair market value of the stock is $400,000. The 200 shares of preferred stock outstanding (par value of $900 and fair market value of $1,000 a share) are owned equally by Yong's children, Hue and Mian. Their basis in the stock is equal to the par value. Now that the children have become adults, Yong wants to encourage them to participate in the management of Jade. He believes that owning common stock would provide the children an incentive to become dedicated members of management. Therefore, the corporation recalls all of the preferred stock and issues Hue and Mian each 250 shares of common. Yong receives 200 shares of preferred stock in exchange for 500 shares of common stock. What is the taxable income each shareholder must recognize on the stock exchanges? What is each shareholder's basis in the new stock received?

32. Svet is the holder of a $200,000 bond issued by Palm Corporation. Due to cash-flow problems, Palm would like to eliminate its bonds. It is having trouble making the required quarterly interest payments. Palm exchanges nonvoting common stock with a market value of $210,000 for Svet's bonds. What are the tax consequences of this exchange to Svet and Palm?

Issue ID

Communications

33. Beach Corporation has been operating at substantial deficits for the past three years. It has been unable to service its bond obligations for the last two years, and this year it has been having difficulty meeting its mortgage and equipment loan payments. The prospects of Beach recovering from its current financial problems look doubtful. Beach's president, Sandy Jones, asks your advice regarding the possibilities of restructuring the corporation. Write Sandy a memo explaining her choices in restructuring Beach.

Issue ID

34. Acquiring Corporation is interested in merging with Target Corporation because Target has a large NOL and excess credit carryovers. Acquiring is a very profitable corporation in the entertainment industry, and Target is in the retail clothing business. Target is owned equally by 20 shareholders. In exchange for 30% of Acquiring stock and $100,000, Target transfers all of its assets, liabilities, and tax attributes to Acquiring. Target then distributes the Acquiring stock to 15 of its shareholders in exchange for 100% of their Target stock. The other 5 shareholders receive cash in exchange for their Target stock. Acquiring sells all of the inventory and fixtures associated with the retail clothing business and uses the gutted stores to sell entertainment merchandise. What are the tax issues to be considered in these transactions?

Issue ID

35. Assume the same facts as in Problem 34, except that three days after the shareholders receive the Acquiring stock, 10 of them sell it to an unrelated party for its fair market value. Discuss the tax consequences of this transaction.

Issue ID

36. Jack and Jill are the sole shareholders of Playco, a corporation that develops and manufactures interactive games for young children. They have developed some very interesting games but have had substantial problems manufacturing and marketing their products. Due to these problems, Playco has never shown a profit. Its current NOL is $300,000. Jack and Jill cannot afford to invest any more in Playco, and the banks are not willing to increase their lines of credits.

Sellco, a widely held corporation, is a distributor of prepackaged foods. It has approached Playco regarding a merger. Sellco has been very successful in marketing its products to children and thinks it could be successful with Playco's products. What issues need to be considered before a merger between Playco and Sellco takes place?

37. Ruby Corporation completed a restructuring transaction with Gold Corporation on August 31 of the current year. Gold distributed 30% of Ruby's stock to its shareholders in exchange for all of its own stock. Just prior to completion of the reorganization, Gold had assets worth $500,000, liabilities of $150,000, and an NOL carryover of $300,000.

*Handwritten margin notes:*

> Olympus Curset <100000>
> — in Acc 150000
> Sub → Acc <210 000>
> E&P 150000
> curret <100000>
> Divide 80000
> return of 30000
> Cap
> → Take oths to next
> yr & can offset
> +ve E&P bal.
>
> _____
>
> NOL Examples
>
> Corp A 9/1/03 Corp B
> Sept 1st NOL
> 80000
> TI 500000
> NOL can
> be used
> against post merger income
> 30% it adj against
> ½ × 8000 = 500000
> remaining NOL is c/f

The Federal long-term tax-exempt rate was 10%. What is the amount of NOL that Ruby may use in the current year? How much will it be able to utilize in the next tax year?

38. Phoenix Corporation merged into Olympus Corporation on July 15 of the current year. Phoenix had an accumulated deficit of $210,000 in its E & P account, and Olympus had accumulated $150,000 in its E & P account. At the end of the current year, Olympus showed an operating loss and, therefore, a current E & P loss of $100,000. Despite this loss, Olympus distributed $80,000 its shareholders. To what extent is this distribution taxable to the Olympus shareholders?

39. On December 31, 2002, Tulip Corporation has a capital loss carryforward of $100,000 and excess credits of $30,000. On this day it merges with Lilly Corporation by exchanging all of its assets for $1,750,000 of stock and cash. Tulip then distributes the cash and stock to its shareholders. This causes an ownership change and subjects Lilly to the § 382 limitation. For the year ending December 31, 2003, Lilly computes its taxable income before application of any carryovers to be $500,000. Of this amount, $420,000 is operating income, and $80,000 is capital gains. Determine Lilly's tax liability for 2003 and its carryovers (capital losses and excess credits) to 2004. Assume that the applicable long-term tax-exempt rate is 8%.

**Decision Making**

**Communications**

40. Disc Corporation is contemplating the acquisition of Density Corporation. Disc is interested in Density because it has a valuable patent used in the process of manufacturing of CDs. Density is a young company and has yet to show substantial profits (accumulated E & P of $28,000). However, Disc thinks it can turn Density around by replacing Density's inexperienced managers with a more mature management team. The value of Density is currently estimated at $800,000, and it has a basis in its assets of $500,000. Disc's president asks you to illustrate (with diagrams) the possible tax-free reorganizations of Disc and Density.

   a. Assume that the patent held by Density is transferable.
   b. Assume that the patent held by Density is *not* transferable.

## Research Problems

*Note: Solutions to Research Problems can be prepared by using the **RIA Checkpoint® Student Edition** online research product, or the **CCH U.S. Master Tax Guide Plus**™ online Federal tax research database, which is available to accompany this text. It is also possible to prepare solutions to the Research Problems by using tax research materials found in a standard tax library.*

**Communications**

**Research Problem 1.** Exterminator Corporation was a small, closely held business that provided pest control services to commercial businesses. Generally, Exterminator's clients purchased three- or six-month contracts with full payment due when the contracts were signed. When the contract payments were collected, they were treated as liabilities and converted to income only when the services were actually provided. This is the customary industry practice and is accepted by the IRS as proper reporting.

A few years ago, a large national corporation, Terminator, Inc., moved into Exterminator's territory and cut into its business. As a matter of fact, Exterminator accumulated a $300,000 NOL. Realizing that the only way to survive was to merge with Terminator, Exterminator shareholders exchanged 100% of their stock and received a 5% interest in Terminator in a transaction qualifying as a "Type C" reorganization. At the time of the reorganization, Exterminator had a fair market value of $600,000, service liabilities of $100,000, other liabilities of $50,000, and adjusted basis in its assets of $150,000. After the acquisition, Terminator provided all services to the Exterminator customers and converted the liabilities into income. Terminator treated the income as recognized built-in gain when computing the yearly § 382 limitation. Upon audit, the IRS disallowed this treatment. The IRS is not questioning the timing of income recognition but rather whether these prepaid pre-change amounts constituted built-in gains within the meaning of § 382. Prepare a memo for Terminator's tax file explaining your findings.

**Communications**

**Research Problem 2.**   Las Vegas Corporation is in the business of developing software used exclusively by multinational corporations. Among its assets are innovative software, valuable trademarks, outstanding corporate name recognition, and a large NOL carryover. These assets make Las Vegas a very appealing takeover prospect to Santa Fe Corporation. Santa Fe is a little known corporation that distributes software products to corporate clients. It is the largest business of its kind and is quite profitable.

After entering into negotiations, Santa Fe learns that Las Vegas's trademarks are not transferable. With further planning, the combination is expected to take place on June 30 of next year.

The president of Santa Fe, Darla Threestars, has requested your expert advice on two matters. First, Ms. Threestars would like to know what type of reorganization would be most effective in acquiring Las Vegas. Second, will the § 381 NOL limitations apply after the reorganization? Santa Fe is subject to the alternative minimum tax (AMT) each year and assumes this situation will continue in the future. Does § 381 only limit the amount of NOL that can offset regular tax in the first year, or does it also apply to the AMT?

Draft a letter to Darla Threestars explaining your conclusions. Her address is 1235 Pinto Drive, Santa Fe, NM 87505.

**Research Problem 3.**   Tapir Corporation manufactures and sells chemical products globally. In 2002, Python Corporation, a holding company whose subsidiaries sell plastic products, made a tender offer to buy all of Tapir's stock. Tapir's shareholders agreed to dispose of their stock in Tapir if the transfer qualified as a tax-free reorganization. Python created a subsidiary corporation, Coral, by transferring assets and its own stock in exchange for all of Coral's stock. Coral then merged into Tapir by transferring all of its assets (including its holdings of Python stock) to Tapir Corporation. Tapir distributed Python stock in exchange for its shareholders' stock in Tapir. The Tapir stock then was distributed to Coral. Coral was liquidated by exchanging the Tapir stock for all of Python's stock in Coral. Tapir Corporation became a subsidiary of Python, and the former Tapir shareholders are now shareholders of Python. After the merger, Tapir deducted its legal fees and investment banking fees incurred in connection with the merger. Upon audit in 2004, the IRS disallows the deduction of the fees. Does this transaction qualify as a tax-free reorganization? Are the legal fees and investment banking fees deductible, or should they be capitalized?

**Research Problem 4.**   As part of an integrated plan, Manchester Corporation creates Bedford Corporation as a wholly owned subsidiary. Then, Manchester acquires all of Bismark Corporation by merging Bedford into Bismark. After this transaction, Bedford no longer exists, and Manchester owns all of the Bismark stock valued at $1 million. Bismark shareholders received Manchester stock valued at $700,000 and $300,000 of cash for their shares of Bismark. Lastly, Bismark merges into Manchester in a statutory merger.

Thus, Manchester owns all of the assets of Bismark, and 70% of the Bismark shareholders are now Manchester shareholders. Explain whether this step transaction restructuring qualifies as a tax-free reorganization. Support your position with citations to primary tax sources.

**Internet Activity**

*Use the tax resources of the Internet to address the following questions. Do not restrict your search to the World Wide Web, but include a review of newsgroups and general reference materials, practitioner sites and resources, primary sources of the tax law, chat rooms and discussion groups, and other opportunities.*

**Research Problem 5.**   The merger of Hewlett-Packard and Compaq received unfavorable press. Using the Internet, find two articles discussing the objections that were raised to this merger. Provide a one-page summary of your findings, and indicate whether you think the objections were valid.

**Research Problem 6.**   Select one of the bankruptcies mentioned at the beginning of this chapter. Use the Internet to find two articles on the bankruptcy you selected. Provide a one-page summary of these articles.

**Research Problem 7.**   There are many mergers and acquisitions taking place that are not discussed at the beginning of this chapter. Use the Internet to identify two reorganizations that have been completed since December 2002. Write a one-page summary of the two restructurings you selected. Be sure to describe the structure of the restructuring (that is, stock for assets, stock for stock, etc.).

**Research Problem 8.** Using an Internet tax service or other Internet sources, make a list of recent cases that you have found in the merger and acquisition area of the tax law. E-mail the list (using proper citations) to your professor.

# Consolidated Tax Returns

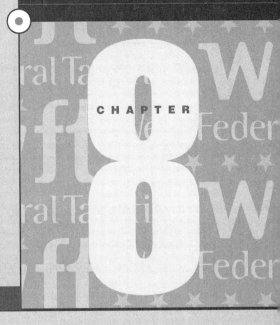

## LEARNING OBJECTIVES

*After completing Chapter 8, you should be able to:*

### LO.1
Apply the fundamental concepts of consolidated tax returns.

### LO.2
Identify the sources of the rules for consolidated taxable income.

### LO.3
Recognize the major advantages and disadvantages of filing consolidated tax returns.

### LO.4
Describe the corporations that are eligible to file on a consolidated basis.

### LO.5
Explain the compliance aspects of consolidated returns.

### LO.6
Compute a parent's investment basis in a subsidiary.

### LO.7
Account for intercompany transactions of a consolidated group.

### LO.8
Identify limitations that restrict the use of losses and credits of group members derived in separate return years.

### LO.9
Derive deductions and credits on a consolidated basis.

### LO.10
Demonstrate tax planning opportunities available to consolidated groups.

http://wft.swlearning.com

## OUTLINE

# Context of the Consolidated Return Rules

To this point, the discussion has centered on the computation of the tax liability of individual corporations under the regular tax calculation, along with specific penalty taxes and the alternative minimum tax. This is an appropriate approach to the study of corporate taxation, as more than 90 percent of the roughly 5 million U.S. corporations are closely held (i.e., either by a small group of operators/investors or by members of the same family).

Although some of these family businesses operate in a multiple-corporation environment, the vast majority of the assets held by businesses nationwide are owned by no more than 10,000 large corporate conglomerates. These corporations conduct the bulk of the country's "big business" and generate most of the taxable income earned by corporate taxpayers. In addition, these corporate groups face some special tax rules, which are the subject of this chapter.

## MOTIVATIONS TO CONSOLIDATE

Corporate conglomerates are present in every aspect of life. The local dairy or bakery is likely to be owned by General Mills or General Foods. Oil and insurance companies own movie-making corporations. Professional sports teams are corporate cousins of the newspapers and television/radio stations that carry their games. The same corporate group that produces night lights for a child's nursery may manufacture control equipment for bombers and other elements of the Defense Department's arsenal.

What brings together these sometimes strange corporate bedfellows? For the most part, nontax motivations provide the strongest incentives for multiple-corporation acquisitions and holdings. Among the many commonly encountered motivations are the following.

- A desire to isolate assets of other group members from the liabilities of specific operating divisions (e.g., to gain limited liability for a tobacco or asbestos company within an operating conglomerate).

- A need to carry out specific estate planning objectives (e.g., by transferring growth or high-risk assets to younger-generation shareholders).
- A wish to isolate the group's exposure to losses and liabilities incurred in joint ventures with "outside" entities (especially when such venturers are not based in the United States).
- A perception that separate divisions/group members will be worth more on the market if they maintain unique identities or otherwise avoid a commingling of assets and liabilities with other group members (e.g., where a trade name or patent is especially valuable or carries excessive goodwill in the marketplace).
- Conversely, an attempt to shield the identities of a subsidiary's true owners from the public where negative goodwill exists (e.g., with respect to the consequences of a nuclear or industrial accident, or the use of a long-held name of an oil or tobacco company).

---

**ETHICAL CONSIDERATIONS** | **Sheltering Corporate Assets**

Should corporations be able to shelter their assets from marketplace liabilities through a capital restructuring? The first large corporations to spin off subsidiaries to isolate high-risk assets and their related liabilities from the main business were financial institutions (e.g., risky loans to debtors in exploratory industries or underdeveloped countries) and utilities (e.g., nuclear power facilities). Today, conglomerates involved in developing health care procedures or turning out such products as tobacco and industrial equipment protect the bulk of the entity's assets by isolating product-liability risks in subsidiaries.

Given the "deep pockets" mentality of many juries and government agencies, merger or consolidation is a prudent reaction by the corporate community. But shouldn't a society's largest risks be shared among all of its players? And should the tax laws be used to foster the isolation of such risk into shallow and insulated corporate pockets?

In many states, "tort reform" would further limit the business entity's exposure to/accountability for malpractice and product warranty claims. Your state's CPA society asks you to lobby legislators in favor of such a measure. Will you take the assignment?

---

**LO.1**

Apply the fundamental concepts of consolidated tax returns.

Although nontax concerns may be the primary reason for the creation of many conglomerates, tax incentives may also play a role. To a large extent, these incentives can be found in the rules that control the filing of **consolidated returns.** In general terms, the IRS allows certain corporate groups to be treated as a single entity for Federal income tax purposes. This enables the group to use available tax exemptions and brackets optimally among its members and to shelter the income of profitable members with the losses of other members. Thus, through the consolidated return rules, corporate taxpayers have an opportunity to manage the combined tax liability of the members of the group.

The consolidated return rules may be available to a taxpayer as a result of various business decisions.

- A consolidated return may result from a merger, acquisition, or other corporate combination (discussed in Chapter 7).

**EXAMPLE 1**

When Dover Corporation acquires all of the stock of Edwards Corporation, a new corporate group, Dover and Edwards Corporation, is formed. The two group members can elect to file their tax return on a consolidated basis. ■

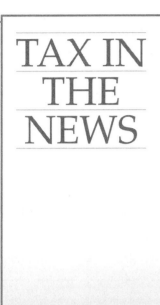

- A group of business taxpayers may be restructured to comply with changes in regulatory requirements, meet the demands of a competitive environment, or gain economies of scale and operate more efficiently in a larger arrangement. Consequently, an election to file a consolidated return becomes available.

**EXAMPLE 2**

External Corporation, a retailer, acquires Internal Corporation, a wholesaler, in an effort to control its flow of inventory in unstable economic times. The two group members can elect to file their tax returns on a consolidated basis. ■

- The taxpayers may be seeking to gain tax and other financial advantages that are more readily available to corporate combinations.

**EXAMPLE 3**

Over the next three years, Mary Corporation will be selling a number of its business assets at a loss. If Norbert Corporation acquires all of Mary's stock and the group elects to file its tax returns on a consolidated basis, Norbert will be able to combine its gains from the sale of business property with Mary's losses in computing the group's consolidated § 1231 gain/loss for the year. ■

### SOURCE AND PHILOSOPHY OF CONSOLIDATED RETURN RULES

Some form of consolidated corporate tax return has been allowed for Federal purposes since World War I. At that time, the Treasury became suspicious that conglomerates were shifting taxable income to a number of smaller entities to avoid the high marginal rates of the excess profits tax that had been imposed to finance the war effort. Thus, the consolidated return rules can be seen as perhaps the earliest effort of the IRS to limit the tax benefits available to multiple corporations.

<table>
<tr><td>

*EXAMPLE 4*

</td><td>

Assume that the marginal Federal income tax rate is 10% on the first $100,000 of taxable income and 15% on any taxable income in excess of $100,000. The additional five percentage points constitute a war profits tax, and the revenue raised is used for the war effort.

Further assume that the tax law includes no restrictions on the tax computations of related corporations. A corporation with annual taxable income of $1 million can eliminate its entire exposure to the war profits tax by splitting its business evenly among 10 separate corporations. ■

</td></tr>
</table>

**LO.2**

Identify the sources of the rules for consolidated taxable income.

At various times since World War I, Congress has modified the pertinent Regulations and imposed a higher tax rate on consolidated groups to increase the cost of making the consolidation election. During the Great Depression, when it feared "too much" income was being sheltered within consolidated groups, Congress suspended the application of the rules for most taxpayers. On other occasions, including the present, complex limitations were placed on the use and timing of positive tax benefits, such as net operating loss (NOL) carryovers, that were acquired in a corporate consolidation. Congress imposed these limits to discourage profitable corporations from "trafficking" in businesses that had generated net losses.

Currently, Congress has delegated most of its legislative authority involving consolidated returns to the Treasury. As a result, the majority of the rules that affect consolidated groups are found in the Regulations. The Code provisions dealing with consolidated returns are strictly definitional in nature and broad in scope,[1] while the related Regulations dictate the computational and compliance requirements of the group.[2]

As discussed in Chapter 1, "legislative" Regulations of this sort carry the full force and effect of law. Challenges to the content of these Regulations seldom are supported by the courts. Consequently, taxpayers generally participate actively in the hearings process in an effort to have their interpretations included in the final Regulations.

The length and detail of these Regulations make the consolidated return rules among the most complex in the entire Federal income tax law. For the most part, the underlying objective of the rules remains one of organizational neutrality; that is, a group of closely related corporations should have neither a tax advantage nor a disadvantage relative to taxpayers who file separate corporate returns.

---

**ETHICAL CONSIDERATIONS**    **Delegating Authority to the Nonelected**

In no other area of the tax law has Congress given the Treasury such leeway in crafting both major principles and details as in the area of consolidated returns. Since Treasury staff members are not elected officials, this delegation of authority might appear to be a shirking of congressional duty and a dangerous assignment of legislative power to an isolated group of individuals.

To what extent should Congress delegate its powers over the country's largest businesses (not only the largest players in the global economy but also the largest contributors to campaign and reelection funds)? Can the delegation of congressional powers to Washington-based civil servants, who are virtually immune to the checks and balances of the election process, be healthy for all taxpayers?

---

[1] §§ 1501–1505.
[2] Reg. §§ 1.1501–1, 1.1502–0 through 1.1502–100, 1.1503–1 through 1.1503–2T, and 1.1504–1.

You are a member of the House Ways and Means Committee, and your chances of reelection are jeopardized when you must take a position on a consolidated tax return issue: Taxes on old-line manufacturers would increase, while those on more environmentally friendly, high-tech industries would fall. Should you avoid the debate altogether by deferring the issue to the Regulations process?

---

The derivation of a set of consolidated financial statements for a conglomerate and the computation of its consolidated taxable income correspond only slightly. The equity approach followed for financial accounting purposes has a role in the consolidated return rules, but exceptions to accounting conventions are both critical and numerous. Thus, a knowledge of financial accounting consolidation procedures is not necessarily of great assistance in computing consolidated taxable income, nor is a lack of familiarity with accounting conventions a hindrance.

**EXAMPLE 5**

Dividends paid by SubCo to its 100% owner, Parent Corporation, are eliminated from the separate taxable income computations of both group members in deriving consolidated taxable income. This treatment parallels the eliminating entry that is made in developing the group's consolidated financial statements.

Later, SubCo sells an asset to its 100% owner, Parent Corporation, at a tax and accounting gain of $100,000. The asset appreciates by another $20,000 before Parent sells it to an unrelated party, Outsider Corporation.

No tax or accounting gain is reported by the group members until the ultimate sale by Parent to Outsider. In constructing the consolidated financial statements, Parent realizes a $120,000 gain. For tax purposes, however, SubCo is assigned $100,000 of the gain, and Parent recognizes only "its" $20,000. ■

**LO.3**

Recognize the major advantages and disadvantages of filing consolidated tax returns.

# Assessing Consolidated Return Status

As Concept Summary 8–1 illustrates, all of the members of a corporate group must meet three broad requirements to be eligible to elect to file a consolidated income tax return: (1) The corporations must meet the statutory ownership requirements to be classified as an affiliated group.[3] (2) The corporations must be eligible to make a consolidation election.[4] (3) The group must meet various tax accounting and compliance requirements in making and maintaining the election.[5]

Before making an election to file consolidated tax returns, related taxpayers must weigh the related advantages and disadvantages.

The potential advantages of filing consolidated returns are many.

- The operating and capital loss carryovers of one group member may be used to shelter the corresponding income of other group members.
- The taxation of all intercompany dividends may be eliminated.
- Recognition of income from certain intercompany transactions can be deferred.
- Certain deductions and credits may be optimized by using consolidated amounts in computing pertinent limitations (e.g., the deductions for charitable contributions and dividends received, and foreign tax credits).

---

[3]§§ 1504(a)(1) and (2).
[4]This is a negative definition, rooted in §§ 1504(b) through (f).

[5]See especially Reg. §§ 1.1502–75, –76, and –77.

Concept Summary 8–1

## The Consolidated Return Election

| Member of affiliated group? | Eligible to file consolidated return? | Met compliance requirements? |
|---|---|---|
| • Stock ownership<br>• Identifiable parent | • Not an ineligible corporation | • Forms 851, 1122<br>• Group tax year |

### GROUP CAN ELECT TO FILE CONSOLIDATED RETURN

**Advantages**

• Taxable income computations allow the taxpayer to offset losses of one group member against income of others.
• Deferred income recognition from certain intercompany sales.
• Group computation of alternative minimum tax, credits, and deductions can reduce overall taxes by fully utilizing statutory floors and ceilings.

**Disadvantages**

• Deriving group taxable income may prevent the use of some membersí losses or credits.
• Binding election with additional compliance requirements.
• Deferred loss recognition from certain intercompany sales.
• Certain Code limitations are applied on a group basis (e.g., tax brackets and exemptions).

* The tax basis of investments in the stock of subsidiaries is increased as the members contribute to consolidated taxable income.
* The alternative minimum tax (AMT) attributes of all group members can be used in deriving consolidated alternative minimum taxable income (AMTI). This can reduce the adjusted current earnings (ACE) adjustment and optimize other AMT preferences and adjustments.
* The share holdings of all group members can be used in meeting other statutory requirements.[6]

Consolidated returns also have a number of potential disadvantages.

* The election is binding on all subsequent tax years of the group members, unless either the makeup of the affiliated group changes or the IRS consents to a revocation of the election.
* Capital and operating losses of one group member are applied against the corresponding income of the other group members even when assigning the losses to separate return years would produce a greater tax benefit. The benefit might be due, for instance, to rate discounts or changes in tax rates.
* Recognition of losses from certain intercompany transactions is deferred.

---

[6]E.g., for purposes of the § 165(g)(3) ordinary deduction for losses from worthlessness of securities. For the 80% corporate control requirement of § 351, see the discussion in Chapter 3.

- Using consolidated amounts in computing the limitations may decrease the amounts of certain deductions and credits.
- Return elections made by the parent (e.g., to claim a § 901 credit for foreign tax payments rather than a deduction) are binding on all members of the filing group for the year.
- The tax basis of investments in the stock of subsidiaries is decreased when the members generate operating losses and by distributions from members' E & P.
- The requirement that all group members use the parent's tax year creates short tax years for the subsidiaries. As a result, a subsidiary's income may be bunched together needlessly, and one of the years of its charitable contribution and loss carryforward periods may be lost.
- Additional administrative costs may be incurred in complying with the consolidated return Regulations.

**EXAMPLE 6**     The following taxpayers should consider filing consolidated returns.

- Major Insurance Corporation generates billions of dollars of taxable income every year. Independent Movie Productions, Ltd., is concerned with artistic integrity, and its annual taxable loss totals $10 to $15 million per year. The accumulated losses are of no use to Independent, but Major can use them to effect an immediate tax reduction at its 35% marginal tax rate.
- Every year, Parent contributes $1.2 million of its $10 million taxable income to charity. Thus, because of the 10% limitation, it cannot deduct the full amount of the gift in computing taxable income. SubCo generates $3 million of taxable income every year, and it makes no charitable contributions. By filing a consolidated return with SubCo, Parent can deduct its full gift against consolidated taxable income.

On the other hand, certain corporations would make unattractive consolidated return partners.

- Parent sells an asset to SubCo at a $500,000 realized loss. As shown in Example 5, this loss cannot be recognized by the consolidated group until the asset subsequently is sold to Outsider.
- ParentCo holds a large NOL carryforward, and SubCo generates a steady level of taxable income every year. Both corporations are involved in international commerce and make significant tax payments to other countries. SubCo would use these payments to compute a foreign tax credit. But if the corporations file a consolidated return, ParentCo effectively makes the tax accounting elections for the group. It is likely that the ParentCo group will claim the foreign tax credits as deductions against consolidated taxable income, so as to use the NOL carryforward more quickly. ■

## Electing Consolidated Return Status

A corporation can join in a consolidated tax return if it meets three requirements, as shown in Concept Summary 8–1.

- It must be a member of an **affiliated group.**
- It cannot be ineligible to file on a consolidated basis.
- It must meet the initial and ongoing compliance requirements specified in the Code and Regulations.

## AFFILIATED GROUP

An affiliated group exists when one corporation owns at least 80 percent of the voting power and stock value of another corporation.[7] This stock ownership test must be met on every day of the tax year. Multiple tiers and chains of corporations are allowed as long as the group has an identifiable parent corporation (i.e., at least 80 percent of one corporation must be owned by another).

**EXAMPLE 7**

Two corporate group structures are illustrated below. Both meet the 80% stock ownership test, but the structure on the right is not an affiliated group because there is no identifiable parent entity.

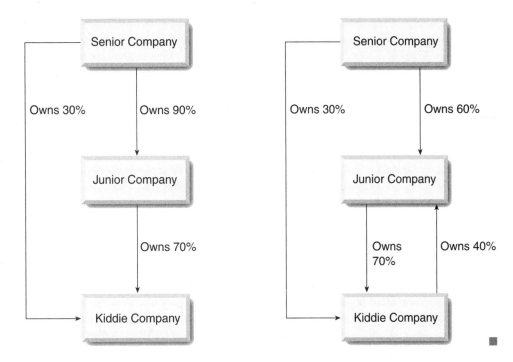

Members of an affiliated group can file tax returns in either of two ways.

* File a separate tax return for each member of the group and claim a 100 percent dividends received deduction for payments passing among them.
* Elect to file income tax returns on a consolidated basis. No 100 percent dividends received deduction is allowed for payments among group members.

Table 8–1 provides additional details as to the tax effects of making a consolidated return election.

A Federal election to form a consolidated group may not be binding for state income tax purposes. Some states allow only separate return filing, and others may define the members of an electing group or tax their income differently than the Federal rules do. See Chapter 15 for additional discussion of the multistate taxation of related corporations.

An affiliated group is similar but not identical to a *parent-subsidiary controlled group*, as discussed in Chapter 2. Members of a controlled group are required to share a number of tax benefits, including the following.

---

[7]§§ 1504(a)(1) and (2).

■ **TABLE 8–1**
Comparison of Tax Effects
Available to Affiliated Group

| Attribute | Treatment If Consolidated Returns Are Filed | Treatment If Separate Returns Are Filed |
|---|---|---|
| Tax year | All companies use the parent's tax year. | Companies use various tax years. |
| Change to common tax year | Required, no IRS permission needed. | Requires IRS permission. |
| Returns of acquired companies | Separate returns through date of consolidation, then join in consolidated return. | Continue filing for each company's tax year. No extra returns needed. |
| Intercompany dividend | Eliminated, not taxed. | Include in taxable income, then claim dividends received deduction. |
| Lower tax brackets | Share one set of rates among the group. | Share one set of rates among the group. |
| Accumulated earnings credit, $150,000/$250,000 floor | Share one floor among the group. | Share one floor among the group. |
| Liability for tax | Each company liable for the entire consolidated tax liability. | Each company liable only for its own tax. |
| Statute of limitations | Extension for one company applies to all in the group. | Each company retains its own statute of limitations. |
| Accounting methods | Need not conform to parent. | Need not conform to parent. |
| NOLs, capital gains/losses, § 1231 gains/losses, charitable contribution deductions, dividends received deductions, foreign tax credit payments and baskets, etc. | Computed on a consolidated basis. | Computed separately for each company. |
| Gain/loss on intercompany transactions | Deferred. | Not deferred. |
| Basis of parent's investment | Changes due to subsidiary operating gain/loss, taxes, and distributions. | No adjustments. |

- Discounted marginal tax rates on the first $75,000 of taxable income.[8]
- The $150,000 or $250,000 accumulated earnings credit.[9]
- The $40,000 exemption in computing the alternative minimum tax liability.[10]

In addition, members of a controlled group must defer the recognition of any realized loss on intercompany sales until a sale is made at a gain to a nongroup member.[11] Similarly, any gain on the sale of depreciable property between members of a controlled group is recognized as ordinary income.[12]

A parent-subsidiary controlled group exists when one corporation owns at least 80 percent of the voting power or stock value of another corporation on the last day of the tax year.[13] Multiple tiers of subsidiaries and chains of ownership are allowed, as long as the group has an identifiable parent corporation.

---

[8] §§ 11(b)(1) and 1561(a)(1).
[9] §§ 535(c)(2) and 1561(a)(2).
[10] §§ 55(d)(2) and 1561(a)(3).
[11] §§ 267(a)(1), (b)(3), and (f).

[12] §§ 1239(a) and (c).
[13] § 1563(a)(1). For this purpose, stock attribution rules apply. In addition, all stock options are considered to be exercised by their holders. §§ 1563(d)(1) and (e)(1) through (3).

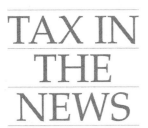

## SOME STATES DON'T ALLOW CONSOLIDATION

Some states have been hesitant to allow a corporate conglomerate doing business within their boundaries to make a consolidation election when computing state taxable income. Perhaps these states question their constitutional ability to tax the income generated by an affiliate that is incorporated elsewhere. Another consideration may be that consolidation would permit losses generated in other states to be applied against taxable income originating within the state.

There is no real consensus among the states as to how to tax a group consolidated for Federal tax purposes. Some states require the group to make a separate election to file on a consolidated basis. Others reserve the right to force the consolidation treatment on a Federal group for state purposes. The diversity that exists is evident in the following table showing a sample of state rules applicable to consolidated returns.

| State | Consolidation Allowed? |
|---|---|
| Alabama | A Federal electing group can make a separate election to file on a consolidated basis for state purposes. With no such election, all must file separate returns. |
| Alaska | If the group files consolidated returns for Federal purposes, it must do so for state purposes. |
| Arizona | A Federal electing group can elect to file on a consolidated basis in the state. The state can require a consolidated return to protect its revenues. |
| Arkansas | A Federal electing group can elect to file a consolidated return in the state so long as it shows some Arkansas taxable income. |
| Connecticut | A Federal electing group can elect to file a consolidated return in the state, but it is called a "combined return." |
| Delaware | No consolidation allowed. |
| District of Columbia | Consolidation allowed only with prior approval of the revenue department. |
| Louisiana | The state can require a consolidated return, but the taxpayer cannot elect to file one. |
| Mississippi | The state can require a consolidated return. The taxpayer can elect to file a consolidated return only with respect to affiliates whose income is generated solely within the state. |

The tax effects brought about by electing to file on a consolidated basis include all of the benefit-sharing effects of controlled group membership. In addition, membership in a consolidated group leads to a much more complex set of controlling tax rules, as discussed in the remainder of this chapter.

**EXAMPLE 8**

ParentCo owns all of the stock of SubCo, and TopCo owns all of the stock of BottomCo. Both pairs of corporations constitute affiliated groups, as well as controlled groups. ParentCo and SubCo elect to file Federal income tax returns on a consolidated basis. TopCo and BottomCo do not so elect. Consequently, they file separate Federal income tax returns.

Both groups share the lower tax rates on the first $75,000 of combined taxable income—ParentCo and SubCo because they file a combined tax return, and TopCo and BottomCo because of the controlled group rules. Neither group can deduct a loss realized on an intercompany sale. But accounting for the taxable income of the consolidated group is much more complex, as indicated by the rules summarized in Table 8–1. ■

The most important differences between an affiliated group and a parent-subsidiary controlled group include the following. In each case, the affiliated group definition is more difficult to meet.

- The 80 percent stock ownership test applies to voting power *and* value for the affiliated group, but only to voting power *or* value for the controlled group. This difference can be important when preferred stock or other shares with voting or liquidation limitations are involved, as in a business succession plan.
- The stock attribution rules applied in meeting the controlled group stock ownership test are not required for the affiliated group definition. In an affiliated group, the identifiable parent corporation itself must meet the 80 percent test.
- Affiliated group members must meet the stock ownership tests on *every day* of the tax year. The corresponding controlled group tests are applied only on the last day of the year.[14]

## LO.4

Describe the corporations that are eligible to file on a consolidated basis.

## ELIGIBILITY FOR THE CONSOLIDATION ELECTION

The Code lists a number of corporations that may *not* use a consolidated return to report their taxable income.[15] Thus, these corporations cannot be used to meet the stock ownership tests, and their taxable incomes cannot be included in a consolidated return. Some of the most frequently encountered entities that are ineligible for consolidated return status include:

- Corporations established outside the United States or in a U.S. possession.
- Tax-exempt (charitable) corporations.[16]
- Insurance companies.
- Partnerships, trusts, estates, limited liability entities, and any other noncorporate entities.[17]

**EXAMPLE 9**

In the first ownership structure in the accompanying figure, Phillips, Rhesus, Todd, and Valiant form an affiliated group, with Phillips as the parent, under the stock ownership rules. Valiant, a life insurance company, cannot be included in a consolidated return, however, so the consolidation election is available only to Phillips, Rhesus, and Todd. In the second structure, Phillips, Rhesus, and Todd form an affiliated group, and all of them can be included in a properly executed consolidated return. Phillips is the identifiable parent of the group. Rhesus and Todd essentially form a brother-sister group below Phillips.

---

[14]§§ 1501 and 1563(b)(1).

[15]§ 1504(b).

[16]This includes any entity that is exempt from tax under § 501. See Chapter 14 for a discussion of the qualification of organizations for exempt status.

[17]Some less frequently encountered entities also are prohibited from filing on a consolidated basis. These include regulated investment companies (mutual funds) and real estate investment trusts. §§ 1504(b)(4) through (7).

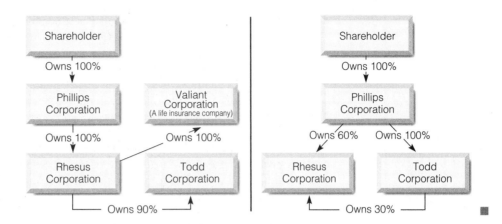

LO.5

Explain the compliance aspects of consolidated returns.

## COMPLIANCE REQUIREMENTS

An eligible entity that meets the stock ownership test can be included in a consolidated group if several compliance requirements are met.

**The Initial Consolidated Return.** The first consolidated tax return must meet certain requirements.

- The Form 1120 for the tax year of the consolidated group should include the taxable results of the operations of all of the members of the consolidated group.[18] This return is filed in lieu of the separate returns of the group members.[19] The identified group then continues to file on a consolidated basis until an eligible group no longer exists or an election to "de-consolidate" is made.[20]
- A Form 1122 should be attached to the first consolidated tax return for each of the subsidiaries included in the group.[21] This form represents a consent by the affiliate to be included in the consolidated group.

The election must be made no later than the extended due date of the parent's return for the year. Only in the case of an inadvertent error can the election to consolidate be rescinded once this extended due date passes.

**EXAMPLE 10**

Parent Corporation owns 100% of the stock of SubCo. Both corporations use calendar tax years and file separate returns. The entities wish to file on a consolidated basis starting with the tax return for 2003. Parent Corporation does not file to obtain an extended due date for its 2003 return.

If the consolidation election is to be effective, Parent must file a Form 1120 that includes the taxable income of the two corporations by March 15, 2004. SubCo must execute a Form 1122 and attach it to the consolidated Form 1120.

---

[18]A consolidation election is inferred, even when specific aspects of pertinent forms are completed incorrectly, as long as the members' combined operations are reported on the Form 1120. *American Pacific Whaling Co. v. Comm.*, 35–1 USTC ¶9065, 14 AFTR 887, 74 F.2d 613 (CA–9, 1935).

[19]Reg. § 1.1502–75(a)(1).

[20]Reg. § 1.1502–75(c). The IRS permits such an election only rarely, on the parent's assertion of (1) a good-cause reason to disengage from consolidated status or (2) a substantial change in the tax law that adversely affects the consolidated tax liability.

[21]Reg. § 1.1502–75(b).

Now assume that Parent Corporation files a complete consolidated Form 1120 on March 3, 2004. On March 5, 2004, the Supreme Court issues a decision that will have a considerable adverse effect on the group's 2006–2009 taxable incomes. If Parent and SubCo file separate 2003 returns by March 15, 2004 (or by some later date if an extension to file is obtained in a timely fashion), the IRS will ignore the consolidation election.

If Parent and SubCo fail to file separate returns in this manner, the election to consolidate is in force for all future years, or until the IRS approves Parent's application to revoke it. ▪

An application to terminate the consolidation election must be filed at least 90 days prior to the extended due date of the consolidated return.[22] Generally, when a subsidiary leaves an ongoing consolidated group, it must wait five years before it can reenter the group.[23]

**Subsequent Consolidated Returns.**   Each consolidated tax return must include Form 851, Affiliations Schedule. This report identifies all of the corporations in the electing group, summarizes pertinent shareholdings and stock ownership changes that occurred during the tax year, and lists the estimated tax payments made by the group members for the year. Affiliates joining an existing consolidated group need not file a Form 1122, though.

Consolidated tax returns are due on the fifteenth day of the third month following the close of the group's tax year (this is March 15 for a calendar year taxpayer). A six-month extension to file the return can be obtained by executing Form 7004, but an estimated payment of the remaining tax liability for the group must accompany the extension application.

**Liability for Taxes.**   Group members are jointly and severally liable for the entire consolidated tax liability.[24] This rule applies to interest and penalties imposed as a result of audits as well as to tax liabilities. Furthermore, the IRS is not bound to follow internal agreements among group members in apportioning the liability.[25]

**EXAMPLE 11**

Parent Corporation, a calendar year taxpayer, acquired 100% of the stock of calendar year SubCo on December 20, 2001. The group filed on a consolidated basis from that date until December 31, 2003, when all of the SubCo stock was sold to Foreign Corporation.

An IRS audit determined that Parent owed an additional $10 million in Federal income taxes, relating to a sale it made on December 30, 2001. By mid-2004, however, Parent's cash-flow difficulties had brought it close to bankruptcy and forced it to cease activities.

Due to the consolidation election, the IRS can assess the delinquent taxes from SubCo (and Foreign Corporation) in 2003. SubCo is liable for the full amount of any consolidated tax liability, even when it is not the source of the income that led to the tax. ▪

Starting with the third consolidated return year, estimated tax payments must be made on a consolidated basis.[26] Prior to that year, estimates can be computed and paid on either a separate or a consolidated basis.

Regular tax liability is computed applying the graduated tax rates to consolidated taxable income, following the requirements of controlled group status. In this regard, contributions to the actual payment of the tax liability often are arranged to correspond to contributions to consolidated taxable income.

---

[22]Reg. § 1.1502–75(c)(1)(i).
[23]§ 1504(a)(3); Rev.Proc. 2002–32, 2002–1 C.B. 959.
[24]Reg. § 1.1502–6(a).

[25]Reg. § 1.1502–6(c).
[26]Reg. § 1.1502–5(a)(1).

**EXAMPLE 12**

Parent Corporation owns 100% of the stock of SubCo, and the two corporations file a consolidated tax return beginning in Year 2. Over the course of a five-year period, the corporations generate the following taxable income/(loss). The low marginal rates that apply to the group's first $75,000 of taxable income might be assigned in various ways.

| Year | Parent's Taxable Income | SubCo's Taxable Income | Low Brackets Assigned to Parent | Low Brackets Assigned to SubCo |
|---|---|---|---|---|
| 1 | $100,000 | ($ 10,000) | $37,500 | $37,500 |
| 2 | 100,000 | (10,000) | 75,000 | –0– |
| 3 | 50,000 | 10,000 | 65,000 | 10,000 |
| 4 | (15,000) | 10,000 | 65,000 | 10,000 |
| 5 | 100,000 | 100,000 | 37,500 | 37,500 |

In Year 1, the consolidated group has not yet been formed. Separate returns are filed, and the low tax brackets are apportioned equally between the two entities. Once consolidated returns begin to be filed in Year 2, the indicated elections are made. For Year 2, all of the low brackets are assigned to Parent, rather than wasting any on SubCo, which has a negative taxable income. For Years 3 and 4, the majority of the low brackets are assigned to Parent, because the group believes that Parent's taxable income is more likely to be adjusted upward on an audit. The apportionment is made to create a cushion for Parent in the event that additional tax liability occurs after the initial return is filed. When group members' taxable incomes are close in value and/or exceed $75,000 in total, as in Year 5, a simple equal apportionment of the low brackets is suggested. ■

Benefits accruing from the graduated corporate tax rates are apportioned equally among the group members unless all members consent to some other method through an annual election. The most commonly used tax-sharing agreements are the *relative taxable income* and *relative tax liability* methods. Under the relative taxable income method,[27] the consolidated tax liability is allocated among the members based on their relative amounts of separate taxable income. When the relative tax liability method is used,[28] the consolidated tax liability is allocated based on the relative hypothetical separate tax liabilities of the members. IRS permission is required for the group to change from one allocation method to another.

**EXAMPLE 13**

The Parent consolidated group reports the following results for the tax year. Assume a 35% marginal tax rate.

| | Parent | SubOne | SubTwo | SubThree | Consolidated |
|---|---|---|---|---|---|
| Ordinary income | $400 | $100 | $–0– | ($ 20) | $480 |
| Capital gain/loss | –0– | –0– | 100 | (25) | 75 |
| § 1231 gain/loss | 50 | –0– | (50) | –0– | –0– |
| Separate taxable incomes | $450 | $100 | $ 50 | ($ 20) | |
| | | | | with a $25 capital loss carryover | |
| Consolidated taxable income | | | | | $555 |

---

[27]§ 1552(a)(1); Reg. § 1.1552–1(a)(1).

[28]§ 1552(a)(2); Reg. § 1.1552–1(a)(2).

| | Parent | SubOne | SubTwo | SubThree | Consolidated |
|---|---|---|---|---|---|
| Consolidated tax liability | | | | | $194 |
| Foreign tax credit, from SubOne | | | | | (19) |
| Net tax due | | | | | $175 |

If the group has consented to the relative taxable income method, the consolidated tax liability is allocated as follows.

| | Separate Taxable Income | Allocation Ratio | Allocated Tax Due |
|---|---|---|---|
| Parent | $450 | 450/600 | $131 |
| SubOne | 100 | 100/600 | 29 |
| SubTwo | 50 | 50/600 | 15 |
| SubThree | –0– | –0– | –0– |
| Totals | $600 | | $175 |

The results are different if the relative tax liability method is in effect. Specifically, SubOne gets an immediate tax benefit for the tax credit that it brings to the group. Under neither method, though, does SubThree get any tax benefit from the losses that it brings to the consolidated group.

| | Separate Taxable Income | Separate Tax Liability | Allocation Ratio | Allocated Tax Due |
|---|---|---|---|---|
| Parent | $450 | $157.5 | 157.5/191 | $144 |
| SubOne | 100 | 16.0* | 16/191 | 15 |
| SubTwo | 50 | 17.5 | 17.5/191 | 16 |
| SubThree | –0– | –0– | –0– | –0– |
| Totals | $600 | $191.0 | | $175 |

* After applying foreign tax credit

Alternative minimum tax (AMT) liability is computed on the basis of consolidated AMTI. The group is allowed only one $40,000 AMT exemption, which is phased out at a rate of 25 percent of the amount by which consolidated AMTI exceeds $150,000. Similarly, the AMT adjustment for adjusted current earnings (ACE), which is 75 percent of the excess of ACE over pre-ACE AMTI, is computed using consolidated amounts.

**Tax Accounting Periods and Methods.**   All the members of a consolidating group must use the parent's tax year.[29] As a result, the group may be required to file a short-year return for the first year a subsidiary is included in the consolidated return, so that the parent's year-end can be adopted.

---

[29]Reg. § 1.1502–76(a)(1).

When a mid-year acquisition occurs, both short years are used in tracking the carryforward period of unused losses and credits. Short-year income and deductions are apportioned between the pre- and post-acquisition periods. The apportionment may be done either on a daily basis or as the items are recorded for financial accounting purposes, at the election of the corporation being acquired.[30]

**EXAMPLE 14**

All of the stock of calendar year SubCo is acquired by Parent Corporation on July 15, 2003. The corporations elect to file a consolidated return immediately upon the acquisition.

SubCo had generated a long-term capital loss in its 2000 tax year. As of January 1, 2004, only one year remains in the five-year carryforward period for the capital loss.

According to SubCo's financial accounting records, $400,000 of its $1 million accounting and taxable income for the year was generated in 2003 after the acquisition. At SubCo's election, either $400,000 (the "books" apportionment method) or $465,753 [(170 postacquisition days/365 days) × $1 million income] (the "daily" method) can be included in the first consolidated return. ■

Members of a consolidated group can continue to use the tax accounting methods that were in place prior to the consolidation election.[31] Thus, the members of a consolidated group may use different accounting methods. On the other hand, because the $5 million gross-receipts test with respect to use of the cash method of accounting is applied on a consolidated basis,[32] some of the group members may need to switch from the cash to the accrual method of tax accounting.

**LO.6**

Compute a parent's investment basis in a subsidiary.

## Stock Basis of Subsidiary

Upon acquiring a subsidiary, the parent corporation records a stock basis on its tax balance sheet equal to the acquisition price. At the end of every consolidated return year, the parent records one or more adjustments to this stock basis, as in the financial accounting "equity" method. This treatment prevents double taxation of gain (or deduction of loss) upon the ultimate disposal of the subsidiary's shares.[33] The adjustments are recorded on the last day of the consolidated return year or on the (earlier) date of the disposal of the shares.[34]

In this regard, positive adjustments to stock basis include:

* An allocable share of consolidated taxable income for the year.
* An allocable share of the consolidated operating or capital loss of a subsidiary that could not utilize the loss through a carryback to a prior year.

Negative adjustments to stock basis include:

* An allocable share of a consolidated taxable loss for the year.
* An allocable share of any carryover operating or capital losses that are deducted on the consolidated return and have not previously reduced stock basis.
* Dividends paid by the subsidiary to the parent out of E & P.

---

[30]Reg. § 1.1502–76(b)(4).
[31]Reg. § 1.1502–17(a).
[32]§§ 448(a)(1) and (c)(2).
[33]This procedure parallels the accounting for tax basis in a partnership or S corporation. See Chapters 10 and 12.

[34]Reg. § 1.1502–32(a). Basis adjustments also are allowed when necessary to determine a tax liability (e.g., when member stock is bought or sold). Prop.Reg. § 1.1502–32(c)(4).

**EXAMPLE 15**

Parent Corporation acquired all of the stock of SubCo on January 1, 2002, for $1 million. The parties immediately elected to file consolidated tax returns. SubCo had a taxable loss of $100,000 in 2002, but it generated $40,000 taxable income in 2003 and $65,000 in 2004. SubCo paid a $10,000 dividend in mid-2004.

Parent has the following stock bases in SubCo on the last day of each of the indicated years.

**2002**  $900,000                     **2003**  $940,000                     **2004**  $995,000 ■

When accumulated postacquisition taxable losses of the subsidiary exceed the acquisition price, an **excess loss account** is created.[35] This account (1) allows the consolidated return to recognize the losses of the subsidiary in the current year and (2) enables the group to avoid the need to reflect a negative stock basis on its tax-basis balance sheet. If the subsidiary stock is redeemed or sold to a nongroup member while an excess loss account exists, the seller recognizes the balance of the account as capital gain income.[36]

**EXAMPLE 16**

Parent Corporation acquired all of the stock of SubCo early in Year 1, for $100,000. As a result of SubCo's operations, the group records the amounts listed.

| Year | Operating Gain/(Loss) | Stock Basis | Excess Loss Account |
|------|----------------------|-------------|---------------------|
| 1 | ($ 40,000) | $60,000 | $  –0– |
| 2 | (80,000) | –0– | 20,000 |
| 3 | 30,000 | 10,000 | –0– |

If Parent sells the SubCo stock for $50,000 at the end of Year 2, Parent recognizes a $70,000 capital gain ($50,000 amount realized – $0 adjusted basis in stock + $20,000 recovery of excess loss account). If the sale takes place at the end of Year 3, the capital gain is $40,000.[37] ■

To limit the recognition effects of an excess loss account, the group may elect instead to reduce the parent's basis of any remaining stock or indebtedness of the subsidiary that is held after the triggering disposition.[38] After the bases of these other investments have been reduced to zero, the seller recognizes only the balance of the excess loss account.

In a chain of more than one tier of subsidiaries, the computation of the stock basis amounts starts with the lowest-level subsidiary, then proceeds up the ownership structure to the parent's holdings. In this regard, there is no such concept as consolidated E & P. Rather, each entity accounts for its own share of consolidated taxable income on an annual basis, immediately recognizing within E & P any gain or loss on intercompany transactions and reducing E & P by an allocable share of the consolidated tax liability.[39]

---

[35]Reg. § 1.1502–19.
[36]Reg. §§ 1.1502–19(a)(1) and (2).
[37]Technically, the Year 3 subsidiary income is first used to eliminate the excess loss account (i.e., before it creates new stock basis). Reg. § 1.1502–32(e)(3).

[38]Reg. § 1.1502–19(a)(6).
[39]Reg. § 1.1502–33(d). In the absence of an election to use some other allocation method, the consolidated tax liability is allocated to each group member according to the relative taxable income method.

■ **FIGURE 8–1**
Computing
Consolidated
Taxable
Income

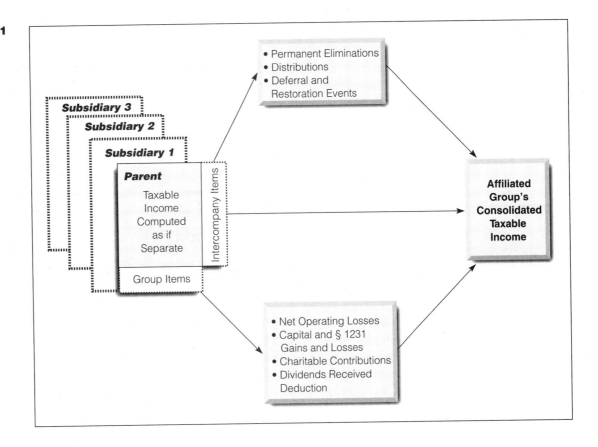

## Computing Consolidated Taxable Income

When an affiliated group computes its taxable income for the year, it does not simply add together the separate taxable income amounts of its members. Two groups of transactions are removed from the members' tax returns and receive special treatment. Then the special items are recombined with the remaining items of members' taxable incomes to obtain the group's consolidated taxable income for the year. Figure 8–1 illustrates how consolidated taxable income is constructed using this sequential approach.

1. Taxable income is computed for each member on a separate basis.
2. "Group items" and "intercompany items" are isolated and receive special treatment.
3. The remaining separate incomes are combined with the group and intercompany items, resulting in consolidated taxable income.

The Code requires this computational procedure to accomplish several goals.

- Certain transactions are accounted for on a consolidated basis (e.g., charitable contributions and capital gains and losses). This requires that the transactions be isolated from the separate tax returns and computed on a groupwide basis.
- Gains and losses from certain intercompany transactions are deferred until a later tax year. Consequently, they are removed from the tax returns of the members that generated them.
- A few intercompany transactions (e.g., dividend payments) are removed from the taxable income calculation altogether, never to appear in a consolidated return.

■ **FIGURE 8–2**
Consolidated Taxable
Income Worksheet

| | Separate Taxable Income | Adjustments | Post-adjustment Amounts |
|---|---|---|---|
| Parent information | _____ | _____ | _____ |
| Subsidiary information | _____ | _____ | _____ |
| Group-basis transactions | _____ | _____ | _____ |
| Deferral/restoration events | _____ | _____ | _____ |
| Consolidated taxable income | | | _____ |

*Permanent eliminations.　　**Group-basis transaction.　　†Deferral/restoration event.

## COMPUTATIONAL PROCEDURE

The remainder of this chapter will follow the computational procedure suggested in Figure 8–1. Figure 8–2 presents a skeleton worksheet for this computational procedure to be used in examples throughout the remainder of this chapter. Additional information is added to the worksheet for every additional subsidiary. In each case, the starting point for this procedure is the separate taxable incomes of all the group members. Adjustments then are made for group and intercompany items, as indicated in the footnotes to the worksheet.

**EXAMPLE 17**

Parent Corporation owns 100% of the stock of SubCo. This year, Parent's taxable income amounted to $100,000, while SubCo generated a $40,000 taxable loss. There were no transactions between the two corporations, and they incurred no capital or § 1231 gains/losses, charitable contributions, dividend income, or other items that are accounted for on a group basis. Accordingly, no adjustments are required, and consolidated taxable income is $60,000.

| | Separate Taxable Income | Adjustments | Post-adjustment Amounts |
|---|---|---|---|
| Parent information | $100,000 | _____ | $100,000 |
| SubCo information | (40,000) | _____ | (40,000) |
| Group-basis transactions | _____ | _____ | _____ |
| Deferral/restoration events | _____ | _____ | _____ |
| Consolidated taxable income | | | $ 60,000 |

*Permanent eliminations.　　**Group-basis transaction.　　†Deferral/restoration event.

## LO.7

Account for intercompany
transactions of a consolidated
group.

## TYPICAL INTERCOMPANY TRANSACTIONS

**General Rules.**　When one member of a consolidated group engages in a transaction with another member of the group, an intercompany transaction occurs. In contrast to the financial accounting treatment of most such transactions, the most commonly encountered items *remain in* the members' separate taxable incomes and therefore cancel each other out on a consolidated basis. For instance, when one group member performs services for another member during the year, the purchaser of the services incurs a deductible expenditure, while the service provider generates includible income. The net result is a zero addition to consolidated taxable income.[40]

---

[40]Reg. §§ 1.1502–13(a)(1)(i) and (b)(1).

This two-step procedure prevents the group from avoiding any related-party loss disallowances. Furthermore, when the members involved in the transaction are using different tax accounting methods, the payor's deduction for the expenditure is deferred until the year in which the recipient recognizes the related gross income.[41]

**EXAMPLE 18**

In the current year, Parent Corporation provided consulting services to its 100%-owned subsidiary, SubCo, under a contract that requires no payments to Parent until next year. Both parties use the accrual method of tax accounting. The services that Parent rendered are valued at $100,000. In addition, Parent purchased $15,000 of supplies from SubCo.

Including these transactions, Parent's taxable income for the year amounted to $500,000. SubCo reported $150,000 of separate taxable income. The group is not required to make any eliminating adjustments. The members' deductions incurred offset the income included by the other party to the intercompany transaction. The consolidated taxable income includes both Parent's $15,000 deduction for supplies and SubCo's $15,000 gross receipts from the sale, so the consolidated taxable income computation *de facto* results in an elimination similar to the kind made in financial accounting. No further adjustment is needed.

| | Separate Taxable Income | Adjustments | Post-adjustment Amounts |
|---|---|---|---|
| Parent information | $500,000 | ———— | $500,000 |
| SubCo information | 150,000 | ———— | 150,000 |
| Group-basis transactions | ———— | ———— | ———— |
| Deferral/restoration events | ———— | ———— | ———— |
| Consolidated taxable income | | | $650,000 |

*Permanent eliminations.  **Group-basis transaction.  †Deferral/restoration event.

**EXAMPLE 19**

Continue with the facts of the previous example, except that Parent is a cash basis taxpayer. Since Parent will not recognize the $100,000 of service income earned in the current year until the next tax period, SubCo's related deduction also is deferred until the following year. Thus, the intercompany item—SubCo's deduction—must be eliminated from consolidated taxable income. Additional record keeping is required to keep track of this intercompany transaction (and all others like it), so that the deduction is claimed in the appropriate year.

| | Separate Taxable Income | Adjustments | Post-adjustment Amounts |
|---|---|---|---|
| Parent information | $500,000 | ———— | $500,000 |
| SubCo information | 150,000 | + $100,000 due to use of different tax accounting methods | 250,000 |
| Group-basis transactions | ———— | ———— | ———— |
| Deferral/restoration events | ———— | ———— | ———— |
| Consolidated taxable income | | | $750,000 |

*Permanent eliminations.  **Group-basis transaction.  †Deferral/restoration event.

---

[41]§§ 267(a)(2) and (b)(3); Reg. § 1.1502–13(b)(2).

Several other rules also apply to intercompany transactions. Certain deferral/restoration events require adjusting computations among tax years; these provisions are addressed in a later section of the chapter. Dividends received from other group members are eliminated from the recipients' separate taxable incomes, and no dividends received deduction is allowed.[42] When the distribution is comprised of noncash assets, the subsidiary payor realizes (but defers recognition of) any gain on the distributed property until the asset leaves the group, and the (eliminated) dividend amount equals the fair market value of the asset.[43]

**EXAMPLE 20**

Parent Corporation received a $50,000 cash dividend from 100%-owned SubCo in the current year. Including this item, Parent's separate taxable income amounted to $200,000, and SubCo reported $240,000 separate taxable income.

Parent cannot claim a dividends received deduction for this payment, but the dividend is eliminated in computing consolidated taxable income. No elimination is required for SubCo, as dividend payments are nondeductible.

| | Separate Taxable Income | Adjustments | Post-adjustment Amounts |
|---|---|---|---|
| Parent information | $200,000 | – $50,000 dividend received from SubCo* | $150,000 |
| SubCo information | 240,000 | ———— | 240,000 |
| Group-basis transactions | ———— | ———— | ———— |
| Deferral/restoration events | ———— | ———— | ———— |
| Consolidated taxable income | | | $390,000 |

*Permanent eliminations.    **Group-basis transaction.    †Deferral/restoration event.

Realized gains and losses from other intercompany transactions involving stock or debt of group members are treated as deferral events, which are discussed later in the chapter.[44] Several other permanent eliminations are delineated in the Regulations.[45]

**LO.8**

Identify limitations that restrict the use of losses and credits of group members derived in separate return years.

**Members' Net Operating Losses.**   Most often, the election to file consolidated returns is motivated by the parent corporation's desire to use the positive tax attributes of the subsidiary corporation, especially its NOLs. A number of provisions, however, discourage corporate acquisitions that are solely tax motivated. These include §§ 381 and 382, which limit the current-year and overall use of NOL carryovers by parties in a tax-favored reorganization (see Chapter 7), and §§ 269 and 482, which allow the IRS to reallocate income and deduction items of related parties that allegedly distort taxable income.

The usual corporate NOL computations are available for the losses of the consolidated group. Excessive losses are carried back 2 years and then forward 20 years, although the parent may elect to forgo the carryback deductions for all

---

[42]Reg. § 1.1502–14(a)(1). If the distribution exceeds the payor's E & P, the stock basis of the payor is reduced. When the basis reaches zero, an excess loss account is created. Reg. § 1.1502–14(a)(2). Dividends received from nongroup members may result in a dividends received deduction; they constitute a group-basis item (discussed later in the chapter).

[43]§§ 301(b)(1) and (d); 311(b)(1); Reg. §§ 1.1502–14(c)(1) and –14T; Ltr.Rul. 8922096.
[44]Reg. §§ 1.1502–14(b) through (e).
[45]Reg. §§ 1.1502–15 through –19.

members of the group. The NOL is derived after removing any consolidated charitable contribution deduction and capital gain or loss from consolidated taxable income. These items are removed because they have their own carryover periods and rules.[46] The consolidated dividends received deduction remains a part of the consolidated NOL.[47]

**EXAMPLE 21**

Parent Corporation and SubCo have filed consolidated returns since both entities were incorporated in 2001. Neither group member incurred any capital gain or loss transactions during 2001–2003, nor did they make any charitable contributions. Taxable income computations for the members include the following.

| Year | Parent's Taxable Income | SubCo's Taxable Income | Consolidated Taxable Income |
|------|------------------------|------------------------|------------------------------|
| 2001 | $100,000 | $ 40,000 | $140,000 |
| 2002 | 100,000 | (40,000) | 60,000 |
| 2003 | 100,000 | (140,000) | ? |
| 2004 | 100,000 | 210,000 | ? |

The 2003 consolidated loss of $40,000 can be carried back to offset 2001 consolidated taxable income. Alternatively, Parent can elect to carry the loss forward to 2004, forgoing any carryback computation. This might be appropriate given an increase in statutory tax rates effective for 2004 or an application of the AMT in 2001 and 2002.

Examine SubCo's 2003 NOL of $140,000. The amount resulted from the following combination of transactions for the year. Unused contributions and capital gain/loss items are subject to their own carryover periods, and they constitute group-basis items, as identified in Figure 8–1.

| | |
|---|---|
| Operating loss | ($ 140,000) |
| Net capital gain | 15,000 |
| Charitable contributions | 20,000 |
| Separate taxable income | (125,000) |

Complications arise, however, when the corporations enter or depart from a consolidated group, so that members' operating losses are either incurred in a "separate return year" and deducted in a "consolidated return year," or vice versa. A variety of restrictions limit the availability of such deductions to discourage profitable corporations from acquiring unprofitable entities simply to file immediate refund claims based on loss and credit carryforwards. Figure 8–3 summarizes the applicable limitations.

In any case where the members of a consolidated group change over time, the taxpayer must apportion the consolidated NOL among the group members. When more than one group member generates a loss for the consolidated year, the following formula is used to apportion the loss among the electing group's members.

$$\frac{\text{Member's separate NOL}}{\text{Members' aggregate NOLs}} \; \otimes \; \text{Consolidated NOL} \; \ominus \; \text{Member's apportioned NOL}$$

---

[46]For instance, no election is available that would enable the parent to forgo the net capital loss carryback.

[47]Reg. § 1.1502–21(f).

■ **FIGURE 8–3**
Limitations on Use of Net Operating Losses

| Year of Loss | Year Reported | Applicable Rules |
|---|---|---|
| Consolidated | Consolidated | • Carry back 2 years, forward 20; parent can elect to carry forward only.<br>• § 382 limitations apply if ownership change occurs. |
| Consolidated | Separate | • Carry back/forward only the member's apportioned loss to its separate return.<br>• Offspring rule may allow carryback of apportioned loss to year/return prior to member's existence.<br>• Departing group member takes apportioned loss with it. |
| Separate | Consolidated | • Group's deduction of member's loss carryforward is limited to member's current-year or cumulative contribution to consolidated taxable income. This limit does not apply to a group's parent.<br>• § 382 limitations apply if ownership change occurs. |

**EXAMPLE 22**

Parent Corporation and SubCo have filed consolidated returns since 2002. Both entities were incorporated in 2001. Neither group member incurred any capital gain or loss transactions during 2001–2004, nor did they make any charitable contributions. Taxable income computations for the members are listed below.

| Year | Parent's Taxable Income | SubCo's Taxable Income | Consolidated Taxable Income |
|---|---|---|---|
| 2001* | $100,000 | $ 40,000 | N/A |
| 2002** | 100,000 | (40,000) | $60,000 |
| 2003** | 100,000 | (140,000) | ? |
| 2004** | 100,000 | 210,000 | ? |

*Separate return year.     **Consolidated return year.

In 2003, SubCo can carry back the entire $40,000 consolidated NOL to its separate 2001 tax year, because it is solely responsible for generating the loss. SubCo files for the refund of taxes that result from the carryback, and it alone receives the refund.[48]

Alternatively, Parent could elect to forgo the carryback of the 2003 consolidated loss, thereby preserving the loss deduction for the group's subsequent years. In that case, the 2004 tax reduction from the $40,000 NOL deduction would be claimed merely by filing the 2004 consolidated tax return, and Parent would receive the refund on behalf of the group. ■

In years when a group member files a separate return, only the apportioned NOL may be carried over.

---

[48]Reg. §§ 1.1502–78(b)(1) and (c), Example 4.

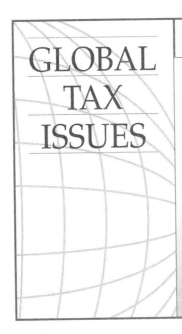

## GLOBAL TAX ISSUES

### CONSOLIDATED RETURNS AND NOLS

Very few countries besides the United States allow the use of consolidated returns. In the view of most countries, tax deductions for operating losses should be used only by those who generated them, not by some sister or other related corporation. This is as much a social principle (the sanctity of the corporate entity) as a revenue-raising provision (NOL deductions mean lower tax collections).

The way European business is conducted makes this result more understandable, as the tax laws of the various countries must ensure that operating losses generated in Tedesco, for instance, are not shifted to Cadenza and converted to deductions there.

This restrictive approach to the trading of operating loss deductions is found in U.S. multistate tax law as well, where tax-oriented border incentives can be especially important. Some states (like Pennsylvania) have, over a specified time period, disallowed the use of loss carryovers of any sort, whereas others (like Ohio) require the taxpayer to deduct only losses assigned to the taxpayer's in-state operations. Multistate tax issues are addressed in Chapter 15.

---

**EXAMPLE 23**

Parent Corporation, SubOne, and SubTwo have filed consolidated returns since 2002. All of the entities were incorporated in 2001. None of the group members incurred any capital gain or loss transactions during 2001–2004, nor did they make any charitable contributions. Taxable income computations for the members are listed below.

| Year | Parent's Taxable Income | SubOne's Taxable Income | SubTwo's Taxable Income | Consolidated Taxable Income |
|------|------------------------|-------------------------|-------------------------|-----------------------------|
| 2001* | $100,000 | $100,000 | $ 40,000 | N/A |
| 2002** | 100,000 | 100,000 | (40,000) | $160,000 |
| 2003** | 100,000 | (60,000) | (120,000) | ? |
| 2004** | 100,000 | 100,000 | 210,000 | ? |

*Separate return year.     **Consolidated return year.

If Parent does not elect to forgo the carryback of the 2003 consolidated NOL of $80,000, both subsidiaries can carry losses back to their 2001 separate return years and receive separate refunds. SubOne can carry back a $26,667 loss [(SubOne's NOL $60,000/aggregate NOLs $180,000) × consolidated NOL $80,000], and SubTwo can carry back a $53,333 loss. ■

Under the so-called offspring rule, the consolidated group can use a carryback loss that is apportioned to a member of the electing group, even though that member was not in existence in the carryback year.[49] If the member joined the group immediately upon its incorporation, but cannot use an apportioned loss in the carryback period because it was not in existence, that loss is still available to the group.[50]

---

[49]Reg. § 1.1502–79(a)(2).
[50]Prop.Reg. § 1.1502–21(b)(2)(ii)(B) restricts the use of this loss to the parent, if the carryback year is a separate return year for the parties.

**EXAMPLE 24**

Parent Corporation, SubOne, and SubTwo have filed consolidated returns since 2002. The first two entities were incorporated and consolidated in 2001, and SubTwo came into existence in 2002 through an asset spin-off from Parent. None of the group members incurred any capital gain or loss transactions during 2001–2004, nor did they make any charitable contributions. Taxable income computations for the members are listed below.

| Year | Parent's Taxable Income | SubOne's Taxable Income | SubTwo's Taxable Income | Consolidated Taxable Income |
|------|-------------------------|-------------------------|-------------------------|-----------------------------|
| 2001* | $100,000 | $ 40,000 | — | $140,000 |
| 2002* | 100,000 | 100,000 | ($ 40,000) | 160,000 |
| 2003* | 100,000 | (60,000) | (120,000) | ? |
| 2004* | 100,000 | 100,000 | 210,000 | ? |

*Consolidated return year.

If Parent does not elect to forgo the carryback of the 2003 consolidated NOL of $80,000, SubOne can carry its $26,667 loss back to 2001. SubTwo's $53,333 share of the loss can also be carried back to 2001 and used by members of the consolidated group. Under the offspring rule, SubTwo is treated as being a member of the group for the entire *group* carryback period because its existence is rooted in Parent's assets. ■

When a corporation leaves a consolidated group, it takes with it any apportioned share of any unused loss carryforwards, to be used on its subsequent separate returns.

**EXAMPLE 25**

Parent Corporation, SubOne, and SubTwo have filed consolidated returns since 2001, the year in which all of the entities were incorporated. None of the group members incurred any capital gain or loss transactions during 2001–2004, nor did they make any charitable contributions. Taxable income computations for the members are listed below.

| Year | Parent's Taxable Income | SubOne's Taxable Income | SubTwo's Taxable Income | Consolidated Taxable Income |
|------|-------------------------|-------------------------|-------------------------|-----------------------------|
| 2001* | $100,000 | $100,000 | $ 40,000 | $240,000 |
| 2002* | 100,000 | 100,000 | (40,000) | 160,000 |
| 2003* | 100,000 | (60,000) | (120,000) | ? |
| 2004** | 100,000 | 100,000 | 210,000 | N/A |

*Consolidated return year.    **Separate return year.

Parent elects to forgo any loss carryback for the group's 2003 operations. On the first day of the 2004 tax year, a non-U.S. investor purchases all of the stock of SubTwo. On its 2004 separate return, SubTwo can deduct its $53,333 share of the 2003 NOL carryforward.[51] ■

---

[51]SubTwo cannot take the entire $120,000 NOL that is attributable to it. Reg. §§ 1.1502–79(a)(1)(ii) and (b)(2)(ii). Losses and carryovers must first be absorbed within the current consolidated return year before any loss apportionment occurs.

When an NOL is carried forward from a separate return year onto a consolidated return, another set of limitations, known as the **separate return limitation year (SRLY)** rules, applies.[52] The consolidated return can include an NOL carryforward from the member's SRLY period only to the extent of the lesser of its (1) current-year or (2) cumulative positive contribution to current-year consolidated income.[53]

The SRLY limitations never apply to the electing group's identifiable parent.[54] Nor do they apply to a member that met all of the eligibility and stock ownership tests for consolidated return status, but never was included in a consolidation election.

**EXAMPLE 26**

Parent Corporation and SubCo have filed consolidated returns since 2002. Both entities were incorporated in 2001. Neither group member incurred any capital gain or loss transactions during 2001–2004, nor did they make any charitable contributions. Taxable income computations for the members are listed below.

| Year | Parent's Taxable Income | SubCo's Taxable Income | Consolidated Taxable Income |
|------|------|------|------|
| 2001* | $100,000 | ($40,000) | N/A |
| 2002** | 100,000 | (10,000) | $90,000 |
| 2003** | 100,000 | 15,000 | ? |
| 2004** | 100,000 | 70,000 | ? |

*Separate return year.     **Consolidated return year.

The thrust of the SRLY rules is to limit Parent's deduction of SubCo's losses from a separate return year against consolidated income. Accordingly, none of SubCo's separate return loss from 2001 can be deducted in computing 2002 consolidated taxable income; the deduction is limited to the lesser of SubCo's current-year (zero) or cumulative (zero) contribution to consolidated taxable income.

In computing 2003 consolidated taxable income, the SubCo SRLY loss deduction is limited to $5,000, the lesser of SubCo's current-year ($15,000) or cumulative ($5,000) contribution to consolidated taxable income. The remaining SRLY deduction reduces consolidated taxable income beginning in 2004. ■

**EXAMPLE 27**

Parent Corporation and SubCo have filed consolidated returns since 2002. Both entities were incorporated in 2001. Neither group member incurred any capital gain or loss transactions during 2001–2004, nor did they make any charitable contributions. Taxable income computations for the members are listed below.

| Year | Parent's Taxable Income | SubCo's Taxable Income | Consolidated Taxable Income |
|------|------|------|------|
| 2001* | ($ 40,000) | $100,000 | N/A |
| 2002** | (100,000) | (10,000) | ($110,000) |
| 2003** | 20,000 | 165,000 | ? |
| 2004** | 100,000 | 70,000 | ? |

*Separate return year.     **Consolidated return year.

---

[52]Reg. § 1.1502–21(c). The SRLY rules apply to capital loss and credit carryforwards as well.

[53]Prop.Reg. § 1.1502–21(c).
[54]Reg. § 1.1502–1(f)(2)(i), known as the "lonely parent" rule.

The 2003 consolidated return can include a deduction for Parent's entire 2001 NOL of $40,000. The deduction is not limited to the lesser of Parent's current-year ($20,000) or cumulative (zero) contribution to consolidated taxable income. SRLY rules do not apply to the group's parent. ■

When both the SRLY rules and a § 382 limitation apply because an ownership change has occurred (see Chapter 7), the § 382 provisions override the SRLY limits.[55]

**EXAMPLE 28**

The Parent consolidated group includes SubTwo, which was acquired as part of a § 382 ownership change. SubTwo brought with it to the group a $180,000 NOL carryforward, $125,000 of which is available this year under the SRLY rules due to SubTwo's positive contribution to the group's taxable income. The § 382 limitation with respect to SubTwo is $100,000. Accordingly, only $100,000 of the SubTwo NOL can be used to reduce consolidated taxable income this year.

If the § 382 limitation had been $200,000 instead, the full $180,000 NOL deduction would have been allowed. The § 382 rules prevail even with respect to SRLY losses that overlap with the same tax year. ■

**LO.9**

Derive deductions and credits on a consolidated basis.

## COMPUTATION OF GROUP ITEMS

Several income and deduction items are derived on a consolidated-group basis. Therefore, statutory limitations and allowances are applied to the group as though it were a single corporation. This computational convention allows group members to match various types of gains and losses and to increase specific limitations, required by the Code, in a manner that optimizes the overall tax benefit.

Specifically, the following items are computed on a group basis with the usual C corporation tax effects applied to the combined group amounts (see Chapter 2).

- Net capital gain/loss.
- Section 1231 gain/loss.
- Casualty/theft gain/loss.
- Charitable contributions.
- Dividends received deduction.
- Net operating loss.

Following the computational procedure of Figures 8–1 and 8–2, all of the group-basis items are removed from each member's separate taxable income. Then, using the consolidated taxable income figure to that point, statutory limitations are applied to determine group-basis gains, losses, income, and deductions.

**EXAMPLE 29**

Parent Corporation's current-year taxable income included $300,000 net income from operations and a $50,000 net long-term capital gain. Parent also made a $40,000 contribution to State University. Accordingly, its separate taxable income amounted to $315,000.

| | |
|---|---|
| Income from operations | $300,000 |
| Capital gain income | +50,000 |
| Charitable contribution (maximum) | −35,000 |
| Separate taxable income | $315,000 |

[55]Reg. §§ 1.1502–15(g) and –21(g).

SubCo generated $170,000 income from operations and incurred a $45,000 short-term capital loss. Thus, its separate taxable income was $170,000, and aggregate separate taxable income for the group amounted to $485,000.

Upon consolidation, a larger amount of Parent's charitable contribution is deductible, and its capital gain is almost fully sheltered from current-year tax.

| | Separate Taxable Income | Adjustments | Post-adjustment Amounts |
|---|---|---|---|
| Parent information | $315,000 | – $50,000 capital gain income** | $300,000 |
| | | + $35,000 charitable contribution deduction** | |
| SubCo information | 170,000 | $45,000 short-term capital loss** | 170,000 |
| Group-basis transactions | | + $5,000 net long-term capital gain | –35,000 |
| | | – $40,000 charitable contribution deduction (maximum for group is $47,500) | |
| Deferral/restoration events | | | |
| Consolidated taxable income | | | $435,000 |
| *Permanent eliminations. | **Group-basis transaction. | †Deferral/restoration event. | |

Computing these items on a group basis does not always result in a reduction of aggregate group taxable income. Nevertheless, the possibility of using the group-basis computations may affect transactions by group members late in the tax year when it becomes apparent that planning opportunities may be available. It may also encourage the taxpayer to seek out fellow group members that bring complementary tax attributes to the consolidated return.

**EXAMPLE 30**

Parent Corporation owns 15% of the stock of Outsider Corporation throughout the year. Outsider paid a $150,000 dividend to Parent during the year. Parent also generated $400,000 of taxable operating income and sold a § 1231 asset at a $10,000 gain. Parent's separate taxable income is computed below.

| | |
|---|---|
| Operating income | $ 400,000 |
| Dividend income | +150,000 |
| § 1231 gain | +10,000 |
| Dividends received deduction (70%) | –105,000 |
| Separate taxable income | $ 455,000 |

A 10% owner of Outsider, SubCo also received a $100,000 dividend. SubCo's operations produced a $20,000 net taxable loss for the year, and it sold a § 1231 asset at a $4,000 loss. Thus, SubCo's separate taxable income is computed as follows.

| | | |
|---|---|---|
| Operating income | ($ 20,000) | |
| Dividend income | +100,000 | |
| § 1231 loss | −4,000 | |
| Dividends received deduction[56] | −53,200 | |
| Separate taxable income | $ 22,800 | |

A consolidated return increases the group's dividends received deduction,[57] but it wastes the opportunity to claim SubCo's § 1231 loss as an ordinary deduction.

| | Separate Taxable Income | Adjustments | Post-adjustment Amounts |
|---|---|---|---|
| Parent information | $455,000 | − $150,000 dividend received from Outsider** | $400,000 |
| | | − $10,000 § 1231 gain** | |
| | | + $105,000 dividends received deduction** | |
| SubCo information | 22,800 | − $100,000 dividend received from Outsider** | (20,000) |
| | | + $4,000 § 1231 loss | |
| | | + $53,200 dividends received deduction | |
| Group-basis transactions | | + $250,000 dividend received from Outsider | +81,000 |
| | | − $175,000 dividends received deduction (70% × $250,000) | |
| | | + $6,000 § 1231 gain | |
| Deferral/restoration events | | | |
| Consolidated taxable income | | | $461,000 |

*Permanent eliminations.    **Group-basis transaction.    †Deferral/restoration event.

Other items computed on a consolidated basis include all elements of the general business and research credits, any recapture of those credits, the foreign tax credit, the percentage depletion deduction, and all elements of AMTI.

## DEFERRAL AND RESTORATION EVENTS

A special class of intercompany transactions receives deferral treatment under the Regulations.[58] The gain or loss realized on these transactions is removed from consolidated taxable income until a **restoration event** occurs. The purpose of this "matching rule" is to prevent group members from accelerating loss deductions that relate to sales of assets within the group. Generally, the loss is deductible only when control of the asset leaves the electing group.

---

[56]Limited to 70% of taxable income before the deduction. § 246(b)(1).

[57]The group cannot apply an 80% rate for the dividends received deduction, even though aggregate group ownership in Outsider Corporation now exceeds 20%. Reg. § 1.1502–26(a)(1)(i).

[58]Reg. §§ 1.1502–13(c) through (h) and –13T.

Deferral/restoration treatment applies to sales of assets or the performance of services among group members. The entire deferred gain or loss is restored to the consolidated taxable income computation when, say, the asset is transferred outside the group through a subsequent sale. Full gain or loss restoration can also be triggered under the "acceleration rule" when the transferor of the property leaves the group or the consolidation election is terminated. Generally, the restored gain or loss is recognized in the same manner as it would have been on the initial transfer.[59] Asset basis and holding periods "start over," reflecting the purchaser's intermediary acquisition.[60] The installment method is not available for any deferral/restoration transaction.[61]

**EXAMPLE 31**

Parent Corporation sold a plot of land to SubCo in the current year for $100,000. Parent had acquired the land 10 years ago for $40,000. The consolidated return also reflects the operating results of the parties: Parent generated $10,000 income, and SubCo produced a $100,000 gain.

This intercompany transaction is a deferral event: Parent's $60,000 realized gain is deferred through an elimination in the computation of consolidated taxable income. SubCo's basis in the land is $100,000, and its holding period in the land begins with this year's purchase. The $60,000 gain is recognized when SubCo sells the land to Outsider Corporation.

|  | Separate Taxable Income | Adjustments | Post-adjustment Amounts |
|---|---|---|---|
| Parent information | $ 70,000 | ———— | $ 70,000 |
| SubCo information | 100,000 | ———— | 100,000 |
| Group-basis transactions |  |  |  |
| Deferral/restoration events |  | – $60,000 gain on intercompany sale to SubCo† | –60,000 |
| Consolidated taxable income |  |  | $110,000 |
| *Permanent eliminations.    **Group-basis transaction.    †Deferral/restoration event. | | | |

SubCo sold the land to Outsider for $110,000 in a year in which its operating income totaled $60,000 (exclusive of the restoration event, the sale of the land), and Parent's operating income amounted to $170,000.

|  | Separate Taxable Income | Adjustments | Post-adjustment Amounts |
|---|---|---|---|
| Parent information | $170,000 | ———— | $170,000 |
| SubCo information | 70,000 | ———— | 70,000 |
| Group-basis transactions |  |  |  |
| Deferral/restoration events |  | + $60,000 restored gain on Parent's sale to SubCo† | +60,000 |
| Consolidated taxable income |  |  | $300,000 |
| *Permanent eliminations.    **Group-basis transaction.    †Deferral/restoration event. | | | |

[59]Sections 267 and 1239 may convert other types of gain into ordinary income. See especially Reg. §§ 1.267(f)–1T and –2T and 1.1239–1(a) and (b)(3).

[60]Reg. § 1.1502–13(g).
[61]Reg. § 1.1502–13(c)(1)(ii).

Any deferred gain or loss on a transfer is recognized upon the earliest restoration event to occur. Other potential restoration events include the following.

- The acquiring group member claims a cost recovery deduction for the asset.[62]
- A nongroup member's installment note is transferred among group members (e.g., with the transferred asset itself).

Generally, the deferral/restoration rules are attractive to the group when intercompany sales take place at a gain. When such sales generate losses, however, the mandatory nature of the rules may become burdensome. Consequently, the Regulations allow an election that overrides the deferral/restoration rules. With the election, all intercompany gains and losses are immediately includible or deductible.[63] The election remains in force until the IRS consents to its revocation.

**LO.10**

Demonstrate tax planning opportunities available to consolidated groups.

**Tax Planning Considerations**

## CHOOSING CONSOLIDATED RETURN PARTNERS

Taxpayers should optimize their overall tax benefits when choosing consolidated return partners. Within the limitations of the rules discussed earlier in the chapter, attributes of potential target corporations might include some of the following.

- Loss and credit carryovers.
- Passive activity income, loss, or credits.
- Gains that can be deferred through intercompany sales.
- Contributions to consolidated ACE adjustments.
- Excess limitation amounts (e.g., with respect to charitable contributions).
- Section 1231 gains, losses, and lookback profiles.

## CONSOLIDATION VERSUS 100 PERCENT DIVIDENDS RECEIVED DEDUCTION

When adequate ownership is held, a 100 percent dividends received deduction is available for payments received from subsidiaries with whom a consolidated return is *not* filed. Thus, this tax benefit is still available when the taxpayer wishes to affiliate with an insurance company, foreign entity, or other ineligible corporation. A taxpayer that cannot find potential group partners with the desired level of complementary tax attributes may also take advantage of this benefit.

## PROTECTING THE GROUP MEMBERS' LIABILITY FOR TAX PAYMENTS

Because all group members are responsible for consolidated tax liabilities, interest, and penalties, target subsidiaries and their (present and potential) shareholders should take measures to protect their separate interests.

**EXAMPLE 32**

Return to the facts of Example 11. Exposure by SubCo and its successive shareholders to tax (and all other) liabilities of Parent Corporation should be minimized by including appropriate clauses in purchase contracts and related documents. For instance, (1) Foreign Corporation could alter its negotiating position so that it pays less to acquire the SubCo

---

[62]Reg. §§ 1.1502–13(d)(1) and –13T(l). The deferred gain is restored to consolidated taxable income over a period of years, using the ACRS, MACRS, or other cost recovery method that the acquiring group member employs. Thus, the present value of the tax on this

restored gain is reduced when the purchaser uses slower methods of cost recovery.

[63]Reg. § 1.1502–13(c)(3).

## CONCEPT SUMMARY 8–2

### The Consolidated Tax Return

1. Groups of corporations form for a variety of tax and nontax reasons. The election to file Federal income tax returns on a consolidated basis allows certain group members to use their positive tax attributes (e.g., loss or credit carryovers) to offset negative tax attributes (e.g., positive taxable income) of other members.

2. Consolidated tax returns are limited to eligible corporations that satisfy stock ownership tests and meet various compliance requirements. For instance, all group members must conform their tax years to that of the parent of the group. Group members may use different tax accounting methods, however.

3. Group members are jointly and severally liable for the overall tax liability of the group. For the most part, computations of estimated tax liabilities must be made on a consolidated basis.

4. The stock basis of a subsidiary is derived from the acquisition price of the stock, increased by the taxable income (or decreased by the losses) of the subsidiary, and decreased by dividend distributions. An excess loss account is created when aggregate losses of the subsidiary exceed both the purchase price and ensuing income amounts. The excess loss account is recaptured as capital gain when the subsidiary stock is disposed of.

5. Under the § 382 or SRLY rules, NOL carryforwards may be deferred when they relate to subsidiaries acquired by the group. When both restrictions apply, the § 382 rules prevail.

6. In computing consolidated taxable income, certain items, such as charitable contributions and § 1231 gains and losses, are computed on a consolidated basis, while other gains and losses are deferred until later tax periods. The group is subject to severe restrictions in using any operating losses of a subsidiary that has been acquired or disposed of.

stock, or (2) SubCo might attempt to recover any Parent taxes that it pays through courts other than the Tax Court. ■

A short tax year may be created when a member with a nonmatching tax year joins or leaves the group. When this occurs, the group should consider measures to limit the ensuing negative tax consequences. For instance, additional income can be accelerated into the short year of acquisition. This will reduce any loss carryforwards when the carryover period is effectively shortened due to the takeover. The group should also make suitable income-allocation elections in assigning income to the short year. Finally, group estimated tax payments should be computed using both consolidated and separate liability amounts to determine the more beneficial method. In this way, only the minimum quarterly tax payments are made, and the benefits of the time value of money are maximized.

### ELECTING TO POSTPONE RECOGNITION OF THE EXCESS LOSS ACCOUNT

An election to reduce the investment basis of remaining subsidiary stock and debt (i.e., upon disposition of shares when an excess loss account exists) may be attractive when the remaining shares are not likely to be sold in the near future. In that case, the present value of the tax on any resulting increased gain will be low. The election may also be used to offset any recognition of the postponed gain upon debt repayments or stock sales when future operating losses are anticipated. The election generally is not attractive when operating loss carryforwards are available in the current year. These can be used to shelter the gain recognized on recovery of the excess loss account.

**EXAMPLE 33**

Parent Corporation owns preferred stock of SubCo with a basis of $10,000. Parent's basis in its common stock investment in SubCo has been eliminated through SubCo's operating losses; in fact, Parent holds a $6,000 excess loss account for SubCo.

Parent sells the SubCo common for $9,000. Thus, it must recognize a $15,000 capital gain on the sale. Alternatively, Parent can elect to recognize only a $9,000 gain on the sale and to reduce its basis in the SubCo preferred to $4,000. ■

## KEY TERMS

| | | |
|---|---|---|
| Affiliated group, 8–8 | Excess loss account, 8–18 | Separate return limitation year (SRLY), 8–27 |
| Consolidated return, 8–3 | Restoration event, 8–30 | |

## PROBLEM MATERIALS

### Discussion Questions

1. The restructuring of a conglomerate usually occurs for nontax reasons (e.g., to increase market share or stock price). What are some other market-driven reasons to form controlled and affiliated groups?

**Decision Making**

2. Describe how a corporate entity might be restructured to enable the resulting group to qualify for a consolidation election. [Hint: Recall the corporate changes discussed in Chapter 7, such as the "A" reorganization.]

3. The Federal government is again running a budget deficit. Do the consolidation rules aid or hinder the balancing of the Federal budget?

**Communications**

4. You are the tax member of a consulting team that is presenting ideas for a possible restructuring to a client. The client has heard that filing consolidated tax returns can produce savings. Prepare for the client an outline on the pros and cons of filing a consolidated return.

5. The election to consolidate cannot be made unless the affiliates meet three threshold tests. What are those tests? How can the group members satisfy them so that the election can occur?

**Issue ID**

6. Black, Brown, and Red Corporations are considering a corporate restructuring that would allow them to file Federal income tax returns on a consolidated basis. Black holds significant NOL carryforwards from several years ago. Brown has always been profitable and is projected to remain so. Red has been successful, but its product cycles are mature and operating losses are likely to begin three years from now and last for a decade. What tax issues should the corporations consider before electing to file on a consolidated basis?

**Issue ID**

7. Continue with the facts presented in Question 6. In addition, assume that Brown Corporation has a history of making large, continuous charitable contributions in its community. In the next three years, Brown's largest investment assets will be priced such that they will be attractive candidates for sale. Modify your list of tax issues to include these considerations.

8. Give three examples of operating entities that cannot join a consolidated group.

9. The Flamingo Group cannot decide whether to start to file on a consolidated basis for Federal income tax purposes, effective for its tax year beginning January 1, 2004. Its computational study of the effects of consolidation is taking longer than expected. What is the latest date by which the group must make this critical decision?

10. The Penguin Group cannot decide whether to cease to file on a consolidated basis for Federal income tax purposes, effective for its tax year beginning January 1, 2004. Its computational study of the effects of such a "de-consolidation" is taking longer than expected. What is the latest date by which the group must make this critical decision?

11. Lavender and Azure began to file a calendar year consolidated return for tax year 2003. The group never extends the due date of its tax returns. Lavender acquires all of the stock of Rose on January 1, 2004, and immediately joins the filing election. All of the Rose stock is sold to another investor at the end of 2006. Explain the significance of the following dates. Which of your answers can change if the taxpayers so elect?
    a. March 15, 2004.
    b. January 1, 2005.
    c. March 15, 2005.
    d. January 1, 2012.

12. Parent Corporation and its wholly owned subsidiary, Child Corporation, file Federal tax returns on a separate basis. Parent manufactures postage meters, and Child provides mail-order services to a cross section of clients in the state.

    Parent uses a calendar tax year, while Child files using an April 30 year-end. Parent's gross receipts for the year total $10 million, and Child's are $2.5 million. Identify some tax issues as to accounting periods and methods that the group would face if the corporations elect to consolidate.

13. In a memo to the tax research file, summarize the most important positive and negative adjustments made by a parent corporation to the stock basis of its subsidiary.

14. In December 2003, Parent Corporation renders services worth $250,000 to its wholly owned subsidiary, Child Corporation. Both entities use calendar tax years. Parent uses accrual tax accounting, while Child employs the cash method of accounting. The entities have been filing on a consolidated basis since Child was incorporated many years ago.

    Parent's operations for 2003 resulted in a $2 million loss. Parent sends Child an invoice for the services in December 2003, and Child pays it in January 2004. What tax consequences are the parties trying to accomplish?

15. SubOne Corporation brought a $2 million NOL carryforward into a group of corporations that elected to file on a consolidated basis as of the beginning of this year. Combined results for the year generated $10 million taxable income, $500,000 of which was attributable to SubOne's activities for the year. Has SubOne been a good consolidation partner?

16. Parent and Child Corporations have filed on a consolidated basis since the mid-1970s. Junior Corporation was formed at the beginning of this year through an asset split-off from Parent. Operations this year resulted in a $2 million operating loss, one-fourth of which can be traced to Junior. Should Junior join the consolidated group this year? Will the group be able to carry back and claim a refund for the $500,000 NOL that is attributable to Junior?

17. Beige owned all of the stock of White when the two corporations were formed a decade ago. The group immediately elected to file on a consolidated basis. The management team of White now has purchased the company from the parent and intends to carry on and expand the business into new markets. When White left the Beige consolidated group, the group held a $3 million NOL carryforward, $800,000 of which was attributable to White operations under formulas used by all of the parties. White will generate $300,000 on each of its first five years' worth of separate returns.

    Advise White as to who "owns" the carryforwards after the corporate division.

18. Junior was a member of the Rice consolidated group for many years. It left the group effective for the 2003 tax year. In 2000, Junior sold a plot of land to Parent at a $600,000 realized loss. Recognition of that loss by the group was deferred under the intercompany sale rule. As a departing group member, does Junior have any right to take the loss with it to be used on its subsequent separate returns? Prepare a memo for the tax research file, outlining the arguments both in Junior's favor and in the remaining group's favor.

## Problems

19. Apply the controlled and affiliated group rules to determine whether a parent-subsidiary controlled group or an affiliated group exists in each of the following independent situations. Circle Y for yes and N for no.

| Situation | Parent-Subsidiary Controlled Group? | | Affiliated Group? | |
|---|---|---|---|---|
| a. Throughout the year, Parent owns 65% of the stock of SubCo. | Y | N | Y | N |
| b. Throughout the year, Parent owns 85% of SubCo's outstanding stock, worth 75% of SubCo's market value. | Y | N | Y | N |
| c. For 11 months, Parent owns 75% of the stock of SubCo. For the last month of the tax year, Parent owns 100% of the SubCo stock. | Y | N | Y | N |

20. Senior Corporation owns all of the stock of Junior, Ltd., a corporation that has been declared bankrupt and has no net assets. Junior still owes $1 million to Wholesale, Inc., one of its suppliers, and $2.5 million to the IRS for unpaid Federal income taxes. Senior and Junior have always filed Federal income tax returns on a consolidated basis. What is Senior's exposure concerning Junior's outstanding liabilities?

21. Parent and Sub Corporations file their Federal income tax returns on a consolidated basis. Parent, a calendar year taxpayer, owns all of the outstanding stock of Sub. The consolidation election was effective in January 2003. Both companies are profitable, and tax projections for the future appear below. How much must be remitted to the IRS for estimated payments in each year?

| Tax Year | Parent's Federal Tax Estimate | Sub's Federal Tax Estimate |
|---|---|---|
| 2003 | $500 | $100 |
| 2004 | 500 | 175 |
| 2005 | 600 | 240 |
| 2006 | 650 | 290 |

22. ParentCo owns all of DaughterCo, and the group files its Federal income tax returns on a consolidated basis. Both taxpayers are subject to the AMT this year due to active operations in the oil and gas development industry. No intercompany transactions were incurred this year. If the affiliates filed separate returns, they would report the following amounts.

| Company | Adjusted Current Earnings (ACE) | AMT Income before the ACE Adjustment |
|---|---|---|
| ParentCo | $1,200,000 | $500,000 |
| DaughterCo | 150,000 | 300,000 |

How does the consolidation election affect the overall AMT liability of the group?

23. The Parent consolidated group reports the following results for the tax year. Determine each member's share of the consolidated tax liability, assuming that the members all have consented to use the relative taxable income method. Assume a 35% marginal tax rate.

| | Parent | SubOne | SubTwo | SubThree | Consolidated |
|---|---|---|---|---|---|
| Ordinary income | $700 | $200 | $ 20 | ($30) | $ 890 |
| Capital gain/loss | –0– | –0– | 40 | (25) | 15 |
| § 1231 gain/loss | 150 | –0– | (55) | –0– | 95 |
| Separate taxable incomes | $850 | $200 | $ 5 | ($30) | |
| | | | | with a $25 capital loss carryover | |
| Consolidated taxable income | | | | | $1,000 |
| Consolidated tax liability | | | | | $ 350 |
| Energy tax credit, from SubOne | | | | | (44) |
| Net tax due | | | | | $ 306 |

24. Assume the same facts as in Problem 23, except that the group members have adopted the relative tax liability tax-sharing method.

25. Senior, Ltd., acquires all of the stock of JuniorCo for $20 million at the beginning of 2003. The group immediately elects to file income tax returns on a consolidated basis. Senior's operations generate a $50 million profit every year. In 2004, JuniorCo pays its parent a $3 million dividend. Operating results for JuniorCo are as follows.

| 2003 | $4 million |
|---|---|
| 2004 | $1 million |
| 2005 | $10 million |

   a. Compute Senior's basis in the JuniorCo stock as of the end of 2003, 2004, and 2005.
   b. Same as (a), except that the 2004 tax year produced a $6 million NOL.
   c. Same as (a), except that the 2004 tax year produced a $40 million NOL.

26. Compute consolidated taxable income for the calendar year Teal Group, which elected consolidated status immediately upon creation of the two member corporations in January 2003. All recognized income relates to the consulting services of the firms. No intercompany transactions were completed during the indicated years.

| Year | Teal Corporation | Orange Corporation |
|---|---|---|
| 2003 | $250,000 | ($ 10,000) |
| 2004 | 250,000 | (70,000) |
| 2005 | 250,000 | (235,000) |
| 2006 | 250,000 | 10,000 |

27. Compute consolidated taxable income for the calendar year Moose Group, which elected consolidated status immediately upon the creation of the two member corporations on January 1, 2003. All recognized income is ordinary in nature, and no intercompany transactions were completed during the indicated years.

| Year | Moose Corporation | Elk Corporation |
|---|---|---|
| 2003 | $250,000 | $ 10,000 |
| 2004 | 250,000 | (200,000) |
| 2005 | 250,000 | (400,000) |
| 2006 | 250,000 | 25,000 |

28. Black, Brown, and Red Corporations have filed on a consolidated, calendar year basis for many years. At the beginning of the 2004 tax year, the group elects to de-consolidate. The group's $4 million NOL carryforward can be traced in the following manner: one-half to Black's operations and one-quarter each to Brown's and Red's. How will Red treat the NOL on its 2004 separate tax return?

29. The Parent consolidated group includes SubTwo, which was acquired as part of a § 382 ownership change. SubTwo brought with it to the group a large NOL carryforward, $500,000 of which is available this year under the SRLY rules due to SubTwo's positive contribution to the group's taxable income. The § 382 limitation with respect to SubTwo is $400,000. How much of SubTwo's NOL can be used this year to reduce consolidated taxable income?

30. Child Corporation joined the Thrust consolidated group in 2003. At the time it joined the group, Child held a $400,000 NOL carryforward. On a consolidated basis, the members of Thrust generated significant profits for many years.

    Child's operating results during the first few consolidated return years were as follows.

    | 2003 | ($200,000) |
    | 2004 | 90,000 |
    | 2005 | 115,000 |

    The § 382 rules do not apply to the group.

    How will Child's NOLs affect consolidated taxable income for these years? Is any refund available with respect to the NOL that Child brought into the group?

31. Parent Corporation sold a plot of undeveloped land to SubCo this year for $100,000. Parent had acquired the land several years ago for $20,000. The consolidated return also reflects the operating results of the parties: Parent generated $130,000 income from operations, and SubCo produced a $20,000 operating loss.
    a. Use the computational worksheet of Figure 8–2 to derive the group members' separate taxable incomes and the group's consolidated taxable income.
    b. Same as (a), except that SubCo sold the land to Outsider Corporation for $110,000 in a subsequent year, when its operating income totaled $30,000 (exclusive of the sale of the land), and Parent's operating income amounted to $90,000.

32. SubCo sold an asset to Parent at a tax and accounting gain of $300,000. The asset appreciated by another $20,000 before Parent sold it to an unrelated party, Outsiders, Inc.
    a. Compute the realized financial accounting and recognized taxable income of the group members for these transactions, indicating the date upon which the gain is triggered and the member that includes the gain.
    b. Same as (a), except that the asset declines in value by $20,000 while it is in Parent's hands.

## Research Problems

*Note: Solutions to Research Problems can be prepared by using the **RIA Checkpoint® Student Edition** online research product, or the **CCH U.S. Master Tax Guide Plus™** online Federal tax research database, which is available to accompany this text. It is also possible to prepare solutions to the Research Problems by using tax research materials found in a standard tax library.*

**Communications**

**Research Problem 1.**   Kite is the parent of a group of corporations that files on a consolidated basis. The other group members are Lite and Mite. The group claimed an NOL carryback deduction based solely on expenses incurred to carry out the members' product liability programs. Kite could deduct all of its separate product liability expenses (PLEs), but separately Lite and Mite could not, because of a lack of sufficient other net taxable income.

| Member | Separate Taxable Income before PLEs | PLE for Tax Year | Separate Deduction for PLE |
|---|---|---|---|
| Kite | $1,000,000 | $ 350,000 | $ 350,000 |
| Lite | 2,000,000 | 3,000,000 | 2,000,000 |
| Mite | 4,000,000 | 7,000,000 | 4,000,000 |
| Totals | $7,000,000 | $10,350,000 | $6,350,000 |

The group wants to deduct the full $10,350,000 in PLE deductions for the year so that it can create a $3,350,000 consolidated NOL carryback to a prior tax year and receive an immediate tax refund. This result would seem to follow from the consolidated tax return rules. The IRS wants to limit the deduction to the aggregate of the separate company amounts, $6,350,000. Kite is incorporated in the jurisdiction of the First Circuit Court of Appeals.

Kite's tax director, Clara Trask, asks your opinion as to whether the $10,350,000 deduction will hold up under audit. Respond to her in the form of a letter. Kite's address is 600 Bearpath Road, Falmouth, ME 04105.

**Research Problem 2.** The calendar year Thor Group files its Federal income tax returns on a consolidated basis. The group's members elected to file on a consolidated basis because some of them were generating income, while others were generating losses. To utilize the deductions for the losses, the group began filing a consolidated return.

Now market conditions have changed. Currently, group members are all producing positive Federal taxable incomes. Various groups of shareholders desire to purchase the affiliates of the now-profitable group. If this occurs, the group will no longer meet the ownership requirements for consolidation starting in tax year 2004.

Is it possible to effect a de-consolidation of the group for tax year 2003? Why not just file separate returns for each member of the group for that year? The parent would claim the 100% dividends received deduction on its own return, and this should void the election.

The breakup of the group will take place by the end of June 2004, so no consolidated group will exist for that calendar tax year. But, by using the suggested strategy, the de-consolidation can be effective all the way back to January 2003. Do you agree?

**Communications**

**Research Problem 3.** The Cardinal Group had filed on a consolidated basis for several years. Parent Cardinal, Ltd., had a wholly owned subsidiary, Swallow, Inc. The group used a calendar tax year.

On January 25, 2002, Heron acquired all of the stock of Cardinal, including its ownership in Swallow, an important supplier for Heron's manufacturing process. All parties in the new group intended to file on a consolidated basis immediately and, indeed, used consolidated amounts in filing the 2002 Heron Group return on September 10, 2003.

During the audit of Heron Group's 2002 tax return, the IRS disallowed the use of the consolidated method because no Form 1122s had ever been filed for the affiliates in the new group. In a memo to the tax research file, summarize the possibilities for the Heron Group to be granted an extension to elect consolidated return status.

**Internet Activity**

*Use the tax resources of the Internet to address the following questions. Do not restrict your search to the World Wide Web, but include a review of newsgroups and general reference materials, practitioner sites and resources, primary sources of the tax law, chat rooms and discussion groups, and other opportunities.*

**Research Problem 4.** Go to the IRS Web site to find out how many consolidated returns are filed in a tax year. Which industries file the most consolidated returns? Send this information to your professor in an e-mail message.

**Research Problem 5.**  Look at the financial statements of a conglomerate with several affiliates. Use the footnotes to the statements to determine the tax savings produced by the election to consolidate.

**Research Problem 6.**  Determine whether the income tax laws of your state, and those of two of its neighbors, allow Federal affiliated groups to file consolidated returns. How are NOL carrybacks treated by your state?

# Taxation of International Transactions

CHAPTER 9

LEARNING OBJECTIVES

After completing Chapter 9, you should be able to:

## LO.1
Understand the framework underlying the U.S. taxation of cross-border transactions.

## LO.2
Understand the interaction between Internal Revenue Code provisions and tax treaties.

## LO.3
Apply the rules for sourcing income and deductions into U.S. and foreign categories.

## LO.4
Explain how foreign currency exchange affects the tax consequences of international transactions.

## LO.5
Work with the U.S. tax provisions affecting U.S. persons earning foreign-source income, including the rules relating to export property tax incentives, cross-border asset transfers, antideferral provisions, and the foreign tax credit.

## LO.6
Apply the U.S. tax provisions concerning nonresident alien individuals and foreign corporations.

http://wft.swlearning.com

## O U T L I N E

---

**LO.1**

Understand the framework underlying the U.S. taxation of cross-border transactions.

# Overview of International Taxation

**G**lobal trade is an integral part of the U.S. economy. In 2001, U.S. exports and imports of goods and services totaled $998 billion and $1.36 trillion, respectively. This international trade creates significant U.S. tax consequences for both U.S. and foreign entities. In the most recent year for which data are available, U.S. corporations reported $147 billion in foreign-source income, paid $48 billion in taxes to foreign governments, and claimed foreign tax credits in excess of $37 billion. Foreign corporations reported $3.2 billion in income subject to U.S. taxation and paid $1.2 billion in U.S. taxes. U.S. corporations controlled by foreign owners reported $43 billion in U.S. taxable income.

Cross-border transactions create the need for special tax considerations for both the United States and its trading partners. From a U.S. perspective, international tax laws should promote the global competitiveness of U.S. enterprises and at the same time protect the tax revenue base of the United States. These two objectives sometimes conflict, however. The need to deal with both contributes to the complexity of the rules governing the U.S. taxation of cross-border transactions.

**EXAMPLE 1**

U.S. persons engage in activities outside the United States for many different reasons. Consider two U.S. corporations that have established sales subsidiaries in foreign countries. Dedalus, Inc., operates in Germany, a high-tax country, because customers demand local attention from sales agents. Mulligan, Inc., operates in the Cayman Islands, a low-tax country, simply to shift income outside the United States. U.S. tax law must fairly address both situations with the same law. ■

**■ FIGURE 9–1**
U.S. Taxation of Cross-Border Transactions

|  | **U.S. Person** | **Foreign Person** |
|---|---|---|
| **U.S.-source income** | U.S. domestic taxation | "Inbound" taxation |
| **Foreign-source income** | "Outbound" taxation | Limited U.S. authority to tax |

U.S. international tax provisions are concerned primarily with two types of potential taxpayers: U.S. persons earning foreign-source income and foreign persons earning U.S.-source income.[1] U.S. persons earning U.S.-source income are taxed under the purely domestic provisions of the Internal Revenue Code. Foreign persons earning foreign-source income are not within the taxing jurisdiction of the United States (unless this income is somehow connected to a U.S. trade or business). Figure 9–1 illustrates this categorization.

The United States taxes the worldwide income of U.S. taxpayers. Because foreign governments may also tax some of this income, these taxpayers may be subjected to double taxation. Special provisions such as the foreign tax credit can mitigate this problem. For foreign taxpayers, the United States generally taxes only income earned within its borders. The U.S. taxation of cross-border transactions can be organized in terms of "outbound" and "inbound" taxation. **Outbound taxation** refers to the U.S. taxation of foreign-source income earned by U.S. taxpayers. **Inbound taxation** refers to the U.S. taxation of U.S.-source income earned by foreign taxpayers.

**EXAMPLE 2**

Gator Enterprises, Inc., a U.S. corporation, operates a manufacturing branch in Italy because of customer demand in Italy, local availability of raw materials, and the high cost of shipping finished goods. This branch income is taxed in the United States as part of Gator's worldwide income, but it is also taxed in Italy. Without the availability of a foreign tax credit to mitigate this double taxation, Gator Enterprises would suffer an excessive tax burden and could not compete with local Italian companies. ■

**EXAMPLE 3**

Purdie, Ltd., a corporation based in the United Kingdom, operates in the United States. Although not a U.S. person, Purdie is taxed in the United States on its U.S.-source business income. If Purdie, Ltd., could operate free of U.S. tax, its U.S.-based competitors would face a serious disadvantage. ■

**LO.2**

Understand the interaction between Internal Revenue Code provisions and tax treaties.

# Tax Treaties

The U.S. tax rules governing cross-border transactions are based on both the Internal Revenue Code and **tax treaties.** Tax treaties are bilateral agreements between countries that provide tax relief for those persons covered by the treaties. Tax treaty provisions generally override the treatment otherwise called for under the Internal Revenue Code or foreign tax statutes.

More than 50 income tax treaties between the United States and other countries are in effect (see Exhibit 9–1). These treaties generally provide *taxing rights* with regard to the taxable income of residents of one treaty country who have income

---

[1]The term "person" includes an individual, corporation, partnership, trust, estate, or association. § 7701(a)(1). The terms "domestic" and "foreign" are defined in §§ 7701(a)(4) and (5).

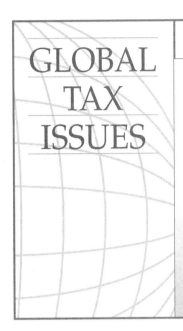

## OTHER COUNTRIES' TAXES ARE STRANGE, TOO

People often complain about the strange provisions or workings of the U.S. Federal income tax system, but other countries can be criticized in the same way. Much of Europe, for example, is less dependent on income taxes than the United States and more dependent on transaction and wealth taxes, and these can take unusual forms. A quick survey of taxes around the globe finds the following.

| | |
|---|---|
| Australia | 68% tax on cigarette purchases |
| China | 80–100% tax on purchase of autos built outside China |
| Costa Rica | 170% tax on purchase of poultry raised outside the country |
| | 96% tax on purchase of foreign dairy products |
| Japan | 1,000% tax on purchase of rice grown outside the country |
| Sweden | 400% tax on purchase of hard liquor |
| Turkmenistan | 100% tax on luxury items, which include mineral water, cotton mittens, saws, blankets, pillows, mattresses |

sourced in the other treaty country. For the most part, neither country is prohibited from taxing the income of its residents. The treaties generally give one country primary taxing rights and require the other country to allow a credit for the taxes paid on the twice-taxed income.

**EXAMPLE 4**

ForCo, Ltd., a resident of a foreign country with which the United States has an income tax treaty, earns income attributable to a permanent establishment (e.g., place of business) in the United States. Under the treaty, the United States has primary taxing rights with regard to this income. The other country can also require that the income be included in gross

■ **EXHIBIT 9–1**

U.S. Income Tax Treaties in Force as of February 2003

| | | |
|---|---|---|
| Australia | Iceland | Pakistan |
| Austria | India | Philippines |
| Barbados | Indonesia | Poland |
| Belgium | Ireland | Portugal |
| Canada | Israel | Romania |
| China | Italy | Russia |
| Commonwealth of | Jamaica | Slovak Republic |
| Independent States* | Japan | South Africa |
| Cyprus | Kazakhstan | Spain |
| Czech Republic | Korea, Republic of | Sweden |
| Denmark | Latvia | Switzerland |
| Egypt | Lithuania | Thailand |
| Estonia | Luxembourg | Trinidad and Tobago |
| Finland | Mexico | Tunisia |
| France | Morocco | Turkey |
| Germany | Netherlands | United Kingdom |
| Greece | New Zealand | Venezuela |
| Hungary | Norway | |

*The income tax treaty between the United States and the former Soviet Union now applies to the countries of Armenia, Azerbaijan, Belarus, Georgia, Kyrgyzstan, Moldova, Tajikistan, Turkmenistan, Ukraine, and Uzbekistan. The Commonwealth of Independent States is an association of many of the former constituent republics of the Soviet Union.

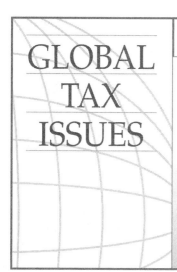

income and can subject the income to its income tax, but it must allow a credit for the taxes paid to the United States on the income. ■

Which country receives primary taxing rights usually depends on the residence of the taxpayer or the presence of a permanent establishment in a treaty country to which the income is attributable. Generally, a permanent establishment is a branch, office, factory, workshop, warehouse, or other fixed place of business.

Most U.S. income tax treaties reduce the withholding tax rate on certain items of investment income, such as interest and dividends. For example, treaties with France and Sweden reduce the withholding on portfolio dividends to 15 percent and on certain interest income to zero. The United States has developed a Model Income Tax Treaty as the starting point for negotiating income tax treaties with other countries.[2]

---

**LO.3**

Apply the rules for sourcing income and deductions into U.S. and foreign categories.

## Sourcing of Income and Deductions

The sourcing of income and deductions inside or outside the United States has a direct bearing on a number of tax provisions affecting both U.S. and foreign taxpayers. For example, foreign taxpayers generally are taxed only on income sourced inside the United States, and U.S. taxpayers receive relief from double taxation under the foreign tax credit rules based on their foreign-source income. Accordingly, an examination of sourcing rules is often the starting point in addressing international tax issues.

### INCOME SOURCED INSIDE THE UNITED STATES

The determination of the source of income depends on the type of income realized (e.g., income from the sale of property versus income for the use of property). This makes the classification of income an important consideration. Section 861 contains

---

[2]Treasury Department Model Income Tax Treaty (September 20, 1996).

source rules for most types of income. Other rules pertaining to the source of income are found in §§ 862–865.

**Interest.**　Interest income received from the U.S. government, from the District of Columbia, and from noncorporate U.S. residents or domestic corporations is sourced inside the United States. There are a few exceptions to this rule. Certain interest received from a U.S. corporation that earned 80 percent or more of its active business income from foreign sources over the prior three-year period is treated as foreign-source income. Interest received on amounts deposited with a foreign branch of a U.S. corporation is also treated as foreign-source income if the branch is engaged in the commercial banking business.

**EXAMPLE 5**　　John holds a bond issued by Delta, a domestic corporation. For the immediately preceding three tax years, 82% of Delta's gross income has been active foreign business income. The interest income that John receives for the current tax year from Delta is foreign-source income. ∎

**Dividends.**　Dividends received from domestic corporations (other than certain U.S. possessions corporations) are sourced inside the United States. Generally, dividends paid by a foreign corporation are foreign-source income. An exception to this rule applies, however, if 25 percent or more of a foreign corporation's gross income for the three tax years immediately preceding the current tax year was effectively connected with the conduct of a U.S. trade or business. In this case, a portion of the dividends received in the tax year is U.S.-source income. This portion is equal to the proportion of gross income effectively connected with the conduct of a U.S. trade or business for the immediately preceding three-year period.

**EXAMPLE 6**　　Ann receives dividend income from the following corporations for the current tax year.

| Amount | Corporation | Effectively Connected U.S. Income for Past 3 Years | U.S.-Source Income |
|--------|-------------|-----------------------------------------------------|--------------------|
| $500 | Green, domestic | 85% | $500 |
| 600 | Brown, domestic | 13% | 600 |
| 300 | Orange, foreign | 92% | 276 |

Because Green Corporation and Brown Corporation are domestic corporations, the dividends they pay are U.S.-source income. Orange Corporation is a foreign corporation meeting the 25% test. Specifically, 92% of Orange Corporation's business income over the prior three years was effectively connected with a U.S. trade or business. Thus, 92% of the dividend from Orange is U.S.-source income. ∎

**Personal Services Income.**　The source of income from personal services is determined by the location in which the services are performed (inside or outside the United States). A limited *commercial traveler* exception is available. Under this exception, personal services income must meet all the following requirements to avoid being classified as U.S.-source income.

- The services must be performed by a nonresident alien who is in the United States for 90 days or less during the taxable year.
- The compensation may not exceed $3,000 in total for the services performed in the United States.

* The services must be performed on behalf of:
    * a nonresident alien, foreign partnership, or foreign corporation that is not engaged in a U.S. trade or business or
    * an office or place of business maintained in a foreign country or possession of the United States by an individual who is a citizen or resident of the United States, a domestic partnership, or a domestic corporation.

**EXAMPLE 7**

Mark, a nonresident alien, is an engineer employed by a foreign oil company. He spent four weeks in the United States arranging the purchase of field equipment for his company. His salary for the four weeks was $3,500. Even though the oil company is not engaged in a U.S. trade or business, and Mark was in the United States for less than 90 days during the taxable year, the income is U.S.-source income because it exceeds $3,000. ■

The issue of whether income is derived from the performance of personal services is important in determining the income's source. The courts have held that a corporation can perform personal services.[3] In addition, in the absence of capital as an income-producing factor, personal services income can arise even though there is no recipient of the services.[4] If payment is received for services performed partly inside and partly outside the United States, the income must be allocated for source purposes on some reasonable basis that clearly reflects income under the facts and circumstances. The number of days worked in each country is generally acceptable.[5]

**Rents and Royalties.**  The source of income received for the use of tangible property is the country in which the property is located. The source of income received for the use of intangible property (e.g., patents, copyrights, secret processes and formulas) is the country in which the property is used.

**Sale or Exchange of Property.**  Generally, the location of real property determines the source of any income derived from the property. Income from the disposition of U.S. real property interests is U.S.-source income.

The source of income from the sale of personal property (assets other than real property) depends on several factors, including the following.

* Whether the property was produced by the seller.
* The type of property sold (e.g., inventory or a capital asset).
* The residence of the seller.

Generally, income, gain, or profit from the sale of personal property is sourced according to the residence of the seller. Income from the sale of purchased inventory, however, is sourced in the country in which the sale takes place.[6]

When the seller has produced the inventory property, the income must be apportioned between the country of production and the country of sale. Gross income is sourced under a 50/50 allocation method unless the taxpayer elects to use the independent factory price (IFP) method or the separate books and records

---

[3]See *British Timken Limited*, 12 T.C. 880 (1949), and Rev.Rul. 60–55, 1960–1 C.B. 270.

[4]See *Robida v. Comm.*, 72–1 USTC ¶9450, 29 AFTR2d 72–1223, 460 F.2d 1172 (CA–9, 1972). The taxpayer was employed in military PXs around the world. He had large slot machine winnings and claimed the foreign earned income exclusion. The IRS challenged the exclusion on the grounds that the winnings were not earned income because there was no recipient of Robida's services. The court,

however, found that, in the absence of capital, the winnings were earned income.

[5]Reg. § 1.861–4(b). See *Stemkowski*, 76 T.C. 252 (1981).

[6]§§ 861(a)(6) and 865. The sale is deemed to take place where title passes. See Reg. § 1.861–7(c) regarding title passage. There has been considerable conflict in this area of tax law. See, for example, *Liggett Group, Inc.*, 58 TCM 1167, T.C.Memo 1990–18.

method. The IFP method may be elected only where an IFP exists.[7] If the manufacturer or producer regularly sells to wholly independent distributors, this can establish an *independent* factory or production price.

Under § 865, income from the sale of personal property other than inventory is sourced at the residence of the seller unless one of the following exceptions applies.

- Gain on the sale of depreciable personal property is sourced according to prior depreciation deductions to the extent of the deductions. Any excess gain is sourced the same as the sale of inventory.
- Gain on the sale of intangibles is sourced according to prior amortization deductions to the extent of the deductions. Contingent payments, however, are sourced as royalty income.
- Gain attributable to an office or fixed place of business maintained outside the United States by a U.S. resident is foreign-source income.
- Income or gain attributable to an office or fixed place of business maintained in the United States by a nonresident is U.S.-source income.

The sourcing of losses is complicated and depends on the nature of the property. Different rules exist for the disposition of stock versus other personal property.[8]

**Transportation and Communication Income.**   Income from transportation beginning *and* ending in the United States is U.S.-source income. Fifty percent of the income from transportation beginning *or* ending in the United States is U.S.-source income, unless the U.S. point is only an intermediate stop. This rule does not apply to personal services income unless the transportation is between the United States and a possession. Income from space and ocean activities conducted outside the jurisdiction of any country is sourced according to the residence of the person conducting the activity.

International communication income derived by a U.S. person is sourced 50 percent in the United States when transmission is between the United States and a foreign country. International communication income derived by foreign persons is foreign-source income unless it is attributable to an office or other fixed place of business in the United States. In that case, it is U.S.-source income.

**Software Income.**   Income from the sale or license of software is sourced depending on how the income is classified. Under Regulation § 1.861–18, a transfer of software is classified as either the transfer of a copyright (e.g., the right to the computer program itself) or the transfer of a copyrighted article (the right to use a copy of the computer program). If the transfer is considered a transfer of a copyright, the income is sourced using the royalty income rules. If the transfer is considered a transfer of a copyrighted article, the income is treated as resulting from a sale of the article and is sourced based on the personal property sales rules.

## INCOME SOURCED OUTSIDE THE UNITED STATES

The provisions for sourcing income outside the United States are not as detailed and specific as those for determining U.S.-source income. Basically, § 862 provides that if interest, dividends, compensation for personal services, income from the use or sale of property, or other income is not U.S.-source income, then it is foreign-source income.

---

[7]§ 863(b)(2), Reg. § 1.863–3, and Notice 89–10, 1989–1 C.B. 631.
[8]See Reg. § 1.861–8(e)(7) and Temp.Reg. § 1.865–1T(a)(1). See Reg. §§ 1.865–2(a)(1) and (2) regarding the source of losses on the disposition of stock.

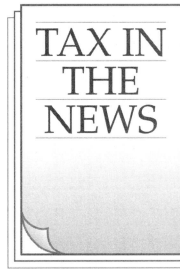

## SOURCING INCOME IN CYBERSPACE

The use of the Internet for more and more consumer and business transactions is posing problems for the taxing authorities. Consumers purchase books, music, clothing, and food from Internet retailers. Businesses negotiate with suppliers via online auctions of products and services. Consultants provide services to their clients over the Web. Very few transactions do not have a counterpart that takes place in cyberspace. The existing income-sourcing rules were developed long before the existence of the Internet, and taxing authorities are finding it challenging to apply these rules to Internet transactions. Where does a sale take place when the Web server is in the Cayman Islands, the seller is in Singapore, and the customer is in Texas? Where is a service performed when all activities take place over the Net? These questions and more will have to be answered by the United States and its trading partners as the Internet economy grows in size and importance.

## ALLOCATION AND APPORTIONMENT OF DEDUCTIONS

The United States levies a tax on *taxable income*. Deductions and losses, therefore, must be allocated and apportioned between U.S.- and foreign-source gross income to determine U.S.- and foreign-source taxable income. Deductions directly related to an activity or property are allocated to classes of income. This is followed by apportionment between the statutory and residual groupings (e.g., foreign versus domestic) on some reasonable basis.[9] A deduction not definitely related to any class of gross income is ratably allocated to all classes of gross income and apportioned between U.S.- and foreign-source income.

**EXAMPLE 8**

Ace, Inc., a domestic corporation, has $2 million gross income and a $50,000 expense, all related to real estate activities. The expense is allocated and apportioned using gross income as a basis as follows.

| | Gross Income | | | Apportionment | |
| | Foreign | U.S. | Allocation | Foreign | U.S. |
|---|---|---|---|---|---|
| Sales | $1,000,000 | $500,000 | $37,500* | $25,000 | $12,500** |
| Rentals | 400,000 | 100,000 | 12,500 | 10,000 | 2,500*** |
| | | | $50,000 | $35,000 | $15,000 |

\*$50,000 × ($1,500,000/$2,000,000).
\*\*$37,500 × ($500,000/$1,500,000).
\*\*\*$12,500 × ($100,000/$500,000).

If Ace could show that $45,000 of the expense was directly related to sales income, the $45,000 would be allocated to that class of gross income, with the remainder allocated and apportioned ratably based on gross income. ■

Interest expense is allocated and apportioned based on the theory that money is fungible. With limited exceptions, interest expense is attributable to all the activities and property of the taxpayer, regardless of the specific purpose for incurring

---

[9]Reg. § 1.861–8.

the debt on which interest is paid.[10] Taxpayers must allocate and apportion interest expense on the basis of assets, using either the fair market value or the tax book value of the assets.[11] Once the fair market value is used, the taxpayer must continue to use this method. Special rules apply in allocating and apportioning interest expense in an affiliated group of corporations.

**EXAMPLE 9**

Fisher, Inc., a domestic corporation, generates U.S.-source and foreign-source gross income for the current year. Fisher's assets (tax book value) are as follows.

| | |
|---|---|
| Assets generating U.S.-source income | $18,000,000 |
| Assets generating foreign-source income | 5,000,000 |
| | $23,000,000 |

Fisher incurs interest expense of $800,000 for the current year. Using the tax book value method, interest expense is apportioned to foreign-source income as follows.

$$\frac{\$5,000,000 \text{ (foreign assets)}}{\$23,000,000 \text{ (total assets)}} \times \$800,000 = \underline{\$173,913}$$

Specific rules also apply to research and development (R & D) expenditures, certain stewardship expenses, legal and accounting fees and expenses, income taxes, and losses. Although U.S. companies incur about 90 percent of their R & D expenditures at U.S. facilities, several billion dollars is spent on foreign R & D each year. The Regulations provide that a portion of a U.S. company's R & D expenditures must be treated as foreign-source expense if the R & D relates to foreign product sales.

## SECTION 482 CONSIDERATIONS

Taxpayers may be tempted to manipulate the source of income and the allocation of deductions arbitrarily to minimize taxation. This manipulation is more easily accomplished between or among related persons. The IRS uses § 482 to counter such actions. The provision gives the IRS the power to reallocate gross income, deductions, credits, or allowances between or among organizations, trades, or businesses owned or controlled directly or indirectly by the same interests. This can be done whenever the IRS determines that reallocation is necessary to prevent the evasion of taxes or to reflect income more clearly. Section 482 is a "one-edged sword" available only to the IRS. The taxpayer cannot invoke it to reallocate income and expenses.[12]

The reach of § 482 is quite broad. The IRS takes the position that a corporation and its sole shareholder who works full-time for the corporation can be treated as two separate trades or businesses for purposes of § 482.[13] Two unrelated shareholders who each owned 50 percent of a corporation were held to be acting in concert for their common good and, thus, together controlled the corporation.[14]

In applying § 482, an arm's length price must be determined to assign the correct profits to related entities. Several alternative methods can be used in determining an

---

[10]Reg. § 1.861–10T(b) describes circumstances in which interest expense can be directly allocated to specific debt. This exception to the fungibility concept is limited to cases in which specific property is purchased or improved with nonrecourse debt.

[11]Reg. § 1.861–9T.

[12]Reg. § 1.482–1(a)(3).

[13]Rev.Rul. 88–38, 1988–1 C.B. 246. But see *Foglesong v. Comm.*, 82–2 USTC ¶9650, 50 AFTR2d 82–6016, 691 F.2d 848 (CA–7, 1982), *rev'g* 77 T.C. 1102 (1981).

[14]See *B. Forman Co., Inc. v. Comm.*, 72–1 USTC ¶9182, 29 AFTR2d 72–403, 453 F.2d 1144 (CA–2, 1972).

## APAs Reduce Uncertainty in Transfer Pricing Disputes

The first APA was approved in January 1991. The IRS reports that 210 APAs have been approved and 190 others are in negotiation. The taxpayers participating in the APA program come from many different industries. The five most represented industries are financial institutions, computer items and software, chemicals, transportation equipment, and electrical equipment.

Only 10 percent of the largest taxpayers involved in international intercompany transactions have participated in the APA process. However, the volume of intercompany transactions represented by these taxpayers constitutes 42 percent of the total dollar value of international intercompany transactions.

The APA process is not simple or quick. The IRS reports that half of the APAs awaiting approval have been pending for more than one year, with 20 percent pending more than two years.

SOURCE: IRS's Advance Pricing Agreement Program, General Accounting Office Report, August 2000.

arm's length price on the sale of tangible or intangible property. The major problem with most pricing methods is that uncontrolled comparable transactions are needed as a benchmark.

An accuracy-related penalty of 20 percent is provided by § 6662 for net § 482 transfer price adjustments (changes in profit allocations by the IRS) for a taxable year that exceed the lesser of $5 million or 10 percent of the taxpayer's gross receipts. In addition, there is a 40 percent penalty for "gross misstatements."

As an aid to reducing pricing disputes, the IRS initiated the Advance Pricing Agreement (APA) program whereby the taxpayer can propose a transfer pricing method for certain international transactions. The taxpayer provides relevant data, which are then evaluated by the IRS. If accepted, the APA provides a safe-harbor transfer pricing method for the taxpayer. Apple Computer, Inc., accomplished the first successful APA submission.

**LO.4**

Explain how foreign currency exchange affects the tax consequences of international transactions.

## Foreign Currency Transactions

The relative value of a foreign currency and the U.S. dollar is described by the foreign exchange rate. Changes in this rate affect the dollar value of foreign property held by the taxpayer, the dollar value of foreign debts, and the dollar amount of gain or loss on a transaction denominated in a foreign currency. Almost every international tax issue requires consideration of currency exchange implications.

**EXAMPLE 10**

Dress, Inc., a domestic corporation, purchases merchandise for resale from Fiesta, Inc., a foreign corporation, for 50,000K (a foreign currency). On the date of purchase, 1K is equal to $1 U.S. (1K:$1). At this time, the account payable is $50,000. On the date of payment by Dress (the foreign exchange date), the exchange rate is 1.25K:$1. In other words, the foreign currency has been devalued in relation to the U.S. dollar, and Dress will pay Fiesta 50,000K, which will cost Dress only $40,000. Dress must record the purchase of the merchandise at $50,000 and recognize a foreign currency gain of $10,000 ($50,000 − $40,000). ∎

In recent years, U.S. currency abroad amounted to more than 50 percent of the U.S. currency in circulation. Taxpayers may find it necessary to translate amounts denominated in foreign currency into U.S. dollars for any of the following purposes.

* Purchase of goods, services, and property.
* Sale of goods, services, and property.
* Collection of foreign receivables.
* Payment of foreign payables.
* Foreign tax credit calculations.
* Recognition of income or loss from foreign branch activities.

The foreign currency exchange rates, however, have no effect on the transactions of a U.S. person who arranges all international transactions in U.S. dollars.

**EXAMPLE 11**

Sellers, Inc., a domestic corporation, purchases goods from Rose, Ltd., a foreign corporation, and pays for these goods in U.S. dollars. Rose then exchanges the U.S. dollars for the currency of the country in which it operates. Sellers has no foreign exchange considerations with which to contend. If instead Rose required Sellers to pay for the goods in a foreign currency, Sellers would have to exchange U.S. dollars to obtain the foreign currency to make payment. If the exchange rate changed from the date of purchase to the date of payment, Sellers would have a foreign currency gain or loss on the currency exchange. ∎

The following concepts are important when dealing with the tax aspects of foreign exchange.

* Foreign currency is treated as property other than money.
* Gain or loss on the exchange of foreign currency is considered separately from the underlying transaction (e.g., the purchase or sale of goods).
* No gain or loss is recognized until a transaction is closed.

## TAX ISSUES

The following major tax issues must be considered when dealing with foreign currency exchange.

* The date of recognition of any gain or loss (see Concept Summary 9–1).
* The source (U.S. or foreign) of the foreign currency gain or loss.
* The character of the gain or loss (ordinary or capital).

## FUNCTIONAL CURRENCY

The Code generally adopted FAS 52, the Financial Accounting Standards Board standard on foreign currency translation. FAS 52 introduced the **functional currency** approach. Under this approach, the currency of the economic environment in which the foreign entity operates generally is to be used as the monetary unit to measure gains and losses.

Under § 985, all income tax determinations are to be made in the taxpayer's functional currency. Generally, a taxpayer's default functional currency is the U.S. dollar. In most cases, a **qualified business unit (QBU)** operating in a foreign country uses that country's currency as its functional currency. A QBU is a separate and clearly identified unit of a taxpayer's trade or business (e.g., a foreign branch). An individual is not a QBU; however, a trade or business conducted by an individual may be a QBU.[15]

---

[15]Reg. § 1.989(a)–1(b).

## CONCEPT SUMMARY 9-1

### Recognition of Foreign Exchange Gain or Loss

| Transaction | Date of Recognition |
| --- | --- |
| Purchase or sale of inventory or business asset | Date of disposition of foreign currency |
| Branch profits | Remittance of branch profits |
| Subpart F income | Receipt of previously taxed income (accumulated E & P) |
| Dividend from current E & P or untaxed accumulated E & P | No exchange gain or loss to recipient |

### BRANCH OPERATIONS

When a foreign branch (QBU) uses a foreign currency as its functional currency, profit or loss is computed in the foreign currency each year and translated into U.S. dollars for tax purposes. The entire amount of profit or loss, not taking remittances into account, is translated using the average exchange rate for the taxable year. Exchange gain or loss is recognized on remittances from the QBU. The U.S. dollar amount of the remittance at the exchange rate in effect on the date of remittance is compared with the U.S. dollar value (basis pool) of the equity pool of the branch. The equity pool comprises the branch's initial capitalization plus contributions to the branch plus undistributed profits minus remittances and losses—all measured in the QBU's functional currency.[16] This exchange gain or loss is ordinary, and it is sourced according to the income to which the remittance is attributable.

### DISTRIBUTIONS FROM FOREIGN CORPORATIONS

An actual distribution of E & P from a foreign corporation is included in income by the U.S. recipient at the exchange rate in effect on the date of distribution. Thus, no exchange gain or loss is recognized. Deemed dividend distributions under Subpart F (discussed later in the chapter) are translated at the average exchange rate for the corporation's tax year to which the deemed distribution is attributable. Exchange gain or loss can result when an actual distribution of this previously taxed income is made.

### FOREIGN TAXES

For purposes of the foreign tax credit, foreign taxes accrued are translated at the average exchange rate for the tax year to which the taxes relate. Under exceptions to this rule, foreign taxes must be translated at the exchange rate in effect when the foreign taxes were paid.[17] If foreign taxes are paid within two years of accrual, and if they differ from the accrued amount merely because of currency exchange fluctuation, no redetermination is required, even though the actual dollar value paid may differ from the accrued amount. In other cases, when the taxes paid differ from the amount accrued, a redetermination is required.

**EXAMPLE 12**

Music, Inc., a domestic corporation, has a foreign branch. Foreign taxes attributable to branch income amount to 5,000K (a foreign currency). The taxes are paid within two years of being

---

[16]Prop.Reg. § 1.987–2.    [17]§§ 986(a)(1)(B) and (C).

accrued. The average foreign exchange rate for the tax year to which the foreign taxes relate is .5K:$1. On the date the taxes are paid, the rate is .6K:$1. No redetermination is required, and Music has foreign taxes of $10,000 for purposes of the foreign tax credit. ■

## SECTION 988 TRANSACTIONS

The disposition of a nonfunctional currency can result in a foreign currency gain or loss under § 988. Section 988 transactions include those in which gain or loss is determined with regard to the value of a nonfunctional currency, such as the following.

- Acquiring (or becoming obligor under) a debt instrument.
- Accruing (or otherwise taking into account) any item of expense or gross income or receipts that is to be paid or received at a later date.
- Entering into or acquiring nearly any forward contract, futures contract, option, or similar investment position.
- Disposing of nonfunctional currency.

Section 988 generally treats exchange gain or loss falling within its provisions as ordinary income or loss. Capital gain or loss treatment may be elected with regard to forward contracts, futures contracts, and options that constitute capital assets in the hands of the taxpayer.

A closed or completed transaction is required. The residence of the taxpayer generally determines the source of a § 988 foreign exchange gain or loss.

**LO.5**

Work with the U.S. tax provisions affecting U.S. persons earning foreign-source income, including the rules relating to export property tax incentives, cross-border asset transfers, antideferral provisions, and the foreign tax credit.

# U.S. Persons with Foreign Income

U.S. taxpayers often "internationalize" gradually over time. A U.S. business may operate on a strictly domestic basis for several years, then explore foreign markets by exporting its products abroad, and later license its products to a foreign manufacturer or enter into a joint venture with a foreign partner. If its forays into foreign markets are successful, the U.S. business may create a foreign subsidiary and move a portion of its operations abroad by establishing a sales or manufacturing facility. A domestically controlled foreign corporation can have significant U.S. tax consequences for the U.S. owners, and any U.S. taxpayer paying foreign taxes must consider the foreign tax credit provisions. Foreign businesses likewise enter the U.S. market in stages. In either case, each step generates increasingly significant international tax consequences.

## EXPORT PROPERTY TAX INCENTIVES

The easiest way for a U.S. enterprise to engage in global commerce is simply to sell U.S.-produced goods and services abroad. These sales can be conducted with little or no foreign presence and allow the business to explore foreign markets without making costly financial commitments to foreign operations. The U.S. tax consequences of simple export sales are straightforward. All such income is taxed in the United States to the U.S. taxpayer. Whether foreign taxes must be paid on this export income depends on the particular law of the foreign jurisdiction and whether the U.S. taxpayer is deemed to have a foreign business presence there (often called a "permanent establishment"). In many cases, such export income is not taxed by any foreign jurisdiction.

To improve the U.S. balance of trade, Congress has used various export tax incentives to encourage exports of U.S.-produced property. In the late 1970s, Congress created the domestic international sales corporation (DISC) provisions that allowed a DISC to defer the tax on a portion of its export income until actual repatriation of the earnings. After the General Agreement on Tariffs and Trade (GATT) charged that the DISC provisions were a prohibited *export subsidy*, the provisions were curtailed. As an alternative, in 1984 the foreign sales corporation (FSC) provisions (§§ 921–927) were enacted to provide similar tax incentives to U.S. exporters while appeasing the GATT members. FSCs were not allowed to defer the tax on export income. Instead, a certain percentage of export income was permanently exempt from U.S. taxation.

In 2000, the United States was forced to repeal the FSC provisions because of a finding by the World Trade Organization (WTO) that the FSC benefits constituted an illegal export subsidy. Congress replaced the FSC with a benefit that excludes **extraterritorial income** from U.S. taxation.[18] The extraterritorial income (ETI) regime preserves the basic incentives provided by the FSC rules. Consequently, it is not surprising that the WTO has found that the ETI provisions also violate its rules. As of January 2003, the United States has yet to repeal the ETI provisions, but the European Union is developing a list of potential trade sanctions.

**Determination of ETI Benefit.** Under the ETI exclusion of § 114, *qualifying foreign trade income* is exempt from U.S. taxation. Qualifying foreign trade income is a specified percentage of *foreign trading gross receipts*. Foreign trading gross receipts are generated from the sale of *qualifying foreign trade property*. Qualifying foreign trade property includes property that meets all three of the following requirements.

- The property is held for sale or lease for direct use, consumption, or disposition outside the United States in the ordinary course of business.
- No more than 50 percent of the property's value may be attributable to the combined market value of components manufactured abroad plus foreign direct labor costs.
- The property must be manufactured, produced, grown, or extracted by the taxpayer, and in the case of property that is manufactured outside the United States, the taxpayer must be a domestic corporation, a U.S. citizen or resident, a foreign corporation that elects to be treated as a domestic corporation, or a partnership with eligible partners.

Qualifying property does not include oil and gas products, intangibles (other than certain qualifying computer software licensed for reproduction outside the United States), and other specified items.[19] The key factors are that the property must be exported, a large portion of the value of the property must be attributable to U.S. components and labor, and the taxpayer must be subject to taxation in the United States.

To qualify for ETI benefits, the taxpayer must meet certain economic process requirements outlined in § 942. These include participating outside the United States in soliciting, negotiating, or making the sales contract relating to the transaction. In addition, the foreign direct costs attributable to the transaction must equal

---

[18]FSC Repeal and Extraterritorial Income Exclusion Act of 2000, Public Law 106–519, and new § 114.

[19]§ 943(a).

or exceed 50 percent of the total direct costs. Small exporters need not meet the foreign economic process requirements when annual foreign trading gross receipts are $5 million or less.

Different pricing methods are provided for determining exempt qualifying foreign trade income. The taxpayer may use whichever of the three following methods maximizes its exempt taxable income.

- 15 percent of foreign trade income (FTI).
- 1.2 percent of foreign trading gross receipts (FTGR) (not exceeding 30 percent of FTI).
- 30 percent of foreign sale and leasing income (FSALI). FSALI is defined in § 941(c) as FTI that is properly allocable to the taxpayer's foreign activities or income from renting foreign trade property for use outside the United States.

The ETI exclusion from gross income is the exempt taxable income plus the ratable share of any disallowed expenses related to the exempt income.

**EXAMPLE 13**

Murphy, Inc., a domestic corporation, manufactures recreational boats. For the current year, it reported the following operating results before consideration of any ETI benefits.

|                    | U.S. Sales | Foreign Sales | Total Sales |
|--------------------|-----------:|--------------:|------------:|
| Gross receipts     | $ 5,000    | $ 500         | $ 5,500     |
| Cost of goods sold | (4,200)    | (360)         | (4,560)     |
| Gross income       | $   800    | $ 140         | $   940     |
| Overhead expenses  | (120)      | (20)          | (140)       |
| Taxable income     | $   680    | $ 120         | $   800     |

Murphy's FTGR are $500, and its FTI is $120. Assume Murphy's FSALI is $50. Murphy can reduce its taxable income by the largest of the three following amounts.

- $18 ($120 FTI × 15%).
- $6 ($500 FTGR × 1.2%).
- $15 ($50 FSALI × 30%).

The $3 in overhead expenses attributable to the excluded taxable income is not deductible [$3 = $20 × ($18/$120)]. Thus, the exclusion from gross income under § 114 is $21 [$18 (reduction in taxable income) + $3 (disallowed overhead expenses)].

Murphy's taxable income after consideration of the ETI exclusion is calculated as follows.

|                                                |          |
|------------------------------------------------|---------:|
| Gross receipts                                 | $ 5,500  |
| Cost of goods sold                             | (4,560)  |
| Gross income before exclusion                  | $   940  |
| ETI exclusion                                  | (21)     |
| Overhead expenses (before disallowed expenses) | (140)    |
| Disallowed overhead expenses                   | 3        |
| Taxable income                                 | $   782  |

| ETHICAL CONSIDERATIONS | **Export Tax Benefits: Unnecessary Subsidy or Important Incentive?** |
|---|---|

By using FSCs, the ETI exclusion, and other export tax incentives, companies can achieve substantial tax savings. Congress hopes these savings will provide economic benefits, including the creation of U.S. jobs. In 1995, for example, Caterpillar, Inc., used FSC benefits to reduce its taxes by $41 million. Some policy makers argue that these tax savings are simply a "giveaway" to corporations. Others point out that the existence of large FSC tax savings, such as Caterpillar's, proves that the incentive is working and that corporations are selling more and more U.S.-produced goods abroad. An unnecessary subsidy or an important incentive: What do you think?

### CROSS-BORDER ASSET TRANSFERS

As part of "going international," a U.S. taxpayer may decide to transfer assets outside the United States so that any foreign business will be conducted outside the U.S. tax jurisdiction. To originate investment through, or transfer investment to, a foreign entity, the U.S. taxpayer must make some sort of transfer to the foreign entity. This may take the form of a cash investment or a transfer of assets of a U.S. entity.

In situations where potential taxable income is transferred to a corporation outside the U.S. taxing jurisdiction, the exchange may trigger a tax. The tax result of transferring property to a foreign corporation depends on the nature of the exchange, the assets involved, the income potential of the property, and the character of the property in the hands of the transferor or transferee. Figure 9–2 summarized the taxation of cross-border asset transfers.

**Outbound Transfers.** As discussed in Chapters 5 and 7, when assets are exchanged for corporate stock in a domestic transaction, realized gain or loss may be deferred rather than recognized. Similarly, deferral treatment may be available when the following "outbound" capital changes occur, i.e., moving corporate business across country borders and outside the United States.

- A U.S. corporation starts up a new corporation outside the United States (§ 351).
- A U.S. corporation liquidates a U.S. subsidiary into an existing foreign subsidiary (§ 332).
- A U.S. corporation incorporates a non-U.S. branch of a U.S. corporation, forming a new foreign corporation (§ 351).
- A foreign corporation uses a stock swap to acquire a U.S. corporation (Type "B" reorganization).
- A foreign corporation acquires substantially all of a U.S. corporation's net assets (Type "C" reorganization).

These otherwise tax-deferred transactions may trigger current taxation when foreign corporations are involved. Under § 367, the general rule is that gain deferral is not allowed when assets are leaving the U.S. taxing jurisdiction. However, a major exception allows continued tax deferral for assets transferred to a foreign corporation to be used in a trade or business carried on outside the United States.

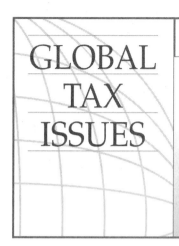

### BOOM IN CROSS-BORDER MERGERS

Recent years have seen an increase in the number of tax-deferred mergers taking place across national borders. Helen of Troy, the publicly traded cosmetics giant, converted itself from a U.S. corporation into a tax haven corporation without triggering any tax for its shareholders. Once outside the U.S. taxing jurisdiction, the company was free from many of the restrictions imposed by U.S. tax law. U.S. taxing authorities responded to this transaction by issuing new regulations [§ 1.367(a)–3(c)] to shut down these so-called inversions unless very strict standards were met. But even after these regulations became law, Chrysler became part of the German corporation DaimlerChrysler in a tax-deferred transaction.

The trade or business exception does not apply to certain "tainted" assets, and the transfer of these assets outside the United States triggers immediate gain (but not loss) recognition. The following are "tainted" assets under § 367.

- Inventory (raw goods, work-in-progress, and finished goods).
- Installment obligations and accounts receivable.
- Foreign currency.
- Property leased by the transferor unless the transferee is the lessee.

These tainted assets are likely to turn over quickly once the asset transfer is completed, and any appreciation is likely to be recognized outside the U.S. taxing jurisdiction. Consequently, § 367 requires recognition of this gain upon transfer of the asset outside the United States.

**EXAMPLE 14**

Amelia, Inc., a domestic corporation, incorporates its profitable Irish manufacturing branch and creates a new wholly owned foreign corporation, St. George, Ltd., to engage in manufacturing activities in Ireland. The transfer qualifies as tax deferred under § 351. The branch assets have always been used in Ireland. Amelia transfers the following branch assets to St. George upon its creation.

■ **FIGURE 9–2**
Taxation of Cross-Border Asset Transfers

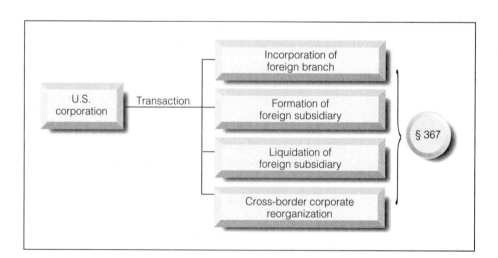

| Asset | Tax Basis | Market Value | Built-in Gain/Loss |
|---|---|---|---|
| Raw materials inventory | $100 | $ 400 | $ 300 |
| Accounts receivable | 200 | 250 | 50 |
| Manufacturing equipment | 450 | 925 | 475 |
| Furniture and fixtures | 150 | 50 | (100) |
| Total | $900 | $1,625 | $ 725 |

Although the $725 in realized gain is deferred under § 351, the gain is potentially taxable under § 367 because the assets are leaving the U.S. taxing jurisdiction. The general rule of § 367 is that all the realized gain is recognized by Amelia. However, because St. George will use the transferred assets in the active conduct of a foreign trade or business, the realized gain remains potentially deferred. As the inventory and accounts receivable are "tainted assets," Amelia must recognize $350 of gain upon the transfer ($300 gain attributable to inventory and $50 gain from the accounts receivable). Gain is recognized on an asset-by-asset basis with no offset for losses on other assets. ■

In addition to gain on the tainted assets listed above, any U.S. depreciation (§§ 1245 and 1250) and other types of recapture potential (e.g., §§ 617, 1252, and 1254) in the assets transferred must be recognized to the extent of gain realized. This provision applies only to appreciated assets for which the depreciation or other deduction has resulted in a tax benefit. The U.S. depreciation is the portion of the depreciation attributable to use of the property in the United States. Prior branch losses are also recaptured to the extent that they are not recaptured under the § 904(f) provisions.

The transfer of intangibles is treated separately under § 367(d) as a transfer pursuant to a sale for contingent payments. These amounts are treated as received by the transferor over the life of the intangible and are ordinary income. They are recognized by the transferor and must be commensurate with the income attributable to the intangible. A subsequent disposition by the transferee triggers income recognition to the initial transferor under § 367.

**Inbound and Offshore Transfers.** One objective of § 367 is to prevent E & P that has accumulated in U.S.-owned foreign corporations from escaping U.S. taxation. Section 367(b) covers the tax treatment of inbound and offshore transfers with regard to stock of a controlled foreign corporation (CFC). (CFCs are discussed in more detail in a later section.) Examples of inbound transactions include the following.

- The liquidation of a foreign corporation into a domestic parent under § 332.
- The acquisition of the assets of a foreign corporation by a domestic corporation in a Type "C" or Type "D" reorganization.

Offshore transfers include the following.

- A foreign corporation acquisition of a first- or lower-tier foreign corporation in exchange for stock of a non-CFC.
- A foreign corporate Type "B," Type "C," or Type "D" acquisition of a foreign corporation in exchange for CFC stock.
- A foreign § 351 transfer of stock or other property in a foreign corporation having a U.S. shareholder.

■ **EXHIBIT 9–2**
OECD Tax Haven Blacklist

**In 2000, the OECD identified these jurisdictions as tax havens that had not cooperated with its campaign to stop harmful global tax practices. As of 2002, only the countries marked with an asterisk remained on the list.**

| | |
|---|---|
| Andorra* | Maldives |
| Anguilla | Marshall Islands* |
| Antigua and Barbuda | Monaco* |
| Aruba | Montserrat |
| Bahamas | Nauru* |
| Bahrain | Netherlands Antilles |
| Barbados | Niue |
| Belize | Panama |
| British Virgin Islands | Samoa |
| Cook Island | Seychelles |
| Dominica | St. Christopher and Nevis |
| Gibraltar | St. Lucia |
| Grenada | St. Vincent and the |
| Guernsey |    Grenadines |
| Isle of Man | Tonga |
| Jersey | Turks and Caicos Islands |
| Liberia* | U.S. Virgin Islands |
| Liechtenstein* | Vanuatu* |

SOURCE: Organization for Economic Cooperation and Development (OECD), *Towards Global Tax Cooperation: Progress in Identifying and Eliminating Harmful Tax Practices*, 2000; and OECD News Release, April 18, 2002.

U.S. persons that are directly or indirectly parties to an inbound or offshore transfer involving stock of a CFC generally recognize dividend income to the extent of their pro rata share of the previously untaxed E & P of the foreign corporation. In some circumstances, income can be deferred by entering into a gain recognition agreement with the IRS.

## TAX HAVENS

Many outbound transfers of assets to foreign corporations are to countries with tax rates higher than or equal to the U.S. rate. Thus, tax avoidance is not the motive for such transfers. Some U.S. corporations, however, make their foreign investment in (or through) a tax haven. A **tax haven** is a country where either locally sourced income or residents are subject to no or low internal taxation. Exhibit 9–2 lists countries classified as tax havens.

One method of potentially avoiding taxation is to invest through a foreign corporation incorporated in a tax haven. Because the foreign corporation is a resident of the tax haven, the income it earns is subject to no or low internal taxes. Tax haven countries may also have provisions limiting the exchange of financial and commercial information.

A tax haven can, in effect, be created by an income tax treaty. For example, under an income tax treaty between Country A and Country B, residents of Country A are subject to a withholding tax of only 5 percent on dividend and interest income sourced in Country B. The United States and Country A have a similar treaty. The United States does not have a treaty with Country B, and the withholding tax is 30 percent. A U.S. corporation can create a foreign subsidiary in Country A and use that subsidiary to make investments in Country B. This practice is referred to as **treaty shopping.** If the Country B investment income had been earned directly

## A MOVE TO THE BEACH FOR U.S. CORPORATIONS SEEKING A VACATION FROM U.S. TAX RULES

A number of U.S.-based companies have decided to cast their lot on the golden shores of Bermuda, reincorporating as Bermuda companies and enjoying Bermuda's low-tax environment. Those with new Bermuda headquarters include such well-known companies as Fruit of the Loom, Cooper Industries, Foster Wheeler, and Ingersoll Rand. Even Accenture, formerly Andersen Consulting, established itself in Bermuda.

Many of these companies argue that U.S. international tax policy creates an environment that damages their ability to compete in the global marketplace. The stock market often rewarded these so-called inversion transactions (i.e., conversion from U.S. to foreign based) with increased stock prices. Although an inversion transaction often entailed a current tax cost, the long-term tax benefits were considered more important. Many other companies were preparing to invert in 2002 when Congress began developing anti-inversion legislation and the public began reacting negatively to these corporate expatriates. During mid-2002, toolmaker Stanley Works called off its previously announced, and very controversial, inversion plans.

by the U.S. corporation, it would be subject to a 30 percent withholding tax. As a result of investing through the foreign subsidiary created in Country A, the U.S. parent corporation pays only 10 percent in foreign taxes on the income earned, that is, 5 percent to Country B and 5 percent to Country A.

In recent years, many countries have enacted "treaty shopping" provisions. Under the provisions, treaty benefits for withholding taxes are not available to a resident corporation unless a certain percentage of its beneficial interests are owned, directly or indirectly, by one or more individual residents of the country in which the corporation is resident. The most controversial article in the U.S. Model Treaty is Article 22, Limitation on Benefits, which is meant to prevent treaty shopping. Article 22 disallows treaty benefits to an entity unless more than 50 percent of the beneficial interest in the entity is owned, directly or indirectly, by one or more individual residents of the treaty country in which the entity is resident.[20]

### FOREIGN CORPORATIONS CONTROLLED BY U.S. PERSONS

To minimize current tax liability, taxpayers often attempt to defer the recognition of taxable income. One way to do this is to shift the income-generating activity to a foreign entity that is not within the U.S. tax jurisdiction. A foreign corporation is the most suitable entity for such an endeavor because, unlike a partnership, it is not a conduit through which income is taxed directly to the owner. Because of the potential for abuse, Congress has enacted various provisions to limit the availability of deferral.

**Controlled Foreign Corporations.** Subpart F, §§ 951–964 of the Code, provides that certain types of income generated by controlled foreign corporations (CFCs) are currently included in gross income by the U.S. shareholders without regard to

---

[20]Additional limitations on the use of treaty benefits are contained in § 894(c).

actual distributions. For Subpart F to apply, the foreign corporation must have been a CFC for an uninterrupted period of 30 days or more during the taxable year. When this is the case, U.S. shareholders must include in gross income their pro rata share of Subpart F income and increase in earnings that the CFC has invested in U.S. property for the tax year. This rule applies to U.S. shareholders who own stock in the corporation on the last day of the tax year or on the last day the foreign corporation is a CFC. The gross income inclusion must be made for their taxable year in which the taxable year of the CFC ends.

**EXAMPLE 15**

Gray, Inc., a calendar year corporation, is a CFC for the entire tax year. Chance Company, a U.S. corporation, owns 60% of Gray's one class of stock for the entire year. Subpart F income is $100,000, and no distributions have been made during the year. Chance, a calendar year taxpayer, includes $60,000 in gross income as a constructive dividend for the tax year. ∎

**EXAMPLE 16**

Gray, Inc., is a CFC until July 1 of the tax year (a calendar year) and earns $100,000 in Subpart F income. Terry, a U.S. citizen, owns 30% of its one class of stock for the entire year. She includes $14,877 [$100,000 × 30% × (181 days/365 days)] in gross income as a constructive dividend for the tax year. ∎

A **CFC** is any foreign corporation in which more than 50 percent of the total combined voting power of all classes of stock entitled to vote or the total value of the stock of the corporation is owned by U.S. shareholders on any day during the taxable year of the foreign corporation. The foreign subsidiaries of most multinational U.S. parent corporations are CFCs. For purposes of determining if a foreign corporation is a CFC, a **U.S. shareholder** is defined as a U.S. person who owns, or is considered to own, 10 percent or more of the total combined voting power of all classes of voting stock of the foreign corporation. Stock owned directly, indirectly, and constructively is counted.

Indirect ownership involves stock held through a foreign entity, such as a foreign corporation, foreign partnership, or foreign trust. This stock is considered to be actually owned proportionately by the shareholders, partners, or beneficiaries. Constructive ownership rules, with certain modifications, apply in determining if a U.S. person is a U.S. shareholder, in determining whether a foreign corporation is a CFC, and for certain related-party provisions of Subpart F.[21]

**EXAMPLE 17**

| Shareholders of Foreign Corporation | Voting Power | Classification |
|---|---|---|
| Alan | 30% | U.S. person |
| Bill | 9% | U.S. person |
| Carla | 40% | Foreign person |
| Dora | 20% | U.S. person |
| Ed | 1% | U.S. person |

Bill is Alan's son. Alan, Bill, and Dora are U.S. shareholders. Alan owns 39%, 30% directly and 9% constructively through Bill. Bill also owns 39%, 9% directly and 30% constructively through Alan. Thus, Bill is a U.S. shareholder. Dora owns 20% directly. The corporation is a CFC because U.S. shareholders own 59% of the voting power. Ed, a U.S. person, owns 1% and is not related to any of the other shareholders. Thus, Ed is not a U.S. shareholder and would not have to include any of the Subpart F income in gross income. If Bill were

---

[21]§§ 958 and 318(a).

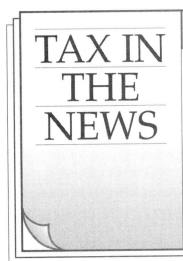

## WHO ARE THESE CFCs?

The 7,500 largest CFCs accounted for $2.7 trillion of the assets and more than $1.7 trillion of the gross receipts of all CFCs for 1996, the latest year for which complete data are available. These CFCs were engaged primarily in manufacturing (39 percent) or finance, insurance, or real estate (30 percent). Although these 7,500 CFCs were incorporated in over 100 different countries, CFCs in the United Kingdom, Canada, Germany, the Netherlands, France, and Japan accounted for over 60 percent of the gross receipts. The number of U.S. multinational corporations with CFCs increased 22 percent from 1990 to 1996. In 1996, CFCs distributed $69 billion of profits to their U.S. parents and other shareholders. A "large" CFC is one having $500 million or more in assets.

SOURCE: *Statistics of Income Bulletin*, Spring 2001.

not related to Alan or to any other U.S. persons who were shareholders, Bill would not be a U.S. shareholder, and the corporation would not be a CFC. ■

U.S. shareholders must include their pro rata share of the applicable income in their gross income only to the extent of their actual ownership. Stock held indirectly (but not constructively) is considered actually owned for this purpose.

**EXAMPLE 18**

Bill, in Example 17, would recognize only 9% of the Subpart F income as a constructive dividend. Alan would recognize 30%, and Dora would recognize 20%. If instead Bill were a foreign corporation wholly owned by Alan, Alan would recognize 39% as a constructive dividend. ■

*Subpart F Income.* A U.S. shareholder of a CFC does not necessarily lose the ability to defer U.S. taxation of income earned by the CFC. Only certain income earned by the CFC triggers immediate U.S. taxation as a constructive dividend. This tainted income, referred to as Subpart F income, can be characterized as income with little or no economic connection with the CFC's country of incorporation. **Subpart F** income consists of the following.

* Insurance income (§ 953).
* Foreign base company income (§ 954).
* International boycott factor income (§ 999).
* Illegal bribes.
* Income derived from a § 901(j) foreign country.

*Insurance Income.* Income attributable to insuring risk of loss outside the country in which the CFC is organized is Subpart F income. This rule precludes U.S. corporations from setting up offshore insurance companies in tax havens to convert expenditures for self-insurance into a deductible insurance premium.

*Foreign Base Company Income.* Foreign base company income (FBCI) provisions target transactions whereby a CFC earns income that lacks any economic connection to its country of organization. There are five categories of FBCI.

* Foreign personal holding company income.
* Foreign base company sales income.

- Foreign base company services income.
- Foreign base company shipping income.
- Foreign base company oil-related income.

Foreign personal holding company (FPHC) income consists of the following.

- Dividends, interest, royalties, rents, and annuities.
- Excess gains over losses from the sale or exchange of property (including an interest in a trust or partnership) that gives rise to FPHC income or that does not give rise to any income.
- Excess of foreign currency gains over foreign currency losses (other than any transaction directly related to the business needs of the CFC).
- Income from notional principal contracts.
- Certain payments in lieu of dividends.

Certain FPHC income does not trigger a Subpart F inclusion under exceptions for same-country payments and active rent and royalty income.

Foreign base company (FBC) sales income is income derived by a CFC where the CFC has very little connection with the process that generates the income and a related party is involved. If the CFC earns income from the sale of property to customers outside the CFC's country of incorporation, and either the supplier or the customer is related to the CFC, such income is FBC sales income.

**EXAMPLE 19**

Ulysses, Ltd., is a CFC organized in the United Kingdom and owned 100% by Joyce, Inc., a U.S. corporation. Ulysses purchases finished inventory from Joyce and sells the inventory to customers in Hong Kong. This sales income constitutes FBC sales income. ∎

An exception applies to property that is manufactured, produced, grown, or extracted in the country in which the CFC was organized or created and also to property sold for use, consumption, or disposition within that country. In both these situations, the CFC has participated in the economic process that generates the income.

**EXAMPLE 20**

If Ulysses, from Example 19, purchases raw materials from Joyce and performs substantial manufacturing activity in the United Kingdom before selling the inventory to customers in Hong Kong, the income is not FBC sales income. Even without the manufacturing activity, sales to customers within the United Kingdom would not produce FBC sales income. ∎

Certain income derived by a branch of the CFC in another country can be deemed FBC sales income. This is the case when the effect of using the branch is the same as if the branch were a wholly owned subsidiary.[22]

FBC services income is income derived from the performance of services for or on behalf of a related person and performed outside the country in which the CFC was created or organized. Income from services performed in connection with the sale of property by a CFC that has manufactured, produced, grown, or extracted such property is not FBC services income.

FBC shipping income includes the following.

- Dividends and interest received from a foreign corporation, to the extent that income is attributable to, or is derived from or in connection with, the shipping activity.
- Income attributable to the use of any aircraft or vessel in foreign commerce.

[22]§ 954(d)(2).

- Income attributable to the performance of services directly related to the use of that aircraft or vessel.
- Income attributable to the sale or exchange of any such aircraft or vessel.

FBC oil-related income is income, other than extraction income, derived in a foreign country by large oil producers in connection with the sale of oil and gas products and sold by the CFC or a related person for use or consumption outside the country in which the oil or gas was extracted.

*Subpart F Income Exceptions.* A *de minimis* rule provides that if the total amount of a foreign corporation's FBCI and gross insurance income for the taxable year is less than the lesser of 5 percent of gross income or $1 million, none of its gross income is treated as FBCI for the tax year. At the other extreme, if a foreign corporation's FBCI and gross insurance income exceed 70 percent of total gross income, all the corporation's gross income for the tax year is treated as Subpart F income.

FBCI and insurance income subject to high foreign taxes are not included under Subpart F if the taxpayer establishes that the income was subject to an effective rate, imposed by a foreign country, of more than 90 percent of the maximum corporate rate under § 11. For example, the rate must be greater than 31.5 percent (90% × 35%), where 35 percent represents the highest U.S. corporate rate.

*Increase in Investment in U.S. Property.* In addition to Subpart F income, U.S. shareholders must include in gross income their pro rata share of the CFC's increase in investment in U.S. property for the taxable year.[23] U.S. property generally includes U.S. real property, debt obligations of U.S. persons, and stock in certain related domestic corporations.

**EXAMPLE 21**

Fleming, Ltd., a CFC, earned no Subpart F income for the taxable year. If Fleming lends $100,000 to Lynn, its sole U.S. shareholder, this debt is considered an investment in U.S. property by Fleming because it now owns a U.S. note receivable. Holding the note triggers a constructive dividend of $100,000 to Lynn. ■

*Distributions of Previously Taxed Income.* Distributions from a CFC are treated as being first from E & P attributable to increases in investment in U.S. property previously taxed as a constructive dividend, second from E & P attributable to previously taxed Subpart F income, and last from other E & P.[24] Thus, distributions of previously taxed income are not taxed again as a dividend but reduce E & P. Any increase in investment in U.S. property is considered attributable first to Subpart F income and thus is not taxed twice.

**EXAMPLE 22**

In the current year, Jet, Inc., a U.S. shareholder, owns 100% of a CFC, from which Jet receives a $100,000 distribution. The CFC's E & P is composed of the following amounts.

- $50,000 attributable to previously taxed increases in investment in U.S. property.
- $30,000 attributable to previously taxed Subpart F income.
- $40,000 attributable to other E & P.

Jet has a taxable dividend of only $20,000, all attributable to other E & P. The remaining $80,000 is previously taxed income. The CFC's E & P is reduced by $100,000. The remaining $20,000 E & P is all attributable to other E & P. ■

---

[23]§ 956.
[24]Prior law included another category of previously taxed income related to investment in excess passive assets under § 956A.

## CONCEPT SUMMARY 9–2

### Income of a CFC That Is Included in Gross Income of a U.S. Shareholder

*Plus all other income, when foreign base company and insurance income exceeds 70% of gross income.

A U.S. shareholder's basis in CFC stock is increased by constructive dividends and decreased by subsequent distributions of previously taxed income. U.S. corporate shareholders who own at least 10 percent of the voting stock of a foreign corporation are allowed an indirect foreign tax credit for foreign taxes deemed paid on constructive dividends included in gross income under Subpart F. The indirect credit also is available for Subpart F income attributable to certain lower-tier foreign corporations. See the foreign tax credit discussion later in this chapter. The various constructive dividend possibilities for CFC income appear in Concept Summary 9–2.

***Dispositions of Stock of a CFC.*** Under the Subpart F provisions, Subpart F income of a CFC is currently taxed to U.S. shareholders to the extent of their pro rata share. This rule, however, does not reach the earnings of the CFC that are not included in the taxable income of the shareholders under Subpart F (e.g., active trade or business income not involving related persons). Section 1248 prevents the gain from the disposition of CFC stock from escaping taxation as ordinary income. This provision requires that gain on the sale or other disposition of stock of a CFC by a U.S. shareholder be treated as dividend income to the extent of the transferor's share of undistributed nonpreviously taxed E & P of the corporation.

**Other Antideferral Provisions.**   Congress has enacted two other provisions to limit the deferral benefits associated with earning investment income through a foreign corporation. Both the foreign personal holding company (FPHC) and the passive foreign investment company (PFIC) rules can trigger constructive dividends to U.S. persons.

A foreign corporation is an FPHC if it meets two requirements.

1. Sixty percent or more of its gross income for the taxable year must be FPHC income, as defined for purposes of Subpart F income. This percentage drops to 50 percent or more after the 60 percent requirement has been met for a tax year. The percentage remains at 50 percent until the foreign corporation does not meet the 50 percent test for three consecutive years or does not meet the stock ownership requirement for an entire tax year.

2. More than 50 percent of the total combined voting power or the total value of the stock of the corporation must be owned, directly or indirectly, at any time during the taxable year by five or fewer individuals who are U.S. persons.[25]

The major distinction between the FPHC tax and the personal holding company (PHC) tax (see Chapter 6) is that the FPHC tax is levied on the U.S. shareholders of an FPHC rather than on the corporation. A pro rata share of the undistributed FPHC income (limited to current E & P) is included in the gross income of U.S. persons who are shareholders of the FPHC. The amount taxable as a constructive dividend to a U.S. shareholder is treated as a contribution to the capital of the corporation and increases the shareholder's basis in the corporation's stock.

Dividends paid can reduce the amount taxable as undistributed FPHC income. In addition, certain income otherwise qualifying as FPHC income is ignored if it is received from a related corporation. U.S. shareholders of a CFC that is also an FPHC are not taxed on the same income under Subpart F and the FPHC provisions. Income falling within both provisions is taxed only under Subpart F.[26]

A PFIC is similar in theory to an FPHC, but the rules are more restrictive. Any level of ownership can subject a U.S. person to taxation under the PFIC provisions if the foreign corporation earns substantial levels of investment income.[27] Foreign mutual funds are often PFICs to their U.S. owners. Similar to FPHCs, income falling under both Subpart F and the PFIC provisions is taxed only under Subpart F.

## THE FOREIGN TAX CREDIT

The United States retains the right to tax its citizens and residents on their world-wide taxable income. This approach can result in double taxation, presenting a potential problem to U.S. persons who invest abroad.

To reduce the possibility of double taxation, Congress enacted the **foreign tax credit (FTC)** provisions. Under these provisions, a qualified taxpayer is allowed a tax credit for foreign income taxes paid. The credit is a dollar-for-dollar reduction of U.S. income tax liability.

For the most recent years data are available, corporations filing U.S. tax returns claimed $37 billion in FTCs and individuals claimed $4.9 billion in FTCs. Income

[25]§ 552.
[26]§ 951(d).

[27]§ 1297.

receipts on U.S. direct investment abroad were $98.3 billion. Without the benefit of the FTC, much of this income would have been subject to double taxation.

**EXAMPLE 23**

Ace Tools, Inc., a U.S. corporation, has a branch operation in Mexico, from which it earns taxable income of $750,000 for the current year. Ace pays income tax of $150,000 on these earnings to the Mexican tax authorities. Ace must also include the $750,000 in gross income for U.S. tax purposes. Assume that, before considering the FTC, Ace owes $255,000 in U.S. income taxes on this foreign-source income. Thus, total taxes on the $750,000 could equal $405,000 ($150,000 + $255,000), a 54% effective rate. But Ace takes an FTC of $150,000 against its U.S. tax liability on the foreign-source income. Ace's total taxes on the $750,000 now are $255,000 ($150,000 + $105,000), a 34% effective rate. ■

The FTC is elective for any particular tax year. If the taxpayer does not "choose" to take the FTC, § 164 allows a deduction for foreign taxes paid or incurred. A taxpayer cannot take a credit and a deduction for the same foreign income taxes.[28] However, a taxpayer can take a deduction in the same year as an FTC for foreign taxes that are not creditable (e.g., non-income taxes).

**The Direct Credit.**   Section 901 provides a direct FTC to U.S. taxpayers that pay or incur a foreign income tax. For purposes of the direct credit, only the taxpayer that bears the legal incidence of the foreign tax is eligible for the credit. Ace Tools in Example 23 would be eligible for the direct credit.

**The Indirect Credit.**   If a U.S. corporation operates in a foreign country through a branch, the direct credit is available for foreign taxes paid. If, however, a U.S. corporation operates in a foreign country through a foreign subsidiary, the direct credit is not available for foreign taxes paid by the foreign corporation. An indirect credit is available to U.S. corporate taxpayers that receive actual or constructive dividends from foreign corporations that have paid foreign income taxes. These foreign taxes are deemed paid by the corporate shareholders in the same proportion as the dividends actually or constructively received bear to the foreign corporation's post-1986 undistributed earnings and profits (E & P).

$$\text{Indirect FTC} = \frac{\text{Actual or constructive dividend}}{\text{Post-1986 undistributed earnings}} \times \text{Post-1986 foreign taxes}$$

Section 78 requires a domestic corporation that chooses the FTC for deemed-paid foreign taxes to *gross up* (add to income) dividend income by the amount of deemed-paid taxes.

**EXAMPLE 24**

Wren, Inc., a domestic corporation, owns 50% of Finch, Inc., a foreign corporation. Wren receives a dividend of $120,000 from Finch. Finch paid foreign taxes of $500,000 on post-1986 E & P. Finch's post-1986 E & P totals $1.2 million. Wren's deemed-paid foreign taxes for FTC purposes are $50,000.

| | |
|---|---|
| Cash dividend from Finch | $120,000 |
| Deemed-paid foreign taxes | |
| $\left(\dfrac{\$120,000}{\$1,200,000} \times \$500,000\right)$ | 50,000 |
| Gross income to Wren | $170,000 |

---

[28]§ 275.

■ **FIGURE 9–3**
Section 902 Ownership
Requirements

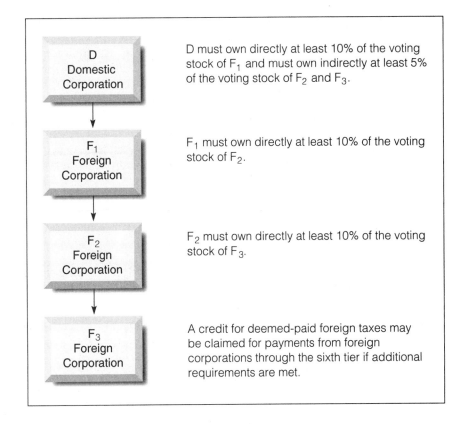

In addition to the $120,000 cash dividend, Wren must include the $50,000 in gross income for the § 78 gross-up adjustment if the FTC is elected. ■

Certain ownership requirements must be met before the indirect credit is available to a domestic corporation. The domestic corporation must own 10 percent or more of the voting stock of the foreign corporation. The credit is also available for deemed-paid foreign taxes of second- and third-tier foreign corporations if the 10 percent ownership requirement is met at the second- and third-tier level. A 5 percent indirect ownership requirement must also be met. The indirect credit is also available for foreign taxes paid by fourth- through sixth-tier foreign corporations if additional requirements are met, including the requirement that these corporations be CFCs. The § 902 ownership requirements are summarized in Figure 9–3.

**FTC Limitations.** To prevent taxpayers from crediting foreign taxes against U.S. taxes levied on U.S.-source taxable income, the FTC is subject to a limitation. The FTC for any taxable year cannot exceed the lesser of two amounts: (1) the actual foreign taxes paid or accrued or (2) the U.S. taxes (before the FTC) on foreign-source taxable income. The FTC limitation is derived in the following manner.

$$\text{FTC limitation} = \frac{\text{Foreign-source taxable income}}{\text{Worldwide taxable income}^{29}} \times \text{U.S. tax before FTC}$$

---

[29]For FTC purposes, the taxable income of an individual, estate, or trust is computed without any deduction for personal exemptions. § 904(b)(1).

**EXAMPLE 25**

Charlotte, a U.S. resident, invests in foreign securities. Her worldwide taxable income (before personal exemptions) for the tax year is $120,000, consisting of $100,000 in salary from a U.S. employer and $20,000 of income from foreign sources. Foreign taxes of $6,000 were withheld by foreign tax authorities. Assume that Charlotte's U.S. tax before the FTC is $33,600. Her FTC is limited to $5,600 [$33,600 × ($20,000/$120,000)]. Her net U.S. tax liability is $28,000. ◼

As Example 25 illustrates, the limitation can prevent the total amount of foreign taxes paid in high-tax jurisdictions from being credited. Taxpayers could overcome this problem by generating additional foreign-source income that is subject to no, or low, foreign taxation.

**EXAMPLE 26**

Compare Domestic Corporation's FTC situations. In one, the corporation has only $500,000 of highly taxed foreign-source income. In the other, Domestic also has $100,000 of low-taxed foreign-source interest income.

|  | Only Highly Taxed Income | With Low-Taxed Interest Income |
|---|---|---|
| Foreign-source income | $500,000 | $600,000 |
| Foreign taxes | 275,000 | 280,000 |
| U.S.-source income | 700,000 | 700,000 |
| U.S. taxes (34%) | 408,000 | 442,000 |
| FTC limitation | 170,000* | 204,000** |

*$408,000 × ($500,000/$1,200,000).
**$442,000 × ($600,000/$1,300,000).

Domestic's foreign taxes increase by only $5,000 ($280,000 − $275,000), but its FTC limitation increases by $34,000. ◼

Example 26 illustrates the *cross-crediting* of foreign taxes from high- and low-taxed foreign income. To prevent this practice, the FTC rules provide for several separate limitation baskets. These provisions require that a separate limitation be calculated for each of certain categories (or baskets) of foreign-source taxable income and the foreign taxes attributable to that income. Section 904(d) provides separate limitation baskets for the following.

* Passive income.
* High withholding tax interest.
* Financial services income.
* Shipping income.
* 10/50 company dividends (dividends from a foreign corporation owned at least 10 percent but not more than 50 percent). A look-through rule applies to dividends paid by 10/50 companies from E & P accumulated in tax years beginning after 2002. The dividends are allocated among the separate baskets based on the ratio of the 10/50 company's post-2002 E & P in that basket to the company's total post-2002 E & P. Dividends paid by 10/50 companies out of E & P accumulated in taxable years beginning before 2003 are assigned to a single 10/50 company basket that applies to all 10/50 companies.[30]
* Dividends from a domestic international sales corporation (DISC) or former DISC to the extent they are treated as foreign-source income.

---

[30]§§ 904(d)(1)(E), (d)(2)(E), and (d)(4).

## CONCEPT SUMMARY 9–3

### Foreign Tax Credit: Separate Income Limitations

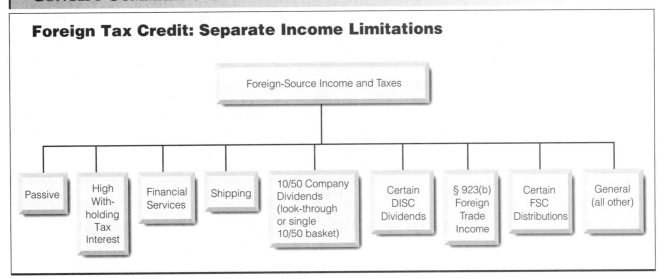

- Taxable income attributable to foreign trade income under § 923(b).
- Distributions from a foreign sales corporation (FSC) or former FSC out of E & P attributable to foreign trade income or qualified interest and carrying charges under § 263(c).

All other foreign-source income is included in a residual (or general) limitation basket. The separate limitations are diagrammed in Concept Summary 9–3.

**EXAMPLE 27**

BenCo, Inc., a U.S. corporation, has a foreign branch in France that earns taxable income of $1,500,000 from manufacturing operations and $600,000 from shipping activities. BenCo also earns French-source high withholding tax interest of $100,000. BenCo pays foreign taxes of $600,000 (40%), $300,000 (50%), and $15,000 (15%), respectively, on this foreign-source income. The corporation also earns $4,000,000 of U.S.-source taxable income, resulting in worldwide taxable income of $6,200,000. BenCo's U.S. taxes before the FTC are $2,108,000 (at 34%). The following tabulation illustrates the effect of the separate limitation baskets on cross-crediting.

| Foreign Income Category | Net Taxable Amount | Foreign Taxes | U.S. Tax before FTC at 34% | FTC with Separate Limits |
|---|---|---|---|---|
| Manufacturing | $1,500,000 | $600,000 | $510,000 | $510,000 |
| Shipping | 600,000 | 300,000 | 204,000 | 204,000 |
| High withholding tax interest | 100,000 | 15,000 | 34,000 | 15,000 |
| Total | $2,200,000 | $915,000 | $748,000 | $729,000 |

Without the separate limitation provisions, the FTC would be the lesser of (1) $915,000 foreign taxes paid or accrued or (2) $748,000 [$2,108,000 × ($2,200,000/$6,200,000)]. The separate limitation provisions reduce the total FTC by $19,000 ($748,000 − $729,000). The effect of the separate limitation rules is that the foreign-source income taxed at the foreign tax rates of 40% and 50% cannot be aggregated with foreign-source income taxed at only 15%. ■

In the case of a CFC, the look-through rules classify any dividend (actual or deemed), interest, rent, or royalty income received from the CFC into separate limitation baskets as if such income were earned directly by the U.S. shareholders of the CFC. A partner's distributive share of partnership income is also generally categorized in separate limitation baskets based on the character of the partnership's income. Additionally, interest, rent, or royalty payments to certain partners are eligible for look-through treatment.

The limitations can result in unused (noncredited) foreign taxes for the tax year. A two-year carryback and a five-year carryforward of excess foreign taxes are allowed. The taxes can be credited in years when the formula limitation for that year exceeds the foreign taxes attributable to the same tax year. The carryback and carryforward provisions are available only within a specific basket. In other words, excess foreign taxes in one basket cannot be carried over unless there is an excess limitation in the same basket for the carryover year.

**Foreign Losses.**   Citizens and residents of the United States who hold foreign investments or operations directly (e.g., through a branch operation) or through a conduit entity (e.g., a partnership) have the opportunity to offset foreign losses against U.S.-source income, thereby reducing the U.S. income tax due on U.S.-source income. If the foreign country in which the loss is generated (sourced) taxes subsequent income from these foreign operations, the FTC could reduce or eliminate any U.S. tax on the income.

To prevent this loss of tax revenue to the United States, tax law provides that the overall foreign losses should be recaptured as U.S.-source income for FTC purposes.[31] This is accomplished by reducing the numerator of the FTC limitation formula. Foreign-source taxable income is reduced by the lesser of (1) the remaining unrecaptured overall foreign loss or (2) 50 percent of foreign-source taxable income for the taxable year (unless the taxpayer elects to recapture a greater percentage). Unrecaptured foreign losses are carried over indefinitely until recaptured.

**EXAMPLE 28**

Shannon, Inc., a domestic corporation, operates a branch in Japan. The earnings record of the branch is as follows.

| Year | Taxable Income (Loss) | Foreign Taxes Paid |
| --- | --- | --- |
| 2000 | ($ 15,000) | –0– |
| 2001 | (20,000) | –0– |
| 2002 | (20,000) | –0– |
| 2003 | 40,000 | $20,000 |

For 2000–2003, Shannon has U.S.-source taxable income of $300,000 each year. Shannon's 2003 U.S. tax liability before the FTC is $115,600. Its overall foreign loss is $55,000 for 2000–2002. The FTC limitation for 2003 is $6,800, $115,600 × {[$40,000 − (50% × $40,000)]/$340,000}. ■

A situation may arise in which overall foreign losses have been incurred and the U.S. taxpayer disposes of trade or business property used predominantly outside the United States before any or all of the loss is recaptured. The provisions described above will not necessarily reach such a situation. The statutory solution to this problem is that upon disposal the U.S. taxpayer generates U.S.-source income. The

---

[31]§ 904(f)(1).

amount of income generated is the lesser of (1) the fair market value of the property less its adjusted basis or (2) the remaining amount of unrecaptured overall foreign losses.[32]

When a taxpayer has a loss for the tax year in one or more foreign-source categories (baskets), the loss must be apportioned pro rata to foreign-source categories with income for the tax year. If there is an overall foreign loss (i.e., foreign losses exceed foreign income in all categories), the overall foreign loss then reduces U.S.-source income. A U.S. loss for the tax year is apportioned pro rata to foreign-source income in each category, but only after the apportionment of any foreign losses to those income categories.

**EXAMPLE 29**

During 2003, Bloom, Inc., a U.S. corporation, incurred a $10,000 loss in its manufacturing activities, $20,000 in shipping income, and $5,000 in high withholding tax interest. The loss in the manufacturing basket is apportioned to the baskets with income as follows:

| Foreign Income Category | Income or Loss | Foreign-Source Taxable Income |
|---|---|---|
| Manufacturing | ($10,000) | $ –0– |
| Shipping | 20,000 | 12,000* |
| High withholding tax interest | 5,000 | 3,000** |
| Total | $15,000 | $15,000 |

*$20,000 − [$10,000 × ($20,000/$25,000)].
**$5,000 − [$10,000 × ($5,000/$25,000)].

In 2004, Bloom earns $25,000 in manufacturing income, $18,000 in shipping income, and $6,000 in high withholding tax interest, so the previously apportioned loss must be reallocated back to the affected baskets as follows:

| Foreign Income Category | Income or Loss | Previously Apportioned Loss | Foreign-Source Taxable Income |
|---|---|---|---|
| Manufacturing | $25,000 | ($10,000) | $15,000 |
| Shipping | 18,000 | 8,000 | 26,000 |
| High withholding tax interest | 6,000 | 2,000 | 8,000 |
| Total | $49,000 | | $49,000 |

**The Alternative Minimum Tax FTC.** For purposes of the alternative minimum tax (AMT), the FTC is limited to the lesser of (1) the credit for regular tax purposes or (2) 90 percent of the tentative minimum tax before the credit. The 10 percent cutback is calculated on the tentative minimum tax without regard to the alternative tax NOL deduction. The FTC limitation is calculated by using foreign-source alternative minimum taxable income (AMTI) in the numerator and worldwide AMTI in the denominator of the formula and the tentative minimum tax rather than the regular tax.

$$\text{AMT FTC limitation} = \frac{\text{Foreign-source AMTI}}{\text{Worldwide AMTI}} \times \text{Tentative minimum tax}$$

[32]§ 904(f)(3).

The taxpayer may elect to use regular foreign-source taxable income in the numerator if it does not exceed total AMTI. The AMT FTC limit must also be determined on a basket-by-basket basis.

**Other Considerations.**   For a foreign levy to qualify for the FTC, it must be a tax, and its predominant character must be that of an income tax in the U.S. sense.[33] A levy is a tax if it is a compulsory payment, rather than a payment for a specific economic benefit such as the right to extract oil. A tax's predominant character is that of an income tax in the U.S. sense if it reaches realized net gain and is not a *soak-up* tax, that is, does not depend on being credited against the income tax of another country. A tax that is levied in lieu of an income tax is also creditable.[34]

**EXAMPLE 30**

JonesCo, a domestic corporation, generates $2 million of taxable income from operations in Larissa, a foreign country. Larissan law levies a tax on income generated in Larissa by foreign residents only in cases in which the country of residence (such as the United States) allows a tax credit for foreign taxes paid. JonesCo will not be allowed an FTC for taxes paid to Larissa, because the foreign tax is a soak-up tax. ■

For purposes of the FTC, foreign taxes are attributable to the year in which they are paid or accrued. Under § 905, taxpayers using the cash method of accounting for tax purposes may elect to take the FTC in the year in which the foreign taxes accrue. The election is binding on the taxpayer for the year in which it is made and for all subsequent years. Foreign taxes generally must be translated to U.S. dollars at the average exchange rate for the tax year to which the taxes relate.[35]

## POSSESSIONS CORPORATIONS

To encourage the economic development of U.S. possessions, Congress enacted a credit provision for income from operations in U.S. possessions. Domestic corporations can elect to receive a § 936 credit against U.S. taxes. The credit is equal to the portion of the U.S. tax attributable to the sum of possession-source taxable income and qualified investment income, even if no tax is paid or due to the possession. This is referred to as a *tax-sparing* credit. No additional credit or deduction is allowed for income taxes actually paid to the possession. A number of pharmaceutical companies, including Eli Lilly Company, have used subsidiaries with operations in Puerto Rico to take advantage of this and local tax benefits. The pharmaceutical and electrical machinery industries receive more than 60 percent of the total § 936 credits allowed.

According to Congressional Budget Office estimates, the § 936 incentive would have triggered a $15 billion revenue loss between 1993 and 1997. For this reason, in 1993, Congress imposed special phaseout limits on the credit. Then, in 1996, it enacted legislation that repealed the credit except for existing claimants.[36] For § 936 corporations conducting an active trade or business in a possession on October 13, 1995, the credit will be phased out by January 1, 2006.

The credit is allowed against the U.S. tax attributable to foreign-source taxable income from the active conduct of a trade or business in a U.S. possession. It is also allowed on the sale or exchange of substantially all the assets used by the domestic corporation in that active trade or business. The credit is not allowed against certain taxes, though, such as the accumulated earnings tax under § 531 and the personal holding company tax under § 541.

---

[33]Reg. § 1.901–2.
[34]§ 903 and Reg. § 1.903–1.

[35]§ 986(a).
[36]§§ 936(j) and 30A.

The credit is not available for income received in the United States unless it is possession-source income received from an unrelated person and is attributable to an active trade or business conducted in a possession. In addition, the credit is not available for income from intangible assets, such as formulas and patents. Intangible property income is includible in taxable income by a domestic corporation as U.S.-source income. If a domestic corporation elects the credit, however, all of its shareholders who are U.S. persons include their pro rata share of that item in gross income as U.S.-source income. In this case, the domestic corporation is not taxed on such income.

**EXAMPLE 31**

A qualified possessions corporation generates the following foreign-source income, on which it pays the following foreign taxes.

| Taxable Income | Source | Foreign Taxes |
| --- | --- | --- |
| $450,000 active trade or business income | Possession | $40,000 |
| $10,000 passive investment income | Possession | –0– |
| $40,000 investment income | Nonpossession | 16,000 |

Assume that the corporation's worldwide taxable income is $500,000 and its U.S. tax before the FTC is $170,000. The § 936 possessions corporation credit is $153,000 (34% × $450,000) before consideration of the § 936 phaseout limitation. The direct FTC is $13,600, the lesser of $16,000 or $13,600 [$170,000 × ($40,000/$500,000)]. ∎

---

**LO.6**

Apply the U.S. tax provisions concerning nonresident alien individuals and foreign corporations.

# U.S. Taxation of Nonresident Aliens and Foreign Corporations

Generally, only the U.S.-source income of nonresident alien individuals and foreign corporations is subject to U.S. taxation. This reflects the reach of the U.S. tax jurisdiction. The constraint, however, does not prevent the United States from also taxing the foreign-source income of nonresident alien individuals and foreign corporations when that income is effectively connected with the conduct of a U.S. trade or business.[37] Concept Summary 9–4 at the end of this section summarizes these tax rules.

## NONRESIDENT ALIEN INDIVIDUALS

A **nonresident alien (NRA)** individual is an individual who is not a citizen or resident of the United States. For example, Queen Elizabeth is an NRA, because she is not a citizen or resident of the United States. Citizenship is determined under the immigration and naturalization laws of the United States.[38] Basically, the citizenship statutes are broken down into two categories: nationality at birth or through naturalization.

**Residency.** Under § 7701(b), a person is a resident of the United States for income tax purposes if he or she meets either the green card test or the substantial presence test. If either of these tests is met for the calendar year, the individual is deemed a U.S. resident for the year.

---

[37]§§ 871, 881, and 882.

[38]Title 8, Aliens and Nationality, *United States Code.*

A foreign person issued a green card is considered a U.S. resident on the first day he or she is physically present in the United States after issuance. The green card is Immigration Form I–551. Newly issued cards are now rose colored, but the form is still referred to as the "green card." Status as a U.S. resident remains in effect until the green card has been revoked or the individual has abandoned lawful permanent resident status.

The substantial presence test is applied to an alien without a green card. It is a mathematical test involving physical presence in the United States. An individual who is physically present in the United States for at least 183 days during the calendar year is a U.S. resident for income tax purposes. This 183-day requirement can also be met over a three-year period that includes the two immediately preceding years and the current year, as long as the individual is present in the United States at least 31 days during the current year.[39] For this purpose, each day of the current calendar year is counted as a full day, each day of the first preceding year as one-third day, and each day of the second preceding year as one-sixth day.

**EXAMPLE 32**

Li, a foreign citizen, was present in the United States for 90 days in 2001, 180 days in 2002, and 110 days in 2003. For Federal income tax purposes, Li is a U.S. resident for 2003, because she was physically present for 185 days [(90 days × ⅙) + (180 days × ⅓) + (110 days × 1)] during the three-year period. ◼

Under the substantial presence test, residence begins the first day the individual is physically present in the United States and ends the last day of physical presence for the calendar year (assuming the substantial presence test is not satisfied for the next calendar year). Nominal presence of 10 days or less can be ignored in determining whether the substantial presence test is met.

The substantial presence test allows for several exceptions. Commuters from Mexico and Canada who are employed in the United States but return home each day are excepted. Also excepted are individuals who are prevented from leaving the United States by medical conditions that arose while the individuals were in the United States. Some individuals are exempt from the substantial presence test, including foreign government-related individuals (e.g., diplomats), qualified teachers, trainees and students, and certain professional athletes.

---

**ETHICAL CONSIDERATIONS**

## Should There Be Some "Heart" in Tax Law?

In determining whether an alien is a U.S. resident for U.S. income tax purposes under the substantial presence test, days on which a medical condition prevents the person from leaving the United States are not counted as days present in the United States. The medical condition (e.g., illness or injury) must have arisen after the NRA arrived in the United States. In other words, it generally must be an unexpected illness or accident. No such exception is available, however, for a family member or other NRA who is significant to the person who becomes ill or injured. Thus, under this rule, the relative or other significant person may have to either risk being classified as a U.S. resident for the tax year or leave the ill person (or accident victim) alone in the United States. Does this limited exception ignore the human element in illness and recovery?

---

[39]§ 7701(b)(3)(A).

**Nonresident Aliens Not Engaged in a U.S. Trade or Business.** Certain U.S.-source income that is *not* effectively connected with the conduct of a U.S. trade or business is subject to a flat 30 percent tax. This income includes dividends, interest, rents, royalties, certain compensation, premiums, annuities, and other fixed, determinable, annual or periodic (FDAP) income. This tax generally is levied by a withholding mechanism that requires the payors of the income to withhold 30 percent of gross amounts.[40] This method eliminates the problems of assuring payment by nonresidents, determining allowable deductions, and, in most instances, the filing of tax returns by nonresidents. Interest received from certain portfolio debt investments, even though U.S.-sourced, is exempt from taxation. Interest earned on deposits with banking institutions is also exempt as long as it is not effectively connected with the conduct of a U.S. trade or business.

Capital gains *not* effectively connected with the conduct of a U.S. trade or business are exempt from tax, as long as the NRA individual was not present in the United States for 183 days or more during the taxable year. If an NRA has not established a taxable year, the calendar year is used. NRAs are not permitted to carry forward capital losses.[41]

**Nonresident Aliens Engaged in a U.S. Trade or Business.** Two important definitions determine the U.S. tax consequences to NRAs with U.S.-source income: "the conduct of a **U.S. trade or business**" and "**effectively connected income**." Specifically, in order for an NRA's noninvestment income to be subject to U.S. taxation, the NRA must be considered engaged in a U.S. trade or business and must earn income effectively connected with that business.

General criteria for determining if a U.S. trade or business exists include the location of production activities, management, distribution activities, and other business functions. Trading in commodities and securities ordinarily does not constitute a trade or business. Dealers, however, need to avoid maintaining a U.S. trading office and trading for their own accounts. Corporations (other than certain personal holding companies) that are not dealers can trade for their own accounts. There are no restrictions on individuals who are not dealers.

The Code does not explicitly define a U.S. trade or business, but case law has defined the concept as activities carried on in the United States that are regular, substantial, and continuous.[42] Once an NRA is considered engaged in a U.S. trade or business, all U.S.-source income other than FDAP and capital gain income is considered effectively connected to that trade or business and is therefore subject to U.S. taxation.

**EXAMPLE 33**

Vito, an NRA, produces wine for export. During the current year, Vito earns $500,000 from exporting wine to unrelated wholesalers in the United States. The title to the wine passes to the U.S. wholesalers in New York. Vito has no offices or employees in the United States. The income from wine sales is U.S.-source income, but because Vito is not engaged in a U.S. trade or business, the income is not subject to taxation in the United States.

Assume that Vito begins operating a hot dog cart in New York City. This activity constitutes a U.S. trade or business. Consequently, all U.S.-source income other than FDAP or capital gain income will be taxed in the United States as income effectively connected

---

[40]§§ 871 and 1441.
[41]§ 871(a)(2).

[42]See, for example, *Higgins v. Comm.*, 312 U.S. 212 (1941) and *Continental Trading, Inc. v. Comm.*, 265 F.2d 40 (1959).

with a U.S. trade or business. Thus, both the hot dog cart profits and the $500,000 in wine income will be taxed in the United States. ■

FDAP and capital gain income may be considered effectively connected income if the assets that generate this income are used in, or held for use in, the trade or business (the asset-use test) or if the activities of the trade or business are a material factor in the production of the income (the business-activities test).[43] As long as FDAP and capital gain income are not effectively connected with a U.S. trade or business, the tax treatment of these income items is the same whether NRAs are engaged in a U.S. trade or business or not.

**EXAMPLE 34**

Ingrid, an NRA, operates a U.S. business. During the year, cash funds accumulate. Ingrid invests these funds on a short-term basis so that they remain available to meet her business needs. Any income earned from these investments is effectively connected income, under the asset-use test. ■

Effectively connected income is taxed at the same rates that apply to U.S. citizens and residents, and deductions for expenses attributable to that income are allowed. NRAs with effectively connected income are also allowed a deduction for casualty and theft losses related to property located within the United States, a deduction for qualified charitable contributions, and one personal exemption. NRAs with income effectively connected with the conduct of a U.S. trade or business may also be subject to the alternative minimum tax.

**Withholding Provisions.**   The 30 percent U.S. tax on FDAP income is generally administered by requiring the payor of the income to withhold the tax and remit it to the U.S. tax authorities. This assures the government of timely collection and relieves it of jurisdictional problems that could arise if it had to rely on recipients residing outside the United States to pay the tax. In recent years, U.S. payors withheld taxes of $3 billion annually from payments to foreign persons. Japanese recipients received the most U.S.-source income, with recipients from the United Kingdom ranked second. As explained earlier, income tax treaties with other countries provide for reduced withholding on certain types of FDAP income (see Exhibit 9–3 for some examples of withholding rates).

## FOREIGN CORPORATIONS

**Definition.**   The classification of an entity as a foreign corporation for U.S. tax purposes is an important consideration. Section 7701(a)(5) defines a foreign corporation as one that is not domestic. A domestic corporation is a corporation that is created or organized in the United States. Thus, though McDonald's is, in reality, a global corporation, it is considered a domestic corporation for U.S. tax purposes, solely because it was organized in the United States.

**Income Not Effectively Connected with a U.S. Trade or Business.**
U.S.-source FDAP income of foreign corporations is taxed by the United States in the same manner as that of NRA individuals—at a flat 30 percent rate. Generally, foreign corporations qualify for the same exemptions from U.S. taxation for investment income as do NRA individuals. The U.S.-source capital gains of foreign

---

[43]§ 864(c).

■ **EXHIBIT 9–3**
Selected Tax Treaty Withholding
Rates

| | Interest | Dividends in General | Dividends Paid by U.S. Subsidiary to a Foreign Parent Corporation |
|---|---|---|---|
| Australia | 10% | 15% | 15% |
| Canada | 10 | 15 | 5 |
| Ireland | 0 | 15 | 5 |
| Japan | 10 | 15 | 10 |
| Mexico | 15 | 15 | 5 |
| Philippines | 15 | 25 | 20 |

SOURCE: IRS Publication 901, *U.S. Tax Treaties.*

corporations are exempt from the Federal income tax if they are not effectively connected with the conduct of a U.S. trade or business.

**Effectively Connected Income.** Foreign corporations conducting a trade or business in the United States are subject to Federal income taxation on any U.S.-source income effectively connected with the trade or business. As with NRAs, any FDAP or capital gain income is not considered effectively connected unless the income meets the asset-use or business-activities test.[44] Foreign corporations are subject to the same tax rates on their effectively connected income as domestic corporations.

**Branch Profits Tax.** The objective of the **branch profits tax** is to afford equal tax treatment to income generated by a domestic corporation controlled by a foreign corporation and to income generated by other U.S. operations controlled by foreign corporations. If the foreign corporation operates through a U.S. subsidiary (a domestic corporation), the income of the subsidiary is taxable by the United States when earned and is also subject to a withholding tax when repatriated (returned as dividends to the foreign parent). Before the branch profits tax was enacted, a foreign corporation with a branch in the United States paid only the initial tax on its U.S. earnings; remittances were not taxed.

In addition to the income tax imposed under § 882 on effectively connected income of a foreign corporation, a tax equal to 30 percent of the **dividend equivalent amount (DEA)** for the taxable year is imposed on any foreign corporation with effectively connected income.[45] The DEA is the foreign corporation's effectively connected earnings for the taxable year, adjusted for increases and decreases in the corporation's U.S. net equity (investment in the U.S. operations). The DEA is limited to current E & P and post-1986 accumulated E & P that is effectively connected, or treated as effectively connected, with the conduct of a U.S. trade or business. U.S. net equity is the sum of money and the aggregate adjusted basis of assets and liabilities directly connected to U.S. operations that generate effectively connected income.

*E X A M P L E   3 5*

Robin, Inc., a foreign corporation, has a U.S. branch operation with the following tax results and other information for the year.

---

[44]§ 864(c).

[45]§ 884.

| | |
|---|---:|
| Pretax earnings effectively connected with a U.S. trade or business | $2,000,000 |
| U.S. corporate tax (at 34%) | 680,000 |
| Remittance to home office | 1,000,000 |
| Increase in U.S. net equity | 320,000 |

Robin's DEA and branch profits tax are computed as follows.

| | |
|---|---:|
| E & P effectively connected with a U.S. trade or business ($2,000,000 − $680,000) | $1,320,000 |
| Less: Increase in U.S. net equity | (320,000) |
| Dividend equivalent amount | $1,000,000 |
| Branch profits tax rate | × 30% |
| Branch profits tax | $   300,000 |

The 30 percent rate of the branch profits tax may be reduced or eliminated by a treaty provision. If a foreign corporation is subject to the branch profits tax, no other U.S. tax is levied on the dividend actually paid by the corporation during the taxable year.

## THE FOREIGN INVESTMENT IN REAL PROPERTY TAX ACT

Prior to 1980, NRAs and foreign corporations could avoid U.S. taxation on gains from the sale of U.S. real estate if the gains were treated as capital gains and were not effectively connected with the conduct of a U.S. trade or business. In the mid-1970s, midwestern farmers pressured Congress to eliminate what they saw as a tax advantage that would allow nonresidents to bid up the price of farmland. This and other concerns about foreign ownership of U.S. real estate led to the enactment of the Foreign Investment in Real Property Tax Act (FIRPTA) of 1980.

Under **FIRPTA**, gains and losses realized by NRAs and foreign corporations from the sale or other disposition of U.S. real property interests are treated as effectively connected with the conduct of a U.S. trade or business even when those individuals or corporations are not actually so engaged. NRA individuals must pay a tax equal to the lesser of two amounts: (1) 26 (or 28) percent of their alternative minimum taxable income or (2) regular U.S. rates on the net U.S. real property gain for the taxable year.[46] For purposes of this provision, losses are taken into account only to the extent they are deductible as business losses, losses on transactions entered into for profit, or losses from casualties and thefts.

**U.S. Real Property Interest (USRPI).**   Any direct interest in real property situated in the United States and any interest in a domestic corporation (other than solely as a creditor) are U.S. real property interests (USRPIs). This definition applies unless the taxpayer can establish that a domestic corporation was not a U.S. real property holding corporation (USRPHC) during the shorter of two periods: (1) the period during which the taxpayer held an interest in the corporation or (2) the five-year period ending on the date on which the interest was disposed of (the base period). A domestic corporation is not a USRPHC if it holds no USRPIs on the date of disposition of its stock and if any USRPIs held by the corporation during the base period were disposed of in a transaction in which gain, if any, was fully recognized.

---

[46]§ 897.

**CONCEPT SUMMARY 9–4**

## U.S. Taxation of NRAs and Foreign Corporations (FCs)

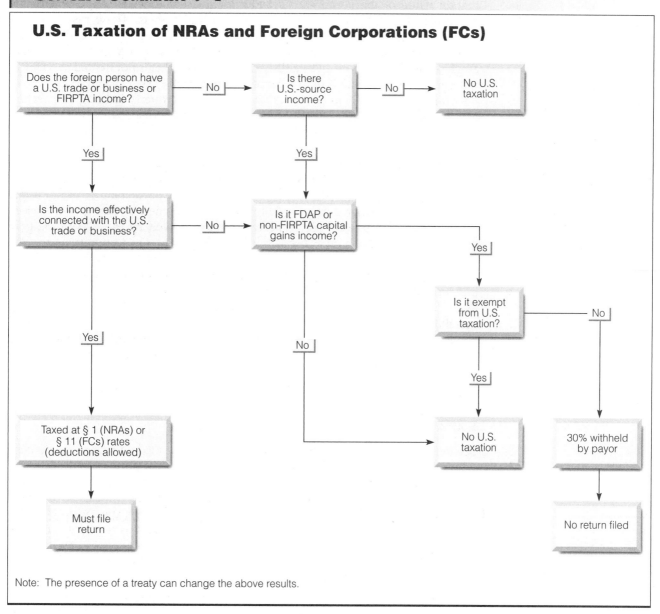

Note:  The presence of a treaty can change the above results.

---

**EXAMPLE 36**

From January 1, 1998, through January 1, 2003, Francis (a foreign investor) held shares in Door, Inc., a U.S. corporation. During this period, Door held two parcels of U.S. real estate and stock of Sash, Inc., another U.S. corporation. Sash also owned U.S. real estate. The two parcels of real estate held directly by Door were disposed of on December 15, 1999, in a nontaxable transaction. Sash disposed of its U.S. real estate in a taxable transaction on January 1, 2003.

An interest in Door is treated as a USRPI because Door did not recognize gain on the December 15, 1999 disposition of the USRPIs. If Door's ownership of U.S. real estate had been limited to its indirect ownership through Sash, an interest in Door would not have constituted a USRPI as of January 2, 2003. This result would occur because Sash disposed of its USRPIs in a taxable transaction in which gain was fully recognized. ■

A USRPHC is any corporation (whether foreign or domestic) where the fair market value of the corporation's USRPIs equals or exceeds 50 percent of the aggregate of fair market value of certain specified assets. These assets are the corporation's USRPIs, its interests in real property located outside the United States, and any other of its assets that are used or held for use in a trade or business. Stock regularly traded on an established securities market is not treated as a USRPI if a person holds no more than 5 percent of the stock.

Gain on a disposition of stock of a foreign real property holding corporation is not subject to tax under FIRPTA. However, gain on a disposition of a USRPI by such a foreign corporation is subject to FIRPTA.

**Withholding Provisions.**    The *FIRPTA* withholding provisions require any purchaser or agent acquiring a USRPI from a foreign person to withhold 10 percent of the amount realized on the disposition.[47] A domestic partnership, trust, or estate with a foreign partner, foreign grantor treated as owner, or foreign beneficiary must withhold 35 percent (or 20 percent where allowed by the IRS) of the gain allocable to that person on a disposition of a USRPI. Foreign corporations are also subject to withholding provisions on certain distributions. Without this withholding, NRAs could sell USRPIs, receiving the sales proceeds outside the United States, and jurisdictional issues could make it difficult for the U.S. tax authorities to collect any U.S. tax that might be due on gains. Certain exceptions to FIRPTA withholding are allowed.

Failure to withhold can subject the purchaser or the purchaser's agent to interest on any unpaid amount.[48] A civil penalty of 100 percent of the amount required to be withheld and a criminal penalty of up to $10,000 or five years in prison can be imposed for willful failure to withhold.[49]

## EXPATRIATION TO AVOID U.S. TAXATION

Section 877 provides for U.S. taxation of U.S.-source income earned by persons who relinquished their U.S. citizenship within 10 years of deriving that income if they gave up their citizenship to avoid U.S. taxation. Furthermore, NRAs who lost U.S. citizenship within a 10-year period immediately preceding the close of the tax year must pay taxes on their U.S.-source income as though they were still U.S. citizens. This provision applies only if the expatriation had as one of its principal purposes the avoidance of U.S. taxes. For 2003, individuals are presumed to have a tax avoidance purpose if they meet either of the following criteria.[50]

- Average annual net income tax for the five taxable years ending before the date of loss of U.S. citizenship is more than $122,000.
- Net worth as of that date is $608,000 or more.

These provisions also apply to "long-term lawful permanent residents" who cease to be taxed as U.S. residents. A long-term permanent resident is an individual (other than a citizen of the United States) who is a lawful permanent resident of the United States in at least 8 taxable years during the 15-year period ending with the taxable year in which the individual either ceases to be a lawful permanent resident of the United States or begins to be treated as a resident of another country under an income tax treaty between the United States and the other country (and does not waive the benefits of the treaty to residents of that country). An exception applies to certain individuals with dual citizenship. Special source rules also apply

---

[47]§ 1445.
[48]§§ 6601, 6621, and 6651.

[49]§§ 6672 and 7202.
[50]The dollar amounts are adjusted for inflation.

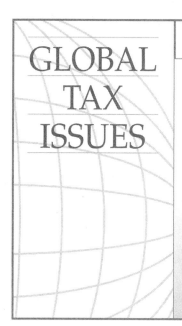

### FILING DEADLINES WHEN YOU'RE OVERSEAS

What if you are situated outside the United States when you file a tax return? Working with a non-U.S. postal service can be challenging even on a good day. The established rule still seems to be that the date of the non-U.S. postmark determines whether the return is filed in a timely manner or whether a failure to file penalty will be assessed (Rev.Rul. 80–218).

The IRS seems to be having some trouble digesting this rule, though. In *Pekar*, 113 TC 158, where the non-U.S. postmark indicated that the return had been mailed before its due date, the IRS seemed to be taking a date-received position with the Tax Court. But the Service admitted its mistake in ITA 2000121085, where the reliance-on-postmark test is applied as expected.

No ruling to date has specifically addressed the application of this rule to a private express delivery service like UPS, but neither the Code nor rulings restrict the when-delivered-to-the-carrier rule to domestic shipments, either. Thus, if a U.S. taxpayer living overseas uses a private delivery service, some form of date stamping is a good idea.

for purposes of expatriate taxation. The expatriate tax will not apply if U.S. taxation of the NRA under the normal provisions applicable to NRAs results in a greater tax liability. Certain expatriate provisions also apply for estate and gift tax purposes.

## Reporting Requirements

The U.S. tax provisions in the international area include numerous reporting requirements. Furthermore, civil and criminal penalties for noncompliance can apply.[51]

A domestic corporation that is 25 percent or more foreign owned must file an information return and maintain certain records where they will be accessible to the IRS.[52] Additionally, any foreign corporation carrying on a trade or business in the United States must file an information return and maintain records in a similar manner.[53]

The U.S. partners of a controlled foreign partnership must also file an information return.[54] A foreign partnership that has gross income that is either U.S.-source or effectively connected with a U.S. trade or business must file a partnership return.[55] Changes in ownership of interests in foreign partnerships (acquisitions or dispositions) must also be reported if a 10 percent or greater interest is involved.[56]

Asset transfers to foreign corporations or partnerships under certain tax-deferred transactions require information returns at the time of the transfer.[57] U.S. taxpayers that control foreign corporations or partnerships must also file annual information returns related to these entities.[58] Creation of, or a transfer to, a foreign trust by a U.S. person necessitates the filing of a Form 3520.[59]

[51]See Chapter 16.
[52]§ 6038A.
[53]§ 6038C.
[54]§ 6038.
[55]§ 6031(e).

[56]§ 6046A.
[57]§ 6038B.
[58]§ 6038.
[59]§ 6048.

**Tax Planning Considerations**

Over time, legislation has tended to reduce the ability to plan transactions and operations in a manner that minimizes tax liability. However, taxpayers who are not limited by the constraints of a particular transaction or operation can use the following suggestions to plan for maximum tax benefits.

### THE FOREIGN TAX CREDIT LIMITATION AND SOURCING PROVISIONS

The FTC limitation is partially based on the amount of foreign-source taxable income in the numerator of the limitation ratio. Consequently, the sourcing of income is extremely important. Income that is taxed by a foreign tax jurisdiction benefits from the FTC only to the extent that it is classified as foreign-source income under U.S. tax law. Thus, elements that affect the sourcing of income, such as the place of title passage, should be considered carefully before a transaction is undertaken.

It may be possible for a U.S. corporation to alleviate the problem of excess foreign taxes by using the following techniques.

- Generate "same basket" foreign-source income that is subject to a tax rate lower than the U.S. tax rate.
- Reduce highly taxed foreign-source income in favor of foreign-source income that is taxed at a lower rate by shifting operations or intangibles.
- Time the repatriation of foreign-source earnings to coincide with excess limitation years.
- Deduct foreign taxes for years when the deduction benefit would exceed the FTC benefit.

A taxpayer who can control the timing of income and loss recognition will want to avoid recognizing losses in years when the loss is apportioned among the FTC limitation baskets. Otherwise, the foreign taxes for which a credit is allowed for the tax year are reduced.

**EXAMPLE 37**

Della, a U.S. person, has U.S.-source taxable income of $200,000, worldwide taxable income of $300,000, and a U.S. tax liability (before the FTC) of $84,000. She receives foreign-source taxable income, pays foreign income taxes, and has an FTC as shown.

| Basket | Amount | Foreign Taxes | FTC Limitation | Allowed FTC |
|---|---|---|---|---|
| Passive | $ 20,000 | $    800 | $ 5,600 | $    800 |
| General | 50,000 | 20,500 | 14,000 | 14,000 |
| High withholding tax interest | 15,000 | 3,000 | 4,200 | 3,000 |
| 10/50 company | 15,000 | 4,500 | 4,200 | 4,200 |
| | $100,000 | $28,800 | | $22,000 |

If Della also suffers a foreign-source loss of $10,000 in the shipping limitation basket, the FTC is reduced by $1,820. The U.S. tax liability before the FTC is $81,200. Of the loss, 50% is apportioned to the general limitation basket, reducing the FTC limitation for this basket to $12,600 [$81,200 × ($45,000/$290,000)], and 15% is apportioned to the 10/50 company basket, reducing the FTC limitation for this basket to $3,780 [$81,200 × ($13,500/$290,000)]. Della would avoid this result if she could defer recognition of the loss to a tax year in which it would not have a negative effect on the FTC. ■

## THE FOREIGN CORPORATION AS A TAX SHELTER

An NRA who is able to hold U.S. investments through a foreign corporation can accomplish much in the way of avoiding U.S. taxation. Capital gains (other than dispositions of U.S. real property interests) are not subject to U.S. taxation. This assumes that they are not effectively connected with a U.S. trade or business. The NRA can dispose of the stock of a foreign corporation that holds U.S. real property and not be subject to taxation under § 897 (FIRPTA). Furthermore, the stock of a foreign corporation is not included in the U.S. gross estate of a deceased NRA, even if all the assets of the foreign corporation are located in the United States.

Caution is advised when the foreign corporation may generate income effectively connected with the conduct of a U.S. trade or business. The income may be taxed at a higher rate than if the NRA individually generated the income. The tradeoff between a higher U.S. tax on this income and protection from the U.S. estate tax and § 897 must be weighed.

## PLANNING UNDER SUBPART F

The *de minimis* rule allows a CFC to avoid the classification of income as FBC income or insurance income and prevents the U.S. shareholder from having to include it in gross income as a constructive dividend. Thus, a CFC with total FBC income and insurance income in an amount close to the 5 percent or $1 million level should monitor income realization to assure that the *de minimis* rule applies for the tax year. At least as important is avoiding the classification of all the gross income of the CFC as FBC income or insurance income. This happens when the sum of the FBC income and gross insurance income for the taxable year exceeds 70 percent of total gross income.

Careful timing of increases in investment in U.S. property can reduce the potential for constructive dividend income to U.S. shareholders. The gross income of U.S. shareholders attributable to increases in investment in U.S. property is limited to the E & P of the CFC.[60] E & P that is attributable to amounts that have been included in gross income as Subpart F income in either the current year or a prior tax year is not taxed again when invested in U.S. property.

## USING THE CHECK-THE-BOX REGULATIONS

The check-the-box Regulations under § 7701 provide a great deal of flexibility for U.S.-based multinational corporations. Corporations are allowed to organize their branches and subsidiaries around the world in ways that optimize both local country and U.S. taxation. For example, a U.S. corporation may choose to treat its subsidiary in the United Kingdom as a partnership or unincorporated branch for U.S. tax purposes (thus taking advantage of loss flow-throughs) and a corporation under United Kingdom law (where certain tax and liability benefits may exist). The flurry of multinational restructurings since the issuance of the check-the-box Regulations has led to some cries of foul by U.S. taxing authorities who claim that these provisions are being used in inappropriate ways. The Treasury Department and the IRS are currently exploring ways to curb some of these perceived abuses.

---

[60]§§ 959(a)(1) and (2).

## TRANSFERRING INTANGIBLE ASSETS OFFSHORE

In many industries, a company's intangible assets, such as licenses and patents, produce a relatively large share of total income. For example, the license to use a software program is much more valuable than the actual disk the customer purchases; thus, a large part of the profit from the sale of software accrues to the license holder.

Unlike manufacturing plants, intangible assets can be easily transferred to related entities outside the United States. Congress recognized this potential, and § 367 requires gain to be recognized if intangibles are transferred outside the United States. To avoid this § 367 "toll charge," companies should consider creating their intangibles offshore so that no subsequent transfer is required. Companies may choose to perform their R & D activities within subsidiaries located in tax haven countries in order to create and keep their valuable intangibles in low-tax jurisdictions.

## KEY TERMS

| | | |
|---|---|---|
| Branch profits tax, 9–39 | FIRPTA, 9–40 | Subpart F, 9–23 |
| CFC (controlled foreign corporation), 9–22 | Foreign tax credit (FTC), 9–27 | Tax haven, 9–20 |
| | Functional currency, 9–12 | Tax treaty, 9–3 |
| Dividend equivalent amount (DEA), 9–39 | Inbound taxation, 9–3 | Treaty shopping, 9–20 |
| | Nonresident alien (NRA), 9–35 | U.S. shareholder, 9–22 |
| Effectively connected income, 9–37 | Outbound taxation, 9–3 | U.S. trade or business, 9–37 |
| Extraterritorial income, 9–15 | Qualified business unit (QBU), 9–12 | |

## PROBLEM MATERIALS

### Discussion Questions

1. Explain why an income tax treaty can be very favorable to a U.S. person who earns investment income from Germany.

2. Will dividends paid by a foreign corporation be treated as foreign-source income in all cases? Explain.

**Issue ID**

**Communications**

3. Write a memo outlining the issues that arise when attempting to source income that is earned from Internet-based activities.

4. Generally, U.S. taxpayers with foreign operations desire to increase foreign-source income and reduce deductions against that foreign-source income in order to increase their FTC limitations. How does § 482 enable the IRS to prevent taxpayers from manipulating the source of income and allocation of deductions? Explain.

5. Explain how a Netherlands branch of a U.S. corporation may use the U.S. dollar as its functional currency.

6. What is a qualified business unit (QBU)? How many QBUs may a single taxpayer have?

7. Explain the purpose of the extraterritorial income exclusion provisions.

8. What are the important concepts to be considered when U.S. assets outside the United States are transferred to foreign persons?

**Communications**

9. Write a memo to a U.S. client explaining why stock of a foreign corporation that it holds may be considered a tax shelter for U.S. tax purposes.

**Decision Making**

10. Eleven unrelated U.S. persons are considering forming a foreign corporation in which they will own equal interests. Will they have to be concerned with the CFC provisions?

**Issue ID**

11. Joanna owns 5% of Axel, a foreign corporation. Joanna's son, Fred, is considering acquiring 15% of Axel from an NRA. The remainder of Axel is owned 27% by unrelated U.S. persons and 53% by unrelated NRAs. Currently, Fred operates (as a sole proprietorship) a manufacturing business that sells goods to Axel for resale outside the United States and outside Axel's country of residence. Joanna is not concerned about the concentration of investment because she expects to sell her stock in Axel in three years at a significant capital gain. Are there tax issues that Joanna and Fred, both U.S. citizens, need to address?

**Issue ID**

12. Molly, Inc., a domestic corporation, owns 15% of PJ, Inc., and 12% of Emma, Inc., both foreign corporations. Molly is paid gross dividends of $35,000 and $18,000 from PJ and Emma, respectively. PJ withheld and paid more than $10,500 in foreign taxes on the $35,000 dividend. PJ's country of residence levies a 20% tax on dividends paid to nonresident corporations. However, the tax rate is increased to 30% if the recipient is a resident of a country that provides an FTC. Taxes of $3,600 are withheld on the dividend from Emma. What tax issues must be considered in determining the availability and amount of the FTC allowed to Molly, Inc.?

13. Amelia, Inc., received a $400 dividend from Bermuda, Ltd., a foreign corporation. Bermuda paid $300 in foreign taxes related to this $400 of distributed earnings. Explain why Amelia's gross income related to this dividend is $700.

14. Carlos, a nonresident alien, is interested in acquiring U.S. real property as an investment. He knows that he will be taxed in the United States on any gains from the disposition of such property if he holds it directly. Will the result be any different if he acquires the real property within a U.S. corporation?

**Issue ID**

15. Old Gear, Inc., a foreign corporation, sells vacuum tubes in several countries, including the United States. In fact, currently 18% of Old Gear's sales income is sourced in the United States (through branches in New York and Miami). Old Gear is considering opening additional branches in San Francisco and Houston in order to increase U.S. sales. What tax issues must Old Gear consider before making this move?

## Problems

16. Miles, a U.S. resident, received the following income items for the current tax year. Identify the source of each income item as either U.S. or foreign.
    a. $1,200 dividend from U.S. Power Company, a U.S. corporation that operates solely in the western United States.
    b. $2,600 dividend from Star Trading Corporation, a U.S. corporation that had total gross income of $2 million from the active conduct of a foreign trade or business for the immediately preceding three tax years. Star's worldwide gross income for the same period was $2.6 million.
    c. $750 dividend from International Consolidated, Inc., a foreign corporation that had gross income of $1.7 million effectively connected with the conduct of a U.S. trade or business for the immediately preceding three tax years. International's worldwide gross income for the same period was $3 million.
    d. $300 interest from a savings account at a Houston bank.
    e. $2,500 interest on Rolan Corporation bonds. Rolan is a U.S. corporation that derived $3 million of its gross income for the immediately preceding three tax years from operation of an active foreign business. Rolan's worldwide gross income for this same period was $3.6 million.

Communications

17. Rita, an NRA, is a professional golfer. She played in 7 tournaments in the United States in the current year and earned $50,000 in prizes from these tournaments. She deposited the winnings in a bank account she opened in Mexico City after her first tournament win. Rita played a total of 30 tournaments for the year and earned $200,000 in total prize money. She spent 40 days in the United States, 60 days in England, 20 days in Scotland, and the rest of the time in South America. Write a letter to Rita explaining how much U.S.-source income she will generate, if any, from her participation in these tournaments and whether any of her winnings are subject to U.S. taxation. Rita's address is AV Rio Branco, 149-4#, Rio de Janeiro, RJ 22421, Brazil.

18. Determine whether the source of income for the following sales is U.S. or foreign.
    a. Kwaku, an NRA, sells stock in Home Depot, a domestic corporation, through a broker in New York.
    b. Chris sells stock in IBM, a domestic corporation, to his brother, Rich. Both Chris and Rich are NRAs, and the sale takes place outside the United States.
    c. Crows, Inc., sells inventory produced in the United States to customers in Europe. Title passes in the international waters of the Atlantic Ocean.
    d. Jordan, Inc., a domestic corporation, manufactures equipment in Taiwan and sells the equipment to customers in the United States.

19. Determine whether the source of income in each of the following situations is U.S. or foreign.
    a. Development, Inc., a U.S. corporation, earns $150,000 in royalty income from Far East, Ltd., a foreign corporation, for the use of several patented processes in Far East's manufacturing business, located in Singapore.
    b. Dora, an NRA, is an employee of a foreign corporation. During the tax year, she spends 50 days in the United States purchasing cloth for her employer, a clothing manufacturer. Her yearly salary is $80,000 (translated to U.S. dollars). She spends a total of 250 days working during the year. Her employer has no other business contacts with the United States.
    c. An NRA sells an apartment building to a U.S. resident. The building is located in Chicago. The closing takes place in the NRA's country of residence.
    d. A domestic corporation sells depreciable personal property that it has been using in its foreign branch operations. The property sells for $180,000, has a tax basis of $75,000, and has been depreciated for tax purposes to the extent of $77,000. The property is located in a foreign country but is sold to another domestic corporation. The sales transaction takes place in the United States.

Decision Making

20. ERP, Inc., produces inventory in its foreign manufacturing plants for sale in the United States. Its foreign manufacturing assets have a tax book value of $3 million and a fair market value of $8 million. Its assets related to the sales activity have a tax book value of $400,000 and a fair market value of $100,000. ERP's interest expense totaled $50,000 for the current year.
    a. What amount of interest expense will be allocated and apportioned to foreign-source income using the tax book value method? What amount of interest expense will be allocated and apportioned to foreign-source income using the fair market method?
    b. If ERP wishes to maximize its FTC, which method should it use?

21. Weight, Inc., a domestic corporation, purchases weight-lifting equipment for resale from HiDisu, a Japanese corporation, for 75 million yen. On the date of purchase, 150 yen is equal to $1 U.S. (Y150:$1). The purchase is made on December 15, 2003, with payment due in 60 days. Weight is a calendar year taxpayer. On December 31, 2003, the foreign exchange rate is Y140:$1. What amount of foreign currency gain or loss, if any, must Weight recognize for 2003 as a result of this transaction?

Issue ID

Communications

22. Carroll Manufacturing, Inc., a calendar year domestic corporation, operates a branch in Ireland. In the current year, the branch generated 750,000 euros in net profit. On December 31 of the current year, one euro equaled 83 cents. The average exchange rate for the current year between the euro and the dollar was 91 cents. Write a memo to the controller of Carroll explaining (1) how and when the Irish profits will be taxed to

Carroll in the United States and (2) under what conditions a foreign currency gain or loss will be recognized.

23. Forrest, Inc., a foreign corporation, pays a dividend to its shareholders on October 31. Harold, Inc., a U.S. corporation and 9% shareholder in Forrest, receives a dividend of 10,000K (a foreign currency). Pertinent exchange rates are as follows.

| | |
|---|---|
| October 31 | .8K:$1 |
| Average for year | .6K:$1 |
| December 31 | 1K:$1 |

What is the dollar amount of the dividend received by Harold, Inc., and does Harold have a foreign exchange gain or loss on receipt of the dividend?

24. Opera, Inc., a domestic corporation, produces music amplifiers. In 2003, it reported the following operating results before consideration of any extraterritorial income (ETI) exclusion benefits.

| | U.S. Sales | Foreign Sales | Total Sales |
|---|---|---|---|
| Gross receipts | $10,000 | $1,000 | $11,000 |
| Cost of goods sold | (8,400) | (720) | (9,120) |
| Gross income | $ 1,600 | $ 280 | $ 1,880 |
| Overhead expenses | (240) | (40) | (280) |
| Taxable income | $ 1,360 | $ 240 | $ 1,600 |

Calculate Opera's taxable income for 2003 assuming it meets the foreign economic process requirements and maximizes its ETI exclusion. Assume Opera's foreign sales and leasing income (FSALI) is $100.

25. WorldCo, a domestic corporation, is planning to incorporate a branch that it has been operating in a foreign country. WorldCo's branch has a large amount of inventory. Discuss the tax results of transferring this inventory to a newly formed foreign corporation.

**Issue ID**

**Communications**

26. Janet, Inc., a domestic corporation, operates a branch in Canada. Over the last 10 years, this branch has generated $40 million in losses. For the last 3 years, however, the branch has been profitable and has earned enough income to entirely offset the prior losses. Most of the assets are fully depreciated, and a net gain would be recognized if the assets were sold. The CFO believes that Janet should incorporate the branch now so that this potential gain can be transferred to a foreign corporation, thereby avoiding U.S. tax and, as an added benefit, avoiding U.S. taxes on future income. Draft an outline of a memo to the CFO addressing the tax issues involved in the proposed transaction.

27. Snowball Enterprises, a domestic corporation, owns 100% of Aussie, Ltd., an Australian corporation. Determine Aussie's Subpart F income for the current year (before any expenses) from the following transactions.
    a. Aussie earned $300,000 from sales of products purchased from Snowball and sold to customers outside Australia.
    b. Aussie earned $500,000 from sales of products purchased from Snowball and sold to customers in Australia.
    c. Aussie earned $200,000 from sales of products purchased from unrelated suppliers and sold to customers in Ireland.
    d. Aussie purchased raw materials from Snowball, used these materials to manufacture finished goods, and sold these goods to customers in New Zealand. Aussie earned $100,000 from these sales.
    e. Aussie earned $60,000 for the performance of warranty services on behalf of Snowball. These services were performed in Japan for customers located in Japan.
    f. Aussie earned $30,000 in dividend income from investments.

28. Radio, Inc., a U.S. corporation, owns 40% of the only class of stock of TV, Inc., a CFC. TV is a CFC until June 1 of the current tax year. Radio has held the stock since TV was organized and continues to hold it for the entire year. Radio and TV are both calendar year taxpayers. TV's Subpart F income for the tax year is $600,000, current E & P is $900,000, and no distributions have been made for the tax year. What amount, if any, must Radio include in gross income under Subpart F for the tax year?

**Issue ID**
**Communications**

29. Mary Beth Alessio, a U.S. citizen, has placed all her investments in a Cayman Island corporation owned 9% by Mary Beth, 42% by another U.S. individual, and 49% by a foreign individual. She pays no income tax in the Cayman Islands on this income. Outline a letter informing Mary Beth of the U.S. tax consequences of her foreign investments. Her address is 941 Windom Lane, Hagerstown, MD 21740.

30. Ben, Inc., a domestic corporation, operates in both Canada and the United States. This year, the business generated taxable income of $300,000 from foreign sources and $100,000 from U.S. sources. All of Ben's foreign-source income is in the general limitation basket. Ben's total worldwide taxable income is $400,000. Ben pays Canadian taxes of $130,000. What is Ben's FTC for the tax year? Assume a 34% U.S. income tax rate.

31. Elmwood, Inc., a domestic corporation, owns 15% of Correy, Ltd., a Hong Kong corporation. The remaining 85% of Correy is owned by Fortune Enterprises, a Canadian corporation. At the end of the current year, Correy has $400,000 in post-1986 undistributed E & P and $200,000 in foreign taxes related to this E & P. On the last day of the year, Correy pays a $30,000 dividend to Elmwood. Elmwood's taxable income before inclusion of the dividend is $200,000. What is Elmwood's tax liability after consideration of the dividend and any allowed FTC, assuming a 34% U.S. tax rate?

**Communications**

32. Your client Nashville Cats, Inc., is engaged in the music production business, with CD production plants in Tennessee and Singapore. The U.S. plant has always produced profits, but the Singapore operation has generated $200,000 in losses since inception. This year, the Singapore operation began producing net profits. Draft a brief memo to John, the CFO of Nashville Cats, explaining why a portion of the current-year foreign-source income must be recharacterized as U.S.-source for FTC limitation purposes.

33. For which of the following foreign income inclusions is a U.S. corporation potentially allowed an indirect FTC under § 902?
    a. Interest income from a 5%-owned foreign corporation.
    b. Interest income from a 60%-owned foreign corporation.
    c. Dividend income from a 5%-owned foreign corporation.
    d. Dividend income from a 60%-owned foreign corporation.

34. Cotton Export, Inc., a domestic corporation, has the following taxable income amounts for the tax year and incurs foreign income taxes as shown.

| Type of Income | Source | Amount | Foreign Taxes |
| --- | --- | --- | --- |
| Sales | Canada | $  800,000 | $336,000 |
|  | U.S. | 300,000 | –0– |
| Financial services income | Canada | 30,000 | 3,000 |
|  | U.S. | –0– | –0– |
| Dividends* | Canada | 12,000 | 3,900** |
|  | U.S.† | 15,000 | –0– |
| Other interest | Canada | 8,000 | 1,200†† |
|  | U.S. | 10,000 | –0– |
|  |  | $1,175,000 | $344,100 |

U.S. taxes before FTC = $399,500.

*From one § 902 non-CFC foreign corporation.
**Included in dividend amount.
†Net of dividends received deduction.
††High withholding tax.

Gross foreign-source sales income is $1.2 million. Deductions allocable to foreign sales income total $350,000, and the apportioned share of deductions not definitely allocable to foreign sales income is $50,000.

Gross foreign-source financial services income is $40,000. Deductions definitely allocable to foreign-source financial services income total $7,000, and the apportioned share of deductions not definitely allocable to foreign sales income is $3,000.

Gross foreign-source dividend income is $13,000. There are no deductions definitely allocable to dividend income. The apportioned share of deductions not definitely allocable to foreign-source dividend income is $1,000. Gross foreign-source "other interest" is $8,700. There are no deductions definitely allocable to other interest income. The apportioned share of deductions not definitely allocable to foreign-source other interest income is $700.

Determine Cotton's FTC by completing the appropriate Form 1118s.

**Decision Making**

35. Harold, Inc., a domestic corporation, earned $500,000 from foreign manufacturing activities on which it paid $150,000 of foreign income taxes. Harold's foreign sales income is taxed at a 45% foreign tax rate. What amount of foreign sales income can Harold earn without generating any excess FTCs for the current year? Assume a 34% U.S. rate.

36. Jones, Inc., a foreign subsidiary of Shirley, Inc., a U.S. corporation, has pretax income of 100,000 euros for 2003. Jones accrues 25,000 euros in foreign taxes on this income. The average exchange rate for the tax year to which the taxes relate is .92 euro:$1. None of the income is Subpart F income. If the net earnings of 75,000 euros are distributed when the exchange rate is 1.02 euro:$1, what are the deemed-paid taxes available to Shirley? Assume that 2003 is Jones's first year of operation.

37. Partin, Inc., a domestic corporation, operates a manufacturing branch in Ireland. During the current year, the manufacturing branch produces a loss of $50,000. Partin also operates a bank in the United Kingdom, where it earns $60,000 in financial services income. Partin paid no foreign income taxes related to the Irish branch, but it paid $15,000 in foreign income taxes related to the financial services income. Partin pays U.S. income taxes at the 34% rate. What is Partin's allowable FTC for the current year?

**Communications**

38. You are the head tax accountant for the Venture Company, a U.S. corporation. The board of directors is considering expansion overseas and asks you to present a summary of the U.S. tax consequences of investing overseas through a foreign subsidiary. Prepare a detailed outline of the presentation you will make to the board.

**Decision Making**

**Communications**

39. Money, Inc., a U.S. corporation, has $500,000 to invest overseas for 2003. For U.S. tax purposes, any additional income earned by Money will be taxed at 34%. Two possibilities for investment are:

a. Invest the $500,000 in common stock of Exco (a foreign corporation). Exco common stock pays a dividend of $3 per share each year. The $500,000 would purchase 10,000 shares (or 10%) of Exco's only class of stock (voting common). Exco expects to earn $10 million before taxes for 2003 and to be taxed at a flat rate of 40%. Its 2003 E & P before taxes is estimated to be $9.4 million. Exco's government does not withhold on dividends paid to foreign investors.

b. Invest the $500,000 in Exco bonds that pay interest at 7% per year. Assume that the bonds will be acquired at par, or face, value. Exco's government withholds 25% on interest paid to foreign investors.

Analyze these two investment opportunities and determine which would give Money the best return after taxes. Be sure to consider the effect of the FTC. Write a memorandum to Money, Inc., advising the corporation of your findings.

40. IrishCo, a manufacturing corporation resident in Ireland, distributes products through a U.S. office. Current-year taxable income from such sales in the United States is $12 million. IrishCo's U.S. office deposits working capital funds short term in certificates of deposit with U.S. banks. Current-year income from these deposits is $100,000.

IrishCo also invests in U.S. securities traded on the New York Stock Exchange. This investing is done by the home office. For the current year, IrishCo has realized capital gains of $200,000 and dividend income of $60,000 from these stock investments. Compute

IrishCo's U.S. tax liability, assuming that the U.S.-Ireland income tax treaty reduces withholding on dividends to 15% and on interest to 5%. Assume a 34% U.S. tax rate.

**Communications**

41. ForCo, Ltd., a foreign corporation, operates a trade or business in the United States. ForCo's U.S.-source income effectively connected with this trade or business is $200,000 for the current year. ForCo's current year E & P is $180,000. ForCo's net U.S. equity was $6.7 million at the beginning of the year and $6.8 million at year-end. ForCo is a resident in a country that has no income tax treaty with the United States. Briefly outline a memo to ForCo's Tax VP reporting ForCo's branch profits tax liability for the current year, along with a planning idea for reducing the branch profits tax.

42. Brenda, an NRA individual, owns 30% of the stock of Jeff, Inc., a U.S. corporation. Jeff's balance sheet on the last day of the taxable year is as follows.

|  |  | Adjusted Basis | Fair Market Value |
|---|---|---|---|
| Cash (used as working capital) |  | $ 200,000 | $ 200,000 |
| Investment in foreign land |  | 300,000 | 800,000 |
| Investment in U.S. real estate: |  |  |  |
| Land |  | 150,000 | 400,000 |
| Buildings | $2,300,000 |  |  |
| Less: Depreciation | 300,000 | 2,000,000 | 5,000,000 |
|  |  | $2,650,000 | $6,400,000 |
| Accounts payable |  | $ 300,000 | $ 300,000 |
| Notes payable |  | 500,000 | 500,000 |
| Capital stock |  | 400,000 | 4,150,000 |
| Retained earnings |  | 1,450,000 | 1,450,000 |
|  |  | $2,650,000 | $6,400,000 |

Brenda was in the United States only 40 days in the tax year. She sold all of her stock in Jeff on the last day of the tax year for $6.4 million. Brenda's adjusted basis in the stock sold was $500,000. She sold the stock for cash. What are the U.S. tax consequences, if any, to Brenda?

43. In Problem 42, what are the U.S. tax consequences, if any, to Brenda if Jeff, Inc., is a foreign corporation instead of a domestic corporation?

**Issue ID**

**Communications**

44. John McPherson is single, an attorney, and a U.S. citizen. He recently attended a seminar where he learned he could give up his U.S. citizenship, move to Bermuda (where he would pay no income tax), and operate his law practice long distance via the Internet with no U.S. tax consequences. Outline a letter informing John of the tax consequences of his proposed actions. His address is 1005 NE 10th Street, Gainesville, GA 32812.

## Research Problems

A THOMSON COMPANY

*Note: Solutions to Research Problems can be prepared by using the RIA Checkpoint® Student Edition online research product, or the CCH U.S. Master Tax Guide Plus™ online Federal tax research database, which is available to accompany this text. It is also possible to prepare solutions to the Research Problems by using tax research materials found in a standard tax library.*

**Research Problem 1.** Jerry Jeff Keen, the CFO of Boots Unlimited, a Texas corporation, has come to you regarding a potential restructuring of business operations. Boots has long manufactured its western boots in plants in Texas and Oklahoma. Recently, Boots has explored the possibility of setting up a manufacturing subsidiary in Ireland, where manufacturing profits are taxed at 10%. Jerry Jeff sees this as a great idea, given that the alternative is to continue all manufacturing in the United States, where profits are taxed at 34%. Boots plans to continue all the cutting, sizing, and hand tooling of leather in its U.S. plants. This material will be shipped to Ireland for final assembly, with the finished product shipped to retail outlets all over Europe and Asia. Your initial concern is whether the income generated by the Irish subsidiary will be considered foreign base company income. Address this issue in a research memo, along with any planning suggestions.

*Partial list of research aids:*
§ 954(d).
Reg. § 1.954–3(a).
*Bausch & Lomb*, 71 TCM 2031, T.C.Memo. 1996–57.

**Research Problem 2.**  A U.S. corporation had the following net taxable income (loss) for the tax year. Its U.S. taxes before the FTC are $600. Determine the FTC limitation for each basket of foreign-source income.

| Source (Basket) | Income (Loss) | Foreign Taxes |
|---|---|---|
| U.S.-source | ($ 68,000) | –0– |
| Foreign-source passive | 70,000 | $21,000 |
| Foreign-source shipping | 30,000 | 6,000 |
| Foreign-source general | (28,000) | –0– |

*Partial list of research aids:*
§ 904(f)(5).
General Explanation of the Tax Reform Act of 1986 (the Bluebook), Joint Committee on Taxation, pp. 909–912.
Instructions accompanying Form 1118, Foreign Tax Credit—Corporations, Dept. of the Treasury, Internal Revenue Service.

**Research Problem 3.**  NewCar.com, Inc., an innovative, Internet-based automobile retailer based in Ghana, is beginning to seek customers in the United States. Currently, it has no sales personnel or assets located in the United States, but it makes a few sales to U.S. customers based on orders over its Web site. NewCar.com is considering sending a few sales agents to the United States to set up sales offices in large cities. The offices will have no inventory and will merely provide a place for the sales agents to meet with interested customers. Ghana has no income tax treaty with the United States. How would you advise NewCar.com, Inc., on the tax consequences of its proposed U.S. venture?

*Partial list of research aids:*
§ 882(a)(1).
*Higgins v. Comm.*, 41–1 USTC ¶9233, 25 AFTR 1160, 61 S.Ct. 475 USSC (1941).
*Continental Trading, Inc. v. Comm.*, 59–1 USTC ¶9316, 3 AFTR2d 923, 265 F.2d 40 (CA–9, 1959).
*Piedras Negras Broadcasting Co.*, 43 BTA 297 (1941), aff'd 127 F.2d 260 (CA–5, 1942).

**Internet Activity**

*Use the tax resources of the Internet to address the following questions. Do not restrict your search to the World Wide Web, but include a review of newsgroups and general reference materials, practitioner sites and resources, primary sources of the tax law, chat rooms and discussion groups, and other opportunities.*

**Research Problem 4.**  The IRS's Web page at **http://www.irs.gov** contains many useful links to publications, tax forms and instructions, and tax revenue statistics. Locate Web pages for at least three other countries' taxing authorities. Indicate the Web address for each of these pages and describe how these Web pages compare with the IRS's page in terms of content and ease of use.

**Research Problem 5.**  Locate the Web page of the Organization for Economic Cooperation and Development (OECD). Find the 2000 report on tax haven countries considered by the OECD to be engaged in harmful tax practices. Using the most recent information available on this Web site, determine which of these countries have agreed to changes in tax policies so as to be removed from the harmful tax haven list.

**Research Problem 6.** Find the text of various tax treaties currently in force in the United States.

a. How does the U.S. income tax treaty with Canada define "permanent establishment" for multinational businesses?

b. How does the U.S. income tax treaty with Japan treat the branch profits tax?

c. List five countries with which the United States has entered into an estate tax treaty.

# Flow-Through Entities

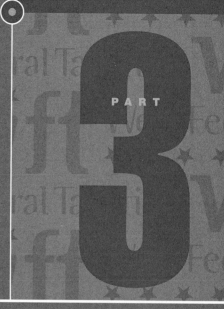

PART

3

Unlike C Corporations, some business entities are taxed under the conduit principle. Generally, this means the tax attributes of various transactions are retained as they flow through the entity to the owners. With limited exceptions, no tax is imposed at the entity level. Part III discusses two types of flow-through entities—partnerships and corporations that make the Subchapter S election.

**CHAPTER 10**

Partnerships: Formation, Operation, and Basis

**CHAPTER 11**

Partnerships: Distributions, Transfer of Interests, and Terminations

**CHAPTER 12**

S Corporations

# Partnerships: Formation, Operation, and Basis

CHAPTER

10

## LEARNING OBJECTIVES

*After completing Chapter 10, you should be able to:*

### LO.1
Discuss governing principles and theories of partnership taxation.

### LO.2
Describe the tax effects of forming a partnership with cash and property contributions.

### LO.3
Identify elections available to a partnership, and specify the tax treatment of expenditures of a newly formed partnership.

### LO.4
Specify the accounting methods available to a partnership and the methods of determining a partnership's tax year.

### LO.5
Calculate partnership taxable income and describe how partnership items affect a partner's income tax return.

### LO.6
Determine a partner's basis in the partnership interest.

### LO.7
Explain how liabilities affect a partner's basis.

### LO.8
Describe the limitations on deducting partnership losses.

### LO.9
Describe the treatment of transactions between a partner and the partnership.

### LO.10
Provide insights regarding advantageous use of a partnership.

http://wft.swlearning.com

## O U T L I N E

# Overview of Partnership Taxation

### FORMS OF DOING BUSINESS—FEDERAL TAX CONSEQUENCES

This chapter and the next two chapters analyze two types of entities that, for some taxpayers, offer certain advantages over regular corporations. These entities are partnerships and S corporations, which are called *flow-through* or *pass-through* entities because the owners of the trade or business choose to avoid treating the enterprise as a separate taxable entity. Instead, the owners are taxed on a proportionate share of the entity's taxable income at the end of each of its taxable years.

Often a partnership may provide tax advantages over a C, or regular, corporation. A partnership is subject to only a single level of taxation, while C corporation income is subject to *double taxation*. Corporate income is taxed at the entity level at rates up to 35 percent. Any after-tax income that is distributed to corporate owners as a dividend is taxed again at the owner level. Though partnership income may be subject to high tax rates at the partner level (currently up to about 38 percent for a partner who is an individual), the resulting tax will likely be lower than a combined corporate-level tax and a second tax on a dividend distribution.

In addition, administrative and filing requirements are usually relatively simple for a partnership, and it offers certain planning opportunities not available to other entities. Both C and S corporations are subject to rigorous allocation and distribution requirements. Generally, each income or loss allocation or distribution is proportionate to the ownership interest of each shareholder. A partnership, though, may

## TAX IN THE NEWS

### PARTNERSHIPS IN THE MOVIES

As movies have become more expensive to produce, many production studios have turned to limited partnerships or limited liability companies (LLCs) as a lucrative source of investment capital. For example, DreamWorks, the Walt Disney Company, and other studios have sold limited partnership (or LLC) interests in various partnerships formed to produce specific movies.

Often the sponsoring studio injects capital for a small (1–5 percent) general partnership interest, and the investors contribute the remaining capital—often many millions of dollars. The partnership agreement spells out the number and types of films the partnership intends to produce and provides a formula for allocating cash flows to the partners. The partnership agreement includes various benefits for the general partner, the studio, such as a preferred allocation of cash flows. For example, the studio may receive the first $1 million per year, distribution fees for marketing the movies, and/or reimbursement of specified amounts of corporate overhead. Any cash remaining after these expenses is allocated under a fixed formula between the general and limited partners. For example, the limited partners may receive 90 percent of remaining cash flows.

Think about bank financing in comparison, and you will see why the studio finds partnerships so appealing: How many banks would allow the general partner to receive reimbursements and allocations before debt principal and interest are paid?

This capital-raising technique has proved so advantageous to the studios that some related industries, such as movie lighting contractors and special effects companies, have also used limited partnerships (or LLCs) to raise capital. The next time you go to a movie, watch the credits at the end and think about the tremendous number of people who invested cash in the movie, hoping for a blockbuster!

adjust its allocations of income and cash flow among the partners each year according to their needs, as long as certain standards, discussed later in this chapter, are met. Also, any previously unrealized income of an S or C corporation, such as appreciation of corporate assets, is taxed at the entity level when the corporation liquidates. However, a partnership generally may liquidate tax-free. Finally, many states impose reporting and licensing requirements on corporate entities, including S corporations. These include franchise or capital stock tax returns that may require annual assessments and costly professional preparation assistance. Partnerships, on the other hand, often have no reporting requirements beyond Federal and state informational tax returns.

For smaller business operations, a partnership enables several owners to combine their resources at low cost. It also offers simple filing requirements, the taxation of income only once, and the ability to discontinue operations relatively inexpensively.

For larger business operations, a partnership offers a unique ability to raise capital with low filing and reporting costs compared to, for example, corporate bond issuances. Special allocations of income and cash-flow items are available in all partnerships to meet the objectives of the owners. The accompanying Tax in the News describes how one industry has used the partnership form as a means of raising capital.

This chapter addresses partnership formation and operations. Chapter 11 focuses on dispositions of partnership interests, partnership distributions, and optional basis adjustments. Chapter 12 discusses the taxation of S corporations.

## WHAT IS A PARTNERSHIP?

A partnership is an association of two or more persons to carry on a trade or business, with each contributing money, property, labor, or skill, and with all expecting to share in profits and losses. A "person" can be an individual, trust, estate, corporation, association, or another partnership.[1] For Federal income tax purposes, a partnership includes a syndicate, group, pool, joint venture, or other unincorporated organization through which any business, financial operation, or venture is carried on. The entity must not be otherwise classified as a corporation, trust, or estate.

The four types of entities that may be taxed as partnerships are general partnerships, limited liability partnerships, limited partnerships, and limited liability companies. A partnership that conducts a service business, such as accounting, law, or medicine, is usually established as either a **general partnership** or a **limited liability partnership (LLP).** A general partnership consists of two or more general partners. Creditors of a general partnership can collect amounts owed them from both the partnership assets and the personal assets of the owner-partners. A general partner can be bankrupted by a malpractice judgment brought against the partnership, even though the partner was not personally involved in the malpractice.

An LLP is a recently created form of entity. In most states, owners of an LLP are treated much like general partners. The primary difference between an LLP and a general partnership is that an LLP partner is not liable for any malpractice committed by other partners. LLPs are discussed in more detail in Chapter 11. The LLP is currently the organizational form of choice for the large accounting firms.

A **limited partnership** is often used for acquiring capital in activities such as real estate development. A limited partnership has at least one general partner and often many limited partners. Typically, only the general partners are personally liable to creditors; each limited partner's risk of loss is restricted to that partner's equity investment in the entity.

An alternative entity form, the **limited liability company (LLC),** is available in all states and the District of Columbia. An LLC combines the corporate benefit of limited liability for the owners with the benefits of partnership taxation, including the single level of tax and special allocations of income, losses, and cash flows. Owners are technically considered to be "members" rather than partners, but a properly structured LLC is treated as a partnership for all tax purposes. Almost all states permit capital-intensive companies as well as nonprofessional service-oriented businesses and some professional service-providing companies to operate as LLCs. This is highly advantageous to a business entity since the LLC can protect each member's assets from being exposed to the entity's debts. As discussed in Chapter 11, application of the partnership tax rules to an LLC can produce some unusual results.

## ELECTIONS RELATED TO PARTNERSHIP STATUS

The IRS's "check-the-box" Regulations allow most unincorporated business entities—such as general partnerships, limited partnerships, LLPs, and LLCs—to select their Federal tax status.[2] If an entity has two or more owners, it generally can choose to be taxed as either a partnership or a C corporation. This provides the entity with flexibility regarding its Federal tax classification. The Regulations, however, do not permit all unincorporated business or investment entities to choose their tax status. Newly formed publicly traded partnerships, for example, must be taxed as corporations.

---

[1]§§ 7701(a)(1) and (a)(2).

[2]Reg. §§ 301.7701–1 to 301.7701–3.

A partnership generally may elect out of the partnership taxation rules if it is involved in one of the following activities:

* Investment (rather than the active conduct of a trade or business).
* Joint production, extraction, or use of property.
* Underwriting, selling, or distributing a specific security issue.[3]

If a proper election is made, the partnership is disregarded for Federal tax purposes, and its operations are reported directly on the owners' tax returns.

<table>
<tr>
<td>

**LO.1**

Discuss governing principles and theories of partnership taxation.

</td>
<td>

## PARTNERSHIP TAXATION

A partnership is not a taxable entity.[4] Rather, the taxable income or loss of the partnership flows through to the partners at the end of the entity's tax year.[5] Partners report their allocable share of the partnership's income or loss for the year on their tax returns. As a result, the partnership itself pays no Federal income tax on its income; instead, the partners' individual tax liabilities are affected by the activities of the entity.

</td>
</tr>
</table>

**EXAMPLE 1**

Adam is a 40% partner in the ABC Partnership. Both Adam's and the partnership's tax years end on December 31. In 2003, the partnership generates $200,000 of ordinary taxable income. However, because the partnership needs capital for expansion and debt reduction, Adam makes no cash withdrawals during 2003. He meets his living expenses by reducing his investment portfolio. Adam is taxed on his $80,000 allocable share of the partnership's 2003 income, even though he received no distributions from the entity during 2003. This allocated income is included in Adam's gross income. ∎

**EXAMPLE 2**

Assume the same facts as in Example 1, except the partnership recognizes a 2003 taxable loss of $100,000. Adam's 2003 adjusted gross income from other sources is reduced by $40,000 because his proportionate share of the loss flows through to him from the partnership. He deducts a $40,000 partnership loss for the year. (Note: Loss limitation rules discussed later in the chapter may result in some or all of this loss being deducted in a later year.) ∎

Many items of partnership income or expense, gain, or loss retain their identity as they flow through to the partners. This separate flow-through of certain items is required because such **separately stated items** *might* affect any two partners' tax liabilities in different ways. When preparing a personal tax return, a partner takes each of these items into account separately.[6] For example, charitable contributions are separately stated because partners need to compute their own personal limitation on charitable contributions. Some partners are able to deduct the entire amount they are allocated. Others are limited in what they can deduct by the amount of their adjusted gross income (AGI).

**EXAMPLE 3**

Beth is a 25% partner in the BR Partnership. The cash basis entity collected sales income of $60,000 during 2003 and incurred $15,000 in business expenses. In addition, it sold a corporate bond for a $9,000 long-term capital gain. Finally, the partnership made a $1,000 contribution to the local Performing Arts Fund drive. The fund is a qualifying charity. BR and all of its partners use a calendar tax year.

For 2003, Beth is allocated ordinary taxable income of $11,250 [($60,000 − $15,000) × 25%] from the partnership. She also is allocated a flow-through of a $2,250 long-term capital gain and a $250 charitable contribution deduction. The ordinary income increases Beth's

---

[3]§ 761(a).
[4]§ 701.

[5]§ 702.
[6]§ 703(a)(1).

gross income. The long-term capital gain and charitable contribution are separately stated because they could be treated differently on her tax return from the way they are treated on the tax returns of the other partners. For example, Beth may have capital losses to offset the capital gain or may be subject to a percentage limitation on charitable contribution deductions for 2003. Other partners may have no capital losses or percentage limitations on charitable contribution deductions. ■

The number of items that are separately reported to the partners varies and depends upon whether the partnership is an **electing large partnership**. A partnership qualifies as a large partnership if it had at least 100 partners during its immediately preceding taxable year and elects simplified reporting of its taxable items. Such partnerships separately report up to 16 different categories of items to their partners. This means that many items are netted at the partnership level. For example, all interest, dividend, and royalty income are combined into one amount, and the electing large partnership reports a share of this amount to each partner. The netting of items at the partnership level makes each partner's tax return easier to complete. Unless otherwise indicated, in this chapter and Chapter 11 assume the partnership is *not* an electing large partnership.

As most partnerships are not electing large partnerships, they may separately report more than 16 categories of items. Some partnership items are netted in these partnerships, but the netting is not as extensive as in electing large partnerships. Pass-through items that are netted in these partnerships include the ordinary income and expenses related to the partnership's trade or business activities. These ordinary income and expense items are netted to produce a single income or loss amount that is passed through to the partners. Most other partnership items are separately stated. For example, net income (loss) from rental real estate activities and net short-term capital gains (losses) are each determined at the partnership level and reported separately to the partners.

Other items that are allocated separately to the partners[7] include recognized gains and losses from property transactions; dividend income; tax preferences and adjustments for the alternative minimum tax; expenditures that qualify for the foreign tax credit; and expenditures that the partners would treat as itemized deductions.

## PARTNERSHIP REPORTING

Even though it is not a taxpaying entity, a partnership must file an information tax return, Form 1065. Look at Form 1065 in Appendix B, and refer to it during the following discussion. The ordinary income and expense items generated by the partnership's trade or business activities are netted to produce a single income or loss amount. The partnership reports this ordinary income or loss from its trade or business activities on Form 1065, page 1. Schedule K (page 3 of Form 1065) accumulates all items that must be separately reported to the partners, including net trade or business income or loss (from page 1). The amounts on Schedule K are allocated to all the partners. Each partner receives a Schedule K–1, which shows that partner's share of partnership items.

**EXAMPLE 4**

The BR Partnership in Example 3 reports its $60,000 sales income on Form 1065, page 1, line 1. The $15,000 of business expenses are reported in the appropriate amounts on page 1, line 2 or lines 9–20. Partnership ordinary income of $45,000 is shown on page 1, line 22,

---

[7]§ 702(a).

and on Schedule K, line 1. The $9,000 net long-term capital gain and the $1,000 charitable contribution are reported only on Schedule K, on lines 4e and 8, respectively.

Beth receives a Schedule K–1 from the partnership that shows her shares of partnership ordinary income of $11,250, long-term capital gain of $2,250, and charitable contributions of $250 on lines 1, 4e, and 8, respectively.

She combines these amounts with similar items from sources other than BR in her personal tax return. For example, if she has a $5,000 long-term capital loss from a stock transaction during the year, her overall net capital loss calculated on Schedule D of her 1040 is $2,750. She evaluates this net amount to determine the amount she may deduct on her Form 1040. She reports the $250 of charitable contributions on her Schedule A. ■

As this example shows, one must look at both page 1 and Schedule K to get complete information regarding a partnership's operations for the year.

Certain items reported on Schedule K are netted and entered on line 1 of the Analysis of Net Income (Loss) on page 4. This total agrees with the total amount on line 9 of Schedule M–1, Reconciliation of Income (Loss) per Books with Income (Loss) per Return. Schedule L generally shows an accounting-basis balance sheet, and Schedule M–2 reconciles beginning and ending partners' capital accounts.

## PARTNER'S OWNERSHIP INTEREST IN A PARTNERSHIP

Each partner typically owns both a **capital interest** and a **profits (loss) interest** in the partnership. A capital interest is measured by a partner's **capital sharing ratio,** which is the partner's percentage ownership of the capital of the partnership. A partner's capital interest can be determined in several ways. The most widely accepted method measures the capital interest as the percentage of net asset value (asset value remaining after payment of all partnership liabilities) a partner would receive on immediate liquidation of the partnership.

A profits (loss) interest is simply the partner's percentage allocation of current partnership operating results. **Profit and loss sharing ratios** are usually specified in the partnership agreement and are used to determine each partner's allocation of partnership ordinary taxable income and separately stated items.[8] The partnership can change its profit and loss allocations at any time simply by amending the partnership agreement.

Each partner's profit, loss, and capital sharing ratios may appear on the partner's Schedule K–1. In many cases, the three ratios are the same. A partner's capital sharing ratio generally equals the partner's profit and loss sharing ratios if all profit and loss allocations, for each year of the partnership's existence, are in the same proportion as the partner's initial contributions to the partnership.

The partnership agreement may, in some cases, provide for a **special allocation** of certain items to specified partners, or it may allocate items in a different proportion from general profit and loss sharing ratios. These items are separately reported to the partner receiving the allocation. For a special allocation to be recognized for tax purposes, it must produce nontax economic consequences to the partners receiving the allocation.[9]

**EXAMPLE 5**

When the George-Helen Partnership was formed, George contributed cash and Helen contributed some City of Iuka bonds that she had held for investment purposes. The partnership agreement allocates all of the tax-exempt interest income from the bonds to Helen as an inducement for her to remain a partner. This is an acceptable special allocation for income

---

[8]§ 704(a).     [9]§ 704(b).

tax purposes; it reflects the differing economic circumstances that underlie the partners' contributions to the capital of the entity. Since Helen would have received the exempt income if she had not joined the partnership, she can retain the tax-favored treatment by means of the special allocation. ■

**EXAMPLE 6**

Assume the same facts as in Example 5. Three years after it was formed, the George-Helen Partnership purchased some City of Butte bonds. The municipal bond interest income of $15,000 flows through to the partners as a separately stated item, so it retains its tax-exempt status. The partnership agreement allocates all of this income to George because he is subject to a higher marginal income tax bracket than is Helen. The partnership also allocates $15,000 more of the partnership taxable income to Helen than to George. These allocations are not effective for income tax purposes because they have no purpose other than reduction of the partners' combined income tax liability. ■

A partner has a **basis in the partnership interest**. When income flows through to a partner from the partnership, the partner's basis in the partnership interest increases. When a loss flows through to a partner, basis is reduced.

**EXAMPLE 7**

Paul contributes $20,000 cash to acquire a 30% capital and profits interest in the Red Robin Partnership. In its first year of operations, the partnership earns ordinary income of $40,000 and makes no distributions to Paul. Paul's initial basis is the $20,000 he paid for the interest. He reports ordinary income of $12,000 (30% × $40,000 partnership income) on his individual return and increases his basis by the same amount, to $32,000. ■

The Code provides for the increase and decrease in a partner's basis so that the income or loss from partnership operations is taxed only once. In Example 7, if Paul sold his interest at the end of the first year for $32,000, he would have no gain or loss. If the Code did not provide for an adjustment of a partner's basis, Paul's basis would be $20,000, and he would be taxed on the gain of $12,000 in addition to being taxed on his $12,000 share of income. In other words, without the basis adjustment, partnership income would be subject to double taxation.

As the following sections discuss in detail, a partner's basis is important for determining the treatment of distributions from the partnership to the partner, establishing the deductibility of partnership losses, and calculating gain or loss on the partner's disposition of the partnership interest.

A partner's basis is not reflected anywhere on the Schedule K–1. Instead, each partner should maintain a personal record of adjustments to basis. Schedule K–1 does reconcile a partner's **capital account,** but the ending capital account balance is rarely the same amount as the partner's basis. Just as the tax and accounting bases of a specific asset may differ, a partner's capital account and basis in partnership interest may not be equal for a variety of reasons. For example, a partner's basis also includes the partner's share of partnership liabilities. These liabilities are not reported as part of the partner's capital account but are included in Item F at the top of the partner's Schedule K–1.

## CONCEPTUAL BASIS FOR PARTNERSHIP TAXATION

The unique tax treatment of partners and partnerships can be traced to two legal concepts that evolved long ago: the **aggregate** (or conduit) **concept** and the **entity concept.** These concepts influence practically every partnership tax rule.

**Aggregate (or Conduit) Concept.**   The aggregate (or conduit) concept treats the partnership as a channel through which income, credits, deductions, and other items flow to the partners. Under this concept, the partnership is regarded as a collection of taxpayers joined in an agency relationship with one another. The imposition of the income tax on individual partners reflects the influence of this doctrine. The aggregate concept has influenced the tax treatment of other pass-through entities, such as S corporations (Chapter 12) and trusts and estates (Chapter 19).

**Entity Concept.**    The entity concept treats partners and partnerships as separate units and gives the partnership its own tax "personality" by (1) requiring a partnership to file an information tax return and (2) treating partners as separate and distinct from the partnership in certain transactions between a partner and the entity. A partner's recognition of capital gain or loss on the sale of the partnership interest illustrates this doctrine.

**Combined Concepts.**    Some rules governing the formation, operation, and liquidation of a partnership contain a blend of both the entity and aggregate concepts.

## ANTI-ABUSE PROVISIONS

As Chapters 10 and 11 reflect, partnership taxation is often flexible. For example, partnership operating income or losses can sometimes be shifted among partners, and partnership capital gains and losses can sometimes be shifted from one partner to another. The Code contains many provisions designed to thwart unwarranted allocations, but the IRS believes opportunities still abound for tax avoidance. As Chapter 11 notes, the IRS has adopted Regulations that allow it to recharacterize transactions that it considers to be "abusive."[10]

**LO.2**

Describe the tax effects of forming a partnership with cash and property contributions.

# Formation of a Partnership: Tax Effects

## GAIN OR LOSS ON CONTRIBUTIONS TO THE PARTNERSHIP

When a taxpayer transfers property to an entity in exchange for valuable consideration, a taxable exchange normally results. Typically, both the taxpayer and the entity realize and recognize gain or loss on the exchange.[11] The gain or loss recognized by the transferor is the difference between the fair market value of the consideration received and the adjusted basis of the property transferred.[12]

In most situations, however, neither the partner nor the partnership recognizes the gain or loss that is realized when a partner contributes property to a partnership in exchange for a partnership interest. Instead, the realized gain or loss is deferred.[13]

There are two reasons for this nonrecognition treatment. First, forming a partnership allows investors to combine their assets toward greater economic goals than could be achieved separately. Only the form of ownership, rather than the amount owned by each investor, has changed. Requiring that gain be recognized on such transfers would make the formation of some partnerships economically unfeasible (e.g., two existing proprietorships are combined to form one larger business). Congress does not want to hinder the creation of valid economic partnerships by requiring gain recognition when a partnership is created. Second, because the partnership interest received is typically not a liquid asset, the partner may

[10]Reg. § 1.701–2.
[11]§ 1001(c).

[12]§ 1001(a).
[13]§ 721.

not have <u>sufficient cash to pay the tax.</u> Thus, deferral of the gain recognizes the economic realities of the business world and <u>follows the wherewithal to pay princi-ple of taxation.</u>

**EXAMPLE 8**

Alicia transfers two assets to the Wren Partnership on the day the entity is created, in exchange for a 60% profit and loss interest worth $60,000. She contributes cash of $40,000 and retail display equipment (basis to her as a sole proprietor, $8,000; fair market value, $20,000). Since an exchange has occurred between two parties, Alicia *realizes* a $12,000 gain on this transaction. The gain realized is the fair market value of the partnership interest of $60,000 less the basis of the assets that Alicia surrendered to the partnership [$40,000 (cash) + $8,000 (equipment)].

Under § 721, Alicia *does not recognize* the $12,000 realized gain in the year of contribution. This makes sense, since all she received from the partnership was an illiquid partnership interest; she received no cash with which to pay any resulting tax liability. ■

**EXAMPLE 9**

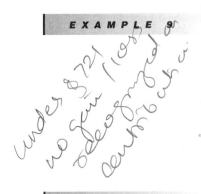

Assume the same facts as in Example 8, except that the equipment Alicia contributes to the partnership has an adjusted basis of $25,000. She has a $5,000 *realized* loss [$60,000 – ($40,000 + $25,000)], but she cannot deduct the loss. Realized losses, as well as realized gains, are deferred by § 721.

Unless it was essential that the partnership receive Alicia's display equipment rather than similar equipment purchased from an outside supplier, Alicia should have considered selling the equipment to a third party. This would have allowed her to deduct a $5,000 loss in the year of the sale. Alicia then could have contributed $60,000 cash (including the proceeds from the sale) for her interest in the partnership, and the partnership would have funds to purchase similar equipment. ■

**EXAMPLE 10**

Five years after the Wren Partnership (Examples 8 and 9) was created, Alicia contributes another piece of equipment to the entity. This property has a basis of $35,000 and a fair market value of $50,000. Alicia will defer the recognition of the $15,000 realized gain. Section 721 is effective whenever a partner makes a contribution to the capital of the partnership. ■

If a partner contributes only capital and § 1231 assets, the partner's holding period in the partnership interest is the same as that partner's holding period for these assets. If cash or other assets that are not capital or § 1231 assets are contrib-uted, the holding period in the partnership interest begins on the date the partner-ship interest is acquired. If multiple assets are contributed, the partnership interest is apportioned, and a separate holding period applies to each portion.

## EXCEPTIONS TO § 721

The nonrecognition provisions of § 721 do not apply where

- appreciated stocks are contributed to an investment partnership;
- the transaction is essentially a taxable exchange of properties;
- the transaction is a disguised sale of properties; or
- the partnership interest is received in exchange for services rendered to the partnership by the partner.

**Investment Partnership.**   If the transfer consists of appreciated stocks and secu-rities and the partnership is an investment partnership, it is possible that the realized gain on the stocks and securities will be recognized by the contributing partner at the time of contribution.[14] This provision prevents multiple investors from using the partnership form to diversify their investment portfolios on a tax-free basis. A similar provision, § 351(e), applies to corporations (see Chapter 3).

**Exchange.**  If a transaction is essentially a taxable exchange of properties, the tax is not deferred under the nonrecognition provisions of § 721.[15]

**EXAMPLE 11**

Sara owns land, and Bob owns stock. Sara would like to have Bob's stock, and Bob wants Sara's land. If Sara and Bob both contribute their property to newly formed SB Partnership in exchange for interests in the partnership, the tax on the transaction appears to be deferred under § 721. The tax on a subsequent distribution by the partnership of the land to Bob and the stock to Sara also appears to be deferred under § 731 (discussed in Chapter 11). According to a literal interpretation of the statutes, no taxable exchange has occurred. Sara and Bob will find, however, that this type of tax subterfuge is not permitted. The IRS will disregard the passage of the properties through the partnership and will hold, instead, that Sara and Bob exchanged the land and stock directly. Thus, the transactions will be treated as any other taxable exchange. ■

**Disguised Sale.**  A similar result occurs in a **disguised sale** of properties. A disguised sale may occur when a partner contributes appreciated property to a partnership and soon thereafter receives a distribution from the partnership. This distribution may be viewed as a payment by the partnership for purchase of the property.[16]

**EXAMPLE 12**

Kim transfers property to the KLM Partnership. The property has an adjusted basis of $10,000 and a fair market value of $30,000. Two weeks later, the partnership makes a distribution of $30,000 cash to Kim. Under the distribution rules of § 731, the distribution would not be taxable to Kim if the basis for her partnership interest prior to the distribution was greater than the $30,000 cash distributed. However, the transaction appears to be a disguised purchase-sale transaction, rather than a contribution and distribution. Therefore, Kim must recognize gain of $20,000 on transfer of the property, and the partnership is deemed to have purchased the property for $30,000. ■

Extensive Regulations under § 707 outline situations in which the IRS will presume a disguised sale has occurred. For example, a disguised sale is presumed to exist if both the following occur:

- A contractual agreement requires a contribution by one partner to be followed within two years by a specified distribution from the partnership.
- The distribution is to be made without regard to partnership profits. In other words, the forthcoming distribution is not subject to significant "entrepreneurial risk."

In some cases, assumption of the partner's liabilities by the partnership may be treated as part of the purchase price paid by the partnership. The IRS can also use a facts and circumstances test to treat a transaction as a disguised sale.

The Regulations also outline situations in which a distribution generally will *not* be deemed to be part of a disguised sale. They include a distribution that occurs more than two years after the property is contributed and a distribution that is deemed "reasonable" in relation to the capital invested by the partner and in relation to distributions made to other partners.

---

[14]§ 721(b).
[15]Reg. § 1.731–1(c)(3).

[16]§ 707(a)(2)(B).

**Services.**    A final exception to the nonrecognition provision of § 721 occurs when a partner receives an interest in the partnership as compensation for services rendered to the partnership. This is not a tax-deferred transaction because services are not treated as "property" that can be transferred to a partnership on a tax-free basis. Instead, the partner performing the services recognizes ordinary compensation income equal to the fair market value of the partnership interest received.[17]

The partnership may deduct the amount included in the service partner's income if the services are of a deductible nature. If the services are not deductible to the partnership, they must be capitalized to an asset account. For example, architectural plans created by a partner are capitalized as part of the structure built with those plans. Alternatively, day-to-day management services performed by a partner for the partnership are usually deductible by the partnership.

| EXAMPLE 13 | Bill, Carl, and Dave form the BCD Partnership, with each receiving a one-third interest in the entity. Dave receives his one-third interest as compensation for tax planning services he will render after the formation of the partnership. The value of a one-third interest in the partnership (for each of the parties) is $20,000. Dave recognizes $20,000 of compensation income, and he has a $20,000 basis in his partnership interest. The same result would occur if the partnership had paid Dave $20,000 for his services and he immediately contributed that amount to the entity for a one-third ownership interest. In either case, the partnership deducts $20,000 in calculating its ordinary business income. ■ |

## TAX ISSUES RELATIVE TO CONTRIBUTED PROPERTY

When a partner makes a tax-deferred contribution of an asset to the capital of a partnership, the tax law assigns a carryover basis to the property.[18] The partnership's basis in the asset is equal to the partner's basis in the property prior to its transfer to the partnership. The partner's basis in the new partnership interest is the same as the partner's basis in the contributed asset. The tax term for this basis concept is *substituted basis*. Thus, two assets are created out of one when a partnership is formed, namely, the property in the hands of the new entity and the new asset (the partnership interest) in the hands of the partner. Both assets are assigned a basis that is derived from the partner's basis in the contributed property.

To understand the logic of these rules, consider what Congress was attempting to accomplish with the deferral approach. Recall that gain or loss is deferred when property is contributed to a partnership in exchange for a partnership interest. The basis amounts are the amounts necessary to allow for recognition of the deferred gain or loss if the property or the partnership interest is subsequently disposed of in a taxable transaction. This treatment is similar to the treatment of assets transferred to a controlled corporation[19] and the treatment of like-kind exchanges.[20]

| EXAMPLE 14 | On June 1, 2003, Luis transfers property to the JKL Partnership in exchange for a one-third interest in the partnership. The property has an adjusted basis to Luis of $10,000 and a fair market value of $30,000 on June 1. Luis has a $20,000 realized gain on the exchange ($30,000 − $10,000), but under § 721, he does not recognize any of the gain. Luis's basis for his partnership interest is the amount necessary to recognize the $20,000 deferred gain if his partnership interest is subsequently sold for its $30,000 fair market value. This amount, $10,000, is referred to as substituted basis. The basis of the property contributed to the partnership is the amount necessary to allow for the recognition of the $20,000 deferred |

---

[17]§ 83(a).
[18]§ 723.

[19]§ 351.
[20]§ 1031.

gain if the property is subsequently sold for its $30,000 fair market value. This amount, also $10,000, is referred to as carryover basis. ■

The holding period for the contributed asset carries over to the partnership. Thus, the partnership's holding period for the asset includes the period during which the partner owned the asset.

**Depreciation Method and Period.** If depreciable property is contributed to the partnership, the partnership is usually required to use the same cost recovery method and life used by the partner. The partnership merely "steps into the shoes" of the partner and continues the same cost recovery calculations. The partnership may not elect under § 179 to immediately expense any part of the basis of depreciable property it receives from the transferor partner.

**Intangible Assets.** If a partner contributes an existing "§ 197" intangible asset to the partnership, the partnership generally will "step into the shoes" of the partner in determining future amortization deductions. Section 197 intangible assets include goodwill, going-concern value, information systems, customer- or supplier-related intangible assets, patents, licenses obtained from a governmental unit, franchises, trademarks, covenants not to compete, and other items.

| EXAMPLE 15 | On September 1, 2001, at a cost of $120,000, James obtained a license to operate a television station from the Federal Communications Commission. The license is effective for 20 years. On January 1, 2003, he contributes the license to the JS Partnership in exchange for a 60% interest. The value of the license is still $120,000 at that time. |
|---|---|

The license is a § 197 asset since it is a license with a term greater than 15 years. The cost is amortized over 15 years. James claims amortization for 4 months in 2001 and 12 months in 2002. Thereafter, the partnership steps into James's shoes in claiming amortization deductions. ■

Intangible assets that do not fall under the § 197 rules are amortized over their useful life, if any.[21]

**Receivables, Inventory, and Losses.** To prevent ordinary income from being converted into capital gain, gain or loss is treated as ordinary when the partnership disposes of either of the following:[22]

- Contributed receivables that were unrealized in the contributing partner's hands at the contribution date. Such receivables include the right to receive payment for goods or services delivered or to be delivered.
- Contributed property that was inventory in the contributor's hands on the contribution date, if the partnership disposes of the property within *five years of the contribution*. For this purpose, inventory includes all tangible property except capital assets and real or depreciable business assets.

| EXAMPLE 16 | Tyrone operates a cash basis retail electronics and television store as a sole proprietor. Ramon is an enterprising individual who likes to invest in small businesses. On January 2 of the current year, Tyrone and Ramon form the TR Partnership. Their partnership contributions are as follows: |
|---|---|

---

[21]Reg § 1.167(a)–3.
[22]§ 724. For this purpose, § 724(d)(2) waives the holding period requirement in defining § 1231 property.

| | Adjusted Basis | Fair Market Value |
|---|---|---|
| From Tyrone: | | |
| Receivables | $ –0– | $ 2,000 |
| Land used as parking lot* | 1,200 | 5,000 |
| Inventory | 2,500 | 5,000 |
| From Ramon: | | |
| Cash | 12,000 | 12,000 |

*The parking lot had been held for nine months at the contribution date.

Within 30 days of formation, TR collects the receivables and sells the inventory for $5,000 cash. It uses the land for the next 10 months as a parking lot, then sells it for $3,500 cash. TR realized the following income in the current year from these transactions:

- Ordinary income of $2,000 from collecting receivables.
- Ordinary income of $2,500 from sale of inventory.
- § 1231 gain of $2,300 from sale of land.

Since the land takes a carryover holding period, it is treated as having been held 19 months at the sale date. ■

A similar rule is designed to prevent a capital loss from being converted into an ordinary loss. Under the rule, if contributed property is disposed of at a loss and the property had a "built-in" capital loss on the contribution date, the loss is treated as a capital loss if the partnership disposes of the property *within five years of the contribution*. The capital loss is limited to the amount of the "built-in" loss on the date of contribution.

**EXAMPLE 17**

Assume the same facts as Example 16, except for the following:

- Tyrone held the land for investment purposes. It had a fair market value of $800 at the contribution date.
- TR used the land as a parking lot for 10 months and sold it for $650.

TR realizes the following income and loss from these transactions:

- Ordinary income of $2,000 from collecting receivables.
- Ordinary income of $2,500 from sale of inventory.
- Capital loss of $400 from sale of land ($1,200 – $800).
- § 1231 loss of $150 from sale of land ($800 – $650).

Since the land was sold within five years of the contribution date, the $400 built-in loss is a capital loss. The postcontribution loss of $150 is a § 1231 loss since TR used the property in its business. ■

## INSIDE AND OUTSIDE BASES

Throughout these chapters, reference is made to the partnership's inside basis and the partners' outside basis. **Inside basis** refers to the adjusted basis of each partnership asset, as determined from the partnership's tax accounts. **Outside basis** represents each partner's basis in the partnership interest. Each partner "owns" a share of the partnership's inside basis for all its assets, and all partners should maintain a record of their respective outside bases.

## CONCEPT SUMMARY 10–1

### Partnership Formation and Basis Computation

1. The *entity concept* treats partners and partnerships as separate units. The nature and amount of entity gains and losses and most partnership tax elections are determined at the partnership level.
2. The *aggregate concept* is used to connect partners and partnerships. It allows income, gains, losses, credits, deductions, etc., to flow through to the partners for separate tax reporting.
3. Sometimes both the *aggregate* and the *entity* concepts apply to the same transaction, but one usually dominates.
4. Generally, partners or partnerships do not recognize gain or loss when property is contributed for capital interests.
5. Partners contributing property for partnership interests take the contributed property's adjusted basis for their *outside basis* in their partnership interest. The partners are said to take a substituted basis in their partnership interest.
6. The partnership will continue to use the contributing partner's basis for the *inside basis* in property it receives. The contributed property is said to take a carryover basis.
7. The holding period of a partner's interest includes that of contributed property when the property was a § 1231 asset or capital asset in the partner's hands. Otherwise, the holding period starts on the day the interest is acquired. The holding period of an interest acquired by a cash contribution starts at acquisition.
8. The partnership's holding period for contributed property includes the contributing partner's holding period.

In many cases—especially on formation of the partnership—the total of all the partners' outside bases equals the partnership's inside bases for all its assets. Differences between inside and outside basis arise when a partner's interest is sold to another person for more or less than the selling partner's share of the inside basis of partnership assets. The buying partner's outside basis equals the price paid for the interest, but the buyer's share of the partnership's inside basis is the same amount as the seller's share of the inside basis.

Concept Summary 10–1 reviews the rules that apply to partnership asset contribution and basis adjustments.

**LO.3**

Identify elections available to a partnership, and specify the tax treatment of expenditures of a newly formed partnership.

### TAX ACCOUNTING ELECTIONS

A newly formed partnership must make numerous tax accounting elections. These elections are formal decisions on how a particular transaction or tax attribute should be handled. Most of these elections must be made by the partnership rather than by the partners individually.[23] The *partnership* makes the elections involving the following items:

- Inventory method.
- Cost or percentage depletion method, excluding oil and gas wells.
- Accounting method (cash, accrual, or hybrid).
- Cost recovery methods and assumptions.
- Tax year.
- Amortization of organization costs and amortization period.
- Amortization of start-up expenditures and amortization period.
- Optional basis adjustments for property (§ 754, discussed in Chapter 11).
- Section 179 deductions for certain tangible personal property.
- Nonrecognition treatment for involuntary conversions gains.
- Election out of partnership rules.

---

[23]§ 703(b).

Each partner is bound by the decisions made by the partnership relative to the elections. If the partnership fails to make an election, a partner cannot compensate for the error by making the election individually.

Though most elections are made by the partnership, each *partner* individually is required to make a specific election on the following relatively narrow tax issues:

- Whether to reduce the basis of depreciable property first when excluding income from discharge of indebtedness.
- Whether to claim cost or percentage depletion for oil and gas wells.
- Whether to take a deduction or a credit for taxes paid to foreign countries and U.S. possessions.

## INITIAL COSTS OF A PARTNERSHIP

In its initial stages, a partnership incurs expenses relating to some or all of the following: forming the partnership (organization costs), admitting partners to the partnership, marketing and selling partnership units to prospective partners (syndication costs), acquiring assets, starting business operations (start-up costs), negotiating contracts, and other items. Many of these expenditures are not currently deductible. However, the Code permits a ratable (i.e., straight-line) amortization of "organization" and "start-up" costs; acquisition costs for depreciable assets are included in the initial basis of the acquired assets; and costs related to some intangible assets may be amortized. "Syndication costs" may be neither amortized nor deducted.

**Organization Costs.**   The partnership may elect to amortize organization costs ratably over a period of 60 months or more, starting with the month in which it began business.[24] The election must be made by the due date (including extensions) of the partnership return for the year it began business.

Organization costs include expenditures that are (1) incident to the creation of the partnership; (2) chargeable to a capital account; and (3) of a character that, if incident to the creation of a partnership with an ascertainable life, would be amortized over that life. These expenditures include accounting fees and legal fees connected with the partnership's formation. To be amortizable, the expenditures must be incurred within a period that starts a reasonable time before the partnership begins business. The period ends with the due date (without extensions) of the tax return for the initial tax year.

Cash method partnerships are not allowed to deduct *in the year incurred* the portion of organization costs that are paid after the end of the first year. The partnership can deduct, in the year of payment, the portion of the expenditures that would have been deductible in a prior year, if they had been paid before that year's end.

**EXAMPLE 18**

The calendar year Bluejay Partnership was formed on May 1, 2002, and immediately started business. Bluejay incurred $720 in legal fees for drafting the partnership agreement and $480 in accounting fees for tax advice of an organizational nature. The legal fees were paid in October 2002. The accounting fees were paid in January 2003. The partnership selected the cash method of accounting and elected to amortize its organization costs.

On its 2002 return, Bluejay deducts $96 of organization costs. No deduction is taken for the accounting fees since the partnership selected the cash method and the fees were paid the following year. On its tax return for 2003, Bluejay deducts organization costs of $304.

[24]§ 709.

|  | Organization Costs Deducted | |
| --- | --- | --- |
|  | **2002** | **2003** |
| [($720 legal fees/60 months) × 8 months] | $96 | |
| [($720 legal fees/60 months) × 12 months] + [($480 accounting fees/60 months) × 20 months] | | $304 |

Note that the 2003 deduction ($304) includes the $64 of accounting fees [($480/60) × 8] that could have been deducted on Bluejay's 2002 tax return if they had been paid by the end of 2002. ■

Costs incurred for the following items are not organization costs:

- Acquiring assets for the partnership.
- Transferring assets to the partnership.
- Admitting partners, other than at formation.
- Removing partners, other than at formation.
- Negotiating operating contracts.
- Syndication costs.

**Start-up Costs.**    Operating costs that are incurred after the entity is formed but before it begins business may not be deducted. Instead, these costs are capitalized. If so elected, they may be amortized over a period of 60 months or more, starting with the month in which the partnership begins business.[25] Such costs include marketing surveys prior to conducting business, pre-operating advertising expenses, costs of establishing an accounting system, and salaries paid to executives and employees before the start of business.

**Acquisition Costs of Depreciable Assets.**    Expenditures may be incurred in changing the legal title in which certain assets are held from that of the contributing partner to the partnership name. These costs include legal fees incurred to transfer assets and transfer taxes imposed by some states. Such costs are added to the partnership's basis for the depreciable assets and increase the amount the partnership may depreciate. As mentioned earlier, the partnership typically determines its depreciation deductions by "stepping into the shoes" of the contributing partner. If additional costs are incurred, though, the additional basis is treated as a new MACRS asset, placed in service on the date the cost is incurred (e.g., the date the asset is transferred to the partnership).

**Syndication Costs.**    Syndication costs are capitalized, but no amortization election is available. Syndication costs include the following expenditures incurred for promoting and marketing partnership interests:

- Brokerage fees.
- Registration fees.
- Legal fees paid for security advice or advice on the adequacy of tax disclosures in the prospectus or placement memo for securities law purposes.
- Accounting fees related to offering materials.
- Printing costs of prospectus, placement memos, and other selling materials.

---

[25]§ 195.

## LO.4

Specify the accounting
methods available to a
partnership and the methods
of determining a partnership's
tax year.

## METHOD OF ACCOUNTING

Like a sole proprietorship, a newly formed partnership may adopt either the cash or the accrual method of accounting, or a hybrid of these two methods.

However, a few special limitations on cash basis accounting apply to partnerships.[26] The cash method of accounting may not be adopted by a partnership that

- has one or more C corporation partners or
- is a tax shelter.

A C corporation partner does *not* preclude cash basis treatment if

- the partnership meets the $5 million gross receipts test described below,
- the C corporation partner(s) is a qualified personal service corporation, such as an incorporated attorney, or
- the partnership is engaged in the business of farming.

A partnership meets the $5 million gross receipts test if it has not received average annual gross receipts of more than $5 million. "Average annual gross receipts" is the average of gross receipts for the three tax years ending with the tax period in question. For new partnerships, the period of existence is used. Gross receipts are annualized for short taxable periods. A partnership must change to the accrual method the first year in which its average annual gross receipts exceed $5 million and must use the accrual method thereafter.

A tax shelter is a partnership whose interests have been sold in a registered offering or a partnership in which 35 percent of the losses are allocated to limited partners.

**EXAMPLE 19**

Jason and Julia are both attorneys. In 2000, each of them formed a professional personal service corporation to operate their separate law practices. In 2003, the two attorneys decide to form the JJ Partnership, which consists of the two professional corporations. In 2003, JJ's gross receipts are $6 million. JJ may adopt the cash method of accounting, since it is a partnership consisting of qualified personal service corporations. Because JJ has no C corporate partners that are not personal service corporations, the cash method is available even though JJ's average annual gross receipts are greater than $5 million. JJ may also adopt the accrual method of accounting or a hybrid of the cash and accrual methods. ■

## TAXABLE YEAR OF THE PARTNERSHIP

Partnership taxable income (and any separately stated items) flows through to each partner at the end of the *partnership's* taxable year. A *partner's* taxable income, then, includes the distributive share of partnership income for any *partnership* taxable year that ends within the partner's tax year.

When all partners use the calendar year, it would be beneficial in present value terms for a profitable partnership to adopt a fiscal year ending with January 31. Why? As Figure 10–1 illustrates, when the adopted year ends on January 31, the reporting of income from the partnership and payment of related taxes can be deferred for up to 11 months. For instance, income earned by the partnership in September 2002 is not taxable to the partners until January 31, 2003. It is reported in the partner's tax return for the year ended December 31, 2003, which is not due

---

[26]§ 448.

■ **FIGURE 10–1**
Deferral Benefit When Fiscal
Year Is Used and All Partners
Are on the Calendar Year

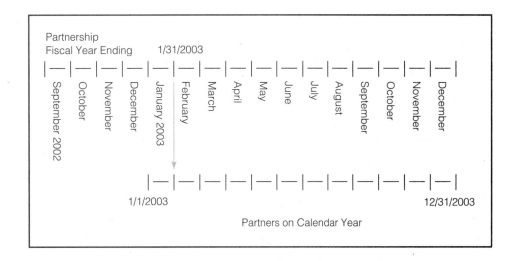

until April 15, 2004. Even though each partner may be required to make quarterly estimated tax payments, some deferral is still possible.

**Required Taxable Years.** To prevent excessive deferral of taxation of partnership income, Congress and the IRS have adopted a series of rules that prescribe the *required* taxable year an entity must adopt if no alternative tax years (discussed on the next page) are available. Three rules are presented in Figure 10–2.[27] The partnership must consider each rule in order. The partnership's required taxable year is the taxable year determined under the first rule that applies.

The first two rules in Figure 10–2 are relatively self-explanatory. Under the **least aggregate deferral rule,** the partnership tests the year-ends that are used by the various partners to determine the weighted-average deferral of partnership income. The year-end that offers the least amount of deferral is the *required tax year* under this rule.

**EXAMPLE 20**

Anne and Bonnie are equal partners in the AB Partnership. Anne uses the calendar year, and Bonnie uses a fiscal year ending August 31. Neither Anne nor Bonnie is a majority partner since neither owns more than 50%. Although Anne and Bonnie are both principal

■ **FIGURE 10–2**
Required Tax Year of
Partnership

| In Order, Partnership Must Use | Requirements |
| --- | --- |
| Majority partners' tax year | • More than 50% of capital *and* profits is owned by partners who have the same taxable year. |
| Principal partners' tax year | • All partners who own 5% or more of capital *or* profits are principal partners. |
|  | • All principal partners must have the same tax year. |
| Year with smallest amount of income deferred | • "Least aggregate deferral rule" (Example 20). |

[27]§ 706(b).

*[handwritten note in margin: if principal partners donot have same tax year than Least deferral rule apportions]*

partners, they do not have the same tax year. Therefore, the general rules indicate that the partnership's required tax year must be determined by the "least aggregate deferral rule." The following computations support August 31 as AB's tax year, since the 2.0 product using that year-end is less than the 4.0 product when December 31 is used.

**Test for 12/31 Year-End**

| Partner | Year Ends | Profit Interest | | Months of Deferral | | Product |
|---------|-----------|-----------------|---|--------------------|---|---------|
| Anne | 12/31 | 50% | × | –0– | = | 0.0 |
| Bonnie | 8/31 | 50% | × | 8 | = | 4.0 |
| Aggregate number of deferral months | | | | | | 4.0 |

**Test for 8/31 Year-End**

| Partner | Year Ends | Profit Interest | | Months of Deferral | | Product |
|---------|-----------|-----------------|---|--------------------|---|---------|
| Anne | 12/31 | 50% | × | 4 | = | 2.0 |
| Bonnie | 8/31 | 50% | × | –0– | = | 0.0 |
| Aggregate number of deferral months | | | | | | 2.0 |

**Alternative Tax Years.**   If the required tax year is undesirable to the entity, two other alternative tax years may be available:

- Establish to the IRS's satisfaction that a *business purpose* exists for a different tax year, usually a natural business year at the end of a peak season or shortly thereafter.
- Elect a tax year so that taxes on partnership income are deferred for not more than *three months* from the *required* tax year.[28] Then, have the partnership maintain with the IRS a prepaid, non-interest-bearing deposit of estimated deferred taxes.[29] This alternative may not be desirable since the deposit is based on the highest individual tax rate plus one percentage point, or 39.6 percent.

## LO.5

Calculate partnership taxable income and describe how partnership items affect a partner's income tax return.

# Operations of the Partnership

An individual, corporation, trust, estate, or another partnership can become a partner in a partnership. Since a partnership is a tax-reporting, rather than a taxpaying, entity for purposes of its Federal (and state) income tax computations, the partnership's income, deductions, credits, and alternative minimum tax (AMT) preferences and adjustments can ultimately be reported and taxed on any of a number of income tax returns (e.g., Forms 1040 [individuals], 1041 [fiduciaries, see Chapter 19], 1120 [C corporations], and 1120S [S corporations]).

A partnership is subject to all other taxes in the same manner as any other business. Thus, the partnership files returns and pays the outstanding amount of pertinent sales taxes, property taxes, and Social Security, unemployment, and other payroll taxes.

---

[28]§ 444.                                    [29]§ 7519.

## MEASURING AND REPORTING INCOME

The partnership's Form 1065 organizes and reports the transactions of the entity for the tax year, and each of the partnership's tax items is reported on Schedule K of that return. Each partner receives a Schedule K–1 that reports the partner's allocable share of partnership income, credits, and preferences for the year. The IRS also receives a copy of each K–1. Form 1065 is due on the fifteenth day of the fourth month following the close of the partnership's tax year; for a calendar year partnership, this is April 15. The partnership must provide a copy of Schedule K–1 to each partner by this same date. However, partners of an electing large partnership must receive their K–1's one month earlier (March 15 for a calendar year partnership).

**Income Measurement.**   The measurement and reporting of partnership income require a two-step approach. Certain items must be netted at the partnership level, and other items must be segregated and reported separately on the partnership return and each partner's Schedule K–1.

Among the many items passed through separately are the following:

- Short- and long-term capital gains and losses.
- Section 1231 gains and losses.
- Charitable contributions.
- Portfolio income items (dividends, interest, and royalties).
- Expenses related to portfolio income.
- Immediately expensed tangible personal property (§ 179).
- Items allocated among the partners in a different ratio from the general profit and loss ratio.
- Recovery of items previously deducted (tax benefit items).
- AMT preference and adjustment items.
- Self-employment income.
- Passive activity items, such as rental real estate income or loss.
- Intangible drilling and development costs.
- Taxes paid to foreign countries and U.S. possessions.
- Nonbusiness and personal items (e.g., alimony, medical, and dental).[30]

The reason for separately reporting the preceding items is rooted in the aggregate or conduit concept. These items affect various exclusions, deductions, and credits at the partner level and must pass through without loss of identity so that the proper tax for each partner may be determined.[31]

A partnership is not allowed the following deductions:

- Net operating losses.
- Depletion of oil and gas interests.
- Dividends received deduction.

In addition, items that are only allowed by legislative grace to individuals, such as standard deductions or personal exemptions, are not allowed to the partnership. Also, if a partnership makes a payment on behalf of a partner, such as for alimony, medical expenses, or other items that constitute itemized deductions to individuals, the partnership treats the payment as a distribution or guaranteed payment (discussed later) to the partner, and the partner determines whether to claim the deduction.

---

[30]§ 702(a).

[31]§ 702(b).

**LE 21**

This year, the TUV Partnership entered into the following transactions:

| | |
|---|---|
| Fees received | $100,000 |
| Salaries paid | 30,000 |
| Cost recovery deductions | 10,000 |
| Supplies, repairs | 3,000 |
| Payroll taxes paid | 9,000 |
| Contribution to art museum | 6,000 |
| Short-term capital gain | 12,000 |
| Passive income (rental operations) | 7,500 |
| Portfolio income (dividends received) | 1,500 |
| Exempt income (bond interest) | 2,100 |
| AMT adjustment (cost recovery) | 3,600 |
| Payment of partner Vern's alimony obligations | 4,000 |

The partnership experienced a $20,000 net loss from operations last year, its first year of business.

The partnership's ordinary income is determined as follows:

| **Nonseparately Stated Items (Ordinary Income)** | |
|---|---|
| Fee income | $100,000 |
| Salaries paid | (30,000) |
| Cost recovery deductions | (10,000) |
| Supplies, repairs | (3,000) |
| Payroll taxes paid | (9,000) |
| Ordinary income | $ 48,000 |

The partnership is not allowed a deduction for last year's $20,000 net operating loss—this item was passed through to the partners in the previous year. Moreover, the partnership is not allowed a deduction for payment of Vern's alimony. This payment is probably handled as a distribution to Vern who may claim it as a deduction *for* AGI as if he had paid it himself.

The partnership's separately stated items are:

| **Separately Stated Items** | |
|---|---|
| Contribution to art museum | $ 6,000 |
| Short-term capital gain | 12,000 |
| Passive income (rental operations) | 7,500 |
| Portfolio income (dividends received) | 1,500 |
| Exempt income (bond interest) | 2,100 |
| AMT adjustment (cost recovery) | 3,600 |

**EXAMPLE 22**

Assume the same facts as in Example 21. Tiwanda is a one-third partner in the TUV Partnership. The partnership will give her a Schedule K–1 on which she will be allocated a one-third share of ordinary income and one-third of each of the separately stated items. Thus, in determining her tax liability on her Form 1040, Tiwanda includes $16,000 of ordinary income, a $2,000 charitable deduction, a $4,000 short-term capital gain, $2,500 of passive rent income, $500 of dividend income, and a $1,200 positive adjustment in computing alternative minimum taxable income. She will disclose her $700 share of tax-exempt interest on the first page of her Form 1040. ■

**Withdrawals.** Capital withdrawals by partners during the year do not affect the partnership's income measuring and reporting process. These items usually are treated as distributions made on the last day of the partnership's tax year. Distributions are discussed in Chapter 11.

**Penalties.** A partner's share of each partnership item should be reported on the partner's tax return in the same manner as presented on the Form 1065. If a partner treats an item differently, the IRS must be notified of the inconsistent treatment.[32] If a partner fails to notify the IRS, a negligence penalty may be added to the tax due.

To encourage the filing of a partnership return, a penalty of $50, per partner, per month (or fraction thereof, but not to exceed five months) is imposed on the partnership for failure to file a complete and timely information return without reasonable cause.[33]

A partnership with 10 or fewer "natural persons" or corporations as partners, where each partner's share of partnership items is the same for all items, is automatically excluded from these penalties.[34]

---

### ETHICAL CONSIDERATIONS

## A Preparer's Responsibility for Partners' Tax Returns

A partnership's tax return preparer is responsible for accurately presenting information supplied by the partnership in that return. If a flow-through amount is significant to a certain partner, the preparer of the *partnership* return can be treated as the preparer of the *partner's* tax return with respect to that item.

If a preparer misstates an item on a partnership return either by taking a position that is not supportable under current law or by willfully misreporting the item, "preparer penalties" can be assessed. Although these penalties are relatively small, their imposition may lead to the preparer's suspension from practice before the IRS or by a state accountancy board.

As an example, assume Stan, a CPA, knowingly reported a $20,000 deduction for fines and penalties (nondeductible items) in determining the JB Partnership's $30,000 income from operations. This amount is allocated equally to partners Joe and Barb. Joe has other income of $35,000; Barb has other income of $1 million. Stan is treated as the preparer of Joe's tax return with respect to the improper $10,000 flow-through item since the fines and penalties are significant relative to Joe's income. Stan is not the preparer of Barb's return since the fines and penalties are not significant to her income.

In a recent case, the preparer of a partnership return was considered to be the preparer of several partners' returns with respect to partnership items flowing through to the partners. The court reached this decision even though the return preparer never met the individual partners, received any direct fees from the partners, or otherwise performed services for them.

Do you believe this is a reasonable approach for allocating responsibility for accurate preparation of a partner's tax return? Why or why not?

---

## PARTNERSHIP ALLOCATIONS

So far, most examples in this chapter have assumed that the partner has the same percentage interest in capital, profits, and losses. Thus, a partner who owns a 25

---

[32]§ 6222.
[33]§ 6698.
[34]§§ 6231(a)(1)(B) and (I). Natural persons for this purpose include individuals who are not nonresident aliens, as well as the estate of a decedent who was not a nonresident alien.

percent interest in partnership capital has been assumed to own 25 percent of partnership profits and 25 percent of partnership losses.

**Economic Effect.**    The partnership agreement can provide that any partner may share capital, profits, and losses in different ratios. For example, a partner could have a 25 percent capital sharing ratio, yet be allocated 30 percent of the profits and 20 percent of the losses of the partnership. Such special allocations have, at times, been used in an attempt to manipulate the allocation of tax benefits among partners. The Regulations[35] are designed to prevent unfair use of such manipulation. Although these rules are too complex to discuss in detail, the general outline of one of these rules—the **economic effect test**—can be easily understood.

In general, the economic effect test requires the following:

- An allocation of income or gain to a partner must increase the partner's capital account, and an allocation of deduction or loss must decrease the partner's capital account.
- When the partner's interest is liquidated, the partner must receive assets that have a fair market value equal to the positive balance in the capital account.
- A partner with a negative capital account must restore that account upon liquidation of the interest. Restoration of a negative capital account can best be envisioned as a contribution of cash to the partnership equal to the negative balance.

These requirements are designed to ensure that a partner bears the economic burden of a loss or deduction allocation and receives the economic benefit of an income or gain allocation.

**EXAMPLE 23**    Eli and Sanjay each contribute $20,000 cash to the newly formed ES Partnership. The partnership uses the cash to acquire a depreciable asset for $40,000. The partnership agreement provides that the depreciation is allocated 90% to Eli and 10% to Sanjay. Other items of partnership income, gain, loss, or deduction are allocated equally between the partners. Upon liquidation of the partnership, property will be distributed to the partners in accordance with their positive capital account balances. Any partner with a negative capital account must restore the capital account upon liquidation. Assume the first-year depreciation on the equipment is $4,000. Also, assume nothing else happens in the first year that affects the partners' capital accounts.

Eli's capital account is $16,400 ($20,000 − $3,600), and Sanjay's capital account has a balance of $19,600 ($20,000 − $400) after the first year of partnership operations. The Regulations require that a hypothetical sale of the asset for its $36,000 adjusted basis on the last day of the year and an immediate liquidation of the partnership should result in Eli and Sanjay receiving distributions equal to their capital accounts. According to the partnership agreement, Eli would receive $16,400, and Sanjay would receive $19,600 of the cash in a liquidating distribution. Eli, therefore, bears the economic burden of $3,600 depreciation since he contributed $20,000 to the partnership and would receive only $16,400 upon liquidation. Likewise, Sanjay's economic burden is $400 since he would receive only $19,600 of his original $20,000 investment. The agreement, therefore, has economic effect. ■

---

[35]Reg. § 1.704–1(b).

| EXAMPLE 24 | Assume the same facts as in Example 23, except that the partnership agreement p that Eli and Sanjay will receive equal amounts of cash upon liquidation of the partnership. The hypothetical sale of the asset for its $36,000 adjusted basis and the immediate liquidation of the partnership would result in each partner receiving $18,000 cash. Since each partner contributed $20,000 to the partnership and each partner would receive $18,000 upon liquidation, each partner bears the economic burden of $2,000 of depreciation. The original 90%/10% allocation of depreciation to the two partners is defective, and the IRS will require that the depreciation be reallocated equally ($2,000 each) to the two partners to reflect the economic burden borne by each partner. ■ |

**Precontribution Gain or Loss.** Certain income, gain, loss, and deductions relative to contributed property may not be allocated under the rules described above. Instead, **precontribution gain or loss** must be allocated among the partners to take into account the variation between the basis of the property and its fair market value on the date of contribution.[36] For nondepreciable property, this means that *built-in* gain or loss on the date of contribution must be allocated to the contributing partner when the property is eventually disposed of by the partnership in a taxable transaction.

| EXAMPLE 25 | Seth and Tim form the equal profit and loss sharing ST Partnership. Seth contributes cash of $10,000, and Tim contributes land purchased two years ago and held for investment. The land has an adjusted basis of $6,000 and fair market value of $10,000 at the contribution date. For accounting purposes, the partnership records the land at its fair market value of $10,000. For tax purposes, the partnership takes a carryover basis of $6,000 in the land. After using the land as a parking lot for five months, ST sells it for $10,600. No other transactions have taken place. |

The accounting and tax gain from the land sale are computed as follows:

|  | Accounting | Tax |
|---|---|---|
| Amount realized | $10,600 | $10,600 |
| Less: Adjusted basis | 10,000 | 6,000 |
| Gain realized | $ 600 | $ 4,600 |
| Gain at contribution date to Tim | –0– | 4,000 |
| Remaining gain (split equally) | $ 600 | $ 600 |

Seth recognizes $300 of the gain ($600 remaining gain ÷ 2), and Tim recognizes $4,300 [$4,000 built-in gain + ($600 remaining gain ÷ 2)]. ■

If the property is depreciable, Regulations describe allowable methods of allocating depreciation deductions.[37]

Concept Summary 10–2 reviews the tax reporting rules for partnership activities.

---

[36]§ 704(c)(1)(A).          [37]Reg. § 1.704–3.

## CONCEPT SUMMARY 10–2

### Tax Reporting of Partnership Activities

| Event | Partnership Level | Partner Level |
|---|---|---|
| 1. Compute partnership ordinary income. | Form 1065, line 22, page 1. Schedule K, Form 1065, line 1, page 3. | Schedule K–1 (Form 1065), line 1, page 1. Each partner's share is passed through for separate reporting. Each partner's basis is increased. |
| 2. Compute partnership ordinary loss. | Form 1065, line 22, page 1. Schedule K, Form 1065, line 1, page 3. | Schedule K–1 (Form 1065), line 1, page 1. Each partner's share is passed through for separate reporting. Each partner's basis is decreased. The amount of a partner's loss deduction may be limited. Losses that may not be deducted are carried forward for use in future years. |
| 3. Separately reported items like portfolio income, capital gain and loss, and § 179 deductions. | Schedule K, Form 1065, various lines, page 3. | Schedule K–1 (Form 1065), various lines, pages 1 and 2. Each partner's share of each item is passed through for separate reporting. |
| 4. Net earnings from self-employment. | Schedule K, Form 1065, line 15, page 3. | Schedule K–1 (Form 1065), line 15, page 2. |

---

**ETHICAL CONSIDERATIONS** | **Built-in Appreciation on Contributed Property**

In the "old days," one partner could contribute cash and another partner could contribute an equal value of appreciated property with no subsequent record-keeping requirements. Future depreciation deductions and gains on sale of the property could be allocated to both partners equally, thereby shifting income from one taxpayer to another. A partner in a lower tax bracket (or with expiring net operating losses and the like) could report the share of the gain on sale of the asset with a relatively low corresponding tax burden.

Section 704(c)(1)(A) was added to the Code to ensure that the partner contributing the property pays tax on any built-in gain. This prevents income shifting among taxpayers and loss of revenue to the IRS.

There is no corresponding provision for S corporations—gains and losses and depreciation expense are allocated among the shareholders without regard to any built-in appreciation on contributed property.

What theory of partnership taxation supports this difference in treatment?

---

| LO.6 | **BASIS OF A PARTNERSHIP INTEREST** |

Determine a partner's basis in the partnership interest.

Previously, this chapter discussed how to compute a partner's adjusted basis when the partnership is formed. It was noted that the partner's adjusted basis in the newly formed partnership usually equals (1) the adjusted basis in any property contributed to the partnership plus (2) the fair market value of any services the partner performed for the partnership (i.e., the amount of ordinary income reported by the partner for services rendered to the partnership).

A partnership interest also can be acquired after the partnership has been formed. The method of acquisition controls how the partner's initial basis is computed. If the partnership interest is purchased from another partner, the purchasing partner's basis is the amount paid (cost basis) for the partnership interest. The basis of a partnership interest acquired by gift is the donor's basis for the interest plus, in certain cases, some or all of the transfer (gift) tax paid by the donor. The basis of a partnership interest acquired through inheritance generally is the fair market value of the interest on the date the partner dies.

After the partner is admitted to the partnership, the partner's basis is adjusted for numerous items. The following operating results *increase* a partner's adjusted basis:

- The partner's proportionate share of partnership income (including capital gains and tax-exempt income).
- The partner's proportionate share of any increase in partnership liabilities. (This provision is discussed in the next section.)

The following operating results *decrease* the partner's adjusted basis in the partnership:

- The partner's proportionate share of partnership deductions and losses (including capital losses).
- The partner's proportionate share of nondeductible expenses.
- The partner's proportionate share of any reduction in partnership liabilities.[38]

Under no circumstances can the partner's adjusted basis for the partnership interest be reduced below zero.

Increasing the adjusted basis for the partner's share of partnership taxable income is logical since the partner has already been taxed on the income. By increasing the partner's basis, the Code ensures that the partner is not taxed again on the income when he or she sells the interest or receives a distribution from the partnership.

It is also logical that the tax-exempt income should increase the partner's basis. If the income is exempt in the current period, it should not contribute to the recognition of gain when the partner either sells the interest or receives a distribution from the partnership.

**EXAMPLE 26**

Yuri is a one-third partner in the XYZ Partnership. His proportionate share of the partnership income during the current year consists of $20,000 of ordinary taxable income and $10,000 of tax-exempt income. None of the income is distributed to Yuri. The adjusted basis of Yuri's partnership interest before adjusting for his share of income is $35,000, and the fair market value of the interest before considering the income items is $50,000.

The unrealized gain inherent in Yuri's investment in the partnership is $15,000 ($50,000 − $35,000) before adjusting for his share of income. Yuri's proportionate share of the income items should increase the fair market value of the interest to $80,000 ($50,000 + $20,000 + $10,000). By increasing the adjusted basis of Yuri's partnership interest to $65,000 ($35,000 + $20,000 + $10,000), the Code ensures that the unrealized gain inherent in Yuri's partnership investment remains at $15,000. This makes sense because the $20,000 of ordinary taxable income is taxed to Yuri this year and should not be taxed again when Yuri either sells his interest or receives a distribution. Similarly, the exempt income is exempt this year and should not increase Yuri's gain when he either sells his interest or receives a distribution from the partnership. ■

---

[38]§§ 705 and 752.

Decreasing the adjusted basis for the partner's share of deductible losses, deductions, and noncapitalizable, nondeductible expenditures is logical for the same reasons. An item that is deductible currently should not contribute to creating a loss when the partnership interest is sold, or a distribution is received from the partnership. Similarly, a noncapitalizable, nondeductible expenditure should never be deductible nor contribute to a loss when a subsequent sale or distribution transaction occurs.

### LO.7

Explain how liabilities affect a partner's basis.

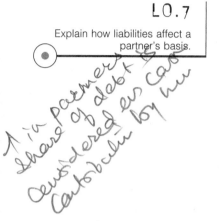

**Liability Sharing.**  A partner's adjusted basis is affected by the partner's share of partnership debt.[39] Partnership debt includes any partnership obligation that creates an asset, results in a deductible expense, or results in a nondeductible, noncapitalizable item at the partnership level. The definition of partnership debt includes most debt that is considered a liability under financial accounting rules except for accounts payable of a cash basis partnership and certain contingent liabilities.

Under § 752, an increase in a partner's share of partnership debt is treated as a cash contribution by the partner to the partnership. A partner's share of partnership debt increases as a result of increases in the total amount of partnership debt. A decrease in a partner's share of partnership debt is treated as a cash distribution from the partnership to the partner. A partner's share of partnership debt decreases as a result of (1) decreases in the total amount of partnership debt and (2) assumption of the partner's debt by the partnership.

**EXAMPLE 27**

Jim and Becky contribute property to form the JB Partnership. Jim contributes cash of $30,000. Becky contributes land with an adjusted basis and fair market value of $45,000, subject to a liability of $15,000. The partnership borrows $50,000 to finance construction of a building on the contributed land. At the end of the first year, the accrual basis partnership owes $3,500 in trade accounts payable to various vendors. Assume no other operating activities occurred.

Partnership debt sharing rules are discussed later in this section, but assuming for simplicity that Jim and Becky share equally in liabilities, the partners' bases in their partnership interests are determined as follows:

| Jim's Basis | | Becky's Basis | |
|---|---|---|---|
| Contributed cash | $30,000 | Basis in contributed land | $ 45,000 |
| Share of debt on land (assumed by partnership) | 7,500 | Less: Debt assumed by partnership | (15,000) |
| | | Share of debt on land (assumed by partnership) | 7,500 |
| Initial basis | $37,500 | Initial basis | $ 37,500 |
| Share of construction loan | 25,000 | Share of construction loan | 25,000 |
| Share of trade accounts payable | 1,750 | Share of trade accounts payable | 1,750 |
| Basis, end of first year | $64,250 | Basis, end of first year | $ 64,250 |

In this case, it is reasonable that the parties have an equal basis, because each is a 50% owner and they contributed property with identical *net* bases and identical *net* fair market values. ∎

**EXAMPLE 28**

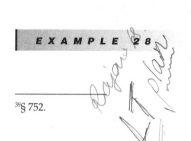

Assume the same facts as in Example 27. In the second year, the partnership generates $70,000 of taxable income from operations and repays both the $50,000 construction loan

---

[39]§ 752.

and the $3,500 trade accounts payable. The taxable income is allocated equally to each partner and increases each partner's basis by $35,000. The $26,750 ($25,000 + $1,750) reduction of each partner's share of liabilities is treated as a cash distribution to each partner and reduces each partner's adjusted basis by that amount. The $72,500 adjusted basis for each partner at the end of the second year is computed as follows:

| Jim's Basis | | Becky's Basis | |
|---|---|---|---|
| Basis, beginning of second year | $ 64,250 | Basis, beginning of second year | $ 64,250 |
| Share of taxable income | 35,000 | Share of taxable income | 35,000 |
| Share of construction loan paid | (25,000) | Share of construction loan paid | (25,000) |
| Share of trade accounts payable paid | (1,750) | Share of trade accounts payable paid | (1,750) |
| Basis, end of second year | $ 72,500 | Basis, end of second year | $ 72,500 |

Two types of partnership debt exist. **Recourse debt** is partnership debt for which the partnership or at least one of the partners is personally liable. This personal liability can exist, for example, through the operation of state law or through personal guarantees that a partner makes to the creditor. Personal liability of a party related to a partner (under attribution rules) is treated as the personal liability of the partner. **Nonrecourse debt** is debt for which no partner (or party related to a partner) is personally liable. Lenders of nonrecourse debt generally require that collateral be pledged against the loan. Upon default, the lender can claim only the collateral, not the partners' personal assets.

How liabilities are shared among the partners depends upon whether the debt is recourse or nonrecourse and when the liability was incurred. For most debt *created* before January 29, 1989, the rules are relatively straightforward. Recourse debt is shared among the partners in accordance with their loss sharing ratios while nonrecourse debt is shared among the partners in accordance with the way they share partnership profits. Although questions arise about the calculation of the profit or loss sharing ratios and the treatment of personal guarantees of debt, the rules for sharing this earlier debt are easy to apply.

The rules for sharing partnership debt created after January 29, 1989, are much more complex. The basic principles of these rules are illustrated below.

*Current Recourse Debt Rules.* Recourse debt created after January 29, 1989, is shared in accordance with a **constructive liquidation scenario.**[40]

Under this scenario, the following events are *deemed* to occur at the end of each taxable year of the partnership:

1. Most partnership assets (including cash) become worthless.
2. The worthless assets are sold at fair market value ($0), and losses on the deemed sales are determined.
3. These losses are allocated to the partners according to their loss sharing ratios. These losses reduce the partners' capital accounts.
4. Any partner with a (deemed) negative capital account balance is treated as contributing cash to the partnership to restore that negative balance to zero.

---

[40]Transition rules (beyond the scope of this text) apply to debt created between January 29, 1989, and December 28, 1991.

5.  The cash deemed contributed by the partners with negative capital balances is used to pay the liabilities of the partnership.
6.  The partnership is deemed to be liquidated immediately, and any remaining cash is distributed to partners with positive capital account balances.

The amount of a partner's cash contribution that would be used (in step 5 above) to pay partnership recourse liabilities is that partner's share of these partnership recourse liabilities.

**EXAMPLE 29**

On January 1 of the current year, Nina and Otis each contribute $20,000 cash to the newly created NO General Partnership. Each partner has a 50% interest in partnership capital, profits, and losses. The first year of partnership operations resulted in the following balance sheet as of December 31:

*[Handwritten margin notes: Assume all assets are worthless loss of 69,000 ; Partners of 69000 ; 195000 ; 0 ; <34500> ; 34500 ; cash <15000> ; Each should contribute 15000 on liquidation]*

|  | Basis | FMV |  | Basis | FMV |
|---|---|---|---|---|---|
| Cash | $12,000 | $12,000 | Recourse payables | $30,000 | $30,000 |
| Receivables | 7,000 | 7,000 | Nina, capital | 19,500 | 19,500 |
| Land and buildings | 50,000 | 50,000 | Otis, capital | 19,500 | 19,500 |
|  | $69,000 | $69,000 |  | $69,000 | $69,000 |

The recourse debt is shared in accordance with the constructive liquidation scenario. All of the partnership assets (including cash) are deemed to be worthless and sold for $0. This creates a loss of $69,000 ($12,000 + $7,000 + $50,000), which is allocated equally between the two partners. The $34,500 loss allocated to each partner creates negative capital accounts of $15,000 each for Nina and Otis. If the partnership were actually liquidated, each partner would contribute $15,000 cash to the partnership; the cash would be used to pay the partnership recourse payables; and the partnership would cease to exist. Because each partner would be required to contribute $15,000 to pay the liabilities, each shares in $15,000 of the recourse payables. Accordingly, Nina and Otis will each have an adjusted basis for their partnership interests of $34,500 ($19,500 + $15,000) on December 31. ■

**EXAMPLE 30**

*[Handwritten margin notes: 60%  40% ; <27600>  <8100> ; 27600  8100 ; Each deemed to contribute cash]*

Assume the same facts as in Example 29, except that the partners allocate partnership losses 60% to Nina and 40% to Otis. The constructive liquidation scenario results in the $69,000 loss being allocated $41,400 to Nina and $27,600 to Otis. As a consequence, Nina's capital account has a negative balance of $21,900, and Otis's account has a negative balance of $8,100. Each partner is deemed to contribute cash equal to these negative capital accounts, and the cash would be used to pay the recourse liabilities under the liquidation scenario. Accordingly, Nina and Otis share $21,900 and $8,100, respectively, in the recourse debt. Note that the debt allocation percentages (73% to Nina and 27% to Otis) are different from the partners' 60%/40% loss sharing ratios. ■

*Current Nonrecourse Debt Rules.*   Nonrecourse debt is allocated in three stages. First, an amount of debt equal to the amount of *minimum gain* is allocated to partners who share in minimum gain. The calculation of minimum gain is complex, and details of the calculation are beyond the scope of this text. In general, minimum gain approximates the amount of nonrecourse (mortgage) liability on a property in excess of the "book" basis of the property. Generally, the "book" basis for a property item is the same as the "tax" basis, although sometimes the amounts are different. For example, the "book" basis for contributed property on the date of contribution is its fair market value at that date, not its "tax" basis.

If a lender forecloses on partnership property, the result is treated as a deemed sale of the property for the mortgage balance. Gain is recognized for at least the

amount of the liability in excess of the property's "book" basis-
gain. Allocation of minimum gain among the partners should b
partnership agreement.

Second, the amount of nonrecourse debt equal to the remaini
*gain* under § 704(c) is allocated to the partner who contributed t
debt to the partnership. For this purpose, the remaining precontribution gain is
the excess of the current nonrecourse debt balance on the contributed property
over the current tax basis of the contributed property.[41] Note that this calculation
is only relevant when the "book" and "tax" bases of the contributed property
are different.

Third, any remaining nonrecourse debt is allocated to the partners in accordance
with one of several different allocation methods. The partnership agreement should
specify which allocation method is chosen. Most often, the profit sharing ratio
is used.

**EXAMPLE 31**

Ted contributes a nondepreciable asset to the TK Partnership in exchange for a one-third
interest in the capital, profits, and losses of the partnership. The asset has an adjusted tax
basis to Ted and the partnership of $24,000 and a fair market value and "book" basis on
the contribution date of $50,000. The asset is encumbered by a nonrecourse note (created
January 1, 2001) of $35,000. Because the "book" basis exceeds the nonrecourse debt, there
is no minimum gain. Under § 704(c) principles, the Regulations provide that the first $11,000
of the nonrecourse debt ($35,000 debt – $24,000 basis) is allocated to Ted. Assume the
partnership allocates the remaining $24,000 nonrecourse debt according to the profit sharing
ratio, and Ted's share is $8,000. Therefore, Ted shares in $19,000 ($11,000 + $8,000) of the
nonrecourse debt.

Ted's basis in his partnership interest is determined as follows:

| | |
|---|---:|
| Substituted basis of contributed property | $ 24,000 |
| Less: Liability assumed by partnership | (35,000) |
| Plus: Allocation of § 704(c) debt | 11,000 |
| Basis before remaining allocation | $    –0– |
| Plus: Allocation of remaining nonrecourse debt | 8,000 |
| Basis in partnership interest | $  8,000 |

The § 704(c) allocation of nonrecourse debt prevents Ted from receiving a deemed
distribution ($35,000) in excess of his basis in property he contributed ($24,000). Without
this required allocation of nonrecourse debt, in some cases, a contributing partner would be
required to recognize gain on a contribution of property encumbered by nonrecourse debt. ■

**Other Factors Affecting Basis Calculations.**   The partner's basis is also affected by (1) postacquisition contributions of cash or property to the partnership;
(2) postacquisition distributions of cash or property from the partnership; and (3)
special calculations that are designed to allow the full deduction of percentage
depletion for oil and gas wells. Postacquisition contributions of cash or property
affect basis in the same manner as contributions made upon the creation of the
partnership. Postacquisition distributions of cash or property reduce basis.

[41]Reg. § 1.704–3.

**EXAMPLE 32**

Ryan is a one-third partner in the ERM Partnership. On January 1, 2003, Ryan's basis in his partnership interest was $50,000. During 2003, the calendar year, accrual basis partnership generated ordinary taxable income of $210,000. It also received $60,000 of tax-exempt interest income from City of Buffalo bonds. It paid $3,000 in nondeductible bribes to local law enforcement officials, so that the police would not notify the Federal government about the products that the entity had imported without paying the proper tariffs. On July 1, 2003, Ryan contributed $20,000 cash and a computer (zero basis to him) to the partnership. Ryan's monthly draw from the partnership is $3,000; this is treated as a distribution and not as a guaranteed payment. The only liabilities that the partnership has incurred are trade accounts payable. On January 1, 2003, the trade accounts payable totaled $45,000; this account balance was $21,000 on December 31, 2003. Ryan shares in one-third of the partnership liabilities for basis purposes.

Ryan's basis in the partnership on December 31, 2003, is $115,000, computed as follows:

| | |
|---|---:|
| Beginning balance | $ 50,000 |
| Share of ordinary partnership income | 70,000 |
| Share of exempt income | 20,000 |
| Share of nondeductible expenditures | (1,000) |
| Ryan's basis in noncash capital contribution | –0– |
| Additional cash contributions | 20,000 |
| Capital withdrawal ($3,000 × 12) | (36,000) |
| Share of net decrease in partnership liabilities [⅓ × ($45,000 − $21,000)] | (8,000) |
| | $115,000 |

**EXAMPLE 33**

Assume the same facts as in Example 32. If Ryan withdraws cash of $115,000 from the partnership on January 1, 2004, the withdrawal is tax-free to him and reduces his basis to zero. The distribution is tax-free because Ryan has recognized his share of the partnership's net income throughout his association with the entity via the annual flow-through of his share of the partnership's income and expense items to his personal tax return. Note that the $20,000 cash withdrawal of his share of the municipal bond interest retains its nontaxable character in this distribution. Ryan receives the $20,000 tax-free because his basis was increased in 2003 when the partnership received the interest income. ■

A partner is required to compute the adjusted basis only when necessary and thus can avoid the inconvenience of making day-to-day calculations of basis. When a partnership interest is sold, exchanged, or retired, however, the partner must compute the adjusted basis as of the date the transaction occurs. Computation of gain or loss requires an accurate calculation of the partner's adjusted basis on the transaction date.

Figure 10–3 summarizes the rules for computing a partner's basis in a partnership interest.

**LO.8**

Describe the limitations on deducting partnership losses.

## LOSS LIMITATIONS

Partnership losses flow through to the partners for use on their tax returns. However, the amount and nature of the losses allowed in a partner's tax computations may be limited. When limitations apply, all or a portion of the losses are held in suspension until a triggering event occurs. Only then can the losses be used to determine the partner's tax liability. No time limit is imposed on such carry-forwards of losses.

■ **FIGURE 10–3**
Partner's Basis in Partnership
Interest

**Basis is generally adjusted in the following order:**

Initial basis. Amount paid for partnership interest, or gift or inherited basis (including share of partnership debt). Amount paid can be amount contributed to the partnership or amount paid to another partner or former partner.

+ Partner's subsequent contributions

+ Since interest acquired, partner's share of the partnership's

- Debt increase
- Taxable income items
- Exempt income items
- Excess of depletion deductions over adjusted basis of property subject to depletion

– Partner's distributions and withdrawals

– Since interest acquired, partner's share of the partnership's

- Debt decrease
- Nondeductible items not chargeable to a capital account
- Special depletion deduction for oil and gas wells
- Loss items

**The basis of a partner's interest can never be negative.**

Three different limitations may apply to partnership losses that are passed through to a partner:

- The first is the overall limitation contained in § 704(d). This limitation allows the deduction of losses only to the extent the partner has adjusted basis for the partnership interest.
- Losses that are deductible under the overall limitation may then be subject to the at-risk limitation of § 465. Losses are deductible under this provision only to the extent the partner is at risk for the partnership interest.
- Any losses that survive this second limitation may be subject to a third limitation, the passive loss rules of § 469.

Only losses that make it through all these applicable limitations are eligible to be deducted on the partner's tax return.

**EXAMPLE 34**

*deduchbluly of 60000*

Meg is a partner in a partnership that does not invest in real estate. On January 1, 2003, Meg's adjusted basis for her partnership interest is $50,000, and her at-risk amount is $35,000. Her share of losses from the partnership for 2003 is $60,000, all of which is passive. She has one other passive income-producing investment that produced $25,000 of passive income during 2003.

Meg will be able to deduct $25,000 of partnership losses on her Form 1040 for 2003. Her deductible loss is calculated as follows:

| Applicable Provision | Deductible Loss | Suspended Loss |
|---|---|---|
| *Basis* Overall limitation | $50,000 | $10,000 |
| At-risk limitation | 35,000 | 15,000 |
| *Passive income* Passive loss limitation | 25,000 | 10,000 |

Meg can deduct only $50,000 under the overall limitation. Of this $50,000, only $35,000 is deductible under the at-risk limitation. Under the passive loss limitation, passive losses can be deducted only against passive income. Thus, Meg can deduct only $25,000 on her return in 2003. ■

**Overall Limitation.**　A partner may only deduct losses flowing through from the partnership to the extent of the partner's adjusted basis in the partnership. A partner's adjusted basis in the partnership is determined at the end of the partnership's taxable year. It is adjusted for distributions and any partnership gains during the year, but it is determined *before considering any losses for the year*.

Losses that cannot be deducted because of this rule are suspended and carried forward (never back) for use against future increases in the partner's adjusted basis. Such increases might result from additional capital contributions, from sharing in additional partnership debts, or from future partnership income.

**EXAMPLE 35**

Carol and Dan do business as the CD Partnership, sharing profits and losses equally. All parties use the calendar year. At the start of the current year, the basis of Carol's partnership interest is $25,000. The partnership sustains an operating loss of $80,000 in the current year. For the current year, only $25,000 of Carol's $40,000 allocable share of the partnership loss can be deducted under the overall limitation. As a result, the basis of Carol's partnership interest is zero as of January 1 of the following year, and Carol must carry forward the remaining $15,000 of partnership losses. ■

**EXAMPLE 36**

Assume the same facts as in Example 35, and that the partnership earns a profit of $70,000 for the next calendar year. Carol reports net partnership income of $20,000 ($35,000 distributive share of income – the $15,000 carryforward loss). The basis of Carol's partnership interest becomes $20,000. ■

In Example 35, Carol's entire $40,000 share of the current-year partnership loss could have been deducted under the overall limitation in the current year if she had contributed an additional $15,000 or more in capital by December 31. Alternatively, if the partnership had incurred additional debt by the end of the current year, Carol's basis might have been increased to permit some or all of the loss to be deducted this year. Thus, if partnership losses are projected for a given year, careful tax planning can ensure their deductibility under the overall limitation.

**At-Risk Limitation.**　Under the at-risk rules, the partnership losses from business and income-producing activities that individual partners and closely held C corporation partners can deduct are limited to amounts that are economically invested in the partnership. Invested amounts include the adjusted basis of cash and property contributed by the partner and the partner's share of partnership earnings that has not been withdrawn.[42] A closely held C corporation exists when five or fewer individuals own more than 50 percent of the entity's stock under appropriate attribution and ownership rules.

When some or all of the partners are personally liable for partnership recourse debt, that debt is included in the adjusted basis of those partners. Usually, those partners also include the debt in their amount at risk.

No partner, however, carries any financial risk on nonrecourse debt. Therefore, as a general rule, partners cannot include nonrecourse debt in their amount at risk even though that debt is included in the adjusted basis of their partnership interest. This rule has an exception, however, that applies in many cases. Real estate nonrecourse financing provided by a bank, retirement plan, or similar party or by a Federal, state, or local government generally is deemed to be at risk.[43] Such debt is termed **qualified nonrecourse debt.** In summary, although the general rule provides that nonrecourse debt is not at risk, the overriding exception may provide that it is deemed to be at risk.

---

[42]§ 465(a).

[43]§ 465(b)(6).

When determining a partner's loss deduction, the overall limitation rule is invoked first. That is, the deduction is limited to the partner's outside basis at the end of the partnership year. Then, the at-risk provisions are applied to see if the remaining loss is still deductible. Suspended losses are carried forward until a partner has a sufficient amount at risk in the activity to absorb them.[44]

**EXAMPLE 37**

*Handwritten notes:*
Invest    5000
+debt     10000
          15000
At risk   15000

Deduct all  11000

Kelly invests $5,000 in the Kelly Green Limited Partnership as a 5% general partner. Shortly thereafter, the partnership acquires the master recording of a well-known vocalist for $250,000 ($50,000 from the partnership and $200,000 secured from a local bank by means of a *recourse* mortgage). Assume Kelly's share of the recourse debt is $10,000, and her basis in her partnership interest is $15,000 ($5,000 cash investment + $10,000 debt share). Since the debt is recourse, Kelly's at-risk amount is also $15,000. Kelly's share of partnership losses in the first year of operations is $11,000. Kelly is entitled to deduct the full $11,000 of partnership losses under both the overall and the at-risk limitations because this amount is less than both her outside basis and at-risk amount. ■

**EXAMPLE 38**

*Handwritten notes:*
Basis   15000
At risk  5000
Can deduct

Assume the same facts as in Example 37, except the bank loan is nonrecourse (the partners have no direct liability under the terms of the loan in the case of a default). Kelly's basis in her partnership interest still is $15,000, but she can deduct only $5,000 of the flow-through loss. The amount she has at risk in the partnership does not include the nonrecourse debt. (The debt does not relate to real estate so it is not qualified nonrecourse debt.) ■

**Passive Activity Rules.** A partnership loss share may be disallowed under the passive activity rules. These rules apply to partners who are individuals, estates, trusts, closely held C corporations, or personal service corporations. The rules require the partners to separate their interests in partnership activities into three groups:

- *Active.* Earned income, such as salary and wages; income or loss from a trade or business in which the partner materially participates; and guaranteed payments received by the partner for services.
- *Portfolio.* Annuity income, interest, dividends, guaranteed payments from a partnership for interest on capital, royalties not derived in the ordinary course of a trade or business, and gains and losses from disposal of investment assets.
- *Passive.* Income from a trade or business activity in which the partner does not materially participate on a regular, continuous, and substantial basis,[45] or income from many rental activities.

Material participation in an activity is determined annually. The burden is on the partner to prove material participation. The IRS has provided a number of objective tests for determining material participation. In general, these tests require the partner to have substantial involvement in daily operations of the activity. Thus, a Maine vacation resort operator investing in a California grape farm or an electrical engineer employed in Virginia investing in an Iowa corn and hog farm may have difficulty proving material participation in the activities.

Rent income from real or personal property generally is passive income, regardless of the partner's level of participation. Exceptions are made for rent income from activities where substantial services are provided (e.g., certain developers, resorts); from hotels, motels, and other transient lodging; from short-term equipment rentals; and from certain developed real estate.

---

[44]§ 465(a)(2).

[45]§§ 469(c)(1) and (2).

Usually, passive activity losses can be offset only against passive activity income.[46] In determining the net passive activity loss for a year, losses and income from all passive activities are aggregated. The amount of suspended losses carried forward from a particular activity is determined by the ratio of the net loss from that activity to the aggregate net loss from all passive activities for the year. A special rule for rental real estate (discussed in the following section) allows a limited $25,000 offset against nonpassive income.[47]

A partner making a taxable disposition of an entire interest in a passive activity takes a full deduction for suspended passive activity losses from that activity in the year of disposal.[48] Suspended losses are deductible against income in the following order: income or gain from the passive activity, net income or gain from all passive activities, and other income. When a passive activity is transferred in a primarily nontaxable exchange (e.g., a like-kind exchange or contribution to a partnership), suspended losses are deductible only to the extent of gains recognized on the transfer. Remaining losses are deducted on disposal of the activity received in the exchange.

**EXAMPLE 39**

Debra has several investments in passive activities that generate aggregate losses of $10,000 in the current year. Debra wants to deduct all of these losses on her current-year tax return. To assure a loss deduction, she needs to invest in some passive activities that generate income. One of her long-time friends, an entrepreneur in the women's apparel business, is interested in opening a new apparel store in a nearby community. Debra is willing to finance a substantial part of the expansion but does not want to get involved with day-to-day operations. Debra also wants to limit any possible loss to her initial investment.

After substantial discussions, Debra and her friend decide to form a limited partnership, which will own the new store. Debra's friend will be the general partner, and Debra will be a limited partner. Debra invests $100,000, and her friend invests $50,000 and sweat equity (provides managerial skills and know-how). Each has a 50% interest in profits and losses. In the first year of operations, the store generates a profit of $30,000. Since Debra's share of the profit ($15,000) is passive activity income, it can be fully utilized against any of her passive activity losses on other investments. Thus, Debra's share of the apparel store profits enables her to obtain a full deduction of her $10,000 of passive activity losses. ■

**Rental Real Estate Losses.** In any one year, individuals can offset up to $25,000 of passive losses from rental real estate against active and portfolio income. The $25,000 maximum is reduced by 50 percent of the difference between the taxpayer's modified AGI and $100,000. Thus, when the taxpayer's modified AGI reaches $150,000, the offset is eliminated.

The offset is available to those who actively (rather than materially) participate in rental real estate activities. Active participation is an easier test to meet. Unlike material participation, it does not require regular, continuous, and substantial involvement with the activity. However, the taxpayer must own at least 10 percent of the fair market value of all interests in the rental property and either contribute to the activity's management decisions in a significant and bona fide way or actively participate in arranging for others to make such decisions.

**EXAMPLE 40**

Raoul invests $10,000 cash in the Sparrow Limited Partnership in the current year for a 10% limited interest in capital and profits. Shortly thereafter, the partnership purchases rental real estate subject to a qualified nonrecourse mortgage of $120,000 obtained from a commercial bank. Raoul has no other passive loss activities during the current year.

[46]§ 469(a)(1).
[47]§ 469(i).

[48]§ 469(g).

*At risk 22000*

Raoul does not participate in any of Sparrow's activities. His share of losses from Sparrow's first year of operations is $27,000. His modified AGI before considering the loss is $60,000. Before considering the loss, Raoul's basis in the partnership interest is $22,000 [$10,000 cash + (10% × $120,000 debt)], and his loss deduction is limited to this amount under the overall limitation. The debt is included in Raoul's amount at risk because it is qualified nonrecourse financing. It may seem that Raoul should be allowed to deduct the $22,000 loss share from portfolio or active income under the rental real estate exception to the passive losses. However, the loss may not be offset against this income because Raoul is not an active participant in the partnership. ■

---

**LO.9**

Describe the treatment of transactions between a partner and the partnership.

# Transactions between Partner and Partnership

Many types of transactions occur between a partnership and one of its partners. The partner may contribute property to the partnership, perform services for the partnership, or receive distributions from the partnership. The partner may borrow money from or lend money to the partnership. Property may be bought and sold between the partner and the partnership. Several of these transactions were discussed earlier in the chapter. The remaining types of partner-partnership transactions are the focus of this section.

## GUARANTEED PAYMENTS

If a partnership makes a payment to a partner, the payment may be a draw against the partner's share of partnership income; a return of some or all of the partner's original capital contribution; or a guaranteed payment, among other treatments. A **guaranteed payment** is a payment for services performed by the partner or for the use of the partner's capital. The payment may not be determined by reference to partnership income. Guaranteed payments are usually expressed as a fixed-dollar amount or as a percentage of capital that the partner has invested in the partnership. Whether the partnership deducts or capitalizes the guaranteed payment depends on the nature of the payment.

**EXAMPLE 41**

David, Donald, and Dale formed the accrual basis DDD Partnership in 2003. According to the partnership agreement, David is to manage the partnership and receive a $21,000 distribution from the entity every year, payable in 12 monthly installments. Donald is to receive an amount that is equal to 18% of his capital account, as it is computed by the firm's accountant at the beginning of the year, payable in 12 monthly installments. Dale is the partnership's advertising specialist. He withdraws approximately 3% of the partnership's net income every month for his personal use. David and Donald receive guaranteed payments from the partnership, but Dale does not. ■

Guaranteed payments resemble the salary or interest payments of other businesses and receive somewhat similar income tax treatment.[49] In contrast to the provision that usually applies to withdrawals of assets by partners from their partnerships, guaranteed payments are deductible (or capitalized) by the entity. Deductible guaranteed payments, like any other deductible expenses of a partnership, can create an ordinary loss for the entity.

---

[49]§ 707(c).

A partner who receives guaranteed payments during a partnership year must include the payments in income as if they were received on the last day of the partnership year. Guaranteed payments are always taxable as ordinary income to the recipient partner.

---

**EXAMPLE 42**

*[handwritten notes: David – guaranteed 21000? Donald – guaranteed – 17000 Dale – withdraws – 20000 withdraws reduce basis]*

Continue with the situation introduced in Example 41. For calendar year 2003, David receives the $21,000 as provided by the partnership agreement, Donald's guaranteed payment for 2003 is $17,000, and Dale withdraws $20,000. Before considering these amounts, the partnership's ordinary income for 2003 is $650,000.

The partnership can deduct its payments to David and Donald, so the final amount of its 2003 ordinary income is $612,000 ($650,000 − $21,000 − $17,000). Thus, each of the equal partners is allocated $204,000 of ordinary partnership income for their 2003 individual income tax returns ($612,000 ÷ 3). In addition, David reports the $21,000 guaranteed payment as income on his 2003 tax return, and Donald similarly includes the $17,000 guaranteed payment in his 2003 income. Dale's partnership draw is deemed to have come from his allocated $204,000 (or from the accumulated partnership income that was taxed in prior years) and is not taxed separately to him. Dale's basis, though, is reduced by the $20,000 distribution. ■

---

**EXAMPLE 43**

Assume the same facts as in Example 42, except that the partnership's tax year ends on March 31, 2004. The total amount of the guaranteed payments is taxable to the partners on that date. Thus, even though David received 9 of his 12 payments for fiscal 2004 in calendar 2003, all of his guaranteed payments are taxable to him in 2004. Similarly, all of Donald's guaranteed payments are taxable to him in 2004 and not when they are received. The deduction for, and the gross income from, guaranteed payments is allowed on the same date that all of the other income and expense items relative to the partnership are allocated to the partners (on the last day of the entity's tax year). ■

## OTHER TRANSACTIONS BETWEEN A PARTNER AND A PARTNERSHIP

Certain transactions between a partner and the partnership are treated as if the partner were an outsider, dealing with the partnership at arm's length.[50] Loan transactions, rental payments, and sales of property between the partner and the partnership are generally treated in this manner. In addition, payments for services are treated this way when the services are short-term technical services that the partner also provides for parties other than the partnership.

---

**EXAMPLE 44**

*[handwritten notes: Land FMV 30000? AB <17000> gain on sale 13000]*

Emilio, a one-third partner in the ABC Partnership, owns a tract of land that the partnership wishes to purchase. The land has a fair market value of $30,000 and an adjusted basis to Emilio of $17,000. If Emilio sells the land to the partnership, he recognizes a $13,000 gain on the sale, and the partnership takes a $30,000 cost basis in the land. If the land has a fair market value of $10,000 on the sale date, Emilio recognizes a $7,000 loss. ■

---

The timing of the deduction for a payment by an accrual basis partnership to a cash basis service partner depends upon whether the payment is a guaranteed payment or a payment to a partner who is treated as an outsider. A guaranteed payment is includible in the partner's income on the last day of the partnership year when it is properly accrued by the partnership, even though the payment may not be made to the partner until the next taxable year. Conversely, the *partner's* method of accounting controls the timing of the deduction if the payment is treated

---

[50]§ 707(a).

as made to an outsider. This is because a deduction cannot be claimed for such amounts until the recipient partner is required to include the amount in income under the partner's method of accounting.[51] Thus, a partnership cannot claim a deduction until it actually makes the payment to the cash basis partner, but it could accrue and deduct a payment due to an accrual basis partner even if payment was not yet made.

**EXAMPLE 45**

Rachel, a cash basis taxpayer, is a partner in the accrual basis RTC Partnership. On December 31, 2003, the partnership accrues but does not pay $10,000 for deductible services that Rachel performed for the partnership during the year. Both Rachel and the partnership are calendar year taxpayers.

If the $10,000 accrual is a guaranteed payment, the partnership deducts the $10,000 in its calendar year ended December 31, 2003, and Rachel includes the $10,000 in her income for the 2003 calendar year. That Rachel is a cash basis taxpayer and does not actually receive the cash in 2003 is irrelevant.

If the payment is classified as a payment to an outsider, the partnership cannot deduct the payment until Rachel actually receives the cash. If, for example, Rachel performs janitorial services (i.e., not in her capacity as a partner) and receives the cash on March 25, 2004, the partnership deducts the payment and Rachel recognizes the income on that date. ■

**Sales of Property.** Certain sales of property fall under special rules. No loss is recognized on a sale of property between a person and a partnership when the person owns, directly or indirectly, more than 50 percent of partnership capital or profits.[52] The disallowed loss may not vanish entirely, however. If the transferee eventually sells the property at a gain, the disallowed loss reduces the gain that the transferee would otherwise recognize.

**EXAMPLE 46**

Barry sells land (adjusted basis to him, $30,000; fair market value, $45,000) to a partnership in which he controls a 60% capital interest. The partnership pays him only $20,000 for the land. Barry cannot deduct his $10,000 realized loss. The sale apparently was not at arm's length, but the taxpayer's intentions are irrelevant. Barry and the partnership are related parties, and the loss is disallowed.

When the partnership sells the land to an outsider at a later date, it receives a sales price of $44,000. The partnership can offset the recognition of its $24,000 realized gain on the subsequent sale ($44,000 sales proceeds − $20,000 adjusted basis) by the amount of the $10,000 prior disallowed loss ($30,000 − $20,000). Thus, the partnership recognizes a $14,000 gain on its sale of the land. ■

Using a similar rationale, any gain that is realized on a sale or exchange between a partner and a partnership in which the partner controls a capital or profit interest of more than 50 percent must be recognized as ordinary income, unless the asset is a capital asset to both the seller and the purchaser.[53]

**EXAMPLE 47**

Kristin purchases some land (adjusted basis, $30,000; fair market value, $45,000) for $45,000 from a partnership in which she controls a 90% profit interest. The land was a capital asset to the partnership. If Kristin holds the land as a capital asset, the partnership recognizes a $15,000 capital gain. However, if Kristin is a land developer and the property is not a capital asset to her, the partnership must recognize $15,000 ordinary income from the sale, even though the property was a capital asset to the partnership. ■

[51]§ 267(a)(2).
[52]§ 707(b).

[53]§ 707(b)(2).

## CONCEPT SUMMARY 10–3

### Partner-Partnership Transactions

1. Partners can transact business with their partnerships in a nonpartner capacity. These transactions include such things as the sale and exchange of property, rentals, loans of funds, etc.
2. A payment to a partner may be classified as a guaranteed payment if it is for services or use of the partner's capital and is not based on partnership income. A guaranteed payment may be deductible by the partnership and is included in the partner's income on the last day of the partnership's taxable year.
3. A payment to a partner may be treated as being to an outside (though related) party. Such a payment is deductible or capitalizable by the partnership at the time it must be included in income under the partner's method of accounting.
4. Guaranteed payments and payments to a partner that are treated as being to an outside party are only deductible if the underlying reason for the payment constitutes an ordinary and necessary (rather than capitalizable) business expense.
5. Losses are disallowed between a partner or related party and a partnership when the partner or related party owns more than a 50% interest in the partnership's capital or profits.
6. When there is income from a related-party sale, it is treated as ordinary income if the property is not a capital asset to both the transferor and the transferee.

### PARTNERS AS EMPLOYEES

A partner usually does not qualify as an employee for tax purposes. Thus, a partner receiving guaranteed payments is not regarded as an employee of the partnership for purposes of withholding taxes. Moreover, since a partner is not an employee, the partnership cannot deduct its payments for the partner's fringe benefits. A general partner's distributive share of ordinary partnership income and guaranteed payments for services are generally subject to the Federal self-employment tax.[54]

Concept Summary 10–3 reviews partner-partnership transactions.

### CHOOSING PARTNERSHIP TAXATION

**LO.10**

Provide insights regarding advantageous use of a partnership.

**Tax Planning Considerations**

Concept Summary 10–4 enumerates various factors that the owners of a business should consider in deciding whether to use a C corporation, S corporation, or partnership as a means of doing business. The reader should refer back to this list after reading Chapters 11 (advanced partnership topics) and 12 (S corporations). Chapter 13 includes a more elaborate discussion of the tax effects of various forms of conducting business.

### FORMATION AND OPERATION OF A PARTNERSHIP

Potential partners should be cautious in transferring assets to a partnership to ensure that they are not required to recognize any gain upon the creation of the entity. The nonrecognition provisions of § 721 are relatively straightforward and resemble the provisions under § 351, which permit certain tax-free property transfers to corporations. However, any partner can make a tax-deferred contribution of assets to the entity either at the inception of the partnership or later. This possibility is not available to less-than-controlling shareholders in a corporation.

---

[54] § 1402(a).

## CONCEPT SUMMARY 10–4

### Advantages and Disadvantages of the Partnership Form

The partnership form may be attractive when one or more of the following factors is present:

- The entity is generating net taxable losses and/or valuable tax credits, which will be of use to the owners.
- The owners want to avoid complex corporate administrative and filing requirements.
- Other means of reducing the effects of the double taxation of corporate business income (e.g., compensation to owners, interest, and rental payments) have been exhausted.
- The entity does not generate material amounts of tax preference and adjustment items, which increase the alternative minimum tax liabilities of its owners.
- The entity is generating net passive income, which its owners can use to claim immediate deductions for net passive losses that they have generated from other sources.
- Given the asset holdings and distribution practices of the entity, the possibility of liability under the accumulated earnings and personal holding company taxes is significant.
- The owners wish to make special allocations of certain income or deduction items that are not possible under the C or S corporation forms.
- The owners anticipate liquidation of the entity within a short period of time. Liquidation of a C or S corporation would generate entity-level recognized gains on appreciated property distributed.
- The owners have adequate bases in their partnership interests to facilitate the deduction of flow-through losses and the assignment of an adequate basis to assets distributed in-kind to the partners.

The partnership form may be less attractive when one or more of the following factors is present:

- The tax paid by the individual owners on the entity's income is greater than the tax the entity would pay if it were a C corporation, and the income is not expected to be distributed soon. (If distributed by a C corporation, double taxation would likely occur.)
- The entity is generating net taxable income without distributing any cash to the partners. The owners may not have sufficient cash with which to pay the tax on the entity's earnings.
- The type of income that the entity is generating (e.g., business and portfolio income) is not as attractive to its owners as net passive income would be because the owners could use net passive income to offset the net passive losses that they have generated on their own.
- The entity is in a high-exposure business, and the owners desire protection from personal liability. An LLC or LLP structure may be available, however, to limit personal liability.
- The owners want to avoid Federal self-employment tax.

The partners should anticipate the tax benefits and pitfalls that are presented in Subchapter K and should take appropriate actions to resolve any potential problems before they arise. Typically, all that is needed is an appropriate provision in the partnership agreement (e.g., with respect to differing allocation percentages for gains and losses). Recall, however, that a special allocation of income, expense, or credit items in the partnership agreement must satisfy certain requirements before it is acceptable to the IRS.

### TRANSACTIONS BETWEEN PARTNERS AND PARTNERSHIPS

Partners should be careful when engaging in transactions with the partnership to ensure that no negative tax results occur. A partner who owns a majority of the partnership generally should not sell property at a loss to the partnership because

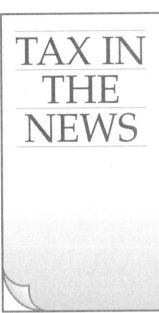

### PARTNERSHIPS AROUND THE WORLD—AND BEYOND

Technology continues to act as a catalyst—and incentive—for the creation of joint ventures. From Web kiosks at gas stations to global satellite networks, high-tech companies are forging alliances to bring technology to consumers.

Both Microsoft and AOL Time Warner have teamed up with various gas stations, pizza parlors, and numerous other retail outlets to offer programming. These ventures appear to be spurred by a desire to capture larger shares of the ever-expanding advertising market.

Meanwhile, the largest U.S. telecommunications companies are continuing to align themselves with partners in foreign markets: each wants to have the widest possible service coverage area so it can offer efficient communications and computer networking to business clients with a global presence.

Other partnerships have been formed by media and cable companies to offer digital satellite television services on numerous channels to customers for a monthly rental fee. And several partnerships have formed to establish satellite-based Web communications around the world.

the loss is disallowed. Similarly, a majority partner should not sell a capital asset to the partnership at a gain, if the asset is to be used by the partnership as other than a capital asset. The gain on this transaction is taxed as ordinary income to the selling partner rather than as capital gain.

As an alternative to selling property to a partnership, the partner should consider a lease arrangement. The partner recognizes rent income, and the partnership has a rent expense. A partner who needs more cash immediately can sell the property to an outside third party; then the third party can lease the property to the partnership for a fair rental.

The timing of the deduction for payments by accrual basis partnerships to cash basis partners varies depending on whether the payment is a guaranteed payment or is treated as a payment to an outsider. If the payment is a guaranteed payment, the deduction occurs when the partnership makes the accrual. If the payment is treated as a payment to an outsider, the actual date the payment is made controls the timing of the deduction.

## DRAFTING THE PARTNERSHIP AGREEMENT

Although a written partnership agreement is not required, many rules governing the tax consequences to partners and their partnerships refer to such an agreement. Remember that a partner's distributive share of income, gain, loss, deduction, or credit is determined in accordance with the partnership agreement. Consequently, if taxpayers operating a business in partnership form want a measure of certainty as to the tax consequences of their activities, a carefully drafted partnership agreement is crucial. An agreement that sets forth the obligations, rights, and powers of the partners should prove invaluable in settling controversies among them and provide some degree of certainty as to the tax consequences of the partners' actions.

## KEY TERMS

Aggregate concept, 10–8

Basis in partnership interest, 10–8

Capital account, 10–8

Capital interest, 10–7

Capital sharing ratio, 10–7

Constructive liquidation scenario, 10–29

Disguised sale, 10–11

Economic effect test, 10–24

Electing large partnership, 10–6

Entity concept, 10–8

General partnership, 10–4

Guaranteed payment, 10–37

Inside basis, 10–14

Least aggregate deferral rule, 10–19

Limited liability company (LLC), 10–4

Limited liability partnership (LLP), 10–4

Limited partnership, 10–4

Nonrecourse debt, 10–29

Outside basis, 10–14

Precontribution gain or loss, 10–25

Profit and loss sharing ratios, 10–7

Profits (loss) interest, 10–7

Qualified nonrecourse debt, 10–34

Recourse debt, 10–29

Separately stated item, 10–5

Special allocation, 10–7

Syndication costs, 10–17

## PROBLEM MATERIALS

### Discussion Questions

1. Distinguish between the entity concept and the aggregate or conduit concept of partnership taxation.

2. Dan is an attorney who is financially quite successful. Mary is a real estate developer who has little cash for investment. The two decide to buy some real estate. Dan will contribute the money to buy the properties and have veto power over which properties to purchase. Mary will make all other decisions. Profits and losses from the operation will be shared equally.
   a. Is this a partnership for tax purposes? Why or why not?
   b. Would your answer change if Dan had no veto power and was to receive a guaranteed 10% annual return on his money?

*Issue ID*

*Decision Making*

3. Justin and Tiffany will contribute property to form the equal TJ Partnership. Justin will contribute cash of $20,000 plus land with a fair market value of $80,000 and an adjusted basis of $65,000. Tiffany currently operates a sole proprietorship with assets valued at $100,000 and an adjusted basis of $125,000. Tiffany can either contribute these assets to the partnership or sell them to Sanford Salvage for their fair market value and then contribute the $100,000 cash to the partnership. The partnership needs assets similar to those owned by Tiffany, but it can purchase new assets for $110,000. Describe the tax consequences of the formation to Tiffany, Justin, and the partnership. Be sure to discuss how the results would differ if Tiffany sells the property rather than contributing it.

*Issue ID*

4. Gerald owns property (basis of $120,000 and value of $240,000) that he plans to contribute to the GMW Partnership in exchange for a one-third interest. What issues arise if the partnership distributes $60,000 of cash to Gerald three months after the property contribution? What techniques can be used to minimize the risk that any adverse tax consequences might arise?

5. What types of expenditures might a new partnership incur? How will these costs be treated for Federal tax purposes?

*Issue ID*

6. Browne and Red, both C corporations, formed the BR Partnership on January 1, 2002. Neither Browne nor Red is a personal service corporation, and BR is not a tax shelter. BR's gross receipts were $4.6 million, $5 million, and $6 million, respectively, for the three tax years ending in 2002, 2003, and 2004. Describe the methods of accounting available to BR in each tax year.

7. What effect does the contribution of property subject to a liability have on the basis of the contributing partner's interest? What is the effect on the basis of the other partners' interests?

8. Discuss the adjustments that must be made to a partner's basis in the partnership interest. When are such adjustments made?

9. Describe the three limitations that apply to the deductibility of a loss from a partnership, and indicate the order in which these limitations are applied.

10. What are guaranteed payments?

**Issue ID**

11. Sam has operated a microbrewery (sole proprietorship) in southern Oregon for the past 15 years. The business has been highly profitable lately, and demand for the product will soon exceed the amount Sam can produce with his present facilities. Marcie, a long-time fan of the brewery, has offered to invest $1.5 million for equipment to expand production. The assets and goodwill of the brewery are currently worth $1 million (tax basis is only $200,000). Sam will continue to manage the business. He is not willing to own less than 50% of whatever arrangement they arrive at. What issues should Sam and Marcie address and document before finalizing their venture?

12. Discuss the advantages and disadvantages of the partnership entity form compared with the C corporation form.

13. Comment on the validity of the following statements:
    a. Since a partnership is not a taxable entity, it is not required to file any type of tax return.
    b. Each partner can choose a different method of accounting and depreciation computation in determining the gross income from the entity.
    c. Generally, a transfer of appreciated property to a partnership results in recognized gain to the contributing partner at the time of the transfer.
    d. A partner can carry forward, for an unlimited period of time, the share of any partnership operating losses that exceed the partner's basis in the entity, provided the partner retains an ownership interest in the partnership.
    e. When a partner renders services to the entity in exchange for an unrestricted interest, that partner does not recognize any gross income.
    f. Losses on sales between a partner and the partnership <u>always</u> are nondeductible.
    g. A partnership may choose a year that results in the least aggregate deferral of tax to the partners, unless the IRS requires the use of an alternative tax year under the "business purpose" test.
    h. A partner's basis in a partnership interest includes that partner's share of partnership recourse and nonrecourse liabilities.
    i. Built-in loss related to nondepreciable property contributed to a partnership must be allocated to the contributing partner to the extent the loss is eventually recognized by the partnership.
    j. Property that was held as inventory by a contributing partner, but is a capital asset in the hands of the partnership, results in a capital gain if the partnership immediately sells the property.

## Problems

14. Kate and Drew form an equal partnership with a cash contribution of $70,000 from Kate and a property contribution (adjusted basis of $60,000 and a fair market value of $70,000) from Drew.
    a. How much gain, if any, must Kate recognize on the transfer? Must Drew recognize any gain?
    b. What is Kate's basis in her partnership interest?
    c. What is Drew's basis in his partnership interest?
    d. What basis does the partnership take in the property transferred by Drew?

Decision Making

15. James and Lynne form an equal partnership with a cash contribution of $40,000 from James and a property contribution (adjusted basis of $60,000 and a fair market value of $40,000) from Lynne.
    a. How much gain or loss, if any, does Lynne realize on the transfer? May Lynne recognize any gain or loss?
    b. What is James's basis in his partnership interest?
    c. What is Lynne's basis in her partnership interest?
    d. What basis does the partnership take in the property transferred by Lynne?
    e. Are there more effective ways to structure the formation?

16. Three years after the H&L Partnership is formed, Lewis, a 25% partner, contributes an additional $75,000 cash and land he has held for investment. Lewis's basis in the land is $20,000, and its fair market value is $25,000. His basis in the partnership interest was $60,000 before this contribution. The partnership uses the land as a parking lot for four years and then sells it for $45,000.
    a. How much gain or loss does Lewis recognize on the contribution?
    b. What is Lewis's basis in his partnership interest immediately following this contribution?
    c. How much gain or loss does H&L recognize on this contribution?
    d. What is H&L's basis in the property it receives from Lewis?
    e. How much gain or loss does the partnership recognize on the later sale of the land, and what is the character of the gain or loss? How much is allocated to Lewis?

Decision Making

17. Nate and Ashley are equal members of the NA Partnership, formed on June 1 of the current year. Nate contributed land that his father gave him three years ago. Nate's father purchased the land in 1980 for $40,000. The land was worth $70,000 at the date of the gift. The fair market value of the land was $100,000 at the date it was contributed to the partnership.

    Ashley has significant experience developing real estate. After the partnership is formed, she will prepare a plan for developing the property and secure zoning approvals for the partnership. She would normally bill a third party $40,000 for these efforts. Ashley will also contribute $60,000 cash in exchange for her 50% interest in the partnership. The value of her 50% interest is $100,000.
    a. How much gain or income will Nate recognize on his contribution of the land to the partnership? What is the character of any gain or income recognized?
    b. What basis will Nate take in his partnership interest?
    c. How much gain or income will Ashley recognize on the formation of the partnership? What is the character of any gain or income recognized?
    d. What basis will Ashley take in her partnership interest?
    e. Construct an opening balance sheet for the partnership reflecting the partnership's basis in assets and the fair market value of these assets.
    f. Outline any planning opportunities that may minimize current taxation to any of the parties.

Decision Making

18. Continue with the facts presented in Problem 17. At the end of the first year, the partnership distributes $40,000 cash to Nate. No distribution is made to Ashley.
    a. Under general tax rules, how would the payment to Nate be treated?
    b. How much income or gain would Nate recognize as a result of the payment?
    c. Under general tax rules, what basis would the partnership take in the land Nate contributed?
    d. What alternative treatment might the IRS try to impose?
    e. Under the alternative treatment, how much income or gain would Nate recognize?
    f. Under the alternative treatment, what basis would the partnership take in the land contributed by Nate?
    g. How can the transaction be restructured to minimize risk of IRS recharacterization?

19. The SJ Partnership was formed to acquire land and subdivide it as residential housing lots. On July 1, 2003, Sarah contributed land valued at $200,000 to the partnership in exchange for a 50% interest. She had purchased the land in 1998 for $160,000 and held it for investment purposes (capital asset). The partnership holds the land as inventory.

On the same date, Joe contributed land valued at $200,000 that he had purchased in 1997 for $240,000. He also became a 50% owner. Joe is a real estate developer, but he held this land personally for investment purposes. The partnership holds this land as inventory.

In 2004, the partnership sells the land contributed by Sarah for $220,000. In 2005, the partnership sells half of the subdivided real estate contributed by Joe for $88,000. The other half is finally sold in 2010 for $110,000.

a. What is each partner's initial basis in his or her partnership interest?

b. What is the amount of gain or loss recognized on the sale of the land contributed by Sarah? What is the character of this gain or loss?

c. What is the amount of gain or loss recognized in 2005 and 2010 on the sale of the land contributed by Joe? What is the character of this gain or loss?

20. The partnership agreement for the SJ Partnership in Problem 19 provides that all gains and losses are allocated equally between the partners unless otherwise required under the tax law.

a. How will the gains or losses determined in (b) and (c) in Problem 19 be allocated to each of the partners?

b. Calculate each partner's basis in his or her partnership interest at December 31, 2010. Assume the partnership has no transactions through the end of the year 2010 other than the transactions described in Problem 19. Why are these balances the same or different?

21. The cash basis Sparrow Partnership incurred the following costs in 2003, the partnership's initial year of operations:

| | |
|---|---|
| Legal fees for preparing partnership agreement | $ 3,000 |
| Printing costs for preparing documents used to help sell the partnership interests | 16,000 |
| Accounting fees for tax advice of an organizational nature | 5,000 |
| Pre-opening expenses to establish office, set up accounting systems, advertise for business, etc. | 20,000 |

All of these costs were paid in 2003, except for $1,000 of the legal fees, which were not paid until 2004. If the partnership begins business in July 2003, how much can Sparrow deduct in that year? In 2004? What elections must the partnership make in its initial tax return to secure the deductions?

22. The Owl Partnership was formed on May 1 of the current year and admitted Harry and Ron as equal partners on that date. The partners contributed $150,000 cash each and borrowed $300,000 from a local bank to establish a specialty book store. The partners spent May and June buying inventory, equipment, supplies, and advertising for their "Grand Opening" on July 1. The partnership will use the accrual method of accounting. The partnership incurred the following costs during its first year of operations:

- Purchased all assets of Floomish & Botts of New York, including:

| | |
|---|---|
| Inventory | $120,000 |
| Shop fixtures, racks, shelves, etc. | 50,000 |
| Store building | 200,000 |

- Other costs:

| | |
|---|---|
| Additional inventory | $400,000 |
| Transfer tax to acquire building | 10,000 |
| Building renovation costs | 50,000 |
| Legal fees to form partnership | 12,000 |
| Advertising for "Grand Opening" | 9,000 |
| Advertising after opening | 5,000 |

| | |
|---|---:|
| Consulting fees for establishing accounting system | $ 8,000 |
| Additional equipment rental, eight months at $3,000/month | 24,000 |
| Utilities at $500 per month | 4,000 |
| Salaries to sales clerks | 40,000 |
| Payments to Harry and Ron for services ($3,500/month each for six months, beginning in July) | 42,000 |
| Tax return preparation expense | 6,000 |

- Revenues during the year included the following:

| | |
|---|---:|
| Sales revenues | $750,000 |
| Interest income on bank balances | 2,000 |

- Inventory remaining at the end of the year was valued at $80,000 on a FIFO basis.

a. Determine how each of the above costs and revenues is treated by the partnership, and identify the period over which the costs can be deducted, if any.
b. Calculate the amortization deduction for any amortizable costs.
c. Identify any elections the partnership should make on its initial tax return.

23. Justin, Kara, and Lindsey form the JKL Partnership on January 1 of the current year. Justin is a 50% partner, and Kara and Lindsey are each 25% partners. Each partner and JKL use the cash method of accounting. For reporting purposes, Justin uses a calendar year, Kara uses an October 31 fiscal year, and Lindsey uses a June 30 fiscal year. What is JKL's required tax year under the least aggregate deferral method?

24. Lisa and Lori are equal members of the Redbird Partnership. They are real estate investors who formed the partnership several years ago with equal cash contributions. Redbird then purchased a piece of land.

On January 1 of the current year, to acquire a one-third interest in the entity, Lana contributed to the partnership some land she had held for investment. Lana purchased the land three years ago for $30,000; its fair market value at the contribution date was $40,000. No special allocation agreements were in effect before or after Lana was admitted to the partnership. The Redbird Partnership holds all land for investment.

Immediately before Lana's property contribution, the balance sheet of the Redbird Partnership was as follows:

| | Basis | FMV | | Basis | FMV |
|---|---|---|---|---|---|
| Land | $5,000 | $80,000 | Lisa, capital | $2,500 | $40,000 |
| | | | Lori, capital | 2,500 | 40,000 |
| | $5,000 | $80,000 | | $5,000 | $80,000 |

a. At the contribution date, what is Lana's basis in her interest in the Redbird Partnership?
b. When does the partnership's holding period begin for the contributed land?
c. On June 30 of the current year, the partnership sold the land contributed by Lana for $40,000. How much is the recognized gain or loss, and how is it allocated among the partners?
d. Prepare a balance sheet reflecting basis and fair market value for the partnership immediately after the land sale described in (c). Assume no other transactions occurred during the tax year.

25. Assume the same facts as in Problem 24, with the following exceptions.

- Lana purchased the land three years ago for $50,000. Its fair market value was $40,000 when it was contributed to the partnership.
- Redbird sold the land contributed by Lana for $34,000.

a. How much is the recognized gain or loss, and how is it allocated among the partners?

b. Prepare a balance sheet reflecting basis and fair market value for the partnership immediately after the land sale. Also prepare schedules that support the amount in each partner's capital account.

26. Earl and Zelda are equal partners in the accrual basis EZ Partnership. At the beginning of the current year, Earl's capital account has a balance of $10,000, and the partnership has recourse debts of $30,000 payable to unrelated parties. All partnership recourse debt is shared equally between the partners. The following information about EZ's operations for the current year is obtained from the partnership's records:

| | |
|---|---|
| Taxable income | $10,000 |
| § 1231 gain | 6,000 |
| Long-term capital gain | 2,000 |
| Short-term capital loss | 600 |
| Charitable contribution to Red Cross | 200 |
| Cash distribution to Earl | 14,000 |
| Payment of Earl's medical expenses | 6,000 |

Assume that year-end partnership debt payable to unrelated parties is $40,000.

a. If all transactions are reflected in his beginning capital and basis in the same manner, what is Earl's basis in the partnership interest at the beginning of the year?

b. If all transactions are reflected in his beginning capital and basis in the same manner, what is Earl's basis in the partnership interest at the end of the current year?

27. The BAG Partnership reported the following items during the current tax year:

| | |
|---|---|
| Taxable income | $200,000 |
| Municipal bond interest income | 8,000 |
| Gain on sale of real estate | 80,000 |

Taxable income includes $20,000 of income from collection of cash basis accounts receivable contributed by 50% partner Barry at the beginning of the year.

The municipal bond income was earned on bonds contributed by 25% partner Aaron. None of the interest was accrued on the contribution date. The partnership agreement provides that all this income will be specially allocated to Aaron this year, and no offsetting allocation will be made now or later.

The real estate gain resulted from the sale of a parcel of land contributed by 25% partner Geneva. When the property was contributed, it was valued at $120,000 and Geneva's basis was $80,000. Assume the real estate is a capital asset to both Geneva and the partnership.

Prepare a schedule showing how each item is allocated to each of the three partners. Assume the partnership will maintain capital account balances and perform all other record keeping required to meet the substantial economic effect requirements of § 704(b).

28. The SS Partnership is owned equally by Sid and Sal. Sal's basis is $20,000 at the beginning of the tax year. Sid's basis is $12,000 at the beginning of the year. SS reported the following income and expenses for the current tax year:

| | |
|---|---|
| Sales revenue | $200,000 |
| Cost of sales | 110,000 |
| Guaranteed payment to Sid | 30,000 |
| Depreciation expense | 15,000 |
| Utilities | 20,000 |
| Rent | 16,000 |
| Interest income | 3,000 |
| Tax-exempt interest income | 6,000 |
| Payment to Medical Center Hospital for Sal's medical expenses | 10,000 |

*[handwritten margin notes top:] Guaranteed paymnt does not affect the basis*

*[handwritten left margin:]*
*separately stated*
*Basis for both*
*Beg. 20000  20000*
*+ ordin 4500  4500*
*+ int. 1500  1500*
*+ tax  3000  3000*
*Dis. <10000>*
*19000  21000*

a. Determine the ordinary partnership income and separately stated items for the partnership.

b. Calculate Sal's basis in her partnership interest at the end of the tax year. What items should Sal report on her Federal income tax return?

c. Calculate Sid's basis in his partnership interest at the end of the tax year. What items should Sid report on his Federal income tax return?

29. Assume the same facts as in Problem 28, except that partnership revenues were $160,000 instead of $200,000.

a. Redetermine the ordinary income and separately stated items for the partnership.

b. Calculate Sal's basis in her partnership interest at the end of the tax year. How much income or loss should Sal report on her Federal income tax return?

c. Calculate Sid's basis in his partnership interest at the end of the tax year. How much income or loss should Sid report on his Federal income tax return?

**Decision Making**

*[handwritten left margin:]*
*outside basis  24000*
*At risk  24000*
*last yr  Current yr*
*24000  120000*
*<24000>  0.000 25%*
*0 —> <6000>*
*Suspended  4000*

30. As of January 1 of last year, Don's outside basis and at-risk limitation for his 25% interest in the DEF Partnership were $24,000. Don and the partnership use the calendar year for tax purposes. The partnership incurred an operating loss of $120,000 for last year and a profit of $40,000 for the current year. Don is a material participant in the partnership.

a. How much loss, if any, may Don recognize for last year?

b. How much net reportable income must Don recognize for the current year?

c. What is Don's basis in the partnership as of December 31 of last year?

d. What is Don's basis in the partnership as of December 31 of the current year?

e. What year-end tax planning would you suggest to ensure that Don can deduct his share of partnership losses?

*[handwritten left margin:]*
*→ on return —*
*ordinane*
*int incume*
*Tax exemp income*
*guaranteed paynt*
*Separately.*
*Guranteed P*
*Int incme*
*Tax exempn*
*Distribution*

31. Fred and Manuel each contribute $100,000 to the newly formed FM Partnership in exchange for a 50% interest. The partnership uses the available funds to acquire equipment costing $160,000 and to fund current operating expenses. The partnership agreement provides that depreciation will be allocated 95% to Fred and 5% to Manuel. All other items of income and loss will be allocated equally between the partners. Upon liquidation of the partnership, property will be distributed to the partners in accordance with their capital account balances. Any partner with a negative capital account must contribute cash in the amount of the negative balance to restore the capital account to $0.

In its first year, the partnership reported an ordinary loss (before depreciation) of $40,000 and depreciation expense of $32,000. In its second year, operations broke even (no gain or loss), and the partnership reported depreciation expense of $51,200. On the first day of the third year, the partnership sold the equipment for $120,000 and distributed the cash in accordance with the partnership agreement. The partnership was liquidated at this time.

a. Calculate the partners' bases in their partnership interests at the end of the first and second tax years. Are any losses suspended?

b. Calculate the partners' bases in their partnership interests after reflecting any gain or loss on disposal of the equipment.

c. How will partnership cash balances be distributed to the partners on liquidation?

d. Does the allocation provided in the partnership agreement have economic effect?

e. What observation can you make regarding the value of a deduction to each partner?

32. Rick and Cheryl each contributed $30,000 cash to the cash basis RC Partnership. The partnership uses $50,000 of the cash to purchase a depreciable asset. The partnership agreement provides that depreciation is allocated 75% to Rick and 25% to Cheryl. All other items of partnership income, gain, loss, or deduction are allocated equally between the two partners. During the first year of operations, the partnership produces $15,000 of income before depreciation and deducts $10,000 of depreciation. At the end of the first year, the partnership sells the depreciable asset for its $40,000 book value and liquidates. Assume nothing else happens in the first year that affects the partners' capital accounts.

a. How much cash is distributed to each partner in the liquidating distribution under the economic effect test?

b. If the partnership distributes $8,000 cash to Cheryl on June 30 of the current year, how much cash is distributed to each partner in the liquidating distribution under the economic effect test?

**Decision Making**

**Communications**

33. Your client, the Williams Institute of Technology (WIT), is a 60% partner in the Research Industries Partnership (RIP). WIT is located at 76 Bradford Lane, St. Paul, MN 55164. The controller, Jeanine West, has sent you the following note and a copy of WIT's 2002 Schedule K–1 from the partnership.

**Excerpt from client's note:**

"RIP expects its 2003 operations to include the following:

| | |
|---|---|
| Net loss from operations | $200,000 |
| Capital gain from sale of land | 100,000 |

The land was contributed by DASH, the other partner, when its value was $260,000. The partnership sold the land for $300,000. The partnership used this cash to repay all the partnership debt and pay for operating expenditures, which a tax partner in your firm has said RIP can deduct this year. The net loss of $200,000 reflects that deduction.

We want to be sure we can deduct our full share of this loss, but we do not believe we will have enough basis. We are a material participant in this partnership's activities."

| Items Reported on the 2002 Schedule K–1 | |
|---|---|
| WIT's share of partnership recourse liabilities | $90,000 |
| WIT's ending capital account balance | 30,000 |

Draft a letter to the controller that describes the following:

- WIT's allocation of partnership items.

- WIT's basis in the partnership interest following the allocation.

- Any limitations on loss deductions.

- Any recommendations you have that would allow WIT to claim the full amount of losses in 2003.

Assume WIT's 2002 K–1 accurately reflects the information needed to compute its basis in the partnership interest. Also assume the operating expenditures are fully deductible this year, as the partner said.

Your client has experience researching issues in the Internal Revenue Code, so you may use some citations. However, be sure the letter is written in layperson's terms and cites are minimized.

34. Lee, Brad, and Rick form the LBR Partnership on January 1 of the current year. In return for a 25% interest, Lee transfers property (basis of $15,000, fair market value of $17,500) subject to a nonrecourse liability of $10,000. The liability is assumed by the partnership. Brad transfers property (basis of $16,000, fair market value of $7,500) for a 25% interest, and Rick transfers cash of $15,000 for the remaining 50% interest. (See Example 27 in the text.) Assume the partnership allocates all "third tier" nonrecourse liabilities in accordance with profit sharing ratios.

a. How much gain must Lee recognize on the transfer?

b. What is Lee's basis in his partnership interest?

c. How much loss may Brad recognize on the transfer?

d. What is Brad's basis in his partnership interest?

e. What is Rick's basis in his partnership interest?

f. What basis does the LBR Partnership take in the property transferred by Lee?

g. What is the partnership's basis in the property transferred by Brad?

*[Handwritten marginal notes:]*

Liability Sharing
Lee · basis 15000
— lia. 20000
+ his share 8750
3750

25    25    50
Lee   Brad   Rick
FMV 17500   7500   15000 cash
AB 15000   16000
lia 10000

Basis
AB 15000   16000   15000
lia (5000)   2500   5000
   7500   18500   20000

Liability in excess
FMV 27500    20000 debt
AB 15000
Nonre 20000
   5000   5000   3750
stays with 8750   3750
Lee    8750

a. 0
c. 0   15000+16000+15000
e. 7500
d. 8750

See in the back

35. Assume the same facts as in Problem 34, except that the property contributed by Lee has a fair market value of $27,500 and is subject to a nonrecourse mortgage of $20,000. (See Example 31 in the text.)
    a. What is Lee's basis in his partnership interest?
    b. How much gain must Lee recognize on the transfer?
    c. What is Brad's basis in his partnership interest?
    d. What is Rick's basis in his partnership interest?
    e. What basis does the LBR Partnership take in the property transferred by Lee?

36. The MGP General Partnership was created on January 1 of the current year by having Melinda, Gabe, and Pat each contribute $10,000 cash to the partnership in exchange for a one-third interest in partnership income, gains, losses, deductions, and credits. On December 31 of the current year, the partnership balance sheet reads as follows:

|  | Basis | FMV |  | Basis | FMV |
|---|---|---|---|---|---|
| Assets | $60,000 | $75,000 | Recourse debt | $30,000 | $30,000 |
|  |  |  | Melinda, capital | 14,000 | 19,000 |
|  |  |  | Gabe, capital | 14,000 | 19,000 |
|  |  |  | Pat, capital | 2,000 | 7,000 |
|  |  |  |  | $60,000 | $75,000 |

Pat's capital account is less than Melinda's and Gabe's capital accounts because Pat has withdrawn more cash than the other partners.

How do the partners share the recourse debt as of December 31 of the current year?

37. Kim and Craig plan to form the KC General Partnership by the end of the current year. The partners will each contribute $30,000 cash, and in addition, the partnership will borrow $140,000 from First State Bank. The partnership's land will serve as collateral, and both partners will be required to personally guarantee the debt.

    The tentative agreement provides that 75% of operating income, gains, losses, deductions, and credits will be allocated to Kim for the first five years the partnership is in existence. The remaining 25% is allocated to Craig. Thereafter, all partnership items will be allocated equally. The agreement also provides that capital accounts will be properly maintained and that each partner must restore any deficit in the capital account upon the partnership's liquidation.

    The partners would like to know, before the end of the tax year, how the $140,000 liability will be allocated for basis purposes. Using the format (1) facts, (2) issues, (3) conclusion, and (4) law and analysis, draft a memo to the tax planning file for the KC Partnership that describes how the debt will be shared between the partners for purposes of computing the adjusted basis of each partnership interest.

38. Chris Elton is a 15% partner in the Cardinal Partnership, which is a lessor of residential rental property. Her share of the partnership's losses for the current year is $70,000. Immediately before considering the deductibility of this loss, Chris's capital account (which, in this case, corresponds to her basis excluding liabilities) reflected a balance of $40,000. Her share of partnership recourse liabilities is $10,000, and her share of the nonrecourse liabilities is $6,000. The nonrecourse liability was obtained from an unrelated bank and is secured solely by the real estate.

    Chris is also a partner in the Bluebird Partnership, which has generated income from long-term (more than 30 days) equipment rental activities. Chris's share of Bluebird's income is $23,000. Chris performs substantial services for Bluebird and spends several hundred hours a year working for the Cardinal Partnership.

    Chris's modified adjusted gross income before considering partnership activities is $100,000. Your manager has asked you to determine how much of the $70,000 Cardinal loss Chris can deduct on her current calendar year return. Using the format (1) facts, (2) issues, (3) conclusion, and (4) law and analysis, draft a memo to the client's tax file describing the loss limitations. Be sure to identify the Code sections under which losses are suspended.

39. Fred and Fran are equal partners in the calendar year F&F Partnership. Fred uses a fiscal year ending June 30, and Fran uses a calendar year. Fred receives an annual guaranteed payment of $50,000 from F&F. F&F's taxable income (after deducting Fred's guaranteed payment) was $40,000 for 2003 and $50,000 for 2004.

   a. What is the aggregate amount of income from the partnership that Fred must report for his tax year ending June 30, 2004?

   b. What is the aggregate amount of income from the partnership that Fran must report for her tax year ending December 31, 2004?

   c. Assume Fred's annual guaranteed payment is increased to $60,000 starting on January 1, 2004, and the partnership's taxable income for 2003 and 2004 is the same (i.e., $40,000 and $50,000, respectively). What is the aggregate amount of income from the partnership that Fred must report for his tax year ending June 30, 2004?

40. Ned, a 50% partner in the MN Partnership, is to receive a payment of $35,000 for services. He will also be allocated 50% of the partnership's profits or losses. After deducting the payment to Ned, the partnership has a loss of $25,000. Ned's basis in his partnership interest was $10,000 before these items.

   a. How much, if any, of the $25,000 partnership loss will be allocated to Ned?

   b. What is the net income from the partnership that Ned must report on his Federal income tax return?

   c. What is Ned's basis in his partnership interest following the guaranteed payment and loss allocation?

41. Four Lakes Partnership is owned by four sisters. Anne holds a 70% interest; each of the others owns 10%. Anne sells investment property to the partnership for its fair market value of $100,000 (Anne's basis is $150,000).

   a. How much loss, if any, may Anne recognize?

   b. If the partnership later sells the property for $160,000, how much gain must it recognize?

   c. If Anne's basis in the investment property was $20,000 instead of $150,000, how much, if any, gain would she recognize on the sale, and how would the gain be characterized?

**See Appendix F for Comprehensive Tax Return Problem—Form 1065**

## Research Problems

*Note: Solutions to Research Problems can be prepared by using the **RIA Checkpoint® Student Edition** online research product, or the **CCH U.S. Master Tax Guide Plus™** online Federal tax research database, which is available to accompany this text. It is also possible to prepare solutions to the Research Problems by using tax research materials found in a standard tax library.*

**Communications**

**Research Problem 1.**   Your clients, Mark Henderson and John Burton, each contributed $10,000 cash to form the Realty Management Partnership, a limited partnership. Mark is the general partner, and John is the limited partner. The partnership used the $20,000 cash to make a down payment on a building. The rest of the building's $200,000 purchase price was financed with an interest-only nonrecourse loan of $180,000, which was obtained from an independent third-party bank.

   The partnership allocates all partnership items equally between the partners except for the MACRS deductions and building maintenance, which are allocated 70% to John and 30% to Mark. The partnership definitely wishes to satisfy the "economic effect" requirements of Reg. §§ 1.704–1 and 1.704–2 and will reallocate MACRS, if necessary, to satisfy the requirements of the Regulations.

Under the partnership agreement, liquidation distributions will be paid in proportion to the partners' positive capital account balances. Capital accounts are maintained as required in the Regulations. Mark has an unlimited obligation to restore his capital account while John is subject to a qualified income offset provision.

Assume all partnership items, except for MACRS, will net to zero throughout the first three years of the partnership operations. Also, assume that each year's MACRS deduction will be $10,000 (to simplify the calculations).

Draft a letter to the partnership evaluating the allocation of MACRS in each of the three years under Reg. §§ 1.704–1 and 1.704–2. The partnership's address is 53 East Marsh Ave., Smyrna, GA 30082. Do not address the "substantial" test.

**Research Problem 2.** Margaret and Henry formed the equal Brown Partnership on January 1 of the current year. Margaret contributed $30,000 cash. Henry contributed depreciable equipment with a basis of $12,000 and a fair market value (book value) of $30,000. Under the partnership agreement, the partners will each be allocated 50% of partnership income, gain, loss, deductions, and credit, except to the extent amounts must be specially allocated under § 704(c).

a. How much gain would the partnership report, and how would that gain be allocated if the property was sold immediately following the contribution for $32,000? (Ignore cost recovery in this question only.)

b. How much book and tax depreciation would each partner report during the year under the "traditional method" outlined in Reg. § 1.704–3? Prepare book and tax capital account reconciliations to assist you. Assume depreciation deductions for the property will be claimed on a straight-line basis using a 10-year life (10% per year). Ignore half-year conventions.

c. If the partnership sold the equipment for $28,000 at the beginning of the second year [after cost recovery allocations determined in (b) for the prior year], how much gain would be allocated to each party? Assume there is no additional cost recovery allocation in Year 2. What difficulty arises with this allocation?

d. The traditional method with curative allocations provides an alternative method that could be used in (b) and (c) to adjust for any inappropriate result. Demonstrate the effect of this method in a book and tax capital account reconciliation.

**Research Problem 3.** Fred and Grady have formed the FG Partnership to operate a retail establishment selling antique household furnishings. Fred is the general partner, and Grady is the limited partner. Both partners contribute $15,000 to form the partnership. The partnership uses the $30,000 contributed by the partners and a recourse loan of $100,000 obtained from an unrelated third-party lender to acquire $130,000 of initial inventory.

The partners believe they will have extensive losses in the first year due to advertising and initial cash-flow requirements. Fred and Grady have agreed to share losses equally. To make sure the losses can be allocated to both partners, they have included a provision in the partnership agreement requiring each partner to restore any deficit balance in his partnership capital account upon liquidation of the partnership.

Fred was also willing to include a provision that requires him to make up any deficit balance within 90 days of liquidation of the partnership. As a limited partner, Grady argued that he should not be subject to such a time requirement. The partners compromised and included a provision that requires Grady to restore a deficit balance in his capital account within two years of liquidation of the partnership. No interest will be owed on the deferred restoration payment.

Determine whether FG will be able to allocate the $100,000 recourse debt equally to the two partners to ensure they will be able to deduct their respective shares of partnership losses.

*Use the tax resources of the Internet to address the following questions. Do not restrict your search to the World Wide Web, but include a review of newsgroups and general reference materials, practitioner sites and resources, primary sources of the tax law, chat rooms and discussion groups, and other opportunities.*

**Research Problem 4.** Print an article posted by a law firm that comments on pitfalls to avoid in drafting partnership agreements. Ideally, use the home page of a firm that has offices in your state.

**Research Problem 5.** Use the search feature on your favorite news site on the Web (e.g, CNNfn, ABC News, Time's Pathfinder site, etc.) and search for news on partnerships, LLCs, or limited partnerships. What entities did you find that are taking advantage of the partnership entity form? (Be sure these entities are truly legal partnerships. Some entities called "partnerships" by the news media actually involve transfers of stock or formation of a corporation to manage the joint venture.)

**Research Problem 6.** Find the home page of a partnership that seems to be soliciting financing from new partners. Comment on the portrayal of the pertinent tax law that is included in the materials, especially with respect to the at-risk rules and the passive activity limitations.

# Partnerships: Distributions, Transfer of Interests, and Terminations

## LEARNING OBJECTIVES

*After completing Chapter 11, you should be able to:*

**LO.1**
Determine the tax treatment of proportionate nonliquidating distributions from a partnership to a partner.

**LO.2**
Determine the tax treatment of proportionate distributions that liquidate a partnership.

**LO.3**
Describe the tax treatment that applies to distributions treated as disguised sales and distributions of marketable securities and precontribution gain property.

**LO.4**
Describe the general concepts governing tax treatment of disproportionate distributions.

**LO.5**
Determine the tax treatment under § 736 of payments from a partnership to a retiring or deceased partner.

**LO.6**
Calculate the selling partner's amount and character of gain or loss on the sale or exchange of a partnership interest.

**LO.7**
Describe tax issues related to other dispositions of partnership interests.

**LO.8**
Calculate the optional adjustments to basis under § 754.

**LO.9**
Outline the methods of terminating a partnership.

**LO.10**
Describe the special considerations of a family partnership.

**LO.11**
Describe the application of partnership provisions to limited liability companies (LLCs) and limited liability partnerships (LLPs).

# OUTLINE

The previous chapter examined the tax effects of partnership formation and operation. Most operating transactions of a partnership present few tax problems; under the aggregate theory of partnership taxation, revenues earned and expenses paid by the partnership flow through to the tax returns of the partners. If the partners are individuals, the transactions are then handled like other individual tax matters.

However, a number of special tax provisions, many of them complex, govern the effects of the following transactions, which are discussed in this chapter:

- Nonliquidating distributions, which in most cases create no recognized gain or loss to the partner receiving the distribution. This treatment contrasts with that of corporate distributions, which may result in dividend income to the shareholder.
- Liquidating distributions, after which the recipient of the distribution is no longer a partner. The general rule here is that gain or loss is not recognized by either the liquidated partner or the partnership. There are exceptions, however, and these may result in gains or losses that are usually capital in nature.
- Sale of a partnership interest to a new or existing partner. This results in the selling partner receiving a return of capital and capital gain or loss. The result follows the entity theory, and the tax treatment is similar to that of a stock sale made by a shareholder in a C or S corporation. Under certain circumstances, however, the aggregate theory may partially govern the results, causing the selling partner to recognize some ordinary income or loss.

This chapter discusses an optional election a partnership may make concerning adjustments to basis when a partnership interest is sold. Partnership terminations and special problems associated with family partnerships are also explained. The chapter closes with discussions of two specialized business forms, limited liability companies and limited liability partnerships.

# Distributions from a Partnership

The tax treatment of distributions from a partnership to a partner was introduced in Chapter 10 in the context of routine cash withdrawals (or "draws") and cash distributions from a continuing partnership to a continuing partner. These draws and distributions reduce the partner's outside basis by the amount of the cash received. The partnership's inside basis in assets is similarly reduced.

**EXAMPLE 1**

Bill is a partner in the BB Partnership. The basis in his partnership interest is $10,000. The partnership distributes $3,000 cash to Bill at the end of the year. Bill does not recognize any gain on the distribution and reduces his basis by $3,000 (the amount of the distribution) to $7,000. Bill's basis in the cash he received is $3,000, and the partnership's inside basis for its assets is reduced by the $3,000 cash distributed. ■

The result in Example 1 arises whether or not a similar distribution is made to other partners. In a partnership, it is not critical that all partners receive a distribution at the same time as long as capital account balances are maintained appropriately, and final distributions are in accordance with ending capital account balances (see Chapter 10). Capital account maintenance requirements ensure that each partner eventually receives the proper amount, even though current distributions are not in accordance with ownership percentages.

A distribution from the partnership to a partner may consist of cash or partnership property. All distributions, cash and property, fall into two distinct categories:

- Liquidating distributions.
- Nonliquidating distributions.

Whether a distribution is a **liquidating** or **nonliquidating distribution** depends solely on whether the partner remains a partner in the partnership after the distribution is made. A *liquidating* distribution occurs either (1) when a partnership itself liquidates and distributes all of its property to its partners or (2) when an ongoing partnership redeems the interest of one of its partners. This second type of liquidating distribution occurs, for example, when a partner retires from a partnership, or when a deceased partner's interest is liquidated. The two types of liquidating distributions receive differing tax treatment, as later sections of the chapter will explain.

A *nonliquidating* distribution is any distribution from a continuing partnership to a continuing partner—that is, any distribution that is not a liquidating distribution. Nonliquidating distributions are of two types: draws or partial liquidations. A *draw* is a distribution of a partner's share of current or accumulated partnership profits that have been taxed to the partner in current or prior taxable years of the partnership. A *partial liquidation* is a distribution that reduces the partner's interest in partnership capital but does not liquidate the partner's entire interest in the partnership. The distinction between the two types of nonliquidating distributions is largely semantic, since the basic tax treatment typically does not differ.

**EXAMPLE 2**

Kay joins the calendar year KLM Partnership on January 1, 2003, by contributing $40,000 cash to the partnership in exchange for a one-third interest in partnership capital, profits, and losses. Her distributive share of partnership income for the year is $25,000. If the partnership distributes $65,000 ($25,000 share of partnership profits + $40,000 initial capital contribution) to Kay on December 31, 2003, the distribution is a nonliquidating distribution as long as Kay continues to be a partner in the partnership. This is true even though Kay receives her share of profits plus her entire investment in the partnership. In this case, $25,000 is considered a draw, and the remaining $40,000 is a partial liquidation of Kay's interest. If, instead, the partnership is liquidated or Kay ceases to be a partner in the ongoing partnership, the $65,000 distribution is a liquidating distribution.  ■

A payment from a partnership to a partner is not necessarily treated as a distribution. For example, as discussed in Chapter 10, a partnership may pay interest or rent to a partner for use of the partner's capital or property, make a guaranteed payment to a partner, or purchase property from a partner. If a payment *is* treated as a distribution, it is not necessarily treated under the general tax deferral rules that apply to most partnership distributions. In certain circumstances, the partner may recognize capital gain (or loss) and ordinary income (or loss) when a distribution is received from the partnership.

Finally, a distribution may be either proportionate or disproportionate. In a **proportionate distribution,** a partner receives the appropriate share of certain ordinary income-producing assets of the partnership. A **disproportionate distribution** occurs when the distribution increases or decreases the distributee partner's interest in certain ordinary income-producing assets. The tax treatment of disproportionate distributions is very complex.

The initial discussion and examples in this chapter describe the treatment of proportionate current and liquidating distributions. Special rules related to property distributions are discussed next. Then a brief overview of the rules pertaining to disproportionate distributions is presented.

## PROPORTIONATE NONLIQUIDATING DISTRIBUTIONS

**LO.1**

Determine the tax treatment of proportionate nonliquidating distributions from a partnership to a partner.

In general, neither the partner nor the partnership recognizes gain or loss when a proportionate nonliquidating distribution occurs.[1] The partner usually takes a carryover basis for the assets distributed.[2] The distributee partner's outside basis is reduced (but not below zero) by the amount of cash and the adjusted basis of property distributed to the partner by the partnership.[3] The details of the taxation of such distributions are discussed below and are summarized in Concept Summary 11–1. The following examples illustrate the situation and show that a distribution does not change a partner's overall economic position.

**EXAMPLE 3**

Jay is a one-fourth partner in the SP Partnership. His basis in his partnership interest is $40,000 on December 31, 2003. The fair market value of the interest is $70,000. The partnership distributes $25,000 cash to him on that date. The distribution is not taxable to Jay or the partnership. The distribution reduces Jay's adjusted basis in the partnership to $15,000 ($40,000 – $25,000), and the fair market value of his partnership interest is, arguably, reduced to $45,000 ($70,000 – $25,000).  ■

**EXAMPLE 4**

Assume the same facts as in Example 3, except that, in addition to the $25,000 cash, the partnership distributes land with an adjusted basis to the partnership of $13,000 and a fair market value of $30,000 on the date of distribution. The distribution is not taxable to Jay or the partnership. Jay reduces his basis in the partnership to $2,000 [$40,000 – ($25,000 + $13,000)] and takes a carryover basis of $13,000 in the land. The fair market value of Jay's

---

[1] §§ 731(a) and (b).
[2] § 732(a)(1).

[3] § 733.

remaining interest in the partnership is, arguably, reduced to $15,000 [$70,000 − ($25,000 + $30,000)].

If Jay had sold his partnership interest for $70,000 rather than receiving the distributions, he would have realized and recognized gain of $30,000 ($70,000 selling price − $40,000 outside basis). Because he has not recognized any gain or loss on the distribution of cash and land, he should still have the $30,000 of deferred gain to recognize at some point in the future. This is exactly what will happen. If Jay sells the cash, land, and remaining partnership interest on January 1, 2004, the day after the distribution, he realizes and recognizes gains of $17,000 ($30,000 − $13,000) on the land and $13,000 ($15,000 − $2,000) on the partnership interest. These gains total $30,000, which is the amount of the original deferred gain. ■

Note the difference between the tax theory governing distributions from C corporations and partnerships. In a C corporation, a distribution from current or accumulated income (earnings and profits) is taxable as a dividend to the shareholder, and the corporation does not receive a deduction for the amount distributed. This is an example of corporate income being subject to double taxation. In a partnership, a distribution from current or accumulated profits is not taxable because Congress has decided that partnership income should be subject to only a single level of taxation. Because a partner pays taxes when the share of income is earned by the partnership, this income is not taxed again when distributed.

These results make sense under the entity and aggregate concepts. The entity concept is applicable to corporate dividends, so any amount paid as a dividend is treated as a transfer by the corporate entity to the shareholder and is taxed accordingly. Under the aggregate theory, though, a partner receiving a distribution of partnership income is treated as merely receiving something already owned. Whether the partner chooses to leave the income in the partnership or receive it in a distribution makes no difference.

**Gain Recognition.** A partner recognizes gain from a proportionate nonliquidating distribution to the extent that the cash received exceeds the outside basis of the partner's interest in the partnership.[4]

*(handwritten margin note: Cash received exceeds the basis → gain is recognized)*

Samantha is a one-third partner in the SMP Partnership. Her basis in this ownership interest is $50,000 on December 31, 2003, after accounting for the calendar year partnership's 2003 operations and for Samantha's 2003 capital contributions. On December 31, 2003, the partnership distributes $60,000 cash to Samantha. She recognizes a $10,000 gain from this distribution ($60,000 cash received − $50,000 basis in her partnership interest). Most likely, this gain is taxed as a capital gain.[5] ■

While distributions *from* current and accumulated earnings are taxed differently to shareholders and partners, cash distributions *in excess* of accumulated profits are taxed similarly for corporate shareholders and partners in partnerships. Both shareholders and partners are allowed to recover the cumulative capital invested in the entity tax-free.

Recall from Chapter 10 that the reduction of a partner's share of partnership debt is treated as a distribution of cash from the partnership to the partner. A reduction of a partner's share of partnership debt, then, first reduces the partner's

---

[4] § 731(a)(1).
[5] § 731(a). If the partnership holds any "hot assets," however, Samantha will probably recognize some ordinary income. See § 751(b)

and the related discussion of ordinary income ("hot") assets and disproportionate distributions later in this chapter.

basis in the partnership. Any reduction of a share of debt in excess of a partner's basis in the partnership is taxable to the partner as a gain.

*Any reduction of a share of debt*

| EXAMPLE 6 |

Returning to the facts of Example 5, assume that Samantha's $50,000 basis in her partnership interest included a $60,000 share of partnership liabilities. If the partnership repays all of its liabilities, Samantha is treated as receiving a $60,000 distribution from the partnership. The first $50,000 of this distribution reduces her basis to $0. The last $10,000 distributed creates a taxable gain to her of $10,000. ■

A distribution of marketable securities can also be treated as a distribution of cash. Determining the treatment of such distributions is complicated, though, since several exceptions may apply and the basis in the distributed stock must be calculated. Such distributions are discussed later under Property Distributions with Special Tax Treatment: Marketable Securities.

**Loss Recognition.**   The distributee partner cannot recognize a loss on a proportionate nonliquidating distribution. This loss is deferred because tax law typically does not permit losses to be recognized until the loss is certain to occur and the amount is known. After the nonliquidating distribution, the partner still owns the partnership interest, which has an indeterminate future value. Only when a final liquidating distribution is received is the loss certain and known in amount—and potentially deductible.

*No loss recognized on distribution*

| EXAMPLE 7 |

Henry has a $50,000 basis in his partnership interest. Assume that on December 31 he receives a distribution of $10,000 cash. As a result of the distribution, the basis in the partnership interest is reduced to $40,000.

Henry knows the partnership has fallen on hard times and that future distributions will probably not amount to more than a few hundred dollars. He does not recognize a loss, even though a loss probably exists. The amount of the loss is not fixed and determinable since he still owns the partnership interest. ■

**Property Distributions.**   In general, a distributee partner does not recognize gain from a property distribution. If the basis of property distributed by a partnership exceeds the partner's basis in the partnership interest, the distributed asset takes a substituted basis. This ensures that the partner does not receive asset basis that is not "paid for."

| EXAMPLE 8 |

*basis in P/S is used & asset is = P/S int.*

Mary has a $50,000 basis in her partnership interest. The partnership distributes land it owns with a basis and a fair market value of $60,000. Mary does not recognize any gain on this distribution because it is a distribution of property. However, Mary should not be allowed to take a carryover basis of $60,000 in the land, when her basis in her partnership interest is only $50,000. Therefore, the Code provides that Mary takes a substituted basis of $50,000 in the land. Her basis in her partnership interest is reduced by the basis she takes in the asset received, or $50,000. Therefore, Mary has a $50,000 basis in the land and a $0 basis in her partnership interest, and she recognizes no gain on this distribution. ■

The rule that no gain or loss is recognized on a property distribution from a partnership has several exceptions. These situations may arise for either a current or a liquidating distribution, so discussion of these exceptions is deferred until all the general rules are discussed (see Property Distributions with Special Tax Treatment later in the chapter).

**Ordering Rules.** When the inside basis of the distributed assets exceeds the distributee partner's outside basis, the Code requires that the assets be deemed distributed in the following order:

- Cash is distributed first.
- Unrealized receivables and inventory are distributed second.
- All other assets are distributed last.

**Unrealized receivables** are receivables that have a value to the partnership, but for which the related income has not yet been realized or recognized under the partnership's method of accounting. The term *unrealized receivables* applies only to amounts that will ultimately be realized and recognized as ordinary income. If the partnership uses the cash method of accounting, trade receivables from services or sales are unrealized receivables. If the partnership uses the accrual method, they are not. Unrealized receivables include receivables from the sales of ordinary income property and rights to payments for services. For some purposes, unrealized receivables also include ordinary recapture income that would arise if the partnership sold its depreciable assets. Installment gains are unrealized receivables if the gain will be taxed as ordinary income when realized.

Inventory, for purposes of these ordering rules, includes any partnership assets except cash, capital, or § 1231 assets. For example, all accounts receivable are considered to be inventory, although only cash basis receivables are "unrealized receivables."

Since the partner typically does not recognize a gain from a *property* distribution, the Code provides that the partner's basis for property received cannot exceed the partner's basis in the partnership interest immediately before the distribution. For each level of asset distribution, the relevant adjustments are made to the partner's basis in the interest. In other words, after a cash distribution, the partner's basis in the interest is recomputed before determining the effect of a distribution of unrealized receivables or inventory. The basis is again recomputed before determining the effect of a distribution of other assets. If the remaining outside basis at the end of any step is insufficient to cover the entire inside basis of the assets in the next step, that remaining outside basis is allocated among the assets within that class.[6]

**EXAMPLE 9** Sally has a $48,000 basis in her partnership interest. On September 10, 2003, the partnership distributes to her cash of $12,000, cash basis receivables with an inside basis of $0 and a fair market value of $10,000, and a parcel of land with a basis to the partnership of $60,000 and a fair market value of $100,000. Sally has a realized gain on the distribution of $74,000 ($12,000 + $10,000 + $100,000 − $48,000). None of that gain is recognized, however, since the $12,000 cash distribution does not exceed her $48,000 adjusted basis for her partnership interest. In determining the basis effects of the distribution, the cash is treated as being distributed first, reducing Sally's adjusted basis to $36,000 ($48,000 − $12,000). The receivables are distributed next, taking a $0 carryover basis to Sally. Her adjusted basis remains at $36,000. The land is distributed last, taking a substituted basis of $36,000 and reducing her adjusted basis for her partnership interest to $0. ■

When more than one asset in a particular class is distributed, special rules apply. For most proportionate nonliquidating distributions, if the partner's remaining adjusted basis for the partnership interest is less than the partnership's adjusted basis for the distributed assets in the particular class, the partner's adjusted basis for each distributed asset is computed by following three steps:

---

[6]§ 732.

Step 1   Each distributed asset within the class initially takes a carryover basis.

Step 2   Then, this carryover basis for each of these assets is reduced in proportion to their respective amounts of unrealized depreciation (amount that carryover basis is greater than fair market value). Under no circumstances, however, can the basis of any asset be reduced below its fair market value in step 2.

Step 3   Any remaining decrease in basis is allocated among all the distributed assets in the class in proportion to their respective adjusted bases (as determined in step 2).

**EXAMPLE 10**

Assume the same facts as in Example 9, except that Sally receives two parcels of land, rather than a single parcel. The partnership's basis for the parcels is $15,000 for Parcel 1 and $45,000 for Parcel 2. Each parcel has a fair market value of $30,000. Sally has a realized gain on the distribution of $34,000 ($12,000 + $10,000 + $60,000 − $48,000). None of that gain is recognized, however, because the $12,000 cash distribution does not exceed her $48,000 adjusted basis.

As in Example 9, Sally takes a $12,000 basis for the cash and a $0 carryover basis for the receivables and has a $36,000 adjusted basis for her partnership interest after these two items are distributed. Because two parcels of land are distributed, and because Sally's remaining $36,000 adjusted basis for her partnership interest is less than the partnership's $60,000 total basis for the two parcels of land, Sally's adjusted basis for each parcel of land is computed by following these steps:

Step 1   She initially takes a carryover basis of $15,000 for Parcel 1 and $45,000 for Parcel 2.

Step 2   She reduces the basis of Parcel 2 to its lower fair market value of $30,000. The basis for Parcel 1 is not adjusted in this step because Parcel 1 has a fair market value greater than its basis.

Step 3   The remaining $9,000 difference between her $36,000 basis for the partnership interest and the $45,000 ($15,000 + $30,000) basis for the land parcels after step 2 is allocated to the two parcels in proportion to their respective bases (as computed in step 2). Therefore, the amount of the step 3 basis reduction allocated to Parcel 1 is:

$$9,000 \times \frac{\$15,000}{\$45,000} = \$3,000$$

Sally's basis for Parcel 1 is $12,000 ($15,000 − $3,000). The amount of the step 3 basis reduction allocated to Parcel 2 is:

$$9,000 \times \frac{\$30,000}{\$45,000} = \$6,000$$

Sally's basis for Parcel 2 is $24,000 ($30,000 − $6,000). ∎

**EXAMPLE 11**

Assume the same facts as in Example 10, and that Sally sells both parcels of land early in 2004 for their fair market values, receiving proceeds of $60,000 ($30,000 + $30,000). She also collects $10,000 from the cash basis receivables. Now she recognizes all of the $34,000 gain that she deferred upon receiving the property from the partnership [$60,000 amount realized − $36,000 basis for the two parcels ($12,000 + $24,000) + $10,000 collected − $0 basis for the receivables]. ∎

Review the tax results of Examples 9 and 10. Although Sally does not recognize any of the gain she realizes from the distribution, she has a zero outside basis for her partnership interest. If Sally expects the partnership to generate net losses in the near future, she will *not* find this zero basis attractive. She may be unable to deduct her share of these future losses when they flow through to her on the last day of the partnership's subsequent tax year.

The low basis that Sally has assigned to the parcels of land is of no significant detriment to her if she does not intend to sell the land in the near future. Since land does not generate cost recovery deductions, the substituted basis is used only to determine Sally's gain or loss upon her disposition of the land in a taxable sale or exchange.

Concept Summary 11–1 reviews the general rules that apply to proportionate nonliquidating partnership distributions.

---

**ETHICAL CONSIDERATIONS**

## Arranging Tax-Advantaged Distributions

The Sparrow Partnership plans to distribute $200,000 cash to its partners at the end of the year. Marjorie is a 40 percent partner and would receive $80,000. Her basis in the partnership is only $10,000, however, so she would be required to recognize a $70,000 gain if she receives a cash distribution. She has asked the partnership instead to purchase a parcel of land she has found on which she will build her retirement residence. The partnership will then distribute that land to her. Under the partnership distribution rules, Marjorie would take a $10,000 basis in land worth $80,000. Her basis in the partnership would be reduced to $0, and the $70,000 deferred gain would be recognized only if she sells the land. Do you think this is an appropriate transaction?

---

**LO.2**

Determine the tax treatment of proportionate distributions that liquidate a partnership.

## PROPORTIONATE LIQUIDATING DISTRIBUTIONS

Proportionate liquidating distributions consist of a single distribution or a series of distributions that result in the termination of the partner's entire interest in the partnership. If the partnership continues in existence after the partner's interest is liquidated, the rules of § 736 govern the classification of the liquidating payments. These rules are discussed later in the chapter. Other rules apply, however, if the partner's interest is liquidated because the partnership is also liquidating. This section examines the latter type of liquidating distribution.

The partnership itself does not recognize either gain or loss on a proportionate liquidating distribution. The following discussion outlines rules for allocation of basis and possible gain/loss recognition by partners. These rules are summarized in Concept Summary 11–2 at the end of this section.

**Gain Recognition and Ordering Rules.**   When a partnership liquidates, the liquidating distributions to a partner usually consist of an interest in several or all of the partnership assets. The gain recognition and ordering rules parallel those for nonliquidating distributions, except that the partner's *entire* basis in the partnership interest is allocated to the assets received in the liquidating distribution, unless the partner is required to recognize a loss. A loss may be recognized when *only* cash, unrealized receivables, or inventory is received in the distribution. As a result of the ordering rules, the basis of some assets may be adjusted upward or downward to absorb the partner's remaining outside basis. Unrealized receivables or inventory are never "stepped up," although they may be "stepped down."

The general ordering and gain recognition rules for a proportionate liquidating distribution are summarized as follows:

## CONCEPT SUMMARY 11–1

### Proportionate Nonliquidating Distributions (General Rules)

1. Neither the distributee partner nor the partnership recognizes any gain or loss on a proportionate nonliquidating distribution. However, if cash distributed exceeds the distributee partner's outside basis, gain is recognized. Property distributions generally do not result in gain recognition.
2. The distributee partner usually takes the same basis in the distributed property that the property had to the partnership (carryover basis). However, where the inside basis of distributed property exceeds the partner's outside basis, the basis assigned to the distributed property cannot exceed that outside basis (substituted basis).
3. Gain recognized by the distributee partner on a proportionate nonliquidating distribution is capital in nature.
4. Loss is never recognized on a proportionate nonliquidating distribution.

#### Calculations

1. Partner's outside basis. _____
2. Less: Cash distributed to partner. _____
3. Gain recognized by partner (excess of Line 2 over Line 1). _____
4. Partner's remaining outside basis (Line 1 – Line 2). If less than $0, enter $0. _____
5. Partner's basis in unrealized receivables and inventory distributed (enter lesser of Line 4 or the partnership's inside basis in the unrealized receivables and inventory). _____
6. Basis available to allocate to other property distributed (Line 4 – Line 5). _____
7. Partnership's inside basis of other property distributed. _____
8. Basis to partner of other property distributed (enter lesser of Line 6 or Line 7). _____
9. Partner's remaining outside basis (Line 6 – Line 8). _____

- Cash is distributed first and results in a capital gain if the amount distributed exceeds the partner's basis in the partnership interest. The cash distributed reduces the liquidated partner's outside basis dollar for dollar. The partner's basis cannot be reduced below zero.
- The partner's remaining outside basis is then allocated to unrealized receivables and inventory up to an amount equal to the partnership's adjusted bases in those properties. If the partnership's bases in the unrealized receivables and inventory exceed the partner's remaining outside basis, the remaining outside basis is allocated to the unrealized receivables and inventory.
- Finally, if the liquidating partner has any outside basis left, that basis is allocated to the other assets received.[7]

**EXAMPLE 12**    When Tara's basis in her partnership interest is $70,000, she receives cash of $15,000, a proportionate share of inventory, and a building in a distribution that liquidates both the partnership and her entire partnership interest. The inventory has a basis to the partnership of $20,000 and a fair market value of $30,000. The building's basis is $8,000, and the fair market value is $12,000. The building is not subject to depreciation recapture. Under these circumstances, Tara recognizes no gain or loss. After reducing Tara's $70,000 basis by the $15,000 cash received, the remaining $55,000 is allocated first to the inventory and then to the building. The basis of the inventory in Tara's hands is $20,000, and the basis of the building is $35,000. ∎

[7]§§ 731 and 732.

When more than one asset in a particular class is distributed in a proportionate liquidating distribution, special rules may apply. If the partner's remaining basis for the partnership interest is less than the partnership's basis for the distributed assets in the particular class, the partner's basis for each distributed asset is computed as illustrated previously in Example 10. If, however, the partner's remaining basis for the partnership interest is greater than the partnership's basis for the distributed assets in the "other assets" class, the partner's basis for each remaining distributed asset is computed by following three steps:

*Step 1* Each distributed asset within the "other assets" class initially takes a carryover basis.

*Step 2* Then, this carryover basis for each of these assets is increased in proportion to their respective amounts of unrealized appreciation (amount that fair market value is greater than carryover basis). Under no circumstances, however, can the basis of any asset be increased above its fair market value in step 2.

*Step 3* Any remaining increase in basis is allocated among all the distributed assets in the "other assets" class in proportion to their respective fair market values.

**EXAMPLE 13**

Assume the same facts as in Example 12, except that Tara receives two parcels of land, rather than a building. The partnership's basis for the parcels is $2,000 for Parcel 1 and $6,000 for Parcel 2. Each parcel has a fair market value of $6,000.

Tara takes a $15,000 basis for the cash and a $20,000 carryover basis for the inventory. She has a $35,000 basis for her partnership interest after these two items are distributed. Because two parcels of land are distributed, and because Tara's remaining $35,000 basis for her partnership interest exceeds the partnership's $8,000 basis for the two parcels of land, Tara's basis for each parcel of land is computed by following these steps:

*Step 1* She initially takes a carryover basis of $2,000 for Parcel 1 and $6,000 for Parcel 2.

*Step 2* She increases the basis of Parcel 1 by $4,000 to its fair market value of $6,000. The basis for Parcel 2 is not affected in this step because Parcel 2 has a fair market value equal to its basis.

*Step 3* Tara's $23,000 ($35,000 − $6,000 − $6,000) remaining basis for her partnership interest is allocated to each land parcel in proportion to each parcel's respective $6,000 fair market value. Therefore, $11,500 [($6,000/$12,000) × $23,000] is allocated to each parcel. Tara's basis in Parcel 1 is $17,500 ($2,000 + $4,000 + $11,500). Her basis in Parcel 2 is $17,500 ($6,000 + $11,500). ■

**Loss Recognition.**   The distributee partner may also recognize a *loss* on a liquidating distribution. The partner recognizes a loss if both of the following are true:

1. The partner receives *only* cash, unrealized receivables, or inventory.   *and*
2. The partner's outside basis in the partnership interest exceeds the partnership's inside basis for the assets distributed. This excess amount is the loss recognized by the distributee partner.[8]

The word "only" is important. A distribution of any other property precludes recognition of the loss.

**EXAMPLE 14**

When Ramon's outside basis is $40,000, he receives a liquidating distribution of $7,000 cash and a proportionate share of inventory having a partnership basis of $3,000 and a fair market

---

[8]§ 731(a)(2).

value of $10,000. Ramon is not allowed to "step up" the basis in the inventory, so it is allocated a $3,000 carryover basis. Ramon's unutilized outside basis is $30,000 ($40,000 – $7,000 – $3,000). Since he received a liquidating distribution of *only* cash and inventory, he recognizes a capital loss of $30,000 on the liquidation. ■

<table>
<tr><td>**E X A M P L E    1 5**</td><td>Assume the same facts as in Example 14, except that in addition to the cash and inventory, Ramon receives the desk he used in the partnership. The desk has an adjusted basis of $100 to the partnership. Applying the rules outlined above to this revised fact situation produces the following results:</td></tr>
</table>

*Step 1*  Cash of $7,000 is distributed to Ramon and reduces his outside basis to $33,000.

*Step 2*  Inventory is distributed to Ramon. He takes a $3,000 carryover basis in the inventory and reduces his outside basis in the partnership to $30,000.

*Step 3*  The desk is distributed to Ramon. Since the desk is a § 1231 asset and not cash, an unrealized receivable, or inventory, he cannot recognize a loss. Therefore, Ramon's remaining basis in his partnership interest is allocated to the desk. He takes a $30,000 basis for the desk. ■

What can Ramon do with a $30,000 desk? If he continues to use it in a trade or business, he can depreciate it. Once he has established his business use of the desk, he could sell it and recognize a large § 1231 loss. If the loss is isolated in the year of the sale, it is an ordinary loss. Thus, with proper planning, no liquidated partner should be forced to recognize a capital loss instead of an ordinary loss.

Gain recognized by the withdrawing partner on the subsequent disposition of inventory is always ordinary income, unless the disposition occurs more than five years after the distribution.[9] The withdrawing partner's holding period for all other property received in a liquidating distribution includes the partnership's related holding period.

Concept Summary 11–2 outlines the general rules that apply to proportionate liquidating partnership distributions.

## PROPERTY DISTRIBUTIONS WITH SPECIAL TAX TREATMENT

**LO.3**

Describe the tax treatment that applies to distributions treated as disguised sales and distributions of marketable securities and precontribution gain property.

Recall that a distribution from a partnership to a partner usually does not result in taxable gain. This section discusses three exceptions in which a proportionate distribution, either liquidating or nonliquidating, may result in gain to the partner.

**Disguised Sales.**  As discussed in Chapter 10, a disguised sale is a transaction in which a partner contributes appreciated property to a partnership and soon thereafter receives a distribution of cash or property from the partnership. If the IRS determines the payment is part of a "purchase" of the property, rather than a distribution from the partnership, the usual sale or exchange rules apply. The partner is treated as having sold the property and must report a gain on the sale. The partnership takes a cost basis in the property purchased. See Chapter 10 for additional discussion.

**Marketable Securities.**  The fair market value of a marketable security distributed to a partner is generally treated as a cash distribution.[10] Some or all of the value of the security over the partner's outside basis prior to the distribution is a taxable gain. The partner must assign a basis to the security received in the distribution, so the distribution ordering rules must be taken into account.

---

[9]§ 735(a)(2).    [10]§ 731(c).

## CONCEPT SUMMARY 11–2

### Proportionate Liquidating Distributions When the Partnership Also Liquidates (General Rules)

1. Generally, neither the distributee partner nor the partnership recognizes gain or loss when a partnership liquidates. However, a partner recognizes gain if the cash received exceeds the partner's outside basis. A partner recognizes loss when (a) the partner receives only cash, unrealized receivables, or inventory and (b) the partner's outside basis is greater than the partnership's inside basis of the assets distributed.
2. A partner's basis in distributed assets must be determined in a certain order. Cash is distributed first, inventory and unrealized receivables second, and all other assets last. Assets in the last category take a substituted basis equal to the distributee partner's remaining outside basis.
3. Gain or loss recognized by a distributee partner in a distribution that liquidates a partnership is usually capital in nature.

#### Calculations

| | |
|---|---|
| 1. Partner's outside basis. | _____ |
| 2. Less: Cash distributed to partner. | _____ |
| 3. Gain recognized by partner (excess of Line 2 over Line 1). | _____ |
| 4. Partner's remaining outside basis (Line 1 – Line 2). If less than $0, enter $0. | _____ |
| 5. Partner's basis in unrealized receivables and inventory distributed (enter lesser of Line 4 or the inside basis in the unrealized receivables and inventory). | _____ |
| 6. Basis to partner of other property distributed (Line 4 – Line 5). | _____ |
| 7. Loss recognized by partner (if no other property was distributed, enter amount from Line 6). | _____ |
| 8. Partner's remaining outside basis. | $0 |

The term *marketable securities* is broadly defined and includes almost any debt or equity interest that is actively traded, including options, futures contracts, and derivatives. Marketable securities are *not* treated as cash if (1) they were originally contributed by the partner to whom they are now distributed (certain exceptions apply to this provision), (2) the property was not a marketable security when acquired by the partnership, or (3) the partner is an eligible partner of an investment partnership, as defined in Chapter 10.

The primary purpose of this rule is to stop the tax avoidance that otherwise would occur if a partnership purchased marketable securities with the intent of immediately distributing them to the partner. As the preceding Ethical Considerations indicated, a partnership can purchase property desired by a partner, distribute that property to the partner, and allow the partner to defer tax on any appreciation inherent in the partnership interest. Section 731(c) was enacted to prevent a partnership from arranging such a transaction with marketable securities.

If, on the distribution date, the marketable security is appreciated, it probably was not acquired by the partnership in an effort to assist the distributee partner in reducing the tax on the distribution. The portion of the security value treated as cash is reduced by a proportionate share of the appreciation inherent in the distributed security. The amount of the reduction is the excess of (1) the partner's share of appreciation in this particular security before the distribution over (2) the partner's share of appreciation in the portion of the security retained by the partnership. This results in a deferral of gain for this portion of the appreciation.

The "reduction" is intended to take into account the partnership's intent, or lack thereof, to reduce the partner's gains.

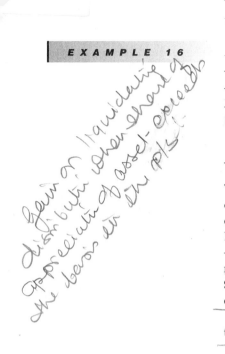

**EXAMPLE 16**

Assume the A to Z Partnership has the following balance sheet:

|  | Basis | FMV |  | Basis | FMV |
|---|---|---|---|---|---|
| ZYX Corporation security | $4,000 | $10,000 | Andy, capital | $ 500 | $ 2,000 |
| Land | 1,000 | 10,000 | Other partners, capital | 4,500 | 18,000 |
| Total | $5,000 | $20,000 | Total | $5,000 | $20,000 |

The partnership distributes $2,000 (value) of the ZYX stock to 10% partner Andy in liquidation of his partnership interest. The amount of the distribution is the $2,000 fair market value of the stock reduced by Andy's decrease in his share of the inside appreciation in the stock. Before the distribution, Andy's share of appreciation in this stock was $600 [10% × ($10,000 − $4,000)]. *His share* of appreciation in the stock retained by the partnership is $0, since he no longer owns an interest in the partnership. The $2,000 value of the stock is reduced by $600 ($600 appreciation before − $0 after distribution). Andy is treated as if he received a cash distribution of $1,400.

Andy's outside basis was $500 before the distribution. The $1,400 deemed cash distribution triggers gain recognition of $900. ■

The distributee partner's basis in the security is the sum of (1) the basis in the stock as determined under the regular distribution rules (see the discussion under Ordering Rules above) and (2) the gain recognized on the distribution.

**EXAMPLE 17**

In Example 16, the stock would take a substituted basis of $500 to Andy under the distribution ordering rules. This basis is the lesser of the partnership's inside basis in the stock of $800 (20% × $4,000) or Andy's outside basis of $500 (see Concept Summary 11–2). The recognized gain of $900 increases Andy's basis in the stock to $1,400 ($500 + $900).

This basis determination preserves the inherent built-in gain in Andy's partnership interest. Before the distribution, Andy has $1,500 of appreciation in his interest ($2,000 − $500). After considering the $900 gain on the stock distribution, he should have $600 of untaxed appreciation. The stock value is $2,000, and Andy's basis is $1,400, so the untaxed appreciation is the expected $600 amount. ■

Unless otherwise indicated, the remaining examples in this chapter assume the partnership is not distributing marketable securities.

**Precontribution Gain.** Taxable gains may arise on a distribution of property to a partner where precontribution (built-in) gains exist. Specifically, if a partner contributes appreciated property to a partnership, the contributing partner recognizes gain in two situations:

1. If the contributed appreciated property is distributed to another partner within seven years of the contribution date, the contributing partner recognizes the remaining net precontribution gain on the property.[11] The contributing partner's basis in the partnership interest is increased by the amount

---

[11]§ 704(c)(1)(B).

of gain recognized. Also, the basis of the distributed property is increased by this same amount to prevent double taxation of this precontribution gain when the distributee partner later sells the asset.

**EXAMPLE 18**

*40000 FMV*
*(10000) AB*
*30000*
*distributed next yr*
*to another partner*
*Buit in gain to Rod*

In 2003, Rod contributes nondepreciable property with an adjusted basis of $10,000 and a fair market value of $40,000 to the RTCO Partnership in exchange for a one-fourth interest in profits and capital. In 2004, when the property's fair market value is $50,000, the partnership distributes the property to Tom, another one-fourth partner. Since the property was contributed to the partnership within seven years of the date the property was distributed, and precontribution gain of $30,000 ($40,000 – $10,000) was attributable to the property, the built-in gain on the property is taxable to Rod. Therefore, Rod must pay tax on the $30,000 built-in gain in 2004, the year the property was distributed to Tom. Rod increases his basis in his partnership interest by the $30,000 gain recognized. Tom also increases his basis in the property received by $30,000.

Note that if the partnership sells the property to an unrelated third party for $40,000 in 2004, the result is the same for Rod. Under § 704(c)(1)(A), recognized built-in gains must be allocated to the partner who contributed the property, and the partner's outside basis is increased accordingly. ■

2. The second situation occurs where the partnership distributes *any* property other than cash to a partner within seven years after *that* partner contributes appreciated property to the partnership. In this case, the partner recognizes the lesser of (a) the remaining net precontribution (built-in) gain or (b) the excess of the fair market value of the distributed property over the partner's basis in interest before the distribution.[12] The distributee partner's basis in his or her partnership interest is increased by the amount of gain recognized. To maintain a parity between inside and outside basis, the partnership is allowed to increase its basis in the precontribution gain property remaining in the partnership.

   An exception applies if the partner originally contributed the distributed property. The partnership is merely returning property to the original contributor, and the partner is not required to recognize built-in gain. The general rules that govern property distributions apply.

**EXAMPLE 19**

In 2001, Bill contributes land to the BMC Partnership. His basis in the land was $16,000. The fair market value at the contribution date was $40,000. In 2003, the partnership distributes other property with an adjusted basis of $16,000 and fair market value of $65,000 to Bill. Bill's basis in his partnership interest was $12,000 immediately before the distribution. Since Bill contributed precontribution gain property within seven years of receiving the distribution of other property, he recognizes gain on the distribution. The maximum he must recognize is the net precontribution gain, or $24,000 ($40,000 fair market value – $16,000 adjusted basis of property contributed). He compares this amount to the excess of the fair market value of the distributed property over his basis in his partnership interest, or $53,000 ($65,000 fair market value of property – $12,000 adjusted basis in interest prior to distribution).

Since the $24,000 precontribution gain is less than the $53,000 inherent gain, Bill recognizes gain of $24,000. His basis in his partnership interest increases by the $24,000 gain recognized to $36,000, and the partnership's basis in the "precontribution gain" property Bill originally contributed also increases by $24,000 to $40,000. ■

---

[12]§ 737.

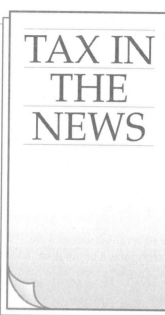

### SIMPLIFYING PARTNERSHIP TAXATION—A LOSING BATTLE?

Partnership taxation has become increasingly complex over the past decade. The tax treatment of a distribution differs depending on the type of property being distributed, the appreciation inherent in the property, who the property is distributed to, and how the partnership originally acquired the property. Liability sharing rules vary depending on the type of liability, the type of partner (general or limited), and when the liability was created. And the "substantial economic effect" rules include numerous pages of guidelines on when and how to allocate income and loss among the partners.

Various parties, including the Joint Committee on Taxation, several members of Congress, and the American Bar Association, have called for simplification of the rules. Yet none of the tax legislation enacted recently has simplified partnership taxation. Also, the IRS is currently considering additional changes in the Regulations that will add considerable complexity to this already difficult area. Pundits speculate that simplification in the partnership area will be slow in coming because most necessary changes would result in a net revenue loss to the government.

**EXAMPLE 20**

Assume the same facts as in Example 19, except that Bill's basis in his partnership interest was $60,000 before the distribution. In this case, the excess value of the distributed property is only $5,000 ($65,000 − $60,000), so Bill only recognizes gain of $5,000, with corresponding adjustments to the basis of his partnership interest and the partnership's basis in the precontribution gain property.

The remaining precontribution gain of $19,000 ($24,000 − $5,000) is charged to Bill at some point in the future if the partnership sells the precontribution gain property or distributes it to another partner within seven years of its contribution. Some or all of the remaining precontribution gain may also be recognized if other appreciated property is distributed to Bill within seven years of the original contribution. ■

If the distribution occurs more than seven years after the original contribution, Bill recognizes no gain, and the distribution is handled under the general distribution rules described earlier in this section.

**LO.4**

Describe the general concepts governing tax treatment of disproportionate distributions.

## DISPROPORTIONATE DISTRIBUTIONS

An additional exception to the general gain and loss nonrecognition rule arises when a partnership makes a "disproportionate distribution" of assets. A disproportionate distribution occurs when a partnership makes a distribution of cash or property to a partner and that distribution increases or decreases the distributee partner's proportionate interest in certain of the partnership's ordinary income-producing assets.

These ordinary income-producing assets, called **hot assets,** include substantially **appreciated inventory** and unrealized receivables. Unrealized receivables are rights to receive future amounts that will result in ordinary income when the income is recognized. Inventory, as the term is used here, has a much broader meaning than usual. It includes all assets that are not cash, capital, or § 1231 assets. Substantially appreciated inventory is inventory that has a fair market value in excess of 120 percent of the partnership's adjusted basis for the inventory.

The taxation of disproportionate distributions is based on the aggregate theory of taxation. Under this theory, each partner is deemed to own a proportionate share of the underlying assets of the partnership. In line with this concept, each partner is responsible for recognizing and reporting the proportionate share of ordinary income potential of these assets, such as would arise on the sale of substantially appreciated inventory or on the collection of cash basis receivables.

Section 751(b) maintains each partner's proportionate share of ordinary income by recasting any transaction in which a disproportionate distribution of hot assets is made. If the distributee partner receives less than a proportionate share of hot assets, the transaction is treated as if two separate events occurred: (1) the partnership made a distribution of some of the hot assets to the distributee partner, and (2) that partner immediately sold these hot assets back to the partnership. The partner recognizes ordinary income on the sale of the hot assets, and the partnership takes a cost basis for the hot assets purchased.

**EXAMPLE 21**

The balance sheet of the AB Partnership is as follows on December 31, 2003:

|  | Basis | FMV |  | Basis | FMV |
|---|---|---|---|---|---|
| Cash | $26,000 | $26,000 | Amanda, capital | $13,000 | $26,000 |
| Unrealized receivables | –0– | 26,000 | Bob, capital | 13,000 | 26,000 |
| Total | $26,000 | $52,000 | Total | $26,000 | $52,000 |

Amanda and Bob are equal partners in the partnership. The partnership makes a liquidating distribution of the unrealized receivables to Amanda and the cash to Bob. Since the unrealized receivables are a hot asset, Amanda has received more than her proportionate share of the hot asset, and Bob has received less than his proportionate share. As Bob received less than his proportionate share of hot assets, § 751 recasts the transaction into two separate events. First, Bob is deemed to receive a current distribution of his 50% share of hot assets (basis = $0; fair market value = $13,000), which he then immediately sells back to the partnership for $13,000 of the cash. Bob recognizes $13,000 ordinary income on the sale, and the partnership takes a $13,000 basis in the receivables purchased. The remaining $13,000 cash received by Bob reduces his adjusted basis for his partnership interest to $0 ($13,000 cash distributed – $13,000 adjusted basis).

Amanda receives both the $13,000 receivables that the partnership purchased from Bob and her share of the remaining $13,000 unrealized receivables. She takes a substituted basis of $13,000 in the receivables and reduces her adjusted basis for her partnership interest to $0. When she collects all $26,000 of the receivables, she will recognize $13,000 of ordinary income ($26,000 cash collected – $13,000 basis for receivables).

Although the mechanical rules of § 751(b) are complicated, the application of the rules in this example has ensured that each partner eventually recognizes his or her $13,000 share of ordinary income. Bob recognizes his share at the time the partnership is liquidated. Amanda's share is recognized when she collects the unrealized receivables. ■

Although most of the problems and examples in this text involve proportionate distributions, be aware that disproportionate distributions occur frequently in practice. The calculation of ordinary income in disproportionate distributions can become extremely complex. These more difficult calculations are not discussed in this text.

## Deferring Partners' Taxes by Delaying Liquidation

Partnerships often use the liabilities included in a partner's basis to shield losses claimed by the partners. By including a share of the partnership's liabilities in basis, the partner may be able to claim ordinary losses greatly in excess of the capital contributions. When the liabilities are repaid or forgiven, the partner is treated as receiving a distribution of cash and recognizes capital gain treatment on the payment or forgiveness of the debt. This is not a bad planning technique—it provides ordinary losses now and capital gains later!

If the capital gain recognition could be deferred for an extended period, the partners would really be ecstatic. Recently, a large national brokerage firm used such a delaying tactic. Investors originally contributed $200,000 each for an interest in a partnership syndicated by the firm. The partners claimed losses from the partnership far in excess of their original contribution. The property owned by the partnership declined in value, and for various reasons, the partners sued

the brokerage firm. In settlement, the firm agreed to loan the partnership up to $20 million and to continue to manage the property for up to 15 years. The partnership used the cash to distribute about $100,000 to each of the partners and to pay off other existing debt.

The partners will continue to hold their partnership interests during the 15 years the general partner manages the property. Debt still exists, so the partners still have basis in their partnership interests, and the partnership still exists, although the partners' interests in the partnership are virtually worthless. Thus, the partners have received losses and then substantial cash distributions and will be able to defer the capital gain on release of liabilities for another 15 years. Example 7 showed that a partner cannot recognize a loss prior to termination. Now it seems a partner cannot be forced to recognize a gain prior to termination. What do you think of this arrangement?

# Liquidating Distributions to Retiring or Deceased Partners

Payments made by an ongoing partnership in complete liquidation of a retiring partner's interest are classified as either *income* or *property* payments by § 736. Payments made to a successor to the interest of a deceased partner are similarly classified by § 736.[13] It is critical to observe that § 736 only classifies the payments. Other Code Sections provide the rules for computing the tax effects of these payments. Although these payments can be made in cash, property, or both cash and property, this discussion assumes that all payments are made in cash.

From a practical standpoint, the partnership and the retiring partner negotiate a total buyout package. The retiring partner expects compensation for the partner's proportionate share of the fair market value of each partnership asset. The partner also expects to be compensated for a share of the partnership's going-concern value. *Property* payments [called § 736(b) payments] represent the former type of buyout provision, and *income* payments [§ 736(a) payments] typically represent the latter. Once the total buyout price is determined, § 736 provides rules for determining the allocation between income and property payments, but leaves some room for negotiation between the partner and the partnership over which component of the buyout represents each type of payment.

[13]A successor is typically the estate of the deceased or the party who inherits the decedent's interest.

These paragraphs and Example 22 describe only the general effects of § 736 and do not cover all the nuances of the provision. In general, property payments [§ 736(b) payments] are cash distributions paid by the partnership to the partner in exchange for the partner's interest in partnership assets. The partnership may not deduct these amounts. If the partnership owns no hot assets, the property payment is treated under the normal proportionate distribution rules. If the partnership owns certain hot assets (e.g., depreciation recapture or substantially appreciated inventory), and the retiring partner receives only cash, the distribution is not proportionate. In this case, the property payments to the partner are allocated between cash payments for the partner's share of (1) hot assets and (2) other assets. The hot asset portion is treated as if it were a proportionate distribution of all hot assets and a sale back to the partnership, as illustrated in Example 21. The income recognized in the hot asset sale is ordinary income, and the gain or loss recognized on the rest of the property payments is capital gain or loss.

Income payments [§ 736(a) payments] are treated as a partner's distributive share of partnership income or, alternatively, as a guaranteed payment to the retiring partner. Recall from Chapter 10 that the partner receiving a guaranteed payment recognizes ordinary income. Depending on whether the amount is a distributive share or a guaranteed payment, either (1) the remaining partners report a lesser share of partnership income (distributive share), or (2) the partnership deducts the guaranteed payment.

**EXAMPLE 22**

Pamela receives cash of $15,000 in liquidation of her partnership interest, in which she has a basis of $10,000. The partnership owns no hot assets. After following all the classification requirements of § 736, $12,000 of this amount is classified as a property payment, and $3,000 is classified as a guaranteed payment. The $12,000 property payment is treated as a distribution from the partnership in exchange for her partnership interest, so Pamela recognizes a $2,000 capital gain on this part of her liquidation proceeds ($12,000 property payment − $10,000 basis in interest). She recognizes $3,000 ordinary income for the guaranteed payment, and the partnership deducts the same amount. ■

## PROPERTY PAYMENTS

Cash payments made for the partner's pro rata share of the fair market value of each partnership asset are classified as § 736(b) payments. The following items are not treated as § 736(b) payments, however, if (1) the partnership is primarily a service provider (i.e., "capital is not a material income-producing factor for the partnership") and (2) the retiring or deceased partner was a general partner in the partnership:

- Payments made for the partner's pro rata share of unrealized receivables. For purposes of this rule, unrealized receivables do not include potential depreciation recapture.
- Payments made for the partner's pro rata share of the partnership goodwill, unless the partnership agreement states that the payments are for goodwill. This exception applies only to payments for goodwill that exceed the partner's pro rata share of the partnership's inside basis for goodwill.
- Certain annuities and lump-sum payments made to retiring partners or deceased partner's successors.

If such payments are made by a service-oriented partnership to a general partner, they are classified as § 736(a) payments.

**EXAMPLE 23**

The ABC Partnership has the following balance sheet at the end of the current tax year:

|  | Basis | FMV |  | Basis | FMV |
|---|---|---|---|---|---|
| Cash | $36,000 | $36,000 | Anne, capital | $15,000 | $27,000 |
| Unrealized receivables | –0– | 18,000 | Bonnie, capital | 15,000 | 27,000 |
| Land | 9,000 | 27,000 | Cindy, capital | 15,000 | 27,000 |
| Total | $45,000 | $81,000 | Total | $45,000 | $81,000 |

Partner Anne is a general partner retiring from the service-oriented partnership. She receives $36,000 cash, none of which is stated to be for goodwill. Since the fair market value of Anne's share of the three recorded assets is only $27,000 (⅓ × $81,000), the $9,000 excess payment is for unstated goodwill.

The payment Anne receives for her interest in the cash and land is a § 736(b) property payment. This payment is $21,000, consisting of $12,000 paid for the cash (⅓ × $36,000) and $9,000 paid for Anne's share of the fair market value of the land (⅓ × $27,000). The remaining cash of $15,000 is for her $6,000 interest in the unrealized receivables and for $9,000 unstated goodwill and is a § 736(a) payment. ■

Section 736(b) payments for "nonhot" assets are treated first as a return of the partner's outside basis in the partnership.[14] Once the entire basis is returned, any additional amounts are taxed to the partner as capital gain. If the cash distributions are not sufficient to return the partner's entire outside basis, the shortfall is taxed to the partner as a capital loss.[15]

**EXAMPLE 24**

In Example 23, the property payment of $21,000 cash includes amounts for Anne's share of land and cash only, neither of which is a hot asset. If Anne's outside basis is $15,000, she recognizes capital gain of $6,000 [($12,000 + $9,000) – $15,000] on the distribution. However, if Anne's outside basis is $25,000, she recognizes a $4,000 capital loss on the distribution [($12,000 + $9,000) – $25,000]. The partnership cannot deduct any part of the $21,000 property payment. ■

If part of the property payment is for the partner's share of hot assets, the § 736(b) payment is allocated between the portion related to hot assets and the portion related to other assets. The portion of the payment *not* related to hot assets is treated as described in Example 24. The portion of the payment related to hot assets is treated as discussed earlier under Disproportionate Distributions. Distributions that are disproportionate to the partner's share of hot assets of the partnership are treated as two separate transactions:

- First, the partner's proportionate share of hot assets is deemed to be distributed. A partner cannot step up the basis in hot assets, so on the distribution, the hot assets take the lesser of the partnership's inside basis for the hot assets or the partner's outside basis in the interest.
- Second, these hot assets are deemed to be sold back to the partnership at fair market value. A portion of the § 736(b) payment is allocated to the partnership's deemed purchase of the hot assets.

---

[14]§§ 736(b) and 731(a)(1).                    [15]§ 731(a)(2).

**EXAMPLE 25**

If, in Example 23, Anne was a limited partner or the partnership was capital-intensive, the entire payment of $36,000 is a § 736(b) property payment. The $36,000 payment is allocated between hot assets and other assets. The payment for cash and land is a payment for Anne's other assets, as is the payment for partnership goodwill. The payment for the unrealized receivables, however, is a payment for Anne's share of the partnership's hot assets.

The partnership is treated first as distributing Anne's $6,000 proportionate share of unrealized receivables. Anne's carryover basis in the receivables is $0.

Anne then resells the unrealized receivables to the partnership for their $6,000 fair market value. She reports $6,000 of ordinary income on this sale. The partnership now has a basis of $6,000 in its $18,000 of accounts receivable.

The partnership paid Anne $36,000. Of this amount, $6,000 is to "repurchase" her share of receivables; the remaining $30,000 is in exchange for the partnership's other assets ($12,000 for cash + $9,000 for land + $9,000 for goodwill). Anne calculates and reports a $15,000 capital gain ($30,000 payment − $15,000 basis) in addition to the $6,000 ordinary income. ■

## INCOME PAYMENTS

All payments that are not classified as § 736(b) property payments are categorized as § 736(a) income payments. These income payments are further classified into two categories. Payments that are *not* determined by reference to partnership income are treated as guaranteed payments. They are fully taxable as ordinary income to the distributee partner and are fully deductible by the continuing partnership.

Section 736(a) income payments that are determined by reference to partnership income are treated as distributive shares of that income (i.e., an allocation of partnership income for the year). They are taxed to the distributee partner according to their character to the partnership. Thus, for example, they may be taxed as capital gain as well as ordinary income.[16] Since this capital gain and ordinary income are allocated to the liquidated partner, the payments reduce the amount of partnership capital gain and ordinary income allocated to the remaining partners.[17]

**EXAMPLE 26**

Continue with the same facts as in Example 23 where the partnership is service oriented. The $6,000 cash payment ($18,000 × ⅓) for Anne's pro rata share of the unrealized receivables is classified as a § 736(a) income payment, as is the $9,000 payment for unstated goodwill.

Because the $15,000 § 736(a) income payment ($6,000 + $9,000) is not determined by reference to partnership income, the payment is classified as a guaranteed payment. It is included as ordinary income on Anne's tax return and is deductible by the partnership. ■

The following table summarizes the taxation results of Examples 23 through 26, for a partnership where capital is not a material income-producing factor and where it is. In both cases, Anne's basis in her partnership interest was $15,000 before the distribution.

| | Tax Character to Anne | Deduction to ABC |
|---|---|---|
| **Service-oriented partnership:** | | |
| § 736(b) (Example 24) | $ 6,000 capital gain | None |
| § 736(a) (Example 26) | 15,000 ordinary income | $15,000 |
| Total gain | $21,000 | |

---

[16]§ 702(b).

[17]Reg. § 1.736–1(a)(4).

| | Tax Character to Anne | | Deduction to ABC |
|---|---|---|---|
| **Capital-intensive partnership:** | | | |
| § 736(b) (Example 25) | $15,000 | capital gain | None |
| § 736(b) (Example 25) | 6,000 | ordinary income | None |
| § 736(a) (Example 25) | –0– | ordinary income | None |
| Total gain | $21,000 | | |

As this table illustrates, the characterization under § 736 does not change the overall gain: in both cases Anne recognizes total gain of $21,000. This is appropriate since she receives $36,000 cash against a basis of $15,000.

The character of Anne's income differs solely as a result of the characterization of goodwill. For the service-oriented partnership with unstated goodwill, the payment for goodwill results in ordinary income to the partner. For the capital-intensive partnership, or if the partner is a limited partner, goodwill results in capital gain.

From the partnership's point of view, it is entitled to a deduction for goodwill payments only if it is a service partnership and the retiring partner is a general partner, and then only if the goodwill payment is not stated in the partnership agreement.

The partnership's position also differs as a result of the treatment of unrealized receivables. As a service partnership, it can claim a current deduction for the amount of the distribution related to the receivables. As a capital-intensive partnership, ABC has a cost basis in the receivables when it is deemed to repurchase them from Anne. When the receivables are collected, the partnership's ordinary income is reduced.

## SERIES OF PAYMENTS

Frequently, the partnership and retiring partner agree that the buyout payment may be made over several years in specified installments. This minimizes the negative cash-flow impact on the partnership and allows the retiring partner to maximize the dollar amount of the buyout arrangement. In certain cases, such as where a retiring partner has been instrumental in developing a business relationship with specific clients, the parties can agree that the buyout payments will be determined by reference to the future income generated by those clients or by reference to overall partnership income, rather than being fixed in amount. If the partners deal at arm's length and specifically agree to the §§ 736(a) and (b) allocation and timing of each class of payment, the agreement normally controls.[18] In the absence of an agreement classifying the payments under § 736, Regulations specify classification rules for each payment. In either situation, certain tax planning opportunities arise that are beyond the scope of this text.

Concept Summary 11–3 reviews the rules for liquidating distributions under § 736.

**LO.6**

Calculate the selling partner's amount and character of gain or loss on the sale or exchange of a partnership interest.

# Sale of a Partnership Interest

A partner can sell or exchange a partnership interest, in whole or in part. The transaction can be between the partner and a third party; in this case, it is similar in concept to a sale of corporate stock. Or, as described in the last section, the

---

[18]Reg. § 1.736–1(b)(5).

| CONCEPT SUMMARY 11–3 |
| --- |

### Liquidating Distributions of Cash When the Partnership Continues

1. Payments made by an ongoing partnership to a liquidating partner are classified as § 736(a) income payments or as § 736(b) property payments.
2. Section 736(b) property payments are payments made for the liquidated partner's share of partnership assets.
3. If the partnership is a service provider and the partner is a general partner, payments made for the liquidated partner's share of certain unrealized receivables, certain goodwill that is not provided for in the partnership agreement, and certain annuity payments are classified as § 736(a) income payments.
4. Section 736(a) income payments are the payments mentioned in Item 3 above and any other payments that are not classified as § 736(b) property payments.
5. To the extent the § 736(b) property payment is for the partner's share of partnership hot assets, the partner is deemed to have received and sold his or her share of such assets to the partnership. The partner reports ordinary income on this transaction, and the partnership will have a cost basis in the hot asset.
6. To the extent the § 736(b) property payments are classified as a payment for the partner's share of the partnership's "nonhot" assets, the payment is taxed as a return of the partner's outside basis. Any excess cash received over the partner's outside basis is taxed as capital gain.
7. Section 736(a) income payments are further classified as either guaranteed payments or distributive shares. Guaranteed payments are taxable as ordinary income to the partner and are deductible by the partnership. Distributive shares retain the same tax character to the partner as they had to the partnership. Distributive shares paid to the liquidated partner are excludible from the continuing partners' tax returns.

transaction can be between the partner and the partnership, in which case it is similar in concept to a redemption of corporate stock by the entity. The transfer of a partnership interest produces different results from the transfer of corporate stock because both the entity and aggregate concepts apply to the partnership situation, whereas only the entity concept applies to a sale of stock. The effect of the different rules is that gain or loss resulting from a sale of a partnership interest may be divided into capital gain or loss and ordinary income or loss.

### GENERAL RULES

Generally, the sale or exchange of a partnership interest results in gain or loss, measured by the difference between the amount realized and the selling partner's adjusted basis in the partnership interest.[19]

**Liabilities.** In computing the amount realized and the adjusted basis of the interest sold, the selling partner's share of partnership liabilities must be determined, as discussed in Chapter 10. The purchasing partner includes any assumed indebtedness as a part of the consideration paid for the partnership interest.[20]

*EXAMPLE 27* Cole originally contributed $50,000 in cash for a one-third interest in the CDE Partnership. During the time Cole was a partner, his share of partnership income was $90,000, and he withdrew $60,000 cash. Cole's capital account balance is now $80,000, and partnership

---

[19]§ 741.    [20]§ 742.

liabilities are $45,000, of which Cole's share is $15,000. Cole's outside basis is $95,000 ($80,000 capital account + $15,000 share of partnership debts).

Cole sells his partnership interest to Stephanie for $110,000 cash, with Stephanie assuming Cole's share of partnership liabilities. The total amount realized by Cole is $125,000 ($110,000 cash received + $15,000 of partnership debts transferred to Stephanie). Cole's gain on the sale is $30,000 ($125,000 realized − adjusted basis of $95,000).

Stephanie's adjusted basis for her partnership interest is the purchase price of $125,000 ($110,000 cash paid + $15,000 assumed partnership debt). ■

**Income Allocation.**  When a partner sells an entire interest in the partnership:

- income for the partnership interest for the tax year is allocated between the buying partner and the selling partner, and
- the partnership's tax year "closes" with respect to the selling partner.

The closing of the tax year causes the selling partner to report the share of income on the sale date rather than at the end of the partnership's tax year.

The selling partner's basis is adjusted for the allocated income or loss before the partner calculates the gain or loss on the sale of the interest.

**EXAMPLE 28**

On September 30, 2003, Erica sells her 20% interest in the Evergreen Partnership to Jason for $25,000. Erica is a calendar year taxpayer. Evergreen owns no hot assets, and its tax year ends on June 30.

Before the sale, Erica's basis in the partnership interest is $8,000. Her share of partnership income is $10,000 for the period she owned the partnership interest. Since the partnership's tax year closes with respect to Erica, she must report $10,000 of income on her 2003 tax return. Her basis in the partnership interest is increased to $18,000, and she recognizes a $7,000 capital gain on the sale.

Note that Erica will also report income from Evergreen's tax year ending on June 30, 2003, on her 2003 tax return. ■

There are several acceptable methods of determining the partner's share of income.[21] Under one method, the partnership merely prorates annual income and allocates an amount to the buying and selling partners based on the number of days (or months) in the partnership's tax year in which they were partners. Another method is called the *interim closing of the books* method. As the name implies, the partnership determines its actual income through the date the selling partner sold the interest and allocates a proportionate share of that income to the partner. If partnership earnings are seasonal, the two methods can produce vastly different results.

**EXAMPLE 29**

Larissa sold her 40% interest in the Owl Partnership to Megan on July 1 of the current tax year. Both Larissa and the partnership report on a calendar year basis. The partnership's income was $60,000 through June 30, and its income for the last half of the year was $2,000. Under the annual proration method, the partnership's income for the year is $62,000, of which 40%, or $24,800, is allocated to the 40% interest. Based on the number of months each was a partner, both Larissa and Megan report income of $12,400 for the current year.

Under the interim closing method, Larissa is allocated 40% of $60,000, or $24,000, and Megan is allocated 40% of $2,000, or $800 of partnership income. ■

If the partnership uses the cash method for certain items such as interest, taxes, rent, or other amounts that accrue over time, it must allocate these items to each

---

[21]§ 706(d)(1) and Regulations thereunder.

day in the tax year over which they economically accrue and use the interim closing method for these items in determining the amount allocated to a selling partner.[22]

The partnership is not required to issue a Schedule K–1 to the selling partner until the normal filing of its tax return. The partner, though, is required to include the share of partnership income as of the sale date. Consequently, the partner may have to obtain an extension for filing his or her personal return until the partnership provides a Schedule K–1. If the partnership uses an IRS-approved fiscal year and the partner uses a calendar year, income bunching may occur, as described in Example 28.

**Tax Reporting.**   Partners who sell or exchange a partnership interest must promptly notify the partnership of the transfers. After notification is received, the partnership may be required to file an information statement with the IRS for the calendar year in which the transfers took place. The statement lists the names and addresses of the transferors and transferees. The partnership provides all parties with a copy of the statement.

## EFFECT OF HOT ASSETS

A major exception to capital gain or loss treatment on the sale or exchange of a partnership interest arises when a partnership has hot assets. As noted previously, *hot assets* are *unrealized receivables* and *inventory*, assets that, when collected or disposed of by the partnership, would cause it to recognize ordinary income. When a partner sells the interest in a partnership, it is as if the partnership had sold its hot assets and allocated to the selling partner the partner's proportionate share of the ordinary income or loss created by the sale. The primary purpose of this rule is to prevent a partner from converting ordinary income into capital gain through the sale of a partnership interest.[23]

**Unrealized Receivables.**   The term "unrealized receivables" generally has the same meaning as in the earlier discussion of disproportionate distributions. As previously noted, unrealized receivables include the accounts receivable of a cash basis partnership and, for sale or exchange purposes, depreciation recapture potential.[24]

EXAMPLE 30

The cash basis Thrush Partnership owns only a $10,000 receivable for rendering health care advice. Its basis in the receivable is zero because no income has been recognized. This item is a hot asset because ordinary income is not generated until Thrush collects on the account.

Jacob, a 50% partner, sells his interest to Mark for $5,000. If Jacob's basis in his partnership interest is $0, his total gain is $5,000. The entire gain is attributable to Jacob's share of the unrealized receivable, so his gain is taxed as ordinary income. ■

Depreciation recapture represents ordinary income the partnership would recognize if it sold depreciable property. Under the aggregate theory, the selling partner's share of depreciation recapture potential is treated as an unrealized receivable and is taxed to the selling partner as ordinary income, rather than capital gain. (Recall that depreciation recapture is *not* treated as an unrealized receivable for § 736 purposes, discussed previously.)

---

[22]§ 706(d)(2).
[23]§ 751(a).

[24]§ 751(a)(1).

**EXAMPLE 31**

Andrew sells his 40% interest in the accrual basis Wren Partnership. The partnership has a depreciable business asset that it originally purchased for $25,000. The asset now has an adjusted basis of $15,000 and a market value of $30,000. Depreciation recapture potential is $10,000 ($25,000 − $15,000). In this case, Wren holds a $10,000 unrealized receivable with a zero basis and a $20,000 ($30,000 − $10,000) nonhot asset with an adjusted basis of $15,000. If Wren sold the asset for $30,000, it would recognize $10,000 of ordinary income and $5,000 of § 1231 gain. Therefore, Andrew recognizes $4,000 ($10,000 × 40%) of ordinary income when he sells his partnership interest. ■

The effect of the hot asset rule is that a partner selling an interest in a partnership with hot assets must usually recognize both ordinary income (loss) and capital gain (loss).

**EXAMPLE 32**

Ahmad sells his interest in the equal ABC Partnership to Dave for $17,000 cash. On the sale date, the partnership's cash basis balance sheet reflects the following:

|  | Basis | FMV |  | Basis | FMV |
|---|---|---|---|---|---|
| Cash | $10,000 | $10,000 | Liabilities | $ 9,000 | $ 9,000 |
| Accounts receivable (for services) | –0– | 30,000 | Capital accounts |  |  |
| Nonhot assets | 14,000 | 20,000 | Ahmad | 5,000 | 17,000 |
|  |  |  | Beth | 5,000 | 17,000 |
|  |  |  | Chris | 5,000 | 17,000 |
| Total | $24,000 | $60,000 | Total | $24,000 | $60,000 |

The total amount realized by Ahmad is $20,000 ($17,000 cash price + $3,000 of debt assumed by Dave). Since Ahmad's basis for his partnership interest is $8,000 ($5,000 capital account + $3,000 debt share), the total gain recognized on the sale is $12,000 ($20,000 − $8,000).

Because the partnership has an unrealized receivable, the hot asset rule applies. If ABC sold the accounts receivable for $30,000, Ahmad's proportionate share of the ordinary income recognized on this sale would be $10,000 ($30,000 × ⅓). Consequently, $10,000 of the $12,000 recognized gain on the sale relates to Ahmad's interest in the unrealized receivables and is taxed to him as ordinary income. The remaining gain of $2,000 is taxed to him as a capital gain.

Note that under the hot asset rule, Ahmad still reports $12,000 of income or gain; the hot asset rule merely reclassifies part of the gain as ordinary income. The effect of the rule is that the partnership's inherent ordinary income is allocated to the partner who earned it. ■

**EXAMPLE 33**

Assume the same facts as in Example 32, except that Ahmad's basis in his partnership interest is $10,000. Under these circumstances, Ahmad's capital gain or loss is zero. Ahmad still has $10,000 of ordinary income because of the unrealized receivables.

If Ahmad's basis in the partnership interest is $11,000 (instead of $10,000), an unusual result occurs. Ahmad has a $9,000 overall gain ($20,000 amount realized − $11,000 basis). The receivables generate $10,000 of ordinary income, and Ahmad recognizes a capital *loss* of $1,000 on the rest of the sale. ■

**Inventory.** For a sale or exchange of a partnership interest, the term *inventory* includes all partnership property except money, capital assets, and § 1231 assets. Receivables of an accrual basis partnership are included in the definition of inventory, since they are neither capital assets nor § 1231 assets.[25] This definition also is broad enough to include all items considered to be unrealized receivables.

---

[25]§ 751(d).

## CONCEPT SUMMARY 11–4

### Sale of a Partnership Interest

1. A partnership interest is a capital asset and generally results in capital gain or loss on disposal.
2. The outside bases of the selling and buying partners, as well as the pertinent selling price and purchase price, include an appropriate share of partnership debt.
3. Partnership income or loss for the interest is allocated between the selling and buying partners. The selling partner's basis is adjusted before the gain or loss on the sale is calculated.
4. The partnership's tax year closes with respect to the selling partner on the sale date; the seller reports partnership income at that time, and income "bunching" may occur.
5. When hot assets are present, the selling partner's overall gain or loss is reclassified into a capital gain or loss portion and an ordinary income or loss amount related to the partnership's underlying hot assets.
6. Hot assets consist of unrealized receivables and inventory.
7. Unrealized receivables include amounts earned by a cash basis taxpayer from services rendered. They also include depreciation recapture potential that would result if an asset were sold at a gain.
8. Inventory includes all partnership property except cash, capital assets, and § 1231 assets. Inventory also includes unrealized receivables.

---

**EXAMPLE 34**

Jan sells her one-third interest in the JKL Partnership to Matt for $20,000 cash. On the sale date, the partnership balance sheet reflects the following:

|  | Basis | FMV |  | Basis | FMV |
|---|---|---|---|---|---|
| Cash | $10,000 | $10,000 | Jan, capital | $15,000 | $20,000 |
| Inventory | 21,000 | 30,000 | Kelly, capital | 15,000 | 20,000 |
| Nonhot assets | 14,000 | 20,000 | Lynn, capital | 15,000 | 20,000 |
| Total | $45,000 | $60,000 | Total | $45,000 | $60,000 |

The overall gain on the sale is $5,000 ($20,000 − $15,000). Jan's share of the appreciation in the inventory is $3,000 [($30,000 − $21,000) × ⅓]. Therefore, she recognizes $3,000 of ordinary income because of the inventory and $2,000 of capital gain from the rest of the sale. ∎

Concept Summary 11–4 enumerates the rules that apply to sales of partnership interests.

---

**LO.7**

Describe tax issues related to other dispositions of partnership interests.

# Other Dispositions of Partnership Interests

Partnership interests may be reduced or terminated, and partnerships liquidated, in a variety of other ways, including the following:

- Transfer of the interest to a corporation when the partners control the corporation after the transfer.
- Transfer of the interest to a corporation when the partners *do not* control the corporation after the transfer.
- Like-kind exchanges.
- Death of a partner.
- Gifts.

## TRANSFERS TO A CORPORATION

Transfers of a partnership interest to a corporation may take place when one or all partners are ready to retire from the business; they may exchange the partnership interest for stock in an existing corporation and cease to be involved in the day-to-day operations of the business. Alternatively, many partnerships incorporate simply to obtain the protection from liability or other advantages of the corporate form and make no real changes in business operations. Incorporation may occur at a time when the business is expanding and wants to obtain equity capital from issuing shares to outsiders. The corporate form may also provide tax advantages for a successful business that prefers to retain some earnings for internal expansion without having them taxed at the high individual tax rates of the owners.

Recall from Chapter 3 the controlled corporation rules of § 351. These rules provide that gain or loss is not recognized on the transfer of property to a corporation solely in exchange for stock in that corporation if, immediately after the exchange, the stockholders are in control of the corporation.

In many cases, including most of those in which an existing partnership is incorporated and continues to operate, § 351 conditions are met, and the transfer of the partnership interest to the corporation is a nontaxable exchange. If the partners transferring the property do not satisfy the 80 percent control requirements of § 351, they recognize gain or loss on the transfer according to standard rules for sales or exchanges.

If the partnership interest transferred represents 50 percent or more of the total interest in capital or profits, the partnership is terminated. Partnership termination is discussed later in the chapter.

**Incorporation Methods.**   Consider the situation where the partners decide to incorporate an existing partnership by creating a new corporation owned entirely by the partners. At least three alternative methods are available for structuring the incorporation transaction:

- Each partner's interest is transferred to the corporation in exchange for stock under the usual § 351 rules. As a result, the partnership terminates, and the corporation owns all partnership assets and liabilities. The corporation takes a substituted basis for the assets, and the old partners have a substituted basis for the stock.
- The partnership transfers all of its assets to the corporation in exchange for stock and the assumption of partnership liabilities. The stock then is distributed to the partners (generally in a liquidating distribution) in proportion to their partnership interests. The corporation takes a carryover basis for the assets, and the old partners have a substituted basis for the stock.
- The partnership makes a pro rata distribution of all of its assets and liabilities to its partners in complete liquidation. The partners then transfer their undivided interests in the assets and liabilities to the corporation in exchange for stock under § 351. The corporation's basis for the assets is the substituted basis of those assets to the partners. The partners have a substituted basis for the stock.

Assuming that existing partnership debt does not exceed the basis of transferred assets, none of the three incorporation methods generates a recognized gain or loss. They may, however, result in different inside and outside basis amounts. Thus, selecting the appropriate incorporation method is crucial.

## LIKE-KIND EXCHANGES

The nontaxable like-kind exchange rules do not apply to the exchange of interests in different partnerships.[26] These exchanges are fully taxable under the sale or exchange rules discussed previously. However, an exchange of interests in the same partnership is generally a nontaxable event.[27]

## DEATH OF A PARTNER

If a partner dies, the taxable year of the partnership closes with respect to that partner on the date of death.[28] The deceased partner's share of partnership income or loss is computed to that date and is reported on the partner's final Form 1040.

In professional partnerships, local law may prohibit an estate or other successor from continuing as a partner (beyond a certain time period). In most cases, the remaining partners want to buy out or liquidate the deceased partner's interest in the partnership. The previously discussed rules pertaining to sales and liquidations of partnership interests apply to these transactions.

## GIFTS

Generally, the donor of a partnership interest recognizes neither gain nor loss. If the donor's entire interest is transferred, all items of partnership income, loss, deduction, or credit attributable to the interest are prorated between the donor and donee.

The taxable year of the partnership does not close with respect to the donor, however, so the donor reports his or her share of partnership income or loss at the end of the partnership's tax year.

As the following Ethical Considerations indicates, the gift of an interest in a partnership owning unrealized receivables can be problematic.

---

**ETHICAL CONSIDERATIONS** | **Assignment of Income**

Jim is a partner in a cash basis partnership that specializes in personal injury matters. Cases are accepted on a contingent fee basis. If the client wins, the firm gets 30 percent of the recovery. If the client loses, no fee results. Just before a large judgment is awarded, Jim gives half of his partnership interest to his son, an attorney. The son recognizes as income the portion of the award attributable to the partnership interest he received as a gift. What is Jim trying to accomplish? Will it work?

---

**L0.8**

Calculate the optional adjustments to basis under § 754.

# Optional Adjustments to Property Basis

When a partner purchases a partnership interest, the purchase price reflects what the acquiring partner believes the interest in the partnership is worth. This price reflects, to a large extent, the value the partner placed on the partnership assets.

---

[26]§ 1031(a)(2)(D).
[27]Rev.Rul. 84–52, 1984–1 C.B. 157.

[28]§ 706(c)(2)(A).

Because the value of the assets probably differs from their inside bases, a discrepancy exists between the purchasing partner's outside basis and that partner's share of the inside basis of partnership assets.

If the partnership makes an **optional adjustment election (§ 754 election),** the inside basis of the partnership property can be adjusted to reflect the purchase price paid by the partner. If the election is not made, the statute produces some inequitable results.

**EXAMPLE 35**

A partnership owns a building with an adjusted basis of $450,000 and a fair market value of $900,000. George buys a one-third interest in the partnership for $300,000 (an amount equal to one-third of the value of the building). The partnership does not make an election under § 754. Although the price George paid for the interest was based on fair market value, the building's depreciation continues to be determined on the partnership's related adjusted basis of $450,000, of which George's share is only $150,000. ■

**EXAMPLE 36**

In contrast, assume that the building in Example 35 had an adjusted basis of $600,000 and a fair market value of $300,000. Assume also that George purchased the one-third interest for $100,000 (an amount equal to one-third of the value of the building). Although the purchase price was based on fair market value, George obtains the benefit of *double* depreciation deductions since these deductions are calculated on the adjusted basis of the depreciable property ($600,000), which is twice the property's market value. ■

A result similar to that in Example 35 can take place when a partnership purchases a retiring partner's interest with a cash payment that is greater than that partner's outside basis for the partnership interest. Without a § 754 election, the partnership cannot increase the adjusted basis of its assets for the excess cash paid to the retiring partner.[29]

An optional adjustment-to-basis election can be made for any year in which a transfer or distribution occurs by attaching a statement to a timely filed partnership return (including extensions).[30] An election is binding for the year for which it is made and for all subsequent years, unless the IRS consents to its revocation. Permission to revoke is granted for business reasons, such as a substantial change in the nature of the business or a significant increase in the frequency of interest transfers. Permission is not granted if it appears the primary purpose is to avoid downward adjustments to basis otherwise required under the election.

## ADJUSTMENT: SALE OR EXCHANGE OF AN INTEREST

If the § 754 optional adjustment-to-basis election is in effect and a partner's interest is sold to or exchanged with a third party, or a partner dies, the partnership adjusts the basis of its assets as illustrated in the following calculation:[31]

| | |
|---|---|
| Transferee's outside basis in the partnership | $ xxx |
| Less: Transferee's share of the inside basis of all partnership property | (xxx) |
| Adjustment | $ xxx |

If the amount calculated is positive, the partnership increases the adjusted basis of its assets. If the amount is negative, the basis of the assets is decreased. In either

[29]§§ 743(a) and 734(a), respectively.
[30]§ 754.

[31]§ 743(b).

case, the adjustment affects the basis of partnership property with respect to the transferee partner only. When a portion of the optional adjustment results in a step-up of depreciable property, the transferee partner generally must depreciate this amount as if it were a newly acquired asset. The transferee partner, therefore, shares in the depreciation taken by the partnership on the original asset and, in addition, reports all of the depreciation taken on the basis created by the optional adjustment.

The partner's basis in each property item for which an optional adjustment has been made equals the partner's share of the inside basis for the property item plus or minus the partner's optional basis adjustment that is allocated to that property.

**EXAMPLE 37**

*Optional adj wanted to basis* (handwritten)

Keith is a member of the KLM Partnership, and all partners have equal interests in capital and profits. The partnership has made an optional adjustment-to-basis election. Keith's interest is sold to Shawn for $76,000. The balance sheet of the partnership immediately before the sale shows the following:

|  | Basis | FMV |  | Basis | FMV |
|---|---|---|---|---|---|
| Cash | $ 15,000 | $ 15,000 | Capital accounts |  |  |
| Depreciable assets | 150,000 | 213,000 | Keith | $ 55,000 | $ 76,000 |
|  |  |  | Leif | 55,000 | 76,000 |
|  |  |  | Marta | 55,000 | 76,000 |
| Total | $165,000 | $228,000 | Total | $165,000 | $228,000 |

The adjustment is the difference between the basis of Shawn's interest in the partnership and his share of the adjusted basis of partnership property. The basis of Shawn's interest is his purchase price, or $76,000. His one-third share of the adjusted basis of partnership property is $55,000 ($165,000 × ⅓). The optional adjustment that is added to the basis of partnership property is $21,000.

| | |
|---|---|
| Transferee's outside basis in partnership | $ 76,000 |
| Less: Transferee's share of inside basis of all partnership property | (55,000) |
| Increase | $ 21,000 |

The $21,000 basis increase is treated as a new depreciable asset. Depreciation on this asset is allocated to Shawn. If the partnership later sells all the underlying assets, Shawn's share of the gain takes into account the remaining (undepreciated) balance of the $21,000 step-up. ■

## ADJUSTMENT: PARTNERSHIP DISTRIBUTIONS

Optional adjustments to basis are also available to the partnership when property is distributed to a partner. If a § 754 optional adjustment-to-basis election is in effect, the basis of partnership property is *increased* by the following:[32]

- Any gain recognized by a distributee partner.
- The excess of the partnership's adjusted basis for any distributed property over the adjusted basis of that property in the hands of the distributee partner.

---

[32]§ 734(b).

Conversely, the basis of partnership property is *decreased* by the following:

- Any loss recognized by a distributee partner.
- In the case of a liquidating distribution, the excess of the distributee partner's adjusted basis of any distributed property over the basis of that property to the partnership.

**EXAMPLE 38**

Rena has a basis of $50,000 in her partnership interest and receives a building with an adjusted basis to the partnership of $120,000 in termination of her interest. (The partnership has no hot assets.) The building's basis in Rena's hands is $50,000 under the proportionate liquidating distribution rules. If an optional adjustment-to-basis election is in effect, the partnership increases the basis of its remaining property by $70,000.

| | |
|---|---|
| Partnership's adjusted basis in distributed property | $120,000 |
| Less: Distributee's basis in distributed property | (50,000) |
| Increase | $ 70,000 |

**EXAMPLE 39**

Assume the same facts as in Example 38, except the partnership's basis in the building was $40,000. Rena's basis in the building is still $50,000, and the partnership reduces the basis of its remaining property by $10,000.

| | |
|---|---|
| Distributee's basis in distributed property | $ 50,000 |
| Less: Partnership's adjusted basis in distributed property | (40,000) |
| Decrease | $ 10,000 |

Although these rules may seem confusing at first reading, understanding the theory on which they are based helps to clarify the situation. Section 734(b) assumes that the inside basis for all partnership assets equals the outside basis for all of the partners' interests immediately before the distribution. When this equality exists both before and after a distribution, no adjustment to the basis of partnership property is necessary. However, when the equality does not exist after the distribution, an adjustment can bring the inside and outside bases back into equality. This is the adjustment that is made by the two increases and the two decreases described in the bulleted lists above.

**EXAMPLE 40**

Assume the Cardinal Partnership has an inside basis of $12,000 for its assets, which have a fair market value of $15,000. Aaron, Bill, and Carmen each have outside bases of $4,000 for their partnership interests. If the partnership liquidates partner Aaron's interest with a $5,000 cash distribution, the resulting balance sheet is unbalanced as follows:

| | Inside (Assets) | | Outside (Capital) |
|---|---|---|---|
| Before | $12,000 | = | $12,000 |
| Distribution | (5,000) | ≠ | (4,000) |
| After | $ 7,000 | ≠ | $ 8,000 |

This unbalanced situation can be eliminated by adding $1,000 to the inside basis of the formula. Note that this is the same amount as the gain that Aaron recognizes on the distribution ($5,000 cash − $4,000 outside basis = $1,000 gain). Therefore, by adding the amount of

Aaron's gain to the inside basis of the partnership assets, the inside basis = outside basis formula is back in balance.

| Inside (Assets) | | Outside (Capital) |
|---|---|---|
| $7,000 | ≠ | $8,000 |
| +1,000 | | |
| $8,000 | = | $8,000 |

Note that if the partnership liquidates Aaron's interest with a distribution of land having a $5,000 inside basis, the same unbalanced situation occurs. Although this transaction does not create any recognized gain for Aaron, the $1,000 optional adjustment is the excess of the $5,000 inside basis of the distributed property over the $4,000 substituted basis of that property to Aaron. ■

The two optional adjustment decreases are also explained by this type of analysis.

The basis adjustments created by distributions affect the bases of all remaining partnership properties. Therefore, any depreciation deductions taken on such basis adjustments are allocated to all partners remaining in the partnership after the distribution. *The partnership* also takes these basis adjustments into account in determining any gains or losses on subsequent sales of partnership properties.

---

**LO.9**

Outline the methods of terminating a partnership.

# Termination of a Partnership

When does a partnership's final tax year end? Technically, it ends when the partnership terminates, which occurs on either of the following events:

- No part of the business continues to be carried on by any of the partners in a partnership.
- Within a 12-month period, there is a sale or exchange of 50 percent or more of the partnership's capital and profits.[33]

The partnership terminates and its tax year closes when the partnership incorporates or when one partner in a two-party partnership buys out the other partner, thereby creating a sole proprietorship. A termination also occurs when the partnership ceases operations and liquidates.

The partnership taxable year usually does not close upon the death of a partner or upon the liquidation of a partner's interest, unless the liquidation of the interest of one partner in a two-partner partnership effectively terminates the partnership on the liquidation date. However, the partnership year will close in respect to the deceased or liquidated partner.[34] The deceased or liquidated partner's share of partnership income or loss is computed to the date of death or liquidation and reported on the partner's tax return for the year in which the death or liquidation occurs.

The partnership year does not close upon the entry of a new partner to the partnership. It also does not close upon the sale or exchange of an existing partnership interest unless the transaction results in 50 percent or more of the interests in the partnership capital and profits being sold within a 12-month period.

---

[33]§ 708(b)(1).

[34]§ 706(c)(2)(A).

**EXAMPLE 41**

Partner Olaf, who held a one-third interest in the Oriole Partnership, died on November 20, 2003. The partnership uses an approved fiscal year ending September 30. Olaf used a calendar year. The partnership agreement does not contain a buy-sell provision that is triggered upon the death of a partner. The partnership's tax year does not close with Olaf's death. The partnership tax year does close, however, with respect to Olaf. His share of partnership income or loss for the period from October 1, 2003, to November 20, 2003, is reported on his final Form 1040. The partnership income or loss from November 21, 2003, to September 30, 2004, is taxed to Olaf's estate or other successor. Income from the fiscal year ending September 30, 2003, is reported on Olaf's final income tax return, which covers the period from January 1 to November 20, 2003.

A **technical termination of a partnership** occurs when the partnership business operations continue but the partnership terminates because there has been a sale or exchange of the requisite 50 percent capital and profits interests within 12 months. If the same interest (less than 50 percent) is sold more than once, only one sale is considered in determining whether more than 50 percent has been sold within 12 months. The terminated partnership is deemed to liquidate by transferring its assets and liabilities to a newly formed partnership, which continues its business operations.[35] A technical termination may have numerous consequences, such as changing the taxable year of the new partnership or the cost recovery methods to be used by the new partnership.

**L0.10**

Describe the special considerations of a family partnership.

# Other Issues

## FAMILY PARTNERSHIPS

Family partnerships are owned and controlled primarily by members of the same family. Such partnerships may be established for a variety of reasons. A daughter may have a particular expertise that, coupled with her parents' abilities, allows them to establish a successful business. Often, however, the primary reason for establishing a family partnership is the desire to save taxes. If the parents are in higher marginal tax brackets than the children, family tax dollars are saved by funneling some of the parents' income to the children.

Nevertheless, valid family partnerships are difficult to establish for tax purposes. A basic tenet of tax law is that income must be taxed to the person who performs the services or owns the capital that generates the income. A parent, therefore, cannot transfer only a profits interest to a child and expect the transfer to be recognized for tax purposes.

---

[35]Reg. § 1.708–1(b).

## TAX IN THE NEWS

### FAMILY LIMITED PARTNERSHIPS FOR ESTATE PLANNING

One of the most widely used estate planning tools in recent times has been the family limited partnership. The parents form a partnership with business or other assets and then give their children or grandchildren an interest in the partnership equivalent to the unified credit. Additional tax-free gifts of $11,000 per donee can also be made annually ($22,000 if the parents elect gift splitting).

The appeal of the family partnership has increased considerably in recent years since the IRS issued a Revenue Ruling stating that a minority discount could be applied to gifts made by family members. A minority discount allows the nominal fair market value of a business interest to be reduced to account for the fact that the owner would have difficulty selling it for the cash value of the underlying assets since the purchaser would not have management control over these assets. With a minority discount of 30 percent, for example, a gift with a nominal fair market value of $15,714 could be eligible for the full $11,000 annual exclusion. With such a minority discount, a $1 million interest in a partnership could be transferred by a married couple to three children in only about two-thirds of the time it would take to transfer it without the discount. This strategy is particularly useful for assets that are expected to appreciate in value.

**Capital versus Services.** Because of the concern that family partnerships are established primarily for tax avoidance purposes, a family member is recognized as a partner only in the following cases:

- Capital is a material income-producing factor in the partnership, and the family member's capital interest is acquired in a bona fide transaction (even if by gift or purchase from another family member) in which ownership and control are received.
- Capital is not a material income-producing factor, but the family member contributes substantial or vital services.[36]

If a partnership derives a substantial portion of its gross income from the use of capital, such as inventories or investments in plant, machinery, or equipment, the capital is considered to be a material income-producing factor. Ordinarily, capital is not a material income-producing factor if the partnership's income consists principally of fees, commissions, or other compensation for personal services performed by partners or employees.

**Children as Partners.** When capital is a material income-producing factor and a partnership interest is transferred by gift or sale to a child who is under age 14, the kiddie tax may apply. Under the kiddie tax, some of the dependent child's distributive share of partnership income may be taxed at the parent's tax rate, unless the income share constitutes earned income. Regardless of age, if the child provides bona fide services to a partnership and the income share constitutes earned income, the parent-partner's tax rate is avoided.

**EXAMPLE 42**

Karen operates a first-floor-window-washing business in a summer lakeside resort city. Relatively small amounts of capital are required to operate the sole proprietorship (buckets,

---

[36]§ 704(e).

sponges, squeegees, etc.). During the summer, Karen normally hires middle and high school students to wash windows. Her 13-year-old daughter and 12-year-old son want to work in the business during the summer to earn money for spending and for college. Each obtains the necessary summer work permit. Karen creates the KDS Partnership and gives each child a 5% interest.

Karen figures that if her children were paid an hourly rate, about 5% of KDS's profits would be distributed to them as wages. Karen believes that an ownership interest will help the children learn what running a profitable business entails and prepare them for an active business life after their education is completed.

Since capital is not a material income-producing factor in the business, and the children's profit percentages approximate what they would earn if they were paid an hourly rate, all of the income is classified as earned income. Thus, the kiddie tax is avoided. ■

**Gift of Capital Interest.**   If a family member acquires a capital interest by gift in a family partnership in which capital is a material income-producing factor, only part of the income may be allocated to this interest. First, the donor of the interest is allocated an amount of partnership income that represents reasonable compensation for services to the partnership. Then, the remaining income is divided among the partners in accordance with their capital interests in the partnership. An interest purchased by one family member from another is considered to be created by gift for this purpose.[37]

**EXAMPLE 43**

A partnership in which a parent transferred a 50% interest by gift to a child generated a profit of $90,000. Capital is a material income-producing factor. The parent performed services valued at $20,000. The child performed no services. Under these circumstances, $20,000 is allocated to the parent as compensation. Of the remaining $70,000 of income attributable to capital, at least 50%, or $35,000, is allocated to the parent. ■

**LO.11**

Describe the application of partnership provisions to limited liability companies (LLCs) and limited liability partnerships (LLPs).

## LIMITED LIABILITY COMPANIES

Owners of small businesses often wish to combine the limited liability of a corporation with the pass-through provisions of a partnership. S corporations, described in Chapter 12, provide some of these advantages. The limited liability company (LLC) is a form of entity that goes further in combining partnership taxation with limited personal liability for all owners of the entity. All of the states and the District of Columbia have passed legislation permitting the establishment of LLCs.

**Taxation of LLCs.**   A properly structured LLC with two or more owners is taxed as a partnership. Since none of the LLC members is personally liable for any debts of the entity, the LLC is effectively treated as a limited partnership with no general partners. This may result in unusual application of partnership taxation rules. The IRS has not specifically ruled on most aspects of LLC taxation, so several of the following comments are based on speculation about how a partnership with no general partners would be taxed.

- Formation of a new LLC is treated in the same manner as formation of a partnership. Generally, no gain or loss is recognized by the LLC member or the LLC, the member takes a substituted basis in the LLC interest, and the LLC takes a carryover basis in the assets it receives.
- Contributed property with built-in gains or losses is subject to the partnership allocation rules (see the discussion of § 704 under Partnership Allocations

---

[37]§ 704(e)(3).

in Chapter 10). Also, an LLC member contributing built-in gain property can be subject to tax on certain distributions within seven years of the contribution, as mentioned earlier in this chapter.

- In allocating liabilities to the members for basis purposes, liabilities are generally treated as if they are nonrecourse. This occurs because under the entity's legal structure, generally none of the members individually bears the economic risk of loss on a liability.
- An LLC's income and losses are allocated under § 704. Special allocations are permitted, as long as they meet the requirements outlined in Chapter 10.
- Losses are subject to the three deductibility limitations described in Chapter 10: A loss must meet the basis, at-risk, and passive loss limitations to be currently deductible. Since the debt is generally considered nonrecourse to each of the members, it may not be included in the at-risk limitation unless it qualifies as "qualified nonrecourse financing." Also, the IRS has not issued final guidance as to whether a member is treated as a material or active participant of an LLC for passive loss purposes. Presumably, passive or active status will be based on the time the member spends in LLC activities.
- The available taxable years and initial elections discussed in Chapter 10 are applicable to an LLC.
- Transactions between an LLC and its members are treated as described in Chapter 10.
- The rules described in this chapter for distributions, sales of an interest, and retirement of a member's interest under § 736 all apply to an LLC. An LLC can make an election under § 754 to adjust the inside basis of its assets to reflect changes in the member's outside bases resulting from sales of interests or distributions from the entity. Note that a distribution of appreciated property from a C or S corporation would result in taxable gain to the entity, whereas such property takes a carryover or substituted basis when distributed from an LLC.

**Converting to an LLC.** A partnership can convert to an LLC with few, if any, tax ramifications: the old elections of the partnership continue, and the partners retain their bases and ownership interests in the new entity. However, a C or an S corporation that reorganizes as an LLC is treated as having liquidated prior to forming the new entity. The transaction is taxable to both the corporation and the shareholders.

**Advantages of an LLC.** An LLC offers certain advantages over a limited partnership, including the following:

- Generally, none of the owners of an LLC are personally liable for the entity's debts. General partners in a limited partnership have personal liability for partnership recourse debts.
- Limited partners cannot participate in the management of the partnership. All owners of an LLC have the legal right to participate in the entity's management.

The advantages of an LLC over an S corporation are discussed in Chapter 13.

**Disadvantages of an LLC.** The disadvantages of an LLC stem primarily from the entity's relative newness. There is no established body of case law interpreting the various state statutes, so the application of specific provisions is uncertain. An additional uncertainty for LLCs that operate in more than one jurisdiction is which state's law will prevail and how it will be applied.

Among other factors, statutes differ from state to state as to the type of business an LLC can conduct—particularly as to the extent to which certain service-providing firms can operate as LLCs. A service entity may find it can operate as an LLC in one state but not in another.

Despite these uncertainties, LLCs are being formed at increasing rates.

## LIMITED LIABILITY PARTNERSHIPS

Earlier in the chapter, limited partnerships were discussed. Another entity, a limited liability partnership (LLP), has a similar name but quite a different nature. In 1991, Texas became the first state to allow professionals to organize their practices as registered LLPs. Since then, other states have adopted similar legislation. The difference between a general partnership and an LLP is small, but very significant. Recall that general partners are jointly and severally liable for all partnership debts. In some states, partners in a registered LLP are jointly and severally liable for contractual liability (i.e., they are treated as general partners for commercial debt). They are also always personally liable for their own malpractice or other torts. They are not, however, personally liable for the malpractice and torts of their partners. As a result, the exposure of their personal assets to lawsuits filed against other partners and the partnership is considerably reduced.

An LLP must have formal documents of organization and register with the state. Because the LLP is a general partnership in other respects, it does not have to pay any state franchise taxes on its operations—an important difference between LLPs and LLCs in states that impose franchise taxes on LLCs. LLPs are taxed as partnerships under Federal tax statutes.

The IRS has ruled that the conversion of a general partnership into a registered LLP is a continuation of the old partnership for tax purposes, if all the general partners become LLP partners and hold the same proportionate interests in the LLP that they held in the general partnership. This means that all the old partnership's elections continue in the LLP, including accounting methods, the taxable year-end, and the § 754 election.[38]

## ANTI-ABUSE REGULATIONS

The IRS has issued Regulations that allow it to disregard the form of a partnership transaction when it believes that the transaction (or series of transactions) is abusive.[39] Under the Regulation, a transaction is abusive if it satisfies two tests. First, it must have a principal purpose of substantially reducing the present value of the partners' aggregate Federal tax liability. In addition, the potential tax reduction must be inconsistent with the intent of Subchapter K. If the IRS disregards the form of a transaction, it will recast the transaction in a manner that reflects the transaction's underlying economic arrangement.

It is often difficult to determine whether a proposed transaction will substantially reduce the present value of the partners' aggregate tax liability. Partners may not know their personal tax situations until the transaction occurs and the partner's tax return is completed. Practitioners are concerned that the IRS could try to use "perfect hindsight" to determine if a transaction should be recast. This could make it difficult to anticipate the ultimate tax treatment of many partnership transactions.

The IRS says it will not recast transactions that are bona fide business arrangements and offers several examples in the Regulation. The IRS has also announced

---

[38]Ltr.Ruls. 9229016, 9420028, and 9426038.    [39]Reg. § 1.701–2.

that a field examiner cannot invoke the Regulation without approval. Review by a partnership specialty group within the IRS is required before the IRS will challenge a taxpayer's treatment of a transaction under this Regulation.

**Tax Planning Considerations**

## SALES AND EXCHANGES OF PARTNERSHIP INTERESTS

**Delaying Ordinary Income.**   A partner planning to dispose of a partnership interest in a taxable transaction might consider either an installment sale or a pro rata distribution of hot assets, followed by a sale of the remaining interest in the partnership. Although the partner will have ordinary income if these hot assets are sold at a later date, the partner can spread the income over more than one tax year by controlling the disposal dates.

**Basis Adjustment for Transferee.**   If a partnership interest is acquired by purchase, the purchaser may want to condition the acquisition on the partnership's promise to make an election to adjust the basis of partnership assets. Making the election under § 754 results in the basis in the partner's ratable share of partnership assets being adjusted to reflect the purchase price. Failure to do so could result in the loss of future depreciation deductions or could convert ordinary losses into capital losses.

## PLANNING PARTNERSHIP DISTRIBUTIONS

**General Guidelines.**   In planning for any partnership distributions, be alert to the following possibilities:

- When gain recognition is undesirable, ascertain that cash distributions from a partnership, including any debt assumptions or repayments, do not exceed the basis of the receiving partner's interest.
- Distributions of marketable securities may also result in gain, but the current gain can be minimized if the securities *are* appreciated.
- When a partner is to receive a liquidating distribution and the full basis of the interest will not be recovered, the partner's capital loss can be ensured by providing that the only assets received by the partner are cash, unrealized receivables, and inventory. If a capital loss is undesirable, however, the partnership should also distribute a capital or § 1231 asset that will take the partner's remaining basis in the interest. This may result in a more desirable ordinary deduction or loss in the future.
- Current and liquidating distributions may result in ordinary income recognition for either the receiving partner or the partnership if hot assets are present. When such income is undesirable, consider making a distribution of hot assets pro rata to the receiving partner.
- If precontribution gain property is contributed to a partnership, gain to the contributing partner can be further deferred if the partnership waits seven years before (1) distributing the gain property to another partner or (2) distributing other partnership property to the gain partner if the value of the other property exceeds the gain partner's basis in the partnership.
- When the partnership agreement initially is drafted, consider including provisions that govern liquidating distributions of partnership income and property. The specifics of the agreement generally will be followed by the IRS if these and other relevant points are addressed early in the life of the entity.

**Valuation Problems.**   Both the IRS and the courts usually consider the value of a partner's interest or any partnership assets agreed upon by all partners to be correct. Thus, when planning the sale or liquidation of a partnership interest, the results of the bargaining process should be documented. To avoid valuation problems on liquidation, include a formula or agreed-upon valuation procedure in the partnership agreement or in a related buy-sell agreement.

## COMPARING SALES TO LIQUIDATIONS

When a partner disposes of an entire interest in a partnership for a certain sum, the *before-tax* result of a sale of that interest to another partner or partners is the same as the liquidation of the interest under § 736. In other words, if both transactions result in the partner receiving the same amount of pre-tax dollars, the partner should be ambivalent about which form the transaction takes unless one form offers tax savings that the other does not.

The *after-tax* result of a sale of a partnership interest and a liquidation of a partner's interest by an ongoing partnership may differ considerably. One difference occurs when the payment for that interest is extended over several years. When a partner sells the partnership interest to another partner, the selling partner can postpone the recognition of income under the installment sale rules. These rules are very restrictive and require that gain and income be recognized at least as quickly as the proportionate share of the receivable is collected. However, in a liquidation, more flexibility may be available. Under § 736, the § 736(b) payments for partnership property can be made before the income payments under § 736(a). Furthermore, the § 736(b) payments can be treated as a return of basis first with gain recognized only after the distributee partner has received amounts equal to the basis. This treatment results in a deferral of gain and income recognition under § 736 that is not available under the installment sale provisions.

**Payments for Goodwill.**   The partner who purchases a partnership interest often pays an amount that can be attributed, in part, to partnership goodwill. Purchased goodwill is included in a purchasing partner's outside basis for the partnership interest. The partner cannot amortize the goodwill unless (1) the asset qualifies as a § 197 intangible, amortizable over 15 years, and (2) the partnership makes an election under § 754 to adjust the basis of partnership assets to reflect the purchase price paid. In many cases, the purchasing partner will not obtain a tax benefit from the goodwill until the partnership interest is disposed of.

Under § 736, amounts paid by a service partnership for a general partner's share of partnership goodwill can be treated as a § 736(a) payment. If this payment is a guaranteed payment, it is deductible by the partnership. If it is a distributive share, it is excludible from the income stream of the remaining partners. In effect, this is also like a deduction. If (1) capital is a material income-producing factor of the partnership or (2) the distributee partner was a limited partner, payments for goodwill constitute § 736(b) property payments. These payments are not deductible by the partnership and result in increased capital gain (or decreased capital loss) to the retiring partner.

**Termination of Partnership.**   A partnership terminates if 50 percent or more of the total interest in partnership capital and profits is sold within a 12-month period. A liquidation under § 736, however, is not considered a sale or exchange under this rule. Therefore, a partnership can liquidate a partner's interest without terminating a three-partner partnership, even if the liquidated partner had a 98 percent interest in partnership capital and profits immediately before the liquidating distribution.

A sale and a liquidation of a partnership interest also differ in other respects that are beyond the scope of this text. The point to remember is that differences exist that may result in considerable after-tax savings for the partners. Careful planning can result in a properly structured transaction.

## OTHER PARTNERSHIP ISSUES

**Choice of Entity.**   The partnership liquidation rules demonstrate the general superiority of the partnership form to that of the C corporation in the final stage of the business's life:

- A service partnership can effectively claim deductions for its payment to a retiring general partner for goodwill.
- The partnership liquidation itself is not a taxable event. Under corporate rules, however, liquidating distributions and sales in preparation for a distribution are fully taxable.
- Tax liability relative to the liquidation is generated at the partner level, but only upon a recognition event (such as receipt of cash in excess of basis, or sale of an asset received in a distribution). The timing of this event is usually under the control of the (ex-)partner. In this manner, the tax obligations can be placed into the most beneficial tax year and rate bracket.

**Family Partnerships.**   If possible, make certain that very young and elderly members of a family partnership contribute services to the entity, so as to justify their income allocations. These services can comprise the most routine facets of the business, including monitoring and operating copy and fax machines and providing ongoing maintenance of the indoor and outdoor landscaping environments. Although no more than a market level of compensation can be assigned for this purpose, the services themselves constitute evidence of the active role that the partner plays in the operations of the entity.

Since there is no equivalent of the kiddie tax for elderly taxpayers, retention of the founding members of the partnership past the nominal retirement age often facilitates the income-shifting goals of the family.

## KEY TERMS

| | | |
|---|---|---|
| Appreciated inventory, 11–16 | Nonliquidating distribution, 11–3 | Section 754 election, 11–30 |
| Disproportionate distribution, 11–4 | Optional adjustment election, 11–30 | Technical termination of partnership, 11–34 |
| Hot assets, 11–16 | | |
| Liquidating distribution, 11–3 | Proportionate distribution, 11–4 | Unrealized receivables, 11–7 |

## PROBLEM MATERIALS

### Discussion Questions

1. Discuss the types of proportionate distributions from a partnership and describe, in general terms, the tax consequences of each.

2. How is the basis determined for property received in a proportionate liquidating or nonliquidating distribution?

Issue ID

3. The SueBart Partnership distributes the following assets to partner Bart:

   • $10,000 cash.

   • An account receivable with a $10,000 value and a $0 basis to the partnership.

   • A parcel of land with a $10,000 value and a $2,000 basis to the partnership.

   What issues must be considered in determining the tax treatment of the distribution?

4. Describe, in general terms, two types of assets considered "hot assets." When is characterization as a "hot asset" relevant?

5. Distinguish between the treatment of § 736 income and property payments. What are the tax consequences of such payments to the retiring partner, the remaining partners, and the partnership?

6. What is the character of a gain or loss recognized on the sale or exchange of a partnership interest, and how is it determined?

7. Identify amounts that are included in the sales proceeds of a partner selling an interest in the partnership to an unrelated third party. How is the character of the selling partner's gain or loss determined?

Issue ID

8. Discuss the rationale for the basis adjustment election under § 754. Distinguish between the basis adjustments allowed for a sale of a partnership interest by a partner and for distributions of property from the partnership to a partner. When could an unfavorable result occur because of a § 754 election?

9. Which taxpayer makes the optional adjustment-to-basis election, how is the election made, and what is the effect of the election on tax reporting in future years?

Issue ID

10. Tiring of the daily grind and uncertainty associated with the home construction industry, Tim is considering selling his partnership interest to Una, who is not a current member of the partnership. Tim, Una, and Tim's partners are concerned about the tax ramifications of the transaction. What potential tax consequences should be called to the attention of all parties involved?

11. What is a family partnership? Under what circumstances can a family member be a partner in such a partnership? What income allocation is required?

12. If a limited liability company (LLC) incurs debt from an independent third-party bank, how do you think that debt should be treated under the liability-sharing rules discussed in Chapter 10?

13. To what extent are the personal assets of a general partner, limited partner, or member of an LLC subject to (a) contractual liability claims, such as trade accounts payable, and (b) malpractice claims against the entity? Answer the question for partners or members in a general partnership, LLP, nonprofessional LLC, and limited partnership.

Issue ID

14. Jim is retiring from the JSU general services partnership. He is trying to decide whether to sell his 51% interest in the partnership to the other partners or to the partnership. Under either scenario, payments would be paid to Jim over several years and would include amounts in exchange for Jim's share of partnership goodwill. Explain why the method selected may make a difference for tax purposes to Jim, JSU, and the other partners.

## Problems

15. Andrew's outside basis in his interest in the ABC Partnership is $100,000. In a proportionate nonliquidating distribution, the partnership distributes to him cash of $25,000, inventory (fair market value of $30,000, basis to the partnership of $20,000), and land (fair market value of $60,000, basis to the partnership of $30,000). The partnership continues in existence.

a. Does the partnership recognize any gain or loss as a result of this distribution? *No*
b. Does Andrew recognize any gain or loss as a result of this distribution? *No*
c. Calculate Andrew's basis in the land, in the inventory, and in his partnership interest immediately following the distribution.

16. When Peggy's outside basis in the PQR Partnership is $25,000, the partnership distributes to her $10,000 cash, an account receivable (fair market value of $70,000, inside basis to the partnership of $0), and a parcel of land (fair market value of $30,000, inside basis to the partnership of $20,000). Peggy remains a partner in the partnership, and the distribution is proportionate to the partners.
   a. Determine the recognized gain or loss to the partnership as a result of this distribution.
   b. Determine the recognized gain or loss to Peggy as a result of the distribution.
   c. Determine Peggy's basis in the land, account receivable, and PQR Partnership after the distribution.

17. In each of the following independent cases in which the partnership owns no hot assets, indicate:

   • Whether the partner recognizes gain or loss.

   • Whether the partnership recognizes gain or loss.

   • The partner's adjusted basis for the property distributed.

   • The partner's outside basis in the partnership after the distribution.

   a. Martha receives $70,000 cash in partial liquidation of her interest in the partnership. Martha's outside basis for her partnership interest immediately before the distribution is $60,000.
   b. Randy receives $30,000 cash and land with an inside basis to the partnership of $25,000 (value $20,000) in partial liquidation of his interest. Randy's outside basis for his partnership interest immediately before the distribution is $65,000.
   c. Assume the same facts as in (b), except that Randy's outside basis for his partnership interest immediately before the distribution is $40,000.
   d. Curt receives $40,000 cash and an account receivable with a basis of $0 and a fair market value of $30,000 in partial liquidation of his partnership interest. His basis was $50,000 before the distribution. All partners received proportionate distributions.

18. Assume the facts of Problem 17. In each independent case, are additional planning opportunities available to the partnership to maximize its inside basis in its assets? If so, by how much can the basis be increased? What is the effect of any basis increase to the distributee partner or the other partners?

19. Tom's basis in his partnership interest is $41,000. In a proportionate nonliquidating distribution, Tom receives $20,000 cash and two inventory items with bases of $20,000 each to the partnership. The values of the inventory items are $30,000 and $10,000.
   a. How much gain or loss, if any, must Tom recognize on the distribution?
   b. What basis will Tom take in each inventory item?

20. Sam Stevens is a 40% partner in the calendar year Stevens-Stuart Partnership. On January 1, 2003, his basis in his partnership interest is $25,000, including his $13,000 share of partnership liabilities. The partnership has no taxable income or loss for the current year. Stevens-Stuart repays all liabilities before the end of 2003 from cash on hand. In a nonliquidating distribution, the partnership distributes $15,000 cash on December 15. It also distributes inventory proportionately to all partners. Sam receives inventory with a basis of $8,000 and a fair market value of $6,000. In January 2004, Sam, your client, asks your advice regarding treatment of 2003 operations and distributions. Using the format (1) facts, (2) issues, and (3) conclusion and analysis, draft a letter to Sam at the Stevens-Stuart Partnership (1622 E. Henry Street, St. Paul, MN 55163) that addresses the following points:
   a. How much gain or loss does the partnership recognize as a result of 2003 activities?
   b. How much gain or loss must Sam recognize in 2003?

**Decision Making**

**Communications**

c. What is Sam's basis in inventory received?

d. What is Sam's basis in his partnership interest at the end of 2003?

Issue ID

21. Walden is a 40% partner in the WXY Partnership. He became a partner three years ago when he contributed land with a value of $40,000 and a basis of $20,000 (current value is $90,000). Xavier and Yolanda each contributed $30,000 cash for a 30% interest. Walden's basis in his partnership interest is currently $40,000; the other partners' bases are each $30,000. The partnership has the following assets:

|  | Basis | FMV |
|---|---|---|
| Cash | $ 60,000 | $ 60,000 |
| Accounts receivable | –0– | 80,000 |
| Marketable securities | 20,000 | 70,000 |
| Land | 20,000 | 90,000 |
| Total | $100,000 | $300,000 |

The partnership will make a distribution of $150,000 in value to the partners before the end of the current year, but the type of property that will be distributed has not been determined. Describe the tax effects on the partners in each of the following independent distribution alternatives:

a. WXY distributes a $45,000 interest in the land each to Yolanda and Xavier and $60,000 of accounts receivable to Walden.

b. WXY distributes $60,000 cash to Walden, $45,000 of marketable securities to Yolanda, and $45,000 of accounts receivable to Xavier.

c. WXY distributes a $36,000 interest in the land and $24,000 of accounts receivable to Walden and $27,000 of cash and $18,000 of accounts receivable each to Xavier and Yolanda.

Issue ID

22. Use the assets and partners' bases from Problem 21. Assume the partnership distributes all its assets in a liquidating distribution. In deciding the allocation of assets, what issues should the partnership consider to minimize each partner's taxable gains?

23. In each of the following independent liquidating distributions in which the partnership also liquidates, determine the amount and character of any gain or loss to be recognized by each partner and the basis of each asset (other than cash) received. In each case, assume distributions of hot assets are proportionate to the partners.

a. Roxanne has a partnership basis of $23,000 and receives a distribution of $40,000 in cash.

b. Barry has a partnership basis of $30,000 and receives $12,000 cash and a capital asset with a basis to the partnership of $23,000 and a fair market value of $16,000.

c. Jason has a partnership basis of $20,000 and receives $7,000 cash, inventory with a basis to the partnership of $8,000, and a capital asset with a partnership basis of $12,000. The inventory and capital asset have fair market values of $9,000 and $10,000, respectively.

d. Marie has a partnership basis of $25,000 and receives a distribution of $10,000 cash and an account receivable with a basis of $0 to the partnership (value is $3,000).

Decision Making

24. The basis of Lee's partnership interest is $75,000. Lee receives a pro rata liquidating distribution consisting of $42,000 cash and his proportionate share of inventory with a basis of $45,000 to the partnership and a fair market value of $52,000. Assume the partnership also liquidates.

a. How much gain or loss, if any, must Lee recognize as a result of the distribution?

b. What basis will Lee take in the inventory?

c. If the inventory is sold two years later for $48,000, what are the tax consequences to Lee?

d. What are the tax consequences to the partnership as a result of the liquidating distribution?

e. Is any planning technique available to the partnership to avoid any "lost basis" results?

f. Would your answer to (b) change if this had been a nonliquidating distribution?

**Decision Making**

25. Assume the same facts as in Problem 24, except that Lee's basis in the partnership is $130,000 instead of $75,000.
    a. How much gain or loss, if any, must Lee recognize on the distribution?
    b. What basis will Lee take in the inventory?
    c. What are the tax consequences to the partnership?
    d. Can you recommend an alternative distribution?
    e. Would your answer to (a) or (b) change if this had been a nonliquidating distribution?

26. Julie's basis in her partnership interest is $108,000. In a proportionate distribution in liquidation of the partnership, Julie receives $50,000 cash and two parcels of land with bases of $20,000 each to the partnership. The partnership holds both parcels of land for investment, and the parcels have fair market values of $10,000 and $30,000.
    a. How much gain or loss, if any, must Julie recognize on the distribution?
    b. What basis will Julie take in each parcel?
    c. If the land had been held as inventory by the partnership, what effect, if any, would it have on your responses to (a) and (b)?

**Decision Making**

27. Assume the same facts as in Problem 26, except that Julie receives $50,000 cash and a desk having a basis of $1,200 to the partnership and a fair market value of $2,000.
    a. How much loss, if any, may Julie recognize on the distribution?
    b. What basis will Julie take in the desk?
    c. Suppose Julie's 15-year-old son uses the desk for his personal use for one year before Julie sells it for $100. How much loss may Julie recognize on the sale of the desk? What tax planning procedures could have prevented this result?

28. Use the approach introduced in Concept Summary 11–2 to derive the realized and recognized gain or loss for the two owners of the dissolving GH Partnership and the bases of the distributed assets, given the following facts:

| | **Partner George (⅔)** | **Partner Hazel (⅓)** |
| --- | --- | --- |
| Basis in interest | $100,000 | $15,000 |
| Cash received | 40,000 | 20,000 |
| Inventory received | | |
| Market value | 12,000 | 6,000 |
| Basis to GH | 6,000 | 3,000 |
| Building and equipment received | | |
| Market value | 180,000 | 90,000 |
| Basis to GH | 144,000 | 72,000 |
| Depreciation recapture potential | | |
| Amount | 16,000 | 8,000 |
| Basis to GH | –0– | –0– |

29. In 2000, Gabriella contributed land with a basis of $16,000 and a fair market value of $25,000 to the Meadowlark Partnership in exchange for a 25% interest in capital and profits. In 2003, the partnership distributes this property to Juanita, also a 25% partner, in a nonliquidating distribution. The fair market value has increased to $30,000 at the time the property is distributed. Juanita's and Gabriella's bases in their partnership interests are each $40,000 at the time of the distribution.
    a. How much gain or loss, if any, does Gabriella recognize on the distribution to Juanita? What is Gabriella's basis in her partnership interest following the distribution?
    b. What is Juanita's basis in the land she received in the distribution?

c. How much gain or loss, if any, does Juanita recognize on the distribution? What is Juanita's basis in her partnership interest following the distribution?

d. How much gain or loss would Juanita recognize if she later sells the land for its $30,000 fair market value? Is this result equitable?

e. Would your answers to (a) and (b) change if Gabriella originally contributed the property to the partnership in 1992?

30. Winston contributed a tract of undeveloped land to the Nightingale Partnership in 1999. He originally paid $20,000 for the property in 1983, but its value was $70,000 at the date of the contribution. In 2003, the partnership distributes another parcel of land to Winston; the land has a basis to the partnership of $30,000. The fair market value of the distributed property is $100,000 in 2003. Winston's basis in his partnership interest is $60,000 immediately before the distribution.

a. How much gain or loss, if any, does Winston recognize on the distribution?

b. What is Winston's basis in his partnership interest following the distribution?

c. What is Winston's basis in the property he receives in the distribution?

d. After the distribution, what is the partnership's basis in the property originally contributed by Winston?

e. Would your answers to (b), (c), and (d) change if Winston originally contributed the property to the partnership in 1993?

31. The FABB Partnership distributes a marketable security to 25% partner Fred in complete liquidation of his interest in the partnership. Use the following facts to answer the questions that follow:

• The partnership's basis in the security is $10,000, and its value is $20,000. The partnership did not own any of this particular security following the distribution.

• Fred's basis in the partnership interest is $7,500 immediately prior to the distribution.

• Fred is a general partner, and capital is a material income-producing factor to the partnership.

• The partnership owns no hot assets.

a. How is the security classified under § 736?

b. What is the amount of the security distribution that is treated as a cash distribution?

c. How much gain does Fred report on the distribution?

d. What is Fred's basis in the security he receives in the distribution?

32. Maurice is a 10% general partner in the Chartreuse Partnership, which provides consulting services. The partnership distributes $100,000 cash to Maurice in complete liquidation of his partnership interest. Maurice's share of partnership unrealized receivables immediately before the distribution is $40,000. The partnership has no other hot assets. Assume none of the cash payment is for goodwill. Maurice's basis for his partnership interest immediately before the distribution is $50,000.

a. How is the cash payment treated under § 736?

b. How much gain or loss must Maurice recognize on the distribution, and what is the character of these amounts?

c. How does the partnership treat the distribution to Maurice?

d. What planning opportunities might the partnership wish to consider?

e. How would your answers to the above questions change if Maurice were a limited partner?

33. ALF Partnership has three equal partners. One of them, Art, sells his interest to his partner, Lou, for $65,000 cash and the assumption of Art's share of partnership liabilities. On the sale date, the partnership's cash basis balance sheet reflects the following. Assume that capital accounts reflect the partners' bases in their partnership interests, excluding liabilities.

**Decision Making**

|  | Basis | FMV |  | Basis | FMV |
|---|---|---|---|---|---|
| Cash | $120,000 | $120,000 | Note payable | $ 15,000 | $ 15,000 |
| Accounts receivable | –0– | 60,000 | Capital accounts |  |  |
| Capital assets | 15,000 | 30,000 | Art | 40,000 | 65,000 |
|  |  |  | Lou | 40,000 | 65,000 |
|  |  |  | Fran | 40,000 | 65,000 |
| Total | $135,000 | $210,000 | Total | $135,000 | $210,000 |

a. What is the total amount realized by Art on the sale?
b. How much, if any, ordinary income must Art recognize on the sale?
c. How much capital gain must Art report?
d. What is Lou's basis in the partnership interest acquired?
e. If the partnership makes an election to adjust the bases of the partnership assets to reflect the sale, what adjustment is made?

34. Assume in Problem 33 that Art's partnership interest is not sold to another partner. Instead, the partnership makes a liquidating distribution of $65,000 cash to Art, and the remaining partners assume his share of the liabilities. How much gain or loss must Art recognize and how is it characterized? Assume Art is a general partner and capital is not a material income-producing factor to the partnership.

35. Dad is the owner of a 60% general partner interest in the Consulting Services Partnership, in which capital is *not* a material income-producing factor. Two unrelated partners each own 20% partnership interests. Dad's basis in his partnership interest is $300,000.

Dad's son, Dean, worked for the partnership on a part-time basis while he was in college and has shown a strong aptitude for the business. Dad would like to retire and allow Dean to take over the business, but he needs to dispose of his partnership interest for its $600,000 value to do so. The partnership has adequate liquidity to make this distribution.

Dad's share of the partnership's unrealized receivables from services (no depreciation recapture, $0 basis) is $225,000. The partnership has a favorable tax year-end, so the other partners want to make sure the partnership does not terminate. Dean is the beneficiary of a trust fund established by his grandmother. He now receives about $60,000 a year and will control the $750,000 principal amount in four years, when he reaches age 30.

Dad is considering two courses of action:

- Dad can sell his interest to Dean on an installment basis with a balloon payment of the $600,000 principal balance at the end of four years. Dean would pay Dad adequate interest (for purposes of OID and imputed interest rules) on the deferred balance each year. Under this arrangement, the entire 60% interest is deemed to be sold for tax purposes at the time the installment contract is consummated, although gain is deferred until payments are made.

- Dad can allow the partnership to redeem his partnership interest immediately. To structure a transition to the son, the partnership would enter into an employment arrangement with Dean, whereby Dean vests in a 10% interest in the partnership each year for six years in exchange for services rendered to the partnership.

Draft a letter to Dad Thomas (1329 Mesquite Boulevard, Amarillo, TX 79109) addressing the consequences of each proposed alternative. Consider the impact to Dad, the partnership, and Dean.

36. At the end of last year, Ben, a 40% partner in the four-person BBJR Partnership, has an outside basis of $50,000 in the partnership, including a $40,000 share of partnership debt. Ben's share of the partnership's § 1245 recapture potential is $25,000. All parties use the calendar year. Describe the income tax consequences to Ben in each of the following independent situations that take place in the current year:

a. On the first day of the tax year, Ben sells his partnership interest to Marilyn for $80,000 cash and the assumption by Marilyn of the appropriate share of partnership liabilities.

b. Ben dies after a lengthy illness on April 1 of the current year. Ben's brother immediately takes Ben's place in the partnership.

37. Briefly discuss how your responses in Problem 36 would change if the BBJR Partnership had $200,000 of unrealized receivables at the end of the current year, including the § 1245 recapture potential.

38. Daryl, a partner in the cash basis DLL Partnership, has a 30% interest in partnership profits and losses. The partnership's balance sheet at the end of the current year is as follows:

|  | Basis | FMV |  | Basis | FMV |
|---|---|---|---|---|---|
| Cash | $ 25,000 | $ 25,000 | Daryl, capital | $ 54,000 | $135,000 |
| Receivables | –0– | 240,000 | Larry, capital | 63,000 | 157,500 |
| Land | 155,000 | 185,000 | Lewis, capital | 63,000 | 157,500 |
| Total | $180,000 | $450,000 | Total | $180,000 | $450,000 |

Daryl sells his interest in the DLL Partnership to Arnold at the end of the current year for cash of $135,000.

a. How much income must Daryl report on his tax return for the current year from the sale, and what is its nature?

b. If the partnership does not make an optional adjustment-to-basis election, what are the type and amount of income that Arnold must report in the next year when the receivables are collected?

c. If the partnership did make an optional adjustment-to-basis election, what are the type and amount of income that Arnold must report in the next year when the receivables are collected (assuming no other transactions in the next year)? The land (which is used in the DLL Partnership's business) is sold for $225,000?

39. For each of the following independent fact patterns, indicate whether a termination of the partnership has occurred for tax purposes. Assume no other partnership interests are sold either one year before or one year after the transactions described.

a. Polly sells her interest in capital and profits of the MPQ Partnership. She owns a 68% interest in capital and a 48% interest in the partnership profits.

b. Rick and Ron are equal partners in the R & R Partnership. Ron dies on January 15, 2003. Rick purchases Ron's interest from his estate on March 15, 2003. Answer for January 15, 2003.

c. Answer (b), for March 15, 2003.

d. Fred, a 58% partner in the profitable F & D Partnership, gives his entire interest to his son on July 1, 2003.

e. Carol, Cora, and Chris are equal partners in the Canary Partnership. On January 22, 2003, Cora sells her entire interest to Ted. On December 29, 2003, Carol sells a 15% interest to Earl. On January 25, 2004, Chris sells his interest to Frank.

40. Peggy and Cindy, parent and child, operate a local apparel shop as a partnership. The PC Partnership earned a profit of $80,000 in the current year. Cindy's equal partnership interest was acquired by gift from Peggy. Assume that capital is a material income-producing factor and that Peggy manages the day-to-day operations of the shop without any help from Cindy. Reasonable compensation for Peggy's services is $30,000.

a. How much of the partnership income is allocated to Peggy?

b. What is the maximum amount of partnership income that can be allocated to Cindy?

c. Assuming that Cindy is five years old, has no other income, and is claimed as a dependent by Peggy, how is Cindy's income from the partnership taxed?

## Research Problems

A THOMSON COMPANY

*Note: Solutions to Research Problems can be prepared by using the **RIA Checkpoint® Student Edition** online research product, or the **CCH U.S. Master Tax Guide Plus**™ online Federal tax research database, which is available to accompany this text. It is also possible to prepare solutions to the Research Problems by using tax research materials found in a standard tax library.*

Decision Making

**Research Problem 1.**   Your client, Paul, is a one-third general partner in the service-oriented Magpie Partnership. He would like to retire from the partnership at the end of the current year and asks your help in structuring the buyout transaction.

   Based on interim financial data and revenue projections for the remainder of the year, the partnership's balance sheet is expected to approximate the following at year-end:

|  | Basis | FMV |  | Basis | FMV |
|---|---|---|---|---|---|
| Cash | $ 60,000 | $ 60,000 | Maggie, capital | $ 60,000 | $150,000 |
| Accounts receivable | –0– | 180,000 | Paul, capital | 60,000 | 150,000 |
| Land (capital asset) | 120,000 | 210,000 | Iris, capital | 60,000 | 150,000 |
| Total assets | $180,000 | $450,000 | Total capital | $180,000 | $450,000 |

   Although the partnership has some cash on hand, the amount is not adequate to purchase Paul's entire interest in the current year. The partnership has proposed to pay Paul, in liquidation of his partnership interest, according to the following schedule:

| December 31, 2003 | $50,000 |
|---|---|
| December 31, 2004 | $50,000 |
| December 31, 2005 | $50,000 |

   Paul has agreed to the above payment schedule, but the parties are not sure of the tax consequences of the buyout and have temporarily halted negotiations to consult with their tax advisers. Paul has come to you to discuss the possible income tax ramifications of the buyout and to make sure he negotiates the most advantageous position possible.

   a. If the buyout agreement between Paul and Magpie is silent as to the treatment of each payment, how will each payment be treated by Paul and the partnership?
   b. As Paul's adviser, what payment schedule do you recommend that Paul negotiate to minimize his current tax liability?
   c. Now assume you are the tax adviser for the partnership. What payment schedule would you propose to ensure that the remaining partners receive the earliest possible deductions?
   d. What additional planning opportunity might you recommend to the partnership?

**Research Problem 2.**   The accrual basis JB Partnership had a § 754 election in effect when partner Jill sold her 40% interest to Krista for $200,000. Krista's share of the inside basis of partnership assets was $120,000 following the acquisition. The total step-up, then, is $80,000. The basis and fair market value of JB's assets are shown below. If the partnership sold the equipment, the entire $20,000 gain would be § 1245 recapture. Using the basis allocation rules of § 755 and the Regulations thereunder, calculate the amount of the total adjustment to be allocated to each of the partnership's assets.

| Item | FMV | Basis before §754 Adjustment |
|---|---|---|
| Cash | $ 80,000 | $ 80,000 |
| Receivable | 80,000 | –0– |
| Equipment | 120,000 | 100,000 |
| Land | 220,000 | 120,000 |
| Total assets | $500,000 | $300,000 |

**Research Problem 3.**   The Western States Partnership is a cash basis general partnership that reports on a calendar year. The partnership was formed in 1996 and consists of 19 partners. Sarah has a 10% capital and profits interest in the partnership, and each of the other partners owns a 5% capital and profits interest.

During an audit of Jason, a 5% partner, in November 2003, the IRS disagrees with the handling of a $200 charitable deduction that was claimed on his 2001 tax return. This amount was reported by Western States on the charitable deduction line of Jason's Schedule K–1. On a schedule attached to each partner's K–1 for 2001, Western States indicated that it made a $4,000 deductible contribution to a foreign charity and reported that amount on the charitable deduction line of the partnership's Schedule K. The IRS properly contends that contributions to foreign-based charities are not deductible. It seeks to adjust the returns of Jason and any other partners who claimed a deduction for this contribution.

a.  Can the IRS adjust Jason's tax return for this item? Must the IRS audit each of the other partners' returns to determine which partners claimed the incorrect deduction?

b.  Assume the partnership has not designated a Tax Matters Partner (TMP). Which partner, if any, must fulfill this role?

c.  When is the latest date that the IRS can bring a proceeding on this issue with Jason? Assume the partnership filed the 2001 Form 1065 on April 10, 2002.

d.  Assume Jason recognized that the contribution was made to a foreign charity and did not deduct it on his return. What should Jason have done when filing his 2001 tax return to indicate his disagreement with the tax treatment of the item on the Schedule K–1?

**Internet Activity**

**Communications**

*Use the tax resources of the Internet to address the following questions. Do not restrict your search to the World Wide Web, but include a review of newsgroups and general reference materials, practitioner sites and resources, primary sources of the tax law, chat rooms and discussion groups, and other opportunities.*

**Research Problem 4.**   Print an article written by a tax adviser discussing the merits of the family limited partnership. Write a memo discussing one of the following issues.

a.  The effects of Revenue Ruling 93–12 on the use of the entity.

b.  The effects of § 704(e) on income computations for the entity.

c.  The accuracy of the computations made by the author in the article.

Your memo should include a summary of the findings presented in the article and a summary and discussion of your thoughts. For example, you may wish to address situations in which family limited partnerships may be beneficial or pitfalls in structuring such an entity.

**Research Problem 5.**   On what form or attachment does a partnership report that it has made a § 754 election? Prepare such a form using the facts of Example 38 in the text.

**Research Problem 6.**   Download a copy of the legislation with which your state began to allow the formation of limited liability companies.

# S Corporations

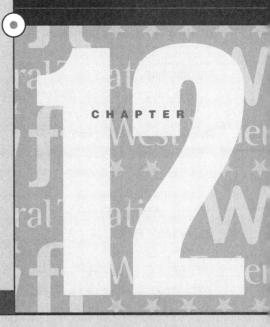

*After completing Chapter 12, you should be able to:*

**L O . 1**
Explain the tax effects that S corporation status has on shareholders.

**L O . 2**
Identify corporations that qualify for the S election.

**L O . 3**
Understand how to make an S election.

**L O . 4**
Explain how an S election can be terminated.

**L O . 5**
Compute nonseparately stated income and identify separately stated items.

**L O . 6**
Allocate income, deductions, and credits to shareholders.

**L O . 7**
Understand how distributions to S corporation shareholders are taxed.

**L O . 8**
Calculate a shareholder's basis in S corporation stock.

**L O . 9**
Explain the tax effects that losses have on shareholders.

**L O . 1 0**
Compute the built-in gains tax.

**L O . 1 1**
Compute the passive investment income penalty tax.

## LO.1

Explain the tax effects that S corporation status has on shareholders.

# Introduction

**A**n individual establishing a business has a number of choices as to the form of business entity under which to operate. Chapters 2 through 7 outline many of the rules, advantages, and disadvantages of operating as a regular corporation. Chapters 10 and 11 discuss the partnership entity, and Chapter 11 covers the limited liability company (LLC) and limited liability partnership (LLP) forms.

Another alternative, the **S corporation**, provides many of the benefits of partnership taxation and at the same time gives the owners limited liability protection from creditors. The S corporation rules, which are contained in **Subchapter S** of the Internal Revenue Code (§§ 1361–1379), were enacted to minimize the role of tax considerations in the entity choice that businesspeople face. Thus, S status combines the legal environment of C corporations with taxation similar to that applying to partnerships. S corporation status is obtained through an election by a *qualifying* corporation with the consent of its shareholders.

S corporations are treated as corporations under state law. They are recognized as separate legal entities and generally provide shareholders with the same liability protection afforded by C corporations. For Federal income tax purposes, however, taxation of S corporations resembles that of partnerships. As with partnerships, the income, deductions, and tax credits of an S corporation flow through to shareholders annually, regardless of whether dividends are paid. Thus, income is taxed at the shareholder level and not at the corporate level. Dividends paid by the corporation are distributed tax-free to shareholders to the extent that the distributed earnings were previously taxed to the shareholders. Further, C corporation penalty taxes like the accumulated earnings tax, personal holding company tax, and alternative minimum tax do not apply to an S corporation.

Although the Federal tax treatment of S corporations and partnerships is similar, it is not identical. For instance, liabilities affect an owner's basis differently, and S corporations may incur a tax liability at the corporate level. Furthermore, an S corporation may not allocate income like a partnership, and distributions of appreciated property are taxable in an S corporation situation (see Concept Summary 12–2 later in this chapter). In addition, a variety of C corporation provisions apply to S corporations. For example, the liquidation of C and S corporations is taxed in the same way. As a rule, where the S corporation provisions are silent, C corporation rules apply.

Today, the choice of a flow-through entity is often between an S corporation (a Federal tax entity) and an LLC (a state tax entity). Although an S corporation resembles an LLC, there are differences. A two-or-more-member LLC operates under partnership tax principles, whereas, as just explained, partnership taxation rules do not always apply to an S corporation.

## AN OVERVIEW OF S CORPORATIONS

Since the inception of S corporations in 1958, their popularity has waxed and waned with changes in the tax law. Before the Tax Reform Act of 1986, their ranks grew slowly. In contrast, in the two years following the 1986 law change, the population of S corporations exploded, increasing by 52 percent. By 1993, more than 1.9 million businesses were filing S corporation returns—48 percent of all corporate returns filed in that year. This rapid growth was driven by a change in the relationship of individual and corporate tax rates. Prior to 1986, maximum individual rates were higher than maximum corporate rates. Following the 1986 tax act, the relationship reversed. After 1993, maximum individual income tax rates were increased again, now exceeding the maximum corporate rate (by 4.6 percentage points). In 2003, this difference is 3.6 percentage points (38.6% − 35%).

The growth in the number of S corporation elections has continued even though the individual income tax rate has remained above the corporate rate. In 1986, only 24.1 percent of corporations were S corporations, but now over half of the country's 5 million corporations have elected S status. The IRS estimates that S corporations will be the fastest-growing choice of business tax entity through 2005. As the following examples illustrate, S corporations can be advantageous even when the top individual tax rate exceeds the top corporate tax rate.

**EXAMPLE 1**

Assume that an S corporation earns $300,000 in 2003, the marginal individual tax rate applicable to shareholders is 38.6%, the applicable marginal corporate tax rate is 34%, and all after-tax income is distributed currently. The entity's available after-tax earnings, compared with those of a similar C corporation, are as follows.

|  | C Corporation | S Corporation |
| --- | --- | --- |
| Earnings | $ 300,000 | $ 300,000 |
| Less: Corporate tax | (102,000) | –0– |
| Available for distribution | $ 198,000 | $ 300,000 |
| Less: Tax at owner level | (76,428) | (115,800) |
| Available after-tax earnings | $ 121,572 | $ 184,200 |

The S corporation generates an extra $62,628 of after-tax earnings ($184,200 − $121,572), when compared with a similar C corporation. The C corporation might be able to reduce this disadvantage, however, by paying out its earnings as compensation, rents, or interest expense. Tax at the owner level can also be deferred or avoided by not distributing after-tax earnings. ■

## S CORPORATION ELECTIONS CONTINUE TO GROW

The S corporation remains the single most popular type of business entity. Since 1986, the number of S corporations has grown at an average annual rate of 9.9 percent; in contrast, the number of other corporations has declined by 1.2 percent on average each year. In 1999, for example, the number of S corporation elections grew by more than 5.3 percent to 2.7 million or 55.2 percent of all corporations, up from nearly 2.6 million (53.4 percent) for 1998.

More than 301,800 new S elections were made in 1999, even though some had speculated that limited liability companies (LLCs) would replace S corporations as the most popular choice. In 1999, there were 589,403 filing LLCs, up from 470,657 in 1998.

Less than half of 1 percent of S corporations reported some Federal income tax in 1999, with 78 percent or $359 million from the built-in gains tax. Nearly 99 percent of the S corporations had 10 or fewer shareholders.

SOURCE: Information from Kelly Bennett, "S Corporation Returns, 1999," *Statistics of Income Bulletin*, Vol. 21, No. 4, Spring 2002, pp. 59–110.

**EXAMPLE 2**

Assume that a new corporation elects S status and incurs a net operating loss (NOL) of $300,000. The shareholders of the corporation may use their proportionate shares of the NOL to offset other taxable income in the current year, providing an immediate tax savings. In contrast, a newly formed C corporation is required to carry the NOL forward for up to 20 years and does not receive any tax benefit in the current year. Hence, an S corporation can accelerate NOL deductions and thereby provide greater present value for tax savings generated by the loss. ■

### WHEN TO ELECT S CORPORATION STATUS

The planner begins by determining the appropriateness of an S election. The following factors should be considered.

- If shareholders have high marginal rates relative to C corporation rates, it may be desirable to avoid S corporation status. Although a C corporation will be subject to double taxation, the effect of the tax can be minimized by taking profits out as salary. Likewise, profits of the corporation may be taken out by the shareholders as capital gain income through stock redemptions, liquidations, or sales of stock to others. Alternatively, profits may be paid out as dividends in years when the shareholders have less other income. Any distribution of profits or sale of stock can be deferred to a later year, thereby reducing the present value of shareholder taxes. Finally, shareholder-level tax on corporate profits can be eliminated by a step-up in basis of the stock upon the shareholder's death.
- S corporation status allows shareholders to realize tax benefits from corporate losses immediately—an important consideration in new business enterprises where losses are common. Thus, if corporate NOLs are anticipated and there is unlikely to be corporate income over the near term to offset with the NOLs, S corporation status is advisable. However, the deductibility of the losses to shareholders must also be considered. The at-risk and passive loss limitations apply to losses generated by an S corporation. In addition, as discussed later in this chapter, shareholders may not deduct losses in excess

of the basis in their stock. Together these limits may significantly reduce the benefits of an S election in a loss setting.

- If the entity electing S corporation status is currently a C corporation, any NOL carryovers from prior years cannot be used in an S corporation year. Even worse, S corporation years reduce the 20-year carryover period. Also, the corporation may be subject to some corporate-level taxes if it elects S status (see the discussion of the built-in gains tax later in this chapter).
- Distributions of earnings from C corporations are usually taxed as ordinary income. In contrast, because S corporations are flow-through entities, all deduction and income items retain any special tax characteristics when they are reported on shareholders' returns. Whether this consideration favors S status depends upon the character of income and deductions of the S corporation.
- The S corporation rules impose significant requirements for qualifying as an S corporation. When electing S status, one should consider whether any of these requirements are likely to be violated at some point in the future.
- State and local tax laws also should be considered when making the S election. Although an S corporation usually escapes Federal income tax, it may not be immune from state and local taxes. State taxation of S corporations varies. Some states, including Michigan, treat them the same as C corporations, resulting in a corporate tax liability from an income or franchise tax.
- The choice of S corporation status is affected by a variety of other factors. For example, the corporate alternative minimum tax (see Chapter 6) may be avoided in an S corporation. An in-depth discussion of entity choice is provided in Chapter 13.

**LO.2**

Identify corporations that qualify for the S election.

# Qualifying for S Corporation Status

## DEFINITION OF A SMALL BUSINESS CORPORATION

To achieve S corporation status, a corporation *first* must qualify as a **small business corporation**. A small business corporation has the following characteristics.

- Is a domestic corporation (incorporated and organized in the United States).
- Is an eligible corporation (see below for ineligible types).
- Issues only one class of stock.
- Is limited to a maximum of 75 shareholders (35 shareholders before 1997).
- Has only individuals, estates, and certain trusts as shareholders.
- Has no nonresident alien shareholder.

Unlike other provisions in the tax law (e.g., § 1244), no maximum or minimum dollar sales or capitalization restrictions apply to small business corporations.

If each of the above requirements is met, then the entity can elect S corporation status. The small business corporation definition is discussed in detail in the following paragraphs.

**Ineligible Corporations.** Small business corporation status is not permitted for foreign corporations, certain banks, insurance companies, and Puerto Rico or possessions corporations. Prior to 1997, small business corporations were prohibited from being members of affiliated groups. Now, ownership of up to 100 percent of

---

## TAX IN THE NEWS

### FLEXIBILITY WITH QSSSs

An S corporation may have a wholly owned subsidiary, an opportunity that offers flexibility in tax planning. Called a qualified Subchapter S subsidiary (QSSS), the subsidiary is not treated as a separate entity for Federal income tax purposes; therefore, all of its assets, liabilities, and items of income, deductions, and credits are treated as belonging to the parent.

A number of advantages and tax planning opportunities accrue to the group. First, an S corporation may separate its lines of business. By dividing the operations among wholly owned subsidiaries, it can insulate certain businesses from liabilities of other businesses.

Second, a profitable S corporation can make a QSSS election with respect to a nonprofitable company. Generally, when a company continually loses money, the losses may not be deductible by the shareholder because of lack of sufficient basis in the company. The QSSS election causes the nonprofitable company's stock to be a contribution of capital by the shareholder as a tax-free exchange. The deemed liquidation under § 332 creates a carryover basis, and any suspended losses of the new subsidiary are carried over. Thus, outside basis is looked at as a whole, and these suspended losses may be used against the profit of the other company.

SOURCES: Adapted from F. J. Fisher, "Qualified Subchapter S Subsidiaries: Greater Flexibility for Real Estate Practitioners," *The Real Estate Digest*, March 1999, pp. 87–91; N. S. Lindholm and S. S. Karlinsky, "The Benefits and Burdens of QSubs," *The Tax Adviser*, July 1999, pp. 490–496.

---

a C corporation is permitted. In addition, small business corporations are permitted (after 1996) to have wholly owned S corporation subsidiaries.[1]

Any domestic corporation that is not an ineligible corporation can be a qualified Subchapter S corporation subsidiary (QSSS), if the S corporation holds 100 percent of its stock and elects to treat the subsidiary as a QSSS. The QSSS is viewed as a division of the parent, so the parent S corporation can own a QSSS through another QSSS. QSSSs are treated as disregarded entities under the check-the-box rules (see Chapter 10). They have a separate existence for legal purposes, but they exist only within the parent S corporation for tax purposes.

**One Class of Stock.**    A small business corporation may have only one class of stock issued and outstanding.[2] This restriction permits differences in voting rights, but not differences in distribution or liquidation rights.[3] Thus, two classes of common stock that are identical except that one class is voting and the other is nonvoting would be treated as a single class of stock for small business corporation purposes. In contrast, voting common stock and voting preferred stock (with a preference on dividends) would be treated as two classes of stock. Authorized and unissued stock or treasury stock of another class does not disqualify the corporation. Likewise, unexercised stock options, phantom stock, stock appreciation rights, warrants, and convertible debentures usually do not constitute a second class of stock.

The determination of whether stock provides identical rights as to distribution and liquidation proceeds is made based on the provisions governing the operation of the corporation. These *governing provisions* include the corporate charter, articles

---

[1]§ 1361(b)(3)(B).
[2]§ 1361(b)(1)(D).

[3]§ 1361(c)(4).

of incorporation, bylaws, applicable state law, and binding agreements relating to distribution and liquidation proceeds. Employment contracts, loan agreements, and other commercial contracts are *not* considered governing provisions.[4] Such contracts will not violate the one-class-of-stock requirement unless their principal purpose is to circumvent the requirement.

> **EXAMPLE 3**
>
> Blue, a small business corporation, has two equal shareholders, Smith and Jones. Both shareholders are employed by Blue and have binding employment contracts with the corporation. The compensation paid by Blue to Jones under her employment contract is reasonable. The compensation paid to Smith under his employment contract, however, is excessive, resulting in a constructive dividend. Smith's employment contract was not prepared to circumvent the one-class-of-stock requirement. Because employment contracts are not considered governing provisions, Blue has only one class of stock. ∎

Although the one-class-of-stock requirement seems straightforward, it is possible for debt to be reclassified as stock, resulting in unexpected loss of S corporation status.[5] To mitigate concern over possible reclassification of debt as a second class of stock, the law provides a set of *safe-harbor* provisions.

First, straight debt *issued in an S corporation year* will not be treated as a second class of stock and will not disqualify the S election.[6] The characteristics of straight debt include the following:

- The debtor is subject to a written, unconditional promise to pay on demand or on a specified date a sum certain in money.
- The interest rate and payment date are not contingent on corporate profit, management discretion, or similar factors.
- The debt is not convertible into stock.
- The debt is held by a creditor who is an individual (other than a nonresident alien), an estate, or a qualified trust.
- Straight debt can be held by creditors actively and regularly engaged in the business of lending money.

In addition to straight debt under the safe-harbor rules, short-term unwritten advances from a shareholder that do not exceed $10,000 in the aggregate at any time during the corporation's taxable year generally are not treated as a second class of stock. Likewise, debt that is held by stockholders in the same proportion as their stock is not treated as a second class of stock, even if it would be reclassified as equity otherwise.[7] If safe-harbor debt is transferred to a nonqualifying creditor or if the debt instrument is modified significantly after its issue, the safe harbors may no longer apply.

**Number of Shareholders.**   A small business corporation is limited to 75 shareholders (35 before 1997). If shares of stock are owned jointly by two individuals, they will generally be treated as separate shareholders. However, a husband and wife are considered one shareholder. Similarly, a widower or widow and his or her spouse's estate are treated as a single shareholder.[8] The treatment of a husband and wife as a single shareholder can have unexpected consequences in a divorce, as illustrated in the following example.

---

[4]Reg. §§ 1.1361–1(l)(2).
[5]Refer to the discussion of debt-versus-equity classification in Chapter 3.

[6]§ 1361(c)(5)(A).
[7]Reg. § 1.1361–1(l)(4).
[8]§ 1361(c)(1).

**EXAMPLE 4**

Fred and Wilma (husband and wife) jointly own 10 shares in Marlins, Inc., an S corporation, with the remaining 90 shares outstanding owned by 74 other shareholders. Fred and Wilma get divorced; pursuant to the property settlement approved by the court, the 10 shares held by Fred and Wilma are divided between them—5 to each. Before the divorce settlement, Marlins had 75 shareholders under the small business corporation rules. After the settlement, it has 76 shareholders and no longer qualifies as a small business corporation. ■

**Type of Shareholder Limitation.**   Small business corporation shareholders may be resident individuals, estates, certain trusts, and certain tax-exempt organizations.[9] This limitation prevents partnerships, corporations, limited liability companies, limited liability partnerships, and IRAs from owning stock. Partnership and corporate shareholders could easily circumvent the 75-shareholder limitation as illustrated in the following example.

**EXAMPLE 5**

Saul and 80 of his close friends wish to form an S corporation. Saul reasons that if he and his friends form a partnership, the partnership can then form an S corporation and act as a single shareholder, thereby avoiding the 75-shareholder rule. Saul's plan will not work because partnerships cannot own stock in a small business corporation. ■

Although partnerships and corporations cannot own small business corporation stock, small business corporations can be partners in a partnership or shareholders in a corporation. This ability allows the 75-shareholder requirement to be bypassed in a limited sense. For example, if two small business corporations, each with 75 shareholders, form a partnership, then the shareholders of both corporations can enjoy the limited liability conferred by S corporation status and a single level of tax on partnership profits.

**Nonresident Aliens.**   Nonresident aliens cannot own stock in a small business corporation.[10] That is, individuals who are not U.S. citizens *must live in the United States* to own S corporation stock. Shareholders with nonresident alien spouses in community property states[11] therefore cannot own S corporation stock because the nonresident alien spouse would be treated as owning half of the community property.[12] Similarly, if a resident alien shareholder moves outside the United States, the S election will be terminated.

---

**ETHICAL CONSIDERATIONS** | **Extortion Payments**

Burt is the custodian at Quaker Inn, an S corporation in Grand Isle, Louisiana. Over the years, he has received a total of 276 shares of stock in the corporation through bonus payments.

While listening to a debate on television about a national health care plan, Burt decides that the company's health coverage is unfair. He is concerned about this because his wife is seriously ill.

---

[9]§ 1361(b)(1)(B).

[10]§ 1362(b)(1)(C).

[11]Assets acquired by a married couple are generally considered community property in these states: Louisiana, Texas, New Mexico, Arizona, California, Washington, Idaho, Nevada, Wisconsin, and (if elected by the spouses) Alaska.

[12]See *Ward v. U.S.*, 81–2 USTC ¶9674, 48 AFTR2d 81–5942, 661 F.2d 226 (Ct.Cls., 1981), where the court found that the stock was owned as community property. Since the taxpayer-shareholder (a U.S. citizen) was married to a citizen and resident of Mexico, the nonresident alien prohibition was violated. If the taxpayer-shareholder had held the stock as separate property, the S election would have been valid.

During the second week in December, Burt informs the president of Quaker that he would like a Christmas bonus of $75,000, or else he will sell 10 shares of his stock to one of his relatives who is a nonresident alien. As a C corporation, Quaker's income tax would be about $136,000.

Can you defend Burt's position?

---

**LO.3**

Understand how to make an S election.

## MAKING THE ELECTION

To become an S corporation, a *small business corporation* (defined above) must file a valid election with the IRS. The election is made on Form 2553 (see Appendix B). For the election to be valid, it must be filed on a timely basis and all shareholders must consent. For S corporation status to apply in the current tax year, the election must be filed either in the previous year or on or before the fifteenth day of the third month of the current year.[13]

**EXAMPLE 6**

In 2003, a calendar year C corporation in Auburn, Alabama, decides to become an S corporation beginning January 1, 2004. The S corporation election can be made at any time in 2003 or by March 15, 2004. An election after March 15, 2004, will not be effective until the 2005 tax year. ■

Even if the 2½-month deadline is met, a current election is not valid unless the corporation qualifies as a small business corporation for the *entire* tax year. Otherwise, the election will be effective for the following tax year. Late current-year elections, after the 2½-month deadline, may be considered timely if there is reasonable cause for the late filing.

A corporation that does not yet exist cannot make an S corporation election.[14] Thus, for new corporations, a premature election may not be effective. A new corporation's 2½-month election period begins at the earliest occurrence of any of the following events: (1) when the corporation has shareholders, (2) when it acquires assets, or (3) when it begins doing business.[15]

**EXAMPLE 7**

Several individuals acquire assets on behalf of Rock Corporation on June 29, 2003, and begin doing business on July 3, 2003. They subscribe to shares of stock, file articles of incorporation for Rock, and become shareholders on July 7, 2003. The S election must be filed no later than 2½ months after June 29, 2003 (on or before September 12) to be effective for 2003. ■

The IRS can correct errors in electing S status, where a taxpayer can show that the mistake was inadvertent, the entity otherwise was qualified to be an S corporation, and it acted as if it were an S corporation. Under certain conditions, automatic relief is granted without the need for a letter ruling request and the normal user fee.

Further, the IRS has the authority to honor S elections that were not filed by the deadline. The company must have a reasonable cause for missing the statutory deadline. This relief is available not only for the initial election to become an S corporation, but also for the qualified Subchapter S subsidiary (QSSS), qualified Subchapter S trust (QSST), and electing small business trust (ESBT) elections.

Sufficient reasonable cause might occur, for example, where both the corporation's accountant and its attorney failed to file the election because each believed

---

[13]§ 1362(b).
[14]See, for example, *T.H. Campbell & Bros., Inc.*, 34 TCM 695, T.C.Memo. 1975–149; Ltr.Rul. 8807070.

[15]Reg. § 1.1372–2(b)(1). Also see, for example, *Nick A. Artukovich*, 61 T.C. 100 (1973).

the other had done so, or because there was miscommunication as to who was responsible for filing.

## SHAREHOLDER CONSENT

A qualifying election requires the consent of all of the corporation's shareholders.[16] Consent must be in writing, and it must generally be filed by the election deadline. However, while no statutory authority exists for obtaining an extension of time for filing an S election (Form 2553), a shareholder may receive an extension of time to file consent. A consent extension is available only if Form 2553 is filed on a timely basis, reasonable cause is given, and the interests of the government are not jeopardized.[17]

**EXAMPLE 8**

Vern and Yvonne decide to convert their C corporation into a calendar year S corporation for 2004. At the end of February 2004 (before the election is filed), Yvonne travels to Ukraine and forgets to sign a consent to the election. Yvonne will not return to the United States until June and cannot be reached by fax or e-mail. Vern files the S election on Form 2553 and also requests an extension of time to file Yvonne's consent to the election. Vern indicates that there is a reasonable cause for the extension: a shareholder is out of the country. Since the government's interest is not jeopardized, the IRS probably will grant Yvonne an extension of time to file the consent. Vern must file the election on Form 2553 on or before March 15, 2004, for the election to be effective for the 2004 calendar year. ■

Both husband and wife must consent if they own their stock jointly (as joint tenants, tenants in common, tenants by the entirety, or community property). This requirement has led to considerable taxpayer grief—particularly in community property states where the spouses may not realize that their stock is jointly owned as a community asset.

**EXAMPLE 9**

Three shareholders, Amy, Monty, and Dianne, incorporate in January and file Form 2553. Amy is married and lives in California. Monty is single and Dianne is married; both live in South Carolina. Because Amy is married and lives in a community property state, her husband also must consent to the S election. South Carolina is not a community property state, so Dianne's husband need not consent. ■

Finally, for current-year S elections, persons who were shareholders during any part of the taxable year before the election date, but were not shareholders when the election was made, must also consent to the election.[18]

**EXAMPLE 10**

On January 15, 2003, the stock of Columbus Corporation (a calendar year C corporation) was held equally by three individual shareholders: Jim, Sally, and LuEllen. On that date, LuEllen sells her interest to Jim and Sally. On March 14, 2003, Columbus Corporation files Form 2553. Jim and Sally indicate their consent by signing the form. Columbus cannot become an S corporation until 2004 because LuEllen did not indicate consent. Had all three shareholders consented by signing Form 2553, S status would have taken effect as of January 1, 2003. ■

---

[16]§ 1362(a)(2).
[17]Rev.Rul. 60–183, 1960–1 C.B. 625; *William Pestcoe*, 40 T.C. 195 (1963); Reg. § 1.1362–6(b)(3)(iii).

[18]§ 1362(b)(2)(B)(ii).

**LO.4**

Explain how an S election can be terminated.

## LOSS OF THE ELECTION

An S election remains in force until it is revoked or lost. Election or consent forms are not required for future years. However, an S election can terminate if any of the following occurs.

- Shareholders owning a majority of shares (voting and nonvoting) voluntarily revoke the election.
- A new shareholder owning more than one-half of the stock affirmatively refuses to consent to the election.
- The corporation no longer qualifies as a small business corporation.
- The corporation does not meet the passive investment income limitation.

Each of these conditions is discussed in detail in this section.

**Voluntary Revocation.** A **voluntary revocation** of the S election requires the consent of shareholders owning a majority of shares on the day that the revocation is to be made.[19] A revocation filed up to and including the fifteenth day of the third month of the tax year is effective for the entire tax year, unless a later date is specified. Similarly, unless an effective date is specified, revocation made after the first 2½ months of the current tax year is effective for the following tax year.

**EXAMPLE 11**

The shareholders of Petunia Corporation, a calendar year S corporation, voluntarily revoke the S election on January 5, 2003. They do not specify a future effective date in the revocation. Assuming the revocation is properly executed and timely filed, Petunia will be a C corporation for the entire 2003 calendar year. If the election is not made until June 2003, Petunia will remain an S corporation in 2003 and will become a C corporation at the beginning of 2004. ■

A corporation can revoke its S status *prospectively* by specifying a future date when the revocation is to be effective. A revocation that designates a future effective date splits the corporation's tax year into a short S corporation year and a short C corporation year. The day on which the revocation occurs is treated as the first day of the C corporation year. The corporation allocates income or loss for the entire year on a pro rata basis, based on the number of days in each short year.

**EXAMPLE 12**

Assume the same facts as in the preceding example, except that Petunia designates July 1, 2003, as the revocation date. Accordingly, June 30, 2003, is the last day of the S corporation's tax year. The C corporation's tax year runs from July 1, 2003 to December 31, 2003. Any income or loss for the 12-month period is allocated evenly between the two short years, because the two short years lasted an equal number of days. ■

Rather than using pro rata allocation, the corporation can elect to compute actual income or loss attributable to the two short years. This election requires the consent of everyone who was a shareholder at any time during the S corporation's short year and everyone who owns stock on the first day of the C corporation's year.[20]

**Loss of Small Business Corporation Status.** If an S corporation fails to qualify as a small business corporation at any time after the election has become effective, its status as an S corporation ends. The termination occurs on the day

---

[19]§ 1362(d)(1).

[20]§ 1362(e)(3).

that the corporation ceases to be a small business corporation.[21] Thus, if the corporation ever has more than 75 shareholders, a second class of stock, or a nonqualifying shareholder, or otherwise fails to meet the definition of a small business corporation, the S election is immediately terminated.

**EXAMPLE 13**

Peony Corporation has been a calendar year S corporation for three years. On August 13, 2003, one of its 75 shareholders sells *some* of her stock to an outsider. Peony now has 76 shareholders, and it ceases to be a small business corporation. For 2003, Peony is an S corporation through August 12, 2003, and a C corporation from August 13 to December 31, 2003. ■

**Passive Investment Income Limitation.**   The Code provides a **passive investment income (PII)** limitation for S corporations that were previously C corporations or for S corporations that have merged with C corporations. If an S corporation has C corporation E & P and passive income in excess of 25 percent of its gross receipts for three consecutive taxable years, the S election is terminated as of the beginning of the fourth year.[22]

**EXAMPLE 14**

For 2000, 2001, and 2002, Diapason Corporation, a calendar year S corporation, received passive income in excess of 25% of its gross receipts. If Diapason holds accumulated E & P from years in which it was a C corporation, its S election is terminated as of January 1, 2003. ■

PII includes dividends, interest, rents, gains and losses from sales of securities, and royalties net of investment deductions. Rents are not considered PII if the corporation renders significant personal services to the occupant.

**EXAMPLE 15**

Violet Corporation owns and operates an apartment building. The corporation provides utilities for the building, maintains the lobby, and furnishes trash collection for tenants. These activities are not considered significant personal services, so any rent income earned by the corporation will be considered PII.

Alternatively, if Violet also furnishes maid services to its tenants (personal services beyond what normally would be expected from a landlord in an apartment building), the rent income would no longer be PII. ■

**ETHICAL CONSIDERATIONS**   **A Voluntary "Involuntary" Termination**

Hirschman, Inc., a calendar year S corporation, would like to terminate its S election immediately. However, March 15 has passed, so any voluntary termination will not be effective until the first day of the following tax year. One shareholder, Elena Muñoz, suggests an involuntary termination. She wants to sell several shares of her stock to a nonresident alien.

Elena has come to you, Hirschman's tax adviser. You have briefed her on the tax effects that the sale would have on the other shareholders. Elena then asks you for some additional advice: Is such a voluntary "involuntary" termination of an S election ethical?

[21]§ 1362(d)(2)(B).

[22]§ 1362(d)(3)(A)(ii).

■ **FIGURE 12–1**
Flow-Through of Separate Items
of Income and Loss to
S Corporation Shareholders

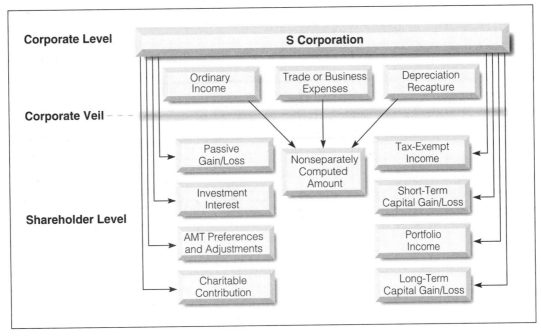

**Reelection after Termination.**   After an S election has been terminated, the corporation must wait five years before reelecting S corporation status. The five-year waiting period is waived if:

- there is a more-than-50-percent change in ownership of the corporation after the first year for which the termination is applicable, or
- the event causing the termination was not reasonably within the control of the S corporation or its majority shareholders.

## Operational Rules

S corporations are treated much like partnerships for tax purposes. With a few exceptions,[23] S corporations generally make tax accounting and other elections at the corporate level. Each year, the S corporation determines nonseparately stated income or loss and separately stated income, deductions, and credits. These items are taxed only once, at the shareholder level. All items are allocated to each shareholder based on average ownership of stock throughout the year. The *flow-through* of each item of income, deduction, and credit from the corporation to the shareholder is illustrated in Figure 12–1.

[23]A few elections can be made at the shareholder level (e.g., the choice between a foreign tax deduction or credit).

**LO.5**

Compute nonseparately stated
income and identify separately
stated items.

## COMPUTATION OF TAXABLE INCOME

Subchapter S taxable income or loss is determined in a manner similar to the tax rules that apply to partnerships, except that S corporations can amortize organizational expenditures[24] and must recognize gains, *but not losses*, on distributions of appreciated property to shareholders.[25] Other special provisions affecting only the computation of C corporation income, such as the dividends received deduction, do not extend to S corporations.[26] Finally, as with partnerships, certain deductions of individuals are not permitted, including alimony payments, personal moving expenses, certain dependent care expenses, the personal exemption, and the standard deduction.

In general, S corporation items are divided into (1) nonseparately stated income or loss and (2) separately stated income, losses, deductions, and credits that could affect the tax liability of any shareholder in a different manner, depending on other factors in the shareholder's tax situation. In essence, nonseparate items are aggregated into an undifferentiated amount that constitutes Subchapter S taxable income or loss. An S corporation's separately stated items are identical to those separately stated by partnerships. These items retain their tax attributes on the shareholder's return. Separately stated items are listed on Schedule K of the 1120S. They include the following.

- Tax-exempt income.
- Long-term and short-term capital gains and losses.
- Section 1231 gains and losses.
- Charitable contributions (no grace period).
- Passive gains, losses, and credits.
- Certain portfolio income.
- Section 179 expense deduction.
- Tax preferences and adjustments for the alternative minimum tax.
- Depletion.
- Foreign income or loss.
- Wagering gains or losses.
- Recoveries of tax benefit items.
- Intangible drilling costs.
- Investment interest, income, and expenses.

**EXAMPLE 16**

The following is the 2003 income statement for Jersey, Inc., an S corporation.

| | | |
|---|---:|---:|
| Sales | | $ 40,000 |
| Less cost of sales | | (23,000) |
| Gross profit on sales | | $ 17,000 |
| Less: Interest expense | $1,200 | |
|     Charitable contributions | 400 | |
|     Advertising expenses | 1,500 | |
|     Other operating expenses | 2,000 | (5,100) |
| | | $ 11,900 |
| Add: Tax-exempt interest | $ 300 | |
|     Dividend income | 200 | |
|     Long-term capital gain | 500 | 1,000 |
| Less: Short-term capital loss | | (150) |
| Net income per books | | $ 12,750 |

---

[24]§§ 248 and 1363(b).
[25]§ 1363(d).

[26]§ 703(a)(2).

Subchapter S taxable income for Jersey is calculated as follows, using net income for book purposes as a starting point.

| | | |
|---|---:|---:|
| Net income per books | | $12,750 |
| *Separately stated items* | | |
| Deduct: Tax-exempt interest | $300 | |
| Dividend income | 200 | |
| Long-term capital gain | 500 | (1,000) |
| Subtotal | | $11,750 |
| Add: Charitable contributions | $400 | |
| Short-term capital loss | 150 | 550 |
| Subchapter S taxable income | | $12,300 |

The $12,300 of Subchapter S taxable income, as well as each of the five separately stated items, are divided among the shareholders based upon their stock ownership. ■

## LO.6

Allocate income, deductions, and credits to shareholders.

## ALLOCATION OF INCOME AND LOSS

Each shareholder is allocated a pro rata portion of nonseparately stated income or loss and all separately stated items. The pro rata allocation method assigns an equal amount of each of the S items to each day of the year. If a shareholder's stock holding changes during the year, this allocation assigns the shareholder a pro rata share of each item for *each* day the stock is owned. On the date of transfer, the transferor (and not the transferee) is considered to own the stock.[27]

The per-day allocation must be used, unless the shareholder disposes of his or her entire interest in the entity.[28] In case of a complete termination, a short year may result, as discussed on the next page. If a shareholder dies during the year, his or her share of the pro rata items up to the date of death is reported on the final individual income tax return.

**EXAMPLE 17**

Assume in Example 16 that Pat, a shareholder, owned 10% of Jersey's stock for 100 days and 12% for the remaining 265 days. Using the required per-day allocation method, Pat's share of the S corporation items is as follows.

| | Schedule K Totals | Pat's Share 10% | Pat's Share 12% | Pat's Schedule K–1 Totals |
|---|---:|---:|---:|---:|
| Subchapter S taxable income | $12,300 | $337 | $1,072 | $1,409 |
| Tax-exempt interest | 300 | 8 | 26 | 34 |
| Dividend income | 200 | 5 | 17 | 22 |
| Long-term capital gain | 500 | 14 | 44 | 58 |
| Charitable contributions | 400 | 11 | 35 | 46 |
| Short-term capital loss | 150 | 4 | 13 | 17 |

---

[27]Reg. § 1.1377–1(a)(2)(ii).

[28]§§ 1366(a)(1) and 1377(a)(1).

Pat's share of the Subchapter S taxable income is the total of $12,300 \times [0.10 \times (100/365)]$ plus $12,300 \times [0.12 \times (265/365)]$, or $1,409. Each of the Schedule K–1 totals from the right-hand column flows through to the appropriate lines on Pat's individual income tax return (Form 1040). ■

**EXAMPLE 18**

If Pat in Example 17 dies after owning the stock 100 days, his share of the S corporation items is reported on his final individual income tax return (Form 1040). Thus, only the items in the column labeled 10% in Example 17 are reported on Pat's final tax return. S corporation items that occur after Pat's death most likely would flow through to the income tax return of Pat's estate (Form 1041). ■

**The Short-Year Election.**  If a shareholder's interest is completely terminated by disposition or death during the tax year, all shareholders holding stock during the year and the corporation may elect to treat the S taxable year as two taxable years. The first year ends on the date of the termination. Under this election, an interim closing of the books is undertaken, and the shareholders report their shares of the S corporation items as they occurred during the short tax year.[29]

The short-year election provides an opportunity to shift income, losses, and credits between shareholders. The election is desirable in circumstances where more loss can be allocated to taxpayers with higher marginal rates.

**EXAMPLE 19**

Alicia, the owner of all of the shares of an S corporation, transfers her stock to Cindy halfway through the tax year. There is a $100,000 NOL for the entire tax year, but $30,000 of the loss occurs during the first half of the year. Without a short-year election, $50,000 of the loss is allocated to Alicia, and $50,000 is allocated to Cindy. If the corporation makes the short-year election, Cindy is allocated $70,000 of the loss. Of course, the sales price of the stock would probably be increased to recognize the tax benefits being transferred from Alicia to Cindy. ■

In the case of the death of a shareholder, a short-year election prevents the income and loss allocation to a deceased shareholder from being affected by post-death events.

**EXAMPLE 20**

Joey and Karl equally own Rose, Inc., a calendar year S corporation. Joey dies on June 29 of a year that is not a leap year. Rose has income of $250,000 for January 1 through June 29 and $750,000 for the remainder of the year. Without a short-year election, the income is allocated by assigning an equal portion of the annual income of $1 million to each day (or $2,739.73 per day) and allocating the daily portion between the shareholders. Joey is allocated 50% of the daily income for the 180 days from January 1 to June 29, or $246,575.70 [($2,739.73/2) \times 180]. Joey's *estate* is allocated 50% of the income for the 185 days from June 30 to December 31, or $253,425.02 [($2,739.73/2) \times 185].

If the short-year election is made, the income of $250,000 from January 1 to June 29 is divided equally between Joey and Karl, so that each is taxed on $125,000. The income of $750,000 from June 30 to December 31 is divided equally between Joey's estate and Karl, or $375,000 to each. ■

## TAX TREATMENT OF DISTRIBUTIONS TO SHAREHOLDERS

The amount of any distribution to an S corporation shareholder is equal to the cash plus the fair market value of any other property distributed. How the distribution is taxed depends upon whether the S corporation has **accumulated earnings and profits** (AEP, described in Chapter 4) from previous C corporation years.

---

[29]§ 1377(a)(2).

**No AEP from C Corporation Years.**   If the S corporation has never been a C corporation or if it has no AEP from C corporation years, the distribution is a tax-free recovery of capital to the extent that it does not exceed the shareholder's adjusted basis in the stock of the S corporation. When the amount of the distribution exceeds the adjusted basis of the stock, the excess is treated as a gain from the sale or exchange of property (capital gain in most cases).

**EXAMPLE 21**

Twirl, Inc., a calendar year S corporation, has no AEP. During the year, Juan, an individual shareholder of the corporation, receives a cash distribution of $12,200 from Twirl. Juan's basis in his stock is $9,700. Juan recognizes a capital gain of $2,500, the excess of the distribution over the stock basis ($12,200 − $9,700). The remaining $9,700 is tax-free, but it reduces Juan's basis in his stock to zero. ■

**AEP from C Corporation Years.**   S corporations with AEP from C corporation years blend the entity and conduit approaches to taxation. This blending treats distributions of pre-election (C corporation) and postelection (S corporation) earnings differently. Distributions of C corporation AEP are taxed as dividends, while distributions of previously taxed S corporation earnings are tax-free to the extent of the shareholder's adjusted basis in the stock.

Concept Summary 12–1 outlines the taxation of distributions. These rules are intended to prevent two problems that result when a C corporation has been converted to an S corporation.

- Tax manipulation could result in AEP from the C corporation years being withdrawn without taxation, since S corporation shareholders are taxed on income, not on distributions.
- On the other hand, double taxation could occur. Earnings from the S corporation years might both flow to the shareholders' tax returns as income and be taxed as dividends as if the corporation were a C corporation.

A special account is used to track undistributed earnings of an S corporation that have been taxed to shareholders previously. Distributions from this account, known as the **accumulated adjustments account (AAA), are tax-free.** Essentially, the AAA is the cumulative total of undistributed nonseparately and separately stated items for S corporation taxable years beginning after 1982. Thus, the account parallels the calculation of C corporation AEP. Calculation of the AAA applies to all S corporations, but the AAA is most important to those that have been C corporations. The AAA provides a mechanism to ensure that the earnings of an S corporation are taxed to shareholders only once.

The AAA is computed by making adjustments in the order specified in Exhibit 12–1. Its balance is determined at the end of each year rather than at the time distributions are made. When more than one distribution occurs in the same year, a pro rata portion of each distribution is treated as having been made out of the AAA.

In calculating the amount in the AAA for purposes of determining the tax treatment of current-year distributions, the net negative adjustments (e.g., the excess of losses and deductions over income) for that tax year are ignored.

A shareholder has a proportionate interest in the AAA, regardless of the size of his or her stock basis.[30] However, since the AAA is a corporate account, no connection exists between the prior accumulated S corporation income and any specific shareholder.[31] Thus, the benefits of the AAA can be shifted from one shareholder to another shareholder. For example, when one S shareholder transfers stock to another

---

[30]§ 1368(c).

[31]§ 1368(e)(1)(A).

### ■ EXHIBIT 12–1
Adjustments to the Corporate AAA

*Increase by:*

1. Schedule K items other than tax-exempt income.
2. Nonseparately computed income.
3. Depletion in excess of basis in the property.

*Decrease by:*

4. Adjustments other than distributions (e.g., losses, deductions).
5. Any portion of a distribution that is considered to be tax-free from AAA (but not below zero).

NOTE: When the combination of items 1 through 4 results in a negative number, the AAA is adjusted first for the distribution and then for the adjustments in items 1 through 4.

shareholder, any AAA on the purchase date may be distributed tax-free to the purchaser. Similarly, issuing additional stock to a new shareholder in an S corporation having AAA dilutes the account relative to the existing shareholders.

The AAA (unlike the stock basis) can have a negative balance. All losses decrease the AAA balance, even those in excess of the shareholder's stock basis. However, *distributions* may not make the AAA negative or increase a negative balance.

**Distribution Ordering Rules.**   A cash distribution from an S corporation with AEP comes first from the AAA (limited to stock basis). The distribution is then deemed to be made from **previously taxed income (PTI)**[32] generated under old S corporation rules (pre-1983). Distributions from the AAA and PTI are tax-free. The remaining distribution is taxed as a dividend to the extent of AEP. After AEP is fully distributed, any residual amount is applied against the shareholder's remaining stock basis. This amount is a tax-free recovery of capital.[33] Any distributions in excess of stock basis are taxed as capital gains. See Concept Summary 12–1.

**EXAMPLE 22**

Salvia, a calendar year S corporation, distributes $1,300 cash to its only shareholder, Otis, on December 31, 2003. Otis's basis in his stock is $1,400, his AAA is $500, and the corporation has AEP of $750 on December 31, 2003.

According to the distribution ordering rules, the first $500 is a tax-free recovery of basis from the AAA. The next $750 is a taxable dividend distribution from AEP. Finally, the remaining $50 of cash is a tax-free recovery of basis. Immediately after the distribution, Salvia has no AAA or AEP, and Otis's stock basis equals $850.

| | Corporate AAA | Corporate AEP | Otis's Stock Basis* |
|---|---|---|---|
| Balance, 12/31/2003 | $ 500 | $ 750 | $1,400 |
| Distribution ($1,300) | (500) | (750) | (50) |
| Basis adjustment for AAA distribution | | | (500) |
| Balance, 12/31/2003 | $ –0– | $ –0– | $ 850 |

*Details of basis adjustments are discussed later in the chapter.

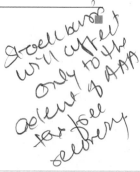

---

[32]§§ 1368(c)(1) and (e)(1). Before 1983, an account similar to the AAA was in place, namely, previously taxed income (PTI). Any S corporations in existence before 1983 may have PTI, which currently may be distributed tax-free.

[33]§ 1368(c).

## CONCEPT SUMMARY 12–1

### Classification Procedures for Distributions from an S Corporation

| Where Earnings and Profits Exist | Where No Earnings and Profits Exist |
| --- | --- |
| 1. Distributions are tax-free to the extent of the AAA.* | 1. Distributions are nontaxable to the extent of adjusted basis in stock. |
| 2. Any PTI from pre-1983 tax years can be distributed tax-free. | 2. Excess is treated as gain from a sale or exchange of stock (capital gain in most cases). |
| 3. The remaining distribution constitutes ordinary dividend from AEP.† | |
| 4. Distributions are tax-free to the extent of the other adjustments account (OAA). | |
| 5. Any residual amount is applied as a tax-free reduction in basis of stock. | |
| 6. Excess is treated as gain from a sale or exchange of stock (capital gain in most cases). | |

*Once stock basis reaches zero, any distribution from the AAA is treated as a gain from the sale or exchange of stock. Thus, basis is an upper limit on what a shareholder may receive tax-free.
†The AAA bypass election is available to pay out AEP before reducing the AAA [§ 1368(e)(3)].

**EXAMPLE 23**

Assume the same facts as in the preceding example. During the following year, Salvia has no earnings and distributes $1,000 to Otis. Of the distribution, $850 is a tax-free recovery of basis, and $150 is taxed to Otis as a capital gain. ■

With the consent of all of its shareholders, an S corporation can elect to have a distribution treated as if it were made from AEP rather than from the AAA. This mechanism is known as an AAA **bypass election**. This election may be desirable for distributions in years when S corporation shareholders have low marginal tax rates.

**EXAMPLE 24**

Collett, a calendar year S corporation, has AEP of $12,000 and a balance of $20,000 in the AAA. Collett Corporation may elect to distribute the AEP first, creating a $12,000 dividend for its shareholders, before using the AAA. ■

**Schedule M–2.** S corporations report changes in the AAA on Schedule M–2 of Form 1120S; this schedule appears on the next page. Schedule M–2 contains a column labeled **Other adjustments account (OAA)**. This account includes items that affect basis but not the AAA, such as tax-exempt income and any related nondeductible expenses. For example, life insurance proceeds received and insurance premiums paid are traced through the OAA. Distributions are made from the OAA after AEP and the AAA are depleted to zero. Distributions from the OAA are generally tax-free recoveries of capital.

**EXAMPLE 25**

During 2003, Sparrow, an S corporation, records the following items.

| | | |
| --- | --- | --- |
| AAA, beginning of the year | $ 8,500 | AAA |
| Previously taxed income, beginning of the year | 6,250 | PTI |
| Ordinary income | 25,000 | AAA |
| Tax-exempt interest | 4,000 | OAA |
| Key employee life insurance proceeds received | 5,000 | OAA |
| Payroll penalty expense | 2,000 | AAA |
| Charitable contributions | 3,000 | AAA |

*[handwritten: 2-19]*

*[handwritten note: — Property div]*

| | |
|---|---|
| Unreasonable compensation | $ 5,000 |
| Premiums on key employee life insurance | 2,100 |
| Distributions to shareholders | 16,000 |

*[handwritten right margin: ( ) AAA, AAA, OAA, AAA, AAA]*

*[handwritten: + Capital gain]*

Sparrow's Schedule M–2 for the current year appears as follows.

*[handwritten left margin: On purchase of asset loss is not subtracted from AAA on purchase but on sale of asset loss is recognized & AAA is reduced by loss]*

| Schedule M-2 | Analysis of Accumulated Adjustments Account, Other Adjustments Account, and Shareholders' Undistributed Taxable Income Previously Taxed | | |
|---|---|---|---|
| | **(a)** Accumulated adjustments account | **(b)** Other adjustments account | **(c)** Shareholders' undistributed taxable income previously taxed |
| 1 Balance at beginning of tax year . . . | 8,500 | | 6,250 |
| 2 Ordinary income from page 1, line 21 . . | 25,000 | | |
| 3 Other additions . . . . . . . . . | | 9,000** | |
| 4 Loss from page 1, line 21. . . . . . | ( ) | | |
| 5 Other reductions . . . . . . . . | ( 10,000* ) | ( 2,100 ) | |
| 6 Combine lines 1 through 5 . . . . . | 23,500 | 6,900 | |
| 7 Distributions other than dividend distributions . | 16,000 | | |
| 8 Balance at end of tax year. Subtract line 7 from line 6 | 7,500 | 6,900 | 6,250 |

*[handwritten above table: offset basis]*

\* $2,000 (payroll penalty) + $3,000 (charitable contributions) + $5,000 (unreasonable compensation).

\*\* $4,000 (tax-exempt interest) + $5,000 (life insurance proceeds).

### Effect of Terminating the S Election.

Normally, distributions to shareholders from a C corporation are taxed as dividends to the extent of E & P. However, any distribution of *cash* by a corporation to shareholders during a one-year period[34] following S election termination receives special treatment. Such a distribution is treated as a tax-free recovery of stock basis to the extent that it does not exceed the AAA.[35] Since *only* cash distributions reduce the AAA during this *postelection termination period*, a corporation should not make property distributions during this time. Instead, the entity should sell property and distribute the proceeds to shareholders. However, post-termination distributions that are charged against the OAA do not get tax-free treatment. To take advantage of post-termination benefits, an S corporation should maintain both the AAA and the OAA, although S corporations without AEP are not required to do so.

**EXAMPLE 26**

Quinn, the sole shareholder of Roman, Inc., a calendar year S corporation, elects during 2003 to terminate the S election, effective January 1, 2004. As of the end of 2003, Roman has an AAA of $1,300. Quinn can receive a nontaxable distribution of cash during a post-termination period of approximately one year to the extent of Roman's AAA. Although a cash distribution of $1,300 during 2004 would be nontaxable to Quinn, it would reduce the adjusted basis of his stock. ■

**LO.7**

Understand how distributions to S corporation shareholders are taxed.

## TAX TREATMENT OF PROPERTY DISTRIBUTIONS BY THE CORPORATION

An S corporation recognizes a gain on any distribution of appreciated property (other than in a reorganization) in the same manner as if the asset had been sold to the shareholder at its fair market value.[36] The corporate gain is passed through to the shareholders. The character of the gain—capital gain or ordinary income—depends upon the type of asset being distributed. There is an important reason for this gain recognition rule. Without it, property might be distributed tax-free (other than for certain recapture items) and later sold without income recognition to the shareholder because the shareholder's basis equals the asset's fair market value.

---

[34]The period is *approximately* one year in length. The post-termination transition period is discussed later in the chapter.

[35]§§ 1371(e) and 1377(b).

[36]§ 311(b).

## TAX IN THE NEWS

### AAA versus OAA

The accumulated adjustments account (AAA) is the cumulative net amount on which the S corporate shareholders have paid tax. This account is determined at the corporate level and not at the shareholder level. When stock is transferred from one person to another, it is likely that the shareholder's tax basis in his or her stock will not be a pro rata portion of the total of the AAA plus capital stock. One cannot conclude, therefore, that a distribution is tax-free by merely looking at the AAA amount.

The OAA also appears in Schedule M–2 of Form 1120S. The OAA contains a running balance of those items that neither increase nor decrease the AAA, but are not properly debited or credited to AEP (e.g., tax-exempt income and related expenses). In the case of shareholder distributions, the OAA is charged only after the AAA and AEP are exhausted.

Once an S election is terminated, a special rule applies to cash distributions during an approximately one-year period at the end of the last S corporation year. Cash distributions during this transition period are tax-free recoveries of basis to the shareholders, *but only to the extent of any AAA.* But post-termination distributions that are charged against the OAA do not get tax-free treatment. There appears to be no policy reason why S corporation post-termination distributions should not be permitted to be paid from both the OAA and the AAA.

SOURCE: Adapted from B. I. W. Raby and W. C. Raby, "S Corporation AAA and OAA—Alphabet Soup or Taxpayer Stew?" *Tax Notes,* February 12, 1998, pp. 1013–1016.

---

The S corporation does not recognize a loss when distributing assets that are worth less than their basis. As with gain property, the shareholder's basis is equal to the asset's fair market value. Thus, the potential loss is postponed until the shareholder sells the stock of the S corporation. Since loss property receives a step-down in basis without any loss recognition by the S corporation, distributions of loss property should be avoided. See Concept Summary 12–2.

**EXAMPLE 27**

Turnip, Inc., an S corporation for 10 years, distributes a tract of land held as an investment to Chang, its majority shareholder. The land was purchased for $22,000 many years ago and is currently worth $82,000. Turnip recognizes a capital gain of $60,000, which increases the AAA by $60,000. The gain appears on Turnip's Schedule K, and a proportionate share of it passes through to the shareholders' tax returns. Then the property dividend reduces the AAA by $82,000 (the fair market value). The tax consequences are the same for appreciated property, whether it is distributed to the shareholders and they dispose of it, or the corporation sells the property and distributes the proceeds to the shareholders.

If the land had been purchased for $82,000 and was currently worth $22,000, Chang takes a $22,000 basis in the land. The $60,000 realized loss is not recognized at the corporate level. The loss does not reduce Turnip's AAA. Only when the S corporation sells the asset does it recognize the loss and reduce AAA. ∎

**EXAMPLE 28**

Assume the same facts as in the previous example, except that Turnip is a C corporation or a partnership. The partner's basis in the partnership is $15,000.

## CONCEPT SUMMARY 12–2

### Distribution of Property

|  | Appreciated Property | Depreciated Property |
|---|---|---|
| S corporation | Realized gain is recognized by the corporation, which passes it through to the shareholders. Such gain increases a shareholder's stock basis, generating a basis in the property equal to FMV. On the distribution, the shareholder's stock basis is reduced by the FMV of the property (but not below zero). | Realized loss is not recognized. The shareholder assumes an FMV basis in the property. |
| C corporation | Realized gain is recognized under § 311(b) and increases E & P (net of tax). The shareholder has a taxable dividend to the extent of E & P. | Realized loss is not recognized. The shareholder assumes an FMV basis in the property. |
| Partnership | No gain to the partnership or partner. The partner takes a carryover basis in the asset, but the asset basis is limited to the partner's basis in the partnership. | Realized loss is not recognized. The partner takes a carryover basis in the asset, but the asset basis is limited to the partner's basis in the partnership. |

*[Handwritten notes in left margin:]*

Distribution of property

AB    22 000
FMV   82 000
gain  60 000

AB    82 000
FMV   22 000
loss  60 000

|  | Appreciated Property | | |
|---|---|---|---|
|  | S Corporation | C Corporation | Partnership |
| Entity gain/loss | $60,000 | $60,000 | $ –0– |
| Owner's gain/loss/dividend | 60,000 | 82,000* | –0– |
| Owner's basis in land | 82,000 | 82,000 | 15,000 |
|  | Property That Has Declined in Value | | |
|  | S Corporation | C Corporation | Partnership |
| Entity gain/loss | $ –0– | $ –0– | $ –0– |
| Owner's gain/loss/dividend | –0– | 22,000* | –0– |
| Owner's basis in land | 22,000 | 22,000 | 15,000** |

*Assume sufficient E & P.
**Basis in property cannot exceed basis in partnership interest.

### SHAREHOLDER'S BASIS

**LO.8**

Calculate a shareholder's basis in S corporation stock.

The calculation of the initial tax basis of stock in an S corporation is similar to that for the basis of stock in a C corporation and depends upon the manner in which the shares are acquired (e.g., gift, inheritance, purchase, exchange under § 351, etc.). Once the initial tax basis is determined, various transactions during the life of the corporation affect the shareholder's basis in the stock. Although each shareholder is required to compute his or her own basis in the S shares, neither Form 1120S nor Schedule K–1 provides a place for deriving this amount.

A shareholder's basis is increased by stock purchases and capital contributions. Operations during the year cause the following upward adjustments to basis.[37]

- Nonseparately computed income.
- Separately stated income items (e.g., nontaxable income).
- Depletion in excess of basis in the property.

Basis then is reduced by distributions not reported as income by the shareholder (e.g., an AAA or PTI distribution). Next, the following items reduce basis (*but not below zero*).

- Nondeductible expenses of the corporation (e.g., fines, penalties, illegal kickbacks).
- Nonseparately computed loss.
- Separately stated loss and deduction items.

As under the partnership rule, basis is first increased by income items; then it is decreased by distributions and finally by losses.[38] Pass-through items (other than distributions) that reduce stock basis are governed by special ordering rules. Noncapital, nondeductible expenditures reduce stock basis before losses or deductible items. A taxpayer may irrevocably elect to have deductible items pass through before any noncapital, nondeductible items. In most cases, this election is advantageous.

**EXAMPLE 29**

In its first year of operations, Iris, Inc., a calendar year S corporation in Clemson, South Carolina, earns income of $2,000. On February 2 in its second year of operations, Iris distributes $2,000 to Marty, its sole shareholder. During the remainder of the second year, the corporation incurs a $2,000 loss.

Under the S corporation ordering rules, the $2,000 distribution is tax-free AAA to Marty, and the $2,000 loss is *not* passed through because the stock basis cannot be reduced below zero. ■

A shareholder's basis in the stock can never be reduced below zero. Once stock basis is zero, any additional basis reductions from losses or deductions, but *not* distributions, decrease (but not below zero) the shareholder's basis in loans made to the S corporation. Any excess of losses or deductions over both bases is *suspended* until there are subsequent bases. Once the basis of any debt is reduced, it is later increased (only up to the original amount) by the subsequent *net* increase resulting from *all* positive and negative basis adjustments. The debt basis is adjusted back to the original amount before any increase is made in the stock basis.[39] A distribution in excess of stock basis does not reduce any debt basis. If a loss and a distribution occur in the same year, the loss reduces the stock basis last, *after* the distribution.

**EXAMPLE 30**

Stacey, a sole shareholder, has a $7,000 stock basis and a $2,000 basis in a loan that she made to a calendar year S corporation. At the beginning of 2003, the corporation's AAA balance is $0. Subchapter S ordinary income for 2003 is $8,200. During 2003, the corporation received $2,000 of tax-exempt interest income.

Cash of $17,300 is distributed to Stacey on November 15, 2003. As a result, Stacey's basis in her stock is zero, and her loan basis is still $2,000 at the end of 2003, because only losses and deductions (and not distributions) reduce loan basis. Stacey recognizes a $100 gain ($17,300 − $17,200).

---

[37]§ 1367(a).
[38]Reg. § 1.1367–1(f).

[39]§ 1367(b)(2).

| | Corporate AAA | Stacey's Stock Basis | Stacey's Loan Basis |
|---|---|---|---|
| Beginning balance | $ –0– | $ 7,000 | $2,000 |
| Subchapter S net income | 8,200 | 8,200 | –0– |
| Tax-exempt income | –0– | 2,000 | –0– |
| Subtotal | $ 8,200 | $ 17,200 | $2,000 |
| Distribution ($17,300) | (8,200) | (17,200) | –0– |
| Ending balance | $ –0– | $ –0– | $2,000 |

Although stock basis cannot be reduced below zero, the $100 excess distribution does not reduce Stacey's loan basis. ■

The basis rules for an S corporation are similar to the rules for determining a partner's interest basis in a partnership. However, a partner's basis in the partnership interest includes the partner's direct investment plus a *ratable share* of any partnership liabilities.[40] If a partnership borrows from a partner, the partner receives a basis increase as if the partnership had borrowed from an unrelated third party.[41] In contrast, except for loans from the shareholder to the corporation, corporate borrowing has no effect on S corporation shareholder basis. Loans from a shareholder to the S corporation have a tax basis only for the shareholder making the loan.

The fact that a shareholder has guaranteed a loan made to the corporation by a third party has no effect upon the shareholder's loan basis, unless payments actually have been made as a result of that guarantee.[42] If the corporation defaults on indebtedness and the shareholder makes good on the guarantee, the shareholder's indebtedness basis is increased to that extent.[43]

If a loan's basis has been reduced and is not restored, income is recognized when the S corporation repays the shareholder. If the corporation issued a note as evidence of the debt, repayment constitutes an amount received in exchange for a capital asset, and the amount that exceeds the shareholder's basis is entitled to capital gain treatment.[44] However, if the loan is made on open account, the repayment constitutes ordinary income to the extent that it exceeds the shareholder's basis in the loan. Each repayment is prorated between the gain portion and the repayment of the debt.[45] Thus, a note should be given to ensure capital gain treatment for the income that results from a loan's repayment.

Since the basis rule requires that corporate income be used to restore debt basis before it can be used to restore stock basis, a double tax on current income can result. Any current income distributed, after both debt and stock basis have been reduced to zero, is taxed as capital gain because it is considered a return of capital, but only to the extent of stock basis.

**EXAMPLE 31**

Sammy is a 57% owner of Falcon, an S corporation in Brooklyn, New York. At the beginning of 2003, his stock basis is zero. Sammy's basis in a $12,000 loan made to Falcon and evidenced

[40]§ 752(a).

[41]Reg. § 1.752–1(e).

[42]See, for example, *Estate of Leavitt*, 90 T.C. 206 (1988), aff'd 89–1 USTC ¶9332, 63 AFTR2d 89–1437, 875 F.2d 420 (CA–4, 1989); *Selfe v. U.S.*, 86–1 USTC ¶9115, 57 AFTR2d 86–464, 778 F.2d 769 (CA–11, 1985); *James K. Calcutt*, 91 T.C. 14 (1988).

[43]Rev.Rul. 70–50, 1970–1 C.B. 178.

[44]*Joe M. Smith*, 48 T.C. 872 (1967), aff'd and rev'd in 70–1 USTC ¶9327, 25 AFTR2d 70–936, 424 F.2d 219 (CA–9, 1970); Rev.Rul. 64–162, 1964–1 C.B. 304.

[45]Rev.Rul. 68–537, 1968–2 C.B. 372.

by Falcon's note has been reduced to $0 by prior losses. During the year, his net share of corporate taxable income is $11,000, which first is applied to increase his debt basis up to $11,000. At the end of the year, he receives a $13,000 distribution, which is treated as a capital gain because he has no stock basis. Sammy has been double taxed. ■

**EXAMPLE 32**

Gomez and Winn have suspended losses at the beginning of the year from their insolvent S corporation, Crocus, Inc. Crocus is a partner in a real estate partnership that realized $4 million in discharge-of-indebtedness (DOI) income. Crocus's share of the DOI income is $2 million, which is not recognized by the corporation. The DOI income does not pass through to the shareholders and does not increase their stock basis. The suspended losses cannot be deducted by the shareholders. (A Supreme Court decision[46] allowed this deduction before October 11, 2001, but Congress plugged this double-benefit loophole in 2002. This change in the law should raise taxes collected by about $1.09 billion over the next 10 years.) ■

**LO.9**

Explain the tax effects that losses have on shareholders.

## TREATMENT OF LOSSES

**Net Operating Loss.** One major advantage of an S election is the ability to pass through any net operating loss (NOL) of the corporation directly to the shareholders. A shareholder can deduct an NOL for the year in which the S corporation's tax year ends. The corporation is not entitled to any deduction for the NOL. A shareholder's basis in the stock is reduced to the extent of any pass-through of the NOL, and the shareholder's AAA is reduced by the same deductible amount.[47]

**EXAMPLE 33**

An S corporation in Chapel Hill, North Carolina, incurs a $20,000 NOL for the current year. At all times during the tax year, the stock was owned equally by the same 10 shareholders. Each shareholder is entitled to deduct $2,000 against other income for the tax year in which the corporate tax year ends. ■

Deductions for an S corporation's NOL pass-through cannot exceed a shareholder's adjusted basis in the stock *plus* the basis of any loans made by the shareholder to the corporation. If a taxpayer is unable to prove the tax basis, the NOL pass-through can be denied.[48] As noted previously, once a shareholder's adjusted stock basis has been eliminated by an NOL, any excess NOL is used to reduce the shareholder's basis for any loans made to the corporation (*but never below zero*). The basis for loans is established by the actual advances made to the corporation, and not by indirect loans.[49] If the shareholder's basis is insufficient to allow a full flow-through and there is more than one type of loss (e.g., in the same year the S corporation incurs both a passive loss and a net capital loss), the flow-through amounts are determined on a pro rata basis.

**EXAMPLE 34**

Ralph is a 50% owner of an S corporation for the entire year. His stock basis is $10,000, and his shares of the various corporate losses are as follows.

| | |
|---|---|
| Ordinary loss from operations | $8,000 |
| Capital loss | 5,000 |
| § 1231 loss | 3,000 |
| Passive loss | 2,000 |

---

[46]*Gitlitz v. Comm.*, 531 U.S. 206 (2001), 2001–1 USTC ¶50,147, 87 AFTR2d 2001–417, 121 S.Ct. 701.
[47]§§ 1368(a)(1)(A) and (e)(1)(A).

[48]See *Donald J. Sauvigne*, 30 TCM 123, T.C.Memo. 1971–30.
[49]*Ruth M. Prashker*, 59 T.C. 172 (1972); *Frederick G. Brown v. U.S.*, 83–1 USTC ¶9364, 52 AFTR2d 82–5080, 706 F.2d 755 (CA–6, 1983).

Based upon a pro rata approach, the total $10,000 allocable flow-through would be split among the various losses as follows.

$$\text{Ordinary loss} = \frac{\$8,000}{\$18,000} \times \$10,000 = \$\ 4,444.44$$

$$\text{Capital loss} = \frac{\$5,000}{\$18,000} \times \$10,000 = \$\ 2,777.78$$

$$\S\ 1231 \text{ loss} = \frac{\$3,000}{\$18,000} \times \$10,000 = \$\ 1,666.67$$

$$\text{Passive loss} = \frac{\$2,000}{\$18,000} \times \$10,000 = \underline{\$\ 1,111.11}$$

Total allocated loss                                    $10,000.00

The distribution adjustments made by an S corporation during a tax year are taken into account *before* applying the loss limitation for the year. Thus, distributions during a year reduce the adjusted basis for determining the allowable loss for the year, but the loss for the year does *not* reduce the adjusted basis for purposes of determining the tax status of the distributions made during the year.

**EXAMPLE 35**

Pylon, Inc., a calendar year S corporation, is partly owned by Doris, who has a beginning stock basis of $10,000. During the year, Doris's share of a long-term capital gain (LTCG) is $2,000, and her share of an ordinary loss is $9,000. If Doris receives a $6,000 distribution, her deductible loss is calculated as follows.

| | |
|---|---|
| Beginning stock basis | $10,000 |
| Add: LTCG | 2,000 |
| Subtotal | $12,000 |
| Less: Distribution | (6,000) |
| Basis for loss limitation purposes | $ 6,000 |
| Deductible loss | ($ 6,000) |
| Unused loss | ($ 3,000) |

Doris's stock now has a basis of zero. ■

A shareholder's share of an NOL may be greater than both stock basis and loan basis. A shareholder is entitled to carry forward a loss to the extent that the loss for the year exceeds basis. Any loss carried forward may be deducted *only* by the *same* shareholder if and when the basis in the stock of or loans to the corporation is restored.[50]

**EXAMPLE 36**

Dana has a stock basis of $4,000 in an S corporation. He has loaned $2,000 to the corporation and has guaranteed another $4,000 loan made to the corporation by a local bank. Although his share of the S corporation's NOL for the current year is $9,500, Dana may deduct only $6,000 of the NOL on his individual tax return. Dana may carry forward $3,500 of the NOL, to be deducted when the basis in his stock or loan to the corporation is restored. Dana has a zero basis in both the stock and the loan after the flow-through of the $6,000 NOL. ■

---

[50]§ 1366(d).

Any loss carryover due to insufficient basis remaining at the end of an approximately one-year post-termination transition period is *lost forever*. The post-termination period includes the 120-day period beginning on the date of any determination pursuant to an audit of a taxpayer that follows the termination of the S corporation's election and that adjusts a Subchapter S item.[51] Thus, if a shareholder has a loss carryover, he or she should increase the stock or loan basis and flow through the loss before disposing of the stock.

Net operating losses from C corporation years cannot be utilized at the corporate level (except with respect to built-in gain, discussed later in this chapter), nor can they be passed through to the shareholders. Further, the carryforward period continues to run during S status.[52] Consequently, the S election may not be appropriate for a C corporation with NOL carryforwards. When a corporation is expecting losses in the future, an S election should be made *before* the loss years.

**At-Risk Rules.** S corporation shareholders, like partners, are limited in the amount of NOL they may deduct by their "at-risk" amounts. The rules for determining at-risk amounts are similar, but not identical, to the partner at-risk rules. These rules apply to the shareholders, but not to the corporation. An amount at risk is determined separately for each shareholder. The amount of the corporate losses that are passed through and deductible by the shareholders is not affected by the amount the corporation has at risk.

A shareholder usually is considered at risk with respect to an activity to the extent of cash and the adjusted basis of other property contributed to the S corporation, any amount borrowed for use in the activity for which the taxpayer has personal liability for payment from personal assets, and the net fair market value of personal assets that secure nonrecourse borrowing. Any losses that are suspended under the at-risk rules are carried forward and are available during the post-termination transition period. The S stock basis limitations and at-risk limitations are applied before the passive activity limitations.[53]

**EXAMPLE 37**

Shareholder Ricketts has a basis of $35,000 in his S corporation stock. He takes a $15,000 nonrecourse loan from a local bank and lends the proceeds to the S corporation. Ricketts now has a stock basis of $35,000 and a debt basis of $15,000. However, due to the at-risk limitation, he can deduct only $35,000 of losses from the S corporation. ■

**Passive Losses and Credits.** Section 469 provides that net passive losses and credits are not deductible when incurred and must be carried over to a year when there is passive income. Thus, one must be aware of three major classes of income, losses, and credits—active, portfolio, and passive. S corporations are not directly subject to the limits of § 469, but corporate rental activities are inherently passive, and other activities of an S corporation may be passive unless the shareholder(s) materially participate(s) in operating the business. An S corporation may engage in more than one such activity. If the corporate activity is rental or the shareholders do not materially participate, any passive losses or credits flow through. The shareholders are able to apply the losses or credits only against their income from other passive activities.

A shareholder's stock basis is reduced by passive losses that flow through to the shareholder, even though the shareholder may not be entitled to a current deduction due to the passive loss limitations. The existence of material participation

---

[51]§ 1377(b)(1).
[52]§ 1371(b).

[53]Reg. § 1.469–2T(d)(6).

is determined at the shareholder level. There are seven tests for material participation, including a need to participate in the activity for more than 500 hours during the taxable year.[54]

**EXAMPLE 38**

Heather is a 50% owner of an S corporation engaged in a passive activity. A nonparticipating shareholder, she receives a salary of $6,000 for services as a result of the passive activity. Heather has $6,000 of earned income as a result of the salary. The $6,000 salary creates a $6,000 deduction/passive loss, which flows through to the shareholders. Heather's $3,000 share of the loss may not be deducted against the $6,000 of earned income. Under § 469(e)(3), earned income is not taken into account in computing the income or loss from a passive activity. ■

**LO.10**

Compute the built-in gains tax.

## TAX ON PRE-ELECTION BUILT-IN GAIN

Normally, an S corporation does *not* pay an income tax, since all items flow through to the shareholders. But an S corporation that was previously a C corporation may be required to pay a built-in gains tax, a LIFO recapture tax, or a passive investment income tax.

Without the **built-in gains tax** (§ 1374), it would be possible to avoid the corporate double tax on disposition of appreciated property by electing S corporation status.

**EXAMPLE 39**

Zinnia, Inc., a C corporation, owns a single asset with a basis of $100,000 and a fair market value of $500,000. If Zinnia sells this asset and distributes the cash to shareholders, there will be two levels of tax, one at the corporate level and one at the shareholder level. Alternatively, if Zinnia distributes the asset to shareholders, a double tax will still result, since a C corporation is taxed on an implicit gain in the distribution of the appreciated property. The shareholders have a dividend equal to the property's fair market value. In an attempt to avoid the double tax, Zinnia elects S corporation status. It then sells the asset and distributes the proceeds to shareholders. Without the § 1374 tax, the gain would be taxed only once, at the shareholder level. The distribution of the sales proceeds would be a tax-free reduction of the AAA. ■

The § 1374 tax generally applies to C corporations converting to S status after 1986. It is a *corporate-level* tax on any built-in gain recognized when the S corporation disposes of an asset in a taxable disposition within 10 calendar years after the date on which the S election took effect.

**General Rules.** The base for the § 1374 tax includes any unrealized gain on appreciated assets (e.g., real estate, cash basis receivables, and goodwill) held by a corporation on the day it elects S status. The highest corporate tax rate (currently 35 percent) is applied to the unrealized gain when any of the assets are sold. Furthermore, the gain on sale (net of the § 1374 tax)[55] passes through as a taxable gain to shareholders.

**EXAMPLE 40**

Assume the same facts as in the preceding example. Section 1374 imposes a corporate-level tax that must be paid by Zinnia if it sells the asset after electing S status. Upon sale of the asset, the corporation owes a tax of $140,000 ($400,000 × 35%). The shareholders have a $260,000 taxable gain ($400,000 − $140,000). Hence, the built-in gains tax effectively imposes a double tax on Zinnia and its shareholders. ■

---

[54]Reg. § 1.469–5T(a).                    [55]§ 1366(f)(2).

The maximum amount of gain that is recognized over the 10-year period is limited to the *aggregate net* built-in gain of the corporation at the time it converted to S status. Thus, at the time of the S election, unrealized gains of the corporation are offset against unrealized losses. The net amount of gains and losses sets an upper limit on the tax base for the built-in gains tax. Any appreciation after the conversion to S status is subject to the regular S corporation pass-through rules.

**EXAMPLE 41**

Quadrant, Inc., is a former C corporation whose first S corporation year began on January 1, 2003. At that time, Quadrant had two assets: X, with a value of $1,000 and a basis of $400, and Y, with a value of $400 and a basis of $600. The net unrealized built-in gain as of January 1, 2003, is $400. If asset X is sold for $1,200 during 2003, and asset Y is retained, the recognized built-in gain is limited to $400. The additional $200 of appreciation after electing S status is not part of the built-in gain. ■

Loss assets on the date of conversion reduce the maximum built-in gain and any potential tax under § 1374.[56] In addition, built-in losses and built-in gains are netted each year to determine the annual § 1374 tax base. Thus, an incentive exists to contribute loss assets to a corporation before electing S status. However, the IRS indicates that contributions of loss property within two years before the earlier of the date of conversion or the date of filing an S election are presumed to have a tax avoidance motive and will not reduce the corporation's net unrealized built-in gain.

**EXAMPLE 42**

Donna owns all the stock of an S corporation, which in turn owns two assets on the S conversion date: asset 1 (basis of $5,000 and fair market value of $2,500) and asset 2 (basis of $1,000 and fair market value of $5,000). The S corporation has a potential net realized built-in gain of $1,500 (i.e., the built-in gain of $4,000 in asset 2 reduced by the built-in loss of $2,500 in asset 1). However, if Donna contributed the loss asset to the corporation within two years before the S election, the built-in gain potential becomes $4,000, i.e., the loss asset cannot be used to reduce built-in gain. ■

The amount of built-in gain recognized in any year is limited to an "as if" taxable income for the year, computed as if the corporation were a C corporation. Any built-in gain that escapes taxation due to the taxable income limitation is carried forward and recognized in future tax years. Thus, a corporation can defer § 1374 tax liability whenever it has a low or negative taxable income.

**EXAMPLE 43**

Assume the same facts as in Example 41, except that if Quadrant were a C corporation, its taxable income in 2003 would be $300. The amount of built-in gain subject to tax in 2003 is $300. The excess built-in gain of $100 is carried forward and taxed in 2004 (assuming adequate C corporation taxable income in that year). There is no statutory limit on the carryforward period, but the gain would effectively expire at the end of the 10-year recognition period applicable to all built-in gains (except for installment sales after March 25, 1990).[57] ■

Gains on sales or distributions of all assets by an S corporation are presumed to be built-in gains unless the taxpayer can establish that the appreciation accrued after the conversion to S status. Thus, it may be advisable to obtain an independent appraisal when converting a C corporation to an S corporation. Certainly, a memorandum should be prepared listing the fair market values of all assets, along with the methods used to arrive at the values.

Normally, tax attributes of a C corporation do *not* carry over to a converted S corporation. For purposes of the tax on built-in gain, however, certain carryovers

---

[56]§§ 1374(c)(2) and (d)(1).

[57]§ 1374(d)(7); Notice 90–27, 1990–1 C.B. 336.

CONCEPT SUMMARY 12–3

---

### Calculation of the Built-in Gains Tax Liability

Step 1.    Select the smaller of built-in gain or taxable income (C corporation rules).*

Step 2.    Deduct unexpired NOLs and capital losses from C corporation tax years.

Step 3.    Multiply the tax base obtained in step 2 by the top corporate income tax rate.

Step 4.    Deduct any business credit carryforwards and AMT credit carryovers arising in a C corporation tax year from the amount obtained in step 3.

Step 5.    The corporation pays any tax resulting from step 4.

*Any net recognized built-in gain in excess of taxable income is carried forward to the next year, as long as the next year is within the 10-year recognition period.

---

are allowed. In particular, an S corporation can offset built-in gains with unexpired NOLs or capital losses from C corporation years.

**EXAMPLE 44**

Maple Corporation elects S status, effective for calendar year 2003. Maple has a $10,000 NOL carryover when it elects S status. As of January 1, 2003, one of Maple's capital assets has a basis of $50,000 and a fair market value of $110,000. Early in 2004, the asset is sold for $110,000. Maple recognizes a $60,000 built-in gain when the asset is sold. However, Maple's NOL reduces the built-in gain from $60,000 to $50,000. Thus, only $50,000 is subject to the built-in gains tax. ■

**EXAMPLE 45**

An S corporation has a built-in gain of $100,000, taxable income of $90,000, and other items as shown below. The built-in gain tax liability is calculated as follows.

| | |
|---|---:|
| Lesser of taxable income or built-in gain | $ 90,000 |
| Less: NOL carryforward from C year | (12,000) |
| Capital loss carryforward from C year | (8,000) |
| Tax base | $ 70,000 |
| Highest corporate income tax rate | × 0.35 |
| Tentative tax | $ 24,500 |
| Less: Business credit carryforward from C year | (4,000) |
| Built-in gains tax liability | $ 20,500 |

The $10,000 realized (but not taxed) built-in gain in excess of taxable income must be carried forward to the next year, as long as the next year is within the 10-year recognition period. ■

Concept Summary 12–3 summarizes the calculation of the built-in gains tax.

**LIFO Recapture Tax.**    When a corporation uses the FIFO method for its last year before making the S election, any built-in gain is recognized and taxed as the inventory is sold. A LIFO-basis corporation does not recognize this gain unless the corporation invades the LIFO layer during the 10-year recognition period. To preclude deferral of gain recognition under LIFO, any LIFO recapture amount at the time of the S election is subject to a corporate-level tax.

The taxable LIFO recapture amount equals the excess of the inventory's value under FIFO over the LIFO value. No negative adjustment is allowed if the LIFO value is higher than the FIFO value. The resulting tax is payable in four equal installments, with the first payment due on or before the due date for the corporate return for the last C corporation year (without regard to any extensions). The remaining three installments must be paid on or before the due dates of the succeeding corporate returns. No interest is due if payments are made by the due dates, and no estimated taxes are due on the four tax installments. The basis of the LIFO inventory is adjusted to account for this LIFO recapture amount, but the AAA is not decreased by payment of the tax.

**EXAMPLE 46**

Engelage Corporation converts from a C corporation to an S corporation at the beginning of 2003. Engelage used the LIFO inventory method in 2002 and had an ending LIFO inventory of $110,000 (FIFO value of $190,000). Engelage must add $80,000 of LIFO recapture amount to its 2002 taxable income, resulting in an increased tax liability of $28,000 ($80,000 × 35%). Thus, Engelage must pay one-fourth of the tax (or $7,000) with its 2002 corporate tax return. The three succeeding installments of $7,000 each are paid with Engelage's next three tax returns. ■

**LO.11**

Compute the passive investment income penalty tax.

## PASSIVE INVESTMENT INCOME PENALTY TAX

A tax is imposed on the excess passive income of S corporations that possess AEP from C corporation years. The tax rate is the highest corporate rate for the year (35 percent in 2003). The rate is applied to excess net passive income (ENPI), which is determined using the following formula:

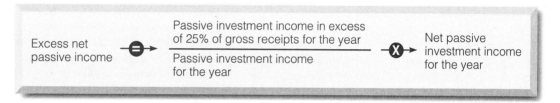

Passive investment income (PII) includes gross receipts derived from royalties, passive rents, dividends, interest, annuities, and sales and exchanges of stocks and securities.[58] Only the net gain from the disposition of capital assets (other than stocks and securities) is taken into account in computing gross receipts. Net passive income is passive income reduced by any deductions directly connected with the production of that income. Any passive income tax reduces the amount the shareholders must take into income.

The excess net passive income cannot exceed the C corporate taxable income for the year before considering any NOL deduction or the special deductions allowed by §§ 241–250 (except the organizational expense deduction of § 248).[59]

**EXAMPLE 47**

At the end of 2003, Barnhardt Corporation, an S corporation, has gross receipts totaling $264,000 (of which $110,000 is PII). Expenditures directly connected to the production of the PII total $30,000. Therefore, Barnhardt has net PII of $80,000 ($110,000 − $30,000), and its PII for tax year 2003 exceeds 25% of its gross receipts by $44,000 [$110,000 PII − (25% × $264,000)]. Excess net passive income (ENPI) is $32,000, calculated as follows.

$$\text{ENPI} = \frac{\$44,000}{\$110,000} \times \$80,000 = \$32,000$$

Barnhardt's PII tax for 2003 is $11,200 ($32,000 × 35%). ■

---

[58]§ 1362(d)(3)(D)(i).          [59]§§ 1374(d)(4) and 1375(a) and (b).

## OTHER OPERATIONAL RULES

Several other points may be made about the possible effects of various Code provisions on S corporations.

- An S corporation is required to make estimated tax payments with respect to tax exposure because of any recognized built-in gain and excess passive investment income.
- An S corporation may own stock in another corporation, but an S corporation may not have a C corporation shareholder. An S corporation is *not* eligible for a dividends received deduction.
- An S corporation is *not* subject to the 10 percent of taxable income limitation applicable to charitable contributions made by a C corporation.
- Any family member who renders services or furnishes capital to an S corporation must be paid reasonable compensation. Otherwise, the IRS can make adjustments to reflect the value of the services or capital.[60] This rule may make it more difficult for related parties to shift Subchapter S taxable income to children or other family members.
- Although § 1366(a)(1) provides for a flow-through of S items to a shareholder, it does not create self-employment income.[61] Compensation for services rendered to an S corporation is, however, subject to FICA taxes.

**EXAMPLE 48**

Cody and Dana each own one-third of a fast-food restaurant, and their 14-year-old son owns the other shares. Both parents work full-time in the restaurant operations, but the son works infrequently. Neither parent receives a salary this year, when the taxable income of the S corporation is $160,000. The IRS can require that reasonable compensation be paid to the parents to prevent the full one-third of the $160,000 from being taxed to the son. Otherwise, this would be an effective technique to shift earned income to a family member to reduce the total family tax burden. Furthermore, low or zero salaries can reduce FICA taxes due to the Federal government. ■

- An S corporation is placed on the cash method of accounting for purposes of deducting business expenses and interest owed to a cash basis related party.[62] Thus, the timing of the shareholder's income and the corporate deduction must match.
- The S election is not recognized by the District of Columbia and several states, including Connecticut, Michigan, New Hampshire, and Tennessee. Thus, some or all of the entity's income may be subject to a state-level income tax.
- If § 1244 stock is issued to an S corporation, the S corporation and its shareholders may not treat losses on such stock as ordinary losses, notwithstanding § 1363, which provides that the taxable income of an S corporation must be computed in the same manner as that of an individual. However, an S corporation may issue § 1244 stock to its shareholders to obtain ordinary loss treatment.
- Losses may be disallowed due to a lack of a profit motive. If the activities at the corporate level are not profit motivated, the losses may be disallowed under the hobby loss rule of § 183.[63]

---

[60]§ 1366(e). In addition, beware of an IRS search for the "real owner" of the stock under Reg. § 1.1373–1(a)(2).
[61]Rev.Rul. 59–221, 1959–1 C.B. 225.

[62]§ 267(b).
[63]*Michael J. Houston*, 69 TCM 2360, T.C.Memo. 1995–159; *Mario G. De Mendoza, III*, 68 TCM 42, T.C.Memo. 1994–314.

**Tax Planning Considerations**

## WHEN THE ELECTION IS ADVISABLE

Effective tax planning with S corporations begins with the determination of whether the election is appropriate. In this context, one should consider the following factors.

- Are losses from the business anticipated? If so, the S election may be highly attractive because these losses pass through to the shareholders.
- What are the tax brackets of the shareholders? If the shareholders are in high individual income tax brackets, it may be desirable to avoid S corporation status and have profits taxed to the corporation at lower C rates (e.g., 15 percent or 25 percent). However, the income still is not in the owners' hands.
- When the immediate pass-through of Subchapter S taxable income is avoided, profits of the corporation may later be taken out by the shareholders as capital gain income through stock redemptions, some liquidating distributions, or sales of stock to others; received as dividend distributions in low tax bracket years; or negated by a partial or complete step-up in basis upon the death of the shareholder.[64] On the other hand, if the shareholders are in low individual income tax brackets, the pass-through of corporate profits has less effect, and the avoidance of the corporate income tax becomes the paramount consideration. Under these circumstances, the S election could be highly attractive. Although an S corporation usually escapes Federal taxes, it may not be immune from state and local taxes imposed on corporations or from several Federal penalty taxes.
- Does a C corporation have an NOL carryover from a prior year? Such a loss cannot be used in an S year (except for purposes of the built-in gains tax). Even worse, S years count in the 20-year carryover limitation. Thus, even if the S election is made, one might consider terminating the election before the carryover limitation expires. Such a termination would permit the loss to be utilized by what is now a C corporation.
- Both individuals and C corporations are subject to the alternative minimum tax. Many of the tax preference and adjustment items are the same, but some apply only to corporate taxpayers while others are limited to individuals. The alternative minimum tax adjustment relating to adjusted current earnings could create havoc with some C corporations (refer to Chapter 6). S corporations themselves are not subject to this tax.
- Some C corporations must convert from the cash method to the accrual method of accounting (refer to Chapter 2).
- S corporations and partnerships have lost some of the flexibility in the choice of their accounting period (see also Chapter 10).
- By taxing C corporations on nonliquidating and liquidating distributions of appreciated property (refer to Chapter 5), the effect of double taxation is reinforced.
- The modifications made to § 382 (refer to Chapter 7) have imposed severe restrictions on the carryover of NOLs.

Since the S election may or may not provide the shareholders with tax advantages, one must consider all of the provisions that affect the owners.

**EXAMPLE 49**

Tracey has a basis of $500,000 in his business assets, including some land, which is subject to a liability of $700,000. Tracey transfers all of the assets of the business to a newly formed corporation, Red, Inc., in exchange for all of the stock in Red. Red elects to be taxed as an S

---

[64]See the discussion of § 1014 in Chapter 18.

corporation. Red incurs ordinary losses as follows: Year 1, $50,000; Year 2, $80,000; Year 3, $90,000. Tracey deducts the losses to offset income from other sources. Red is audited in Year 3.

- Tracey must recognize a $200,000 gain upon the incorporation of Red under § 357(c), because the liabilities exceed his basis in the assets. Tracey's basis in the Red stock is zero: $500,000 (basis of Tracey's assets) − $700,000 (liabilities assumed by Red) + $200,000 (gain recognized to Tracey).
- Because Tracey's basis in the Red stock is zero, he is not entitled to deduct any of the losses for Year 1, Year 2, or Year 3.
- Because Tracey was actively involved in his business, had he not incorporated, he could have offset total losses of $220,000 against other ordinary income. Moreover, the $200,000 gain upon the incorporation of his business would not have arisen. Thus, the incorporation and S election increased Tracey's taxable income by $420,000. ■

The choice of the form of doing business often is dictated by other factors. For example, many businesses cannot qualify for the S election—due to the possibility of a public offering or a need for substantial capital inflow—or would find the partnership or limited liability company forms more practical. Therefore, freedom of action based on tax considerations may not be an attainable goal. Comparative tax attributes of partnerships, S corporations, and C corporations are examined fully in Chapter 13.

## MAKING A PROPER ELECTION

Once the parties have decided the election is appropriate, it becomes essential to ensure that the election is made properly.

- Make sure all shareholders consent. If any doubt exists concerning the shareholder status of an individual, it would be wise to have that party issue a consent anyway.[65] Too few consents are fatal to the election; the same cannot be said for too many consents.
- Be sure that the election is timely and properly filed. Either hand carry the election to an IRS office or send it by certified or registered mail. The date used to determine timeliness is the postmark date, not the date the IRS receives the election. A copy of the election should become part of the corporation's permanent files.
- Be careful to ascertain when the timely election period begins to run for a newly formed corporation. An election made too soon (before the corporation is in existence) is worse than one made too late. If serious doubts exist as to when this period begins, filing more than one election might be considered a practical means of guaranteeing the desired result.
- It still is beneficial for an S corporation to issue § 1244 stock (refer to Chapter 3). This type of stock allows the original shareholder to obtain an ordinary deduction for a loss on the sale or worthlessness of the stock, rather than long-term capital loss treatment. Shareholders have nothing to lose by complying with § 1244.

## PRESERVING THE ELECTION

Recall that an election can be lost intentionally or unintentionally in several ways, and that a five-year waiting period generally is imposed before another S election is available. To preserve an S election, the following points should be kept in mind.

---

[65]See *William B. Wilson*, 34 TCM 463, T.C.Memo. 1975–92.

- As a starting point, all parties concerned should be made aware of the various transactions that lead to the loss of an election.
- Watch for possible disqualification of a small business corporation. For example, the divorce of a shareholder, accompanied by a property settlement, could violate the 75-shareholder limitation. The death of a shareholder could result in a nonqualifying trust becoming a shareholder. The latter circumstance might be avoided by utilizing a buy-sell agreement or binding the deceased shareholder's estate to turn in the stock to the corporation for redemption or, as an alternative, to sell it to the surviving shareholders.[66]
- Make sure a new majority shareholder (including the estate of a deceased shareholder) does not file a refusal to continue the election.
- Watch for the passive investment income limitation. Avoid a consecutive third year with excess passive income if a corporation has Subchapter C accumulated earnings and profits. In this connection, assets that produce passive investment income (e.g., stocks and bonds, certain rental assets) might be retained by the shareholders in their individual capacities and thereby kept out of the corporation.
- Do not transfer stock to a nonresident alien.
- Do not issue a second class of stock.

---

**ETHICAL CONSIDERATIONS**   **A Divorce Threatens S Status**

Golden Cowrie, Inc., has operated successfully as an S corporation for eight years in Greer, South Carolina. In July 2003, the company had 75 shareholders, but one of the shareholders, Morrie Williams, is considering obtaining a divorce. Both Morrie and his wife, Kristy, own shares in the corporation.

Morrie discusses the situation with the board of directors, who offer several suggestions.

- Morrie should postpone the divorce until 2004, while the company tries to purchase all of the stock of one of the smaller owners.

- Morrie and Kristy should remain married indefinitely for the good of the S election.
- Two of the unmarried shareholders will be encouraged to marry for the "benefit of the company."
- The company will continue to list Morrie and Kristy as married on Form 1120S after they divorce.

The S election saves the group about $320,000 each year. How would you counsel Morrie to respond to the board's proposals?

---

## PLANNING FOR THE OPERATION OF THE CORPORATION

Operating an S corporation to achieve optimum tax savings for all parties involved requires a great deal of care and, most important, an understanding of the applicable tax rules.

**Accumulated Adjustments Account.**   Although the corporate-level accumulated adjustments account (AAA) is used primarily by an S corporation with accumulated earnings and profits (AEP) from a Subchapter C year, all S corporations should maintain an accurate record of the AAA. Because there is a grace period

---

[66]See Chapter 18 for a discussion of buy-sell agreements. Most such agreements do not create a second class of S stock. Rev.Rul. 85–161, 1985–2 C.B. 191; *Portage Plastics Co. v. U.S.*, 72–2 USTC ¶9567, 30 AFTR2d 72–5229, 470 F.2d 308 (CA–7, 1973).

for distributing the AAA after termination of the S election, the parties must be in a position to determine the balance of the account.

**EXAMPLE 50**

Nobles, Inc., an S corporation during 2002, has no AEP from a Subchapter C year. Over the years, Nobles made no attempt to maintain an accurate accounting for the AAA. In 2003, the S election is terminated, and Nobles has a grace period for distributing the AAA tax-free to its shareholders. A great deal of time and expense may be necessary to reconstruct the AAA balance in 2003. ■

When AEP is present, a negative AAA may cause double taxation of S corporation income. With a negative AAA, a distribution of current income restores the negative AAA balance to zero, but is considered to be a distribution in excess of AAA and is taxable as a dividend to the extent of AEP. Distributions during the year reduce the stock basis for determining the allowable loss for the year, but the loss does *not* reduce the stock basis for determining the tax status of distributions made during the year. In determining the tax treatment of distributions by an S corporation having AEP, any net adjustments (e.g., excess of losses and deductions over income) for the tax year are ignored.

The AAA bypass election may be used to reduce exposure to the accumulated earnings tax or personal holding company tax in post-S years. This bypass election allows AEP to be distributed instead.

**EXAMPLE 51**

Zebra, Inc., an S corporation during 2002, has a significant amount in its AEP account. The shareholders expect to terminate the election in 2003, when Zebra will be subject to the lower corporate income tax rates. Since Zebra as a C corporation may be subject to the accumulated earnings penalty tax in 2003, the shareholders may wish to use the AAA bypass election to distribute some or all of the AEP. Of course, any distributions of the AEP account in 2002 would be taxable to the shareholders. ■

A net loss allocated to a shareholder reduces the AAA. This required adjustment should encourage an S corporation to make annual distributions of net income to avoid the reduction of an AAA by a future net loss.

**Salary Structure.**   The amount of salary paid to a shareholder-employee of an S corporation can have varying tax consequences and should be considered carefully. Larger amounts might be advantageous if the maximum contribution allowed for the shareholder-employee under the corporation's retirement plan has not been reached. Smaller amounts may be beneficial if the parties are trying to shift taxable income to lower-bracket shareholders, reduce payroll taxes, curtail a reduction of Social Security benefits, or restrict losses that do not pass through because of the basis limitation.

A strategy of decreasing compensation and correspondingly increasing distributions to shareholder-employees often results in substantial savings in employment taxes. However, a shareholder of an S corporation cannot always perform substantial services and arrange to receive distributions rather than compensation so that the corporation may avoid paying employment taxes. The IRS may deem the shareholder to be an employee, with any distributions recharacterized as wages subject to FICA and FUTA taxes.[67] In effect, the IRS requires that reasonable compensation be paid to shareholder-employees. For planning purposes, some level of

---

[67]Rev.Rul. 74–44, 1974–1 C.B. 287; *Spicer Accounting, Inc. v. U.S.,* 91–1 USTC ¶50,103, 66 AFTR2d 90–5806, 918 F.2d 90 (CA–9, 1990); *Radtke v. U.S.,* 90–1 USTC ¶50,113, 65 AFTR2d 90–1155, 895 F.2d 1196 (CA–7, 1990).

compensation should be paid to all shareholder-employees to avoid any recharacterization of nonpassive distributions as deductible salaries—especially in personal service corporations.

The IRS can require that reasonable compensation be paid to family members who render services or provide capital to the S corporation. The IRS also can adjust the items taken into account by family-member shareholders to reflect the value of services or capital they provided. Refer to Example 48.

Unreasonable compensation traditionally has not been a problem for S corporations, but deductible compensation under § 162 reduces an S corporation's taxable income, which is relevant to the built-in gains tax. Compensation may be one of the larger items that an S corporation can use to reduce taxable income to minimize any built-in gains penalty tax. Thus, IRS agents may attempt to classify compensation as unreasonable to increase the § 1374 tax.

**Loss Considerations.**   A net loss in excess of tax basis may be carried forward and deducted only by the same shareholder in succeeding years. Thus, before disposing of the stock, a shareholder should increase the basis of such stock/loan to flow through the loss. The next shareholder does not obtain the loss carryover.

Any unused loss carryover in existence upon the termination of the S election may be deducted only in the next tax year and is limited to the individual's *stock* basis (not loan basis) in the post-termination year.[68] The shareholder may wish to purchase more stock to increase the tax basis in order to absorb the loss.

The NOL provisions create a need for sound tax planning during the last election year and the post-termination transition period. If it appears that the S corporation is going to sustain an NOL or use up any loss carryover, each shareholder's basis should be analyzed to determine if it can absorb the share of the loss. If basis is insufficient to absorb the loss, further investments should be considered before the end of the post-termination transition year. Such investments can be accomplished through additional stock purchases from the corporation, or from other shareholders, to increase basis. This action ensures the full benefit from the NOL carryover.

**EXAMPLE 52**

A calendar year C corporation has an NOL of $20,000 in 2002. The corporation makes a valid S election in 2003 and has another $20,000 NOL in that year. At all times during 2003, the stock of the corporation was owned by the same 10 shareholders, each of whom owned 10% of the stock. Tim, one of the 10 shareholders, has an adjusted basis of $1,800 at the beginning of 2003. None of the 2002 NOL may be carried forward into the S year. Although Tim's share of the 2003 NOL is $2,000, the deduction for the loss is limited to $1,800 in 2003 with a $200 carryover. ∎

**Avoiding the Passive Investment Income Tax.**   Too much passive investment income (PII) may cause an S corporation to incur a § 1375 penalty tax and/or terminate the S election. Several planning techniques can be used to avoid both of these unfavorable events. Where a small amount of AEP exists, an AAA bypass election may be appropriate to purge the AEP, thereby avoiding the passive income tax altogether. Alternatively, the corporation might reduce taxable income below the excess net passive income; similarly, PII might be accelerated into years in which there is an offsetting NOL. In addition, the tax can be avoided if the corporation manufactures needed gross receipts. By increasing gross receipts without increasing PII, the amount of PII in excess of 25 percent of gross receipts is reduced. Finally,

---

[68] § 1366(d)(3).

performing significant services or incurring significant costs with respect to rental real estate activities can elevate the rent income to nonpassive.

**EXAMPLE 53**

An S corporation has paid a passive income penalty tax for two consecutive years. In the next year, the corporation has a large amount of AAA. If the AEP account is small, a bypass election may be appropriate to purge the corporation of the AEP. Without any AEP, no passive income tax applies, and the S election is not terminated. Any distribution of AEP to the shareholders constitutes taxable dividends, however.

Another alternative is to manufacture a large amount of gross receipts without increasing PII through an action such as a merger with a grocery store. If the gross receipts from the grocery store are substantial, the amount of the PII in excess of 25% of gross receipts is reduced. ∎

**Managing the Built-in Gains Tax.**   A taxable income limitation encourages an S corporation to create deductions or accelerate deductions in the years that built-in gains are recognized. Although the postponed built-in gain is carried forward to future years, the time value of money makes the postponement beneficial. For example, payment of compensation, rather than a distribution, creates a deduction that reduces taxable income and postpones the built-in gains tax.

**EXAMPLE 54**

Mundy, Inc., an S corporation converted from a C corporation, has built-in gain of $110,000 and taxable income of $120,000 before payment of salaries to its two shareholders. If Mundy pays at least $120,000 in salaries to the shareholders (rather than a distribution), taxable income will drop to zero, and the built-in gains tax is postponed. Thus, Mundy needs to keep the salaries as high as possible to postpone the built-in gains tax in future years and reap a benefit from the time value of money. Of course, paying the salaries may increase the payroll tax burden if the salaries are below FICA and FUTA limits. ∎

Giving built-in gain property to a charitable organization does not trigger the built-in gains tax. However, the built-in gain may be a preference item at the shareholder level for purposes of the alternative minimum tax. To reduce or eliminate the built-in gains tax, built-in *loss* property may be sold in the same year that built-in gain property is sold. Generally, the taxpayer should sell built-in loss property in a year when an equivalent amount of built-in gain property is sold. Otherwise, the built-in loss could be wasted.

**EXAMPLE 55**

Green Corporation elects S status effective for calendar year 2002. As of January 1, 2002, Green's only asset has a basis of $40,000 and a fair market value of $100,000. If this asset is sold for $120,000 in 2003, Green recognizes an $80,000 gain, of which $60,000 is subject to the corporate built-in gains tax. The other $20,000 of gain is subject to the S corporation pass-through rules and bypasses the corporate income tax.

Unless the taxpayer can show otherwise, any appreciation existing at the date of the sale or exchange is presumed to be preconversion built-in gain. Therefore, Green incurs a built-in gain of $80,000 unless it can prove that the $20,000 gain developed after the effective date of the election. ∎

**Controlling Adjustments and Preference Items.**   The individual alternative minimum tax (AMT) affects more taxpayers than ever before, because the tax base has expanded and the difference between regular tax rates and the individual AMT rate has been narrowed. In an S corporation setting, tax preferences flow through proportionately to the shareholders, who, in computing the individual AMT, treat the preferences as if they were directly realized. Thus, the S corporation may not take advantage of the AMT exemption available to a small corporation.

A flow-through of tax preferences can be a tax disaster for a shareholder who is an "almost-AMT taxpayer." Certain steps can be taken to protect such a shareholder from being pushed into the AMT. For example, a large S corporation preference from tax-exempt interest on private activity bonds could adversely affect an "almost-AMT taxpayer." Certain adjustment and preference items are subject to elections that can remove them from a shareholder's AMT computation. Certain positive adjustments can be removed from a shareholder's alternative minimum taxable income base if the S corporation elects to capitalize and amortize certain expenditures over a prescribed period of time. These expenditures include excess intangible drilling and development expenditures, research and experimental costs, mining exploration and development expenditures, and circulation expenses.

Other corporate choices can protect an "almost-AMT shareholder." Using a slower method of cost recovery (rather than a more accelerated method) can be beneficial to certain shareholders. Many of these decisions and elections may generate conflicts of interest, however, with other shareholders who are not so situated and would not suffer from the flow-through of adjustments and tax preference items.

**EXAMPLE 56**

Tallis, Ltd., an S corporation, is owned equally by Ann, Bob, and Chris. Ann and Bob are subject to a 40% net state and Federal marginal tax rate, while Chris is subject to the AMT. Tallis put the following into service this year.

- Depreciable assets: MACRS deductions per shareholder, $14,290; AMT cost recovery per shareholder, $10,714.
- Mining exploration costs: Regular tax deduction per shareholder, $30,000; AMT deduction per shareholder, $20,000.

Ann and Bob favor the larger regular tax deductions. Chris would like Tallis to elect to use the AMT deduction amounts for regular tax purposes. If the corporation does this, it eliminates the shareholders' related AMT adjustments for the lives of these assets. At the same time, the election does away with Chris's individual-level AMT on these items. Thus, Tallis's tax choice is between:

- Larger deductions at no AMT cost for Ann and Bob.
- Lower deductions and a higher tax base for all shareholders, which would save Chris the related AMT. ■

**Allocation of Tax Items.** If a shareholder dies or stock is transferred during the taxable year, tax items may be allocated under the pro rata approach or the per-books method. Without the per-books election, a shareholder's pro rata share of tax items is determined by assigning an equal portion of each item to each day of the tax year and then dividing that portion pro rata among the shares outstanding on the transfer day.

With the consent of all affected shareholders and the corporation, an S corporation can elect to allocate tax items according to the permanent records using normal tax accounting rules. The allocation is made as if the taxable year consists of two taxable years. The first portion ends on the date of termination. On the day the shares are transferred, the shares are considered owned by the disposing shareholder. The selected method may be beneficial to the terminating shareholder and harmful to the acquiring shareholder. An election might result in a higher allocation of losses to a taxpayer who is better able to utilize the losses. In the case of the death of a shareholder, a per-books election prevents the income and loss allocation to a deceased shareholder from being affected by postdeath events.

**Termination Aspects.**    It is always advisable to avoid accumulated earnings and profits (AEP) in an S corporation. There is the ever-present danger of terminating the election because of excess passive investment income in three consecutive years. Further, the § 1375 penalty tax is imposed on excess passive net income. Thus, one should try to eliminate such AEP through a dividend distribution or liquidation of the S corporation with a subsequent reincorporation. If the AEP account is small, to eliminate the problem all of the shareholders may consent under § 1368(e)(3) to have distributions treated as made first from AEP rather than from the AAA (the AAA bypass election).

If the shareholders of an S corporation decide to terminate the election other than through voluntary revocation, they should make sure that the disqualifying act possesses substance. When the intent of the parties is obvious and the act represents a technical noncompliance rather than a real change, the IRS may be able to disregard it and keep the parties in S status.[69]

**Liquidation of an S Corporation.**    S corporations are subject to many of the same liquidation rules applicable to C corporations (refer to Chapter 5). In general, the distribution of appreciated property to S shareholders in complete liquidation is treated as if the property were sold to the shareholders in a taxable transaction. Unlike a C corporation, however, the S corporation incurs no incremental tax on the liquidation gains, because such gains flow through to the shareholders subject only to the built-in gains tax of § 1374. Any corporate gain increases the shareholder's stock basis by a like amount and reduces any gain realized by the shareholder when he or she receives the liquidation proceeds. Thus, an S corporation usually avoids the double tax that is imposed on C corporations. However, when an S corporation liquidates, all of its special tax attributes disappear (e.g., AAA, AEP, PTI, C corporation NOLs, suspended losses).

## KEY TERMS

| | | |
|---|---|---|
| Accumulated adjustments account (AAA), 12–17 | Other adjustments account (OAA), 12–19 | S corporation, 12–2 |
| Accumulated earnings and profits (AEP), 12–16 | Passive investment income (PII), 12–12 | Small business corporation, 12–5 |
| Built-in gains tax, 12–28 | Previously taxed income (PTI), 12–18 | Subchapter S, 12–2 |
| Bypass election, 12–19 | | Voluntary revocation, 12–11 |

## PROBLEM MATERIALS

### Discussion Questions

1. What dollar sales and capitalization restrictions apply to an S corporation?

2. May an S corporation own a subsidiary and obtain a dividends received deduction for any dividends? May an S corporation own an S corporation subsidiary? May an S corporation be a member of a consolidated tax return?

---

[69]See *Clarence L. Hook*, 58 T.C. 267 (1972).

3. Bob Roman, the major owner of an S corporation, approaches you for some tax planning help. He would like to exchange some real estate in a like-kind transaction under § 1031 for some real estate that may have some environmental liabilities. Prepare a letter to Bob outlining your suggestion. Bob's address is 8411 Huron Boulevard, West Chester, PA 19382.

4. On March 2, 2003, the two 50% shareholders of a calendar year corporation decide to elect S status. One of the shareholders, Terry, had purchased her stock from a previous shareholder (a nonresident alien) on January 18, 2003. Identify any potential problems for Terry or the corporation.

5. Elvis Samford calls you and says that his two-person S corporation was involuntarily terminated in February 2002. He asks you if they can make a new election because of the law changes in 1997. Draft a memo for the file dated September 8, 2003, outlining what you told Elvis.

6. Can "too much" passive income affect an S election? How?

7. Using the categories in the following legend, classify each transaction as a plus (+) or minus (–) on Schedule M–2 of Form 1120S. An answer might look like one of these: "+AAA" or "–PTI."

| **Legend** | |
| --- | --- |
| PTI | = Shareholders' undistributed taxable income previously taxed |
| AAA | = Accumulated adjustments account |
| OAA | = Other adjustments account |
| NA | = No direct effect on Schedule M–2 |

   a. Receipt of tax-exempt interest income.
   b. Unreasonable compensation determined.
   c. Section 1245 recapture income.
   d. Distribution of nontaxable income (PTI) from 1981.
   e. Nontaxable life insurance proceeds.
   f. Expenses related to tax-exempt securities.
   g. Charitable contributions.
   h. Business gifts in excess of $25.
   i. Nondeductible fines and penalties.
   j. Selling expenses.

8. Collett's S corporation has a small amount of accumulated earnings and profits (AEP), requiring the use of the more complex distribution rules. His accountant tells him that this AEP forces the maintenance of the AAA figure each year. Identify relevant tax issues facing Collett.

9. Caleb Hudson owns 10% of an S corporation. He is confused with respect to his AAA and stock basis. Write a brief memo dated November 1, 2003, to Caleb identifying the key differences between AAA and his stock basis.

10. For each of the following independent statements, indicate whether the transaction will increase (+), decrease (–), or have no effect (*NE*) on the adjusted basis of a shareholder's stock in an S corporation.
   a. Expenses related to tax-exempt income.
   b. Long-term capital gain.
   c. Nonseparately computed loss.
   d. Section 1231 gain.
   e. Depletion *not* in excess of basis.
   f. Separately computed income.
   g. Nontaxable return-of-capital distribution by the corporation.
   h. Selling expenses.

      i. Business gifts in excess of $25.
      j. Section 1245 gain.
      k. Dividends received by the S corporation.
      l. LIFO recapture tax at S election.
      m. Recovery of bad debt.
      n. Short-term capital loss.
      o. Corporate dividends out of AAA.

**Issue ID**

11. A C corporation that owns a subsidiary converts to an S corporation, but does not liquidate the subsidiary or convert it to a qualified Subchapter S subsidiary (QSSS). Several years later the subsidiary is liquidated. Point out any tax problems.

**Decision Making**

12. One of your clients is considering electing S status. Texas, Inc., is a six-year-old company with two equal shareholders, both of whom paid $30,000 for their stock. Going into 2003, Texas has a $110,000 NOL carryforward from prior years. Estimated income is $40,000 for 2003 and $25,000 for each of the next three years. Should Texas make an S election for 2003?

## Problems

13. An S corporation's profit and loss statement for 2003 shows net profits of $90,000 (book income). The corporation has three equal shareholders. From supplemental data, you obtain the following information about items that are included in the $90,000.

| | |
|---|---|
| Selling expenses | $21,200 |
| Tax-exempt interest | 2,000 |
| Dividends received | 9,000 |
| § 1231 gain | 6,000 |
| § 1250 gain | 12,000 |
| Recovery of bad debts | 4,000 |
| Long-term capital loss | 6,000 |
| Salary to owners (each) | 10,000 |
| Cost of goods sold | 95,000 |

  a. Compute Subchapter S taxable income or loss for 2003.
  b. What would be the portion of taxable income or loss for Chang, one of the shareholders?

14. Saul, Inc., a calendar year S corporation, incurred the following items for 2003.

| | |
|---|---|
| Sales | $130,000 |
| § 1250 gain | 12,000 |
| Short-term capital gain | 30,000 |
| Cost of goods sold | 42,000 |
| Municipal bond interest income | 7,000 |
| Administrative expenses | 15,000 |
| Depreciation expense | 17,000 |
| Charitable contributions | 14,000 |

Calculate Saul's nonseparately computed income.

15. Zebra, Inc., a calendar year S corporation, incurred the following items for 2003.

| | |
|---|---|
| Sales | $100,000 |
| Cost of goods sold | 40,000 |
| Depreciation expense | 10,000 |

| | |
|---|---|
| Administrative expenses | $ 5,000 |
| § 1231 gain | 21,000 |
| § 1250 gain | 20,000 |
| Short-term capital loss from stock sale | 6,000 |
| Long-term capital loss from stock sale | 4,000 |
| Long-term capital gain from stock sale | 15,000 |
| Charitable contributions | 4,500 |

Sammy is a 40% shareholder throughout the year.
  a. Calculate Sammy's share of nonseparately computed income.
  b. Calculate Sammy's share of any net long-term capital gain.

16. Noon, Inc., a calendar year S corporation, is equally owned by Ralph and Thomas. Thomas dies on April 1 (not a leap year), and his estate selects a March 31 fiscal year. Noon has $400,000 of income for January 1 through March 31 and $600,000 for the remainder of the year.
  a. Determine how income is allocated to Ralph and Thomas under the pro rata approach.
  b. Determine how income is allocated to Ralph and Thomas under the per-books method.

17. During 2003, Joy, the sole shareholder of a calendar year S corporation, received a distribution of $16,000. On December 31, 2002, Joy's stock basis was $4,000. The corporation earned $11,000 ordinary income during the year. Calculate the amount and type of income Joy recognizes in 2003.

18. Goblins, Inc., a calendar year S corporation, has $90,000 of AEP. Tobias, the sole shareholder, has an adjusted basis of $80,000 in his stock with a zero balance in the AAA. Determine the tax aspects if a $90,000 salary is paid to Tobias.

19. Assume the same facts as in Problem 18, except that Tobias receives a dividend of $90,000.

20. During the year, a calendar year S corporation in Stillwater, Oklahoma, has a positive AMT adjustment of $66,000 for mining exploration costs, an excess depletion tax preference of $96,000, and a certified pollution control facility positive adjustment of $36,000. The firm's positive ACE adjustment is $102,000. If Pam Epstein is a one-third shareholder, what effect do these items have on her individual tax return?

21. Individuals Adam and Bonnie form an S corporation, with Adam contributing cash of $100,000 for a 50% interest and Bonnie contributing appreciated ordinary income property with an adjusted basis of $20,000 and a fair market value of $100,000.
  a. Determine Bonnie's initial basis in her stock, assuming that she receives a 50% interest.
  b. The S corporation sells the property for $120,000. Determine Adam's and Bonnie's stock basis after the sale.
  c. Determine Adam's and Bonnie's gain or loss if the company is liquidated.

22. In 2003, Ourso, Inc., an S corporation with one shareholder, has a loss of $55,000 and makes a distribution of $70,000 to the shareholder, Bip Wallace. Bip's stock basis at the beginning of the year is $100,000. Write a memo dated October 21, 2003, to your manager discussing any problem that may result and the possible solution.

23. Fabrizius, Inc., an S corporation in Saint Cloud, Minnesota, had a balance in AAA of $100,000 and AEP of $55,000 on December 31, 2003. During 2004, Fabrizius distributes $70,000 to its shareholders, while sustaining a loss of $60,000. Determine any balance in the AAA and the AEP account.

24. At the beginning of the year, Malcolm, a 50% shareholder of a calendar year S corporation, has a stock basis of $22,000. During the year, the corporation has taxable income of $32,000. The following data are obtained from supplemental sources.

*Handwritten (left margin):*

Stock basis 22000
+ ½ taxable in  16000
+ Dividend in.  6000
+ Tax exp.  9000
+ 1231 gain  3500
+ Charitable  (2500)
— Political Cont  (4000)
— STCL  (6000)
+ STCL...  8000
— Distribution  6000
Ending Basis  41000

Beg AAA  40000
+ Taxable in.  32000
+ Dividend.  12000
+ STCG  6000
+ & 1231 gain  7000
— Charitable  (5000)
— political.  (8000)
— STCL.  (12000)
  72000
— Distrib  6000
  66000

Only T-E income goes to
other adj

Basis  24000
30% of Tax at loss
  80000 × 30%.  (24000)
30% of Cap loss
  20000 × 30%  (6000)

Ord loss × basis
Total loss
  24000 × 24000 = (19200)
  30000

Cap 6000 × 24000 = (4800)
  30000 =

24000 - 19200 = 4800 Tax loss
  Ch loss

6000 - 4800 = 1200 Cap loss
  Ch

*Handwritten (top right):* Special ... use it as Invest income for deduction

*Printed (middle):*

| | | |
|---|---|---|
| Dividends received | ½ | $12,000 |
| Tax-exempt interest | ½ | 18,000 |
| Short-term capital gain | ½ | 6,000 |
| § 1245 gain | | 10,000 |
| § 1231 gain | | 7,000 |
| Charitable contributions | | 5,000 |
| Political contributions | | 8,000 |
| Short-term capital loss | | 12,000 |
| Dividends to Malcolm | | 6,000 |
| Selling expense | | 14,000 |
| Beginning AAA | | 40,000 |

a. Compute Malcolm's ending stock basis.
b. Compute ending AAA.  *This is for equity*

25. Money, Inc., a calendar year S corporation in Denton, Texas, has two unrelated shareholders, each owning 50% of the stock. Both shareholders have a $400,000 stock basis as of January 1, 2003. At the beginning of 2003, Money has AAA of $300,000 and AEP of $600,000. During 2003, Money has operating income of $100,000. At the end of the year, Money distributes securities worth $1 million, with an adjusted basis of $800,000. Determine the tax effects of these transactions.

26. Assume the same facts as in Problem 25, except that the two shareholders consent under § 1368(e)(3) (the AAA bypass election) to distribute AEP first.

27. Red Dragon, Inc., is an S corporation with a sizable amount of AEP from a C corporation year. The S corporation has $300,000 of investment income and $300,000 of investment expenses in 2003. The company makes cash distributions to enable its sole shareholder to pay her taxes. What are the tax aspects to consider?

**Issue ID**

28. On January 1, Bobby and Alicia own equally all of the stock of an electing S corporation called Prairie Dirt Delight. The company has a $60,000 loss for the year (not a leap year). On the 219th day of the year, Bobby sells his half of the stock to his son, Bubba. How much of the $60,000 loss, if any, is allocated to Bubba?

**Communications**

29. A calendar year S corporation has a taxable loss of $80,000 and a capital loss of $20,000. Ms. Muhammad owns 30% of the corporate stock and has a $24,000 basis in her stock. Determine the amounts of the taxable loss and capital loss, if any, that flow through to Ms. Muhammad. Prepare a tax memo for the files dated December 3, 2003.

30. Marjorie is a shareholder in a calendar year S corporation in Tazewell, Tennessee. At the beginning of the year, her stock basis is $10,000, her share of AAA is $2,000, and her share of corporate AEP is $5,000. She receives a $6,000 distribution, and her share of S items includes a $2,000 long-term capital gain and a $9,000 ordinary loss. Determine the effects of these events on AAA, stock basis, and AEP.

31. Crew Corporation elects S status effective for tax year 2003. As of January 1, 2003, Crew's assets were appraised as follows.

| | Adjusted Basis | Fair Market Value |
|---|---|---|
| Cash | $ 16,010 | $ 16,010 |
| Accounts receivable | –0– | 55,400 |
| Inventory (FIFO) | 70,000 | 90,000 |
| Investment in land | 110,000 | 195,000 |
| Building | 220,000 | 275,000 |
| Goodwill | –0– | 93,000 |

In each of the following situations, calculate any built-in gains tax, assuming that the highest corporate tax rate is 35%.

    a. During 2003, Crew collects $40,000 of the accounts receivable and sells 80% of the inventory for $99,000.

    b. In 2004, Crew sells the land held for investment for $203,000.

    c. In 2005, the building is sold for $270,000.

32. During 2003, BlyteCo, an S corporation in Flint, Michigan, recognizes a built-in gain of $80,000 and a built-in loss of $10,000. BlyteCo also holds an unexpired NOL from a C corporation year of $8,000. It generates $65,000 ordinary income. Calculate any built-in gains tax.

33. An S corporation with substantial AEP has operating revenues of $410,000, taxable interest income of $390,000, operating expenses of $260,000, and deductions attributable to the interest of $150,000. Calculate any § 1375 penalty tax payable.

34. At the end of 2003, Brew, an S corporation, has gross receipts of $190,000 and gross income of $170,000. Brew has AEP of $22,000 and taxable income of $30,000. It has passive investment income of $100,000, with $40,000 of expenses directly related to the production of passive investment income. Calculate Brew's excess net passive income and any § 1375 penalty tax.

35. Savoy, Inc., in Auburn, Alabama, is an accrual basis S corporation with three equal shareholders. The three cash basis shareholders have the following stock basis at the beginning of 2003: Andre, $18,000; Crum, $22,000; and Barbara, $28,000. Savoy has the following income and expense items during 2003.

| | |
|---|---|
| Net tax operating loss | $30,000 |
| Short-term capital gain | 37,500 |
| Long-term capital loss | 6,000 |
| Nondeductible fees and penalties | 3,000 |

The electing corporation distributes $5,000 cash to each of the shareholders during the tax year. Calculate the shareholders' stock bases at the end of 2003.

36. Yates Corporation in Cutoff, Louisiana, elects S status, effective for calendar year 2003. Yates' only asset has a basis of $50,200 and a fair market value of $110,400 as of January 1, 2003. The asset is sold at the end of 2003 for $130,800. What are the tax aspects of this transaction for Mark Farris, a 60% owner of the company?

**Issue ID**

37. Bonnie and Clyde each own one-third of a fast-food restaurant, and their 13-year-old daughter owns the other shares. Both parents work full-time in the restaurant, but the daughter works infrequently. Neither Bonnie nor Clyde receives a salary during the year, when the taxable income of the S corporation is $180,000. An IRS agent estimates that reasonable salaries for Bonnie, Clyde, and the daughter are $30,000, $35,000, and $10,000, respectively. What adjustments would you expect the IRS to impose upon these taxpayers?

**Communications**

38. Friedman, Inc., an S corporation, holds some highly appreciated land and inventory, and some marketable securities that have declined in value. It anticipates a sale of these assets and a complete liquidation of the company over the next two years. Arnold Schwartz, the CFO, calls you, asking how to treat these transactions. Prepare a tax memo dated June 18, 2003, indicating what you told Arnold over the phone.

39. Claude Bergeron sold 1,000 shares of Ditta, Inc., an S corporation located in Concord, North Carolina, for $8,000. He has a stock basis of $105,000 in the shares. Assuming that Claude is single and that he is the original owner of these § 1244 stock shares, calculate the appropriate tax treatment of any gain or loss. If he sold the stock for $201,000, could he obtain a 50% exclusion under § 1202 for any gain?

40. Opal, the owner of *all* of the shares of an S corporation in Richmond, Virginia, transfers all of the stock to Will at the middle of the tax year. There is a $200,000 NOL for the entire year, but $130,000 of the loss occurs during the first half of the year. With a short-year election, how much of the loss is allocated to Will?

---

**See Appendix F for Comprehensive Tax Return Problem—Form 1120S**

---

## Research Problems

*Note: Solutions to Research Problems can be prepared by using the **RIA Checkpoint® Student Edition** online research product, or the **CCH U.S. Master Tax Guide Plus™** online Federal tax research database, which is available to accompany this text. It is also possible to prepare solutions to the Research Problems by using tax research materials found in a standard tax library.*

**Research Problem 1.** Ewing Ballman owned a major league baseball team (the Rattlers), which was an S corporation. In 1993, Ballman sold 49% of his stock to Avon Fogel. Fogel also bought an option to purchase more of the stock. In 1997, Fogel purchased 2% more of the shares of the team, but later he encountered financial problems. In 2000, Ballman loaned $34 million to the team; then the Rattlers lent the money to Fogel, secured by his stock shares. Fogel's stock was auctioned off, but no acceptable bids were obtained. Fogel defaulted on the $34 million loan and signed a waiver allowing the Rattlers to take his stock and options. The Rattlers claimed that the collateral had no value and deducted the full amount of the loan. Ballman deducted the losses on his 2001 tax return. Do you agree with Ballman's action?

**Research Problem 2.** Paul and Jane Dingy own an S corporation that operates several restaurants in Santa Cruz, California. Paul and Jane provide various services for the S corporation. On their individual tax return, the couple reported negative net earnings for self-employment on the basis of a large loss from the S corporation. Can S corporation pass-through items be included in calculating the self-employment liability of the owners?

*Partial list of research aids:*
§ 1402(a).
§ 1366.

**Research Problem 3.** Peter Sleiman entered into a lease agreement with Blockbuster Video, Inc., to purchase land, build a video rental store, and lease the property to Blockbuster. Sleiman formed an S corporation and assigned his rights under the lease to the corporation, REE, Inc. REE then obtained bank loans of approximately $1 million, pledging the property that the S corporation had purchased as collateral under the contract. Sleiman personally guaranteed the corporation's loans, but the banks never asked him for repayment. Does Sleiman get a $1 million step-up in basis for the guaranteed loans?

*Partial list of research aids:*
*Selfe v. U.S.*, 86–1 USTC ¶9115, 75 AFTR2d 86–464, 778 F.2d 769 (CA–11, 1985).
*Plantation Patterns, Inc. v. Comm.*, 72–2 USTC ¶9494, 29 AFTR2d 72–1408, 462 F.2d 712 (CA–5, 1972).

**Internet Activity**

*Use the tax resources of the Internet to address the following questions. Do not restrict your search to the World Wide Web, but include a review of newsgroups and general reference materials, practitioner sites and resources, primary sources of the tax law, chat rooms and discussion groups, and other opportunities.*

**Research Problem 4.** Go to both the U.S. Tax Court and the U.S. Court of Appeals sites and find a recent decision involving an S corporation. Prepare a summary of each decision.

**Research Problem 5.** Use a spreadsheet program to graph the growth in the number of S corporation returns filed. Obtain data for these years: 1975, 1980, 1985, 1990, 1995, 2000, and 2005 (projected).

**Research Problem 6.**   Find a question about S corporation tax planning that has been posted to a newsgroup. Submit to the group your answer to the query. Make a copy of the question and answer.

# Advanced Tax Practice Considerations

PART

4

A specialist in taxation must cope with the procedural aspects of tax administration and practice. Furthermore, the specialist may be confronted with a variety of technical subjects. These include tax considerations in choosing a form for operating a business, the unique rules applicable to tax-exempt entities, and multistate dealings. The following chapters, therefore, reflect a cross section of the myriad problems often encountered in tax practice.

http://wft.swlearning.com

# Comparative Forms of Doing Business

## LEARNING OBJECTIVES

*After completing Chapter 13, you should be able to:*

**LO.1**
Identify the principal legal and tax forms for conducting a business.

**LO.2**
Appreciate the relative importance of nontax factors in making business decisions.

**LO.3**
Distinguish between the forms for conducting a business according to whether they are subject to single taxation or double taxation.

**LO.4**
Identify techniques for avoiding double taxation and for controlling the entity tax.

**LO.5**
Understand the applicability and the effect of the conduit and entity concepts on contributions to the entity, operations of the entity, entity distributions, passive activity loss and at-risk rules, and special allocations.

**LO.6**
Analyze the effect of the disposition of a business on the owners and the entity for each of the forms for conducting a business.

http://wft.swlearning.com

## O U T L I N E

**A** variety of factors, both tax and nontax, affect the choice of the form of business entity. The form that is appropriate at one point in the life of an entity and its owners may not be appropriate at a different time.

**EXAMPLE 1**

Eva is a tax practitioner in Kentwood, the Dairy Center of the South. Many of her clients are dairy farmers. She recently had tax planning discussions with two of her clients, Jesse, a Line Creek dairy farmer, and Larry, a Spring Creek dairy farmer.

Jesse recently purchased his dairy farm. He is 52 years old and just retired after 30 years of service as a chemical engineer at an oil refinery in Baton Rouge. Eva recommended that he incorporate his dairy farm and elect S corporation status for Federal income tax purposes.

Larry has owned his dairy farm since 1997. He inherited it from his father. At that time, Larry retired after 20 years of service in the U.S. Air Force. He has a master's degree in Agricultural Economics from LSU. His farm is incorporated, and shortly after the date of incorporation, Eva had advised him to elect S corporation status. She now advises him to revoke the S election. ∎

Example 1 raises a number of interesting questions. Does Eva advise all of her dairy farmer clients to initially elect S corporation status? Why has she advised Larry to revoke his S election? Will she advise Jesse to revoke his S election at some time in the future? Will she advise Larry to make another S election at some time in the future? Why did she not advise Larry to terminate his corporate status? Could Larry and Jesse have achieved the same tax consequences for their dairy farms if they had operated the farms as partnerships instead of incorporating? Does the way the farm is acquired (e.g., purchase versus inheritance) affect the choice of business entity for tax purposes?

**TAX IN THE NEWS**

## TAX REFORM: HOW EASY IS IT?

Athletes quite often distinguish between "talking the talk" and "walking the walk." At various times, many politicians have called for replacing the complex Internal Revenue Code with one that is fairer, more efficient, and easier to use. But "talking" tax reform is easier than "walking" it into practice.

In doing their "walking," would-be tax reformers need to take a number of factors into consideration:

- To be acceptable and worth the effort, any replacement for the current Code must foster a faster-growing economy and restore public confidence in the tax system.
- Although tax reform is on the President's to-do list, he appears to give it a lower priority than committed tax reformers do. When former Treasury Secretary Paul O'Neill talked about putting forth a proposal next year, for example, a White House spokesman stated that "there is no timetable" for such a proposal.
- Succeeding at tax reform requires both brainpower and political agility. Tax reform will succeed only with the cooperation of Congress.

Before beginning on any tax reform adventure, the reformers would have to address several questions including the following:

- Is the same amount of tax money to be collected?
- Is income or spending to be taxed?
- Are the rich to pay more or less than they do today?
- How are corporate profits to be taxed?
- What can be sacrificed to reduce the size of the tax code?
- What popular tax breaks are taxpayers willing to give up?

SOURCE: Adapted from David Wessel, "Talking Tax Reform Is Easier Than Doing It," *Wall Street Journal*, May 16, 2002, p. A2.

This chapter provides the basis for comparatively analyzing the tax consequences of business decisions for five types of tax entities (sole proprietorship, partnership, corporation, S corporation, and limited liability company). Understanding the comparative tax consequences for the different types of entities and being able to apply them effectively to specific fact patterns can lead to effective tax planning, which is exactly what Eva was doing with her two clients. As the following discussion illustrates, a variety of potential answers may exist for each of the questions raised by Eva's advice.

**LO.1**

Identify the principal legal and tax forms for conducting a business.

# Forms of Doing Business

## PRINCIPAL FORMS

The principal *legal* forms for conducting a business entity are a sole proprietorship, partnership, limited liability company, and corporation.[1] From a *Federal income tax*

---

[1]A business entity can also be conducted in the form of a trust or estate. These two forms are not discussed in this chapter. See the discussion of the income taxation of trusts and estates in Chapter 19.

perspective, these same forms are available with the corporate form being divided into two types (S corporation and C or regular corporation). In most instances, the legal form and the tax form are the same. In some cases, however, the IRS may attempt to tax a business entity as a form different from its legal form. This reclassification normally takes one of two possible approaches:

- The IRS ignores the corporate form and taxes the owners directly (the corporate entity lacks substance).
- The IRS ignores the partnership form and taxes the partnership as if it were a corporation.

The IRS may try to reclassify a corporation for several reasons. One reason is to prevent taxpayers from taking advantage of the disparity between the corporate and individual tax rates. The highest corporate statutory rate now is lower than the highest individual statutory rate (35 percent versus 38.6 percent). In addition, the specific corporate and individual rates applicable to a particular taxpayer may produce a greater spread than 3.6 percent (38.6% − 35%). For example, an individual may be in the 38.6 percent bracket, and the corporation may be in the 15 percent, 25 percent, or 34 percent bracket. Another reason for taxing the owners directly is to make them ineligible for favorable taxation of certain fringe benefits (see the subsequent discussion in Favorable Treatment of Certain Fringe Benefits).

In the case of a partnership, reclassification of a partnership as if it were a corporation can subject the business entity to double taxation. In addition, the resultant loss of conduit status prevents partnership losses from being passed through to the tax returns of the partners.

The taxpayer generally is bound for tax purposes by the legal form that is selected. A major statutory exception to this is the ability of an S corporation to receive tax treatment similar to that of a partnership.[2] In addition, taxpayers sometimes can control which set of tax rules will apply to their business operations. The "check-the-box" Regulations provide an elective procedure that enables certain entities to be classified as partnerships for Federal income tax purposes even though they have corporate characteristics.[3] These Regulations have greatly simplified the determination of entity classification.

An individual conducting a sole proprietorship files Schedule C of Form 1040. If more than one trade or business is conducted, a separate Schedule C is filed for each trade or business. A partnership files Form 1065. A corporation files Form 1120, and an S corporation files Form 1120S.

## LIMITED LIABILITY COMPANY

A **limited liability company (LLC)** is a hybrid business form that combines the corporate characteristic of limited liability for the owners with the tax characteristics of a partnership.[4] All of the states now permit this legal form for conducting a business.

The most frequently cited benefit of an LLC is the limited liability of the owners. Compared to the other forms of ownership, LLCs offer additional benefits, including the following:

---

[2]§§ 1361 and 1362.
[3]Reg. §§ 301.7701–1 through –4, and –6. Note that if the business has only one owner, the elective procedure enables the entity to be classified as a sole proprietorship.

[4]Depending on state law, an LLC may be organized as a limited liability corporation or a limited liability partnership.

*S corporation*

- Greater flexibility in terms of the number of owners, types of owners, special allocation opportunities, and capital structure.
- Inclusion of entity debt in the owner's basis for an ownership interest.
- More liberal requirements on deferral of recognition of gain on contributions of appreciated property by an owner (determined under § 721 rather than § 351).
- For securities law purposes, an ownership interest in an LLC is not necessarily a security.

*C corporation*

- Ability to pass tax attributes through to the owners.
- Absence of double taxation.

*Limited partnership*

- Right of all owners to participate in the management of the business.
- Ability of all owners to have limited liability (no need for a general partner).
- For securities law purposes, an ownership interest in an LLC is not necessarily a security (the interest of a limited partner normally is classified as a security).

*General partnership*

- Ability of owners to have limited liability.
- Greater continuity of life.
- Limitation on an owner's ability to withdraw from the business.

Among the disadvantages associated with LLCs are the following:

- Absence of a developed body of case law on LLCs.
- Frequent absence of continuity of life (e.g., limited to 30 years by many states) and free transferability of interests.
- Requirement in most states that there be at least two owners.
- Inability to qualify for § 1244 ordinary loss treatment.

---

**ETHICAL CONSIDERATIONS**   **Avoiding Double Taxation with an LLC**

Bryan operates his business as a C corporation. He is the only shareholder. The accumulated E & P is $800,000. Starting next year, he plans on distributing $200,000. In future years, he intends to distribute all of the annual earnings. Recognizing that the distribution would be taxed as dividend income, he has developed the following tax strategy:

- Sell the corporate assets to himself for the fair market value.
- Have the corporation invest the sales proceeds in a mutual fund.
- Contribute the assets to an LLC and operate his business in this legal form.

Evaluate Bryan's proposal to avoid double taxation.

---

As previously discussed, the tax form for a business entity may be different from the legal form. The mere passage of a state law providing for an entity called an LLC does not ensure that the entity will be taxed as a partnership.

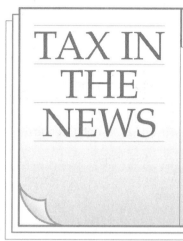

## PROFESSIONAL SERVICE FIRMS AND ORGANIZATIONAL FORM

Many professional service firms (e.g., accountants, architects, lawyers) have chosen to become limited liability partnerships (LLPs). In the accounting profession, this includes all of the Big 4 (i.e., Deloitte & Touche, Ernst & Young, KPMG, and PricewaterhouseCoopers) and most regional and local accounting firms.

An LLP helps to provide protection for the purely personal assets of the partners. Under the LLP organizational structure, the only partners whose personal assets are at risk to pay a judgment are those actually involved in the negligence or wrongdoing at issue. Note, however, that the entity is still responsible for the full judgment. Thus, the capital of the entity is still at risk.

---

**LO.2**

Appreciate the relative importance of nontax factors in making business decisions.

# Nontax Factors

Taxes are only one of many factors to consider in making any business decision. Above all, any business decision should make economic sense.

**EXAMPLE 2**

Albert is considering investing $10,000 in a limited partnership. He projects that he will be able to deduct the $10,000 within the next two years (his share of partnership losses). Since Albert's marginal tax rate is 35%, the deductions will produce a positive cash-flow effect of $3,500 ($10,000 × 35%). However, there is a substantial risk that he will not recover any of his original investment. If this occurs, his negative cash flow from the investment in the limited partnership is $6,500 ($10,000 − $3,500). Albert must decide if the investment makes economic sense. ■

## CAPITAL FORMATION

The ability of an entity to raise capital is a factor that must be considered. A sole proprietorship is subject to obvious limitations. Compared to the sole proprietorship, the partnership has a greater opportunity to raise funds through the pooling of owner resources.

**EXAMPLE 3**

Adam and Beth decide to form a partnership, AB. Adam contributes cash of $200,000, and Beth contributes land with an adjusted basis of $60,000 and a fair market value of $200,000. The partnership is going to construct an apartment building at a cost of $800,000. AB pledges the land and the building to secure a loan of $700,000. ■

The limited partnership offers even greater potential than the general partnership form because a limited partnership can secure funds from investors (limited partners).

**EXAMPLE 4**

Carol and Dave form a limited partnership, CD. Carol contributes cash of $200,000, and Dave contributes land with an adjusted basis of $60,000 and a fair market value of $200,000. The partnership is going to construct a shopping center at a cost of $5 million. Included in this cost is the purchase price of $800,000 for land adjacent to that contributed by Dave. Thirty limited partnership interests are sold for $100,000 each to raise $3 million. CD also pledges the shopping center (including the land) and obtains nonrecourse creditor financing of $2 million. ■

Both the § 465 at-risk provision and the § 469 passive activity loss provision have reduced the tax attractiveness of investments in real estate, particularly in the limited partnership form. In effect, the tax consequences have a critical effect on the economic consequences.[5]

Of the different forms of business entities, the corporate form offers the greatest ease and potential for obtaining owner financing because it can issue additional shares of stock. The ultimate examples of this form are the large public companies that are listed on the stock exchanges.

## LIMITED LIABILITY

A corporation offers its owners limited liability under state law. This absence of personal liability on the part of the owners is the most frequently cited advantage of the corporate form.

**EXAMPLE 5**

Ed, Fran, and Gabriella each invest $25,000 for all the shares of stock of Brown Corporation. Brown obtains creditor financing of $100,000. Brown is the defendant in a personal injury suit resulting from an accident involving one of its delivery trucks. The court awards a judgment of $2.5 million to the plaintiff. The award exceeds Brown's insurance coverage by $1.5 million. Even though the judgment will probably result in Brown's bankruptcy, the shareholders will have no personal liability for the unpaid corporate debts. ■

Limited liability is not available to all corporations. For many years, state laws did not permit professional individuals (e.g., accountants, attorneys, architects, and physicians) to incorporate. Even though professionals are now allowed to incorporate, the statutes do not provide limited liability for the performance of professional services.

Even if state law provides for limited liability, the shareholders of small corporations may have to forgo this benefit. Quite often, such a corporation may be unable to obtain external financing (e.g., a bank loan) unless the shareholders guarantee the loan.

The limited partnership form provides limited liability to the limited partners. Their liability is limited to the amount invested plus any additional amount that they agreed to invest. However, the general partner (or partners) has unlimited liability.

**EXAMPLE 6**

Hazel, the general partner, invests $250,000 in HIJ, a limited partnership. Iris and Jane, the limited partners, each invest $50,000. While the potential loss for Iris and Jane is limited to $50,000 each, Hazel's liability is unlimited. ■

Indirectly, it may be possible to provide the general partner with limited liability by having a corporation as the general partner (see Figure 13–1). When the entity is structured this way, the general partner (the corporation) has limited its liability under the corporate statutes. Therefore, individual A is protected from personal liability by being merely the shareholder of Corporation A. Prior to the issuance of the check-the-box Regulations, it was necessary to structure the entity very carefully in order to avoid the limited partnership being classified as an association

---

[5]See the related discussions in Chapters 10 and 11. For a comprehensive discussion of these provisions, see Chapter 11 in *West Federal Taxation: Individual Income Taxes.*

■ **FIGURE 13–1**
Limited Partnership with a
Corporate General Partner

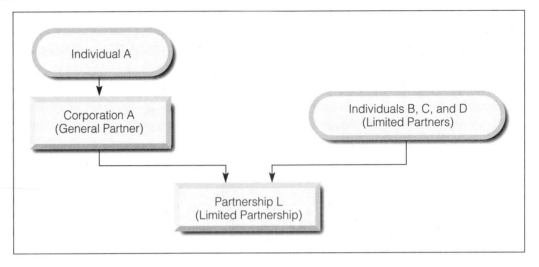

and taxed as a corporation. With the check-the-box Regulations, the limited partnership depicted in Figure 13–1 can be taxed as a partnership.[6]

## OTHER FACTORS

Other nontax factors may be significant in selecting an organization form including the following:

- Estimated life of the business.
- Number of owners and their roles in the management of the business.
- Freedom of choice in transferring ownership interests.
- Organizational formality including the related cost and extent of government regulation.

**LO.3**

Distinguish between the forms for conducting a business according to whether they are subject to single taxation or double taxation.

# Single versus Double Taxation

## OVERALL IMPACT ON ENTITY AND OWNERS

The sole proprietorship, partnership, and LLC are subject to *single* taxation. This result occurs because the owner(s) and the entity generally are not considered separate for tax purposes. Thus, the tax liability is levied at the owner level rather than at the entity level.

On the other hand, the corporate form is subject to *double* taxation. This is frequently cited as the major tax disadvantage of the corporate form. Under double taxation, the entity is taxed on the earnings of the corporation, and the owners are taxed on distributions to the extent they are made from corporate earnings.

---

[6]See the discussions of limited partnerships in Chapter 11. Also see
Rev.Proc. 89–12, 1989–1 C.B. 798 and Rev.Rul. 88–76, 1988–2 C.B. 360.

The S corporation provides a way to attempt to avoid double taxation and to subject the earnings to a lower tax rate (the actual individual tax rate may be lower than the actual corporate tax rate). However, the ownership structure of an S corporation is restricted in both the number and type of shareholders. In addition, statutory exceptions subject the entity to taxation in certain circumstances. To the extent these exceptions apply, double taxation may result. Finally, the distribution policy of the S corporation may encounter difficulties with the *wherewithal to pay* concept.

**EXAMPLE 7**

Hawk Corporation has been operating as an S corporation since it began its business two years ago. For both of the prior years, Hawk incurred a tax loss. Hawk has taxable income of $75,000 for 2003 and expects that its earnings will increase each year in the foreseeable future. Part of this earnings increase will result from Hawk's expansion into other communities in the state. Since most of this expansion will be financed internally, no dividend distributions will be made to the shareholders.

Assuming all of Hawk's shareholders are in the 30% tax bracket, their tax liability for 2003 will be $22,500 ($75,000 × 30%). Although the S corporation election will avoid double taxation, the shareholders will have a wherewithal to pay problem. In addition, the actual tax liability for 2003 would have been less if Hawk had not been an S corporation [(15% × $50,000) + (25% × $25,000) = $13,750]. ■

The data in Example 7 can be used to illustrate two additional tax concepts. First, the current wherewithal to pay problem could be resolved by terminating the S corporation election. The tax liability would then be imposed at the corporate level. Since the corporation does not intend to make any dividend distributions, double taxation at the present time would be avoided. Terminating the election will also reduce the overall shareholder-corporation tax liability by $8,750 ($22,500 − $13,750).[7] Second, tax decisions on the form of business organization should consider more than the current taxable year. If the S election is terminated, another election will not be available for five years. If the earnings exceed the expansion needs, Hawk could encounter an accumulated earnings tax problem (at a 38.6 percent tax rate) if it is a C corporation. Thus, the decision to revoke the election should have at least a five-year time frame. Perhaps a better solution would be to retain the election and distribute enough dividends to the S corporation shareholders to enable them to pay the shareholder tax liability.

Two other variables that relate to the adverse effect of double taxation are the timing and form of corporate distributions. If no distributions are made in the short run, then only single taxation occurs in the short run.[8] To the extent that double taxation does occur in the future, the cash-flow effect should be discounted to the present. Second, when the distribution is made, is it in the form of a dividend or a return of capital (a stock redemption or a complete liquidation)?[9]

**EXAMPLE 8**

Gray Corporation has taxable income of $100,000 for 2003. Gray's tax liability is $22,250. All of Gray's shareholders are in the 30% bracket. If dividends of $77,750 are distributed in 2003, the shareholders will have a tax liability of $23,325 ($77,750 × 30%). The combined corporation-shareholder tax liability is $45,575 ($22,250 + $23,325) for a combined effective tax rate of 45.6%. ■

---

[7]The absence of distributions to shareholders could create an accumulated earnings tax problem under § 531. However, as long as earnings are used to finance expansion, the "reasonable needs" provision will be satisfied, and the corporation will avoid any accumulated earnings tax.

[8]This assumes there is no accumulated earnings tax problem. See the subsequent discussion of distributions in Minimizing Double Taxation.

[9]See the coverage of dividends in Chapter 4 and the coverage of stock redemptions and complete liquidations in Chapter 5.

■ **FIGURE 13–2**
Bar Graph Illustration of
Dividend versus Stock
Redemption

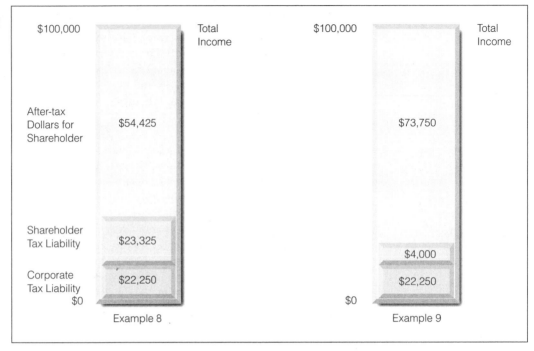

| | Example 8 | Example 9 |
|---|---|---|

**EXAMPLE 9**

Assume the same facts as in Example 8, except that the form of the distribution is a stock redemption and the basis for the redeemed shares is $57,750. The shareholders have a recognized gain of $20,000 and a tax liability of $4,000 ($20,000 × 20% beneficial capital gain rate). The combined corporation-shareholder tax liability is $26,250 ($22,250 + $4,000) for a combined effective tax rate of 26.25%. ■

The differences in the tax consequences in Examples 8 and 9 are even more obvious when illustrated in bar graph form (see Figure 13–2).

## ALTERNATIVE MINIMUM TAX

All of the forms of business are directly or indirectly subject to the alternative minimum tax (AMT).[10] For the sole proprietorship and the C corporation, the effect is direct (the AMT liability calculation is attached to the tax form that reports the entity's taxable income—Form 1040 or Form 1120). For the partnership, LLC, and S corporation, the effect is indirect (the tax preferences and adjustments are passed through from the entity to the owners, and the AMT liability calculation is not attached to the tax form that reports the entity's taxable income—Form 1065 or Form 1120S).

When compared with the other forms of business, the C corporation appears to have a slight advantage. The corporate AMT rate of 20 percent is less than the individual AMT rates of 26 and 28 percent. An even better perspective is provided by comparing the maximum AMT rate with the maximum regular rate for both the individual and the corporation. For the individual, the AMT rate is 72.5 percent (28%/38.6%) of the maximum regular rate. The AMT rate for the corporation is

---

[10]§ 55.

57 percent (20%/35%) of the maximum regular rate. Therefore, on the basis of comparative rates, the C corporation does have an advantage. In addition, as presented below, under certain circumstances, a C corporation is exempt from the AMT.

The apparent corporate AMT rate advantage may be more than offset by the AMT adjustment that applies only to the C corporation. This is the adjustment for adjusted current earnings (ACE). The amount of the adjustment is 75 percent of the excess of ACE over unadjusted alternative minimum taxable income (AMTI). If unadjusted AMTI exceeds ACE for the tax year, the adjustment is negative.[11]

If the ACE adjustment continually causes the C corporation to be subject to the AMT, the owners should consider electing S corporation status if the eligibility requirements can be satisfied. Since the S corporation does not have this item as an adjustment, it may be possible to reduce the tax liability.

The AMT does not apply to small corporations for tax years beginning after December 31, 1997. For this purpose, a C corporation is classified as a small corporation if it had average annual gross receipts of not more than $5 million for the three-year period beginning after December 1993. A corporation will continue to be classified as a small corporation if its average annual gross receipts for the three-year period preceding the current tax year and any intervening three-year periods do not exceed $7.5 million. Tax legislation enacted in 1998 provided an additional opportunity for a C corporation to be classified as a small corporation. A C corporation automatically is classified as a small corporation in its first year of existence.

If the AMT is going to apply for the taxable year, the entity should consider accelerating income into the current taxable year and delaying deductions so that the resultant increased taxable income will be taxed at the lower AMT rate. For the C corporation, the potential rate differential is 15 percent (20 percent AMT rate versus 35 percent regular rate). For the individual taxpayer (i.e., as a sole proprietor, as a partner, or as an S corporation shareholder), the potential tax rate differential is 10.6 percent (28 percent highest AMT rate versus 38.6 percent regular rate). A present value analysis should be used to assure that the acceleration of income and delaying of deductions do not increase actual tax liabilities.

## STATE TAXATION

In selecting a form for doing business, the determination of the tax consequences should not be limited to Federal income taxes. Consideration should also be given to state income taxes and, if applicable, local income taxes.[12]

The S corporation provides a good illustration of this point. Suppose that the forms of business being considered are a limited partnership or a corporation. An operating loss is projected for the next several years. The owners decide to operate the business in the corporate form. The principal nontax criterion for the decision is the limited liability attribute of the corporation. The owners consent to an S corporation election, so the corporate losses can be passed through to the shareholders to deduct on their individual tax returns. However, assume that state law does not permit the S corporation election on the state income tax return. Thus, the owners will not receive the tax benefits of the loss deductions that would have been available on their state income tax returns if they had chosen the limited partnership form. As a result of providing limited liability to the owner who would

---

[11]§§ 56(c)(1) and (f). See the discussion of the corporate AMT in Chapter 6.

[12]See the discussion of multistate corporate taxation in Chapter 15.

have been the general partner for the limited partnership, the loss deduction at the state level is forgone.

**LO.4**

Identify techniques for avoiding double taxation and for controlling the entity tax.

# Controlling the Entity Tax

Of the five forms of business entities, it appears at first glance that only the corporation needs to be concerned with controlling the entity tax. If control is defined in the narrow sense of double taxation, then this issue is restricted to the corporate form. However, from the broader perspective of controlling the tax liability related to the business entity's profits, whether that tax is imposed at the entity or the owner level, all five business forms are encompassed.

Techniques that can be used to minimize the current-period tax liability include the following:

1. Distribution policy.
2. Recognizing the interaction between the regular tax liability and the AMT liability.
3. Utilization of special allocations.
4. Favorable treatment of certain fringe benefits.
5. Minimizing double taxation.

Some of the techniques apply to all five forms of business entities. Others apply to only one of the five forms. Even those that apply to all do not minimize taxes equally for all forms. Since the first three techniques are discussed elsewhere in this chapter, only the last two are discussed here.

## FAVORABLE TREATMENT OF CERTAIN FRINGE BENEFITS

Ideally, a fringe benefit produces the following tax consequences:

* Deductible by the entity (employer) that provides the fringe benefit.
* Excludible from the gross income of the taxpayer (employee) who receives the fringe benefit.

From the perspective of the owner or owners of an entity, when the entity provides such favorably taxed fringe benefits to an owner, the benefits are paid for with *before-tax* dollars.

**EXAMPLE 10**

Rocky, the owner of Rocky's Ranch, a C corporation in the 34% tax bracket, is provided with meals and lodging that qualify for exclusion treatment under § 119. The annual cost of the meals and lodging to Rocky's Ranch is $10,000. Since the cost is deductible in calculating the taxable income of Rocky's Ranch on Form 1120, the after-tax cost to the corporation is only $6,600 [$10,000 − (34% × $10,000)]. Since the $10,000 is excluded in calculating Rocky's gross income, there is no additional tax cost at the owner level. If Rocky had paid for the meals and lodging himself, no deduction would have been permitted because these expenditures are nondeductible personal expenditures. Thus, from Rocky's perspective, the receipt of excludible meals and lodging of $10,000 is equivalent to receiving a distribution from the corporation of $15,385 [$10,000/(100% − 35%)], assuming he is in the 35% tax bracket. ■

Not all favorably taxed fringe benefits receive exclusion treatment. Although not as attractive to the recipient, another approach provided in the Code is deferral treatment (e.g., pension plans and profit sharing plans).

Example 10 illustrates how certain fringe benefits can be used to benefit the owner of an entity and at the same time have a beneficial impact on the combined tax liability of the entity and the owner. In recognition of this, Congress has enacted various nondiscrimination provisions that generally negate favorable tax treatment if the fringe benefit program is discriminatory. In addition, the Code includes several statutory provisions that make the favorably taxed fringe benefit treatment available only to *employees* (e.g., group term life insurance, meal and lodging exclusion).[13]

The IRS defines the term *employee* restrictively. For the owner of a business entity to be treated as an employee, the entity must be a corporation.[14] For this purpose, an S corporation is treated as a partnership, and a greater-than-2 percent shareholder is treated as a partner.[15]

Classification of an owner as a nonemployee produces two negative results. First, the deduction for the cost of the fringe benefit to the entity is disallowed at the entity level. Second, the owner whose fringe benefit has been paid for by the entity must include the cost of the fringe benefit in gross income.

## MINIMIZING DOUBLE TAXATION

Only the corporate form is potentially subject to double taxation. Several techniques are available for eliminating or at least reducing the second layer of taxation:

- Making distributions to the shareholders that are deductible to the corporation.
- Not making distributions to the shareholders.
- Making distributions that qualify for return of capital treatment at the shareholder level.
- Making the S corporation election.

**Making Deductible Distributions.** Use of the first technique requires careful advance planning. Typical distribution forms that will result in a deduction to the corporation are (1) salary payments to shareholder-employees, (2) lease rental payments to shareholder-lessors, and (3) interest payments to shareholder-creditors. Recognizing the tax benefit of this technique, the IRS scrutinizes these types of transactions carefully. All three types are evaluated in terms of *reasonableness*.[16] In addition, the interest payments may result in the IRS raising the **thin capitalization** issue and reclassifying some or all of the debt as equity.[17] IRS success with either approach raises the specter of double taxation.

**EXAMPLE 11**

Donna owns all the stock of Green and is also the chief executive officer. Green's taxable income before salary payments to Donna is as follows:

| | |
|---|---|
| 2001 | $ 80,000 |
| 2002 | 50,000 |
| 2003 | 250,000 |

---

[13]§§ 79 and 119.

[14]Reg. § 1.79–0(b). The IRS has not been completely successful with respect to this position.

[15]§ 1372(a).

[16]§ 162(a)(1). *Mayson Manufacturing Co. v. Comm.*, 49–2 USTC ¶9467, 38 AFTR 1028, 178 F.2d 115 (CA–6, 1949); *Harolds Club v. Comm.*, 65–1 USTC ¶9198, 15 AFTR2d 241, 340 F.2d 861 (CA–9, 1965).

[17]§ 385; Rev.Rul. 83–98, 1983–2 C.B. 40; *Bauer v. Comm.*, 84–2 USTC ¶9996, 55 AFTR2d 85–433, 748 F.2d 1365 (CA–9, 1984).

During the year, Donna receives a monthly salary of $3,000. In December of each year, she reviews the operations for the year and determines the year-end bonus to be paid to the key officers (only Donna for bonus purposes). Donna's yearly bonuses are as follows:

| | |
|---|---|
| 2001 | $ 44,000 |
| 2002 | 14,000 |
| 2003 | 214,000 |

The obvious purpose of Green's bonus program is to reduce the corporate taxable income to zero and thereby avoid double taxation. The examination of Green's tax return by the IRS would likely result in a deduction disallowance for unreasonable compensation. ■

**EXAMPLE 12**

Tom and Vicki each contribute $20,000 to TV Corporation for all the stock of TV. In addition, they each loan $80,000 to TV. The loan is documented by formal notes, the interest rate is 7%, and the maturity date is 10 years from the date of the loan.

The notes provide the opportunity for the corporation to make payments of $5,600 each year to both Tom and Vicki and for the payments not to be subject to double taxation. That is, the interest payments are includible in the gross income of Tom and Vicki, but are deductible by TV in calculating its taxable income. At the time of repayment in 10 years, neither Tom nor Vicki will have any gross income from the repayment since the $80,000 amount realized is equal to the basis for the note of $80,000 (return of capital concept).

If the IRS succeeded in reclassifying the notes as equity, Tom and Vicki's includible gross income of $5,600 each would remain the same (interest income would be reclassified as dividend income). However, because the dividend payments are not deductible by TV, the corporation's taxable income would increase by $11,200 ($5,600 × 2). To make matters worse, the repayment of the notes in 10 years would not qualify for return of capital treatment and would likely result in dividend income treatment for Tom and Vicki. ■

## Not Making Distributions.

Double taxation will not occur unless the corporation makes (actual or deemed) distributions to the shareholders. A closely held corporation that does not make distributions will eventually encounter an accumulated earnings tax problem unless the reasonable needs requirement is satisfied. When making distribution policy decisions each year, the board of directors should be apprised of any potential accumulated earnings tax problem and take the appropriate steps to eliminate it. The accumulated earnings tax rate of 38.6 percent in 2003 is the same as the maximum tax bracket for individual taxpayers.[18]

**EXAMPLE 13**

According to an internal calculation made by Dolphin Corporation, its accumulated taxable income is $400,000. The board of directors would prefer not to declare any dividends, but is considering a dividend declaration of $400,000 to avoid the accumulated earnings tax. All of the shareholders are in the 35% bracket.

If a dividend of $400,000 is declared, the tax cost to the shareholders is $140,000 ($400,000 × 35%). If a dividend is not declared and the IRS assesses the accumulated earnings tax, the tax cost to the corporation for the accumulated earnings tax would be $154,400 ($400,000 × 38.6%).

To make matters worse, Dolphin will have incurred the accumulated earnings tax cost without getting any funds out of the corporation to the shareholders. If the unwise decision were now made to distribute the remaining $245,600 ($400,000 – $154,400) to the shareholders, the additional tax cost at the shareholder level would be $85,960 ($245,600 × 35%). Therefore, the combined shareholder-corporation tax cost would be $240,360 ($154,400 + $85,960). This

---

[18]§ 531. See the discussion of the accumulated earnings tax in Chapter 6.

## REDUCING OR ELIMINATING DOUBLE TAXATION

A major disadvantage of the C corporation is the potential for double taxation. Among the proposals being considered by the Bush administration is a plan to reduce or eliminate double taxation of C corporation profits.

This objective could be achieved by either of the following:

* Permitting the corporation to take a partial or full deduction for dividends paid.
* Permitting the shareholders to take a partial or full exclusion for dividends received.

According to estimates, full elimination of double taxation would cost the Federal government $485 billion over a 10-year period. This heavy loss of revenue probably means that double taxation will not completely disappear. The Bush administration favors the second approach.

SOURCE: Adapted from Jackie Calmes and John D. McKinnon, "With Deficits Back in the Picture, Bush Agenda Faces Big Test," *Wall Street Journal*, November 11, 2002, p. A1.

is 172% ($240,360/$140,000) of the tax cost that would have resulted from an initial dividend distribution of $400,000. ■

Assuming that the accumulated earnings tax can be avoided (e.g., a growth company whose reasonable needs justify its no dividend policy), a policy of no distributions to shareholders can avoid the second layer of taxation forever. This will occur if the shares of stock are bequeathed to the taxpayer's beneficiaries. As a result of the step-up in basis rules for inherited property, the basis of the stock for the beneficiaries will be the fair market value at the date of the decedent's death rather than the decedent's basis.

**Return of Capital Distributions.**   The magnitude of the effect of double taxation can be reduced if the corporate distributions to the shareholders can qualify for return of capital rather than dividend treatment. For an ongoing corporation, the stock redemption provisions offer an opportunity to reduce the includible gross income at the shareholder level. The corporate liquidation provisions can be used if the business entity will cease to operate in corporate form. Under redemption and liquidation rules, the distribution may be treated as a sale of some or all of the shareholder's stock resulting in a tax-free recovery of basis and capital gain.

**EXAMPLE 14**

Copper Corporation makes a distribution of $400,000 to its shareholders. Mark and Kate, two of the shareholders, each receive $25,000. The form of the distribution permits the shareholders to surrender a certain number of shares of stock. The potential exists that the distribution can qualify for stock redemption treatment at the shareholder level. Mark satisfies the requirements for a substantially disproportionate distribution under § 302. Kate does not because she is in control of the corporation after the distribution (she owns 60% of the stock). Assuming Mark's basis for the shares redeemed is $20,000, he has a capital gain of $5,000 ($25,000 − $20,000). Kate has dividend income of $25,000. She must allocate her stock basis among her remaining shares. ■

**Electing S Corporation Status.**   Electing S corporation status generally eliminates double taxation by making the corporation a tax reporter rather than a

## C CORPORATIONS VERSUS S CORPORATIONS

Are there more C corporations than S corporations? If you answered yes, you are right, but not by much. According to IRS data, 47 percent of all corporations are S corporations. Most S corporations (81 percent) have only one or two shareholders.

When it comes to share of corporate net income, C corporations win hands down. C corporations report 82 percent of net income.

taxpayer. Therefore, the only tax levy is at the shareholder level. Factors to consider in making this election include the following:

- Are all the shareholders willing to consent to the election?
- Can the qualification requirements under § 1361 be satisfied at the time of the election?
- Since the qualification requirements become maintenance requirements, can these requirements continue to be satisfied?
- For what period will the conditions that make the election beneficial continue to prevail?
- Will the corporate distribution policy create wherewithal to pay problems at the shareholder level?

**EXAMPLE 15**

Emerald Corporation commenced business in January 2003. The two shareholders, Diego and Jaime, are both in the 30% tax bracket. The following operating results are projected for the first five years of operations:

| 2003 | ($   50,000) |
|------|------|
| 2004 | 400,000 |
| 2005 | 600,000 |
| 2006 | 800,000 |
| 2007 | 1,000,000 |

The corporation plans to expand rapidly. Therefore, no distributions will be made to shareholders. In addition, beginning in 2004, preferred stock will be offered to a substantial number of investors to help finance the expansion.

If the S corporation election is made for 2003, the $50,000 loss can be passed through to Diego's and Jaime's tax returns. Therefore, the cash-flow effect would be $15,000 ($50,000 × 30%). Assume that the election is either revoked or is involuntarily terminated at the beginning of 2004 as a result of the issuance of the preferred stock. The corporate tax liability for 2004 would be $136,000 ($400,000 × 34%).

If the S corporation election is not made for 2003, the $50,000 loss will be a net operating loss. The amount can be carried forward to reduce the 2004 corporate taxable income to $350,000 ($400,000 − $50,000). The resultant tax liability is $119,000 ($350,000 × 34%).

Should the S corporation election be made for just the one-year period? The answer is unclear. With an assumed after-tax rate of return to Diego and Jaime of 10%, the value of the $15,000 one year hence is $16,500 ($15,000 × 110%). Even considering the time value of money, the combined corporation-shareholder negative cash-flow effect of $119,500 ($136,000 − $16,500) in the case of an S election is about the same as the $119,000 corporate tax liability that would result for a regular corporation. The negative cash flow is even greater when related accounting and/or legal fees are considered. ■

LO.5

Understand the applicability and the effect of the conduit and entity concepts on contributions to the entity, operations of the entity, entity distributions, passive activity loss and at-risk rules, and special allocations.

# Conduit versus Entity Treatment

Under the **conduit concept,** the entity is viewed as merely an extension of the owners. Under the **entity concept,** the entity is regarded as being separate and distinct from its owners. The effects that these different approaches have in the following areas are examined for the partnership (and LLC), C corporation, and S corporation:

* Recognition at time of contribution to the entity.
* Basis of ownership interest.
* Results of operations.
* Recognition at time of distribution.
* Passive activity losses.
* At-risk rules.
* Special allocations.

The sole proprietorship is not analyzed separately because the owner and the business are in essence the same. In one circumstance, however, a tax difference does occur. Recognition does not occur when an owner contributes an asset to a sole proprietorship. Thus, the basis generally is a carryover basis. However, if the asset is a personal use asset, the sole proprietorship's basis is the *lower of* the adjusted basis or the fair market value at the date of contribution. Also note that if a personal use asset is contributed to a partnership or corporation, this *lower of* rule applies.

## EFFECT ON RECOGNITION AT TIME OF CONTRIBUTION TO THE ENTITY

Since the conduit approach applies for the partnership and LLC, § 721 provides for no recognition on the contribution of property to the partnership or LLC in exchange for an ownership interest. Section 721 protects both a contribution associated with the formation of the partnership or LLC and later contributions. The partnership or LLC has a carryover basis for the contributed property, and the owners have a carryover basis for their ownership interests.[19]

Since the entity approach applies for the corporation, the transfer of property to a corporation in exchange for its stock is a taxable event. However, if the § 351 control requirement is satisfied, no gain or loss is recognized. In this case, both the corporate property and the shareholders' stock will have a carryover basis.[20] This control requirement makes it more likely that shareholders who contribute appreciated property to the corporation *after* the formation of the corporation will recognize gain.

To the extent that the fair market value of property contributed to the entity at the time of formation is not equal to the property's adjusted basis, a special allocation may be desirable. With a special allocation, the owner contributing the property receives the tax benefit or detriment for any recognized gain or loss that subsequently results because of the initial difference between the adjusted basis and the fair market value. For the partnership or LLC, this special allocation treatment is mandatory. No such allocation is available for the C corporation form, since the gain or loss is recognized at the corporation level rather than at the shareholder

---

[19]See the pertinent discussion in Chapter 10.

[20]See the pertinent discussion in Chapter 3.

level. For the S corporation, no such allocation is available. The recognized gain or loss will be reported on the shareholders' tax returns based on their stock ownership.

**E X A M P L E   1 6**

Khalid contributes land with an adjusted basis of $10,000 and a fair market value of $50,000 for a 50% ownership interest. At the same time, Tracy contributes cash of $50,000 for the remaining 50% ownership interest. Because the entity is unable to obtain the desired zoning, it subsequently sells the land for $50,000.

If the entity is a C corporation, Khalid has a realized gain of $40,000 ($50,000 − $10,000) and a recognized gain of $0 resulting from the contribution. His basis for his stock is $10,000, and the corporation has a basis for the land of $10,000. The corporation has a realized and recognized gain of $40,000 ($50,000 − $10,000) when it sells the land. Thus, what should have been Khalid's recognized gain becomes the corporation's taxable gain. There is no way that the corporation can directly allocate the recognized gain to Khalid. The corporation could distribute the land to Khalid and let him sell the land, but the distribution may be taxable to Khalid as a dividend, and gain may be recognized at the corporate level on the distribution.

If the entity is a partnership or LLC, the tax consequences are the same as in the C corporation illustration except for the $40,000 recognized gain on the sale of the land. The partnership or LLC has a realized and recognized gain of $40,000 ($50,000 − $10,000). However, even though Khalid's share of profits and losses is only 50%, all of the $40,000 recognized gain is allocated to him. If the entity is an S corporation, the tax consequences are the same as in the C corporation illustration except that Khalid reports $20,000 of the recognized gain on his tax return and Tracy reports $20,000 also. ■

## EFFECT ON BASIS OF OWNERSHIP INTEREST

In a partnership or LLC, since the owner is the taxpayer, profits and losses of the entity affect the owner's basis in the entity interest. Likewise, the owner's basis is increased by the share of entity liability increases and is decreased by the share of entity liability decreases. This liability effect enables the owner to potentially benefit from the leverage concept. Accordingly, the owner's basis changes frequently.[21]

For the C corporation, the corporation is the taxpayer. Therefore, the shareholder's basis for the stock is not affected by corporate profits and losses or corporate liability increases or decreases.

The treatment of an S corporation shareholder falls in between that of the owner of a partnership or LLC interest and the C corporation shareholder. The S corporation shareholder's stock basis is increased by the share of profits and decreased by the share of losses, but it is not affected by corporate liability increases or decreases. Thus, unlike the owner of a partnership or LLC interest, the S corporation shareholder does not potentially benefit from the leverage concept.

**E X A M P L E   1 7**

Peggy contributes cash of $100,000 to an entity for a 30% ownership interest. The entity borrows $50,000 and repays $20,000 of this amount by the end of the taxable year. The profits for the year are $90,000.

If the entity is a partnership or LLC, Peggy's basis at the end of the period is $136,000 ($100,000 investment + $9,000 share of net liability increase + $27,000 share of profits). If Peggy is a C corporation shareholder instead, her stock basis is $100,000 ($100,000 original investment). If the corporation is an S corporation, Peggy's stock basis is $127,000 ($100,000 + $27,000). ■

---

[21]§§ 705 and 752.

## EFFECT ON RESULTS OF OPERATIONS

The entity concept is responsible for producing potential double taxation for the C corporation form (the corporation is taxed on its earnings, and the shareholders are taxed on the distribution of earnings). Thus, from the perspective of taxing the results of operations, the entity concept appears to be a disadvantage for the corporation. However, whether the entity concept actually produces disadvantageous results depends on the following:

- Whether the corporation generates positive taxable income.
- The tax rates that apply for the corporation and for the shareholders.
- The distribution policy of the corporation.

As discussed previously, techniques exist for getting cash out of the corporation to the shareholders without incurring double taxation (e.g., compensation payments to shareholder-employees, lease rental payments to shareholder-lessors, and interest payments to shareholder-creditors). Since these payments are deductible to the corporation, they reduce corporate taxable income. If the payments can be used to reduce corporate taxable income to zero, the corporation will have no tax liability.

The maximum individual tax bracket (38.6 percent) does exceed the maximum corporate tax bracket (35 percent). However, in a specific situation, the corporate tax rates that apply may be greater than or less than the applicable individual rates. This opportunity for the corporation to be subject to a lower tax rate is less likely to be available for personal service corporations. There, the only rate available is 35 percent.[22]

Double taxation can occur only if distributions are made to the shareholders. Thus, if no distributions (actual or constructive) are made and if the entity can avoid the accumulated earnings tax (e.g., based on the statutory credit or the reasonable needs adjustment) and the personal holding company tax (e.g., the corporation primarily generates active income), only one current level of taxation will occur. If distributions do occur in the future with respect to current earnings, the resultant tax liability should be discounted for the interim period. If the distribution can qualify for return of capital treatment (stock redemption or liquidation) rather than dividend treatment, the shareholder tax liability is decreased. Ideally, taxation of the earnings at the shareholder level can be avoided permanently if the stock passes through the decedent shareholder's estate.

Application of the entity concept does result in the earnings components losing their identity when they are passed through to shareholders in the form of dividends. This may produce a negative result for net long-term capital gains, as the potential beneficial capital gain treatment is lost. Since capital gains lose their identity when passed through in the form of dividends, they cannot be used to offset capital losses at the shareholder level. An even more negative result is produced when dividends are paid out of tax-exempt income. Tax-exempt income is excludible in calculating corporate taxable income, but is included in calculating current earnings and profits. Thus, what should not be subject to taxation (an exclusion) is taxed because of the entity concept.

The partnership, the LLC, and the S corporation use the conduit concept in reporting the results of operations. Any item that is subject to special treatment on the taxpayer-owners' tax return is reported separately to the owners. Other items are netted and reported as taxable income. Thus, taxable income merely represents those income and deduction items that are not subject to special treatment.[23]

---

[22]§ 11(b)(2).

[23]§§ 701, 702, 1363, and 1366.

Many of the problems that the entity concept may produce for the C corporation form are not present for the partnership, LLC, or S corporation. Included in this category are double taxation, problems with the reasonableness requirement, and loss of identity of the income or expense item at the owner level.

Only the partnership and LLC completely apply the conduit concept in reporting the results of operations. In several circumstances, the S corporation is subject to taxation at the corporate level, including the tax on built-in gains and the tax on certain passive investment income.[24] This limited application of the entity concept necessitates additional planning to attempt to avoid taxation at the corporate level.

## EFFECT ON RECOGNITION AT TIME OF DISTRIBUTION

The application of the conduit concept results in distributions not being taxed to the owners. The application of the entity concept produces the opposite result. Therefore, distributions can be made to partners, to LLC owners, or to S corporation shareholders tax-free, whereas the same distribution would produce dividend income treatment for C corporation shareholders.

In this regard, a distinction must be made between distributions of earnings and other distributions for the S corporation. The S corporation generally is treated as a conduit with respect to its operations. However, as previously discussed, in several cases the entity concept is applied, and the S corporation becomes a taxpayer rather than merely a tax reporter. In effect, the conduit concept applies to S corporation operations unless otherwise specified in Subchapter S of the Code. Since distributions of earnings are included in the operations category, they are subject to conduit treatment through the application of the accumulated adjustments account (AAA).[25] Distributions in excess of earnings qualify for return of capital treatment.

A combination entity/conduit concept applies to property distributions to S corporation shareholders. As discussed above, the conduit concept applies with respect to the shareholder. However, if the property distributed is appreciated property, § 311(b) provides that the realized gain is recognized at the corporate level (same treatment as a C corporation). This corporate-level gain recognition is an application of the entity concept. Then, however, the conduit concept is applied to the pass-through of the gain to the shareholders.

**EXAMPLE 18**

Tan, an S corporation, is equally owned by Leif and Matt. Tan distributes two parcels of land to Leif and Matt. Tan has a basis of $10,000 for each parcel. Each parcel has a fair market value of $15,000. The distribution results in a $10,000 ($30,000 − $20,000) recognized gain for Tan. Leif and Matt each report $5,000 of the gain on their individual income tax returns. ■

Stock redemptions and complete liquidations are not covered by the provisions of Subchapter S. Therefore, the tax consequences of an S corporation stock redemption are determined under the C corporation provisions in § 302, while those for a complete liquidation are determined under the C corporation provisions in §§ 331 and 336.

## EFFECT ON PASSIVE ACTIVITY LOSSES

The passive activity loss rules apply to the partnership, LLC, and S corporation, but apply to the C corporation only for personal service corporations and closely held corporations. A *closely held corporation* is defined as one that meets the stock

---

[24]§§ 1374 and 1375.    [25]§ 1368.

ownership requirement under the personal holding company provisions. That is, more than 50 percent of the value of the outstanding stock at any time during the last half of the taxable year is owned by or for not more than five individuals. The definition of a personal service corporation is modified slightly from the standard definition under § 269A. A corporation is classified as a § 469 *personal service corporation* only if the following requirements are satisfied:

- The principal activity of the corporation is the performance of personal services.
- The services are substantially performed by owner-employees.
- Owner-employees own more than 10 percent in value of the stock of the corporation.

The general passive activity loss rules apply to the personal service corporation. Therefore, passive activity losses cannot be offset against either active income or portfolio income. For the closely held corporation, the application of the passive activity rules is less harsh. Although passive activity losses cannot be offset against portfolio income, they can be offset against active income.

The statutory language of § 469(a)(2), which describes the taxpayers subject to the passive activity loss rules, does not mention the partnership, LLC, or S corporation. Instead, it mentions the individual taxpayer. Since the conduit concept applies, the passive activity results are separately stated at the partnership, LLC, or S corporation level and are passed through to the owners with the identity maintained.

## EFFECT OF AT-RISK RULES

The at-risk rules of § 465 apply to the partnership, LLC, and S corporation. Although the statutory language of § 465(a) mentions none of these, the conduit concept that applies to these entities results in the application of § 465. Section 465 also applies to closely held C corporations (defined the same as under the passive activity loss rules). However, exceptions are available for closely held corporations that are actively engaged in equipment leasing or are defined as qualified C corporations.

The application of the at-risk rules produces a harsher result for the partnership and the LLC than for the S corporation. This occurs because the partnership and the LLC, in the absence of § 465, would have a greater opportunity to use the leveraging concept.

**EXAMPLE 19**

Walt is the general partner, and Ira and Vera are the limited partners in the WIV limited partnership. Walt contributes land with an adjusted basis of $40,000 and a fair market value of $50,000 for his partnership interest, and Ira and Vera each contribute cash of $100,000 for their partnership interests. They agree to share profits and losses equally. To finance construction of an apartment building, the partnership obtains $600,000 of nonrecourse financing [not qualified nonrecourse financing under § 465(b)(6)] using the land and the building as the pledged assets. Each partner's basis for the partnership interest is as follows:

|  | Walt | Ira | Vera |
|---|---|---|---|
| Contribution | $ 40,000 | $100,000 | $100,000 |
| Share of nonrecourse debt | 200,000 | 200,000 | 200,000 |
| Basis | $240,000 | $300,000 | $300,000 |

Without the at-risk rules, Ira and Vera could pass through losses up to $300,000 each even though they invested only $100,000 and have no personal liability for the nonrecourse debt. However, the at-risk rules limit the loss pass-through to the at-risk basis, which is $100,000 for Ira and $100,000 for Vera. Note that the at-risk rules can also affect the general partner. Since Walt is not at risk for the nonrecourse debt, his at-risk basis is $40,000. If the mortgage were recourse debt, his at-risk basis would be $640,000 ($40,000 + $600,000). Thus, as a result of the at-risk rules, leveraging is available only for recourse debt for partners who have potential personal liability. ■

**EXAMPLE 20**

Assume the same facts as in Example 19, except that the entity is an S corporation and Walt receives 20% of the stock and Ira and Vera each receive 40%. The basis for their stock is as follows:

| | |
|---|---|
| Walt | $ 40,000 |
| Ira | 100,000 |
| Vera | 100,000 |

The nonrecourse debt does not affect the calculation of stock basis. The stock basis for each shareholder would remain the same even if the debt were recourse debt. Only direct loans by the shareholders increase the ceiling on loss pass-through (basis for stock plus basis for loans by shareholders). ■

## EFFECT OF SPECIAL ALLOCATIONS

An advantage of the conduit concept over the entity concept is the ability to make special allocations. Special allocations are not permitted for the C corporation form. Indirectly, however, the corporate form may be able to achieve results similar to those produced by special allocations through payments to owners (e.g., salary payments, lease rental payments, and interest payments) and through different classes of stock (e.g., preferred, common). However, even in these cases, the breadth of the treatment and the related flexibility are less than that achievable under the conduit concept.

Although the S corporation is a conduit, it is treated more like a C corporation than a partnership or an LLC with respect to special allocations. This treatment results from the application of the per-share and per-day rule in § 1377(a). Although the S corporation is limited to one class of stock, it can still use the payments to owners procedure. However, the IRS has the authority to reallocate income among members of a family if fair returns are not provided for services rendered or capital invested.[26]

**EXAMPLE 21**

The stock of an S corporation is owned by Debra (50%), Helen (25%), and Joyce (25%). Helen and Joyce are Debra's adult children. Debra is in the 35% bracket, and Helen and Joyce are in the 15% bracket. Only Debra is an employee of the corporation. She is paid an annual salary of $20,000, whereas employees with similar responsibilities in other corporations earn $100,000. The corporation generates earnings of approximately $200,000 each year.

It appears that the reason Debra is paid a low salary is to enable more of the earnings of the S corporation to be taxed to Helen and Joyce, who are in lower tax brackets. Thus, the IRS could use its statutory authority to allocate a larger salary to Debra. ■

The partnership and LLC have many opportunities to use special allocations, including the following:

- The ability to share profits and losses differently from the share in capital.
- The ability to share profits and losses differently.

[26]§ 1366(e).

- The special allocation required under § 704(c) for the difference between the adjusted basis and the fair market value of contributed property.
- The special allocation of any item permitted under § 704(a) if the substantial economic effect rule of § 704(b) is satisfied.
- The optional adjustment to basis permitted under § 754 and calculated under § 734 that results from distributions.
- The optional adjustment to basis permitted under § 754 and calculated under § 743 that results from an acquisition by purchase, taxable exchange, or inheritance.

---

**LO.6**

Analyze the effect of the disposition of a business on the owners and the entity for each of the forms for conducting a business.

# Disposition of a Business or an Ownership Interest

A key factor in evaluating the tax consequences of disposing of a business is whether the disposition is viewed as the sale of an ownership interest or as a sale of assets. Generally, the tax consequences are more favorable if the transaction is treated as a sale of the ownership interest.

## SOLE PROPRIETORSHIP

Regardless of the form of the transaction, the sale of a sole proprietorship is treated as the sale of individual assets. Thus, gains and losses must be calculated separately. Classification as capital gain or ordinary income depends on the nature and holding period of the individual assets. Ordinary income property such as inventory will result in ordinary gains and losses. Section 1231 property such as land, buildings, and machinery used in the business will produce § 1231 gains and losses (subject to depreciation recapture under §§ 1245 and 1250). Capital assets such as investment land and stocks qualify for capital gain or loss treatment.

If the amount realized exceeds the fair market value of the identifiable assets, the excess is attributed to goodwill, which produces capital gain for the seller. If instead the excess payment is attributed to a covenant not to compete, the related gain is classified as ordinary income rather than capital gain. Thus, the seller prefers the excess to be attributed to goodwill.

Unless the legal protection provided by a covenant not to compete is needed, the buyer is neutral as to whether the excess is attributed to goodwill or a covenant. Both goodwill and a covenant are § 197 intangibles and are amortized over a 15-year statutory period.

**EXAMPLE 22**

Seth, who is in the 35% tax bracket, sells his sole proprietorship to Wilma for $600,000. The identifiable assets are as follows:

|                          | Adjusted Basis | Fair Market Value |
| ------------------------ | -------------- | ----------------- |
| Inventory                | $ 20,000       | $ 25,000          |
| Accounts receivable      | 40,000         | 40,000            |
| Machinery and equipment* | 125,000        | 150,000           |
| Buildings**              | 175,000        | 250,000           |
| Land                     | 40,000         | 100,000           |
|                          | $400,000       | $565,000          |

*Potential § 1245 recapture of $50,000.
**Potential § 1250 recapture of $20,000.

The sale produces the following results for Seth:

|  | Gain (Loss) | Ordinary Income | § 1231 Gain | Capital Gain |
|---|---|---|---|---|
| Inventory | $ 5,000 | $ 5,000 | | |
| Accounts receivable | –0– | | | |
| Machinery and equipment | 25,000 | 25,000 | | |
| Buildings | 75,000 | 20,000 | $ 55,000 | |
| Land | 60,000 | | 60,000 | |
| Goodwill | 35,000 | | | $35,000 |
| | $200,000 | $50,000 | $115,000 | $35,000 |

If the sale is structured this way, Wilma can deduct the $35,000 paid for goodwill over a 15-year period. If instead Wilma paid the $35,000 to Seth for a covenant not to compete for a period of seven years, she still would amortize the $35,000 over a 15-year period. However, this would result in Seth's $35,000 capital gain being reclassified as ordinary income. If the covenant has no legal relevance to Wilma, in exchange for treating the payment as a goodwill payment, she should negotiate for a price reduction that reflects the benefit of the tax on capital gains to Seth. ■

## PARTNERSHIP AND LIMITED LIABILITY COMPANY

The sale of a partnership or LLC can be structured as the sale of assets or as the sale of an ownership interest. If the transaction takes the form of an asset sale, it is treated the same as for a sole proprietorship (described above). The sale of an ownership interest is treated as the sale of a capital asset under § 741 (subject to ordinary income potential under § 751 for unrealized receivables and substantially appreciated inventory). Thus, if capital gain treatment can produce beneficial results for the taxpayer (e.g., has capital losses to offset or has beneficially treated net capital gain), the sale of an ownership interest is preferable.

From the buyers' perspective, the form does not produce different tax consequences. If the transaction is an asset purchase, the basis for the assets is the amount paid for them. Assuming the buyers intend to continue to operate in the partnership or LLC form, the assets can be contributed to the entity under § 721. Therefore, the owners' basis for their entity interest is equal to the purchase price for the assets. Likewise, if ownership interests are purchased, the owners' basis is the purchase price, and the entity's basis for the assets is the purchase price since the original entity will have terminated.[27]

A problem may arise if an individual purchases an entity interest from another partner or limited liability entity owner and the amount paid exceeds the new owner's pro rata share of the entity's basis for the assets. If the new owner does not acquire at least a 50 percent capital and profits interest, the old entity may not terminate.[28]

**EXAMPLE 23**

Paul purchases Sandra's partnership interest for $100,000. He acquires both a 20% capital interest and a 20% interest in profits and losses. At the purchase date, the assets of the partnership are as follows:

---

[27]§ 708(b)(1)(B).

[28]§§ 708(b)(1)(A) and (B).

|  | Adjusted Basis | Fair Market Value |
|---|---|---|
| Cash | $ 10,000 | $ 10,000 |
| Inventory | 30,000 | 35,000 |
| Accounts receivable | 15,000 | 15,000 |
| Machinery and equipment | 70,000 | 90,000 |
| Buildings | 100,000 | 150,000 |
| Land | 175,000 | 200,000 |
|  | $400,000 | $500,000 |

In effect, Paul paid $100,000 for his 20% share of partnership assets ($500,000 × 20%). His basis for his partnership interest reflects the purchase price of $100,000. However, Paul's proportionate share of the partnership assets is based on the partnership's adjusted basis for the assets of $400,000 (i.e., $400,000 × 20% = $80,000). Since Paul's acquisition of his ownership interest from Sandra did not result in a termination of the partnership, the partnership's adjusted basis for the assets does not change. Therefore, if the partnership were to liquidate all of its assets immediately for $500,000, Paul's share of the recognized gain of $100,000 ($500,000 − $400,000) would be $20,000 ($100,000 × 20%). This result occurs even though Paul paid fair market value for his partnership interest.

The Code does provide an opportunity to rectify this inequity to Paul. If the partnership elects the optional adjustment to basis under § 754, the operational provisions of § 743 will result in Paul having a special additional basis for each of the appreciated partnership assets. The amount is the excess of the amount Paul effectively paid for each of the assets over his pro rata share of the partnership's basis for the assets.

|  | Amount Paid (20% Share) | Pro Rata Share of Adjusted Basis | Special Basis Adjustment |
|---|---|---|---|
| Cash | $ 2,000 | $ 2,000 | $ –0– |
| Inventory | 7,000 | 6,000 | 1,000 |
| Accounts receivable | 3,000 | 3,000 | –0– |
| Machinery and equipment | 18,000 | 14,000 | 4,000 |
| Buildings | 30,000 | 20,000 | 10,000 |
| Land | 40,000 | 35,000 | 5,000 |
|  | $100,000 | $80,000 | $20,000 |

Therefore, if the partnership sells the inventory, Paul's share of the ordinary income is $1,000 ($5,000 × 20%). He then reduces this amount by his special additional basis of $1,000. Thus, the net effect, as it equitably should be, is $0 ($1,000 − $1,000). ■

As Example 23 illustrates, the optional adjustment to basis election under § 754 provides a way to avoid the aforementioned problem. However, four additional factors need to be considered. First, the election must be made by the partnership (or LLC), not just by the acquiring partner. Therefore, the acquiring partner should obtain a written agreement from the other partners indicating they will consent to the § 754 election. Second, the election is a continuing election. Thus, while the election benefits an acquiring partner if the partnership assets are appreciated at the date of acquisition, it produces detrimental consequences (i.e., a negative special basis adjustment) if the adjusted basis exceeds the fair market value of the assets at the acquisition date. Third, the election not only activates the operational provisions of § 743, it also activates the operational provisions of § 734 with respect to partnership distributions. Fourth, if the members of the partnership change frequently, record keeping can become complex.

---

| **ETHICAL CONSIDERATIONS** | **Modifying the Legal Form of a Sales Transaction and the Allocation of the Sales Price** |

Ted has an ownership interest in two businesses. He owns a radio station as a sole proprietorship and has a 75 percent interest in a general partnership that owns a TV station. The remaining 25 percent is owned by his elderly uncle, Frank. The fair market values of the radio station and the TV station substantially exceed the owners' bases for their ownership interests.

Aqua, Inc., has made an offer to purchase the ownership interests in the radio station and the TV station, with 40 percent of the purchase price allocated to the radio station and 60 percent to the TV station. The offer is valid only if both entities are sold to Aqua. Ted feels that it is preferable taxwise to sell the assets of the entities, rather than the ownership interests. For a 2 percent discount, he is able to structure the transaction as an asset sale rather than a sale of ownership interests. In addition, he has the purchase price reallocated 60 percent to the radio station and 40 percent to the TV station. This allocation will provide him with a greater cash-flow benefit. Ted informs Uncle Frank only about the final offer as restructured, not the initial offer.

Evaluate the restructuring of the sales transaction from a business and an ethical perspective.

---

## C CORPORATION

The sale of the business held by a C corporation can be structured as either an asset sale or a stock sale. The stock sale has the dual advantage to the seller of being less complex both as a legal transaction and as a tax transaction. It also has the advantage of providing a way to avoid double taxation. Finally, the gain or loss on the sale of the stock is a capital gain or loss to the shareholder.

*EXAMPLE 24*

Jane and Zina each own 50% of the stock of Purple Corporation. They have owned the business for 10 years. Jane's basis for her stock is $40,000, and Zina's basis for her stock is $60,000. They agree to sell the stock to Rex for $300,000. Jane has a long-term capital gain of $110,000 ($150,000 – $40,000), and Zina has a long-term capital gain of $90,000 ($150,000 – $60,000). Rex has a basis for his stock of $300,000. Purple's basis for its assets does not change as a result of the stock sale. ■

Structuring the sale of the business as a stock sale may produce detrimental tax results for the purchaser. As Example 24 illustrates, the basis of the corporation's assets is not affected by the stock sale. If the fair market value of the stock exceeds the corporation's adjusted basis for its assets, the purchaser is denied the opportunity to step up the basis of the assets to reflect the amount in effect paid for them through the stock acquisition. Note that this is similar to the problem at the partnership (or LLC) level if the § 754 election is not made.

For an asset sale, the seller of the business can be either the corporation or the shareholders. If the seller is the corporation, the corporation sells the business (the assets), pays any debts not transferred, and makes a liquidating distribution to the shareholders. If the sellers are the shareholders, the corporation pays any debts that will not be transferred and makes a liquidating distribution to the shareholders; then the shareholders sell the business.

Regardless of the approach used for an asset sale, double taxation will occur. The corporation is taxed on the actual sale of the assets and is taxed as if it had sold the assets when it makes the liquidating distribution of the assets to the shareholders who then sell the assets. The shareholders are taxed when they receive cash or assets distributed in-kind by the corporation.

The asset sale resolves the purchaser's problem of not being able to step up the basis of the assets to their fair market value. The basis for each asset is the amount paid for it. In order to operate in corporate form (assuming the purchaser is not a corporation), the purchaser needs to transfer the property to a corporation in a § 351 transaction.

From the perspective of the seller, the ideal form of the transaction is a stock sale. Conversely, from the purchaser's perspective, the ideal form is an asset purchase. Thus, a conflict exists between the buyer's and the seller's objectives regarding the form of the transaction. Therefore, the bargaining ability of the seller and the purchaser to structure the sale as a stock sale or an asset sale, respectively, has become more critical.

Rather than selling the entire business, an owner may sell his or her ownership interest. Since the form of the transaction is a stock sale, the results for the selling shareholder will be the same as if all the shareholders had sold their stock (i.e., capital gain or capital loss to the shareholder).

## S CORPORATION

Since the S corporation is a corporation, it is subject to the provisions for a C corporation discussed previously. Either an asset sale at the corporate level or a liquidating distribution of assets produces recognition at the corporate level. However, under the conduit concept applicable to the S corporation, the recognized amount is taxed at the shareholder level. Therefore, double taxation is avoided directly (only the shareholder is involved) for a stock sale and indirectly (the conduit concept ignores the involvement of the corporation) for an asset sale.

See Concept Summary 13–1 for a summary of the tax consequences of the disposition of a business.

# Overall Comparison of Forms of Doing Business

See Concept Summary 13–2 for a detailed comparison of the tax consequences of the following forms of doing business: sole proprietorship, partnership, limited liability company, S corporation, and C corporation.

**Tax Planning Considerations**  The chapter began with an example that illustrated the relationship between tax planning and the choice of business form; it also raised a variety of questions about the advice given by the tax practitioner. By this time, the student should be able to develop various scenarios supporting the tax advice given. The actual fact situations that produced the tax adviser's recommendations were as follows:

- Jesse's experience in the dairy industry consists of raising a few heifers during the last five years he was employed. Eva anticipates that Jesse will have tax losses for the indeterminate future. In choosing between the partnership and the S corporation forms, Jesse indicated that he and his wife must have limited liability associated with the dairy farm.

## Tax Treatment of Disposition of a Business

| Form of Entity | Form of Transaction | Tax Consequences | |
|---|---|---|---|
| | | Seller | Buyer |
| Sole proprietorship | Sale of individual assets. | Gain or loss is calculated separately for the individual assets. Classification as capital or ordinary depends on the nature and holding period of the individual assets. If amount realized exceeds the fair market value of the identifiable assets, the excess is allocated to goodwill (except to the extent identified with a covenant not to compete), which is a capital asset. | Basis for individual assets is the allocated cost. Prefers that any excess of purchase price over the fair market value of identifiable assets be identified with a covenant not to compete if the covenant has legal utility. Otherwise, the buyer is neutral since both goodwill and covenants are amortized over a 15-year statutory period. |
| | Sale of the business. | Treated as if a sale of the individual assets (as above). | Treated as if a purchase of the individual assets (as above). |
| Partnership and limited liability company | Sale of individual assets. | Treatment is the same as for the sole proprietorship. | Treatment is the same as for the sole proprietorship. If the intent is to operate in partnership or LLC form, the assets can be contributed to a partnership or LLC under § 721. |
| | Sale of ownership interest. | Entity interest is treated as the sale of a capital asset under § 741 (subject to ordinary income potential under § 751 for unrealized receivables and substantially appreciated inventory). | Basis for new owner's ownership interest is the cost. The new entity's basis for the assets is also the pertinent cost (i.e., contributed to the entity under § 721), since the original entity will have terminated. |
| C corporation | Sale of corporate assets by corporation (i.e., corporation sells assets, pays debts, and makes liquidating distribution to the shareholders). | Double taxation occurs. Corporation is taxed on the sale of the assets with the gain or loss determination and the classification as capital or ordinary treated the same as for the sole proprietorship. Shareholders calculate gain or loss as the difference between the stock basis and the amount received from the corporation in the liquidating distribution. Capital gain or loss usually results, since stock typically is a capital asset. | Basis for individual assets is the allocated cost. If the intent is to operate in corporate form, the assets can be contributed to a corporation under § 351. |
| | Sale of corporate assets by the shareholders (i.e., corporation pays debts and makes liquidating distribution to the shareholders). | Double taxation occurs. At the time of the liquidating distribution to the shareholders, the corporation is taxed as if it had sold the assets. Shareholders calculate gain or loss as the difference between the stock basis and the fair market value of the assets received from the corporation in the liquidating distribution. Capital gain or loss usually results, since stock typically is a capital asset. | Same as above. |

| Form of Entity | Form of Transaction | Tax Consequences | |
|---|---|---|---|
| | | Seller | Buyer |
| | Sale of corporate stock. | Enables double taxation to be avoided. Since the corporation is not a party to the transaction, there are no tax consequences at the corporate level. Shareholders calculate gain or loss as the difference between the stock basis and the amount received for the stock. Capital gain or loss usually results, since stock typically is a capital asset. | Basis for the stock is its cost. The basis for the corporate assets is not affected by the stock purchase. |
| S corporation | Sale of corporate assets by corporation. | Recognition occurs at the corporate level on the sale of the assets with the gain or loss determination and the classification as capital or ordinary treated the same as for the sole proprietorship. Conduit concept applicable to the S corporation results in the recognized amount being taxed at the shareholder level. Double taxation associated with the asset sale is avoided, because the shareholder's stock basis is increased by the amount of gain recognition and decreased by the amount of loss recognition. Shareholders calculate gain or loss as the difference between the stock basis and the amount received from the corporation in the liquidating distribution. Capital gain or loss usually results, since stock typically is a capital asset. | Basis for individual assets is the allocated cost. If the intent is to operate in corporate form (i.e., as an S corporation), the assets can be contributed to a corporation under § 351. |
| | Sale of corporate assets by the shareholders. | At the time of the liquidating distribution to the shareholders, recognition occurs at the corporation level as if the corporation had sold the assets. The resultant tax consequences for the shareholders and the corporation are the same as for the sale of corporate assets by the S corporation. | Same as above. |
| | Sale of corporate stock. | Same as the treatment for the sale of stock of a C corporation. | Same as the treatment for the purchase of stock of a C corporation. |

## CONCEPT SUMMARY 13–2

### Tax Attributes of Different Forms of Business (Assume Partners and Shareholders Are All Individuals)

| | Sole Proprietorship | Partnership/Limited Liability Company* | S Corporation** | Regular (C) Corporation*** |
|---|---|---|---|---|
| Restrictions on type or number of owners | One owner. The owner must be an individual. | Must have at least 2 owners. | Only individuals, estates, and certain trusts can be owners. Maximum number of shareholders limited to 75. | None, except some states require a minimum of 2 shareholders. |
| Incidence of tax | Sole proprietorship's income and deductions are reported on Schedule C of the individual's Form 1040. A separate Schedule C is prepared for each business. | Entity not subject to tax. Owners in their separate capacity subject to tax on their distributive share of income. Entity files Form 1065. | Except for certain built-in gains and passive investment income when earnings and profits are present from C corporation tax years, entity not subject to Federal income tax. S corporation files Form 1120S. Shareholders are subject to tax on income attributable to their stock ownership. | Income subject to double taxation. Entity subject to tax, and shareholder subject to tax on any corporate dividends received. Corporation files Form 1120. |
| Highest tax rate | 38.6% at individual level. | 38.6% at owner level. | 38.6% at shareholder level. | 35% at corporate level plus 38.6% on any corporate dividends at shareholder level. |
| Choice of tax year | Same tax year as owner. | Selection generally restricted to coincide with tax year of majority owners or principal owners, or to tax year determined under the least aggregate deferral method. | Restricted to a calendar year unless IRS approves a different year for business purposes or other exceptions apply. | Unrestricted selection allowed at time of filing first tax return. |
| Timing of taxation | Based on owner's tax year. | Owners report their share of income in their tax year with or within which the entity's tax year ends. Owners in their separate capacities are subject to payment of estimated taxes. | Shareholders report their shares of income in their tax year with or within which the corporation's tax year ends. Generally, the corporation uses a calendar year, but see "Choice of tax year" above. Shareholders may be subject to payment of estimated taxes. Corporation may be subject to payment of estimated taxes for the taxes imposed at the corporate level. | Corporation subject to tax at close of its tax year. May be subject to payment of estimated taxes. Dividends will be subject to tax at the shareholder level in the tax year received. |

| | Sole Proprietorship | Partnership/Limited Liability Company* | S Corporation** | Regular (C) Corporation*** |
|---|---|---|---|---|
| Basis for allocating income to owners | Not applicable (only one owner). | Profit and loss sharing agreement. Cash basis items of cash basis entities are allocated on a daily basis. Other entity items are allocated after considering varying interests of owners. | Pro rata share based on stock ownership. Shareholder's pro rata share is determined on a daily basis, according to the number of shares of stock held on each day of the corporation's tax year. | Not applicable. |
| Contribution of property to the entity | Not a taxable transaction. | Generally not a taxable transaction. | Is a taxable transaction unless the § 351 requirements are satisfied. | Is a taxable transaction unless the § 351 requirements are satisfied. |
| Character of income taxed to owners | Retains source characteristics. | Conduit—retains source characteristics. | Conduit—retains source characteristics. | All source characteristics are lost when income is distributed to owners. |
| Basis for allocating a net operating loss to owners | Not applicable (only one owner). | Profit and loss sharing agreement. Cash basis items of cash basis entities are allocated on a daily basis. Other entity items are allocated after considering varying interests of owners. | Prorated among shareholders on a daily basis. | Not applicable. |
| Limitation on losses deductible by owners | Investment plus liabilities. | Owner's investment plus share of liabilities. | Shareholder's investment plus loans made by shareholder to corporation. | Not applicable. |
| Subject to at-risk rules | Yes, at the owner level. Indefinite carryover of excess loss. | Yes, at the owner level. Indefinite carryover of excess loss. | Yes, at the shareholder level. Indefinite carryover of excess loss. | Yes, for closely held corporations. Indefinite carryover of excess loss. |
| Subject to passive activity loss rules | Yes, at the owner level. Indefinite carryover of excess loss. | Yes, at the owner level. Indefinite carryover of excess loss. | Yes, at the shareholder level. Indefinite carryover of excess loss. | Yes, for closely held corporations and personal service corporations. Indefinite carryover of excess loss. |
| Tax consequences of earnings retained by entity | Taxed to owner when earned and increases his or her investment in the sole proprietorship. | Taxed to owners when earned and increases their respective interests in the entity. | Taxed to shareholders when earned and increases their respective bases in stock. | Taxed to corporation as earned and may be subject to penalty tax if accumulated unreasonably. |
| Nonliquidating distributions to owners | Not taxable. | Not taxable unless money received exceeds recipient owner's basis in entity interest. Existence of § 751 assets may cause recognition of ordinary income. | Generally not taxable unless the distribution exceeds the shareholder's AAA or stock basis. Existence of accumulated earnings and profits could cause some distributions to be dividends. | Taxable in year of receipt to extent of earnings and profits or if exceeds basis in stock. |

| | Sole Proprietorship | Partnership/Limited Liability Company* | S Corporation** | Regular (C) Corporation*** |
|---|---|---|---|---|
| Capital gains | Taxed at owner level with opportunity to use alternative tax rate. | Conduit—owners must account for their respective shares. | Conduit, with certain exceptions (a possible penalty tax)—shareholders must account for their respective shares. | Taxed at corporate level with a maximum 35% rate. No other benefits. |
| Capital losses | Only $3,000 of capital losses can be offset each tax year against ordinary income. Indefinite carryover. | Conduit—owners must account for their respective shares. | Conduit—shareholders must account for their respective shares. | Carried back three years and carried forward five years. Deductible only to the extent of capital gains. |
| § 1231 gains and losses | Taxable or deductible at owner level. Five-year lookback rule for § 1231 losses. | Conduit—owners must account for their respective shares. | Conduit—shareholders must account for their respective shares. | Taxable or deductible at corporate level only. Five-year lookback rule for § 1231 losses. |
| Foreign tax credits | Available at owner level. | Conduit—passed through to owners. | Generally conduit—passed through to shareholders. | Available at corporate level only. |
| § 1244 treatment of loss on sale of interest | Not applicable. | Not applicable. | Available. | Available. |
| Basis treatment of entity liabilities | Includible in interest basis. | Includible in interest basis. | Not includible in stock basis. | Not includible in stock basis. |
| Built-in gains | Not applicable. | Not applicable. | Possible corporate tax. | Not applicable. |
| Special allocations to owners | Not applicable (only one owner). | Available if supported by substantial economic effect. | Not available. | Not applicable. |
| Availability of fringe benefits to owners | None. | None. | None unless a 2%-or-less shareholder. | Available within antidiscrimination rules. |
| Effect of liquidation/ redemption/ reorganization on basis of entity assets | Not applicable. | Usually carried over from entity to owner unless a § 754 election is made, excessive cash is distributed, or more than 50% of the capital interests are transferred within 12 months. | Taxable step-up to fair market value. | Taxable step-up to fair market value. |
| Sale of ownership interest | Treated as the sale of individual assets. Classification of recognized gain or loss depends on the nature of the individual assets. | Treated as the sale of an entity interest. Recognized gain or loss is classified as capital under § 741, subject to ordinary income treatment under § 751. | Treated as the sale of corporate stock. Recognized gain is classified as capital gain. Recognized loss is classified as capital loss, subject to ordinary loss treatment under § 1244. | Treated as the sale of corporate stock. Recognized gain is classified as capital gain. Recognized loss is classified as capital loss, subject to ordinary loss treatment under § 1244. |

| | Sole Proprietorship | Partnership/Limited Liability Company* | S Corporation** | Regular (C) Corporation*** |
|---|---|---|---|---|
| Distribution of appreciated property | Not taxable. | No recognition at the entity level. | Recognition at the corporate level to the extent of the appreciation. Conduit—amount of recognized gain is passed through to shareholders. | Taxable at the corporate level to the extent of the appreciation. |
| Splitting of income among family members | Not applicable (only one owner). | Difficult—IRS will not recognize a family member as an owner unless certain requirements are met. | Rather easy—gift of stock will transfer tax on a pro rata share of income to the donee. However, IRS can make adjustments to reflect adequate compensation for services. | Same as an S corporation, except that donees will be subject to tax only on earnings actually or constructively distributed to them. Other than unreasonable compensation, IRS generally cannot make adjustments to reflect adequate compensation for services and capital. |
| Organizational costs | Start-up expenditures are amortizable over 60 months. | Amortizable over 60 months. | Same as partnership. | Same as partnership. |
| Charitable contributions | Limitations apply at owner level. | Conduit—owners are subject to deduction limitations in their own capacities. | Conduit—shareholders are subject to deduction limitations in their own capacities. | Limited to 10% of taxable income before certain deductions. |
| Alternative minimum tax | Applies at owner level. AMT rates are 26% and 28%. | Applies at the owner level rather than at the entity level. AMT preferences and adjustments are passed through from the entity to the owners. | Applies at the shareholder level rather than at the corporate level. AMT preferences and adjustments are passed through from the S corporation to the shareholders. | Applies at the corporate level. AMT rate is 20%. Exception for small corporations. |
| ACE adjustment | Does not apply. | Does not apply. | Does not apply. | The adjustment is made in calculating AMTI. The adjustment is 75% of the excess of adjusted current earnings over unadjusted AMTI. If the unadjusted AMTI exceeds adjusted current earnings, the adjustment is negative. |
| Tax preference items | Apply at owner level in determining AMT. | Conduit—passed through to owners who must account for such items in their separate capacities. | Conduit—passed through to shareholders who must account for such items in their separate capacities. | Subject to AMT at corporate level. |

*Refer to Chapters 10 and 11 for additional details on partnerships and limited liability companies.
**Refer to Chapter 12 for additional details on S corporations.
***Refer to Chapters 2 through 9 for additional details on regular (C) corporations.

- Larry was born and raised on his father's dairy farm. Both his education and his Air Force managerial experience provide him with useful tools for managing his business. However, Larry inherited his farm when milk prices were at a low for the modern era. Since none of her dairy farm clients were generating tax profits at that time, Eva anticipated Larry would operate his dairy farm at a loss. Larry, like Jesse, felt that limited liability was imperative. Thus, he incorporated the dairy farm and made the S corporation election.

  For the first two years, Larry's dairy farm produced tax losses. Since then, the dairy farm has produced tax profits large enough to absorb the losses. Larry anticipates that his profits will remain relatively stable in the $50,000 to $75,000 range. Since he is in the 30 percent marginal tax bracket and anticipates no dividend distributions to him from the corporation, his tax liability associated with the dairy farm will be less if he terminates the S corporation election.

As Jesse and Larry's example illustrates, selection of the proper business form can result in both nontax and tax advantages. Both of these factors should be considered in making the selection decision. Furthermore, this choice should be reviewed periodically, since a proper business form at one point in time may not be the proper form at a different time. Note that another business form Eva could have considered for Jesse is the LLC.

In looking at the tax attributes, consideration should be given to the tax consequences of the following:

- Contribution of assets to the entity by the owners at the time the entity is created and at later dates.
- Taxation of the results of operations.
- Distributions to owners.
- Disposition of an ownership interest.
- Termination of the entity.

## KEY TERMS

| | | |
|---|---|---|
| Conduit concept, 13–17 | Limited liability company (LLC), 13–4 | Thin capitalization, 13–13 |
| Entity concept, 13–17 | | |

## PROBLEM MATERIALS

### Discussion Questions

1. What are the principal legal forms for conducting a business entity? What are the principal Federal income tax forms for doing so?

2. A corporation is one of the legal forms that can be used to conduct a business. Discuss why the corporate form is divided into S corporations and C corporations for Federal income tax purposes.

3. Discuss the business and tax advantages of a limited liability company.

4. What are the advantages of a limited liability company compared with a general partnership?

5. All of the Big 4 accounting firms changed their ownership form from a general partnership to a limited liability partnership. Discuss the legal and tax ramifications of this modification of ownership form.

6. Several taxpayers would like to conduct a business in partnership form with all of the owners having limited liability. Can a partnership, other than a limited liability partnership, be structured so that this objective is accomplished? If so, are there any tax pitfalls?

7. Samuel is evaluating the idea of opening a lawn-servicing business. Discuss the nontax factors that he should consider in choosing a form of business entity.

**Decision Making** 8. Gary is an entrepreneur who likes to be actively involved in his business ventures. He is going to invest $400,000 in a business that he projects will produce a tax loss of approximately $75,000 per year in the short run. However, once consumers become aware of the new product being sold by the business and the quality of the service it provides, he is confident the business will generate a profit of at least $100,000 per year. Gary has substantial other income (from both business ventures and investment activities) each year. Advise Gary on the business form he should select for the short run. He will be the sole owner.

**Decision Making** 9. Sam is trying to decide whether he should operate his business as a C corporation or as an S corporation. Due to potential environmental hazard problems, it is imperative that the business have limited liability. Sam is leaning toward the S corporation form because it avoids double taxation. However, he is concerned that he may encounter difficulty several years in the future when he may want to issue some preferred stock to his son as a way of motivating him to remain active in the business. Sue, a friend of his, says that he can maintain maximum flexibility by operating as a C corporation. According to her, Sam can avoid double taxation by paying himself a salary equal to the before-tax earnings. As Sam's tax adviser, what is your advice to him?

10. How does classification of a distribution as a dividend or as a return of capital affect the extent to which a C corporation and its shareholders are subject to double taxation?

11. What AMT adjustment applies only to the corporate taxpayer? Does it apply to both C corporations and S corporations?

12. Violet Corporation, a C corporation in the 34% tax bracket, is going to be subject to the AMT this year. Armen, Violet's president, has heard that it can be advantageous to accelerate income and defer deductions into a year in which the taxpayer is subject to the AMT. He wonders about the logic of doing this since it would increase Violet's total Federal income tax liability. Violet does not expect to be subject to the AMT next year, but will remain in the 34% tax bracket. Clarify this planning approach for Armen.

13. Mary and Richert are establishing a retail business that will have outlets in six cities in a southeastern state. Since they project that the business will generate losses in at least the first three-year period, they want an entity form that will permit them to pass the entity losses through to their individual tax returns for both Federal and state income tax purposes. They have narrowed their choices to an S corporation and a limited liability company. Advise them on selecting an entity form.

14. "A favorably taxed fringe benefit is one that is deductible by the employer who provides it and is excludible from the gross income of the employee who receives it." Discuss the extent to which this statement is correct.

**Issue ID** 15. Tan, Inc., a C corporation that has been in existence for five years, has accumulated E & P of $990,000. It projects future earnings to continue at about $200,000 per year. David, Tan's sole shareholder and CEO, receives an annual salary of $400,000. David would like Tan to continue its current dividend policy. What issues do David and Tan need to consider if their objective is to avoid double taxation?

16. What techniques can the shareholders of a C corporation use to reduce taxable income and avoid double taxation? What can the IRS do to respond?

**Decision Making**

17. Liane owns land and a building that she has been using in her sole proprietorship. She is going to incorporate her sole proprietorship as a C corporation. Liane is trying to decide whether to contribute the land and building to the corporation or to lease them to the corporation. The net income of the sole proprietorship for the past five years has averaged $200,000. Advise Liane on the tax consequences.

18. For a C corporation, what is a return of capital distribution? What are the tax consequences to the shareholder?

19. Martin Corporation has been operating for 10 years and has earned taxable income of approximately $100,000 each year. Martin has not distributed any dividends in the past nor does it intend to do so in the near future. What negative tax result may occur because of this policy? Describe a set of circumstances for Martin that would avoid this negative result.

**Decision Making**

20. Arnold is going to conduct his business in corporate form. What factors should he consider in deciding whether to operate as a C corporation or as an S corporation?

**Issue ID**

21. Tammy and Arnold own 40% of the stock of Roadrunner, an S corporation. The other 60% is owned by 74 other family members (all are single). Tammy and Arnold have agreed to a divorce and are in the process of negotiating a property settlement. Identify the relevant tax issues for Tammy and Arnold.

22. Susan is going to contribute a truck to her wholly owned business. She purchased the truck five years ago for $26,000 and used it exclusively for personal purposes during this period. The fair market value of the truck is $11,000. Are the tax consequences different if she contributes the truck to an S corporation in which she is a 15% shareholder rather than a C corporation in which she is a 15% shareholder?

23. How are the nonrecognition rules for contributions of property to a partnership by a partner similar to those for contributions of property to a corporation by a shareholder? How are they different?

24. Why are special allocations either permitted or required for the partners in a partnership, yet are not permitted for the shareholders in a C corporation or an S corporation?

25. Entity liabilities have an effect on the calculation of a partner's basis for his or her partnership interest. Yet entity liabilities do not have any effect on a corporate shareholder's calculation of his or her stock basis. What is the reason for this difference in tax treatment?

26. Identify the effect of each of the following on a partner's basis for a partnership interest and a shareholder's (both C corporation and S corporation) basis for stock:

    • Profits.

    • Losses.

    • Liability increase.

    • Liability decrease.

    • Contribution of assets.

27. The conduit concept applies to the S corporation. Are there any circumstances in which the S corporation is a taxpayer rather than merely a tax reporter?

28. Distinguish between the tax treatment of a distribution of earnings and the treatment of other distributions of an S corporation.

29. A partner's ability to pass through and deduct his or her share of the partnership loss is limited by the partnership interest basis. Does the Code further limit the loss pass-through and deduction with the § 465 at-risk rules? In this regard, what effect do the § 469 passive activity loss rules have?

**Decision Making**

30. Sandra and Renee each own 50% of the stock of Olive, a C corporation. They have decided to dispose of their ownership interests in the corporation, and a substantial gain will result. Sandra thinks they should sell their stock whereas Renee thinks they should first liquidate the corporation and then sell the assets. Advise them on the consequences of each approach.

**Issue ID**

31. Vladimir owns all the stock of Ruby. The fair market value of the stock (and Ruby's assets) is about four times his adjusted basis for the stock. Vladimir is negotiating with an investor group for the sale of the corporation. Identify the relevant tax issues for Vladimir.

32. Using the legend provided, indicate which form of business entity each of the following characteristics describes. Some of the characteristics may apply to more than one form of business entity.

---
**Legend**
---

SP = Applies to sole proprietorship

P  = Applies to partnership

S  = Applies to S corporation

C  = Applies to C corporation

---

  a. Has limited liability.
  b. Greatest ability to raise capital.
  c. Subject to double taxation.
  d. Not subject to double taxation.
  e. Subject to accumulated earnings tax.
  f. Limit on types and number of shareholders.
  g. Has unlimited liability.
  h. Sale of the business can be subject to double taxation.
  i. Profits and losses affect the basis for an ownership interest.
  j. Entity liabilities affect the basis for an ownership interest.

33. Using the legend provided, indicate which form of business entity each of the following characteristics describes. Some of the characteristics may apply to more than one form of business entity.

---
**Legend**
---

P  = Applies to partnership

S  = Applies to S corporation

C  = Applies to C corporation

---

The basis for an ownership interest is:
  a. Increased by an investment by the owner.
  b. Decreased by a distribution to the owner.
  c. Increased by entity profits.
  d. Decreased by entity losses.
  e. Increased as the entity's liabilities increase.
  f. Decreased as the entity's liabilities decrease.

34. Green Partnership, a general partnership, has many opportunities to use special allocations. One of the special allocations available to Green is the optional adjustment to basis election under §§ 754 and 743 when a new partner acquires a partnership interest from an existing partner. Discuss the relevant factors that should be considered before making this election.

## Problems

35. A business entity has the following assets and liabilities on its balance sheet:

|  | Net Book Value | Fair Market Value |
|---|---|---|
| Assets | $675,000 | $950,000 |
| Liabilities | 100,000 | 100,000 |

The business entity has just lost a product liability suit with damages of $5 million being awarded to the plaintiff. Although the business entity will appeal the judgment, legal counsel indicates the judgment is highly unlikely to be overturned by the appellate court. The product liability insurance carried by the business has a policy ceiling of $3 million. What is the amount of liability of the entity and its owners if the form of the business entity is:
   a. A sole proprietorship?
   b. A partnership?
   c. A C corporation?
   d. An S corporation?

36. Red, White, Blue, and Orange have taxable income as follows:

| Corporation | Taxable Income |
|---|---|
| Red | $    84,000 |
| White | 330,000 |
| Blue | 700,000 |
| Orange | 30,000,000 |

   a. Calculate the marginal tax rate and the effective tax rate for each of the C corporations.
   b. Explain why the marginal tax rate for a C corporation can exceed 35%, but the effective tax rate cannot do so.

**Decision Making**

**Communications**

37. Amy and Jeff Barnes are going to operate their florist shop as a partnership or as an S corporation. After paying salaries of $45,000 to each of the owners, the shop's earnings are projected to be about $60,000. The earnings are to be invested in the growth of the business. Write a letter to Amy and Jeff Barnes (5700 Redmont Highway, Washington, D.C. 20024) advising them as to which of the two entity forms they should select.

**Decision Making**

38. Jack, an unmarried taxpayer, is going to establish a manufacturing business. He anticipates that the business will be profitable immediately due to a patent that he holds. He anticipates that profits for the first year will be about $200,000 and will increase at a rate of about 20% per year for the foreseeable future. He will be the sole owner of the business. Advise Jack on the form of business entity he should select. Assume Jack will be in the 35% tax bracket.

**Decision Making**

39. Silver Corporation will begin operations on January 1. Earnings for the next five years are projected to be relatively stable at about $100,000 per year. The shareholders of Silver are in the 30% tax bracket.
   a. Assume that Silver will reinvest its after-tax earnings in the growth of the company. Should Silver operate as a C corporation or as an S corporation?
   b. Assume that Silver will distribute its after-tax earnings each year to its shareholders. Should Silver operate as a C corporation or as an S corporation?

40. Mabel and Alan, who are in the 35% tax bracket, recently acquired a fast-food franchise. Each of them will work in the business and receive a salary of $100,000. They anticipate

that the annual profits of the business, after deducting salaries, will be approximately $300,000. The entity will distribute enough cash each year to Mabel and Alan to cover their Federal income taxes associated with the franchise.

a. What amount will the entity distribute if the franchise operates as a C corporation?

b. What amount will the entity distribute if the franchise operates as an S corporation?

c. What will be the amount of the combined entity/owner tax liability in (a) and (b)?

41. Parrott is a closely held corporation owned by 10 shareholders (each has 10% of the stock). Selected financial information provided by Parrott follows:

| | |
|---|---|
| Taxable income | $5,250,000 |
| Positive AMT adjustments (excluding ACE adjustment) | 425,000 |
| Negative AMT adjustments | (30,000) |
| Tax preferences | 6,000,000 |
| Retained earnings | 850,000 |
| Accumulated E & P | 775,000 |
| ACE adjustment | 720,000 |

a. Calculate Parrott's tax liability if Parrott is a C corporation.

b. Calculate Parrott's tax liability if Parrott is an S corporation.

c. How would your answers in (a) and (b) change if Parrott is not closely held (e.g., 5,000 shareholders with no shareholder owning more than 2% of the stock)?

**Decision Making**

42. Falcon Corporation, an offshore drilling company, is going to sell real estate that it no longer needs. The real estate is located in Grand Isle, Louisiana. The adjusted basis for the real estate is $400,000 ($700,000 – $300,000 MACRS straight-line depreciation), and the fair market value is $500,000. ADS straight-line depreciation would have been $275,000. The buyer of the real estate would like to close the transaction prior to the end of the calendar year. Falcon is uncertain whether the tax consequences would be better if it sold the real estate this year or next year and is considering the following options:

- $500,000 in cash payable on December 31, 2003.

- The sale will be closed on December 31, 2003, with the consideration being a $500,000 note issued by the buyer. The maturity date of the note is January 2, 2004, with the real estate being pledged as security.

Falcon projects its taxable income for 2003 and 2004 to be $400,000 (gross receipts of about $9.5 million) without the sale of the real estate. Falcon also has other AMT adjustments and tax preferences of $425,000 in 2003, which it does not expect to recur in 2004. Falcon's accounting period is the calendar year. Determine the tax consequences to Falcon under either option and recommend which option Falcon should select.

43. Three unmarried sisters own and operate a dairy farm. They live on the farm and take their meals on the farm for the "convenience of the employer." The fair market value of their lodging is $30,000, and the fair market value of their meals is $18,000. The meals are prepared for them by the farm cook who prepares their meals along with those of the five other farm employees.

a. Determine the tax consequences of the meals and lodging to the sisters if the farm is incorporated.

b. Determine the tax consequences of the meals and lodging to the sisters if the farm is not incorporated.

44. A business entity's taxable income before the cost of certain fringe benefits paid to owners and other employees is $400,000. The amounts paid for these fringe benefits are as follows:

|  | **Owners** | **Other Employees** |
|---|---|---|
| Group term life insurance | $20,000 | $40,000 |
| Meals and lodging incurred for the convenience of the employer | 50,000 | 75,000 |
| Pension plan | 30,000* | 90,000 |

*H.R. 10 (Keogh) plan for partnership and S corporation.

The business entity is equally owned by four owners.
  a. Calculate the taxable income of the business entity if the entity is a partnership, a C corporation, or an S corporation.
  b. Determine the effect on the owners for each of the three business forms.

45. Fawn, a C corporation, has taxable income of $200,000 before paying salaries to the two shareholder-employees, Gus and Janet. Fawn follows a policy of distributing all after-tax earnings to the shareholders.
  a. Determine the tax consequences for Fawn, Gus, and Janet if the corporation pays salaries to Gus and Janet as follows:

| **Option 1** | | **Option 2** | |
|---|---|---|---|
| Gus | $120,000 | Gus | $45,000 |
| Janet | 80,000 | Janet | 30,000 |

  b. Is Fawn likely to encounter any tax problems associated with either option?

46. Swallow, a C corporation, is owned by Sandra (50%) and Fran (50%). Sandra is the president, and Fran is the vice president for sales. Late in 2002, Swallow encounters working capital difficulties. Thus, Sandra and Fran each loan the corporation $300,000 on a 6% note that is due in five years with interest payable annually.
  a. Determine the tax consequences to Swallow, Sandra, and Fran for 2003 if the notes are classified as debt.
  b. Determine the tax consequences to Swallow, Sandra, and Fran for 2003 if the notes are classified as equity.

**Decision Making**

47. Marci and Jennifer each own 50% of the stock of Lavender, a C corporation. After paying each of them a "reasonable" salary of $125,000, the taxable income of Lavender is normally around $600,000. The corporation is about to purchase a $2 million shopping mall ($1.5 million allocated to the building and $500,000 allocated to the land). The mall will be rented to tenants at a net rent income (i.e., includes rental commissions, depreciation, etc.) of $500,000 annually. Marci and Jennifer will contribute $1 million each to the corporation to provide the cash required for the acquisition. Their CPA has suggested that Marci and Jennifer purchase the shopping mall as individuals and lease it to Lavender for a fair rental of $300,000. Both Marci and Jennifer are in the 38.6% tax bracket. The acquisition will occur on January 2, 2003. Determine whether the shopping mall should be acquired by Lavender or by Marci and Jennifer in accordance with their CPA's recommendation. Assume the depreciation on the shopping mall in 2003 is $37,000.

48. Rose, Inc., has taxable income of $400,000 for 2003. It has used up the accumulated earnings credit and has no additional "reasonable needs of the business" for the current tax year.
  a. Determine the total potential tax liability for Rose if it declares no dividends.
  b. Determine the total potential tax liability for Rose if it declares and pays dividends equal to the after-tax earnings.
  c. Determine the total potential tax liability for Rose in (a) and (b) if Rose is an S corporation.

**Decision Making**

49. Eagle Corporation has been an electing S corporation since its incorporation 10 years ago. During the first three years of operations, it incurred total losses of $250,000. Since then Eagle has generated earnings of approximately $150,000 each year. None of the

earnings have been distributed to the three equal shareholders, Claire, Lynn, and Todd, because the corporation has been in an expansion mode. At the beginning of 2003, Claire sells her stock to Nell for $400,000. Nell has reservations about the utility of the S election. Therefore, Lynn, Todd, and Nell are discussing whether the election should be continued. They expect the earnings to remain at approximately $150,000 each year. However, since they perceive that the expansion period is over and Eagle has adequate working capital, they may start distributing the earnings to the shareholders. All of the shareholders are in the 30% tax bracket. Advise the three shareholders on whether the S election should be maintained.

**Communications**

50. Bob Bentz and Carl Pierce each own 50% of the stock of Deer, Inc., a C corporation. When the corporation was organized, Bob contributed cash of $200,000, and Carl contributed land with an adjusted basis of $125,000 and a fair market value of $240,000. Deer assumed Carl's $40,000 mortgage on the land. In addition to the capital contributions, Bob and Carl each loaned the corporation $75,000. The maturity date of the loan is in 10 years, and the interest rate is 8%, the same as the Federal rate.
    a. Determine the tax consequences to Bob, Carl, and Deer of the initial contribution of assets, the shareholder loans, and the annual interest payments if the loans are classified as debt.
    b. The same as (a) except the loans are reclassified as equity.
    c. You and Bob met over lunch to discuss the tax consequences of the capital contributions and loans he and Carl made to Deer, Inc. Prepare a memo for the files on your discussion.

51. Buddy and Bobby form a business entity with each contributing the following property:

|  | **Buddy** | **Bobby** |
| --- | --- | --- |
| Cash | $150,000 | |
| Land | | $150,000* |

*Fair market value. Adjusted basis is $90,000.

Four months later, the land is sold for $165,000 because the local commission refused to rezone the land from commercial to residential. The proceeds are to be applied toward the purchase of another parcel of land to be used for real estate development. Determine the tax consequences to the entity and to the owners from the formation of the business entity and the sale of the land if the entity is:
    a. A partnership.
    b. An S corporation.
    c. A C corporation.
    d. Is it possible to structure the disposition of the land and the subsequent acquisition of other land so that the realized gain on the disposition can be deferred?

52. Alicia contributes $25,000 to a business entity in exchange for a 20% ownership interest. During the first year of operations, the entity earns a profit of $150,000, and at the end of that year, it has liabilities of $60,000.
    a. Calculate Alicia's basis for her stock if the entity is a C corporation.
    b. Calculate Alicia's basis for her stock if the entity is an S corporation.
    c. Calculate Alicia's basis for her partnership interest if the entity is a partnership.

53. An entity engages in the following transactions during the taxable year:

   • Sells stock held for three years as an investment for $30,000 (adjusted basis of $20,000).

   • Sells land used in the business for $65,000. The land has been used as a parking lot and originally cost $40,000.

   • Receives tax-exempt interest on municipal bonds of $5,000.

   • Receives dividends on IBM stock of $8,000.

Describe the effect of these transactions on the entity and the owners of the entity if the entity is:

   a. A partnership.
   b. A C corporation.
   c. An S corporation.

54. Swift Corporation distributes land to Sam and cash to Allison in exchange for part of their stock. Other shareholders do not redeem any of their stock. Swift's basis for the land is $12,000 (fair market value is $30,000). Sam surrenders shares of stock that have a basis of $16,000. Prior to the stock redemption, Sam owned 20% of the Swift stock, and after the redemption, he owns 10%. At the same time, Swift distributes $45,000 cash to Allison. Allison surrenders shares of stock that have a basis to her of $25,000. Prior to the stock redemption, Allison owned 70% of the Swift stock, and after the redemption, she owns 55%. Determine the tax consequences to Swift, Sam, and Allison if Swift is:
   a. A C corporation.
   b. An S corporation.

55. Yellow, a personal service corporation, has the following types of income and losses for 2003:

| | |
|---|---|
| Active income | $190,000 |
| Portfolio income | 15,000 |
| Passive activity losses | 170,000 |

   a. Calculate Yellow's taxable income for 2003.
   b. Assume that instead of being a personal service corporation, Yellow is a closely held corporation. Calculate Yellow's taxable income for 2003.

56. Rosa contributes $50,000 to a business entity in exchange for a 10% ownership interest. Rosa materially participates in the entity. The business entity incurs a loss of $900,000 for 2003 and has liabilities at the end of the year of $700,000. Of this amount, $150,000 is for recourse debt, and $550,000 is for nonrecourse debt.
   a. Assume the business entity is a partnership. How much of Rosa's share of the loss can be deducted on her 2003 income tax return? What is Rosa's basis for her partnership interest at the end of 2003?
   b. Assume the business entity is a C corporation. How much of Rosa's share of the loss can be deducted on her 2003 income tax return? What is Rosa's basis for her stock at the end of 2003?

57. Megan owns 60% and Vern owns 40% of a business entity. For 2003, the entity has a tax loss of $100,000. The owners would like to share profits with 60% for Megan and 40% for Vern and to share losses with 90% for Vern and 10% for Megan. Determine the tax consequences for 2003 if the entity is:
   a. A partnership.
   b. A C corporation.
   c. An S corporation.

58. Emily and Freda are negotiating with George to purchase the business that he operates in corporate form (Pelican, Inc.). The assets of Pelican, Inc., a C corporation, are as follows:

| Asset | Basis | FMV |
|---|---|---|
| Cash | $ 20,000 | $ 20,000 |
| Accounts receivable | 50,000 | 50,000 |
| Inventory | 100,000 | 110,000 |
| Furniture and fixtures* | 150,000 | 170,000 |
| Building** | 200,000 | 250,000 |
| Land | 40,000 | 150,000 |

*Potential depreciation recapture under § 1245 is $45,000.
**The straight-line method was used to depreciate the building. The balance in the accumulated depreciation account is $340,000.

George's basis for the stock of Pelican, Inc., is $560,000. George is in the 30% tax bracket, and Pelican, Inc., is in the 34% tax bracket.

a. Assume that Emily and Freda purchase the stock of Pelican from George and that the purchase price is $908,000. Determine the tax consequences to Emily and Freda, Pelican, and George.

b. Assume that Emily and Freda purchase the assets from Pelican and that the purchase price is $908,000. Determine the tax consequences to Emily and Freda, Pelican, and George.

c. Assume that the purchase price is $550,000 because the fair market value of the building is $150,000, and the fair market value of the land is $50,000. Also, assume that no amount is assigned to goodwill. Emily and Freda purchase the stock of Pelican from George. Determine the tax consequences to Emily and Freda, Pelican, and George.

**Decision Making**

59. Linda is the owner of a sole proprietorship. The entity has assets as follows:

| Asset | Basis | FMV |
|---|---|---|
| Cash | $10,000 | $10,000 |
| Accounts receivable | –0– | 25,000 |
| Office furniture and fixtures* | 15,000 | 17,000 |
| Building** | 75,000 | 90,000 |
| Land | 60,000 | 80,000 |

\*Potential depreciation recapture under § 1245 of $5,000.
\*\*The straight-line method of depreciation has been used to depreciate the building.

Linda sells the business for $260,000 to Juan.

a. Determine the tax consequences to Linda, including the classification of any recognized gain or loss.

b. Determine the tax consequences to Juan.

c. Advise Juan on how the purchase agreement could be modified to produce more beneficial tax consequences for him.

**Decision Making**

60. Gail and Harry own the GH Partnership, which has conducted business for 10 years. The bases for their partnership interests are $100,000 for Gail and $150,000 for Harry. GH Partnership has the following assets:

| Asset | Basis | FMV |
|---|---|---|
| Cash | $ 10,000 | $ 10,000 |
| Accounts receivable | 30,000 | 28,000 |
| Inventory | 25,000 | 26,000 |
| Building* | 100,000 | 150,000 |
| Land | 250,000 | 400,000 |

\*The straight-line method has been used to depreciate the building. Accumulated depreciation is $70,000.

Gail and Harry sell their partnership interests to Keith and Liz for $307,000 each.

a. Determine the tax consequences of the sale to Gail, Harry, and GH Partnership.

b. From a tax perspective, would it matter to Keith and Liz whether they purchase Gail's and Harry's partnership interests or the partnership assets from GH Partnership?

**Decision Making**
**Communications**

61. Bill Evans is going to purchase either the stock or the assets of Dane Corporation. All of the Dane stock is owned by Chuck. Bill and Chuck agree that Dane is worth $750,000. The tax basis for Dane's assets is $410,000. Write a letter to Bill advising him on whether he should negotiate to purchase the stock or the assets. Also, prepare a memo for the files. Bill's address is 100 Village Green, Chattanooga, TN 37403.

## Research Problems

**Internet Activity**

*Use the tax resources of the Internet to address the following questions. Do not restrict your search to the World Wide Web, but include a review of newsgroups and general reference materials, practitioner sites and resources, primary sources of the tax law, chat rooms and discussion groups, and other opportunities.*

**Research Problem 1.**   Find an anecdote about a professional consulting firm that recently converted to LLP status. Are the firm and its competition and clients agreeable to the conversion of operating status?

**Research Problem 2.**   When did your state adopt LLC legislation? When did it receive IRS approval to apply partnership tax law to the entities?

**Research Problem 3.**   Find an article describing how a specific business put together its employee fringe benefit package in light of the limitations presented by the tax law and its form of operation.

**Research Problem 4.**   Determine whether your state income tax system permits an S corporation election.

# Exempt Entities

**CHAPTER 14**

## LEARNING OBJECTIVES

*After completing Chapter 14, you should be able to:*

### LO.1
Identify the different types of exempt organizations.

### LO.2
Enumerate the requirements for exempt status.

### LO.3
Know the tax consequences of exempt status, including the different consequences for public charities and private foundations.

### LO.4
Determine which exempt organizations are classified as private foundations.

### LO.5
Recognize the taxes imposed on private foundations and calculate the related initial tax and additional tax amounts.

### LO.6
Determine when an exempt organization is subject to the unrelated business income tax and calculate the amount of the tax.

### LO.7
List the reports exempt organizations must file with the IRS and the related due dates.

### LO.8
Identify tax planning opportunities for exempt organizations.

# O U T L I N E

Ideally, any entity that generates profit would prefer not to be subject to the Federal income tax. All of the types of entities discussed in Chapter 13 are subject to the Federal income tax at one level (e.g., sole proprietorships, partnerships, S corporations, and LLCs generally are subject only to single taxation) or more (e.g., C corporations are subject to double taxation). In contrast, entities classified as **exempt organizations** may be able to escape Federal income taxation altogether.

Churches are among the types of organizations that are exempt from Federal income tax. Nevertheless, one must be careful not to conclude that anything labeled a church will qualify for exempt status.

During the 1970s and 1980s, a popular technique for attempting to avoid Federal income tax was the establishment of so-called mail-order churches. For example, in one scheme, a nurse obtained a certificate of ordination and a church charter from an organization that sold such documents.[1] The articles of incorporation stated that the church was organized exclusively for religious and charitable purposes, including a religious mission of healing the spirit, mind, emotions, and body. The nurse was the church's minister, director, and principal officer. Taking a vow of poverty, she transferred all her assets, including a house and car, to the church. The church assumed all of the nurse's liabilities, including the mortgage on her house and her credit card bills. The nurse continued to work at a hospital and deposited her salary in the church's bank account. The church provided her with a living allowance sufficient to maintain or improve her previous standard of living. She was also permitted to use the house and car for personal purposes.

The IRS declared that such organizations were shams and not bona fide churches. For a church to be tax-exempt under § 501(c)(3), none of its net earnings may be used to the benefit of any private shareholder or individual. In essence, the organization should serve a public rather than a private interest. Though the

---

[1]Rev.Rul. 81–94, 1981–1 C.B. 330.

**EQUITABLE TREATMENT OF CHARITIES**

The IRS audit rate has been declining across the board, and the rate has been especially low for tax-exempt entities. According to a report from the General Accounting Office, the IRS audited only 1 out of every 233 returns (less than one-half of 1 percent) of tax-exempts during 2001.

But times are changing. The IRS plans more audits of tax-exempts this year. Random audits of the various types of tax-exempts will be conducted to obtain foundational data for identifying areas of noncompliance. These data will then be used in the future in selecting tax-exempts to audit. The intent is to make the audit process more effective and more efficient.

courts have consistently upheld the IRS position, numerous avoidance schemes such as this have been attempted.

As discussed in Chapter 1, the major objective of the Federal tax law is to raise revenue. If revenue raising were the only objective, however, the Code would not contain provisions that permit certain organizations to be either partially or completely exempt from Federal income tax. Social considerations may also affect the tax law. This objective bears directly on the decision by Congress to provide for exempt organization tax status. The House Report on the Revenue Act of 1938 explains:

> The exemption from taxation of money or property devoted to charitable and other purposes is based upon the theory that the Government is compensated for the loss of revenue by its relief from the financial burden which would otherwise have to be met by appropriations from public funds, and by the benefits resulting from the promotion of the general welfare.[2]

Recognizing this social consideration objective, Subchapter F (Exempt Organizations) of the Code (§§ 501–530) provides the authority under which certain organizations are exempt from Federal income tax. Exempt status is not open-ended in that two general limitations exist. First, the nature or scope of the organization may result in it being only partially exempt from tax.[3] Second, the organization may engage in activities that are subject to special taxation.[4]

---

**LO.1**

Identify the different types of exempt organizations.

## Types of Exempt Organizations

An organization qualifies for exempt status *only* if it fits into one of the categories provided in the Code. Examples of qualifying exempt organizations and the specific statutory authority for their exempt status are listed in Exhibit 14–1.[5]

---

[2]See 1939–1 (Part 2) C.B. 742 for a reprint of H.R. No. 1860, 75th Congress, 3rd Session.

[3]See the subsequent discussion of Unrelated Business Income Tax.

[4]See the subsequent discussions of Prohibited Transactions and Taxes Imposed on Private Foundations.

[5]Section 501(a) provides for exempt status for organizations described in §§ 401 and 501. The orientation of this chapter is toward organizations that conduct business activities. Therefore, the exempt organizations described in § 401 (qualified pension, profit sharing, and stock bonus trusts) are outside the scope of the chapter and are not discussed.

■ **EXHIBIT 14–1**
Types of Exempt Organizations

| Statutory Authority | Brief Description | Examples or Comments |
|---|---|---|
| § 501(c)(1) | Federal and related agencies. | Commodity Credit Corporation, Federal Deposit Insurance Corporation, Federal Land Bank. |
| § 501(c)(2) | Corporations holding title to property for and paying income to exempt organizations. | Corporation holding title to college fraternity house. |
| § 501(c)(3) | Religious, charitable, educational, scientific, literary, etc., organizations. | Boy Scouts of America, Red Cross, Salvation Army, Episcopal Church, United Fund, University of Richmond. |
| § 501(c)(4) | Civic leagues and employee unions. | Garden club, tenants' association promoting tenants' legal rights in entire community, League of Women Voters. |
| § 501(c)(5) | Labor, agricultural, and horticultural organizations. | Teachers' association, organization formed to promote effective agricultural pest control, organization formed to test soil and to educate community members in soil treatment, garden club. |
| § 501(c)(6) | Business leagues, chambers of commerce, real estate boards, etc. | Chambers of Commerce, American Plywood Association, National Football League (NFL), Professional Golfers Association (PGA) Tour, medical association peer review board, organization promoting acceptance of women in business and professions. |
| § 501(c)(7) | Social clubs. | Country club, rodeo and riding club, press club, bowling club, college fraternities. |
| § 501(c)(8) | Fraternal beneficiary societies. | Lodges. Must provide for the payment of life, sickness, accident, or other benefits to members or their dependents. |
| § 501(c)(9) | Voluntary employees' beneficiary associations. | Provide for the payment of life, sickness, accident, or other benefits to members, their dependents, or their designated beneficiaries. |
| § 501(c)(10) | Domestic fraternal societies. | Lodges. Must not provide for the payment of life, sickness, accident, or other benefits; and must devote the net earnings exclusively to religious, charitable, scientific, literary, educational, and fraternal purposes. |
| § 501(c)(11) | Local teachers' retirement fund associations. | Only permitted sources of income are amounts received from (1) public taxation, (2) assessments on teaching salaries of members, and (3) income from investments. |
| § 501(c)(12) | Local benevolent life insurance associations, mutual or cooperative telephone companies, etc. | Local cooperative telephone company, local mutual water company, local mutual electric company. |
| § 501(c)(13) | Cemetery companies. | Must be operated exclusively for the benefit of lot owners who hold the lots for burial purposes. |
| § 501(c)(14) | Credit unions. | Other than credit unions exempt under § 501(c)(1). |
| § 501(c)(15) | Mutual insurance companies. | Mutual fire insurance company, mutual automobile insurance company. |
| § 501(c)(16) | Corporations organized by farmers' cooperatives for financing crop operations. | Related farmers' cooperative must be exempt from tax under § 521. |
| § 501(c)(19) | Armed forces members' posts or organizations. | Veterans of Foreign Wars (VFW), Reserve Officers Association. |
| § 501(c)(20) | Group legal service plans. | Provided by a corporation for its employees. |
| § 501(d) | Religious and apostolic organizations. | Communal organization. Members must include pro rata share of the net income of the organization in their gross income as dividends. |
| § 501(e) | Cooperative hospital service organizations. | Centralized purchasing organization for exempt hospitals. |
| § 501(f) | Cooperative service organization of educational institutions. | Organization formed to manage universities' endowment funds. |
| § 529 | Qualified tuition programs. | Prepaid tuition and educational savings programs. |
| § 530 | Coverdell Education Savings Accounts. | Qualified education savings accounts. |

LO.2

Enumerate the requirements
for exempt status.

# Requirements for Exempt Status

Exempt status frequently requires more than mere classification in one of the categories of exempt organizations. Many of the organizations that qualify for exempt status share the following characteristics.

- The organization serves some type of *common good*.[6]
- The organization is *not* a *for-profit* entity.[7]
- *Net earnings* do not benefit the members of the organization.[8]
- The organization does not exert *political influence*.[9]

## SERVING THE COMMON GOOD

The underlying rationale for all exempt organizations is that they serve some type of *common good*. However, depending on the type of the exempt organization, the term *common good* may be interpreted broadly or narrowly. If the test is interpreted broadly, the group being served is the general public or some large subgroup thereof. If it is interpreted narrowly, the group is the specific group referred to in the statutory language. One of the factors in classifying an exempt organization as a private foundation is the size of the group it serves.

## NOT-FOR-PROFIT ENTITY

The organization may not be organized or operated for the purpose of making a profit. For some types of exempt organizations, the *for-profit prohibition* appears in the statutory language. For other types, the prohibition is implied.

## NET EARNINGS AND MEMBERS OF THE ORGANIZATION

What uses are appropriate for the net earnings of a tax-exempt organization? The logical answer would seem to be that the earnings should be used for the exempt purpose of the organization. However, where the organization exists for the good of a specific group of members, such an open-ended interpretation could permit net earnings to benefit specific group members. Therefore, the Code specifically prohibits certain types of exempt organizations from using their earnings in this way.

> . . . no part of the net earnings . . . inures to the benefit of any private shareholder or individual.[10]

In other instances, a statutory prohibition is unnecessary because the definition of the exempt organization in the Code effectively prevents such use.

> . . . the net earnings of which are devoted exclusively to religious, charitable, scientific, literary, educational, and fraternal purposes.[11]

---

[6]See, for example, §§ 501(c)(3) and (4).
[7]See, for example, §§ 501(c)(3), (4), (6), (13), and (14).
[8]See, for example, §§ 501(c)(3), (6), (7), (9), (10), (11), and (19).

[9]See, for example, § 501(c)(3).
[10]§ 501(c)(6).
[11]§ 501(c)(10).

## POLITICAL INFLUENCE

Religious, charitable, educational, etc., organizations are generally prohibited from attempting to influence legislation or participate in political campaigns. Participation in political campaigns includes participation both *on behalf of* a candidate and *in opposition to* a candidate.

Only in limited circumstances are such exempt organizations permitted to attempt to influence legislation. See the subsequent discussion under Prohibited Transactions.

---

<table>
<tr><td>

**LO.3**

Know the tax consequences of exempt status, including the different consequences for public charities and private foundations.

</td></tr>
</table>

# Tax Consequences of Exempt Status: General

An organization that is appropriately classified as one of the types of exempt organizations is generally exempt from Federal income tax. Four exceptions to this general statement exist, however. An exempt organization that engages in a *prohibited transaction* or is a so-called *feeder organization* is subject to tax. If the organization is classified as a *private foundation*, it may be partially subject to tax. Finally, an exempt organization is subject to tax on its *unrelated business taxable income.*

In addition to being exempt from Federal income tax, an exempt organization may be eligible for other benefits, including the following.

- The organization may be exempt from state income tax, state franchise tax, sales tax, or property tax.
- The organization may receive discounts on postage rates.
- Donors of property to the exempt organization may qualify for charitable contribution deductions on their Federal and state income tax returns. However, *not* all exempt organizations are qualified charitable contribution recipients (e.g., gifts to the National Football League, PGA Tour, and Underwriters Laboratories are not deductible).

## PROHIBITED TRANSACTIONS

Engaging in a § 503 prohibited transaction can produce three negative results. First, part or all of the organization's income may be subject to Federal income tax. Second and even worse, the organization may forfeit its exempt status. Finally, intermediate sanctions may be imposed on certain exempt organization insiders.

**Failure to Continue to Qualify.**   Organizations initially qualify for exempt status only if they are organized as indicated in Exhibit 14–1. The initial qualification requirements then effectively become maintenance requirements. Failure to continue to meet the qualification requirements results in the loss of the entity's exempt status.

New Faith, Inc., is an excellent example of an exempt organization that failed to continue to qualify for tax exemption.[12] The stated purposes of the organization were to feed and shelter the poor. In its application for exempt status, New Faith indicated that it would derive its financial support from donations, bingo games, and raffles. The IRS approved the exempt status.

New Faith's only source of income was the operation of several lunch trucks, which provided food to the general public in exchange for scheduled "donations." Evidence provided by the organization to the Tax Court did not show that the

---

[12]*New Faith, Inc.*, 64 TCM 1050, T.C.Memo. 1992–601.

food from the lunch trucks was provided free of charge or at reduced prices. In addition, no evidence was presented to show that the people who received food for free or at below-cost prices were impoverished or needy. The court concluded that the primary purpose of the activity was the conduct of a trade or business. It upheld the IRS's revocation of New Faith's exempt status.

**Election Not to Forfeit Exempt Status for Lobbying.** Organizations exempt under § 501(c)(3) (religious, charitable, educational, etc., organizations) generally are prohibited from attempting to influence legislation (lobbying activities) or from participating in political campaigns.[13] Any violation can result in the forfeiture of exempt status.

Certain § 501(c)(3) exempt organizations are permitted to engage in lobbying activities on a limited basis.[14] Eligible for such treatment are most § 501(c)(3) exempt organizations (educational institutions, hospitals, and medical research organizations; organizations supporting government schools; organizations publicly supported by charitable contributions; certain organizations that are publicly supported by various sources including admissions, sales, gifts, grants, contributions, or membership fees; and certain organizations that support certain types of public charities). Churches, their integrated auxiliaries, and *private foundations* are not permitted to engage in lobbying activities, however.

An eligible § 501(c)(3) organization must make an affirmative election to participate in lobbying activities on a limited basis. The lobbying expenditures of electing § 501(c)(3) organizations are subject to a ceiling. Exceeding the ceiling can lead to the forfeiture of exempt status. Even when the ceiling is not exceeded, a tax may be imposed on some of the lobbying expenditures (discussed subsequently).

Two terms are key to the calculation of the ceiling amount: **lobbying expenditures** and **grass roots expenditures**. Lobbying expenditures are made for the purpose of influencing legislation through either of the following.

- Attempting to affect the opinions of the general public or any segment thereof.
- Communicating with any legislator or staff member or with any government official or staff member who may participate in the formulation of legislation.

Grass roots expenditures are made for the purpose of influencing legislation by attempting to affect the opinions of the general public or any segment thereof.

The statutory ceiling is imposed on both lobbying expenditures and grass roots expenditures and is computed as follows.

- 150% × Lobbying nontaxable amount = Lobbying expenditures ceiling.
- 150% × Grass roots nontaxable amount = Grass roots expenditures ceiling.

The *lobbying nontaxable amount* is the lesser of (1) $1 million or (2) the amount determined in Figure 14–1.[15] The *grass roots nontaxable amount* is 25 percent of the lobbying nontaxable amount.[16]

An electing exempt organization is assessed a tax on **excess lobbying expenditures** as follows.[17]

- 25% × Excess lobbying expenditures = Tax liability.

Excess lobbying expenditures are the greater of the following.[18]

---

[13]§ 501(c)(3). In recognition of the influence of technology, even a single Internet link to a partisan political site will taint the exempt entity.

[14]§ 501(h). An affirmative election to lobby must be made.

[15]§ 4911(c)(2).

[16]§ 4911(c)(4).

[17]§ 4911(a)(1).

[18]§ 4911(b).

■ **FIGURE 14–1**

Calculation of Lobbying
Nontaxable Amount

| Exempt Purpose Expenditures | Lobbying Nontaxable Amount Is |
|---|---|
| Not over $500,000 | 20% of exempt purpose expenditures* |
| Over $500,000 but not over $1 million | $100,000 + 15% of the excess of exempt purpose expenditures over $500,000 |
| Over $1 million but not over $1.5 million | $175,000 + 10% of the excess of exempt purpose expenditures over $1 million |
| Over $1.5 million | $225,000 + 5% of the excess of exempt purpose expenditures over $1.5 million |

*Exempt purpose expenditures generally are the amounts paid or incurred for the taxable
year to accomplish the following purposes: religious, charitable, scientific, literary, educational, fostering national or international amateur sports competition, or the prevention of
cruelty to children or animals.

- Excess of the lobbying expenditures for the taxable year over the lobbying
  nontaxable amount.
- Excess of the grass roots expenditures for the taxable year over the grass
  roots nontaxable amount.

**EXAMPLE 1**

Tan, Inc., a qualifying § 501(c)(3) organization, incurs lobbying expenditures of $500,000 for
the taxable year and grass roots expenditures of $0. Exempt purpose expenditures for the
taxable year are $5 million. Tan elects to be eligible to make lobbying expenditures on a
limited basis.

Applying the data in Figure 14–1, the lobbying nontaxable amount is $400,000 [$225,000
+ 5%($5,000,000 − $1,500,000)]. The ceiling on lobbying expenditures is $600,000 (150% ×
$400,000). Therefore, the $500,000 of lobbying expenditures are under the permitted $600,000.
However, the election results in the imposition of tax on the excess lobbying expenditures
of $100,000 ($500,000 lobbying expenditures − $400,000 lobbying nontaxable amount). The
resulting tax liability is $25,000 ($100,000 × 25%). ■

A § 501(c)(3) organization that makes disqualifying lobbying expenditures is
subject to a 5 percent tax on the lobbying expenditures for the taxable year. A 5
percent tax may also be levied on the organization's management. The tax is
imposed on management only if the managers knew that making the expenditures
was likely to result in the organization no longer qualifying under § 501(c)(3), and
if the managers' actions were willful and not due to reasonable cause. The tax
does not apply to private foundations (see the subsequent discussion).[19] Concept
Summary 14–1 capsulizes the rules on influencing legislation.

**Intermediate Sanctions.**   Prior to 1996, the IRS had only two options available
for dealing with exempt organizations (other than private foundations) engaging
in prohibited transactions. First, it could attempt to subject part or all of the organization's income to Federal income tax. Second, it could revoke the exempt status of
the organization. For private foundations, an additional option was available. The
IRS could impose certain taxes on private foundations for engaging in so-called
prohibited transactions (see Concept Summary 14–3 later in the chapter).

Tax legislation enacted in 1996 added another option to the IRS toolbox—
**intermediate sanctions**—for so-called public charities.[20] The intermediate sanctions
take the form of excise taxes imposed on disqualified persons (any individuals

---

[19]§ 4912.     [20]§ 4958.

## CONCEPT SUMMARY 14–1

### Exempt Organizations and Influencing Legislation

| Factor | Tax Result |
| --- | --- |
| Entity subject to rule | § 501(c)(3) organization. |
| Effect of influencing legislation | Subject to tax on lobbying expenditures under § 4912. Forfeit exempt status under § 501(c)(3). Not eligible for exempt status under § 501(c)(4). |
| Effect of electing to make lobbying expenditures | Permitted to make limited lobbying expenditures. Subject to tax under § 4911. |

who are in a position to exercise substantial influence over the affairs of the organization) who engage in *excess benefit transactions* and on exempt organization managers who participate in such a transaction knowing that it is improper. Such excess benefit transactions include transactions in which a disqualified person engages in a non-fair-market-value transaction with the exempt organization or receives unreasonable compensation.

The excise tax on the disqualified person is imposed at a rate of 25 percent of the excess benefit. For the exempt organization manager, the excise tax is imposed at a rate of 10 percent of the excess benefit (unless such participation is not willful and is due to reasonable cause) with a statutory ceiling of $10,000 for any excess benefit transaction. These excise taxes are referred to as first-level taxes.

A second-level tax is imposed on the disqualified person if the excess benefit transaction is not corrected within the taxable period. This excise tax is imposed at a rate of 200 percent of the excess benefit.

### FEEDER ORGANIZATIONS

A **feeder organization** carries on a trade or business for the benefit of an exempt organization and remits its profits to the exempt organization. Such organizations are not exempt from Federal income tax. This provision is intended to prevent an entity whose primary purpose is to conduct a trade or business for profit from escaping taxation merely because all of its profits are payable to one or more exempt organizations.[21]

Some income and activities are *not* subject to the feeder organization rules.[22]

- Rent income that would be excluded from the definition of the term *rent* for purposes of the unrelated business income tax (discussed subsequently).
- A trade or business where substantially all the work is performed by volunteers.
- The trade or business of selling merchandise where substantially all the merchandise has been received as contributions or gifts.

Concept Summary 14–2 highlights the consequences of exempt status.

---

[21]§ 502(a).

[22]§ 502(b).

---

### CONCEPT SUMMARY 14–2

## Consequences of Exempt Status

| | |
|---|---|
| General | Exempt from Federal income tax.<br>Exempt from most state and local income, franchise, sales, and property taxes.<br>Qualify for reductions in postage rates.<br>Gifts to the organization often can be deducted by donor. |
| Exceptions | May be subject to Federal income tax associated with the following.<br>• Engaging in a prohibited transaction.<br>• Being a feeder organization.<br>• Being a private foundation.<br>• Generating unrelated business taxable income. |

---

LO.4

Determine which exempt
organizations are classified as
private foundations.

# Private Foundations

## TAX CONSEQUENCES OF PRIVATE FOUNDATION STATUS

Certain exempt organizations are classified as **private foundations.** This classification produces two negative consequences. First, the classification may have an adverse impact on the contributions received by the donee exempt organization. Contributions may decline because the tax consequences for donors may not be as favorable as if the entity were not a private foundation.[23] Second, the classification may result in taxation at the exempt organization level. The reason for this less beneficial tax treatment is that private foundations define common good more narrowly and therefore are seen as not being supported by, and operated for the good of, the public.

**Definition of a Private Foundation.**    The following § 501(c)(3) organizations are *not* private foundations.[24]

1. Churches; educational institutions; hospitals and medical research organizations; charitable organizations receiving a major portion of their support from the general public or the United States, a state, or a political subdivision thereof that is operated for the benefit of a college or university; and governmental units (favored activities category).
2. Organizations that are broadly supported by the general public (excluding disqualified persons), by governmental units, or by organizations described in (1) above.
3. Entities organized and operated exclusively for the benefit of organizations described in (1) or (2) [a supporting organization].
4. Entities organized and operated exclusively for testing for public safety.

To meet the broadly supported requirement in (2) above, both the following tests must be satisfied.

- External support test.
- Internal support test.

---

[23]§ 170(e)(1)(B)(ii).                    [24]§ 509(a).

**PRIVATE FOUNDATION INVESTMENT STRATEGY**

The founders of Hewlett-Packard established two foundations: the David and Lucile Packard Foundation and the William and Flora Hewlett Foundation. Although the two foundations were in agreement in opposing HP's acquisition of Compaq Computer, they have adopted different investment strategies for foundation assets.

The Packard Foundation holds stock only in HP and in an HP spin-off, Agilent Technologies. As a result, with the substantial downturn in the market for technology stock, the foundation's endowment declined from a peak of $18 billion in 2000 to $6.2 billion by the end of 2001.

The Hewlett Foundation has a more diversified investment strategy. In preparation for an infusion of HP shares from the estate of William Hewlett, who died in 2001, the foundation reduced its HP holdings to 2 percent of its portfolio. Laurance Hougland, the foundation's chief financial officer, plans to continue to diversify the portfolio as the foundation receives installments of HP stock from the estate. Without this continued diversification, the foundation's HP holdings would ultimately make up 50 percent of the portfolio.

The investment performance of a foundation's endowment can have a substantial impact on its activities. The Packard Foundation has reduced its grant making from $615 million in 2000 to a budgeted $250 million for 2002. With its more diversified portfolio, the Hewlett Foundation has better weathered the market downturn.

SOURCE: Adapted from David Bank, "Foundations Divide Over Need to Diversify," *Wall Street Journal*, February 14, 2002, p. C1.

Under the *external support test*, more than one-third of the organization's support each taxable year *normally* must come from the three groups listed in (2) above, in the following forms.

- Gifts, grants, contributions, and membership fees.
- Gross receipts from admissions, sales of merchandise, performance of services, or the furnishing of facilities in an activity that is not an unrelated trade or business for purposes of the unrelated business income tax (discussed subsequently). However, such gross receipts from any person or governmental agency in excess of the greater of $5,000 or 1 percent of the organization's support for the taxable year are not counted.

The *internal support test* limits the amount of support *normally* received from the following sources to one-third of the organization's support for the taxable year.[25]

- Gross investment income (gross income from interest, dividends, rents, and royalties).
- Unrelated business taxable income (discussed subsequently) minus the related tax.

---

[25]Reg. § 1.509(a)–3(c) generally requires that the external and internal support tests be met in each of the four preceding tax years.

<table>
<tr><td>EXAMPLE 2</td><td colspan="2">Lion, Inc., a § 501(c)(3) organization, received the following support during the taxable year.</td></tr>
</table>

| | |
|---|---:|
| Governmental unit A for services rendered | $30,000 |
| Governmental unit B for services rendered | 20,000 |
| General public for services rendered | 20,000 |
| Gross investment income | 15,000 |
| Contributions from individual substantial contributors (disqualified persons) | 15,000 |

For purposes of the *external support test*, the support from A is counted only to the extent of $5,000 (greater of $5,000 or 1% of $100,000 support). Likewise, for B, only $5,000 is counted as support. Thus, the total countable support is $30,000 ($20,000 from the general public + $5,000 + $5,000), and Lion fails the test for the taxable year ($30,000/$100,000 = 30%; need > 33.3%). The $15,000 received from disqualified persons is excluded from the numerator but is included in the denominator.

In calculating the *internal support test*, only the gross investment income of $15,000 is included in the numerator. Thus, the test is satisfied ($15,000/$100,000 = 15%; cannot > 33%) for the taxable year.

Since Lion did not satisfy both tests, it does not qualify as an organization that is broadly supported. ■

The intent of the two tests is to exclude from private foundation status those § 501(c)(3) organizations that are responsive to the general public rather than to the private interests of a limited number of donors or other persons.

Examples of § 501(c)(3) organizations that would be classified as private foundations, except that they receive broad public support, include the United Fund, the Girl Scouts, university alumni associations, symphony orchestras, and the PTA.

## LO.5

Recognize the taxes imposed on private foundations and calculate the related initial tax and additional tax amounts.

## TAXES IMPOSED ON PRIVATE FOUNDATIONS

In general, a private foundation is exempt from Federal income tax. However, because a private foundation is usually not a broadly, publicly supported organization, it may be subject to the following taxes.[26]

- Tax based on investment income.
- Tax on self-dealing.
- Tax on failure to distribute income.
- Tax on excess business holdings.
- Tax on investments that jeopardize charitable purposes.
- Tax on taxable expenditures.

These taxes restrict the permitted activities of private foundations. Two levels of tax may be imposed on the private foundation and the foundation manager: an initial tax and an additional tax. The initial taxes (first-level), with the exception of the tax based on investment income, are imposed because the private foundation engages in so-called *prohibited transactions*. The additional taxes (second-level) are imposed only if the prohibited transactions are not corrected within a statutory time period.[27] See Concept Summary 14–3 for additional details.

The tax on a failure to distribute income will be used to illustrate how expensive these taxes can be and the related importance of avoiding their imposition. Both an initial (first-level) tax and an additional (second-level) tax may be imposed on

---

[26]§§ 4940–4945.    [27]§ 4961.

## CONCEPT SUMMARY 14–3

### Taxes Imposed on Private Foundations

| Type of Tax | Code Section | Purpose | Private Foundation | | Foundation Manager | |
|---|---|---|---|---|---|---|
| | | | Initial Tax | Additional Tax | Initial Tax | Additional Tax |
| On investment income | § 4940 | Audit fee to defray IRS expenses. | 2%* | | | |
| On self-dealing | § 4941 | Engaging in transactions with disqualified persons. | 5%** | 200%** | 2.5%† | 50%† |
| On failure to distribute income | § 4942 | Failing to distribute adequate amount of income for exempt purposes. | 15% | 100% | | |
| On excess business holdings | § 4943 | Investments that enable the private foundation to control unrelated businesses. | 5% | 200% | | |
| On jeopardizing investments | § 4944 | Speculative investments that put the private foundation's assets at risk. | 5% | 25% | 5%†† | 5%† |
| On taxable expenditures | § 4945 | Expenditures that should not be made by private foundations. | 10% | 100% | 2.5%†† | 50%† |

  * May be possible to reduce the tax rate to 1%. In addition, an exempt operating foundation [see §§ 4940(d)(2) and 4942(j)(3)] is not subject to the tax.
 ** Imposed on the disqualified person rather than the foundation.
  † Subject to a statutory ceiling of $10,000.
 †† Subject to a statutory ceiling of $5,000.

a private nonoperating foundation for failure to distribute a sufficient portion of its income. The initial tax is imposed at a rate of 15 percent on the undistributed income for the taxable year that is not distributed by the end of the following taxable year. The initial tax is imposed on such undistributed income for each year until the IRS assesses the tax.

The additional tax is imposed at a rate of 100 percent on the amount of the inadequate distribution that is not distributed by the assessment date. The additional tax is effectively waived if the undistributed income is distributed within 90 days after the mailing of the deficiency notice for the additional tax. Extensions of this period may be obtained.

*Undistributed income* is the excess of the distributable amount (in effect, the amount that should have been distributed) over qualifying distributions made by the entity. The distributable amount is the excess of the minimum investment return over the sum of (1) the unrelated business income tax and (2) the excise tax based on net investment income.[28] The minimum investment return is 5 percent of the excess of the fair market value of the foundation's assets over the unpaid debt associated with acquiring or improving these assets. The foundation's assets

---

[28]§ 4940.

employed directly in carrying on the foundation's exempt purpose are not used in making this calculation.

**EXAMPLE 3**

Gold, Inc., a private foundation, has undistributed income of $80,000 for the taxable year 2000. It distributes $15,000 of this amount during 2001 and an additional $45,000 during 2002. An IRS deficiency notice is mailed to Gold on August 5, 2003. The initial tax is $12,750 [($65,000 × 15%) + ($20,000 × 15%)].

At the date of the deficiency notice, no additional distributions have been made from the 2000 undistributed income. Therefore, since the remaining undistributed income of $20,000 has not been distributed by August 5, 2003, an additional tax of $20,000 ($20,000 × 100%) is imposed.

If Gold distributes the $20,000 of undistributed income for 2000 within 90 days of the deficiency notice, the additional tax is waived. Without this distribution, however, the foundation will owe $32,750 in taxes. ■

**LO.6**

Determine when an exempt organization is subject to the unrelated business income tax and calculate the amount of the tax.

# Unrelated Business Income Tax

As explained in the previous section, private foundations are subject to excise taxes for certain actions. One of these excise taxes penalizes the private foundation for using the foundation to gain control of unrelated businesses (tax on excess business holdings). However, *unrelated business* has different meanings for purposes of that excise tax and for the unrelated business income tax.

The **unrelated business income tax (UBIT)** is designed to treat the entity as if it were subject to the corporate income tax. Thus, the rates that are used are those applicable to a corporate taxpayer.[29] In general, **unrelated business income** is derived from activities not related to the exempt purpose of the exempt organization. The tax is levied because the organization is engaging in substantial commercial activities.[30] Without such a tax, nonexempt organizations (regular taxable business entities) would be at a substantial disadvantage when trying to compete with the exempt organization. Thus, the UBIT is intended to neutralize the exempt entity's tax advantage.[31]

**EXAMPLE 4**

Historic, Inc., is an exempt private foundation. Its exempt activity is to maintain a restoration of eighteenth-century colonial life (houses, public buildings, taverns, businesses, and craft demonstrations) that is visited by more than a million people each year. A fee is charged for admission to the "restored area." In addition to this "museum" activity, Historic operates two hotels and three restaurants that are available to the general public. The earnings from the hotel and restaurant business are used to defray the costs of operating the "museum" activity.

The "museum" activity is not subject to the Federal income tax, except to the extent of any tax liability for any of the aforementioned excise taxes that are levied on private foundations. However, even though the income from the hotel and restaurant business is used for exempt purposes, that income is unrelated business income and is subject to the UBIT. ■

The UBIT applies to all organizations that are exempt from Federal income tax under § 501(c), except Federal agencies. In addition, the tax applies to state colleges and universities.[32]

---

[29]§ 511(a)(1).
[30]§ 512(a)(1).

[31]Reg. § 1.513–1(b).
[32]§ 511(a)(2) and Reg. § 1.511–2(a)(2).

A materiality exception generally exempts an entity from being subject to the UBIT if such income is insignificant. See the later discussion of the $1,000 statutory deduction generally available to all exempt organizations.

---

| **ETHICAL CONSIDERATIONS** | **Unfair Competition: Exempt Entity versus Taxable Entity** |
| --- | --- |

Ted has operated a travel agency as an S corporation for nearly 20 years. Over the past two years, he has noticed a decline in the volume of his business, especially in overseas tours.

In a conversation with a former client, Rob, at a college football game, Ted learns that Rob is scheduled to take a tour to Israel that his church is sponsoring. Rob also mentions that during the past summer, he went on a tour to the United Kingdom that was sponsored by his college alumni society.

Ted is perplexed as to how he can compete with these tax-exempt organizations for the overseas tour business. He is aware that such organizations generally are not subject to Federal income tax while his travel agency must pay Federal income tax.

Evaluate the equity of the tax treatment of these tax-exempt organizations versus that of Ted's travel agency.

---

## UNRELATED TRADE OR BUSINESS

An exempt organization may be subject to the UBIT in the following circumstances.[33]

- The organization conducts a trade or business.
- The trade or business is not substantially related to the exempt purpose of the organization.
- The trade or business is regularly carried on by the organization.

The Code specifically exempts the following activities from classification as an unrelated trade or business. Thus, even if all of the above factors are present, the activity is not classified as an unrelated trade or business.

- The individuals performing substantially all the work of the trade or business do so without compensation (e.g., an orphanage operates a retail store for sales to the general public, and all the work is done by volunteers).
- The trade or business consists of selling merchandise, and substantially all of the merchandise has been received as gifts or contributions (e.g., thrift shops).
- For § 501(c)(3) organizations and for state colleges or universities, the trade or business is conducted primarily for the convenience of the organization's members, students, patients, officers, or employees (e.g., a laundry operated by the college for laundering dormitory linens and students' clothing, a college bookstore).
- For most employee unions, the trade or business consists of selling to members, at their usual place of employment, work-related clothing and equipment and items normally sold through vending machines, snack bars, or food-dispensing facilities.

**Definition of Trade or Business.**   Trade or business, for this purpose, is broadly defined. It includes any activity conducted for the production of income

---

[33]§ 513(a) and Reg. § 1.513–2(a).

through the sale of merchandise or the performance of services. An activity need not generate a profit to be treated as a trade or business. The activity may be part of a larger set of activities conducted by the organization, some of which may be related to the exempt purpose. Being included in a larger set does not cause the activity to lose its identity as an unrelated trade or business.[34]

**EXAMPLE 5**

Health, Inc., is an exempt hospital that operates a pharmacy. The pharmacy provides medicines and supplies to the patients in the hospital (i.e., it contributes to the conduct of the hospital's exempt purpose). In addition, the pharmacy sells medicines and supplies to the general public. The activity of selling to the general public constitutes a trade or business for purposes of the UBIT. ∎

**Not Substantially Related to the Exempt Purpose.** Exempt organizations frequently conduct unrelated trades or businesses to provide income to help defray the costs of conducting the exempt purpose (like the hotel and restaurant business in Example 4). Providing financial support for the exempt purpose will not prevent an activity from being classified as an unrelated trade or business and thereby being subject to the UBIT.

To be related to the accomplishment of the exempt purpose, the conduct of the business activities must be causally related and contribute importantly to the exempt purpose. Whether a causal relationship exists and the degree of its importance are determined by examining the facts and circumstances. One must consider the size and extent of the activities in relation to the nature and extent of the exempt function that the activities serve.[35]

**EXAMPLE 6**

Art, Inc., an exempt organization, operates a school for training children in the performing arts. As an essential part of that training, the children perform for the general public. The children are paid at the minimum wage for the performances, and Art derives gross income by charging admission to the performances.

The income from admissions is not income from an unrelated trade or business, because the performances by the children contribute importantly to the accomplishment of the exempt purpose of providing training in the performing arts. ∎

**EXAMPLE 7**

Assume the facts are the same as in Example 6, except that four performances are conducted each weekend of the year. Assume that this number of performances far exceeds that required for training the children. Thus, the part of the income derived from admissions for these excess performances is income from an unrelated trade or business. ∎

The trade or business may sell merchandise that has been produced as part of the accomplishment of the exempt purpose. The sale of such merchandise is normally treated as related to the exempt purpose. However, if the merchandise is not sold in substantially the same state it was in at the completion of the exempt purpose, the gross income subsequently derived from the sale of the merchandise is income from an unrelated trade or business.[36]

**EXAMPLE 8**

Help-Self, Inc., an exempt organization, conducts programs for the rehabilitation of the handicapped. One of the programs includes training in radio and television repair. Help-Self

---

[34]Reg. § 1.513–1(b).
[35]Reg. § 1.513–1(d).

[36]Reg. § 1.513–1(d)(4)(ii).

derives gross income by selling the repaired items. The income is substantially related to the accomplishment of the exempt purpose. ■

An asset or facility used in the exempt purpose may also be used in a nonexempt purpose. Income derived from use for a nonexempt purpose is income from an unrelated trade or business.[37]

**EXAMPLE 9**

Civil, Inc., an exempt organization, operates a museum. As part of the exempt purpose of the museum, educational lectures are given in the museum's theater during the operating hours of the museum. In the evening, when the museum is closed, the theater is leased to an individual who operates a movie theater. The lease income received from the individual who operates the movie theater is income from an unrelated trade or business. ■

**Special Rule for Corporate Sponsorship Payments.** The term *unrelated trade or business* does not include the soliciting and receiving of qualified sponsorship payments.[38]

A payment qualifies as a qualified sponsorship payment if it meets the following requirements.

- There is no arrangement or expectation that the trade or business making the payment will receive any substantial benefit other than the use or acknowledgment of its name, logo, or product lines in connection with the activities of the exempt organization.
- Such use or acknowledgment does not include advertising the payor's products or services.
- The payment does not include any payment for which the amount is contingent upon the level of attendance at one or more events, broadcast ratings, or other factors indicating the degree of public exposure to one or more events.

**EXAMPLE 10**

Pets, Inc., a manufacturer of cat food, contributes $25,000 to Feline Care, Inc., an exempt organization that cares for abandoned cats. In return for the contribution, Feline agrees to put Pets' corporate logo in its monthly newsletter to donors. Under these circumstances, the $25,000 payment is a qualified sponsorship payment and is not subject to the UBIT. ■

**EXAMPLE 11**

Assume the same facts as in Example 10, except that Feline agrees to endorse Pets' cat food in its monthly newsletter by stating that it feeds only Pets' cat food to its cats. The $25,000 is not a qualified sponsorship payment and is subject to the UBIT. ■

**Special Rule for Bingo Games.** A special provision applies in determining whether income from bingo games is from an unrelated trade or business. Under this provision, a *qualified bingo game* is not an unrelated trade or business if both of the following requirements are satisfied.[39]

- The bingo game is legal under both state and local law.
- Commercial bingo games (conducted for a profit motive) ordinarily are not permitted in the jurisdiction.

**EXAMPLE 12**

Play, Inc., an exempt organization, conducts weekly bingo games. The laws of the state and municipality in which Play conducts the games expressly provide that exempt organizations may conduct bingo games, but do not permit profit-oriented entities to do so. Since both

---

[37]Reg. § 1.513–1(d)(4)(iii) addresses the allocation of expenses to exempt and nonexempt activities.

[38]§ 513(i).
[39]§ 513(f).

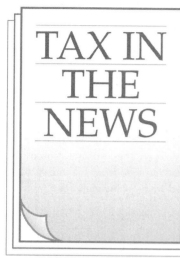

## GAMBLING: GOING BEYOND BINGO

The revenue generated by the unrelated business income tax (UBIT) is increasing for two reasons: tax-exempt organizations are expanding their unrelated business activities, and the IRS is stepping up its scrutiny in this area. Illustrative of the latter are the IRS regulations on travel tours sponsored by tax-exempt organizations.

The Code clearly defines when bingo games sponsored by tax-exempts are not subject to the UBIT. The treatment for other gambling activities sponsored by tax-exempts comes under the general UBIT rules, however, rather than under the special rules for bingo games. Therefore, unless the gambling activity (e.g., a casino night) is conducted by volunteers, the sponsoring tax-exempt entity can expect to encounter the UBIT. More IRS audits are expected in 2003 and subsequent years in this area.

of the requirements for bingo games are satisfied, the bingo games conducted by Play are not an unrelated trade or business. ∎

**EXAMPLE 13**

Game, Inc., an exempt organization, conducts weekly bingo games in City X and City Y. State law expressly permits exempt organizations to conduct bingo games. State law also provides that profit-oriented entities may conduct bingo games in X, which is a resort community. Several businesses regularly conduct bingo games there.

The bingo games conducted by Game in Y are not an unrelated trade or business. However, the bingo games that Game conducts in X are an unrelated trade or business, because commercial bingo games are regularly permitted to be conducted there. ∎

**Special Rule for Distribution of Low-Cost Articles.**   If an exempt organization distributes low-cost items as an incidental part of its solicitation for charitable contributions, the distributions may not be considered an unrelated trade or business. A low-cost article is one that costs $8.00 for 2003 (indexed annually) or less. Examples of such items are pens, stamps, stickers, stationery, and address labels. If more than one item is distributed to a person during the calendar year, the costs of the items are combined.[40]

**Special Rule for Rental or Exchange of Membership Lists.**   If an exempt organization conducts a trade or business that consists of either exchanging with or renting to other exempt organizations the organization's donor or membership list (mailing lists), the activity is not an unrelated trade or business.[41]

**Other Special Rules.**   Other special rules are used in determining whether each of the following activities is an unrelated trade or business.[42]

* Qualified public entertainment activities (e.g., a state fair).
* Qualified convention and trade show activities.
* Certain services provided at cost or less by a hospital to other small hospitals.
* Certain pole rentals by telephone or electric companies.

[40]§ 513(h)(1)(A).
[41]§ 513(h)(1)(B).

[42]§§ 513(d), (e), and (g).

■ **FIGURE 14–2**

Tax Formula for Unrelated
Business Taxable Income

| |
| --- |
| Gross unrelated business income |
| − Deductions |
| = Net unrelated business income |
| ± Modifications |
| = Unrelated business taxable income |

## UNRELATED BUSINESS INCOME

Even when an exempt organization conducts an unrelated trade or business, a tax is assessed only if the exempt organization regularly conducts the activity and the business produces unrelated business income.

**Regularly Carried on by the Organization.** An activity is classified as unrelated business income only if it is regularly carried on by the exempt organization. This provision assures that only activities that are actually competing with taxable organizations are subject to the unrelated business income tax. Accordingly, factors to be considered in applying the *regularly carried on* test include the frequency of the activity, the continuity of the activity, and the manner in which the activity is pursued.[43]

**EXAMPLE 14**

Silver, Inc., an exempt organization, owns land that is located next to the state fairgrounds. During the 10 days of the state fair, Silver uses the land as a parking lot and charges individuals attending the state fair for parking there. The activity is not regularly carried on. ■

**EXAMPLE 15**

Black, Inc., an exempt organization, has its offices in the downtown area. It owns a parking lot adjacent to its offices on which its employees park during the week. On Saturdays, it rents the spaces in the parking lot to individuals shopping or working in the downtown area. Black is conducting a business activity on a year-round basis, even though it is only for one day per week. Thus, an activity is regularly being carried on. ■

**Unrelated Business Income Defined.** Unrelated business income is generally that derived from the unrelated trade or business, reduced by the deductions directly connected with the conduct of the unrelated trade or business.[44]

## UNRELATED BUSINESS TAXABLE INCOME

**General Tax Model.** The model for unrelated business taxable income (UBTI) appears in Figure 14–2.

*Positive adjustments*[45]

1. A charitable contribution deduction is permitted without regard to whether the charitable contributions are associated with the unrelated trade or business. However, to the extent the charitable contributions deducted in calculating net unrelated business income (see Figure 14–2) exceed 10 percent of UBTI (without regard to the charitable contribution deduction), the excess is treated as a positive adjustment.

---

[43]§ 512(a)(1) and Reg. § 1.513–1(c).
[44]§ 512(a)(1).

[45]§§ 512(a)(1) and (b) and Reg. § 1.512(b)–1.

**EXAMPLE 16**

Brown, Inc., an exempt organization, has UBTI of $100,000 (excluding any modifications associated with charitable contributions). Total charitable contributions (all associated with the unrelated trade or business) are $13,000. Assuming that the $13,000 is deducted in calculating net unrelated business income, the excess of $3,000 [$13,000 − 10%($100,000)] is a positive adjustment in calculating UBTI. ∎

2. Unrelated debt-financed income net of the unrelated debt-financed deductions (see the subsequent discussion of Unrelated Debt-Financed Income).
3. Certain net interest, annuity, royalty, and rent income received by the exempt organization from an organization it controls (80 percent test). This provision overrides the modifications for these types of income (negative adjustment 3).

*Negative adjustments*

1. Income from dividends, interest, and annuities net of all deductions directly related to producing such income.
2. Royalty income, regardless of whether it is measured by production, gross income, or taxable income from the property, net of all deductions directly related to producing such income.
3. Rent income from real property and from certain personal property net of all deductions directly related to producing such income. Personal property rents are included in the negative adjustment only if the personal property is leased with the real property. In addition, the personal property rent income must be incidental (does not exceed 10 percent of the gross rent income under the lease) to be used in computing the negative adjustment. In both of the following cases, however, none of the rent income is treated as a negative adjustment.
   * More than 50 percent of the rent income under the lease is from personal property.
   * Rent income is calculated using the tenant's profits.

**EXAMPLE 17**

Beaver, Inc., an exempt organization, leases land and a building (realty) and computers (personalty) housed in the building. Under the lease, $46,000 of the rent is for the land and building, and $4,000 is for the computers. Expenses incurred for the land and building are $10,000. The net rent income from the land and building of $36,000 ($46,000 − $10,000) and the income from the computers of $4,000 are negative adjustments. ∎

**EXAMPLE 18**

Assume the same facts as in Example 17, except that the rent income is $35,000 from the land and building and $15,000 from the computers. Since the rent income from the computers exceeds $5,000 (10% × $50,000) and is not incidental, it is not a negative adjustment. ∎

**EXAMPLE 19**

Assume the same facts as in Example 17, except that the rent income is $20,000 from the land and building and $30,000 from the computers. Since more than 50% of the rent income under the lease is from the computers, neither the rent income from the land and building nor that from the computers is a negative adjustment. ∎

If the lessor of real property provides significant services to the lessee, such income, for this purpose, is not rent income.
4. Gains and losses from the sale, exchange, or other disposition of property *except for* inventory.

**EXAMPLE 20**

Beaver, the owner of the land, building, and computers in Example 17, sells these assets for $450,000. Their adjusted basis is $300,000. Beaver's recognized gain of $150,000 is a negative adjustment. ■

5. Certain research income net of all deductions directly related to producing that income.
6. The charitable contribution deduction is permitted without regard to whether the charitable contributions are associated with the unrelated trade or business. Therefore, to the extent that the charitable contributions exceed those deducted in calculating net unrelated business income (see Figure 14–2), the excess is a negative adjustment in calculating UBTI. In making this calculation, be aware that the 10 percent of UBTI (without regard to the charitable contribution deduction) limit still applies (see positive adjustment 1).

**EXAMPLE 21**

Canine, Inc., an exempt organization, has unrelated business taxable income of $100,000 (excluding any modifications associated with charitable contributions). The total charitable contributions are $9,000, of which $7,000 (those associated with the unrelated trade or business) has been deducted in calculating net unrelated business income. Therefore, the remaining $2,000 of charitable contributions is a negative adjustment in calculating UBTI. ■

7. A specific deduction of $1,000 is permitted.

**EXAMPLE 22**

Petit Care, Inc., an exempt organization, has net unrelated business income of $800. Since Petit will receive a specific deduction of $1,000, its UBTI is $0. Therefore, its income tax liability is $0. ■

After UBTI is determined, that amount is subject to tax using the regular corporate tax rates.

**EXAMPLE 23**

Patient, Inc., an exempt organization, has UBTI of $500,000. Patient's income tax liability is $170,000 ($500,000 UBTI × 34% corporate tax rate). ■

## UNRELATED DEBT-FINANCED INCOME

In the formula for calculating the tax on unrelated business income (see Figure 14–2), unrelated debt-financed income is one of the positive adjustments. Examples of income from debt-financed property include rent income from real estate or tangible personal property, dividends from corporate stock, and gains from the disposition of debt-financed property. Gains from unrelated business income property are also included to the extent the gains are not otherwise treated as unrelated business income.

In terms of the UBIT, the positive adjustment for unrelated debt-financed income is a significant one. Without this provision, a tax-exempt organization could use borrowed funds to acquire unrelated business or investment property and use the untaxed (i.e., exempt) earnings from the acquisition to pay for the property.

**Definition of Debt-Financed Income.** **Debt-financed income** is the gross income generated from debt-financed property. *Debt-financed property* is all property of the exempt organization that is held to produce income and on which there is acquisition indebtedness, *except* for the following.[46]

---

[46]§ 514(b).

- Property where substantially all (at least 85 percent) of the use is for the achievement of the exempt purpose of the exempt organization.[47]
- Property whose gross income is otherwise treated as unrelated business income.
- Property whose gross income is from the following sources and is not otherwise treated as unrelated business income.
  - Income from research performed for the United States or a Federal governmental agency, or a state or a political subdivision thereof.
  - For a college, university, or hospital, income from research.
  - For an organization that performs fundamental (i.e., not applied) research for the benefit of the general public, income from research.
- Property used in an activity that is not an unrelated trade or business.

If the 85 percent test is not satisfied, only the portion of the property that is *not* used for the exempt purpose is debt-financed property.

**EXAMPLE 24**   Deer, Inc., an exempt organization, owns a five-story office building on which there is acquisition indebtedness. Three of the floors are used for Deer's exempt purpose. The two other floors are leased to Purple Corporation. In this case, the *substantially all* test is not satisfied. Therefore, 40% of the office building is debt-financed property, and 60% is not. ■

Certain land that is acquired by an exempt organization for later exempt use is excluded from debt-financed property if the following requirements are satisfied.[48]

- The principal purpose of acquiring the land is for use (substantially all) in achieving the organization's exempt purpose.
- This use will begin within 10 years of the acquisition date.
- At the date when the land is acquired, it is located in the *neighborhood* of other property of the organization for which substantially all the use is for achieving the organization's exempt purpose.

Even if the third requirement is not satisfied, the land still is excluded from debt-financed property if it is converted to use for achieving the organization's exempt purpose within the 10-year period. Qualification under this provision will result in a refund of taxes previously paid. If the exempt organization is a church, the 10-year period becomes a 15-year period, and the neighborhood requirement is waived.

**Definition of Acquisition Indebtedness.**   Acquisition indebtedness is debt sustained by the exempt organization in association with the acquisition of property. More precisely, *acquisition indebtedness* consists of the unpaid amounts of the following for debt-financed property.[49]

- Debt incurred in acquiring or improving the property.
- Debt incurred before the property was acquired or improved, but which would not have been incurred without the acquisition or improvement.
- Debt incurred after the property was acquired or improved, but which would not have been incurred without the acquisition or improvement.

---

[47]Reg. § 1.514(b)–1(b)(1)(ii).
[48]§ 514(b)(3).
[49]§ 514(c)(1). Educational organizations can exclude certain debt incurred for real property acquisitions from classification as acquisition indebtedness.

**EXAMPLE 25**

Red, Inc., an exempt organization, acquires land for $100,000. To finance the acquisition, Red mortgages the land and receives loan proceeds of $80,000. Red leases the land to Duck Corporation. The mortgage is acquisition indebtedness. ■

**EXAMPLE 26**

Rose, Inc., an exempt organization, makes improvements to an office building that it rents to Bird Corporation. Excess working capital funds are used to finance the improvements. Rose is later required to mortgage its laboratory building, which it uses for its exempt purpose, to replenish working capital. The mortgage is acquisition indebtedness. ■

**Portion of Debt-Financed Income and Deductions Treated as Unrelated Business Taxable Income.** Once the amount of the debt-financed income and deductions is determined, one must ascertain what portion thereof constitutes unrelated debt-financed income and deductions. Unrelated debt-financed income increases unrelated business taxable income, and unrelated debt-financed deductions decrease unrelated business taxable income.

The calculation is made for each debt-financed asset. The gross income from the property is multiplied by the following percentage.[50]

$$\frac{\text{Average acquisition indebtedness for the property}}{\text{Average adjusted basis of the property}} = \text{Debt/basis percentage}$$

This percentage cannot exceed 100. If debt-financed property is disposed of during the taxable year at a gain, average acquisition indebtedness in the formula is replaced with highest acquisition indebtedness. *Highest acquisition indebtedness* is the largest amount of acquisition indebtedness for the property during the 12-month period preceding the date of disposition.[51]

Deductions are allowed for expenses directly related to the debt-financed property and the income from it. Cost recovery deductions must apply the straight-line method. Once allowable deductions are determined, this amount is multiplied by the debt/basis percentage.[52]

**EXAMPLE 27**

White, Inc., an exempt organization, owns an office building that it leases to Squirrel Corporation for $120,000 per year. The average acquisition indebtedness is $300,000, and the average adjusted basis is $500,000. Since the office building is debt-financed property, the gross unrelated debt-financed income is:

$$\frac{\$300,000}{\$500,000} \times \$120,000 = \$72,000.$$

If White's expenses associated with the office building lease (including straight-line cost recovery) equal $50,000, then allowable deductions are:

$$\frac{\$300,000}{\$500,000} \times \$50,000 = \$30,000.$$

Thus, White's net unrelated debt-financed income is $42,000 ($72,000 − $30,000). ■

**Average Acquisition Indebtedness.** The *average acquisition indebtedness* for debt-financed property is the average amount of the outstanding debt for the taxable year (ignoring interest) during the portion of the year the property is held by the exempt organization. This amount is calculated by summing the outstanding debt on the first day of each calendar month the property is held by the exempt

---

[50]§ 514(a)(1).
[51]§ 514(c)(7).

[52]§ 514(a)(3).

organization. Then this total is divided by the number of months the property is held by the organization.[53]

**EXAMPLE 28**

On August 12, Yellow, Inc., an exempt organization, acquires an office building that is debt-financed property for $500,000. The initial mortgage on the property is $400,000. The principal amount of the debt on August 12 and on the first of each subsequent month is as follows.

| Month | Principal Amount |
| --- | --- |
| August 12 | $  400,000 |
| September 1 | 380,000 |
| October 1 | 360,000 |
| November 1 | 340,000 |
| December 1 | 320,000 |
| Total | $1,800,000 |

Average acquisition indebtedness is $360,000 ($1,800,000 ÷ 5 months). August is treated as a full month. ■

**Average Adjusted Basis.**   The *average adjusted basis* of debt-financed property is calculated by summing the adjusted bases of the property on the first and last days during the taxable year the property is held by the exempt organization and then dividing by two.[54]

**EXAMPLE 29**

Assume the facts are the same as in Example 28. In addition, during the taxable year, depreciation of $5,900 is deducted. The average adjusted basis is $497,050 [($500,000 + $494,100) ÷ 2]. ■

Concept Summary 14–4 presents the rules concerning the UBIT.

---

**LO.7**

List the reports exempt organizations must file with the IRS and the related due dates.

# Reporting Requirements

## OBTAINING EXEMPT ORGANIZATION STATUS

Not all exempt organizations are required to obtain IRS approval for their exempt status. Among those required by statute to do so are organizations exempt under §§ 501(c)(3), 501(c)(9), and 501(c)(20).[55] Even in these cases, exceptions are provided (e.g., churches).

Even when not required to obtain IRS approval, most exempt organizations do apply for exempt status. Typically, an organization does not want to assume that it qualifies for exempt status and describe itself in that way to the public, only to have the IRS rule later that it does not qualify. Organizations exempt under § 501(c)(3) use Form 1023 [Application for Recognition of Exemption under Section 501(c)(3)]. Form 1024 [Application for Recognition of Exemption under Section 501(a)] is used by most other types of exempt organizations.

If an organization is required to obtain IRS approval for its exempt status and does not do so, it does not qualify as an exempt organization.

---

[53]§ 514(c)(7) and Reg. § 1.514(a)–1(a)(3). A partial month is treated as a full month.

[54]§ 514(a)(1) and Reg. § 1.514(a)–1(a)(2).
[55]§§ 505(c), 508(a), and 508(c).

## CONCEPT SUMMARY 14–4

### Unrelated Business Income Tax

| | |
|---|---|
| Purpose | To tax the entity on unrelated business income as if it were subject to the corporate income tax. |
| Applicable tax rates | Corporate tax rates. |
| Exempt organizations to which applicable | All organizations exempt under § 501(c), except Federal agencies. |
| Entities subject to the tax | The organization conducts a trade or business; the trade or business is not substantially related to the exempt purpose of the organization; and the trade or business is regularly carried on by the organization. |
| Exceptions to the tax | • All the work is performed by volunteers. |
| | • Substantially all of the merchandise being sold has been received by gift. |
| | • For § 501(c)(3) organizations, the business is conducted primarily for the benefit of the organization's members, students, patients, officers, or employees. |
| | • For most employee unions, the trade or business consists of selling to members work-related clothing and equipment and items normally sold through vending machines, snack bars, or food-dispensing facilities. |
| $1,000 provision | If the gross income from an unrelated trade or business is less than $1,000, it is not necessary to file a return associated with the unrelated business income tax. |

---

**ETHICAL CONSIDERATIONS**　　**Tax-Exempt Bingo**

---

Assist, Inc., is a § 501(c)(3) exempt organization. Its mission is to help feed and clothe the homeless. Assist does this through providing a shelter, clothes closet, and soup kitchen for the homeless in the inner city.

Donations (i.e., both cash and property) are the principal source of Assist's revenue. Contributions result from mailings and from help kettles located outside area supermarkets. In addition, Assist sponsors bingo games on Friday and Saturday evenings. Approximately 30 percent of Assist's revenue comes from the bingo games.

You are a new member of Assist's board of directors. You are an employee (recently promoted to manager) of an accounting firm, and you specialize in the financial services industry. Over lunch with one of your firm's partners (your unofficial mentor), you mention your service on Assist's board of directors. She provides you with information on the usual Federal income tax reporting requirements of exempt organizations [i.e., Form 1023: Application for Recognition of Exemption under Section 501(a); Form 990: Return of Organization Exempt from Income Tax, or Form 990–PF: Return of Private Foundation; and Form 990–T: Exempt Organization Business Income Tax Return].

You later ask Al Marin, Assist's foundation manager, who was the driving force behind the creation of Assist 15 years ago, for copies of these forms. He provides you with a copy of Form 1023 and a copy of Form 990–PF for the past three years. He says the CPA who served on the board prior to you told him that it was not necessary for Assist to file any Federal tax returns associated with the bingo games because Assist is tax-exempt. Therefore, no disclosures regarding the bingo games are made on any of these forms.

You are aware that bingo games are illegal in your state. You are also aware that many tax-exempt organizations in your city and in other locales in the state conduct bingo games. The police "look the other way" as long as the sponsor is a tax-exempt organization. In fact, several local churches are Assist's biggest bingo game competitors. How should you respond?

## ANNUAL FILING REQUIREMENTS

Most exempt organizations are required to file an annual information return.[56] The return is filed on Form 990 (Return of Organization Exempt from Income Tax). The following exempt organizations need not file Form 990.[57]

* Federal agencies.
* Churches.
* Organizations whose annual gross receipts do not exceed $25,000.
* Private foundations.

Private foundations are required to file Form 990–PF (Return of Private Foundation). Form 990–PF requires more information than Form 990.

The due date for Form 990 or Form 990–PF is the fifteenth day of the fifth month after the end of the taxable year. These returns are filed with the appropriate IRS Service Center based on the location of the exempt organization's principal office. Requests for extensions on filing are made by filing Form 2758 (Applications for Extension of Time).

**EXAMPLE 30**

Green, Inc., a § 501(c)(3) organization, has a fiscal year that ends June 30, 2003. The due date for the annual return is November 15, 2003. If Green were a calendar year entity, the due date for the 2003 annual return would be May 15, 2004. ∎

Exempt organizations that are subject to the UBIT may be required to file Form 990–T (Exempt Organization Business Income Tax Return). The return must be filed if the organization has gross income of at least $1,000 from an unrelated trade or business. The due date for the return is the fifteenth day of the fifth month after the end of the taxable year.

If an exempt organization is subject to any of the excise taxes imposed on private foundations, Form 4720 (Return of Certain Excise Taxes on Charities and Other Persons) must be filed. The return is filed with the private foundation's Form 990–PF.

**EXAMPLE 31**

During the year, the First Church of Kentwood receives parishioner contributions of $450,000. Of this amount, $125,000 is designated for the church building fund. First Church is not required to file an annual return (Form 990) because churches are exempt from doing so. In addition, it is not required to file Form 990–T because it has no unrelated business income.

Colonial, Inc., is an exempt private foundation. Gross receipts for the year total $800,000, of which 40% is from admission fees paid by members of the general public who visit Colonial's museum of eighteenth-century life. The balance is endowment income and contributions from the founding donor. Because Colonial is a private foundation, it must file Form 990–PF.

Orange, Inc., is an exempt organization and is not a private foundation. Gross receipts for the year are $20,000. None of this amount is unrelated business income. Orange is not required to file Form 990 because its annual gross receipts do not exceed $25,000.

Restoration, Inc., is an exempt private foundation. Gross receipts for the year are $20,000. None of this amount is unrelated business income. Restoration must file Form 990–PF because private foundations are not eligible for the $25,000 filing exception.

During the year, the Second Church of Port Allen receives parishioner contributions of $300,000. In addition, the church has unrelated business income of $5,000. Second Church is not required to file Form 990 because churches are exempt from doing so. Form 990–T

---

[56]§ 6033(a)(1).

[57]§ 6033(a)(2).

must be filed, however, because churches are not exempt from the UBIT and Second Church has exceeded the $1,000 floor. ■

## DISCLOSURE REQUIREMENTS

As a result of new consumer-friendly rules, exempt entities must make more information readily available to the general public.[58] Prior to the issuance of these rules, the disclosure requirements could be satisfied by making the information available for public inspection during regular business hours at the principal office of the exempt entity.

Copies of the following now must be made available to the general public.

- Form 990.
- Form 1023 (or Form 1024).

Copies of the three most recent returns of the Form 990 must be made available.

If an individual requests a copy in person, the exempt entity must provide a copy immediately. If the request is received in writing or by e-mail or fax, the copy must be provided within 30 days. The copy must be provided without charge, except for a reasonable fee for reproduction and mailing costs.

If the exempt entity has made the forms widely available to the general public, it is not required to fill individual requests. One technique for making the forms widely available is to put them on the Internet. Individual requests can also be disregarded if the exempt entity can show the request is part of a harassment campaign.

Private foundations must make Form 990–PF available for public inspection. The effective date for the disclosure requirements for private foundations is after March 12, 2000.[59]

<table>
<tr><td>LO.8

Identify tax planning opportunities for exempt organizations.</td></tr>
</table>

**Tax Planning Considerations**

## GENERAL

Exempt organizations provide at least two potential tax benefits. First, the entity may be exempt from Federal income tax. Second, contributions to the entity may be deductible by the donor.

An organization that qualifies as an exempt organization may still be subject to certain types of Federal income tax, including the following.

- Tax on prohibited transactions.
- Tax on feeder organizations.
- Tax on private foundations.
- Tax on unrelated business income.

Therefore, classification as an exempt organization should not be interpreted to mean that the organization need not be concerned with any Federal income tax. Such a belief can result in the organization engaging in transactions that produce a substantial tax liability.

An organization is exempt from taxation only if it fits into one of the categories enumerated in the Code. Thus, particular attention must be given to the qualification requirements. These requirements must continue to be satisfied to avoid termination of exempt status (in effect they are now maintenance requirements).

---

[58]§ 6104(d), Reg. § 301.6104(d), and T.D. 8818 (April 1999).
[59]An Internet source of Forms 990 and 990–PF and other relevant materials on exempt entities is **http://www.guidestar.com**.

## MAINTAINING EXEMPT STATUS

To maintain exempt status, the organization must satisfy both an organizational test and an operational test. The organizational test requires that the entity satisfy the statutory requirements for exempt status on paper. The operational test ensures that the entity does, in fact, satisfy the statutory requirements for exempt status.

*King Shipping Consum., Inc.* (Zion Coptic Church, Inc.) indicates that it is usually much easier to satisfy the organizational test than the operational test.[60] Zion's stated purpose was to engage in activities usually and normally associated with churches. Based on this, the IRS approved Zion's exempt status as a § 501(c)(3) organization.

Zion's real intent, however, was to smuggle illegal drugs into the country and to distribute them for profit. The church's justification for the drugs was that it used marijuana in its sacrament. During a four-month period, however, the police confiscated 33 tons of marijuana from church members. The IRS calculated that, even assuming the maximum alleged church membership of several thousand, each member would have had to smoke over 33 pounds of marijuana during the four-month confiscation period.

The court concluded that Zion's real purpose was to cloak a large commercial drug smuggling operation. Since this activity was inconsistent with the religious purpose for exempt status, the court upheld the IRS's revocation of Zion's exempt status and the deficiency assessment of approximately $1.6 million.

## PRIVATE FOUNDATION STATUS

Exempt organizations that can qualify as public charities receive more beneficial tax treatment than do those that qualify as private foundations. Thus, if possible, the organization should be structured to qualify as a public charity. The following can result when an exempt organization is classified as a private foundation.

- Taxes may be imposed on the private foundation.
  - Tax based on investment income.
  - Tax on self-dealing.
  - Tax on failure to distribute income.
  - Tax on excess business holdings.
  - Tax on investments that jeopardize charitable purposes.
  - Tax on taxable expenditures.
- Donors may receive less favorable tax deduction treatment under § 170 than they would if the exempt organization were not a private foundation.

**EXAMPLE 32**

David has undeveloped land ($25,000 adjusted basis, $100,000 fair market value) that he is going to contribute to one of the following exempt organizations: Blue, Inc., a public charity, or Teal, Inc., a private nonoperating foundation. David has owned the land for five years.

David asks the manager of each organization to describe the tax benefits of contributing to that organization. He tells them he is in the 35% tax bracket and his AGI exceeds $250,000.

Based on the data provided by the managers, David decides to contribute the land to Blue, Inc. He calculates the amount of the charitable contribution under each option as follows.[61]

---

[60]58 TCM 574, T.C.Memo. 1989–593.
[61]See Chapter 2 of this text and Chapter 10 in *West Federal Taxation: Individual Income Taxes*.

## CONCEPT SUMMARY 14–5

### Private Foundation Status

| | Exempt Organization Is | |
|---|---|---|
| | **A Private Foundation** | **Not a Private Foundation** |
| Reason for classification | Does not serve the common good because it lacks an approved exempt purpose or does not receive broad public financial support. | Serves the common good. |
| Eligible for exempt status? | Yes | Yes |
| Most beneficial charitable contribution deduction treatment available to donors? | Depends. No, if the private foundation is classified as a private *nonoperating* foundation. | Yes |
| Subject to excise taxes levied on prohibited transactions? | Yes | No |
| Subject to tax on unrelated business income? | Yes | Yes |

| Donee | Contribution Deduction | Tax Rate | Contribution Borne by U.S. Government |
|---|---|---|---|
| Blue | $100,000 | 35% | $35,000 |
| Teal | 25,000 ($100,000 − $75,000) | 35% | 8,750 |

One method of avoiding private foundation status is to have a tax-exempt purpose that results in the organization not being classified as a private foundation (the *organization* approach). If this is not feasible, it may be possible to operate the organization so that it receives broad public support and thereby avoids private foundation status (the *operational* approach).

If the organization is a private foundation, care must be exercised to avoid the assessment of a tax liability on prohibited transactions. This objective can best be achieved by establishing controls that prevent the private foundation from engaging in transactions that trigger the imposition of the taxes. If an initial tax is assessed, corrective actions should be implemented to avoid the assessment of an additional tax. See Concept Summary 14–5.

### UNRELATED BUSINESS INCOME TAX

If the exempt organization conducts an unrelated trade or business, it may be subject to tax on the unrelated business income. Worse yet, the unrelated trade or business could result in the loss of exempt status if the IRS determines that the activity is the primary purpose of the organization. Thus, caution and planning should be used to eliminate the latter possibility and to minimize the former.

One approach that can be used to avoid the imposition of the UBIT is to establish a taxable subsidiary to conduct the unrelated trade or business. With a subsidiary, the revenues and expenses of the exempt organization can be separated from those of the unrelated trade or business. When the subsidiary remits its after-tax profits to the exempt organization in the form of dividends, the dividends will not be taxable to the exempt organization. In addition, having a taxable subsidiary conduct the unrelated trade or business avoids the possibility that the IRS will consider the unrelated business income to be an excessive percentage of the total revenues of the exempt organization. Such a view can lead to the IRS questioning the exempt organization's right to retain its exempt status.

Another approach to avoiding the UBIT is to fail the definition of an unrelated trade or business. This is accomplished by *not* satisfying at least one of the following requirements.

- The organization conducts a trade or business.
- The trade or business is not substantially related to the exempt purpose of the organization.
- The trade or business is regularly carried on by the organization.

Even if the definitional requirements for an unrelated trade or business appear to be satisfied, the negative adjustments in calculating unrelated business taxable income (see Figure 14–2) can be used to minimize the tax liability.

Rental activities best illustrate the necessity of careful planning to avoid including the income from the activity in calculating unrelated business taxable income. The income from the rental of real property by an exempt organization is not part of unrelated business taxable income. However, leases must be drafted so as to preserve the negative adjustment and avoid the UBIT prevalent in the following circumstances.

- If personal property is leased with real property and more than 50 percent of the rent income under the lease is from personal property, all the rent income is included in calculating unrelated business taxable income.
- If rent income from real property is calculated completely, or in part, based on the profits of the lessee (unless the calculation is based on a fixed percentage of sales or receipts), the rent income is included in calculating unrelated business taxable income.
- If the lessor of real property provides significant services to the lessee, the income is not treated as rent income and thus is included in the computation of unrelated business taxable income.
- If the rent income is received from an organization that the exempt organization controls (80 percent), the income is included in calculating unrelated business taxable income.
- To the extent the rent income is classified as unrelated debt-financed income, it is included in calculating unrelated business taxable income.

## KEY TERMS

| | | |
|---|---|---|
| Debt-financed income, 14–21 | Grass roots expenditure, 14–7 | Unrelated business income, 14–14 |
| Excess lobbying expenditure, 14–7 | Intermediate sanctions, 14–8 | Unrelated business income tax (UBIT), 14–14 |
| Exempt organization, 14–2 | Lobbying expenditure, 14–7 | |
| Feeder organization, 14–9 | Private foundation, 14–10 | |

## PROBLEM MATERIALS

### Discussion Questions

1. A C corporation that conducts a business is subject to double taxation whereas a church is subject only to single taxation. Evaluate this statement.

2. Why are certain organizations either partially or completely exempt from Federal income tax?

3. Which of the following organizations qualify for exempt status?
   a. Tulane University.
   b. Virginia Qualified Tuition Program.
   c. Red Cross.
   d. Disneyland.
   e. Ford Foundation. *qualify*
   f. Jacksonville Chamber of Commerce.
   g. Colonial Williamsburg Foundation.
   h. Professional Golfers Association (PGA) Tour.
   i. Green Bay Packers.
   j. Cleveland Indians.

4. Identify the statutory authority under which each of the following is exempt from Federal income tax.
   a. Kingsmill Country Club.
   b. Shady Lawn Cemetery.
   c. Amber Credit Union.
   d. Veterans of Foreign Wars.
   e. Boy Scouts of America.
   f. United Fund.
   g. Federal Deposit Insurance Corporation.
   h. Bruton Parish Episcopal Church.
   i. PTA.
   j. National Press Club.

5. Adrenna is the treasurer for two exempt organizations. One exempt organization pays no Federal income taxes for 2003, and the other pays Federal income taxes of $100,000 for 2003. Discuss potential reasons for this difference in tax results.

6. In addition to exemption from Federal income tax, for what other benefits may an exempt organization be eligible?

7. What negative tax consequences may be associated with an exempt organization engaging in § 503 prohibited transactions?

**Issue ID**

8. Rex is the chief executive officer of Helping People, Inc., a § 501(c)(3) exempt organization located in Mobile, Alabama. He and the organization's board of directors are concerned about the effect that proposed legislation would have on the organization's budget and its ability to carry out its mission. They are discussing a proposal to have a law firm in Washington, D.C., aid in opposing the legislation. What tax issues are relevant to Helping People, Inc., as it makes this decision?

9. The IRS can impose intermediate sanctions on a public charity if its gross unrelated business income exceeds two-thirds of its gross income or if less than 50% of its net unrelated business income is used in carrying out its tax-exempt mission. Evaluate this statement.

10. The Living Museum is a tax-exempt organization. Dolphin Corporation, a wholly owned subsidiary of the Living Museum, sells boats. Dolphin remits all of its earnings each year to its parent. Is Dolphin exempt from Federal income tax because it is a subsidiary of a tax-exempt organization and remits all of its earnings to a tax-exempt organization?

11. What types of activities are not subject to the tax imposed on feeder organizations?

12. What is a private foundation, and what are the disadvantages of an exempt organization being classified as a private foundation?

13. Which of the following exempt organizations could be private foundations?
    a. Bruton Parish Episcopal Church.
    b. Our Lady Catholic Church.
    c. Kentwood Community Hospital.

d. National Football League (NFL). *Prt fundation exist two went for players*
e. Southeastern Louisiana University Alumni Association. *Contrl by two Deyrn*
f. United Fund.
g. Burr's Foundation.

14. Describe the external support test and the internal support test for a private foundation.

15. What types of taxes may be levied on a private foundation? Why are the taxes levied?

16. What is the purpose of the tax on the investment income of a private foundation? Discuss the applicable tax rates.

17. At the end of the tax year, a private foundation has excess business holdings of $100,000. This is the first year that the private foundation has had any excess business holdings. What are the tax consequences to the private foundation?

18. During the tax year, a private foundation makes speculative investments of $700,000 that are classified as jeopardizing investments. What are the tax consequences to the private foundation?

19. A private foundation has taxable expenditures of $200,000. What are the tax consequences to the private foundation?

**Issue ID**

20. Welcome, Inc., a tax-exempt organization, receives 25% of its support from disqualified persons. Another disqualified person has agreed to match this support if Welcome will appoint him to the organization's board of directors. What tax issues are relevant to Welcome as it makes this decision?

21. An exempt organization has unrelated business taxable income of $400,000 and total earnings of $1 million. Why is only the $400,000 subject to the Federal income tax?

**Issue ID**

22. First Church has been selling cards and small books in the church tower. A contribution box is provided in which payments are to be deposited. To increase church revenues, a task force is evaluating setting up a gift shop in the church parish house. What tax issues are relevant to the task force as it makes its decision?

23. An exempt hospital operates a pharmacy that is staffed by a pharmacist 24 hours per day. The pharmacy serves only hospital patients. Is the pharmacy an unrelated trade or business?

**Decision Making**

24. An exempt hospital receives as a gift from a wealthy donor all the shares of stock of Compute, Inc., a retail computer chain. Because the chain is very profitable and its CEO has offered to continue to manage it, the hospital has decided to operate the chain rather than sell the stock. All of the chain's profits will be used in carrying out the exempt mission of the hospital. Advise the hospital on whether better tax consequences can be achieved by operating the chain as a subsidiary or as a division of the hospital corporation.

25. To which of the following tax-exempt organizations may the unrelated business income tax apply?
    a. Red Cross.
    b. Salvation Army.
    c. United Fund.
    d. College of William and Mary.
    e. Rainbow, Inc., a private foundation.
    f. Federal Land Bank.

*All of them except (f) rest of them would have UBIT*

26. Discuss the significance of the "regularly carried on" test as it relates to the unrelated business income tax.

**Issue ID**

27. An exempt organization is considering conducting bingo games on Thursday nights as a way of generating additional revenue to support its exempt purpose. Before doing so, however, the president of the organization has come to you for advice regarding the effect on the organization's exempt status and whether the net income from the bingo games will be taxable. Identify the relevant tax issues.

28. Define each of the following with respect to unrelated debt-financed property:
    a. Debt-financed income.
    b. Debt-financed property.
    c. Acquisition indebtedness.
    d. Average acquisition indebtedness.
    e. Average adjusted basis.

29. Tom is the treasurer of the City Garden Club, a new garden club. A friend, who is the treasurer of the garden club in a neighboring community, tells Tom that it is not necessary for the garden club to file a request for exempt status with the IRS. Has Tom received correct advice?

**Issue ID**

30. Abby recently became the treasurer of First Church. The church has been in existence for three years and has never filed anything with the IRS. Identify any reporting responsibilities Abby might have as church treasurer.

31. Robin, Inc., a private foundation, generated $22,000 of gross receipts this year. Must Robin file an annual information return? If so, what form should be used?

32. Shane and Brittany are treasurers for § 501(c)(3) exempt organizations. Neither exempt organization is a church. Each year Shane's exempt organization files a Form 990 while Brittany's exempt organization files a Form 990–PF. Discuss the public disclosure requirements for each exempt organization.

## Problems

33. Match the following exempt organizations with the statutory authority under which exempt status is granted. The statutory authority may apply to more than one exempt organization.

| Exempt Organizations | Statutory Authority |
|---|---|
| Girl Scouts | § 501(c)(1) |
| Catholic Church | § 501(c)(2) |
| National Football League (NFL) | § 501(c)(3) |
| American Red Cross | § 501(c)(4) |
| Salvation Army | § 501(c)(5) |
| United Fund | § 501(c)(6) |
| Bill and Melinda Gates Foundation | § 501(c)(7) |
| University of Richmond | § 501(c)(8) |
| Underwriters Laboratories (UL) | § 501(c)(9) |
| PGA Tour | § 501(c)(10) |
| Veterans of Foreign Wars (VFW) | § 501(c)(11) |
| Dallas Rodeo Club | § 501(c)(12) |
| PTA | § 501(c)(13) |
| Toano Cemetery Association | § 501(c)(14) |
| Alpha Chi Omega Sorority | § 501(c)(15) |
| Green, Inc., Legal Services Plan | § 501(c)(16) |
| National Press Club | § 501(c)(19) |
| Federal Deposit Insurance Corporation (FDIC) | § 501(c)(20) |
| League of Women Voters | § 501(d) |

**Decision Making**

34. Research, Inc., a § 501(c)(3) medical research organization, makes lobbying expenditures of $1.2 million. Research incurs exempt purpose expenditures of $20 million in carrying out its medical research mission.

a. Determine the tax consequences to Research if it does not elect to be eligible to participate in lobbying activities on a limited basis.

b. Determine the tax consequences to Research if it does elect to be eligible to participate in lobbying activities on a limited basis.

c. In light of pending health care legislation, Research is considering increasing its lobbying expenditures by 50% annually. Advise Research whether this is a wise thing to do from a tax perspective.

35. Choice, Inc., a § 501(c)(3) organization, pays unreasonable compensation to Monica, the treasurer of Choice. Monica's compensation is $275,000. Assume reasonable compensation would be $185,000.

a. Determine any adverse tax consequences for Choice, Inc.

b. Determine any adverse tax consequences for Monica.

**Decision Making**

**Communications**

36. Roadrunner, Inc., is an exempt medical organization. Quail, Inc., a sporting goods retailer, is a wholly owned subsidiary of Roadrunner. Roadrunner inherited the Quail stock last year from a major benefactor of the medical organization. Quail's taxable income is $400,000. Quail will remit all of its earnings, net of any taxes, to Roadrunner to support the exempt purpose of the parent.

a. Is Quail subject to Federal income tax? If so, calculate the liability.

b. Arthur Morgan, the treasurer of Roadrunner, has contacted you regarding minimizing or eliminating Quail's tax liability. He would like to know if the tax consequences would be better if Quail were liquidated into Roadrunner. Write a letter to Morgan that contains your advice. Roadrunner's address is 500 Rouse Tower, Rochester, NY 14627.

c. Would your answer in (a) change if Roadrunner had acquired the Quail stock by purchase rather than by inheritance? Discuss.

**Communications**

37. Cardinal, Inc., a § 501(c)(3) organization, received support from the following sources.

| | |
|---|---|
| Governmental unit A for services rendered | $ 6,000 |
| General public for services rendered | 80,000 |
| Gross investment income | 40,000 |
| Contributions from disqualified persons | 20,000 |
| Contributions from other than disqualified persons | 95,000 |

a. Does Cardinal satisfy the test for receiving broad public support?

b. Is Cardinal a private foundation?

c. Arnold Horn, Cardinal's treasurer, has asked you to advise him on whether Cardinal is a private foundation. Write a letter to him in which you address the issue. His address is 250 Bristol Road, Charlottesville, VA 22903.

38. Gray, Inc., a private foundation, has the following items of income and deductions.

| | |
|---|---|
| Interest income | $24,000 |
| Rent income | 60,000 |
| Dividend income | 20,000 |
| Royalty income | 10,000 |
| Unrelated business income | 75,000 |
| Rent expenses | 18,000 |
| Unrelated business expenses | 10,000 |

Gray is not an exempt operating foundation and is not eligible for the 1% tax rate.

a. Calculate the net investment income.

b. Calculate the tax on net investment income.

c. What is the purpose of the tax on net investment income?

39. Eagle, Inc., a private foundation, has been in existence for 10 years. During this period, Eagle has been unable to satisfy the requirements for classification as a private operating foundation. At the end of 2002, it had undistributed income of $280,000. Of this amount, $120,000 was distributed in 2003, and $160,000 was distributed during the first quarter of 2004. The IRS deficiency notice was mailed on August 1, 2005.
    a. Calculate the initial tax for 2002, 2003, and 2004.
    b. Calculate the additional tax for 2005.

**Decision Making**

40. Otis is the CEO of Rectify, Inc., a private foundation. Otis invests $500,000 (80%) of the foundation's investment portfolio in derivatives. Previously, the $500,000 had been invested in corporate bonds with an AA rating that earned 7% per annum. If the derivatives investment works as Otis's investment adviser claims, the annual earnings could be as high as 20%.
    a. Determine if Rectify is subject to any of the taxes imposed on private foundations.
    b. If so, calculate the amount of the initial tax.
    c. If so, calculate the amount of the additional tax if the act causing the imposition of the tax is not addressed within the correction period.
    d. Are Otis and the foundation better off financially if the prohibited transaction, if any, is addressed within the correction period?

41. The board of directors of Pearl, Inc., a private foundation, consists of Alice, Beth, and Carlos. They vote unanimously to provide a $100,000 grant to Doug, their business associate. The grant is to be used for travel and education and does not qualify as a permitted grant to individuals (i.e., it is a taxable expenditure under § 4945). Each director knows that Doug was selected for the grant because he is a friend of the organization and that the grant is a taxable expenditure.
    a. Calculate the initial tax imposed on the private foundation.
    b. Calculate the initial tax imposed on the foundation manager (i.e., board of directors).

**Communications**

42. The Open Museum is an exempt organization that operates a gift shop. The museum's annual operations budget is $2.5 million. Gift shop sales generate a profit of $750,000. Another $500,000 of endowment income is generated. Both the income from the gift shop and the endowment income are used to support the exempt purpose of the museum. The balance of $1.25 million required for annual operations is provided through admission fees. Wayne Davis, a new board member, does not understand why the museum is subject to tax at all, particularly since the profits are used in carrying out the mission of the museum. The museum's address is 250 Oak Avenue, Peoria, IL 61625.
    a. Calculate the amount of unrelated business income.
    b. Assume that the endowment income is reinvested rather than being used to support annual operations. Calculate the amount of unrelated business income.
    c. As the museum treasurer, write a letter to Wayne explaining the reason for the tax consequences. Mr. Davis's address is 45 Pine Avenue, Peoria, IL 61625.

**Communications**

43. Salmon, Inc., an exempt organization, has unrelated business taxable income of $20 million.
    a. Calculate Salmon's unrelated business income tax.
    b. Prepare an outline of a presentation you are going to give to the new members of Salmon's board on why Salmon is subject to the UBIT even though it is an exempt organization.

44. For each of the following organizations, determine the amount of the UBIT.
    a. AIDS, Inc., an exempt charitable organization that provides support for individuals with AIDS, operates a retail medical supply store open to the general public. The net income of the store, before any Federal income taxes, is $325,000.
    b. The local Episcopal Church operates a retail gift shop. The inventory consists of the typical items sold by commercial gift shops in the city. The director of the gift shop estimates that 80% of the gift shop sales are to tourists and 20% are to church members. The net income of the gift shop, before the salaries of the three gift shop

employees and any Federal income taxes, is $300,000. The salaries of the employees total $80,000.

c. Education, Inc., a private university, has vending machines in the student dormitories and academic buildings on campus. In recognition of recent tuition increases, the university has adopted a policy of merely trying to recover its costs associated with the vending machine activity. For the current year, however, the net income of the activity, before any Federal income taxes, is $75,000.

*[handwritten: Not taxed.]*

d. Worn, Inc., an exempt organization, provides food for the homeless. It operates a thrift store that sells used clothing to the general public. The thrift shop is staffed by four salaried employees. All of the clothes it sells are received as contributions. The $100,000 profit generated for the year by the thrift shop is used in Worn's mission of providing food to the homeless.

*[handwritten: Sells 100% cost donated Not taxed]*

e. Small, Inc., an exempt organization, has unrelated business income of $900 and unrelated business expenses of $400.

*[handwritten: under 1000 exemption]*

45. Medium, Inc., an exempt organization, has unrelated business income of $3,700 and unrelated business expenses of $2,900. Calculate the amount of the UBIT.

Communications

46. Falcon Basketball League, an exempt organization, is a youth basketball league for children ages 12 through 14. The league has been in existence for 30 years. In the past, revenue for operations has been provided through community fund-raising and the sale of snacks at the games by the parents. Due to a projected revenue shortfall of approximately $5,000, the governing board has decided to charge admission to the basketball games of $1.00 for adults and $0.50 for children.

a. Will the admission charge affect Falcon's exempt status?

b. What are the tax consequences to Falcon of the net income from snack sales and the new admission fee?

c. As the volunteer treasurer of the Falcon League, prepare a memo for the board in which you explain the effect, if any, of the admission fee policy on Falcon's exempt status.

*[handwritten: Can charge. NO only for people come there. Not tax]*

47. Upward, Inc., a § 501(c)(3) organization that provides training programs for welfare recipients, has the following income and expenses from the sale of products associated with the training program.

| | |
|---|---|
| Gross income from sales | $800,000 |
| Cost of goods sold | 200,000 |
| Advertising and selling expenses | 50,000 |

*[handwritten: 800,000 (200,000) (50,000) 550,000 − 1000 = 549,000 × tax = 186,660]*

Calculate Upward's unrelated business income tax:

a. If the sale of the training program products is substantially related to Upward's exempt purpose.

b. If the sale of the training program products is not substantially related to Upward's exempt purpose.

48. Save the Squirrels, Inc., a § 501(c)(3) organization that feeds the squirrels in municipal parks, receives a $100,000 contribution from Animal Feed, Inc., a corporation that sells animal feed. In exchange for the contribution, Save the Squirrels will identify Animal Feed as a major supporter in its monthly newsletter.

a. If Save the Squirrels receives no other similar payments, calculate its unrelated business income tax.

b. Calculate Save the Squirrels' unrelated business income tax if Save the Squirrels agrees to identify Animal Feed as a major supporter and to include a half-page advertisement for Animal Feed products in its monthly newsletter as a result of that contribution.

49. Faith Church is exempt from Federal income taxation under § 501(c)(3). To supplement its contribution revenue, it holds bingo games on Saturday nights. It has the licenses and permits required to do so. The net income from the bingo games is $75,000. These

funds are used to support the ministry of the church. Faith Church is located in a resort city where bingo games can be conducted by churches, charities, and for-profit entities.
a. Will conducting the bingo games affect the exempt status of Faith Church?
b. Calculate the Federal tax liability, if any, associated with the bingo games.

50. Fish, Inc., an exempt organization, has unrelated business taxable income of $400,000 (excluding the deduction for charitable contributions). During the year, it makes charitable contributions of $45,000, of which $38,000 are associated with the unrelated trade or business.
a. Calculate unrelated business taxable income.
b. Assume that the charitable contributions are $39,000, of which $38,000 are associated with the unrelated trade or business. Calculate unrelated business taxable income.

51. Comfort, Inc., an exempt hospital, is going to operate a pharmacy that will be classified as an unrelated trade or business. Comfort establishes the pharmacy as a wholly owned subsidiary. During the current year, the subsidiary generates taxable income of $200,000 and pays dividends of $125,000 to Comfort.
a. What are the tax consequences to the subsidiary?
b. What are the tax consequences to Comfort?

52. Tranquility, Inc., an exempt organization, leases factory equipment to Blouses, Inc. Blouses is a taxable entity that manufactures blouses for distribution through up-scale department stores. Blouses owns the land and building where it conducts its manufacturing operations. The original cost of the building to Blouses was $800,000, and the cost recovery deduction for the current year is $20,512. Rent income to Tranquility for the factory equipment is $300,000, and the related expenses are $170,000. Calculate Tranquility's unrelated business taxable income.

53. Seniors, Inc., an exempt organization, leases an office building to Copper Corporation for $150,000. Seniors previously had used the building as its headquarters. Now, however, Seniors has constructed a new headquarters building, enabling it to lease the first building to Copper. Calculate the amount of unrelated business income and the effect on unrelated business taxable income.

54. Education, Inc., an exempt organization that provides educational services, has the following gains and losses from property transactions.

- $50,000 loss on the sale of land and a building. The building had been used in carrying out Education's exempt purpose, but is no longer needed due to a contraction in the geographic area served.

- $5,000 gain on the sale of land and a building. The building had initially been acquired to lease to a national retailer. Due to a reduction in the number of its stores, the national retailer canceled the lease at the end of last year.

- $45,000 gain on the sale of investment land.

- $20,000 loss on the sale of computers. The computers had been leased to Teachers, Inc., an unrelated exempt organization. Prior to leasing the computers, Education had used them in carrying out its exempt purpose.

Determine the effect of these transactions on Education's unrelated business taxable income.

55. Benevolent, Inc., an exempt organization, owns the following properties.

| Property | Basis | Acquisition Indebtedness | % Used in Exempt Purpose |
| --- | --- | --- | --- |
| Building A | $400,000 | $300,000 | 100% |
| Building B | 500,000 | –0– | 60 |
| Building C | 600,000 | 200,000 | 90 |
| Building D | 700,000 | 500,000 | 70 |

Calculate the adjusted basis to Benevolent of its debt-financed property.

56. Fix, Inc., an exempt organization, owns a one-story building. Fix's adjusted basis for the building is $900,000. Of the building's total area of 10,000 square feet, the front portion (approximately 3,000 square feet) is used in carrying out Fix's exempt purpose. The remainder of the building is leased for $300,000 each year to Belts, Inc., a taxable entity, to use for storing its inventory. The unamortized balance of a mortgage relating to the original acquisition of the building is $600,000. Determine the portion of the adjusted basis that is treated as debt-financed property and the amount of the mortgage that is acquisition indebtedness.

57. Rust, Inc., an exempt organization, acquires a building for $800,000 on September 1, 2003. The principal amount of the related mortgage on September 1 and on the first day of the following months is as follows.

| September | $600,000 |
|-----------|----------|
| October   | 595,000  |
| November  | 590,000  |
| December  | 585,000  |

Depreciation deducted during 2003 was $7,400. Rust leases the building to Build Corporation.
a. Calculate the average acquisition indebtedness for the building.
b. Calculate the average adjusted basis for the building.
c. Calculate the debt/basis percentage.

58. Seagull, Inc., a § 501(c)(3) exempt organization, uses a tax year that ends on October 31, 2003. Seagull's gross receipts are $600,000, and related expenses are $580,000.
a. Is Seagull required to file an annual Form 990?
b. If so, what is the due date?

59. Education, Inc., a § 501(c)(3) organization, is a private foundation with a tax year that ends on June 30, 2003. Gross receipts for the fiscal year are $180,000, and the related expenses are $160,000.
a. Is Education required to file an annual information return?
b. If so, what form is used?
c. If so, what is the due date?
d. How would your answers in (a), (b), and (c) change if Education is an exempt organization that is not a private foundation?

60. Historic Burg is an exempt organization that operates a museum depicting eighteenth-century life. Sally gives the museum an eighteenth-century chest that she has owned for 10 years. Her adjusted basis is $55,000, and the chest's appraised value is $100,000. Sally's adjusted gross income is $300,000. Calculate Sally's charitable contribution deduction if Historic Burg is:
a. A private operating foundation.
b. A private nonoperating foundation.

## Research Problems

*Note: Solutions to Research Problems can be prepared by using the **RIA Checkpoint® Student Edition** online research product, or the **CCH U.S. Master Tax Guide Plus**™ online Federal tax research database, which is available to accompany this text. It is also possible to prepare solutions to the Research Problems by using tax research materials found in a standard tax library.*

**Research Problem 1.** Allied Fund, a charitable organization exempt under § 501(c)(3), has branches located in each of the 50 states. Allied is not a private foundation. Rather than having each of the state units file an annual return with the IRS, Allied would like to file a single return that reports the activities of all of its branches. Is this permissible? What is the due date of the return?

*Partial list of research aids:*
§ 6033.
§ 6072.
Reg. § 1.6033–2(d).

**Research Problem 2.** Heal, Inc., a tax-exempt hospital, was sold to its shareholders for $6.6 million. The IRS determined that the fair market value of the hospital was $7.8 million. An IRS agent is proposing that the tax-exempt status of the hospital be revoked because the sale of the hospital to the shareholders for less than the fair market value resulted in "private inurement" to them. Evaluate the IRS's proposal.

**Research Problem 3.** The Shark Club, an exempt organization, conducts bingo games on the weekends. Profit entities are prohibited from conducting bingo games in the state, but tax-exempt organizations are permitted to do so. Shark uses the net profits from the bingo games in carrying out its tax-exempt mission.

The bingo games are conducted by volunteers. However, the volunteers are permitted to accept tips from the players. Tipping by players is a frequent occurrence.

Determine whether Shark is subject to the unrelated business income tax on its bingo activities.

**Communications**

**Research Problem 4.** City Hospital, a tax-exempt hospital, has purchased a sports and fitness center located about three miles from the hospital. It is a state-of-the-art fitness center that includes an open fitness room with cardiovascular and strength equipment, an indoor track, exercise rooms, racquetball and tennis courts, an aquatic area with two pools, a nutrition center/juice bar, and tanning beds. The hospital's overall goals for the center are to enhance cardiovascular, physical, and psychosocial function, reduce morbidity and mortality, improve quality of life, and promote compliance with a lifelong prevention program.

The membership of the center will consist of three segments of the community: the general public, employees, and former rehabilitation patients. Each group will be charged a monthly fee and an initiation fee with a reduced fee provided for employees. Within each category, the fees vary depending on the member's age and restrictions on availability of the facilities during specific hours. The hospital hired a professional consulting firm to conduct a survey of the community to ensure that the fee structure would achieve its goal of making the center facilities available to an economic cross section of the community.

You have been contacted by Anne Dexter, the chief financial officer for the hospital. She is concerned that some or perhaps all of the revenue from the sports and fitness center will be classified as unrelated business income and therefore be subject to the unrelated business income tax. Write a letter to Ms. Dexter that contains your findings, and prepare a memo for the tax files. City Hospital's address is 1000 Board Street, Billings, MT 59101.

**Research Problem 5.** A volunteer fire department located in Green County holds tax-exempt status. As a way of raising funds to support its fire-fighting activities, the department obtained the permission of the owners of three taverns located in Green County to place "tip jars" in the taverns. A tip jar is a gambling device from which patrons purchase sealed pieces of paper containing numbers, series of numbers, or symbols that may entitle the patron to cash or other prizes. The tip jars are legal under state law and under the county ordinance for tax-exempt organizations.

Under the county ordinance, the tax-exempt organization must receive at least 70% of the net proceeds after the winnings are paid, and the business where the tip jar is located must receive no more than 30%. Under the arrangement with the three taverns, the volunteer fire department received 80%.

The three taverns included the 20% they received in their gross income in calculating their taxable income. Since the volunteer fire department is tax-exempt, it did not pay Federal income taxes on the 80% it received.

The IRS determines that the tip jar income received by the volunteer fire department is unrelated business income and issues a deficiency notice. Evaluate the position of the IRS.

**Internet Activity**

**Communications**

*Use the tax resources of the Internet to address the following questions. Do not restrict your search to the World Wide Web, but include a review of newsgroups and general reference materials, practitioner sites and resources, primary sources of the tax law, chat rooms and discussion groups, and other opportunities.*

**Research Problem 6.**   Download an application for tax-exempt status that would be filed with the IRS. Write a one-page letter to an organization that is contemplating the filing of such an application. The letter should walk through the application and highlight the information that must be provided and the estimated time required to comply with the directives of the form.

**Research Problem 7.**   Summarize a recent newspaper or magazine story that relates a perceived abuse of the § 501(c)(3) provisions by a business owner or politician.

**Research Problem 8.**   Determine if the Bill and Melinda Gates Foundation is a private foundation. Print a copy of its Form 990 or Form 990–PF.

# Multistate Corporate Taxation

CHAPTER

15

*After completing Chapter 15, you should be able to:*

## LO.1
Illustrate the computation of a multistate corporation's state tax liability.

## LO.2
Define nexus and explain its role in state income taxation.

## LO.3
Distinguish between allocation and apportionment of a multistate corporation's taxable income.

## LO.4
Describe the nature and treatment of business and nonbusiness income.

## LO.5
Discuss the sales, payroll, and property apportionment factors.

## LO.6
Apply the unitary method of state income taxation.

## LO.7
Discuss the states' income tax treatment of S corporations.

## LO.8
Describe other commonly encountered state and local taxes on businesses.

## LO.9
Recognize tax planning opportunities available to minimize a corporation's state and local tax liability.

http://wft.swlearning.com

**O U T L I N E**

Although most of this text concentrates on the effects of the Federal income tax law upon the computation of a taxpayer's annual tax liability, a variety of tax bases apply to most business taxpayers. For instance, a multinational corporation may be subject to tax in a number of different countries (see Chapter 9). Similarly, the taxpayer may be subject to a county-level wheel tax on its business vehicles, a state sales or use tax on many of its asset purchases, and state and local income or franchise taxes on its net income or on the privilege of doing business in the taxing jurisdiction. Indeed, estimates are that about 40 percent of the tax dollars paid by business taxpayers go to state and local authorities.

Businesses operate in a multistate environment for a variety of reasons. For the most part, nontax motivations drive such location decisions as where to build new plants or distribution centers or whether to move communications and data processing facilities and corporate headquarters. For instance, a business typically wants to be close to its largest markets and to operate in a positive private- and public-sector business climate, where it has access to well-trained and reasonably priced labor, suppliers and support operations, sources of natural resources and well-educated personnel, and highway and airport facilities.

Many location decisions, though, are motivated by multistate tax considerations.

- The taxpayer's manufacturing, wholesaling, sales, retailing, and credit operations each may be centered in a different state to take advantage of various economic development incentives created by politicians.

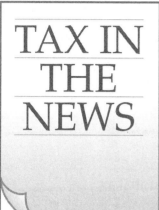

SEARCHING FOR NEW TAXPAYERS

In recent years, state and local taxes have grown to constitute about 40 percent of most businesses' tax liabilities. Likewise, as revenue pressures continue to increase, state and local governments have become more aggressive in identifying new taxpayers and new taxable transactions. Most states now devote more resources to auditing and litigating sales/use tax issues than to enhancing income tax revenues.

For instance, current taxpayers in some states receive questionnaires from the department of revenue, asking them to identify their three most important competitors in the state. The governments use this information to make certain that all taxpayers present in the state are subject to applicable income and sales/use taxes.

- Mail-order and other catalog operations blur the traditional jurisdictional boundaries for buyer and seller alike. Often advertising campaigns boast "no sales tax payable."
- Similarly, the ability to transfer sales and purchase orders, pricing information, and other data via telephone lines, the Internet, and satellite transmissions may tempt the taxpayer to overlook traditional applications of the property and sales tax base. For instance, is computer software tangible (and subject to property tax) or intangible property? Is canned software, transferred via the Internet, rather than by disk, subject to sales tax? Which jurisdiction's property tax should apply to a communications satellite?
- In addition to flying over virtually the entire country, the major airlines depart from and land in the majority of the states. Which state's income tax should apply to the ticket income? Should sales or income tax apply to sales of movies or liquor while the plane is airborne?
- Local political concerns lead to a multiplicity of tax rules as politicians attempt to serve their constituents by introducing a variety of special tax incentives. This variety can be confusing, however. Taxpayers may have difficulty determining whether they qualify for energy or enterprise zone credits, S corporation status, exemptions from sales tax liability or income tax withholding, or passive loss relief at the local level.
- Politicians have a strong incentive to impose new tax burdens on visitors and others who have no direct say in their reelection. Thus, it is increasingly common to see tourist and hotel-bed taxes on convention delegates, city payroll taxes on commuters, and the use of obscure tax formulas that otherwise discriminate against those with limited contact in the area.
- Each jurisdiction in which the entity is subject to tax represents a geometrical increase in compliance responsibilities. For instance, how many tax returns must be filed by a three-shareholder S corporation operating in 15 states?
- Various states and localities have adopted revenue-raising statutes that vary in sophistication and operate on different time schedules. For instance, only a few states have adopted an alternative minimum tax, and states that impose the tax have tended to select different bases. In addition, the aggressiveness with which departments of revenue enforce their tax statutes varies greatly from state to state, even in a context of ongoing pressure to enhance revenues. Accordingly, the taxpayer must deal with a patchwork of germane taxing and enforcement provisions in an environment that is often uncertain.

This chapter reviews the basic tax concepts that are predominant among most states that impose a tax based on net income and discusses the major areas in which tax planning can reduce a corporation's overall state tax burden.

Most of this chapter is devoted to a discussion of state taxes that are based on income. Each state is free to identify its corporate tax by a different term. Not all of the states that impose a tax on corporate income call the tax an "income tax." Rather, some states refer to their tax on corporate income as a franchise tax,[1] a business tax, a license tax, or a business profits tax.

| ETHICAL CONSIDERATIONS | **Encouraging Economic Development through Tax Concessions** |

The tax professional occasionally is in a position to negotiate with a state or city taxing jurisdiction to garner tax relief for a client as an incentive to locate a plant or distribution center in that geographic area. In times when construction budgets are high and interstate competition is fierce, such tax concessions can be significant.

For instance, to encourage a business to build a large distribution center in the area, community leaders might be agreeable to (1) paying for roads, sewer, water, and other improvements through taxpayer bonds; (2) reducing property taxes by 50 percent for the first 10 years of the center's operations; and (3) permanently excluding any distribution-related vehicles and equipment from the personal property tax.

The community would grant the concessions even though the influx of new workers would place a great strain on public school facilities and likely necessitate improvements in traffic patterns and other infrastructure. Local residents, even those who obtain jobs at the new facility, and the tax adviser may wonder whether the tax concessions are supportable in light of these changes in the community's quality of life.

Take the position of a large employer that has been located in the area for more than 50 years. By how much should it be willing to absorb the tax increases that result when economic development concessions are used to attract new, perhaps temporary, businesses to the area? Should higher "impact fees" be assessed on new developments? Does your analysis change if the new business competes with the long-time resident for sales? For employees? For political power?

# Overview of Corporate State Income Taxation

Forty-six states and the District of Columbia impose a tax based on a corporation's taxable income. Since each state is free to create its own tax provisions, the tax practitioner could be faced with 47 entirely different state tax provisions.[2] Fortunately, however, to simplify the filing of tax returns and increase compliance with state tax laws, the majority of states "piggyback" onto the Federal income tax base. This means they have adopted *en masse* part or all of the Federal provisions governing the definition of income and the allowance of various exemptions, exclusions, and deductions. None of the states, however, has piggybacked its tax collections with the IRS.

---

[1]Although a franchise tax in some states is a business privilege tax based on a corporation's capital stock or net worth, several states use that term for the tax that they impose on a corporation's net income.

[2]Although the District of Columbia is not a state, it operates in much the same manner as a state and imposes a tax based on income.

Four states impose no corporate income tax at all: Nevada, South Dakota, Washington, and Wyoming. Corporations, however, are subject to a business and occupation tax in Washington. Several states base the tax on gross receipts, and Michigan uses a form of value added tax.

## UP TO BAT FOR THE STATE TREASURY, IT'S A-ROD!

One state has released figures showing the revenue effects of having professional sports teams based in the area. These data may be useful in justifying the public financing of large stadium projects for privately owned sports teams.

Wisconsin, a small state, collects about $6 billion in personal income taxes each year. Of this amount, about $4 million is attributable to members of the Green Bay Packers and around $300,000 to their opponents' players. Another $1.3 million is estimated to come from the conduct of summer training camps for other NFL teams. NBA players also contribute significantly to the state's income tax collections: around $1.6 million for Milwaukee Bucks players and $1.1 million for their opponents. As the Milwaukee Brewers operate on a low salary scale budget, their team members pay $1.2 million in income taxes and their opponents $1.8 million.

The Wisconsin Department of Revenue cited recent payments by several prominent players as examples of its computations.

- Alex Rodriguez, Texas Rangers, paid $330,000.
- Brett Favre, Green Bay Packers, paid $52,500.
- Jeromy Burnitz, Milwaukee Brewers, paid $14,300.
- Ray Allen, Milwaukee Bucks, paid $41,000.

Athletes and their advisers can use this information when negotiating contracts. It may be easier to recruit a free agent athlete to play in Texas, Florida, or Washington, where personal income taxes are low or nonexistent, than in high-tax states like Massachusetts, Minnesota, and Wisconsin. California, because it houses many professional teams, has a high marginal income tax schedule. It enforces its laws aggressively and collects about $100 million from professional athletes every year.

**LO.1**

Illustrate the computation of a multistate corporation's state tax liability.

## COMPUTING STATE TAXABLE INCOME

In more than 40 of the states that impose a corporate income tax, the starting point in computing the tax base is taxable income as reflected on the Federal corporate income tax return (Form 1120). These states typically use either taxable income before the net operating loss and special deductions (line 28) or taxable income itself (line 30). Those states whose computation of state taxable income is not coupled to the Federal tax return have their own state-specific definitions of gross and taxable income. Nonetheless, even these states typically adopt most Federal income and deduction provisions.

Although Federal tax law plays a significant role in the computation of state taxable income, there is a wide disparity in both the methods used to determine a state's taxable income and the tax rates imposed on that income. Accordingly, increasing the number of states in which a corporation is subject to tax causes the complexity of determining the corporation's state income tax liability to rise exponentially.

The formula used by a multistate corporation to determine its tax liability in a typical state is illustrated in Figure 15–1.

## OPERATIONAL IMPLICATIONS

Generally, the accounting period and methods used by a corporation for state tax purposes must be consistent with those used on the Federal return. States often

**■ FIGURE 15–1**
Computing Corporate State
Income Tax Liability

|  | Starting point in computing taxable income* |
|---|---|
| ± | State modification items |
|  | State tax base |
| ± | Total net allocable income/(loss) (nonbusiness income) |
|  | Total apportionable income/(loss) (business income) |
| × | State's apportionment percentage |
|  | Income apportioned to the state |
| ± | Income/(loss) allocated to the state |
|  | State taxable income/(loss) |
| × | State tax rate |
|  | Gross income tax liability for state |
| − | State's tax credits |
|  | Net income tax liability for the state |

*Most states use either line 28 or line 30 of the Federal corporate
income tax return (Form 1120). In other states, the corporation
is required to identify and report each element of income and
deduction on the state return.

apply different rules, however, in identifying the members of a group filing a consolidated return and the income of each group member that is subject to tax.

As the starting point for computing state taxable income often is directly related to the Federal taxable income amount, most states also piggyback onto the IRS's audit process. Consequently, virtually all of the states that levy an income tax require notification of the final settlement of a Federal income tax audit. State authorities then adjust the originally calculated state tax liability appropriately.

## STATE MODIFICATIONS

Federal taxable income generally is used as the starting point in computing the state's income tax base, but numerous state adjustments or modifications are often made to Federal taxable income to:

- Reflect differences between state and Federal tax statutes.
- Remove income that a state is constitutionally prohibited from taxing.

The required modifications to Federal taxable income vary significantly among the states. Accordingly, this discussion is limited to the most common additions and subtractions that the states require. Exhibit 15–1 lists the most frequently encountered modifications. In computing the taxable income for a given state, only a selected number of these modifications may be applicable.

**EXAMPLE 1**

Blue Corporation is subject to tax only in State A. The starting point in computing A taxable income is Federal taxable income. Modifications then are made to reflect, among other provisions, the exempt status of interest on A obligations, all dividends received from in-state corporations, and the disallowance of a deduction for state income taxes. Blue generated the following income and deductions this year.

■ **EXHIBIT 15–1**
Common State Modifications

---

### Addition Modifications

* Interest income received on state and municipal obligations and any other interest income that is exempt from Federal income tax. For this purpose, some states exempt interest earned on their own obligations.

* Expenses deducted in computing Federal taxable income that are directly or indirectly related to U.S. obligations.

* Income-based franchise and income taxes imposed by any state and the District of Columbia that were deducted in computing Federal taxable income.

* The amount by which the Federal deductions for depreciation, amortization, or depletion exceed those permitted by the state.

* The amount by which the state gain or loss from the disposal of assets differs from the Federal gain or loss. Due to the difference in permitted depreciation methods and other adjustments, a corporation's assets may have different Federal and state tax bases. This adjustment is not necessary if the state and Federal basis provisions are identical.

Adjustments required as a result of different elections being made for state and Federal purposes. Examples of such elections include the methods under which income from installment sales or long-term contracts is determined.

Federal net operating loss deduction. This modification is not required by states in which the starting point in the computation of taxable income is Federal income before special deductions.

### Subtraction Modifications

* Interest on U.S. obligations or obligations of Federal agencies to the extent included in Federal taxable income but exempt from state income taxes under U.S. law.

* Expenses that are directly or indirectly related to the state and municipal interest that is taxable for state purposes.

* Refunds of franchise and income taxes imposed by any state and the District of Columbia, to the extent included in Federal taxable income.

* The amount by which the state deductions for depreciation, amortization, or depletion exceed the deductions permitted for Federal tax purposes.

Adjustments required as a result of different elections being made for state and Federal purposes, as above.

Dividends received from certain out-of-state corporations, to the extent included in Federal taxable income.

Net operating loss deduction as determined for state tax purposes.

Deduction for Federal income tax paid.

---

*Required by most states.

---

| | |
|---|---:|
| Sales | $1,500,000 |
| Interest on Federal obligations | 50,000 |
| Interest on municipal obligations of State B | 100,000 |
| Dividends received from 50%-owned State A corporations | 200,000 |
| Total income | $1,850,000 |

| | |
|---|---:|
| Expenses related to Federal obligations | $ 1,000 |
| Expenses related to municipal obligations | 5,000 |
| State income tax expense | 50,000 |
| Depreciation allowed for Federal tax purposes (the deduction allowed for state purposes is $300,000) | 400,000 |
| Other allowable deductions | 1,000,000 |
| Total deductions | $1,456,000 |

Blue's taxable income for Federal and state purposes is $139,000 and $295,000, respectively.

### Federal Taxable Income

| | |
|---|---:|
| Sales | $1,500,000 |
| Interest on Federal obligations | 50,000 |
| Dividends received from domestic corporations | 200,000 |
| Total income | $1,750,000 |
| Expenses related to Federal obligations | $ 1,000 |
| State income tax expense | 50,000 |
| Depreciation | 400,000 |
| Other allowable deductions | 1,000,000 |
| Total deductions | $1,451,000 |
| Taxable income before special deductions | $ 299,000 |
| Less: Dividends received deduction (80% × $200,000) | 160,000 |
| Federal taxable income | $ 139,000 |

### State A Taxable Income

| | |
|---|---:|
| Federal taxable income | $139,000 |
| **Addition Modifications** | |
| Interest on State B obligations | 100,000 |
| State income tax expense | 50,000 |
| Excess depreciation deduction allowed for Federal purposes ($400,000 – $300,000) | 100,000 |
| Expenses related to Federal obligations | 1,000 |
| **Subtraction Modifications** | |
| Expenses related to State B obligations | (5,000) |
| Dividends from in-state corporations included in Federal taxable income ($200,000 – $160,000) | (40,000) |
| Interest on Federal obligations | (50,000) |
| State A taxable income | $295,000 |

**EXAMPLE 2**

Continue with the facts of Example 1, except that the $100,000 of municipal interest was generated from State A obligations. The computation of Federal taxable income is unaffected by this change. Since A exempts interest on its own obligations from taxation, Blue's A taxable income is $200,000.

| State A Taxable Income | |
| --- | --- |
| Federal taxable income | $139,000 |
| **Addition Modifications** | |
| State income tax expense | 50,000 |
| Excess depreciation deduction allowed for Federal purposes ($400,000 – $300,000) | 100,000 |
| Expenses related to Federal obligations | 1,000 |
| **Subtraction Modifications** | |
| Dividends from in-state corporations included in Federal taxable income ($200,000 – $160,000) | (40,000) |
| Interest on Federal obligations | (50,000) |
| State A taxable income | $200,000 |

## THE UDITPA AND THE MULTISTATE TAX COMMISSION

The Uniform Division of Income for Tax Purposes Act (**UDITPA**) is a model law relating to the assignment of income among the states for corporations that maintain operations in more than one state (multistate corporations). Many states have adopted the provisions of the UDITPA, either by joining the Multistate Tax Compact or by modeling their laws after the provisions of the UDITPA.

The **Multistate Tax Commission (MTC),** which is appointed by the member states of the Multistate Tax Compact, writes regulations and other rules that interpret the UDITPA. When a new MTC rule or regulation is created, the member states propose its adoption to their respective legislatures. The majority of member states adopt the regulations with no exceptions or only minor changes.[3]

**LO.2**

Define nexus and explain its role in state income taxation.

## JURISDICTION TO IMPOSE TAX: NEXUS AND PUBLIC LAW 86-272

The state in which a business is incorporated has the jurisdiction to tax the corporation, regardless of the volume of its business activity within the state. Whether a state can tax the income of a business that is incorporated in another state usually depends on the relationship between the state and the corporation.

**Nexus** describes the degree of business activity that must be present before a taxing jurisdiction has the right to impose a tax on an out-of-state entity's income. State law defines the measure of the relationship that is necessary to create nexus. Typically, sufficient nexus is present when a corporation derives income from sources within the state, owns or leases property in the state, employs personnel in the state, or has physical or financial capital there. **Public Law 86–272** limits the states' right to impose an income tax on interstate activities.[4] This Federal law prohibits a state from taxing a business whose only connection with the state is to solicit orders for sales of tangible personal property that is sent outside the state for approval or rejection. If approved, the orders must be filled and shipped by the business from a point outside the state.

---

[3]Many of the states that are not members of the Multistate Tax Compact also model their laws after the UDITPA and the MTC regulations.

[4]15 U.S.C. 381–385.

Only the sales of tangible personal property are immune from taxation under the law, however. Leases, rentals, and other dispositions of tangible personal property are not protected activities. Moreover, dispositions of real property and intangible property, as well as sales of services, are not protected by Public Law 86–272. In this regard, each state constructs its own definition of tangible and intangible property. Thus, since property ownership is not a protected activity, providing company-owned fax, copy, or computer equipment to an out-of-state salesperson may create nexus with a state, even though the salesperson merely solicits sales orders there.

An activity that consists merely of solicitation is immune from taxation. The statute does not define the term *solicitation*, but the Supreme Court has held that *solicitation of orders* includes any explicit verbal request for orders and any speech or conduct that implicitly invites an order.[5] The Court also created a *de minimis* rule, allowing immunity from nexus where a limited amount of solicitation occurs.

Exhibit 15–2 summarizes the activities that the MTC has identified as being directly related to solicitation (protected activities) and activities unrelated to solicitation (which establish income tax nexus for the entity).

**Independent Contractors.**   Public Law 86–272 extends immunity to certain in-state activities conducted by an independent contractor that would not be permitted if performed directly by the taxpayer. Generally, an independent contractor may engage in the following limited activities without establishing nexus for the principal: (1) soliciting sales, (2) making sales, and (3) maintaining a sales office.

LO.3

Distinguish between allocation and apportionment of a multistate corporation's taxable income.

# Allocation and Apportionment of Income

A corporation that conducts business activities in more than one state must determine the portion of its net income that is subject to tax by each state. A corporation that has established sufficient nexus with another state generally must both **allocate** and **apportion** its income.

*Apportionment* is a means by which a corporation's business income is divided among the states in which it conducts business. Under an apportionment procedure, a corporation determines allowable income and deductions for the company as a whole and then apportions some of its net income to a given state, according to an approved formula.

*Allocation* is a method under which specific components of a corporation's income, net of related expenses, are directly assigned to a certain state. Allocation differs from apportionment in that allocable income is assigned to one state, whereas apportionable income is divided among several states. Nonapportionable (nonbusiness) income generally includes:

* Income or losses derived from the sale of nonbusiness real or tangible property, or
* Income or losses derived from rentals and royalties from nonbusiness real or tangible personal property.

This income normally is allocated to the state where the property that generated the income or loss is located.

---

[5]*Wisconsin Department of Revenue v. William Wrigley, Jr., Co.*, 112 S.Ct. 2447 (1992).

■ **EXHIBIT 15–2**

Common Nexus Definitions
under Public Law 86–272

**General rule:** P.L. 86–272 immunity applies where the sales representative's activities are ancillary to the order-solicitation process.

## Activities That Usually Do Not Create Nexus under P.L. 86–272

* Advertising campaigns.

* Carrying free samples only for display or distribution.

* Owning or furnishing automobiles to salespersons.

* Passing inquiries or complaints on to the home office.

* Checking customers' inventories for reorder.

* Maintaining a sample or display room for two weeks or less during the year.

## Activities Usually Sufficient to Establish Nexus

* Making repairs or providing maintenance.

* Collecting delinquent accounts; investigating creditworthiness.

* Installation or supervision of installation.

* Conducting training classes, seminars, or lectures for persons other than sales personnel.

* Approving or accepting orders.

* Picking up or replacing damaged or returned property.

* Hiring, training, or supervising personnel other than sales employees.

* Providing shipping information and coordinating deliveries.

* Carrying samples for sale, exchange, or distribution in any manner for consideration or other value.

* Owning, leasing, maintaining, or otherwise using any of the following facilities or property in the state: real estate; repair shop; parts department; employment office; purchasing office; warehouse; meeting place for directors, officers, or employees; stock of goods; telephone answering service; or mobile stores (i.e., trucks with driver-salespersons).

* Maintaining an office for an employee, including an office in the home.

As Figure 15–1 indicated, total allocable (nonapportionable) income or loss typically is removed from corporate net income before the state's apportionment percentage is applied. The nonapportionable income or loss assigned to a state then is combined with the income apportionable to that state to arrive at total income subject to tax in the state.

**EXAMPLE 3**

Green Corporation conducts business in States N, O, P, and Q. Green's $900,000 taxable income is comprised of $800,000 apportionable income and $100,000 allocable income generated from transactions conducted in State Q. Green's sales, property, and payroll are evenly divided among the four states, and the states all employ an identical apportionment formula. Accordingly, $200,000 of Green's income is taxable in each of States N, O, and P. Green is subject to income tax on $300,000 of income in State Q.

| | |
|---|---|
| Apportionable income | $800,000 |
| Apportionment percentage (apportionable income is divided equally among the four states) | × 25% |
| Income apportioned to each state | $200,000 |

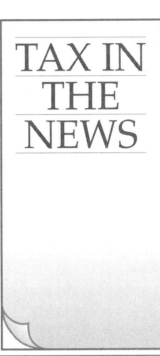

## TAX IN THE NEWS

### WHERE WILL WE BEE TAXED?

Nexus definitions remain the most controversial aspect of state and local taxation today. In a service-based economy that depends upon electronic and other paperless transfers of information, it may be difficult for a taxing jurisdiction to find and measure nexus. For instance, assume that a toy retailer uses Billy the Bee as its national mascot. Billy appears in all of the chain's print and television advertisements, and his image has become synonymous with the retailer's operations. The retailer has a store in State A, but all of its bank accounts, inventory, and intangible assets (including the copyrights on Billy the Bee) are in another state. Does the toy chain have any tax exposure in A? Specifically, does the presence of an intangible asset (Billy's image), a financial asset (the flow of receivables in and out of the state), or an electronic presence (the flow of orders and inventory management to headquarters over the Internet) create nexus?

Or suppose that the Do It Yourself Partnership operates a retail hardware store chain, as well as the in-store credit card operations for the chain. The credit card operations are limited to State Q, but the stores are located in nearly every state. Is the income from the credit card operations subject to tax outside Q because of its relationship with the multistate partnership?

|                     | State N   | State O   | State P   | State Q   |
|---------------------|-----------|-----------|-----------|-----------|
| Income apportioned  | $200,000  | $200,000  | $200,000  | $200,000  |
| Income allocated    | –0–       | –0–       | –0–       | 100,000   |
| Taxable income      | $200,000  | $200,000  | $200,000  | $300,000  |

## THE APPORTIONMENT PROCEDURE

Apportionment assumes that the production of business income is linked to business activity, and the laws of each state define a number of factors believed to indicate the amount of corporate activity conducted within the state. However, apportionment often does not provide a uniform division of an organization's income based on its business activity, because each state is free to choose the type and number of factors that it believes are indicative of the business activity conducted within its borders. Therefore, a corporation may be subject to state income tax on more or less than 100 percent of its income.

An equally incongruous consequence of apportionment may occur when the operations in a state result in a loss.

**EXAMPLE 4**

Red Corporation's operations include two manufacturing facilities, located in States A and B, respectively. The plant located in A generated $500,000 of income, and the plant located in B generated a loss of $200,000. Therefore, Red's total taxable income is $300,000.

By applying the statutes of each state, Red determines that its apportionment factors for A and B are .65 and .35, respectively. Accordingly, Red's income is apportioned to the states as follows.

Income apportioned to State A: .65 × $300,000 = $195,000

Income apportioned to State B: .35 × $300,000 = $105,000

Red is subject to tax in B on $105,000 of income, even though the operations conducted in that state resulted in a loss. ∎

## LO.4
Describe the nature and treatment of business and nonbusiness income.

## BUSINESS AND NONBUSINESS INCOME

*Business income* is assigned among the states by using an apportionment formula. In contrast, *nonbusiness income* either is apportioned or allocated to the state in which the income-producing asset is located. For instance, income derived from the rental of nonbusiness real property generally is allocated to the state in which the property is located.

**EXAMPLE 5**

TNT Corporation, a manufacturer of explosive devices, is a multistate taxpayer that has nexus with States P and Q. During the taxable year, TNT's net sales of explosive devices were $900,000; $600,000 of these sales were made in P and $300,000 were made in Q. The corporation also received $90,000 from the rental of nonbusiness real property located in P.

Both states employ a three-factor apportionment formula under which sales, property, and payroll are equally weighted. However, the states do not agree on the definition of apportionable income. Under P's tax provisions, nonbusiness rent income is allocable and business income is apportionable, while Q requires a corporation to apportion all of its (business and nonbusiness) income. The sales factor (the ratio of in-state sales to total sales) for each of the states is computed as follows.

$$\text{State P: } \frac{\$600{,}000 \text{ (sales in State P)}}{\$900{,}000 \text{ (total sales)}} = 66.67\%$$

$$\text{State Q: } \frac{\$300{,}000 \text{ (sales in State Q)}}{\$990{,}000 \text{ (total sales)}^*} = 30.30\%$$

*Since rent income is treated as business income, rents are included in the denominator of the sales factor. ∎

**EXAMPLE 6**

Continue with the facts of Example 5, except that the rent income was generated from property located in Q, rather than from property located in P. Although the sales factor for P remains the same, the sales factor for Q changes.

$$\text{State P: } \frac{\$600{,}000 \text{ (sales in State P)}}{\$900{,}000 \text{ (total sales)}} = 66.67\%$$

$$\text{State Q: } \frac{\$390{,}000 \text{ (sales in State Q)}}{\$990{,}000 \text{ (total sales)}} = 39.39\%$$

Due to the composition of the sales factor in the two states, TNT's income never is perfectly apportioned: the aggregate of the sales factors is either more or less than 100%. ∎

Business income arises from the taxpayer's regular course of business or constitutes an integral part of the taxpayer's regular business.[6] In determining whether an item of income is (apportionable) business income, state courts have developed a variety of approaches to determine what constitutes a taxpayer's "regular course of business."[7]

---

[6]MTC Reg. IV.1.(a).
[7]*Atlantic Richfield Co. v. State of Colorado and Joseph F. Dolan*, 601 P.2d 628 (Colo.S.Ct., 1979); *Appeal of A. Epstein and Sons, Inc.* (Cal.State Bd. of Equalization, 1984).

A few states, including Connecticut and New Jersey, fail to distinguish between business and nonbusiness income. In these states, all of a corporation's income is deemed to be business income and subject to apportionment.

**EXAMPLE 7**

Scarlet Corporation is subject to income tax in several states. Scarlet earned $2.5 million from the sales of its products and $1 million from the sale of assets that were unrelated to its regular business operations.

In the states that distinguish between business and nonbusiness income, $2.5 million of Scarlet's income is apportioned to the state according to the state's apportionment formula. The gain on the sale of the nonbusiness assets is allocated to the state in which the assets were located. In the states that subject a corporation's entire income to apportionment, $3.5 million ($2,500,000 + $1,000,000) is apportioned to the states in which the taxpayer conducts business. ■

Nonbusiness income is "all income other than business income."[8] Usually, nonbusiness income comprises passive and portfolio income, such as dividends, interest, rents, royalties, and certain capital gains. However, passive or portfolio income may be classified as business income when the acquisition, management, and disposition of the underlying property constitute an integral part of the taxpayer's regular business operation.

**EXAMPLE 8**

Gray Corporation owns and operates two manufacturing facilities, one in State A and the other in State B. Due to a temporary decline in sales, Gray has rented 10% of its A facility to an unaffiliated corporation. Gray generated $100,000 net rent income and $900,000 income from manufacturing.

Both A and B classify such rent income as allocable nonbusiness income. By applying the statutes of each state, as discussed in the next section, Gray determines that its apportionment factors are 0.40 for A and 0.60 for B. Gray's income attributable to each state is determined as shown below.

| **Income Subject to Tax in State A** | |
| --- | ---: |
| Taxable income | $1,000,000 |
| Less: Allocable income | (100,000) |
| Apportionable income | $  900,000 |
| Times: Apportionment factor | 40% |
| Income apportioned to State A | $  360,000 |
| Plus: Income allocated to State A | 100,000 |
| Income subject to tax in State A | $  460,000 |
| **Income Subject to Tax in State B** | |
| Taxable income | $1,000,000 |
| Less: Allocable income | (100,000) |
| Apportionable income | $  900,000 |
| Times: Apportionment factor | 60% |
| Income apportioned to State B | $  540,000 |
| Plus: Income allocated to State B | –0– |
| Income subject to tax in State B | $  540,000 |

---

[8]UDITPA § 1(e).

**EXAMPLE 9**

Continue with the facts of Example 8, but assume that B does not distinguish between business and nonbusiness income. Thus, all of Gray's income is apportionable.

Gray properly determines that its apportionment factors are 0.40 for A and 0.58 for B. Since the apportionment factors used by the two states are derived differently, Gray's income that is subject to tax does not equal 100%.

| | |
|---|---|
| **Income Subject to Tax in State A** | $ 460,000 |
| **Income Subject to Tax in State B** | |
| Apportionable income | $1,000,000 |
| Times: Apportionment factor | 58% |
| Income apportioned to State B | $ 580,000 |

Due to differences in the states' definitions of apportionable and allocable income, $1.04 million of Gray's $1 million Federal taxable income is subject to state income taxation. ■

**LO.5**

Discuss the sales, payroll, and property apportionment factors.

## APPORTIONMENT FACTORS: ELEMENTS AND PLANNING

Business income is apportioned among the states by determining the appropriate apportionment percentage for each state that has a right to tax the entity. To determine the apportionment percentage for each state, a ratio is established for each of the factors included in the state's apportionment formula. Each ratio is calculated by comparing the level of a specific business activity within a state to the total corporate activity of that type. The ratios then are summed, averaged, and appropriately weighted (if required) to determine the corporation's apportionment percentage for a specific state.

Although apportionment formulas vary among jurisdictions, the traditional three-factor formula equally weights sales, property, and payroll.[9] However, most of the states now use a modified three-factor formula, where the sales factor receives more than a one-third weight. The use of a higher-weighted sales factor tends to pull a larger percentage of an out-of-state corporation's income into the taxing jurisdiction of the state, because the corporation's major activity within the state—the sales of its products—is weighted more heavily than are its payroll and property activities. Overweighting the sales factor, however, provides tax relief for corporations that are domiciled in the state. Those corporations generally own significantly more property and incur more payroll costs (factors that are given less weight in the apportionment formula) within the state than do out-of-state corporations.

**EXAMPLE 10**

Musk Corporation realized $500,000 of taxable income from the sales of its products in States A and B. Musk's activities in both states establish nexus for income tax purposes. Musk's sales, payroll, and property in the states include the following.

| | State A | State B | Total |
|---|---|---|---|
| Sales | $1,250,000 | $750,000 | $2,000,000 |
| Property | 2,500,000 | –0– | 2,500,000 |
| Payroll | 1,500,000 | –0– | 1,500,000 |

---

[9]Certain industries, such as financial institutions, insurance companies, air and motor carriers, pipeline companies, and public utilities, typically are required to use special apportionment formulas.

If State B uses an equally weighted three-factor apportionment formula, $62,500 of Musk's taxable income is apportioned to B.

| | | |
|---|---|---|
| Sales ($750,000/$2,000,000) | = | 37.5% |
| Property ($0/$2,500,000) | = | –0– |
| Payroll ($0/$1,500,000) | = | –0– |
| Sum of apportionment factors | | 37.5% |
| Average | ÷ | 3 |
| Apportionment factor for State B | | 12.5% |
| Taxable income | × | $500,000 |
| Income apportioned to State B | | $ 62,500 |

If State B uses a double-weighted sales factor in its three-factor apportionment formula, $93,750 of Musk's taxable income is apportioned to B.

| | | | | |
|---|---|---|---|---|
| Sales ($750,000/$2,000,000) | = | 37.5% × 2 | = | 75% |
| Property ($0/$2,500,000) | = | | | –0– |
| Payroll ($0/$1,500,000) | = | | | –0– |
| Sum of apportionment factors | | | | 75% |
| Average | | | ÷ | 4 |
| Apportionment factor for State B | | | | 18.75% |
| Taxable income | | | × | $500,000 |
| Income apportioned to State B | | | | $ 93,750 |

When a state uses a double-weighted sales factor, typically a larger percentage of an out-of-state corporation's income is subject to tax in the state. Here, an additional $31,250 ($93,750 – $62,500) of Musk's income is subject to tax in B. ■

A single-factor apportionment formula consisting solely of a sales factor is even more detrimental to an out-of-state corporation than an apportionment factor that double weights the sales factor.[10]

**EXAMPLE 11**

PPR Corporation, a retailer of paper products, owns retail stores in States A, B, and C. A uses a three-factor apportionment formula under which the sales, property, and payroll factors are equally weighted. B uses a three-factor apportionment formula under which sales are double weighted. C employs a single-factor apportionment factor, based solely on sales.

PPR's operations generated $800,000 of apportionable income, and its sales, payroll activity, and average property owned in each of the three states are as follows.

| | State A | State B | State C | Total |
|---|---|---|---|---|
| Sales | $500,000 | $400,000 | $300,000 | $1,200,000 |
| Payroll | 100,000 | 125,000 | 75,000 | 300,000 |
| Property | 150,000 | 250,000 | 100,000 | 500,000 |

$280,000 of PPR's apportionable income is assigned to A.

---

[10]Currently, Illinois, Iowa, Nebraska, and Texas require the use of a single-factor apportionment formula.

| | | | |
|---|---|---|---|
| Sales ($500,000/$1,200,000) | = | 41.67% | |
| Payroll ($100,000/$300,000) | = | 33.33% | |
| Property ($150,000/$500,000) | = | 30.00% | |
| Sum of apportionment factors | | 105.00% | |
| Average | ÷ | 3 | |
| Apportionment factor for State A | | 35.00% | |
| Apportionable income | × | $800,000 | |
| Income apportioned to State A | | $280,000 | |

$316,640 of PPR's apportionable income is assigned to B.

| | | | | |
|---|---|---|---|---|
| Sales ($400,000/$1,200,000) | = | 33.33% × 2 | = | 66.66% |
| Payroll ($125,000/$300,000) | | | = | 41.67% |
| Property ($250,000/$500,000) | | | = | 50.00% |
| Sum of apportionment factors | | | | 158.33% |
| Average | | | ÷ | 4 |
| Apportionment factor for State B | | | | 39.58% |
| Apportionable income | | | × | $800,000 |
| Income apportioned to State B | | | | $316,640 |

$200,000 of PPR's apportionable income is assigned to C.

| | | |
|---|---|---|
| Sales ($300,000/$1,200,000) | = | 25.00% |
| Sum of apportionment factors | | 25.00% |
| Average | ÷ | 1 |
| Apportionment factor for State C | | 25.00% |
| Apportionable income | × | $800,000 |
| Income apportioned to State C | | $200,000 |

**Summary**

| | |
|---|---|
| Income apportioned to State A | $280,000 |
| Income apportioned to State B | 316,640 |
| Income apportioned to State C | 200,000 |
| Total income apportioned | $796,640 |

Due to the variations in the apportionment formulas employed by the various states, only 99.58% ($796,640/$800,000) of PPR's income is apportioned to the states in which it is subject to tax. ■

## THE SALES FACTOR

The **sales factor** is a fraction, whose numerator is the corporation's total sales in the state during the tax period. The denominator is the corporation's total sales everywhere during the tax period. Gross sales for this purpose generally are net of returns, allowances, and discounts. Moreover, interest income, service charges, and carrying charges are included in the sales factor. Federal and state excise taxes and state sales taxes are included in the factor, if these taxes are either passed on to the buyer or included in the selling price of the goods.

Since the sales factor is a component in the formula used to apportion a corporation's business income to a state, only sales that generate business income are includible in the fraction. The "sales" factor actually resembles a "receipts" factor since it also generally includes business income from the sale of inventory or services, interest, dividends, rentals, royalties, sales of assets, and other business income. Income on Federal obligations, however, is not included in the sales factor.

When the sale involves capital assets, some states require that the gross proceeds, rather than the net gain or loss, be included in the fraction. Most states allow incidental or occasional asset sales and sales of certain intangible assets to be excluded from gross receipts.[11]

In determining the numerator of the sales factor, most states follow the UDITPA's "ultimate destination concept," under which tangible asset sales are assumed to take place at the point of delivery, not at the location at which the shipment originates.

**EXAMPLE 12**

Olive Corporation, whose only manufacturing plant is located in State A, sells its products to residents of A through its local retail store. Olive also ships its products to customers in States B and C. The products that are sold to residents of A are assigned to A, while the products that are delivered to B and C are assigned to B and C, respectively. ∎

**Dock Sales.**   **Dock sales** occur where a purchaser uses its owned or rented vehicles, or a common carrier with which it has made arrangements, to take delivery of the product at the seller's shipping dock. Most states apply the destination test to dock sales in the same manner as it is applied to other sales. Thus, if the seller makes dock sales to a purchaser that has an out-of-state location to which it returns with the product, the sale is assigned to the purchaser's state.

**Throwback Rule.**   Out-of-state sales that are not subject to tax in the destination state are pulled back into the origination state if that state has adopted a **throwback rule.** This rule is an exception to the destination test. The rule provides that, when a corporation is not subject to tax in the destination state or the purchaser is the U.S. government, the sales are treated as in-state sales of the origination state, and the actual destination of the product is disregarded. Consequently, when the seller is immune from tax in the destination state under Public Law 86–272, the sales are considered to be in-state sales of the origination state if that state has a throwback provision.

The throwback rule seems inappropriate when the sale is made to a purchaser in a foreign country, where the transaction is subject to a gross-receipts tax (but no income tax). In these cases, the taxpayer truly is subject to double taxation, as state taxes increase but no Federal foreign tax credit is available. Nonetheless, most of the throwback states fail to distinguish between U.S. and foreign throwback sales.

**EXAMPLE 13**

Braun Corporation's entire operations are located in State A. Seventy percent ($700,000) of Braun's sales are made in A, and the remaining 30% ($300,000) are made in State B. Braun's solicitation of sales in B is limited to mailing a monthly catalog to its customers in that state. However, Braun employees do pick up and replace damaged merchandise in State B.

The pickup and replacement of damaged goods establish nexus with A. Braun's activities in B are sufficient (as determined by A's law) to subject Braun to a positive tax, based on its income. Therefore, Braun is permitted to apportion its income between A and B. However, B's interpretation of activities necessary to create nexus is less strict than that imposed by

---

[11]MTC Reg. IV.18.(c).

A; in B, the mere pickup and replacement of damaged goods do not subject a corporation's income to tax.

Braun's taxable income is $900,000. Both A and B impose a 10% corporate income tax and include only the sales factor in their apportionment formulas. If A has not adopted a throwback rule, Braun's effective state income tax rate is 7%.

| | Apportionment Factors | Net Income | Tax Rate | Tax |
|---|---|---|---|---|
| State A | 70% | $900,000 | 10% | $63,000 |
| State B | * | 900,000 | 10% | –0– |
| Total tax liability | | | | $63,000 |
| Effective state income tax rate: $63,000/$900,000 = | | | | 7% |

*As determined under B's laws, Braun's income is not apportionable to State B, because insufficient nexus is present.

If A has adopted a throwback rule, Braun does not benefit from its lack of nexus with B, because the sales in B are considered to be in-state sales of A. Thus, Braun's effective tax rate is 10%.

| | Apportionment Factors | Net Income | Tax Rate | Tax |
|---|---|---|---|---|
| State A | 100% | $900,000 | 10% | $90,000 |
| State B | –0– | 900,000 | 10% | –0– |
| Total tax liability | | | | $90,000 |
| Effective state income tax rate: $90,000/$900,000 = | | | | 10% |
| Tax increase due to throwback provision ($90,000 – $63,000) | | | | $27,000 |

## THE PAYROLL FACTOR

The **payroll factor** is determined by comparing the compensation paid for services rendered within a state to the total compensation paid by the corporation. Generally, the payroll factor is a fraction, whose numerator is the total amount that a corporation paid or accrued for compensation in a state during the tax period. The denominator is the total amount paid or accrued by the corporation for compensation during the tax period. For purposes of the payroll factor, compensation includes wages, salaries, commissions, and any other form of remuneration paid or accrued to employees for personal services. Compensation may also include the value of board, rent, housing, lodging, and other benefits or services furnished to employees by the taxpayer in return for personal services, if these amounts constitute Federal gross income.

Payments made to an independent contractor or any other person who is not properly classifiable as an employee generally are excluded from the numerator and denominator of the payroll factor. Some states exclude from the payroll factor the compensation paid to corporate officers.

Several states provide that earnings paid to a cash or deferred compensation plan, excluded from Federal gross income under § 401(k), are to be included in the numerator and the denominator of the payroll factor. Accordingly, the total compensation that is included in the denominator of a corporation's payroll factor may vary among the states in which the corporation's income is apportioned.

**EXAMPLE 14**

Mice Corporation's sales office and manufacturing plant are located in State A. Mice also maintains a manufacturing plant and sales office in State C. For purposes of apportionment, A defines payroll as all compensation paid to employees, including contributions to § 401(k) deferred compensation plans. Under the statutes of C, neither compensation paid to officers nor contributions to § 401(k) plans are included in the payroll factor. Mice incurred the following personnel costs.

|  | State A | State C | Total |
| --- | --- | --- | --- |
| Wages and salaries for employees other than officers | $350,000 | $250,000 | $600,000 |
| Salaries for officers | 150,000 | 100,000 | 250,000 |
| Contributions to § 401(k) plans | 30,000 | 20,000 | 50,000 |
| Total | $530,000 | $370,000 | $900,000 |

The payroll factor for State A is computed as follows.

$$\frac{\$530,000}{\$900,000} = 58.89\%$$

Since C excludes from the payroll factor any compensation paid to officers and contributions to § 401(k) plans, C's factor is computed as follows.

$$\frac{\$250,000}{\$600,000} = 41.67\%$$

The aggregate of Mice's payroll factors is 100.56% (58.89% + 41.67%). In certain cases, the sum of a corporation's payroll factors may be significantly more or less than 100%. ■

The compensation of an employee normally is not split between two or more states during the year, unless he or she is transferred or changes positions during the year. Instead, each employee's compensation is allocated to only one state. Under the UDITPA, compensation is treated as paid in the state (it is included in the numerator of the payroll factor) in which the services are primarily performed.

When an employee's services are performed in more than one state, his or her compensation is attributed to the employee's base of operations or, if there is no base of operations in any state in which some part of the service is performed, to the place from which the services are directed or controlled. When no services are performed in the state that serves as the base of operations or the place from which the services are directed, the employee's compensation is attributed to his or her state of residency.[12]

**EXAMPLE 15**

Geese Corporation has its headquarters and a manufacturing plant in State A. Reggie, a resident of State Y, works at the A manufacturing plant. His compensation is included in the numerator of A's payroll factor, as the service is performed entirely in A. ■

Only compensation that is related to the production of apportionable income is included in the payroll factor. Accordingly, in those states that distinguish between business and nonbusiness income, compensation related to the operation, maintenance, protection, or supervision of nonbusiness income is not includible in the payroll factor.

---

[12]UDITPA § 14.

**EXAMPLE 16**

Dog Corporation, a manufacturer of automobile parts, is subject to tax in States X and Y. Dog incurred the following payroll costs.

|  | State X | State Y | Total |
|---|---|---|---|
| Wages and salaries for officers and personnel of manufacturing facilities | $450,000 | $350,000 | $800,000 |
| Wages and salaries for personnel involved in nonbusiness rental activities | 50,000 | –0– | 50,000 |

If both states distinguish between business and nonbusiness income in determining apportionable income and include officers' compensation in the payroll factor, Dog's payroll factors are computed as follows.

Payroll factor for State X: $450,000/$800,000 = 56.25%

Payroll factor for State Y: $350,000/$800,000 = 43.75%

**EXAMPLE 17**

Continue with the facts of Example 16, but assume that Y defines apportionable income as the corporation's total income (business and nonbusiness income). Dog's payroll factor for X remains unchanged, but its payroll factor for Y is reduced.

Payroll factor for State X: $450,000/$800,000 = 56.25%

Payroll factor for State Y: $350,000/$850,000* = 41.18%

*$800,000 (compensation related to business income) + $50,000 (compensation related to nonbusiness income).

Compensation related to the operation, maintenance, protection, or supervision of property used in the production of both apportionable and nonapportionable income or losses generally is prorated between business and nonbusiness sources.

**EXAMPLE 18**

Tall Corporation, a manufacturer of paper products, operates paper mills in States A and B. In addition, the corporation owns nonbusiness rental real property in A. Tall incurred the following compensation expenses.

|  | State A | State B | Total |
|---|---|---|---|
| Wages and salaries for mill employees | $1,200,000 | $1,500,000 | $2,700,000 |
| Wages and salaries for administrative staff | 600,000 | 500,000 | 1,100,000 |
| Compensation of officers | 800,000 | 400,000 | 1,200,000 |

Ten percent of the time spent by the administrative staff located in A and 5% of the time spent by officers located in A are devoted to the operation, maintenance, and supervision of the nonbusiness rental property. Both states exclude such rent income from the definition of apportionable income.

*Payroll factor for State A*

$$\frac{\$2,500,000 \ [\$1,200,000 + 90\%(\$600,000) + 95\%(\$800,000)]}{\$4,900,000 \ [\$2,700,000 + 90\%(\$600,000) + \$500,000 + 95\%(\$800,000) + \$400,000]} = 51.02\%$$

*Payroll factor for State B*

$$\frac{\$2,400,000 \ (\$1,500,000 + \$500,000 + \$400,000)}{\$4,900,000 \ [\$2,700,000 + 90\%(\$600,000) + \$500,000 + 95\%(\$800,000) + \$400,000]} = 48.98\%$$

## THE PROPERTY FACTOR

The **property factor** generally is a fraction, whose numerator is the average value of the corporation's real property and its tangible personal property owned and used or rented and used in the state during the taxable year. The denominator is the average value of all of the corporation's real property and its tangible personal property owned or rented and used during the taxable year, wherever it is located. In this manner, a state's property factor reflects the extent of total property usage by the taxpayer in the state.

For this purpose, property includes land, buildings, machinery, inventory, equipment, and other real and tangible personal property, other than coins or currency.[13] Other types of property that may be included in the factor are construction in progress (even though it does not yet contribute to the production of income), offshore property, outer space property (satellites), and partnership property.

In the case of property that is in transit between locations of the taxpayer or between a buyer and seller, the assets are included in the numerator of the destination state. With respect to mobile or movable property, such as construction equipment, trucks, and leased equipment, which is both in- and outside the state during the tax period, the numerator of a state's property factor generally is determined on the basis of the total time that the property was within the state.

Space satellites used in the communication industry generally are included in the numerator of the property factor based on the ratio of earth stations serviced. For example, if a satellite is being serviced by earth stations located in San Francisco, Chicago, New York, and Houston, 25 percent of the cost of the satellite is included in the numerator of the property factor for each of the four corresponding states.

Property owned by the corporation typically is valued at its average original or historical cost plus the cost of additions and improvements, but without adjusting for depreciation. Some states allow property to be included at net book value or adjusted tax basis. The value of the property usually is determined by averaging the values at the beginning and end of the tax period. Alternatively, some states allow or require the amount to be calculated on a monthly basis if annual computation results in or requires substantial distortions.

**EXAMPLE 19**

Blond Corporation, a calendar year taxpayer, owns property in States A and B. Both A and B require that the average value of assets be included in the property factor. A requires that the property be valued at its historical cost, and B requires that the property be included in the property factor at its net book value.

| Account Balances at January 1 | | | |
|---|---|---|---|
| | **State A** | **State B** | **Total** |
| Inventories | $ 150,000 | $ 100,000 | $ 250,000 |
| Building and machinery (cost) | 200,000 | 400,000 | 600,000 |
| Accumulated depreciation for building and machinery | (150,000) | (50,000) | (200,000) |
| Land | 50,000 | 100,000 | 150,000 |
| Total | $ 250,000 | $ 550,000 | $ 800,000 |

---

[13]MTC Reg. IV.10.(a).

| Account Balances at December 31 | | | |
|---|---|---|---|
| | **State A** | **State B** | **Total** |
| Inventories | $ 250,000 | $ 200,000 | $ 450,000 |
| Building and machinery (cost) | 200,000 | 400,000 | 600,000 |
| Accumulated depreciation for building and machinery | (175,000) | (100,000) | (275,000) |
| Land | 50,000 | 100,000 | 150,000 |
| Total | $ 325,000 | $ 600,000 | $ 925,000 |

| State A Property Factor | | | |
|---|---|---|---|
| **Historical Cost** | **January 1** | **December 31** | **Average** |
| Property in State A | $ 400,000* | $ 500,000** | $ 450,000 |
| Total property | 1,000,000† | 1,200,000†† | 1,100,000 |

  * $150,000 + $200,000 + $50,000.
 ** $250,000 + $200,000 + $50,000.
  † $250,000 + $600,000 + $150,000.
†† $450,000 + $600,000 + $150,000.

Property factor for State A: $\dfrac{\$450,000}{\$1,100,000} = 40.91\%$

| State B Property Factor | | | |
|---|---|---|---|
| **Net Book Value** | **January 1** | **December 31** | **Average** |
| Property in State B | $550,000 | $600,000 | $575,000 |
| Total property | 800,000 | 925,000 | 862,500 |

Property factor for State B: $\dfrac{\$575,000}{\$862,500} = 66.67\%$

Due to the variations in the property factors, the aggregate of Blond's property factors equals 107.58%. ■

Leased property, when included in the property factor, is valued at eight times its annual rental. Annual rentals may include payments, such as real estate taxes and insurance, made by the lessee in lieu of rent.

**EXAMPLE 20**

Jasper Corporation is subject to tax in States D and G. Both states require that leased or rented property be included in the property factor at eight times the annual rental costs, and that the average historical cost be used for other assets. Information regarding Jasper's property and rental expenses follows.

| **Average Historical Cost** | |
|---|---|
| Property located in State D | $ 750,000 |
| Property located in State G | 450,000 |
| Total property | $1,200,000 |

| **Lease and Rental Expenses** | |
|---|---|
| State D | $ 50,000 |
| State G | 150,000 |
| Total | $ 200,000 |

*Property factor for State D*

$$\frac{\$1,150,000\ [\$750,000 + 8(\$50,000)]}{\$2,800,000\ [\$1,200,000 + 8(\$200,000)]} = 41.07\%$$

*Property factor for State G*

$$\frac{\$1,650,000\ [\$450,000 + 8(\$150,000)]}{\$2,800,000\ [\$1,200,000 + 8(\$200,000)]} = 58.93\%$$  ∎

Only property that is used in the production of apportionable income is includible in the numerator and denominator of the property factor. In this regard, idle property and property that is used in producing nonapportionable income generally are excluded. However, property that is temporarily idle or unused generally remains in the property factor.

## LO.6

*Apply the unitary method of state income taxation.*

# The Unitary Theory

The **unitary theory** developed in response to the early problems that states faced in attributing the income of a multistate business among the states in which the business was conducted. Originally, this theory was applied to justify apportionment of the income of multiple operating divisions within a single company. Over the years, however, the concept has been extended to require the combined reporting of certain affiliated corporations, including those outside the United States.

When two affiliated corporations are subject to tax in different states, each entity must file a return and report its income in the state in which it conducts business. Each entity reports its income separately from that of its affiliated corporations. In an effort to minimize overall state income tax, multistate entities have attempted to separate the parts of the business that are carried on in the various states.

**EXAMPLE 21**

Arts Corporation owns a chain of retail stores located in several states. To enable each store to file and report the income earned only in that state, each store was organized as a separate subsidiary in the state in which it did business. In this manner, each store is separately subject to tax only in the state in which it is located. ∎

Since most states attempt to allocate as much income to in-state sources as possible, several states have adopted the *unitary* approach to computing state taxable income. Under this method, a corporation is required to file a "combined return" that includes the results from all of the operations of the related corporations, not just from those that transacted business in the state. In this manner, the unitary method allows a state to apply formula apportionment to a firm's nationwide or worldwide unitary income. To include the activities of the corporation's subsidiaries in the apportionment formula, the state must determine that the subsidiaries' activities are an integral part of a unitary business and, as a result, are subject to apportionment.

## WHAT IS A UNITARY BUSINESS?

A unitary business operates as a unit and cannot be segregated into independently operating divisions. The operations are integrated, and each division depends on or contributes to the operation of the business as a whole. It is not necessary that each unit operating within a state contribute to the activities of all divisions outside the state. The unitary theory ignores the separate legal existence of the entities and focuses instead on practical business realities. Accordingly, the separate entities are treated as a single business for state income tax purposes, and the apportionment formula is applied to the combined income of the unitary business.

**EXAMPLE 22**

Continue with the facts of Example 21. Arts manufactured no goods, but conducted central management, purchasing, distributing, advertising, and administrative departments. The subsidiaries carried on a purely intrastate business, and they paid for the goods and services received at the parent company's cost, plus overhead. Arts and the subsidiaries constitute a unitary business due to their unitary operations (purchasing, distributing, advertising, and administrative functions). Accordingly, in states that have adopted the unitary method, the income and apportionment factors of the entire unitary group are combined and apportioned to the states in which at least one member of the group has nexus. ■

**EXAMPLE 23**

Crafts Corporation organized its departments as separate corporations on the basis of function: mining copper ore, refining the ore, and fabricating the refined copper into consumer products. Even though the various steps in the process are operated substantially independently of each other with only general supervision from Crafts's executive offices, Crafts is engaged in a single unitary business. Its various divisions are part of a large, vertically structured enterprise, in which each business segment needs the products or raw materials provided by another. The flow of products between the affiliates also provides evidence of functional integration, which generally requires some form of central decision or policy making, another characteristic of a unitary business. ■

Notice that the application of the unitary theory is based on a series of subjective observations about the organization and operation of the taxpayer's businesses, whereas the availability of Federal controlled and affiliated group status is based on objective, mechanical ownership tests. About half of the states require or allow unitary reporting, a somewhat smaller number than in the early 1980s.

## TAX EFFECTS OF THE UNITARY THEORY

Use of the unitary approach by a state eliminates several of the planning techniques that could be used to shift income between corporate segments to avoid or minimize state taxes. In addition, the unitary approach usually results in a larger portion of the corporation's income being taxable in states where the compensation, property values, and sales prices are high relative to other states. This occurs because the larger in-state costs (numerators in the apportionment formula) include in the tax base a larger portion of the taxable income within the state's taxing jurisdiction. This has an adverse effect upon the corporation's overall state tax burden if the states in which the larger portions are allocated impose a high tax rate relative to the other states in which the business is conducted.

The presence of a unitary business is favorable when losses of unprofitable affiliates may be offset against the earnings of profitable affiliates. It also is favorable when income earned in a high-tax state may be shifted to low-tax states due to the use of combined apportionment factors.

**EXAMPLE 24**

Rita Corporation owns two subsidiaries, Arts and Crafts. Arts, located in State K, generated taxable income of $700,000. During this same period, Crafts, located in State M, generated a loss of $400,000. If the subsidiaries are independent corporations, Arts is required to pay K tax on $700,000 of income. However, if the corporations constitute a unitary business, the incomes, as well as the apportionment factors, of the two entities are combined. As a result, the combined income of $300,000 ($700,000 − $400,000) is apportioned to unitary states K and M. ■

**E X A M P L E   2 5**

Everett Corporation, a wholly owned subsidiary of Dan Corporation, generated $1 million taxable income. Everett's activities and sales are restricted to State P, which imposes a 10% income tax. Dan's income for the taxable period is $1.5 million. Dan's activities and sales are restricted to State Q, which imposes a 5% income tax. Both states use a three-factor apportionment formula that equally weights sales, payroll, and property. Sales, payroll, and average property for each of the corporations are as follows.

|  | **Everett Corporation** | **Dan Corporation** | **Total** |
|---|---|---|---|
| Sales | $3,000,000 | $7,000,000 | $10,000,000 |
| Payroll | 2,000,000 | 3,500,000 | 5,500,000 |
| Property | 2,500,000 | 4,500,000 | 7,000,000 |

If the corporations are independent entities, the overall state income tax liability is $175,000.

| | | |
|---|---|---|
| State P (10% × $1,000,000) | = | $100,000 |
| State Q (5% × $1,500,000) | = | 75,000 |
| Total state income tax | | $175,000 |

If the corporations are members of a unitary business, the income and apportionment factors are combined in determining the income tax liability in unitary states P and Q. As a result of the combined reporting, the overall state income tax liability is reduced.

**State P Income Tax**

| | | | |
|---|---|---|---|
| Total apportionable income | | | $2,500,000 |
| Apportionment formula | | | |
| Sales ($3,000,000/$10,000,000) | = | 30.00% | |
| Payroll ($2,000,000/$5,500,000) | = | 36.36% | |
| Property ($2,500,000/$7,000,000) | = | 35.71% | |
| Total | | 102.07% | |
| Average (102.07% ÷ 3) | | | × 34.02% |
| State P taxable income | | | $   850,500 |
| Tax rate | | | × 10% |
| State P tax liability | | | $85,050 |

**State Q Income Tax**

| | | | |
|---|---|---|---|
| Total apportionable income | | | $2,500,000 |
| Apportionment formula | | | |
| Sales ($7,000,000/$10,000,000) | = | 70.00% | |
| Payroll ($3,500,000/$5,500,000) | = | 63.64% | |
| Property ($4,500,000/$7,000,000) | = | 64.29% | |
| Total | | 197.93% | |
| Average (197.93% ÷ 3) | | | × 65.98% |
| State Q taxable income | | | $1,649,500 |
| Tax rate | | | × 5% |
| State Q tax liability | | | 82,475 |
| Total state income tax, if unitary | | | $167,525 |
| Total state income tax, if nonunitary | | | 175,000 |
| Tax reduction from unitary combined reporting | | | $   7,475 |

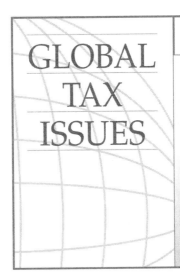

GLOBAL TAX ISSUES

## WATER'S EDGE IS NOT A DAY AT THE BEACH

As a result of pressure from the business community, the Federal government, and foreign countries, most of the states that impose an income tax on a unitary business's worldwide operations permit a multinational business to elect **water's edge** unitary reporting as an alternative to worldwide unitary filing.

The water's edge provision permits a multinational corporation to elect to limit the reach of the state's taxing jurisdiction over out-of-state affiliates to activities occurring within the boundaries of the United States. The decision to make a water's edge election may have a substantial effect on the tax liability of a multinational corporation. For instance, a water's edge election usually cannot be revoked for a number of years without permission from the appropriate tax authority. Moreover, corporations making this election may be assessed an additional tax for the privilege of excluding out-of-state entities from the combined report.

The results of unitary reporting would have been detrimental if Q had imposed a higher rate of tax than P, because a larger percentage of the corporation's income is attributable to Q when the apportionment factors are combined. ∎

By identifying the states that have adopted the unitary method and the criteria under which a particular state defines a unitary business, a taxpayer may reduce its overall state tax by restructuring its corporate relationships to create or guard against a unitary relationship. For instance, an independent business enterprise can be made unitary by exercising day-to-day operational control and by centralizing functions, such as marketing, financing, accounting, and legal services.

### CONSOLIDATED AND COMBINED RETURNS

As discussed in Chapter 8, an affiliated group of corporations may file a consolidated return if all members of the group consent. Once such a return has been filed, the group must continue to file on a consolidated basis as long as it remains in existence, or until permission to file separate returns has been obtained. The consolidated return essentially treats the controlled corporations as a single taxable entity. Thus, the affiliated group pays only one tax, based upon the combined income of its members after certain adjustments (e.g., net operating losses) and eliminations (e.g., intercompany dividends and inventory profits).

Several states permit affiliated corporations to file a consolidated return if such a return has been filed for Federal purposes. The filing of a consolidated return is mandatory in only a few states.

Usually, only corporations that are subject to tax in the state can be included in a consolidated return unless specific requirements are met or the state permits the inclusion of corporations without nexus.

Do not confuse elective consolidated returns with required combined returns in unitary states. A combined return is filed in every unitary state in which one or more unitary members have nexus. The computations reflect apportioned and allocated income of the unitary members, resulting in a summary of the taxable income of the entities in each state. The combined method chiefly permits the unitary taxpayer to develop the summary of assigned taxable incomes, which is accepted by (and disclosed to) all of the states.

| CONCEPT SUMMARY 15–1 |
| --- |

### Principles of Multistate Corporate Taxation

1. Taxability of an organization's income in a state other than the one in which it is incorporated depends on the laws, regulations, and judicial interpretations of the other state; the nature and level of the corporation's activity in, or contacts with, that state; and, to a limited extent, the application of P.L. 86–272.
2. Each state has adopted its own multistate income tax laws, regulations, methods, and judicial interpretations; consequently, the nonuniformity of state income taxing provisions provides a multitude of planning techniques that allow a multistate corporation to reduce its overall state tax liability legally.
3. The apportionment procedure is used to assign the income of a multistate taxpayer to the various states in which business is conducted. Generally, nonbusiness income is allocated, rather than apportioned, directly to the state in which the nonbusiness income-generating assets are located.
4. The various state apportionment formulas offer planning opportunities in that more or less than 100% of the taxpayer's income may be subjected to state income tax.
5. Most states employ an equally weighted three-factor apportionment formula. In some states, the sales factor is doubled, and occasionally only the sales factor is used in apportioning multistate taxable income. Generally, the greater the relative weight assigned to the sales factor, the greater the tax burden on out-of-state taxpayers.
6. The sales factor is based upon the destination concept except where a throwback rule applies. The payroll factor generally includes compensation that is included in Federal gross income, but some states include excludible fringe benefits. An employee's compensation usually is not divided among states. The property factor is derived using the average undepreciated historical costs for the assets and eight times the rental value of the asset.
7. The unitary theory may require the taxpayer to include worldwide activities and holdings in the apportionment factors. A water's edge election can limit these amounts to U.S. transactions.

---

**LO.7**

Discuss the states' income tax treatment of S corporations.

## Taxation of S Corporations

The majority of the 46 states that impose a corporate income tax have special provisions, similar to the Federal law, that govern the taxation of S corporations. As of 2003, only a few states—Connecticut, Michigan, New Hampshire, Tennessee, and Texas—and the District of Columbia do not provide special (no corporate-level tax) treatment for Federal S corporations. In addition, Massachusetts imposes a corporate-level tax on S corporations that have gross receipts in excess of $6 million, and California assesses a 1.5 percent tax on the Federal taxable income of an S corporation.

In the non-S election states, a Federal S corporation generally is subject to tax in the same manner as a regular C corporation. Accordingly, if a multistate S corporation operates in any of these states, it is subject to state income tax and does not realize one of the primary benefits of S status—the avoidance of double taxation. Other potential tax-related benefits of the S election, including the pass-through of net operating losses and the reduction in the rate of tax imposed on individual and corporate taxpayers, may be curtailed.

**EXAMPLE 26**

Bryan, an S corporation, has established nexus in States A and B. A recognizes S status, while B does not. Bryan generated $600,000 of ordinary business income and $100,000 of dividends that were received from corporations in which Bryan owns 50% of the stock. Bryan's State B apportionment percentage is 50%.

For B tax purposes, Bryan must first compute its income as though it were a regular corporation and then apportion the resulting income to B. Assuming that B has adopted the Federal provisions governing the dividends received deduction, Bryan's income, determined as though it were a C corporation, is $620,000 [$600,000 + (100% − 80%) × $100,000]. Accordingly, Bryan is subject to corporate income tax in B on $310,000 ($620,000 × 50% apportionment percentage) of taxable income. ■

Most states impose a different tax rate for corporate and individual taxpayers. Assuming that the state recognizes the entity's S status, if the corporation is generating income and the state corporate tax rate is higher than the rate imposed on individuals, an S election reduces the overall state tax liability. Where the state has a graduated tax rate structure, the difference between the corporate and individual tax rates must be analyzed in light of the amount of the corporation's income and the marginal tax rate under which the shareholders fall.

## ELIGIBILITY

All of the states that recognize S status permit a corporation to be treated as an S corporation for state purposes only if the corporation has a valid Federal S election in place. Generally, the filing of a Federal S election is sufficient to render the corporation an S corporation for state tax purposes. In most states, an entity that is an S corporation for Federal tax purposes automatically is treated as an S corporation for state tax purposes. A few states permit the entity to *elect out* of its S status for state purposes.

## CORPORATE-LEVEL TAX

Although S corporations generally are not taxable entities, Federal income tax liability may arise if the corporation has excess passive investment income or built-in gains. Several states have adopted similar provisions, and, therefore, an S corporation is exempt from the related state income tax only to the extent that it is exempt from corresponding Federal income taxes. In the majority of these states, the imposition of Federal income taxes generates a corporate-level tax for state purposes to the extent that corporate income is allocated or apportioned to the state.

**EXAMPLE 27**

Amp, an S corporation, has nexus with States X and Y, both of which recognize S status. X imposes a corporate-level tax on S corporations to the extent that the corresponding Federal tax applies. Amp is subject to the § 1374 tax. This year, its Federal excessive passive income is $60,000. The amount of income subject to tax in X depends on Amp's apportionment percentage for X.

If Amp's State X apportionment percentage is 50%, Amp is subject to a corporate-level tax in X on $30,000 of passive income ($60,000 × 50%). ■

A few states deviate from the Federal S corporation provisions and provide that an S corporation is entirely exempt from state income tax only if all of its shareholders are residents of the state. In these states, an S corporation is taxed on the portion of its income that is attributable to nonresident shareholders. Some of these states permit the S corporation to escape corporate-level tax on this income if its nonresident shareholders sign a form, agreeing to pay state tax on their share of the corporation's income. Moreover, about half of the states require the corporation to withhold taxes on the nonresident shareholders' portions of the entity's income.

**EXAMPLE 28**

ARGO, an S corporation, is subject to income tax only in Vermont. On the last day of its taxable year, 40% of ARGO's stock is held by nonresident shareholders. To the extent that

ARGO's stock is held by resident shareholders, the corporation is not subject to income tax. Accordingly, ARGO is not subject to tax on 60% of its income.

The corporation *is* subject to tax on the remaining 40% of its income. ARGO may be able to avoid this corporate-level tax by withholding Vermont income tax for its nonresident shareholders. ■

## COMPOSITE TAX RETURN

In an effort to decrease compliance burdens and simplify the filing process for nonresident shareholders of S corporations, several states allow an S corporation to file a single income tax return and pay the resulting tax on behalf of some or all of its nonresident shareholders. State requirements for the filing of a composite or "block" return vary substantially.

| LO.8 |
| --- |
| Describe other commonly encountered state and local taxes on businesses. |

# Other State and Local Taxes

## STATE AND LOCAL SALES AND USE TAXES

Forty-five states and the District of Columbia impose a consumers' sales tax on retail sales of tangible personal property for use or consumption. For most states, the sales and use tax is the chief source of revenue, surpassing even the individual income tax.

In many of these states, in-state localities, including cities, towns, school districts, or counties, also have the power to levy a sales tax. A consumers' sales tax is a tax imposed directly on the purchaser who acquires the asset at retail; the tax is measured by the price of the sale. The vendor or retailer merely acts as a collection agent for the state.

The use tax, which may be imposed either as a separate tax or as an extension of the sales tax, is designed to complement the sales tax. The purpose of the use tax is to prevent consumers from evading sales tax by purchasing goods outside the state for in-state use and to provide an equitable sales environment between in-state and out-of-state retailers.

All of the states exempt certain items, such as prescriptions and medical devices, from the tax. Several states provide that selected services are subject to tax.

Sales and use taxes are imposed on the final consumer of the taxable item. Sales by manufacturers, producers, and processors usually are exempt from the tax because these transactions are made in anticipation of a resale. Hence, sales to retailers who will resell the item to the ultimate consumer generally are exempt from the sales tax.

Certain sales to manufacturers, producers, and processors also are exempt in the majority of states. The exemptions applicable to such taxpayers usually include one or more of the following.

- Containers and other packing, packaging, and shipping materials actually used to transfer merchandise to customers of the purchaser.
- Tangible personal property that becomes an ingredient or component part of an article of tangible personal property destined for sale.
- Tangible personal property (other than fuel or electricity) that is consumed or destroyed or loses its identity in the manufacture of tangible personal property destined for sale.

## YOU PICK: CLICKS OR BRICKS?

The sales tax issue of the decade has to do with the definition of nexus for sales and use tax purposes among the states. Where is the sales/use tax payable in the following situation?

Carol, a Mississippi resident, uses her home computer, connected to the Internet via Virginia-based America Online, to purchase a wedding present from Crate and Barrel, a retailer based in Illinois. The gift is wrapped and shipped directly to the bride and groom, who live in Oregon. AOL's routing of Carol's connection used computer servers in Arkansas and Indiana. Crate and Barrel's customer service and distribution center handling the order is in Missouri. Carol used a California credit card to pay for the purchase, which was delivered by Georgia-based UPS.

Sales and use tax rules generally subject a taxable transaction to an "ultimate user" test, but so many states have been a part of this sale that it may be difficult to determine just who the final user of the merchandise might be.

Add to this a politically popular "no new taxes on the Internet" pledge that business has convinced Congress to enforce through 2007. But does exempting Internet sales from sales/use tax give Internet retailers an unfair advantage over "bricks and mortar" businesses that must collect sales tax on the sales that they make? These retailers have invested in physical stores and merchandise and make up most downtown and shopping mall areas. Why should we allow a full tax holiday for "clicks and mortar" Internet sellers, which have invested in just-in-time inventories and intangible assets like e-commerce Web software?

Will the next step in the saga look like this? Crate and Barrel will set up computer kiosks in all of its stores so that customers can browse the merchandise in a hands-on manner, then place a sales-tax-free order on one of the terminals. This is progress?

---

- Machines and specific processing equipment and repair parts or replacements exclusively and directly used in manufacturing tangible personal property.

The states apply a separate set of nexus rules that generally subject *more* businesses to the sales/use tax than are caught by income tax nexus rules. The Supreme Court has held that the regular solicitation of sales by independent brokers establishes sufficient nexus to require a nonresident seller to register and collect the use tax, even though the seller does not have regular employees, agents, and an office or other place of business in the state.[14] As a result, a corporation may be required to collect sales and use taxes in a state where it is immune from the imposition of an income tax.

### LOCAL PROPERTY TAXES

Property taxes, a major source of revenue at the city and county level, are referred to as *ad valorem* taxes because they are based on the value of property that is located in the state on a specific date. Generally, that date fixes taxable ownership, situs (location), and the valuation of the property. Nonetheless, to avoid tax evasion,

---

[14]*Scripto, Inc. v. Carson*, 80 S.Ct. 619 (1960).

## TAX IN THE NEWS

### TAX HOLIDAY—FOR WHOM?

Many counties and states have adopted "tax amnesty" strategies and found them to be useful. The arrangement usually allows delinquent taxpayers and nonfilers to submit outstanding returns with "no questions asked." Often penalties for late payment are waived, and occasionally interest is waived as well. From the government's perspective, the objective is to pick up back taxes and to enter into the database those who have come forward to claim the amnesty. "Hunting down" those who do not file tax returns can be quite costly. Thus, the government is seeking the annuity of taxes that will come its way from future tax returns, once the errant taxpayer has been identified.

A similar ploy is the "tax holiday" granted by various jurisdictions to encourage consumer spending. Starting out as a mere variation on the amnesty idea, a tax holiday is a period in which no sales/use tax is imposed. The week before school starts or the week before Thanksgiving often is targeted for this purpose, perhaps to jumpstart a lagging economy by accelerating the shopping season. But a jurisdiction may realize a net reduction in sales volume if taxpayers plan their purchasing binges so as to maximize the tax savings. A tax holiday will backfire and reduce net tax collections if the holiday lasts "too long," if it applies to "too many" or "too expensive" goods, or if consumers plan "too well" for its coming.

personal property that is temporarily outside the state may be taxed at the domicile of the owner.

Property taxes can take the form of either real property taxes or personal property taxes. States apply different tax rates and means of assessment to the two classes of property. The methods of assessing the value of the real and tangible property also vary in different taxing jurisdictions.

Although a personal property tax may be imposed on both intangible and tangible property, most states limit the tax to tangible property. The distinction between the various items of personal property is important because special rates, computations, or exemptions apply to certain types of property. For instance, inventory constitutes tangible personal property, but is exempt from taxation in most states.

### OTHER TAXES

States may impose a variety of other state and local taxes on corporations, including incorporation or entrance fees or taxes; gross receipt taxes; stock transfer taxes; realty transfer and mortgage recording taxes; license taxes; and franchise taxes based on net worth or capital stock outstanding.

An *incorporation tax* is an excise tax for the corporate privilege conferred on the business. At the time the business is incorporated, the state generally imposes a fee or tax for the privilege of conducting business within the state as a corporation. Similarly, an out-of-state corporation usually must pay an entrance fee or tax before it can transact business in a state other than its state of incorporation.

Some states base the incorporation tax on the par value of the authorized stock. To prevent tax evasion, a few of these states impose a similar fee or tax on subsequent increases in the corporation's authorized stock. Where the incorporation fee or tax is based on the amount of authorized stock, the tax may be based on the total amount of the stock, even though the corporation conducts business in several states.

A *license tax* is an excise tax on the privilege of engaging in a certain business, occupation, or profession. A state may impose business, occupational, or professional license taxes as a means of generating revenue or regulating the activities of the business, occupation, or profession for the public welfare.

Stock and realty transfer and mortgage recording taxes are nonrecurring taxes that are imposed at the time of recording or transfer. *Stock transfer taxes* are imposed on the transfer of shares or certificates of stock of domestic and foreign corporations. The tax typically is based on the number of shares transferred and the par or market value of the stock. Generally, the following stock transfers are exempt from the transfer tax: original issues, deposits of stock as security for a loan, and transfers to a broker for sale or purchase.

The base of the *realty transfer tax* usually is measured by the consideration paid or to be paid for the realty. The *mortgage recording tax* may be based on the actual consideration given, the value of the property, or the debt to be secured by the instrument.

Typically, a *capital stock tax* is an excise tax imposed on a domestic corporation for the privilege of existing as a corporation or imposed on an out-of-state corporation, either for the privilege of doing business or for the actual transaction of business within the state. This annual tax usually is based on the book value of the corporation's net worth, including capital, surplus, and retained earnings. In a few states, a corporation is subject to a *franchise tax* only to the extent that the tax exceeds the corporate income tax, but in the majority of states, the entity is subject to both taxes.

The majority of capital stock taxes are apportioned if the corporation does business or maintains an office in another state. In some states, however, the tax is levied on the entire authorized or issued capital stock of a domestic corporation, even though the corporation may be engaged in business in other states. For corporations based in other states, the tax is imposed only on the capital that is employed in the state as determined by an apportionment formula.

**EXAMPLE 29**

The balance sheet of Bull, a domestic corporation of State A, at the end of its taxable year is as follows.

| | |
|---|---|
| Cash | $100,000 |
| Equipment (net of $50,000 accumulated depreciation) | 150,000 |
| Building (net of $75,000 accumulated depreciation) | 225,000 |
| Land | 125,000 |
| Total assets | $600,000 |
| Accounts payable and other short-term liabilities | $100,000 |
| Long-term liabilities | 200,000 |
| Capital stock | 50,000 |
| Paid-in capital in excess of par value | 50,000 |
| Retained earnings | 200,000 |
| Total liabilities and equity | $600,000 |

A imposes a 2% franchise tax based on the entire net worth of a domestic corporation. Bull is subject to a franchise tax in A of $6,000 ($600,000 assets − $300,000 liabilities = $300,000 net worth × 2% rate). ■

**EXAMPLE 30**

Continue with the facts of Example 29, except that A subjects a domestic corporation to tax only on the capital that is employed in the state. Bull properly determines its A apportionment percentage as 20%. In this case, Bull's A franchise tax liability is $1,200 ($300,000 net worth × 20% apportionment percentage = $60,000 capital employed in A × 2% rate). ■

**Tax Planning Considerations**

The inconsistencies in the tax laws and rates among the states not only complicate state tax planning, but also provide the nucleus of pertinent planning opportunities. Although several tax planning devices are available to a corporation that does business in only one state, most planning techniques are directed toward corporations that do business or maintain property in more than one state. All suggested tax planning strategies should be reviewed in light of practical business considerations and the additional administrative and other costs that may be incurred, because simply minimizing state taxes may not be prudent from a business perspective.

**LO.9**

Recognize tax planning opportunities available to minimize a corporation's state and local tax liability.

## SELECTING THE OPTIMAL STATE IN WHICH TO OPERATE

Because the states employ different definitions of the amount and type of activity necessary to establish nexus, a company has some latitude in selecting the states by which it will be taxed. When a corporation has only a limited connection with a high-tax state, it may abandon that activity by electing an alternative means of accomplishing the same result. For example, if providing a sales representative with a company-owned computer constitutes nexus in an undesired state, the company could eliminate its connection with that state by reimbursing sales personnel for equipment expenses, instead of providing a company computer. Similarly, when nexus is caused by conducting customer training sessions or seminars in the state, the corporation could bypass this connection. This can be done by sending the personnel to a nearby state in which nexus clearly has been established or in which the activity would not constitute nexus.

In addition, when sufficient activity originates from the repair and maintenance of the corporation's products or the activities performed by the sales representatives within the state, the organization could incorporate the service or sales divisions. This would invalidate a nonunitary state's right to tax the parent corporation's income; only the income of the service or sales divisions would be subject to tax. However, this technique will be successful only if the incorporated division is a *bona fide* business operation. Therefore, the pricing of any sales or services between the new subsidiary and the parent corporation must be at arm's length, and the operations of the new corporation preferably should result in a profit.

Although most planning techniques are employed to disconnect a corporation's activities from an undesirable state, they can also be utilized to create nexus in a desirable state. For example, when the presence of a company-owned computer creates nexus in a desirable state, the corporation could provide its sales representatives in that state with company-owned equipment, rather than reimbursing or providing increased compensation for equipment costs.

Establishing nexus in a state is advantageous, for instance, when that state has a lower tax rate than the state in which the income currently is taxed, or when losses or credits become available to reduce tax liabilities in the state.

**EXAMPLE 31**

Bird Corporation generates $500,000 of taxable income from selling goods; specifically, 40% of its product is sold in State A and 60% in State B. Both states levy a corporate income tax and include only the sales factor in their apportionment formulas. The tax rate in A is 10%; B's rate is only 3%. Bird's manufacturing operation is located in A; therefore, the corporation's income is subject to tax in that state. Currently, Bird is immune from tax under Public Law 86–272 in B. Since A has adopted a throwback provision, Bird incurs $50,000 of state income taxes.

| | Apportionment Formula | Net Income | Tax Rate | Tax |
|---|---|---|---|---|
| State A | 100/100 | $500,000 | 10% | $50,000 |
| State B | 0/100 | 500,000 | 3% | –0– |
| Total tax liability | | | | $50,000 |

Because B imposes a lower tax rate than A, Bird substantially reduces its state tax liability if sufficient nexus is created with B.

| | Apportionment Formula | Net Income | Tax Rate | Tax |
|---|---|---|---|---|
| State A | 40/100 | $500,000 | 10% | $20,000 |
| State B | 60/100 | 500,000 | 3% | 9,000 |
| Total tax liability | | | | $29,000 |

A corporation may benefit by storing inventory in a low- or no-tax state because the average property value in the state in which the manufacturing operation is located is reduced significantly. When the manufacturing operation is located in a high-tax state, the establishment of a distribution center in a low- or no-tax state may reduce the overall state tax liability.

**EXAMPLE 32**

Trill Corporation realized $200,000 of taxable income from selling its product in States A and B. Trill's manufacturing plant, product distribution center, and warehouses are located in A. The corporation's activities within the two states are as follows:

| | State A | State B | Total |
|---|---|---|---|
| Sales | $500,000 | $200,000 | $700,000 |
| Property | 300,000 | 50,000 | 350,000 |
| Payroll | 100,000 | 10,000 | 110,000 |

Trill is subject to tax in A and B. Both states utilize a three-factor apportionment formula that equally weights sales, property, and payroll; however, A imposes a 10% corporate income tax, while B levies a 3% tax. Trill incurs a total income tax liability of $17,575.

| | Apportionment Formulas | | | | | |
|---|---|---|---|---|---|---|
| | **State A** | | | **State B** | | |
| Sales | $500,000/$700,000 | = | 71.43% | $200,000/$700,000 | = | 28.57% |
| Property | $300,000/$350,000 | = | 85.71% | $50,000/$350,000 | = | 14.29% |
| Payroll | $100,000/$110,000 | = | 90.91% | $10,000/$110,000 | = | 9.09% |
| Total | | | 248.05% | | | 51.95% |
| Apportionment factor (totals/3) | | | 82.68% | | | 17.32% |
| Income apportioned to the state ($200,000 × apportionment factor) | | | $165,360 | | | $34,640 |
| Tax rate | | | × 10% | | | × 3% |
| Tax liability | | | $ 16,536 | | | $ 1,039 |
| Total tax liability | | | | $17,575 | | |

**EXAMPLE 33**

Continue with the facts of Example 32, and further assume that Trill's product distribution center and warehouse operations were acquired for $200,000 and the payroll of these operations is $20,000. Ignoring all nontax considerations, Trill could reduce its tax liability by $3,514 (a 20% reduction) by moving its distribution center, warehouses, and applicable personnel to B.

|  | State A | State B | Total |
|---|---|---|---|
| Sales | $500,000 | $200,000 | $700,000 |
| Property | 100,000 | 250,000 | 350,000 |
| Payroll | 80,000 | 30,000 | 110,000 |

| | Apportionment Formulas | | | | |
|---|---|---|---|---|---|
| | State A | | | State B | |
| Sales | $500,000/$700,000 | = 71.43% | $200,000/$700,000 | = | 28.57% |
| Property | $100,000/$350,000 | = 28.57% | $250,000/$350,000 | = | 71.43% |
| Payroll | $80,000/$110,000 | = 72.73% | $30,000/$110,000 | = | 27.27% |
| Total | | 172.73% | | | 127.27% |
| Apportionment factor (totals/3) | | 57.58% | | | 42.42% |
| Income apportioned to the state ($200,000 × apportionment factor) | | $115,160 | | | $84,840 |
| Tax rate | | × 10% | | | × 3% |
| Tax liability | | $ 11,516 | | | $ 2,545 |
| Total tax liability | | | $14,061 | | |
| Tax imposed before move to State B | | | 17,575 | | |
| Tax reduction due to move | | | $ 3,514 | | |

## RESTRUCTURING CORPORATE ENTITIES

One of the major objectives of state tax planning is to design the proper mix of corporate entities. An optimal mix of entities often generates the lowest combined state income tax for the corporation. Ideally, the income from all of the entities will be subject to a low tax rate or no tax at all. However, this generally is not possible. Consequently, the goal of designing a good corporate combination often is to situate the highly profitable entities in states that impose a low (or no) income tax.

**Matching Tax Rates and Corporate Income.**   When the corporation must operate in a high-tax state, divisions that generate losses should also be located there. Alternatively, unprofitable or less profitable operations can be merged into profitable operations to reduce the overall income subject to tax in the state. An ideal candidate for this type of merger may be a research and development subsidiary that is only marginally profitable, but is vital to the parent corporation's strategic goals. By using computer simulation models, a variety of different combinations can be tested to determine the optimal corporate structure.

**Passive Investment Companies.**   The creation of a **passive investment company** is another restructuring technique utilized to minimize a corporation's state tax burden. Nonbusiness or passive income generally is allocated to the state in which the income-producing asset is located, rather than apportioned among the states in which the corporation does business. Therefore, significant tax savings may be realized when nonbusiness assets are located in a state that either does not levy an income tax or provides favorable tax treatment for passive income. The corporation need not be domiciled in the state to benefit from these favorable provisions. Instead, the tax savings can be realized by forming a passive investment subsidiary to hold the intangible assets and handle the corporation's investment activities. The passive investment subsidiary technique usually produces the desired result in any no-tax state. Delaware, however, often is selected for this purpose due to its other corporate statutory provisions and favorable political, business, and legal climate.

Delaware does not impose an income tax upon a corporation whose only activity within the state is the maintenance and management of intangible investments and the collection and distribution of income from such investments or from tangible property physically located in another state. Consequently, trademarks, patents, stock, and other intangible property can be transferred to a Delaware corporation whose activity is limited to collecting passive income. The assets can be transferred to the subsidiary without incurring a Federal income tax under § 351 (see Chapter 3).

However, to receive the desired preferential state tax treatment, the holding company's activities within the state must be sufficient to establish nexus in the state. The passive investment company should avoid performing any activity outside the state that may result in establishing nexus with another state. In addition, the formation of the subsidiary must be properly implemented to assure the legal substance of the operation. The passive investment company must have a physical office, and it must function as an independent operation. Ensuring nexus and proper formation is not difficult since numerous consulting organizations are available to furnish new passive investment companies with all of the elements necessary to fulfill these requirements.

Because the subsidiary's activities are confined to Delaware (or some other no- or low-tax state), and its operations generate only passive income, its income will not be taxed in any nonunitary state. Moreover, most states exclude dividends from taxation or otherwise treat them favorably; therefore, the earnings of a passive investment subsidiary can be distributed as a dividend to the parent at a minimal tax cost. If the state in which the parent is located does not levy the full income tax on dividends received, the entire measure of passive income may escape taxation.

Formation of a passive investment subsidiary also may favorably affect the parent corporation's apportionment formula in nonunitary states because the passive income earned by the subsidiary is excluded from the numerator of its sales factor.

**EXAMPLE 34**

Purple Corporation generates $800,000 of taxable income; $600,000 is income from its manufacturing operations, and $200,000 is dividend income from passive investments. All of Purple's sales are made, and assets are kept, in State A, which imposes a 10% corporate income tax and permits a 100% deduction for dividends received from subsidiaries. The corporation is not subject to tax in any other state. Consequently, Purple incurs $80,000 of income tax (tax base $800,000 × tax rate 10%).

If Purple creates a passive investment subsidiary in State B, which does not impose an income tax upon a corporation whose only activity within the state is the maintenance and management of passive investments, Purple's tax liability is reduced by $20,000 (a 25% decrease). Since passive income is nonbusiness income (which is allocated for state tax purposes to the state in which it is located), the income earned from its passive investments is not subject to tax in A.

## TAX IN THE NEWS

### HOLDING COMPANIES MAKE OTHER STATES ANGRY

A tax dollar saved in one state is a tax dollar lost in another. That's how some state tax administrators and observers view the use of the passive investment holding company. According to a spokesman for the Multistate Tax Commission, the average state income tax rate paid by larger conglomerates fell from about 9.6 percent in 1980 to about 5.2 percent currently. That isn't fair, says the Secretary of Revenue in North Carolina, who points out that as corporate income tax revenue declines, income and sales/use taxes on individuals must be increased to make up the difference.

The Delaware version of the investment holding company is the culprit largely responsible. By locating intangible assets such as trademarks and income-generating investment assets in tax-friendly states like Delaware, corporations can achieve major tax savings. The list of companies taking advantage of the Delaware holding company provisions includes such familiar names as Kmart, Home Depot, Circuit City, Staples, The Gap, Limited, and Burger King.

Although many state authorities are working hard to have the courts or Congress scale back the use of these shelters, passive investment companies remain a viable course of action.

| | State A (Purple Corporation) | State B (Passive Investment Company) |
|---|---|---|
| Taxable income | $600,000 | $200,000 |
| Tax rate | × 10% | × –0–* |
| Tax liability | $ 60,000 | $ –0– |
| Total tax liability | | $ 60,000 |
| Tax imposed without restructuring | | 80,000 |
| Tax reduction due to use of subsidiary | | $ 20,000 |

*B does not impose an income tax on a passive investment corporation.

The income earned by the subsidiary from its passive investments can be distributed to Purple as a dividend without incurring a tax liability because A allows a 100% deduction for dividends that are received from subsidiary corporations. ■

These desired results, however, will not be fully available in states that view the entire corporate operation as being unitary. Since those states require combined reporting, the income earned by the passive investment subsidiary is included in the corporation's apportionable or allocable income.

### SUBJECTING THE CORPORATION'S INCOME TO APPORTIONMENT

When a multistate organization is domiciled in a high-tax state, some of its apportionable income is eliminated from the tax base in that state. In light of the high tax rate, this may result in significant tax savings. Apportioning income will be especially effective where the income that is attributed to the other states is not subject to income tax. The income removed from the taxing jurisdiction of the domicile state entirely escapes state income taxation when the state to which the income is attributed (1) does not levy a corporate income tax; (2) requires a higher level of activity necessary to subject an out-of-state company to taxation than that adopted by the state of domicile; or (3) is prohibited under Public Law 86–272 from taxing the income (assuming that the domicile state has not adopted a throwback provision). Thus, the right to apportion income may provide substantial benefits because the out-of-state sales are excluded from the numerator of the sales factor and may not be taxed in another state.

However, to acquire the right to apportion its income, the organization must have sufficient activities in, or contacts with, one or more other states. Whether the type and amount of activities and/or contacts are considered adequate is determined by the domicile state's nexus rules. Therefore, a corporation should analyze its current activities in, and contacts with, other states to determine which, if any, activities or contacts could be redirected so that the corporation gains the right to apportion its income.

---

**ETHICAL CONSIDERATIONS**    **Can You Be a Nowhere Adviser?**

The intent of much of today's multistate income tax planning is to create so-called nowhere sales, such that the income from the transaction is not subject to tax in any state. Suppose, for instance, that a sale is made from Georgia (a state with no throwback rule) into Nevada (the place of ultimate destination, but a state with no income tax). No state-level income tax liability is generated. Is it ethical for a tax adviser to suggest such a strategy? Could you propose the establishment of a sales office in a nonthrowback state, thereby avoiding state income tax on a transaction that is fully taxable under Federal rules?

---

## PLANNING WITH APPORTIONMENT FACTORS

**Sales Factor.**    The sales factor often yields the greatest planning opportunities for a multistate corporation. In-state sales include those to purchasers with a destination point in that state; sales delivered to out-of-state purchasers are included in the numerator of the sales factor of the destination state. However, to be permitted to exclude out-of-state sales from the sales factor of the origination state, the seller generally must substantiate the shipment of goods to an out-of-state location. Therefore, the destinations of sales that a corporation makes and the means by which the goods are shipped must be carefully reviewed. The corporation's overall state tax can possibly be reduced by establishing a better record-keeping system or by manipulating the numerator of the sales factor by changing the delivery location or method.

For example, a corporation may substantially reduce its state tax if the delivery location of its sales is changed from a state in which the company is taxed to one in which it is not. This technique may not benefit the corporation if the state in which the sales originate has adopted the throwback rule.

**Property Factor.**    Because most fixed assets are physically stationary in nature, the property factor is not so easily manipulated. Nonetheless, significant tax savings can be realized by establishing a leasing subsidiary in a low- or no-tax state. If the property is located in a state that does not include leased assets in the property factor, the establishment of a subsidiary from which to lease the property eliminates the assets from the property factor in the parent's state.

Permanently idle property generally is excluded from the property factor. Accordingly, a corporation should identify and remove such assets from the property factor to ensure that the factor is not distorted. It is equally important to identify and remove nonbusiness assets from the property factor in states that distinguish between business and nonbusiness income.

**EXAMPLE 35**

Quake Corporation's property holdings were as follows.

|  | State A | Total |
| --- | --- | --- |
| Equipment (average historical cost) | $1,200,000 | $2,000,000 |
| Accumulated depreciation (average) | 800,000 | 1,000,000 |

Twenty percent of the equipment in State A is fully depreciated and is idle. Assuming that A includes property in the factor at historical cost, Quake's property factor is 54.55% [($1,200,000 − $240,000 idle property)/($2,000,000 − $240,000)]. If the idle property is not removed from the property factor, Quake's property factor in A is incorrectly computed as 60% ($1,200,000/$2,000,000). ■

**Payroll Factor.**  The payroll factor provides planning potential where several corporate employees spend substantial periods of time outside their state of employment, or the corporation is able to relocate highly paid employees to low- or no-tax states. Use of an independent contractor who works for more than one principal, however, can be beneficial under certain circumstances. Since the commissions paid to independent contractors are excluded from the payroll factor, the taxpayer may reduce its payroll factor in a high-tax state.

**EXAMPLE 36**

Yellow Corporation's total payroll costs are $1.4 million. Of this amount, $1 million was attributable to State A, a high-tax state. Yellow's payroll factor in A is 71.43% ($1,000,000/$1,400,000).

Assuming that $200,000 of the A compensation had been paid to sales representatives and that Yellow replaced its sales force with independent contractors, Yellow's payroll factor in A would be reduced to 66.67% [($1,000,000 − $200,000)/($1,400,000 − $200,000)]. ■

## SALES/USE TAXES ON CAPITAL CHANGES

The tax adviser must be aware of the impact that sales and use taxes may have on a transaction that might otherwise be free from income tax. For example, although the transfer of property to a controlled corporation in exchange for its stock generally is not subject to corporate income taxes, several states provide that such transfers constitute taxable sales for sales and use tax purposes. Similarly, a corporate reorganization may be structured to avoid the imposition of income taxes, but under the statutes of several states, such transfers are considered to be taxable sales and, accordingly, will be subject to sales and use taxes.

## CAPITAL STOCK TAXATION

Capital stock tax liabilities can be significant for capital-intensive taxpayers to the extent that they reinvest a large portion of retained earnings (the tax base) in productive assets. If all nontax factors are equal, a taxpayer with sizable exposure to a capital stock tax should consider the following techniques.

- Funding expansion with debt, rather than retained earnings.
- Funding subsidiary operations with debt, rather than direct capital contributions.
- Regularly paying dividends to parent companies that are domiciled in tax-favored states, such as Delaware.

## KEY TERMS

Allocate, 15–10

Apportion, 15–10

Dock sales, 15–18

Multistate Tax Commission (MTC), 15–9

Nexus, 15–9

Passive investment company, 15–36

Payroll factor, 15–19

Property factor, 15–22

Public Law 86–272, 15–9

Sales factor, 15–17

Throwback rule, 15–18

UDITPA, 15–9

Unitary theory, 15–24

Water's edge election, 15–27

## PROBLEM MATERIALS

### Discussion Questions

1. As a staff member of the governor of your state, you are charged with bringing new business into the jurisdiction and with keeping the industry and services that are already there. List some of the tax incentives that your Department of Revenue might provide to help meet these goals.

2. In most states, corporate taxable income is computed by reference to a series of statutes and rulings that impose a unique definition of the tax base. Evaluate the validity of this statement.

3. Distinguish between the UDITPA and the MTC as sources of state income tax guidance.

4. What is the precedential value of rulings and regulations issued by the Multistate Tax Commission, a voluntary body with no legislative authority?

5. List the principles by which one state gains authority under its own constitution and under the U.S. Constitution to tax the in-state activities of a conglomerate doing business in a number of jurisdictions.

6. Sales representative Jones is based in Utah, where the operating plants and corporate headquarters of her employer also are located. She visits customers in Colorado for a day, soliciting orders for the seashells that she sells. The orders are approved in Utah, and the shells are shipped from Oregon within a week. Are these sales subject to the Colorado corporate income tax?

7. Continue with the facts of Question 6. In processing her orders, Jones regularly reviews the credit standing of the customer and decides whether the order should be billed on company credit or sent COD (cash on delivery). Are these sales subject to the Colorado corporate income tax?

8. Evaluate the following comment: A multistate business must allocate its income from sales among the states in which it operates. Divided in this manner, taxes are payable to states according to the income allocation.

**Issue ID**

9. If you were a state legislator, would you push for your state to adopt a double-weighted sales or sales-factor-only apportionment formula? Why?

10. In computing the corporate income taxes for an Arizona-based client, should a single large sale in July, in which merchandise was shipped to a customer in New Mexico, be included in the Arizona sales factor?

11. Continue with the facts of Question 10. Another large shipment was made to a customer in South Dakota, a state that does not impose any corporate income tax. Is this sale to be included in the Arizona sales factor?

12. Evaluate the following comment: The unitary concept is similar to the idea of the Federal consolidated return.

13. Parent Corporation wants to acquire Junior, Inc., in a merger transaction. Parent's advisers are consulting statutory and judicial law under § 368 to make certain that the transaction is classified as a reorganization. What advice can you offer the parties to the deal?

**Communications**

14. Your client, Ecru Limited, is considering an expansion of its sales operations, but it fears adverse resulting tax consequences. Write a memo for the tax research file identifying the planning opportunities presented by the ability of a corporation to terminate or create nexus. Be certain to discuss the *Wrigley* case in your analysis.

**Communications**

15. Your client, Royal Corporation, generates significant interest income from its working capital liquid investments. Write a memo for the tax research file discussing the planning opportunities presented by establishing a passive investment company. Support your memo with a diagram of the resulting flow of assets and income.

**Decision Making**

16. Mollusk Corporation generates $70 million taxable income per year, all in State F, where its marginal state tax rate is 8%. The taxable income includes $20 million in interest income from Treasury bills. How might Mollusk reduce its state tax liability? Suggest three alternatives Mollusk should consider. Ignore any nontax considerations.

## Problems

17. For each of the following independent cases, indicate whether the circumstances call for an addition modification (*A*), a subtraction modification (*S*), or no modification (*N*) in computing state taxable income. Then indicate the amount of any modification. The starting point in computing State Q taxable income is the year's Federal taxable income.
    a. Q income taxes, deducted on the Federal return as a business expense = $10,000.
    b. State R income taxes, deducted on the Federal return as a business expense = $10,000.
    c. Federal income taxes paid = $30,000.
    d. Refund received from last year's Q income taxes = $3,000.
    e. Local property taxes, deducted on the Federal return as a business expense = $7,000.
    f. Federal cost recovery = $10,000, and Q cost recovery = $15,000.
    g. Federal cost recovery = $15,000, and Q cost recovery = $10,000.
    h. An asset was sold for $18,000; its purchase price was $20,000. Accumulated Federal cost recovery = $11,000, and accumulated Q cost recovery = $8,000.
    i. Federal investment tax credit = $0, and Q investment tax credit = $5,000.
    j. Dividend income received from State R corporation = $10,000, subject to a Federal dividends received deduction of 70%.

18. Perk Corporation is subject to tax only in State A. Perk generated the following income and deductions.

| | |
|---|---|
| Federal taxable income | $200,000 |
| State A income tax expense | 15,000 |
| Refund of State A income tax | 13,000 |
| Depreciation allowed for Federal tax purposes | 200,000 |
| Depreciation allowed for state tax purposes | 180,000 |

Federal taxable income is the starting point in computing A taxable income. State income taxes are not deductible for A tax purposes. Determine Perk's A taxable income.

19. Flip Corporation is subject to tax only in State X. Flip generated the following income and deductions. State income taxes are not deductible for X income tax purposes.

| | |
|---|---|
| Sales | $4,000,000 |
| Cost of sales | 2,250,000 |
| State X income tax expense | 110,000 |
| Depreciation allowed for Federal tax purposes | 300,000 |
| Depreciation allowed for state tax purposes | 250,000 |
| Interest on Federal obligations | 20,000 |
| Interest on X obligations | 50,000 |
| Expenses related to X obligations | 7,000 |

   a. The starting point in computing the X income tax base is Federal taxable income. Derive this amount.
   b. Determine Flip's X taxable income, assuming that interest on X obligations is exempt from X income tax.
   c. Determine Flip's taxable income, assuming that interest on X obligations is subject to X income tax.

20. Jest Corporation owns and operates two facilities that manufacture paper products. One of the facilities is located in State D, and the other is located in State E. Jest generated $2.5 million of taxable income, comprised of $2 million of income from its manufacturing facilities and a $500,000 gain from the sale of nonbusiness property, located in E. E does not distinguish between business and nonbusiness income, but D apportions only business income. Jest's activities within the two states are outlined below.

| | State D | State E | Total |
|---|---|---|---|
| Sales of paper products | $4,500,000 | $5,800,000 | $10,300,000 |
| Property | 600,000 | 1,500,000 | 2,100,000 |
| Payroll | 1,200,000 | 1,900,000 | 3,100,000 |

   Both D and E utilize a three-factor apportionment formula, under which sales, property, and payroll are equally weighted. Determine the amount of Jest's income that is subject to income tax by each state.

21. Assume the same facts as Problem 20, except that, under the statutes of both D and E, only business income is subject to apportionment.

22. Millie Corporation has nexus in States A and B. Millie's activities for the year are summarized below.

| | State A | State B | Total |
|---|---|---|---|
| Sales | $1,200,000 | $ 300,000 | $1,500,000 |
| Property | | | |
| Average cost | 500,000 | 300,000 | 800,000 |
| Average accumulated depreciation | (300,000) | (100,000) | (400,000) |
| Payroll | 2,400,000 | 100,000 | 2,500,000 |
| Rent expense | 10,000 | 25,000 | 35,000 |

   Determine the apportionment factors for A and B, assuming that A uses a three-factor apportionment formula under which sales, property (net depreciated basis), and payroll are equally weighted, and B employs a single-factor formula that consists solely of sales. State A has adopted the UDITPA with respect to the inclusion of rent payments in the property factor.

23. Assume the facts of Problem 22, except that A uses a single-factor apportionment formula that consists solely of sales, and B uses a three-factor apportionment formula that equally weights sales, property (at historical cost), and payroll. State B does not include rent payments in the property factor.

24. Assume the facts of Problem 22, except that both states employ a three-factor formula, under which sales are double weighted. The basis of the property factor in A is historical cost, while the basis of this factor in B is the net depreciated basis. Neither A nor B includes rent payments in the property factor.

25. Falcon Corporation operates in two states, as indicated below. This year's operations generated $300,000 of apportionable income.

|          | State A    | State B    | Total      |
|----------|-----------|-----------|-----------|
| Sales    | $500,000  | $400,000  | $900,000  |
| Property | 300,000   | 50,000    | 350,000   |
| Payroll  | 100,000   | 10,000    | 110,000   |

Compute Falcon's State A taxable income, assuming that State A apportions income based on a:
   a. Three-factor formula.
   b. Double-weighted sales factor.
   c. Sales factor only.

26. Tootie Corporation operates in two states, as indicated below. All goods are manufactured in State A. Determine the sales to be assigned to both states in computing Tootie's sales factor for the year. Both states follow the UDITPA and the MTC regulations in this regard.

| Sales shipped to A locations | $200,000 |
|---|---|
| Sales shipped to B locations | 190,000 |
| Interest income from Tootie's B checking accounts | 3,000 |
| Rental income from excess space in A warehouse | 13,000 |
| Interest income from Treasury bills in Tootie's B brokerage account, holding only idle cash from operations | 15,000 |
| One-time sale of display equipment to B purchaser | 45,000 |
| Royalty received from holding patent, licensed to B user | 70,000 |

27. State E applies a throwback rule to sales, while State F does not. State G has not adopted an income tax to date. Orange Corporation, headquartered in E, reported the following sales for the year. All of the goods were shipped from Orange's E manufacturing facilities. Orange's degree of operations is sufficient to establish nexus only in E and F. Determine its sales factor in those states.

| Customer | Customer's Location | This Year's Sales |
|----------|--------------------|-------------------|
| ShellTell, Inc. | E | $ 64,000,000 |
| Tourists, Ltd. | F | 40,000,000 |
| PageToo Corp. | G | 30,000,000 |
| U.S. Department of Interior | All 50 states | 18,000,000 |
| Total | | $152,000,000 |

28. Aqua Corporation is subject to tax in States G, H, and I. Aqua's compensation expense includes the following.

|  | State G | State H | State I | Total |
|---|---|---|---|---|
| Salaries and wages for nonofficers | $200,000 | $400,000 | $100,000 | $700,000 |
| Officers' salaries | –0– | –0– | 250,000 | 250,000 |
| Total |  |  |  | $950,000 |

Officers' salaries are included in the payroll factor for G and I, but not for H. Compute Aqua's payroll factors for G, H, and I.

29. Judy, a regional sales manager, has her office in State U. Her region includes several states, as indicated in the sales report below. Judy is compensated through straight commissions on the sales in her region and a fully excludible cafeteria plan conveying various fringe benefits to her. Determine how much of Judy's $150,000 commissions and $40,000 fringe benefit package is assigned to the payroll factor of State U.

| State | Sales Generated | Judy's Time Spent There |
|---|---|---|
| U | $3,000,000 | 20% |
| V | 4,000,000 | 55% |
| X | 5,000,000 | 25% |

30. Justine Corporation operates manufacturing facilities in State G and State H. In addition, the corporation owns nonbusiness rental property in H. Justine incurred the following compensation expenses.

|  | State G | State H | Total |
|---|---|---|---|
| Manufacturing wages | $475,000 | $200,000 | $675,000 |
| Administrative wages | 95,000 | 65,000 | 160,000 |
| Officers' salaries | 180,000 | 80,000 | 260,000 |

Thirty percent of the time spent by the administrative staff located in H and 15% of the time spent by officers located in H are devoted to the operation, maintenance, and supervision of the rental property. G includes all income in the definition of apportionable income, while H excludes nonbusiness income from apportionable income. Only G includes officers' compensation in the payroll factor. Determine Justine's payroll factors for G and H.

31. Kim Corporation, a calendar year taxpayer, has manufacturing facilities in States A and B. A summary of Kim's property holdings follows.

|  | Beginning of Year | | |
|---|---|---|---|
|  | State A | State B | Total |
| Inventory | $ 300,000 | $ 200,000 | $ 500,000 |
| Plant and equipment | 2,500,000 | 1,500,000 | 4,000,000 |
| Accumulated depreciation: plant and equipment | (1,200,000) | (500,000) | (1,700,000) |
| Land | 600,000 | 600,000 | 1,200,000 |
| Rental property* | 900,000 | 300,000 | 1,200,000 |
| Accumulated depreciation: rental property | (200,000) | (50,000) | (250,000) |

|  | End of Year | | |
|---|---|---|---|
|  | State A | State B | Total |
| Inventory | $ 400,000 | $ 150,000 | $ 550,000 |
| Plant and equipment | 2,500,000 | 1,200,000 | 3,700,000 |
| Accumulated depreciation: plant and equipment | (1,500,000) | (450,000) | (1,950,000) |
| Land | 600,000 | 400,000 | 1,000,000 |
| Rental property* | 950,000 | 300,000 | 1,250,000 |
| Accumulated depreciation: rental property | (300,000) | (100,000) | (400,000) |

*Unrelated to Kim's regular business operations.

Determine Kim's property factors for the two states, assuming that the statutes of both A and B provide that average historical cost of business property is to be included in the property factor.

32. Assume the facts of Problem 31, except that nonbusiness income is apportionable in B.

**Decision Making**

33. Crate Corporation, a calendar year taxpayer, has established nexus with numerous states. On December 3, Crate sold one of its two facilities in State X. The cost of this facility was $800,000.

   On January 1, Crate owned property with a cost of $3 million, $1.5 million of which was located in X. On December 31, Crate owned property with a cost of $2.2 million, $600,000 of which was located in X.

   X law allows the use of average annual or monthly amounts in determining the property factor. If Crate wants to minimize the property factor in X, which method should be used to determine the property factor there?

**Decision Making**

**Communications**

34. True Corporation, a wholly owned subsidiary of Trumaine Corporation, generated a $500,000 taxable loss in its first year of operations. True's activities and sales are restricted to State A, which imposes an 8% income tax. Trumaine's income for the taxable period is $1 million. Trumaine's activities and sales are restricted to State B, which imposes an 11% income tax. Both states use a three-factor apportionment formula that equally weights sales, payroll, and property, and both require a unitary group to file on a combined basis. Sales, payroll, and average property for each corporation are as follows.

|  | True Corporation | Trumaine Corporation | Total |
|---|---|---|---|
| Sales | $2,500,000 | $4,000,000 | $6,500,000 |
| Property | 1,000,000 | 2,500,000 | 3,500,000 |
| Payroll | 800,000 | 1,200,000 | 2,000,000 |

True and Trumaine have been found to be members of a unitary business.
   a. Determine the overall state income tax for the unitary group.
   b. Determine aggregate state income tax for the entities if they were nonunitary.
   c. Incorporate this analysis in a letter to Trumaine's board of directors. Corporate offices are located at 1234 Mulberry Lane, Chartown, AL 35298.

35. Gerald Corporation is part of a three-corporation unitary business. The group has a water's edge election in effect with respect to unitary State Q. State B does not apply the unitary concept with respect to its corporate income tax laws. Nor does Despina, a European country to which Geraldine paid a $4 million value added tax this year.

   Geraldine was organized in Despina and conducts all of its business there. Given the summary of operations that follows, determine Gerald's and Elena's sales factors in B and Q.

| Corporation | Customer's Location | Sales |
|---|---|---|
| Gerald | B | $10,000,000 |
| | Q | 15,000,000 |
| Elena | Q | 20,000,000 |
| Geraldine | Despina | 25,000,000 |

**Communications**

36. Hernandez, which has been an S corporation since inception, is subject to tax in States Y and Z. On Schedule K of its Federal Form 1120S, Hernandez reported ordinary income of $500,000 from its business, taxable interest income of $10,000, capital loss of $30,000, and $40,000 of dividend income from a corporation in which it owns 30%.

    Both states apportion income by use of a three-factor formula that equally weights sales, payroll, and the average cost of property; both states treat interest and dividends as business income. In addition, both Y and Z follow Federal provisions with respect to the determination of taxable income for a corporation. Y recognizes S status, but Z does not. Based on the following information, write a memo to the shareholders of Hernandez, detailing the amount of taxable income on which Hernandez will pay tax in Y and Z. Hernandez corporate offices are located at 5678 Alabaster Circle, Koopville, KY 47697.

| | State Y | State Z |
|---|---|---|
| Sales | $1,000,000 | $800,000 |
| Property (average cost) | 500,000 | 200,000 |
| Payroll | 800,000 | 300,000 |

37. Using the following information from the books and records of Grande Corporation, determine Grande's total sales that are subject to State C's sales tax. Grande operates a retail hardware store.

| | |
|---|---|
| Sales to C consumers, general merchandise | $700,000 |
| Sales to C consumers, crutches and other medical supplies | 111,000 |
| Sales to consumers in State D, via mail order | 84,000 |
| Purchases from suppliers | 55,000 |

38. As a retailer, Granite Corporation sells software programs manufactured and packaged by other parties. Granite also purchases computer parts, assembles them as specified by a customer in a purchase order, and sells them as operating stand-alone computers. All of Granite's operations take place in State F, which levies a 6% sales tax. Results for the current year are as follows.

| | |
|---|---|
| Sales of software | $1,400,000 |
| Purchases of computer parts | 1,700,000 |
| Sales of computer systems | 3,500,000 |
| Purchases of office supplies | 60,000 |
| Purchases of packaging materials for the computer systems | 7,500 |
| Purchases of tools used by computer assemblers | 52,000 |

    a. What is Granite's own sales tax expense for the year?
    b. How much F sales tax must Granite collect and pay over to the state on behalf of other taxpayers subject to the tax?

39. Wayne Corporation is subject to State A's franchise tax. The tax is imposed at a rate of 3% of the corporation's net worth that is apportioned to the state by use of a two-factor (sales and property equally weighted) formula. The property factor includes real and tangible personal property, valued at historical cost as of the end of the taxable year.

Forty percent of Wayne's sales are attributable to A, and $300,000 of the cost of Wayne's tangible personal property is located in A.

Determine the A franchise tax payable by Wayne this year, given the following end-of-the-year balance sheet.

| | | |
|---|---|---|
| Cash | | $ 500,000 |
| Equipment | $1,000,000 | |
| Accumulated depreciation | (300,000) | 700,000 |
| Furniture and fixtures | $ 200,000 | |
| Accumulated depreciation | (50,000) | 150,000 |
| Intangible assets | | 350,000 |
| Total assets | | $1,700,000 |
| Accounts and taxes payable | | $ 600,000 |
| Long-term debt | | 350,000 |
| Common stock | | 1,000 |
| Additional paid-in capital | | 249,000 |
| Retained earnings | | 500,000 |
| Total liabilities and equity | | $1,700,000 |

**Decision Making**

40. Dread Corporation operates in a high-tax state. The firm asks you for advice on a plan to outsource overhead work done in its home state to independent contractors. This work now costs the company $350,000 in wages and benefits. Dread's total payroll for the year is $2 million, of which $1.5 million is for work currently done in the home state.

## Research Problems

**Internet Activity**

**Communications**

*Use the tax resources of the Internet to address the following questions. Do not restrict your search to the World Wide Web, but include a review of newsgroups and general reference materials, practitioner sites and resources, primary sources of the tax law, chat rooms and discussion groups, and other opportunities.*

**Research Problem 1.**   Send an e-mail message to the secretary of revenue for your home state, proposing adoption of one of the following provisions that does not currently exist in your state. Justify your proposal with a numerical example.
   a. Increase the apportionment weight for the sales factor.
   b. Exempt computer and communications technology from the apportionment weight for the property factor.
   c. Adopt a throwback rule for the sales factor.
   d. Tax advertising expenditures under the sales/use tax.
   e. Tax the income of an investment subsidiary set up by a domestic taxpayer.
   f. Add a "nexus team" to find the taxpayers operating in your state, but based in Ohio, Illinois, or Arizona.

**Research Problem 2.**   For your state and one of its neighbors, determine the following. (Place your data in a chart and e-mail your finding to your professor.)
   a. To what extent does each state follow the rulings of the Multistate Tax Commission?
   b. What is each state's apportionment formula, with factors and weightings?

**Research Problem 3.**   Diagram the legislative process through which a tax law change would be adopted in your state. Then diagram the judicial path that a tax case would take in your state (e.g., circuit court → appeals court → state supreme court).

# Tax Administration and Practice

CHAPTER

16

http://wft.swlearning.com

## O U T L I N E

**F**ew events arouse so much fear in the typical individual or corporation as the receipt of a letter from the Internal Revenue Service (IRS), notifying the taxpayer that prior years' tax returns are to be the subject of an audit. Almost immediately, calls are made to the tax adviser. Advice is sought as to what to reveal (or not reveal) in the course of the audit, how to delay or avoid the audit, and how friendly one should be with the auditor when he or she ultimately arrives.

Indeed, many tax practitioners' reputations with their clients have been made or broken by the way they are observed to behave under the pressure of an audit situation. The strategy and tactics of audits—including such seemingly unimportant issues as whether the tax adviser brings donuts or other refreshments to the audit session, the color of his or her suit and tie, and the most effective negotiation techniques—are the subject of both cocktail party banter and scholarly review.

In actuality, the practitioner can render valuable services to the taxpayer in an audit context, thereby assuring that tax payments for the disputed years are neither under- nor over-reported, as part of an ongoing tax practice. In this regard, the adviser must appreciate the following.

- The elements of the Treasury's tax administration process and opportunities for appeal within the structure of the IRS.
- The extent of the negative sanctions that can be brought to bear against taxpayers whose returns are found to have been inaccurate.
- The ethical and professional constraints on the advice tax advisers can give and the actions they can take on behalf of their clients, within the context of an adversarial relationship with the IRS.

## Tax Administration

The Treasury has delegated the administration and enforcement of the tax laws to its subsidiary agency, the IRS. In this process, the Service is responsible for providing adequate information, in the form of publications and forms with instructions, to taxpayers so that they can comply with the laws in an appropriate manner. The IRS

## SHOULD THE IRS BE LARGER?

What is the optimal size of the IRS? The IRS maintains in congressional testimony that it can produce three to four dollars of revenue for every dollar spent on its ongoing operations. Actually, the rate of return might be higher, especially for special projects that the Service itself devises and undertakes. As the agency becomes more proficient with computers and more aggressive in finding and treating nonfilers, the temptation to enlarge the Service increases as well.

Given concerns about the return of a Federal deficit and an underground economy measured in the hundreds of billions of dollars, one might expect the number of IRS operatives to keep increasing, even though it already is one of the largest Federal agencies, with a staff of more than 90,000. Yet, the last few presidents have found that pledges to cut back the size of government also apply to the IRS (i.e., the public does not apply such a rate of return test itself).

Thus, the IRS must live within its budget allocations and reallocate the resources that it now has. Can a stepped-up education campaign, further reliance on electronic filing, and an overall consumer-friendly operation produce significant revenue increases for the IRS?

also identifies delinquent tax payments and carries out assessment and collection procedures under the restrictions of due process and other constitutional guarantees.

In meeting these responsibilities, the Service conducts audits of selected tax returns. Fewer than 0.5 percent of all individual tax returns are subjected to audit in a given tax year. However, certain types of both taxpayers and income—including, for instance, high-income individuals (about 3 percent), cash-oriented businesses, real estate transactions, and estate- and gift-taxable transfers (15 to 30 percent)—are subject to much higher probabilities of audit. One's residence also affects the chances of audit, ranging from about 1.5 percent in California to under 0.2 percent in Georgia.

Recently, much of the IRS's effort has been devoted to developing statutory and administrative requirements relative to information reporting and document matching. For instance, when a taxpayer engages in a like-kind exchange or sells a personal residence, various parties to the transaction are required to report the nature and magnitude of the transaction to the IRS. Later the Treasury's computers determine whether the transaction has been reported properly by comparing the information reported by the third parties with the events included on the relevant taxpayers' returns for the year.

In addition, the IRS has been placing increasing pressure on the community of tax advisers. Severe penalties may be assessed on those who have prepared the appropriate return when the Service's interpretation of applicable law conflicts with that of the preparer.

The IRS processes over 125 million individual income tax returns every year, about 40 million of which are filed electronically. It collects more than $2 trillion in tax revenues and pays refunds to about 100 million taxpayers every year.

Current operational strategies of the IRS include the following.

- Focusing on taxpayer education.
- Developing a "customer first" orientation in working with individual taxpayers.

■ **FIGURE 16–1**
IRS National Office Organization

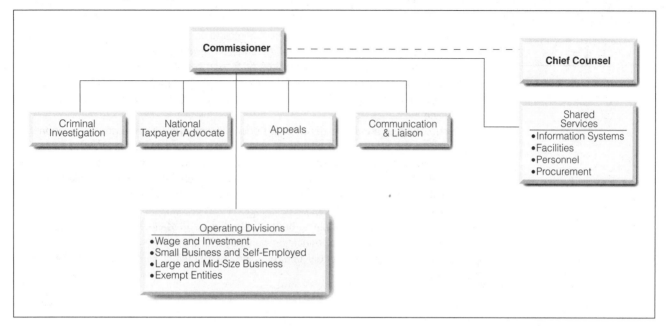

* Adapting to the changing cultural and linguistic needs of the public.
* Accelerating the modernization of equipment and operating methods.
* Making the Regulations and tax procedures as simple and fair as possible.

The IRS believes that, under these principles, the taxpayer will benefit in a number of ways.

* Taxpayers will spend significantly less time dealing with the IRS.
* The IRS will issue refunds more rapidly.
* Taxpayers will have more filing and payment choices.
* Taxpayers will pay less interest.

## LO.1

Describe the organization and structure of the IRS.

## ORGANIZATIONAL STRUCTURE OF THE IRS

The structure of the IRS is moving toward that illustrated in Figure 16–1. The IRS Commissioner, a presidential appointee, has organized the day-to-day operations of the agency into four divisions, conducted using regional and district offices. Table 16–1 provides estimates of the workload of each operating division. Administrative functions, such as those relating to personnel and computer issues, are organized on a shared-services model, managed from the national office. Broader functions, such as litigation, investigations, and taxpayer relations, are managed at the national level as well.

The Chief Counsel, another presidential appointee, is the head legal officer of the IRS. The Chief Counsel's office provides legal advice to the IRS and guidance to the public on matters pertaining to the administration and enforcement of the tax laws. For instance, the Chief Counsel's duties include establishing uniform nationwide interpretative positions on the law, drafting tax guide material for taxpayers and IRS personnel, issuing technical rulings to taxpayers, and providing advice and technical assistance to IRS personnel. The Chief Counsel reports to the Commissioner and represents the IRS in all litigation before the Tax Court.

■ **TABLE 16–1**
IRS Operating Divisions: Tax
Year 2000 Estimates

| | **Wage and Investment** | **Small Business and Self-Employed** | **Large and Mid-Size Businesses (Assets > $10 Million)** | **Exempt Entities (Charities, Retirement Plans, Governments)** |
|---|---|---|---|---|
| **Type of return filed** | 1040 with only wage and investment income (no Schedule C, E, F, or Form 2106) | 1040 Schedules C and F, Forms 1120, 1120S, and 1065 | 1040 Schedules C and F, Forms 1120, 1120S, and 1065 | Form 990 and various payroll forms |
| **Number of filers** | 90 million, 116 million taxpayers | 45 million | 210,000 | 3 million entities, 1.9 million pay tax |
| **Annual income tax liabilities** | $265 billion | $816 billion | $466 billion | $94 billion |
| **Payroll taxes, withholdings paid** | $38 billion | $562 billion | $712 billion | $198 billion |
| **Notes** | Fewer than half use a paid tax preparer. Only 2% earn >$100,000 per year, 85% earn <$50,000, 28% earn <$10,000. | Pay in over 40% of all cash received by the IRS 4–60 annual transactions with the IRS | Further organized into industry segments to handle complex filing requirements About 10% are audited every year; some deal with IRS agents year-round. | Control about $7 trillion in assets |

## LO.2

Identify the various administrative pronouncements issued by the IRS and explain how they can be used in tax practice.

## IRS PROCEDURE—LETTER RULINGS

When a tax issue is controversial or a transaction involves considerable tax dollars, the taxpayer often wishes to obtain either assurance or direction from the IRS as to the treatment of the event. The **letter ruling** process is an effective means of dealing directly with the IRS while in the planning stages of a large or otherwise important transaction.

Rulings issued by the National Office provide a written statement of the position of the IRS concerning the tax consequences of a course of action contemplated by the taxpayer. Letter rulings do not have the force and effect of law, but they do provide guidance and support for taxpayers in similar transactions. The IRS will issue rulings only on uncompleted, actual (rather than hypothetical) transactions or on transactions that have been completed before the filing of the tax return for the year in question.

In certain circumstances, the IRS will not issue a ruling. It ordinarily will not rule in cases that essentially involve a question of fact.[1] For example, no ruling will be issued to determine whether compensation paid to employees is reasonable in amount and therefore allowable as a deduction.[2]

A letter ruling represents the current opinion of the IRS on the tax consequences of a transaction with a given set of facts. IRS rulings are not unchangeable. They are frequently declared obsolete or are superseded by new rulings in response to tax law changes. However, revocation or modification of a ruling is usually not applied retroactively to the taxpayer who received the ruling, if it was relied on

---

[1]Rev.Proc. 2003–1, I.R.B. No. 1, 1.

[2]Rev.Proc. 2003–3, I.R.B. No. 1, 113.

in good faith and if the facts in the ruling request were in agreement with the completed transaction. The IRS may revoke any ruling if, upon subsequent audit, the agent finds a misstatement or omission of facts or substantial discrepancies between the facts in the ruling request and the actual situation.

A ruling may be relied upon only by the taxpayer who requested and received it. It must be attached to the tax return for the year in question.

Letter rulings benefit both the IRS and the taxpayer. Not only do they help promote a uniform application of the tax laws, but they may also reduce the potential for litigation or disputes with IRS agents. In addition, they make the IRS aware of significant transactions being consummated by taxpayers. A fee is charged for processing a ruling request.

## IRS PROCEDURE—OTHER ISSUANCES

In addition to issuing unpublished letter rulings and published rulings and procedures, the IRS issues determination letters and technical advice memoranda.

A Director orders a **determination letter** for a completed transaction when the issue involved is covered by judicial or statutory authority, Regulations, or rulings. Determination letters are issued for various death, gift, income, excise, and employment tax matters.

**EXAMPLE 1**

True Corporation recently opened a car clinic and has employed numerous mechanics. The corporation is not certain whether its educational reimbursement plan is nondiscriminatory. True may request a determination letter from the appropriate Director. ■

**EXAMPLE 2**

Assume the same facts as in Example 1. True would like to establish a pension plan that qualifies for the tax advantages of § 401(k). To determine whether the plan qualifies, True should request and obtain a determination letter from the IRS. ■

**EXAMPLE 3**

A group of physicians plans to form an association to construct and operate a hospital. The determination letter procedure is appropriate to ascertain whether the group is subject to the Federal income tax or is tax-exempt. ■

A **technical advice memorandum (TAM)** is issued by the National Office to a Director and/or Regional Commissioner in response to a specific request by an agent, Appellate Conferee, or Director. The taxpayer may request a TAM if an issue in dispute is not treated by the law or precedent and/or published rulings or Regulations. TAMs are also appropriate when there is reason to believe that the IRS is not administering the tax law consistently. For example, a taxpayer may inquire why an agent proposes to disallow a certain expenditure when agents in other districts permit the deduction. Technical advice requests arise from the audit process, whereas ruling requests are issued before any IRS audit.

The IRS is now testing a new written determination approach, the technical expedited advice memorandum (TEAM), to be used during an office or field audit. The TEAM is designed to reflect the position of the IRS in a shorter time than the TAM now requires. This quicker response time is possible because the following occur before a TEAM request is submitted.

- The taxpayer and the IRS agree to a set of facts for the case.
- The parties conduct a presubmission conference, with attorneys for both sides in attendance.

- Technology, including e-mails and faxes, is used to gather facts as part of the process.
- The IRS holds an internal strategic planning meeting, discussing potential responses to various holdings that could be issued as part of the TEAM.

If the TEAM pilot is successful, the new procedure could see wider usage in coming years.

## ADMINISTRATIVE POWERS OF THE IRS

**Examination of Records.** The Code authorizes the IRS to examine the taxpayer's books and records as part of the process of determining the correct amount of tax due. The IRS can also require the persons responsible for the return to appear and to produce any necessary books and records.[3] Taxpayers are required to maintain certain record-keeping procedures and retain the records necessary to facilitate the audit.

**Burden of Proof.** If the taxpayer meets the record-keeping requirement and substantiates income and deductions properly, the IRS bears the burden of proof in establishing a tax deficiency during litigation. The taxpayer must have cooperated with the IRS regarding reasonable requests for information, documents, meetings, and interviews. For individual taxpayers, the IRS's burden of proof extends to penalties and interest amounts that it assesses in a court proceeding with the taxpayer.[4]

**Assessment and Demand.** The Code permits the IRS to assess a deficiency and to demand payment for the tax. However, no assessment or effort to collect the tax may be made until 90 days after a statutory notice of a deficiency (a *90-day letter*) is issued. The taxpayer therefore has 90 days to file a petition to the U.S. Tax Court, effectively preventing the deficiency from being assessed or collected pending the outcome of the case.[5]

Following assessment of the tax, the IRS issues a notice and demand for payment. The taxpayer is usually given 30 days after the notice and demand for payment to pay the tax.

If the IRS believes the assessment or collection of a deficiency is in jeopardy, it may assess the deficiency and demand immediate payment.[6] The taxpayer can avoid (*stay*) the collection of the jeopardy assessment by filing a bond for the amount of the tax and interest. This action prevents the IRS from selling any property it has seized.

**Collection.** If the taxpayer neglects or refuses to pay the tax after receiving the demand for payment, a lien in favor of the IRS is placed on all property (realty and personalty, tangible and intangible) belonging to the taxpayer.

The levy power of the IRS is very broad. It allows the IRS to garnish (*attach*) wages and salary and to seize and sell all nonexempt property by any means. After a 30-day notice period, the IRS can make successive seizures on any property owned by the taxpayer until the levy is satisfied.[7] A taxpayer's principal residence

---

[3] § 7602.
[4] §§ 7491(a)(1), (a)(2)(B), and (c).
[5] §§ 6212 and 6213.
[6] § 6861. A jeopardy assessment is appropriate, for instance, where the IRS fears that the taxpayer will flee the country or destroy valuable property.

[7] The taxpayer can keep certain personal and business property and a minimal amount of his or her income as a subsistence allowance, even if a lien is outstanding. These amounts are indexed for inflation. § 6334.

is exempt from the levy process, unless the disputed tax, interest, and penalty exceed $5,000 and a U.S. District Court judge approves of the seizure.[8]

If property is transferred and any related tax is not paid, the subsequent owners of the property may be liable for the tax. For example, if an estate is insolvent and unable to pay the estate tax, the executor or the beneficiaries may be liable for the payment.[9]

## LO.3

Describe the audit process, including how returns are selected for audit and the various types of audits.

## THE AUDIT PROCESS

**Selection of Returns for Audit.**    The IRS utilizes mathematical formulas to select tax returns that are most likely to contain errors and yield substantial amounts of additional tax revenues upon audit. The IRS does not openly disclose all of its audit selection techniques. However, some observations can be made regarding the probability of a return's selection for audit.

- Certain groups of taxpayers are subject to audit more frequently than others. These groups include individuals with gross income in excess of $100,000, self-employed individuals with substantial business income and deductions, and cash businesses where the potential for tax evasion is high.

**EXAMPLE 4**    Tracey owns and operates a liquor store. As nearly all of her sales are for cash, Tracey might be a prime candidate for an audit by the IRS. Cash transactions are easier to conceal than those made on credit. ■

---

**ETHICAL CONSIDERATIONS**

## Do You Live in an Audit-Friendly Part of the Country?

Tax advisers have long suspected that the area of the country in which taxpayers live is one of the most important factors determining their susceptibility to audit. Theoretically, why should taxpayers living in Las Vegas be more likely to be audited than those living in Baltimore? Aren't all tax returns created equal?

Not even close. For the roughly one million individual income tax returns that are audited every year, the taxpayer's zip code partly determines not only the probability of being audited, but also the chances of success in reaching compromises with the IRS as the audit is settled.

The official IRS answer to this problem is that "[a]ny perceived 'geographic' variations result from other factors, such as differences in compliance levels, taxpayer behavior, and economic and business trends." But are Phoenix taxpayers more likely to cheat than those in Des Moines?

When a tax return is audited and the tax liability is not changed, has the government's money been wasted? Are auditors in the low-audit-rate areas lazier or less productive than those who produce more dollars for the government?

---

- If a taxpayer has been audited in a past year and the audit led to the assessment of a substantial deficiency, the IRS often makes a return visit.
- An audit might materialize if information returns (e.g., Form W–2, Form 1099) are not in substantial agreement with the income reported on the taxpayer's return. Obvious discrepancies do not necessitate formal audits and usually can be handled by correspondence with the taxpayer.

---

[8]§§ 6334(a)(13)(A) and (e)(1).

[9]§ 6901.

- If an individual's itemized deductions are in excess of norms established for various income levels, the probability of an audit increases. Certain deductions (e.g., casualty and theft losses, business use of the home, tax-sheltered investments) are sensitive areas, as the IRS realizes that many taxpayers determine the amount of the deduction incorrectly or may not be entitled to the deduction at all.
- The filing of a refund claim by the taxpayer may prompt an audit of the return.
- Some returns are selected because the IRS has targeted a specific industry or type of tax return for in-depth review. This enables examiners to develop special skills and interests applicable to those returns. In the Industry Specialization Program (ISP), returns might be selected from retailers, energy developers, or health care operations for special review. In the Market Segment Specialization Program (MSSP), specialized auditors focus on returns that show passive losses, involve construction activities, or include legal or consulting income.
- Information is often obtained from other sources (e.g., other government agencies, news items, informants). The IRS then applies its own judgment and experience, and it may audit the return to address such questions as, Why did dividend income increase so much this year? Why did mortgage interest payments decrease? How did the taxpayer pay for such a large vacation home, sold this year?
- The IRS can pay rewards to persons who provide information that leads to the detection and punishment of those who violate the tax laws. The rewards are paid at the discretion of a Director and cannot exceed 15 percent of the taxes, fines, and penalties recovered as a result of such information.[10]

**EXAMPLE 5**

Phil reports to the police that burglars broke into his home while he was out of town and took a shoe box containing $25,000 in cash, among other things. A representative of the IRS reading the newspaper account of the burglary might wonder why Phil kept such a large amount of cash in a shoe box at home. ■

**EXAMPLE 6**

After 15 years, Betty is discharged by her employer, Dr. Franklin. Shortly thereafter, the IRS receives a letter from Betty informing it that Franklin keeps two sets of books, one of which substantially understates his cash receipts. ■

The statistical models used by the IRS to select individual tax returns for audit come from random audits of a small number of taxpayers, who are required to document every entry that they made on the Form 1040. The latest round of these National Research Program audits took place in early 2003 and resulted in the construction of new Discriminant Information Function (DIF) scores that project the amount of revenue that the IRS will gain from pursuing tax returns with various statistical profiles. The higher the DIF score, the better the return to the IRS from pursuing the audit, and the higher the probability of selection for an examination.

These data-seeking audits have been delayed since the late 1980s as a result of taxpayer complaints to Congress about the stress that they create.[11] But the data from the older DIF models no longer match our service-based, information-powered

---

[10]§ 7623 and Reg. § 301.7623–1T.

[11]The IRS planned to conduct the National Research Program audits less obtrusively than in the past. The program would involve about 49,000 returns. About 8,000 of these returns were to be analyzed without contacting the taxpayer, and another 9,000 taxpayers would be contacted only by mail with queries about one or two items. The rest of the sample would consist largely of proprietors, partners, and farmers (i.e., those using Schedules C, E, and F). Only about 1,700 returns were to be subjected to "line-by-line" review.

## IRS Inside Information

There is nothing like turnover in the IRS Commissioner's office to produce leaks of new information about how the IRS really works. In conjunction with his recent farewell speech, outgoing Commissioner Rossotti revealed some interesting statistics, including the following.

- The IRS gets a budget of 41 cents per return to collect taxes. This is 10 percent less than it received in real terms just five years ago. In the meantime, tax planning efforts by taxpayers have accelerated, and Congress has passed almost 300 new tax laws.
- The 10 percent "cut" in IRS appropriations translates into a 28 percent decline in resources dedicated to audits, collections, and investigations.
- For some types of tax understatements, four in five "tax cheats" escape detection because of this underfunding.
- The IRS can follow up on only 20 percent of all income understatements by partners and partnerships because the document matching program is underfunded.
- Budget restrictions have meant that only 17,000 of the 82,000 taxpayers identified as using offshore accounts to evade taxes can be pursued.
- Fiscal 2001 estimates show roughly a 10 percent decline in the number of corporations, partnerships, and high-income individuals being audited.

Observers critical of Commissioner Rossotti's work have questioned the large amounts paid to consultants to reengineer the structure of the IRS, replacing a geographically based system with one based on the type of return filed. One former commissioner said about Rossotti, "I just wish he had spent more money on revenue agents and less on consultants." Others suggest that his dedication to customer service came at a cost of decreasing quality in audit and enforcement activities.

---

economy. "Too many" audits using the older DIF scores to select the returns have concluded with "no change." Consequently, updating the underlying models has become essential.

Many individual taxpayers mistakenly assume that if they do not hear from the IRS within a few weeks after filing their return or if they have received a refund check, no audit will be forthcoming. As a practical matter, most individual returns are examined about two years from the date of filing. If not, they generally remain unaudited. All large corporations, however, are subject to annual audits.

**Verification and Audit Procedures.**   The filed tax return is immediately reviewed for mathematical accuracy. A check is also made for deductions, exclusions, etc., that are clearly erroneous. One obvious error would be the failure to comply with the 7.5 percent limitation on the deduction for medical expenses.

Almost 5 percent of all individual returns show a math error. In such cases, the Service Center merely sends the taxpayer revised computations and a bill or refund as appropriate. Taxpayers usually are able to settle such matters through direct correspondence with the IRS without the necessity of a formal audit.

*Office audits* are conducted by a representative of the Director's Office, either in the office of the IRS or through correspondence. Individual returns with few or no items of business income are usually handled through the office audit procedure. In most instances, the taxpayer is required merely to substantiate a deduction, credit, or item of income that appears on the return. The taxpayer presents documentation in the form of canceled checks, invoices, etc., for the items in question.

The *field audit* procedure is commonly used for corporate returns and for returns of individuals engaged in business or professional activities. This type of audit generally involves a more complete examination of a taxpayer's transactions.

A field audit is conducted by IRS agents at the office or home of the taxpayer or at the office of the taxpayer's representative. The agent's work may be facilitated by a review of certain tax workpapers and discussions with the taxpayer's representative about items appearing on the tax return. Table 16–2 summarizes key audit information.

Prior to or at the initial interview, the IRS must provide the taxpayer with an explanation of the audit process that is the subject of the interview and describe the taxpayer's rights under that process. If the taxpayer clearly states at any time during the interview the desire to consult with an attorney, CPA, or enrolled agent or any other person permitted to represent the taxpayer before the IRS, then the IRS representative must suspend the interview.[12]

Any officer or employee of the IRS must, upon advance request, allow a taxpayer to make an audio recording of any in-person interview with the officer or employee concerning the determination and collection of any tax.

**Settlement with the Revenue Agent.**   Following an audit, the IRS agent may either accept the return as filed or recommend certain adjustments. The **Revenue Agent's Report (RAR)** is reviewed by the agent's group supervisor and the Review Staff within the IRS. In most instances, the agent's proposed adjustments are approved. However, the Review Staff or group supervisor may request additional information or raise new issues.

Agents must adhere strictly to IRS policy as reflected in published rulings, Regulations, and other releases. The agent cannot settle an unresolved issue based upon the probability of winning the case in court. Usually, issues involving factual questions can be settled at the agent level, and it may be advantageous for both the taxpayer and the IRS to reach agreement at the earliest point in the settlement process. For example, it may be to the taxpayer's advantage to reach agreement at the agent level and avoid any further opportunity for the IRS to raise new issues.

If agreement is reached upon the proposed deficiency, the taxpayer signs Form 870 (Waiver of Restrictions on Assessment and Collection of Deficiency in Tax). One advantage to the taxpayer of signing Form 870 at this point is that interest stops accumulating on the deficiency 30 days after the form is filed.[13] When this form is signed, the taxpayer effectively waives the right to receive a statutory notice of deficiency (90-day letter) and to subsequently petition the Tax Court. In addition, it is no longer possible for the taxpayer later to go to the IRS Appeals Division. The signing of Form 870 at the agent level generally closes the case. However,

**■ TABLE 16–2**
IRS Audit Information by Type
(Returns Filed in 1999)

| | Conducted (Number) | Conducted (Percent) |
| --- | --- | --- |
| Correspondence audit | 803,000 | 52.9% |
| Office audit | 506,000 | 33.3% |
| Field audit | 210,000 | 13.8% |

---

[12]§ 7521(b).

[13]§ 6601(c).

■ **FIGURE 16–2**
Income Tax Appeal Procedure

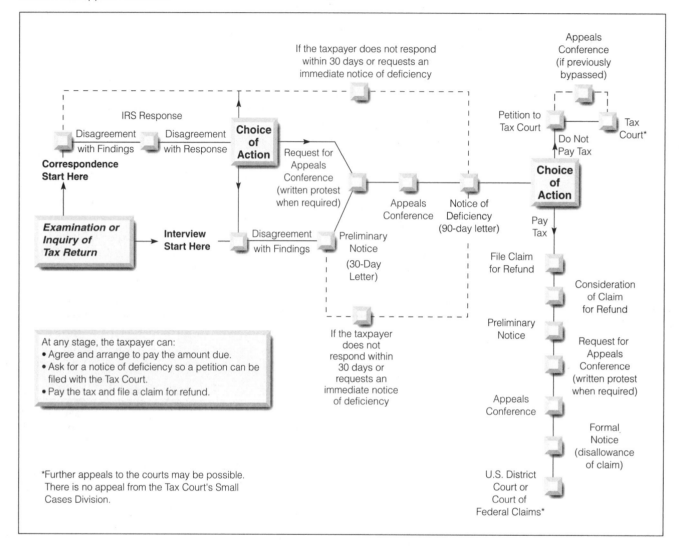

the IRS is not restricted by Form 870 and may assess additional deficiencies if deemed necessary.

## THE TAXPAYER APPEAL PROCESS

**LO.4**

Explain the taxpayer appeal process, including various settlement options available.

If agreement cannot be reached at the agent level, the taxpayer receives a copy of the Revenue Agent's Report and a **30-day letter.** The taxpayer has 30 days to request an administrative appeal. If an appeal is not requested, a **90-day letter** is issued. Figure 16–2 illustrates the taxpayer's alternatives when a disagreement with the IRS persists.

A taxpayer who wishes to appeal must make an appropriate request to the Appeals Division. The request must be accompanied by a written protest except in the following cases.

- The proposed tax deficiency does not exceed $10,000 for any of the tax periods involved in the audit.
- The deficiency resulted from a correspondence or office audit (i.e., not as a result of a field audit).

The Appeals Division is authorized to settle all tax disputes based on the hazards of litigation (the chances of winning in court). Since the Appeals Division has final settlement authority until a 90-day letter has been issued, the taxpayer may be able to negotiate a settlement. In addition, an overall favorable settlement may be reached by "trading" disputed issues. The Appeals Division occasionally may raise new issues if the grounds are substantial and of significant tax impact.

Both the Appeals Division and the taxpayer have the right to request technical advice memoranda from the National Office of the IRS. A TAM that is favorable to the taxpayer is binding on the Appeals Division. Even if the TAM is favorable to the IRS, the Appeals Division may nevertheless settle the case based on the hazards of litigation.

**EXAMPLE 7**

At the time Terri is audited, the corporation that she controls had advances outstanding to her in the amount of $80,000. The IRS field agent held that these advances were constructive dividends to her (refer to the discussion in Chapter 4). Some facts point toward this result (e.g., the corporation is closely held, Terri has made no repayments, and the loan balance has increased over several years). Other facts, however, appear to indicate that these advances are bona fide loans (e.g., a written instrument provides for interest, Terri has the independent means of repayment, and the corporation has a good dividend-paying record).

The Appeals Division and Terri's representative assess the hazards of litigation as being 50% for each side. Thus, if Terri chooses to take the issue to court, she would have an even chance of winning or losing her case. Based on this assessment, both sides agree to treat $40,000 of the advance as a dividend and $40,000 as a bona fide loan. The agreement enables Terri to avoid $40,000 of dividend income (the loan portion) and saves her the cost of litigating the issue.

Thus, by going to the Appeals Division, Terri obtained a satisfactory settlement otherwise unobtainable from the agent. ■

Taxpayers who file a petition with the U.S. Tax Court have the option of having the case heard before the more informal Small Cases Division if the amount of tax in dispute does not exceed $50,000.[14] If the Small Cases Division is used, neither party may appeal the case.

The economic costs of a settlement offer from the Appeals Division should be weighed against the costs of litigation and the probability of winning the case. The taxpayer should also consider the impact of the settlement upon the tax liability for future periods in addition to the years under audit.

If a settlement is reached with the Appeals Division, the taxpayer is required to sign Form 870–AD. Interest stops running on the deficiency when the Appeals Division accepts the Form 870–AD. According to the IRS, this settlement is binding upon both parties unless fraud, malfeasance, concealment, or misrepresentation of material fact has occurred. Nevertheless, the question of whether this settlement form prevents the taxpayer from filing a subsequent refund claim and suit for refund has been litigated with conflicting results.[15]

---

[14]§ 7463(a).
[15]Compare *Stair v. U.S.*, 75–1 USTC ¶9463, 35 AFTR2d 75–1515, 516 F.2d 560 (CA–2, 1975), with *Unita Livestock Corp. v. U.S.*, 66–1 USTC ¶9193, 17 AFTR2d 254, 355 F.2d 761 (CA–10, 1966).

## OFFERS IN COMPROMISE AND CLOSING AGREEMENTS

The IRS can negotiate a compromise if the taxpayer's ability to pay the tax is doubtful. If the taxpayer is financially unable to pay the total amount of the tax, a Form 656 (Offer in Compromise) is filed with the Memphis Internal Revenue Service Center or the Brookhaven Internal Revenue Service Center in Holtsville, New York, depending on the location of the taxpayer. An **offer in compromise** is appropriate in the following circumstances.[16]

- There is doubt as to the taxpayer's liability for the tax (i.e., disputed issues still exist).
- There is doubt as to the collectibility of the tax (i.e., the taxpayer's net worth and earnings capacity are low).
- Payment of the disputed amount would constitute an economic hardship for the taxpayer. For instance, the taxpayer is incapable of earning a living because of a long-term illness or disability, or liquidation of the taxpayer's assets to pay the amount due would leave the taxpayer unable to meet basic living expenses.

The IRS investigates the offer by evaluating the taxpayer's financial ability to pay the tax. In some instances, the compromise settlement includes an agreement for final settlement of the tax through payments of a specified percentage of the taxpayer's future earnings. This settlement procedure usually entails lengthy negotiations with the IRS, but the presumption is that the agency will find terms upon which to enter into a compromise with the taxpayer. The IRS is charged to use a "liberal acceptance policy" in compromising with taxpayers and to increase educational efforts so that taxpayer rights and obligations are better known.

The IRS has statutory authority to enter into a written agreement allowing taxes to be paid on an installment basis if that arrangement facilitates the tax collection. The agency encourages its employees to use installment plans, and an individual is guaranteed the right to use an installment agreement when the amount in dispute does not exceed $10,000. The taxpayer uses Form 9465 to initiate the installment plan.

The IRS provides an annual statement accounting for the status of the agreement. The agreement may later be modified or terminated because of (1) inadequate information, (2) subsequent change in financial condition, or (3) failure to pay an installment when due or to provide requested information.[17]

A **closing agreement** is binding on both the taxpayer and the IRS except upon a subsequent showing of fraud, malfeasance, or misrepresentation of a material fact.[18] The closing agreement may be used when disputed issues carry over to future years. It may also be employed to dispose of a dispute involving a specific issue for a prior year or a proposed transaction involving future years. If, for example, the IRS is willing to make substantial concessions in the valuation of assets for death tax purposes, it may require a closing agreement from the recipient of the property to establish the income tax basis of the assets.

**LO.5**

Determine the amount of interest on a deficiency or a refund and when it is due.

## INTEREST

**Determination of the Interest Rate.**   Congress sets the interest rates applicable to Federal tax underpayments (deficiencies) and overpayments (refunds) close to the rates available in financial markets. The Code provides for the rates to be

---

[16]§ 7122 and Reg. § 301.7122–1T(b).
[17]§ 6159.

[18]§ 7121(b).

determined quarterly.[19] Thus, the rates that are determined during March are effective for the following April through June.

IRS interest is based on the Federal short-term rates published periodically by the IRS in Revenue Rulings. They are based on the average market yield on outstanding marketable obligations of the United States with remaining maturity of three years or less.

For noncorporate taxpayers, the interest rate applicable to *both* overpayments and underpayments is 5 percent for the first quarter of 2003. For most corporate taxpayers, the rate is 4 percent for overpayments and 5 percent for underpayments. Corporations with large overpayments or underpayments are subject to different rates.

**Computation of the Amount of Interest.** Interest is compounded daily.[20] Depending on the applicable interest rate, daily compounding doubles the payable amount over a period of five to eight years.

Tables for determining the daily compounded amount are available from the IRS and on the Internet. The tables ease the burden of those who prepare late returns where additional taxes are due.[21]

**IRS Deficiency Assessments.** Interest usually accrues from the unextended due date of the return until 30 days after the taxpayer agrees to the deficiency by signing Form 870. If the taxpayer does not pay the amount shown on the IRS's notice and demand (tax bill) within 30 days, interest again accrues on the deficiency.

**Refund of Taxpayer's Overpayments.** If an overpayment is refunded to the taxpayer within 45 days after the date the return is filed or is due, no interest is allowed. When the taxpayer files an amended return or makes a claim for refund of a prior year's tax (e.g., when net operating loss carrybacks result in refunds of a prior year's tax payments), however, interest is authorized from the original due date of the return through the date when the amended return is filed. In general, taxpayers applying for refunds receive interest as follows.

- When a return is filed after the due date, interest on any overpayment accrues from the date of filing. However, no interest is due if the IRS makes the refund within 45 days of the date of filing.

**EXAMPLE 8**

Naomi, a calendar year taxpayer, files her 2002 return on December 1, 2003. The return reflects an overwithholding of $2,500. On June 8, 2004, Naomi receives a refund of her 2002 overpayment. Interest on the refund began to accrue on December 1, 2003 (not April 15, 2003). ■

**EXAMPLE 9**

Assume the same facts as in Example 8, except that the refund is paid to Naomi on January 5, 2004 (rather than June 8, 2004). No interest is payable by the IRS, since the refund was made within 45 days of the filing of the return. ■

- In no event will interest accrue on an overpayment unless the return that is filed is in "processible form." Generally, this means that the return must contain enough information in a readable format to enable the IRS to identify the taxpayer and to determine the tax (and overpayment) involved.

---

[19]§ 6621.
[20]§ 6622.

[21]Rev.Proc. 95–17, 1995–1 C.B. 556.

## TAX IN THE NEWS

### THE IRS STRIVES TO BECOME CONSUMER-FRIENDLY

When country singer Willie Nelson was found guilty of underreporting his Federal income taxes, chiefly due to his involvement in real estate tax shelters, the total deficiency, including taxes, interest, and penalties, came to $16.7 million. The IRS intended to collect the full amount by forcing auctions of Nelson's most valuable possessions, placing claims on royalties from his recordings, encouraging him to make television commercials for fast-food outlets, and prompting him to sue his prior tax advisers for offsetting damages (to be paid directly to the IRS). Three years of such collections totaled only about $4 million.

As part of a nationwide effort to expand the use of the offer in compromise program, the IRS then settled with Nelson for total collections of $9 million, to be paid over a five-year period, with no future liens or collection activities. An IRS spokesperson asserted that the broader use of the compromise powers indicated the agency was "willing to settle for something less than the entire amount . . . to be more reasonable with taxpayers" having difficulty finding the full deficiency amount. As more taxpayers are having such difficulties, the IRS seems willing to collect what it can, rather than haggle in court for years to collect the "last penny" due.

- In the case of a carryback (e.g., net operating loss, capital loss, tax credit), interest on any refund begins to accrue on the due date of the return (disregarding extensions) for the year in which the carryback arises. Even then, however, no interest accrues until a return is filed or, if the return has been filed, if the IRS pays the refund within 45 days.

**EXAMPLE 10**

Top Corporation, a calendar year taxpayer, incurs a net operating loss during 2003 that it can carry back to tax year 2001 and obtain a refund. On December 27, 2004, Top files a claim for refund. The earliest that interest can begin to accrue in this situation is March 15, 2004, but since the return was not filed until December 27, 2004, the later date controls. If, however, the IRS pays the refund within 45 days of December 27, 2004, no interest need be paid. ■

**LO.6**

Discuss the various penalties that can be imposed on acts of noncompliance by taxpayers and return preparers.

### TAXPAYER PENALTIES

To promote and enforce taxpayer compliance with the U.S. voluntary self-assessment system of taxation, Congress has enacted a comprehensive array of penalties.

Tax penalties may involve both criminal and civil offenses. Criminal tax penalties are imposed only after the usual criminal process, in which the taxpayer is entitled to the same constitutional guarantees as nontax criminal defendants. Normally, a criminal penalty provides for imprisonment. Civil tax penalties are collected in the same manner as other taxes and usually provide only for monetary fines. Criminal and civil penalties are not mutually exclusive; therefore, both types of sanctions may be imposed on a taxpayer.

The Code characterizes tax penalties as additions to tax; thus, they cannot subsequently be deducted by the taxpayer.

*Ad valorem penalties* are additions to tax that are based upon a percentage of the owed tax. *Assessable penalties*, on the other hand, typically include a flat dollar amount. Assessable penalties are not subject to review by the Tax Court, but ad valorem penalties are subject to the same deficiency procedures that apply to the underlying tax.

**Failure to File and Failure to Pay.** For a failure to file a tax return by the due date (including extensions), a penalty of 5 percent per month (up to a maximum of 25 percent) is imposed on the amount of tax shown as due on the return, with a minimum penalty amount of $100.[22] If the failure to file is attributable to fraud, the penalty becomes 15 percent per month, to a maximum of 75 percent of the tax.[23]

For a failure to pay the tax due as shown on the return, a penalty of 0.5 percent per month (up to a maximum of 25 percent) is imposed on the amount of the tax. The penalty is doubled if the taxpayer fails to pay the tax after receiving a deficiency assessment.

In all of these cases, a fraction of a month counts as a full month. These penalties relate to the net amount of the tax due.

Obtaining an extension for filing a tax return does not by itself extend the date by which the taxes due must be paid. Thus, an application for an extended due date for a tax return almost always is accompanied by a payment by the taxpayer of a good faith estimate of the taxes that will be owed with the return when it is filed by the extended due date. If the taxpayer does not make such a good faith estimate and payment, the extension itself may be voided by the IRS (e.g., when the return is filed by the extended due date with a much larger amount due than had been estimated).

**EXAMPLE 11**

Conchita uses an automatic four-month extension for the filing of her 2003 tax return. Thus, the return is due on August 15, 2004, not on April 15. Conchita's application for the extension includes a $5,000 check, the amount that she estimates her 2003 return will show as owing for the year when she files it in August. ■

During any month in which both the failure to file penalty and the failure to pay penalty apply, the failure to file penalty is reduced by the amount of the failure to pay penalty.

**EXAMPLE 12**

Jason files his tax return 10 days after the due date. Along with the return, he remits a check for $3,000, which is the balance of the tax he owes. Disregarding any interest liabilities, Jason's total penalties are as follows.

| | | |
|---|---:|---:|
| Failure to pay penalty (½% × $3,000) | | $ 15 |
| Failure to file penalty (5% × $3,000) | $150 | |
| Less failure to pay penalty for the same period | 15 | |
| Failure to file penalty | | 135 |
| Total penalties | | $150 |

The penalties for one full month are imposed even though Jason was delinquent by only 10 days. Unlike the method used to compute interest, any part of a month is treated as a whole month. ■

These penalties can be avoided if the taxpayer shows that the failure to file and/or failure to pay was due to reasonable cause and not due to willful neglect. The Code is silent on what constitutes reasonable cause, and the Regulations do

---

[22]§ 6651(a).                                    [23]§ 6651(f).

little to clarify this important concept.[24] Reasonable cause for failure to pay is presumed under the automatic four-month extension (Form 4868) when the additional tax due is not more than 10 percent of the tax liability shown on the return. In addition, the courts have ruled on some aspects of **reasonable cause.**

- Reasonable cause was found where the taxpayer relied on the advice of a competent tax adviser given in good faith, the facts were fully disclosed to the adviser, and he or she considered that the specific question represented reasonable cause.[25] No reasonable cause was found, however, where the taxpayer delegated the filing task to another, even when that person was an accountant or an attorney.[26]
- Among the reasons not qualifying as reasonable cause were lack of information on the due date of the return,[27] illness that did not incapacitate a taxpayer from completing a return,[28] refusal of the taxpayer's spouse to cooperate for a joint return,[29] and ignorance or misunderstanding of the tax law.[30]

**Accuracy-Related Penalties.**   Major civil penalties relating to the accuracy of tax return data, including misstatements stemming from taxpayer negligence and improper valuation of income and deductions, are coordinated under the umbrella term **accuracy-related penalties.**[31] This consolidation of related penalties into a single levy eliminates the possibility that multiple penalties will apply to a single understatement of tax.

The accuracy-related penalties each amount to 20 percent of the portion of the tax underpayment that is attributable to one or more of the following infractions.

- Negligence or disregard of rules and regulations.
- Substantial understatement of tax liability.
- Substantial valuation overstatement.
- Substantial valuation understatement.

The penalties apply only where the taxpayer fails to show a reasonable basis for the position taken on the return.[32]

**Negligence.**   For purposes of this accuracy-related penalty, **negligence** includes any failure to make a reasonable attempt to comply with the provisions of the tax law. The penalty also applies to any disregard (whether careless, reckless, or intentional) of rules and regulations.[33] The penalty can be avoided upon a showing of reasonable cause and that the taxpayer acted in good faith.[34]

The negligence penalty applies to *all* taxes, except when fraud is involved. A negligence penalty may be assessed when the taxpayer fails to report gross income, overstates deductions, or fails to keep adequate records. When the taxpayer takes a nonnegligent position on the return that is contrary to a judicial precedent or published pronouncement of the IRS, the penalty is waived if the taxpayer has a

---

[24]Reg. § 301.6651–1(c)(1) likens reasonable cause to the exercise of "ordinary business care and prudence" on the part of the taxpayer.

[25]*Estate of Norma S. Bradley*, 33 TCM 70, T.C.Memo. 1974–17.

[26]*U.S. v. Boyle*, 85–1 USTC ¶13,602, 55 AFTR2d 85–1535, 105 S.Ct. 687 (USSC, 1985).

[27]*Beck Chemical Equipment Co.*, 27 T.C. 840 (1957).

[28]*Jacob Gassman*, 26 TCM 213, T.C.Memo. 1967–42, and *Babetta Schmidt*, 28 T.C. 367 (1957). Compare *Estate of Kirchner*, 46 B.T.A. 578 (1942).

[29]*Electric and Neon, Inc.*, 56 T.C. 1324 (1971).

[30]*Stevens Brothers Foundation, Inc.*, 39 T.C. 93 (1965).

[31]§ 6662.

[32]Temporary Regulations issued as TD 8533, 1994–1 C.B. 307. Most tax professionals measure this standard as a one-fourth probability of prevailing in court.

[33]§ 6662(c).

[34]§ 6664(c)(1).

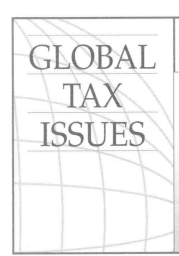

## GLOBAL TAX ISSUES

### ADVANCE PRICING AGREEMENTS REDUCE INTERNATIONAL UNCERTAINTY

Two of the more severe accuracy-related penalties involve the transfer pricing issues surrounding the IRS's application of § 482. Transfer pricing issues are particularly difficult—and important—in an international context because multiple taxing authorities are involved. Consequently, taxpayers have begun to negotiate international transfer pricing agreements in advance with the IRS and other countries. Obtaining one of these *advance pricing agreements (APAs)* can require a substantial amount of work from the taxpayer, but the certainty they bring is valuable.

An estimated 400 APAs have been completed with the United States, and the IRS offers a simpler APA process for small businesses.

reasonable basis for the interpretation and has disclosed the disputed position on Form 8275.

**Substantial Understatement of Tax Liability.** The understatement penalty is designed to strike at middle- and high-income taxpayers who are tempted to play the so-called audit lottery.[35] Some taxpayers take questionable and undisclosed positions on their tax returns in the hope that the return will not be selected for audit. Disclosing the positions would have called attention to the return and increased the probability of audit.

A substantial understatement of a tax liability transpires when the understatement exceeds the larger of 10 percent of the tax due or $5,000 ($10,000 for a C corporation). The understatement to which the penalty applies is the difference between the amount of tax required to be shown on the return and the amount of tax actually shown on the return.

The penalty is avoided under any of the following circumstances.

- The taxpayer has **substantial authority** for the treatment.[36]
- The relevant facts affecting the treatment are adequately disclosed in the return by attaching Form 8275.
- The IRS has not borne its burden of proof as to matters of fact in resolving a tax dispute in a court proceeding. This shift of the burden of proof does not relieve the taxpayer of documentation requirements, and it is limited to taxpayers of modest means.[37] The taxpayer retains the burden of proof in all proceedings prior to a court hearing, but the burden is on the IRS where fraud or a frivolous tax return is involved.

**Penalty for Overvaluation.** The objective of the overvaluation penalty is to deter taxpayers from inflating values (or basis), usually of charitable contributions of property, to reduce income taxes.[38]

---

[35]§ 6662(b)(2).
[36]Review the discussion related to Footnote 52 in Chapter 1.
[37]The shifting of the burden is not available if the taxpayer's net worth exceeds $7 million or if the taxpayer employs more than 500 persons.

[38]§§ 6662(b)(3) and (h).

- The penalty is 20 percent of the additional tax that would have been paid had the correct valuation (or basis) been used.
- The penalty applies only when the valuation (or basis) used is 200 percent or more of the correct valuation (or basis). The penalty is doubled if the valuation is overstated by 400 percent or more.
- The penalty applies only to the extent that the resulting income tax underpayment exceeds $5,000 ($10,000 for C corporations).

**EXAMPLE 13**

Gretchen (a calendar year taxpayer) purchased a painting for $10,000. Years later, when the painting is worth $18,000 (as later determined by the IRS), Gretchen donates the painting to an art museum. Based on the appraisal of a cousin who is an amateur artist, she deducts $40,000 for the donation. Since Gretchen was in the 30% tax bracket, overstating the deduction by $22,000 results in a tax underpayment of $6,600.

Gretchen's penalty for overvaluation is $1,320 [20% × $6,600 (the underpayment that resulted from using $40,000 instead of $18,000)]. ■

The substantial valuation overstatement penalty is avoided if the taxpayer can show reasonable cause and good faith. However, when the overvaluation involves *charitable deduction property*, the taxpayer must show two *additional* facts.

- The claimed value of the property is based on a qualified appraisal made by a qualified appraiser.
- The taxpayer made a good faith investigation of the value of the contributed property.[39]

Based on these criteria, Gretchen in Example 13 would find it difficult to avoid the penalty. A cousin who is an amateur artist does not meet the definition of a qualified appraiser. Likewise, she apparently has not made a good faith investigation of the value of the contributed property.

**Penalty for Undervaluation.** When attempting to minimize the income tax, it is to the benefit of taxpayers to *overvalue* deductions. When attempting to minimize transfer taxes (estate and gift taxes), however, executors and donors may be inclined to *undervalue* the assets transferred. A lower valuation reduces estate and gift taxes. An accuracy-related penalty is imposed for substantial estate or gift tax valuation understatements.[40] As with other accuracy-related penalties, reasonable cause and good faith on the part of the taxpayer are a defense.

- The penalty is 20 percent of the additional transfer tax that would have been due had the correct valuation been used on Form 706 (estate tax return) or Form 709 (gift and generation-skipping tax return).
- The penalty applies only if the value of the property claimed on the return is 50 percent or less than the amount determined to be correct. The penalty is doubled if the reported valuation was 25 percent or less than the correct determination.
- The penalty applies only to an additional transfer tax liability in excess of $5,000.

---

[39]§ 6664(c)(2).            [40]§ 6662(b)(5).

---

| ETHICAL CONSIDERATIONS | **Good Faith Valuations** |
|---|---|

When dealing with the undervaluation penalty, the tax adviser may shift from being in adversarial alliance with the taxpayer to being a mediator for the court. Good faith value estimates, especially for family-owned businesses, can easily vary by as much as the 50 percentage points specified for the penalty. Even a gross undervaluation can occur when someone in the business other than the donor or decedent is a particularly talented entrepreneur, an effective sales representative, and/or the founder of the company; similarly, a business may be substantially undervalued when a minority equity interest is involved, or an intangible asset conveys a sizable nominal amount of goodwill to the valuation.

Because most taxpayers are highly averse to incurring any nondeductible penalties, the client may be tempted to compromise on the business valuation "too soon" (i.e., when the return is filed), eliminating any possibility of a more favorable valuation being presented before the Appeals Division or a court. Keeping in mind all of the potential taxpayer and preparer penalties that might apply, the tax professional should stick with a good faith appraisal of the business value, no matter what its nominal amount.

How would you react if your client, a composer, wanted to deduct $100,000 for the contribution of an obscure manuscript to the Symphony Society? What if your (first) appraiser placed the value of the manuscript at $15,000? What course of action would you propose to the client concerning the deduction? Any consequent penalties?

---

**Civil Fraud Penalty.** A 75 percent civil penalty is imposed on any underpayment resulting from **fraud** by the taxpayer who has filed a return.[41] For this penalty, the burden of proof *is on the IRS* to show by a preponderance of the evidence that the taxpayer had a specific intent to evade a tax.

Once the IRS has initially established that fraud has occurred, the taxpayer then bears the burden of proof to show by a preponderance of the evidence the portion of the underpayment that is not attributable to fraud.

Although the Code and Regulations do not provide any assistance in ascertaining what constitutes civil fraud, it is clear that mere negligence on the part of the taxpayer (however great) will not suffice. Fraud has been found in cases of manipulation of the books,[42] substantial omissions from income,[43] and erroneous deductions.[44]

> **EXAMPLE 14**

Frank underpaid his income tax by $90,000. The IRS can prove that $60,000 of the underpayment was due to fraud. Frank responds by a preponderance of the evidence that $30,000 of the underpayment was not due to fraud. The civil fraud penalty is $45,000 (75% × $60,000). ■

If the underpayment of tax is partially attributable to negligence and partially attributable to fraud, the fraud penalty is applied first.

**Criminal Penalties.** In addition to civil fraud penalties, the Code contains numerous criminal sanctions that carry various monetary fines and/or imprisonment. The difference between civil and criminal fraud is often one of degree. A characteristic of criminal fraud is the presence of willfulness on the part of the taxpayer. Thus, § 7201, dealing with attempts to evade or defeat a tax, contains the following language.

---

[41]§ 6663. As noted later in the chapter, underpayments traceable to fraudulent acts are not subject to a statute of limitations.

[42]*Dogget v. Comm.*, 60–1 USTC ¶9342, 5 AFTR2d 1034, 275 F.2d 823 (CA–4, 1960).

[43]*Harvey Brodsky*, 21 TCM 578, T.C.Memo. 1962–105.

[44]*Lash v. Comm.*, 57–2 USTC ¶9725, 51 AFTR 492, 245 F.2d 20 (CA–1, 1957).

Any person who *willfully* attempts in any manner to evade or defeat any tax imposed by this title or the payment thereof shall, in addition to other penalties provided by law, be guilty of a felony and, upon conviction thereof, shall be fined not more than $100,000 ($500,000 in the case of a corporation), or imprisoned not more than five years, or both, together with the costs of prosecution. [Emphasis added.]

As to the burden of proof, the IRS must show that the taxpayer was guilty of willful evasion "beyond the shadow of any reasonable doubt."

**Failure to Pay Estimated Taxes.**    A penalty is imposed for a failure to pay estimated income taxes. The penalty applies to individuals and corporations and is based on the rate of interest in effect for deficiency assessments.[45] The penalty also applies to trusts and certain estates that are required to make estimated tax payments. The penalty is not imposed if the tax due for the year (less amounts withheld and credits) is less than $500 for corporations, $1,000 for all others. For employees, an equal part of withholding is deemed paid on each due date.

Quarterly payments are to be made on or before the fifteenth day of the fourth month (April 15 for a calendar year taxpayer), sixth month, ninth month, and the first month of the following year. Corporations must make the last quarterly payment by the twelfth month of the same year.

An individual's underpayment of estimated tax is the difference between the estimates that were paid and the least of (1) 90 percent of the current-year tax, (2) 100 percent of the prior-year tax (the tax year must have been a full 12 months, and a return must have been filed), and (3) 90 percent of the tax that would be due on an annualized income computation for the period running through the end of the quarter. When the taxpayer's prior-year adjusted gross income (AGI) exceeds $150,000, the required payment percentage for the prior-year alternative is 110 percent.

A corporation's underpayment of estimated tax is the difference between the estimates that were paid and the least of (1) the current-year tax, (2) the prior-year tax, and (3) the tax on an annualized income computation using one of three methods of computation sanctioned by the Code. For the prior-year alternative, (1) the prior tax year must have been a full 12 months, (2) a nonzero tax amount must have been generated for that year, and (3) large corporations (taxable income of $1 million or more in any of the three immediately preceding tax years) can use the alternative only for the first installment of a year.

In computing the penalty, Form 2210 (Underpayment of Estimated Tax by Individuals) or Form 2220 (Underpayment of Estimated Tax by Corporations) is used.

**False Information with Respect to Withholding.**    Withholding from wages is an important element of the Federal income tax system, which is based on a pay-as-you-go approach. One way employees might hope to avoid this withholding would be to falsify the information provided to the employer on Form W–4 (Employee Withholding Allowance Certificate). For example, by overstating the number of exemptions, income tax withholdings could be cut or completely eliminated.

To encourage compliance, a civil penalty of $500 applies when a taxpayer claims withholding allowances based on false information. The criminal penalty for willfully failing to supply information or for willfully supplying false or fraudulent

---

[45]§§ 6655 (corporations) and 6654 (other taxpayers). Other computations can avoid the penalty. See §§ 6654(d)(2) and (k), 6655(e) and (i).

information in connection with wage withholding is an additional fine of up to $1,000 and/or up to one year of imprisonment.[46]

### Failure to Make Deposits of Taxes and Overstatements of Deposits.
When business is not doing well or cash-flow problems develop, employers have a great temptation to "borrow" from Uncle Sam. One way this can be done is to fail to pay to the IRS the amounts that have been withheld from the wages of employees for FICA and income tax purposes. The IRS does not appreciate being denied the use of these funds and has a number of weapons at its disposal to discourage the practice.

- A penalty of up to 15 percent of any underdeposited amount not paid, unless the employer can show that the failure is due to reasonable cause and not to willful neglect.[47]
- Various criminal penalties.[48]
- A 100 percent penalty if the employer's actions are willful.[49] The penalty is based on the amount of the tax evaded (i.e., not collected, or not accounted for or paid over). Since the penalty is assessable against the "responsible person" of the business, more than one party may be vulnerable (e.g., the president and treasurer of a corporation). Although the IRS may assess the penalty against several persons, it cannot collect more than the 100 percent due.
- In addition to these penalties, the actual tax due must be remitted. An employer remains liable for the amount that should have been paid, even if the withholdings have not been taken out of the wages of its employees.[50]

## LO.7

Understand the rules governing the statute of limitations on assessments and on refunds.

## STATUTES OF LIMITATIONS

A **statute of limitations** defines the period of time during which one party may pursue against another party a cause of action or other suit allowed under the governing law. Failure to satisfy any requirement provides the other party with an absolute defense should the statute be invoked. Inequity would result if no limits were placed on such suits. Permitting an extended period of time to elapse between the initiation of a claim and its pursuit could place the defense at a serious disadvantage. Witnesses may have died or disappeared; records or other evidence may have been discarded or destroyed.

**Assessment and the Statute of Limitations.** In general, any tax that is imposed must be assessed within three years of the filing of the return (or, if later, the due date of the return).[51] Some exceptions to this three-year limitation exist.

- If no return is filed or a fraudulent return is filed, assessments can be made at any time. There is, in effect, no statute of limitations in these cases.
- If a taxpayer omits an amount of gross income in excess of 25 percent of the gross income stated on the return, the statute of limitations is increased to six years. The courts have interpreted this rule as including only items affecting income and not the omission of items affecting cost of sales.[52] In addition, gross income includes capital gains in the *gross* income amount (not reduced by capital losses).

---

[46]§§ 6682 and 7205.
[47]§ 6656.
[48]See, for example, § 7202 (willful failure to collect or pay over a tax).
[49]§ 6672.

[50]§ 3403.
[51]§§ 6501(a) and (b)(1).
[52]*The Colony, Inc. v. Comm.*, 58–2 USTC ¶9593, 1 AFTR2d 1894, 78 S.Ct. 1033 (USSC, 1958).

**EXAMPLE 15**

During 1998, Jerry had the following income transactions (all of which were duly reported on his timely filed return).

| | | |
|---|---|---|
| Gross receipts | | $ 480,000 |
| Cost of sales | | (400,000) |
| Net business income | | $  80,000 |
| Capital gains and losses | | |
| Capital gain | $ 36,000 | |
| Capital loss | (12,000) | 24,000 |
| Total income | | $ 104,000 |

Jerry retains your services in 2003 as a tax consultant. It seems that he inadvertently omitted some income on his 1998 return and he wishes to know if he is "safe" under the statute of limitations. The six-year statute of limitations would apply, putting Jerry in a vulnerable position only if he omitted more than $129,000 on his 1998 return [($480,000 + $36,000) × 25%]. ∎

- The statute of limitations may be extended by mutual consent of a Director and the taxpayer. This extension covers a definite period and is made by signing Form 872 (Consent to Extend the Time to Assess Tax). The extension is frequently requested by the IRS when the lapse of the statutory period is imminent and the audit has not been completed. This practice is often applied to audits of corporate taxpayers and explains why many corporations have more than three "open years."

Special rules relating to assessment are applicable in the following situations.

- Taxpayers (corporations, estates, etc.) may request a prompt assessment of the tax.
- The assessment period for capital loss and net operating loss carrybacks generally relates to the determination of tax in the year of the loss or unused credit rather than in the carryback years.

If the IRS issues a statutory notice of deficiency to the taxpayer, who then files a Tax Court petition, the statute is suspended on both the deficiency assessment and the period of collection until 60 days after the decision of the Tax Court becomes final. The statute is also suspended when the taxpayer is "financially disabled"; that is, the taxpayer has been rendered unable to manage his or her financial affairs by a physical or mental impairment that is likely to last for a year or more or to cause the taxpayer's death. The statute continues to run if another party is authorized to act for the taxpayer in financial matters.[53]

### Refund Claims and the Statute of Limitations.

To receive a tax refund, the taxpayer is required to file a valid refund claim. The official form for filing a claim is Form 1040X for individuals and Form 1120X for corporations. If the refund claim does not meet certain procedural requirements, the IRS may reject the claim with no consideration of its merit.

---

[53]"Equitable tolling" or suspension of the statute of limitations has been allowed by the courts when attributable to a taxpayer disability or IRS misconduct. See *Brockamp v. Comm.*, 97–1 USTC ¶50,216, 79 AFTR2d 97–986, 117 S.Ct. 849 (USSC, 1997). §§ 6501(c)(4) and 6511(h).

- A separate claim must be filed for each taxable period.
- The grounds for the claim must be stated in sufficient detail.
- The statement of facts must be sufficient to permit the IRS to evaluate the merits of the claim.

The refund claim must be filed within three years of the filing of the tax return or within two years following the payment of the tax if this period expires on a later date.[54]

**EXAMPLE 16**

On March 10, 2000, Louise filed her 1999 income tax return reflecting a tax of $10,500. On July 10, 2001, she filed an amended 1999 return showing an additional $3,000 of tax that was then paid. On May 19, 2003, she filed a claim for refund of $4,500.

Assuming that Louise is correct in claiming a refund, how much tax can she recover? The answer is only $3,000. Because the claim was not filed within the three-year period, Louise is limited to the amount she actually paid during the last two years. ∎

Special rules are available for claims relating to bad debts and worthless securities. A seven-year period of limitations applies in lieu of the normal three-year rule.[55] The extended period is provided in recognition of the inherent difficulty of identifying the exact year in which a bad debt or security becomes worthless.

**LO.8**

Summarize the legal and ethical guidelines that apply to those engaged in tax practice.

## Tax Practice

### THE TAX PRACTITIONER

**Definition.**   Who is a tax practitioner? What service does the practitioner perform? To begin defining the term *tax practitioner*, one should consider whether the individual is qualified to practice before the IRS. Generally, practice before the IRS is limited to CPAs, attorneys, and persons who have been enrolled to practice before the IRS (called **enrolled agents [EAs]**). In most cases, EAs are admitted to practice only if they pass an examination administered by the IRS. CPAs and attorneys are not required to take this examination and are automatically admitted to practice if they are in good standing with the appropriate licensing board regulating their profession.

Persons other than CPAs, attorneys, and EAs may be allowed to practice before the IRS in limited situations. Circular 230 (entitled "Rules Governing the Practice of Attorneys and Agents Before the Internal Revenue Service") issued by the Treasury Department permits certain notable exceptions.

- A taxpayer may always represent himself or herself. A person may also represent a member of the immediate family if no compensation is received for such services.
- Regular full-time employees may represent their employers.
- Corporations may be represented by any of their bona fide officers.
- Partnerships may be represented by any of the partners.
- Trusts, receiverships, guardianships, or estates may be represented by their trustees, receivers, guardians, or administrators or executors.
- A taxpayer may be represented by whoever prepared the return for the year in question. However, such representation cannot proceed beyond the agent level.

---

[54]§§ 6511(a) and 6513(a).

[55]§ 6511(d)(1).

**EXAMPLE 17**

Joel is currently undergoing audit by the IRS for tax years 2000 and 2001. He prepared the 2000 return himself but paid AddCo, a bookkeeping service, to prepare the 2001 return. AddCo may represent Joel only in matters concerning 2001. However, even for 2001, AddCo would be unable to represent Joel at an Appeals Division proceeding. Joel could, of course, represent himself, or he could retain a CPA, attorney, or EA to represent him in matters concerning both years under examination. ■

**Rules Governing Tax Practice.**   Circular 230 further prescribes the rules governing practice before the IRS. The following are some of the most important rules imposed on CPAs, attorneys, and EAs.

- A prohibition against taking a position on a tax return unless there is a *realistic possibility* of the position being sustained on its merits. Generally, the realistic possibility standard is met when a person knowledgeable in the tax law would conclude that the position has at least a one-in-three probability of prevailing in court.
- A prohibition against taking frivolous tax return positions.
- A requirement that nonfrivolous tax return positions that fail the realistic possibility standard be disclosed in the return (i.e., using Form 8275).
- A requirement to inform clients of penalties likely to apply to return positions and of ways such penalties can be avoided.
- A requirement to make known to a client any error or omission the client may have made on any return or other document submitted to the IRS.
- A duty to submit records or information lawfully requested by the IRS.
- An obligation to exercise due diligence in preparing and filing tax returns accurately.
- A restriction against unreasonably delaying the prompt disposition of any matter before the IRS.
- A restriction against charging the client "an unconscionable fee" for representation before the IRS.
- A restriction against representing clients with conflicting interests.

Anyone can prepare a tax return or render tax advice, regardless of his or her educational background or level of competence. Likewise, nothing prevents the "unlicensed" tax practitioner from advertising his or her specialty, directly soliciting clients, or otherwise violating any of the standards of conduct controlling CPAs, attorneys, and EAs. Nevertheless, some restraints do govern all parties engaged in rendering tax returns for the general public.

- A person who holds himself or herself out to the general public as possessing tax expertise could be liable to the client if services are performed in a negligent manner. At a minimum, the practitioner is liable for any interest and penalties the client incurs because of the practitioner's failure to exercise due care.
- If a practitioner agrees to perform a service (e.g., prepare a tax return) and subsequently fails to do so, the aggrieved party may be in a position to obtain damages for breach of contract.
- The IRS requires all persons who prepare tax returns for a fee to sign as preparer of the return.[56] Failure to comply with this requirement could result in penalty assessment against the preparer.

---

[56]Reg. § 1.6065–1(b)(1). Rev.Rul. 84–3, 1984–1 C.B. 264, contains a series of examples illustrating when a person is deemed to be a preparer of the return.

- The Code prescribes various penalties for the deliberate filing of false or fraudulent returns. These penalties apply to a tax practitioner who either was aware of the situation or actually perpetrated the false information or the fraud.[57]
- Penalties are prescribed for tax practitioners who disclose to third parties information they have received from clients in connection with the preparation of tax returns or the rendering of tax advice.[58]

**EXAMPLE 18**

Sarah operates a tax return preparation service. Her brother-in-law, Butch, has just taken a job as a life insurance salesman. To help Butch find contacts, Sarah furnishes him with a list of the names and addresses of all of her clients who report AGI of $10,000 or more. Sarah is subject to penalties. ■

- All nonattorney tax practitioners should avoid becoming engaged in activities that constitute the unauthorized practice of law. If they engage in this practice (e.g., by drafting legal documents for a third party), action could be instituted against them in the appropriate state court by the local or state bar association. What actions constitute the unauthorized practice of law is largely undefined, though, and such charges are filed only rarely today.

**Preparer Penalties.** The Code also provides for penalties to discourage improper actions by tax practitioners.

1. A $250 penalty for understatements due to taking unrealistic positions.[59] Unless the position is adequately disclosed on the tax return, the penalty is imposed if two conditions are satisfied.

   - Any part of any understatement of tax liability on any return or claim for refund is due to a position that did not have a realistic possibility of being sustained on its merits.
   - Any person who was an income tax return preparer for that return or claim knew (or should have known) of this position.

   The penalty can be avoided by showing reasonable cause and by showing that the preparer acted in good faith.

2. A $1,000 penalty for willful and reckless conduct.[60] The penalty applies if any part of the understatement of a taxpayer's liability on a return or claim for refund is due to:

   - The preparer's willful attempt to understate the taxpayer's tax liability in any manner.
   - Any reckless or intentional disregard of IRS rules or regulations by the preparer.

   Adequate disclosure can avoid the penalty. If both this penalty and the unrealistic position penalty (see item 1 above) apply to the same return, the total penalty cannot exceed $1,000.

3. A $1,000 ($10,000 for corporations) penalty per return or document is imposed against persons who aid in the preparation of returns or other documents that they know (or have reason to believe) would result in an

---

[57]§ 7206.
[58]§ 7216.

[59]§ 6694(a).
[60]§ 6694(b).

understatement of the tax liability of another person.[61] Clerical assistance in the preparation process does not incur the penalty.

If this penalty applies, neither the unrealistic position penalty (item 1) nor the willful and reckless conduct penalty (item 2) is assessed.

4. A $50 penalty is assessed against the preparer for failure to sign a return or furnish the preparer's identifying number.[62]
5. A $50 penalty is assessed if the preparer fails to furnish a copy of the return or claim for refund to the taxpayer.
6. A $500 penalty may be assessed if a preparer endorses or otherwise negotiates a check for refund of tax issued to the taxpayer.

**Privileged Communications.**   Communications between an attorney and client have long been protected from disclosure to other parties (such as the IRS and the tax courts). A similar privilege of confidentiality extends to tax advice between a taxpayer and tax practitioner, as we used that term above. The privilege is not available for matters involving criminal charges or questions brought by other agencies, such as the Securities and Exchange Commission.[63] Nor is it allowed in matters involving promoting or participating in tax shelters.

A taxpayer will likely want to protect documents such as the tax adviser's research memo detailing the strengths and weaknesses of a tax return position or a conversation about an appeals strategy. The confidentiality privilege should be interpreted in the following manner.

- The privilege is often available when an attorney or CPA completes a tax return for the taxpayer. But some courts have restricted the attorney's privilege in this context on the ground that the tax professional is conducting accounting work, not offering legal advice. Others assert that the confidentiality privilege is waived when the taxpayer discloses financial data on the tax return. To the contrary, if the tax professional is providing traditional legal advice to help the client decide what to disclose on a tax return, the privilege should be available.
- The privilege for CPAs applies only to tax advice. Attorneys can still exercise the privilege concerning advice rendered as a business consultant, estate/ financial planner, and so on.
- About a third of the states offer a similar confidentiality privilege for CPAs, but outside the Federal tax appeals process, protection is not yet the norm.
- The privilege is not available for tax accrual workpapers prepared as part of an independent financial audit.

Thus, the CPA needs to exercise care to ensure that the privilege of confidentiality will apply to his or her tax work. Taking the following steps can help.

- Segregate the time spent and documents produced in rendering services for tax compliance from the time and documents devoted to tax advice. Doing this will protect the privilege from being waived as to the tax advice.
- Explain the extent of the privilege to the client—specify what will and will not be protected from the IRS in a dispute.
- Do not inadvertently waive the privilege, say, by telling "too much" to the IRS or to a third party who is not protected by the privilege.
- Indemnify the CPA for time spent protecting and enforcing the privilege once it is challenged.

---

[61]§ 6701.
[62]§ 6695.

[63]§ 7525(a)(1).

## AICPA STATEMENTS ON STANDARDS FOR TAX SERVICES

Tax practitioners who are CPAs, attorneys, or EAs must abide by the codes or canons of professional ethics applicable to their respective professions. The various codes and canons have much in common with and parallel the standards of conduct set forth in Circular 230.[64]

The AICPA has issued a series of Statements on Standards for Tax Services (SSTSs). The Statements are enforceable standards of professional practice for AICPA members working in state or Federal tax practice. The SSTSs comprise part of the AICPA's Code of Professional Conduct. Together with the provisions of Circular 230 and the penalty provisions of the Code, the SSTSs make up a set of guidelines for the conduct of the tax practitioner who is also a CPA. Other sources of descriptions of professional ethics are issued by state bar associations and CPA societies, the American Bar Association, and the associations of enrolled agents.

Key provisions of some of the SSTSs are presented below.

**Statement No. 1: Tax Return Positions.** Under certain circumstances, a CPA may take a position that is contrary to that taken by the IRS. To do so, however, the CPA must have a good faith belief that the position has a realistic possibility of being sustained administratively or judicially on its merits if challenged.

The client should be fully advised of the risks involved and the penalties that may result if the position taken by the CPA is not successful. The client should also be informed that disclosure on the return may avoid some or all of these penalties.

In no case, though, should the CPA exploit the audit lottery. That is, the CPA should not take a questionable position based on the probabilities that the client's return will not be chosen by the IRS for audit. Furthermore, the CPA should not "load" the return with questionable items in the hope that they might aid the client in a later settlement negotiation with the IRS.

**Statement No. 2: Questions on Returns.** A CPA should make a reasonable effort to obtain from the client, and provide, appropriate answers to all questions on a tax return before signing as preparer. Reasonable grounds may exist for omitting an answer.

- The information is not readily available, and the answer is not significant in computing the tax.
- The meaning of the question as it applies to a particular situation is genuinely uncertain.
- The answer to the question is voluminous.

The fact that an answer to a question could prove disadvantageous to the client does not justify omitting the answer.

**Statement No. 3: Procedural Aspects of Preparing Returns.** In preparing a return, a CPA may in good faith rely without verification on information furnished by the client or by third parties. However, the CPA should make reasonable inquiries if the information appears to be incorrect, incomplete, or inconsistent. In this regard, the CPA should refer to the client's returns for prior years whenever appropriate.

---

[64]For an additional discussion of tax ethics, see Raabe, Whittenburg, and Sanders, *West's Federal Tax Research*, 6th ed. (South-Western/Thomson Learning, 2003), especially Chapters 1 and 13.

**EXAMPLE 19**

A CPA can normally take a client's word for the validity of dependency exemptions. But suppose a recently divorced client wants to claim his three children as dependents (when he does not have custody). You must act in accordance with § 152(e)(2) in preparing the return, and this will require evidence of a waiver by the custodial parent. Without this waiver, you should not claim the dependency exemptions on your client's tax return. ■

**EXAMPLE 20**

While preparing a client's income tax return for 2003, you review her income tax return for 2002. In comparing the dividend income reported on the 2002 Schedule B with that received in 2003, you note a significant decrease. Further investigation reveals the variation is due to a stock sale in 2003 that was unknown to you until now. Thus, the review of the 2002 return has unearthed a transaction that should be reported on the 2003 return. ■

If the Code or Regulations require certain types of verification (as is the case with travel and entertainment expenditures), the CPA must advise the client of these rules. Further, inquiry must be made to ascertain whether the client has complied with the verification requirements.

**Statement No. 4: Estimates.** A CPA may prepare a tax return using estimates received from a taxpayer if it is impracticable to obtain exact data. The estimates must be reasonable under the facts and circumstances as known to the CPA. When estimates are used, they should be presented in such a manner as to avoid the implication of greater accuracy than exists.

**Statement No. 5: Recognition of Administrative Proceeding or Court Decision.** As facts may vary from year to year, so may the position taken by a CPA. In these types of situations, the CPA is not bound by an administrative or judicial proceeding involving a prior year.

**EXAMPLE 21**

Upon audit of Ramon Corporation's income tax return for 2001, the IRS disallowed $18,000 of the $400,000 salary paid to its president and sole shareholder on the grounds that it is unreasonable [§ 162(a)(1)]. You are the CPA who has been engaged to prepare Ramon's income tax return for 2003. Again the corporation paid its president a salary of $400,000 and chose to deduct this amount. Because you are not bound for 2003 by what the IRS deemed reasonable for 2001, the full $400,000 can be claimed as a salary deduction. ■

Other problems that require a CPA's use of judgment include reclassification of corporate debt as equity (thin capitalization) and corporate accumulations beyond the reasonable needs of the business (for the penalty tax under § 531).

**Statement No. 6: Knowledge of Error.** A CPA should promptly advise a client upon learning of an error in a previously filed return or upon learning of a client's failure to file a required return. The advice can be oral or written and should include a recommendation of the corrective measures, if any, to be taken. The error or other omission should not be disclosed to the IRS without the client's consent.

If the past error is material and is not corrected by the client, the CPA may be unable to prepare the current year's tax return. This situation might occur if the error has a carryover effect that prevents the CPA from determining the correct tax liability for the current year.

**EXAMPLE 22**

In preparing a client's 2003 income tax return, you discover that final inventory for 2002 was materially understated. First, you should advise the client to file an amended return for 2002 reflecting the correct amount in final inventory. Second, if the client refuses to make

## CONCEPT SUMMARY 16–1

### Tax Administration and Practice

1. The Internal Revenue Service (IRS) enforces the tax laws of the United States. Its size and form of organization reflect its various responsibilities relative to taxpayer interaction, litigation, and collection, as well as its internal functions.

2. The IRS issues various pronouncements, communicating its position on certain tax issues. These pronouncements promote the uniform enforcement of the tax law among taxpayers and among the internal divisions of the IRS. Taxpayers should seek such rulings and memoranda when the nature or magnitude of a pending transaction requires a high degree of certainty in the planning process.

3. IRS audits can take several forms. Taxpayers are selected for audit based on the probable net dollar return to the Treasury from the process. Offers in compromise and closing agreements can be a useful means of completing an audit without resorting to litigation.

4. Certain IRS personnel are empowered to consider the hazards of litigation in developing a settlement with the taxpayer during the audit process.

5. The IRS pays interest to taxpayers on overpaid taxes, starting essentially 45 days after the due date of the return, in amounts tied to the Federal short-term rate. Interest paid to the IRS on underpayments is similarly based on the Federal rate, starting essentially on the due date of the return. Interest for both purposes is compounded daily.

6. The Treasury assesses penalties when the taxpayer fails to file a required tax return or pay a tax. Penalties also are assessed when an inaccurate return is filed due to negligence or other disregard of IRS rules. Tax preparers are subject to penalties for assisting a taxpayer in filing an inaccurate return, failing to follow IRS rules in an appropriate manner, or mishandling taxpayer data or funds.

7. Statutes of limitations place outer boundaries on the timing and amounts of proposed amendments to completed tax returns that can be made by the taxpayer or the IRS.

8. Tax practitioners must operate under constraints imposed on them by codes of ethics or pertinent professional societies and by Treasury Circular 230. These rules also define the parties who can represent others in an IRS proceeding.

9. A limited privilege of confidentiality exists between taxpayer and tax preparer.

this adjustment, you should consider whether the error will preclude you from preparing a substantially correct return for 2003. Because this will probably be the case (the final inventory for 2002 becomes the beginning inventory for 2003), you should withdraw from the engagement.

If the client corrects the error, you may proceed with the preparation of the tax return for 2003. You must assure yourself that the error is not repeated. ■

**Statement No. 8: Advice to Clients.** In providing tax advice to a client, the CPA must use judgment to assure that the advice reflects professional competence and appropriately serves the client's needs. No standard format or guidelines can be established to cover all situations and circumstances involving written or oral advice by the CPA.

The CPA may communicate with the client when subsequent developments affect previous advice on significant matters. However, the CPA cannot be expected to assume responsibility for initiating the communication, unless he or she is assisting a client in implementing procedures or plans associated with the advice. The CPA may undertake this obligation by specific agreement with the client.

## STRATEGIES IN SEEKING AN ADMINISTRATIVE RULING

**Determination Letters.**   In many instances, the request for an advance ruling or a determination letter from the IRS is a necessary or desirable planning strategy. The receipt of a favorable ruling or determination reduces the risk associated with a transaction when the tax results are in doubt. For example, the initiation or amendment of a qualified pension or profit sharing plan should be accompanied by a determination letter from a Director. Otherwise, on subsequent IRS review, the plan may not qualify, and the tax deductibility of contributions to the plan will be disallowed. In some instances, the potential tax effects of a transaction are so numerous and of such consequence that proceeding without a ruling is unwise.

**Letter Rulings.**   In some cases, it may not be necessary or desirable to request an advance ruling. For example, it is generally not desirable to request a ruling if the tax results are doubtful and the company is committed to complete the transaction in any event. If a ruling is requested and negotiations with the IRS indicate that an adverse determination will be forthcoming, it is usually possible to have the ruling request withdrawn. However, the National Office of the IRS may forward its findings, along with a copy of the ruling request, to a Director. In determining the advisability of a ruling request, the taxpayer should consider the potential exposure of other items in the tax returns of all "open years."

A ruling request may delay the consummation of a transaction if the issues are novel or complex. Frequently, a ruling can be processed within six months, although in some instances a delay of a year or more may be encountered.

**Technical Advice Memoranda.**   A taxpayer in the process of contesting a proposed deficiency with the Appeals Division should consider requesting a technical advice memorandum from the National Office of the IRS. If the memorandum is favorable to the taxpayer, it is binding on the Appeals Division. The request may be particularly appropriate when the practitioner feels that the agent or Appeals Division has been too literal in interpreting an IRS ruling.

## CONSIDERATIONS IN HANDLING AN IRS AUDIT

As a general rule, a taxpayer should attempt to settle disputes at the earliest possible stage of the administrative appeal process. It is usually possible to limit the scope of the examination by furnishing pertinent information requested by the agent. Extraneous information or fortuitous comments may result in the opening of new issues and should be avoided. Agents usually appreciate prompt and efficient responses to inquiries, since their performance may in part be judged by their ability to close or settle assigned cases.

To the extent possible, it is advisable to conduct the investigation of field audits in the practitioner's office, rather than the client's office. This procedure permits greater control over the audit investigation and facilitates the agent's review and prompt closure of the case.

Many practitioners feel that it is generally not advisable to have clients present at the scheduled conferences with the agent, since the client may give emotional or gratuitous comments that impair prompt settlement. If the client is not present, however, he or she should be advised of the status of negotiations. The client makes the final decision on any proposed settlement.

---

| ETHICAL CONSIDERATIONS | **Should the Client Attend an Audit?** |
| --- | --- |

Whether the client should be present during an audit is a matter of some debate. Certainly, the client's absence tends to slow down the negotiating process because the taxpayer must make all final decisions on settlement terms and is the best source of information for open questions of fact. Nevertheless, most practitioners discourage their clients from attending audits or conferences with the Appeals Division involving an income tax dispute. Ignorance of the law and of the conventions of the audit process can make the taxpayer a "loose cannon" that can do more harm than good if unchecked. All too often, a client will "say too much" in the presence of a government official.

In reality, though, by discouraging clients from attending the audit, practitioners may be interfering with the IRS's func-

tion of gathering evidence, depending on what precisely the taxpayer is being prevented from saying. To many practitioners, a "wrong" answer is one that increases taxes, not one that misrepresents the truth. A popular saying among tax advisers is "Don't tell me more than I want to know." Although this philosophy is supportable under various professional codes of conduct, it is hardly defensible in the larger scheme of things.

In your opinion, under what circumstances should the client attend such a session? To what degree should the tax professional "coach" the client as to how to behave in that setting? Or do a taxpayer's rights include the right to increase his or her own tax liability?

---

**Preparing for the Audit.**  The tax professional must prepare thoroughly for the audit or Appeals proceeding. Practitioners often cite the following steps as critical to such preparations. Carrying out a level of due diligence in preparing for the proceeding is part of the tax professional's responsibility in representing the client.

- Make certain that both sides agree on the issues to be resolved in the audit. The goal here is to limit the agent's list of open issues.
- Identify all of the facts underlying the issues in dispute, including those favorable to the IRS. Gather evidence to support the taxpayer's position, and evaluate the evidence supporting the other side.
- Research current tax law authorities as they bear on the facts and open issues. Remember that the IRS agent is bound only by Supreme Court cases and IRS pronouncements. Determine the degree of discretion that the IRS is likely to have in disposing of the case.
- Prepare a list of points supporting and contradicting the taxpayer's case. Include both minor points bearing little weight and core principles. Short research memos will also be useful in the discussion with the agent. Points favoring the taxpayer should be mentioned during the discussion and "entered into the record."
- Prepare tax and interest computations showing the effects of points that are in dispute, so that the consequences of closing or compromising an issue can be readily determined.
- Determine a "litigation point" (i.e., at which the taxpayer will withdraw from further audit negotiation and pursue the case in the courts). This position should be based on the dollars of tax, interest, and penalty involved, the chances of prevailing in various trial-level courts, and other strategies discussed with the taxpayer. One must have an "end game" strategy for the audit, and thorough tax research is critical in developing that position in this context.

**Offers in Compromise.**  The IRS is encouraging the use of offers in compromise to a greater degree than ever before as part of its "consumer-friendly" approach to its enforcement obligations and its efforts to bring more nonfilers into compliance with the tax system.

Both parties to a tax dispute may find a compromise offer useful because it conclusively settles all of the issues covered by the agreement and may include a favorable payment schedule for the taxpayer.

On the other hand, several attributes of an offer in compromise may work to the detriment of the taxpayer. Just as the IRS no longer can raise new issues as part of the audit proceedings against the taxpayer, he or she cannot contest or appeal any such agreement. As part of the offer process, the taxpayer must disclose all relevant finances and resources, including details he or she might not want the government to know. Furthermore, both parties are bound to the filing positions established by the compromise for five tax years, a level of inflexibility that may work against a taxpayer whose circumstances change over time.

**Documentation Issues.**   The tax practitioner's workpapers should include all research memoranda, and a list of resolved and unresolved issues should be continually updated during the course of the IRS audit. Occasionally, agents request access to excessive amounts of accounting data in order to engage in a so-called fishing expedition. Providing blanket access to working papers should be avoided. Workpapers should be carefully reviewed to minimize opportunities for the agent to raise new issues not otherwise apparent. It is generally advisable to provide the agent with copies of specific workpapers upon request.

In unusual situations, a Special Agent may appear to gather evidence in the investigation of possible criminal fraud. When this occurs, the taxpayer should be advised to seek legal counsel to determine the extent of his or her cooperation in providing information to the agent. Further, it is frequently desirable for the tax adviser to consult personal legal counsel in such situations. If the taxpayer receives a Revenue Agent's Report (RAR), it generally indicates that the IRS has decided not to initiate criminal proceedings. The IRS usually does not take any action upon a tax deficiency until the criminal matter has been resolved. If, for whatever reasons, the criminal action is dropped, the 75 percent civil fraud penalty normally is assessed.

## LITIGATION CONSIDERATIONS

During the process of settlement with the IRS, the taxpayer must assess the economic consequences of possible litigation. Specifically, the probability of winning in court should be weighed against the costs of litigating the dispute (legal, support, and court costs). In some instances, taxpayers become overly emotional and do not adequately consider the economic and psychological costs of litigation.

Signing Form 870 or Form 870–AD precludes the use of the Tax Court as a forum for future litigation. In that event, the taxpayer's only recourse is to pay the taxes and sue for a refund upon denial of a claim for refund. The Tax Court was established to provide taxpayers an opportunity to litigate issues without first paying the tax on the deficiency. Some taxpayers, however, prefer to litigate the case in a Federal District Court or the Court of Federal Claims, since the payment of tax effectively stops the running of interest on the deficiency.

In selecting a proper tax forum, consideration should be given to the decisions of the various courts in related cases. The Tax Court follows the decisions of Courts of Appeals if the court is one to which the taxpayer may appeal.[65] For example, if an individual is in the jurisdiction of the Fifth Circuit Court of Appeals and that

---

[65]*Jack E. Golsen*, 54 T.C. 742 (1970).

court has issued a favorable opinion on the same issue that currently confronts the taxpayer, the Tax Court will follow this opinion in deciding the taxpayer's case, even if previous Tax Court decisions have been adverse.

If the issue involves a question in which equity is needed, strategy may dictate the choice of a Federal District Court (where a jury trial is obtainable) or the Court of Federal Claims, which has frequently given greater weight to equity considerations than to strict legal precedent.

## PENALTIES

Penalties are imposed upon a taxpayer's failure to file a return or pay a tax when due. These penalties can be avoided if the failure is due to reasonable cause and not due to willful neglect. Reasonable cause, however, has not been liberally interpreted by the courts and should not be relied upon in the routine situation.[66] A safer way to avoid the failure to file penalty is to obtain from the IRS an extension of time for filing the return.

The penalty for failure to pay estimated taxes can become quite severe. Often trapped by the provision are employed taxpayers with outside income. They may forget about the outside income and assume the amount withheld from wages and salaries is adequate to cover their liability. Not only does April 15 provide a real shock (in terms of the additional tax owed) for these persons, but a penalty situation may have evolved. One way for an employee to mitigate this problem (presuming the employer is willing to cooperate) is described in the following example.

**EXAMPLE 23**

Patty, a calendar year taxpayer, is employed by Finn Corporation and earns (after withholding) a monthly salary of $4,000 payable at the end of each month. Patty also receives income from outside sources (interest, dividends, and consulting fees). After some quick calculations in early October, Patty determines that she has underestimated her tax liability by $7,500 and will be subject to the penalty for the first two quarters of the year and part of the third quarter. Patty, therefore, completes a new Form W–4 in which she arbitrarily raises her income tax withholding by $2,500 a month. Finn accepts the Form W–4, and as a result, an extra $7,500 is paid to the IRS on Patty's account for the payroll period from October through December.

Patty avoids penalties for the underpayment for the first three quarters because withholding of taxes is allocated pro rata over the year involved. Thus, a portion of the additional $7,500 withheld in October–December is assigned to the January 1–April 15 period, the April 16–June 15 period, etc. Had Patty merely paid the IRS an additional $7,500 in October, the penalty would still have been assessed for the earlier quarters. ■

## KEY TERMS

| | | |
|---|---|---|
| Accuracy-related penalty, 16–18 | Negligence, 16–18 | Statute of limitations, 16–23 |
| Closing agreement, 16–14 | Ninety-day letter, 16–12 | Substantial authority, 16–19 |
| Determination letter, 16–6 | Offer in compromise, 16–14 | Technical advice memorandum (TAM), 16–6 |
| Enrolled agent (EA), 16–25 | Reasonable cause, 16–18 | Thirty-day letter, 16–12 |
| Fraud, 16–21 | Revenue Agent's Report (RAR), 16–11 | |
| Letter ruling, 16–5 | | |

[66]*Dustin v. Comm.*, 72–2 USTC ¶9610, 30 AFTR2d 72–5313, 467 F.2d 47 (CA–9, 1972), *aff'g* 53 T.C. 491 (1969).

## PROBLEM MATERIALS

### Discussion Questions

1. Evaluate this statement: A tax professional must be very familiar with the IRS's operations and organization.

2. Describe the current organization, management structure, and operations of the IRS.

3. What is the IRS? What responsibilities is it charged to carry out?

4. Carol takes some very aggressive positions on her tax return. She maintains, "With the downsizing of the government, my chances of getting caught are virtually zero." Is Carol's approach correct?

5. Identify several of the most important techniques that the IRS currently emphasizes in carrying out its enforcement responsibilities.

*Issue ID*

6. Should the IRS audit more or fewer returns every year? What issues would you consider in this regard if you were a politician? A wealthy individual?

*Communications*

7. Your tax supervisor has informed you that the firm has received an unfavorable answer to a ruling request. In a memo to the supervisor, describe the appropriate weight that she should assign to the holding in the ruling.

8. Summarize the rules as to the burden of proof when the IRS assesses additional tax, penalties, and interest.

9. Sarah tells you, "I was worried about getting audited on the tax return I filed two months ago, but I received my refund check today, so the IRS must agree with my figures." Comment.

10. Many tax professionals encourage their clients to pursue tax disputes through the judicial system. But the courts hear only several hundred tax cases in a typical year. Identify some advantages and disadvantages of settling a tax case within IRS channels (i.e., with the auditor or the Appeals Division).

11. Which taxpayers should try to settle tax disputes with the Small Cases Division of the U.S. Tax Court?

*Decision Making*

12. What bearing should the interest rate currently in effect have on each of the following situations?
    a. Whether a taxpayer litigates in the U.S. Tax Court or the Court of Federal Claims.
    b. The penalty for underpayment of estimated taxes.

13. On February 10, 2004, Quon, a calendar year taxpayer, files her 2003 income tax return on which she claims a $1,200 refund. If Quon receives her refund check on May 2, 2004, will it include any interest? Explain.

14. For the completion and filing of his 2003 income tax return, Ron retains the services of a CPA. Because of a particularly hectic tax season, the CPA does not complete and file the return until June 2004. Is Ron excused from the failure to file and pay penalties under the reasonable cause exception? Would it make any difference if Ron were entitled to a refund?

15. Indicate whether each of the following statements is true or false.
    a. The government never pays a taxpayer interest on an overpayment of tax.
    b. Penalties paid to the IRS are an itemized deduction on an individual's tax return, but net of the 2%-of-AGI floor.
    c. An extension of time for filing a return results in an automatic extension of time for paying the tax.
    d. The IRS can compromise on the amount of tax liability if there is doubt as to the taxpayer's ability to pay.

    e. The statute of limitations for assessing a tax never extends beyond three years from the filing of a return.

    f. A taxpayer's claim for a refund is not subject to a statute of limitations.

16. In each of the following cases, distinguish between the terms.
    a. Offer in compromise and closing agreement.
    b. Failure to file and failure to pay.
    c. Ninety-day letter and thirty-day letter.
    d. Negligence and fraud.
    e. Criminal and civil penalties.

17. When Maggie accepted employment with Martin Corporation, she completed a Form W–4 listing 14 exemptions. Since Maggie was single and had no dependents, she misrepresented her situation on Form W–4. What penalties, if any, might the IRS impose upon Maggie?

**Decision Making**

18. Why should the taxpayer be "let off the hook" and no longer be subject to audit exposure once the applicable statute of limitations has expired? Do statutes of limitations protect the government? Other taxpayers?

**Issue ID**

19. The disclosures about Enron, Tyco, and WorldCom have changed the regulation of the accounting profession. Who regulates the behavior of tax return preparers? Where are the constraints on the behavior of tax professionals to be found?

20. Lorraine, a vice president of Scott Corporation, prepared and filed the corporate Form 1120 for 2002. This return is being audited by the IRS in 2004.
    a. May Lorraine represent Scott during the audit?
    b. Can Lorraine's representation continue beyond the agent level (e.g., before the Appeals Division)?

21. Indicate which codes, canons, and other bodies of ethical statements apply to each of the following tax practitioners.
    a. CPAs who are members of the AICPA.
    b. CPAs who are not members of the AICPA.
    c. Attorneys.
    d. Enrolled agents.
    e. Tax preparers who are not CPAs, EAs, or attorneys.

## Problems

22. Compute the failure to pay and failure to file penalties for John, who filed his 2003 income tax return on November 10, 2004, paying the $8,000 amount due. On April 1, 2004, John had received a four-month extension of time in which to file his return. He has no reasonable cause for failing to file his return by August 16 or for failing to pay the tax that was due on April 15, 2004. John's failure to comply with the tax laws was not fraudulent.

23. Orville, a cash basis, calendar year taxpayer, filed his income tax return 70 days after the due date. Orville never extended his return, and he paid the taxes that were due when he filed the return. What penalty will Orville incur, and how much will he have to pay if his additional tax is $3,000? Disregard any interest he must pay.

24. Rhoda, a calendar year individual taxpayer, files her 2003 return on December 11, 2004. She did not obtain an extension for filing her return, and the return reflects additional income tax due of $7,000.
    a. What are Rhoda's penalties for failure to file and to pay?
    b. Would your answer to (a) change if Rhoda, before the due date of the return, had retained a CPA to prepare the return and it was the CPA's negligence that caused the delay?

25. Kim underpaid her taxes by $15,000. Of this amount, $9,500 was due to negligence on her part, as her record-keeping system is highly inadequate. Determine the amount of any negligence penalty.

26. Dana underpaid her taxes by $250,000. A portion of the underpayment was shown to be attributable to Dana's negligence ($200,000). A court found that a portion of that deficiency constituted civil fraud ($110,000). Compute the total fraud and negligence penalties incurred.

27. Olivia, a calendar year taxpayer, does not file her 2003 return until October 4, 2004. At this point, she pays the $7,000 balance due on her 2003 tax liability of $70,000. Olivia did not apply for and obtain any extension of time for filing the 2003 return. When questioned by the IRS on her delinquency, Olivia asserts: "If I was too busy to file my regular tax return, I was too busy to request an extension."
   a. Is Olivia liable for any penalties for failure to file and for failure to pay?
   b. If so, compute the penalty amounts.

28. Compute the overvaluation penalty for each of the following independent cases involving the taxpayer's reporting of the fair market value of charitable contribution property. In each case, assume a marginal income tax rate of 35%.

| | Taxpayer | Corrected IRS Value | Reported Valuation |
|---|---|---|---|
| a. | Individual | $ 30,000 | $ 50,000 |
| b. | C corporation | 30,000 | 50,000 |
| c. | S corporation | 40,000 | 50,000 |
| d. | Individual | 150,000 | 250,000 |
| e. | Individual | 150,000 | 500,000 |
| f. | C corporation | 150,000 | 900,000 |

29. Compute the undervaluation penalty for each of the following independent cases involving the executor's reporting of the value of a closely held business in the decedent's gross estate. In each case, assume a marginal estate tax rate of 50%.

| | Reported Value | Corrected IRS Valuation |
|---|---|---|
| a. | $20,000 | $ 25,000 |
| b. | 80,000 | 150,000 |
| c. | 80,000 | 250,000 |
| d. | 80,000 | 530,000 |

30. Arnold made a charitable contribution of property that he valued at $70,000. He deducted this amount as an itemized deduction on his tax return. The IRS can prove that the real value of the property is $55,000. Arnold is in the 30% income tax bracket. Determine Arnold's overvaluation penalty.

31. Marla owns and operates a tavern. Because she had been keeping "two sets of books," one for herself and one for the benefit of the IRS, she has been charged with civil fraud in the District Court. The IRS assesses an additional $75,000 in taxes, but Marla shows by a preponderance of the evidence that two-thirds of that amount was due to mere negligence, not to her fraudulent actions. Compute Marla's civil fraud tax penalty in this matter.

32. Moose, a former professional athlete, now supplements his income by signing autographs at collectors' shows. Unfortunately, Moose has not been conscientious about reporting all of this income on his tax return. Now the IRS has charged him with additional taxes of $80,000 due to negligence in his record keeping and $20,000 due to an intent to defraud the U.S. government of income taxes. No criminal fraud charges are brought against Moose. The District Court finds by a preponderance of the evidence that only half of the $20,000 underpayment was due to Moose's fraudulent action; the

remainder was due to mere negligence. Compute the accuracy-related and civil fraud penalties in this matter.

33. Trudy's AGI last year was $170,000. Her Federal income tax came to $50,000, which she paid through a combination of withholding and estimated payments. This year, her AGI will be $270,000, with a projected tax liability of $85,000, all to be paid through estimates. Ignore the annualized income method. Compute Trudy's quarterly estimated payment schedule for this year.

34. Kold Corporation estimates that its 2004 taxable income will be $500,000. Thus, it is subject to a flat 34% income tax rate and incurs a $170,000 liability. For each of the following independent cases, compute Kold's minimum quarterly estimated tax payments that will avoid an underpayment penalty.
    a. For 2003, taxable income was ($100,000). Kold carried back all of this loss to prior years and exhausted the entire net operating loss in creating a zero 2003 liability.
    b. For 2003, taxable income was $300,000, and tax liability was $102,000.
    c. For 2002, taxable income was $2 million, and tax liability was $680,000. For 2003, taxable income was $300,000, and tax liability was $102,000.

**Decision Making**

**Communications**

35. The Scooter Company, owned equally by Julie (chair of the board of directors) and Jeff (company president), is in very difficult financial straits. Last month, Jeff used the $100,000 withheld from employee paychecks for Federal payroll and income taxes to pay off a creditor who threatened to cut off all supplies. To keep the company afloat, Jeff used these government funds willfully for the operations of the business, but even that effort was not enough. The company missed the next two payrolls, and today other creditors took action to shut down Scooter altogether. How much will the IRS assess in taxes and penalties in this matter, and from whom? How can you as a tax professional best offer service to Julie, Jeff, and Scooter? Address these matters in a memo for the tax research file.

36. What is the applicable statute of limitations in each of the following independent situations?
    a. No return was filed by the taxpayer.
    b. The taxpayer incurred a bad debt loss that she failed to claim.
    c. A taxpayer inadvertently omitted a large amount of gross income.
    d. Same as (c), except that the omission was deliberate.
    e. A taxpayer innocently overstated her deductions by a large amount.

37. Suzanne (a calendar year taxpayer) had the following transactions, all of which were properly reported on a timely filed return.

| | | |
|---|---|---|
| Gross receipts | | $ 960,000 |
| Cost of sales | | (800,000) |
| Gross profit | | $ 160,000 |
| Capital gain | $ 72,000 | |
| Capital loss | (24,000) | 48,000 |
| Total income | | $ 208,000 |

   a. Presuming the absence of fraud, how much of an omission from gross income is required before the six-year statute of limitations applies?
   b. Would it matter if cost of sales had been inadvertently overstated by $100,000?
   c. How does the situation change in the context of fraud by Suzanne?

**Decision Making**

38. On April 2, 2002, Mark filed his 2001 income tax return, which showed a tax due of $40,000. On June 1, 2004, he filed an amended return for 2001 that showed an additional tax of $12,000. Mark paid the additional amount. On May 18, 2005, Mark filed a claim for a refund of $18,000.

a. If Mark's claim for a refund is correct in amount, how much tax will he recover?
b. What is the period that interest runs with respect to Mark's claim for a refund?
c. How would you have advised him differently?

39. Carol owed $4,000 in Federal income tax when she filed her Form 1040 for 2003. She attached a Post-It note to the 1040 saying, "My inventory computations on last year's return were wrong so I paid $1,000 too much in tax." Carol then included a check for $3,000 with the Form 1040 for 2003. Write a memo to the tax research file commenting on Carol's actions.

40. Rod's Federal income tax returns (Form 1040) for the indicated three years were prepared by the following persons.

| Year | Preparer |
|------|----------|
| 2002 | Rod |
| 2003 | Ann |
| 2004 | Cheryl |

Ann is Rod's next-door neighbor and owns and operates a pharmacy. Cheryl is a licensed CPA and is engaged in private practice. In the event Rod is audited and all three returns are examined, who may represent him before the IRS at the agent level? Who may represent Rod before the Appeals Division?

41. Discuss which penalties, if any, might be imposed on the tax adviser in each of the following independent circumstances. In this regard, assume that the tax adviser:
a. suggested to the client various means by which to acquire excludible income.
b. suggested to the client various means by which to conceal cash receipts from gross income.
c. suggested to the client means by which to improve her cash flow by delaying for six months or more the deposit of the employee's share of Federal employment taxes.
d. kept in his own safe deposit box the concealed income of item (b).
e. failed, because of pressing time conflicts, to conduct the usual review of the client's tax return. The IRS later discovered that the return included fraudulent data.
f. failed, because of pressing time conflicts, to conduct the usual review of the client's tax return. The IRS later discovered a mathematical error in the computation of the personal exemption.

42. Compute the preparer penalty that the IRS could assess on Gerry in each of the following independent cases.
a. On March 21, the copy machine was not working, so Gerry gave original returns to her 30 clients that day without providing any duplicates for them. Copies for Gerry's files and for use in preparing state tax returns had been made on March 20.
b. Because Gerry extended her vacation a few days, she missed the Annual Tax Update seminar that she usually attends. As a result, she was unaware that Congress had changed a law affecting limited partnerships. The change affected the transactions of 20 of Gerry's clients, all of whom understated their tax as a result.
c. Gerry heard that the IRS was increasing its audits of corporations that hold assets in a foreign trust. As a result, Gerry instructed the intern who prepared the initial drafts of the returns for three corporate clients to leave blank the question about such trusts. Not wanting to lose his position, the intern, a senior accounting major at State University, complied with Gerry's instructions.

43. You are the chair of the Ethics Committee of your state's CPA Licensing Commission. Interpret controlling AICPA authority in addressing the following assertions by your membership.
a. When a CPA has reasonable grounds for not answering an applicable question on a client's return, a brief explanation of the reason for the omission should not be provided, because it would flag the return for audit by the IRS.

b. If a CPA discovers during an IRS audit that the client has a material error in the return under examination, he should immediately withdraw from the engagement.
c. If the client tells you that she had contributions of $500 for unsubstantiated cash donations to her church, you should deduct an odd amount on her return (e.g., $499), because an even amount ($500) would indicate to the IRS that her deduction was based on an estimate.
d. If a CPA knows that the client has a material error in a prior year's return, he should not, without the client's consent, disclose the error to the IRS.
e. If a CPA's client will not correct a material error in a prior year's return, the CPA should not prepare the current year's return for the client.

## Research Problems

*Note: Solutions to Research Problems can be prepared by using the **RIA Checkpoint® Student Edition** online research product, or the **CCH U.S. Master Tax Guide Plus™** online Federal tax research database, which is available to accompany this text. It is also possible to prepare solutions to the Research Problems by using tax research materials found in a standard tax library.*

**Communications**

**Research Problem 1.** The Bird Estate committed tax fraud when it purposely understated the value of the business created and operated by the decedent, Beverly Bird. Executor Wilma Holmes (1111 East Michigan Avenue, Charleston, WV 44333) admitted to the Tax Court that she had withheld several contracts and formulas that, had they been disclosed to the valuation experts used by the government and the estate, would have added $1 million in value to the business and over half that amount in Federal estate tax liabilities. Summary data include the following.

| | Reported on Form 706 | Other Amounts |
|---|---|---|
| Gross estate | $12 million | $1 million understatement |
| Deductions on original return | 2 million | |
| Interest on estate tax deficiency, professional fees incurred during administration period | | 400,000 |

Holmes asks you for advice in computing the fraud penalty. Ignore interest amounts. She wonders whether to take the 75% civil penalty against the full $1 million understatement or against the $600,000 net amount that the taxable estate would have increased had the administrative expenses been incurred prior to the filing date of the Form 706. Write Holmes, an experienced CPA with an extensive tax practice, a letter stating your opinion.

*Partial list of research aids:*
§ 6663.
*Estate of Emanuel Trompeter*, 111 T.C. 57 (1998).

**Communications**

**Research Problem 2.** The IRS has issued a summons for the tax file held by CPA Ann Whitman for her clients, the Harberts. The file consists of paper and electronic spreadsheets in which Whitman detailed some tax computations using assumptions that the IRS would find to be "too aggressive." In addition, the file includes notes from meetings with the Harberts, income and balance sheet data as to their personal assets, and other technical correspondence, including e-mail messages. In a memo to the tax research file, summarize the current status of the law as to whether the privilege of confidentiality protects these documents from the government.

**Communications**

**Research Problem 3.** Blanche Creek (111 Elm Avenue, Patriotville, IN 40123) has engaged your firm because she has been charged with failure to file her 2001 Federal Form 1040. Blanche maintains that the "reasonable cause" exception should apply. During the entire tax filing season in 2002, she was under a great deal of stress at work and in her personal life. As a result, Blanche developed a sleep disorder, which was treated through a combination of pills and counseling.

Your firm ultimately prepared the 2001 tax return for Blanche, but it was filed far beyond the due date. Blanche is willing to pay the delinquent tax and related interest. However, she feels that the failure to pay penalty is unfair as she was ill. Consequently, she could not be expected to keep to the usual deadlines for filing.

Write a letter to Blanche concerning these matters.

**Research Problem 4.**   Max and Annie are roommates sharing an apartment. Although they know each other well, they have respect for each other's privacy. Thus, when Max's 2000 Form 1040 was audited by the IRS, he made no mention of the audit to Annie.

When Annie was clearing the answering machine that they shared, she heard the following message: "Max, this is Richard, the IRS auditor. My figures show that you owe the government $10,000 in taxes and another $4,500 in penalties and interest."

When Annie brought up the message during dinner conversation that night, Max was furious. How could the IRS be so careless as to broadcast this news to a stranger? Didn't he have any privacy and confidentiality rights? Max calls you to determine whether he might have a case against the IRS or Richard, the agent.

**Internet Activity**

*Use the tax resources of the Internet to address the following questions. Do not restrict your search to the World Wide Web, but include a review of newsgroups and general reference materials, practitioner sites and resources, primary sources of the tax law, chat rooms and discussion groups, and other opportunities.*

**Research Problem 5.**   Find an article in which a tax professional describes the confidentiality privilege available under the Code for a CPA tax adviser. Then construct a list of "Confidentiality Dos and Don'ts for the CPA."

**Research Problem 6.**   Find an article that discusses these terms: realistic possibility, reasonable basis, frivolous return. Summarize the article in an e-mail to your professor.

**Research Problem 7.**   Corporations with large estimated tax overpayments and underpayments are subject to special interest rates. (a) Find in the Code how these rates are determined. (b) List such rates that have been in effect for the last six calendar quarters.

# Family Tax Planning

**PART 5**

Family tax planning has as its objective the minimization of *all* taxes imposed on the family unit. Carrying out this objective requires familiarity with the rules applicable to transfers by gift and by death. These rules must then be applied to reduce the transfer tax burden. Also to be considered are the income tax consequences of the transfers made. Finally, entities created as a result of these transfers (trusts and estates) are subject to unique income tax rules.

**CHAPTER 17**

The Federal Gift and Estate Taxes

**CHAPTER 18**

Family Tax Planning

**CHAPTER 19**

Income Taxation of Trusts and Estates

# The Federal Gift and Estate Taxes

**CHAPTER**

**17**

## LEARNING OBJECTIVES

*After completing Chapter 17, you should be able to:*

**LO.1**
Understand the nature of the Federal gift and estate taxes.

**LO.2**
Work with the Federal gift tax formula.

**LO.3**
Work with the Federal estate tax formula.

**LO.4**
Explain the operation of the Federal gift tax.

**LO.5**
Illustrate the computation of the Federal gift tax.

**LO.6**
Review the components of the gross estate.

**LO.7**
Describe the components of the taxable estate.

**LO.8**
Determine the Federal estate tax liability.

**LO.9**
Appreciate the role of the generation skipping transfer tax.

http://wft.swlearning.com

## O U T L I N E

## Transfer Taxes—In General

Until now, this text has dealt primarily with the various applications of the Federal income tax. Also important in the Federal tax structure are various excise taxes that cover transfers of property. Sometimes called transaction taxes, excise taxes are based on the value of the property transferred, not on the income derived from the property. Two such taxes—the Federal gift tax and the Federal estate tax—are the central focus of Chapters 17 and 18.

The importance of being familiar with rules governing transfer taxes can be shown with a simple illustration.

**EXAMPLE 1**

After 20 years of marriage to George, Helen decides to elope with Mark, a bachelor and long-time friend. Helen and Mark travel to a country in the Caribbean where Helen obtains a divorce, and she and Mark are married. Fifteen years later in 2003, Helen dies. Her will leaves all of her property (estimated value of $3 million) to Mark. Under the unlimited marital deduction (discussed later in the chapter), Helen's estate has no tax to pay. ∎

But the marital deduction applies only to transfers between husband and wife. Suppose the jurisdiction where Helen and Mark live does not recognize the validity of divorces granted by the Caribbean country involved. If this is the case, Helen and Mark are not married because Helen was never legally divorced from George. If Mark is not Helen's spouse, no marital deduction is available. Disregarding any administration expenses, Helen's estate must pay an estate tax of $924,200.

**LO.1**

Understand the nature of the Federal gift and estate taxes.

### NATURE OF THE TAXES

Before the enactment of the Tax Reform Act of 1976, Federal law imposed a tax on the gratuitous transfer of property in one of two ways. If the transfer occurred during the owner's life, it was subject to the Federal gift tax. If the property passed by virtue of the death of the owner, the Federal estate tax applied. The two taxes were governed by different rules including separate sets of tax rates. As Congress felt that lifetime transfers of wealth should be encouraged, the gift tax rates were lower than the estate tax rates.

## AN ERRATIC APPROACH TO TRANSFER TAXES

Congressional policy toward transfer taxes has been highly erratic.

- Before the Tax Reform Act of 1976, the lower gift tax rates favored transfers by gift.
- The Tax Reform Act of 1976 took a neutral approach. It established a new unified transfer tax that applied the same tax rates to transfers by gift and transfers by death.
- The Tax Relief Reconciliation Act of 2001, once fully implemented, obviously favors transfers by death as the estate tax is to be phased out, while the gift tax is retained.

Clearly, Congress has not been consistent in its tax treatment of lifetime (i.e., gift tax) and death (i.e., estate tax) transfers.

The Tax Reform Act of 1976 significantly changed the approach taken by the Federal gift and estate taxes. Much of the distinction between life and death transfers was eliminated. Instead of subjecting these transfers to two separate tax rate schedules, the Act substituted a **unified transfer tax** that covered all gratuitous transfers. Thus, gifts were subject to a gift tax at the same rates as those applicable to transfers at death. In addition, the law eliminated the prior exemptions allowed under each tax and replaces them with a unified tax credit.

The Tax Relief Reconciliation Act of 2001 made further changes. First, the top rates applicable to both taxes are lowered. Second, by scheduled increases in the unified tax credit applicable to estates, the estate tax will be eliminated by year 2010, but the gift tax is retained. For budget reasons, all changes made by the 2001 Act are eliminated after December 31, 2010 (referred to as a "sunset" provision). Thus, the estate tax is reincarnated for transfers by death after 2010.

The estate tax differs in several respects from the typical **inheritance tax** imposed by many states and some local jurisdictions. First, the Federal estate tax is imposed on the decedent's entire estate. It is a tax on the right to pass property at death. Inheritance taxes are taxes on the right to receive property at death and are therefore levied on the heirs. Second, the relationship of the heirs to the decedent usually has a direct bearing on the inheritance tax. In general, the more closely related the parties, the larger the exemption and the lower the applicable rates.[1] Except for transfers to a surviving spouse that may result in a marital deduction, the relationship of the heirs to the decedent has no effect on the Federal estate tax.

The Federal gift tax is imposed on the right to transfer property by one person (the donor) to another (the donee) for less than full and adequate consideration. The tax is payable by the donor.[2] If the donor fails to pay the tax when due, the donee may be held liable for the tax to the extent of the value of the property received.[3]

**Persons Subject to the Tax.**   To determine whether a transfer is subject to the Federal gift tax, first ascertain if the donor is a citizen or resident of the United

---

[1]For example, one state's inheritance tax provides an exemption of $50,000 for surviving spouses, with rates ranging from 5% to 10% on the taxable portion. In contrast, an exemption of only $1,000 is provided for strangers (persons unrelated to the deceased), with rates ranging from 14% to 18% on the taxable portion. Other exemptions and rates between these extremes cover beneficiaries variously related to the decedent.

[2]§ 2502(c).

[3]§ 6324(b). Known as the doctrine of transferee liability, this rule also operates to enable the IRS to enforce the collection of other taxes (e.g., income tax, estate tax).

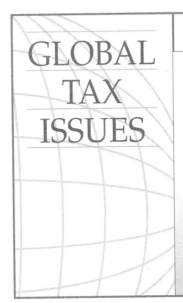

GLOBAL TAX ISSUES

## EXPATRIATION TO AVOID U.S. TAXES

Much media attention has recently been given to wealthy individuals who renounce their U.S. citizenship and move to another country to avoid U.S. taxes. These expatriates select a country where citizenship is easily available and low, if any, income and estate taxes are imposed.

Will this so-called expatriation to avoid taxes work? One difficulty for those who voluntarily renounce U.S. citizenship is that §§ 877 and 2107 continue to apply to their income tax and estate tax for a 10-year period. The taxpayer involved may avoid the application of these provisions by showing that the giving up of citizenship did not have as one of its principal purposes the avoidance of taxes.

Thus, the expatriation procedure will not be effective for at least 10 years. But even after this period, any income may still be subject to the Federal income tax if it is sourced in the United States. Likewise, assets located in the United States will probably be subject to the estate tax at death.

States. If the donor is not a citizen or a resident, it is important to determine whether the property involved in the gift was situated within the United States.

The Federal gift tax is applied to all transfers by gift of property wherever located by individuals who, at the time of the gift, were *citizens* or *residents* of the United States. The term "United States" includes only the 50 states and the District of Columbia; it does not include U.S. possessions or territories.[4] For a U.S. citizen, the place of residence at the time of the gift is irrelevant.

For individuals who are neither citizens nor residents of the United States, the Federal gift tax is applied only to gifts of property situated within the United States.[5] A gift of intangible personal property (stocks and bonds) by a nonresident alien usually is not subject to the Federal gift tax.[6]

A gift by a corporation is considered a gift by the individual shareholders. A gift to a corporation is generally considered a gift to the individual shareholders. In certain cases, however, a gift to a charitable, public, political, or similar organization may be regarded as a gift to the organization as a single entity.[7]

The Federal estate tax is applied to the entire estate of a decedent who, at the time of death, was a resident or citizen of the United States. If the decedent was a U.S. citizen, the residence at death makes no difference.[8]

If the decedent was neither a resident nor a citizen of the United States at the time of death, the Federal estate tax is imposed on the value of any property located within the United States. In that case, the tax determination is controlled by a separate subchapter of the Internal Revenue Code.[9] In certain instances, the tax consequences outlined in the Code may have been modified by death tax conventions (treaties) between the United States and various foreign countries.[10] Further

---

[4]§ 7701(a)(9).

[5]§ 2511(a).

[6]§§ 2501(a)(2) and (3). But see § 2511(b) and Reg. §§ 25.2511–3(b)(2), (3), and (4) for exceptions.

[7]Reg. §§ 25.0–1(b) and 25.2511–1(h)(1). But note the exemption from the Federal gift tax for certain transfers to political organizations discussed later.

[8]§ 2001(a).

[9]Subchapter B (§§ 2101 through 2108) covers the estate tax treatment of decedents who are neither residents nor citizens. Subchapter A

(§§ 2001 through 2057) covers the estate tax treatment of those who are either residents or citizens.

[10]At present, the United States has death tax conventions with the following countries: Australia, Austria, Canada, Denmark, Finland, France, Germany, Greece, Ireland, Italy, Japan, Netherlands, Norway, Republic of South Africa, Sweden, Switzerland, and the United Kingdom. The United States has gift tax conventions with Australia, Austria, Denmark, France, Germany, Japan, and the United Kingdom.

coverage of this area is beyond the scope of this text. The following discussion . limited to the tax treatment of decedents who were residents or citizens of the United States at the time of death.[11]

**LO.2**

Work with the Federal gift tax formula.

**Formula for the Gift Tax.**   Like the income tax, which uses taxable income (not gross income) as a tax base, the gift tax usually does not apply to the full amount of the gift. Deductions and the annual exclusion may be allowed to arrive at an amount called the **taxable gift.** However, unlike the income tax, which does not consider taxable income from prior years, *prior taxable gifts* must be added in arriving at the tax base to which the unified transfer tax rate is applied. Otherwise, the donor could start over again each year with a new set of progressive rates.

**EXAMPLE 2**

Don makes taxable gifts of $1 million in 1986 and $1 million in 2003. Presuming no other taxable gifts and *disregarding the effect of the unified tax credit*, Don must pay a tax of $345,800 (see Appendix A, page A–7) on the 1986 transfer and a tax of $780,800 (see Appendix A, page A–9) on the 2003 transfer (using a tax base of $2 million). If the 1986 taxable gift had not been included in the tax base for the 2003 gift, the tax would have been $345,800. The correct tax liability of $780,800 is more than twice $345,800! ■

Because the gift tax is cumulative in effect, a credit is allowed against the gift taxes paid (or deemed paid) on prior taxable gifts included in the tax base. The deemed paid credit is explained later in the chapter.

**EXAMPLE 3**

Assume the same facts as in Example 2. Don will be allowed a credit of $345,800 against the gift tax of $780,800. Thus, his gift tax liability for 2003 becomes $435,000 ($780,800 – $345,800). ■

In 1982, the annual exclusion was increased from $3,000 to $10,000 and in 2002 from $10,000 to $11,000. By allowing larger amounts to be exempt from the gift tax, taxpayer compliance may improve, as the tax will apply only to larger, planned gifts and not to day-to-day transfers. As noted in Chapter 1, the result is to ease the audit function of the IRS. Effective for years after 1998, the annual exclusion is indexed to account for *significant* inflation.

The formula for the gift tax is summarized in Figure 17–1. (Note: Section [§] references are to the portion of the Internal Revenue Code involved.)

**LO.3**

Work with the Federal estate tax formula.

**Formula for the Federal Estate Tax.**   The Federal unified transfer tax at death, commonly known as the Federal estate tax, is summarized in Figure 17–2. (Note: Section [§] references are to the portion of the Internal Revenue Code involved.)

The reason post-1976 taxable gifts are added to the taxable estate to arrive at the tax base goes back to the scheme of the unified transfer tax. Starting in 1977, all transfers, whether lifetime or by death, were to be treated the same. Consequently, taxable gifts made after 1976 must be accounted for upon the death of the donor. Note that the possible double tax effect of including these gifts is mitigated by allowing a credit against the estate tax for the gift taxes previously paid or deemed paid.

**Role of the Unified Tax Credit.**   Before the unified transfer tax, the gift tax allowed a $30,000 specific exemption for the lifetime of the donor. A comparable

---

[11]Further information concerning Subchapter B (§§ 2101 through 2108) can be obtained from the relevant Code Sections (and the related Treasury Regulations). See also the Instructions to Form 706NA (U.S. Estate Tax Return of Nonresident Not a Citizen of the U.S.).

| | | |
|---|---|---|
| Determine whether the transfers are considered gifts by referring to §§ 2511 through 2519; list the fair market value of only the covered transfers | | $xxx,xxx |
| Determine the deductions allowed by § 2522 (charitable) and § 2523 (marital) | $xx,xxx | |
| Claim the annual exclusion (per donee) under § 2503(b), if available | 11,000 | xx,xxx |
| Taxable gifts [as defined by § 2503(a)] for the current period | | $ xx,xxx |
| Add: Taxable gifts from prior years | | xx,xxx |
| Total of current and past taxable gifts | | $ xx,xxx |
| Compute the gift tax on the total of current and past taxable gifts by using the rates in Appendix A | | $ x,xxx |
| Subtract: Gift tax paid or deemed paid on past taxable gifts and the unified tax credit | | xxx |
| Gift tax due on transfers during the current period | | $ xxx |

■ **FIGURE 17–2**
Formula for the Federal Estate Tax

| | | |
|---|---|---|
| Gross estate (§§ 2031–2046) | | $xxx,xxx |
| Subtract: | | |
| Expenses, indebtedness, and taxes (§ 2053) | $xx | |
| Losses (§ 2054) | xx | |
| Charitable bequests (§ 2055) | xx | |
| Marital deduction (§§ 2056 and 2056A) | xx | |
| Deduction for family-owned business interests (§ 2057) | xx | x,xxx |
| Taxable estate (§ 2051) | | $ xx,xxx |
| Add: Post-1976 taxable gifts [§ 2001(b)] | | x,xxx |
| Tax base | | $xxx,xxx |
| Tentative tax on total transfers [§ 2001(c)] | | $ xx,xxx |
| Subtract: | | |
| Unified transfer tax on post-1976 taxable gifts (gift taxes paid or deemed paid) | $xx | |
| Tax credits (including the unified tax credit) (§§ 2010–2016) | xx | x,xxx |
| Estate tax due | | $ xxx |

$60,000 exemption was allowed for estate tax purposes. The purpose of these exemptions was to allow donors and decedents to transfer modest amounts of wealth without being subject to the gift and estate taxes. Unfortunately, inflation took its toll, and more taxpayers became subject to these transfer taxes than Congress believed was appropriate. The congressional solution was to rescind the exemptions and replace them with the **unified tax credit.**[12]

---

[12]§§ 2010 and 2505.

**■ TABLE 17–1**

Phase-in of Unified Tax Credit (Applicable to Both Gift and Estate Taxes)

| Year of Gift or Death | Amount of Credit | Exclusion Amount |
|---|---|---|
| 1977 | $ 30,000 | $ 120,667 |
| 1978 | 34,000 | 134,000 |
| 1979 | 38,000 | 147,333 |
| 1980 | 42,500 | 161,563 |
| 1981 | 47,000 | 175,625 |
| 1982 | 62,800 | 225,000 |
| 1983 | 79,300 | 275,000 |
| 1984 | 96,300 | 325,000 |
| 1985 | 121,800 | 400,000 |
| 1986 | 155,800 | 500,000 |
| 1987 through 1997 | 192,800 | 600,000 |
| 1998 | 202,050 | 625,000 |
| 1999 | 211,300 | 650,000 |
| 2000 and 2001 | 220,550 | 675,000 |
| 2002 | 345,800 | 1,000,000 |

Table 17–1 reflects the unified tax credit applicable to transfers by gift and by death from 1977 through 2002. The Tax Relief Reconciliation Act of 2001 froze the credit applicable to the gift tax at $345,800 (exclusion amount of $1 million). By increasing the exclusion amount, the estate tax is scheduled to be phased out as shown in Table 17–2.

The **exclusion amount** (also termed **exemption equivalent**) is the amount of the transfer that will pass free of the gift or estate tax by virtue of the credit.

**EXAMPLE 4**

In 2003, Janet makes a taxable gift of $1 million. Presuming she has made no prior taxable gifts, Janet will not owe any gift tax. Under the tax rate schedules (see Appendix A, page A–9), the tax on $1 million is $345,800, which is the exact amount of the credit allowed.[13] ■

The Tax Reform Act of 1976 allowed donors one last chance to use the $30,000 specific exemption on lifetime gifts. If, however, the exemption was used on gifts made after September 8, 1976 (and before January 1, 1977), the unified tax credit must be reduced by 20 percent of the exemption utilized.[14] The credit must be adjusted whether the gift tax or the estate tax is involved. No adjustment is necessary for post-1976 gifts since the specific exemption was no longer available for such transfers.

**■ TABLE 17–2**

Scheduled Increases in Exclusion Amount Applicable to Estate Taxes

| Year of Death | Exclusion Amount |
|---|---|
| 2003 | $1,000,000 |
| 2004 and 2005 | 1,500,000 |
| 2006 through 2008 | 2,000,000 |
| 2009 | 3,500,000 |
| 2010 | Estate tax repealed |

---

[13]The rate schedules are contained in § 2001(c). Neither the credit nor the rate schedule is subject to indexation.

[14]§§ 2010(c) and 2505(c).

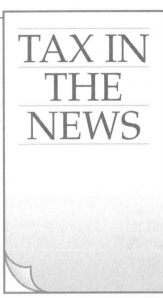

## WHAT ARE THE CHANCES?

Under the Tax Relief Reconciliation Act of 2001, the estate tax is scheduled to be phased out by 2010. Even more fantastic, a "sunset" provision in the Act reincarnates this tax as of January 1, 2011. (The "sunset" provision was mandated due to budget considerations.)

What are the chances that all of these provisions will take effect as scheduled? Hopefully, not very high! The sunset reincarnation is particularly absurd and makes meaningful estate planning impossible. Tax practitioners are placed in the ridiculous posture of advising clients to live at least until 2010 but to be sure and die before 2011.

Bills that would rescind the sunset provision have been introduced in Congress. If enacted, the legislation would kill the estate tax for good (as of 2010) and keep it from coming back. Such proposals, however, are not likely to succeed. There is strong support for retaining some form of the estate tax. Perhaps an acceptable compromise would be a version that provides a generous exclusion amount and contains relief provisions to help preserve family businesses.

**EXAMPLE 5**

Net of the annual exclusion, Myrtle, a widow, made gifts of $10,000 in June 1976 and $20,000 in December 1976. Assume Myrtle has never used any of her specific exemption and chooses to use the full $30,000 to cover the 1976 gifts. Under these circumstances, the unified tax credit will be reduced by $4,000 (20% × $20,000). The use of the specific exemption on transfers made before September 9, 1976, has no effect on the credit. ■

## VALUATION FOR ESTATE AND GIFT TAX PURPOSES

The value of the property on the date of its transfer generally determines the amount that is subject to the gift tax or the estate tax. Under certain conditions, however, an executor can elect to value estate assets on the **alternate valuation date** (§ 2032).

The alternate valuation date election was designed as a relief provision to ease the economic hardship that could result when estate assets decline in value over the six months after the date of death. If the election is made, all assets of the estate are valued six months after death *or* on the date of disposition if this occurs earlier.[15] The election covers *all* assets in the gross estate and cannot be applied to only a portion of the property.

**EXAMPLE 6**

Robert's gross estate consists of the following property:

|  | Value on Date of Death | Value Six Months Later |
|---|---|---|
| Land | $  800,000 | $  840,000 |
| Stock in Brown Corporation | 900,000 | 700,000 |
| Stock in Green Corporation | 500,000 | 460,000 |
| Total | $2,200,000 | $2,000,000 |

---

[15]§ 2032(a). For this purpose, the term "disposition" is broadly defined. It includes the transfer of property to an heir to satisfy a bequest and the use of property to fund a testamentary trust.

If Robert's executor elects the alternate valuation date, the estate must be valued at $2,000,000. It is not permissible to value the land at its date of death value ($800,000) and choose the alternate valuation date for the rest of the gross estate. ∎

**EXAMPLE 7**

*[handwritten note: Sale of asset - No alternative evaluation]*

Assume the same facts as in Example 6, except that the executor sells the stock in Green Corporation for $480,000 four months after Robert's death. If the alternate valuation date is elected, the estate must be valued at $2,020,000 ($840,000 + $700,000 + $480,000). As to the Green stock, the value on its date of disposition controls because that date occurred prior to the six months' alternate valuation date. ∎

The alternate valuation date election is not available unless the estate must file a Form 706 (Estate Tax Return). When an estate is required to file a Form 706 is discussed later in this chapter.

The election of the alternate valuation date must decrease the value of the gross estate *and* decrease the estate tax liability.[16] The reason for this last requirement is that the income tax basis of property acquired from a decedent will be the value used for estate tax purposes (discussed further in Chapter 18).[17] Without a special limitation, the alternate valuation date could be elected solely to add to income tax basis.

**EXAMPLE 8**

*[handwritten note: Marital deduction - No Estate tax]*

Al's gross estate is comprised of assets with a date of death value of $1 million and an alternate valuation date value of $1.1 million. Under Al's will, all of his property passes outright to Jean (Al's wife). Because of the marital deduction, no estate tax results regardless of which value is used. But if the alternate valuation date could be elected, Jean would have an income tax basis of $1.1 million in the property acquired from Al. ∎

The alternate valuation date cannot be elected in Example 8 for two reasons, either of which would suffice. First, the alternate valuation date will not decrease Al's gross estate. Second, the election will not decrease Al's estate tax liability. Thus, his estate must use the date of death valuation of $1 million. As a result, Jean's income tax basis in the property received from Al is $1 million.

Another valuation option available for estate tax purposes is the special use valuation method. Election of this method is limited to certain situations involving interests in closely held businesses (usually farms). Special use valuation is discussed in Chapter 18.

## KEY PROPERTY CONCEPTS

When property is transferred either by gift or by death, the form of ownership can have a direct bearing on any transfer tax consequences. Understanding the different forms of ownership is necessary for working with Federal gift and estate taxes.

**Undivided Ownership.**　Assume Dan and Vicky own an undivided but equal interest in a tract of land. Such ownership can fall into any of four categories: joint tenancy, tenancy by the entirety, tenancy in common, or community property.

If Dan and Vicky hold ownership as **joint tenants** or **tenants by the entirety,** the right of survivorship exists. This means that the last tenant to survive receives full ownership of the property. Thus, if Dan predeceases Vicky, the land belongs entirely to Vicky. None of the land will pass to Dan's heirs or will be subject to administration by Dan's executor. A tenancy by the entirety is a joint tenancy between husband and wife.

---

[16]§ 2032(c).　　　　　　　　　　[17]§ 1014(a).

If Dan and Vicky hold ownership as **tenants in common** or as community property, death does not defeat an owner's interest. Thus, if Dan predeceases Vicky, Dan's one-half interest in the land will pass to his estate or heirs.

Community property interests arise from the marital relationship. Normally, all property acquired after marriage, except by gift or inheritance, by husband and wife residing in a community property state becomes part of the community. The following states have the community property system in effect: Louisiana, Texas, New Mexico, Arizona, California, Washington, Idaho, Nevada, Wisconsin, and (by election of the spouses) Alaska. All other states follow the common law system of ascertaining a spouse's rights to property acquired after marriage.

**Partial Interests.**   Interests in assets can be divided in terms of rights to income and principal. Particularly when property is placed in trust, it is not uncommon to carve out various income interests that must be accounted for separately from the ultimate disposition of the property itself.

**EXAMPLE 9**

Under Bill's will, a ranch is to be placed in trust, life estate to Sam, Bill's son, with remainder to Sam's children (Bill's grandchildren). Under this arrangement, Sam is the life tenant and, as such, is entitled to the use of the ranch (including any income) during his life. Upon Sam's death, the trust terminates, and its principal passes to his children. Thus, Sam's children receive outright ownership in the ranch when Sam dies. ■

## LO.4

Explain the operation of the Federal gift tax.

# The Federal Gift Tax

## GENERAL CONSIDERATIONS

**Requirements for a Gift.**   For a gift to be complete under state law, the following elements must be present.

- A donor competent to make the gift.
- A donee capable of receiving and possessing the property.
- Donative intent on behalf of the donor.
- Actual or constructive delivery of the property to the donee or the donee's representative.
- Acceptance of the gift by the donee.

**Incomplete Transfers.**   The Federal gift tax does not apply to transfers that are incomplete. Thus, if the transferor retains the right to reclaim the property or has not really parted with the possession of the property, a taxable event has not taken place.

**EXAMPLE 10**

Lesly creates a trust, income payable to Mary for life, remainder to Paul. Under the terms of the trust instrument, Lesly can revoke the trust at any time and repossess the trust principal and the income earned. No gift takes place on the creation of the trust; Lesly has not ceased to have dominion and control over the property. ■

**EXAMPLE 11**

Assume the same facts as in Example 10, except that one year after the transfer, Lesly relinquishes his right to terminate the trust. At this point, the transfer becomes complete, and the Federal gift tax applies. ■

**Business versus Personal Setting.**   In a business setting, full and adequate consideration is apt to exist. Regulation § 25.2512–8 provides that "a sale, exchange, or other transfer of property made in the ordinary course of business (a transaction that is bona fide, at arm's length, and free of any donative intent) will be considered as made for an adequate and full consideration in money or money's worth." If the parties are acting in a personal setting, however, a gift usually is the result.

**EXAMPLE 12**

Grace loans money to Debby in connection with a business venture. About a year later, Grace forgives part of the loan. Grace probably has not made a gift to Debby if she and Debby are unrelated parties.[18] ■

**EXAMPLE 13**

Assume the same facts as in Example 12, except that Grace and Debby are mother and daughter and no business venture is involved. If the loan itself was not actually a disguised gift, the later forgiveness is probably a gift. ■

Regulation § 25.2512–8 also holds that valuable consideration (such as would preclude a gift result) does not include a payment or transfer based on "love and affection . . . promise of marriage, etc." Consequently, property settlements in consideration of marriage (i.e., pre- or antenuptial agreements) are regarded as gifts.

Do not conclude that the presence of *some* consideration is enough to preclude Federal gift tax consequences. Again, the answer may rest on whether the transfer occurred in a business setting.

**EXAMPLE 14**

Peter sells Bob some real estate for $40,000. Unknown to Peter, the property contains valuable mineral deposits and is really worth $200,000. Peter may have made a bad business deal, but he has not made a gift of $160,000 to Bob. ■

**EXAMPLE 15**

Assume the same facts as in Example 14, except that Peter and Bob are father and son. In addition, Peter is very much aware that the property is worth $200,000. Peter has made a gift of $160,000 to Bob. ■

---

**ETHICAL CONSIDERATIONS** | **What Constitutes Support?**

When Earl's daughter, Clara, turns 40, he gives her a Mercedes convertible as a birthday present. Clara is married and has a family of her own. She is a licensed orthopedic surgeon and maintains a successful practice in the field of sports medicine.

Earl does not regard the transfer as being subject to the gift tax. As a parent, he is merely satisfying his obligation of support. Such obligation includes providing your child with transportation. Is Earl's reasoning sound?

---

**Certain Excluded Transfers.** Transfers to political organizations are exempt from the application of the Federal gift tax.[19] This provision in the Code made unnecessary the previous practice whereby candidates for public office established

---

[18]The forgiveness could result in taxable income to Debby under § 61(a)(12).

[19]§ 2501(a)(5).

multiple campaign committees to maximize the number of annual exclusions available to their contributors. As noted later, an annual exclusion of $11,000 for each donee passes free of the Federal gift tax.

The Federal gift tax does not apply to tuition payments made to an educational organization (e.g., a college) on another's behalf. Nor does it apply to amounts paid on another's behalf for medical care.[20] In this regard, the law is realistic since it is unlikely that most donors would recognize these items as transfers subject to the gift tax. The payments, however, must be made directly to the provider (e.g., doctor, hospital, college). There is no requirement that the beneficiary of the service (e.g., patient, student) qualify as a dependent of the person making the payment.

Satisfying an obligation of support is not subject to the gift tax. Thus, no gift takes place when parents pay for their children's education because one of the obligations of parents is to educate their children. What constitutes an obligation of support is determined by applicable state law.

**Lifetime versus Death Transfers.**   Be careful to distinguish between lifetime (inter vivos) and death (testamentary) transfers.

**EXAMPLE 16**

Dudley buys a 12-month certificate of deposit (CD) from State Bank and lists ownership as follows: "Dudley, payable on proof of death to Faye." Nine months later, Dudley dies. When the CD matures, Faye collects the proceeds from State Bank. No gift takes place when Dudley invests in the CD; Faye has received a mere expectancy (i.e., to obtain ownership of the CD upon Dudley's death). At any time before his death, Dudley may withdraw the funds or delete Faye's name from the account, thereby cutting off her expectancy. Furthermore, no gift occurs upon Dudley's death as the CD passes to Faye by testamentary disposition. As noted later, the CD will be included in Dudley's gross estate as property in which the decedent had an interest (§ 2033). ■

The arrangement used in Example 16, known as a **Totten trust**, is very similar in effect to a revocable trust (see Example 10 above). Both carry the advantage of avoiding the probate estate (see Chapter 18). A Totten trust, however, is simpler to use in the case of bank accounts and securities, and it avoids the need of having to create a formal trust.

## TRANSFERS SUBJECT TO THE GIFT TAX

Whether a transfer is subject to the Federal gift tax depends upon the application of §§ 2511 through 2519 and the applicable Regulations.

**Gift Loans.**   To understand the tax ramifications of gift loans, an illustration is helpful.

**EXAMPLE 17**

Before his daughter (Denise) leaves for college, Victor lends her $300,000. Denise signs a note that provides for repayment in five years. The loan contains no interest element, and neither Victor nor Denise expects any interest to be paid. Following Victor's advice, Denise invests the loan proceeds in income-producing securities. During her five years in college, she uses the income from the investments to pay for college costs and other living expenses. On the maturity date of the note, Denise repays the $300,000 she owes Victor. ■

---

[20]§ 2503(e).

In a gift loan arrangement, the following consequences ensue.

- Victor has made a gift to Denise of the interest element. The amount of the gift is determined by the difference between the amount of interest charged (in this case, none) and the market rate (as determined by the yield on certain U.S. government securities).
- The interest element is included in Victor's gross income and is subject to the Federal income tax.
- Denise may be allowed an income tax deduction for the interest element, but may benefit from this result only if she is in a position to itemize her deductions *from* adjusted gross income.

The Code defines a gift loan as "any below-market loan where the foregoing [sic] of interest is in the nature of a gift."[21] Unless tax avoidance was one of the principal purposes of the loan, special limitations apply if the gift loan does not exceed $100,000. In such a case, the interest element may not exceed the borrower's net investment income.[22] Furthermore, if the net investment income does not exceed $1,000, it is treated as zero. Under a $1,000 *de minimis rule*, the interest element is disregarded.

**Certain Property Settlements (§ 2516).** Normally, the settlement of certain marital rights is not regarded as being for consideration and is subject to the Federal gift tax.[23] As a special exception to this general approach, Congress enacted § 2516. By this provision, transfers of property interests made under the terms of a written agreement between spouses in settlement of their marital or property rights are deemed to be for adequate consideration. These transfers are exempt from the Federal gift tax if a final decree of divorce is obtained within the three-year period beginning on the date one year before the parties entered into the agreement. Likewise excluded are transfers to provide a reasonable allowance for the support of minor children (including legally adopted children) of a marriage. The agreement need not be approved by the divorce decree.

**Disclaimers (§ 2518).** A **disclaimer** is a refusal by a person to accept property that is designated to pass to him or her. The effect of the disclaimer is to pass the property to someone else.

**EXAMPLE 18**

Earl dies without a will and is survived by a son, Andy, and a grandson, Jay. At the time of his death, Earl owned real estate that, under the applicable state law, passes to the closest lineal descendant, Andy in this case. If, however, Andy disclaims his interest in the real estate, state law provides that the property passes to Jay. At the time of Earl's death, Andy has considerable property of his own, and Jay has none. ∎

Why might Andy want to consider disclaiming his inheritance and have the property pass directly from Earl to Jay? By doing so, an extra transfer tax may be avoided. If the disclaimer does not take place (i.e., Andy accepts the inheritance) and the property eventually passes to Jay (either by gift or by death), the later transfer is subject to the application of either the gift tax or the estate tax.

For many years, whether a disclaimer was effective in avoiding a Federal transfer tax depended on the application of state law. To illustrate by using the

---

[21]§ 7872(f)(3).

[22]Net investment income has the same meaning given to the term by § 163(d). Generally, net investment income is investment income (e.g., interest, dividends) less related expenses.

[23]Reg. § 25.2512–8.

facts of Example 18, if state law determined that the real estate was deemed to have passed through Andy despite his disclaimer after Earl's death, the Federal gift tax applied. In essence, Andy was treated as if he had inherited the property from Earl and then given it to Jay. As state law was not always consistent in this regard and sometimes was not even known, the application or nonapplication of Federal transfer taxes depended on where the parties lived. To remedy this situation and provide some measure of uniformity, § 2046 (relating to disclaimers for estate tax purposes) and § 2518 (relating to disclaimers for gift tax purposes) were added to the Code.

In the case of the gift tax, when the requirements of § 2518 are met and Andy issues a timely lifetime disclaimer (refer to Example 18), the property is treated as if it goes directly from Earl to Jay. Since the property is not treated as passing through Andy (regardless of what state law holds), it is not subject to the Federal gift tax.

The tax law also permits the Federal gift tax to be avoided in cases of a partial disclaimer of an undivided interest.

**EXAMPLE 19**

Assume the same facts as in Example 18, except that Andy wishes to retain half of the real estate for himself. If Andy makes a timely disclaimer of an undivided one-half interest in the property, the Federal gift tax does not apply to the portion passing to Jay. ∎

To be effective, the disclaimer must be timely made. Generally, this means no later than nine months after the right to the property arose. Furthermore, the person making the disclaimer must not have accepted any benefits or interest in the property.

**Other Transfers Subject to Gift Tax.**　Other transfers that may carry gift tax consequences (e.g., the exercise of a power of appointment, the creation of joint ownership) are discussed and illustrated in connection with the Federal estate tax.

## ANNUAL EXCLUSION

**In General.**　The first $11,000 of gifts made to any one person during any calendar year (except gifts of future interests in property) is excluded in determining the total amount of gifts for the year.[24] The **annual exclusion** applies to all gifts of a present interest made during the calendar year in the order in which they are made until the $11,000 exclusion per donee is exhausted. For a gift in trust, each beneficiary of the trust is treated as a separate person for purposes of the exclusion.

A **future interest** is defined as one that will come into being (as to use, possession, or enjoyment) at some future date. Examples of future interests include such rights as remainder interests that are commonly encountered when property is transferred to a trust. A *present interest* is an unrestricted right to the immediate use, possession, or enjoyment of property or of the income.

**EXAMPLE 20**

During the current year, Laura makes the following cash gifts: $8,000 to Rita and $12,000 to Maureen. Laura may claim an annual exclusion of $8,000 with respect to Rita and $11,000 with respect to Maureen. ∎

**EXAMPLE 21**

By a lifetime gift, Ron transfers property to a trust with a life estate (with income payable annually) to June and remainder upon June's death to Albert. Ron has made two gifts: one

---

[24]§ 2503(b).

to June of a life estate and one to Albert of a remainder interest. (The valuation of each of these gifts is discussed in Chapter 18.) The life estate is a present interest and qualifies for the annual exclusion. The remainder interest granted to Albert is a future interest and does not qualify for the exclusion. Note that Albert's interest does not come into being until some future date (on the death of June). ■

Although Example 21 indicates that the gift of an income interest is a present interest, this is not always the case. If a possibility exists that the income beneficiary may not receive the immediate enjoyment of the property, the transfer is of a future interest.

**EXAMPLE 22**

Assume the same facts as in Example 21, except that the income from the trust need not be payable annually to June. It may, at the trustee's discretion, be accumulated and added to the principal. Since June's right to receive the income from the trust is conditioned on the trustee's discretion, it is not a present interest. No annual exclusion is allowed. The mere possibility of diversion is enough. It would not matter if the trustee never exercised the discretion to accumulate and did, in fact, distribute the trust income to June annually. ■

**Trust for Minors.** Section 2503(c) offers an important exception to the future interest rules just discussed. Under this provision, a transfer for the benefit of a person who has not attained the age of 21 years on the date of the gift may be considered a gift of a present interest. This is true even though the minor is not given the unrestricted right to the immediate use, possession, or enjoyment of the property. For the exception to apply, the following conditions must be satisfied.

- Both the property and its income may be expended by or for the benefit of the minor before the minor attains the age of 21.
- Any portion of the property or its income not expended by the time the minor reaches the age of 21 shall pass to the minor at that time.
- If the minor dies before attaining the age of 21, the property and its income will be payable either to the minor's estate or as the minor may designate under a general power of appointment (discussed later in the chapter).

The exception allows a trustee to accumulate income on behalf of a minor beneficiary without converting the income interest to a future interest.

**EXAMPLE 23**

Bret places property in trust, income payable to Billy until he reaches 21, remainder to Billy or Billy's estate. Under the terms of the trust instrument, the trustee is empowered to accumulate the trust income or apply it toward Billy's benefit. In either event, the accumulated income and principal must be paid to Billy whenever he reaches 21 years of age or to whomever Billy designates in his will if he dies before reaching that age. The conditions of § 2503(c) are satisfied, and Bret's transfer qualifies for the annual exclusion. Billy's interest is a present interest. ■

**Contributions to Qualified Tuition Programs.** For income tax purposes, § 529 plans have become the best of all possible worlds. Although no up-front deduction is allowed,[25] income earned by the fund accumulates free of income tax, and distributions are not taxed if they are used for higher education purposes. A special provision allows a donor to enjoy a gift tax advantage by using five years of annual exclusions.[26]

---

[25]Depending on the taxpayer's home state, some (or all) of the deduction may be allowed for *state* income tax purposes.

[26]§ 529(c)(2)(B). Subsection (A) protects against future interest treatment.

| | |
|---|---|
| **E X A M P L E   2 4** | Trevor and Audry would like to start building a college education fund for their 10-year-old granddaughter, Loni. In 2003, Trevor contributes $110,000 to the designated carrier of their state's § 529 plan. By electing to split the gift and using five annual exclusions [2 (number of donors) × $11,000 (annual exclusion) × 5 years = $110,000], no taxable gift results. (The gift-splitting election is discussed in detail later in this chapter.) ■ |

Making the five-year election precludes Trevor and Audry from using any annual exclusion on gifts to Loni for the next four years.[27] If either donor dies before the period is up, the annual exclusions are allocated pro rata in computing the gross estate.

The election does not, however, impair the availability of the annual exclusion as to gifts to *other* donees.

## DEDUCTIONS

In arriving at taxable gifts, a deduction is allowed for transfers to certain qualified charitable organizations. On transfers between spouses, a marital deduction may be available. Since both the charitable and marital deductions apply in determining the Federal estate tax, these deductions are discussed later in the chapter.

**LO.5**

Illustrate the computation of the Federal gift tax.

## COMPUTING THE FEDERAL GIFT TAX

**The Unified Transfer Tax Rate Schedule.**   The top rates of the unified transfer tax rate schedule originally reached as high as 70 percent (see Appendix A, page A–4). Over the years, these top rates have been reduced to 55 percent. Under the Tax Relief Reconciliation Act of 2001, the top rate is reduced to 50 percent, and further reductions are scheduled for future years.[28] Keep in mind that the unified transfer tax rate schedule applies to all transfers (by gift or death) after 1976 and before 2010. Different rate schedules apply for pre-1977 gifts (see Appendix A, page A–11) and pre-1977 deaths (see Appendix A, page A–10).

**The Deemed Paid Adjustment.**   Review the formula for the gift tax in Figure 17–1, and note that the tax base for a current gift includes *all* past taxable gifts. The effect of the inclusion is to force the current taxable gift into a higher bracket due to the progressive nature of the unified transfer tax rates (refer to Example 2). To mitigate such double taxation, the donor is allowed a credit for any gift tax previously paid or deemed paid (refer to Example 3).

Limiting the donor to a credit for the gift tax *actually paid* on pre-1977 taxable gifts would be unfair. Pre-1977 taxable gifts were subject to a lower set of rates (see Appendix A, page A–11) than those in the unified transfer tax rate schedule. As a consequence, the donor is allowed a *deemed paid* credit on pre-1977 taxable gifts. This is the amount that would have been due under the unified transfer tax rate schedule had it been applicable. *Post-1976* taxable gifts *also* are subject to the deemed paid adjustment since the same rate schedule may not be involved in all gifts. Compare the variation in rates in Appendix A, pages A–4, A–5, A–6, A–7, A–8, and A–9. For post-1976 taxable gifts, it is entirely possible that the deemed paid credit allowed could be *less* than the gift tax that was actually paid.

---

[27]Trevor and Audry could resort to § 2503(e)(2)(A) to avoid any gift at all. As mentioned earlier, a *direct* payment of tuition to certain educational institutions is exempt from the gift tax. But this rule does not help to build an education fund for future use, as § 529 does. Recall that Loni, the granddaughter, is only 10 years old.

[28]§ 2001(c)(2)(B). Scheduled reductions in the maximum tax rates are as follows: 49% (2003); 48% (2004); 47% (2005); 46% (2006); and 45% (2007, 2008, 2009). As to the 2003 rates, see Appendix A, page A–9.

| EXAMPLE 25 | In early 1976, Lisa made taxable gifts of $500,000, upon which a Federal gift (see Appendix A, page A–11) was paid. Assume Lisa makes further taxable gi[ in 2003. The unified transfer tax on the 2003 gifts is determined as follows. |

| | | |
|---|---|---|
| Taxable gifts made in 2003 | | $1,700,000 |
| Add: Taxable gifts made in 1976 | | 500,000 |
| Total of current and past taxable gifts | | $2,200,000 |
| Unified transfer tax on total taxable gifts per Appendix A, page A–9 [$780,800 + 49%($2,200,000 − $2,000,000)] | | $ 878,800 |
| Subtract: | | |
| Deemed paid tax on pre-1977 taxable gifts per Appendix A, page A–9 | $155,800 | |
| Unified tax credit for 2003 | 345,800 | (501,600) |
| Gift tax due on the 2003 taxable gift | | $ 377,200 |

Note that the gift tax actually paid on the 1976 transfer was $109,275. Nevertheless, Lisa is allowed a deemed paid credit on the gift of $155,800, considerably different from what was paid. ■

**The Election to Split Gifts by Married Persons.** To understand the reason for the gift-splitting election of § 2513, consider the following situations:

| EXAMPLE 26 | Dick and Margaret are husband and wife and reside in Michigan, a common law state. Dick has been the only breadwinner in the family, and Margaret has no significant property of her own. Neither has made any prior taxable gifts or has used the $30,000 specific exemption previously available for pre-1977 gifts. In 2003, Dick makes a gift to Leslie of $2,022,000. Presuming the election to split gifts did not exist, Dick's gift tax is as follows. |

| | |
|---|---|
| Amount of gift | $2,022,000 |
| Subtract: Annual exclusion | (11,000) |
| Taxable gift | $2,011,000 |
| Gift tax on $2,011,000 per Appendix A, page A–9 [$780,800 + (49% × $11,000)] | $ 786,190 |
| Subtract: Unified transfer tax credit for 2003 | (345,800) |
| Gift tax due on the 2003 taxable gift | $ 440,390 |

| EXAMPLE 27 | Assume the same facts as in Example 26, except that Dick and Margaret always have resided in California (a community property state). Even though Dick is the sole breadwinner, income from personal services generally is community property. Consequently, the gift to Leslie probably involves community property. If this is the case, the gift tax is as follows. |

| | Dick | Margaret |
|---|---|---|
| Amount of gift | $1,011,000 | $1,011,000 |
| Subtract: Annual exclusion | 11,000 | 11,000 |
| Taxable gift | $1,000,000 | $1,000,000 |
| Gift tax on $1,000,000 per Appendix A, page A–9 | $ 345,800 | $ 345,800 |
| Subtract: Unified transfer tax credit for 2003 | 345,800 | 345,800 |
| Gift tax due on the 2003 taxable gift | $ –0– | $ –0– |

As the results of Examples 26 and 27 indicate, married donors residing in community property jurisdictions possessed a significant gift tax advantage over those residing in common law states. To rectify this inequity, the Revenue Act of 1948 incorporated into the Code the predecessor to § 2513. Under this provision, a gift made by a person to someone other than his or her spouse may be considered, for Federal gift tax purposes, as having been made one-half by each spouse. Returning to Example 26, Dick and Margaret could treat the gift passing to Leslie as being made one-half by each of them. They may do this even though the cash belonged to Dick. As a result, the parties are able to achieve the same tax consequence as in Example 27.

To split gifts, the spouses must be legally married to each other at the time of the gift. If they are divorced later in the calendar year, they may still split the gift if neither marries anyone else during that year. They both must indicate on their separate gift tax returns their consent to have all gifts made in that calendar year split between them. In addition, both must be citizens or residents of the United States on the date of the gift. A gift from one spouse to the other spouse cannot be split. Such a gift might, however, be eligible for the marital deduction.

The election to split gifts is not necessary when husband and wife transfer community property to a third party. It is available, however, if the gift consists of the separate property of one of the spouses. Generally, separate property is property acquired before marriage and property acquired after marriage by gift or inheritance. The election, then, is not limited to residents of common law states.

## PROCEDURAL MATTERS

Having determined which transfers are subject to the Federal gift tax and the various deductions and exclusions available to the donor, the procedural aspects of the tax should be considered. The following sections discuss the return itself, the due dates for filing and paying the tax, and other related matters.

**The Federal Gift Tax Return.**   For transfers by gift, a Form 709 (U.S. Gift Tax Return) must be filed whenever the gifts for any one calendar year exceed the annual exclusion or involve a gift of a future interest. A Form 709 need not be filed, however, for transfers between spouses that are offset by the unlimited marital deduction regardless of the amount of the transfer.[29]

| | |
|---|---|
| **EXAMPLE 28** | In 2003, Larry makes five gifts, each in the amount of $11,000, to his five children. If the gifts do not involve future interests, a Form 709 need not be filed to report the transfers. ■ |

| | |
|---|---|
| **EXAMPLE 29** | During 2003, Esther makes a gift of $22,000 cash of her separate property to her daughter. To double the amount of the annual exclusion allowed, Jerry (Esther's husband) is willing to split the gift. Since the § 2513 election can be made only on a gift tax return, a form must be filed even though no gift tax will be due as a result of the transfer. Useful for this purpose is Form 709–A (U.S. Short Form Gift Tax Return). This form is available to simplify the gift-splitting procedure. ■ |

In Example 29, no gift tax return would be necessary if the transfer consisted of community property. Since two donors are now involved, the cap for filing becomes more than $22,000, rather than more than $11,000.

Presuming a gift tax return is due, it must be filed on or before the fifteenth day of April following the year of the gift.[30] As is the case with other Federal taxes,

---

[29]§ 6019(a)(2).                    [30]§ 6075(b)(1).

---

**CONCEPT SUMMARY 17–1**

### Federal Gift Tax Provisions

1. The Federal gift tax applies to all gratuitous transfers of property made by U.S. citizens or residents. In this regard, it does not matter where the property is located.
2. In the eyes of the IRS, a gratuitous transfer is one not supported by full and adequate consideration. If the parties are acting in a business setting, such consideration usually exists. If, however, purported sales are between family members, a gift element may be suspected.
3. If one party lends money to another and intends some or all of the interest element to be a gift, the arrangement is categorized as a gift loan. To the extent that the interest provided for is less than the market rate, three tax consequences result. First, a gift has taken place between the lender and the borrower as to the interest element. Second, income may result to the lender. Third, an income tax deduction may be available to the borrower.
4. Property settlements can escape the gift tax if a divorce occurs within a prescribed period of time.
5. A disclaimer is a refusal by a person to accept property designated to pass to that person. The effect of a disclaimer is to pass the property to someone else. If certain conditions are satisfied, the issuance of a disclaimer will not be subject to the Federal gift tax.
6. Except for gifts of future interests, a donor is allowed an annual exclusion of $11,000. The future interest limitation does not apply to certain trusts created for minors.
7. The election to split a gift enables a married couple to be treated as two donors. The election doubles the annual exclusion and makes the unified tax credit available to the nonowner spouse.
8. The election to split gifts is not necessary if the property is jointly owned by the spouses. That is the case when the property is part of the couple's community.
9. In determining the tax base for computing the gift tax, all prior taxable gifts must be added to current taxable gifts. Thus, the gift tax is cumulative in nature.
10. Gifts are reported on Form 709 or Form 709–A. The return is due on April 15 following the year of the gift.

---

when the due date falls on Saturday, Sunday, or a legal holiday, the date for filing the return is the next business day. Note that the filing requirements for Form 709 have no correlation to the accounting year used by a donor for Federal income tax purposes. Thus, a fiscal year taxpayer must follow the April 15 rule for any reportable gifts. If sufficient reason is shown, the IRS is authorized to grant reasonable extensions of time for filing the return.[31]

# The Federal Estate Tax

The following discussion of the estate tax coincides with the formula that appeared earlier in the chapter in Figure 17–2. The key components in the formula are the gross estate, the taxable estate, the tax base, and the credits allowed against the tentative tax. This formula can be summarized as follows:

---

[31]§ 6081. Under § 6075(b)(2), an extension of time granted to a calendar year taxpayer for filing an income tax return automatically extends the due date of a gift tax return.

L0.6

Review the components of the
gross estate.

## GROSS ESTATE

Simply stated, the **gross estate** includes all property subject to the Federal estate tax. This depends on the provisions of the Internal Revenue Code as supplemented by IRS pronouncements and the judicial interpretations of Federal courts.

In contrast to the gross estate, the **probate estate** is controlled by state (rather than Federal) law. The probate estate consists of all of a decedent's property subject to administration by the executor or administrator of the estate. The administration is supervised by a local court of appropriate jurisdiction (usually designated as a probate court). An executor (or executrix) is the decedent's personal representative appointed under the decedent's will. When a decedent dies without a will or fails to name an executor in the will (or that person refuses to serve), the local probate court appoints an administrator (or administratrix).

The probate estate is frequently smaller than the gross estate. It contains only property owned by the decedent at the time of death and passing to heirs under a will or under the law of intestacy (the order of distribution for those dying without a will). As noted later, such items as the proceeds of many life insurance policies become part of the gross estate but are not included in the probate estate.

All states provide for an order of distribution in the event someone dies without a will. After the surviving spouse, who receives some or all of the estate, the preference is usually in the following order: down to lineal descendants (e.g., children, grandchildren), up to lineal ascendants (e.g., parents, grandparents), and out to collateral relations (e.g., brothers, sisters, aunts, and uncles).

**Property Owned by the Decedent (§ 2033).**   Property owned by the decedent at the time of death is included in the gross estate. The nature of the property or the use to which it was put during the decedent-owner's lifetime has no significance as far as the estate tax is concerned. Thus, personal effects (such as clothing), stocks, bonds, furniture, jewelry, works of art, bank accounts, and interests in businesses conducted as sole proprietorships and partnerships are all included in the deceased owner's gross estate. No distinction is made between tangible and intangible, depreciable and nondepreciable, business and personal assets. However, a deceased spouse's gross estate does not include the surviving spouse's share of the community property.

The application of § 2033 is illustrated as follows:

**EXAMPLE 30**   Irma dies owning some City of Denver bonds. The fair market value of the bonds plus any interest accrued to the date of Irma's death is included in her gross estate. Although interest on municipals is normally not taxable under the Federal income tax, it is property owned by Irma at the time of death. However, any interest accrued after death is not part of Irma's gross estate. ■

**EXAMPLE 31**   Sharon dies on April 8, 2003, at a time when she owns stock in Robin Corporation and Wren Corporation. On March 3 of this year, both corporations authorized a cash dividend payable on May 2. Robin's dividend is payable to shareholders of record as of April 3. Wren's date of record is April 11. Sharon's gross estate includes the following: the stock in Robin Corporation, the stock in Wren Corporation, and the dividend on the Robin stock. It does not include the dividend on the Wren stock. ■

**EXAMPLE 32**

Ray dies holding some promissory notes issued to him by his son. In his will, Ray forgives these notes, relieving the son of the obligation to make any payments. The fair market value of these notes is included in Ray's gross estate. ■

**EXAMPLE 33**

At the time of his death on a business trip, Ray was a consulting engineer for Falcon Corporation. Ray's estate receives a distribution from Falcon's qualified pension plan of $1,100,000 consisting of the following:

| | |
|---|---|
| Falcon's contributions | $450,000 |
| Ray's contributions | 350,000 |
| Income earned by the plan | 300,000 |

Ray's estate also receives $150,000 from Hawk Insurance Company. The payment represents the maturity value of term life insurance from a group plan Falcon maintains for its employees. As to these amounts, Ray's gross estate includes $1,250,000 ($1,100,000 + $150,000). For income tax purposes, however, $750,000 ($450,000 + $300,000) is subject to tax, while $500,000 ($350,000 + $150,000) is not.[32] ■

**Dower and Curtesy Interests (§ 2034).** In its common law (nonstatutory) form, dower generally gave a surviving widow a life estate in a portion of her husband's estate (usually the real estate he owned) with the remainder passing to their children. Most states have modified and codified these common law rules, and the resulting statutes often vary between jurisdictions. In some states, for example, by statute, a widow is entitled to outright ownership of a percentage of her deceased husband's real estate and personal property. Curtesy is a similar right held by the husband in his wife's property that takes effect in the event he survives her. Most states have abolished the common law curtesy concept and have, in some cases, substituted a modified statutory version.

Dower and curtesy rights are incomplete interests and may never materialize. Thus, if a wife predeceases her husband, the dower interest in her husband's property is lost.

**EXAMPLE 34**

Martin dies without a will, leaving an estate of $2.1 million. Under state law, Belinda (Martin's widow) is entitled to one-third of his property. The $700,000 Belinda receives is included in Martin's gross estate. Depending on the nature of the interest Belinda receives in the $700,000, this amount could qualify Martin's estate for a marital deduction. (This possibility is discussed at greater length later in the chapter. For the time being, however, the focus is on what is or is not included as part of the decedent's gross estate.) ■

**Adjustments for Gifts Made within Three Years of Death (§ 2035).** At one time, all taxable gifts made within three years of death were included in the donor's gross estate unless it could be shown that the gifts were not made in contemplation of death. The prior rule was intended to preclude tax avoidance since the gift tax and estate tax rates were separate and the former was lower than

---

[32]Retirement plan benefits [H.R. 10 or Keogh plans, IRAs, Roths, § 401(k), § 403(b)(1)] are invariably subject to estate tax. Usually, the benefits are included in the gross estate under § 2033, as was the case in Example 33. If the payout is in the form of an annuity, § 2039 applies (see later in the chapter).

the latter. When the gift and estate tax rates were combined into the unified transfer tax, the reason for the rule for gifts in contemplation of death largely disappeared. The three-year rule has, however, been retained for the following items:

- Inclusion in the gross estate of any gift tax paid on gifts made within three years of death. Called the *gross-up* procedure, it prevents the gift tax amount from escaping the estate tax.
- Any property interests transferred by gift within three years of death that would have been included in the gross estate by virtue of the application of § 2036 (transfers with a retained life estate), § 2037 (transfers taking effect at death), § 2038 (revocable transfers), and § 2042 (proceeds of life insurance). All except § 2037 are discussed later in the chapter.

**EXAMPLE 35**

Before her death in 2003, Jennifer made the following taxable gifts.

| Year of Gift | Nature of the Asset | Fair Market Value | | Gift Tax Paid |
|---|---|---|---|---|
| | | Date of Gift | Date of Death | |
| 1992 | Hawk Corporation stock | $100,000 | $ 150,000 | $  –0– |
| 2001 | Policy on Jennifer's life | 80,000 (cash value) | 1,000,000 (face value) | –0– |
| 2002 | Land | 800,000 | 810,000 | 16,000 |

Jennifer's *gross estate* includes $1,016,000 [$1,000,000 (life insurance proceeds) + $16,000 (gross-up for the gift tax on the 2002 taxable gift)] as to these transfers. Referring to the formula for the estate tax (see Figure 17–2), the other post-1976 taxable gifts are added to the *taxable estate* (at the fair market value on the date of the gift) in arriving at the tax base. Jennifer's estate is allowed a credit for the gift tax paid (or deemed paid) on the 2002 transfer. ■

The three-year rule also applies in testing for qualification under § 303 (stock redemptions to pay death taxes and administration expenses), § 2032A (special valuation procedures), and § 6166 (extensions of time to pay death taxes). All these provisions are discussed in Chapter 18.

**Transfers with a Retained Life Estate (§ 2036).**   Code §§ 2036 through 2038 were enacted on the premise that the estate tax can be avoided on lifetime transfers only if the decedent does not retain control over the property. The logic of this approach is somewhat difficult to dispute. One should not be able to escape the tax consequences of property transfers at death while remaining in a position to enjoy some or all of the fruits of ownership during life.

Under § 2036, the value of any property transferred by the deceased during lifetime for less than adequate consideration must be included if either of the following was retained:

- The possession or enjoyment of, or the right to the income from, the property.
- The right, either alone or in conjunction with any person, to designate the persons who shall possess or enjoy the property or the income.

"The possession or enjoyment of, or the right to the income from, the property," as it appears in § 2036(a)(1), is considered to have been retained by the decedent to the extent that such income, etc., is to be applied toward the discharge of a legal obligation of the decedent. The term "legal obligation" includes a legal obligation of the decedent to support a dependent during the decedent's lifetime.[33]

The following examples illustrate the practical application of § 2036.

**EXAMPLE 36**

Carl's will passes all of his property to a trust, income to Alan for his life (Alan is given a life estate). Upon Alan's death, the principal goes to Melissa (Melissa is granted a remainder interest). On Alan's death, none of the trust property is included in his gross estate. Although Alan held a life estate, § 2036 is inapplicable because he was not the transferor (Carl was) of the property. Section 2033 (property owned by the decedent) causes any income distributions Alan was entitled to receive at the time of his death to be included in his gross estate. ■

**EXAMPLE 37**

By deed, Nora transfers the remainder interest in her ranch to Marcia, retaining for herself the right to continue occupying the property until death. Upon Nora's death, the fair market value of the ranch is included in her gross estate. Furthermore, Nora is subject to the gift tax. The amount of the gift is the fair market value of the ranch on the date of the gift less the portion applicable to Nora's retained life estate. (See Chapter 18 for the way this gift is determined.) ■

**Revocable Transfers (§ 2038).** Another type of lifetime transfer that is drawn into a decedent's gross estate is covered by § 2038. The gross estate includes the value of property interests transferred by the decedent (except to the extent that the transfer was made for full consideration) if the enjoyment of the property transferred was subject, at the date of the decedent's death, to any power of the decedent to *alter, amend, revoke, or terminate* the transfer. This includes the power to change the beneficiaries or the power to accelerate or increase any beneficiary's enjoyment of the property.

The capacity in which the decedent could exercise the power is immaterial. If the decedent gave property in trust, making him- or herself the trustee with the power to revoke the trust, the property is included in his or her gross estate. If the decedent named another person as trustee with the power to revoke, but reserved the power to later appoint him- or herself trustee, the property is also included in his or her gross estate. If, however, the power to alter, amend, revoke, or terminate was held at all times solely by a person other than the decedent and the decedent did not reserve a right to assume these powers, the property is not included in the decedent's gross estate.

The Code and the Regulations make it clear that one cannot avoid inclusion in the gross estate under § 2038 by relinquishing a power within three years of death.[34] Recall that § 2038 is one of several types of situations listed as exceptions to the usual rule excluding gifts made within three years of death from the gross estate.

In the event § 2038 applies, the amount includible in the gross estate is the portion of the property transferred that is subject, at the decedent's death, to the decedent's power to alter, amend, revoke, or terminate.

The classic § 2038 situation results from the use of a revocable trust.

**EXAMPLE 38**

Maria creates a trust, life estate to her children, remainder to her grandchildren. Under the terms of the trust, Maria reserves the right to revoke the trust and revest the trust principal and income in herself. As noted in Example 10, the creation of the trust does not result in a gift because the transfer is not complete. However, if Maria dies still retaining the power to revoke, the trust is included in her gross estate under § 2038. ■

---

[33]Reg. § 20.2036–1(b)(2).

[34]§ 2038(a)(1) and Reg. § 20.2038–1(e)(1).

In application, the provisions related to incomplete transfers (§§ 2036 and 2038) tend to overlap. It is not unusual to find that either or both of these Sections apply to a particular transfer.

**Annuities (§ 2039).**    Annuities can be divided by their origin into commercial and noncommercial contracts. Noncommercial annuities are issued by private parties and, in some cases, charitable organizations that do not regularly issue annuities. The two varieties have much in common, but noncommercial annuities present special income tax problems and are not treated further in this discussion.

Regulation § 20.2039–1(b)(1) defines an annuity as representing "one or more payments extending over any period of time." According to the Regulation, the payments may be equal or unequal, conditional or unconditional, periodic or sporadic. Annuity contracts that terminate upon the death of the person covered (i.e., annuitant) are designated as straight-life annuities. Other contracts provide for a survivorship feature (e.g., reduced payments to a surviving spouse).

In the case of a straight-life annuity, nothing is included in the gross estate of the annuitant at death. Section 2033 (property in which the decedent had an interest) does not apply because the annuitant's interest in the contract is terminated by death. Section 2036 (transfers with a retained life estate) does not cover the situation; a transfer made for full consideration is specifically excluded from § 2036 treatment. A commercial annuity is presumed to have been purchased for full consideration unless some evidence exists to indicate that the parties were not acting at arm's length.

**EXAMPLE 39**    Arnold purchases a straight-life annuity that will pay him $12,000 a month when he reaches age 65. Arnold dies at age 70. Except for the payments he received before his death, nothing relating to this annuity affects Arnold's gross estate. ∎

In the case of a survivorship annuity, the estate tax consequences under § 2039(a) are usually triggered by the death of the first annuitant. The amount included in the gross estate is the cost from the same company of a comparable annuity covering the survivor at his or her attained age on the date of the deceased annuitant's death.

**EXAMPLE 40**    Assume the same facts as in Example 39, except that the annuity contract provides for Veronica to be paid $6,000 a month for life as a survivorship feature. Veronica is 62 years of age when Arnold dies. Under these circumstances, Arnold's gross estate includes the cost of a comparable contract that provides an annuity of $6,000 per month for the life of a female, age 62. ∎

Full inclusion of the survivorship element in the gross estate is subject to an exception under § 2039(b). The amount includible is to be based on the proportion of the deceased annuitant's contribution to the total cost of the contract. This is expressed by the following formula:

$$\frac{\text{Decedent's contribution to purchase price}}{\text{Total purchase price of the annuity}} \times \text{Value of the annuity (or refund) at decedent's death} = \text{Amount includible in the deceased annuitant's gross estate}$$

**EXAMPLE 41**

Assume the same facts as in Example 40, except that Arnold and Veronica are husband and wife and have always lived in a community property state. The premiums on the contract were paid with community funds. Since Veronica contributed half of the cost of the contract, only half of the amount determined under Example 40 is included in Arnold's gross estate. ■

The result reached in Example 41 is not unique to community property jurisdictions. The outcome would have been the same in a noncommunity property state if Veronica had furnished half of the consideration from her own funds.

**Joint Interests (§§ 2040 and 2511).**   Recall that joint tenancies and tenancies by the entirety are characterized by the right of survivorship. Thus, upon the death of a joint tenant, title to the property passes to the surviving tenant. None of the property is included in the *probate* estate of the deceased tenant. In the case of tenancies in common and community property, death does not defeat an ownership interest. Further, the deceased owner's interest is part of the probate estate.

The Federal *estate tax treatment* of tenancies in common or of community property follows the logical approach of taxing only the portion of the property included in the deceased owner's probate estate. Thus, if Homer, Wilma, and Thelma are tenants in common in a tract of land, each owning an equal interest, and Homer dies, only one-third of the value of the property is included in the gross estate. This one-third interest is also the same amount that passes to Homer's heirs.

**EXAMPLE 42**

Homer, Wilma, and Thelma acquire a tract of land, ownership listed as tenants in common, each party furnishing $200,000 of the $600,000 purchase price. When the property is worth $900,000, Homer dies. If Homer's undivided interest in the property is 33⅓%, the gross estate *and* probate estate each include $300,000. ■

Unless the parties have provided otherwise, each tenant is deemed to own an interest equal to the portion of the original consideration he or she furnished. The parties in Example 42 could have provided that Homer would receive an undivided half interest in the property although he contributed only one-third of the purchase price. In that case, Wilma and Thelma have made a gift to Homer when the tenancy was created, and Homer's gross estate and probate estate each include $450,000.

For certain joint tenancies, the tax consequences are different. All of the property is included in the deceased co-owner's gross estate unless it can be proved that the surviving co-owners contributed to the cost of the property.[35] If a contribution can be shown, the amount to be *excluded* is calculated by the following formula:

$$\frac{\text{Surviving co-owner's contribution}}{\text{Total cost of the property}} \times \text{Fair market value of the property}$$

In computing a survivor's contribution, any funds received as a gift *from the deceased co-owner* and applied to the cost of the property cannot be counted. However, income or gain from gift assets can be counted.

If the co-owners receive the property as a gift *from another*, each co-owner is deemed to have contributed to the cost of his or her own interest.

The preceding rules can be illustrated as follows.

**EXAMPLE 43**

Keith and Steve (father and son) acquire a tract of land, ownership listed as joint tenancy with right of survivorship. Keith furnished $400,000 and Steve $200,000 of the $600,000 purchase price. Of the $200,000 provided by Steve, $100,000 had previously been received

---

[35]§ 2040(a).

as a gift from Keith. When the property is worth $900,000, Keith dies. Because only $100,000 of Steve's contribution can be counted (the other $100,000 was received as a gift from Keith), Steve has furnished only one-sixth ($100,000/$600,000) of the cost. Thus, Keith's gross estate must include five-sixths of $900,000, or $750,000. This presumes Steve can prove that he did in fact make the $100,000 contribution. In the absence of such proof, the full value of the property is included in Keith's gross estate. Keith's death makes Steve the immediate owner of the property by virtue of the right of survivorship. None of the property is part of Keith's probate estate. ■

**EXAMPLE 44**

Francis transfers property to Irene and Martin as a gift, listing ownership as joint tenancy with the right of survivorship. Upon Irene's death, one-half of the value of the property is included in the gross estate. Since the property was received as a gift and the donees are equal owners, each is considered to have furnished half of the consideration. ■

To simplify the joint ownership rules for *married persons*, § 2040(b) provides for an automatic inclusion rule upon the death of the first joint-owner spouse to die. Regardless of the amount contributed by each spouse, one-half of the value of the property is included in the gross estate of the spouse who dies first. The special rule eliminates the need to trace the source of contributions and recognizes that any inclusion in the gross estate is neutralized by the marital deduction.

**EXAMPLE 45**

In 1992, Hank purchases real estate for $100,000 using his separate funds and listing title as "Hank and Louise, joint tenants with the right of survivorship." Hank predeceases Louise 10 years later when the property is worth $300,000. If Hank and Louise are husband and wife, Hank's gross estate includes $150,000 (½ of $300,000) as to the property. ■

**EXAMPLE 46**

Assume the same facts as in Example 45, except that Louise (instead of Hank) dies first. Presuming the value at the date of death to be $300,000, Louise's gross estate includes $150,000 as to the property. In this regard, it is of no consequence that Louise did not contribute to the cost of the real estate. ■

In both Examples 45 and 46, inclusion in the gross estate of the first spouse to die is neutralized by the unlimited marital deduction allowed for estate tax purposes (see the discussion of § 2056 later in the chapter). Under the right of survivorship, the surviving joint tenant obtains full ownership of the property. The marital deduction generally is allowed for property passing from one spouse to another.

Whether a *gift* results when property is transferred into some form of joint ownership depends on the consideration furnished by each of the contributing parties for the ownership interest acquired.

**EXAMPLE 47**

Brenda and Sarah purchase real estate as tenants in common, each furnishing $400,000 of the $800,000 cost. If each is an equal owner in the property, no gift has occurred. ■

**EXAMPLE 48**

Assume the same facts as in Example 47, except that of the $800,000 purchase price, Brenda furnishes $600,000 and Sarah furnishes only $200,000. If each is an equal owner in the property, Brenda has made a gift to Sarah of $200,000. ■

**EXAMPLE 49**

Martha purchases real estate for $900,000, the title to the property being listed as follows: "Martha, Sylvia, and Dan as joint tenants with the right of survivorship." If under state law the mother (Martha), the daughter (Sylvia), and the son (Dan) are deemed to be equal owners in the property, Martha is treated as having made gifts of $300,000 to Sylvia and $300,000 to Dan. ■

Several important *exceptions* exist to the general rule that gift treatment is triggered by the creation of a joint ownership with disproportionate interests resulting from unequal consideration. First, if the transfer involves a joint bank account, there is no gift at the time of the contribution.[36] If a gift occurs, it is when the noncontributing party withdraws the funds provided by the other joint tenant. Second, the same rule applies to the purchase of U.S. savings bonds. Again, any gift tax consequences are postponed until the noncontributing party appropriates some or all of the proceeds for his or her individual use.

**EXAMPLE 50**

Cynthia deposits $400,000 in a bank account under the names of Cynthia and Carla as joint tenants. Both Cynthia and Carla have the right to withdraw funds from the account without the other's consent. Cynthia has not made a gift to Carla when the account is established. ■

**EXAMPLE 51**

Assume the same facts as in Example 50. At some later date, Carla withdraws $100,000 from the account for her own use. At this point, Cynthia has made a gift to Carla of $100,000. ■

**EXAMPLE 52**

Wesley purchases a U.S. savings bond that he registers in the names of Wesley and Harriet. After Wesley dies, Harriet redeems the bond. No gift takes place when Wesley buys the bond. In addition, Harriet's redemption is not treated as a gift since the bond passed to her by testamentary disposition (Harriet acquired the bond by virtue of surviving Wesley) and not through a lifetime transfer. However, the fair market value of the bond is included in Wesley's gross estate under § 2040. ■

---

**ETHICAL CONSIDERATIONS**

## A Joint Bank Account and a Subsequent Marriage

Horace, a well-to-do widower, wants to marry Fran, his much younger secretary. Fran is agreeable to marriage but would like to achieve some degree of financial independence. Upon advice of his attorney, Horace uses $1.5 million to establish a bank account listing himself and Fran as joint tenants. Horace and Fran are married, and shortly thereafter she withdraws the $1.5 million and places the funds in a new account in her name only.

If the transfer from Horace to Fran took place before their marriage, it generates a Federal gift tax. The position of the IRS is that premarital settlements are gifts because they are not supported by adequate consideration. If the transfer from Horace to Fran took place after marriage, a gift tax is avoided due to the application of the marital deduction.

Has Horace successfully avoided the Federal gift tax?

---

**Powers of Appointment (§§ 2041 and 2514).** A **power of appointment** is a power to determine who shall own or enjoy, at the present or in the future, the property subject to the power. It must be created by another and does not include a power created or retained by the decedent when he or she transferred his or her own property.

Powers of appointment fall into one of two classifications: *general* and *special*. A general power of appointment is one in which the decedent could have appointed himself, his creditors, his estate, or the creditors of his estate. In contrast, a special power enables the holder to appoint to others but *not* to herself, her creditors, her estate, or the creditors of her estate. Assume, for example, that Don has the power

---

[36]Reg. § 25.2511–1(h)(4).

to designate how the principal of the trust will be distributed among Edie, Frank, and Georgia. At this point, Don's power is only a special power of appointment. If Don is given the further right to appoint the principal to himself, what was a special power of appointment becomes a general power.

Three things can happen to a power of appointment: exercise, lapse, and release. Exercising the power involves appointing the property to one or all of the parties designated. A lapse occurs upon failure to exercise a power. Thus, if Don fails to indicate how the principal of a trust will be distributed among Edie, Frank, and Georgia, Don's power of appointment will lapse, and the principal will pass in accordance with the terms of the trust instrument. A release occurs if the holder relinquishes a power of appointment.

Powers of appointment have the following transfer tax consequences.

1. No tax implications result from the exercise, lapse, or release of a special power of appointment.
2. The exercise, lapse, or release of a general power of appointment created after October 21, 1942, during life or upon the death of the holder causes the fair market value of the property (or income interest) subject to the power to be a gift or to be included in the holder's gross estate.
3. In connection with (2), a holder is not considered to have had a general power of appointment if he or she had a right to consume or invade for his or her own benefit, as long as that right is limited by an ascertainable standard. The standard must relate to the holder's health, education, support, or maintenance. A power to use the property for the "comfort, welfare, or happiness" of the holder is not an ascertainable standard and therefore is a general power of appointment.

The following examples illustrate these rules.

**EXAMPLE 53**

Justin, Monica's father, leaves his property in trust, life estate to Monica and remainder to whichever of Monica's children she decides to appoint in her will. Monica's power is not a general power of appointment because she cannot exercise it in favor of herself. Thus, regardless of whether Monica exercises the power or not, none of the trust property subject to the power is included in her gross estate. ■

**EXAMPLE 54**

Assume the same facts as in Example 53. In addition to having the testamentary power to designate the beneficiary of the remainder interest, Monica is given a power to direct the trustee to pay to her from time to time as much of the principal as she might request "for her support." Although Monica now has a power that she can exercise in favor of herself, it is not a general power of appointment. The power is limited to an ascertainable standard. Thus, none of the property subject to these powers is subject to the gift tax or is included in Monica's gross estate at her death. ■

**Life Insurance (§ 2042).**   Under § 2042, the gross estate includes the proceeds of life insurance on the decedent's life if (1) they are receivable by the estate, (2) they are receivable by another for the benefit of the estate, or (3) the decedent possessed an incident of ownership in the policy.

Life insurance on the life of another owned by a decedent at the time of death is included in the gross estate under § 2033 (property in which the decedent had an interest) and not under § 2042. The amount includible is the replacement value of the policy.[37] Under these circumstances, inclusion of the face amount of the policy is inappropriate as the policy has not yet matured.

---

[37]Reg. § 20.2031–8(a)(1).

**EXAMPLE 55**

At the time of his death, Luigi owned a life insurance policy on the life of Benito, face amount of $500,000 and replacement value of $50,000, with Sofia as the designated beneficiary. Since the policy has not matured at Luigi's death, § 2042 is inapplicable. However, § 2033 (property in which the decedent had an interest) compels the inclusion of $50,000 (the replacement value) in Luigi's gross estate. If Luigi and Sofia owned the policy as community property, only $25,000 is included in Luigi's gross estate. ∎

The term *life insurance* includes whole life policies, term insurance, group life insurance, travel and accident insurance, endowment contracts (before being paid up), and death benefits paid by fraternal societies operating under the lodge system.[38]

As just noted, proceeds of insurance on the life of the decedent receivable by the executor or administrator or payable to the decedent's estate are included in the gross estate. The estate need not be specifically named as the beneficiary. Assume, for example, the proceeds of the policy are receivable by an individual beneficiary and are subject to an obligation, legally binding upon the beneficiary, to pay taxes, debts, and other charges enforceable against the estate. The proceeds are included in the decedent's gross estate to the extent of the beneficiary's obligation. If the proceeds of an insurance policy made payable to a decedent's estate are community assets and, under state law, one-half belongs to the surviving spouse, only one-half of the proceeds will be considered as receivable by or for the benefit of the decedent's estate.

Proceeds of insurance on the life of the decedent not receivable by or for the benefit of the estate are includible if the decedent at death possessed any of the incidents of ownership in the policy. In this connection, the term *incidents of ownership* means not only the ownership of the policy in a technical legal sense but also, generally speaking, the right of the insured or his or her estate to the economic benefits of the policy. Thus, it also includes the power to change beneficiaries, revoke an assignment, pledge the policy for a loan, or surrender or cancel the policy.[39]

**EXAMPLE 56**

At the time of death, Broderick was the insured under a policy (face amount of $1 million) owned by Gregory with Demi as the designated beneficiary. Broderick took out the policy five years ago and immediately transferred it as a gift to Gregory. Under the assignment, Broderick transferred all rights in the policy except the right to change beneficiaries. Broderick died without having exercised this right, and the policy proceeds are paid to Demi. Under § 2042(2), Broderick's retention of an incident of ownership in the policy (i.e., the right to change beneficiaries) causes $1 million to be included in his gross estate. ∎

Assuming that the deceased-insured holds the incidents of ownership in a policy, how much is included in the gross estate if the insurance policy is a community asset? Only one-half of the proceeds becomes part of the deceased spouse's gross estate.

In determining whether a policy is *community property* or what portion of it might be so classified, state law controls. The states appear to follow one of two general approaches. Under the inception of title approach, the classification depends on when the policy was originally purchased. If purchased before marriage, the policy is separate property regardless of how many premiums were paid after marriage with community funds. However, if the noninsured spouse is not the

---

[38]Reg. § 20.2042–1(a)(1). As to travel and accident insurance, see *Comm. v. Estate of Noel*, 65–1 USTC ¶12,311, 15 AFTR2d 1397, 85 S.Ct. 1238 (USSC, 1965). As to employer-sponsored group term life insurance, see Example 33 earlier in this chapter.

[39]Reg. § 20.2042–1(c)(2).

beneficiary of the policy, he or she may be entitled to reimbursement from the deceased-insured spouse's estate for half of the premiums paid with community funds. The inception of title approach is followed in at least three states: Louisiana, Texas, and New Mexico.

Some community property jurisdictions classify a policy using the tracing approach: the nature of the funds used to pay premiums controls. Thus, a policy paid for 20 percent with separate funds and 80 percent with community funds is 20 percent separate property and 80 percent community property. The point in time when the policy was purchased makes no difference. Conceivably, a policy purchased after marriage with the premiums paid exclusively from separate funds is classified entirely as separate property. The tracing approach appears to be the rule in California and Washington.

Merely purchasing a life insurance contract with someone else designated as the beneficiary does not constitute a *gift*. As long as the purchaser still owns the policy, nothing has really passed to the beneficiary. Even on the death of the insured-owner, no gift takes place. The proceeds paid to the beneficiary constitute a testamentary and not a lifetime transfer. But consider the following possibility.

**EXAMPLE 57**

Kurt purchases an insurance policy on his own life that he transfers to Olga. Kurt retains no interest in the policy (such as the power to change beneficiaries). In these circumstances, Kurt has made a gift to Olga. Furthermore, if Kurt continues to pay the premiums on the transferred policy, each payment constitutes a separate gift. ■

Under certain conditions, the death of the insured may constitute a gift to the beneficiary of part or all of the proceeds. This occurs when the owner of the policy is not the insured.

**EXAMPLE 58**

Randolph owns an insurance policy on the life of Frank, with Tracy as the designated beneficiary. Up until the time of Frank's death, Randolph retained the right to change the beneficiary of the policy. The proceeds paid to Tracy by the insurance company by reason of Frank's death constitute a gift from Randolph to Tracy.[40] ■

**EXAMPLE 59**

Hubert and Carrie live in a community property state. With community funds, Hubert purchases an insurance policy with a face amount of $1 million on his own life and designates Ann as the revocable beneficiary. On Hubert's death, the proceeds of the policy are paid to Ann. If under state law Hubert's death makes the transfer by Carrie complete, Carrie has made a gift to Ann of $500,000. Since the policy is community property, Carrie is the owner of only one-half of the policy. Furthermore, one-half of the proceeds of the policy ($500,000) is included in Hubert's gross estate under § 2042. ■

**LO.7**

Describe the components of the taxable estate.

## TAXABLE ESTATE

After the gross estate has been determined, the next step is to determine the taxable estate. By virtue of § 2051, the **taxable estate** is the gross estate less the following: expenses, indebtedness, and taxes (§ 2053); losses (§ 2054); charitable transfers (§ 2055); the marital deduction (§§ 2056 and 2056A); and qualified family-owned business interest deduction (§ 2057). As previously noted, the charitable and marital deductions also have gift tax ramifications (§§ 2522 and 2523).

---

[40]*Goodman v. Comm.*, 46–1 USTC ¶10,275, 34 AFTR 1534, 156 F.2d 218 (CA–2, 1946).

**Expenses, Indebtedness, and Taxes (§ 2053).**    A deduction is allowed for funeral expenses; expenses incurred in administering property; claims against the estate; and unpaid mortgages and other charges against property, whose value is included in the gross estate (without reduction for the mortgage or other indebtedness).

Expenses incurred in administering community property are deductible only in proportion to the deceased spouse's interest in the community.[41]

Administration expenses include commissions of the executor or administrator, attorney's fees of the estate, accountant's fees, court costs, and certain selling expenses for disposition of estate property.

Claims against the estate include property taxes accrued before the decedent's death, unpaid income taxes on income received by the decedent before he or she died, and unpaid gift taxes on gifts made by the decedent before death.

Amounts that may be deducted as claims against the estate are only for enforceable personal obligations of the decedent at the time of death. Deductions for claims founded on promises or agreements are limited to the extent that the liabilities were contracted in good faith and for adequate and full consideration. However, a pledge or subscription in favor of a public, charitable, religious, or educational organization is deductible to the extent that it would have constituted an allowable deduction had it been a bequest.[42]

Deductible funeral expenses include the cost of interment, the burial plot or vault, a gravestone, perpetual care of the grave site, and the transportation expense of the person bringing the body to the place of burial. If the decedent had, before death, acquired cemetery lots for him- or herself and family, no deduction is allowed, but the lots are not included in the decedent's gross estate under § 2033 (property in which the decedent had an interest).

**Losses (§ 2054).**    Section 2054 permits an estate tax deduction for losses from casualty or theft incurred during the period when the estate is being settled. As is true with casualty or theft losses for income tax purposes, any anticipated insurance recovery must be taken into account in arriving at the amount of the deductible loss. Unlike the income tax, however, the deduction is not limited by a floor ($100) or a percentage amount (the excess of 10 percent of adjusted gross income). If the casualty occurs to property after it has been distributed to an heir, the loss belongs to the heir and not to the estate. If the casualty occurs before the decedent's death, it should be claimed on the appropriate Form 1040. The fair market value of the property (if any) on the date of death plus any insurance recovery is included in the gross estate.

As is true of certain administration expenses, a casualty or theft loss of estate property can be claimed as an income tax deduction on the fiduciary return of the estate (Form 1041). But a double deduction prohibition applies, and claiming the income tax deduction requires a waiver of the estate tax deduction.[43]

**Transfers to Charity (§§ 2055 and 2522).**    A deduction is allowed for the value of property in the decedent's gross estate that is transferred by the decedent through testamentary disposition to (or for the use of) any of the following.

1. The United States or any of its political subdivisions.
2. Any corporation or association organized and operated exclusively for religious, charitable, scientific, literary, or educational purposes.
3. Various veterans' organizations.

---

[41]*U.S. v. Stapf*, 63–2 USTC ¶12,192, 12 AFTR2d 6326, 84 S.Ct. 248 (USSC, 1963).

[42]§ 2053(c)(1)(A) and Reg. § 20.2053–5.
[43]§ 642(g).

The organizations just described are identical to those that qualify for the Federal gift tax deduction under § 2522. With the following exceptions, they are also the same organizations that qualify a donor for an income tax deduction under § 170.

- Certain nonprofit cemetery associations qualify for income tax but not estate and gift tax purposes.
- Foreign charities may qualify under the estate and gift tax but not under the income tax.

No deduction is allowed unless the charitable bequest is specified by a provision in the decedent's will or the transfer was made before death and the property is subsequently included in the gross estate. Generally speaking, a deduction does not materialize when an individual dies intestate (without a will). The amount of the bequest to charity must be mandatory and cannot be left to someone else's discretion. It is, however, permissible to allow another person—such as the executor of the estate—to choose which charity will receive the specified donation. Likewise, a bequest may be expressed as an alternative and still be effective if the noncharitable beneficiary disclaims (refuses) the intervening interest before the due date for the filing of the estate tax return (nine months after the decedent's death plus any extensions of time granted for filing).

**Marital Deduction (§§ 2056, 2056A, and 2523).**   The **marital deduction** originated with the Revenue Act of 1948 as part of the same legislation that permitted married persons to secure the income-splitting advantages of filing joint income tax returns. The purpose of these statutory changes was to eliminate the major tax variations that existed between taxpayers residing in community property and common law states. The marital deduction was designed to provide equity in the estate and gift tax areas.

In a community property state, for example, no marital deduction generally was allowed, since the surviving spouse already owned one-half of the community and that portion was not included in the deceased spouse's gross estate. In a common law state, however, most if not all of the assets often belonged to the breadwinner of the family. When that spouse died first, all of these assets were included in the gross estate. Recall that a dower or curtesy interest (regarding a surviving spouse's right to some of the deceased spouse's property) does not reduce the gross estate. To equalize the situation, therefore, a marital deduction, usually equal to one-half of all separate assets, was allowed upon the death of the first spouse.

Ultimately, Congress decided to dispense with these historical justifications and recognize husband and wife as a single economic unit. Consistent with the approach taken under the income tax, spouses are considered as one for transfer tax purposes. By making the marital deduction unlimited in amount, neither the gift tax nor the estate tax is imposed on outright interspousal transfers of property. The unlimited marital deduction even includes one spouse's share of the community property transferred to the other spouse.

Under § 2056, the marital deduction is allowed only for property that is included in the deceased spouse's gross estate *and* that passes or has passed to the surviving spouse. In determining whether the parties are legally married, look to state law (see Example 1 earlier). Property that *passes* from the decedent to the surviving spouse includes any interest received as (1) the decedent's heir or donee; (2) the decedent's surviving tenant by the entirety or joint tenant; (3) the appointee under the decedent's exercise (or lapse or release) of a general power of appointment; or (4) the beneficiary of insurance on the life of the decedent.

**EXAMPLE 60**

At the time of his death in the current year, Matthew owned an insurance policy on his own life (face amount of $500,000) with Minerva (his wife) as the designated beneficiary. Matthew and Minerva also owned real estate (worth $600,000) as tenants by the entirety (Matthew had furnished all of the purchase price). As to these transfers, $800,000 ($500,000 + $300,000) is included in Matthew's gross estate, and this amount represents the property that passes to Minerva for purposes of the marital deduction.[44] ■

Disclaimers can affect the amount passing to the surviving spouse. If, for example, the surviving spouse is the remainderperson under the will of the deceased spouse, a disclaimer by another heir increases the amount passing to the surviving spouse. This, in turn, will increase the amount of the marital deduction allowed to the estate of the deceased spouse.

A problem arises when a property interest passing to the surviving spouse is subject to a mortgage or other encumbrance. In this case, only the net value of the interest after reduction by the amount of the mortgage or other encumbrance qualifies for the marital deduction. To allow otherwise results in a double deduction since a decedent's liabilities are separately deductible under § 2053.

**EXAMPLE 61**

In his will, Oscar leaves real estate (fair market value of $500,000) to his wife. If the real estate is subject to a mortgage of $100,000 (upon which Oscar was personally liable), the marital deduction is limited to $400,000 ($500,000 − $100,000). The $100,000 mortgage is deductible under § 2053 as an obligation of the decedent (Oscar). ■

However, if the executor is required under the terms of the decedent's will or under local law to discharge the mortgage out of other assets of the estate or to reimburse the surviving spouse, the payment or reimbursement is an additional interest passing to the surviving spouse.

**EXAMPLE 62**

Assume the same facts as in Example 61, except that Oscar's will directs that the real estate is to pass to his wife free of any liabilities. Accordingly, Oscar's executor pays off the mortgage by using other estate assets and distributes the real estate to Oscar's wife. The marital deduction now becomes $500,000. ■

Federal estate taxes or other death taxes paid out of the surviving spouse's share of the gross estate are not included in the value of property passing to the surviving spouse. Therefore, it is usually preferable for the deceased spouse's will to provide that death taxes be paid out of the portion of the estate that does not qualify for the marital deduction.

Certain interests in property passing from the deceased spouse to the surviving spouse are referred to as **terminable interests.** Such an interest will terminate or fail after the passage of time, upon the happening of some contingency, or upon the failure of some event to occur. Examples are life estates, annuities, estates for terms of years, and patents. A terminable interest will not qualify for the marital deduction if another interest in the same property passed from the deceased spouse to some other person. By reason of the passing, that other person or his or her heirs may enjoy part of the property after the termination of the surviving spouse's interest.[45]

---

[44]Inclusion in the gross estate falls under § 2042 (proceeds of life insurance) and § 2040 (joint interests). Although Matthew provided the full purchase price for the real estate, § 2040(b) requires inclu- sion of only one-half of the value of the property when one spouse predeceases the other.

[45]§§ 2056(b)(1) and 2523(b)(1).

EXAMPLE 63

Vicky's will places her property in trust, life estate to her husband, Brett, remainder to Andrew or his heirs. The interest passing from Vicky to Brett does not qualify for the marital deduction. It will terminate on Brett's death, and Andrew or his heirs will then possess or enjoy the property. ∎

EXAMPLE 64

Assume the same facts as in Example 63, except that Vicky created the trust during her life. No marital deduction is available for gift tax purposes for the same reason as in Example 63.[46] ∎

The justification for the terminable interest rule can be illustrated by examining the possible results of Examples 63 and 64. Without the rule, Vicky could have passed property to Brett at no cost because of the marital deduction. Yet, on Brett's death, none of the property would have been included in his gross estate. Section 2036 (transfers with a retained life estate) would not apply to Brett since he was not the original transferor of the property. The marital deduction should not be available in situations where the surviving spouse can enjoy the property and still pass it to another without tax consequences. The marital deduction merely postpones the transfer tax on the death of the first spouse and operates to shift any such tax to the surviving spouse.

The terminable interest rule can be avoided under a *power of appointment exception*.[47] Under the exception, a property interest passing from the deceased spouse to the surviving spouse qualifies for the marital deduction (and is not considered a terminable interest) if the surviving spouse is granted a general power of appointment over the property. Thus, the exercise, release, or lapse of the power during the survivor's life or at death will be subject to either the gift or the death tax.[48] If Examples 63 and 64 are modified to satisfy this condition, the life estate passing from Vicky to Brett is not a terminable interest and will qualify for the marital deduction.

As previously noted, the purpose of the terminable interest rule is to ensure that property not taxed to the transferor-spouse (due to the marital deduction) will be subject to the gift or estate tax upon disposition by the transferee-spouse.

Consistent with the objective of the terminable interest rule, another exception offers an alternative means for obtaining the marital deduction. Under this provision, the marital deduction is allowed for transfers of **qualified terminable interest property** (commonly referred to as **QTIP**). This is defined as property that passes from one spouse to another by gift or at death and for which the transferee-spouse has a qualifying income interest for life.

For a donee or a surviving spouse, a qualifying income interest for life exists under the following conditions:

- The person is entitled for life to all of the income from the property (or a specific portion of it), payable at annual or more frequent intervals.
- No person (including the spouse) has a power to appoint any part of the property to any person other than the surviving spouse during his or her life.[49]

If these conditions are met, an election can be made to claim a marital deduction as to the QTIP. For estate tax purposes, the executor of the estate makes the election on Form 706 (the Federal estate tax return). For gift tax purposes, the donor spouse

---

[46]Both Examples 63 and 64 contain the potential for a qualified terminable interest property (QTIP) election discussed later in this section.

[47]For the estate tax, see § 2056(b)(5). The gift tax counterpart is in § 2523(e).

[48]§§ 2514 and 2041.

[49]§§ 2523(f) and 2056(b)(7).

makes the election on Form 709 (the Federal gift tax return). The election is irrevocable.

If the election is made, a transfer tax is imposed upon the QTIP when the transferee-spouse disposes of it by gift or upon death. If the disposition occurs during life, the gift tax applies, measured by the fair market value of the property as of that time.[50] If no lifetime disposition takes place, the fair market value of the property on the date of death (or alternate valuation date if applicable) is included in the gross estate of the transferee-spouse.[51]

**EXAMPLE 65**

In 1980, Clyde dies and provides in his will that certain assets (fair market value of $800,000) are to be transferred to a trust under which Gertrude (Clyde's wife) is granted a life estate with the remainder passing to their children upon Gertrude's death. Presuming all of the preceding requirements are satisfied and Clyde's executor so elects, his estate receives a marital deduction of $800,000. ■

**EXAMPLE 66**

Assume the same facts as in Example 65, with the further stipulation that Gertrude dies in 2003 when the trust assets are worth $1.4 million. This amount is included in her gross estate. ■

Because the estate tax is imposed on assets not physically included in the probate estate, the law allows the liability for those assets to be shifted to the heirs. The amount to be shifted is determined by comparing the estate tax liability both with and without the inclusion of the QTIP. This right of recovery can be canceled by a provision in the deceased spouse's will.[52]

The major difference between the power of appointment and the QTIP exceptions to the terminable interest rules relates to the control the surviving spouse has over the principal of the trust. In the power of appointment situation, the surviving spouse can appoint the principal to him- or herself (or to his or her estate). Only if this power is not exercised will the property pass as specified in the deceased spouse's will. In the QTIP situation, however, the surviving spouse has no such control. If the QTIP election is made, the principal must pass as prescribed by the transferor (the donor in the case of a lifetime transfer or the decedent in the case of a death transfer).

In the case of a nonresident alien whose spouse is a U.S. citizen, the marital deduction is allowed for estate and gift tax purposes. Property passing to a surviving spouse who is not a U.S. citizen is not eligible for the estate tax marital deduction.[53] Similarly, no gift tax marital deduction is allowed where the spouse is not a U.S. citizen. However, the annual exclusion for these gift transfers is increased to $112,000 (up from $110,000 in 2002).[54]

For the estate tax, an exception exists for certain transfers to a surviving spouse who is not a U.S. citizen.[55] If the transfer is to a *qualified domestic trust*, the marital deduction is allowed. A qualified domestic trust must meet the following conditions.[56]

- The trust instrument provides that all trustees must be U.S. citizens or domestic corporations.
- The surviving spouse is entitled to all income from the trust payable at least annually.

---

[50] § 2519.
[51] § 2044.
[52] § 2207A(a).
[53] § 2056(d)(1).

[54] § 2523(i).
[55] § 2056(d)(2).
[56] § 2056A.

- The trust must be subject to the estate tax upon the death of the surviving spouse.
- The executor makes an irrevocable election for the trust on the deceased spouse's estate tax return.

The reason for the qualified domestic trust exception is to guarantee that the marital deduction property will not escape estate taxes on the death of the surviving spouse. This would be possible if the property and spouse are outside the jurisdiction of the U.S. tax laws.

**Qualified Family-Owned Business Deduction (§ 2057).**  Originally classified as an exclusion from the gross estate, the predecessor to § 2057 (enacted in 1997 as § 2033A) was converted into a deduction by the IRS Restructuring and Reform Act of 1998. Belatedly, Congress recognized that the exclusion approach contained many flaws and fell short in providing the relief desired for small businesses.

Applicable to the estates of U.S. residents or citizens dying after 1997, the provision allows for a deduction of up to $675,000 for a **qualified family-owned business interest (QFOBI)**.[57] The deduction is available only for estate tax purposes and is not available for the gift tax or the tax on generation skipping transfers.

Unfortunately, the deduction allowed must be coordinated with the exemption equivalent. In no event may a combination of these items exceed $1,300,000.[58]

**EXAMPLE 67**

Bert dies in 2003 when the exclusion amount (exemption equivalent) is $1,000,000 (see Table 17–2 earlier in the chapter). Bert's estate includes $1,200,000 of QFOBI. If his estate elects to claim the maximum deduction of $675,000, the exclusion amount must be reduced to $625,000 to stay within the $1,300,000 limit.  ■

Moreover, the exemption equivalent cannot exceed the amount allowed for that year.

**EXAMPLE 68**

Tracy dies in 2003 when the exclusion amount is $1,000,000. Tracy's estate includes QFOBI of $250,000. If her estate elects to claim the deduction, the exclusion amount is limited to $1,000,000 and not $1,050,000 ($1,300,000 − $250,000).  ■

Because the business deduction is intended to alleviate the need for small businesses to liquidate to pay estate taxes, its provisions are restrictive and very detailed. Although detail leads to complexity, Congress has no intention of allowing this provision to be manipulated so as to permit widespread estate tax avoidance.

The deduction applies only when the value of the QFOBI exceeds 50 percent of the adjusted gross estate.[59] It must be increased by certain gifts of the interest made to family members during the decedent's lifetime.[60] The adjusted gross estate is the gross estate less deductible claims and mortgages under §§ 2053(a)(1) and (2) (see Chapter 18).[61]

The QFOBI can be a sole proprietorship or complete or partial ownership in an entity (i.e., partnership, corporation).

To ensure that the business is truly operated by the decedent (or family), several tests must be satisfied.

---

[57]§ 2057(a)(2). The $675,000 amount is *not* subject to indexation.
[58]§ 2057(a)(3).
[59]§ 2057(e).
[60]§ 2057(b).
[61]§ 2057(c).

- The decedent (or family member) must have owned and materially participated in the business for at least five of the eight years prior to death.
- A qualified heir must materially participate in the business for at least 5 years in an 8-year period during the 10 years following the decedent's death.

For both pre- and post-death purposes, "material participation" is intended to carry the same meaning as it does in satisfying the requirement for electing § 2032A. This provision deals with special use valuation and is discussed in Chapter 18.

"Qualified heir" includes heirs who are family members. The term also includes an active employee of the business if the person held this status for a period of at least 10 years before the decedent's death.

The deduction is intended to keep the business intact for the benefit of the deceased owner's family. Consequently, it is not surprising that the tax savings are taken back (i.e., recaptured) when this objective is compromised. The effect of recapture is to yield an additional estate tax equivalent to the tax that would have resulted had the deduction not been utilized.[62]

Recapture can be triggered by any of the following events.

- The qualified heir ceases to meet the material participation requirements.
- The business is disposed of to outsiders.
- The business is removed from the United States, or the qualified heir loses U.S. citizenship.

Full recapture (100 percent) is required if the disqualifying act occurs during the first six years after the owner's death. Thereafter, the recapture percentage is reduced by 20 percent for each additional year. Thus, the recapture potential disappears if the business continues in the family for more than 10 years.

The deduction is an elective provision. The election is made by the executor of the owner's estate. The election must be accompanied by an agreement executed by the qualifying heirs accepting liability as to recapture consequences, should they take place.

Under the Tax Relief Reconciliation Act of 2001, the QFOBI deduction is repealed for tax years after 2003.

**LO.8**

Determine the Federal estate tax liability.

## COMPUTING THE FEDERAL ESTATE TAX

Once the taxable estate has been determined, post-1976 taxable gifts are added to arrive at the tax base. Note that pre-1977 taxable gifts do not enter into the computation of the tax base.

**EXAMPLE 69**

Joyce dies in 2003, leaving a taxable estate of $1,800,000. During her life, Joyce made taxable gifts as follows: $50,000 in 1975 and $100,000 in 1982. For estate tax purposes, the Federal estate tax base becomes $1,900,000 determined as follows: $1,800,000 (taxable estate) + $100,000 (taxable gift made in 1982). ∎

With the unified transfer tax rate schedule contained in § 2001(c), the tentative tax on the tax base is computed. Using the facts in Example 69, the tentative tax on $1,900,000 is $735,800 [$555,800 + (45% × $400,000)]—see Appendix A, page A–9.

All available estate tax credits are subtracted from the tentative estate tax to arrive at the estate tax (if any) that is due.

---

[62]§ 2057(f).

## ESTATE TAX CREDITS

**Unified Tax Credit (§ 2010).**    Recall from previous discussion of this credit that the amount of the credit allowed depends upon the year of the transfer. Returning to Example 69, the credit allowed on the gift in 1982 was $62,800. Since the exemption equivalent of this amount is $225,000 (refer to Table 17–1), no gift tax was due on the transfer. On Joyce's death in 2003, however, the unified tax credit is $345,800, which is less than the tentative tax of $735,800 (refer to the discussion following Example 69). Disregarding the effect of any other estate tax credits, Joyce's estate owes a tax of $390,000 [$735,800 (tentative tax on a tax base of $1,900,000) – $345,800 (unified tax credit for 2003)].

An adjustment to the unified tax credit is necessary if any portion of the specific exemption was utilized on gifts made after September 8, 1976, and before January 1, 1977. In this regard, refer to Example 5.

**Credit for State Death Taxes (§ 2011).**    The Code allows a limited credit for the amount of any death tax actually paid to any state (or to the District of Columbia) attributable to any property included in the gross estate. Like the credit for foreign death taxes paid, this provision mitigates the harshness of subjecting the same property to multiple death taxes.

The credit allowed is limited to the lesser of the amount of tax actually paid or the amount provided for in a table contained in § 2011(b). (See Appendix A, page A–12.) The table amount is based on the adjusted taxable estate, which for this purpose is the taxable estate less $60,000. No credit is allowed if the adjusted taxable estate is $40,000 or less.

**EXAMPLE 70**    Butch's taxable estate is $98,000, and the state of appropriate jurisdiction imposes a death tax of $1,500 on this amount. Since the adjusted taxable estate is $38,000 ($98,000 – $60,000), none of the $1,500 paid qualifies for the state death tax credit. ■

The Tax Relief Reconciliation Act of 2001 phases out § 2011 starting in 2002 at the rate of 25 percent per year. Thus, the credit allowed is 75 percent for 2002, 50 percent for 2003, and 25 percent for 2004.

**EXAMPLE 71**    Ann's taxable estate is $200,000, and the state of appropriate jurisdiction imposes a death tax of $3,000 on this amount. Because the adjusted taxable estate is $140,000 ($200,000 – $60,000), the table amount limits the death tax credit to $1,200. For 2003, the amount allowed is $600 (50% × $1,200). ■

As Examples 70 and 71 illustrate, the credit allowed by § 2011 may be less than the amount of state death taxes paid. The reverse is possible but usually is not the case. Most states make sure that the minimum tax payable to the jurisdiction is at least equal to the credit allowed by the table. Sometimes this result is accomplished by a soak-up (pickup or sponge) tax superimposed on the regular inheritance tax. Thus, if the regular inheritance tax yields $2,500, but the maximum credit allowed by the table is $3,200, a soak-up tax would impose an additional $700 in state death taxes. In other states, the state death tax liability depends entirely upon the amount allowed for Federal death tax purposes under the table. In the previous illustration, the state death tax would be an automatic $3,200.

**Credit for Tax on Prior Transfers (§ 2013).**    Suppose Nancy owns some property that she passes at death to Lisa. Shortly thereafter, Lisa dies and passes the property to Rita. Assuming both estates are subject to the Federal estate tax, the successive deaths result in a multiple effect. To mitigate the possible multiple

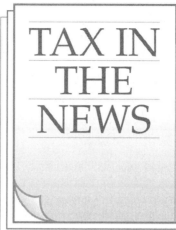

taxation that might result, § 2013 provides relief in the form of a credit for a death tax on prior transfers. In the preceding hypothetical case, Lisa's estate may be able to claim as an estate tax credit some of the taxes paid by Nancy's estate.

The credit is limited to the lesser of the following amounts:

1. The amount of the Federal estate tax attributable to the transferred property in the transferor's estate.
2. The amount of the Federal estate tax attributable to the transferred property in the decedent's estate.

To apply the limitations, certain adjustments must be made that are not covered in this text.[63] However, it is not necessary for the transferred property to be identified in the present decedent's estate or for it to be in existence at the time of the present decedent's death. It is sufficient that the transfer of property was subjected to the Federal estate tax in the estate of the transferor and that the transferor died within the prescribed period of time.

If the transferor dies within two years after or before the present decedent's death, the credit is allowed in full (subject to the preceding limitations). If the transferor died more than two years before the decedent, the credit is a certain percentage: 80 percent if the transferor died within the third or fourth year preceding the decedent's death, 60 percent if within the fifth or sixth year, 40 percent if within the seventh or eighth year, and 20 percent if within the ninth or tenth year.

**EXAMPLE 72**

Under Nancy's will, Lisa inherits property. One year later Lisa dies. Assume the estate tax attributable to the inclusion of the property in Nancy's gross estate was $15,000 and the estate tax attributable to the inclusion of the property in Lisa's gross estate is $12,000. Under these circumstances, Lisa's estate claims a credit against the estate tax of $12,000 (refer to limitation 2). ■

**EXAMPLE 73**

Assume the same facts as in Example 72, except that Lisa dies three years after Nancy. The applicable credit is now 80% of $12,000, or $9,600. ■

**Credit for Foreign Death Taxes (§ 2014).**   A credit is allowed against the estate tax for any estate, inheritance, legacy, or succession tax actually paid to a foreign country. For purposes of this provision, the term *foreign country* means not only

---

[63]See the instructions to Form 706 and Reg. §§ 20.2013–2 and –3.

---

## CONCEPT SUMMARY 17–2

### Federal Estate Tax Provisions

1. The Federal gift and estate taxes are both excise taxes on the transfer of wealth.
2. The starting point for applying the Federal estate tax is to determine which assets are subject to tax. Such assets comprise a decedent's gross estate.
3. The gross estate generally will not include any gifts made by the decedent within three years of death. It does include any gift tax paid on these transfers.
4. Based on the premise that one should not continue to enjoy or control property and not have it subject to the estate tax, certain incomplete transfers are included in the gross estate.
5. Upon the death of a joint tenant, the full value of the property is included in the gross estate unless the survivor(s) made a contribution toward the cost of the property. Spouses are subject to a special rule that calls for automatic inclusion of half of the value of the property in the gross estate of the first tenant to die. The creation of joint ownership is subject to the gift tax when a tenant receives a lesser interest in the property than is warranted by the consideration furnished.
6. A power of appointment is the right to determine who shall own or enjoy, at the present or in the future, the property subject to the power. The exercise, lapse, or release of a general power of appointment during the life of the holder is subject to the gift tax. If the exercise, lapse, or release occurs at death, the property subject to the power is included in the holder's gross estate. If, however, a special power of appointment is involved, no gift or estate tax consequences result.
7. If the decedent is the insured, life insurance proceeds are included in the gross estate if either of two conditions is satisfied. First, the proceeds are paid to the estate or for the benefit of the estate. Second, the decedent possessed incidents of ownership (e.g., the right to change beneficiaries) over the policy.
8. In moving from the gross estate to the taxable estate, certain deductions are allowed. Under § 2053, deductions are permitted for various administration expenses (e.g., executor's commissions, funeral costs), debts of the decedent, and certain unpaid taxes. Casualty and theft losses incurred during the administration of an estate can be deducted in arriving at the taxable estate.
9. Charitable transfers are deductible if the designated organization holds qualified status with the IRS at the time of the gift or upon death.
10. Transfers to a spouse qualify for the gift or estate tax marital deduction. Except as noted in (11), such transfers are subject to the terminable interest limitation.
11. The terminable interest limitation will not apply if the transferee-spouse is given a general power of appointment over the property or the QTIP election is made. In the case of a lifetime transfer, the donor-spouse makes the QTIP election. In the case of a testamentary transfer, the executor of the estate of the deceased spouse has the election responsibility.
12. The tax base for determining the estate tax is the taxable estate plus all post-1976 taxable gifts. All available credits are subtracted from the tax.
13. Of prime importance in the tax credit area is the unified tax credit. Except for large taxable transfers, the unified tax credit varies and depends upon the year of death.
14. Other Federal estate tax credits include credits for state death taxes, tax on prior transfers, and foreign death taxes.
15. If due, a Federal estate tax return (Form 706) must be filed within nine months of the date of the decedent's death.

states in the international sense but also possessions or political subdivisions of foreign states and possessions of the United States.

The credit is allowed for death taxes paid with respect to (1) property situated within the foreign country to which the tax is paid, (2) property included in the decedent's gross estate, and (3) the decedent's estate. No credit is allowed for interest or penalties paid in connection with foreign death taxes.

The credit is limited to the lesser of the following amounts:

1. The amount of the foreign death tax attributable to the property situated in the country imposing the tax and included in the decedent's gross estate for Federal estate tax purposes.
2. The amount of the Federal estate tax attributable to particular property situated in a foreign country, subject to death tax in that country, and included in the decedent's gross estate for Federal estate tax purposes.

Both of these limitations may require certain adjustments to arrive at the amount of the allowable credit. These adjustments are illustrated in the Regulations and are not discussed in this text.[64] In addition to the credit for foreign death taxes under the provisions of Federal estate tax law, similar credits are allowable under death tax conventions with a number of foreign countries.[65] If a credit is allowed under either the provisions of law or the provisions of a convention, the credit that is most beneficial to the estate should be claimed.

### PROCEDURAL MATTERS

A Federal estate tax return, if required, is due nine months after the date of the decedent's death.[66] The time limit applies to all estates regardless of the nationality or residence of the decedent. Not infrequently, an executor will request and obtain from the IRS an extension of time for filing Form 706 (estate tax return).[67] Also available is an *automatic* six-month extension of time to file the estate tax return. To receive the extension, the executor must file Form 4768 [Application for Extension of Time to File a Return and/or Pay U.S. Estate (and Generation-Skipping Transfer) Taxes].

The filing requirements parallel the exclusion amounts of the unified tax credit available for each year (refer to Table 17–1). The filing requirements may be lower when the decedent has made taxable gifts after 1976 or has utilized any of the $30,000 specific gift tax exemption after September 8, 1976.

| EXAMPLE 74 | Carlos dies in 2003, leaving a gross estate of $1,000,000. If Carlos did not make any post-1976 taxable gifts or use the specific gift tax exemption after September 8, 1976, his estate need not file Form 706. ▪ |

| EXAMPLE 75 | Assume the same facts as in Example 74, except that Carlos made a taxable gift of $20,000 in 1980. Since the filing requirement now becomes $980,000 [$1,000,000 (the regular filing requirement for 2003) − $20,000 (the post-1976 taxable gift)], Carlos's estate must file Form 706. ▪ |

**LO.9**

Appreciate the role of the generation skipping transfer tax.

# The Generation Skipping Transfer Tax

In order to prevent partial avoidance of Federal gift and estate taxes on large transfers, the tax law imposes an additional generation skipping transfer tax.

---

[64]Reg. §§ 20.2014–2 and –3.
[65]For the list of countries with which the United States has death tax conventions, refer to Footnote 10.

[66]§ 6075(a).
[67]§ 6081.

## THE PROBLEM

Previously, by structuring the transaction carefully, it was possible to bypass a generation of transfer taxes.

**EXAMPLE 76**

Under his will, Edward creates a trust, life estate to Stephen (Edward's son) and remainder to Ava (Edward's granddaughter) upon Stephen's death. Edward is subject to the Federal estate tax, but no tax results on Stephen's death. Stephen held a life estate, but § 2036 does not apply because he was not the grantor of the trust. Nor does § 2033 (property owned by the decedent) come into play because Stephen's interest disappeared upon his death. The ultimate result is that the property in trust skips a generation of transfer taxes. ∎

**EXAMPLE 77**

Amy gives assets to Eric (her grandson). Called a direct skip, the gift would circumvent any transfer taxes that would have resulted had the assets been channeled through Eric's parents. ∎

## THE SOLUTION

The generation skipping transfer tax (GSTT) is imposed when a younger generation is bypassed in favor of a later generation.[68] The GSTT applies to lifetime transfers by gift and to transfers by death. The tax rate imposed is the highest rate under the gift and estate tax schedule, or 50 percent. Consequently, the GSTT does not permit the use of the graduated rate structure.

The application of the GSTT depends upon the type of arrangement involved. In Example 76, the GSTT would be imposed upon the death of Stephen (the life tenant). The tax, however, is levied against the trust. In effect, it reduces the amount that is distributed to Ava (the remainderperson).

In Example 77, the GSTT is imposed upon Amy when the gift is made to Eric. In this situation, not only will Amy be subject to the GSTT but the amount of the tax represents an additional gift to Eric.[69] Thus, if a gift is a direct skip (such as Example 77), the total transfer tax (the GSTT plus the gift tax) may exceed what the donee receives.

Though the GSTT seemingly yields a confiscatory result, every grantor is entitled to a $1,200,000 exemption.[70] The exemption can be applied to whichever transfers the grantor (or personal representative of the grantor) chooses. Any appreciation attributable to the exempted portion of the transfer is not subject to the GSTT.

**EXAMPLE 78**

Assume the same facts as in Example 76, except that the trust created by Edward contained assets valued at $1,120,000. Ten years later when Stephen dies, the trust is now worth $3 million. If the exemption of $1,120,000 is used upon the creation of the trust, no GSTT results upon Stephen's death. ∎

Under the Tax Relief Reconciliation Act of 2001, after 2003 the GSTT exemption becomes the exclusion amount applicable to the Federal estate tax. Like the estate tax, therefore, the GSTT is scheduled to be phased out by 2010.

**Tax Planning Considerations**

Tax planning for the Federal gift and estate tax is discussed in Chapter 18 in connection with family tax planning.

---

[68]The generation skipping transfer tax provisions are contained in §§ 2601–2663 of the Code.

[69]§ 2515.

[70]Before 1999, the exemption was $1 million and was not indexed for inflation.

## KEY TERMS

| | | |
|---|---|---|
| Alternate valuation date, 17–8 | Joint tenants, 17–9 | Taxable estate, 17–30 |
| Annual exclusion, 17–14 | Marital deduction, 17–32 | Taxable gift, 17–5 |
| Disclaimers, 17–13 | Power of appointment, 17–27 | Tenants by the entirety, 17–9 |
| Exclusion amount, 17–7 | Probate estate, 17–20 | Tenants in common, 17–10 |
| Exemption equivalent, 17–7 | Qualified family-owned business interest (QFOBI), 17–36 | Terminable interests, 17–33 |
| Future interest, 17–14 | | Totten trust, 17–12 |
| Gross estate, 17–20 | Qualified terminable interest property (QTIP), 17–34 | Unified tax credit, 17–6 |
| Inheritance tax, 17–3 | | Unified transfer tax, 17–3 |

## PROBLEM MATERIALS

### Discussion Questions

1. Why can the unified transfer tax be categorized as an excise tax? In this regard, how does it differ from an income tax?

2. Over the years, has congressional tax policy toward estate and gift taxes been consistent? Explain.

3. What are the major differences between the Federal estate tax and the typical inheritance tax levied by some states?

4. In connection with the Federal gift tax, comment on each of the following.
   a. Upon whom it is imposed.
   b. When it is applicable to a nonresident alien.
   c. When it is applicable to property located outside the United States.

**Issue ID**

5. Evita is a citizen and resident of Costa Rica. She has investments in U.S. property consisting of unimproved land in South Carolina and stock in Ford Motor Company held by her Miami brokerage firm. If Evita makes a gift of these assets to her son (also a citizen and resident of Costa Rica), what U.S. tax consequences result?

**Issue ID**

6. To avoid the Federal estate and gift taxes, John, a U.S. citizen, sells his home in Los Angeles and moves to Uruguay. John buys a home in Montevideo where he currently resides. Will John's actions succeed in avoiding Federal estate and gift taxation? Explain.

7. Evaluate the propriety of the following statement: "The Tax Relief Reconciliation Act of 2001 eliminated the Federal estate tax."

8. What is the relationship, if any, between the *unified transfer tax credit*, the *exclusion amount*, and the *exemption equivalent*?

9. What is the justification for the alternate valuation date election?

10. The alternate valuation date cannot be used unless its election decreases the value of the gross estate *and* decreases the estate tax liability. Why are these conditions imposed?

11. What are the similarities between each of the following?
    a. Joint tenancy and tenancy by the entirety.
    b. Tenancy in common and community property.
    c. Tenancy by the entirety and community property.

12. Bertha gives her son a Jaguar automobile on his fortieth birthday. The transfer is not subject to the Federal gift tax because Bertha is satisfying her obligation of support. Do you agree?

Online quizzing @ WFT Interactive Study Center

13. Can a loan between related parties ever carry gift tax ramifications? Explain.

14. Under Leon's will, all of his property is to pass to his son, Jody. Jody is a widower, and his only survivor is a daughter, Brenda. Jody has considerable wealth of his own and is in poor health. Do you recognize an attractive estate tax option for the parties?

15. Section 2503(c) of the Code contains special rules dealing with trusts for minors.
    a. What nontax purpose is served by these trusts for minors?
    b. What is the tax advantage?

16. In connection with the gift-splitting provision of § 2513, comment on the following:
    a. What it was designed to accomplish.
    b. How the election is made.
    c. Its utility in a community property jurisdiction.

17. In connection with the filing of a Federal gift tax return, comment on the following:
    a. No Federal gift tax is due.
    b. The § 2513 election to split gifts is to be used.
    c. A gift of a future interest is involved.
    d. The donor uses a fiscal year for Federal income tax purposes.
    e. The donor obtained from the IRS an extension of time for filing his or her Federal income tax return.

18. Distinguish between the following:
    a. The gross estate and the taxable estate.
    b. The gross estate and the probate estate.

19. Discuss the estate tax treatment of the following items:
    a. A dower interest claimed by the surviving spouse of the decedent.
    b. A dividend that has been declared but not paid on stock owned by the decedent.
    c. Interest accrued but unpaid on city bonds owned by the decedent.
    d. A note receivable due from a relative but forgiven in the decedent's will.

20. In what situations does § 2035 cause inclusion in the gross estate of a donor/decedent?

21. At the time of Emile's death, he was a joint tenant with Colette in a parcel of real estate. With regard to the inclusion in Emile's gross estate under § 2040, comment on the following independent assumptions:
    a. Emile and Colette received the property as a gift from Douglas.
    b. Colette provided all of the purchase price of the property.
    c. Colette's contribution was received as a gift from Emile.
    d. Emile's contribution was derived from income generated by property he received as a gift from Colette.

22. With regard to "life insurance," comment on the following.
    a. What the term includes (i.e., types of policies).
    b. The meaning of "incidents of ownership."
    c. When a gift occurs upon maturity of the policy.
    d. When § 2033 (property in which the decedent had an interest) can apply as to a policy.

23. At the time of death, the decedent owned real estate that was subject to a mortgage.
    a. How does the mortgage affect the taxable estate?
    b. Can the mortgage affect the amount of any marital deduction allowed? Explain.
    c. Can the mortgage affect the amount of any charitable deduction allowed? Explain.

24. A qualified charity for estate and gift tax purposes is the same as one for Federal income tax purposes. Do you agree with this statement?

25. In terms of the QTIP (qualified terminable interest property) election, comment on the following:
    a. Who makes the election.
    b. What the election accomplishes.
    c. The tax effect of the election upon the death of the surviving spouse.

26. Tim and Ann are husband and wife. Tim dies first. Discuss the marital deduction result for each of the following situations.
    a. In his will, Tim exercised a special power of appointment in favor of Ann.
    b. Tim and Ann owned land (that Ann had purchased) as tenants in the entirety.
    c. Ann is the owner and beneficiary of a policy on Tim's life.
    d. Ann is the designated beneficiary of IRAs held by Tim.

27. a. What is the reason for the recapture feature of the $675,000 deduction for small business?
    b. When does the recapture take place, and how much is recaptured?
    c. Who is responsible for the additional estate tax liability that results?

28. What effect, if any, might the phaseout of § 2011 have on the revenue receipts of some states?

**Issue ID**

29. Would the credit for tax on prior transfers (§ 2013) ever apply in the husband and wife-type of situation? Explain.

30. Did the Tax Relief Reconciliation Act of 2001 have any impact on the GSTT provisions? Explain.

31. Which of the following provisions are scheduled to be indexed for inflation?
    a. The annual exclusion.
    b. The unified transfer tax rate schedules.
    c. The unified tax credit.
    d. The $675,000 deduction for small business.
    e. The generation skipping transfer tax exemption.

## Problems

32. An estate holds the following assets.

| | Fair Market Value | |
| --- | --- | --- |
| | On Date of Death | Six Months Later |
| Land | $1,100,000 | $1,150,000 |
| Stock in Oriole Corporation | 900,000 | 700,000 |
| Stock in Kingfisher Corporation | 800,000 | 750,000 |

The executor of the estate sells the Oriole stock for $710,000 three months after the decedent's death and sells the Kingfisher stock for $760,000 seven months after the decedent's death. Death occurred in January 2003.
    a. If the § 2032 election is made, how much is included in the gross estate?
    b. Would your answer to part (a) change if the Oriole stock was not sold but, instead, was distributed to an heir in satisfaction of a bequest in the decedent's will? Explain.
    c. What value should be included in the gross estate if the § 2032 election is not made?

33. In which, if any, of the following independent situations could the alternate valuation date *not be* elected in 2003? In all cases, Rudy and Ashley are husband and wife, and Rudy dies first.
    a. Rudy's will passes all of his property to Ashley.
    b. Rudy's will passes one-half of his property to Ashley and the other half to the city of Boise, Idaho.
    c. The election would decrease the estate tax liability but increase the value of the gross estate.
    d. Rudy's gross estate is $995,000.
    e. Rudy's gross estate is $995,000. Rudy made a taxable gift of $20,000 four years ago.

34. In each of the following independent situations, indicate whether the transfer by Phillip is, or could be, subject to the Federal gift tax.

    a. Phillip makes a contribution to an influential political figure.

    b. Phillip makes a contribution to Crow Corporation, of which he is not a shareholder.

    c. In consideration of his upcoming marriage to Teri, Phillip establishes a savings account in Teri's name.

    d. Same as (c). After their marriage, Phillip establishes a joint checking account in the names of "Phillip and Teri."

    e. Same as (d). One year after the checking account is established, Teri withdraws all of the funds.

    f. Phillip exercises a special power of appointment in favor of Teri.

    g. Phillip enters into an agreement with Teri whereby he will transfer property to her in full satisfaction of her marital rights. One month after the agreement, the transfer occurs. Later Phillip and Teri are divorced.

    h. Phillip purchases U.S. savings bonds, listing ownership as "Phillip and Teri." Several years later, and after Phillip's death, Teri redeems the bonds.

35. In each of the following independent situations, indicate whether the transfer by Jeff is, or could be, subject to the Federal gift tax.

    a. Jeff purchases real estate and lists title as "Jeff and Chris as joint tenants." Jeff and Chris are brothers.

    b. Same as (a), except that Jeff and Chris are husband and wife.

    c. Jeff creates a revocable trust with Chris as the designated beneficiary.

    d. Same as (c). One year after creating the trust, Jeff releases all power to revoke the trust.

    e. Jeff takes out an insurance policy on his life, designating Chris as the beneficiary.

    f. Same as (e). Two years later, Jeff dies and the policy proceeds are paid to Chris.

    g. Jeff takes out an insurance policy on the life of Gretchen and designates Chris as the beneficiary. Shortly thereafter, Gretchen dies and the policy proceeds are paid to Chris.

    h. Jeff pays for Chris's college tuition.

36. In March 2001, Chester and Louise enter into a property settlement under which Chester agrees to pay $900,000 to Louise in return for the release of her marital rights. The payment is to be made in three annual installments of $300,000 each, commencing in 2001. The parties are divorced in 2002, but Chester dies in 2003 before the third and last installment can be made. In January 2004, Chester's executor pays Louise the $300,000 balance due. Discuss the transfer tax consequences of these transactions.

37. Jesse dies intestate (i.e., without a will) in May 2002. Jesse's major asset is a tract of land. Under applicable state law, Jesse's property will pass to Lorena, who is his only child. In December 2002, Lorena disclaims one-half of the property. In June 2003, Lorena disclaims the other half interest. Under state law, Lorena's disclaimer results in the property passing to Arnold (Lorena's only child). The value of the land (in its entirety) is as follows: $2 million in May 2002; $2.1 million in December 2002; and $2.2 million in June 2003. Discuss the transfer tax ramifications of these transactions.

38. In 2003, Marsha makes a gift of stock (fair market value of $1.2 million) to her adult daughter. Marsha has never made any prior taxable gifts. Marsha's husband, Paul, previously made a taxable gift of $500,000 in early 1976 on which he paid a gift tax of $109,275. At the time of the gift, Paul was not married to Marsha.

    a. Determine the amount of the gift tax on the 2003 transfer if the § 2513 election is not made.

    b. If the § 2513 election is made.

39. When Pat died on August 4, 2003, she owned the following property.

| | Fair Market Value |
| --- | --- |
| Stock in Maroon Corporation | $1,100,000 |
| Stock in Crimson Corporation | 800,000 |
| City of Davenport Bonds | 500,000 |

Maroon Corporation and Crimson Corporation each declared a cash dividend on July 1, 2003. The Maroon dividend was payable to shareholders of record as of August 1, 2003, while the Crimson dividend used a record date of August 5.

In early September 2003, Pat's executor received the following amounts: Maroon dividend of $8,800, Crimson dividend of $7,200, and interest of $6,250 ($250 accrued since August 4) on City of Davenport bonds. As to these items, how much is included in Pat's gross estate?

40. Curt dies in late 2003. Previously, he was involved in the following transfers.

    • Using marketable securities, in 1990 Curt created a revocable trust naming his wife as the beneficiary. In early 2003, when the securities are worth $900,000, Curt relinquishes the power to revoke the trust.

    • In 2001, Curt made a gift to his daughter of an insurance policy on his life. The policy has a maturity value of $80,000.

    • In 2002, Curt made a gift to his son of stock worth $340,000. The transfer resulted in a gift tax of $35,000. The stock is worth $290,000 on the date of Curt's death.

    • In 1999, Curt paid off the mortgage on his mother's personal residence. The payment resulted in a gift tax of $12,000.

    As to these transactions, how much is included in Curt's gross estate?

**Decision Making**

41. In 1976, Irma created a revocable trust with securities worth $300,000. National Trust Company was designated as the trustee. Under the terms of the trust, Irma retained a life estate with remainder to her children. In 2001, Irma releases her right to revoke the trust. Irma dies in 2003 when the trust assets have a fair market value of $1.2 million.
    a. What, if any, are Irma's gift tax consequences in 1976?
    b. What, if any, is included in Irma's gross estate in 2003?
    c. Would your answer to (b) change if Irma *also* released her life estate in 2001? Explain.

42. In 1996, Felix and Zoe purchased a commercial single-premium annuity. Felix furnished 70% of the cost, and Zoe provided 30%. Under the terms of the policy, Felix is to receive $120,000 per year for his life. If Felix predeceases Zoe, she is to receive $90,000 per year for her life.
    a. If Felix dies in 2003 when the survivorship feature is worth $800,000, how much, if any, is included in his gross estate?
    b. What is included in Zoe's estate when she dies after Felix?

43. In 1980, Darcy purchased real estate for $600,000, listing title as "Darcy and Kirk, equal tenants in common." Darcy predeceases Kirk in 2003 when the property is worth $1.2 million. Darcy and Kirk are mother and son.
    a. Are there any gift tax consequences in 1980?
    b. Are there any estate tax consequences in 2003?
    c. Would the answers to (a) and (b) change if Darcy and Kirk were wife and husband (not mother and son)? Explain.

44. In 1990, Bertha purchased an office building for $1.2 million listing title as "Bertha and Barney, joint tenants with the right of survivorship." In the same year, as a wedding present to Barney and his new wife, Teri, Bertha gives them her former home (worth $600,000). Title to the home is recorded as "Barney and Teri, tenants by the entirety with the right of survivorship." In 2003, Barney is killed in a skiing accident and is survived by his mother (Bertha) and wife (Teri). If at the time of Barney's death the office building has a value of $1.5 million and the residence is worth $900,000, what is included in his gross estate as to these properties? Did any gift tax consequences ensue in 1990?

45. In 1991, Gabe purchased realty for $1.4 million and listed title to the property as "Gabe and Nelda, joint tenants with right of survivorship." Nelda predeceases Gabe in 2003 when the realty is worth $2 million. Gabe and Nelda are brother and sister.
    a. What, if any, are the gift tax consequences in 1991?
    b. What, if any, are the estate tax consequences in 2003?

46. Assume the same facts as in Problem 45, except that Gabe and Nelda are husband and wife.
    a. What, if any, are the gift tax consequences in 1991?
    b. What, if any, are the estate tax consequences in 2003?

**Decision Making**

**Communications**

47. Mike Edwards would like to make a lifetime transfer in trust of $1 million to his son, Keith, and accomplish the following objectives.

    • Avoid any death tax on the deaths of Mike, Keith, and Bette (Keith's wife).

    • Give Keith the right to determine what portion of the remainder should be allocated between Bette and their children.

    • Give Keith some additional security by allowing him to reach the principal should the need materialize.

    • Prevent Keith from squandering all of the principal to the detriment of Bette or her children.

    Write a letter to Mike recommending a course of action. Mike's address is 4320 Richmond Avenue, Syracuse, NY 13244.

48. In each of the following independent situations, determine how much, if any, should be included in Eric's gross estate.
    a. Hope, Eric's wife, owns a policy on Eric's life (maturity value of $200,000). Upon Eric's death, the proceeds are paid to Ward, Hope's son, who is the designated beneficiary.
    b. Eric owns a policy on Hope's life (maturity value of $200,000 and current value of $40,000) with Ward, Eric's son, as the designated beneficiary.
    c. Assume the same facts as in (b) except that Eric's estate (not Ward) is the designated beneficiary.
    d. Upon Eric's death, Ward collected $200,000 on a policy he owned on Eric's life. The policy was originally taken out by Eric and was given by him to Ward two years ago.

49. Prior to his marriage to Camille, Terrence purchased an insurance policy on his life (maturity value of $200,000) with his mother as the designated beneficiary. Ten years later, Terrence predeceases Camille, and the policy proceeds are paid to his mother. Premiums paid on the policy originated 60% from Terrence's separate property and 40% from community funds. Discuss the tax consequences of this situation if all parties live in:
    a. California.
    b. Texas.

50. Comment on how each of the following independent situations should be handled for estate tax purposes.
    a. At the time of his death, $18,000 of Homer's church pledge was unpaid. Homer's executor paid the pledge during the administration of the estate.
    b. At the time of her death, Saleha (a widow) owned 10 cemetery lots (each worth $5,000), which she had purchased many years before for herself and her family.
    c. At the time of his death, Stanley was delinquent in the payment of back Federal income taxes. Stanley's executor pays the taxes from assets of the estate.

51. At the time of his death in the current year, Jerome owned the following real estate.

| | |
|---|---|
| Tract A | $1,000,000 |
| Mortgage on tract A | (200,000) |
| Tract B | 700,000 |
| Mortgage on tract B | (100,000) |

Under Jerome's will, both tracts of land pass to Janice (Jerome's surviving spouse). However, Jerome's will directs the executor to pay off the mortgage on tract B from the remainder interest passing to the children.

a. How much marital deduction will Jerome's estate be allowed?

b. What is the deduction for indebtedness under § 2053?

52. In 1985, Brad places in trust $500,000 worth of securities. Under the terms of the trust instrument, Wanda (Brad's wife) is granted a life estate, and on Wanda's death, the remainder interest passes to Brad and Wanda's children (as Wanda determines in her will). Upon Wanda's death in 2003, the trust assets are valued at $2 million.

a. How much, if any, marital deduction will be allowed on the gift made in 1985?

b. How much, if any, of the trust will be included in Wanda's gross estate upon her death?

53. Assume the same facts as in Problem 52, except that Brad made the QTIP election when the trust was created. Further assume that Wanda has no choice as to which of her children will receive the remainder interest upon her death.

a. How much, if any, marital deduction will be allowed on the gift made in 1985?

b. How much, if any, of the trust will be subject to the Federal estate tax upon Wanda's later death?

54. In each of the following independent situations, determine the exclusion amount that is available.

| Decedent | Year of Death | QFOBI Election |
|---|---|---|
| Sam | 1999 | $675,000 |
| Helen | 2003 | 600,000 |
| Art | 2000 | 500,000 |

55. Determine the state death tax credit that will be allowed under § 2011 in each of the following independent situations. All deaths occur in 2003.

a. The taxable estate is $90,000. The state death tax paid is $2,000.

b. The adjusted taxable estate is $840,000. The state death tax paid is $32,000.

c. The adjusted taxable estate is $1,040,000. The state death tax paid is $18,500.

d. The adjusted taxable estate is $900,000. The state death tax is a soak-up (sponge) tax that is paid.

56. Under Martina's will, Paige (Martina's sister) inherits property. Three years later Paige dies. Determine Paige's credit for tax on prior transfers based on the following assumptions.

a. The estate tax attributable to the inclusion of the property in Martina's gross estate is $400,000, and the estate tax attributable to the inclusion of the property in Paige's gross estate is $480,000.

b. The estate tax attributable to the inclusion of the property in Martina's gross estate is $500,000, and the estate tax attributable to the inclusion of the property in Paige's gross estate is $450,000.

57. In each of the following independent situations, determine the decedent's final estate tax liability (net of any unified tax credit).

| | Decedent | | | |
|---|---|---|---|---|
| | Meg | Caleb | Lily | Buzz |
| Year of death | 1998 | 1999 | 2000 | 2003 |
| Taxable estate | $600,000 | $900,000 | $1,000,000 | $ 900,000 |
| Post-1976 taxable gifts— | | | | |
| Made in 1985 | 500,000 | — | — | — |
| Made in 1987 | — | 700,000 | — | — |
| Made in 1999 | — | — | 800,000 | — |
| Made in 2002 | — | — | — | 1,000,000 |

> See Appendix F for Comprehensive Tax Return Problems—
> Form 706 and Form 709.

## Research Problems

A THOMSON COMPANY

*Note: Solutions to Research Problems can be prepared by using the **RIA Checkpoint® Student Edition** online research product, or the **CCH U.S. Master Tax Guide Plus™** online Federal tax research database, which is available to accompany this text. It is also possible to prepare solutions to the Research Problems by using tax research materials found in a standard tax library.*

**Research Problem 1.**   In 2001, Carol, a widow, makes substantial gifts of marketable securities (stocks and bonds) to her adult children (Peter and Susan). As a result of these transfers, Carol incurs and pays a Federal gift tax of $4 million. Carol dies in 2003 leaving an estate of inconsequential value. Carol's executor files a Form 706 for her estate reflecting a gross estate of slightly in excess of $4 million. The estate tax of $1.8 million that is attributable to the $4 million is not paid as the estate has no available funds.

Upon investigation by the IRS, the $1.8 million estate tax shortfall is assessed against Peter and Susan under the rules pertaining to transferee liability. Are Peter and Susan liable for the estate tax? Why or why not?

*Partial list of research aids:*
§§ 2035(c), (d)(3)(C), and 6324(a).

**Research Problem 2.**   Florence Thomas, a 74-year-old widow, died on January 4, 2003, from heart failure. After suffering a mild stroke around Christmas of the prior year, Florence decided to do some of the planning she had been postponing.

On December 29, 2002, Florence drew up 16 checks on an account she had at Union National Bank. The first 15 were in the amount of $11,000 each and were made out to immediate family members (sons, daughters, grandchildren). The sixteenth check was for $50,000 and was made payable to St. Alban's Episcopal Church. All 16 checks were mailed to the payees on the same day as written (i.e., December 29, 2002).

Discuss the Federal income, gift, and estate tax ramifications of the transfers made by Florence.

*Partial list of research aids:*
§§ 102, 170, 2031, 2033, and 2503(b).
Reg. §§ 20.2031–5 and 25.2511–2(b).
*Estate of Spiegel,* 12 T.C. 524 (1949).
*Estate of Belcher,* 83 T.C. 227 (1984).
*Estate of Gagliardi,* 89 T.C. 1207 (1987).
*Estate of Metzger,* 100 T.C. 204 (1993), *aff'd* 94–2 USTC ¶60,179, 74 AFTR2d 94–7486, 38 F.3d 118 (CA–4, 1994).
*Estate of Sarah H. Newman,* 111 T.C. 81 (1998).

**Research Problem 3.**   In 1996, Anne, a 70-year-old widow, creates an irrevocable trust naming her five adult grandchildren as the beneficiaries. The assets transferred in trust consist of marketable securities (worth $600,000) and Anne's personal residence (worth $390,000). Bill, Anne's younger brother and a practicing attorney, is designated as the trustee. Other provisions of the trust are noted below.

- Bill is given the discretion to distribute the income of the trust to the beneficiaries based upon their need or to add it to corpus. He also is granted the power to terminate the trust, liquidate its assets, and distribute the proceeds to the beneficiaries.

- The trust is to last for Anne's lifetime or, if sooner, until termination by Bill.

- Upon the termination of the trust, the principal and any accumulated income are to be distributed to the beneficiaries (i.e., Anne's grandchildren).

For 1996, Anne filed a Form 709 to report the transfers in trust and paid the Federal gift tax.

After its transfer in trust and up to the time of her death, Anne continued to occupy the residence. Although she paid no rent, she maintained the property, making all necessary repairs and paying the annual property taxes. Anne never discussed the matter of her continued occupancy of the residence with either Bill or the beneficiaries of the trust.

During the existence of the trust, Bill made no distributions to the beneficiaries. All trust income was accumulated and added to corpus.

On Anne's death in 2003, the value of the trust is $1,620,000, broken down as follows: marketable securities and cash ($1,080,000) and personal residence ($540,000). Shortly thereafter, Bill liquidates the trust and distributes the proceeds to the beneficiaries.

What are the estate tax consequences of these transactions to Anne?

*Partial list of research aids:*
§ 2036.
*Guynn v. U.S.,* 71–1 USTC ¶12,742, 27 AFTR2d 71–1653, 437 F.2d 1148 (CA–4, 1971).
*Estate of Eleanor T. R. Trotter,* 82 TCM 633, T.C.Memo. 2001–250.

**Research Problem 4.**   In 1996, John Letts dies and is survived by his widow (Mildred) and two adult children. Under the terms of his will, most of his property passes to a trust, life estate to Mildred, remainder to their children. John designated Mildred and their children as executors of his estate.

The executors filed a Form 706 that reflected no taxes due because of the allowance of the marital deduction. On page 2 of Form 706, the executors indicated that the QTIP election of § 2056(b)(7) *was not* being made. John Letts's Form 706 was timely filed but never audited by the IRS.

In 2002, Mildred dies, and her will names her children as executors. Mildred's estate includes none of the trust created by John, as the QTIP election was not made. Mildred's life estate is not subject to inclusion under § 2036(a)(2), as she was not the grantor of the trust. The parties admit that John's estate should not have claimed a marital deduction, as what passed to Mildred was a terminable interest. The error, inadvertent as it was, cannot be corrected since the statute of limitations precludes filing an amended Form 706 for John Letts's estate.

Does the IRS have any recourse?

*Partial list of research aids:*
§ 2044.
*Barry S. Glass,* 87 T.C. 1087 (1986).
*Estate of Mildred Geraldine Letts,* 109 T.C. 290 (1997).

**Internet Activity**

*Use the tax resources of the Internet to address the following questions. Do not restrict your search to the World Wide Web, but include a review of newsgroups and general reference materials, practitioner sites and resources, primary sources of the tax law, chat rooms and discussion groups, and other opportunities.*

**Research Problem 5.**   The ultimate design of the Tax Relief Reconciliation Act of 2001 is to repeal the estate tax but retain the gift tax. While the Act and accompanying Conference Committee Report are silent as to why Congress intended this result, it was based on concerns raised by several legal commentators. Using the Internet, locate and comment on one (or more) of these commentaries.

**Research Problem 6.**   Find a calculator on the World Wide Web that will estimate the Federal estate or gift tax liability. Use this device to check your answer to one of the problems that you have completed in this chapter.

**Research Problem 7.**   Plenty of tax advice about § 529 plans can be found on the Web. Do these articles address related Federal estate tax consequences? What do they recommend in this regard to potential donors?

# Family Tax Planning

CHAPTER

18

*After completing Chapter 18, you should be able to:*

### LO.1
Use various established concepts in carrying out the valuation process.

### LO.2
Apply the special use valuation method in appropriate situations.

### LO.3
Identify problems involved in valuing an interest in a closely held business.

### LO.4
Compare the income tax basis rules applying to property received by gift and by death.

### LO.5
Plan gifts so as to minimize gift taxes and avoid estate taxes.

### LO.6
Make gifts so as to avoid income taxes for the donor.

### LO.7
Reduce probate costs in the administration of an estate.

### LO.8
Apply procedures that reduce estate tax consequences.

### LO.9
Obtain liquidity for an estate.

**B**roadly speaking, *family tax planning* involves the use of various procedures that minimize the effect of taxation on transfers within the family unit. As such, planning involves a consideration not only of transfer taxes (i.e., gift and estate) but also of the income tax ramifications to both the transferor (i.e., donor or decedent) and the transferees (i.e., donees or heirs).

The valuation of the transferred property also is an essential element of family tax planning. The gift tax is based on the fair market value of the property on the date of the transfer. For the Federal estate tax, the fair market value on the date of the owner's death or the alternate valuation date (if available and elected) controls.

**LO.1**

Use various established concepts in carrying out the valuation process.

# Valuation Concepts

The central focus of this chapter concerns the valuation of property involved in transfers by gift and by death.

## VALUATION IN GENERAL

The Internal Revenue Code refers to "value" and "fair market value," but does not discuss these terms at length.[1] Section 2031(b) comes closest to a definition when it treats the problem of stocks and securities for which no sales price information (the usual case with closely held corporations) is available. In such situations, "the value thereof shall be determined by taking into consideration, in addition to all other factors, the value of stock or securities of corporations engaged in the same or similar line of business which are listed on an exchange."

Regulation § 20.2031–1(b) is more specific in defining fair market value as "the price at which property would change hands between a willing buyer and a willing seller, neither being under any compulsion to buy or to sell and both having reasonable knowledge of relevant facts." The same Regulation makes clear that the fair market value of an item of property is not determined by a forced sale price.

---

[1]See, for example, §§ 1001(b), 2031(a), and 2512(a). Sections 2032A(e)(7) and (8) set forth certain procedures for valuing farms and interests in closely held businesses.

Nor is the fair market value determined by the sale price of the item in a market other than that in which the item is most commonly sold to the public. Sentiment should not play a part in the determination of value. Suppose, for example, the decedent's daughter is willing to pay $500 for a portrait of her mother. If the painting is really worth $200 (i.e., what the general public would pay), then that should be its value.

The item's location must also be considered. Thus, the fair market value of property that generally is obtained by the public in a retail market is the price at which the property (or comparable items) would be sold at retail.

**EXAMPLE 1**

At the time of his death, Don owned three automobiles. The automobiles are included in Don's gross estate at their fair market value on the date of his death or on the alternate valuation date (if elected). The fair market value of the automobiles is determined by looking at the price a member of the general public would pay for automobiles of approximately the same description, make, model, age, condition, etc. The price a dealer in used cars would pay for these automobiles is inappropriate, because an automobile is an item obtainable by the public in a retail market. ■

If tangible personalty is sold as a result of an advertisement in the classified section of a newspaper and the property is of a type often sold in this manner, or if the property is sold at a public auction, the price for which it is sold is presumed to be the retail sales price of the item at the time of the sale. The retail sales price is also used if the sale is made within a reasonable period following the valuation date, and market conditions affecting the value of similar items have not changed substantially.[2] Tangible personalty includes all property except real estate and intangible property.

## VALUATION OF SPECIFIC ASSETS

**Stocks and Bonds.**   If there is a market for stocks and bonds on a stock exchange, in an over-the-counter market, or otherwise, the mean between the highest and lowest quoted selling prices on the valuation date is the fair market value per unit. A special rule applies if no sales occurred on the valuation date but did occur on dates within a reasonable period before and after the valuation date. The fair market value is the weighted average of the means between the highest and the lowest sales prices on the nearest date before and the nearest date after the valuation date. The average is weighted *inversely* by the respective number of trading days between the selling dates and the valuation date.[3]

**EXAMPLE 2**

Carla makes a gift to Antonio of shares of stock in Green Corporation. The transactions involving this stock that occurred closest to the date of the gift took place two trading days before the date of the gift at a mean selling price of $10 and three trading days after the gift at a mean selling price of $15. The $12 fair market value of each share of Green stock is determined as follows.

$$\frac{(3 \times \$10) + (2 \times \$15)}{5} = \$12$$

■

If no transactions occurred within a reasonable period before and after the valuation date, the fair market value is determined by taking a weighted average of the means between the bona fide bid and asked prices on the nearest trading

---

[2]Rev.Proc. 65–19, 1965–2 C.B. 1002.

[3]Reg. §§ 20.2031–2(b) and 25.2512–2(b).

dates before and after the valuation date. However, both dates must be within a reasonable period of time.

If no actual sales prices or bona fide bid and asked prices are available for dates within a reasonable period relative to the valuation date, the mean between the highest and lowest available sales prices or bid and asked prices on that date may be taken as the value.

In many instances, there are no established market prices for securities. This lack of information is typically the case with stock in closely held corporations. Problems unique to valuing interests in closely held businesses are discussed later in this chapter.

**Notes Receivable.**   The fair market value of notes, secured or unsecured, is the amount of unpaid principal plus interest accrued to the valuation date, unless the parties (e.g., executor, donor) establish a lower value or prove the notes are worthless. Factors such as a low interest rate and a distant maturity date are relevant in showing that a note is worth less than its face amount. Crucial elements in proving that a note is entirely or partially worthless are the financial condition of the borrower and the absence of any value for the property pledged or mortgaged as security for the obligation.[4]

**EXAMPLE 3**

At the time of his death, Ira held a note (face amount of $50,000) issued by his son, Kevin. Although Kevin is solvent, he is relieved of the obligation because Ira forgives the note in his will. Presuming the note is payable on demand, it is included in Ira's gross estate at $50,000 plus accrued interest. If the note is not due immediately and/or the interest provided for is under the current rate, a discount may be in order, and the fair market value of the note would be less than $50,000. The burden of proof in supporting a discount for the note is on the executor. ■

**Insurance Policies and Annuity Contracts.**   The value of a life insurance policy on the life of a person other than the decedent, or the value of an annuity contract issued by a company regularly engaged in selling annuities, is the cost of a comparable contract.[5]

**EXAMPLE 4**

Paul purchased a joint and survivor annuity contract from an insurance company (i.e., a commercial contract). Under the contract's terms, Paul is to receive payments of $120,000 per year for his life. Upon Paul's death, his wife (Kate) is to receive $90,000 annually for her life. Ten years after purchasing the annuity, when Kate is 40 years old, Paul dies. The value of the annuity contract on the date of Paul's death [and the amount includible in Paul's gross estate under § 2039(a)] is the amount the insurance company would charge in the year of Paul's death for an annuity that would pay $90,000 annually for the life of a female 40 years of age. ■

**EXAMPLE 5**

At the time of her death, Lana owns an insurance policy (face amount of $500,000) on the life of her son, Sam. No further payments need be made on the policy (e.g., it is a single premium policy or a paid-up policy). The value of the policy on the date of Lana's death (and the amount includible in her gross estate under § 2033 as property owned by the decedent) is the amount the insurance company would charge in the year of her death for a single premium contract (face amount of $500,000) on the life of someone Sam's age. ■

Determining the value of an insurance policy by using the amount charged for a comparable policy is more difficult when, on the date of valuation, the contract

---

[4]Reg. §§ 20.2031–4 and 25.2512–4.    [5]Reg. §§ 20.2031–8(a)(1) and 25.2512–6(a).

has been in force for some time and further premium payments are to be made. In such a case, the value may be approximated by adding to the interpolated terminal reserve the proportionate part of the gross premium last paid before the valuation date that covers the period extending beyond that date.[6]

The valuation of annuities issued by parties *not regularly engaged in the sale of annuities* (i.e., noncommercial contracts) requires the use of special tables issued by the IRS.

**Life Estates, Terms for Years, Reversions, and Remainders.**    As with noncommercial annuities, the valuation of life estates, income interests for a term of years, reversions, and remainders involves the use of tables.

Because life expectancies change, the IRS is required to issue new tables at least every 10 years.[7] The current tables were issued in April 1999 and are effective for transfers beginning in May of that year.[8] The tables contain 50 different possible rates (ranging from 4.2 percent to 14 percent), but *only a portion of the tables is reproduced* in Appendix A.

The tables provide only the remainder factor. If the income interest (life estate) has also been transferred, the factor to be used is one minus the remainder factor.

| | |
|---|---|
| **EXAMPLE 6** | Matt transfers $1 million in trust, specifying a life estate to Rita, remainder to Rick on Rita's death. The gift took place on January 6, 2003, when Rita was age 35. Assume that the appropriate rate is 6.8%. Using the table extract in Appendix A (Table S) for a person age 35 under the 6.8% column, the value of the remainder interest is $96,380 (.09638 × $1,000,000). The life estate factor is .90362 (1.00000 − .09638). Thus, Matt has made a gift to Rita of $903,620 and a gift to Rick of $96,380. ▪ |

In computing the value of an income interest for a term of years, a different table is used. Again, the table furnishes the remainder factor. The income interest factor is the difference between one and the remainder factor. *Only a portion of the tables is reproduced* in Appendix A.

| | |
|---|---|
| **EXAMPLE 7** | On December 30, 2003, Julia transfers $200,000 by gift to a trust. Under the terms of the trust, income is payable to Paul for eight years. After the eight-year period, the trust terminates, and the trust principal passes to Sara. For the month in which the trust was created, the appropriate rate was 7.4%. The present worth of $1 due at the end of eight years is $0.564892. Thus, Julia has made a gift to Sara of $112,978.40 (.564892 × $200,000) and a gift to Paul of $87,021.60 (.435108 × $200,000). ▪ |

What is the significance of dividing a gift into several distinct parts? This is important in determining the applicability of the annual exclusion and the marital deduction. Under the facts of Example 6, an annual exclusion probably would be allowed for the gift to Rita but not for the interest passing to Rick (because of the future interest limitation). If Rita is Matt's wife, no marital deduction is allowed because the life estate is a terminable interest. As noted in Chapter 17, however, this problem could be cured with a qualified terminable interest property (QTIP) election.

---

[6]The terminal reserve value of a life insurance policy generally approximates the policy's cash surrender value. For an illustration on how to arrive at the interpolated terminal reserve value, see Reg. § 20.2031–8(a)(3) (Ex. 3).

[7]§ 7520.

[8]The valuation factors in the tables represent 120% of whatever the Federal mid-term rate is for the month of the valuation date.

**LO.2**

Apply the special use valuation method in appropriate situations.

## REAL ESTATE AND THE SPECIAL USE VALUATION METHOD

Proper valuation principles usually require that real estate be valued at its most suitable (i.e., "best" or "highest") use. Section 2032A, however, permits an executor to elect to value certain classes of real estate used in farming or in connection with a closely held business at its "current" use, rather than the most suitable use. The major objective of the **special use value** election is to provide a form of limited relief to protect the heirs against the possibility of having to sell a portion of the family farm to pay estate taxes.

**EXAMPLE 8**

At the time of his death, Rex owned a dairy farm on the outskirts of a large city. For farming purposes, the property's value is $500,000 (the current use value).[9] As a potential site for a shopping center, however, the property is worth $1.2 million (the most suitable use value). The executor of Rex's estate can elect to include only $500,000 in the gross estate. ■

The special use valuation procedure permits a reduction of no more than $840,000 in estate tax valuation in 2003 ($820,000 for 2002). Prior to 1999, the reduction was limited to $750,000. Beginning in 1999, the amount is subject to indexation.

**EXAMPLE 9**

At the time of her death in 2003, Wanda owned a farm with a most suitable use value of $2.5 million but a current use value of $1.3 million. Assuming the property qualifies under § 2032A and the special use valuation election is made, Wanda's gross estate must include $1,660,000. Only $840,000 can be excluded under § 2032A. ■

The special use valuation election is available if *all* of the following conditions are satisfied.

- At least 50 percent of the adjusted value of the gross estate consists of *real* or *personal* property devoted to a qualifying use (used for farming or in a closely held business) at the time of the owner's death.[10]
- The *real* property devoted to a qualifying use comprises at least 25 percent of the adjusted value of the gross estate.
  For purposes of satisfying both the 50 percent test (above) and the 25 percent test, the qualifying property is considered at its most suitable use value. Thus, in Example 8, the property would be treated as if it had a value of $1.2 million (not $500,000). The adjusted value of the gross estate is the gross estate less certain unpaid mortgages and other indebtedness.
- The qualifying property passes to a qualifying heir of the decedent. Qualifying heirs are certain family members as set forth in § 2032A(e)(2).
- The *real* property has been owned by the decedent or the decedent's family for five out of the eight years ending on the date of the decedent's death and was devoted to a qualifying use during that period.
- The decedent or a member of the decedent's family participated materially in the operation of the farm or business during the five-year period specified above.[11]

---

[9]Sections 2032A(e)(7) and (8) set forth various methods of valuation to be applied in arriving at current use value.

[10]§§ 2032A(b)(1)(A) and (b)(2). For a definition of "farm" and "farming," see §§ 2032A(e)(4) and (5).

[11]§ 2032A(b)(1)(C)(ii). "Material participation" is defined in § 2032A(e)(6).

Section 2032A(c) provides that the estate tax savings derived from the special use valuation method are recaptured from the heir, if he or she disposes of the property or ceases to use it as qualifying use property within a period of 10 years from the date of the decedent's death.

---

**ETHICAL CONSIDERATIONS** | **A Temporary Election?**

Roy is the executor and sole heir of his uncle's estate. The estate's major asset is a peach orchard located on the outskirts of a large metropolitan area. Because the suburbs are expanding, the value of the orchard has increased much more than that of similar agricultural use property. Several of Roy's friends who are knowledgeable in real estate matters tell him that in several years the land may be worth double or triple its present value. Roy owns his own orchard and will have no difficulty satisfying the qualified use requirements of § 2032A.

Roy makes the special use election for his uncle's property. Although he has no intention of keeping the property as an orchard for 10 years, he reasons: "Why pay estate taxes today that you can put off until tomorrow?" Has Roy acted properly?

---

**EXAMPLE 10**

Assume the same facts as in Example 9. Further assume that by electing § 2032A, Wanda's estate tax liability was reduced by $245,000. Three years after Wanda's death, Otis (the qualifying heir) leases the farm to an unrelated party. At this point, Otis must pay the $245,000 additional estate tax liability that would have been imposed had § 2032A not been utilized. ■

In the event recapture occurs, the qualifying heir may *elect* to increase the income tax basis of the property by the amount of the recapture. If the election is made, however, interest on the additional estate tax due must be paid.[12]

In this regard, the Code gives the IRS security for compliance with the terms of § 2032A by placing a special lien on the qualifying property.[13]

**LO.3**

Identify problems involved in valuing an interest in a closely held business.

## VALUATION PROBLEMS WITH A CLOSELY HELD BUSINESS

**General Guidelines.** Revenue Ruling 59–60 sets forth the approach, methods, and factors to be considered in valuing the shares of closely held corporations for gift and estate tax purposes.[14] The following factors, although not all-inclusive, are fundamental and require careful analysis in each case.

- The nature of the business and the history of the enterprise from its inception.
- The economic outlook in general and the condition and outlook of the specific industry in particular.
- The book value of the stock and the financial condition of the business.
- The earning capacity of the company.
- The company's dividend-paying capacity.
- Whether the enterprise has goodwill or other intangible value.

---

[12]§ 1016(c).
[13]§ 6324B.

[14]1959–1 C.B. 237. See also Reg. § 20.2031–2(f).

- The prices and number of shares of the stock sold previously and the size of the block of stock to be valued.
- The market price of stocks issued by corporations in the same or a similar line of business and actively traded in a free and open market, either on an exchange or over-the-counter.

Some of these factors are discussed in depth in the pages to follow.

**Goodwill Aspects.** If a closely held corporation's record of past earnings is higher than is usual for the industry, the IRS is apt to claim the presence of goodwill as a corporate asset.

**EXAMPLE 11**

Adam owned 70% of the stock of White Corporation, with the remaining 30% held by various family members. Over the past five years, White Corporation has generated average net profits of $200,000, and on the date of Adam's death, the book value of the corporation's stock was $500,000. If the IRS identifies 8% as an appropriate rate of return, one approach to the valuation of White stock would yield the following result.

| | |
|---|---:|
| Average net profit for the past five years | $ 200,000 |
| 8% of the $500,000 book value | 40,000 |
| Excess earnings over 8% | $ 160,000 |
| Value of goodwill (5 × $160,000) | $ 800,000 |
| Book value | 500,000 |
| Total value of the White stock | $1,300,000 |

Thus, the IRS might contend that the stock should be included in Adam's gross estate at 70 percent of $1,300,000, or $910,000. If the estate wishes to argue for a lower valuation, relevant factors might include any of the following.

- The average net profit figure for the past five years ($200,000) may not be representative. Perhaps it includes some extraordinary gains that normally do not occur or are extraneous to the business conducted by the corporation. An example might be a windfall profit for a specific year because of an unusual market situation. The corporation may have recognized a large gain from an appreciated investment held for many years. The figure may fail to take into account certain expenses that normally would be incurred but for some justifiable reason have been deferred. In a family business during periods of expansion and development, it is not uncommon to find an unusually low salary structure. Profits might be considerably less if the owner-employees of the business were being paid the true worth of their services.
- The appropriate rate of return for this type of business may not be 8 percent. If it is higher, there would be less goodwill because the business is not as profitable as it seems.
- If Adam was a key person in the operation of White Corporation, could some or all of any goodwill developed by the business be attributed to his efforts? If so, is it not reasonable to assume that the goodwill might be seriously impaired by Adam's death?

**Other Factors.** Aside from the issue of goodwill, the valuation of closely held stock must take other factors into account. For example, consider the percentage of ownership involved. If the percentage represents a *minority interest* and the corporation has a poor dividend-paying record, a substantial discount is in order.[15] The justification for the discount is the general inability of the holder of the minority interest to affect corporate policy, particularly with respect to the distribution of dividends. At the other extreme is an interest large enough to represent control, either actual or effective. Considered alone, a controlling interest calls for valuation at a premium.[16]

A controlling interest may be so large, however, that the disposition of the stock within a reasonable period of time after the valuation date could have a negative effect on the market for such shares. The **blockage rule** recognizes what may happen to per-unit value when a large block of shares is marketed at one time.[17] Most often, the rule is applied to stock that has a recognized market. The rule permits a discount from the amount at which smaller lots are selling on or about the valuation date.[18] Although the blockage rule may have a bearing on the valuation of other assets, it is more frequently applied to stocks and securities.[19]

Because most stock in closely held corporations does not trade in a recognized market, a discount for *lack of marketability* may be in order. The discount recognizes the costs that would be incurred in creating a market for such shares to effect their orderly disposition.[20] The discount could be significant considering typical underwriting expenses and other costs involved in going public.

Closely related to the reasons that an asset's marketability might be impaired is the possibility of built-in income tax consequences. In one case, the value of stock in a holding company was significantly discounted because of the income tax that would ensue if the holding company distributed its major asset to its shareholders.[21]

**Resolving the Valuation Problem for Stock in Closely Held Corporations.** Since the valuation of closely held stock is subject to so many variables, planning should be directed toward bringing about some measure of certainty.

**EXAMPLE 12**

Polly wants to transfer some of her stock in Brown Corporation to a trust formed for her children. She would also like to make a substantial contribution to her alma mater, State University. At present, the Brown stock is owned entirely by Polly and has never been traded on any market or otherwise sold or exchanged. Brown's past operations have proved profitable, and Brown has established a respectable record of dividend distributions. Based on the best available information and taking into account various adjustments (e.g., discount for lack of marketability), Polly feels each share of Brown stock possesses a fair market value of $120. ∎

If Polly makes a gift of some of the stock to the trust set up for the children and uses the $120 per share valuation, what assurance is there that the IRS will

---

[15]See, for example, *Jack D. Carr*, 49 TCM 507, T.C.Memo. 1985–19.

[16]*Helvering v. Safe Deposit and Trust Co. of Baltimore, Exr. (Estate of H. Walters)*, 38–1 USTC ¶9240, 21 AFTR 12, 95 F.2d 806 (CA–4, 1938), *aff'g* 35 B.T.A. 259 (1937).

[17]Reg. § 20.2031–2(e).

[18]See, for example, *Estate of Robert Damon*, 49 T.C. 108 (1967).

[19]In *Estate of David Smith*, 57 T.C. 650 (1972), the estate of a now-famous sculptor successfully argued for the application of the blockage rule to 425 sculptures included in the gross estate. See also *Estate of Georgia T. O'Keeffe*, 63 TCM 2699, T.C.Memo. 1992–210.

[20]See, for example, *Estate of Mark S. Gallo*, 50 TCM 470, T.C.Memo. 1985–363. In this case, the taxpayer also argued that a bad product image (i.e., the Thunderbird, Ripple, and Boone's Farm brands) would depress the value of the stock. Since the trend was toward better wines, association with cheaper products had a negative consumer impact. Not emphasized were the enormous profits that the sale of the cheap wines generated!

[21]*Estate of Artemus D. Davis*, 110 T.C. 530 (1998). The major asset held by the holding company was a considerable block of substantially appreciated stock in the Winn-Dixie supermarket chain.

accept this figure? If the IRS is successful in increasing the fair market value per share, Polly could end up with additional gift tax liability.

Polly could hedge against any further gift tax liability. Concurrently with the gift of stock to the trust formed for the children, Polly could make an outright transfer of some of the shares to State University, thereby generating an income tax deduction. Polly would base the income tax deduction on the value used for gift tax purposes. If the IRS later raises the value and assesses more gift tax, Polly can file an amended income tax return, claim a larger charitable contribution deduction, and obtain an offsetting income tax refund. To carry out this hedge, Polly would derive the amount of her gift of Brown stock by comparing her prevailing gift tax and income tax brackets for the year of the transfers. By virtue of the charitable deduction allowed for gift tax purposes by § 2522 (discussed in Chapter 17), no gift tax liability is incurred for the stock transferred to State University.

**The Buy-Sell Agreement and Valuation.**    The main objective of a **buy-sell agreement** is to effect the orderly disposition of a business interest without the risk of the interest falling into the hands of outsiders. Moreover, a buy-sell agreement can ease the problems of estate liquidity and valuation.

Two types of buy-sell agreements exist: **entity** and **cross-purchase** arrangements. Under the entity type, the business itself (partnership or corporation) agrees to buy out the interest of the withdrawing owner (partner or shareholder). For a corporation, this normally takes the form of a stock redemption plan set up to qualify for income tax purposes under either § 302(b) or § 303. By making use of these provisions, corporate distributions can qualify for sale or exchange treatment rather than being treated as dividends (see Chapter 5). Under a cross-purchase agreement, the surviving owners (partners or shareholders) agree to buy out the withdrawing owner. The structures of the most typical buy-sell agreements are illustrated in Figure 18–1.

**EXAMPLE 13**

Iris, Ned, and Hal are equal and unrelated shareholders in Blue Corporation, and all three share in Blue's management. All agree to turn in their stock to the corporation for redemption at $100 per share if any one of them withdraws (by death or otherwise) from the business. Shortly thereafter, Hal dies, and the estate redeems the Blue stock at the agreed-upon price of $100 per share. ■

**EXAMPLE 14**

Assume the same facts as in Example 13, except that the agreement is the cross-purchase type under which each shareholder promises to buy a share of the withdrawing shareholder's interest. When Hal dies, the estate sells the Blue stock to Iris and Ned for $100 per share. ■

Will the $100 per share paid to Hal's estate determine the amount to be included in his gross estate? The answer is *yes*, subject to the following conditions.

- The price is the result of a bona fide business agreement.
- The agreement is not a device to transfer property to family members.
- The agreement is comparable to other arrangements entered into by persons dealing at arm's length.[22]

---

[22]§ 2703.

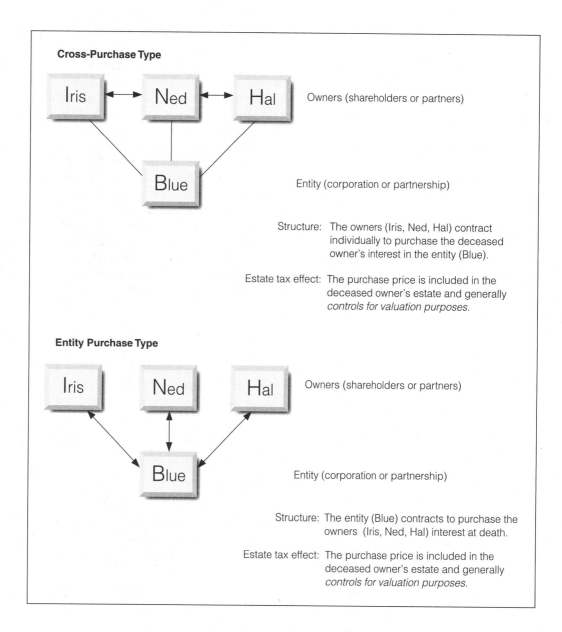

**■ FIGURE 18–1**
Structures of Typical
Buy-Sell Agreements

---

| ETHICAL CONSIDERATIONS | **Income Tax Consequences from a Botched Buy-Sell Agreement** |

Rohm, Turner, and Walker are equal shareholders in Crane Corporation. They agree that if any one of them withdraws from the business, by death or otherwise, the remaining shareholders will purchase the departing shareholder's interest.

When Rohm dies, Turner and Walker lack the funds to buy his interest from the estate. Consequently, they have Crane Corporation redeem the stock. Since Turner and Walker have received nothing from this transaction, they feel it has no income tax consequences for them.

Do you agree with Turner and Walker? Why or why not?

**Estate Freezes—Corporations.**    Over the years, owners of closely held businesses have searched for ways to transfer the major value of the business to their heirs while retaining some security interest. The typical approach with corporations has been for the owner to retain preferred stock and make gifts of common stock to the family. The approach freezes the amount that will be included in the owner's gross estate to the value of the preferred stock. Any post-gift appreciation in the business is attributed to the common stock and is *not* part of the owner's gross estate.

Under current law, some degree of the **estate freeze** is permitted.[23] Unfortunately, current law is designed to maximize the amount of the gift made by the donor upon the creation of the freeze. Generally, the retained interest is valued at zero, thereby resulting in the transfer of the *full* value of the business.

**EXAMPLE 15**

Quinn owns all of the stock in Robin Corporation valued as follows: $4 million common stock and $1 million preferred stock. The preferred stock is noncumulative, does not have a redemption date, and possesses no liquidation preference. Quinn gives the common stock to his adult children and retains the preferred stock. Quinn has made a gift to the children of $5 million. The $1 million worth of preferred stock Quinn retained is treated as having no value. ■

Special rules apply if the preferred stock is cumulative, has a redemption date, or carries certain other preferential rights. These rules allow some value to be assigned to the preferred stock, thereby reducing the amount of the gift. The adjustments can become complex and are not discussed further in the text.

The estate freeze rules *do not apply* to transfers of the following assets.

* Retained interests for which market quotations are readily available.
* Retained interests that are the same as those transferred (e.g., common stock, a partnership interest in which all partners share equally).

The response of the business community to the current estate freeze rules has not been positive. Consider some of the inherent disadvantages.

* Although the retained interest is deemed to be a gift, it is also included in the donor's gross estate upon death. In Example 15, therefore, the preferred stock is included in Quinn's gross estate upon his subsequent death.
* The donor loses the use of any gift tax paid on the retained interest.

The estate freeze does, however, escape later estate taxation on any post-transfer appreciation that develops.

**EXAMPLE 16**

Assume the same facts as in Example 15. Quinn dies 10 years after the gift when the Robin Corporation common and preferred stock are worth $10 million and $1 million, respectively. Quinn's estate includes only $1 million for the preferred stock. The $6 million appreciation on the common stock ($10 million − $4 million) has escaped a transfer tax. ■

**Estate Freezes—Partnerships.**    Due to the statutory limitations imposed on estate freezes using corporations, the adoption of a family limited partnership (FLP) to carry out an estate freeze has become popular. A common scenario is for grandparents to form an FLP to hold a closely held business or other assets that can be expected to appreciate (e.g., real estate). The grandparents make themselves general partners and over a period of years make gifts of limited partnership interests to their children and grandchildren.

---

[23]§ 2701.

## USE OF FLPs REQUIRES CAUTION

An estate planner must exercise care when using a family limited partnership (FLP). Considering the decidedly negative attitude of the IRS, the planner must be prepared to take a defensive posture in the event of challenge. The following guidelines may be helpful.

- Avoid the appearance that tax avoidance is the only motivation for using the FLP. For example, more efficient management of the property involved is a proper business justification.
- Depending on the nature of the assets involved, temper the amount of the discount claimed. For example, taking a discount of more than 30 percent for a partnership with marketable securities is inviting IRS scrutiny.
- Be able to support the claimed discount with an appraisal.
- Avoid creating the arrangement in a "deathbed" setting.
- Allow some time to elapse between the creation of the partnership and the gifts of the limited interests.
- Try to avoid funding the partnership with personal use assets (e.g., personal residence).
- Recognize the existence of the arrangement. For example, a general partner should not claim the partnership income if it belongs to the limited partners.

In valuing gifts of limited partnership interests, generous discounts (from 25 percent to 60 percent) are made for lack of marketability and a minority interest. As the grandparents are the general partners, they remain in control of the business (i.e., the FLP).

At one point, the IRS contended that a discount for a minority interest was not available as long as the business was held fully within the family unit (e.g., grandparents, children, grandchildren). After losing on the issue in several court cases, the IRS conceded that the valuation discount is available.[24]

The overall expectation underlying the FLP approach is that a lesser value of the business can be transferred by gift than would be the case if everything is passed by death. The key to success, however, is the acceptability of the discounts used to value the gifts. Overly generous discount percentages could result in vulnerability to the penalty for undervaluation.[25]

In light of what happened to the estate freeze of corporate stock previously discussed, it is not unlikely that Congress might enact statutory limitations on the use of FLPs.

Valuation concepts are reviewed in Concept Summary 18–1.

## Income Tax Concepts

Family tax planning also involves an assessment of the income tax positions of the transferor (the donor or decedent) and the transferee (the donee or heir).

---

[24]Rev.Rul. 93–12, 1993–1 C.B. 202, rescinding Rev.Rul. 81–253, 1981–1 C.B. 187.

[25]§ 6662(b)(5). See the discussion of accuracy-related penalties in Chapter 16.

---

**CONCEPT SUMMARY 18–1**

## Valuation Concepts

1. Fair market value is "the price at which property would change hands between a willing buyer and a willing seller, neither being under any compulsion to buy or to sell and both having reasonable knowledge of relevant facts."
2. Special rules govern the valuation of life insurance policies and annuity contracts. In the case of unmatured life insurance policies, value depends on whether the policies are paid up or not. Use of the IRS valuation tables is necessary when the annuities are issued by parties not regularly engaged in selling annuities.
3. The IRS valuation tables must be used to value multiple interests in property. Such interests include income for a term of years, life estates, and remainders.
4. Section 2032A provides valuation relief for the estates of persons who hold real estate used in farming or in connection with a closely held business. If the requirements of the provision are met and if the executor elects, the property can be valued at its *current use* rather than its *most suitable use*.
5. Determining the value of the stock in a closely held corporation presents unique problems. The presence or absence of *goodwill* at the corporate level has a direct bearing on the stock being valued. A discount may be in order for any of the following: a minority interest, lack of marketability, and the application of the blockage rule. The IRS will contend that a premium attaches to an interest that represents control of the corporation.
6. A properly structured buy-sell agreement will control the value to be assigned a deceased owner's interest in a partnership or a corporation.
7. An estate tax freeze is useful in avoiding post-transfer appreciation that develops on the partnership or corporate interest involved. However, the donor must consider the gift tax consequences that result when the freeze is created.

---

**LO.4**

Compare the income tax basis rules applying to property received by gift and by death.

## BASIS OF PROPERTY ACQUIRED BY GIFT

The income tax basis of property acquired by gift depends on whether the donee sells the property for a gain or for a loss and, in certain cases, on when the gift occurred.

- If the gift took place after 1920 and before 1977, the donee's basis for gain is the donor's adjusted basis plus any gift tax paid on the transfer (but not to exceed the fair market value on the date of the gift). The basis for loss is the lower of the basis for gain or the fair market value of the property on the date of the gift.
- If the gift took place after 1976, the donee's basis for gain is the donor's adjusted basis plus only the gift tax attributable to the appreciation of the property to the point of the gift. For this purpose, use the *taxable gift* amount (i.e., gift less annual exclusion). The basis for loss is the lesser of the basis for gain or the fair market value of the property on the date of the gift.[26]

**EXAMPLE 17**

In 1975, Norm receives stock as a gift from Lana. The stock cost Lana $20,000 and was worth $100,000 on the date of the gift. As a result of the transfer, Lana paid a gift tax of $10,000. Norm's income tax basis for gain or loss is $30,000 [$20,000 (Lana's basis) + $10,000 (gift tax paid by Lana)]. Norm does not have a different basis for loss; the fair market value of the property on the date of the gift ($100,000) is not less than the basis for gain ($30,000). ■

---

[26]§§ 1015(a) and (d).

### CARRYOVER BASIS—WILL IT EVER HAPPEN?

Pursuant to the Tax Relief Reconciliation Act of 2001, the Federal estate tax is to be phased out by the end of 2009. If the phaseout takes place as planned, what will be the impact on the current "step-up" and "step-down" rules of § 1014? Different basis rules will come into play, and § 1014 will cease to apply.

Under new Code § 1022, scheduled to become effective in 2010, an heir will receive a carryover basis from a decedent. With certain exceptions, the basis determination rules governing property transferred by gift will also apply to transfers by death. For basis purposes, therefore, donees and heirs will be treated much the same.

As noted in Chapter 17, however, whether the estate tax will ever be entirely eliminated is uncertain.

**EXAMPLE 18**

Assume the same facts as in Example 17, except that the gift takes place in 2003. Only the portion of the gift tax that is attributable to the appreciation can be considered. This portion is determined as follows:

$$\frac{\$80,000 \text{ (appreciation)}}{\$89,000 \text{ (taxable gift)}} = 90\% \text{ (rounded)}$$

Consequently, Norm's income tax basis is $29,000.

| | |
|---|---|
| Lana's basis | $20,000 |
| Allowable gift tax adjustment (90% × $10,000) | 9,000 |
| Basis for gain and loss | $29,000 |

The effect of the rule illustrated in Example 18 is to deny a donee any increase in basis for the gift tax attributable to the donor's adjusted basis.

Because the donee usually assumes the donor's basis in the property, transfers by gifts are considered carryover situations. Consistent with this approach, the donee's holding period includes that of the donor.[27]

## BASIS OF PROPERTY ACQUIRED BY DEATH

**General Rule.** Except as otherwise noted in the following sections, the income tax basis of property acquired from a decedent is the fair market value on the date of death or, if elected, on the alternate valuation date. When property has appreciated in value between acquisition and date of death, a **step-up in** income tax **basis** occurs for the estate or heir of the deceased owner. A step-up in basis means that appreciation existing at death escapes the application of the Federal income tax.

**EXAMPLE 19**

Upon her death in 2003, Nancy owned real estate (adjusted basis of $200,000) worth $800,000 that she leaves to Jack. Assuming that the alternate valuation date is not elected, Jack's income tax basis in the property becomes $800,000. Thus, a subsequent sale of the real estate by Jack for $800,000 results in no gain or loss to him.

---

[27]§ 1223(2).

**EXAMPLE 20**

Assume the same facts as in Example 19, except that, shortly before her death, Nancy sells the real estate for $800,000. Nancy has a taxable gain of $600,000 for income tax purposes. ■

By contrasting Examples 19 and 20, one can see that the rules place a premium on holding appreciated property until death, to take advantage of the step-up in basis rule. The same cannot be said for property that has declined in value. Here, death causes a **step-down in basis.** This result should be avoided if selling the property would generate a deductible income tax loss.

**EXAMPLE 21**

Upon his death in 2003, Wes held stock as an investment with an adjusted basis of $200,000 and a fair market value of $120,000. Because only $120,000 is included in the gross estate, the basis of the stock to the estate or heir is this amount. Had Wes sold the stock before his death, a deduction for some or all of the $80,000 loss might have been available. ■

The holding period to the estate or heir of property acquired from a decedent is automatically treated as long term.[28]

If the property does not pass through a decedent's estate, there is no step-up (or step-down) in income tax basis.

**EXAMPLE 22**

In 1980, Aaron and Sandra (brother and sister) purchased land for $200,000, listing title as "joint tenants with the right of survivorship." Each furnished one-half of the purchase price. In 2003, when the land is worth $600,000, Aaron dies. Under § 2040 (see Chapter 17), Aaron's estate includes $300,000 as to the land. Sandra's income tax basis in the land is $400,000, determined as follows: $100,000 (Sandra's original cost basis) + $300,000 (amount passing through Aaron's estate). ■

**Community Property.**    Although there is usually no change in basis for property that is not part of a decedent's gross estate (see Example 22 above), a special exception applies to community property. In such situations, the surviving spouse's half of the community takes the same basis as the half included in the deceased spouse's gross estate.[29] The following examples illustrate the reason for and the effect of this special rule.

**EXAMPLE 23**

Leif and Rosa were husband and wife and lived in a common law state. At the time of Leif's death, he owned assets (worth $1.6 million with a basis to him of $200,000), which he bequeathed to Rosa. Presuming the transfer qualifies under § 2056, Leif's estate is allowed a marital deduction of approximately $1.6 million. As the property passes through Leif's estate, Rosa receives a step-up in basis to $1.6 million. ■

**EXAMPLE 24**

Assume the same facts as in Example 23, except that Leif and Rosa had always lived in California (a community property state). If the $1.6 million of assets are community property, only one-half of this value is included in Leif's gross estate. Because the other half does not pass through Leif's estate (it already belongs to Rosa), is it fair to deny Rosa a new basis in it? Therefore, allowing the surviving spouse's share of the community to take on a basis equal to the half included in the deceased spouse's gross estate equalizes the income tax result generally achieved in common law states through the use of the marital deduction.

---

[28]§ 1223(11).                                             [29]§ 1014(b)(6).

By giving Rosa an income tax basis of $1.6 million ($800,000 for Leif's half passing to her plus $800,000 for her half) and including only $800,000 in Leif's gross estate, the tax outcome is the same as in Example 23. ∎

### Step-Up in Basis and the One-Year Rule.

To understand the need for § 1014(e), consider the following situation.

**EXAMPLE 25**

Gary and Hazel are husband and wife and reside in a common law state. When the couple learns that Hazel has a terminal illness, Gary transfers property (basis of $100,000 and fair market value of $400,000) to her as a gift. Hazel dies shortly thereafter, and under the provisions of her will, the property returns to Gary. ∎

If it were not for § 1014(e), what have the parties accomplished? No gift tax occurs on the transfer from Gary to Hazel because of the application of the marital deduction. Upon Hazel's death, her bequest to Gary does not generate any estate tax because the inclusion of the property in her gross estate is offset by the marital deduction. Through the application of the general rule of § 1014, Gary ends up with the same property, with its basis stepped up to $400,000. Thus, the procedure enables Gary to get a "free" increase in income tax basis of $300,000.

When applicable, § 1014(e) forces Gary (the original donor) to assume the property with the same basis it had to Hazel immediately before her death. Hazel's basis would have been determined under § 1015 (basis of property acquired by gift). The basis would have been $100,000 (donor's adjusted basis) plus any gift tax adjustment (none in this case) and any capital additions made by the donee (none in this case), or $100,000. If § 1014(e) applies to Example 25, Gary ends up where he started (with $100,000) in terms of income tax basis.

For § 1014(e) to be operative, the following conditions must be satisfied.

* The decedent must have received appreciated property as a gift during the one-year period ending with his or her death.
* The property is acquired from the decedent by the donor (or the donor's spouse).

Example 25 concerns a transfer between spouses, but the application of § 1014(e) is not so limited. The provision applies with equal effect if, for example, the donor-heir were a daughter of the donee-decedent. In such cases, moreover, the technique used in Example 25 might be susceptible to the imposition of gift or estate taxes, because of the unavailability of the marital deduction.

### Income in Respect of a Decedent.

Income in respect of a decedent (IRD) is income earned by a decedent to the point of his or her death but not reportable on the final income tax return under the method of accounting used. IRD is most frequently applicable to decedents using the cash basis of accounting. IRD also occurs, for example, when a taxpayer at the time of death held installment notes receivable on which the gain has been deferred. For both cash and accrual taxpayers, IRD is increasingly including postdeath distributions from retirement plans [e.g., traditional IRA, § 401(k), H.R. 10 (Keogh), § 403(b)(1), qualified plan]. With the exception of Roth IRAs, distributions from retirement plans invariably contain an income component that has not yet been subject to income tax.

IRD is included in the gross estate at its fair market value on the appropriate valuation date. However, the income tax basis of the decedent transfers to the estate or heirs. Neither a step-up nor a step-down in basis is possible as is true of

## CONCEPT SUMMARY 18–2

### Income Tax Concepts

1. The income tax basis of property acquired by gift is the donor's basis with appropriate adjustment for any gift tax paid. With built-in loss situations, the income tax basis is the fair market value of the property on the date of the gift.
2. The income tax basis of property acquired through the death of the owner is its fair market value on the appropriate estate tax valuation date.
3. No step-up in basis is allowed if the property returns to the donor or donor's spouse within one year.
4. Items of income in respect of a decedent do not undergo a step-up or step-down in basis.
5. The value used for estate tax purposes is presumed to establish basis for income tax purposes. This presumption can be rebutted, but only with great difficulty.

property received by death.[30] Furthermore, the recipient of IRD must classify it in the same manner (e.g., ordinary income, capital gain) as the decedent would have.[31]

**How Conclusive Is the Value Used for Estate Tax Purposes?**   Suppose a value is used for estate tax purposes and reflected on the estate tax return. At some future date, an heir to the property included in the gross estate believes the value used for estate tax purposes was incorrect. An heir might desire a change in value for countless reasons, including the following.

- The property is sold. Higher value leads to higher basis and less income tax gain.
- The property is depreciable. More basis means larger depreciation deductions.
- A home equity loan is obtained. With a higher value, a larger loan is allowed.
- If the heir is a charitable organization, higher value could improve its fund-raising potential.

Is there any chance of success in arguing for a different value and thereby changing the income tax basis? The answer is yes, but with definite reservations.

If the statute of limitations has not lapsed for the estate tax return, the heir may try for a higher income tax basis by having the estate tax valuation raised. Any new valuation, however, requires both cooperation from the decedent's executor and acceptance by the IRS.

If the statute of limitations has lapsed for the estate tax return, the success of the heir's challenge depends on the following factors.

- The value reflected on the estate tax return and accepted by the IRS is presumed to be correct.[32] The heir must rebut the presumption.
- To rebut the presumption of correctness, it is important to determine by what means the property was originally valued. Did the valuation result from a unilateral determination by the IRS, or was it the result of a carefully considered compromise between the estate and the IRS? The presumption is more difficult for the heir to overcome in the latter instance.

---

[30]§ 1014(c).

[31]§ 691(a)(3). See Chapter 19 for a further discussion of IRD. Example 11 in Chapter 19 specifically deals with the IRD classification of distributions from retirement plans.

[32]Rev.Rul. 54–97, 1954–1 C.B. 113; *H. B. Levy*, 17 T.C. 728 (1951); and *Malcolm C. Davenport*, 6 T.C. 62 (1946).

- Did the heir have a hand in setting the original value? If so, allowing the value to be changed now would seem to give the heir an unfair advantage. The heir used or influenced the use of a lower value for estate tax purposes (thereby eliminating estate taxes) and now wants a higher value for income tax purposes (thereby reducing a recognized gain).[33]
- Even if the concept of fairness is not applicable because the heir was not involved in setting the original value, justification for a new value must be produced.

**LO.5**

*Plan gifts so as to minimize gift taxes and avoid estate taxes.*

# Gift Planning

One of the ways to carry out family tax planning is to start a program of lifetime giving. The objectives of such a program are to minimize transfer taxes while keeping income tax consequences in mind.

## MINIMIZING GIFT TAXES

The Federal gift tax can be avoided through proper use of the annual exclusion. Because a new annual exclusion is available each year, spacing gifts over multiple years increases the amount that can be transferred free of gift tax.

**EXAMPLE 26**

Starting in 1997, Cora makes gifts in the amount of the annual exclusion to each of her five grandchildren. Through 2003, Cora will have transferred $360,000 [$10,000 (annual exclusion for 1997–2001) × 5 (number of donees) × 5 (number of years at $10,000 annual exclusion) + $11,000 (annual exclusion for 2002 on) × 5 (number of donees) × 2 (number of years at $11,000 annual exclusion)] with no gift tax consequences. ∎

For married donors, the § 2513 election to split gifts can double the amount of a tax-free transfer.

**EXAMPLE 27**

Assume the same facts as in Example 26, except that Cora is married to Leon. If Leon consents to the § 2513 elections, Cora can transfer $720,000 [$20,000 (annual exclusion for two donors for 1997–2001) × 5 (number of donees) × 5 (number of years at $20,000 annual exclusion) + $22,000 (annual exclusion for 2002 on) × 5 (number of donees) × 2 (number of years at $22,000 annual exclusion)] with no gift tax consequences. ∎

From a practical standpoint, many donors who want to take advantage of the annual exclusion do not wish to give cash or near-cash assets (e.g., marketable securities). Where the value of the gift property substantially exceeds the amount of the annual exclusion, as is often the case with real estate, gifts of a partial interest are an attractive option.

**EXAMPLE 28**

Seth and Kate want to give a parcel of unimproved land to their three adult children and five grandchildren as equal owners. The land has an adjusted basis of $100,000, is held by Seth and Kate as community property, and has an appraised value of $352,000 as of December 19, 2003. On December 23, 2003, Seth and Kate convey a one-half undivided interest in the land to their children and grandchildren as tenants in common. This is followed by a transfer

---

[33]In *William A. Beltzer*, 74–1 USTC ¶9373, 33 AFTR2d 74–1173, 495 F.2d 211 (CA–8, 1974), *aff'g* 73–2 USTC ¶9512, 32 AFTR2d 73–5250 (D.Ct.Neb., 1973), the concept of fairness was *invoked against the* *taxpayer* since, as the executor of the estate, he had been instrumental in setting the original value reported on the death tax return.

of the remaining one-half interest on January 5, 2004. Neither transfer causes gift tax because each is fully offset by annual exclusions of $176,000 [$22,000 (annual exclusion for two donors) × 8 (number of donees)]. Thus, in a period of less than two weeks, Seth and Kate transfer $352,000 in value free of any Federal tax consequences. ◼

Further examination of Example 28 leads to the following observations.

* No income tax consequences ensue from the gift. However, had Seth and Kate first sold the land and made a gift of the cash proceeds, recognized gain of $252,000 [$352,000 (selling price) – $100,000 (adjusted basis)] would have resulted.
* The § 2513 election to split gifts is not necessary because the land was community property. If the land had been held by one of the spouses as separate property, the election would have been necessary to generate the same $352,000 of exclusions. The annual exclusion for 2004 is assumed to remain at $11,000.
* Good tax planning generally dictates that sizable gifts of property be supported by reliable appraisals. In the case of successive gifts of partial interests in the same property, multiple appraisals should be obtained to cover each gift. This advice was not followed in Example 28 due to the short interval between gifts. Barring exceptional circumstances, the value of real estate will not change over a period of less than two weeks.

## MINIMIZING ESTATE TAXES

Aside from the annual exclusion, do lifetime gifts offer any tax advantages over transfers at death? Someone familiar with the tax law applicable to asset transfers would answer "no" to this question. Under the unified transfer tax scheme, the tax rates and credit are the same. Consequently, there seems to be no transfer tax difference between transfer by gift and at death. However, as the following discussion shows, lifetime transfers may be preferable to those at death.

**Avoiding a Transfer Tax on Future Appreciation.**   If property is expected to appreciate in value, a gift removes the appreciation from the donor's gross estate.

**EXAMPLE 29**

In 1986, Wilma transfers an insurance policy on her life to Karen, the designated beneficiary. At the time of the transfer, the policy had a fair market value of $50,000 and a face amount of $1 million. Wilma dies in 2003, and the insurance company pays the $1 million proceeds to Karen. By making the gift, Wilma has kept $950,000 in value from being subject to a transfer tax. ◼

Besides life insurance, other assets that often appreciate in value include real estate, art objects, and special collections (e.g., rare books, coins, and stamps).

**Preparing for the Special Use Valuation Method.**   The § 2032A election is not available for valuing transfers by gift. Yet, if its use is planned in estate tax situations, gifts of nonqualifying property may aid in meeting the requirements of § 2032A. Recall that one of the requirements of § 2032A is that qualified use property must constitute at least 50 percent of the adjusted value of the gross estate.

**EXAMPLE 30**

In 1998, Floyd's estate includes the following.

|  | Fair Market Value |
| --- | --- |
| Farm operated by Floyd with current use value of $250,000 | $2,000,000 |
| Stock in a local bank | 1,400,000 |
| Marketable securities and cash | 800,000 |

At this point, Floyd's estate does not qualify for the § 2032A election. The qualifying property [$2,000,000 (farm)] does not equal or exceed 50% of the adjusted gross estate [$2,000,000 (farm) + $1,400,000 (bank stock) + $800,000 (marketable securities and cash)]. ■

**EXAMPLE 31**

Continuing with the facts of Example 30, Floyd makes a gift of one-half of the bank stock in 1999. He dies in 2003 with no change in asset values. Floyd's estate now qualifies for § 2032A treatment since $2,000,000 (farm) is 50% or more of $3,500,000 [$2,000,000 (farm) + $700,000 (bank stock) + $800,000 (marketable securities and cash)]. The election enables the estate to value the farm at $250,000 (current use). As a result, the estate tax on $840,000 in value is saved. ■

Care must be taken to avoid gifts of property within three years of death. Though such gifts usually are not included in the gross estate of the donor for estate tax purposes, they are counted when testing for the percentage requirements of § 303 (stock redemptions to pay death taxes and administration expenses—refer to Chapter 5), § 2032A, and § 6166 (extension of time to pay estate taxes in installments—discussed later in this chapter).[34]

**EXAMPLE 32**

Assume the same facts as in Example 31, except that the gift occurs in 2001 (not 1999). Although only $700,000 of the bank stock is included in Floyd's gross estate for estate tax purposes, $1,400,000 is used for the percentage requirements of the special use valuation provisions. As a result, the estate fails to qualify for the election. ■

**Avoiding State Transfer Taxes.** Another element that may favor lifetime over death transfers is the state's transfer tax system. All states impose some type of death tax, but only a few impose a gift tax. Thus, a gift may completely avoid a state transfer tax.

The states currently imposing a state gift tax include Connecticut, Louisiana, North Carolina, and Tennessee. Unfortunately, this could lead to multiple taxation of the same transfer. Unlike the *state death* tax credit (see the discussion of § 2011 in Chapter 17), the Code does not allow a credit for state gift taxes paid. In fact, the only credit allowed against the Federal gift tax is the unified transfer tax credit.

**Effect of Gift Taxes Paid.** As to taxable gifts that generate a tax, consider the time value of the gift taxes paid. Since the donor loses the use of these funds, the predicted interval between the gift (and the imposition of the gift tax) and death (the imposition of the estate tax) may make the gift less attractive.

**EXAMPLE 33**

In 1997, Gail makes a gift that results in a gift tax of $100,000. She dies five years later. Presuming a 10% rate of return, the gift tax paid would have been worth $161,051 at Gail's death. Therefore, Gail has lost $61,051 by making the gift. ■

---

[34]§§ 2035(c)(1) and (2).

The analysis used in Example 33 requires refinement to yield a meaningful result. Variables that need to be questioned or interjected include the following.

- The life expectancy of the donor at the time of the gift. Actuarial tables can provide a start, but this kind of information must be adjusted for the general health and lifestyle of the donor. In any event, accurately predicting when a specific person will die is more chance than science.
- The interest factor used. Anticipating even short-rate changes, erratic at best, becomes mere guesswork as the time interval increases.
- Any change in the value of the property from the point of gift to the date of death. Appreciation in value during this interval makes the gift look like a wise choice. The opposite is true if value declines.
- The income tax ramifications of the gift. A donor escapes any post-transfer income yielded by the property. Thus, the income tax burden is shifted away from the donor to the donee.

Finally, a present value analysis must consider the estate tax effect of any gift tax paid. Except for gifts within three years of death (see Chapter 17), the gift tax paid itself is not subject to estate tax. Referring to Example 33, the $100,000 in gift taxes paid escapes inclusion in Gail's gross estate.

**LO.6**

Make gifts so as to avoid income taxes for the donor.

## INCOME TAX CONSIDERATIONS

**Income Shifting.**   One way to lower the overall tax burden on the family unit is to shift income from high-bracket taxpayers to lower-bracket family members. To accomplish this shifting, however, income-producing property must be transferred.

If a gift of property is to shift income to the donee, the transfer must be *complete*. Continued control over the property by the donor may lead the IRS to question the finality of the gift.

**EXAMPLE 34**

Gloria, subject to a 38.6% marginal income tax rate, owns all of the stock in Orange, an S corporation. Gloria transfers by gift 60% of the Orange stock to her four children. The children range in age from 14 to 19 years and are all in the 10% income tax bracket. After the transfer, Gloria continues to operate the business. No shareholder meetings are held. Except for reporting 60% of the pass-through of Orange's profits, Gloria's children have no contact with the business. Aside from the salary paid to Gloria, Orange makes no cash distributions to its shareholders. ■

The situation posed in Example 34 occurs frequently and is fraught with danger. If the purported gift by Gloria lacks economic reality and Gloria is the true economic owner of all of Orange's stock, the pass-through to the children is disregarded.[35] The profits are taxed to Gloria at her 38.6 percent rate rather than to the children at their 10 percent rates. Consequently, the transfer has not accomplished the intended shifting of income.

What can be done to make the transfer in Example 34 tax-effective? First, a distribution of dividends would provide some economic benefit to the children. As the transfer is currently constituted, all that the children have received as a result of the gift is an economic detriment, because they must pay income taxes on their share of Orange's pass-through of profits. Second, some steps should be taken to recognize and protect the interests of the children as donees. One way to do this is to make use of the state's Uniform Gifts to Minors Act.[36] Gloria could

---

[35]*Michael F. Beirne*, 52 T.C. 210 (1969) and 61 T.C. 268 (1973).

[36]*Donald O. Kirkpatrick*, 36 TCM 1122, T.C.Memo. 1977–281.

designate a family member as the custodian of the stock. The custodian would have a fiduciary responsibility to safeguard the interests of the children. Once the children reach age 21 and the custodianship relationship ends, shareholder meetings should be encouraged. That the children do not actively participate in the business of Orange is of no consequence, as long as they are given the opportunity to do so.

As was true in Example 34, income shifting techniques assume that the donee is in a lower tax bracket than the donor. When the donee is under age 14, however, kiddie tax treatment can neutralize the income tax effect of a gift. Under this provision, certain unearned income (e.g., interest, dividends) of a child is taxed at the marginal rate applicable to the parent.[37] In Example 34, suppose one of Gloria's children was not yet 14 years old. Giving Orange stock to the child would not serve any purpose. Even if the transfer was complete and the child recognized the profit pass-through, the applicable rate would be 38.6 percent, not 10 percent. Once the child reaches age 14, however, kiddie tax treatment no longer applies.

**Income Tax Consequences to the Donor.** Generally, a gift of property results in no income tax consequences to the donor. Two important exceptions, however, involve installment notes receivable and U.S. savings bonds.

A gift of an installment note receivable is a taxable disposition, and the donor is treated as if the note had been sold for its fair market value.[38] As a result, the donor recognizes the deferred profit.

**EXAMPLE 35**

In 2001, Adam sells real estate (basis of $200,000) to Norm (an unrelated party) for $800,000. Norm (the obligor) issues two notes of $400,000 each, one due in 2002 and one due in 2003. Adam (the obligee) does not elect out of the installment method. In 2002 and before the first note becomes due, Adam gives both notes to his son, Sam. On this date, the notes have a fair market value of $760,000. As a result of the gift to Sam, Adam recognizes a gain of $560,000 [$760,000 (fair market value of the notes) – $200,000 (Adam's unrecovered basis)]. ■

A gift of U.S. savings bonds is not effective unless the bonds are re-registered in the donee's name. This forces the donor to recognize any deferred income accrued on the bonds. The result may surprise donors who expect to postpone the recognition of interest income until the bonds are redeemed. Thus, the donor who desires to avoid income tax consequences should avoid gifts of installment notes receivable and U.S. savings bonds.

For purposes of contrasting tax results, what happens if these properties are passed by death?

- Installment notes receivable are taxed to whoever collects the notes (the estate or heirs).[39] If the notes are forgiven or canceled by the decedent's will, the income is taxed to the estate.
- Deferred interest income on U.S. savings bonds is taxed to whoever redeems the bonds (the estate or heirs).
- Recapture potential disappears at death.[40] The estate or heirs take the property free of any recapture potential existing at the time of the owner's death.

**Carryover Basis Situations.** When considering the income tax effect of a transfer on the donee or heir, the basis rules of §§ 1014 and 1015 warrant close examination. When appreciated property is involved, receiving the property from a decedent is preferred to a lifetime transfer.

---

[37]§ 1(g).
[38]§ 453B(a).
[39]§ 453B(c).

[40]§§ 1245(b)(1) and 1250(d)(1). Contrast this result with what happens when § 1245 or § 1250 property is transferred by gift. Here, the recapture potential carries over to the donee.

**EXAMPLE 36**

Keith plans to transfer unimproved real estate (basis of $200,000 and fair market value of $800,000) to his daughter, Esther. If the property passes by death, Esther's basis is $800,000. If the property passes by gift, her income tax basis (presuming no gift tax adjustment) is $200,000. The step-up effect of § 1014 provides Esther with an additional basis of $600,000. ■

**EXAMPLE 37**

Keith plans to transfer unimproved real estate (basis of $300,000 and fair market value of $150,000) to his daughter, Esther. If the property passes by death, Esther's basis is $150,000. If the property passes by gift, her income tax basis is $150,000 for losses and $300,000 for gains. Receiving the property as a gift, therefore, might be more advantageous to Esther than the complete step-down in basis under § 1014. ■

For Keith, the options posed by Example 37 are not attractive. By making a gift or passing the property by death, Keith sacrifices the potential loss deduction of $150,000. Presuming he holds the land as an investment, he can use the capital loss to offset capital gains or apply it against ordinary income to the extent of $3,000 per year. Unused capital losses can be carried over indefinitely but will not survive Keith's death.

# Estate Planning

Estate planning considers the nontax and tax aspects of death. In the nontax area are the various steps that can be taken to reduce the costs of probating an estate. In the tax area, the focus is on controlling the amount of the gross estate and maximizing estate tax deductions.

**LO.7**

Reduce probate costs in the administration of an estate.

## PROBATE COSTS

The probate estate consists of all properties subject to administration by an executor. The administration is conducted under the supervision of a local court, usually called a probate court. In certain states, probate functions are performed by county courts, surrogate courts, or orphan's courts.

**Probate costs** include attorney fees, accountant fees, appraisal and inventory fees, court costs, expenses incident to the disposition of assets and satisfaction of liabilities, litigation costs needed to resolve will contests, and charges for the preparation of tax returns. The total amount of probate costs cannot be accurately predicted because so many variables are involved. A conservative range might be from 5 to 15 percent of the amount of the probate estate.

Many procedures can be used to reduce the probate estate and thereby save probate costs, including the following.

- Owning property as joint tenants (or tenants by the entirety) with right of survivorship. Upon death, the property passes to the surviving tenant and generally is not subject to probate.
- Making life insurance payable to a beneficiary other than the estate.
- Utilizing a revocable trust. Upon the death of the creator, the trust becomes irrevocable and is not subject to probate. The revocable trust is often popularly referred to as a **living trust.**
- Listing bank accounts and title to securities by use of the Totten trust arrangement. As noted in Chapter 17, the designation "payable on proof of death" passes title to the property if the listed beneficiary survives the owner. A Totten trust arrangement has the same effect as a revocable trust but avoids the need to create a formal trust.

## HOW LONG SHOULD PROBATE TAKE?

Although Marilyn Monroe died on August 5, 1962, her estate is still in probate. Surely, a probate that has already continued for over 40 years must establish some kind of record!

The trouble stems from the wording of Marilyn's will. According to its terms, equal shares of the estate went to her psychoanalyst and her manager. The psychoanalyst then left his half to a mental health care center, while the manager's portion went to his children.

The manager's children dispute the transfer to the medical institution. They contend that Marilyn's intent was to benefit persons, not organizations.

Why all of the controversy? Perhaps it is because the estate generates annual income of more than $1 million!

Another advantage of bypassing the probate estate is that the beneficiary can obtain immediate possession and enjoyment of the property. The probate process can become prolonged, and the heir may have to await the final settlement of the estate before getting the property.

In terms of probate costs, the ownership of out-of-state real estate can cause horrendous problems. Out-of-state ownership is not uncommon with decedents who have relocated after retirement or who maintain vacation homes.

**EXAMPLE 38**

After retirement and five years before his death, Ted moved from Nebraska to Arizona. At death, Ted still owns a rental house in Nebraska and a vacation home in Idaho. To clear title to these properties, Ted's executor must institute ancillary probate proceedings in Nebraska and Idaho. This will result in additional attorney fees and court costs. ■

The solution to the dilemma posed in Example 38 is to dispose of these properties before death. Although this may generate some legal fees, they will be far less than the cost of ancillary probate proceedings.

**LO.8**

Apply procedures that reduce estate tax consequences.

## CONTROLLING THE AMOUNT OF THE GROSS ESTATE

Unlike the probate estate, the gross estate determines what property is subject to the Federal estate tax. In fact, many of the steps taken to reduce the probate estate will not have a similar effect on the gross estate—see the discussion of §§ 2036 and 2038 in Chapter 17.

Valuation procedures sometimes can be applied to control the amount of the gross estate. The special use valuation method of § 2032A can be elected when the estate consists of real estate used in farming or in connection with a closely held business. When the estate comprises assets that have declined in value shortly after death, the use of the alternate valuation date of § 2032 (see Chapter 17) is advised.

## PROPER HANDLING OF ESTATE TAX DEDUCTIONS

Estate taxes can be reduced either by decreasing the size of the gross estate or by increasing the total allowable deductions. The lower the taxable estate, the less estate tax is generated. Planning with deductions involves the following considerations.

- Making proper use of the marital deduction.
- Working effectively with the charitable deduction.
- Optimizing other deductions and losses allowed under §§ 2053 and 2054.

**Approaches to the Marital Deduction.**   When planning for the estate tax marital deduction, both tax and nontax factors are taken into account. Two major tax goals guide the planning. They are the *equalization* and *deferral* approaches.

- Attempt to equalize the estates of both spouses. Clearly, for example, the estate tax on $2 million is more than double the estate tax on $1 million [compare $780,800 with $691,600 ($345,800 × 2)].
- Based on the time value of taxes deferred, try to postpone estate taxation as long as possible. Also keep in mind the possible effect of the Tax Relief Reconciliation Act of 2001. If, as proposed, the estate tax is phased out, the exclusion amount (i.e., exemption equivalent) for the *estate tax credit increases.* The scheduled increases are to $1.5 million for 2004 and 2005, $2 million for 2006 to 2008, and $3.5 million for 2009. See the discussion in connection with Tables 17–1 and 17–2 in Chapter 17.

Barring certain circumstances, the deferral approach generally is preferable. By maximizing the marital deduction on the death of the first spouse to die, taxes are saved, and the surviving spouse can trim his or her future estate by entering into a program of lifetime giving. By making optimum use of the annual exclusion, considerable amounts can be shifted without incurring *any* transfer tax.

Tax planning must remain flexible and be tailored to the individual circumstances of the parties involved. The equalization approach may be most attractive in the following situations.

- Both spouses are of advanced age and/or in poor health, and neither is expected to survive the other for a prolonged period of time.
- The spouse who is expected to survive has considerable assets of his or her own. Keep in mind that the transfer tax rate schedules are progressive in nature.
- Because of appreciation, property worth $250,000 today when it passes to the surviving spouse may be worth $1 million five years later when the survivor dies.

**The Marital Deduction—Sophistication of the Deferral Approach.**   When saving estate taxes for the family unit is the sole consideration, the equalization and deferral approaches can be combined with maximum effect.

**EXAMPLE 39**

At the time of his death in 2003, Vito had never made any taxable gifts. Under Vito's will, his *disposable estate* of $3 million passes to his wife, Zina.[41]  ■

**EXAMPLE 40**

Assume the same facts as in Example 39, except that Vito's will provides as follows: $1 million to the children and the remainder ($2 million) to Zina.  ■

From a tax standpoint, which is the better plan? Although no estate tax results from either arrangement, Example 39 represents an overfunding in terms of the marital deduction. Why place an additional $1 million in Zina's potential estate when it can pass free of tax to the children through the application of the $345,800

---

[41]For this purpose, the *disposable estate* includes the gross estate less all deductions (e.g., debts, administration, and funeral expenses) except the marital deduction. The term is not in the Code but is useful in evaluating tax options.

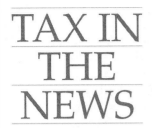

## HOW TO SAVE TAXES BY PROTECTING THE ENVIRONMENT

What do Ted Turner, Robert Redford, Clint Eastwood, and James Baker (former secretary of state) have in common? Besides being celebrities and financially well-to-do, all have issued **conservation easements** in some or all of the real estate they own. By this means, any "scenic view" that currently exists is preserved. The owner is precluded from obstructing the view by further development of the property. Allegedly, the transfer of the easement is motivated by the owner's desire to "conserve the environment." Realistically, the transfer is largely tax motivated.

The steps involved in creating a conservation easement and the tax consequences that ensue are as follows.

- After the easement is drafted, the owner transfers it to a conservation trust. Usually, the trust is already in existence, having been created by an environmental group, and operates under the auspices of a local government agency.
- The owner obtains a generous appraisal as to the value of the easement transferred.
- The owner claims the value of the easement as an income tax deduction.
- The value of the property retained (e.g., residence, vacation home) is accordingly reduced by the value of the easement for ad valorem property tax purposes.
- Upon the owner's death, the gross estate includes the property at a discounted value due to the restrictions contained in the easement.

In summary, the conservation easement saves income, property, and estate taxes. The donor receives all of this plus the aura of being hailed as an environmentalist.[42]

unified tax credit available for 2003? (The exemption equivalent of $345,800 is $1 million.) The exclusion amount (exemption equivalent) is known as the *bypass amount*. The arrangement in Example 40 is preferred because it avoids unnecessary concentration of wealth in Zina's estate.

On occasion, disclaimers can be used to effect the deferral approach.

**EXAMPLE 41**

Upon his death in 2003, Pete had never made any taxable gifts. Under Pete's will, his disposable estate of $2 million passes as follows: $1.2 million to Jim (Pete's adult son) and the remainder ($800,000) to Clare (Pete's surviving spouse). Shortly after Pete's death, Jim issues a disclaimer as to $200,000 of his $1.2 million bequest. This amount, therefore, passes to Clare as the remainderperson under Pete's will. ∎

Jim's disclaimer avoids an estate tax on $200,000. The result is an increase of $200,000 in the marital deduction and the elimination of *any* estate tax upon Pete's death.

**Effectively Working with the Charitable Deduction.** As a general guide to obtaining overall tax savings, lifetime charitable transfers are preferred over testamentary dispositions. For example, an individual who gives $20,000 to a qualified charity during his or her life secures an income tax deduction, avoids any gift tax, and reduces the gross estate by the amount of the gift. By way of contrast, if

---

[42]If the contribution of the conservation easement occurs postmortem (i.e., after the death of the owner), the estate can claim a § 2055(f) charitable contribution. It then can elect, under § 2031(c), to *exclude* up to 40% of the value of the land subject to the easement. In computing the amount of the exclusion, the value of the land must be reduced by the charitable contribution allowed.

the $20,000 is willed to charity, no income tax deduction is available, and the amount of the gift is includible in the decedent's gross estate (though later deducted for estate tax purposes). In short, the lifetime transfer provides a double tax benefit (income tax deduction plus reduced estate taxes) at no gift tax cost. The testamentary transfer merely neutralizes the effect of the inclusion of the property in the gross estate (inclusion under § 2033 and then deduction under § 2055).

To ensure that an estate tax deduction is allowed for a charitable contribution, the designated recipient must fall within the classifications set forth in § 2055. The status of the organization on the date the transfer becomes effective controls, and not the date the will authorizing the transfer was executed.

**EXAMPLE 42**

In 1982, Lisa drew up and executed a will in which she provided for $100,000 to pass to the Rose Academy, a nonprofit educational organization described in § 2055(a)(2) and, at that time, approved by the IRS as a qualified recipient. In 1984, the qualified status of the academy was revoked for practicing racial discrimination in the enrollment of its student body.[43] Lisa dies in 2003, and the executor of her estate, being compelled to satisfy the provisions of the will, transfers $100,000 to the academy. ■

Even though Lisa may have been unaware of the action taken by the IRS in 1984, her estate is not allowed a charitable deduction. The recipient was no longer qualified on the date of Lisa's death. It may be that Lisa, even if she had known about the probable loss of the charitable deduction, would still have wished the bequest carried out as originally conceived. If not, it is easy to see that the error was of Lisa's own making because of her failure to review her estate planning situation.

One way to circumvent the quandary posed by Example 42 (other than changing Lisa's will before her death) is to express the charitable bequest in more flexible terms. The transfer to the academy could have been conditioned on the organization's continued status as a qualified recipient at the time of Lisa's death. Alternatively, Lisa's will may grant her executor the authority to substitute a different, but comparable, charitable organization *that is qualified* in the event of the disqualification of the named group.

On occasion, a charitable bequest depends on the issuance of a disclaimer by a noncharitable heir. Such a situation frequently arises with special types of property or collections, which the decedent may feel a noncharitable heir should have a choice of receiving.

**EXAMPLE 43**

Megan specified in her will that her valuable art collection is to pass to her son or, if the son refuses, to a designated and qualified art museum. At the time the will was drawn, Megan knew that her son was not interested in owning the collection. If, after Megan's death, the son issues a timely disclaimer, the collection passes to the museum, and Megan's estate takes a charitable deduction for its death tax value. ■

**EXAMPLE 44**

Dick's will specifies that one-half of his disposable estate is to pass to his wife and the remainder of his property to a specified qualified charitable organization. If the wife issues a timely disclaimer after Dick's death, all of the property passes to the charity and qualifies for the § 2055 charitable deduction. ■

Has the son in Example 43 acted wisely if he issues the disclaimer in favor of the museum? Although such a disclaimer will provide Megan's estate with a

---

[43]Most of the organizations that are qualified recipients (which will permit the donor a charitable deduction) are listed in IRS Publication 78. This compilation, revised and supplemented from time to time, addresses § 170 (income tax deduction) transfers. Publication 78, with the exceptions noted in Chapter 17, also applies to § 2055 (estate tax deduction) and § 2522 (gift tax deduction) transfers.

deduction for the value of the art collection, consider the income tax deduction alternative. If the son accepts the bequest, he can still dispose of the collection (and fulfill his mother's philanthropic objectives) through a lifetime donation to the museum. At the same time, he obtains an income tax deduction under § 170. Whether this saves taxes for the family depends on a comparison of the mother's estate tax bracket with the estimated income tax bracket of the son. If the value of the collection runs afoul of the percentage limitations of § 170(b)(1), the donations could be spread over more than one year. If this is done, and to protect against the contingency of the son's dying before the entire collection is donated, the son can neutralize any potential death tax consequences by providing in his will for the undonated balance to pass to the museum.

The use of a disclaimer in Example 44 would be sheer folly. It would not reduce Dick's estate tax; it would merely substitute a charitable deduction for the marital deduction. Whether the wife issues a disclaimer or not, no estate taxes will be due. The wife should accept her bequest and, if she is so inclined, make lifetime gifts of it to a qualified charity. In so doing, she generates an income tax deduction for herself.

### Proper Handling of Other Deductions and Losses under §§ 2053 and 2054.

Many § 2053 and § 2054 deductions and losses may be claimed either as estate tax deductions or as income tax deductions by the estate on the fiduciary return (Form 1041), but not both.[44] The income tax deduction is not allowed unless the estate tax deduction is waived. It is possible for these deductions to be apportioned between the two returns.

<table>
<tr><td>LO.9</td><td></td></tr>
<tr><td>⊙ Obtain liquidity for an estate.</td><td></td></tr>
</table>

## PROVIDING ESTATE LIQUIDITY

**Recognizing the Problem.** Even with effective predeath family tax planning directed toward a minimization of transfer taxes, the smooth administration of an estate necessitates a certain degree of liquidity. After all, probate costs will be incurred, and most important of all, death taxes must be satisfied. In the meantime, the surviving spouse and dependent beneficiaries may need financial support. Without funds to satisfy these claims, estate assets may have to be sold at sacrifice prices, and most likely, the decedent's scheme of testamentary disposition will be defeated.

**EXAMPLE 45**

At the time of Myrtle's death, her estate was made up almost entirely of a large ranch currently being operated by Jim, one of Myrtle's two sons. Because the ranch had been in the family for several generations and was a successful economic unit, Myrtle hoped that Jim would continue its operation and share the profits with Bob, her other son. Unfortunately, Bob, on learning that his mother had died without a will, demanded and obtained a partition and sale of his share of the property. Additional land was sold to pay for administration expenses and death taxes. After all of the sales had taken place, the portion remaining for Jim could not be operated profitably, and he was forced to give up the family ranch activity. ∎

What type of predeath planning might have avoided the result reached in Example 45? Certainly, Myrtle should have recognized and provided for the cash needs of the estate. Life insurance payable to her estate, although it adds to the estate tax liability, could have eased or solved the problem. This presumes that Myrtle was insurable or that the cost of the insurance would not be prohibitive.

---

[44]§ 642(g) and Reg. § 20.2053–1(d).

Furthermore, Myrtle made a serious error in dying without a will. A carefully drawn will could have precluded Bob's later course of action and perhaps kept much more of the ranch property intact. The ranch could have been placed in trust, life estate to Jim and Bob, remainder to their children. With such an arrangement, Bob would have been unable to sell the principal (the ranch).

Being able to defer the payment of death taxes may be an invaluable option for an estate that lacks cash or near-cash assets (e.g., marketable securities). In this connection, two major possibilities exist.

- The discretionary extension of time (§ 6161).
- The extension of time when the estate consists largely of an interest in a closely held business (§ 6166).

**Discretionary Extension of Time to Pay Estate Taxes—§ 6161.**   Currently, an executor or administrator may request an extension of time for paying the death tax for a period not to exceed 10 years from the date fixed for the payment. The IRS grants such requests whenever there is "reasonable cause." Reasonable cause is not limited to a showing of undue hardship. It includes cases in which the executor or administrator is unable to marshal liquid assets readily because they are located in several jurisdictions. It also includes situations where the estate is largely made up of assets in the form of payments to be received in the future (e.g., annuities, copyright royalties, contingent fees, or accounts receivable), or where the assets that must be liquidated to pay the estate tax must be sold at a sacrifice or in a depressed market.

**Extension of Time When the Estate Consists Largely of an Interest in a Closely Held Business—§ 6166.**   Congress always has been sympathetic to the plight of an estate that consists of an interest in a closely held business. The immediate imposition of the estate tax in such a situation may force the liquidation of the business at distress prices or cause the interest to be sold to outside parties.

A possible resolution of the problem is to use § 6166, which requires the IRS to accept a 15-payment procedure (5 interest-only payments, followed by 10 installment payments of the estate tax). This delay can enable the business to generate enough income to buy out the deceased owner's interest without disruption of operations or other financial sacrifice.

To meet the requirements of § 6166, the decedent's interest in a farm or other closely held business must exceed 35 percent of the decedent's adjusted gross estate.[45] The adjusted gross estate is the gross estate less the sum allowable as deductions under § 2053 (expenses, indebtedness, and taxes) and § 2054 (casualty and theft losses during the administration of an estate).

An interest in a closely held business includes the following.[46]

- Any sole proprietorship.
- An interest in a partnership carrying on a trade or business, if 20 percent of the capital interest in the partnership is included in the gross estate *or* the partnership has 45 or fewer partners.
- Stock in a corporation carrying on a trade or business, if 20 percent or more of the value of the voting stock of the corporation is included in the gross estate *or* the corporation has 45 or fewer shareholders.[47]

---

[45]§ 6166(a)(1).
[46]§ 6166(b)(1).
[47]The change to 45 or fewer partners or shareholders was made by the Tax Relief Reconciliation Act of 2001. It is effective for decedents dying in 2002 and beyond. For decedents dying before 2002, the rule was 15 or fewer partners or shareholders.

## CONCEPT SUMMARY 18–3

### Estate and Gift Planning

1. In reducing (or eliminating) gift taxes, one can take advantage of the annual exclusion and the election to split gifts. In the case of a single asset with high value (e.g., land), annual gifts of partial interests should be considered.
2. Gifts can reduce later estate taxes. This is accomplished by giving away assets that will appreciate in value (e.g., life insurance policies, art works, rare collections).
3. Timely gifts can help an estate qualify for § 2032A (special use valuation method), § 6166 (15-year payout of estate taxes), and § 303 (stock redemptions to pay death taxes). To be effective, the gift must avoid the three-year rule of § 2035.
4. Gifts can relieve the income tax burden on the family unit. This objective is accomplished by shifting the income from the gift property to family members who are in a lower income tax bracket. In this regard, make sure the gift is *complete* and circumvents kiddie tax treatment.
5. Avoid gifts of property that result in income tax consequences to the donor.
6. Potential *probate costs* can be an important consideration in meaningful estate planning. Some procedures that reduce these costs include joint tenancies with the right of survivorship, living trusts, and predeath dispositions of out-of-state real estate. Keep in mind that most of these procedures *do not reduce estate taxes*.
7. A program of lifetime gifts and proper use of valuation techniques will reduce a decedent's *gross estate*. Further planning can reduce the *taxable estate* by proper handling of estate tax deductions.
8. For a married decedent, the most important deduction is the *marital deduction*. The two major approaches to the marital deduction are the *equalization* and *deferral* approaches.
9. Whether the equalization approach or the deferral approach is emphasized, make use of the *bypass amount*.
10. Lifetime charitable contributions are preferable to transfers by death. The lifetime contributions provide the donor with an income tax deduction, and the amount donated is not included in the gross estate.
11. The *disclaimer* procedure can be used to control (either lower or raise) the amount of the marital deduction. It also can be used to increase the amount of the charitable deduction.
12. Gift planning can help ease potential *estate liquidity* problems (see item 3 above). After death, § 6166 can be useful if the estate qualifies. The provision allows installment payments of deferred estate taxes over an extended period of time.

In meeting the preceding requirements, a decedent and his or her surviving spouse are treated as one owner (shareholder or partner) if the interest is held as community property, tenants in common, joint tenants, or tenants by the entirety. Attribution from family members is allowed.[48]

**EXAMPLE 46**

Decedent Bonnie held a 15% capital interest in the Wren Partnership. Her son holds another 10%. Wren had 46 partners including Bonnie and her son. Since the son's interest is attributed to Bonnie, the estate is deemed to hold a 25% interest, and Wren (for purposes of § 6166) has only 45 partners. ■

In satisfying the more-than-35 percent test for qualification under § 6166, interests in more than one closely held business are aggregated when the decedent's gross estate includes 20 percent or more of the value of each such business.[49]

**EXAMPLE 47**

Henry's estate includes stock in Green Corporation and Brown Corporation, each of which qualifies as a closely held business. If the stock held in each entity represents 20% or more

---

[48]As described in § 267(c)(4).

[49]§ 6166(c).

of the total value outstanding, the stocks can be combined for purposes of the more-than-35% test. ■

If the conditions of § 6166 are satisfied and the provision is elected, the following results transpire.

- No payments on the estate tax attributable to the inclusion of the interest in a closely held business in the gross estate need be made with the first five payments. Then, annual installments are made over a period not longer than 10 years.
- From the outset, interest at the rate of 2 percent is paid.[50] Originally, the 2 percent rate of interest applied only to the first $1 million of estate tax value. Since the estate tax value amount has been indexed for inflation, for 2003 it is $1,120,000 (it was $1,100,000 for 2002).
- Acceleration of deferred payments may be triggered upon the disposition of the interest or failure to make scheduled principal or interest payments.[51]

In qualifying for § 6166, prune the potential estate of assets that may cause the 35 percent test to be failed. In this regard, lifetime gifts of such assets as marketable securities and life insurance should be considered.[52]

Some of the estate planning procedures covered in the last part of this chapter appear in Concept Summary 18–3.

## KEY TERMS

| | | |
|---|---|---|
| Blockage rule, 18–9 | Entity buy-sell agreement, 18–10 | Special use value, 18–6 |
| Buy-sell agreement, 18–10 | Estate freeze, 18–12 | Step-down in basis, 18–16 |
| Conservation easements, 18–27 | Living trust, 18–24 | Step-up in basis, 18–15 |
| Cross-purchase buy-sell agreement, 18–10 | Probate costs, 18–24 | |

## PROBLEM MATERIALS

### Discussion Questions

1. Discuss the relevance of the following in defining "fair market value" for Federal gift and estate tax purposes.
   a. § 2031(b).
   b. The definition contained in Reg. § 20.2031–1(b).
   c. A forced sale price.
   d. The location of the property being valued.
   e. The sentimental value of the property being valued.
   f. The wholesale price of the property.
   g. Tangible personalty sold as a result of an advertisement in the classified section of a newspaper.

**Issue ID**

2. Marvin's daughter is a student at an exclusive private women's college. Each year that she attends, Marvin has her sign a note for $20,000 to cover books, tuition, and room and board. Fifteen years after the daughter graduates, Marvin dies without a will. The

---

[50]§ 6601(j)(1).
[51]§ 6166(g).

[52]A gift within three years of death is not effective for this purpose. § 2035(c)(2).

notes are found in his safe deposit box. Although the daughter has become a successful business executive, Marvin never discussed the notes with her or made any attempts at collection. What are the pertinent tax issues? [Note: In answering this question, a review of the earlier part of Chapter 17 might prove useful.]

3. When Pierce dies, one of the assets of his estate is a note receivable from Geena in the amount of $50,000. In valuing this note, what effect, if any, do the following factors have?
   a. The interest on the note is 2%.
   b. No collateral for the note exists.
   c. The maturity date is in five years.
   d. Geena is Pierce's daughter, and Pierce forgives the note in his will.
   e. No one knows where Geena is.

4. Comment on the valuation of each of the following items.
   a. An annuity contract issued by a party not regularly engaged in issuing such contracts.
   b. An annuity contract issued by an insurance company.
   c. A single premium life insurance policy.
   d. A life insurance policy, not recently issued, on which future premiums need to be made.

5. With a transfer of securities worth $1 million, Julius creates a trust. Under the terms of the trust, Courtney is granted a life estate with the remainder interest passing to Margaret.
   a. Has Julius made one or two gifts? What difference does it make?
   b. How is the gift to Margaret determined?
   c. How is the gift to Courtney determined?

6. In connection with § 2032A, comment on the following.
   a. The reason for the provision.
   b. Distinguish between "most suitable" and "special" use. Where do "best," "current," and "highest" use fit in?
   c. The amount of valuation that can be excluded under this provision.
   d. The relevance of the term "material participation."

7. Eight years after the § 2032A election is made, the qualified heir sells the qualified property.
   a. What estate taxes result?
   b. What income taxes result?

8. A program of lifetime giving can help an estate qualify for the special use valuation election of § 2032A.
   a. Explain how this advice can succeed.
   b. What could go wrong?

9. In determining the value of goodwill attributable to stock in a closely held corporation, comment on the following factors.
   a. The corporation's average profit figure includes large gains not related to the business conducted.
   b. The family members who own and run the business have been paid adequate salaries by the corporation.
   c. The rate of return used by the IRS for this type of business is too high.
   d. The deceased owner was active in the operation of the business.

10. What effect, if any, will each of the following factors have on the valuation of stock in a closely held corporation?
    a. The "blockage rule."
    b. A minority interest is involved.
    c. A majority interest is involved.
    d. The cost the corporation would incur in going public.
    e. The income tax consequences upon disposition of the stock.

11. A renowned artist dies. Explain what factors might have a bearing on the valuation of oil paintings included in her gross estate.

12. During the same year, a donor gives stock in a closely held corporation to family members and to a qualified charitable organization. In terms of tax planning, what might such a procedure accomplish?

13. In terms of buy-sell agreements, comment on the following.
    a. The type of agreement that envisions a stock redemption.
    b. An agreement where the price set will control for estate tax purposes.

14. In determining the income tax basis of property acquired by gift, when are the donor's gift tax consequences irrelevant?

15. What role does "fair market value" play in determining the income tax basis of property acquired by gift? Of property acquired by death (i.e., inherited)?

16. In terms of income tax basis, comment on the following.
    a. The surviving spouse's share of community property.
    b. The surviving tenant's share of property held in joint tenancy.
    c. Property a donor reacquires by inheritance from a donee-decedent.
    d. Property received that is classified as income in respect of a decedent (IRD).

17. Jonathan Rand is distressed about the basis of some land he inherited five years ago and recently sold for a large gain. He feels that the value placed on the property is too low. Consequently, he requests your advice as to whether he is bound by this value.
    a. Write a letter to Jonathan regarding this matter. Jonathan's address is 326 Wisteria Avenue, Charlotte, NC 28223.
    b. Include in the letter a list of further information you will need before you can assess the probability of success in challenging the value used by the estate.

18. In terms of saving future estate taxes, comment on the advisability of making gifts of the following assets.
    a. An insurance policy on the life of the donor. The beneficiary is the donor's son.
    b. Same as (a), but the beneficiary is the donor's estate.
    c. Same as (a), but the beneficiary is the donor's spouse.
    d. Marketable securities. The donor hopes to have his estate qualify under § 2032A.
    e. A valuable art collection.

19. Rita and Larry Owen own all of the stock in Crow Company, an S corporation. In order to shift income, they are proposing making gifts of some of the stock to their children: Lisa (age 17), Mike (age 16), Lori (age 15), and Donald (age 13). They request your advice on how to make these gifts effective for tax purposes.
    a. Write a letter to Rita and Larry on this matter. The Owens' address is 408 Commerce Street, Kingston, RI 02881.
    b. Prepare a memo for your firm's files.

20. How do the income tax consequences differ depending on whether the following assets are transferred by gift or by death?
    a. Installment note receivable.
    b. U.S. savings bond.
    c. Depreciable property with recapture potential under § 1245 or § 1250.

21. Charles Horn wants his daughter Sharon to get stock that he owns in Crimson Corporation. He acquired the stock two years ago at a cost of $800,000, and it currently has a fair market value of $650,000. Charles has made prior taxable gifts and is in poor health. He seeks your advice as to whether he should gift the stock to Sharon or pass it to her under his will. Charles has a large capital loss carryover and has no prospect for any capital gains.
    a. Write a letter to Charles regarding the tax implications of the alternatives he has suggested. His address is 648 Scenic Drive, Chattanooga, TN 37403.
    b. Prepare a memo for your firm's files on this matter.

22. Dwight is the owner and insured of a life insurance policy. Comment on the probate and gross estate impact of the following options.
    a. Dwight designates his estate as the beneficiary.
    b. Dwight designates his wife as the beneficiary.
    c. Dwight gives the policy to his wife, and she designates his estate as the beneficiary.
    d. Same as (c), except that his wife designates their son as the beneficiary.

23. Ten years ago, Judy retired and moved from New York to Florida. She retained her personal residence in New York as rental property. She also owns a beach house in New Jersey. Should Judy carry out any predeath planning as to the real estate she owns? Explain.

24. In connection with the *bypass amount*, comment on the following.
    a. What is it?
    b. How does it relate to the *exclusion amount*? The *exemption equivalent*?
    c. How can it be utilized in the case of charitable bequests?
    d. In the case of marital bequests?

**Issue ID**

25. Elena, a naturalized U.S. citizen who immigrated from Spain, has accumulated considerable wealth during her lifetime. She is in poor health and probably will not live for more than a few years. For some time, she has wanted to make a large donation to her church but has feared that she might need the funds to live on. Suggest means by which Elena might carry out her wish with a significant tax saving.

**Decision Making**

26. Regarding charitable transfers, comment on the following issues.
    a. A preference for lifetime, rather than testamentary, transfers.
    b. Avoiding the danger that the designated recipient is no longer a "qualified" charity.
    c. The advisability of a surviving spouse issuing a disclaimer as to a bequest when the remainderperson under the will is a qualified charity.
    d. The tax planning utility of issuing scenic conservation easements.

27. Regarding § 6166, comment on the following.
    a. The reason for the provision.
    b. The interest rate.
    c. The schedule of payments.
    d. The recent change made by the Tax Relief Reconciliation Act of 2001.

**Issue ID**

28. The estate of Janet, currently still alive, almost qualifies for an election under § 6166. Janet is not concerned, however, because she plans on giving away her life insurance policy before her death. This, she believes, will allow her estate to meet the requirements of § 6166. Any comment?

29. Although not explicitly stated as such, certain Code provisions implicitly recognize that the owner-decedent of a small business may have a liquidity problem. How is this notion manifested in the following Code provisions?
    a. Small business deduction of § 2057 (see the discussion in Chapter 17).
    b. Special use value election of § 2032A.
    c. Extension of time to pay estate taxes of § 6166.

## Problems

30. When Sarah died, she owned 10,000 shares of Oriole Corporation. The stock is traded in an over-the-counter market. The nearest trades before and after the date of Sarah's death are as follows.

|  | Per Share Mean Selling Price |
| --- | --- |
| Four days before Sarah's death | $210 |
| Six days after Sarah's death | 230 |

Assuming the alternate valuation date is not elected, at what value should the Oriole stock be included in Sarah's gross estate?

31. In 2003, John creates a trust with securities worth $3 million. Under the terms of the trust, Mary (age 40) receives a life estate, while Nolan (age 15) receives the remainder interest. In the month the trust is created, the appropriate interest rate is 7.6%. Determine the value of John's gifts.

32. In 2003, Rita creates a trust with securities worth $2.5 million. Under the terms of the trust, Burl (age 12) receives the income for 15 years, remainder to Tina (age 35). In the month the trust is created, the appropriate interest rate is 7.8%. Determine the value of Rita's gifts.

33. In 2000, Calvin (age 64) creates a trust with property worth $2.1 million. Under the terms of the trust, Calvin retains a life estate with the remainder interest passing to Timothy (Calvin's son) upon Calvin's death.

    Calvin dies in 2003, when the value of the trust is $2.4 million and Timothy is age 30. In the month the trust is created, the appropriate interest rate is 8.0%. In the month Calvin died, the appropriate interest rate is 6.8%. Determine what taxable gifts have occurred.

34. Assume the same facts as in Problem 33. How much, if any, is included in Calvin's gross estate? Refer to Chapter 17 if necessary.

35. Comment on each of the following statements relating to § 2032A.
    a. Section 2032A applies even if the qualifying property is willed by the decedent to a nonfamily member.
    b. If § 2032A applies, current use value (as opposed to most suitable use value) can be used for the qualifying property, but not to exceed a limit on the adjustment of $840,000.
    c. The special use valuation method cannot be used in setting the valuation of a lifetime gift.
    d. Recapture occurs only if the qualifying property is sold.
    e. Lifetime gifts of nonqualifying assets may help in satisfying the 50% and 25% requirements of § 2032A.
    f. In satisfying the 50% and 25% requirements, the qualifying property is valued at most suitable use value.
    g. In the event recapture occurs, the amount of additional value used must be added to the existing income tax basis of the property.

36. Review the discussion of § 2057 (deduction for small business) in Chapter 17. Based on the legend provided below, classify each statement accordingly.

    | Legend | | |
    | --- | --- | --- |
    | B | = | Applies to *both* § 2032A and § 2057 |
    | N | = | Applies to *neither* § 2032A nor § 2057 |
    | E | = | Applies *only* to § 2057 |
    | V | = | Applies *only* to § 2032A |

    a. Provision is elective and need not be used by the estate.
    b. Provision requires the element of material participation.
    c. Provision is subject to indexation (i.e., adjustment for inflation).
    d. The property (or business) must pass to "qualifying heirs."
    e. A "qualifying heir" can include a long-time employee who is not part of the decedent's family.
    f. Any recapture is in full (i.e., 100% of tax)—partial recapture (e.g., 80%) is not possible.

37. At the time of his death, Caleb owns 70% of the stock in Swallow Corporation, with the balance of 30% held by family members. During the past five years, Swallow has generated average net profits of $400,000. On the date of Caleb's death the book value

(corporate net worth) of the Swallow stock is $1 million. An appropriate rate of return for the type of business Swallow conducts is 8%.

a. Presuming that some goodwill exists, what value should be included in Caleb's gross estate for the Swallow stock?

b. What arguments could Caleb's executor make in arguing that the value determined under (a) is too high?

38. Myron owns all of the stock in Tern Corporation. The stock has a value of $2 million for the common and $500,000 for the preferred. The preferred is noncumulative, does not have a redemption value, and carries no liquidation preference. Myron gives the common stock to his adult children and retains the preferred stock. What are Myron's gift tax consequences?

39. Assume the same facts as in Problem 38. Six years after the gift, Myron dies. At that time, the Tern stock is worth $3 million for the common and $500,000 for the preferred. What amount, if any, is included in Myron's gross estate?

40. Polly gives stock to Elton when it has a fair market value of $150,000. Polly acquired the stock several years ago at a cost of $50,000. Determine Elton's income tax basis for gain or loss under each of the following assumptions.

a. The gift occurred in 1976, and Polly paid a gift tax of $8,200.

b. The gift occurred in 2003, and Polly paid a gift tax of $6,000.

41. Ward gives stock to Mona in the current year when the shares have a value of $450,000. Ward acquired the stock several years ago for $500,000. As a result of the transfer, Ward incurs and pays a gift tax of $20,000. Determine Mona's gain or loss if she sells the stock for:

a. $510,000.

b. $440,000.

c. $460,000.

**Decision Making**

**Communications**

42. Virginia and Kim Andrews are married and have always lived in a community property state. Kim (age 76) is terminally ill, while Virginia (age 63) is in good health. Among the assets they own as part of their community are the following investments.

| | Adjusted Basis | Fair Market Value |
|---|---|---|
| Stock in Mallard Corporation | $150,000 | $100,000 |
| Stock in Dove Corporation | 50,000 | 100,000 |

Virginia and Kim need $100,000 to meet current needs and pay Kim's medical expenses.

a. Do you have any suggestions as to which stock Virginia and Kim might sell?

b. Write a letter to them explaining your recommendations. The Andrews live at 1420 Burro Lane, Reno, NV 89557.

c. Prepare a memo on this matter for your firm's client files.

43. In April 2002, George gives Beverly a house (basis of $50,000 and fair market value of $250,000) to be used as her personal residence. As a result of the transfer, George incurs and pays a gift tax of $15,000. Before her death in March 2003, Beverly installs a swimming pool in the backyard at a cost of $20,000. The residence is worth $270,000 on the date of Beverly's death, and her estate does not elect the alternate valuation date. Determine the income tax basis of the property to the heir, based on the following independent assumptions.

a. Under Beverly's will, the residence passes to George.

b. Under Beverly's will, the residence passes to Junior (Beverly's son).

**Decision Making**

44. Elsie and Garth are husband and wife with four married children and six grandchildren. Commencing in December 2003, they would like to transfer a tract of land (worth $616,000) equally to their children (including spouses) and grandchildren as quickly as possible and without making a taxable gift. What do you suggest?

45. At the time of her death, Hortense has an adjusted gross estate of $3.1 million. Her estate includes the family farm, with a most suitable use value of $1.6 million and a current use value of $800,000. The farm is inherited by Phil, Hortense's son, who has worked it for her since 1985. Phil plans to continue farming indefinitely.
    a. Based on the information given, is the § 2032A election available to Hortense's estate?
    b. If so, what value must be used for the farm?
    c. Suppose Hortense had made a gift of securities (fair market value of $150,000) to her cousin six months before her death. Does this fact affect your analysis? Explain.

46. Last year, Dean sold real estate (basis of $80,000) to Paul (an unrelated party) for $200,000, receiving $40,000 in cash and Paul's notes for the balance. The notes carry a 10% rate of interest and mature annually at $16,000 each year over a period of 10 years. Dean did not elect out of the installment method for reporting the gain on the sale. Before any of the notes mature and when the notes have a total fair market value of $150,000, Dean gives them to Shelley. Disregarding the interest element, what are Dean's income tax consequences as a result of the gift?

47. At the time of her death in the current year, Monica held the following assets.

|  | Fair Market Value |
| --- | --- |
| Personal residence (title listed as "Monica and Philip, tenants by the entirety with right of survivorship") | $800,000 |
| Savings account (listed as "Monica and Rex, joint tenants with right of survivorship") | 40,000 |
| Unimproved real estate (title listed as "Monica and Rex, equal tenants in common") | 300,000 |
| Insurance policy on Monica's life, issued by Lavender Company (Monica's estate is the designated beneficiary) | 200,000 |
| Insurance policy on Monica's life, issued by Crimson Company (Rex is the designated beneficiary) | 400,000 |
| Living trust created by Monica five years ago (life estate to Philip, remainder to Rex) | 700,000 |

Assuming Philip and Rex survive Monica, how much is included in Monica's *probate estate*?

**Decision Making**

48. During their marriage, Brenda and Victor have operated a business together. Each has managed to accumulate approximately $650,000 of income-producing property. Because she is 10 years younger and in better health, Brenda is expected to survive Victor. Upon the death of the survivor, they want their property to pass to their adult children.
    Outline an estate plan for Victor that would accomplish the following objectives.

    • Give Brenda maximum income protection.

    • Avoid a concentration of wealth in Brenda's estate that would cause an estate tax liability on her later death.

    • Avoid estate taxes on Victor's prior death.

    Neither Brenda nor Victor has made any prior taxable gifts. Victor has a niece, Julia, who is a practicing attorney and is familiar with the state's trust laws. Victor has close ties with Julia as he financed her education.
    In this connection, consider §§ 2036 and 2041 (discussed in Chapter 17).

49. In the following independent situations, describe the effect of a disclaimer on the estate tax positions of the parties. Assume all decedents die in 2003.
    a. Jan's will passes $1,125,000 to Kim (her son) and the remainder of her assets to Horace (Jan's husband). Kim disclaims $125,000.

b. Rebecca's will passes $1,200,000 to Les (Rebecca's husband) and the remaining $900,000 to Junior (Rebecca's son). Les disclaims $100,000.

c. Wesley's will passes $1,350,000 to Nadine (Wesley's wife) and the remainder to the Salvation Army. Nadine disclaims $350,000.

50. At the time of his death, Clint had an adjusted gross estate of $2.1 million. Included in the estate is a 15% capital interest in a partnership valued at $800,000. Except for Clint's daughter Phoebe, none of the other 48 partners are related to him. Phoebe holds a 10% capital interest.

a. Does Clint's estate qualify for the § 6166 election?

b. Suppose that one year prior to his death, Clint gave $200,000 cash to Phoebe. Does this change your analysis?

51. At the time of her death, Victoria had an adjusted gross estate of $1.5 million. Included in the estate were the following business interests.

| | Fair Market Value |
|---|---|
| A 40% capital interest in the RH Partnership | $300,000 |
| A 25% interest (i.e., 250 shares out of 1,000) in Olive Corporation | 200,000 |
| A catering service operated as a sole proprietorship | 150,000 |

The RH Partnership has 42 partners while Olive Corporation has a total of 40 shareholders. None of the other partners or shareholders are related to Victoria. Can Victoria's estate qualify for an election under § 6166? Explain.

## Research Problems

A THOMSON COMPANY

*Note: Solutions to Research Problems can be prepared by using the* **RIA Checkpoint® Student Edition** *online research product, or the* **CCH U.S. Master Tax Guide Plus™** *online Federal tax research database, which is available to accompany this text. It is also possible to prepare solutions to the Research Problems by using tax research materials found in a standard tax library.*

**Research Problem 1.** At the time of his death in 1998, Kevin Garth owned 8,000 shares in Cimarron Corporation. Cimarron is a closely held C corporation whose stock has never been traded. Under Kevin's will, half of his stock interest (i.e., 4,000 shares) passes to his surviving spouse, Louise. In completing and filing the estate tax return (Form 706), Kevin's executor treats the 8,000 shares of Cimarron stock as a minority interest and assigns a value of $2,000 to each share.

In early 1999, Cimarron redeems all of Louise's shares for $10 million ($2,500 per share). As her basis in the stock is $8 million (4,000 × $2,000), the redemption results in a gain of $2 million ($10 million redemption amount − $8 million basis). The gain is a long-term capital gain that generates a tax of $400,000 ($2 million gain × 20% maximum long-term capital gain tax rate).

In late 1999, Louise dies, and her estate is administered. In completing her estate tax return, Louise's executor claims a $400,000 deduction under § 2053(a)(3). This reflects the claim against the estate for the income taxes resulting from the stock redemption. The executor also prepares Louise's final income tax return (Form 1040). The return reports the $2 million gain. When the return is filed, the $400,000 tax on the gain is paid to the IRS.

In 2000, Kevin's Form 706 is audited by the IRS. Among the adjustments made and agreed to by the estate is an increase in the valuation of the Cimarron stock from $2,000 to $3,000 a share. When the executor of Louise's estate learns of this change, he files an amended income tax return for tax year 1999. What was previously reported as a gain of $2 million from the redemption is now shown as a loss of $2 million ($12 million basis − $10 million redemption amount). In due course, Louise's estate receives a refund from the IRS of the income taxes previously overpaid.

In 2001, Louise's Form 706 is audited by the IRS. Among the adjustments proposed is a disallowance of the $400,000 deduction claimed under § 2053(a)(3).

On what basis can the adjustment proposed by the IRS against Louise's estate be justified? How should the estate argue against the adjustment?

*Partial list of research aids:*
*Ithaca Trust Co. v. U.S.*, 1 USTC ¶386, 7 AFTR 8856, 49 S.Ct. 291 (USSC, 1929).
*Estate of Smith v. Comm.*, 2000–1 USTC ¶50,147, 84 AFTR2d 99–7393, 198 F.3d 515 (CA–5, 1999).
*Estate of Evelyn M. McMorris*, 77 TCM 1552, T.C.Memo. 1999–82.

**Research Problem 2.** In 1992, Troy wins the Connecticut LOTTO grand prize of $15 million. The LOTTO contest is governed by the following rules.

- The prize money is to be paid in 20 equal annual installments (in this case, $750,000 per year) with no interest provided for.

- The rights to the prize award are not assignable. If a winner dies during the payout period, however, the remaining installment payments are to be made to the winner's duly appointed executor.

- The prize award is not specifically funded or guaranteed by any state agency. It constitutes a general obligation of the state of Connecticut.

Troy dies in 1994 after having received two payments of $750,000 each. Troy's estate includes the present value of the remaining $13.5 million prize award in the estate at $4,860,000. This is determined by using the IRS table amount of $6,750,000 and discounting it for absence of security (i.e., no separate funding or guarantee of payment by a state agency) and lack of marketability (i.e., the award cannot be assigned). The table used is that issued by the IRS in Reg. § 20.2031–7 under the authority of § 7520. The table is to be used in valuing, among other income interests, private (i.e., noncommercial) annuity contracts.

Upon audit of the estate tax return, the IRS disputes the deviation from the table amount. The IRS argues that the absence-of-security discount is inappropriate because the state of Connecticut has never defaulted on any of its LOTTO obligations. Furthermore, the lack-of-marketability discount is inappropriately applied to annuity-type situations. Unlike stocks and bonds and other ownership interests, private annuities are not subject to marketplace valuation procedures.

Who should prevail? The taxpayer or the IRS?

*Partial list of research aids:*
§§ 2039 and 7520.
Reg. § 20.7520–3(b).
*O'Reilly v. Comm.*, 92–2 USTC ¶60,111, 70 AFTR2d 92–6211, 973 F.2d 1403 (CA–8, 1992).
*Shackleford v. U.S.*, 99–2 USTC ¶60,356, 84 AFTR2d 99–5902 (D.Ct.Calif, 1999), *aff'd* by 88 AFTR2d 2001–5658, 262 F.3d 1028 (CA–9, 2001).
*Estate of Gribauskas*, 116 T.C. 142 (2001).

**Issue ID**

**Research Problem 3.** Norman and Lydia Gates are husband and wife and have always lived in California. In 1982, they formed Oriole Corporation to engage in the restaurant supply business. Oriole's authorized stock of 1,000 shares was issued equally (500 shares each) to Norman and Lydia.

In 1996, Lydia predeceases Norman. By her will, 450 of the Oriole shares are placed in trust, life estate to Norman, remainder to their children. Under the terms of the trust, Norman is granted a testamentary general power of appointment. The power enables Norman, through a designation in his will, to appoint the trust corpus to whomever he chooses, including his own estate or the creditors of his estate.

In 2002, Norman dies intestate (i.e., without a will). Since Norman never exercised the power of appointment, the 450 shares of Oriole Corporation in Lydia's trust are distributed to her children. Norman's *probate estate*, however, does not include these shares but does include the 500 shares of Oriole that he owned outright.

How much of the Oriole stock should be included in Norman's *gross estate*? How should the stock be valued?

*Partial list of research aids:*
§§ 2031, 2033, 2041(b), 2044, and 2056(b)(5) and (7).
*Estate of Harriet R. Mellinger*, 112 T.C. 26 (1999).
*Estate of Aldo Fontana*, 118 T.C. 318 (2002).

**Internet Activity**

*Use the tax resources of the Internet to address the following questions. Do not restrict your search to the World Wide Web, but include a review of newsgroups and general reference materials, practitioner sites and resources, primary sources of the tax law, chat rooms and discussion groups, and other opportunities.*

**Research Problem 4.** Locate a professional firm or association that regularly does asset appraisals. Under which codes of behavioral conduct does that entity operate?

**Research Problem 5.** The Tax Relief Reconciliation Act of 2001 enacted new Code § 1022. Scheduled to become effective in 2010, this provision largely revokes the step-up and step-down in income tax basis that an heir gets in property received from a decedent. Using the Internet, locate and review § 1022. Are there any exceptions to the new rules that impose a "carryover basis" upon the heirs? Elaborate.

# Income Taxation of Trusts and Estates

CHAPTER 19

## LEARNING OBJECTIVES

*After completing Chapter 19, you should be able to:*

### LO.1
Use working definitions with respect to trusts, estates, beneficiaries, and other parties.

### LO.2
Identify the steps in determining the accounting and taxable income of a trust or estate and the related taxable income of the beneficiaries.

### LO.3
Illustrate the uses and implications of distributable net income.

### LO.4
Use the special rules that apply to trusts where the creator (grantor) of the trust retains certain rights.

http://wft.swlearning.com

## OUTLINE

# An Overview of Subchapter J

Taxpayers create trusts for a variety of reasons. Some trusts are established primarily for tax purposes, but most are designed to accomplish a specific financial goal or to provide for the orderly management of assets in case of emergency. Table 19–1 lists some of the more common reasons for creating a trust, and Figure 19–1 illustrates the structure of a typical trust (and estate).

Because a trust is a separate tax entity, its gross income and deductions must be measured, and an annual tax return must be filed. Similarly, when an individual dies, a legal entity is created in the form of his or her estate. This chapter examines the rules related to the income taxation of trusts and estates.

The income taxation of trusts and estates is governed by Subchapter J of the Internal Revenue Code, §§ 641 through 692. Certain similarities are apparent between Subchapter J and the income taxation of individuals (e.g., the definitions of gross income and deductible expenditures), partnerships and limited liability entities (e.g., the conduit principle), and S corporations (e.g., the conduit principle and the trust as a separate taxable entity). Trusts also involve several important new concepts, however, including the determination of *distributable net income* and the *tier system* of distributions to beneficiaries.

■ **TABLE 19–1**
Motivations for Creating a Trust

| Type of Trust | Financial and Other Goals |
|---|---|
| Life insurance trust | Holds life insurance policies on the insured, removes the proceeds of the policies from the gross estate (if an irrevocable trust), and safeguards against receipt of the proceeds by a young or inexperienced beneficiary. |
| "Living" (revocable) trust | Manages assets, reduces probate costs, provides privacy for asset disposition, protects against medical or other emergencies, and provides relief from the necessity of day-to-day management of the underlying assets. |
| Trust for minors | Provides funds for a college education, shifts income to lower-bracket taxpayers, and transfers accumulated income without permanently parting with the underlying assets. |
| "Blind" trust | Holds and manages the assets of the grantor without his/her input or influence (e.g., while the grantor holds political office or some other sensitive position). |
| Retirement trust | Manages asset contributions under a qualified retirement plan. |
| Alimony trust | Manages the assets of an ex-spouse and assures they will be distributed in a timely fashion to specified beneficiaries. |
| Liquidation trust | Collects and distributes the last assets of a corporation that is undergoing a complete liquidation. |

LO.1

Use working definitions with respect to trusts, estates, beneficiaries, and other parties.

## WHAT IS A TRUST?

The Code does not contain a definition of a trust. However, the term usually refers to an arrangement created by a will or by an *inter vivos* (lifetime) declaration through which trustees take title to property for the purpose of protecting or conserving it for the beneficiaries.[1]

Typically, the creation of a trust involves at least three parties: (1) The **grantor** (sometimes referred to as the settlor or donor) transfers selected assets to the trust entity. (2) The trustee, who may be either an individual or a corporation, is charged with the fiduciary duties associated with the trust. (3) The beneficiary is designated to receive income or property from the trust; the beneficiary's rights are defined by state law and by the trust document.

In some situations, fewer than three persons may be involved, as specified by the trust agreement. For instance, an elderly individual who no longer can manage his or her own property (e.g., because of ill health) may create a trust under which he or she is both the grantor and the beneficiary. In this case, a corporate trustee is charged with the management of the grantor's assets.

In another situation, the grantor might designate himself or herself as the trustee of the trust assets. For example, a parent who wants to transfer selected assets to a minor child could use a trust entity to assure that the minor does not waste the property. By naming himself or herself as the trustee, the parent retains virtual control over the property that is transferred.

Under the general rules of Subchapter J, the **grantor trusts** just described are not recognized for income tax purposes. Similarly, when only one party is involved (when the same individual is grantor, trustee, and sole beneficiary of the trust), Subchapter J rules do not apply, and the entity is ignored for income tax purposes.

---
[1]Reg. § 301.7701–4(a).

■ **FIGURE 19–1**
Structure of a Typical Trust and Estate

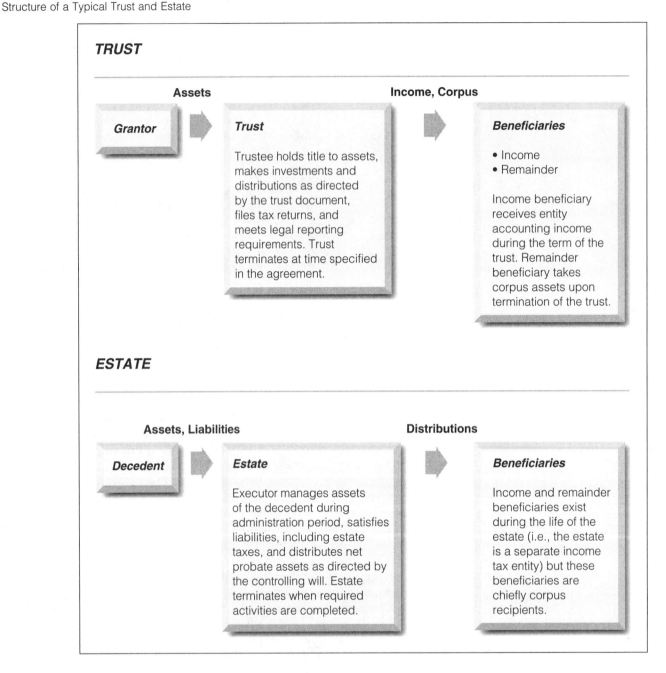

## OTHER DEFINITIONS

When the grantor transfers title of selected assets to a trust, those assets become the **corpus** (body), or principal, of the trust. Trust corpus, in most situations, earns *income*, which may be distributed to the beneficiaries or accumulated for the future by the trustee, as the trust instrument directs.

In the typical trust, the grantor creates two types of beneficiaries: one who receives the accounting income of the trust and one who receives the trust corpus that remains at the termination of the trust entity. Beneficiaries in the former category hold an *income interest* in the trust, and those in the latter category hold a *remainder interest* in the trust's assets. If the grantor retains the remainder interest, the interest is known as a **reversionary interest** (corpus reverts to the grantor when the trust entity terminates).

The trust document establishes the term of the trust. The term may be for a specific number of years (*term certain*) or until the occurrence of a specified event. For instance, a trust might exist (1) for the life of the income beneficiary, in which case the income beneficiary is known as a *life tenant* in trust corpus; (2) for the life of some other individual; (3) until the income or remainder beneficiary reaches the age of majority; or (4) until the beneficiary, or another individual, marries, receives a promotion, or reaches some specified age.

The trustee may be required to distribute the accounting income of the entity according to a distribution schedule specified in the agreement. Sometimes, however, the trustee is given more discretion with respect to the timing and nature of the distributions. If the trustee can determine, within guidelines that may be included in the trust document, either the timing of the income or corpus distributions or the specific beneficiaries who will receive them (from among those identified in the agreement), the trust is called a **sprinkling trust.** Here, the trustee can "sprinkle" the distributions among the various beneficiaries. As discussed in Chapters 17 and 18, family-wide income taxes can be reduced by directing income to those who are subject to lower marginal tax rates. Thus, by giving the trustee a sprinkling power, the income tax liability of the family unit can be manipulated by applying the terms of the trust agreement.

For purposes of certain provisions of Subchapter J, a trust must be classified as either a **simple trust** or a **complex trust.** A simple trust (1) is required to distribute its entire accounting income to designated beneficiaries every year, (2) has no beneficiaries that are qualifying charitable organizations, and (3) makes no distributions of trust corpus during the year. A complex trust is any trust that is not a simple trust.[2] These criteria are applied to the trust every year. Thus, every trust is classified as a complex trust in the year in which it terminates (because it distributes all of its corpus during that year).

## WHAT IS AN ESTATE?

An estate is created upon the death of every individual. The entity is charged with collecting and conserving all of the individual's assets, satisfying all liabilities, and distributing the remaining assets to the heirs identified by state law or the will.

Typically, the creation of an estate involves at least three parties: the decedent, all of whose probate assets are transferred to the estate for disposition; the executor, who is appointed under the decedent's valid will (or the administrator, if no valid will exists); and the beneficiaries of the estate, who are to receive assets or income from the entity, as the decedent has indicated in the will. The executor or administrator holds the fiduciary responsibility to operate the estate as directed by the will, applicable state law, and the probate court.

Recall that the assets that make up the probate estate are not identical to those that constitute the gross estate for transfer tax purposes (refer to Chapter 18). Many gross estate assets are not a part of the probate estate and thus are not subject to disposition by the executor or administrator. For instance, property held by the decedent as a joint tenant passes to the survivor(s) by operation of the applicable

---

[2]Reg. § 1.651(a)–1.

state's property law rather than through the probate estate. Proceeds of insurance policies on the life of the decedent, over which the decedent held the incidents of ownership, are not under the control of the executor or administrator. The designated beneficiaries of the policy receive the proceeds outright under the insurance contract.

An estate is a separate taxable entity. Under certain circumstances, taxpayers may find it profitable to prolong an estate's existence. This situation is likely to arise when the heirs are already in a high income tax bracket and would, therefore, prefer to have income generated by the estate so as to fully use the estate's lower marginal income tax rates. If an estate's existence is unduly prolonged, however, the IRS can terminate it for Federal income tax purposes after the expiration of a reasonable period for completing the duties of administration.[3]

# Nature of Trust and Estate Taxation

In general, the taxable income of a trust or estate is taxed to the entity or to its beneficiaries to the extent that each has received the accounting income of the entity. Thus, Subchapter J creates a modified conduit principle relative to the income taxation of trusts, estates, and their beneficiaries. Whoever receives the accounting income of the entity, or some portion of it, is liable for the income tax that results.

**EXAMPLE 1**

Adam receives 80% of the accounting income of the Zero Trust. The trustee accumulated the other 20% of the income at her discretion under the trust agreement and added it to trust corpus. Adam is liable for income tax only on the amount of the distribution, while Zero is liable for the income tax on the accumulated portion of the income. ■

## FILING REQUIREMENTS

The fiduciary is required to file a Form 1041 (U.S. Income Tax Return for Estates and Trusts) in the following situations.[4]

- For an estate that has gross income of $600 or more for the year.
- For a trust that either has any taxable income or, if there is no taxable income, has gross income of $600 or more.

The fiduciary return (and any related tax liability) is due no later than the fifteenth day of the fourth month following the close of the entity's taxable year. The return is filed with the Internal Revenue Service in either Cincinnati, Ohio, or Ogden, Utah, depending on the U.S. location of the fiduciary's principal place of business.

## TAX ACCOUNTING PERIODS, METHODS, AND PAYMENTS

An estate or trust may use many of the tax accounting methods available to individuals. The method of accounting used by the grantor of a trust or the decedent of an estate need not carry over to the entity.

An estate has the same options for choosing a tax year as any new taxpayer. Thus, the estate of a calendar year decedent dying on March 3 can select any fiscal year or report on a calendar year basis. If the latter is selected, the estate's first taxable year will include the period from March 3 to December 31. If the first or

---

[3]Reg. § 1.641(b)–3(a).                    [4]§ 6012(a).

last tax years are short years (less than one calendar year), income for those years need not be annualized.

To eliminate the possibility of deferring the taxation of fiduciary-source income simply by using a fiscal tax year, virtually all trusts (other than tax-exempt trusts) are required to use a calendar tax year.[5]

Trusts and estates are required to make estimated Federal income tax payments using the same quarterly schedule that applies to individual taxpayers. This requirement applies to estates and grantor trusts only for tax years that end two or more years after the date of the decedent's death. Charitable trusts and private foundations are exempt from estimated payment requirements altogether.[6]

The two-year estimated tax exception for estates recognizes the liquidity problems that an executor often faces during the early months of administering the estate. The exception does not assure, however, that an estate in existence less than 24 months will never be required to make an estimated tax payment.

**EXAMPLE 2**

Juanita died on March 15, 2003. Her executor elected a fiscal year ending on July 31 for the estate. Estimated tax payments will be required from the estate starting with the tax year that begins on August 1, 2004. ∎

## TAX RATES AND PERSONAL EXEMPTION

Congress's desire to stop trusts from being used as income-shifting devices has made the fiduciary entity the highest-taxed taxpayer in the Code. The entity reaches the 38.6 percent marginal rate with only $9,350 of 2003 taxable income, so the grantor's ability to shift income in a tax-effective manner is nearly eliminated. The following table, which lists the 2003 taxes paid by various entities on taxable income of $30,000, shows how expensive the accumulation of income within an estate or trust can be today. Proper income shifting now would move assets *out of* the estate or trust and into the hands of the grantor or beneficiary.

| Filing Status/Entity | Taxable Income | Marginal Income Tax Rate (%) | 2003 Tax Liability |
|---|---|---|---|
| Single | $30,000 | 27 | $ 4,392 |
| Married, filing jointly | 30,000 | 15 | 3,900 |
| C corporation | 30,000 | 15 | 4,500 |
| Trust or estate | 30,000 | 38.6 | 10,538 |

A fiduciary's net long-term capital gains can be taxed at a nominal rate of no more than 20 percent. In addition to the regular income tax, an estate or trust may be subject to the alternative minimum tax.[7]

Both trusts and estates are allowed a personal exemption in computing the fiduciary tax liability. All estates are allowed a personal exemption of $600. The exemption available to a trust depends upon the type of trust involved. A trust that is required to distribute all of its income currently is allowed an exemption of $300. All other trusts are allowed an exemption of $100 per year.[8]

The classification of trusts as to the appropriate personal exemption is similar but not identical to the distinction between simple and complex trusts. The classification as a simple trust is more stringent.

[5] § 645.
[6] § 6654(l).

[7] § 55.
[8] § 642(b).

## EVERYONE GETS WET WHEN YOU SOAK THE RICH

Fiduciary taxation has fallen prey to the "soak the rich" approach to tax reform. In an environment that emphasizes taxes on millionaires, the tax rates that apply to trusts and estates have also increased, and the width of the lower brackets has become so narrow that these entities now are subject to the highest marginal rate structure in U.S. income tax law. Higher tax rates for trusts and estates affect all fiduciary arrangements, however, even those designed for reasons other than tax avoidance.

Perhaps by design, these rate changes have dampened the planning potential of fiduciary entities as a means of shifting income among generations (e.g., from parent to child) or over time (i.e., from the taxpayer's present tax return to a future one). But they have also deepened the tax burden on fixed-income retirees, handicapped individuals, children of divorced parents, and other commonly encountered fiduciary beneficiaries.

Most trust beneficiaries are passive recipients of investment income generated by a stock portfolio managed by a corporate trustee or by the distant managers of the mutual funds in which the funds are invested. In a typical year, a trust enters into very few "new" transactions. For the most part, there is little portfolio turnover, and periodic interest and dividends are collected. The beneficiaries exercise little decision-making authority over the yield or timing of the entity's distributions, which are fixed by the controlling instrument. Under such circumstances, tax rate increases seem to punish the powerless as well as to soak the rich.

**EXAMPLE 3**

Three trusts appear to operate in a similar fashion, but they are subject to different Subchapter J classifications and exemptions.

Trust Alpha is required to distribute all of its current accounting income to Susan. Thus, it is allowed a $300 personal exemption. No corpus distributions or charitable contributions are made during the year. Accordingly, Alpha is a simple trust.

Trust Beta is required to distribute all of its current accounting income; it is allowed a $300 personal exemption. The beneficiaries of these distributions are specified in the trust instrument: one-half of accounting income is to be distributed to Tyrone, and one-half is to be distributed to State University, a qualifying charitable organization. Since Beta has made a charitable distribution for the tax year, it is a complex trust.

The trustee of Trust Gamma can, at her discretion, distribute the current-year accounting income or corpus of the trust to Dr. Chapman. As the trustee is not required to distribute current accounting income, only a $100 personal exemption is allowed. During the current year, the trustee distributed all of the accounting income of the entity to Dr. Chapman, but made no corpus or charitable distributions. Nonetheless, because it lacks the current-year income distribution requirement, Gamma is a complex trust. ■

## ALTERNATIVE MINIMUM TAX

The alternative minimum tax (AMT) may apply to a trust or estate in any tax year. Given the nature and magnitude of the tax preferences, adjustments, and exemptions that determine alternative minimum taxable income (AMTI), however, most trusts and estates are unlikely to incur the tax. Nevertheless, they could be vulnerable if they are actively engaged in cashing out the stock options of a donor/decedent who was a corporate executive.

In general, derivation of AMTI for the entity follows the rules that apply to individual taxpayers. Thus, the corporate ACE adjustment does not apply to fiduciary entities, but AMTI may be created through the application of most of the other AMT preference and adjustment items discussed in Chapter 6.

The entity has a $22,500 annual exemption, similar to that available to a married individual who files a separate return. The exemption phases out at a rate of one-fourth of the amount by which AMTI exceeds $75,000.

A 26 percent alternative minimum tax rate is applied to AMTI, increasing to 28 percent when AMTI in excess of the exemption reaches $175,000. In addition, estimated tax payments for the entity must include any applicable AMT liability.

**LO.2**

Identify the steps in determining the accounting and taxable income of a trust or estate and the related taxable income of the beneficiaries.

# Taxable Income of Trusts and Estates

Generally, the taxable income of an estate or trust is computed similarly to that for an individual. Subchapter J does, however, include several important exceptions and provisions that make it necessary to use a systematic approach to calculating the taxable income of these entities. Figure 19–2 illustrates the procedure implied by the Code, and Figure 19–3 presents a systematic computation method to be followed in this chapter.

■ **FIGURE 19–2**

Accounting Income, Distributable Net Income, and Taxable Income of the Entity and Its Beneficiaries—The Five-Step Procedure

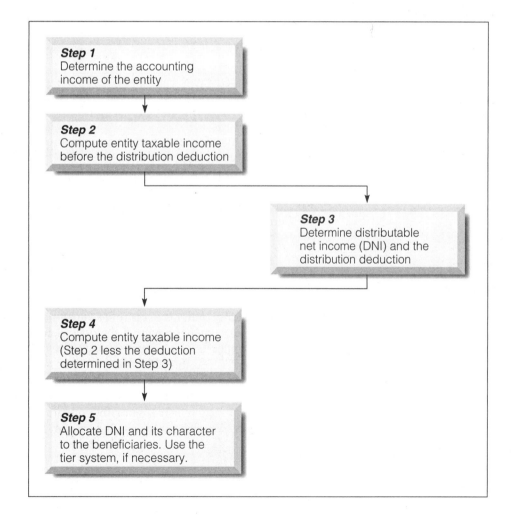

**Step 1**
Determine the accounting income of the entity

**Step 2**
Compute entity taxable income before the distribution deduction

**Step 3**
Determine distributable net income (DNI) and the distribution deduction

**Step 4**
Compute entity taxable income (Step 2 less the deduction determined in Step 3)

**Step 5**
Allocate DNI and its character to the beneficiaries. Use the tier system, if necessary.

■ **FIGURE 19–3**
Computational Template Applying the Five-Step Procedure

| Item | Totals | Accounting Income | Taxable Income | Distributable Net Income/Distribution Deduction |
|------|--------|-------------------|----------------|------------------------------------------------|
| Income | ___ | ___ | ___ | |
| Income | ___ | ___ | ___ | |
| Expense | ___ | ___ | ___ | |
| Expense | ___ | ___ | ___ | |
| Personal exemption | | | ___ | |
| Accounting income/taxable income before the distribution deduction | | ___ | ___ | |
| Exemption | | *Step 1* | *Step 2* | ___ |
| Corpus capital gain/loss | | | | ___ |
| Net exempt income | | | | ___ |
| Distributable net income | | | | ___ |
| Distribution deduction | | | ___ | *Step 3* |
| Entity taxable income | | | ___ | *Step 4* |

Beneficiary taxable income is addressed in *Step 5.*

## ENTITY ACCOUNTING INCOME

The first step in determining the taxable income of a trust or estate is to compute the entity's accounting income for the period. Although this prerequisite is not apparent from a cursory reading of Subchapter J, a closer look at the Code reveals a number of references to the *income* of the entity.[9] Wherever the term *income* is used in Subchapter J without some modifier (e.g., *gross* income or *taxable* income), the statute is referring to the accounting income of the trust or estate for the tax year.

A definition of entity accounting income is critical to understanding the Subchapter J computation of fiduciary taxable income. Under state law, entity accounting income is the amount that the income beneficiary of the simple trust or estate is eligible to receive from the entity. More importantly, the calculation of accounting income is virtually under the control of the grantor or decedent (through a properly drafted trust agreement or will). If the document has been drafted at arm's length, a court will enforce a fiduciary's good faith efforts to carry out the specified computation of accounting income.

Entity accounting income generally is defined by state laws that are derived from the Uniform Principal and Income Act. Most states have adopted some form of the Uniform Act, which essentially constitutes generally accepted accounting principles (GAAP) in the fiduciary tax setting.

---

[9]For example, see §§ 651(a)(1), 652(a), and 661(a)(1).

■ **TABLE 19–2**
Common Allocations of Items to
Income or Corpus

| Allocable to Income | Allocable to Corpus |
|---|---|
| • Ordinary and operating net income from trust assets. | • Depreciation on business assets. |
| • Interest, dividend, rent, and royalty income. | • Casualty gain/loss on income-producing assets. |
| • Stock dividends. | • Insurance recoveries on income-producing assets. |
| • One-half of fiduciary fees/commissions. | • Capital gain/loss on investment assets. |
|  | • Stock splits. |
|  | • One-half of fiduciary fees/commissions. |

By allocating specific items of income and expenditure either to the income beneficiaries or to corpus, the desires of the grantor or decedent are put into effect. Table 19–2 shows typical assignments of revenue and expenditure items to fiduciary income or corpus.

Where the controlling document is silent as to whether an item should be assigned to income or corpus, state law prevails. These allocations are an important determinant of the benefits received from the entity by its beneficiaries and the timing of those benefits.

**EXAMPLE 4**

The Arnold Trust is a simple trust. Mrs. Bennett is its sole beneficiary. In the current year, the trust earns $20,000 in taxable interest and $15,000 in tax-exempt interest. In addition, the trust recognizes an $8,000 long-term capital gain. The trustee assesses a fee of $11,000 for the year. If the trust agreement allocates fees and capital gains to corpus, trust accounting income is $35,000, and Mrs. Bennett receives that amount. Thus, the income beneficiary receives no immediate benefit from the trust's capital gain, and she bears none of the financial burden of the fiduciary's fees.

| | |
|---|---|
| Interest income | $35,000 |
| Long-term capital gain | ± –0–* |
| Fiduciary's fees | ± –0–* |
| Trust accounting income | $35,000 |

*Allocable to corpus.

**EXAMPLE 5**

Assume the same facts as in Example 4, except that the trust agreement allocates the fiduciary's fees to income. The trust accounting income is $24,000, and Mrs. Bennett receives that amount.

| | |
|---|---|
| Interest income | $ 35,000 |
| Long-term capital gain | ± –0–* |
| Fiduciary's fees | –11,000 |
| Trust accounting income | $ 24,000 |

*Allocable to corpus.

**EXAMPLE 6**

Assume the same facts as in Example 4, except that the trust agreement allocates to income all capital gains and losses and one-half of the trustee's commissions. The trust accounting income is $37,500, and Mrs. Bennett receives that amount.

| | |
|---|---|
| Interest income | $35,000 |
| Long-term capital gain | +8,000 |
| Fiduciary's fees | −5,500* |
| Trust accounting income | $37,500 |

*One-half allocable to corpus.

## GROSS INCOME

The gross income of an estate or trust is similar to that of an individual. In determining the gain or loss to be recognized by an estate or trust upon the sale or other taxable disposition of assets, the rules for basis determination are similar to those applicable to other taxpayers. Thus, an estate's basis for property received from a decedent is stepped up or stepped down to gross estate value (refer to Chapter 18 for a more detailed discussion). Property received as a gift (the usual case in trust arrangements) usually takes the donor's basis. Property purchased by the trust from a third party is assigned a basis equal to the purchase price.

**Property Distributions.**   In general, the entity does not recognize gain or loss upon its distribution of property to a beneficiary under the provisions of the will or trust document. The distributed property has the same basis to the beneficiary of the distribution as it did to the estate or trust. Moreover, the distribution absorbs distributable net income (DNI) and qualifies for a distribution deduction (both of which are explained later in this chapter) to the extent of the lesser of the distributed asset's basis to the beneficiary or the asset's fair market value as of the distribution date.[10]

**EXAMPLE 7**

The Howard Trust distributes a painting, basis of $40,000 and fair market value of $90,000, to beneficiary Kate. Kate's basis in the painting is $40,000. The distribution absorbs $40,000 of Howard's DNI, and Howard claims a $40,000 distribution deduction relative to the transaction. ■

**EXAMPLE 8**

Assume the same facts as in Example 7, except that Howard's basis in the painting is $100,000. Kate's basis in the painting is $100,000. The distribution absorbs $90,000 of Howard's DNI, and Howard claims a $90,000 distribution deduction. ■

A trustee or executor can elect to recognize gain or loss with respect to all of its in-kind property distributions for the year. If the election is made, the beneficiary's basis in the asset is equal to the asset's fair market value as of the distribution date. The distribution absorbs DNI and qualifies for a distribution deduction to the extent of the asset's fair market value. However, § 267 can restrict an estate or trust's deduction for such losses.

**EXAMPLE 9**

The Green Estate distributes an antique piano, basis to Green of $10,000 and fair market value of $15,000, to beneficiary Kyle. The executor elects that Green recognize the related $5,000 gain on the distribution. Accordingly, Kyle's basis in the piano is $15,000 ($10,000 basis to Green + $5,000 gain recognized). Without the election, Green would not recognize any gain, and Kyle's basis in the piano would be $10,000. ■

---

[10]§ 643(e).

**EXAMPLE 10**

Assume the same facts as in Example 9, except that Green's basis in the piano is $18,000. The executor elects that Green recognize the related $3,000 loss on the distribution. Accordingly, Kyle's basis in the piano is $15,000 ($18,000 − $3,000). Without the election, Green would not recognize any loss, and Kyle's basis in the piano would be $18,000.

The estate cannot deduct this loss, however. Because an estate and its beneficiaries are related parties, realized losses cannot be recognized immediately.[11] The loss would be recognized if Kyle later sells the piano to a stranger. ∎

**Income in Respect of a Decedent.** The gross income of a trust or estate includes **income in respect of a decedent (IRD)** that the entity received.[12] For a cash basis decedent, IRD includes accrued salary, interest, rent, and other income items that were not constructively received before death. For both cash and accrual basis decedents, IRD includes, for instance, death benefits from qualified retirement plans and deferred compensation contracts.

The tax consequences of IRD are as follows.

* The fair market value of the right to IRD on the appropriate valuation date is included in the decedent's gross estate. Thus, it is subject to the Federal estate tax.[13]
* The decedent's basis in the property carries over to the recipient (the estate or heirs). There is no step-up or step-down in the basis of IRD items.
* The recipient of the income recognizes gain or loss, measured by the difference between the amount realized and the adjusted basis of the IRD in the hands of the decedent. The character of the gain or loss depends upon the treatment that it would have received had it been realized by the decedent before death. Thus, if the decedent would have realized capital gain, the recipient must do likewise.
* Expenses related to the IRD (such as interest, taxes, and depletion) that properly were not reported on the final income tax return of the decedent may be claimed by the recipient. These items are known as **expenses in respect of a decedent.** Typically, such expenses also include fiduciary fees, commissions paid to dispose of estate assets, and state income taxes payable. They are deductible for both Federal estate and income tax purposes, for or from adjusted gross income (AGI) as would have been the case for the decedent.
* If the IRD item would have created an AMT preference or adjustment for the decedent (e.g., with respect to the collection of certain tax-exempt interest by the entity), an identical AMT item is created for the recipient.

**EXAMPLE 11**

Amanda died on July 13 of the current year. On August 2, the estate received a check (before deductions) for $1,200 from Amanda's former employer; this was Amanda's compensation for the last pay period of her life. On November 23, the estate received a $45,000 distribution from the qualified profit sharing plan of Amanda's employer, the full amount to which Amanda was entitled under the plan. Both Amanda and the estate are calendar year, cash basis taxpayers.

The last salary payment and the profit sharing plan distribution constitute IRD to the estate. Amanda had earned these items during her lifetime, and the estate had an enforceable right to receive each of them after Amanda's death. Consequently, the gross estate includes

---

[11]§ 267(b)(13).

[12]§ 691 and the Regulations thereunder. The concept of IRD was introduced in Chapter 18.

[13]To mitigate the effect of double taxation (imposition of both the estate tax and the income tax), § 691(c) allows the recipient an income tax deduction for the incremental estate tax attributable to the net IRD. For individual recipients, this is an itemized deduction, not subject to the 2%-of-AGI floor.

$46,200 with respect to these two items. However, the income tax basis to the estate for these items is not stepped up (from zero to $1,200 and $45,000, respectively) upon distribution to the estate.

The estate must report gross income of $46,200 for the current tax year with respect to the IRD items. The gain recognized upon the receipt of the IRD is $46,200 [$1,200 + $45,000 (amounts realized) − $0 (adjusted bases)]. ■

Including the IRD in both the taxpayer's gross estate and the gross income of the estate may seem harsh. Nevertheless, the tax consequences of IRD are similar to the treatment that applies to all of a taxpayer's earned income. The item is subject to income tax upon receipt, and to the extent that it is not consumed by the taxpayer before death, it is included in the gross estate.

**EXAMPLE 12**

Assume the same facts as in Example 11, except that Amanda is an accrual basis taxpayer. IRD now includes only the $45,000 distribution from the qualified retirement plan. Amanda's last paycheck is included in the gross income of her own last return (January 1 through date of death). The $1,200 salary is already properly recognized under Amanda's usual method of tax accounting. It does not constitute IRD and is not gross income when received by the executor. ■

**EXAMPLE 13**

Assume the same facts as in Example 11. Amanda's last paycheck was reduced by $165 for state income taxes that were withheld by the employer. The $165 tax payment is an expense in respect of a decedent and is allowed as a deduction on *both* Amanda's estate tax return *and* the estate's income tax return. ■

## ORDINARY DEDUCTIONS

As a general rule, the taxable income of an estate or trust is similar to that of an individual. Deductions are allowed for ordinary and necessary expenses paid or incurred in carrying on a trade or business; for the production or collection of income; for the management, conservation, or maintenance of property; and in connection with the determination, collection, or refund of any tax.[14] Reasonable administration expenses, including fiduciary fees and litigation costs in connection with the duties of administration, also are deductible.

The trust or estate must apply the 2 percent-of-AGI floor to many of the § 212 expenses that it incurs. For this purpose, AGI appears to be the greater of (1) the pertinent-year AGI of the grantor of the trust or (2) the AGI of the trust or estate, computed as though the entity were an individual. The floor does not apply, however, to items like fiduciary fees or the personal exemption (i.e., items that would not be incurred by an individual).[15]

Expenses attributable to the production or collection of tax-exempt income are not deductible.[16] The amount of the disallowed deduction is found by using a formula based upon the composition of the income elements of entity accounting income for the year of the deduction. The § 212 deduction is apportioned without regard to the accounting income allocation of such expenses to income or to corpus. The deductibility of the fees is determined strictly by the Code (under §§ 212 and 265), and the allocation of expenditures to income and to corpus is controlled by the trust agreement or will or by state law.

---

[14]§§ 162 and 212.

[15]§§ 67(b) and (e). *O'Neill Trust v. Comm.,* 93–1 USTC ¶50,332, 71 AFTR2d 93–2052, 994 F.2d 302 (CA–6, 1993), *rev'g* 98 T.C. 227 (1992).

[16]§ 265.

## COORDINATE YOUR DEDUCTIONS

The deduction under § 691(c) may be one of the more obscure provisions of the tax Code, but its benefits can add up fast. The deduction is allowed on the tax return of the recipient of income in respect of a decedent (IRD). IRD often is received by the estate of the decedent or a trust that he or she created under the will or during lifetime. The deduction is for the Federal estate tax attributable to the IRD item. For an individual, it is a miscellaneous itemized deduction *not* subject to the 2 percent-of-AGI floor.

Because IRD often includes the value of the survivorship feature on pensions and other retirement plans and assets, the amount subject to the estate tax can be quite high. On top of that, recall from Chapters 17 and 18 that the marginal estate tax rate can be as high as 50 percent. Thus, when computing the current-year income tax for the IRD recipient, the § 691(c) deduction can be extremely valuable in offsetting the IRD received.

For instance, suppose that an IRA balance of $1 million generates $450,000 in attributable estate tax. If the recipient of the IRA takes the net-of-tax distribution in one year, the § 691(c) deduction shelters $450,000 in gross income and may be worth over $170,000 in income taxes saved.

But taking the § 691(c) deduction is more complex than it looks. Because different tax advisers often prepare the Form 706 for the estate and the Form 1040 or 1041 for the IRD recipient, the § 691(c) deduction can get lost altogether or at least be miscomputed. When the IRD is paid out over several years, computing the § 691(c) deduction can become complex. And some tax professionals do not know the law well enough to track down the deduction, while tax software and IRS forms and publications say relatively little about it. One tax attorney believes that the omission or miscalculation of the deduction is "probably the most prevalent error today in respect to estate taxes."

As retirement assets become a larger portion of most gross estates, thanks to a robust stock market and the results of various rollovers from IRAs and qualified plans into the decedent's accounts, IRD and the § 691(c) deduction are likely to be encountered much more frequently in the future.

---

**EXAMPLE 14**

The Silver Trust operates a business and invests idle cash in marketable securities. Its sales proceeds for the current year are $180,000. Expenses for wages, cost of sales, and office administration are $80,000. Interest income recognized is $20,000 from taxable bonds and $50,000 from tax-exempt bonds. The trustee claims a $35,000 fee for its activities. According to the trust agreement, $30,000 of this amount is allocated to the income beneficiaries and $5,000 is allocated to corpus.

| | |
|---|---:|
| Sales income | $180,000 |
| Cost of sales | –80,000 |
| Interest income ($50,000 is exempt) | +70,000 |
| Fiduciary's fees, as allocated | –30,000 |
| Trust accounting income | $140,000 |

The sales proceeds are included in the gross income of the trust under § 61. The costs associated with the business are deductible in full under § 162. The taxable income is included in Silver's gross income under § 61, but the tax-exempt income is excluded under § 103. The fiduciary's fees are deductible by Silver under § 212, but a portion of the deduction is lost because § 265 prohibits deductions for expenses incurred in the generation of tax-exempt income.

Specifically, 50/250 of the fees of $35,000 can be traced to tax-exempt income, so $7,000 of the fees is nondeductible. For purposes of the computation, only the income elements of the year's trust accounting income are included in the denominator. Moreover, the allocation of portions of the fees to income and to corpus is irrelevant in the calculation. The disallowed deduction for fiduciary's fees is computed in the following manner.

$$\$35{,}000^{*} \text{ (total fees paid)} \times \frac{\$50{,}000^{**} \text{ \textit{(exempt} income elements of trust accounting income)}}{\$250{,}000^{**} \text{ \textit{(all} income elements of trust accounting income)}}$$

$$= \$7{,}000 \text{ (amount disallowed)}$$

*All of the fees, and not just those that are allocated to income, are deductible by the trust under § 212.
**The numerator and denominator of this fraction are *not* reduced by expense items allocable to income (e.g., cost of sales). ◼

Under § 642(g), amounts deductible as administration expenses or losses for death tax purposes (under §§ 2053 and 2054) cannot be claimed by the estate for income tax purposes, unless the estate files a waiver of the death tax deduction. Although these expenses cannot be deducted twice, they may be allocated as the fiduciary sees fit between Forms 706 and 1041; they need not be claimed in their entirety on either return.[17] As discussed earlier, the prohibition against double deductions does not extend to expenses in respect of a decedent.

Trusts and estates are allowed cost recovery deductions. However, such deductions are assigned proportionately among the recipients of the entity accounting income.[18]

**EXAMPLE 15**

Lisa and Martin are the equal income beneficiaries of the Needle Trust. Under the terms of the trust agreement, the trustee has complete discretion as to the timing of the distributions from Needle's current accounting income. The trust agreement allocates all depreciation expense to income. In the current year, the trustee distributes 40% of the current trust accounting income to Lisa and 40% to Martin; thus, 20% of the income is accumulated. The depreciation deduction allowable to Needle is $100,000. This deduction is allocated among the trust and its beneficiaries on the basis of the distribution of current accounting income: Lisa and Martin each can claim a $40,000 deduction, and the trust can deduct $20,000. ◼

**EXAMPLE 16**

Assume the same facts as in Example 15, except that the trust agreement allocates all depreciation expense to corpus. Lisa and Martin both still claim a $40,000 depreciation deduction, and Needle retains its $20,000 deduction. The Code assigns the depreciation deduction proportionately to the recipients of entity accounting income. Allocation of depreciation to income or to corpus is irrelevant in determining which party can properly claim the deduction. ◼

When a trust sells property received by transfer from the grantor, the amount of depreciation subject to recapture includes the depreciation claimed by the grantor before the transfer of the property to the trust. However, depreciation recapture potential disappears at death.

[17]Reg. § 1.642(g)–2.    [18]§§ 167(h) and 611(b)(3) and (4).

EXAMPLE 17

Jaime transferred an asset to the Shoulder Trust via a lifetime gift. The asset's total depreciation recapture potential was $40,000. If Shoulder sells the asset at a gain, ordinary income not to exceed $40,000 is recognized by the trust. Had Jaime transferred the asset after his death to his estate through a bequest, the $40,000 recapture potential would have disappeared. ■

## DEDUCTIONS FOR LOSSES

An estate or trust is allowed a deduction for casualty or theft losses that are not covered by insurance or other arrangements. Such losses may also be deductible by an estate for Federal death tax purposes under § 2054. As a result, an estate is not allowed an income tax deduction unless the death tax deduction is waived.[19]

The net operating loss (NOL) deduction is available for estates and trusts (i.e., where trade or business income is generated). The carryback of an NOL may reduce the distributable net income of the trust or estate for the carryback year and therefore affect the amount taxed to the beneficiaries for that year.

Certain losses realized by an estate or trust also may be disallowed, as they are for all taxpayers. Thus, the wash sale provisions of § 1091 disallow losses on the sale or other disposition of stock or securities when substantially identical stock or securities are acquired by the estate or trust within the prescribed 30-day period. Likewise, § 267 disallows certain losses, expenses, and interest with respect to transactions between related taxpayers. Generally, related parties include a trust, its trustee, grantor, and beneficiaries, as well as an estate, its executor, and beneficiaries.

Except for the possibility of unused losses in the year of termination, the net capital losses of an estate or trust are used only on the fiduciary income tax return.[20] The tax treatment of these losses is the same as for individual taxpayers.

## CHARITABLE CONTRIBUTIONS

An estate or complex trust is allowed a deduction for contributions to charitable organizations under certain conditions.

* The contribution is made pursuant to the will or trust instrument, and its amount is determinable using the language of that document.
* The recipient is a qualified organization. For this purpose, qualified organizations include the same charities for which individual and corporate donors are allowed deductions, except that estates and trusts are permitted a deduction for contributions to certain foreign charitable organizations.
* Generally, the contribution is claimed in the tax year it is paid, but a fiduciary can treat amounts paid in the year immediately following as a deduction for the preceding year.[21] Under this rule, estates and complex trusts receive more liberal treatment than individuals or corporations.

Unlike the charitable contribution deductions of individuals and corporations, the deductions of estates and complex trusts are not limited (e.g., to a percentage of taxable or adjusted gross income). Nonetheless, an entity's charitable contribution may not be fully deductible.[22] Specifically, the deduction is limited to amounts

---

[19]See Reg. § 1.642(g)–1 for the required statement waiving the estate tax deduction. In addition, see Reg. §§ 1.165–7(c) and 1.165–8(b), requiring that a statement be filed to allow an income tax deduction for such losses.

[20]§ 642(h).
[21]§ 642(c)(1) and Reg. § 1.642(c)–1(b).
[22]Reg. §§ 1.642(c)–3(b) and (c).

included in the gross income of the entity in the year of the contribution. A contribution is deemed to have been made proportionately from each of the income elements of entity accounting income. Thus, if the entity has tax-exempt income, the contribution is deductible only to the extent that the income elements of entity accounting income for the year of the deduction are included in the entity's gross income.

This rule is similar to that used to limit the § 212 deduction for fiduciary fees and other expenses incurred to generate tax-exempt income. However, if the will or trust agreement requires that the contribution be made from a specific type of income or from the current income from a specified asset, the allocation of the contribution to taxable and tax-exempt income will not be required.

**EXAMPLE 18**

The Capper Trust has 2003 gross rent income of $80,000, expenses attributable to the rents of $60,000, and tax-exempt interest from state bonds of $20,000. Under the trust agreement, the trustee is to pay 30% of the annual trust accounting income to the United Way, a qualifying organization. Accordingly, the trustee pays $12,000 to the charity in 2004 (i.e., 30% × $40,000). The charitable contribution deduction allowed for 2003 is $9,600 [($80,000/$100,000) × $12,000]. ■

**EXAMPLE 19**

Assume the same facts as in Example 18, except that the trust instrument also requires that the contribution be paid from the net rent income. The agreement controls, and the allocation formula need not be applied. The entire $12,000 is allowed as a charitable deduction. ■

**LO.3**

Illustrate the uses and implications of distributable net income.

## DEDUCTION FOR DISTRIBUTIONS TO BENEFICIARIES

The modified conduit approach of Subchapter J is embodied in the deduction allowed to trusts and estates for the distributions made to beneficiaries during the year. Some portion of any distribution that a beneficiary receives from a trust may be subject to income tax on the beneficiary's own return. At the same time, the distributing entity is allowed a deduction for some or all of the distribution. Consequently, the modified conduit principle of Subchapter J is implemented. A good analogy is to the taxability of corporate profits distributed to employees as taxable wages. The corporation is allowed a deduction for the payment, but the employee receives gross income in the form of compensation.

A critical value that is used in computing the amount of the entity's distribution deduction is **distributable net income (DNI).** As it is defined in Subchapter J, DNI serves several functions.

- DNI is the maximum amount of the distribution on which the beneficiaries can be taxed.[23]
- DNI is the maximum amount that the entity can use as a distribution deduction for the year.[24]
- The makeup of DNI carries over to the beneficiaries (the items of income and expenses retain their DNI character in the hands of the distributees).[25]

Subchapter J defines DNI in a circular manner, however. The DNI value is necessary to determine the entity's distribution deduction and therefore its taxable income for the year. Nonetheless, the Code defines DNI as a modification of the

---

[23]§§ 652(a) and 662(a).
[24]§§ 651(b) and 661(c).

[25]§§ 652(b) and 662(b).

entity's taxable income itself. Using the systematic approach to determining the taxable income of the entity and its beneficiaries, as shown earlier in Figure 19–2, first compute *taxable income before the distribution deduction*, modify that amount to determine DNI and the distribution deduction, return to the calculation of *taxable income*, and apply the deduction that has resulted.

*Taxable income before the distribution deduction* includes all of the entity's items of gross income, deductions, gains, losses, and exemptions for the year. Therefore, to compute this amount, (1) determine the appropriate personal exemption for the year and (2) account for all of the other gross income and deductions of the entity.

The next step in Figure 19–2 is the determination of *distributable net income*, computed by making the following adjustments to the entity's *taxable income before the distribution deduction*.[26]

- Add back the personal exemption.
- Add back *net* tax-exempt interest. To arrive at this amount, reduce the total tax-exempt interest by charitable contributions and by related expenses not deductible under § 265.
- Add back the entity's *net* capital losses.
- Subtract any net capital gains allocable to corpus. In other words, the only net capital gains included in DNI are those attributable to income beneficiaries or to charitable contributions.

Since taxable income before the distribution deduction is computed by deducting all of the expenses of the entity (whether they were allocated to income or to corpus), DNI is reduced by expenses that are allocated to corpus. The effect is to reduce the taxable income of the income beneficiaries. The actual distributions to the beneficiaries exceed DNI because the distributions are not reduced by expenses allocated to corpus. Aside from this shortcoming of Subchapter J, DNI offers a good approximation of the current-year economic income available for distribution to the entity's income beneficiaries.

DNI includes the net tax-exempt interest income of the entity, so that amount must be removed from DNI in computing the distribution deduction. Moreover, for estates and complex trusts, the amount actually distributed during the year may include discretionary distributions of income and distributions of corpus permissible under the will or trust instrument. Thus, the distribution deduction for estates and complex trusts is computed as the lesser of (1) the deductible portion of DNI or (2) the taxable amount actually distributed to the beneficiaries during the year. For a simple trust, however, full distribution is always assumed, relative to both the entity and its beneficiaries, in a manner similar to the partnership and S corporation conduit entities.

**EXAMPLE 20**   The Zinc Trust is a simple trust. Because of severe liquidity problems, its 2003 accounting income is not distributed to its sole beneficiary, Mark, until early in 2004. Zinc still is allowed a full distribution deduction for, and Mark still is taxable upon, the entity's 2003 income in 2003. ■

**EXAMPLE 21**   The Pork Trust is required to distribute its current accounting income annually to its sole income beneficiary, Barbara. Capital gains and losses and all other expenses are allocable to corpus. In the current year, Pork incurs the following items.

---

[26]These and other (less common) adjustments are detailed in § 643.

| Dividend income | $25,000 |
|---|---|
| Taxable interest income | 15,000 |
| Tax-exempt interest income | 20,000 |
| Net long-term capital gains | 10,000 |
| Fiduciary's fees | 6,000 |

| Item | Totals | Accounting Income | Taxable Income | Distributable Net Income/ Distribution Deduction |
|---|---|---|---|---|
| Dividend income | $25,000 | $25,000 | $ 25,000 | |
| Taxable interest income | 15,000 | 15,000 | 15,000 | |
| Exempt interest income | 20,000 | 20,000 | | |
| Net long-term capital gain | 10,000 | | 10,000 | |
| Fiduciary fees | 6,000 | | (4,000) | |
| Personal exemption | | | (300) | |
| Accounting income/taxable income before the distribution deduction | | $60,000 | $ 45,700 | $ 45,700 |
| | | Step 1 | Step 2 | |
| Exemption | | | | 300 |
| Corpus capital gain/loss | | | | (10,000) |
| Net exempt income | | | | 18,000 |
| Distributable net income | | | | $ 54,000 |
| Distribution deduction | | | Step 3 | (36,000) |
| Entity taxable income | | | Step 4 | ($ 9,700) |

*Step 1*  Trust accounting income is $60,000; this includes the tax-exempt interest income, but not the fees or the capital gains, pursuant to the trust document. Barbara receives $60,000 from the trust for the current year.

*Step 2*  Taxable income before the distribution deduction is computed as directed by the Code. The tax-exempt interest is excluded under § 103. Only a portion of the fees is deductible because some of the fees are traceable to the tax-exempt income. The trust claims a $300 personal exemption as it is required to distribute its annual trust accounting income.

*Step 3*  DNI and the distribution deduction reflect the required adjustments. The distribution deduction is the lesser of the distributed amount ($60,000) or the deductible portion of DNI ($54,000 – $18,000 net exempt income).

*Step 4*  Finally, return to the computation of the taxable income of the Pork Trust. A simple test should be applied at this point to assure that the proper figure for the trust's taxable income has been determined. On what is Pork to be taxed? Pork has distributed to Barbara all of its gross income except the $10,000 net long-term capital gains. The $300 personal exemption reduces taxable income to $9,700. ■

**EXAMPLE  22**

The Quick Trust is required to distribute all of its current accounting income equally to its two beneficiaries, Faith and the Universal Church, a qualifying charitable organization. Capital gains and losses and depreciation expenses are allocable to income. Fiduciary fees are allocable to corpus. In the current year, Quick incurs various items as indicated.

| Item | Totals | Accounting Income | Taxable Income | Distributable Net Income/ Distribution Deduction |
|---|---|---|---|---|
| Rent income | $100,000 | $100,000 | $100,000 | |
| Expenses—rent income | 30,000 | (30,000) | (30,000) | |
| Depreciation—rent income | 15,000 | (15,000) | | |
| Net long-term capital gain | 20,000 | 20,000 | 20,000 | |
| Charitable contribution | | | (37,500) | |
| Fiduciary fees | 18,000 | | (18,000) | |
| Personal exemption | | | (300) | |
| Accounting income/taxable income before the distribution deduction | | $ 75,000 | $ 34,200 | $34,200 |
| | | **Step 1** | **Step 2** | |
| Exemption | | | | 300 |
| Corpus capital gain/loss | | | | |
| Net exempt income | | | | |
| Distributable net income | | | | $34,500 |
| Distribution deduction | | **Step 3** | (34,500) | |
| Entity taxable income | | **Step 4** | ($    300) | |

*Step 1*  Trust accounting income of $75,000 reflects the indicated allocations of items to income and to corpus. Each income beneficiary receives $37,500.

*Step 2*  In the absence of tax-exempt income, a deduction is allowed for the full amount of the fiduciary's fees. Quick is a complex trust, but since it is required to distribute its full accounting income annually, a $300 exemption is allowed. The trust properly does not deduct any depreciation for the rental property. The depreciation deduction is available only to the recipients of the entity's accounting income for the period. Thus, the deduction is split equally between Faith and the church. The deduction probably is of no direct value to the church, as the church is not subject to the income tax. The trust's charitable contribution deduction is based upon the $37,500 that the charity actually received (one-half of trust accounting income).

*Step 3*  As there is no tax-exempt income, the only adjustment needed to compute DNI is to add back the trust's personal exemption. Subchapter J requires no adjustment for the charitable contribution. DNI is computed only from the perspective of Faith, who also received $37,500 from the trust.

*Step 4*  Perform the simple test (referred to above) to assure that the proper taxable income for the Quick Trust has been computed. All of the trust's gross income has been distributed to Faith and the charity. As is the case with most trusts that distribute all of their annual income, the Quick Trust "wastes" the personal exemption. ∎

## TAX CREDITS

An estate or trust may claim the foreign tax credit to the extent that it is not passed through to the beneficiaries.[27] Similarly, other credits are apportioned between the

---

[27]§§ 642(a)(1) and 901.

estate or trust and the beneficiaries on the basis of the entity accounting income allocable to each.

# Taxation of Beneficiaries

The beneficiaries of an estate or trust receive taxable income from the entity under the modified conduit principle of Subchapter J. Distributable net income determines the maximum amount that can be taxed to the beneficiaries for any tax year. The constitution of DNI also carries over to the beneficiaries (e.g., net long-term capital gains retain their character when they are distributed from the entity to the beneficiary).

The timing of any tax consequences to the beneficiary of a trust or estate presents a problem only when the parties involved use different tax years. A beneficiary includes in gross income an amount based upon the DNI of the trust for any taxable year or years of the entity ending with or within his or her taxable year.[28]

**EXAMPLE 23**

An estate uses a fiscal year ending on March 31 for tax purposes. Its sole income beneficiary is a calendar year taxpayer. For calendar year 2003, the beneficiary reports the income assignable to her for the entity's fiscal year April 1, 2002, to March 31, 2003. If the estate is terminated by December 31, 2003, the beneficiary also includes any trust income assignable to her for the short year. This could result in a bunching of income in 2003. ▨

## DISTRIBUTIONS BY SIMPLE TRUSTS

The amount taxable to the beneficiaries of a simple trust is limited by the trust's DNI. However, since DNI includes net tax-exempt income, the amount included in the gross income of the beneficiaries could be less than DNI. When there is more than one income beneficiary, the elements of DNI are apportioned ratably according to the amount required to be distributed currently to each.

**EXAMPLE 24**

A simple trust has ordinary income of $40,000, a long-term capital gain of $15,000 (allocable to corpus), and a trustee commission expense of $4,000 (payable from corpus). The two income beneficiaries, Allie and Bart, are entitled to the trust's annual accounting income, based on shares of 75% and 25%, respectively. Although Allie receives $30,000 as her share (75% × trust accounting income of $40,000), she is allocated DNI of only $27,000 (75% × $36,000). Likewise, Bart is entitled to receive $10,000 (25% × $40,000), but he is allocated DNI of only $9,000 (25% × $36,000). The $15,000 capital gain is taxed to the trust. ▨

## DISTRIBUTIONS BY ESTATES AND COMPLEX TRUSTS

A problem arises with estates and complex trusts when more than one beneficiary receives a distribution from the entity and the controlling document does not require a distribution of the entire accounting income of the entity.

**EXAMPLE 25**

The trustee of the Wilson Trust has the discretion to distribute the income or corpus of the trust in any proportion between the two beneficiaries of the trust, Wong and Washington. Under the trust instrument, Wong must receive $15,000 from the trust every year. In the current year, the trust's accounting income is $50,000, and its DNI is $40,000. The trustee pays $15,000 to Wong and $25,000 to Washington. ▨

---

[28]§§ 652(c) and 662(c).

How is Wilson's DNI to be divided between Wong and Washington? Several arbitrary methods of allocating DNI between the beneficiaries could be devised. Subchapter J resolves the problem by creating a two-tier system to govern the taxation of beneficiaries in such situations.[29] The tier system determines which distributions will be included in the gross income of the beneficiaries in full, which will be included in part, and which will not be included at all.

Income that is required to be distributed currently, whether or not it is distributed, is categorized as a *first-tier distribution*. All other amounts properly paid, credited, or required to be distributed are *second-tier distributions*.[30] A formula is used to allocate DNI among the appropriate beneficiaries when only first-tier distributions are made and those amounts exceed DNI.

When both first-tier and second-tier distributions are made and the first-tier distributions exceed DNI, the above formula is applied to the first-tier distributions. In this case, none of the second-tier distributions are taxed, because all of the DNI has been allocated to the first-tier beneficiaries.

If both first-tier and second-tier distributions are made and the first-tier distributions do not exceed DNI, but the total of both first-tier and second-tier distributions does exceed DNI, the second-tier beneficiaries recognize income as shown below.

**EXAMPLE 26**

The trustee of the Gray Trust is required to distribute $10,000 per year to both Harriet and Wally, the two beneficiaries of the entity. In addition, he is empowered to distribute other amounts of trust income or corpus at his sole discretion. In the current year, the trust has accounting income of $60,000 and DNI of $50,000. However, the trustee distributes only the required $10,000 each to Harriet and to Wally. The balance of the income is accumulated and added to trust corpus.

In this case, only first-tier distributions have been made, but the total amount of the distributions does not exceed DNI for the year. Although DNI is the maximum amount that is included by the beneficiaries for the year, they can include no more in gross income than is distributed by the entity. Thus, both Harriet and Wally may be subject to tax on $10,000 as their proportionate shares of DNI. ∎

**EXAMPLE 27**

Assume the same facts as in Example 26, except that DNI is $12,000. Harriet and Wally each receive $10,000, but they cannot be taxed in total on more than DNI. Each is taxed on $6,000 [DNI of $12,000 × ($10,000/$20,000 of the first-tier distributions)]. ∎

---

[29]§§ 662(a)(1) and (2).                    [30]Reg. §§ 1.662(a)–2 and –3.

| EXAMPLE 28 | Return to the facts in Example 25. Wong receives a first-tier distribution of $15,000. Second-tier distributions include $20,000 to Wong and $25,000 to Washington. Wilson's DNI is $40,000. The DNI is allocated between Wong and Washington as follows. |
|---|---|

> **(1) First-tier distributions**
>
> | To Wong | $15,000 DNI |
> |---|---|
> | To Washington | –0– |
> | Remaining DNI = $25,000 | |
>
> **(2) Second-tier distributions**
>
> | To Wong | $11,111 DNI [(20/45) × $25,000] |
> |---|---|
> | To Washington | $13,889 DNI [(25/45) × $25,000] |

| EXAMPLE 29 | Assume the same facts as in Example 28, except that accounting income is $80,000 and DNI is $70,000. DNI is allocated between Wong and Washington as follows. |
|---|---|

> **(1) First-tier distributions**
>
> | To Wong | $15,000 DNI |
> |---|---|
> | To Washington | –0– |
> | Remaining DNI = $55,000 | |
>
> **(2) Second-tier distributions**
>
> | To Wong | $20,000 DNI |
> |---|---|
> | To Washington | $25,000 DNI |

**Separate Share Rule.**   For the sole purpose of determining the amount of DNI for a complex trust or estate with more than one beneficiary, the substantially separate and independent shares of different beneficiaries in the trust or estate are treated as *separate* trusts or estates.[31] An illustration shows the need for this special rule.

| EXAMPLE 30 | A trustee has the discretion to distribute or accumulate income on behalf of Greg and Hannah (in equal shares). The trustee also has the power to invade corpus for the benefit of either beneficiary to the extent of that beneficiary's one-half interest in the trust. For the current year, DNI is $10,000. Of this amount, $5,000 is distributed to Greg, and $5,000 is accumulated on behalf of Hannah. In addition, the trustee pays $20,000 from corpus to Greg. Without the separate share rule, Greg is taxed on $10,000 (the full amount of the DNI). With the separate share rule, Greg is taxed on only $5,000 (his share of the DNI) and receives the $20,000 corpus distribution tax-free. The trust is taxed on Hannah's $5,000 share of the DNI that is accumulated. |
|---|---|

The separate share rule is designed to prevent the inequity that results if the corpus payments are treated under the regular rules applicable to second-tier beneficiaries. In Example 30, the effect of the separate share rule is to produce a two-trust result: one trust for Greg and one for Hannah, each with DNI of $5,000. The rule also results in the availability of extra entity personal exemptions and in a greater use of lower entity tax brackets.

## CHARACTER OF INCOME

Consistent with the modified conduit principle of Subchapter J, various classes of income (e.g., dividends, passive or portfolio gain and loss, AMT preferences, and

---

[31]§ 663(c); Reg. § 1.663(c)–1(a).

tax-exempt interest) retain the same character for the beneficiaries that they had when they were received by the entity. If there are multiple beneficiaries *and* if all of the DNI is distributed, a problem arises in allocating the various classes of income among the beneficiaries.

Distributions are treated as consisting of the same proportion as the items that enter into the computation of DNI. This allocation does not apply, however, if local law or the governing instrument specifically allocates different classes of income to different beneficiaries.[32]

If the entity distributes only a part of its DNI, the amount of a specific class of DNI that is deemed distributed must first be determined.

**EXAMPLE 31**

The Baron Trust has DNI of $40,000, including the following: $10,000 of taxable interest, $10,000 of tax-exempt interest, and $20,000 of passive activity income. The trustee distributes, at her discretion, $8,000 to Mike and $12,000 to Nancy.

| | | Income Type | | |
|---|---|---|---|---|
| **Beneficiary** | **Amount Received** | **Taxable Interest** | **Exempt Interest** | **Passive Income** |
| Mike | $ 8,000 | $2,000* | $2,000 | $4,000 |
| Nancy | 12,000 | 3,000 | 3,000 | 6,000 |

*$8,000 distribution/$40,000 total DNI × $10,000 taxable interest in DNI. ∎

**EXAMPLE 32**

Continue with the facts of Example 31. The character of the income that flows through to Mike and Nancy is effective for all other tax purposes. For instance, the $2,000 exempt interest allocated to Mike is used in computing the taxable portion of any Social Security benefits Mike receives. If this exempt interest relates to nonessential activities of the issuing agency, Mike includes a $2,000 AMT preference on his current-year return.

The $4,000 passive activity income that is allocated to Mike is available for offset against passive losses that he has incurred from limited partnerships and rental activities for the year. Similarly, the $3,000 taxable interest income allocated to Nancy can be used to increase the amount of investment interest expense deductible by her in the year of the flow-through. The interest is treated as portfolio income to the same extent as that received directly by the taxpayer. ∎

---

[32]Reg. § 1.662(b)–1 seems to allow special allocations, but see *Harkness v. U.S.*, 72–2 USTC ¶9740, 30 AFTR2d 72–5754, 469 F.2d 310 (Ct.Cls., 1972).

**Special Allocations.**   Under certain circumstances, the parties may modify the character-of-income allocation method set forth above. A modification is permitted only to the extent that the allocation is required in the trust instrument and only to the extent that it has an economic effect independent of the cash-flow and income tax consequences of the allocation.[33]

| EXAMPLE 33 | Return to the facts in Example 31. Assume that the beneficiaries are elderly individuals who have pooled their investment portfolios to avail themselves of the trustee's professional asset management skills. Suppose the trustee has the discretion to allocate different classes of income to different beneficiaries and that she designates $10,000 of Nancy's $12,000 distribution as being from the tax-exempt income. Such a designation *would not be recognized* for tax purposes, and the allocation method of Example 31 must be used. |
|---|---|

Suppose, however, that the trust instrument stipulated that Nancy was to receive all of the income from the tax-exempt securities because she alone contributed the exempt securities to trust corpus. Under this provision, the $10,000 of the nontaxable interest is paid to Nancy. This allocation *is recognized*, and $10,000 of Nancy's distribution is tax-exempt. ■

## LOSSES IN THE TERMINATION YEAR

The ordinary net operating and capital losses of a trust or estate do not flow through to the entity's beneficiaries, as would such losses from a partnership or an S corporation. However, in the year in which an entity terminates its existence, the beneficiaries do receive a direct benefit from the loss carryovers of the trust or estate.[34]

Net operating losses and net capital losses are subject to the same carryover rules that otherwise apply to an individual. Consequently, NOLs can be carried back 2 years and then carried forward 20 years while net capital losses can be carried forward only, and for an indefinite period of time. However, if the entity incurs a negative taxable income in the last year of its existence, the excess of deductions over the entity's gross income is allowed to the beneficiaries (it will flow through to them directly). The net loss is available as a deduction *from* AGI in the beneficiary's tax year with or within which the entity's tax year ends. The amount allowed is in proportion to the relative amount of corpus assets that each beneficiary receives upon the termination of the entity, and it is subject to the 2-percent-of-AGI floor.

Any carryovers of the entity's other losses flow through to the beneficiaries in the year of termination in proportion to the relative amount of corpus assets that each beneficiary receives. The character of the loss carryover is retained by the beneficiary, except that a carryover of a net capital loss to a corporate beneficiary is always treated as short term. Beneficiaries who are individuals use these carryovers as deductions *for* AGI.

| EXAMPLE 34 | The Edgar Estate terminates on December 31, 2004. It had used a fiscal year ending July 31. For the termination year, the estate incurred a $15,000 negative taxable income. In addition, the estate had an unused NOL carryover of $23,000 from the year ending July 31, 2001, and an unused net long-term capital loss carryover of $10,000 from the year ending July 31, 2003. Dawn receives $60,000 of corpus upon termination, and Blue Corporation receives the remaining $40,000. Dawn and Blue are calendar year taxpayers. |
|---|---|

Dawn can claim an itemized deduction of $9,000 [($60,000/$100,000) × $15,000] for the entity's negative taxable income in the year of termination. This deduction is subject to the

[33]Reg. § 1.652(b)–2(b). This is similar to the § 704(b) requirement for partnerships.

[34]Reg. §§ 1.642(h)–1 and –2.

2%-of-AGI floor on her miscellaneous itemized deductions. In addition, Dawn can claim a $13,800 deduction *for* AGI in 2004 (60% × $23,000) for Edgar's NOL carryover, and she can use $6,000 of the estate's net long-term capital loss carryover with her other 2004 capital transactions.

Blue receives ordinary business deductions in 2004 for Edgar's NOLs: $6,000 for the loss in the year of termination and $9,200 for the carryover from fiscal 2001. Moreover, Blue can use the $4,000 carryover of Edgar's net capital losses to offset against its other 2004 capital transactions, although the loss must be treated as short term. ■

### THE SIXTY-FIVE-DAY RULE

Amounts paid or credited to the beneficiaries in the first 65 days of the estate or trust's tax year may be treated as paid on the last day of the preceding taxable year.[35] This provision offers the trustee some flexibility in timing distributions so that entity-level accumulations can be avoided.

**LO.4**

Use the special rules that apply to trusts where the creator (grantor) of the trust retains certain rights.

# Grantor Trusts

A series of special provisions contained in §§ 671 through 679 applies when the grantor of the trust retains beneficial enjoyment or substantial control over the trust property or income. In that event, the grantor is taxed on the trust income, and the trust is disregarded for income tax purposes. The person who is taxed on the income is allowed to claim, on his or her own return, any deductions or credits attributable to the income. Such taxes restrict the grantor's ability to redirect the income recognized from trust corpus to the trust or its beneficiaries. The trustee still files a Form 1041, but no dollar amounts are included on the mostly "blank" return. All income and deduction items are reported on the grantor's Form 1040.

### REVERSIONARY TRUSTS

Creation of virtually any new reversionary trust is subject to the Federal gift tax. If the grantor dies before the income interest expires, the present value of the reversionary interest is included in his or her gross estate under § 2033; thus, a Federal estate tax could also result.

### POWERS RETAINED BY THE GRANTOR

Sections 674 through 677 contain other restrictions on the extent of the powers over the trust that the grantor can retain without incurring grantor trust status. If any of these provisions is violated, the income of the trust is taxed to the grantor, and the usual Subchapter J rules do not apply to the trust.

The grantor is taxed on the income if he or she retains (1) the beneficial enjoyment of corpus or (2) the power to dispose of the trust income without the approval or consent of any adverse party. An adverse party is any person having a substantial beneficial interest in the trust who could be affected adversely by the power the grantor possesses over the trust assets.[36]

---

[35]See Reg. § 1.663(b)–2 for the manner and timing of the election.
[36]§§ 672(a), (b), and 674. See Reg. § 1.672(a)–1 for examples of adverse party situations.

A number of important powers, including the following, will *not* cause such income to be taxed to the grantor.[37]

- To apply the income toward the support of the grantor's dependents (except to the extent that it actually is applied for this purpose).[38]
- To allocate trust income or corpus among charitable beneficiaries.
- To invade corpus on behalf of a designated beneficiary.
- To withhold income from a beneficiary during his or her minority or disability.
- To allocate receipts and disbursements between income and corpus.

The retention by the grantor or a nonadverse party of certain administrative powers over the trust causes the income to be taxed to the grantor. Such powers include those to deal with trust income or corpus for less than full and adequate consideration and to borrow from the trust without providing adequate interest or security.[39]

The grantor of a trust is taxed on the trust's income if he or she (or a nonadverse party) possesses the power to revoke the trust.[40] In addition, a grantor is taxed on all or part of the income of a trust when, without the consent of any adverse party, the income is or, at the discretion of the grantor or a nonadverse party (or both), may be:

- Distributed to the grantor or the grantor's spouse.
- Held or accumulated for future distribution to the grantor or the grantor's spouse.
- Applied to the payment of premiums on insurance policies on the life of the grantor or the grantor's spouse.[41]

**EXAMPLE 35**

Frank creates an irrevocable trust for his children with a transfer of income-producing property and an insurance policy on the life of Marion, his wife. During the year, the trustee uses $3,000 of the trust income to pay the premiums on the policy covering Marion's life. Frank is taxed on $3,000 of the trust's income. ■

Moreover, trust income accumulated for the benefit of someone whom the grantor is *legally obligated* to support is taxed to the grantor but only to the extent that it is actually applied for that purpose.[42]

**EXAMPLE 36**

Melanie creates an irrevocable accumulation trust. Her son, Sean, is the life beneficiary, and the remainder goes to any grandchildren. During the year, the trust income of $8,000 is applied as follows: $5,000 toward Sean's college tuition and other related educational expenses and $3,000 accumulated on Sean's behalf. If, under state law, Melanie has an obligation to support Sean and this obligation includes providing a college education, Melanie is taxed on the $5,000 that is so applied. ■

**Tax Planning Considerations**

Many of the tax planning possibilities for estates and trusts were discussed in Chapter 18. However, several specific tax planning possibilities are available to help minimize the income tax effects on estates and trusts and their beneficiaries.

---

[37]§ 674(b).
[38]§ 677(b).
[39]See Reg. § 1.675–1(b) for a further discussion of this matter.
[40]§ 676.
[41]§ 677(a).

[42]§ 677(b). The taxpayer's legal obligations vary according to state law, financial resources, and family expectations. See *Frederick C. Braun, Jr.*, 48 TCM 210, T.C.Memo. 1984–285, and *Cristopher Stone*, 54 TCM 462, T.C.Memo. 1987–454.

## DON'T TRUST YOUR DICTIONARY

Today, the middle and upper classes are often including trusts in their estate plans. Usually, the purpose of the trust is to spare the survivors the time and effort required to work through a state's probate proceedings.

But planning for death can sometimes lead to confusion about terminology, especially between a living trust and a living will. A "living trust" is typically created to hold the assets of the decedent-to-be, including investments, homestead, and household goods. Assets are retitled in the name of the trustee, who periodically files a Form 1041 for the new entity. The idea underlying the living trust is to reduce the probate estate. This, in turn, lowers the fees for carrying out the probate process. Such fees often total 5 percent or so of the date of death value of the probate assets.

The living trust accomplishes virtually no Federal tax savings. The trust assets are included in the decedent's gross estate, as the living trust is an incomplete transfer under §§ 2036 and 2038. For the most part, the entity is treated as a grantor trust. Because of the retained investment and distribution powers, the donor is still liable for taxes on the taxable income of the fiduciary.

A "living will," on the other hand, is a legal document that conveys powers to relatives and third parties to make medical and financial decisions when the decedent-to-be can no longer do so. More appropriately referred to as a "medical power of attorney," the document expresses the person's wishes as to how and when to reduce specified medical treatments (including directives for removing life support systems).

Various states and estate planners use the terms *living trust* and *living will* differently, and sometimes interchangeably. Consequently, it is important that the *proper* document is used to accomplish the desired goals. Usually, it is "too late" to amend the document once a misunderstanding is discovered!

## A TRUST OR ESTATE AS AN INCOME-SHIFTING DEVICE

The compressed tax rate schedule applicable to Subchapter J entities may have reversed the traditional techniques by which families set aside funds for long-term activities, such as business startups, college education, and home purchases. When the tax rate schedules for trusts and estates were more accommodating, high-income individuals would shift income-producing assets to trusts to take advantage of the lower effective tax rate that would fall on the income accumulated within the trust. The target of the plan, usually a child, would receive the accumulated income (and, perhaps, trust corpus) at a designated age, and more funds would be available because a lower tax rate had been applied over the life of the investment in the trust.

Today, such an income shift would *deplete*, rather than shelter, the family's assets, as the rates falling on individuals are much more graduated than are those applicable to fiduciaries, and the kiddie tax also penalizes attempts to shift taxable income to children. Assuming that the objectives of the plan remain unchanged, possible strategies in view of these rate changes include the following.

- Trust corpus should be invested in growth assets that are low on yield but high on appreciation, so that the trustee can determine the timing of the gain and somewhat control the effective tax rate that applies.
- Trust corpus should be invested in tax-exempt securities, such as municipal bonds and mutual funds that invest in them, to eliminate the tax costs

---

## CONCEPT SUMMARY 19–1

### Principles of Fiduciary Taxation

1. Estates and trusts are temporary entities created to locate, maintain, and distribute assets and to satisfy liabilities according to the wishes of the decedent or grantor as expressed in the will or trust document.
2. Generally, the estate or trust acts as a conduit of the taxable income that it receives. To the extent that the income is distributed by the entity, it is taxed to the beneficiary. Taxable income retained by the entity is taxed to the entity itself.
3. The entity's accounting income must first be determined. Accounting conventions that are stated in the controlling document or, lacking such provisions, in state law allocate specific items of receipt and expenditure either to income or to corpus. Income beneficiaries typically receive payments from the entity that are equal to the accounting income.
4. The taxable income of the entity is computed using the scheme in Figure 19–2. The entity usually recognizes income in respect of a decedent. Deductions for fiduciary's fees and for charitable contributions may be reduced if the entity received any tax-exempt income during the year. Cost recovery deductions are assigned proportionately to the recipients of accounting income. Upon election, realized gain or loss on assets that properly are distributed in kind can be recognized by the entity.
5. A distribution deduction, computationally derived from distributable net income (DNI), is allowed to the entity. DNI is the maximum amount on which entity beneficiaries can be taxed. Moreover, the constitution of DNI is preserved for the recipients of the distributions.
6. Additional taxes are levied under Subchapter J to discourage the retention of excessive administrative powers by the grantor of a trust when the gross income is taxed to a lower-bracket beneficiary.

---

associated with the investment. If this approach is taken, a trust might be unnecessary—the parent should simply retain full control over the assets and invest in the exempt securities in his or her own account.

- The grantor should retain high-yield assets, so that control over the assets is not surrendered when the tax cost is too high.
- Use of trust vehicles should be reserved for cases where professional management of the assets is necessary for portfolio growth and the additional tax costs can be justified.
- An income-shifting strategy may require several steps to achieve the desired result. For instance, the grantor might increase contributions to his or her own qualified retirement plan, thereby sheltering the funds from all tax liabilities. Then the grantor could use the tax dollars saved from these contributions to purchase tax-deferred annuity contracts, savings bonds, exempt securities, or other assets where the tax liabilities are reduced or deferred. The grantor could then either retain these exempt securities as discussed above or transfer them to the trust at a later date.

### INCOME TAX PLANNING FOR ESTATES

As a separate taxable entity, an estate can select its own tax year and accounting methods. The executor of an estate should consider selecting a fiscal year because this will determine when beneficiaries must include income distributions from the estate in their own tax returns. Beneficiaries must include the income for their tax year with or within which the estate's tax year ends. Proper selection of the estate's tax year can result in a smoothing out of income and a reduction of the income taxes for all parties involved.

Caution should be taken in determining when the estate is to be terminated. Selecting a fiscal year for the estate can result in a bunching of income to the beneficiaries in the year in which the estate is closed. Prolonging the termination of an estate can be effective income tax planning, but the IRS carefully examines the purpose of keeping the estate open. Since the unused losses of an estate pass through to the beneficiaries only in the termination year, the estate should be closed when the beneficiaries can enjoy the maximum tax benefit of the losses.

The timing and amounts of income distributions to the beneficiaries also present important tax planning opportunities. If the executor can make discretionary income distributions, he or she should evaluate the relative marginal income tax rates of the estate and its beneficiaries. By timing the distributions properly, the overall income tax liability can be minimized. Care should be taken, however, to time the distributions in light of the estate's DNI.

**EXAMPLE 37**

For several years before his death on March 7, Don had entered into annual deferred compensation agreements with his employer. These agreements collectively called for the payment of $200,000 six months after Don's retirement or death. To provide a maximum 12-month period within which to generate deductions to offset this large item of income in respect of a decedent, the executor or administrator of the estate should elect a fiscal year ending August 31. The election is made simply by filing the estate's first tax return for the short period of March 7 to August 31. ■

**EXAMPLE 38**

Carol, the sole beneficiary of an estate, is a calendar year, cash basis taxpayer. If the estate elects a fiscal year ending January 31, all distributions during the period of February 1 to December 31, 2003, will be reported on Carol's tax return for calendar year 2004 (due April 15, 2005). Thus, assuming estimated tax requirements have otherwise been met, any income taxes that result from a $50,000 distribution made by the estate on February 20, 2003, are deferred until April 15, 2005. ■

**EXAMPLE 39**

Assume the same facts as in Example 38. If the estate is closed on December 15, 2004, the DNI for both the fiscal year ending January 31, 2004, and the final tax year ending December 15, 2004, is included in Carol's tax return for the same calendar year. To avoid the effect of this bunching of income, the estate should not be closed until calendar year 2005. ■

**EXAMPLE 40**

Assume the same facts as in Example 39, except that the estate has a substantial NOL for the period February 1 to December 15, 2004. If Carol is subject to a high income tax rate for calendar year 2004, the estate should be closed in that year so that the excess deductions are passed through to its beneficiary. However, if Carol anticipates being in a higher tax bracket in 2005, the termination of the estate should be postponed. ■

**EXAMPLE 41**

Review Examples 28 and 29 carefully. Note, for instance, the flexibility that is available to the executor or administrator in timing the second-tier distributions of income and corpus of the estate. To illustrate, if Washington is subject to a high tax rate, distributions to him should be minimized except in years when DNI is low. In this manner, Washington's exposure to gross income from the distributions can be controlled so that most of the distributions he receives will be free of income tax. ■

In general, those beneficiaries who are subject to high income tax rates should be made beneficiaries of second-tier (but not IRD) distributions of the estate. Most likely, these individuals will have less need for an additional steady stream of (taxable) income while their income tax savings can be relatively large. Moreover, a special allocation of tax-favored types of income and expenses should be considered. For example, tax-exempt income can be directed more easily to beneficiaries in higher income tax brackets.

---

| **ETHICAL CONSIDERATIONS** | **Should a Tax Adviser Also Be a Trustee?** |

Tax clients need to be counseled on the best use of the trust entity and the proper choice of beneficiary of the trust income. The objectives of the grantor typically will best be served by transferring more power to the trustee; sprinkling powers, in particular, enable the trustee to be sensitive to the short-term and ongoing needs of the various beneficiaries. The client, however, may not appreciate this suggestion when the trust document is drafted. Especially if the tax adviser is the trustee or a co-trustee, the client may balk at the professional's well-intended suggestion that future developments might favor one beneficiary over another in a manner that cannot be anticipated at the time.

Should the source of the estate plan—the tax adviser—also then be designated as the trustee by the grantor? When the adviser serves in that capacity, who is "the client"? Merely the grantor? How about the beneficiaries? And the trust itself?

To avoid any potential for conflict with their clients, some professional firms have adopted a policy of refusing to serve as trustee of a client's trust (or executor of his or her estate). Certainly, surrendering a sprinkling power to a fiduciary who is less sensitive to the tax ramifications of Subchapter J may be costly to all of the parties, but these firms see the preservation of the client relationship as more valuable in the long term.

Although both of her children were attorneys, Jacqueline Kennedy Onassis was careful to make other parties the executor of her estate and the trustees of her fiduciary entities. In more typical estates, though, the grantor must address critical issues: How much power and control over assets and income should be surrendered to "outsiders" through the trust? Which items lend themselves to such transfers of control?

---

## INCOME TAX PLANNING WITH TRUSTS

The great variety of trusts provides the grantor, trustee, and beneficiaries with excellent opportunities for tax planning. Many of the same tax planning opportunities available to the executor of an estate are available to the trustee. For instance, the distributions from a trust are taxable to the trust's beneficiaries to the extent of the trust's DNI. If income distributions are discretionary, the trustee can time the distributions to minimize the income tax consequences to all parties.

## DISTRIBUTIONS OF IN-KIND PROPERTY

The ability of the trustee or executor to elect to recognize the realized gain or loss relative to a distributed noncash asset allows the gain or loss to be allocated to the optimal taxpayer.

**EXAMPLE 42**

The Yorba Linda Estate distributed some stock, basis of $40,000 and fair market value of $41,500, to beneficiary Larry. Yorba Linda is subject to a 15% marginal income tax rate, and Larry is subject to a 30% marginal rate. The executor of Yorba Linda should elect that the entity recognize the related $1,500 realized gain, thereby subjecting the gain to the estate's lower marginal tax rate and reducing Larry's future capital gain income. ∎

## DEDUCTIBILITY OF FIDUCIARY EXPENSES

Many § 2053 and § 2054 estate tax deductions and losses may be claimed either as estate tax deductions or as income tax deductions of the estate on the fiduciary return (Form 1041), at the taxpayer's choice.[43] In such a case, the deduction for income tax purposes is not allowed unless the estate tax deduction is waived. These deductions can be apportioned between the two returns.

An expense deductible for estate tax purposes may not qualify as an income tax deduction. Interest expense incurred to carry tax-exempt bonds is disallowed for income tax purposes. If this expense is not claimed under § 2053 for estate tax purposes, it is completely lost.

Medical expenses incurred by the decedent but unpaid at the time of the decedent's death are covered by a special rule. If paid by the estate during a one-year period beginning with the day after death, the expenses may be claimed as an income tax deduction in the year incurred or as an estate tax deduction, but not both.[44] The choice is between the decedent's appropriate Form 1040 and his or her estate tax return. The expenses may be divided in any way between Form 1040 and the estate tax return.

**EXAMPLE 43**

The executor of Dana's estate pays $5,000 in burial expenses (authorized under local law and approved by the probate court) from estate assets. The $5,000 expense should be claimed on the estate tax return, as it is not deductible at all for income tax purposes. ■

## KEY TERMS

| | | |
|---|---|---|
| Complex trust, 19–5 | Grantor, 19–3 | Reversionary interest, 19–5 |
| Corpus, 19–4 | Grantor trust, 19–3 | Simple trust, 19–5 |
| Distributable net income (DNI), 19–18 | Income in respect of a decedent (IRD), 19–13 | Sprinkling trust, 19–5 |
| Expenses in respect of a decedent, 19–13 | | |

## PROBLEM MATERIALS

### Discussion Questions

**Issue ID**

1. When should a client be counseled to create a trust? What tax motivations might lead to the use of a fiduciary? List important tax and nontax objectives that might be satisfied by the use of a trust created during the taxpayer's lifetime.

2. How many parties are needed to create an estate? A trust? Identify the titles traditionally given to each party.

3. Is it more or less expensive in tax terms for a married couple to shift taxable income via a trust? What if they were to use a C corporation?

4. Evaluate this comment: A fiduciary entity such as a trust or an estate is not subject to the alternative minimum tax, but its beneficiaries are.

---

[43]§ 642(g) and Reg. § 20.2053–1(d).                        [44]§ 213(c).

5. Illustrate the nature and operations of each of the following trusts by creating a fact pattern to match each result. Be specific.
   a. A simple trust.
   b. A complex trust with a $300 personal exemption.
   c. A complex trust with a $100 personal exemption.

6. Using Figure 19–2 as a guide, describe the computation of a fiduciary entity's accounting income, taxable income, and distributable net income.

7. The Lopez Trust is short of cash. It is required to distribute $100,000 to Judith every year, and that payment is due in six weeks. In its asset corpus, Lopez holds a number of stocks that are valued at $100,000. One of them has a tax basis to the trust of $65,000. Assuming that the trust agreement so allows, what are the tax consequences if Lopez distributes this stock to Judith?

**Decision Making**

8. In its first tax year, the Wittmann Estate generated $50,000 of taxable interest income and $20,000 of tax-exempt interest income. It paid fiduciary fees of $3,000. The estate is subject to a 47% marginal estate tax rate and a 30% marginal income tax rate.
   a. How should the executor assign the deductions for the payment of the fees?
   b. How does the 2%-of-AGI floor apply to the fees assigned to the estate's income tax return?

9. The Red Trust generated $50,000 in cost recovery deductions this year. Can Red claim this deduction in computing its entity taxable income?

10. In 2003, the Helpful Trust agreed to make a $50,000 contribution to Local Soup Kitchen, a charitable organization. Helpful's board agreed to the gift at a November 2003 meeting, but the check was not issued until February 20, 2004. Can the trust claim a charitable contribution deduction? If so, describe how Helpful should treat its gift.

**Issue ID**

11. The Flan Trust is scheduled to terminate in two years, when Amy Flan reaches age 30. The trust operated a business several years ago, and it generated a sizable NOL carryforward that the trust has not been able to use. In addition, due to a bearish stock market, the value of the entity's investment portfolio has declined 15% from its purchase price. What issues must you consider in giving Amy and the corporate trustee tax planning advice?

**Issue ID**

12. Harriet wants to transfer some assets to a trust this year; the income beneficiaries will be her two grandchildren. The trust will be used to pay the grandchildren's tuition to private high schools and universities. Upon the younger grandchild's graduation, the trust assets will return to Harriet's ownership. Identify tax issues related to Harriet's plan to use a temporary fiduciary entity.

**Decision Making**

**Communications**

13. Carol wants to set up a trust that will pay her life insurance premiums. She believes that the trust will be able to deduct these premium payments, something that she cannot currently do on her Form 1040. Write a memo to the tax research file addressing Carol's ideas.

## Problems

14. The Purple Trust incurred the following items this year.

| | |
|---|---|
| Taxable interest income | $35,000 |
| Tax-exempt interest income, not on private activity bonds | 50,000 |
| Tax-exempt interest income, on private activity bonds | 60,000 |

Compute Purple's tentative minimum tax for the year. Purple does not have any credits available to reduce the AMT liability.

**Decision Making**

15. The Grouper Trust will incur the following items next year, its first year of existence.

| | |
|---|---|
| Interest income | $70,000 |
| Rent income | 12,000 |
| Cost recovery expense | 9,500 |
| Capital gain income | 40,000 |
| Fiduciary and tax preparation fees | 11,000 |

Betty, the grantor of the trust, is working with you on the language in the trust instrument relative to the derivation of annual accounting income for the entity. She will name Shirley as the sole income beneficiary and Benny as the remainder beneficiary.

a. Suggest language to Betty that will maximize the annual income distribution to Shirley.

b. Suggest language to Betty that will minimize the annual distribution to Shirley and maximize the accumulation on Benny's behalf.

16. Complete the following chart, indicating the comparative attributes of the typical trust and estate by answering yes/no or explaining the differences between the entities where appropriate.

| Attribute | Estate | Trust |
|---|---|---|
| Separate income tax entity | | |
| Controlling document | | |
| Termination date is determinable from controlling document | | |
| Legal owner of assets under fiduciary's control | | |
| Document identifies both income and remainder beneficiaries | | |
| Separate share rules apply | | |
| Generally must use calendar tax year | | |

17. Complete the chart below, indicating trust accounting income for each of the alternatives. For this purpose, use the following information.

| | |
|---|---|
| Interest income, taxable | $70,000 |
| Interest income, tax-exempt | 30,000 |
| Interest income, tax-exempt but AMT preference | 20,000 |
| Long-term capital gain | 25,000 |
| Trustee fee | 6,000 |

| Trust Agreement Provisions | Trust Accounting Income |
|---|---|
| Fees and capital gains allocable to corpus | |
| Capital gains allocable to corpus, one-half of fees allocable to income | |
| Capital gains allocable to income, silent concerning allocation of fees | |
| Fees and exempt income allocable to corpus, silent concerning allocation of capital gain/loss | |

18. Bob is one of the income beneficiaries of the LeMans Estate. This year, as directed by the will, Bob received all of the sales commissions that were earned and payable to LeMans (cash basis) at her death, as well as one of the remaining installment payments. Compute Bob's gross income attributable to LeMans's activities for the current year, given the following financial data.

| | |
|---|---|
| Sales commissions receivable | $50,000 |
| Deferred ordinary gain on installment sale, two payments remaining | 90,000 |

19. Brown incurred the following items.

| | |
|---|---|
| Business income | $75,000 |
| Tax-exempt interest income | 25,000 |
| Payment to charity from 2003 income, paid 3/1/2004 | 20,000 |

Complete the following chart, indicating how the Code treats charitable contributions under the various assumptions.

| Assumption | 2003 Deduction for Contribution |
|---|---|
| Brown is a cash basis individual. | |
| Brown is an accrual basis corporation. | |
| Brown is a trust. | |

20. The Oliver Trust has generated $50,000 in depreciation deductions for the year. Its accounting income is $30,000. In computing this amount, pursuant to the trust document, depreciation was allocated to corpus. Accounting income was distributed at the trustee's discretion: $15,000 to Hernandez and $15,000 to Jackson.
    a. Compute the depreciation deductions that Hernandez, Jackson, and Oliver may claim.
    b. Same as (a), except that depreciation was allocated to income.
    c. Same as (a), except that the trustee distributed $6,000 each to Hernandez and to Jackson and retained the remaining accounting income.
    d. Same as (a), except that Oliver is an estate (and not a trust).

21. The Ricardo Trust is a simple trust that correctly uses the calendar year for tax purposes. Its three income beneficiaries (Lucy, Mark, and Ethel) are entitled to the trust's annual accounting income in shares of one-third each. For the current calendar year, the trust generates ordinary income of $75,000, a long-term capital gain of $15,000 (allocable to corpus), and a trustee commission expense of $9,000 (allocable to corpus). Use the format of Figure 19–3 to address the following items.
    a. How much income is each beneficiary entitled to receive?
    b. What is the trust's DNI?
    c. What is the trust's taxable income?
    d. How much is taxed to each of the beneficiaries?

22. Assume the same facts as in Problem 21, except that the trust instrument allocates the capital gain to income.
    a. How much income is each beneficiary entitled to receive?
    b. What is the trust's DNI?
    c. What is the trust's taxable income?
    d. How much is taxed to each of the beneficiaries?

23. Under the terms of the trust instrument, the trustee has discretion to distribute or accumulate income on behalf of Willie, Sylvia, and Doris in equal shares. The trustee also can invade corpus for the benefit of any of the beneficiaries to the extent of each person's respective one-third interest in the trust.

In the current year, the trust has DNI of $75,000. Distributions were made as follows.

- To Willie: $25,000 from DNI, $15,000 from corpus.
- To Sylvia: $15,000. The remaining $10,000 DNI is accumulated.
- To Doris: $0. The $25,000 DNI is accumulated.

a. How much income is taxed to Willie?
b. To Sylvia?
c. To Doris?
d. To the trust?

24. A trust is required to distribute $100,000 annually to its two equal income beneficiaries, Clare and David. If trust income is not sufficient to pay these amounts, the trustee can invade corpus to the extent necessary. During the current year, the trust generates only taxable interest income and has DNI of $120,000; the trustee distributes $75,000 to Clare and $50,000 to David.

a. How much of the $75,000 distributed to Clare is included in her gross income?
b. How much of the $50,000 distributed to David is included in his gross income?
c. Are these distributions first-tier or second-tier distributions?

25. An estate has $75,000 of DNI, composed of $30,000 in dividends, $20,000 in taxable interest, $15,000 passive activity income, and $10,000 in tax-exempt interest. The trust's two noncharitable income beneficiaries, Brenda and Del, receive $30,000 each. How much of each class of income is deemed to have been distributed to Brenda? To Del?

26. The trustee of the Purple Trust can distribute any amount of accounting income and corpus to the trust's beneficiaries, Lydia and Kent. This year, the trust incurred the following.

| | |
|---|---|
| Taxable interest income | $40,000 |
| Tax-exempt interest income | 60,000 |
| Long-term capital gains—allocable to corpus | 30,000 |
| Fiduciary's fees—allocable to corpus | 10,000 |

The trustee distributed $40,000 to Lydia and $30,000 to Kent.
a. What is Purple's trust accounting income?
b. What is Purple's DNI?
c. What is Purple's taxable income?
d. How much is taxed to each of the beneficiaries?

**Decision Making**

27. Each of the following items was incurred by José, the cash basis, calendar year decedent. Under the terms of the will, Dora took immediate ownership in all of José's assets, except the dividend-paying stock. The estate received José's final paycheck.

Applying the rules for income and deductions in respect of a decedent, indicate on which return each item should be reported: Dora's Form 1040 income tax (*Form 1040*); José's estate's first Form 1041 income tax (*Form 1041*); or José's estate's Form 706 estate tax (*Form 706*). More than one alternative may apply in some cases.

| Item Incurred | Form(s) Reported on |
|---|---|
| a. Wages, last paycheck | _____ |
| b. State income tax withheld on last paycheck | _____ |
| c. Capital gain portion of installment payment received | _____ |
| d. Ordinary income portion of installment payment received | _____ |

| Item Incurred | Form(s) Reported on |
|---|---|
| e. Dividend income, record date was two days prior to José's death | |
| f. Unrealized appreciation on a mutual fund investment | |
| g. Depreciation recapture accrued as of date of death | |
| h. Medical expenses of last illness | |
| i. Apartment building, rents accrued but not collected as of death | |
| j. Apartment building, property tax accrued and assessed but not paid as of death | |

**Decision Making**

**Communications**

28. In each of the following independent cases, write a memo for the tax research file in preparation for a meeting with Gary. In each memo, explain whether the proposed plan meets his objective of shifting income and avoiding the grantor trust rules.
   a. Gary transfers property in trust, income payable to Winnie (his wife) for life, remainder to his grandson. Gary's son is designated as the trustee.
   b. Gary transfers income-producing assets and a life insurance policy to a trust, life estate to his children, remainder to his grandchildren. The policy is on Winnie's life, and the trustee (an independent trust company) is instructed to pay the premiums with income from the income-producing assets. The trust is designated as the beneficiary of the policy.
   c. Gary transfers property in trust. The trust income is payable to Gary's grandchildren, as Winnie sees fit. Winnie and an independent trust company are designated as trustees.
   d. Gary transfers property in trust, income payable to Winnie (Gary's ex-wife), remainder to Gary or his estate upon Winnie's death. The transfer was made in satisfaction of Gary's alimony obligation to Winnie. An independent trust company is designated as the trustee.

29. Determine the tax effects of the indicated losses for the Yellow Estate for both tax years. The estate holds a variety of investment assets, which it received from the decedent, Mrs. Yellow. The estate's sole income and remainder beneficiary is Yellow, Jr.

| Tax Year | Loss Generated |
|---|---|
| 2003 (first tax year) | Taxable income ($300) |
| | Capital loss ($8,000) |
| 2004 (final tax year) | Taxable income ($20,000) |

**Decision Making**

30. Woody wishes to transfer some of the income from his investment portfolio to his daughter, age 6. Woody wants the trust to be able to accumulate income on his daughter's behalf and to meet any excessive expenses associated with the daughter's prep school and private college education. Furthermore, Woody wants the trust to protect his daughter against his own premature death without increasing his Federal gross estate. Thus, Woody provides the trustee with the powers to purchase insurance on his life and to meet tuition, fee, and book expenses of his daughter's education. The trust is created in 1987. A whole life insurance policy with five annual premium payments is purchased during that year. The trustee spends $10,000 for the daughter's college expenses in 2003 (but in no other year). Woody dies in 2005. Has the trust been tax-effective?

31. Complete the following chart, indicating the comparative attributes of the typical simple trust and complex trust by answering yes/no or explaining the differences between the entities where appropriate.

| Attribute | Simple Trust | Complex Trust |
|---|---|---|
| Trust could incur its own tax liability for the year | | |
| Trust generally distributes all of DNI | | |
| Trust can deduct its charitable contributions in the year of, or the year after, payment | | |
| Trust could claim a foreign tax credit | | |
| Maximum tax rate on net long-term capital gains = 20% | | |
| AMT preferences and adjustments flow through to beneficiaries ratably | | |
| Amount of personal exemption | | |

**Decision Making**

**Communications**

32. Your client, Annie O'Toole (22 Beneficiary Lane, Bowling Green, KY 42101), has come to you for some advice regarding gifts of property. She has just learned that she must undergo major surgery, and she would like to make certain gifts before entering the hospital. On your earlier advice, she had established a plan of lifetime giving for four prior years.

   Build a spreadsheet, supplemented by a list of your assumptions, and write a cover letter to Annie, discussing each of the following assets that she is considering using as gifts to family and friends. In doing so, evaluate the income tax consequences of having such property pass through her estate to the designated heir.
   a. Annie plans to give a cottage to her son to fulfill a promise made many years ago. She has owned the cottage for the past 15 years and has a basis in it of $30,000 (fair market value of $20,000).
   b. Annie has $100,000 of long-term capital losses that she has been carrying forward for the past few years. Now she is considering making a gift of $200,000 in installment notes to her daughter. Her basis in the notes is $100,000, and the notes' current fair market value is $190,000.
   c. Annie has promised to make a special cash bequest of $25,000 to her grandson in her will. However, she does not anticipate having that much cash immediately available after her death. Annie requests your advice concerning the income tax consequences to the estate if the cash bequest is settled with some other property.

**See Appendix F for Comprehensive Tax Return Problem—Form 1041**

## Research Problems

*Note: Solutions to Research Problems can be prepared by using the **RIA Checkpoint® Student Edition** online research product, or the **CCH U.S. Master Tax Guide Plus™** online Federal tax research database, which is available to accompany this text. It is also possible to prepare solutions to the Research Problems by using tax research materials found in a standard tax library.*

**Communications**

**Research Problem 1.** Your client, Chuck Konkol, is a self-employed investment adviser who provides services to individuals and small investment clubs for an hourly fee. He is aware of the difficulty that his clients have in deducting payments to him, such as advisory fees, due to the 2%-of-AGI floor on miscellaneous itemized deductions.

   His new client, the Ferguson Trust, wants to be certain that it can deduct such fees in computing entity taxable income. The Ferguson Trust operates in the jurisdiction of the Eighth Circuit Court of Appeals. Konkol asks you to make a presentation to the trust's officers on this subject. Provide a speaker's outline for this purpose, with citations to only the most important statutory and judicial law.

**Decision Making**

**Research Problem 2.** Your client, Celia van Sustern, wants to send her daughter Muffy to private grade school to avoid the problems of crime, drugs, and other roadblocks to Muffy's personal growth. Celia, a resident of Beverly Hills, is fully supported by a trust she set up to manage her investment funds, chiefly given to her 10 years ago by her father. She receives monthly distributions of various amounts, each made only after approval by the trustee.

If Celia convinces the trustee to pay for Muffy's tuition, directly by a check from the trust to the school, are there any income tax consequences to Celia?

*Partial list of research aids:*
§ 677(b).
*Frederick C. Braun, Jr.,* 48 TCM 210, T.C.Memo. 1984–285.

**Communications**

**Research Problem 3.** Laura is the executor of her mother's estate. She is collecting assets and paying off liabilities as she finds them, as she is required to do under the terms of the will. Three months after her mother died, Laura received for the estate a check from her father for back alimony payments that were due her mother at the date of death. The alimony payment was sizable, and Laura had sufficient cash with which to meet the rest of the obligations of the estate, so she distributed $100,000 of the total $300,000 check to herself this year, as the estate's sole beneficiary.

Laura, who lives in Charlotte, North Carolina, has come to you to help her determine the proper income tax treatment for the alimony. She maintains it is a tax-free inheritance from the estate. Summarize your analysis in a memorandum to the tax research file.

*Partial list of research aids:*
§§ 682(b), 691.
*Holloway v. U.S.,* 70–2 USTC ¶9548, 26 AFTR2d 70–5034, 428 F.2d 140 (CA–9, 1970).

**Internet Activity**

*Use the tax resources of the Internet to address the following questions. Do not restrict your search to the World Wide Web, but include a review of newsgroups and general reference materials, practitioner sites and resources, primary sources of the tax law, chat rooms and discussion groups, and other opportunities.*

**Research Problem 4.** Go to the IRS Web site. How many Form 1041s were filed last year? How many Form 1041s were audited last year, at various income levels?

**Research Problem 5.** Find the most recent case decided in your jurisdiction addressing the definition of "support" under § 677(b). Summarize the case and compare it to *Braun,* cited in text footnote 42, in an e-mail to your professor.

**Research Problem 6.** Under the income tax laws of your state applicable to fiduciaries, how are the following items allocated?

- Capital gain.

- Cost recovery.

- Fiduciary fees.

# Tax Rate Schedules and Tables

# 2002 Tax Rate Schedules

## Single—Schedule X

| If taxable income is: Over— | But not over— | The tax is: | of the amount over— |
|---|---|---|---|
| $0 | $ 6,000 | . . . . . . .10% | $0 |
| 6,000 | 27,950 | $ 600.00 + 15% | 6,000 |
| 27,950 | 67,700 | 3,892.50 + 27% | 27,950 |
| 67,700 | 141,250 | 14,625.00 + 30% | 67,700 |
| 141,250 | 307,050 | 36,690.00 + 35% | 141,250 |
| 307,050 | . . . . . . | 94,720.00 + 38.6% | 307,050 |

## Head of household—Schedule Z

| If taxable income is: Over— | But not over— | The tax is: | of the amount over— |
|---|---|---|---|
| $0 | $ 10,000 | . . . . . . .10% | $0 |
| 10,000 | 37,450 | $1,000.00 + 15% | 10,000 |
| 37,450 | 96,700 | 5,117.50 + 27% | 37,450 |
| 96,700 | 156,600 | 21,115.00 + 30% | 96,700 |
| 156,600 | 307,050 | 39,085.00 + 35% | 156,600 |
| 307,050 | . . . . . . | 91,742.50 + 38.6% | 307,050 |

## Married filing jointly or Qualifying widow(er)—Schedule Y–1

| If taxable income is: Over— | But not over— | The tax is: | of the amount over— |
|---|---|---|---|
| $0 | $ 12,000 | . . . . . . .10% | $0 |
| 12,000 | 46,700 | $1,200.00 + 15% | 12,000 |
| 46,700 | 112,850 | 6,405.00 + 27% | 46,700 |
| 112,850 | 171,950 | 24,265.50 + 30% | 112,850 |
| 171,950 | 307,050 | 41,995.50 + 35% | 171,950 |
| 307,050 | . . . . . . | 89,280.50 + 38.6% | 307,050 |

## Married filing separately—Schedule Y–2

| If taxable income is: Over— | But not over— | The tax is: | of the amount over— |
|---|---|---|---|
| $0 | $ 6,000 | . . . . . . .10% | $0 |
| 6,000 | 23,350 | $ 600.00 + 15% | 6,000 |
| 23,350 | 56,425 | 3,202.50 + 27% | 23,350 |
| 56,425 | 85,975 | 12,132.75 + 30% | 56,425 |
| 85,975 | 153,525 | 20,997.75 + 35% | 85,975 |
| 153,525 | . . . . . . | 44,640.25 + 38.6% | 153,525 |

# 2003 Tax Rate Schedules

## Single—Schedule X

| If taxable income is: Over— | But not over— | The tax is: | of the amount over— |
|---|---|---|---|
| $0 | $ 6,000 | . . . . . . .10% | $0 |
| 6,000 | 28,400 | $ 600.00 + 15% | 6,000 |
| 28,400 | 68,800 | 3,960.00 + 27% | 28,400 |
| 68,800 | 143,500 | 14,868.00 + 30% | 68,800 |
| 143,500 | 311,950 | 37,278.00 + 35% | 143,500 |
| 311,950 | . . . . . . | 96,235.50 + 38.6% | 311,950 |

## Head of household—Schedule Z

| If taxable income is: Over— | But not over— | The tax is: | of the amount over— |
|---|---|---|---|
| $0 | $ 10,000 | . . . . . . .10% | $0 |
| 10,000 | 38,050 | $1,000.00 + 15% | 10,000 |
| 38,050 | 98,250 | 5,207.50 + 27% | 38,050 |
| 98,250 | 159,100 | 21,461.50 + 30% | 98,250 |
| 159,100 | 311,950 | 39,716.50 + 35% | 159,100 |
| 311,950 | . . . . . . | 93,214.00 + 38.6% | 311,950 |

## Married filing jointly or Qualifying widow(er)—Schedule Y–1

| If taxable income is: Over— | But not over— | The tax is: | of the amount over— |
|---|---|---|---|
| $0 | $ 12,000 | . . . . . . .10% | $0 |
| 12,000 | 47,450 | $1,200.00 + 15% | 12,000 |
| 47,450 | 114,650 | 6,517.50 + 27% | 47,450 |
| 114,650 | 174,700 | 24,661.50 + 30% | 114,650 |
| 174,700 | 311,950 | 42,676.50 + 35% | 174,700 |
| 311,950 | . . . . . . | 90,714.00 + 38.6% | 311,950 |

## Married filing separately—Schedule Y–2

| If taxable income is: Over— | But not over— | The tax is: | of the amount over— |
|---|---|---|---|
| $0 | $ 6,000 | . . . . . . .10% | $0 |
| 6,000 | 23,725 | $ 600.00 + 15% | 6,000 |
| 23,725 | 57,325 | 3,258.75 + 27% | 23,725 |
| 57,325 | 87,350 | 12,330.75 + 30% | 57,325 |
| 87,350 | 155,975 | 21,338.25 + 35% | 87,350 |
| 155,975 | . . . . . . | 45,357.00 + 38.6% | 155,975 |

# Income Tax Rates—Estates and Trusts

## TAX YEAR 2002

| Taxable Income | | The Tax Is: | Of the Amount |
|---|---|---|---|
| Over— | But Not Over— | | Over— |
| $ 0 | $1,850 | 15% | $ 0 |
| 1,850 | 4,400 | $ 277.50 + 27% | 1,850 |
| 4,400 | 6,750 | 966.00 + 30% | 4,400 |
| 6,750 | 9,200 | 1,671.00 + 35% | 6,750 |
| 9,200 | ......... | 2,528.50 + 38.6% | 9,200 |

## TAX YEAR 2003

| Taxable Income | | The Tax Is: | Of the Amount |
|---|---|---|---|
| Over— | But Not Over— | | Over— |
| $ 0 | $1,900 | 15% | $ 0 |
| 1,900 | 4,500 | $ 285 + 27% | 1,900 |
| 4,500 | 6,850 | 987 + 30% | 4,500 |
| 6,850 | 9,350 | 1,692 + 35% | 6,850 |
| 9,350 | ......... | 2,567 + 38.6% | 9,350 |

# Income Tax Rates—Corporations

| Taxable Income | | Tax Is: | Of the Amount |
|---|---|---|---|
| Over— | But Not Over— | | Over— |
| $ 0 | $ 50,000 | 15% | $ 0 |
| 50,000 | 75,000 | $ 7,500 + 25% | 50,000 |
| 75,000 | 100,000 | 13,750 + 34% | 75,000 |
| 100,000 | 335,000 | 22,250 + 39% | 100,000 |
| 335,000 | 10,000,000 | 113,900 + 34% | 335,000 |
| 10,000,000 | 15,000,000 | 3,400,000 + 35% | 10,000,000 |
| 15,000,000 | 18,333,333 | 5,150,000 + 38% | 15,000,000 |
| 18,333,333 | ............ | 35% | 0 |

# Unified Transfer Tax Rates

## FOR GIFTS MADE AND FOR DEATHS AFTER 1976 AND BEFORE 1982

| If the Amount with Respect to Which the Tentative Tax to Be Computed Is: | The Tentative Tax Is: |
| --- | --- |
| Not over $10,000 | 18 percent of such amount. |
| Over $10,000 but not over $20,000 | $1,800, plus 20 percent of the excess of such amount over $10,000. |
| Over $20,000 but not over $40,000 | $3,800, plus 22 percent of the excess of such amount over $20,000. |
| Over $40,000 but not over $60,000 | $8,200, plus 24 percent of the excess of such amount over $40,000. |
| Over $60,000 but not over $80,000 | $13,000, plus 26 percent of the excess of such amount over $60,000. |
| Over $80,000 but not over $100,000 | $18,200, plus 28 percent of the excess of such amount over $80,000. |
| Over $100,000 but not over $150,000 | $23,800, plus 30 percent of the excess of such amount over $100,000. |
| Over $150,000 but not over $250,000 | $38,800, plus 32 percent of the excess of such amount over $150,000. |
| Over $250,000 but not over $500,000 | $70,800, plus 34 percent of the excess of such amount over $250,000. |
| Over $500,000 but not over $750,000 | $155,800, plus 37 percent of the excess of such amount over $500,000. |
| Over $750,000 but not over $1,000,000 | $248,300, plus 39 percent of the excess of such amount over $750,000. |
| Over $1,000,000 but not over $1,250,000 | $345,800, plus 41 percent of the excess of such amount over $1,000,000. |
| Over $1,250,000 but not over $1,500,000 | $448,300, plus 43 percent of the excess of such amount over $1,250,000. |
| Over $1,500,000 but not over $2,000,000 | $555,800, plus 45 percent of the excess of such amount over $1,500,000. |
| Over $2,000,000 but not over $2,500,000 | $780,800, plus 49 percent of the excess of such amount over $2,000,000. |
| Over $2,500,000 but not over $3,000,000 | $1,025,800, plus 53 percent of the excess of such amount over $2,500,000. |
| Over $3,000,000 but not over $3,500,000 | $1,290,800, plus 57 percent of the excess of such amount over $3,000,000. |
| Over $3,500,000 but not over $4,000,000 | $1,575,800, plus 61 percent of the excess of such amount over $3,500,000. |
| Over $4,000,000 but not over $4,500,000 | $1,880,800, plus 65 percent of the excess of such amount over $4,000,000. |
| Over $4,500,000 but not over $5,000,000 | $2,205,800, plus 69 percent of the excess of such amount over $4,500,000. |
| Over $5,000,000 | $2,550,800, plus 70 percent of the excess of such amount over $5,000,000. |

# Unified Transfer Tax Rates

## FOR GIFTS MADE AND FOR DEATHS IN 1982

| If the Amount with Respect to Which the Tentative Tax to Be Computed Is: | The Tentative Tax Is: |
| --- | --- |
| Not over $10,000 | 18 percent of such amount. |
| Over $10,000 but not over $20,000 | $1,800, plus 20 percent of the excess of such amount over $10,000. |
| Over $20,000 but not over $40,000 | $3,800, plus 22 percent of the excess of such amount over $20,000. |
| Over $40,000 but not over $60,000 | $8,200, plus 24 percent of the excess of such amount over $40,000. |
| Over $60,000 but not over $80,000 | $13,000, plus 26 percent of the excess of such amount over $60,000. |
| Over $80,000 but not over $100,000 | $18,200, plus 28 percent of the excess of such amount over $80,000. |
| Over $100,000 but not over $150,000 | $23,800, plus 30 percent of the excess of such amount over $100,000. |
| Over $150,000 but not over $250,000 | $38,800, plus 32 percent of the excess of such amount over $150,000. |
| Over $250,000 but not over $500,000 | $70,800, plus 34 percent of the excess of such amount over $250,000. |
| Over $500,000 but not over $750,000 | $155,800, plus 37 percent of the excess of such amount over $500,000. |
| Over $750,000 but not over $1,000,000 | $248,300, plus 39 percent of the excess of such amount over $750,000. |
| Over $1,000,000 but not over $1,250,000 | $345,800, plus 41 percent of the excess of such amount over $1,000,000. |
| Over $1,250,000 but not over $1,500,000 | $448,300, plus 43 percent of the excess of such amount over $1,250,000. |
| Over $1,500,000 but not over $2,000,000 | $555,800, plus 45 percent of the excess of such amount over $1,500,000. |
| Over $2,000,000 but not over $2,500,000 | $780,800, plus 49 percent of the excess of such amount over $2,000,000. |
| Over $2,500,000 but not over $3,000,000 | $1,025,800, plus 53 percent of the excess of such amount over $2,500,000. |
| Over $3,000,000 but not over $3,500,000 | $1,290,800, plus 57 percent of the excess of such amount over $3,000,000. |
| Over $3,500,000 but not over $4,000,000 | $1,575,800, plus 61 percent of the excess of such amount over $3,500,000. |
| Over $4,000,000. | $1,880,800, plus 65 percent of the excess of such amount over $4,000,000. |

# Unified Transfer Tax Rates

## FOR GIFTS MADE AND FOR DEATHS IN 1983

| If the Amount with Respect to Which the Tentative Tax to Be Computed Is: | The Tentative Tax Is: |
|---|---|
| Not over $10,000 | 18 percent of such amount. |
| Over $10,000 but not over $20,000 | $1,800, plus 20 percent of the excess of such amount over $10,000. |
| Over $20,000 but not over $40,000 | $3,800, plus 22 percent of the excess of such amount over $20,000. |
| Over $40,000 but not over $60,000 | $8,200, plus 24 percent of the excess of such amount over $40,000. |
| Over $60,000 but not over $80,000 | $13,000, plus 26 percent of the excess of such amount over $60,000. |
| Over $80,000 but not over $100,000 | $18,200, plus 28 percent of the excess of such amount over $80,000. |
| Over $100,000 but not over $150,000 | $23,800, plus 30 percent of the excess of such amount over $100,000. |
| Over $150,000 but not over $250,000 | $38,800, plus 32 percent of the excess of such amount over $150,000. |
| Over $250,000 but not over $500,000 | $70,800, plus 34 percent of the excess of such amount over $250,000. |
| Over $500,000 but not over $750,000 | $155,800, plus 37 percent of the excess of such amount over $500,000. |
| Over $750,000 but not over $1,000,000 | $248,300, plus 39 percent of the excess of such amount over $750,000. |
| Over $1,000,000 but not over $1,250,000 | $345,800, plus 41 percent of the excess of such amount over $1,000,000. |
| Over $1,250,000 but not over $1,500,000 | $448,300, plus 43 percent of the excess of such amount over $1,250,000. |
| Over $1,500,000 but not over $2,000,000 | $555,800, plus 45 percent of the excess of such amount over $1,500,000. |
| Over $2,000,000 but not over $2,500,000 | $780,800, plus 49 percent of the excess of such amount over $2,000,000. |
| Over $2,500,000 but not over $3,000,000 | $1,025,800, plus 53 percent of the excess of such amount over $2,500,000. |
| Over $3,000,000 but not over $3,500,000 | $1,290,800, plus 57 percent of the excess of such amount over $3,000,000. |
| Over $3,500,000. | $1,575,800, plus 60 percent of the excess of such amount over $3,500,000. |

# Unified Transfer Tax Rates

## FOR GIFTS MADE AND FOR DEATHS AFTER 1983 AND BEFORE 2002

| If the Amount with Respect to Which the Tentative Tax to Be Computed Is: | The Tentative Tax Is: |
| --- | --- |
| Not over $10,000 | 18 percent of such amount. |
| Over $10,000 but not over $20,000 | $1,800, plus 20 percent of the excess of such amount over $10,000. |
| Over $20,000 but not over $40,000 | $3,800, plus 22 percent of the excess of such amount over $20,000. |
| Over $40,000 but not over $60,000 | $8,200, plus 24 percent of the excess of such amount over $40,000. |
| Over $60,000 but not over $80,000 | $13,000, plus 26 percent of the excess of such amount over $60,000. |
| Over $80,000 but not over $100,000 | $18,200, plus 28 percent of the excess of such amount over $80,000. |
| Over $100,000 but not over $150,000 | $23,800, plus 30 percent of the excess of such amount over $100,000. |
| Over $150,000 but not over $250,000 | $38,800, plus 32 percent of the excess of such amount over $150,000. |
| Over $250,000 but not over $500,000 | $70,800, plus 34 percent of the excess of such amount over $250,000. |
| Over $500,000 but not over $750,000 | $155,800, plus 37 percent of the excess of such amount over $500,000. |
| Over $750,000 but not over $1,000,000 | $248,300, plus 39 percent of the excess of such amount over $750,000. |
| Over $1,000,000 but not over $1,250,000 | $345,800, plus 41 percent of the excess of such amount over $1,000,000. |
| Over $1,250,000 but not over $1,500,000 | $448,300, plus 43 percent of the excess of such amount over $1,250,000. |
| Over $1,500,000 but not over $2,000,000 | $555,800, plus 45 percent of the excess of such amount over $1,500,000. |
| Over $2,000,000 but not over $2,500,000 | $780,800, plus 49 percent of the excess of such amount over $2,000,000. |
| Over $2,500,000 but not over $3,000,000 | $1,025,800, plus 53 percent of the excess of such amount over $2,500,000. |
| Over $3,000,000* | $1,290,800, plus 55 percent of the excess of such amount over $3,000,000. |

*For large taxable transfers (generally in excess of $10 million) there is a phase-out of the graduated rates and the unified tax credit.

# Unified Transfer Tax Rates

## FOR GIFTS MADE AND FOR DEATHS IN 2002

| If the Amount with Respect to Which the Tentative Tax to Be Computed Is: | The Tentative Tax Is: |
|---|---|
| Not over $10,000 | 18 percent of such amount. |
| Over $10,000 but not over $20,000 | $1,800, plus 20 percent of the excess of such amount over $10,000. |
| Over $20,000 but not over $40,000 | $3,800, plus 22 percent of the excess of such amount over $20,000. |
| Over $40,000 but not over $60,000 | $8,200, plus 24 percent of the excess of such amount over $40,000. |
| Over $60,000 but not over $80,000 | $13,000, plus 26 percent of the excess of such amount over $60,000. |
| Over $80,000 but not over $100,000 | $18,200, plus 28 percent of the excess of such amount over $80,000. |
| Over $100,000 but not over $150,000 | $23,800, plus 30 percent of the excess of such amount over $100,000. |
| Over $150,000 but not over $250,000 | $38,800, plus 32 percent of the excess of such amount over $150,000. |
| Over $250,000 but not over $500,000 | $70,800, plus 34 percent of the excess of such amount over $250,000. |
| Over $500,000 but not over $750,000 | $155,800, plus 37 percent of the excess of such amount over $500,000. |
| Over $750,000 but not over $1,000,000 | $248,300, plus 39 percent of the excess of such amount over $750,000. |
| Over $1,000,000 but not over $1,250,000 | $345,800, plus 41 percent of the excess of such amount over $1,000,000. |
| Over $1,250,000 but not over $1,500,000 | $448,300, plus 43 percent of the excess of such amount over $1,250,000. |
| Over $1,500,000 but not over $2,000,000 | $555,800, plus 45 percent of the excess of such amount over $1,500,000. |
| Over $2,000,000 but not over $2,500,000 | $780,800, plus 49 percent of the excess of such amount over $2,000,000. |
| Over $2,500,000 | $1,025,800, plus 50 percent of the excess of such amount over $2,500,000. |

# Unified Transfer Tax Rates

## FOR GIFTS MADE AND FOR DEATHS IN 2003

| If the Amount with Respect to Which the Tentative Tax to Be Computed Is: | The Tentative Tax Is: |
| --- | --- |
| Not over $10,000 | 18 percent of such amount. |
| Over $10,000 but not over $20,000 | $1,800, plus 20 percent of the excess of such amount over $10,000. |
| Over $20,000 but not over $40,000 | $3,800, plus 22 percent of the excess of such amount over $20,000. |
| Over $40,000 but not over $60,000 | $8,200, plus 24 percent of the excess of such amount over $40,000. |
| Over $60,000 but not over $80,000 | $13,000, plus 26 percent of the excess of such amount over $60,000. |
| Over $80,000 but not over $100,000 | $18,200, plus 28 percent of the excess of such amount over $80,000. |
| Over $100,000 but not over $150,000 | $23,800, plus 30 percent of the excess of such amount over $100,000. |
| Over $150,000 but not over $250,000 | $38,800, plus 32 percent of the excess of such amount over $150,000. |
| Over $250,000 but not over $500,000 | $70,800, plus 34 percent of the excess of such amount over $250,000. |
| Over $500,000 but not over $750,000 | $155,800, plus 37 percent of the excess of such amount over $500,000. |
| Over $750,000 but not over $1,000,000 | $248,300, plus 39 percent of the excess of such amount over $750,000. |
| Over $1,000,000 but not over $1,250,000 | $345,800, plus 41 percent of the excess of such amount over $1,000,000. |
| Over $1,250,000 but not over $1,500,000 | $448,300, plus 43 percent of the excess of such amount over $1,250,000. |
| Over $1,500,000 but not over $2,000,000 | $555,800, plus 45 percent of the excess of such amount over $1,500,000. |
| Over $2,000,000 | $780,800, plus 49 percent of the excess of such amount over $2,000,000. |

# Estate Tax Rates (Before 1977)

| (A) Taxable Estate Equal to or More Than | (B) Taxable Estate Less Than | (C) Tax on Amount in Column (A) | (D) Rate of Tax on Excess Over Amount in Column (A) (Percentage) |
|---|---|---|---|
| 0 | $ 5,000 | 0 | 3 |
| $ 5,000 | 10,000 | $ 150 | 7 |
| 10,000 | 20,000 | 500 | 11 |
| 20,000 | 30,000 | 1,600 | 14 |
| 30,000 | 40,000 | 3,000 | 18 |
| 40,000 | 50,000 | 4,800 | 22 |
| 50,000 | 60,000 | 7,000 | 25 |
| 60,000 | 100,000 | 9,500 | 28 |
| 100,000 | 250,000 | 20,700 | 30 |
| 250,000 | 500,000 | 65,700 | 32 |
| 500,000 | 750,000 | 145,700 | 35 |
| 750,000 | 1,000,000 | 233,200 | 37 |
| 1,000,000 | 1,250,000 | 325,700 | 39 |
| 1,250,000 | 1,500,000 | 423,200 | 42 |
| 1,500,000 | 2,000,000 | 528,200 | 45 |
| 2,000,000 | 2,500,000 | 753,200 | 49 |
| 2,500,000 | 3,000,000 | 998,200 | 53 |
| 3,000,000 | 3,500,000 | 1,263,200 | 56 |
| 3,500,000 | 4,000,000 | 1,543,200 | 59 |
| 4,000,000 | 5,000,000 | 1,838,200 | 63 |
| 5,000,000 | 6,000,000 | 2,468,200 | 67 |
| 6,000,000 | 7,000,000 | 3,138,200 | 70 |
| 7,000,000 | 8,000,000 | 3,838,200 | 73 |
| 8,000,000 | 10,000,000 | 4,568,200 | 76 |
| 10,000,000 | | 6,088,200 | 77 |

# Gift Tax Rates (Before 1977)

| (A) | (B) | (C) | (D) |
|---|---|---|---|
| Amount of Taxable Gifts Equal to or More Than | Amount of Taxable Gifts Less Than | Tax on Amount in Column (A) | Rate of Tax on Excess Over Amount in Column (A) (Percentage) |
| 0 | $ 5,000 | 0 | 2¼ |
| $ 5,000 | 10,000 | $ 112.50 | 5¼ |
| 10,000 | 20,000 | 375.00 | 8¼ |
| 20,000 | 30,000 | 1,200.00 | 10½ |
| 30,000 | 40,000 | 2,250.00 | 13½ |
| 40,000 | 50,000 | 3,600.00 | 16½ |
| 50,000 | 60,000 | 5,250.00 | 18¾ |
| 60,000 | 100,000 | 7,125.00 | 21 |
| 100,000 | 250,000 | 15,525.00 | 22½ |
| 250,000 | 500,000 | 49,275.00 | 24 |
| 500,000 | 750,000 | 109,275.00 | 26¼ |
| 750,000 | 1,000,000 | 174,900.00 | 27¾ |
| 1,000,000 | 1,250,000 | 244,275.00 | 29¼ |
| 1,250,000 | 1,500,000 | 317,400.00 | 31½ |
| 1,500,000 | 2,000,000 | 396,150.00 | 33¾ |
| 2,000,000 | 2,500,000 | 564,900.00 | 36¾ |
| 2,500,000 | 3,000,000 | 748,650.00 | 39¾ |
| 3,000,000 | 3,500,000 | 947,400.00 | 42 |
| 3,500,000 | 4,000,000 | 1,157,400.00 | 44¼ |
| 4,000,000 | 5,000,000 | 1,378,650.00 | 47¼ |
| 5,000,000 | 6,000,000 | 1,851,150.00 | 50¼ |
| 6,000,000 | 7,000,000 | 2,353,650.00 | 52½ |
| 7,000,000 | 8,000,000 | 2,878,650.00 | 54¾ |
| 8,000,000 | 10,000,000 | 3,426,150.00 | 57 |
| 10,000,000 | | 4,566,150.00 | 57¾ |

# Table For Computation of Maximum Credit for State Death Taxes

| (A) | (B) | (C) | (D) |
|---|---|---|---|
| Adjusted Taxable Estate* Equal to or More Than | Adjusted Taxable Estate* Less Than | Credit on Amount in Column (A) | Rate of Credit on Excess Over Amount in Column (A) (Percentage) |
| 0 | $ 40,000 | 0 | None |
| $ 40,000 | 90,000 | 0 | 0.8 |
| 90,000 | 140,000 | $ 400 | 1.6 |
| 140,000 | 240,000 | 1,200 | 2.4 |
| 240,000 | 440,000 | 3,600 | 3.2 |
| 440,000 | 640,000 | 10,000 | 4.0 |
| 640,000 | 840,000 | 18,000 | 4.8 |
| 840,000 | 1,040,000 | 27,600 | 5.6 |
| 1,040,000 | 1,540,000 | 38,800 | 6.4 |
| 1,540,000 | 2,040,000 | 70,800 | 7.2 |
| 2,040,000 | 2,540,000 | 106,800 | 8.0 |
| 2,540,000 | 3,040,000 | 146,800 | 8.8 |
| 3,040,000 | 3,540,000 | 190,800 | 9.6 |
| 3,540,000 | 4,040,000 | 238,800 | 10.4 |
| 4,040,000 | 5,040,000 | 290,800 | 11.2 |
| 5,040,000 | 6,040,000 | 402,800 | 12.0 |
| 6,040,000 | 7,040,000 | 522,800 | 12.8 |
| 7,040,000 | 8,040,000 | 650,800 | 13.6 |
| 8,040,000 | 9,040,000 | 786,800 | 14.4 |
| 9,040,000 | 10,040,000 | 930,800 | 15.2 |
| 10,040,000 | | 1,082,800 | 16.0 |

*Adjusted Taxable Estate = Taxable Estate – $60,000

# Scheduled phaseout:

| Year | Percentage Allowed |
|---|---|
| 2002 ............................. | 75 |
| 2003 ............................. | 50 |
| 2004 ............................. | 25 |

# Valuation Tables (After April 30, 1999)

## TABLE S SINGLE LIFE REMAINDER FACTORS INTEREST RATE

| Age | 6.6% | 6.8% | 7.0% | 7.2% | 7.4% | 7.6% | 7.8% | 8.0% |
|-----|-------|-------|-------|-------|-------|-------|-------|-------|
| 0 | .02700 | .02559 | .02433 | .02321 | .02220 | .02129 | .02047 | .01973 |
| 1 | .01929 | .01782 | .01650 | .01533 | .01427 | .01331 | .01246 | .01168 |
| 2 | .01983 | .01829 | .01692 | .01569 | .01458 | .01358 | .01268 | .01187 |
| 3 | .02065 | .01905 | .01761 | .01632 | .01516 | .01412 | .01317 | .01232 |
| 4 | .02163 | .01996 | .01846 | .01712 | .01590 | .01481 | .01382 | .01292 |
| 5 | .02275 | .02101 | .01945 | .01804 | .01677 | .01562 | .01458 | .01364 |
| 6 | .02398 | .02217 | .02053 | .01906 | .01773 | .01653 | .01544 | .01445 |
| 7 | .02532 | .02343 | .02172 | .02019 | .01880 | .01754 | .01640 | .01536 |
| 8 | .02675 | .02479 | .02301 | .02140 | .01995 | .01864 | .01744 | .01635 |
| 9 | .02832 | .02627 | .02442 | .02274 | .02122 | .01985 | .01859 | .01745 |
| 10 | .03001 | .02788 | .02595 | .02420 | .02262 | .02118 | .01987 | .01867 |
| 11 | .03183 | .02961 | .02760 | .02578 | .02413 | .02262 | .02125 | .02000 |
| 12 | .03377 | .03146 | .02937 | .02748 | .02575 | .02418 | .02275 | .02144 |
| 13 | .03579 | .03339 | .03122 | .02924 | .02744 | .02580 | .02431 | .02294 |
| 14 | .03783 | .03534 | .03308 | .03102 | .02915 | .02744 | .02587 | .02444 |
| 15 | .03986 | .03728 | .03493 | .03279 | .03083 | .02905 | .02742 | .02593 |
| 16 | .04187 | .03919 | .03674 | .03452 | .03248 | .03063 | .02892 | .02736 |
| 17 | .04387 | .04108 | .03855 | .03623 | .03411 | .03218 | .03040 | .02877 |
| 18 | .04588 | .04299 | .04036 | .03795 | .03574 | .03373 | .03187 | .03017 |
| 19 | .04796 | .04496 | .04222 | .03972 | .03742 | .03532 | .03339 | .03161 |
| 20 | .05013 | .04702 | .04418 | .04158 | .03919 | .03700 | .03498 | .03313 |
| 21 | .05242 | .04920 | .04625 | .04354 | .04105 | .03877 | .03667 | .03473 |
| 22 | .05482 | .05147 | .04841 | .04559 | .04301 | .04063 | .03844 | .03642 |
| 23 | .05734 | .05387 | .05069 | .04777 | .04508 | .04260 | .04032 | .03821 |
| 24 | .06001 | .05642 | .05312 | .05008 | .04728 | .04470 | .04232 | .04012 |
| 25 | .06285 | .05913 | .05570 | .05255 | .04964 | .04695 | .04447 | .04218 |
| 26 | .06586 | .06200 | .05845 | .05518 | .05215 | .04936 | .04677 | .04438 |
| 27 | .06907 | .06508 | .06140 | .05800 | .05485 | .05195 | .04925 | .04676 |
| 28 | .07246 | .06833 | .06451 | .06098 | .05772 | .05469 | .05189 | .04929 |
| 29 | .07603 | .07176 | .06780 | .06414 | .06075 | .05761 | .05469 | .05198 |
| 30 | .07978 | .07536 | .07127 | .06748 | .06396 | .06069 | .05766 | .05483 |
| 31 | .08372 | .07915 | .07491 | .07098 | .06733 | .06394 | .06078 | .05785 |
| 32 | .08785 | .08313 | .07875 | .07468 | .07089 | .06737 | .06409 | .06103 |
| 33 | .09220 | .08732 | .08279 | .07858 | .07466 | .07100 | .06759 | .06441 |
| 34 | .09676 | .09173 | .08705 | .08269 | .07862 | .07483 | .07129 | .06798 |

# Valuation Tables (After April 30, 1999, *continued*)

## TABLE S   SINGLE LIFE REMAINDER FACTORS INTEREST RATE

| Age | 6.6% | 6.8% | 7.0% | 7.2% | 7.4% | 7.6% | 7.8% | 8.0% |
|-----|------|------|------|------|------|------|------|------|
| 35 | .10157 | .09638 | .09155 | .08704 | .08283 | .07890 | .07522 | .07179 |
| 36 | .10662 | .10127 | .09628 | .09162 | .08726 | .08319 | .07938 | .07581 |
| 37 | .11193 | .10641 | .10126 | .09645 | .09194 | .08772 | .08377 | .08006 |
| 38 | .11751 | .11183 | .10652 | .10155 | .09689 | .09253 | .08843 | .08459 |
| 39 | .12338 | .11753 | .11206 | .10693 | .10212 | .09761 | .09337 | .08938 |
| 40 | .12955 | .12355 | .11791 | .11262 | .10766 | .10299 | .09860 | .09447 |
| 41 | .13606 | .12989 | .12409 | .11864 | .11352 | .10870 | .10417 | .09989 |
| 42 | .14291 | .13657 | .13061 | .12500 | .11972 | .11475 | .11006 | .10564 |
| 43 | .15010 | .14360 | .13747 | .13171 | .12627 | .12115 | .11631 | .11174 |
| 44 | .15764 | .15098 | .14469 | .13876 | .13317 | .12789 | .12290 | .11819 |
| 45 | .16550 | .15867 | .15223 | .14615 | .14040 | .13496 | .12982 | .12496 |
| 46 | .17370 | .16671 | .16011 | .15387 | .14796 | .14238 | .13708 | .13207 |
| 47 | .18220 | .17505 | .16830 | .16190 | .15584 | .15010 | .14466 | .13950 |
| 48 | .19102 | .18373 | .17682 | .17027 | .16406 | .15817 | .15258 | .14727 |
| 49 | .20018 | .19274 | .18568 | .17898 | .17262 | .16658 | .16084 | .15539 |
| 50 | .20969 | .20210 | .19490 | .18805 | .18155 | .17536 | .16948 | .16388 |
| 51 | .21955 | .21182 | .20448 | .19749 | .19084 | .18452 | .17849 | .17275 |
| 52 | .22973 | .22186 | .21438 | .20726 | .20047 | .19400 | .18784 | .18196 |
| 53 | .24022 | .23222 | .22461 | .21735 | .21043 | .20383 | .19753 | .19151 |
| 54 | .25101 | .24290 | .23516 | .22777 | .22072 | .21399 | .20756 | .20140 |
| 55 | .26212 | .25389 | .24604 | .23853 | .23136 | .22450 | .21793 | .21166 |
| 56 | .27355 | .26522 | .25725 | .24963 | .24233 | .23535 | .22867 | .22227 |
| 57 | .28529 | .27686 | .26879 | .26106 | .25365 | .24656 | .23976 | .23324 |
| 58 | .29731 | .28878 | .28061 | .27278 | .26528 | .25807 | .25116 | .24453 |
| 59 | .30956 | .30095 | .29269 | .28477 | .27716 | .26986 | .26284 | .25610 |
| 60 | .32202 | .31334 | .30500 | .29699 | .28929 | .28190 | .27478 | .26794 |
| 61 | .33473 | .32598 | .31757 | .30948 | .30170 | .29422 | .28701 | .28007 |
| 62 | .34772 | .33892 | .33044 | .32229 | .31443 | .30687 | .29958 | .29255 |
| 63 | .36101 | .35216 | .34363 | .33542 | .32750 | .31986 | .31250 | .30539 |
| 64 | .37456 | .36568 | .35711 | .34884 | .34087 | .33317 | .32574 | .31857 |
| 65 | .38838 | .37947 | .37087 | .36257 | .35455 | .34681 | .33932 | .33208 |
| 66 | .40249 | .39357 | .38496 | .37663 | .36858 | .36079 | .35326 | .34597 |
| 67 | .41694 | .40803 | .39941 | .39107 | .38299 | .37518 | .36761 | .36028 |
| 68 | .43170 | .42281 | .41419 | .40585 | .39777 | .38994 | .38235 | .37499 |
| 69 | .44672 | .43786 | .42927 | .42094 | .41286 | .40503 | .39743 | .39006 |

# Valuation Tables (After April 30, 1999, *continued*)

## TABLE S  SINGLE LIFE REMAINDER FACTORS INTEREST RATE

| Age | 6.6% | 6.8% | 7.0% | 7.2% | 7.4% | 7.6% | 7.8% | 8.0% |
|-----|------|------|------|------|------|------|------|------|
| 70 | .46194 | .45312 | .44456 | .43626 | .42820 | .42038 | .41278 | .40540 |
| 71 | .47727 | .46851 | .46000 | .45174 | .44371 | .43591 | .42832 | .42095 |
| 72 | .49268 | .48399 | .47554 | .46733 | .45934 | .45157 | .44401 | .43666 |
| 73 | .50813 | .49952 | .49114 | .48299 | .47506 | .46733 | .45981 | .45249 |
| 74 | .52367 | .51515 | .50686 | .49879 | .49092 | .48325 | .47578 | .46849 |
| 75 | .53936 | .53095 | .52276 | .51477 | .50698 | .49938 | .49197 | .48474 |
| 76 | .55524 | .54696 | .53888 | .53100 | .52330 | .51579 | .50846 | .50130 |
| 77 | .57132 | .56318 | .55523 | .54747 | .53988 | .53247 | .52523 | .51815 |
| 78 | .58755 | .57957 | .57177 | .56414 | .55668 | .54939 | .54225 | .53527 |
| 79 | .60385 | .59604 | .58840 | .58092 | .57360 | .56644 | .55943 | .55256 |
| 80 | .62007 | .61244 | .60497 | .59765 | .59048 | .58347 | .57659 | .56985 |
| 81 | .63608 | .62864 | .62135 | .61421 | .60721 | .60034 | .59361 | .58701 |
| 82 | .65182 | .64458 | .63748 | .63052 | .62368 | .61698 | .61041 | .60395 |
| 83 | .66728 | .66024 | .65334 | .64656 | .63991 | .63338 | .62696 | .62066 |
| 84 | .68256 | .67574 | .66904 | .66246 | .65599 | .64964 | .64340 | .63727 |
| 85 | .69775 | .69116 | .68467 | .67830 | .67204 | .66587 | .65982 | .65386 |
| 86 | .71272 | .70636 | .70010 | .69394 | .68789 | .68193 | .67606 | .67029 |
| 87 | .72726 | .72114 | .71511 | .70917 | .70333 | .69757 | .69190 | .68632 |
| 88 | .74137 | .73548 | .72968 | .72396 | .71833 | .71279 | .70732 | .70194 |
| 89 | .75503 | .74938 | .74381 | .73832 | .73290 | .72757 | .72231 | .71712 |
| 90 | .76823 | .76281 | .75748 | .75221 | .74702 | .74190 | .73684 | .73186 |
| 91 | .78075 | .77557 | .77046 | .76542 | .76044 | .75553 | .75068 | .74589 |
| 92 | .79235 | .78740 | .78250 | .77767 | .77290 | .76818 | .76353 | .75893 |
| 93 | .80307 | .79832 | .79363 | .78899 | .78441 | .77989 | .77542 | .77100 |
| 94 | .81306 | .80850 | .80401 | .79956 | .79517 | .79082 | .78653 | .78228 |
| 95 | .82254 | .81818 | .81387 | .80961 | .80539 | .80122 | .79710 | .79302 |
| 96 | .83147 | .82729 | .82316 | .81907 | .81503 | .81103 | .80707 | .80315 |
| 97 | .83973 | .83573 | .83176 | .82784 | .82396 | .82012 | .81632 | .81255 |
| 98 | .84750 | .84366 | .83985 | .83609 | .83236 | .82867 | .82502 | .82140 |
| 99 | .85508 | .85140 | .84776 | .84415 | .84057 | .83703 | .83353 | .83005 |
| 100 | .86246 | .85894 | .85546 | .85200 | .84858 | .84519 | .84183 | .83849 |
| 101 | .86974 | .86638 | .86305 | .85975 | .85648 | .85324 | .85003 | .84684 |
| 102 | .87689 | .87369 | .87052 | .86738 | .86426 | .86116 | .85809 | .85505 |
| 103 | .88399 | .88095 | .87793 | .87494 | .87197 | .86903 | .86611 | .86321 |
| 104 | .89157 | .88871 | .88586 | .88304 | .88024 | .87745 | .87469 | .87195 |

# Valuation Tables (After April 30, 1999, *continued*)

## TABLE S   SINGLE LIFE REMAINDER FACTORS INTEREST RATE

| Age | 6.6% | 6.8% | 7.0% | 7.2% | 7.4% | 7.6% | 7.8% | 8.0% |
|-----|------|------|------|------|------|------|------|------|
| 105 | .89898 | .89628 | .89360 | .89094 | .88830 | .88568 | .88307 | .88049 |
| 106 | .90852 | .90605 | .90359 | .90115 | .89873 | .89632 | .89392 | .89154 |
| 107 | .92010 | .91791 | .91573 | .91356 | .91141 | .90927 | .90714 | .90502 |
| 108 | .93814 | .93641 | .93469 | .93298 | .93128 | .92958 | .92790 | .92622 |
| 109 | .96904 | .96816 | .96729 | .96642 | .96555 | .96468 | .96382 | .96296 |

# Valuation Tables (After April 30, 1989)

## TABLE B   TERM CERTAIN REMAINDER FACTORS INTEREST RATE

| Years | 7.4% | 7.6% | 7.8% | 8.0% | 8.2% | 8.4% | 8.6% | 8.8% |
|---|---|---|---|---|---|---|---|---|
| 1 | .931099 | .929368 | .927644 | .925926 | .924214 | .922509 | .920810 | .919118 |
| 2 | .866945 | .863725 | .860523 | .857339 | .854172 | .851023 | .847892 | .844777 |
| 3 | .807211 | .802718 | .798259 | .793832 | .789438 | .785077 | .780747 | .776450 |
| 4 | .751593 | .746021 | .740500 | .735030 | .729610 | .724241 | .718920 | .713649 |
| 5 | .699808 | .693328 | .686920 | .680583 | .674316 | .668119 | .661989 | .655927 |
| 6 | .651590 | .644357 | .637217 | .630170 | .623213 | .616346 | .609566 | .602874 |
| 7 | .606694 | .598845 | .591111 | .583490 | .575982 | .568585 | .561295 | .554112 |
| 8 | .564892 | .556547 | .548340 | .540269 | .532331 | .524524 | .516846 | .509294 |
| 9 | .525971 | .517237 | .508664 | .500249 | .491988 | .483879 | .475917 | .468101 |
| 10 | .489731 | .480704 | .471859 | .463193 | .454703 | .446383 | .438230 | .430240 |
| 11 | .455987 | .446750 | .437717 | .428883 | .420243 | .411792 | .403526 | .395441 |
| 12 | .424569 | .415196 | .406046 | .397114 | .388394 | .379882 | .371571 | .363457 |
| 13 | .395316 | .385870 | .376666 | .367698 | .358960 | .350445 | .342147 | .334060 |
| 14 | .368078 | .358615 | .349412 | .340461 | .331756 | .323288 | .315052 | .307040 |
| 15 | .342717 | .333285 | .324130 | .315242 | .306613 | .298236 | .290103 | .282206 |
| 16 | .319103 | .309745 | .300677 | .291890 | .283376 | .275126 | .267130 | .259381 |
| 17 | .297117 | .287867 | .278921 | .270269 | .261901 | .253806 | .245976 | .238401 |
| 18 | .276645 | .267534 | .258739 | .250249 | .242052 | .234139 | .226497 | .219119 |
| 19 | .257584 | .248638 | .240018 | .231712 | .223708 | .215995 | .208561 | .201396 |
| 20 | .239836 | .231076 | .222651 | .214548 | .206754 | .199257 | .192045 | .185107 |
| 21 | .223311 | .214755 | .206541 | .198656 | .191085 | .183817 | .176837 | .170135 |
| 22 | .207925 | .199586 | .191596 | .183941 | .176604 | .169573 | .162834 | .156374 |
| 23 | .193598 | .185489 | .177733 | .170315 | .163220 | .156432 | .149939 | .143726 |
| 24 | .180259 | .172387 | .164873 | .157699 | .150850 | .144310 | .138065 | .132101 |
| 25 | .167839 | .160211 | .152943 | .146018 | .139418 | .133128 | .127132 | .121416 |
| 26 | .156275 | .148895 | .141877 | .135202 | .128852 | .122811 | .117064 | .111596 |
| 27 | .145507 | .138379 | .131611 | .125187 | .119087 | .113295 | .107794 | .102570 |
| 28 | .135482 | .128605 | .122088 | .115914 | .110062 | .104515 | .099258 | .094274 |
| 29 | .126147 | .119521 | .113255 | .107328 | .101721 | .096416 | .091398 | .086649 |
| 30 | .117455 | .111079 | .105060 | .099377 | .094012 | .088945 | .084160 | .079640 |
| 31 | .109362 | .103233 | .097458 | .092016 | .086887 | .082053 | .077495 | .073199 |
| 32 | .101827 | .095942 | .090406 | .085200 | .080302 | .075694 | .071358 | .067278 |
| 33 | .094811 | .089165 | .083865 | .078889 | .074216 | .069829 | .065708 | .061837 |
| 34 | .088278 | .082867 | .077797 | .073045 | .068592 | .064418 | .060504 | .056835 |
| 35 | .082196 | .077014 | .072168 | .067635 | .063394 | .059426 | .055713 | .052238 |

# Valuation Tables (After April 30, 1989, *continued*)

## TABLE B   TERM CERTAIN REMAINDER FACTORS INTEREST RATE

| Years | 7.4% | 7.6% | 7.8% | 8.0% | 8.2% | 8.4% | 8.6% | 8.8% |
|-------|------|------|------|------|------|------|------|------|
| 36 | .076532 | .071574 | .066946 | .062625 | .058589 | .054821 | .051301 | .048013 |
| 37 | .071259 | .066519 | .062102 | .057986 | .054149 | .050573 | .047239 | .044130 |
| 38 | .066349 | .061821 | .057609 | .053690 | .050045 | .046654 | .043498 | .040560 |
| 39 | .061778 | .057454 | .053440 | .049713 | .046253 | .043039 | .040053 | .037280 |
| 40 | .057521 | .053396 | .049573 | .046031 | .042747 | .039703 | .036881 | .034264 |
| 41 | .053558 | .049625 | .045987 | .042621 | .039508 | .036627 | .033961 | .031493 |
| 42 | .049868 | .046120 | .042659 | .039464 | .036514 | .033789 | .031271 | .028946 |
| 43 | .046432 | .042862 | .039572 | .036541 | .033746 | .031170 | .028795 | .026605 |
| 44 | .043233 | .039835 | .036709 | .033834 | .031189 | .028755 | .026515 | .024453 |
| 45 | .040254 | .037021 | .034053 | .031328 | .028825 | .026527 | .024415 | .022475 |
| 46 | .037480 | .034406 | .031589 | .029007 | .026641 | .024471 | .022482 | .020657 |
| 47 | .034898 | .031976 | .029303 | .026859 | .024622 | .022575 | .020701 | .018986 |
| 48 | .032493 | .029717 | .027183 | .024869 | .022756 | .020825 | .019062 | .017451 |
| 49 | .030255 | .027618 | .025216 | .023027 | .021031 | .019212 | .017552 | .016039 |
| 50 | .028170 | .025668 | .023392 | .021321 | .019437 | .017723 | .016163 | .014742 |
| 51 | .026229 | .023855 | .021699 | .019742 | .017964 | .016350 | .014833 | .013550 |
| 52 | .024422 | .022170 | .020129 | .018280 | .016603 | .015083 | .013704 | .012454 |
| 53 | .022739 | .020604 | .018673 | .016925 | .015345 | .013914 | .012619 | .011446 |
| 54 | .021172 | .019149 | .017322 | .015672 | .014182 | .012836 | .011620 | .010521 |
| 55 | .019714 | .017796 | .016068 | .014511 | .013107 | .011841 | .010699 | .009670 |
| 56 | .018355 | .016539 | .014906 | .013436 | .012114 | .010923 | .009852 | .008888 |
| 57 | .017091 | .015371 | .013827 | .012441 | .011196 | .010077 | .009072 | .008169 |
| 58 | .015913 | .014285 | .012827 | .011519 | .010347 | .009296 | .008354 | .007508 |
| 59 | .014817 | .013276 | .011899 | .010666 | .009563 | .008576 | .007692 | .006901 |
| 60 | .013796 | .012339 | .011038 | .009876 | .008838 | .007911 | .007083 | .006343 |

(Tax forms can be obtained from the IRS web site: **http://www.irs.gov**)

Form **709**

Department of the Treasury
Internal Revenue Service

## United States Gift (and Generation-Skipping Transfer) Tax Return

(Section 6019 of the Internal Revenue Code) (For gifts made during calendar year 2002)

▶ **See separate instructions.**

OMB No. 1545-0020

20**02**

### Part 1—General Information

| 1 Donor's first name and middle initial | 2 Donor's last name | 3 **Donor's social security number** |
|---|---|---|

| 4 Address (number, street, and apartment number) | 5 Legal residence (domicile) (county and state) |
|---|---|

| 6 City, state, and ZIP code | 7 Citizenship |
|---|---|

|   |   | Yes | No |
|---|---|---|---|
| 8 | If the donor died during the year, check here ▶ ☐ and enter date of death................ , ............. . | | |
| 9 | If you received an extension of time to file this Form 709, check here ▶ ☐ and attach the Form 4868, 2688, 2350, or extension letter . | | |
| 10 | Enter the total number of donees listed on Schedule A—count each person only once. ▶ | | |
| 11a | Have you (the donor) previously filed a Form 709 (or 709-A) for any other year? If the answer is "No," do not complete line 11b . | | |
| 11b | If the answer to line 11a is "Yes," has your address changed since you last filed Form 709 (or 709-A)? . . . . . . . . | | |
| 12 | Gifts by husband or wife to third parties. —Do you consent to have the gifts (including generation-skipping transfers) made by you and by your spouse to third parties during the calendar year considered as made one-half by each of you? (See instructions.) (If the answer is "Yes," the following information must be furnished and your spouse must sign the consent shown below. **If the answer is "No," skip lines 13–18 and go to Schedule A.**) . . . . . . . . | | |
| 13 | Name of consenting spouse                              14  SSN | | |
| 15 | Were you married to one another during the entire calendar year? (see instructions) . . . . . . . . . | | |
| 16 | If the answer to 15 is "No," check whether ☐ married ☐ divorced or ☐ widowed, and give date (see instructions) ▶ | | |
| 17 | Will a gift tax return for this calendar year be filed by your spouse? . . . . . . . . . . . . . . | | |
| 18 | **Consent of Spouse**—I consent to have the gifts (and generation-skipping transfers) made by me and by my spouse to third parties during the calendar year considered as made one-half by each of us. We are both aware of the joint and several liability for tax created by the execution of this consent. | | |

Consenting spouse's signature ▶                                              Date ▶

### Part 2—Tax Computation

| | | | |
|---|---|---|---|
| 1 | Enter the amount from Schedule A, Part 3, line 15 . . . . . . . . . | 1 | |
| 2 | Enter the amount from Schedule B, line 3 . . . . . . . . . . . | 2 | |
| 3 | Total taxable gifts (add lines 1 and 2) . . . . . . . . . . . | 3 | |
| 4 | Tax computed on amount on line 3 (see Table for Computing Tax in separate instructions) . . | 4 | |
| 5 | Tax computed on amount on line 2 (see Table for Computing Tax in separate instructions) . . | 5 | |
| 6 | Balance (subtract line 5 from line 4) . . . . . . . . . . . . | 6 | |
| 7 | Maximum unified credit (nonresident aliens, see instructions) . . . . . . . . | 7 | 345,800 | 00 |
| 8 | Enter the unified credit against tax allowable for all prior periods (from Sch. B, line 1, col. C) . . | 8 | |
| 9 | Balance (subtract line 8 from line 7) . . . . . . . . . . . . | 9 | |
| 10 | Enter 20% (.20) of the amount allowed as a specific exemption for gifts made after September 8, 1976, and before January 1, 1977 (see instructions) . . . . . . . . . . . . | 10 | |
| 11 | Balance (subtract line 10 from line 9) . . . . . . . . . . . . | 11 | |
| 12 | Unified credit (enter the smaller of line 6 or line 11) . . . . . . . . . | 12 | |
| 13 | Credit for foreign gift taxes (see instructions) . . . . . . . . . . | 13 | |
| 14 | Total credits (add lines 12 and 13) . . . . . . . . . . . . | 14 | |
| 15 | Balance (subtract line 14 from line 6) (do not enter less than zero) . . . . . . . | 15 | |
| 16 | Generation-skipping transfer taxes (from Schedule C, Part 3, col. H, Total) . . . . . . | 16 | |
| 17 | Total tax (add lines 15 and 16) . . . . . . . . . . . . . | 17 | |
| 18 | Gift and generation-skipping transfer taxes prepaid with extension of time to file . . . . . | 18 | |
| 19 | If line 18 is less than line 17, enter **balance due** (see instructions) . . . . . . . | 19 | |
| 20 | If line 18 is greater than line 17, enter **amount to be refunded** . . . . . . . . . . | 20 | |

**Sign Here**

Under penalties of perjury, I declare that I have examined this return, including any accompanying schedules and statements, and to the best of my knowledge and belief, it is true, correct, and complete. Declaration of preparer (other than donor) is based on all information of which preparer has any knowledge.

▶ Signature of donor                                          Date

**Paid Preparer's Use Only**

| Preparer's signature ▶ | Date | Check if self-employed ▶ ☐ |
|---|---|---|
| Firm's name (or yours if self-employed), address, and ZIP code ▶ | Phone no. ▶ (      ) | |

Attach check or money order here.

For Disclosure, Privacy Act, and Paperwork Reduction Act Notice, see page 12 of the separate instructions for this form.    Cat. No. 16783M    Form **709** (2002)

| SCHEDULE A | Computation of Taxable Gifts (Including Transfers in Trust) |
|---|---|

**A** Does the value of any item listed on Schedule A reflect any valuation discount? If the answer is "Yes," see instructions. .   Yes ☐ No ☐

**B** ☐ ◄ Check here if you elect under section 529(c)(2)(B) to treat any transfers made this year to a qualified state tuition program as made ratably over a 5-year period beginning this year. See instructions. Attach explanation.

**Part 1— Gifts Subject Only to Gift Tax.** *Gifts less political organization, medical, and educational exclusions —see instructions*

| A<br>Item<br>number | B<br>• Donee's name and address<br>• Relationship to donor (if any)<br>• Description of gift<br>• If the gift was made by means of a trust, enter trust's EIN and<br>  attach a description or copy of the trust instrument (see instructions)<br>• If the gift was of securities, give CUSIP number | C<br>Donor's adjusted<br>basis of gift | D<br>Date<br>of gift | E<br>Value at<br>date of gift |
|---|---|---|---|---|
| 1 | | | | |

Total of Part 1 (add amounts from Part 1, column E) . . . . . . . . . . . . . . . ▶

**Part 2—Gifts That are Direct Skips and are Subject to Both Gift Tax and Generation-Skipping Transfer Tax. You must list the gifts in chronological order.** *Gifts less political organization, medical, and educational exclusions—see instructions. (Also list here direct skips that are subject only to the GST tax at this time as the result of the termination of an "estate tax inclusion period." See instructions.)*

| A<br>Item<br>number | B<br>• Donee's name and address<br>• Relationship to donor (if any)<br>• Description of gift<br>• If the gift was made by means of a trust, enter trust's EIN and<br>  attach a description or copy of the trust instrument (see instructions)<br>• If the gift was of securities, give CUSIP number | C<br>Donor's adjusted<br>basis of gift | D<br>Date<br>of gift | E<br>Value at<br>date of gift |
|---|---|---|---|---|
| 1 | | | | |

Total of Part 2 (add amounts from Part 2, column E) . . . . . . . . . . . . . . ▶

**Part 3—Taxable Gift Reconciliation**

| | | | |
|---|---|---|---|
| 1 | Total value of gifts of donor (add totals from column E of Parts 1 and 2) . . . . . . . . . | 1 | |
| 2 | One-half of items ............................................. attributable to spouse (see instructions) | 2 | |
| 3 | Balance (subtract line 2 from line 1) . . . . . . . . . . . . . . . | 3 | |
| 4 | Gifts of spouse to be included (from Schedule A, Part 3, line 2 of spouse's return—see instructions) . . | 4 | |
| | If any of the gifts included on this line are also subject to the generation-skipping transfer tax, check here ▶ ☐ and enter those gifts also on Schedule C, Part 1. | | |
| 5 | Total gifts (add lines 3 and 4) . . . . . . . . . . . . . . . . | 5 | |
| 6 | Total annual exclusions for gifts listed on Schedule A (including line 4, above) (see instructions) . . . | 6 | |
| 7 | Total included amount of gifts (subtract line 6 from line 5) . . . . . . . . . . . . | 7 | |

**Deductions** (see instructions)

| | | | | |
|---|---|---|---|---|
| 8 | Gifts of interests to spouse for which a marital deduction will be claimed, based on items ......................... of Schedule A . . . . . | 8 | | |
| 9 | Exclusions attributable to gifts on line 8 . . . . . . . . . . | 9 | | |
| 10 | Marital deduction—subtract line 9 from line 8 . . . . . . . . | 10 | | |
| 11 | Charitable deduction, based on items .................less exclusions . . | 11 | | |
| 12 | Total deductions—add lines 10 and 11 . . . . . . . . . . . . . | | 12 | |
| 13 | Subtract line 12 from line 7 . . . . . . . . . . . . . . . . . | | 13 | |
| 14 | Generation-skipping transfer taxes payable with this Form 709 (from Schedule C, Part 3, col. H, Total) . | | 14 | |
| 15 | Taxable gifts (add lines 13 and 14). Enter here and on line 1 of the Tax Computation on page 1 . . . | | 15 | |

*(If more space is needed, attach additional sheets of same size.)*

Form 709 (2002)                                                                                          Page **3**

| SCHEDULE A | Computation of Taxable Gifts *(continued)* |
|---|---|

**16  Terminable Interest (QTIP) Marital Deduction.** (See instructions for line 8 of Schedule A.)

If a trust (or other property) meets the requirements of qualified terminable interest property under section 2523(f), and

   **a.** The trust (or other property) is listed on Schedule A, and

   **b.** The value of the trust (or other property) is entered in whole or in part as a deduction on line 8, Part 3 of Schedule A,

then the donor shall be deemed to have made an election to have such trust (or other property) treated as qualified terminable interest property under section 2523(f).

If less than the entire value of the trust (or other property) that the donor has included in Part 1 of Schedule A is entered as a deduction on line 8, the donor shall be considered to have made an election only as to a fraction of the trust (or other property). The numerator of this fraction is equal to the amount of the trust (or other property) deducted on line 10 of Part 3, Schedule A. The denominator is equal to the total value of the trust (or other property) listed in Part 1 of Schedule A.

If you make the QTIP election (see instructions for line 8 of Schedule A), the terminable interest property involved will be included in your spouse's gross estate upon his or her death (section 2044). If your spouse disposes (by gift or otherwise) of all or part of the qualifying life income interest, he or she will be considered to have made a transfer of the entire property that is subject to the gift tax (see Transfer of Certain Life Estates on page 4 of the instructions).

**17  Election Out of QTIP Treatment of Annuities**

☐ ◄ Check here if you elect under section 2523(f)(6) **NOT** to treat as qualified terminable interest property any joint and survivor annuities that are reported on Schedule A and would otherwise be treated as qualified terminable interest property under section 2523(f). (See instructions.) Enter the item numbers (from Schedule A) for the annuities for which you are making this election ►

| SCHEDULE B | Gifts From Prior Periods |
|---|---|

**If you answered "Yes" on line 11a of page 1, Part 1, see the instructions for completing Schedule B. If you answered "No," skip to the Tax Computation on page 1 (or Schedule C, if applicable).**

| A<br>Calendar year or calendar quarter (see instructions) | B<br>Internal Revenue office where prior return was filed | C<br>Amount of unified credit against gift tax for periods after December 31, 1976 | D<br>Amount of specific exemption for prior periods ending before January 1, 1977 | E<br>Amount of taxable gifts |
|---|---|---|---|---|
|  |  |  |  |  |
|  |  |  |  |  |
|  |  |  |  |  |
|  |  |  |  |  |
|  |  |  |  |  |

**1**  Totals for prior periods . . . . . . . . . . . . **1**

**2**  Amount, if any, by which total specific exemption, line 1, column D, is more than $30,000 . . . . . **2**

**3**  Total amount of taxable gifts for prior periods (add amount, column E, line 1, and amount, if any, on line 2). (Enter here and on line 2 of the Tax Computation on page 1.) . . . . . . . . . . . . . . **3**

*(If more space is needed, attach additional sheets of same size.)*                                        Form **709** (2002)

| SCHEDULE C | Computation of Generation-Skipping Transfer Tax |
|---|---|

**Note:** *Inter vivos direct skips that are completely excluded by the GST exemption must still be fully reported (including value and exemptions claimed) on Schedule C.*

### Part 1—Generation-Skipping Transfers

| A<br>Item No.<br>(from Schedule A,<br>Part 2, col. A) | B<br>Value<br>(from Schedule A,<br>Part 2, col. E) | C<br>Split Gifts<br>(enter ½ of col. B)<br>(see instructions) | D<br>Subtract col. C<br>from col. B | E<br>Nontaxable<br>portion of transfer | F<br>Net Transfer<br>(subtract col. E<br>from col. D) |
|---|---|---|---|---|---|
| 1 | | | | | |
| 2 | | | | | |
| 3 | | | | | |
| 4 | | | | | |
| 5 | | | | | |
| 6 | | | | | |

| | Split gifts from<br>spouse's Form 709<br>(enter item number) | Value included<br>from spouse's<br>Form 709 | Nontaxable<br>portion of transfer | Net transfer<br>(subtract col. E<br>from col. D) |
|---|---|---|---|---|
| If you elected gift splitting and your spouse was required to file a separate Form 709 (see the instructions for "Split Gifts"), you must enter all of the gifts shown on Schedule A, Part 2, of your spouse's Form 709 here. | S- | | | |
| In column C, enter the item number of each gift in the order it appears in column A of your spouse's Schedule A, Part 2. We have preprinted the prefix "S-" to distinguish your spouse's item numbers from your own when you complete column A of Schedule C, Part 3. | S- | | | |
| In column D, for each gift, enter the amount reported in column C, Schedule C, Part 1, of your spouse's Form 709. | S- | | | |

(Note: the left cell text spans the rows; the S- entries appear on eight lines: S-, S-, S-, S-, S-, S-, S-, S-)

### Part 2—GST Exemption Reconciliation (Section 2631) and Section 2652(a)(3) Election

Check box ▶ ☐ if you are making a section 2652(a)(3) (special QTIP) election (see instructions)

Enter the item numbers (from Schedule A) of the gifts for which you are making this election ▶ .................

| | | |
|---|---|---|
| 1 | Maximum allowable exemption (see instructions) . . . . . . . . . . . . . | **1** |
| 2 | Total exemption used for periods before filing this return . . . . . . . . . | **2** |
| 3 | Exemption available for this return (subtract line 2 from line 1) . . . . . . . | **3** |
| 4 | Exemption claimed on this return (from Part 3, col. C total, below) . . . . . . . . . | **4** |
| 5 | Exemption allocated to transfers not shown on Part 3, below. **You must attach a Notice of Allocation.** (See instructions.) . . . . . . . . . . . | **5** |
| 6 | Add lines 4 and 5 . . . . . . . . . . . . . . . | **6** |
| 7 | Exemption available for future transfers (subtract line 6 from line 3) . . . . . . . . | **7** |

### Part 3—Tax Computation

| A<br>Item No.<br>(from Schedule<br>C, Part 1) | B<br>Net transfer<br>(from Schedule C,<br>Part 1, col. F) | C<br>GST Exemption<br>Allocated | D<br>Divide col. C<br>by col. B | E<br>Inclusion Ratio<br>(subtract col. D<br>from 1.000) | F<br>Maximum Estate<br>Tax Rate | G<br>Applicable Rate<br>(multiply col. E<br>by col. F) | H<br>Generation-Skipping<br>Transfer Tax<br>(multiply col. B by col. G) |
|---|---|---|---|---|---|---|---|
| 1 | | | | | 50% (.50) | | |
| 2 | | | | | 50% (.50) | | |
| 3 | | | | | 50% (.50) | | |
| 4 | | | | | 50% (.50) | | |
| 5 | | | | | 50% (.50) | | |
| 6 | | | | | 50% (.50) | | |
| | | | | | 50% (.50) | | |
| | | | | | 50% (.50) | | |
| | | | | | 50% (.50) | | |

| Total exemption claimed. Enter here and on line 4, Part 2, above. May not exceed line 3, Part 2, above . . . . . | | **Total generation-skipping transfer tax.** Enter here, on line 14 of Schedule A, Part 3, and on line 16 of the Tax Computation on page 1 . . . . . . . . . . . . . . | |
|---|---|---|---|

*(If more space is needed, attach additional sheets of same size.)*          ✳          Form **709** (2002)

Form **1041**

Department of the Treasury—Internal Revenue Service

**U.S. Income Tax Return for Estates and Trusts** | 2002 | OMB No. 1545-0092

| A Type of entity (see instr.): | For calendar year 2002 or fiscal year beginning , 2002, and ending , 20 | |
|---|---|---|
| ☐ Decedent's estate | Name of estate or trust (If a grantor type trust, see page 11 of the instructions.) | C Employer identification number |
| ☐ Simple trust | | |
| ☐ Complex trust | | D Date entity created |
| ☐ Qualified disability trust | | |
| ☐ ESBT (S portion only) | Name and title of fiduciary | E Nonexempt charitable and split-interest trusts, check applicable boxes (see page 12 of the instructions): |
| ☐ Grantor type trust | | |
| ☐ Bankruptcy estate—Ch. 7 | Number, street, and room or suite no. (If a P.O. box, see page 11 of the instructions.) | |
| ☐ Bankruptcy estate—Ch. 11 | | ☐ Described in section 4947(a)(1) |
| ☐ Pooled income fund | | ☐ Not a private foundation |
| B Number of Schedules K-1 attached (see instructions) | City or town, state, and ZIP code | ☐ Described in section 4947(a)(2) |

F Check applicable boxes: ☐ Initial return ☐ Final return ☐ Amended return ☐ Change in fiduciary's name ☐ Change in fiduciary's address

G Pooled mortgage account (see page 13 of the instructions): ☐ Bought ☐ Sold Date:

**Income**

| | | | |
|---|---|---|---|
| 1 | Interest income | 1 | |
| 2 | Ordinary dividends | 2 | |
| 3 | Business income or (loss) (attach Schedule C or C-EZ (Form 1040)) | 3 | |
| 4 | Capital gain or (loss) (attach Schedule D (Form 1041)) | 4 | |
| 5 | Rents, royalties, partnerships, other estates and trusts, etc. (attach Schedule E (Form 1040)) | 5 | |
| 6 | Farm income or (loss) (attach Schedule F (Form 1040)) | 6 | |
| 7 | Ordinary gain or (loss) (attach Form 4797) | 7 | |
| 8 | Other income. List type and amount | 8 | |
| 9 | **Total income.** Combine lines 1 through 8 | 9 | |

**Deductions**

| | | | |
|---|---|---|---|
| 10 | Interest. Check if Form 4952 is attached ▶ ☐ | 10 | |
| 11 | Taxes | 11 | |
| 12 | Fiduciary fees | 12 | |
| 13 | Charitable deduction (from Schedule A, line 7) | 13 | |
| 14 | Attorney, accountant, and return preparer fees | 14 | |
| 15a | Other deductions **not** subject to the 2% floor (attach schedule) | 15a | |
| b | Allowable miscellaneous itemized deductions subject to the 2% floor | 15b | |
| 16 | **Total.** Add lines 10 through 15b | 16 | |
| 17 | Adjusted total income or (loss). Subtract line 16 from line 9. Enter here and on Schedule B, line 1 ▶ | 17 | |
| 18 | Income distribution deduction (from Schedule B, line 15) (attach Schedules K-1 (Form 1041)) | 18 | |
| 19 | Estate tax deduction (including certain generation-skipping taxes) (attach computation) | 19 | |
| 20 | Exemption | 20 | |
| 21 | **Total deductions.** Add lines 18 through 20 ▶ | 21 | |

**Tax and Payments**

| | | | |
|---|---|---|---|
| 22 | Taxable income. Subtract line 21 from line 17. If a loss, see page 17 of the instructions | 22 | |
| 23 | **Total tax** (from Schedule G, line 7) | 23 | |
| 24 | **Payments: a** 2002 estimated tax payments and amount applied from 2001 return | 24a | |
| b | Estimated tax payments allocated to beneficiaries (from Form 1041-T) | 24b | |
| c | Subtract line 24b from line 24a | 24c | |
| d | Tax paid with extension of time to file: ☐ Form 2758 ☐ Form 8736 ☐ Form 8800 | 24d | |
| e | Federal income tax withheld. If any is from Form(s) 1099, check ▶ ☐ | 24e | |
| | Other payments: **f** Form 2439 ; **g** Form 4136 ; Total ▶ | 24h | |
| 25 | **Total payments.** Add lines 24c through 24e, and 24h ▶ | 25 | |
| 26 | Estimated tax penalty (see page 18 of the instructions) | 26 | |
| 27 | **Tax due.** If line 25 is smaller than the total of lines 23 and 26, enter amount owed | 27 | |
| 28 | **Overpayment.** If line 25 is larger than the total of lines 23 and 26, enter amount overpaid | 28 | |
| 29 | Amount of line 28 to be: **a** Credited to 2003 estimated tax ▶ ; **b** Refunded ▶ | 29 | |

**Sign Here**

Under penalties of perjury, I declare that I have examined this return, including accompanying schedules and statements, and to the best of my knowledge and belief, it is true, correct, and complete. Declaration of preparer (other than taxpayer) is based on all information of which preparer has any knowledge.

▶ 　　　　　　　　　　　　　　　　　▶

Signature of fiduciary or officer representing fiduciary　　Date　　EIN of fiduciary if a financial institution

May the IRS discuss this return with the preparer shown below (see instr.)? ☐ Yes ☐ No

**Paid Preparer's Use Only**

| Preparer's signature ▶ | Date | Check if self-employed ☐ | Preparer's SSN or PTIN |
|---|---|---|---|
| Firm's name (or yours if self-employed), address, and ZIP code ▶ | | EIN | |
| | | Phone no. ( ) | |

For Paperwork Reduction Act Notice, see the separate instructions.　　　Cat. No. 11370H　　　Form **1041** (2002)

Form 1041 (2002)                                                                          Page **2**

| **Schedule A** | **Charitable Deduction.** Do not complete for a simple trust or a pooled income fund. | | |
|---|---|---|---|
| 1 | Amounts paid or permanently set aside for charitable purposes from gross income (see page 19) | **1** | |
| 2 | Tax-exempt income allocable to charitable contributions (see page 19 of the instructions) . . | **2** | |
| 3 | Subtract line 2 from line 1 . . . . . . . . . . . . . . . . . | **3** | |
| 4 | Capital gains for the tax year allocated to corpus and paid or permanently set aside for charitable purposes | **4** | |
| 5 | Add lines 3 and 4 . . . . . . . . . . . . . . . . . . . | **5** | |
| 6 | Section 1202 exclusion allocable to capital gains paid or permanently set aside for charitable purposes (see page 19 of the instructions) | **6** | |
| 7 | **Charitable deduction.** Subtract line 6 from line 5. Enter here and on page 1, line 13 . . . . | **7** | |

| **Schedule B** | **Income Distribution Deduction** | | | |
|---|---|---|---|---|
| 1 | Adjusted total income (see page 19 of the instructions) . . . . . . . . . . . | **1** | | |
| 2 | Adjusted tax-exempt interest . . . . . . . . . . . . . . . . . | **2** | | |
| 3 | Total net gain from Schedule D (Form 1041), line 16, column (1) (see page 20 of the instructions) | **3** | | |
| 4 | Enter amount from Schedule A, line 4 (reduced by any allocable section 1202 exclusion). . . | **4** | | |
| 5 | Capital gains for the tax year included on Schedule A, line 1 (see page 20 of the instructions) | **5** | | |
| 6 | Enter any gain from page 1, line 4, as a negative number. If page 1, line 4, is a loss, enter the loss as a positive number . . . . . . . . . . . | **6** | | |
| 7 | **Distributable net income (DNI).** Combine lines 1 through 6. If zero or less, enter -0- . . . . | **7** | | |
| 8 | If a complex trust, enter accounting income for the tax year as determined under the governing instrument and applicable local law | **8** | | |
| 9 | Income required to be distributed currently . . . . . . . . . . . . . . | **9** | | |
| 10 | Other amounts paid, credited, or otherwise required to be distributed . . . . . . . | **10** | | |
| 11 | Total distributions. Add lines 9 and 10. If greater than line 8, see page 20 of the instructions | **11** | | |
| 12 | Enter the amount of tax-exempt income included on line 11 . . . . . . . . . . | **12** | | |
| 13 | Tentative income distribution deduction. Subtract line 12 from line 11 . . . . . . . | **13** | | |
| 14 | Tentative income distribution deduction. Subtract line 2 from line 7. If zero or less, enter -0- | **14** | | |
| 15 | **Income distribution deduction.** Enter the smaller of line 13 or line 14 here and on page 1, line 18 | **15** | | |

| **Schedule G** | **Tax Computation** (see page 21 of the instructions) | | | |
|---|---|---|---|---|
| 1 | **Tax: a** ☐ Tax rate schedule or ☐ Schedule D (Form 1041) . . | **1a** | | |
| | **b** Tax on lump-sum distributions (attach Form 4972). . . . | **1b** | | |
| | **c** Alternative minimum tax (from Schedule I, line 56). . . . | **1c** | | |
| | **d** **Total.** Add lines 1a through 1c . . . . . . . . . . ▶ | **1d** | | |
| 2a | Foreign tax credit (attach Form 1116) . . . . . . . . . | **2a** | | |
| **b** | Other nonbusiness credits (attach schedule) . . . . . . . | **2b** | | |
| **c** | General business credit. Enter here and check which forms are attached: ☐ Form 3800 ☐ Forms (specify) ▶ ............................ | **2c** | | |
| **d** | Credit for prior year minimum tax (attach Form 8801) . . . . . | **2d** | | |
| 3 | **Total credits.** Add lines 2a through 2d . . . . . . . . . . . . . ▶ | **3** | | |
| 4 | Subtract line 3 from line 1d. If zero or less, enter -0- . . . . . . . . . . | **4** | | |
| 5 | Recapture taxes. Check if from: ☐ Form 4255 ☐ Form 8611. . . . . . . . | **5** | | |
| 6 | Household employment taxes. Attach Schedule H (Form 1040) . . . . . . . . | **6** | | |
| 7 | **Total tax.** Add lines 4 through 6. Enter here and on page 1, line 23 . . . . . . . ▶ | **7** | | |

| | **Other Information** | Yes | No |
|---|---|---|---|
| 1 | Did the estate or trust receive tax-exempt income? If "Yes," attach a computation of the allocation of expenses Enter the amount of tax-exempt interest income and exempt-interest dividends ▶ $ .............................. | | |
| 2 | Did the estate or trust receive all or any part of the earnings (salary, wages, and other compensation) of any individual by reason of a contract assignment or similar arrangement? . . . . . . . . . . | | |
| 3 | At any time during calendar year 2002, did the estate or trust have an interest in or a signature or other authority over a bank, securities, or other financial account in a foreign country? . . . . . . . . . See page 22 of the instructions for exceptions and filing requirements for Form TD F 90-22.1. If "Yes," enter the name of the foreign country ▶ ............................. | | |
| 4 | During the tax year, did the estate or trust receive a distribution from, or was it the grantor of, or transferor to, a foreign trust? If "Yes," the estate or trust may have to file Form 3520. See page 22 of the instructions . | | |
| 5 | Did the estate or trust receive, or pay, any qualified residence interest on seller-provided financing? If "Yes," see page 22 for required attachment . . . . . . . . . . . . . . . . . . . . . | | |
| 6 | If this is an estate or a complex trust making the section 663(b) election, check here (see page 23) . . ▶☐ | | |
| 7 | To make a section 643(e)(3) election, attach Schedule D (Form 1041), and check here (see page 23) . . ▶☐ | | |
| 8 | If the decedent's estate has been open for more than 2 years, attach an explanation for the delay in closing the estate, and check here ▶☐ | | |
| 9 | Are any present or future trust beneficiaries skip persons? See page 23 of the instructions . . . . . . | | |

Form **1041** (2002)

Form 1041 (2002)                                                                                           Page **3**

## Schedule I    Alternative Minimum Tax (see pages 23 through 29 of the instructions)

### Part I—Estate's or Trust's Share of Alternative Minimum Taxable Income

| | | | |
|---|---|---|---|
| 1 | Adjusted total income or (loss) (from page 1, line 17) | 1 | |
| 2 | Interest | 2 | |
| 3 | Taxes | 3 | |
| 4 | Miscellaneous itemized deductions (from page 1, line 15b) | 4 | |
| 5 | Refund of taxes | 5 ( | ) |
| 6 | Depletion (difference between regular tax and AMT) | 6 | |
| 7 | Net operating loss deduction. Enter as a positive amount | 7 | |
| 8 | Interest from specified private activity bonds exempt from the regular tax | 8 | |
| 9 | Qualified small business stock (42% of gain excluded under section 1202) | 9 | |
| 10 | Exercise of incentive stock options (excess of AMT income over regular tax income) | 10 | |
| 11 | Other estates and trusts (amount from Schedule K-1 (Form 1041), line 9) | 11 | |
| 12 | Electing large partnerships (amount from Schedule K-1 (Form 1065-B), box 6) | 12 | |
| 13 | Disposition of property (difference between AMT and regular tax gain or loss) | 13 | |
| 14 | Depreciation on assets placed in service after 1986 (difference between regular tax and AMT) | 14 | |
| 15 | Passive activities (difference between AMT and regular tax income or loss) | 15 | |
| 16 | Loss limitations (difference between AMT and regular tax income or loss) | 16 | |
| 17 | Circulation costs (difference between regular tax and AMT) | 17 | |
| 18 | Long-term contracts (difference between AMT and regular tax income) | 18 | |
| 19 | Mining costs (difference between regular tax and AMT) | 19 | |
| 20 | Research and experimental costs (difference between regular tax and AMT) | 20 | |
| 21 | Income from certain installment sales before January 1, 1987 | 21 ( | ) |
| 22 | Intangible drilling costs preference | 22 | |
| 23 | Other adjustments, including income-based related adjustments | 23 | |
| 24 | Alternative tax net operating loss deduction | 24 ( | ) |
| 25 | Adjusted alternative minimum taxable income. Combine lines 1 through 24 | 25 | |

**Note:** *Complete Part II below before going to line 26.*

| | | | | |
|---|---|---|---|---|
| 26 | Income distribution deduction from line 44 below | 26 | | |
| 27 | Estate tax deduction (from page 1, line 19) | 27 | | |
| 28 | Add lines 26 and 27 | | 28 | |
| 29 | Estate's or trust's share of alternative minimum taxable income. Subtract line 28 from line 25 | | 29 | |

If line 29 is:

- $22,500 or less, stop here and enter -0- on Schedule G, line 1c. The estate or trust is not liable for the alternative minimum tax.
- Over $22,500, but less than $165,000, go to line 45.
- $165,000 or more, enter the amount from line 29 on line 51 and go to line 52.

### Part II—Income Distribution Deduction on a Minimum Tax Basis

| | | | |
|---|---|---|---|
| 30 | Adjusted alternative minimum taxable income (see page 27 of the instructions) | 30 | |
| 31 | Adjusted tax-exempt interest (other than amounts included on line 8) | 31 | |
| 32 | Total net gain from Schedule D (Form 1041), line 16, column (1). If a loss, enter -0- | 32 | |
| 33 | Capital gains for the tax year allocated to corpus and paid or permanently set aside for charitable purposes (from Schedule A, line 4) | 33 | |
| 34 | Capital gains paid or permanently set aside for charitable purposes from gross income (see page 28 of the instructions) | 34 | |
| 35 | Capital gains computed on a minimum tax basis included on line 25 | 35 ( | ) |
| 36 | Capital losses computed on a minimum tax basis included on line 25. Enter as a positive amount | 36 | |
| 37 | Distributable net alternative minimum taxable income (DNAMTI). Combine lines 30 through 36. If zero or less, enter -0- | 37 | |
| 38 | Income required to be distributed currently (from Schedule B, line 9) | 38 | |
| 39 | Other amounts paid, credited, or otherwise required to be distributed (from Schedule B, line 10) | 39 | |
| 40 | Total distributions. Add lines 38 and 39 | 40 | |
| 41 | Tax-exempt income included on line 40 (other than amounts included on line 8) | 41 | |
| 42 | Tentative income distribution deduction on a minimum tax basis. Subtract line 41 from line 40 | 42 | |
| 43 | Tentative income distribution deduction on a minimum tax basis. Subtract line 31 from line 37. If zero or less, enter -0- | 43 | |
| 44 | **Income distribution deduction on a minimum tax basis.** Enter the smaller of line 42 or line 43. Enter here and on line 26 | 44 | |

Form **1041** (2002)

## Part III—Alternative Minimum Tax

| 45 | Exemption amount | | | | | 45 | $22,500 | 00 |
|----|------------------|---|---|---|---|----|---------|-----|
| 46 | Enter the amount from line 29 | | **46** | | | | | |
| 47 | Phase-out of exemption amount | | **47** | $75,000 | 00 | | | |
| 48 | Subtract line 47 from line 46. If zero or less, enter -0- | | **48** | | | | | |
| 49 | Multiply line 48 by 25% (.25) | | | | | 49 | | |
| 50 | Subtract line 49 from line 45. If zero or less, enter -0- | | | | | 50 | | |
| 51 | Subtract line 50 from line 46 | | | | | 51 | | |

52 Go to Part IV of Schedule I to figure line 52 if the estate or trust has a gain on lines 15a and 16 of column (2) of Schedule D (Form 1041) (as refigured for the AMT, if necessary). Otherwise, if line 51 is—
- $175,000 or less, multiply line 51 by 26% (.26).
- Over $175,000, multiply line 51 by 28% (.28) and subtract $3,500 from the result . . . . | 52 | | |

| 53 | Alternative minimum foreign tax credit (see page 28 of the instructions) | 53 | | |
|----|------|----|---|---|
| 54 | Tentative minimum tax. Subtract line 53 from line 52 | 54 | | |
| 55 | Enter the tax from Schedule G, line 1a (minus any foreign tax credit from Schedule G, line 2a) | 55 | | |
| 56 | **Alternative minimum tax.** Subtract line 55 from line 54. If zero or less, enter -0-. Enter here and on Schedule G, line 1c | 56 | | |

## Part IV—Line 52 Computation Using Maximum Capital Gains Rates

**Caution:** *If the estate or trust did not complete Part V of Schedule D (Form 1041), see page 29 of the instructions before completing this part.*

| 57 | Enter the amount from line 51 | | | | 57 | | |
|----|------|---|---|---|----|---|---|
| 58 | Enter the amount from Schedule D (Form 1041), line 21, or line 9 of the Schedule D Tax Worksheet, whichever applies (as refigured for AMT, if necessary) | | **58** | | | | |
| 59 | Enter the amount from Schedule D (Form 1041), line 15d, column (2) (as refigured for AMT, if necessary) | | **59** | | | | |
| 60 | If you did not complete a Schedule D Tax Worksheet for the regular tax or the AMT, enter the amount from line 58. Otherwise, add lines 58 and 59 and enter the **smaller** of that result or the amount from line 4 of the Schedule D Tax Worksheet (as refigured for the AMT, if necessary). | | | | 60 | | |
| 61 | Subtract line 60 from line 57. If zero or less, enter -0- | | | | 61 | | |
| 62 | If line 61 is $175,000 or less, multiply line 61 by 26% (.26). Otherwise, multiply line 61 by 28% (.28) and subtract $3,500 from the result ▶ | | | | 62 | | |
| 63 | Enter the amount from Schedule D (Form 1041), line 26, or line 16 of the Schedule D Tax Worksheet (as figured for the regular tax) | | | | 63 | | |
| 64 | Enter the **smallest** of line 57, line 58, or line 63 | | | | 64 | | |
| 65 | Enter the estate's or trust's allocable portion of qualified 5-year gain, if any, from Schedule D (Form 1041) line 15c, column (2) (as refigured for the AMT, if necessary). | | **65** | | | | |
| 66 | Enter the smaller of line 64 or line 65 | | | | 66 | | |
| 67 | Multiply line 66 by 8% (.08) ▶ | | | | 67 | | |
| 68 | Subtract line 66 from line 64 | | | | 68 | | |
| 69 | Multiply line 68 by 10% (.10) ▶ | | | | 69 | | |
| 70 | Enter the **smaller** of line 57 or line 58 | | | | 70 | | |
| 71 | Enter the amount from line 64 | | | | 71 | | |
| 72 | Subtract line 71 from line 70. If zero or less, enter -0- | | | | 72 | | |
| 73 | Multiply line 72 by 20% (.20) ▶ | | | | 73 | | |
| 74 | Enter the amount from line 57 | | | | 74 | | |
| 75 | Add lines 61, 64, and 72 | | | | 75 | | |
| 76 | Subtract line 75 from line 74 | | | | 76 | | |
| 77 | Multiply line 76 by 25% (.25) ▶ | | | | 77 | | |
| 78 | Add lines 62, 67, 69, 73, and 77 | | | | 78 | | |
| 79 | If line 57 is $175,000 or less, multiply line 57 by 26% (.26). Otherwise, multiply line 57 by 28% (.28) and subtract $3,500 from the result | | | | 79 | | |
| 80 | Enter the **smaller** of line 78 or line 79 here and on line 52 ▶ | | | | 80 | | |

Form **1041** (2002)

| | | OMB No. 1545-0092 |
|---|---|---|
| **SCHEDULE K-1**<br>**(Form 1041)**<br>Department of the Treasury<br>Internal Revenue Service | **Beneficiary's Share of Income, Deductions, Credits, etc.**<br>for the calendar year 2002, or fiscal year<br>beginning ............... , 2002, ending ............... , 20 ........<br>▶ **Complete a separate Schedule K-1 for each beneficiary.** | **2002** |

| Name of trust or decedent's estate | ☐ Amended K-1<br>☐ Final K-1 |
|---|---|

| Beneficiary's identifying number ▶ | Estate's or trust's EIN |
|---|---|
| Beneficiary's name, address, and ZIP code | Fiduciary's name, address, and ZIP code |

| (a) Allocable share item | | (b) Amount | (c) Calendar year 2002 Form 1040 filers enter the amounts in column (b) on: |
|---|---|---|---|
| **1** Interest. . . . . . . . . . . . . . | **1** | | Schedule B, Part I, line 1 |
| **2** Ordinary dividends . . . . . . . . . . | **2** | | Schedule B, Part II, line 5 |
| **3** Net short-term capital gain . . . . . . . | **3** | | Schedule D, line 5 |
| **4** Net long-term capital gain: **a** Total for year . . . | **4a** | | Schedule D, line 12, column (f) |
| **b** 28% rate gain . . . . . . . . | **4b** | | Schedule D, line 12, column (g) |
| **c** Qualified 5-year gain . . . . . . . . . | **4c** | | Line 5 of the worksheet for Schedule D, line 29 |
| **d** Unrecaptured section 1250 gain . . . . . . | **4d** | | Line 11 of the worksheet for Schedule D, line 19 |
| **5a** Annuities, royalties, and other nonpassive income before directly apportioned deductions . . . . | **5a** | | Schedule E, Part III, column (f) |
| **b** Depreciation . . . . . . . . . . | **5b** | | ⎫ |
| **c** Depletion . . . . . . . . . . . . | **5c** | | Include on the applicable line of the appropriate tax form |
| **d** Amortization . . . . . . . . . . | **5d** | | ⎭ |
| **6a** Trade or business, rental real estate, and other rental income before directly apportioned deductions (see instructions) . | **6a** | | Schedule E, Part III |
| **b** Depreciation . . . . . . . . . . | **6b** | | ⎫ |
| **c** Depletion . . . . . . . . . . . . | **6c** | | Include on the applicable line of the appropriate tax form |
| **d** Amortization . . . . . . . . . . | **6d** | | ⎭ |
| **7** Income for minimum tax purposes . . . . . . | **7** | | |
| **8** Income for regular tax purposes (add lines 1, 2, 3, 4a, 5a, and 6a) . . . . . . . . . . . . . . . . | **8** | | |
| **9** Adjustment for minimum tax purposes (subtract line 8 from line 7) | **9** | | Form 6251, line 14 |
| **10** Estate tax deduction (including certain generation-skipping transfer taxes) . . . . . . . . . . | **10** | | Schedule A, line 27 |
| **11** Foreign taxes. . . . . . . . . . . . | **11** | | Form 1040, line 45 or Schedule A, line 8 |
| **12** Adjustments and tax preference items (itemize): | | | |
| **a** Accelerated depreciation . . . . . . . | **12a** | | ⎫ |
| **b** Depletion . . . . . . . . . . . | **12b** | | Include on the applicable line of Form 6251 |
| **c** Amortization . . . . . . . . . . . | **12c** | | ⎭ |
| **d** Exclusion items . . . . . . . . . . | **12d** | | 2003 Form 8801 |
| **13** Deductions in the final year of trust or decedent's estate: | | | |
| **a** Excess deductions on termination (see instructions) | **13a** | | Schedule A, line 22 |
| **b** Short-term capital loss carryover . . . . . . | **13b** ( ) | | Schedule D, line 5 |
| **c** Long-term capital loss carryover . . . . . . | **13c** ( ) | | Schedule D, line 12, columns (f) and (g) |
| **d** Net operating loss (NOL) carryover for regular tax purposes | **13d** ( ) | | Form 1040, line 21 |
| **e** NOL carryover for minimum tax purposes . . . . . | **13e** | | See the instructions for Form 6251, line 27 |
| **f** .................................. | **13f** | | ⎫ Include on the applicable line |
| **g** .................................. | **13g** | | ⎭ of the appropriate tax form |
| **14** Other (itemize): | | | |
| **a** Payments of estimated taxes credited to you . . | **14a** | | Form 1040, line 63 |
| **b** Tax-exempt interest . . . . . . . . . | **14b** | | Form 1040, line 8b |
| **c** .................................. | **14c** | | ⎫ |
| **d** .................................. | **14d** | | |
| **e** .................................. | **14e** | | Include on the applicable line of the appropriate tax form |
| **f** .................................. | **14f** | | |
| **g** .................................. | **14g** | | ⎭ |
| **h** | **14h** | | |

| For Paperwork Reduction Act Notice, see the Instructions for Form 1041. | Cat. No. 11380D | **Schedule K-1 (Form 1041) 2002** |
|---|---|---|

**Form 1065**

Department of the Treasury
Internal Revenue Service

## U.S. Return of Partnership Income

For calendar year 2002, or tax year beginning ........ , 2002, and ending ........ , 20.... .
▶ See separate instructions.

OMB No. 1545-0099

**2002**

| | | |
|---|---|---|
| A Principal business activity | Use the IRS label. Otherwise, print or type. | Name of partnership |
| B Principal product or service | | Number, street, and room or suite no. If a P.O. box, see page 14 of the instructions. |
| C Business code number | | City or town, state, and ZIP code |

D Employer identification number

E Date business started

F Total assets (see page 14 of the instructions)
$

G  Check applicable boxes: **(1)** ☐ Initial return  **(2)** ☐ Final return  **(3)** ☐ Name change  **(4)** ☐ Address change  **(5)** ☐ Amended return
H  Check accounting method: **(1)** ☐ Cash  **(2)** ☐ Accrual  **(3)** ☐ Other (specify) ▶ ...............................................
I  Number of Schedules K-1. Attach one for each person who was a partner at any time during the tax year ▶ ...............................................

**Caution:** *Include **only** trade or business income and expenses on lines 1a through 22 below. See the instructions for more information.*

### Income

| | | | |
|---|---|---|---|
| 1a | Gross receipts or sales | 1a | |
| b | Less returns and allowances | 1b | 1c |
| 2 | Cost of goods sold (Schedule A, line 8) | | 2 |
| 3 | Gross profit. Subtract line 2 from line 1c | | 3 |
| 4 | Ordinary income (loss) from other partnerships, estates, and trusts (attach schedule) | | 4 |
| 5 | Net farm profit (loss) (attach Schedule F (Form 1040)) | | 5 |
| 6 | Net gain (loss) from Form 4797, Part II, line 18 | | 6 |
| 7 | Other income (loss) (attach schedule) | | 7 |
| 8 | **Total income (loss).** Combine lines 3 through 7 | | 8 |

### Deductions (see page 15 of the instructions for limitations)

| | | | |
|---|---|---|---|
| 9 | Salaries and wages (other than to partners) (less employment credits) | | 9 |
| 10 | Guaranteed payments to partners | | 10 |
| 11 | Repairs and maintenance | | 11 |
| 12 | Bad debts | | 12 |
| 13 | Rent | | 13 |
| 14 | Taxes and licenses | | 14 |
| 15 | Interest | | 15 |
| 16a | Depreciation (if required, attach Form 4562) | 16a | |
| b | Less depreciation reported on Schedule A and elsewhere on return | 16b | 16c |
| 17 | Depletion (**Do not deduct oil and gas depletion.**) | | 17 |
| 18 | Retirement plans, etc. | | 18 |
| 19 | Employee benefit programs | | 19 |
| 20 | Other deductions (attach schedule) | | 20 |
| 21 | **Total deductions.** Add the amounts shown in the far right column for lines 9 through 20 | | 21 |

| | | | |
|---|---|---|---|
| 22 | **Ordinary income (loss)** from trade or business activities. Subtract line 21 from line 8 | | 22 |

**Sign Here**

Under penalties of perjury, I declare that I have examined this return, including accompanying schedules and statements, and to the best of my knowledge and belief, it is true, correct, and complete. Declaration of preparer (other than general partner or limited liability company member) is based on all information of which preparer has any knowledge.

▶ _____
Signature of general partner or limited liability company member

▶ _____
Date

May the IRS discuss this return with the preparer shown below (see instructions)? ☐ Yes ☐ No

**Paid Preparer's Use Only**

| Preparer's signature | | Date | | Check if self-employed ▶ ☐ | Preparer's SSN or PTIN |
|---|---|---|---|---|---|
| Firm's name (or yours if self-employed), address, and ZIP code | | | | EIN ▶ | |
| | | | | Phone no. (    ) | |

**For Paperwork Reduction Act Notice, see separate instructions.**          Cat. No. 11390Z          Form **1065** (2002)

Form 1065 (2002) Page **2**

## Schedule A  Cost of Goods Sold (see page 19 of the instructions)

| | | | |
|---|---|---|---|
| 1 | Inventory at beginning of year . . . . . . . . . . . . . . . . . . . . . . | 1 | |
| 2 | Purchases less cost of items withdrawn for personal use . . . . . . . . . . . . | 2 | |
| 3 | Cost of labor. . . . . . . . . . . . . . . . . . . . . . . . . . . | 3 | |
| 4 | Additional section 263A costs *(attach schedule)* . . . . . . . . . . . . . . | 4 | |
| 5 | Other costs *(attach schedule)* . . . . . . . . . . . . . . . . . . . . | 5 | |
| 6 | **Total.** Add lines 1 through 5 . . . . . . . . . . . . . . . . . . . . | 6 | |
| 7 | Inventory at end of year . . . . . . . . . . . . . . . . . . . . . . . | 7 | |
| 8 | **Cost of goods sold.** Subtract line 7 from line 6. Enter here and on page 1, line 2 . . . . | 8 | |

**9a** Check all methods used for valuing closing inventory:

    **(i)** ☐ Cost as described in Regulations section 1.471-3

    **(ii)** ☐ Lower of cost or market as described in Regulations section 1.471-4

    **(iii)** ☐ Other (specify method used and attach explanation) ▶ ----------------------------

  **b** Check this box if there was a writedown of "subnormal" goods as described in Regulations section 1.471-2(c). . . . ▶ ☐

  **c** Check this box if the LIFO inventory method was adopted this tax year for any goods *(if checked, attach Form 970)* . . ▶ ☐

  **d** Do the rules of section 263A (for property produced or acquired for resale) apply to the partnership? . . ☐ **Yes** ☐ **No**

  **e** Was there any change in determining quantities, cost, or valuations between opening and closing inventory? ☐ **Yes** ☐ **No**
    If "Yes," attach explanation.

## Schedule B  Other Information

| | | Yes | No |
|---|---|---|---|
| **1** | What type of entity is filing this return? Check the applicable box: | | |

  **a** ☐ Domestic general partnership        **b** ☐ Domestic limited partnership

  **c** ☐ Domestic limited liability company    **d** ☐ Domestic limited liability partnership

  **e** ☐ Foreign partnership            **f** ☐ Other ▶ ------------------------------

**2** Are any partners in this partnership also partnerships?

**3** During the partnership's tax year, did the partnership own any interest in another partnership or in any foreign entity that was disregarded as an entity separate from its owner under Regulations sections 301.7701-2 and 301.7701-3? If yes, see instructions for required attachment . . . . . . . . . . . . . . . .

**4** Is this partnership subject to the consolidated audit procedures of sections 6221 through 6233? If "Yes," see **Designation of Tax Matters Partner** below . . . . . . . . . . . . . . . . . . . . .

**5** Does this partnership meet **all three** of the following requirements?

  **a** The partnership's total receipts for the tax year were less than $250,000;

  **b** The partnership's total assets at the end of the tax year were less than $600,000; **and**

  **c** Schedules K-1 are filed with the return and furnished to the partners on or before the due date (including extensions) for the partnership return.

    If "Yes," the partnership is not required to complete Schedules L, M-1, and M-2; Item F on page 1 of Form 1065; or Item J on Schedule K-1 . . . . . . . . . . . . . . . . . . . . . . . .

**6** Does this partnership have any foreign partners? If "Yes," the partnership may have to file Forms 8804, 8805 and 8813. See page 20 of the instructions

**7** Is this partnership a publicly traded partnership as defined in section 469(k)(2)? . . . . . . . . . .

**8** Has this partnership filed, or is it required to file, **Form 8264,** Application for Registration of a Tax Shelter? . .

**9** At any time during calendar year 2002, did the partnership have an interest in or a signature or other authority over a financial account in a foreign country (such as a bank account, securities account, or other financial account)? See page 20 of the instructions for exceptions and filing requirements for Form TD F 90-22.1. If "Yes," enter the name of the foreign country. ▶ -----------------------------------------------------

**10** During the tax year, did the partnership receive a distribution from, or was it the grantor of, or transferor to, a foreign trust? If "Yes," the partnership may have to file Form 3520. See page 20 of the instructions . . . .

**11** Was there a distribution of property or a transfer (e.g., by sale or death) of a partnership interest during the tax year? If "Yes," you may elect to adjust the basis of the partnership s assets under section 754 by attaching the statement described under **Elections Made By the Partnership** on page 8 of the instructions . . . . . .

**12** Enter the number of **Forms 8865,** Return of U.S. Persons With Respect to Certain Foreign Partnerships, attached to this return . . . . . . . . . . . . . . . . . . . . . . . . . . ▶ -----------------

## Designation of Tax Matters Partner (see page 21 of the instructions)

Enter below the general partner designated as the tax matters partner (TMP) for the tax year of this return:

| Name of designated TMP ▶ | | Identifying number of TMP ▶ | |
|---|---|---|---|
| Address of designated TMP ▶ | | | |

Form **1065** (2002)

Form 1065 (2002)                                                                            Page **3**

## Schedule K    Partners' Shares of Income, Credits, Deductions, etc.

| | | (a) Distributive share items | | (b) Total amount |
|---|---|---|---|---|

### Income (Loss)

| | | | |
|---|---|---|---|
| **1** | Ordinary income (loss) from trade or business activities (page 1, line 22) . . . . . . . | **1** | |
| **2** | Net income (loss) from rental real estate activities *(attach Form 8825)* . . . . . . | **2** | |
| **3a** | Gross income from other rental activities . . . . . . . . . **3a** | | |
| **b** | Expenses from other rental activities *(attach schedule)* . . . . **3b** | | |
| **c** | Net income (loss) from other rental activities. Subtract line 3b from line 3a . . . | **3c** | |
| **4** | Portfolio income (loss): ▶ **a** Interest income . . . . . . . | **4a** | |
| **b** | Ordinary dividends . . . . . . . . . . . . . . . | **4b** | |
| **c** | Royalty income . . . . . . . . . . . . . . . . | **4c** | |
| **d** | Net short-term capital gain (loss) *(attach Schedule D (Form 1065))* . . . . | **4d** | |
| **e** | **(1)** Net long-term capital gain (loss) *(attach Schedule D (Form 1065))* . . . . . . | **4e(1)** | |
| | **(2)** 28% rate gain (loss) ▶ ................... **(3)** Qualified 5-year gain ▶ .................. | | |
| **f** | Other portfolio income (loss) *(attach schedule)* . . . . . . . . . . . | **4f** | |
| **5** | Guaranteed payments to partners . . . . . . . . . . . . . . | **5** | |
| **6** | Net section 1231 gain (loss) (other than due to casualty or theft) *(attach Form 4797)* . . . | **6** | |
| **7** | Other income (loss) *(attach schedule)* . . . . . . . . . . . . . | **7** | |

### Deductions

| | | | |
|---|---|---|---|
| **8** | Charitable contributions *(attach schedule)* . . . . . . . . . . | **8** | |
| **9** | Section 179 expense deduction *(attach Form 4562)* . . . . . . . . . | **9** | |
| **10** | Deductions related to portfolio income (itemize) . . . . . . . . . | **10** | |
| **11** | Other deductions *(attach schedule)* . . . . . . . . . . . . | **11** | |

### Credits

| | | | |
|---|---|---|---|
| **12a** | Low-income housing credit: | | |
| | **(1)** From partnerships to which section 42(j)(5) applies . . . . . . . . . . | **12a(1)** | |
| | **(2)** Other than on line 12a(1) . . . . . . . . . . . . . . . . | **12a(2)** | |
| **b** | Qualified rehabilitation expenditures related to rental real estate activities *(attach Form 3468)* | **12b** | |
| **c** | Credits (other than credits shown on lines 12a and 12b) related to rental real estate activities | **12c** | |
| **d** | Credits related to other rental activities . . . . . . . . . . . . . | **12d** | |
| **13** | Other credits . . . . . . . . . . . . . . . . . . . | **13** | |

### Investment Interest

| | | | |
|---|---|---|---|
| **14a** | Interest expense on investment debts . . . . . . . . . . . . . | **14a** | |
| **b** | **(1)** Investment income included on lines 4a, 4b, 4c, and 4f above . . . . . . . | **14b(1)** | |
| | **(2)** Investment expenses included on line 10 above . . . . . . . . . . . | **14b(2)** | |

### Self-Employment

| | | | |
|---|---|---|---|
| **15a** | Net earnings (loss) from self-employment . . . . . . . . . . . . | **15a** | |
| **b** | Gross farming or fishing income . . . . . . . . . . . . . . | **15b** | |
| **c** | Gross nonfarm income . . . . . . . . . . . . . . . . | **15c** | |

### Adjustments and Tax Preference Items

| | | | |
|---|---|---|---|
| **16a** | Depreciation adjustment on property placed in service after 1986 . . . . . . | **16a** | |
| **b** | Adjusted gain or loss . . . . . . . . . . . . . . . . | **16b** | |
| **c** | Depletion (other than oil and gas) . . . . . . . . . . . . . | **16c** | |
| **d** | **(1)** Gross income from oil, gas, and geothermal properties . . . . . . . | **16d(1)** | |
| | **(2)** Deductions allocable to oil, gas, and geothermal properties . . . . . . . | **16d(2)** | |
| **e** | Other adjustments and tax preference items *(attach schedule)* . . . . . . . | **16e** | |

### Foreign Taxes

| | | | |
|---|---|---|---|
| **17a** | Name of foreign country or U.S. possession ▶ -------------------------------- | | |
| **b** | Gross income from all sources . . . . . . . . . . . . . . | **17b** | |
| **c** | Gross income sourced at partner level . . . . . . . . . . . . | **17c** | |
| **d** | Foreign gross income sourced at partnership level: | | |
| | **(1)** Passive ▶ --------------- **(2)** Listed categories *(attach schedule)* ▶ ----------- **(3)** General limitation ▶ | **17d(3)** | |
| **e** | Deductions allocated and apportioned at partner level: | | |
| | **(1)** Interest expense ▶ -------------------------- **(2)** Other . . . . . . . . . . ▶ | **17e(2)** | |
| **f** | Deductions allocated and apportioned at partnership level to foreign source income: | | |
| | **(1)** Passive ▶ --------------- **(2)** Listed categories *(attach schedule)* ▶ ----------- **(3)** General limitation ▶ | **17f(3)** | |
| **g** | Total foreign taxes (check one): ▶ Paid ☐ Accrued ☐ . . . . . . . . . | **17g** | |
| **h** | Reduction in taxes available for credit *(attach schedule)* . . . . . . . . | **17h** | |

### Other

| | | | |
|---|---|---|---|
| **18** | Section 59(e)(2) expenditures: **a** Type ▶ ------------------------------------ **b** Amount ▶ | **18b** | |
| **19** | Tax-exempt interest income . . . . . . . . . . . . . . | **19** | |
| **20** | Other tax-exempt income . . . . . . . . . . . . . . . | **20** | |
| **21** | Nondeductible expenses . . . . . . . . . . . . . . . | **21** | |
| **22** | Distributions of money (cash and marketable securities) . . . . . . . . | **22** | |
| **23** | Distributions of property other than money . . . . . . . . . . | **23** | |
| **24** | Other items and amounts required to be reported separately to partners *(attach schedule)* . . . . | | |

Form **1065** (2002)

Form 1065 (2002)                                                                                    Page **4**

## Analysis of Net Income (Loss)

| | | | | | | |
|---|---|---|---|---|---|---|
| **1** | Net income (loss). Combine Schedule K, lines 1 through 7 in column (b). From the result, subtract the sum of Schedule K, lines 8 through 11, 14a, 17g, and 18b . . . . . . . . . . . . . . . | | | | **1** | |

| **2** Analysis by partner type: | **(i)** Corporate | **(ii)** Individual (active) | **(iii)** Individual (passive) | **(iv)** Partnership | **(v)** Exempt organization | **(vi)** Nominee/Other |
|---|---|---|---|---|---|---|
| **a** General partners | | | | | | |
| **b** Limited partners | | | | | | |

**Note:** Schedules L, M-1 and M-2 are not required if Question 5 of Schedule B is answered "Yes."

| **Schedule L** | **Balance Sheets per Books** | Beginning of tax year | | End of tax year | |
|---|---|---|---|---|---|
| | **Assets** | **(a)** | **(b)** | **(c)** | **(d)** |
| **1** | Cash . . . . . . . . . . . | | | | |
| **2a** | Trade notes and accounts receivable . . . . | | | | |
| **b** | Less allowance for bad debts . . . . . | | | | |
| **3** | Inventories . . . . . . . . | | | | |
| **4** | U.S. government obligations . . . . . . | | | | |
| **5** | Tax-exempt securities . . . . . . | | | | |
| **6** | Other current assets (attach schedule) . . . | | | | |
| **7** | Mortgage and real estate loans . . . . . | | | | |
| **8** | Other investments (attach schedule) . . . . | | | | |
| **9a** | Buildings and other depreciable assets . . . | | | | |
| **b** | Less accumulated depreciation . . . . . . | | | | |
| **10a** | Depletable assets . . . . . . . . | | | | |
| **b** | Less accumulated depletion . . . . . . | | | | |
| **11** | Land (net of any amortization) . . . . . | | | | |
| **12a** | Intangible assets (amortizable only). . . . . | | | | |
| **b** | Less accumulated amortization . . . . . | | | | |
| **13** | Other assets (attach schedule) . . . . . | | | | |
| **14** | **Total** assets . . . . . . . . | | | | |
| | **Liabilities and Capital** | | | | |
| **15** | Accounts payable . . . . . . . . | | | | |
| **16** | Mortgages, notes, bonds payable in less than 1 year | | | | |
| **17** | Other current liabilities (attach schedule) . . . | | | | |
| **18** | All nonrecourse loans . . . . . . . | | | | |
| **19** | Mortgages, notes, bonds payable in 1 year or more | | | | |
| **20** | Other liabilities (attach schedule) . . . . . | | | | |
| **21** | Partners' capital accounts . . . . . . | | | | |
| **22** | **Total** liabilities and capital . . . . . . . | | | | |

| **Schedule M-1** | **Reconciliation of Income (Loss) per Books With Income (Loss) per Return** | | |
|---|---|---|---|
| **1** Net income (loss) per books . . . . . | | **6** Income recorded on books this year not included on Schedule K, lines 1 through 7 (itemize): | |
| **2** Income included on Schedule K, lines 1 through 4, 6, and 7, not recorded on books this year (itemize): .................... | | **a** Tax-exempt interest $ .......................... ...................................................... | |
| **3** Guaranteed payments (other than health insurance) . . . . . . . . . . | | **7** Deductions included on Schedule K, lines 1 through 11, 14a, 17g, and 18b, not charged against book income this year (itemize): | |
| **4** Expenses recorded on books this year not included on Schedule K, lines 1 through 11, 14a, 17g, and 18b (itemize): | | **a** Depreciation $ ................................ ...................................................... | |
| **a** Depreciation $ .......................... | | | |
| **b** Travel and entertainment $ ................ | | **8** Add lines 6 and 7 . . . . . . . | |
| .................................................. | | **9** Income (loss) (Analysis of Net Income (Loss), line 1). Subtract line 8 from line 5 . . . . | |
| **5** Add lines 1 through 4 . . . . . . . | | | |

| **Schedule M-2** | **Analysis of Partners' Capital Accounts** | | |
|---|---|---|---|
| **1** Balance at beginning of year . . . . | | **6** Distributions: **a** Cash . . . . . . . | |
| **2** Capital contributed: **a** Cash . . . . . | | **b** Property . . . . . . | |
| | **b** Property . . . . | | **7** Other decreases (itemize): ................... | |
| **3** Net income (loss) per books . . . . . | | ...................................................... | |
| **4** Other increases (itemize): ................ | | **8** Add lines 6 and 7 . . . . . . . | |
| .................................................. | | **9** Balance at end of year. Subtract line 8 from line 5 | |
| **5** Add lines 1 through 4 . . . . . . . | | | |

Form **1065** (2002)

| SCHEDULE K-1<br>(Form 1065)<br>Department of the Treasury<br>Internal Revenue Service | **Partner's Share of Income, Credits, Deductions, etc.**<br>▶ See separate instructions.<br>For calendar year 2002 or tax year beginning , 2002, and ending , 20 | OMB No. 1545-0099<br>20**02** |
|---|---|---|

**Partner's identifying number ▶** | **Partnership's identifying number ▶**

Partner's name, address, and ZIP code | Partnership's name, address, and ZIP code

**A** This partner is a ☐ general partner ☐ limited partner
☐ limited liability company member
**B** What type of entity is this partner? ▶ ............
**C** Is this partner a ☐ domestic or a ☐ foreign partner?

**F** Partner's share of liabilities (see instructions):
Nonrecourse . . . . . . . . $ .................
Qualified nonrecourse financing . $ .................
Other . . . . . . . . . $ .................

| | **(i)** Before change<br>or termination | **(ii)** End of<br>year |
|---|---|---|
| **D** Enter partner's percentage of: | | |
| Profit sharing . . . . . . | ......... % | ......... % |
| Loss sharing . . . . . . . | ......... % | ......... % |
| Ownership of capital . . . | ......... % | ......... % |

**G** Tax shelter registration number . ▶ .................

**H** Check here if this partnership is a publicly traded partnership as defined in section 469(k)(2) . . . . . ☐

**E** IRS Center where partnership filed return:

**I** Check applicable boxes: **(1)** ☐ Final K-1 **(2)** ☐ Amended K-1

**J** Analysis of partner's capital account:

| **(a)** Capital account at<br>beginning of year | **(b)** Capital contributed<br>during year | **(c)** Partner's share of lines<br>3, 4, and 7, Form 1065,<br>Schedule M-2 | **(d)** Withdrawals and<br>distributions | **(e)** Capital account at end of<br>year (combine columns (a)<br>through (d)) |
|---|---|---|---|---|
| | | | ( ) | |

| | **(a)** Distributive share item | | **(b)** Amount | **(c)** 1040 filers enter the<br>amount in column (b) on: |
|---|---|---|---|---|
| **Income (Loss)** | **1** Ordinary income (loss) from trade or business activities . . . | **1** | | See page 6 of Partner's<br>Instructions for Schedule K-1<br>(Form 1065). |
| | **2** Net income (loss) from rental real estate activities . . . . . | **2** | | |
| | **3** Net income (loss) from other rental activities . . . . . . | **3** | | |
| | **4** Portfolio income (loss): | | | |
| | **a** Interest . . . . . . . . . . . . . . . . . . | **4a** | | Sch. B, Part I, line 1 |
| | **b** Ordinary dividends . . . . . . . . . . . . . . . | **4b** | | Sch. B, Part II, line 5 |
| | **c** Royalties . . . . . . . . . . . . . . . . . . | **4c** | | Sch. E, Part I, line 4 |
| | **d** Net short-term capital gain (loss) . . . . . . . . . | **4d** | | Sch. D, line 5, col. (f) |
| | **e (1)** Net long-term capital gain (loss). . . . . . . . . | **4e(1)** | | Sch. D, line 12, col. (f) |
| | **(2)** 28% rate gain (loss) . . . . . . . . . . . . | **4e(2)** | | Sch. D, line 12, col. (g) |
| | **(3)** Qualified 5-year gain . . . . . . . . . . | **4e(3)** | | Line 5 of worksheet for Sch. D, line 29 |
| | **f** Other portfolio income (loss) *(attach schedule)* . . . | **4f** | | Enter on applicable line of your return. |
| | **5** Guaranteed payments to partner . . . . . . . . | **5** | | See page 6 of Partner's<br>Instructions for Schedule K-1<br>(Form 1065). |
| | **6** Net section 1231 gain (loss) (other than due to casualty or theft) | **6** | | |
| | **7** Other income (loss) *(attach schedule)* . . . . . . . . | **7** | | Enter on applicable line of your return. |
| **Deductions** | **8** Charitable contributions (see instructions) *(attach schedule)* . . | **8** | | Sch. A, line 15 or 16 |
| | **9** Section 179 expense deduction. . . . . . . . . | **9** | | See pages 7 and 8 of<br>Partner's Instructions for<br>Schedule K-1 (Form 1065). |
| | **10** Deductions related to portfolio income *(attach schedule)* . . . | **10** | | |
| | **11** Other deductions *(attach schedule)*. . . . . . . . . | **11** | | |
| **Credits** | **12a** Low-income housing credit: | | | |
| | **(1)** From section 42(j)(5) partnerships . . . . . . . . | **12a(1)** | | Form 8586, line 5 |
| | **(2)** Other than on line 12a(1) . . . . . . . . . | **12a(2)** | | |
| | **b** Qualified rehabilitation expenditures related to rental real estate activities . . . . . . . . . . . . . . . | **12b** | | See page 8 of Partner's<br>Instructions for Schedule K-1<br>(Form 1065). |
| | **c** Credits (other than credits shown on lines 12a and 12b) related to rental real estate activities . . . . . . . | **12c** | | |
| | **d** Credits related to other rental activities . . . . . . | **12d** | | |
| | **13** Other credits . . . . . . . . . . . . . . . | **13** | | |

**For Paperwork Reduction Act Notice, see Instructions for Form 1065.** Cat. No. 11394R **Schedule K-1 (Form 1065) 2002**

| (a) Distributive share item | | (b) Amount | (c) 1040 filers enter the amount in column (b) on: |
|---|---|---|---|

**Investment Interest**

| 14a | Interest expense on investment debts . . . . . . . . | 14a | | Form 4952, line 1 |
| b | (1) Investment income included on lines 4a, 4b, 4c, and 4f . . | 14b(1) | | See page 9 of Partner's Instructions for Schedule K-1 (Form 1065). |
| | (2) Investment expenses included on line 10 . . . . . . . | 14b(2) | | |

**Self-employment**

| 15a | Net earnings (loss) from self-employment . . . . . . . . | 15a | | Sch. SE, Section A or B |
| b | Gross farming or fishing income. . . . . . . . . . | 15b | | See page 9 of Partner's Instructions for Schedule K-1 (Form 1065). |
| c | Gross nonfarm income. . . . . . . . . . . . . | 15c | | |

**Adjustments and Tax Preference Items**

| 16a | Depreciation adjustment on property placed in service after 1986 | 16a | | See page 9 of Partner's Instructions for Schedule K-1 (Form 1065) and Instructions for Form 6251. |
| b | Adjusted gain or loss . . . . . . . . . . . . | 16b | | |
| c | Depletion (other than oil and gas) . . . . . . . . . | 16c | | |
| d | (1) Gross income from oil, gas, and geothermal properties . . | 16d(1) | | |
| | (2) Deductions allocable to oil, gas, and geothermal properties | 16d(2) | | |
| e | Other adjustments and tax preference items *(attach schedule)* | 16e | | |

**Foreign Taxes**

| 17a | Name of foreign country or U.S. possession ▶ . . . . . . . . . . . | | | |
| b | Gross income from all sources . . . . . . . . . . | 17b | | |
| c | Gross income sourced at partner level . . . . . . | 17c | | |
| d | Foreign gross income sourced at partnership level: | | | |
| | (1) Passive . . . . . . . . . . . . . | 17d(1) | | |
| | (2) Listed categories *(attach schedule)* . . . . . . . | 17d(2) | | |
| | (3) General limitation . . . . . . . . . . . . | 17d(3) | | |
| e | Deductions allocated and apportioned at partner level: | | | Form 1116, Part I |
| | (1) Interest expense . . . . . . . . . . . | 17e(1) | | |
| | (2) Other . . . . . . . . . . . . . | 17e(2) | | |
| f | Deductions allocated and apportioned at partnership level to foreign source income: | | | |
| | (1) Passive . . . . . . . . . . . . . | 17f(1) | | |
| | (2) Listed categories *(attach schedule)* . . . . . . . | 17f(2) | | |
| | (3) General limitation . . . . . . . . . . . | 17f(3) | | |
| g | Total foreign taxes (check one): ▶ ☐ Paid ☐ Accrued . . . | 17g | | Form 1116, Part II |
| h | Reduction in taxes available for credit *(attach schedule)* . . . | 17h | | Form 1116, line 12 |

**Other**

| 18 | Section 59(e)(2) expenditures: **a** Type ▶ . . . . . . . . . . . . . | | | See page 9 of Partner's Instructions for Schedule K-1 (Form 1065). |
| b | Amount . . . . . . . . . . . . . . . | 18b | | |
| 19 | Tax-exempt interest income . . . . . . . . . . | 19 | | Form 1040, line 8b |
| 20 | Other tax-exempt income. . . . . . . . . . . | 20 | | See pages 9 and 10 of Partner's Instructions for Schedule K-1 (Form 1065). |
| 21 | Nondeductible expenses . . . . . . . . . . | 21 | | |
| 22 | Distributions of money (cash and marketable securities) . . . | 22 | | |
| 23 | Distributions of property other than money . . . . . . | 23 | | |
| 24 | Recapture of low-income housing credit: | | | |
| a | From section 42(j)(5) partnerships . . . . . . . . | 24a | | Form 8611, line 8 |
| b | Other than on line 24a . . . . . . . . . . . | 24b | | |

**Supplemental Information**

25 Supplemental information required to be reported separately to each partner *(attach additional schedules if more space is needed):*

-----------------------------------------------------------------------------------------------------

-----------------------------------------------------------------------------------------------------

-----------------------------------------------------------------------------------------------------

-----------------------------------------------------------------------------------------------------

-----------------------------------------------------------------------------------------------------

-----------------------------------------------------------------------------------------------------

Form **1120-A**
Department of the Treasury
Internal Revenue Service

## U.S. Corporation Short-Form Income Tax Return

For calendar year 2002 or tax year beginning_____, 2002, ending _____, 20____
See separate instructions to make sure the corporation qualifies to file Form 1120-A.

OMB No. 1545-0890

**2002**

| | | |
|---|---|---|
| **A** Check this box if the corp. is a personal service corp. (as defined in Regulations section 1.441-3(c) — see instructions) ☐ | **Use IRS label. Other-wise, print or type.** Name<br><br>Number, street, and room or suite no. (If a P.O. box, see page 7 of instructions.)<br><br>City or town, state, and ZIP code | **B** Employer identification number<br><br>**C** Date incorporated<br><br>**D** Total assets (see page 8 of instructions)<br>$ |

**E** Check applicable boxes:  (1) ☐ Initial return  (2) ☐ Name change  (3) ☐ Address change

**F** Check method of accounting:  (1) ☐ Cash  (2) ☐ Accrual  (3) ☐ Other (specify) ▶

**Income**

| | | |
|---|---|---|
| **1a** Gross receipts or sales | **b** Less returns and allowances | **c** Balance ▶ | **1c** | |
| **2** Cost of goods sold (see page 14 of instructions). | | **2** | |
| **3** Gross profit. Subtract line 2 from line 1c | | **3** | |
| **4** Domestic corporation dividends subject to the 70% deduction | | **4** | |
| **5** Interest | | **5** | |
| **6** Gross rents | | **6** | |
| **7** Gross royalties | | **7** | |
| **8** Capital gain net income (attach Schedule D (Form 1120)) | | **8** | |
| **9** Net gain or (loss) from Form 4797, Part II, line 18 (attach Form 4797) | | **9** | |
| **10** Other income (see page 9 of instructions) | | **10** | |
| **11** **Total income.** Add lines 3 through 10 ▶ | | **11** | |

**Deductions** (See instructions for limitations on deductions.)

| | | |
|---|---|---|
| **12** Compensation of officers (see page 10 of instructions) | **12** | |
| **13** Salaries and wages (less employment credits) | **13** | |
| **14** Repairs and maintenance | **14** | |
| **15** Bad debts | **15** | |
| **16** Rents | **16** | |
| **17** Taxes and licenses | **17** | |
| **18** Interest | **18** | |
| **19** Charitable contributions (see page 11 of instructions for 10% limitation) | **19** | |
| **20** Depreciation (attach Form 4562) | **20** | |
| **21** Less depreciation claimed elsewhere on return | **21a** | **21b** | |
| **22** Other deductions (attach schedule) | **22** | |
| **23** **Total deductions.** Add lines 12 through 22 ▶ | **23** | |
| **24** Taxable income before net operating loss deduction and special deductions. Subtract line 23 from line 11 | **24** | |
| **25** **Less: a** Net operating loss deduction (see page 13 of instructions) | **25a** | |
| **b** Special deductions (see page 13 of instructions) | **25b** | **25c** | |

**Tax and Payments**

| | | |
|---|---|---|
| **26** **Taxable income.** Subtract line 25c from line 24 | **26** | |
| **27** **Total tax** (from page 2, Part I, line 6) | **27** | |
| **28** **Payments:** | | |
| **a** 2001 overpayment credited to 2002 | **28a** | |
| **b** 2002 estimated tax payments | **28b** | |
| **c** Less 2002 refund applied for on Form 4466 | **28c** ( ) Bal ▶ **28d** | |
| **e** Tax deposited with Form 7004 | **28e** | |
| **f** Credit for tax paid on undistributed capital gains (attach Form 2439) | **28f** | |
| **g** Credit for Federal tax on fuels (attach Form 4136). See instructions | **28g** | |
| **h** Total payments. Add lines 28d through 28g | **28h** | |
| **29** Estimated tax penalty (see page 14 of instructions). Check if Form 2220 is attached ▶ ☐ | **29** | |
| **30** **Tax due.** If line 28h is smaller than the total of lines 27 and 29, enter amount owed | **30** | |
| **31** **Overpayment.** If line 28h is larger than the total of lines 27 and 29, enter amount overpaid | **31** | |
| **32** Enter amount of line 31 you want: **Credited to 2003 estimated tax** ▶   Refunded ▶ | **32** | |

**Sign Here**

Under penalties of perjury, I declare that I have examined this return, including accompanying schedules and statements, and to the best of my knowledge and belief, it is true, correct, and complete. Declaration of preparer (other than taxpayer) is based on all information of which preparer has any knowledge.

▶ _____  _____  ▶ _____
Signature of officer          Date          Title

May the IRS discuss this return with the preparer shown below (see instructions)? ☐ **Yes** ☐ **No**

**Paid Preparer's Use Only**

| | | | |
|---|---|---|---|
| Preparer's signature ▶ | | Date | Check if self-employed ☐ | Preparer's SSN or PTIN |
| Firm's name (or yours if self-employed), address, and ZIP code ▶ | | | EIN<br>Phone no. ( ) |

For Paperwork Reduction Act Notice, see page 20 of the instructions.     Cat. No. 11456E     Form **1120-A** (2002)

Form 1120-A (2002)　　　　　　　　　　　　　　　　　　　　　　　　　　　　　Page **2**

## Part I　　Tax Computation (see page 17 of instructions)

| | | |
|---|---|---|
| **1** Income tax. If the corporation is a qualified personal service corporation (see page 17), check here ▶ ☐ | **1** | |
| **2a** General business credit. Check box(es) and indicate which forms are attached. | | |
| ☐ Form 3800　☐ Form(s) (specify) ▶ ............................. | **2a** | |
| **b** Credit for prior year minimum tax (attach Form 8827) . . . . . . . | **2b** | |
| **3** **Total credits.** Add lines 2a and 2b . . . . . . . . . . . | **3** | |
| **4** Subtract line 3 from line 1 . . . . . . . . . . . . . | **4** | |
| **5** Other taxes. Check if from: ☐ Form 4255　☐ Form 8611　☐ Form 8697　☐ Form 8866 | | |
| ☐ Other (attach schedule) . . . . . . . . . . . . | **5** | |
| **6** **Total tax.** Add lines 4 and 5. Enter here and on line 27, page 1 . . . . . . . . . . | **6** | |

## Part II　　Other Information (see page 19 of instructions)

**1** See page 21 and enter the:

**a** Business activity code no. ▶ ............................

**b** Business activity ▶ ............................

**c** Product or service ▶ ............................

**2** At the end of the tax year, did any individual, partnership, estate, or trust own, directly or indirectly, 50% or more of the corporation's voting stock? (For rules of attribution, see section 267(c).) . . . . . . . . . . . ☐ Yes ☐ No

If "Yes," attach a schedule showing name and identifying number.

**3** Enter the amount of tax-exempt interest received or accrued during the tax year . . . . ▶ $ |_____|

**4** Enter total amount of cash distributions and the book value of property distributions (other than cash) made during the tax year . . . . . . . . . . ▶ $ |_____|

**5a** If an amount is entered on line 2, page 1, enter from worksheet on page 14 instr.:

**(1)** Purchases . . . . . . . . |_____|

**(2)** Additional 263A costs (attach schedule) |_____|

**(3)** Other costs (attach schedule) . |_____|

**b** If property is produced or acquired for resale, do the rules of section 263A apply to the corporation? . . . . . ☐ Yes ☐ No

**6** At any time during the 2002 calendar year, did the corporation have an interest in or a signature or other authority over a financial account (such as a bank account, securities account, or other financial account) in a foreign country? ☐ Yes ☐ No

If "Yes," the corporation may have to file Form TD F 90-22.1.

If "Yes," enter the name of the foreign country ▶ ...................

**7** Are the corporation's total receipts (line 1a plus lines 4 through 10 on page 1) for the tax year **and** its total assets at the end of the tax year less than $250,000? . . . . . . . . ☐ Yes ☐ No

If "Yes," the corporation is **not** required to complete Parts III and IV below.

## Part III　　Balance Sheets per Books

| | | (a) Beginning of tax year | | (b) End of tax year | |
|---|---|---|---|---|---|
| **Assets** | **1** Cash . . . . . . . . . | | | | |
| | **2a** Trade notes and accounts receivable . . . . . | | | | |
| | **b** Less allowance for bad debts . . . . . . | ( | ) | ( | ) |
| | **3** Inventories . . . . . . . | | | | |
| | **4** U.S. government obligations . . . . . | | | | |
| | **5** Tax-exempt securities (see instructions) . . . . . | | | | |
| | **6** Other current assets (attach schedule) . . . . | | | | |
| | **7** Loans to shareholders . . . . . | | | | |
| | **8** Mortgage and real estate loans . . . . | | | | |
| | **9a** Depreciable, depletable, and intangible assets . . . . | | | | |
| | **b** Less accumulated depreciation, depletion, and amortization | ( | ) | ( | ) |
| | **10** Land (net of any amortization) . . . . . | | | | |
| | **11** Other assets (attach schedule) . . . . . | | | | |
| | **12** Total assets . . . . . . . . . | | | | |
| **Liabilities and Shareholders' Equity** | **13** Accounts payable . . . . . | | | | |
| | **14** Other current liabilities (attach schedule) . . . . | | | | |
| | **15** Loans from shareholders . . . . . | | | | |
| | **16** Mortgages, notes, bonds payable . . . . | | | | |
| | **17** Other liabilities (attach schedule) . . . . | | | | |
| | **18** Capital stock (preferred and common stock) . . . . | | | | |
| | **19** Additional paid-in capital . . . . . | | | | |
| | **20** Retained earnings . . . . . . . | | | | |
| | **21** Adjustments to shareholders' equity (attach schedule) . | | | | |
| | **22** Less cost of treasury stock . . . . | ( | ) | ( | ) |
| | **23** Total liabilities and shareholders' equity . . . . . | | | | |

## Part IV　　Reconciliation of Income (Loss) per Books With Income per Return

| | | | |
|---|---|---|---|
| **1** Net income (loss) per books . . . . . . | | **6** Income recorded on books this year not included on this return (itemize).................. | |
| **2** Federal income tax per books . . . . . | | | |
| **3** Excess of capital losses over capital gains . . | | **7** Deductions on this return not charged against book income this year (itemize)................ | |
| **4** Income subject to tax not recorded on books this year (itemize) .................. | | | |
| **5** Expenses recorded on books this year not deducted on this return (itemize) | | **8** Income (line 24, page 1). Enter the sum of lines 1 through 5 less the sum of lines 6 and 7 | |

Form **1120-A** (2002)

**Form 1120**
Department of the Treasury
Internal Revenue Service

## U.S. Corporation Income Tax Return

For calendar year 2002 or tax year beginning _____ , 2002, ending _____ , 20 ____
▶ **Instructions are separate. See page 20 for Paperwork Reduction Act Notice.**

OMB No. 1545-0123

**2002**

**A  Check if a:**
1  Consolidated return (attach Form 851) ☐
2  Personal holding co. (attach Sch. PH) ☐
3  Personal service corp. (as defined in Regulations sec. 1.441-3(c) — see instructions) ☐

Use IRS label. Otherwise, print or type.

Name

Number, street, and room or suite no. (If a P.O. box, see page 7 of instructions.)

City or town, state, and ZIP code

**B  Employer identification number**

**C  Date incorporated**

**D  Total assets (see page 8 of instructions)**

**E**  Check applicable boxes:  (1) ☐ Initial return  (2) ☐ Final return  (3) ☐ Name change  (4) ☐ Address change  $

### Income

| | | | |
|---|---|---|---|
| 1a | Gross receipts or sales _____  **b** Less returns and allowances _____  **c** Bal | 1c | |
| 2 | Cost of goods sold (Schedule A, line 8) | 2 | |
| 3 | Gross profit. Subtract line 2 from line 1c | 3 | |
| 4 | Dividends (Schedule C, line 19) | 4 | |
| 5 | Interest | 5 | |
| 6 | Gross rents | 6 | |
| 7 | Gross royalties | 7 | |
| 8 | Capital gain net income (attach Schedule D (Form 1120)) | 8 | |
| 9 | Net gain or (loss) from Form 4797, Part II, line 18 (attach Form 4797) | 9 | |
| 10 | Other income (see page 9 of instructions — attach schedule) | 10 | |
| 11 | **Total income.** Add lines 3 through 10 ▶ | 11 | |

### Deductions (See instructions for limitations on deductions.)

| | | | |
|---|---|---|---|
| 12 | Compensation of officers (Schedule E, line 4) | 12 | |
| 13 | Salaries and wages (less employment credits) | 13 | |
| 14 | Repairs and maintenance | 14 | |
| 15 | Bad debts | 15 | |
| 16 | Rents | 16 | |
| 17 | Taxes and licenses | 17 | |
| 18 | Interest | 18 | |
| 19 | Charitable contributions (see page 11 of instructions for 10% limitation) | 19 | |
| 20 | Depreciation (attach Form 4562)  20 | | |
| 21 | Less depreciation claimed on Schedule A and elsewhere on return  21a | 21b | |
| 22 | Depletion | 22 | |
| 23 | Advertising | 23 | |
| 24 | Pension, profit-sharing, etc., plans | 24 | |
| 25 | Employee benefit programs | 25 | |
| 26 | Other deductions (attach schedule) | 26 | |
| 27 | **Total deductions.** Add lines 12 through 26 ▶ | 27 | |
| 28 | Taxable income before net operating loss deduction and special deductions. Subtract line 27 from line 11 | 28 | |
| 29 | **Less:**  **a** Net operating loss (NOL) deduction (see page 13 of instructions)  29a | | |
| | **b** Special deductions (Schedule C, line 20)  29b | 29c | |

### Tax and Payments

| | | | |
|---|---|---|---|
| 30 | **Taxable income.** Subtract line 29c from line 28 | 30 | |
| 31 | **Total tax** (Schedule J, line 11) | 31 | |
| 32 | Payments: **a** 2001 overpayment credited to 2002  32a | | |
| **b** | 2002 estimated tax payments  32b | | |
| **c** | Less 2002 refund applied for on Form 4466  32c (_____)  **d** Bal ▶ 32d | | |
| **e** | Tax deposited with Form 7004  32e | | |
| **f** | Credit for tax paid on undistributed capital gains (attach Form 2439)  32f | | |
| **g** | Credit for Federal tax on fuels (attach Form 4136). See instructions  32g | 32h | |
| 33 | Estimated tax penalty (see page 14 of instructions). Check if Form 2220 is attached ▶ ☐ | 33 | |
| 34 | **Tax due.** If line 32h is smaller than the total of lines 31 and 33, enter amount owed | 34 | |
| 35 | **Overpayment.** If line 32h is larger than the total of lines 31 and 33, enter amount overpaid | 35 | |
| 36 | Enter amount of line 35 you want: **Credited to 2003 estimated tax** ▶  **Refunded** ▶ | 36 | |

**Sign Here**

Under penalties of perjury, I declare that I have examined this return, including accompanying schedules and statements, and to the best of my knowledge and belief, it is true, correct, and complete. Declaration of preparer (other than taxpayer) is based on all information of which preparer has any knowledge.

▶ _____  _____  ▶ _____
Signature of officer          Date               Title

May the IRS discuss this return with the preparer shown below (see instructions)? ☐ **Yes**  ☐ **No**

**Paid Preparer's Use Only**

| Preparer's signature ▶ | Date | Check if self-employed ☐ | Preparer's SSN or PTIN |
|---|---|---|---|
| Firm's name (or yours if self-employed), address, and ZIP code ▶ | | EIN | Phone no. (    ) |

Cat. No. 11450Q

Form **1120** (2002)

Form 1120 (2002)                  Page **2**

## Schedule A    Cost of Goods Sold (see page 14 of instructions)

| | | | |
|---|---|---|---|
| 1 | Inventory at beginning of year | 1 | |
| 2 | Purchases | 2 | |
| 3 | Cost of labor | 3 | |
| 4 | Additional section 263A costs (attach schedule) | 4 | |
| 5 | Other costs (attach schedule) | 5 | |
| 6 | **Total.** Add lines 1 through 5 | 6 | |
| 7 | Inventory at end of year | 7 | |
| 8 | **Cost of goods sold.** Subtract line 7 from line 6. Enter here and on line 2, page 1 | 8 | |

9a   Check all methods used for valuing closing inventory:

     (i) ☐   Cost as described in Regulations section 1.471-3

     (ii) ☐   Lower of cost or market as described in Regulations section 1.471-4

     (iii) ☐   Other (Specify method used and attach explanation.) ▶ _____

   b   Check if there was a writedown of subnormal goods as described in Regulations section 1.471-2(c) . . . . . . . . ▶ ☐

   c   Check if the LIFO inventory method was adopted this tax year for any goods (if checked, attach Form 970) . . . . . . ▶ ☐

   d   If the LIFO inventory method was used for this tax year, enter percentage (or amounts) of closing inventory computed under LIFO . . . . . . . . . . . . . . . . . . . . 9d | |

   e   If property is produced or acquired for resale, do the rules of section 263A apply to the corporation? . . . . . ☐ Yes   ☐ No

   f   Was there any change in determining quantities, cost, or valuations between opening and closing inventory? If "Yes," attach explanation . . . . . . . . . . . . . . . . . . . . . . . . . . . . . . . . ☐ Yes   ☐ No

## Schedule C    Dividends and Special Deductions (see instructions beginning on page 15)

| | | (a) Dividends received | (b) % | (c) Special deductions (a) × (b) |
|---|---|---|---|---|
| 1 | Dividends from less-than-20%-owned domestic corporations that are subject to the 70% deduction (other than debt-financed stock) | | 70 | |
| 2 | Dividends from 20%-or-more-owned domestic corporations that are subject to the 80% deduction (other than debt-financed stock) | | 80 | |
| 3 | Dividends on debt-financed stock of domestic and foreign corporations (section 246A) | | see instructions | |
| 4 | Dividends on certain preferred stock of less-than-20%-owned public utilities | | 42 | |
| 5 | Dividends on certain preferred stock of 20%-or-more-owned public utilities | | 48 | |
| 6 | Dividends from less-than-20%-owned foreign corporations and certain FSCs that are subject to the 70% deduction | | 70 | |
| 7 | Dividends from 20%-or-more-owned foreign corporations and certain FSCs that are subject to the 80% deduction | | 80 | |
| 8 | Dividends from wholly owned foreign subsidiaries subject to the 100% deduction (section 245(b)) | | 100 | |
| 9 | **Total.** Add lines 1 through 8. See page 16 of instructions for limitation | //// | //// | |
| 10 | Dividends from domestic corporations received by a small business investment company operating under the Small Business Investment Act of 1958 | | 100 | |
| 11 | Dividends from certain FSCs that are subject to the 100% deduction (section 245(c)(1)) | | 100 | |
| 12 | Dividends from affiliated group members subject to the 100% deduction (section 243(a)(3)) | | 100 | |
| 13 | Other dividends from foreign corporations not included on lines 3, 6, 7, 8, or 11 | | //// | //// |
| 14 | Income from controlled foreign corporations under subpart F (attach Form(s) 5471) | | //// | //// |
| 15 | Foreign dividend gross-up (section 78) | | //// | //// |
| 16 | IC-DISC and former DISC dividends not included on lines 1, 2, or 3 (section 246(d)) | | //// | //// |
| 17 | Other dividends | | //// | //// |
| 18 | Deduction for dividends paid on certain preferred stock of public utilities | //// | | |
| 19 | **Total dividends.** Add lines 1 through 17. Enter here and on line 4, page 1 ▶ | | //// | //// |
| 20 | **Total special deductions.** Add lines 9, 10, 11, 12, and 18. Enter here and on line 29b, page 1 . . . . . ▶ | | | |

## Schedule E    Compensation of Officers (see instructions for line 12, page 1, on page 10 of instructions)

Note: *Complete Schedule E only if total receipts (line 1a plus lines 4 through 10 on page 1) are $500,000 or more.*

| (a) Name of officer | (b) Social security number | (c) Percent of time devoted to business | Percent of corporation stock owned | | (f) Amount of compensation |
|---|---|---|---|---|---|
| | | | (d) Common | (e) Preferred | |
| 1 | | % | % | % | |
| | | % | % | % | |
| | | % | % | % | |
| | | % | % | % | |
| | | % | % | % | |

| | | | |
|---|---|---|---|
| 2 | Total compensation of officers | | |
| 3 | Compensation of officers claimed on Schedule A and elsewhere on return | | |
| 4 | Subtract line 3 from line 2. Enter the result here and on line 12, page 1 | | |

Form **1120** (2002)

Form 1120 (2002)                                                                           Page **3**

## Schedule J | Tax Computation (see page 17 of instructions)

1  Check if the corporation is a member of a controlled group (see sections 1561 and 1563) . . . . ▶ ☐

   **Important:** Members of a controlled group, see instructions on page 17.

2a  If the box on line 1 is checked, enter the corporation's share of the $50,000, $25,000, and $9,925,000 taxable income brackets (in that order):

   **(1)** $_____   **(2)** $_____   **(3)** $_____

 b  Enter the corporation's share of: **(1)** Additional 5% tax (not more than $11,750)  $_____

   **(2)** Additional 3% tax (not more than $100,000)  $_____

3  Income tax. Check if a qualified personal service corporation under section 448(d)(2) (see page 17) . . ▶ ☐  **3**

4  Alternative minimum tax (attach Form 4626) . . . . . . . . . . . . . . . . . .  **4**

5  Add lines 3 and 4 . . . . . . . . . . . . . . . . . . . . . . . . . . . .  **5**

6a  Foreign tax credit (attach Form 1118) . . . . . . . . . . .  **6a**

 b  Possessions tax credit (attach Form 5735) . . . . . . . . . .  **6b**

 c  Check: ☐ Nonconventional source fuel credit  ☐ QEV credit (attach Form 8834)  **6c**

 d  General business credit. Check box(es) and indicate which forms are attached.

   ☐ Form 3800   ☐ Form(s) (specify) ▶ _____  **6d**

 e  Credit for prior year minimum tax (attach Form 8827) . . . . . . . . .  **6e**

 f  Qualified zone academy bond credit (attach Form 8860) . . . . . . . .  **6f**

7  **Total credits.** Add lines 6a through 6f  . . . . . . . . . . . . . . . . .  **7**

8  Subtract line 7 from line 5  . . . . . . . . . . . . . . . . . . . . . . .  **8**

9  Personal holding company tax (attach Schedule PH (Form 1120)) . . . . . . . . . .  **9**

10  Other taxes. Check if from: ☐ Form 4255   ☐ Form 8611   ☐ Form 8697

   ☐ Form 8866   ☐ Other (attach schedule) . . . . . . . .  **10**

11  **Total tax.** Add lines 8 through 10. Enter here and on line 31, page 1 . . . . . . . .  **11**

## Schedule K | Other Information (see page 19 of instructions)

| | | Yes | No |
|---|---|---|---|

1  Check method of accounting: **a** ☐ Cash

   **b** ☐ Accrual   **c** ☐ Other (specify) ▶ _____

2  See page 21 of the instructions and enter the:

 a  Business activity code no. ▶ _____

 b  Business activity ▶ _____

 c  Product or service ▶ _____

3  At the end of the tax year, did the corporation own, directly or indirectly, 50% or more of the voting stock of a domestic corporation? (For rules of attribution, see section 267(c).) . . . . . . . . .

   If "Yes," attach a schedule showing: **(a)** name and employer identification number (EIN), **(b)** percentage owned, and **(c)** taxable income or (loss) before NOL and special deductions of such corporation for the tax year ending with or within your tax year.

4  Is the corporation a subsidiary in an affiliated group or a parent-subsidiary controlled group? . . . . . .

   If "Yes," enter name and EIN of the parent corporation ▶ _____

5  At the end of the tax year, did any individual, partnership, corporation, estate, or trust own, directly or indirectly, 50% or more of the corporation's voting stock? (For rules of attribution, see section 267(c).) . . . . . . .
   If "Yes," attach a schedule showing name and identifying number. (Do not include any information already entered in **4** above.) Enter percentage owned ▶ _____

6  During this tax year, did the corporation pay dividends (other than stock dividends and distributions in exchange for stock) in excess of the corporation's current and accumulated earnings and profits? (See sections 301 and 316.) . . .

   If "Yes," file **Form 5452,** Corporate Report of Nondividend Distributions.

   If this is a consolidated return, answer here for the parent corporation and on **Form 851,** Affiliations Schedule, for each subsidiary.

7  At any time during the tax year, did one foreign person own, directly or indirectly, at least 25% of **(a)** the total voting power of all classes of stock of the corporation entitled to vote or **(b)** the total value of all classes of stock of the corporation? . . . . . . . . . . .

   If "Yes," enter: **(a)** Percentage owned ▶ _____

   and **(b)** Owner's country ▶ _____

 c  The corporation may have to file **Form 5472,** Information Return of a 25% Foreign-Owned U.S. Corporation or a Foreign Corporation Engaged in a U.S. Trade or Business. Enter number of Forms 5472 attached ▶ _____

8  Check this box if the corporation issued publicly offered debt instruments with original issue discount . . ▶ ☐

   If checked, the corporation may have to file **Form 8281,** Information Return for Publicly Offered Original Issue Discount Instruments.

9  Enter the amount of tax-exempt interest received or accrued during the tax year ▶ $ _____

10  Enter the number of shareholders at the end of the tax year (if 75 or fewer) ▶ _____

11  If the corporation has an NOL for the tax year and is electing to forego the carryback period, check here ▶ ☐

   If the corporation is filing a consolidated return, the statement required by Regulations section 1.1502-21(b)(3)(i) or (ii) must be attached or the election will not be valid.

12  Enter the available NOL carryover from prior tax years (Do not reduce it by any deduction on line 29a.) ▶ $ _____

13  Are the corporation's total receipts (line 1a plus lines 4 through 10 on page 1) for the tax year **and** its total assets at the end of the tax year less than $250,000? . . . .

   If "Yes," the corporation is not required to complete Schedules L, M-1, and M-2 on page 4. Instead, enter the total amount of cash distributions and the book value of property distributions (other than cash) made during the tax year. ▶ $ _____

**Note:** *If the corporation, at any time during the tax year, had assets or operated a business in a foreign country or U.S. possession, it may be required to attach* **Schedule N (Form 1120),** *Foreign Operations of U.S. Corporations, to this return. See Schedule N for details.*

Form **1120** (2002)

Form 1120 (2002)                                                                                                Page **4**

**Note:** *The corporation is not required to complete Schedules L, M-1, and M-2 if Question 13 on Schedule K is answered "Yes."*

| **Schedule L** | **Balance Sheets per Books** | \multicolumn{2}{c\|}{Beginning of tax year} | \multicolumn{2}{c\|}{End of tax year} |
|---|---|---|---|---|---|
| | **Assets** | (a) | (b) | (c) | (d) |
| 1 | Cash | | | | |
| 2a | Trade notes and accounts receivable | | | | |
| b | Less allowance for bad debts | ( ) | | ( ) | |
| 3 | Inventories | | | | |
| 4 | U.S. government obligations | | | | |
| 5 | Tax-exempt securities (see instructions) | | | | |
| 6 | Other current assets (attach schedule) | | | | |
| 7 | Loans to shareholders | | | | |
| 8 | Mortgage and real estate loans | | | | |
| 9 | Other investments (attach schedule) | | | | |
| 10a | Buildings and other depreciable assets | | | | |
| b | Less accumulated depreciation | ( ) | | ( ) | |
| 11a | Depletable assets | | | | |
| b | Less accumulated depletion | ( ) | | ( ) | |
| 12 | Land (net of any amortization) | | | | |
| 13a | Intangible assets (amortizable only) | | | | |
| b | Less accumulated amortization | ( ) | | ( ) | |
| 14 | Other assets (attach schedule) | | | | |
| 15 | Total assets | | | | |
| | **Liabilities and Shareholders' Equity** | | | | |
| 16 | Accounts payable | | | | |
| 17 | Mortgages, notes, bonds payable in less than 1 year | | | | |
| 18 | Other current liabilities (attach schedule) | | | | |
| 19 | Loans from shareholders | | | | |
| 20 | Mortgages, notes, bonds payable in 1 year or more | | | | |
| 21 | Other liabilities (attach schedule) | | | | |
| 22 | Capital stock:   **a** Preferred stock | | | | |
| | **b** Common stock | | | | |
| 23 | Additional paid-in capital | | | | |
| 24 | Retained earnings—Appropriated (attach schedule) | | | | |
| 25 | Retained earnings—Unappropriated | | | | |
| 26 | Adjustments to shareholders' equity (attach schedule) | | | | |
| 27 | Less cost of treasury stock | | ( ) | | ( ) |
| 28 | Total liabilities and shareholders' equity | | | | |

| **Schedule M-1** | **Reconciliation of Income (Loss) per Books With Income per Return** (see page 20 of instructions) |
|---|---|

| 1 | Net income (loss) per books | | 7 | Income recorded on books this year not included on this return (itemize): | |
| 2 | Federal income tax per books | | | Tax-exempt interest $ ............ | |
| 3 | Excess of capital losses over capital gains | | | ............................ | |
| 4 | Income subject to tax not recorded on books this year (itemize): ............ | | | ............................ | |
| | ............................ | | 8 | Deductions on this return not charged against book income this year (itemize): | |
| 5 | Expenses recorded on books this year not deducted on this return (itemize): | | **a** | Depreciation . . . . $............ | |
| **a** | Depreciation . . . . $............ | | **b** | Charitable contributions $............ | |
| **b** | Charitable contributions $............ | | | ............................ | |
| **c** | Travel and entertainment $............ | | 9 | Add lines 7 and 8 | |
| 6 | Add lines 1 through 5 | | 10 | Income (line 28, page 1)—line 6 less line 9 | |

| **Schedule M-2** | **Analysis of Unappropriated Retained Earnings per Books (Line 25, Schedule L)** |
|---|---|

| 1 | Balance at beginning of year | | 5 | Distributions:   **a** Cash | |
| 2 | Net income (loss) per books | | | **b** Stock | |
| 3 | Other increases (itemize): ............ | | | **c** Property | |
| | ............................ | | 6 | Other decreases (itemize): ............ | |
| | ............................ | | 7 | Add lines 5 and 6 | |
| 4 | Add lines 1, 2, and 3 | | 8 | Balance at end of year (line 4 less line 7) | |

Form **1120** (2002)

Form **1120S**

Department of the Treasury
Internal Revenue Service

# U.S. Income Tax Return for an S Corporation

▶ Do not file this form unless the corporation has timely filed
Form 2553 to elect to be an S corporation.
▶ See separate instructions.

OMB No. 1545-0130

**2002**

For calendar year 2002, or tax year beginning _____ , 2002, and ending _____ , 20 _____

| A Effective date of election as an S corporation | Use IRS label. Other-wise, print or type. | Name | C Employer identification number |
| --- | --- | --- | --- |
| | | Number, street, and room or suite no. (If a P.O. box, see page 11 of the instructions.) | D Date incorporated |
| B Business code no. (see pages 29–31) | | City or town, state, and ZIP code | E Total assets (see page 11) $ |

F Check applicable boxes: (1) ☐ Initial return  (2) ☐ Final return  (3) ☐ Name change  (4) ☐ Address change  (5) ☐ Amended return
G Enter number of shareholders in the corporation at end of the tax year . . . . . . . . . . . . . . . . . . . .

**Caution:** *Include **only** trade or business income and expenses on lines 1a through 21. See page 11 of the instructions for more information.*

### Income

| | | |
| --- | --- | --- |
| 1a Gross receipts or sales _____ b Less returns and allowances _____ | c Bal | **1c** |
| 2 Cost of goods sold (Schedule A, line 8) . . . . . . . . . . | | **2** |
| 3 Gross profit. Subtract line 2 from line 1c . . . . . . . . . | | **3** |
| 4 Net gain (loss) from Form 4797, Part II, line 18 *(attach Form 4797)* . . . . | | **4** |
| 5 Other income (loss) *(attach schedule)*. . . . . . . . . . | | **5** |
| 6 **Total income (loss).** Combine lines 3 through 5 . . . . . . . . ▶ | | **6** |

### Deductions (see page 12 of the instructions for limitations)

| | |
| --- | --- |
| 7 Compensation of officers . . . . . . . . . . . . . | **7** |
| 8 Salaries and wages (less employment credits) . . . . . . . . | **8** |
| 9 Repairs and maintenance . . . . . . . . . . . . . | **9** |
| 10 Bad debts . . . . . . . . . . . . . . . . . | **10** |
| 11 Rents. . . . . . . . . . . . . . . . . . . | **11** |
| 12 Taxes and licenses . . . . . . . . . . . . . . | **12** |
| 13 Interest . . . . . . . . . . . . . . . . . . | **13** |
| 14a Depreciation *(if required, attach Form 4562)* . . . . . . | **14a** |
| b Depreciation claimed on Schedule A and elsewhere on return . . | **14b** |
| c Subtract line 14b from line 14a . . . . . . . . . . . | **14c** |
| 15 Depletion **(Do not deduct oil and gas depletion.)** . . . . . . | **15** |
| 16 Advertising . . . . . . . . . . . . . . . . . | **16** |
| 17 Pension, profit-sharing, etc., plans . . . . . . . . . . | **17** |
| 18 Employee benefit programs. . . . . . . . . . . . . | **18** |
| 19 Other deductions *(attach schedule)* . . . . . . . . . . | **19** |
| 20 **Total deductions.** Add the amounts shown in the far right column for lines 7 through 19 . ▶ | **20** |
| 21 Ordinary income (loss) from trade or business activities. Subtract line 20 from line 6. . . . | **21** |

### Tax and Payments

| | | |
| --- | --- | --- |
| 22 **Tax: a** Excess net passive income tax *(attach schedule)* . . . | **22a** | |
| **b** Tax from Schedule D (Form 1120S) | **22b** | |
| **c** Add lines 22a and 22b (see page 16 of the instructions for additional taxes) . . . . . | | **22c** |
| 23 **Payments: a** 2002 estimated tax payments and amount applied from 2001 return | **23a** | |
| **b** Tax deposited with Form 7004. . . . . . . . . . | **23b** | |
| **c** Credit for Federal tax paid on fuels *(attach Form 4136)* . . . . | **23c** | |
| **d** Add lines 23a through 23c . . . . . . . . . . . ▶ | | **23d** |
| 24 Estimated tax penalty. Check if Form 2220 is attached . . . . . . . . . . ▶ ☐ | | **24** |
| 25 **Tax due.** If the total of lines 22c and 24 is larger than line 23d, enter amount owed. See page 4 of the instructions for depository method of payment . . . . . . . . . . . ▶ | | **25** |
| 26 **Overpayment.** If line 23d is larger than the total of lines 22c and 24, enter amount overpaid ▶ | | **26** |
| 27 Enter amount of line 26 you want: **Credited to 2003 estimated tax** ▶ _____ | Refunded ▶ | **27** |

**Sign Here**

Under penalties of perjury, I declare that I have examined this return, including accompanying schedules and statements, and to the best of my knowledge and belief, it is true, correct, and complete. Declaration of preparer (other than taxpayer) is based on all information of which preparer has any knowledge.

▶ _____  _____  ▶ _____
Signature of officer            Date         Title

May the IRS discuss this return with the preparer shown below (see instructions)? ☐ Yes ☐ No

**Paid Preparer's Use Only**

| Preparer's signature ▶ | Date | Check if self-employed ☐ | Preparer's SSN or PTIN |
| --- | --- | --- | --- |
| Firm's name (or yours if self-employed), address, and ZIP code ▶ | | EIN | |
| | | Phone no. ( ) | |

**For Paperwork Reduction Act Notice, see the separate instructions.**          Cat. No. 11510H          Form **1120S** (2002)

Form 1120S (2002) Page **2**

## Schedule A — Cost of Goods Sold (see page 17 of the instructions)

| | | |
|---|---|---|
| 1 | Inventory at beginning of year | 1 |
| 2 | Purchases | 2 |
| 3 | Cost of labor | 3 |
| 4 | Additional section 263A costs (attach schedule) | 4 |
| 5 | Other costs (attach schedule) | 5 |
| 6 | **Total.** Add lines 1 through 5 | 6 |
| 7 | Inventory at end of year | 7 |
| 8 | **Cost of goods sold.** Subtract line 7 from line 6. Enter here and on page 1, line 2 | 8 |

9a Check all methods used for valuing closing inventory:  (i) ☐ Cost as described in Regulations section 1.471-3

    (ii) ☐ Lower of cost or market as described in Regulations section 1.471-4

    (iii) ☐ Other (specify method used and attach explanation) ▶ ............................................................

  **b** Check if there was a writedown of "subnormal" goods as described in Regulations section 1.471-2(c) . . . . . . . . ▶ ☐

  **c** Check if the LIFO inventory method was adopted this tax year for any goods (if checked, attach Form 970) . . . . . . ▶ ☐

  **d** If the LIFO inventory method was used for this tax year, enter percentage (or amounts) of closing inventory computed under LIFO . . . . . . . . . . . . . . . 9d

  **e** Do the rules of section 263A (for property produced or acquired for resale) apply to the corporation? . . . . ☐ Yes ☐ No

  **f** Was there any change in determining quantities, cost, or valuations between opening and closing inventory? . . ☐ Yes ☐ No
If "Yes," attach explanation.

## Schedule B — Other Information

| | | Yes | No |
|---|---|---|---|
| 1 | Check method of accounting: **(a)** ☐ Cash **(b)** ☐ Accrual **(c)** ☐ Other (specify) ▶ .................... | | |
| 2 | Refer to the list on pages 29 through 31 of the instructions and state the corporation's principal: **(a)** Business activity ▶ ................................ **(b)** Product or service ▶ .......................... | | |
| 3 | Did the corporation at the end of the tax year own, directly or indirectly, 50% or more of the voting stock of a domestic corporation? (For rules of attribution, see section 267(c).) If "Yes," attach a schedule showing: **(a)** name, address, and employer identification number and **(b)** percentage owned . . . . . . . . . . . . . . . | | |
| 4 | Was the corporation a member of a controlled group subject to the provisions of section 1561? . . . . . . . | | |
| 5 | Check this box if the corporation has filed or is required to file **Form 8264,** Application for Registration of a Tax Shelter ▶ ☐ | | |
| 6 | Check this box if the corporation issued publicly offered debt instruments with original issue discount . . ▶ ☐ If so, the corporation may have to file **Form 8281,** Information Return for Publicly Offered Original Issue Discount Instruments. | | |
| 7 | If the corporation: **(a)** was a C corporation before it elected to be an S corporation **or** the corporation acquired an asset with a basis determined by reference to its basis (or the basis of any other property) in the hands of a C corporation **and (b)** has net unrealized built-in gain (defined in section 1374(d)(1)) in excess of the net recognized built-in gain from prior years, enter the net unrealized built-in gain reduced by net recognized built-in gain from prior years (see page 17 of the instructions) . . . . . . . . . . . ▶ $ ................................ | | |
| 8 | Check this box if the corporation had accumulated earnings and profits at the close of the tax year (see page 18 of the instructions) . . . . . . . . . . . . . . . . . . . . ▶ ☐ | | |
| 9 | Are the corporation's total receipts (see page 29 of the instructions) for the tax year **and** total assets at the end of the tax year less than $250,000? If "Yes," the corporation is not required to complete Schedules L and M-1. | | |

**Note:** *If the corporation had assets or operated a business in a foreign country or U.S. possession, it may be required to attach* **Schedule N (Form 1120),** *Foreign Operations of U.S. Corporations, to this return. See Schedule N for details.*

## Schedule K — Shareholders' Shares of Income, Credits, Deductions, etc.

| | (a) Pro rata share items | | (b) Total amount |
|---|---|---|---|
| Income (Loss) | **1** Ordinary income (loss) from trade or business activities (page 1, line 21) . . . . . . . | 1 | |
| | **2** Net income (loss) from rental real estate activities (attach Form 8825) . . . . . . | 2 | |
| | **3a** Gross income from other rental activities . . . . . | 3a | |
| |   **b** Expenses from other rental activities (attach schedule) . | 3b | |
| |   **c** Net income (loss) from other rental activities. Subtract line 3b from line 3a . . . . . | 3c | |
| | **4** Portfolio income (loss): | | |
| |   **a** Interest income . . . . . . . . . . . . . . . | 4a | |
| |   **b** Ordinary dividends . . . . . . . . . . . . . . | 4b | |
| |   **c** Royalty income . . . . . . . . . . . . . . . | 4c | |
| |   **d** Net short-term capital gain (loss) (attach Schedule D (Form 1120S)). . . . . . . . | 4d | |
| |   **e (1)** Net long-term capital gain (loss) (attach Schedule D (Form 1120S)). . . . . . | 4e(1) | |
| |     **(2)** 28% rate gain (loss) ▶ .............. **(3)** Qualified 5-year gain ▶ .................. | | |
| |   **f** Other portfolio income (loss) (attach schedule). . . . . . . . . . . . . . . . | 4f | |
| | **5** Net section 1231 gain (loss) (other than due to casualty or theft) (attach Form 4797) . . | 5 | |
| | **6** Other income (loss) (attach schedule) . . . . . . . . . . . . . . . . . . | 6 | |

Form **1120S** (2002)

| Schedule K | Shareholders' Shares of Income, Credits, Deductions, etc. *(continued)* | | |
|---|---|---|---|

| | **(a)** Pro rata share items | | **(b)** Total amount | |
|---|---|---|---|---|
| **Deductions** | **7** Charitable contributions *(attach schedule)* | **7** | | |
| | **8** Section 179 expense deduction *(attach Form 4562)* | **8** | | |
| | **9** Deductions related to portfolio income (loss) (itemize) | **9** | | |
| | **10** Other deductions *(attach schedule)* | **10** | | |
| **Investment Interest** | **11a** Interest expense on investment debts | **11a** | | |
| | **b (1)** Investment income included on lines 4a, 4b, 4c, and 4f above | **11b(1)** | | |
| | **(2)** Investment expenses included on line 9 above | **11b(2)** | | |
| **Credits** | **12a** Credit for alcohol used as a fuel *(attach Form 6478)* | **12a** | | |
| | **b** Low-income housing credit: | | | |
| | **(1)** From partnerships to which section 42(j)(5) applies | **12b(1)** | | |
| | **(2)** Other than on line 12b(1) | **12b(2)** | | |
| | **c** Qualified rehabilitation expenditures related to rental real estate activities *(attach Form 3468)* | **12c** | | |
| | **d** Credits (other than credits shown on lines 12b and 12c) related to rental real estate activities | **12d** | | |
| | **e** Credits related to other rental activities | **12e** | | |
| | **13** Other credits | **13** | | |
| **Adjustments and Tax Preference Items** | **14a** Depreciation adjustment on property placed in service after 1986 | **14a** | | |
| | **b** Adjusted gain or loss | **14b** | | |
| | **c** Depletion (other than oil and gas) | **14c** | | |
| | **d (1)** Gross income from oil, gas, or geothermal properties | **14d(1)** | | |
| | **(2)** Deductions allocable to oil, gas, or geothermal properties | **14d(2)** | | |
| | **e** Other adjustments and tax preference items *(attach schedule)* | **14e** | | |
| **Foreign Taxes** | **15a** Name of foreign country or U.S. possession ▶ ......................... | | | |
| | **b** Gross income from all sources | **15b** | | |
| | **c** Gross income sourced at shareholder level | **15c** | | |
| | **d** Foreign gross income sourced at corporate level: | | | |
| | **(1)** Passive | **15d(1)** | | |
| | **(2)** Listed categories *(attach schedule)* | **15d(2)** | | |
| | **(3)** General limitation | **15d(3)** | | |
| | **e** Deductions allocated and apportioned at shareholder level: | | | |
| | **(1)** Interest expense | **15e(1)** | | |
| | **(2)** Other | **15e(2)** | | |
| | **f** Deductions allocated and apportioned at corporate level to foreign source income: | | | |
| | **(1)** Passive | **15f(1)** | | |
| | **(2)** Listed categories *(attach schedule)* | **15f(2)** | | |
| | **(3)** General limitation | **15f(3)** | | |
| | **g** Total foreign taxes (check one): ▶ ☐ Paid  ☐ Accrued | **15g** | | |
| | **h** Reduction in taxes available for credit *(attach schedule)* | **15h** | | |
| **Other** | **16** Section 59(e)(2) expenditures: **a** Type ▶ ......................... **b** Amount ▶ | **16b** | | |
| | **17** Tax-exempt interest income | **17** | | |
| | **18** Other tax-exempt income | **18** | | |
| | **19** Nondeductible expenses | **19** | | |
| | **20** Total property distributions (including cash) other than dividends reported on line 22 below | **20** | | |
| | **21** Other items and amounts required to be reported separately to shareholders *(attach schedule)* | | | |
| | **22** Total dividend distributions paid from accumulated earnings and profits | **22** | | |
| | **23** **Income (loss).** (Required only if Schedule M-1 must be completed.) Combine lines 1 through 6 in column (b). From the result, subtract the sum of lines 7 through 11a, 15g, and 16b | **23** | | |

Form **1120S** (2002)

Form 1120S (2002)            Page **4**

**Note:** The corporation is not required to complete Schedules L and M-1 if question 9 of Schedule B is answered "Yes."

**Schedule L**   **Balance Sheets per Books**

| Assets | Beginning of tax year | | End of tax year | |
|---|---|---|---|---|
| | (a) | (b) | (c) | (d) |
| **1** Cash | | | | |
| **2a** Trade notes and accounts receivable | | | | |
| **b** Less allowance for bad debts | | | | |
| **3** Inventories | | | | |
| **4** U.S. Government obligations | | | | |
| **5** Tax-exempt securities | | | | |
| **6** Other current assets (attach schedule) | | | | |
| **7** Loans to shareholders | | | | |
| **8** Mortgage and real estate loans | | | | |
| **9** Other investments (attach schedule) | | | | |
| **10a** Buildings and other depreciable assets | | | | |
| **b** Less accumulated depreciation | | | | |
| **11a** Depletable assets | | | | |
| **b** Less accumulated depletion | | | | |
| **12** Land (net of any amortization) | | | | |
| **13a** Intangible assets (amortizable only) | | | | |
| **b** Less accumulated amortization | | | | |
| **14** Other assets (attach schedule) | | | | |
| **15** Total assets | | | | |
| **Liabilities and Shareholders' Equity** | | | | |
| **16** Accounts payable | | | | |
| **17** Mortgages, notes, bonds payable in less than 1 year | | | | |
| **18** Other current liabilities (attach schedule) | | | | |
| **19** Loans from shareholders | | | | |
| **20** Mortgages, notes, bonds payable in 1 year or more | | | | |
| **21** Other liabilities (attach schedule) | | | | |
| **22** Capital stock | | | | |
| **23** Additional paid-in capital | | | | |
| **24** Retained earnings | | | | |
| **25** Adjustments to shareholders' equity (attach schedule) | | | | |
| **26** Less cost of treasury stock | | ( ) | | ( ) |
| **27** Total liabilities and shareholders' equity | | | | |

**Schedule M-1**   **Reconciliation of Income (Loss) per Books With Income (Loss) per Return**

| | | | | |
|---|---|---|---|---|
| **1** Net income (loss) per books | | **5** Income recorded on books this year not included on Schedule K, lines 1 through 6 (itemize): | |
| **2** Income included on Schedule K, lines 1 through 6, not recorded on books this year (itemize): | | **a** Tax-exempt interest $ ........... | |
| **3** Expenses recorded on books this year not included on Schedule K, lines 1 through 11a, 15g, and 16b (itemize): | | **6** Deductions included on Schedule K, lines 1 through 11a, 15g, and 16b, not charged against book income this year (itemize): | |
| **a** Depreciation $ ........... | | **a** Depreciation $ ........... | |
| **b** Travel and entertainment $ ........... | | | |
| | | **7** Add lines 5 and 6 | |
| **4** Add lines 1 through 3 | | **8** Income (loss) (Schedule K, line 23). Line 4 less line 7 | |

**Schedule M-2**   **Analysis of Accumulated Adjustments Account, Other Adjustments Account, and Shareholders' Undistributed Taxable Income Previously Taxed** (see page 26 of the instructions)

| | (a) Accumulated adjustments account | (b) Other adjustments account | (c) Shareholders' undistributed taxable income previously taxed |
|---|---|---|---|
| **1** Balance at beginning of tax year | | | |
| **2** Ordinary income from page 1, line 21 | | | |
| **3** Other additions | | | |
| **4** Loss from page 1, line 21 | ( ) | | |
| **5** Other reductions | ( ) | ( ) | |
| **6** Combine lines 1 through 5 | | | |
| **7** Distributions other than dividend distributions | | | |
| **8** Balance at end of tax year. Subtract line 7 from line 6 | | | |

Form **1120S** (2002)

**SCHEDULE K-1**
**(Form 1120S)**

Department of the Treasury
Internal Revenue Service

## Shareholder's Share of Income, Credits, Deductions, etc.

▶ See separate instructions.

For calendar year 2002 or tax year
beginning , 2002, and ending , 20

OMB No. 1545-0130

**2002**

Shareholder's identifying number ▶

Corporation's identifying number ▶

Shareholder's name, address, and ZIP code

Corporation's name, address, and ZIP code

A  Shareholder's percentage of stock ownership for tax year (see instructions for Schedule K-1) . . . . . . . ▶ ————————— %
B  Internal Revenue Service Center where corporation filed its return ▶ ------------------------------------
C  Tax shelter registration number (see instructions for Schedule K-1) . . . . . . . . . ▶ ------------------------------
D  Check applicable boxes:  **(1)** ☐ Final K-1   **(2)** ☐ Amended K-1

| | **(a)** Pro rata share items | | **(b)** Amount | **(c)** Form 1040 filers enter the amount in column (b) on: |
|---|---|---|---|---|
| **Income (Loss)** | **1** Ordinary income (loss) from trade or business activities . . . | **1** | | See page 4 of the Shareholder's Instructions for Schedule K-1 (Form 1120S). |
| | **2** Net income (loss) from rental real estate activities . . . . . | **2** | | |
| | **3** Net income (loss) from other rental activities . . . . . . . | **3** | | |
| | **4** Portfolio income (loss): | | | |
| | a  Interest . . . . . . . . . | **4a** | | Sch. B, Part I, line 1 |
| | b  Ordinary dividends . . . . . . . . | **4b** | | Sch. B, Part II, line 5 |
| | c  Royalties . . . . . . . . . | **4c** | | Sch. E, Part I, line 4 |
| | d  Net short-term capital gain (loss). . . . . . . . | **4d** | | Sch. D, line 5, col. (f) |
| | e  **(1)** Net long-term capital gain (loss). . . . . . . . . | **4e(1)** | | Sch. D, line 12, col. (f) |
| | **(2)** 28% rate gain (loss) . . . . . . . . . . | **4e(2)** | | Sch. D, line 12, col. (g) |
| | **(3)** Qualified 5-year gain . . . . . . . . . | **4e(3)** | | Line 5 of worksheet for Sch. D, line 29 |
| | f  Other portfolio income (loss) *(attach schedule)* . . . . . . | **4f** | | *(Enter on applicable line of your return.)* |
| | **5** Net section 1231 gain (loss) (other than due to casualty or theft) | **5** | | See Shareholder's Instructions for Schedule K-1 (Form 1120S). |
| | **6** Other income (loss) *(attach schedule)* . . . . . . . . . | **6** | | *(Enter on applicable line of your return.)* |
| **Deductions** | **7** Charitable contributions *(attach schedule)* . . . . . . . | **7** | | Sch. A, line 15 or 16 |
| | **8** Section 179 expense deduction . . . . . . . . . | **8** | | See pages 5 and 6 of the Shareholder's Instructions for Schedule K-1 (Form 1120S). |
| | **9** Deductions related to portfolio income (loss) *(attach schedule)* . | **9** | | |
| | **10** Other deductions *(attach schedule)* . . . . . . . . . | **10** | | |
| **Investment Interest** | **11a** Interest expense on investment debts . . . . . . . | **11a** | | Form 4952, line 1 |
| | b  **(1)** Investment income included on lines 4a, 4b, 4c, and 4f above | **11b(1)** | | Shareholder's Instructions for Schedule K-1 (Form 1120S). |
| | **(2)** Investment expenses included on line 9 above . . . . . | **11b(2)** | | |
| **Credits** | **12a** Credit for alcohol used as fuel . . . . . . . . | **12a** | | Form 6478, line 10 |
| | b  Low-income housing credit: | | | |
| | **(1)** From section 42(j)(5) partnerships . . . . . . . . | **12b(1)** | | Form 8586, line 5 |
| | **(2)** Other than on line 12b(1) . . . . . . . . . . | **12b(2)** | | |
| | c  Qualified rehabilitation expenditures related to rental real estate activities . . . . . . . . . . . . . . | **12c** | | |
| | d  Credits (other than credits shown on lines 12b and 12c) related to rental real estate activities . . . . . . . . . . | **12d** | | See pages 6 and 7 of the Shareholder's Instructions for Schedule K-1 (Form 1120S). |
| | e  Credits related to other rental activities. . . . . . . . | **12e** | | |
| | **13** Other credits . . . . . . . . . . . | **13** | | |

**For Paperwork Reduction Act Notice, see the Instructions for Form 1120S.**   Cat. No. 11520D   **Schedule K-1 (Form 1120S) 2002**

Schedule K-1 (Form 1120S) 2002                 Page **2**

| (a) Pro rata share items | | (b) Amount | (c) Form 1040 filers enter the amount in column (b) on: |
|---|---|---|---|
| **Adjustments and Tax Preference Items** | | | |
| **14a** Depreciation adjustment on property placed in service after 1986 | 14a | | See page 7 of the Shareholder's Instructions for Schedule K-1 (Form 1120S) and Instructions for Form 6251 |
| **b** Adjusted gain or loss . . . . . . | 14b | | |
| **c** Depletion (other than oil and gas) . . . . . . . . . | 14c | | |
| **d (1)** Gross income from oil, gas, or geothermal properties . . . | 14d(1) | | |
| **(2)** Deductions allocable to oil, gas, or geothermal properties | 14d(2) | | |
| **e** Other adjustments and tax preference items *(attach schedule)* . | 14e | | |
| **Foreign Taxes** | | | |
| **15a** Name of foreign country or U.S. possession ▶ .................... | | | |
| **b** Gross income from all sources . . . . . . . . . . . | 15b | | |
| **c** Gross income sourced at shareholder level . . . . . . | 15c | | |
| **d** Foreign gross income sourced at corporate level: | | | |
| **(1)** Passive . . . . . . . . . . . . . . | 15d(1) | | |
| **(2)** Listed categories *(attach schedule)* . . . . . . . | 15d(2) | | |
| **(3)** General limitation . . . . . . . . . . . | 15d(3) | | |
| **e** Deductions allocated and apportioned at shareholder level: | | | Form 1116, Part I |
| **(1)** Interest expense. . . . . . . . . . . . . | 15e(1) | | |
| **(2)** Other . . . . . . . . . . . . . . . | 15e(2) | | |
| **f** Deductions allocated and apportioned at corporate level to foreign source income: | | | |
| **(1)** Passive . . . . . . . . . . . . . . | 15f(1) | | |
| **(2)** Listed categories *(attach schedule)* . . . . . . . | 15f(2) | | |
| **(3)** General limitation . . . . . . . . . . . | 15f(3) | | |
| **g** Total foreign taxes (check one): ▶ ☐ Paid   ☐ Accrued . . | 15g | | Form 1116, Part II |
| **h** Reduction in taxes available for credit *(attach schedule)* . . . | 15h | | See Instructions for Form 1116 |
| **Other** | | | |
| **16** Section 59(e)(2) expenditures: **a** Type ▶ ........................... | | | See Shareholder's Instructions for Schedule K-1 (Form 1120S). |
| **b** Amount . . . . . . . . . . . . . . . . | 16b | | |
| **17** Tax-exempt interest income . . . . . . . . . . . | 17 | | Form 1040, line 8b |
| **18** Other tax-exempt income . . . . . . . . . . . | 18 | | |
| **19** Nondeductible expenses . . . . . . . . . . . | 19 | | See page 7 of the Shareholder's Instructions for Schedule K-1 (Form 1120S). |
| **20** Property distributions (including cash) other than dividend distributions reported to you on Form 1099-DIV . . . . . | 20 | | |
| **21** Amount of loan repayments for "Loans From Shareholders" . . | 21 | | |
| **22** Recapture of low-income housing credit: | | | |
| **a** From section 42(j)(5) partnerships . . . . . . . . | 22a | | Form 8611, line 8 |
| **b** Other than on line 22a . . . . . . . . . . . . | 22b | | |
| **Supplemental Information** | | | |
| **23** Supplemental information required to be reported separately to each shareholder *(attach additional schedules if more space is needed)*: | | | |

..............................................................................................

..............................................................................................

..............................................................................................

..............................................................................................

..............................................................................................

..............................................................................................

..............................................................................................

..............................................................................................

..............................................................................................

..............................................................................................

..............................................................................................

..............................................................................................

**Schedule K-1 (Form 1120S) 2002**

The words and phrases in this glossary have been defined to reflect their conventional use in the field of taxation. The definitions may therefore be incomplete for other purposes.

## A

**Accelerated cost recovery system (ACRS).** A method in which the cost of tangible property is recovered over a prescribed period of time. The approach disregards salvage value, imposes a period of cost recovery that depends upon the classification of the asset into one of various recovery periods, and prescribes the applicable percentage of cost that can be deducted each year. The modified system is referred to as MACRS. § 168.

**Accelerated depreciation.** Various methods of depreciation that yield larger deductions in the earlier years of the life of an asset than the straight-line method. Examples include the double declining-balance and the sum-of-the-years' digits methods of depreciation.

**Accounting method.** The method under which income and expenses are determined for tax purposes. Important accounting methods include the cash basis and the accrual basis. Special methods are available for the reporting of gain on installment sales, recognition of income on construction projects (the completed contract and percentage of completion methods), and the valuation of inventories (last-in, first-out and first-in, first-out). §§ 446–474. See also *accrual basis, cash basis, completed contract method*, and *percentage of completion method*.

**Accounting period.** The period of time, usually a year, used by a taxpayer for the determination of tax liability. Unless a fiscal year is chosen, taxpayers must determine and pay their income tax liability by using the calendar year (January 1 through December 31) as the period of measurement. An example of a fiscal year is July 1 through June 30. A change in accounting periods (e.g., from a calendar year to a fiscal year) generally requires the consent of the IRS. Some new taxpayers, such as a newly formed corporation, are free to select either an initial calendar or a fiscal year without the consent of the IRS. §§ 441–443. See also *annual accounting period concept*.

**Accrual basis.** A method of accounting that reflects expenses incurred and income earned for any one tax year. In contrast to the cash basis of accounting, expenses need not be paid to be deductible, nor need income be received to be taxable. Unearned income (e.g., prepaid interest and rent) generally is taxed in the year of receipt regardless of the method of accounting used by the taxpayer. § 446(c)(2). See also *accounting method, cash basis*, and *unearned income*.

**Accumulated adjustments account (AAA).** An account that aggregates an S corporation's post-1982 income, loss, and deductions for the tax year (including nontaxable income and nondeductible losses and expenses). After the year-end income and expense adjustments are made, the account is reduced by distributions made during the tax year.

**Accumulated earnings and profits.** Net undistributed tax-basis earnings of a corporation aggregated from March 1, 1913, to the end of the prior tax year. Used to determine the amount of dividend income associated with a distribution to shareholders. See also *current earnings and profits* and *earnings and profits*. § 316 and Reg. § 1.316–2.

**Accumulated earnings credit.** A reduction allowed in arriving at accumulated taxable income, in determining the accumulated earnings tax. See also *accumulated earnings tax* and *accumulated taxable income*.

**Accumulated earnings tax (AET).** A special tax imposed on corporations that accumulate (rather than distribute) their earnings beyond the reasonable needs of the business. The accumulated earnings tax and related interest are imposed on accumulated taxable income in addition to the corporate income tax. §§ 531–537.

**Accumulated taxable income.** The base upon which the accumulated earnings tax is imposed. Generally, it is the taxable income of the corporation as adjusted for certain items (e.g., the Federal income tax, excess charitable contributions, the dividends received deduction) less the dividends paid deduction and the accumulated earnings credit. § 535.

**Accumulating trust.** See *discretionary trust*.

**Accuracy-related penalty.** Major civil taxpayer penalties relating to the accuracy of tax return data, including misstatements stemming from taxpayer negligence and improper valuation of income and deductions, are coordinated under this umbrella term. The penalty usually equals 20 percent of the understated tax liability.

**Acquiescence.** Agreement by the IRS on the results reached in some of the more significant decisions involving tax issues; sometimes abbreviated *Acq.* or *A.* See also *nonacquiescence*.

**Acquisition.** See *corporate acquisition*.

**ACRS.** See *accelerated cost recovery system*.

**Ad valorem tax.** A tax imposed on the value of property. The most common ad valorem tax is that imposed by states, counties, and cities on real estate. Ad valorem taxes can be imposed on personal property as well. See also *personalty*.

**Adjusted basis.** The cost or other basis of property reduced by depreciation allowed or allowable and increased by capital improvements. Other special adjustments are provided in § 1016 and the related Regulations. See also *basis*.

**Adjusted current earnings (ACE).** An adjustment in computing corporate alternative minimum taxable income (AMTI), computed at 75 percent of the excess of adjusted current earnings and profits over AMTI. ACE computations reflect restrictions on the timing of certain recognition events. Exempt interest, life insurance proceeds, and other receipts that are included in earnings and profits but not in taxable income also increase the ACE adjustment. See also *alternative minimum tax* and *earnings and profits*.

**Adjusted gross estate.** The gross estate of a *decedent* reduced by § 2053 expenses (e.g., administration, funeral) and § 2054 losses (e.g., casualty). Necessary in testing for the extension of time for installment payment of estate taxes under § 6166. See also *gross estate*.

**Adjusted gross income (AGI).** A tax determination peculiar to individual taxpayers. Generally, it represents the gross income of an individual, less business expenses and less any appropriate capital gain or loss adjustment. See also *gross income*.

**Adjusted ordinary gross income (AOGI).** A determination peculiar to the *personal holding company tax*. In ascertaining whether a corporation is a personal holding company, personal holding company income divided by adjusted ordinary gross income must equal 60 percent or more. Adjusted ordinary gross income is the corporation's gross income less capital gains, § 1231 gains, and certain expenses. §§ 541 and 543(b)(2). See also *personal holding company income*.

**Adjusted taxable estate.** The taxable estate reduced by $60,000. The adjusted taxable estate is utilized only in applying § 2011 for determining the limit on the credit for state death taxes paid that will be allowed against the Federal estate tax. See also *taxable estate*.

**Administration.** The supervision and winding up of an estate. The administration of an estate runs from the date of an individual's death until all assets have been distributed and liabilities paid.

**Administrator.** A person appointed by the court to administer (manage or take charge of) the assets and liabilities of a decedent (the deceased). See also *executor*.

**Affiliated group.** A parent-subsidiary group of corporations that is eligible to elect to file on a consolidated basis. Eighty percent ownership of the voting power and value of all of the corporations must be achieved on every day of the tax year, and an identifiable parent corporation must exist (i.e., it must own at least 80 percent of another group member without applying attribution rules).

**AFTR.** *American Federal Tax Reports* contain all of the Federal tax decisions issued by the U.S. District Courts, U.S. Court of Federal Claims, U.S. Courts of Appeals, and the U.S. Supreme Court.

**AFTR2d.** The second series of the *American Federal Tax Reports*, dealing with 1954 and 1986 Code case law.

**Aggregate concept.** The theory of partnership taxation under which, in certain cases, a partnership is treated as a mere extension of each partner.

**Alimony.** Alimony deductions result from the payment of a legal obligation arising from the termination of a marital relationship. Payments designated as alimony generally are included in the gross income of the recipient and are deductible *for* AGI by the payer.

**Allocable share of income.** Certain entities receive conduit treatment under the Federal income tax law. This means the earned income or loss is not taxed to the entity, but is allocated to the owners or beneficiaries, regardless of the magnitude or timing of corresponding distributions. The portion of the entity's income that is taxed to the owner or beneficiary is the allocable share of the entity's income or loss for the period. The allocations are determined by (1) the partnership agreement for partners, (2) a weighted-average stock ownership computation for shareholders of an S corporation, and (3) the controlling will or trust instrument for the beneficiaries of an estate or trust.

**Allocate.** The assignment of income for various tax purposes. A *multistate corporation*'s nonbusiness income usually is allocated to the state where the nonbusiness assets are located; it is not *apportioned* with the rest of the entity's income. The income and expense items of an estate or trust are allocated between income and corpus components. Specific items of income, expense, gain, loss, and credit can be allocated to specific partners, if a substantial economic nontax purpose for the allocation is established. See also *apportion* and *substantial economic effect*.

**Alternate valuation date.** Property passing from a *decedent* by death may be valued for death tax purposes as of the date of death or the alternate valuation date. The alternate valuation date is six months from the date of death or the date the property is disposed of by the estate, whichever comes first. To use the alternate valuation date, the *executor* or *administrator* of the estate must make an affirmative election. Election of the alternate valuation date is not available unless it decreases the amount of the gross estate *and* reduces the estate tax liability.

**Alternative minimum tax (AMT).** AMT is a fixed percentage of alternative minimum taxable income (AMTI). AMTI generally starts with the taxpayer's adjusted gross income (for individuals) or taxable income (for other taxpayers). To this amount, the taxpayer (1) adds designated preference items (e.g., interest income on private activity bonds), (2) makes other specified adjustments (e.g., to reflect a longer, straight-line cost recovery deduction), (3) subtracts certain AMT itemized deductions for individuals (e.g., interest incurred on housing but not taxes paid), and (4) subtracts an exemption amount (e.g., $40,000 on a C corporation's return). The taxpayer must pay the greater of the resulting AMT (reduced by only the foreign tax credit) or the regular income tax (reduced by all allowable tax credits). The AMT does not apply to certain small C corporations. AMT preferences and adjustments are assigned to partners and S corporation shareholders.

**Alternative minimum taxable income (AMTI).** The base for computing a taxpayer's *alternative minimum tax*. Generally, the taxable income for the year, modified for AMT adjustments, preferences, and exemptions.

**Amortization.** The tax deduction for the cost or other basis of an intangible asset over the asset's estimated useful life. Examples of amortizable intangibles include patents, copyrights, and leasehold interests. Most intangible assets are amortized over 15 years. § 195. For tangible assets, see *depreciation*. For natural resources, see *depletion*. See also *estimated useful life* and *goodwill*.

**Amount realized.** The amount received by a taxpayer upon the sale or exchange of property. Amount realized is the sum of the cash and the fair market value of any property or services received by the taxpayer, plus any related debt assumed by the buyer. Determining the amount realized is the starting point for arriving at realized gain or loss. § 1001(b). See also *realized gain or loss* and *recognized gain or loss*.

**Annual accounting period concept.** In determining a taxpayer's income tax liability, only transactions taking place during a specified tax year are taken into consideration. For reporting and payment purposes, therefore, the tax life of taxpayers is divided into equal annual accounting periods. See also *accounting period* and *mitigation of the annual accounting period concept*.

**Annual exclusion.** In computing the taxable gifts for the year, each donor excludes the first $11,000 of a gift to each donee. Usually, the annual exclusion is not available for gifts of future interests. § 2503(b). See also *future interest* and *gift splitting*.

**Annuitant.** The party entitled to receive payments from an annuity contract. See also *annuity*.

**Annuity.** A fixed sum of money payable to a person at specified times for a specified period of time or for life. If the party making the payment (i.e., the obligor) is regularly engaged in this type of business (e.g., an insurance company), the arrangement is classified as a commercial annuity. A so-called private annuity involves an obligor that is not regularly engaged in selling annuities (e.g., a charity or family member).

**Anticipatory assignment of income.** See *assignment of income*.

**Appellate court.** For Federal tax purposes, appellate courts include the U.S. Courts of Appeals and the U.S. Supreme Court. If the party losing in the trial (or lower) court is dissatisfied with the result, the dispute may be carried to the appropriate appellate court. See also *Court of Appeals* and *trial court*.

**Apportion.** The assignment of the business income of a multistate corporation to specific states for income taxation. Usually, the apportionment procedure accounts for the property, payroll, and sales activity levels of the various states, and a proportionate assignment of the entity's total income is made, using a three-factor apportionment formula. These activities indicate the commercial domicile of the corporation, relative to that income. Some states exclude nonbusiness income from the apportionment procedure; they *allocate* nonbusiness income to the states where the nonbusiness assets are located. See also *allocate, domicile, nonbusiness income, payroll factor, property factor*, and *sales factor*.

**Appreciated inventory.** In partnership taxation, appreciated inventory is a *hot asset*, and a partner's share of its ordinary income potential must be allocated. If a partner sells an interest in the partnership, ordinary income is recognized to the extent of the partner's share in the partnership's inventory and *unrealized receivables*. The definition of "inventory" is broad enough to include any accounts receivable, including unrealized receivables.

**Arm's length concept.** The standard under which unrelated parties would carry out a transaction. Suppose Bint Corporation sells property to its sole shareholder for $10,000. In determining whether $10,000 is an arm's length price, one would ascertain the amount for which the corporation could have sold the property to a disinterested third party.

**Articles of incorporation.** The legal document specifying a corporation's name, period of existence, purpose and powers, authorized number of shares, classes of stock, and other conditions for operation. The organizers of the corporation file the articles with the state of incorporation. If the articles are satisfactory and other conditions of the law are satisfied, the state will issue a charter recognizing the organization's status as a corporation.

**Assessment.** The process whereby the IRS imposes a tax liability. If, for example, the IRS audits a taxpayer's income tax return and finds gross income understated or deductions overstated, it will assess a deficiency in the amount of the tax that should have been paid in light of the adjustments made. See also *deficiency*.

**Assignment of income.** A procedure whereby a taxpayer attempts to avoid the recognition of income by assigning to another the property that generates the income. Such a procedure will not avoid the recognition of income by the taxpayer making the assignment if it can be said that the income was earned at the point of the transfer. In this case, usually referred to as an anticipatory assignment of income, the income will be taxed to the person who earns it.

**Assumption of liabilities.** In a corporate formation, corporate takeover, or asset purchase, the new owner often takes assets and agrees to assume preexisting debt. Such actions do not create *boot* received on the transaction for the new shareholder, unless there is no *bona fide* business purpose for the exchange, or the principal purpose of the debt assumption is the avoidance of tax liabilities. Gain is recognized to the extent that liabilities assumed exceed the aggregated bases of the transferred assets. § 357.

**At-risk amount.** The taxpayer has an amount at risk in a business or investment venture to the extent that personal assets have been subjected to the risks of the business. Typically, the taxpayer's at-risk amount includes (1) the amount of money or other property that the investor contributed to the venture for the investment, (2) the amount of any of the entity's liabilities for which the taxpayer personally is liable and that relate to the investment, and (3) an allocable share of nonrecourse debts incurred by the venture from third parties in arm's length transactions for real estate investments.

**At-risk limitation.** Generally, a taxpayer can deduct losses related to a trade or business, S corporation, partnership, or investment asset only to the extent of the at-risk amount.

**Attribution.** Under certain circumstances, the tax law applies attribution rules to assign to one taxpayer the ownership interest of another taxpayer. If, for example, the stock of Tree Corporation is held 60 percent by Mary and 40 percent by Sam, Mary may be deemed to own 100 percent of Tree if Sam is her son. In that case, the stock owned by Sam is attributed to Mary. Stated differently, Mary has a 60 percent direct and a 40 percent indirect interest in Tree. It can also be said that Mary is the constructive owner of Sam's interest.

**Audit.** Inspection and verification of a taxpayer's return or other transactions possessing tax consequences. See also *correspondence audit, field audit*, and *office audit*.

**Automobile expenses.** Automobile expenses generally are deductible only to the extent the automobile is used in business or for the production of income. Personal commuting expenses are not deductible. The taxpayer may deduct actual out-of-pocket expenses (including depreciation and insurance), or a standard mileage rate for the tax year. For 2003, per-mile deduction amounts are 36 cents for business use of the auto, 14 cents if in support of charity, 12 cents for medical purposes, and 12 cents for a job-related move.

# B

**Bailout.** Various procedures whereby the owners of an entity can obtain the entity's profits with favorable tax consequences. With corporations, for example, the bailout of corporate profits without dividend consequences might be the desired objective. The alternative of distributing the profits to the shareholders as dividends generally is less attractive since dividend payments are not deductible. See also *preferred stock bailout*.

*Bardahl* **formula.** A formula approved in a Tax Court memorandum decision, used in the context of the accumulated earnings tax to compute the reasonable business needs of the corporation for working capital. Most appropriate were the corporation holds inventory.

**Bargain sale or purchase.** A sale or purchase of property for less than fair market value. The difference between the sale or purchase price and the fair market value of the property may have tax consequences. If, for example, a corporation sells property worth $1,000 to one of its shareholders for $700, the $300 difference probably represents a constructive dividend to the shareholder. Suppose, instead, the shareholder sells the property (worth $1,000) to his or her corporation for $700. The $300 difference probably represents a contribution by the shareholder to the corporation's capital. Bargain sales and purchases among members of the same family may lead to gift tax consequences. See also *constructive dividend*.

**Basis.** The acquisition cost assigned to an asset for income tax purposes. For assets acquired by purchase, basis is cost (§ 1012). Special rules govern the basis of property received by virtue of another's death (§ 1014) or by gift (§ 1015), the basis of stock received on a transfer of property to a controlled corporation (§ 358), the basis of the property transferred to the corporation (§ 362), and the basis of property received upon the liquidation of a corporation (§ 334). See also *adjusted basis*.

**Basis in partnership interest.** The acquisition cost of the partner's ownership interest in the *partnership*. Includes purchase price and associated debt acquired from other partners and in the course of the entity's trade or business.

**Beneficiary.** A party who will benefit from a transfer of property or other arrangement. Examples include the beneficiary of a trust, the beneficiary of a life insurance policy, and the beneficiary of an estate.

**Bequest.** A transfer of personal property by will. To bequeath is to leave such property by will. See also *devise* and *personal property*.

**Blockage rule.** A factor to be considered in valuing a large block of stock. Application of this rule generally justifies a discount in the fair market value since the disposition of a large amount of stock at any one time may depress the value of the shares in the marketplace.

**Bona fide.** In good faith, or real. In tax law, this term is often used in connection with a business purpose for carrying out a transaction. Thus, was there a bona fide business purpose for a shareholder's transfer of a liability to a controlled corporation? § 357(b)(1)(B). See also *business purpose*.

**Book value.** The net amount of an asset after reduction by a related reserve. The book value of machinery, for example, is the amount of the machinery less the reserve for depreciation.

**Boot.** Cash or property of a type not included in the definition of a nontaxable exchange. The receipt of boot causes an otherwise nontaxable transfer to become taxable to the extent of the lesser of the fair market value of the boot or the realized gain on the transfer. For example, see transfers to controlled corporations under § 351(b) and like-kind exchanges under § 1031(b). See also *like-kind exchange* and *realized gain or loss*.

**Branch profits tax.** A tax on the effectively connected earnings and profits of the U.S. branch of a foreign corporation. The tax is levied in addition to the usual § 11 tax, in an amount equal to 30 percent of the dividend equivalent amount. Treaties can override the tax or reduce the withholding percentage. Earnings reinvested in the U.S. operations of the entity are not subject to the tax until repatriation. See also *dividend equivalent amount*.

**Bribes and illegal payments.** Section 162 denies a deduction for bribes or kickbacks, fines, and penalties paid to a government official or employee for violation of law, and two-thirds of the treble damage payments made to claimants for violation of the antitrust law. Denial of a deduction for bribes and illegal payments is based upon the judicially established principle that allowing such payments would be contrary to public policy.

**Brother-sister controlled group.** More than one corporation owned by the same shareholders. If, for example, Clara and Dan each own one-half of the stock in Top Corporation and Bottom Corporation, then Top and Bottom form a brother-sister controlled group.

**B.T.A.** The Board of Tax Appeals was a trial court that considered Federal tax matters. This court is now the U.S. Tax Court.

**Built-in gains tax.** A penalty tax designed to discourage a shift of the incidence of taxation on unrealized gains from a C corporation to its shareholders, via an S election. Under this provision, any recognized gain during the first 10 years of S status generates a corporate-level tax on a base not to exceed the aggregate untaxed built-in gains brought into the S corporation upon its election from C corporation taxable years.

**Burden of proof.** The requirement in a lawsuit to show the weight of evidence and thereby gain a favorable decision. In cases of tax fraud, the burden of proof in a tax case is on the IRS. See also *fraud*.

**Business bad debts.** A tax deduction allowed for obligations obtained in connection with a trade or business that have become either partially or completely worthless. In contrast to nonbusiness bad debts, business bad debts are deductible as business expenses. § 166. See also *nonbusiness bad debt*.

**Business purpose.** A justifiable business reason for carrying out a transaction. Mere tax avoidance is not an acceptable business purpose. The presence of a business purpose is crucial in the area of corporate reorganizations and certain liquidations. See also *bona fide*.

**Buy-sell agreement.** An arrangement, particularly appropriate in the case of a closely held corporation or a partnership, whereby the surviving owners (shareholders or partners) or the entity agrees to purchase the interest of a withdrawing owner. The buy-sell agreement provides for an orderly disposition of an interest in a business and may aid in setting the value of the interest for death tax purposes. See also *cross-purchase buy-sell agreement* and *entity buy-sell agreement*.

**Bypass amount.** The amount that can be transferred by gift or death free of any unified transfer tax. Currently, the by-pass amount is $1,000,000. See also *exemption equivalent amount*.

# C

**C corporation.** A separate taxable entity, subject to the rules of Subchapter C of the Code. This business form may create a double taxation effect relative to its shareholders. The entity is subject to the regular corporate tax and a number of penalty taxes at the Federal level. §§ 301ff.

**Calendar year.** See *accounting period*.

**Capital account.** The financial accounting analog of a partner's tax basis in the entity.

**Capital asset.** Broadly speaking, all assets are capital except those specifically excluded by the Code. Major categories of noncapital assets include property held for resale in the normal course of business (inventory), trade accounts and notes receivable, and depreciable property and real estate used in a trade or business (§ 1231 assets). § 1221. See also *capital gain* and *capital loss*.

**Capital contribution.** Various means by which a shareholder makes additional funds available to the corporation (placed at the risk of the business), sometimes without the receipt of additional stock. If no stock is received, the contributions are added to the basis of the shareholder's existing stock investment and do not generate gross income to the corporation. § 118.

**Capital expenditure.** An expenditure added to the basis of the property improved. For income tax purposes, this generally precludes a full deduction for the expenditure in the year paid or incurred. Any cost recovery in the form of a tax deduction comes in the form of depreciation, depletion, or amortization. § 263.

**Capital gain.** The gain from the sale or exchange of a capital asset. See also *capital asset*.

**Capital interest.** Usually, the percentage of the entity's net assets that a partner would receive on liquidation. Typically determined by the partner's capital sharing ratio.

**Capital loss.** The loss from the sale or exchange of a capital asset. See also *capital asset*.

**Capital sharing ratio.** A partner's percentage ownership of the entity's capital.

**Capital stock tax.** A state-level tax, usually imposed on out-of-state corporations for the privilege of doing business in the state. The tax may be based on the entity's apportionable income or payroll, or on its apportioned net worth as of a specified date.

**Carryover basis.** When a taxpayer exchanges one asset for another, many provisions in the tax law allow the basis assigned to the received asset to be precisely that of the traded asset. Thus, no step-up or -down of basis occurs as a result of the exchange. For instance, when an investor contributes an asset to a corporation or partnership, the entity generally takes a carryover basis in the property. § 723.

**Cash basis.** A method of accounting that reflects deductions as paid and income as received in any one tax year. However, deductions for prepaid expenses that benefit more than one tax year (e.g., prepaid rent and prepaid interest) usually must be spread over the period benefited rather than deducted in the year paid. § 446(c)(1). See also *constructive receipt of income.*

**Cash surrender value.** The amount of money that an insurance policy would yield if cashed in with the insurance company that issued the policy.

**CCH.** Commerce Clearing House (CCH) is the publisher of a tax service and of Federal tax decisions (USTC series).

**Cert. den.** By denying the Writ of Certiorari, the U.S. Supreme Court refuses to accept an appeal from a U.S. Court of Appeals. The denial of *certiorari* does not, however, mean that the U.S. Supreme Court agrees with the result reached by the lower court.

**Certiorari.** Appeal from a U.S. Court of Appeals to the U.S. Supreme Court is by Writ of Certiorari. The Supreme Court need not accept the appeal, and it usually does not (*cert. den.*) unless a conflict exists among the lower courts that must be resolved or a constitutional issue is involved. See also *cert. den.*

**Cf.** Compare.

**Charitable contributions.** Contributions are deductible (subject to various restrictions and ceiling limitations) if made to qualified nonprofit charitable organizations. A cash basis taxpayer is entitled to a deduction solely in the year of payment. Accrual basis corporations may accrue contributions at year-end if payment is properly authorized before the end of the year and payment is made within two and one-half months after the end of the year. § 170.

**Check the box Regulations.** A business entity can elect to be taxed as a partnership, S corporation, or C corporation by indicating its preference on the tax return. Legal structure and operations are irrelevant in this regard. Thus, by using the check-the-box rules prudently, an entity can select the most attractive tax results offered by the Code, without being bound by legal forms. Not available if the entity is incorporated under state law.

**Civil fraud.** See *fraud.*

**Closely held corporation.** A corporation where stock ownership is not widely dispersed. Rather, a few shareholders are in control of corporate policy and are in a position to benefit personally from that policy.

**Closing agreement.** In a tax dispute, the parties sign a closing agreement to spell out the terms under which the matters are settled. The agreement is binding on both the IRS and the taxpayer for the disputed year and for all future years.

**Collapsing.** To disregard a transaction or one of a series of steps leading to a result. See also *step transaction, substance vs. form concept,* and *telescoping.*

**Commissioner of the IRS.** The head of IRS operations, a presidential appointee.

**Common law state.** See *community property.*

**Community property.** Louisiana, Texas, New Mexico, Arizona, California, Washington, Idaho, Nevada, and Wisconsin have community property systems. The rest of the states are common law property jurisdictions. Alsaka residents can elect community property status for assets. The difference between common law and community property systems centers around the property rights possessed by married persons. In a common law system, each spouse owns whatever he or she earns. Under a community property system, one-half of the earnings of each spouse is considered owned by the other spouse. Assume, for example, Hal and Wanda are husband and wife and their only income is the $50,000 annual salary Hal receives. If they live in New York (a common law state), the $50,000 salary belongs to Hal. If, however, they live in Texas (a community property state), the $50,000 salary is owned one-half each by Hal and Wanda. See also *separate property.*

**Complete termination redemption.** See *redemption (complete termination).*

**Completed contract method.** A method of reporting gain or loss on certain long-term contracts. Under this method of accounting, gross income and expenses are recognized in the tax year in which the contract is completed. Reg. § 1.451–3. See also *percentage of completion method.*

**Complex trust.** Not a *simple trust.* Such trusts may have charitable beneficiaries, accumulate income, and distribute corpus. §§ 661–663.

**Concur.** To agree with the result reached by another, but not necessarily with the reasoning or the logic used in reaching the result. For example, Judge Ross agrees with Judges Smith and Tanaka (all being members of the same court) that the income is taxable but for a different reason. Judge Ross would issue a concurring opinion to the majority opinion issued by Judges Smith and Tanaka.

**Condemnation.** The taking of property by a public authority. The taking is by legal action, and the owner of the property is compensated by the public authority.

**Conduit concept.** An approach assumed by the tax law in the treatment of certain entities and their owners. Permits specified tax characteristics to pass through the entity without losing their identity. For example, long-term capital losses realized by a limited liability company are passed through as such to the individual members of the entity. Varying forms of the conduit concept apply for partnerships, trusts, estates, and S corporations. See also *aggregate concept.*

**Consent dividend.** For purposes of avoiding or reducing the penalty tax on the unreasonable accumulation of earnings or the personal holding company tax, a corporation may declare a consent dividend. No cash or property is distributed to the shareholders, although the corporation obtains a dividends paid deduction. The consent dividend is taxed to the shareholders and increases the basis in their stock investment. § 565.

**Conservation easement.** An interest in real property that maintains its natural or pristine condition. Most often it restricts the development of the property. Properly structured, the grant of such an easement can generate an income tax deduction for the donor. If the grant takes place after the owner's death, a § 2055 charitable deduction results, and a portion of the property's value is excluded from the gross estate. § 2031(c).

**Consolidated return.** A procedure whereby certain affiliated corporations may file a single return, combine the tax transactions of each corporation, and arrive at a single income tax liability for the group. The election to file a consolidated return usually is binding on future years. §§ 1501–1505 and related Regulations.

**Consolidation.** The combination of two or more corporations into a newly created corporation. Thus, Apt Corporation and Bye Corporation combine to form Cart Corporation. A consolidation may qualify as a nontaxable reorganization if certain conditions are satisfied. §§ 354 and 368(a)(1)(A).

**Constructive dividend.** A taxable benefit derived by a shareholder from his or her corporation that is not actually called a dividend. Examples include unreasonable compensation, excessive rent payments, bargain purchases of corporate property, and shareholder use of corporate property. Constructive dividends generally are found in closely held corporations. See also *bargain sale or purchase, closely held corporation,* and *unreasonable compensation.*

**Constructive liquidation scenario.** The means by which recourse debt is shared among partners in basis determination.

**Constructive ownership.** See *attribution.*

**Constructive receipt of income.** If income is unqualifiedly available although not physically in the taxpayer's possession, it is subject to the income tax. An example is accrued interest on a savings account. Under the constructive receipt of income concept, the interest is taxed to a depositor in the year available, rather than the year actually withdrawn. The fact that the depositor uses the cash basis of accounting for tax purposes is irrelevant. See Reg. § 1.451–2. See also *cash basis.*

**Continuity of business enterprise.** In a tax-favored reorganization, a shareholder or corporation that has substantially the same investment after an exchange as before should not

be taxed on the transaction. Specifically, the transferee corporation must continue the historic business of the transferor or use a significant portion of the transferor's assets in the new business.

**Continuity of interest test.** In a tax-favored reorganization, a shareholder or corporation that has substantially the same investment after an exchange as before should not be taxed on the transaction. Specifically, the seller must acquire an equity interest in the purchasing corporation equal in value to at least 50 percent of all formerly outstanding stock of the acquired entity.

**Continuity of life or existence.** The death or other withdrawal of an owner of an entity does not terminate the existence of the entity. This is a characteristic of a corporation since the death or withdrawal of a shareholder does not affect the corporation's existence.

**Contributions to the capital of a corporation.** See *capital contribution.*

**Contributory qualified pension or profit sharing plan.** A plan funded with both employer and employee contributions. Since the employee's contributions to the plan are subject to income tax, a later distribution of the contributions to the employee generally is tax-free. See also *qualified pension or profit sharing plan.*

**Control.** Holding a specified level of stock ownership in a corporation. For § 351, the new shareholder(s) must hold at least 80 percent of the total combined voting power of all voting classes of stock. Other tax provisions require different levels of control to bring about desired effects, such as 50 or 100 percent.

**Controlled foreign corporation (CFC).** A non-U.S. corporation in which more than 50 percent of the total combined voting power of all classes of stock entitled to vote or the total value of the stock of the corporation is owned by "U.S. shareholders" on any day during the taxable year of the foreign corporation. For purposes of this definition, a U.S. shareholder is any U.S. person who owns, or is considered to own, 10 percent or more of the total combined voting power of all classes of voting stock of the foreign corporation. Stock owned directly, indirectly, and constructively is used in this measure.

**Controlled group.** A controlled group of corporations is required to share the lower-level corporate tax rates and various other tax benefits among the members of the group. A controlled group may be either a brother-sister or a parent-subsidiary group.

**Corporate acquisition.** The takeover of one corporation by another if both parties retain their legal existence after the transaction. An acquisition can be effected via a stock purchase or through a tax-free exchange of stock. See also *corporate reorganization* and *merger.*

**Corporate liquidation.** Occurs when a corporation distributes its net assets to its shareholders and ceases its legal existence. Generally, a shareholder recognizes capital gain or loss upon the liquidation of the entity, regardless of the corporation's balance in its earnings and profits account. However, the distributing corporation recognizes gain and loss on assets that it distributes to shareholders in kind.

**Corporate reorganization.**   Occurs, among other instances, when one corporation acquires another in a merger or acquisition, a single corporation divides into two or more entities, a corporation makes a substantial change in its capital structure, or a corporation undertakes a change in its legal name or domicile. The exchange of stock and other securities in a corporate reorganization can be effected favorably for tax purposes if certain statutory requirements are followed strictly. Tax consequences include the nonrecognition of any gain that is realized by the shareholders except to the extent of boot received. See also *corporate acquisition* and *merger.*

**Corpus.**   The body or principal of a trust. Suppose, for example, George transfers an apartment building into a trust, income payable to Wanda for life, remainder to Sam upon Wanda's death. Corpus of the trust is the apartment building.

**Correspondence audit.**   An audit conducted by the IRS by mail. Typically, the IRS writes to the taxpayer requesting the verification of a particular deduction or exemption. The completion of a special form or the remittance of copies of records or other support is all that is requested of the taxpayer. See also *audit, field audit,* and *office audit.*

**Court of Appeals.**   Any of 13 Federal courts that consider tax matters appealed from the U.S. Tax Court, a U.S. District Court, or the U.S. Court of Federal Claims. Appeal from a U.S. Court of Appeals is to the U.S. Supreme Court by *Certiorari.* See also *appellate court, Court of Federal Claims,* and *trial court.*

**Court of Federal Claims.**   A trial court (court of original jurisdiction) that decides litigation involving Federal tax matters. Appeal is to the Court of Appeals for the Federal Circuit.

**Credit for prior transfers.**   The death tax credit for prior transfers applies when property is taxed in the estates of different decedents within a 10-year period. The credit is determined using a decreasing statutory percentage, with the magnitude of the credit decreasing as the length of time between the multiple deaths increases. § 2013.

**Criminal fraud.**   See *fraud.*

**Cross-purchase buy-sell agreement.**   Under this type of arrangement, the surviving owners of the business agree to buy out the withdrawing owner. Assume, for example, Ron and Sara are equal shareholders in Tip Corporation. Under a cross-purchase buy-sell agreement, Ron and Sara would contract to purchase the other's interest should that person decide to withdraw from the business. See also *buy-sell agreement* and *entity buy-sell agreement.*

**Current earnings and profits.**   Net tax-basis earnings of a corporation aggregated during the current tax year. A corporate distribution is deemed to be first from the entity's current earnings and profits and then from accumulated earnings and profits. Shareholders recognize dividend income to the extent of the earnings and profits of the corporation. A dividend results to the extent of current earnings and profits, even if there is a larger negative balance in accumulated earnings and profits. § 316 and Reg. § 1.316–2.

**Current use valuation.**   See *special use value.*

**Curtesy.**   A husband's right under state law to all or part of his wife's property upon her death. See also *dower.*

# D

**Death benefit.**   A payment made by an employer to the beneficiary or beneficiaries of a deceased employee on account of the death of the employee.

**Death tax.**   A tax imposed on property transferred by the death of the owner. See also *estate tax* and *inheritance tax.*

**Debt-financed income.**   Included in computations of the *unrelated business income* of an *exempt organization,* the gross income generated from debt-financed property.

**Decedent.**   An individual who has died.

**Deduction.**   The Federal income tax is not imposed upon gross income. Rather, it is imposed upon taxable income. Congressionally identified deductions are subtracted from gross income to arrive at the tax base, taxable income.

**Deductions in respect of a decedent.**   Deductions accrued at the moment of death but not recognizable on the final income tax return of a decedent because of the method of accounting used. Such items are allowed as deductions on the estate tax return and on the income tax return of the estate (Form 1041) or the heir (Form 1040). An example of a deduction in respect of a decedent is interest expense accrued to the date of death by a cash basis debtor.

**Deferred compensation.**   Compensation that will be taxed when received and not when earned. An example is contributions by an employer to a qualified pension or profit sharing plan on behalf of an employee. The contributions will not be taxed to the employee until they are distributed (e.g., upon retirement). See also *qualified pension or profit sharing plan.*

**Deficiency.**   Additional tax liability owed by a taxpayer and assessed by the IRS. See also *assessment* and *statutory notice of deficiency.*

**Deficiency dividend.**   Once the IRS has established a corporation's liability for the personal holding company tax in a prior year, the tax may be reduced or avoided by the issuance of a deficiency dividend under § 547. The deficiency dividend procedure is not available in cases where the deficiency was due to fraud with intent to evade tax or to a willful failure to file the appropriate tax return [§ 547(g)]. Nor does the deficiency dividend procedure avoid the usual penalties and interest applicable for failure to file a return or pay a tax.

**Deficit.**   A negative balance in the earnings and profits account.

**Demand loan.**   A loan payable upon request by the creditor, rather than on a specific date.

**Depletion.** The process by which the cost or other basis of a natural resource (e.g., an oil or gas interest) is recovered upon extraction and sale of the resource. The two ways to determine the depletion allowance are the cost and percentage (or statutory) methods. Under cost depletion, each unit of production sold is assigned a portion of the cost or other basis of the interest. This is determined by dividing the cost or other basis by the total units expected to be recovered. Under percentage (or statutory) depletion, the tax law provides a special percentage factor for different types of minerals and other natural resources. This percentage is multiplied by the gross income from the interest to arrive at the depletion allowance. §§ 613 and 613A.

**Depreciation.** The deduction for the cost or other basis of a tangible asset over the asset's estimated useful life. For intangible assets, see *amortization*. For natural resources, see *depletion*. See also *estimated useful life*.

**Depreciation recapture.** Upon the disposition of depreciable property used in a trade or business, gain or loss is measured by the difference between the consideration received (the amount realized) and the adjusted basis of the property. The gain recognized could be § 1231 gain and qualify for long-term capital gain treatment. The recapture provisions of the Code (e.g., §§ 291, 1245, and 1250) may operate to convert some or all of the previous § 1231 gain into ordinary income. The justification for depreciation recapture is that it prevents a taxpayer from converting a dollar of ordinary deduction (in the form of depreciation) into deferred tax-favored income (§ 1231 or long-term capital gain). The depreciation recapture rules do not apply when the property is disposed of at a loss or via a gift. See also *Section 1231 gains and losses*.

**Determination letter.** Upon the request of a taxpayer, an IRS Director will comment on the tax status of a completed transaction. Determination letters frequently are used to clarify employee status, determine whether a retirement or profit sharing plan qualifies under the Code, and determine the tax-exempt status of certain nonprofit organizations.

**Devise.** A transfer of real estate by will. See also *bequest*.

**Disclaimers.** Rejections, refusals, or renunciations of claims, powers, or property. Section 2518 sets forth the conditions required to avoid gift tax consequences as the result of a disclaimer.

**Discretionary trust.** A trust under which the trustee or another party has the right to accumulate (rather than distribute) the income for each year. Depending on the terms of the trust instrument, the income may be accumulated for future distributions to the income beneficiaries or added to corpus for the benefit of the remainderperson. See also *corpus* and *income beneficiary*.

**Disguised sale.** When a partner contributes property to the entity and soon thereafter receives a distribution from the partnership, the transactions are collapsed, and the distribution is seen as a purchase of the asset by the partnership. § 707(a)(2)(B).

**Disproportionate.** Not pro rata or ratable. Suppose, for example, Fin Corporation has two shareholders, Cal and Dot, each of whom owns 50 percent of its stock. If Fin distributes a cash dividend of $2,000 to Cal and only $1,000 to Dot, the distribution is disproportionate. The distribution would have been proportionate if Cal and Dot had received $1,500 each.

**Disproportionate distribution.** A distribution from a partnership to one or more of its partners in which at least one partner's interest in partnership hot assets is increased or decreased. For example, a distribution of cash to one partner and hot assets to another changes both partners' interest in hot assets and is disproportionate. The intent of rules for taxation of disproportionate distributions is to ensure each partner eventually recognizes his or her proportionate share of partnership ordinary income.

**Disproportionate redemption.** See *redemption (disproportionate)*.

**Dissent.** To disagree with the majority. If, for example, Judge Bird disagrees with the result reached by Judges Crown and Dove (all of whom are members of the same court), Judge Bird could issue a dissenting opinion.

**Distributable net income (DNI).** The measure that determines the nature and amount of the distributions from estates and trusts that the beneficiaries must include in income. DNI also limits the amount that estates and trusts can claim as a deduction for such distributions. § 643(a).

**Distribution deduction.** Used to compute an estate or trust's taxable income for the year. The lesser of the amount distributed to beneficiaries from income, or the deductible portion of distributable net income for the period.

**Distributions in kind.** Transfers of property "as is." If, for example, a corporation distributes land to its shareholders, a distribution in kind has taken place. A sale of land followed by a distribution of the cash proceeds would not be a distribution in kind of the land.

**District Court.** A Federal District Court is a trial court for purposes of litigating Federal tax matters. It is the only trial court in which a jury trial can be obtained. See also *trial court*.

**Dividend.** A nondeductible distribution to the shareholders of a corporation. A dividend constitutes gross income to the recipient if it is from the current or accumulated earnings and profits of the corporation.

**Dividend equivalent amount (DEA).** The amount subject to the branch profits tax, it is equal to the effectively connected earnings and profits of the U.S. branch of a foreign corporation, reduced/(increased) by an increase/(reduction) in U.S. net equity.

**Dividends paid deduction.** Relative to the accumulated earnings and personal holding company taxes, reductions in the tax base are allowed to the extent that the corporation made dividends payments during the year. Thus, this adjustment reduces *accumulated taxable income* and *personal holding company income.*

**Dividends received deduction.**   A deduction allowed a corporate shareholder for dividends received from a domestic corporation. The deduction usually is 70 percent of the dividends received, but it could be 80 or 100 percent depending upon the ownership percentage held by the payee corporation. §§ 243–246.

**Divisive reorganization.**   A corporate division: some of the assets of one corporation are transferred to another corporation in exchange for control of the transferee. Then, in a spin-off or split-off, stock of the transferee is distributed to the transferor's shareholders.

**Dock sale.**   A purchaser uses its owned or rented vehicles to take possession of the product at the seller's shipping dock. In most states, the sale is apportioned to the operating state of the purchaser, rather than the seller. See also *apportion* and *sales factor.*

**Domestic corporation.**   A corporation created or organized in the United States or under the law of the United States or any state. § 7701(a)(4). Only dividends received from domestic corporations qualify for the dividends received deduction (§ 243). See also *foreign corporation.*

**Domicile.**   A person's legal home.

**Donee.**   The recipient of a gift.

**Donor.**   The maker of a gift.

**Double-weighted apportionment formula.**   A means by which the total taxable income of a *multistate corporation* is assigned to a specific state. Usually, the payroll, property, and sales factors are equally treated, and the weighted average of these factors is used in the apportionment procedure. In some states, however, the sales factor may receive a double weight, or it may be the only factor considered. These latter formulas place a greater tax burden on the income of out-of-state corporations. See also *apportion, payroll factor, property factor, sales factor,* and *UDITPA.*

**Dower.**   A wife's right to all or part of her deceased husband's property; unique to common law states as opposed to community property jurisdictions. See also *curtesy.*

# E

**Earned income.**   Income from personal services. Distinguished from passive, portfolio, and other unearned income (sometimes referred to as "active" income). See §§ 469, 911, and the related Regulations.

**Earnings and profits (E & P).**   Measures the economic capacity of a corporation to make a distribution to shareholders that is not a return of capital. Such a distribution results in dividend income to the shareholders to the extent of the corporation's current and accumulated earnings and profits.

**Economic effect test.**   Requirements that must be met before a special allocation may be used by a partnership. The premise behind the test is that each partner who receives an allocation of income or loss from a partnership bears the economic benefit or burden of the allocation.

**Effectively connected income.**   Income of a nonresident alien or foreign corporation that is attributable to the operations of a U.S. trade or business under either the asset-use or the business-activities test.

**Electing large partnership.**   A partnership with 100 or more partners may elect to be subject to simplified tax reporting and audit procedures. The election allows the partnership to combine certain income and expense amounts and report net amounts to the partners. The result is fewer "pass-through" items to the partners, making the partners' tax returns easier to prepare. As an example, an electing large partnership with a long-term capital gain and a short-term capital loss would offset the two amounts and allocate the net amount among the partners.

**Employee stock ownership plan (ESOP).**   A type of qualified profit sharing plan that invests in securities of the employer. In a noncontributory ESOP, the employer usually contributes its shares to a trust and receives a deduction for the fair market value of the stock. Generally, the employee does not recognize income until the stock is sold after its distribution to him or her upon retirement or other separation from service. See also *qualified pension or profit sharing plan.*

**En banc.**   The case was considered by the whole court. Typically, for example, only one of the judges of the U.S. Tax Court will hear and decide on a tax controversy. However, when the issues involved are unusually novel or of wide impact, the case will be heard and decided by the full court sitting *en banc.*

**Energy tax credit–business property.**   A 10 percent tax credit is available to businesses that invest in certain energy property. The purpose of the credit is to create incentives for conservation and to develop alternative energy sources. The credit is available on the acquisition of solar and geothermal property. §§ 46 and 48.

**Enrolled agent (EA).**   A tax practitioner who has gained admission to practice before the IRS by passing an IRS examination.

**Entity.**   An organization or being that possesses separate existence for tax purposes. Examples are corporations, partnerships, estates, and trusts.

**Entity accounting income.**   Entity accounting income is not identical to the taxable income of a trust or estate, nor is it determined in the same manner as the entity's financial accounting income would be. The trust document or will determines whether certain income, expenses, gains, or losses are allocated to the corpus of the entity or to the entity's income beneficiaries. Only the items that are allocated to the income beneficiaries are included in entity accounting income.

**Entity buy-sell agreement.** An arrangement whereby the entity is to purchase a withdrawing owner's interest. When the entity is a corporation, the agreement generally involves a stock redemption on the part of the withdrawing shareholder. See also *buy-sell agreement* and *cross-purchase buy-sell agreement*.

**Entity concept.** Even in so-called flow-through entities, tax accounting elections are made (e.g., a tax year is adopted) and conventions are adopted (e.g., with respect to cost recovery methods) at the entity level. This may seem to violate the *conduit concept*, but such exceptions tend to ease the administration of such conduit taxpayers, especially in the context of a large number of shareholders/partners/members/beneficiaries.

**Equity structure shift.** A tax-free reorganization other than a *divisive reorganization* or *recapitalization*. If there is a more than 50 percent change in the ownership of a loss corporation in an equity structure shift, § 382 limits the use of net operating loss carryovers of the loss corporation. Specifically, the annual net operating loss carryover deduction is limited to the value of the loss corporation immediately before the equity structure shift times the *long-term tax-exempt rate.*

**Escrow.** Money or other property placed with a third party as security for an existing or proposed obligation. Cyd, for example, agrees to purchase Don's stock in Rip Corporation but needs time to raise the necessary funds. Don places the stock with Ernie (the escrow agent), with instructions to deliver it to Cyd when the purchase price is paid.

**Estate.** An entity that locates, collects, distributes, and discharges the assets and liabilities of a decedent.

**Estate freeze.** Procedures directed toward fixing and stabilizing the value of an interest retained in a business, while transferring the growth portion to family members. In the case of a closely held corporation, the estate freeze usually involves keeping the preferred stock and giving away the common stock. The ultimate objective is to reduce estate value when the original owner-donor dies.

**Estate tax.** A tax imposed on the right to transfer property by death. Thus, an estate tax is levied on the decedent's estate and not on the heir receiving the property. See also *death tax* and *inheritance tax.*

**Estimated useful life.** The period over which an asset will be used by the taxpayer. Assets such as collectible artwork do not have an estimated useful life. The estimated useful life of an asset is essential to measuring the annual tax deduction for depreciation and amortization.

**Estoppel.** The process of being stopped from proving something (even if true) in court due to a prior inconsistent action. It is usually invoked as a matter of fairness to prevent one party (either the taxpayer or the IRS) from taking advantage of a prior error.

**Excess lobbying expenditure.** An excise tax is applied on otherwise tax-exempt organizations with respect to the excess of total lobbying expenditure over *grass roots expenditure* for the year.

**Excess loss account.** When a subsidiary has generated more historical losses than its parent has invested in the entity, the parent's basis in the subsidiary is zero, and the parent records additional losses in an excess loss account. This treatment allows the parent to continue to deduct losses of the subsidiary, even where no basis reduction is possible, while avoiding the need to show a negative stock basis on various financial records. If the subsidiary stock is sold while an excess loss account exists, capital gain income usually is recognized to the extent of the balance in the account.

**Excise tax.** A tax on the manufacture, sale, or use of goods; on the carrying on of an occupation or activity; or on the transfer of property. Thus, the Federal estate and gift taxes are, theoretically, excise taxes.

**Exclusion amount.** The value of assets that is equal to the credit allowed for gifts or transfers by death. Thus, if the unified transfer tax credit is $345,800, the exclusion amount is $1,000,000. Often called the *exemption equivalent amount.* See also *bypass amount.*

**Executor.** A person designated by a will to administer (manage or take charge of) the assets and liabilities of a decedent. See also *administrator.*

**Exempt organization.** An organization that is either partially or completely exempt from Federal income taxation. § 501.

**Exemption.** An amount by which the tax base is reduced for all qualifying taxpayers. Individuals can receive personal and dependency exemptions, and taxpayers apply an exemption in computing their alternative minimum taxable income. Often, the exemption amount is phased out as the tax base becomes sizable.

**Exemption equivalent.** The maximum value of assets that can be transferred to another party without incurring any Federal gift or death tax because of the application of the unified tax credit.

**Exemption equivalent amount.** The amount of value (currently $1,000,000) that is the equivalent of the unified transfer tax credit allowed. See also *bypass amount.*

**Expenses in respect of a decedent.** See *deductions in respect of a decedent.*

**Extraterritorial income.** A device by which the U.S. encourages outbound (export) sales, services, and leases. An exclusion from gross income is computed under § 114 for certain transactions of U.S. taxpayers.

## F

**Fair market value.** The amount at which property would change hands between a willing buyer and a willing seller, neither being under any compulsion to buy or to sell, and both having reasonable knowledge of the relevant facts. Reg. § 20.2031–1(b).

**Federal Register.** The first place that the rules and regulations of U.S. administrative agencies (e.g., the U.S. Treasury Department) are published.

**F.3d.** An abbreviation for the third series of the *Federal Reporter,* the official series in which decisions of the U.S. Court of Federal Claims and the U.S. Court of Appeals are published. The second series is denoted F.2d.

**F.Supp.** The abbreviation for *Federal Supplement,* the official series in which the reported decisions of the U.S. Federal District Courts are published.

**Feeder organization.** An entity that carries on a trade or business for the benefit of an *exempt organization.* However, such a relationship does not result in the feeder organization itself being tax-exempt. § 502.

**Fiduciary.** A person who manages money or property for another and who must exercise a standard of care in the management activity imposed by law or contract. A trustee, for example, possesses a fiduciary responsibility to the beneficiaries of the trust to follow the terms of the trust and the requirements of applicable state law. A breach of fiduciary responsibility would make the trustee liable to the beneficiaries for any damage caused by the breach.

**Field audit.** An audit conducted by the IRS on the business premises of the taxpayer or in the office of the tax practitioner representing the taxpayer. See also *audit, correspondence audit,* and *office audit.*

**FIRPTA.** Under the Foreign Investment in Real Property Tax Act, gains or losses realized by nonresident aliens and non-U.S. corporations on the disposition of U.S. real estate create U.S.-source income and are subject to U.S. income tax.

**First-in, first-out (FIFO).** An accounting method for determining the cost of inventories. Under this method, the inventory on hand is deemed to be the sum of the cost of the most recently acquired units. See also *last-in, first-out (LIFO).*

**Fiscal year.** See *accounting period.*

**Flat tax.** In its pure form, a flat tax would eliminate all exclusions, deductions, and credits and impose a one-rate tax on gross income.

**Foreign corporation.** A corporation that is not created in the United States or organized under the laws of one of the states of the United States. § 7701(a)(5). See also *domestic corporation.*

**Foreign currency transaction.** An exchange that could generate a foreign currency gain or loss for a U.S. taxpayer. For instance, if Avery, Inc., contracts to purchase foreign goods, payable in a currency other than U.S. dollars, at a specified date in the future, any change in the exchange rate between the dollar and that currency will generate a foreign currency gain or loss upon completion of the contract. This gain or loss is treated as separate from the underlying transaction; it may create ordinary or capital gain or loss.

**Foreign earned income exclusion.** The Code allows exclusions for earned income generated outside the United States to alleviate any tax base and rate disparities among countries. In addition, the exclusion is allowed for housing expenditures incurred by the taxpayer's employer with respect to the non-U.S. assignment, and self-employed individuals can deduct foreign housing expenses incurred in a trade or business.

**Foreign personal holding company (FPHC).** A foreign corporation in which (1) 60 percent or more of the gross income for the taxable year is FPHC income and (2) more than 50 percent of the total combined voting power or the total value of the stock is owned, directly or indirectly, by five or fewer individuals who are U.S. persons (the U.S. group) at any time during the taxable year. The 60 percent of gross income test drops to 50 percent or more after the 60 percent requirement has been met for one tax year, until the foreign corporation does not meet the 50 percent test for three consecutive years, or the stock ownership requirement is not met for an entire tax year.

**Foreign sales corporation (FSC).** An entity qualifying for a partial exemption of its gross export receipts from U.S. tax. Most FSCs must maintain a presence in a foreign country. In addition, an FSC cannot issue preferred stock, nor can it have more than 25 shareholders.

**Foreign-source income.** Income that is not sourced within the United States. Examples include earnings from the performance of a personal services contract outside the United States, interest received from a non-U.S. corporation, and income from the use of property outside the United States.

**Foreign tax credit or deduction.** A U.S. citizen or resident who incurs or pays income taxes to a foreign country on income subject to U.S. tax may be able to claim some of these taxes as a deduction or a credit against the U.S. income tax. §§ 27, 164, and 901–905.

**Form 706.** The U.S. Estate Tax Return. In certain cases, this form must be filed for a decedent who was a resident or citizen of the United States.

**Form 709.** The U.S. Gift Tax Return.

**Form 709–A.** The U.S. Short Form Gift Tax Return.

**Form 870.** The signing of Form 870 (Waiver of Restriction on Assessment and Collection of Deficiency in Tax and Acceptance of Overassessments) by a taxpayer permits the IRS to assess a proposed deficiency without issuing a statutory notice of deficiency (90-day letter). This means the taxpayer must pay the deficiency and cannot file a petition to the U.S. Tax Court. § 6213(d).

**Form 872.** The signing of this form by a taxpayer extends the applicable statute of limitations. § 6501(c)(4).

**Form 1041.** The U.S. Fiduciary Income Tax Return, required to be filed by estates and trusts. See Appendix B for a specimen form.

**Form 1065.** The U.S. Partnership Return of Income. See Appendix B for a specimen form.

**Form 1120.** The U.S. Corporation Income Tax Return. See Appendix B for a specimen form.

**Form 1120–A.** The U.S. Short-Form Corporation Income Tax Return. See Appendix B for a specimen form.

**Form 1120S.** The U.S. Small Business Corporation Income Tax Return, required to be filed by S corporations. See Appendix B for a specimen form.

**Fraud.** Tax fraud falls into two categories: civil and criminal. Under civil fraud, the IRS may impose as a penalty an amount equal to as much as 75 percent of the underpayment [§ 6651(f)]. Fines and/or imprisonment are prescribed for conviction of various types of criminal tax fraud (§§ 7201–7207). Both civil and criminal fraud involve a specific intent on the part of the taxpayer to evade the tax; mere negligence is not enough. Criminal fraud requires the additional element of willfulness (i.e., done deliberately and with evil purpose). In practice, it becomes difficult to distinguish between the degree of intent necessary to support criminal, rather than civil, fraud. In either situation, the IRS has the burden of proving fraud. See also *burden of proof.*

**Free transferability of interests.** The capability of the owner of an entity to transfer his or her ownership interest to another without the consent of the other owners. It is a characteristic of a corporation since a shareholder usually can freely transfer the stock to others without the approval of the existing shareholders.

**Fringe benefits.** Compensation or other benefits received by an employee that are not in the form of cash. Some fringe benefits (e.g., accident and health plans, group term life insurance) may be excluded from the employee's gross income and thus are not subject to the Federal income tax.

**Functional currency.** The currency of the economic environment in which the taxpayer carries on most of its activities and transacts most of its business.

**Future interest.** An interest that will come into being at some future time. Distinguished from a present interest, which already exists. Assume that Dora transfers securities to a newly created trust. Under the terms of the trust instrument, income from the securities is to be paid each year to Nan for her life, with the securities passing to Steve upon Nan's death. Nan has a present interest in the trust since she is currently entitled to receive the income from the securities. Steve has a future interest since he must wait for Nan's death to benefit from the trust. The *annual exclusion* of $11,000 is not allowed for a gift of a future interest. § 2503(b). See also *annual exclusion* and *gift splitting.*

# G

**General business credit.** The summation of various nonrefundable business credits, including the jobs credit, alcohol fuels credit, and research activities credit. The amount of general business credit that can be used to reduce the tax liability is limited to the taxpayer's net income tax reduced by the greater of (1) the tentative minimum tax or (2) 25 percent of the net regular tax liability that exceeds $25,000. Unused general business credits can be carried back 1 year and forward 20 years. §§ 38 and 39.

**General partner.** A partner who is fully liable in an individual capacity for the debts of the partnership to third parties. A general partner's liability is not limited to the investment in the partnership. See also *limited partner.*

**General partnership.** A partnership that is owned by one or more *general partners.* Creditors of a general partnership can collect amounts owed them from both the partnership assets and the assets of the partners individually.

**General power of appointment.** See *power of appointment.*

**Gift.** A transfer of property for less than adequate consideration. Gifts usually occur in a personal setting (such as between members of the same family). They are excluded from the income tax base but may be subject to a transfer tax.

**Gift splitting.** A special election for Federal gift tax purposes under which husband and wife can treat a gift by one of them to a third party as being made one-half by each. If, for example, Hal (the husband) makes a gift of $22,000 to Sharon, Winnie (the wife) may elect to treat $11,000 of the gift as coming from her. The major advantage of the election is that it enables the parties to take advantage of the non-owner spouse's (Winnie in this case) annual exclusion and unified credit. § 2513. See also *annual exclusion.*

**Gift tax.** A tax imposed on the transfer of property by gift. The tax is imposed upon the donor of a gift and is based on the fair market value of the property on the date of the gift.

**Gifts within three years of death.** Some taxable gifts automatically are included in the gross estate of the donor if death occurs within three years of the gift. § 2035.

**Goodwill.** The reputation and built-up business of a company. For accounting purposes, goodwill has no basis unless it is purchased. In the purchase of a business, goodwill generally is the difference between the purchase price and the value of the assets acquired. The intangible asset goodwill is amortized over 15 years. § 195. See also *amortization.*

**Grantor.** A transferor of property. The creator of a trust is usually referred to as the grantor of the trust.

**Grantor trust.** A trust under which the grantor retains control over the income or corpus (or both) to such an extent that he or she is treated as the owner of the property and its income for income tax purposes. Income from a grantor trust is taxable to the grantor, and not to the beneficiary who receives it. §§ 671–679. See also *reversionary interest.*

**Grass roots expenditure.** Exempt organizations are prohibited from engaging in political activities, but spending incurred to influence the opinions of the general public relative to specific legislation is permitted by the law. See also *excess lobbying expenditure.*

**Green card test.** Form I-551, received from a U.S. consul as a receipt showing that the holder has immigration status in the United States, and used to refute alien status for tax purposes.

**Gross estate.** The property owned or previously transferred by a *decedent* that is subject to the Federal estate tax. Distinguished from the *probate estate*, which is property actually subject to administration by the *administrator* or *executor* of an estate. §§ 2031–2046. See also *adjusted gross estate* and *taxable estate.*

**Gross income.** Income subject to the Federal income tax. Gross income does not include all economic income. That is, certain exclusions are allowed (e.g., interest on municipal bonds). For a manufacturing or merchandising business, gross income usually means gross profit (gross sales or gross receipts less cost of goods sold). § 61 and Reg. § 1.61– 3(a). See also *adjusted gross income* and *taxable income.*

**Gross up.** To add back to the value of the property or income received the amount of the tax that has been paid. For gifts made within three years of death, any gift tax paid on the transfer is added to the gross estate. § 2035.

**Group term life insurance.** Life insurance coverage provided by an employer for a group of employees. Such insurance is renewable on a year-to-year basis, and typically no cash surrender value is built up. The premiums paid by the employer on the insurance are not taxed to the employees on coverage of up to $50,000 per person. § 79 and Reg. § 1.79–1(b).

**Guaranteed payment.** Made by a partnership to a partner for services rendered or for the use of capital, to the extent that the payments are determined without regard to the income of the partnership. The payments are treated as though they were made to a nonpartner and thus are usually deductible by the entity.

**Guardianship.** A legal arrangement under which one person (a guardian) has the legal right and duty to care for another (the ward) and his or her property. A guardianship is established because the ward is unable to act legally on his or her own behalf (e.g., because of minority [he or she is not of age] or mental or physical incapacity).

# H

**Head of household.** An unmarried individual who maintains a household for another and satisfies certain conditions set forth in § 2(b). This status enables the taxpayer to use a set of income tax rates that are lower than those applicable to other unmarried individuals but higher than those applicable to surviving spouses and married persons filing a joint return.

**Heir.** A person who inherits property from a decedent.

**Hobby.** An activity not engaged in for profit. The Code restricts the amount of losses that an individual can deduct for hobby activities so that these transactions cannot be used to offset income from other sources. § 183.

**Holding period.** The period of time during which property has been held for income tax purposes. The holding period is significant in determining whether gain or loss from the sale or exchange of a capital asset is long term or short term. § 1223.

**Hot assets.** Unrealized receivables and substantially appreciated inventory under § 751. When hot assets are present, the sale of a partnership interest or the disproportionate distribution of the assets can cause ordinary income to be recognized.

**H.R. 10 plans.** See *Keogh plans.*

# I

**Imputed interest.** For certain long-term sales of property, the IRS can convert some of the gain from the sale into interest income if the contract does not provide for a minimum rate of interest to be paid by the purchaser. The application of this procedure has the effect of forcing the seller to recognize less long-term capital gain and more ordinary income (interest income). § 483 and the related Regulations.

**In kind.** See *distributions in kind.*

**Inbound taxation.** U.S. tax effects when a non-U.S. person begins an investment or business activity in the U.S.

**Incident of ownership.** An element of ownership or degree of control over a life insurance policy. The retention by an insured of an incident of ownership in a life insurance policy will cause the policy proceeds to be included in the insured's gross estate upon death. § 2042(2) and Reg. § 20.2042–1(c). See also *gross estate* and *insured.*

**Income beneficiary.** The party entitled to income from property. In a typical trust situation, Art is to receive the income for life with corpus or principal passing to Bev upon Art's death. In this case, Art is the income beneficiary of the trust.

**Income in respect of a decedent (IRD).** Income earned by a decedent at the time of death but not reportable on the final income tax return because of the method of accounting that appropriately is utilized. Such income is included in the gross estate and is taxed to the eventual recipient (either the estate or heirs). The recipient is, however, allowed an income tax deduction for the estate tax attributable to the income. § 691.

**Income interest.** The right of a beneficiary to receive distributions from the fiduciary income of a trust or estate.

**Income shifting.** Occurs when an individual transfers some of his or her gross income to a taxpayer who is subject to a lower tax rate, thereby reducing the total income tax liability of the group. Income shifting produces a successful assignment of income. It can be accomplished by transferring income-producing property to the lower-bracket taxpayer or to an effective trust for his or her benefit, or by transferring ownership interests in a family partnership or in a closely held corporation.

**Incomplete transfer.** A transfer made by a decedent during lifetime that, because of certain control or enjoyment retained by the transferor, is not considered complete for Federal estate tax purposes. Thus, some or all of the fair market value of the property transferred is included in the transferor's gross estate. §§ 2036–2038. See also *gross estate* and *revocable transfer*.

**Indexation.** Various components of the tax formula are adjusted periodically for the effects of inflation, so that the effects of the formula are not eroded by price level changes. Tax rate schedules, exemption amounts, and the standard deduction, among other items, are indexed in this manner.

**Individual retirement account (IRA).** Individuals with earned income are permitted to set aside up to 100 percent of that income per year (not to exceed $3,000) for a retirement account. The amount so set aside can be deducted by the taxpayer and is subject to income tax only upon withdrawal. The Code limits the amount of this contribution that can be deducted *for* AGI depending upon the magnitude of the taxpayer's AGI before the IRA contribution is considered. No deduction is allowed for a contribution to a Roth IRA, but withdrawals are completely tax-free. § 219.

**Inheritance tax.** A tax imposed on the right to receive property from a *decedent*. Thus, theoretically, an inheritance tax is imposed on the heir. The Federal estate tax is imposed on the estate. See also *death tax* and *estate tax*.

**Inside basis.** A partnership's basis in each of the assets it owns.

**Installment method.** A method of accounting enabling certain taxpayers to spread the recognition of gain on the sale of property over the collection period. Under this procedure, the seller arrives at the gain to be recognized by computing the gross profit percentage from the sale (the gain divided by the contract price) and applying it to each payment received. § 453.

**Insured.** A person whose life is the subject of an insurance policy. Upon the death of the insured, the life insurance policy matures, and the proceeds become payable to the designated beneficiary. See also *life insurance*.

**Intangible asset.** Property that is a "right" rather than a physical object. Examples are patents, stocks and bonds, goodwill, trademarks, franchises, and copyrights. See also *amortization* and *tangible property*.

**Inter vivos transfer.** A transfer of property during the life of the owner. Distinguished from testamentary transfers, where the property passes at death.

**Interest-free loans.** Bona fide loans that carry no interest (or a below-market rate). If made in a nonbusiness setting, the imputed interest element is treated as a gift from the lender to the borrower. If made by a corporation to a shareholder, a constructive dividend could result. In either event, the lender may recognize interest income. § 7872.

**Intermediate sanctions.** The IRS can assess excise taxes on disqualified persons and organization managers associated with so-called public charities engaging in excess benefit transactions. An excess benefit transaction is one in which a disqualified person engages in a non-fair market value transaction with the exempt organization or receives unreasonable compensation. Prior to the idea of intermediate sanctions, the only option available to the IRS was to revoke the organization's exempt status.

**Internal Revenue Code.** The collected statutes that govern the taxation of income, property transfers, and other transactions in the United States and the enforcement of those provisions. Enacted by Congress, the Code is amended frequently, but it has not been reorganized since 1954. However, because of the extensive revisions to the statutes that occurred with the Tax Reform Act of 1986, Title 26 of the U.S. Code is now known as the Internal Revenue Code of 1986.

**Internal Revenue Service (IRS).** The Federal agency, a division of the Department of the Treasury, charged with administering the U.S. revenue enforcement and collection provisions.

**Interpolated terminal reserve.** The measure used in valuing insurance policies for gift and estate tax purposes when the policies are not paid up at the time of their transfer. Reg. § 20.2031–8(a)(3), Ex. (3).

**Intestate.** The condition when no will exists at the time of death. In such cases, state law prescribes who will receive the decedent's property. The laws of intestate succession generally favor the surviving spouse, children, and grandchildren, and then parents and grandparents and brothers and sisters.

**Investment income.** Consisting of virtually the same elements as portfolio income, a measure by which to justify a deduction for interest on investment indebtedness. See also *investment indebtedness* and *portfolio income*.

**Investment indebtedness.** Debt incurred to carry or incur investments by the taxpayer in assets that will produce portfolio income. Limitations are placed upon interest deductions that are incurred in connection with the debt (generally to the corresponding amount of investment income).

**Investor losses.** Losses on stock and securities. If stocks and bonds are capital assets in the hands of the holder, a capital loss materializes as of the last day of the taxable year in which the stocks or bonds become worthless. Under certain circumstances involving stocks and bonds of affiliated corporations, an ordinary loss is permitted upon worthlessness.

**Involuntary conversion.** The loss or destruction of property through theft, casualty, or condemnation. Any gain realized on an involuntary conversion can, at the taxpayer's election, be deferred for Federal income tax purposes if the owner reinvests the proceeds within a prescribed period of time in property that is similar or related in service or use. § 1033.

**IRA.** See *individual retirement account*.

**Itemized deductions.** Personal and employee expenditures allowed by the Code as deductions from adjusted gross income. Examples include certain medical expenses, interest on home mortgages, and charitable contributions. Itemized deductions are reported on Schedule A of Form 1040. Certain miscellaneous itemized deductions are reduced by 2 percent of the taxpayer's adjusted gross income. In addition, a taxpayer whose adjusted gross income exceeds a certain level (indexed annually) must reduce the itemized deductions by 3 percent of the excess of adjusted gross income over that level. Medical, casualty and theft, and investment interest deductions are not subject to the 3 percent reduction. The 3 percent reduction may not reduce itemized deductions that are subject to the reduction to below 20 percent of their initial amount.

# J

**Jeopardy assessment.** If the collection of a tax appears in question, the IRS may assess and collect the tax immediately without the usual formalities. The IRS can terminate a taxpayer's taxable year before the usual date if it feels that the collection of the tax may be in peril because the taxpayer plans to leave the country. §§ 6851 and 6861–6864.

**Joint and several liability.** Permits the IRS to collect a tax from one or all of several taxpayers. A husband and wife who file a joint income tax return usually are collectively or individually liable for the full amount of the tax liability. The same rule applies to consolidated return partners. § 6013(d)(3).

**Joint tenants.** Two or more persons having undivided ownership of property with the right of survivorship. Right of survivorship gives the surviving owner full ownership of the property. Suppose Betty and Cheryl are joint tenants of a tract of land. Upon Betty's death, Cheryl becomes the sole owner of the property. For the estate tax consequences upon the death of a joint tenant, see § 2040. See also *tenancy by the entirety* and *tenancy in common*.

**Joint venture.** A one-time grouping of two or more persons in a business undertaking. Unlike a partnership, a joint venture does not entail a continuing relationship among the parties. A joint venture is treated like a partnership for Federal income tax purposes. § 7701(a)(2).

# K

**Keogh plans.** Retirement plans available to self-employed taxpayers. They are also referred to as H.R. 10 plans. Under such plans, a taxpayer may deduct each year up to either 20 percent of net earnings from self-employment or $40,000, whichever is less.

**Kiddie tax.** See *tax on unearned income of a child under age 14*.

# L

**Lapse.** The expiration of a right either by the death of the holder or upon the expiration of a period of time. Thus, a power of appointment lapses upon the death of the holder if he or she has not exercised the power during life or at death (through a will).

**Last-in, first-out (LIFO).** An accounting method for valuing inventories for tax purposes. Under this method, it is assumed that the inventory on hand is valued at the cost of the earliest acquired units. § 472. See also *first-in, first-out (FIFO)*.

**Leaseback.** The transferor of property later leases it back. In a sale-leaseback situation, for example, Ron sells property to Sal and subsequently leases the property from Sal. Thus, Ron becomes the lessee and Sal the lessor.

**Least aggregate deferral rule.** A test applied to determine the allowable fiscal year of a *partnership* or *S corporation*. Possible year-ends are tested, and the fiscal year allowed by the IRS is the one that offers the least amount of income deferral to the owners on an individual basis.

**Legacy.** A transfer of cash or other property by will.

**Legal age.** The age at which a person may enter into binding contracts or commit other legal acts. In most states, a minor reaches legal age or majority (comes of age) at age 18.

**Legal representative.** A person who oversees the legal affairs of another; for example, the executor or administrator of an estate or a court-appointed guardian of a minor or incompetent person.

**Legatee.** The recipient of property that is transferred under a will by the death of the owner.

**Lessee.** One who rents property from another. In the case of real estate, the lessee is also known as the tenant.

**Lessor.** One who rents property to another. In the case of real estate, the lessor is also known as the landlord.

**Letter ruling.** The written response of the IRS to a taxpayer's request for interpretation of the revenue laws with respect to a proposed transaction, (e.g., concerning the tax-free status of a reorganization). Not to be relied on as precedent by other than the party who requested the ruling.

**LEXIS.** An online database system through which a tax researcher can obtain access to the Internal Revenue Code, Regulations, administrative rulings, and court case opinions.

**Liabilities in excess of basis.** On the contribution of capital to a corporation, an investor recognizes gain on the exchange to the extent that contributed assets carry liabilities with a face amount in excess of the tax basis of the contributed assets. This rule keeps the investor from holding the investment asset received with a negative basis. § 357(c).

**Life estate.** A legal arrangement under which the beneficiary (the life tenant) is entitled to the income from the property for his or her life. Upon the death of the life tenant, the property is transferred to the holder of the remainder interest. See also *income beneficiary* and *remainder interest*.

**Life insurance.** A contract between the holder of a policy and an insurance company (the carrier) under which the company agrees, in return for premium payments, to pay a specified sum (the face value or maturity value of the policy) to the designated beneficiary upon the death of the insured. See also *insured*.

**Like-kind exchange.**   An exchange of property held for productive use in a trade or business or for investment (except inventory and stocks and bonds) for other investment or trade or business property. Unless non-like-kind property (*boot*) is received, the exchange is fully nontaxable. § 1031.

**Limited liability.**   The liability of an entity and its owners to third parties is limited to the investment in the entity. This is a characteristic of a corporation, as shareholders generally are not responsible for the debts of the corporation and, at most, may lose the amount paid for the stock issued.

**Limited liability company (LLC).**   A form of entity allowed by all of the states. The entity is taxed as a partnership in which all owners of the LLC are treated much like limited partners. There are no restrictions on ownership, all partners may participate in management, and none of the owners has personal liability for the entity's debts.

**Limited liability partnership (LLP).**   A form of entity allowed by many of the states, where a general partnership registers with the state as an LLP. Owners are general partners, but a partner is not liable for any malpractice committed by other partners. The personal assets of the partners are at risk for the entity's contractual liabilities, such as accounts payable. The personal assets of a specific partner are at risk for his or her own professional malpractice and tort liability, and for malpractice and torts committed by those whom he or she supervises.

**Limited partner.**   A partner whose liability to third-party creditors of the partnership is limited to the amount he or she has invested in the partnership. See also *general partner* and *limited partnership*.

**Limited partnership.**   A partnership in which some of the partners are *limited partners*. At least one of the partners in a limited partnership must be a *general partner*.

**Liquidating distribution.**   A distribution by a partnership or corporation that is in complete liquidation of the entity's trade or business activities. Typically, such distributions generate capital gain or loss to the investors without regard, for instance, to the earnings and profits of the corporation or to the partnership's basis in the distributed property. They can, however, lead to recognized gain or loss at the corporate level.

**Liquidation.**   See *corporate liquidation*.

**Living trust.**   A revocable trust. Often touted as a means of avoiding some probate costs.

**Lobbying expenditure.**   An expenditure made for the purpose of influencing legislation. Such payments can result in the loss of the exempt status and the imposition of Federal income tax on an exempt organization.

**Long-term capital gain or loss.**   Results from the sale or other taxable exchange of a capital asset that had been held by the seller for more than one year or from other transactions involving statutorily designated assets, including § 1231 property and patents.

**Long-term tax-exempt rate.**   Used in deriving net operating loss limitations in the context of an equity structure shift. The highest of the Federal long-term interest rates in effect for any of the last three months. § 382.

**Low-income housing credit.**   Beneficial treatment to owners of low-income housing is provided in the form of a tax credit. The calculated credit is claimed in the year the building is placed in service and in the following nine years. § 42. See also *general business credit*.

**Lump-sum distribution.**   Payment of the entire amount due at one time rather than in installments. Such distributions often occur from qualified pension or profit sharing plans upon the retirement or death of a covered employee.

# M

**MACRS.**   See *accelerated cost recovery system (ACRS)*.

**Majority.**   See *legal age*.

**Malpractice.**   Professional misconduct; an unreasonable lack of skill.

**Marital deduction.**   A deduction allowed against the taxable estate or taxable gifts upon the transfer of property from one spouse to another.

**Market value.**   See *fair market value*.

**Meaningful reduction test.**   A decrease in the shareholder's voting control. Used to determine whether a redemption qualifies for sale or exchange treatment.

**Merger.**   The absorption of one corporation by another with the corporation being absorbed losing its legal identity. Flow Corporation is merged into Jobs Corporation, and the shareholders of Flow receive stock in Jobs in exchange for their stock in Flow. After the merger, Flow ceases to exist as a separate legal entity. If a merger meets certain conditions, it is nontaxable to the parties involved. § 368(a)(1)(A). See also *corporate acquisition* and *corporate reorganization*.

**Minimum credit (AET).**   A fixed amount, $150,000 for personal service firms and $250,000 for all others, below which the *accumulated earnings credit* cannot be derived. Assures that small and start-up corporations can generate a minimum amount of earnings before being subject to the accumulated earnings tax (AET).

**Minimum tax.**   See *alternative minimum tax*.

**Minimum tax credit (AMT).**   When a corporation pays an alternative minimum tax (AMT), a minimum tax credit is created on a dollar-for-dollar basis, to be applied against regular tax liabilities incurred in future years. The credit is carried forward indefinitely, but it is not carried back. The effect of the credit for corporate taxpayers alternating between the AMT and regular tax models is to make the AMT liabilities a prepayment of regular taxes. Noncorporate AMT taxpayers are allowed the credit only with respect to the elements of the AMT that reflect timing differences between the two tax models.

**Minority.**   See *legal age.*

**Mitigate.**   To make less severe. See also *mitigation of the annual accounting period concept.*

**Mitigation of the annual accounting period concept.** Various tax provisions that provide relief from the effect of the finality of the annual accounting period concept. For example, the net operating loss carryover provisions allow the taxpayer to apply the negative taxable income of one year against a corresponding positive amount in another tax accounting period. See also *annual accounting period concept.*

**Mortgagee.**   The party who holds the mortgage; the creditor.

**Mortgagor.**   The party who mortgages the property; the debtor.

**Most suitable use value.**   For gift and estate tax purposes, property that is transferred normally is valued in accordance with its most suitable or optimal use. Thus, if a farm is worth more as a potential shopping center, the value as a shopping center is used, even though the transferee (the donee or heir) continues to use the property as a farm. For an exception to this rule concerning the valuation of certain kinds of real estate transferred by death, see *special use value.*

**Multistate corporation.**   A corporation that has operations in more than one of the states of the United States. Issues arise relative to the assignment of appropriate amounts of the entity's taxable income to the states in which it has a presence. See also *allocate, apportion, nexus,* and *UDITPA.*

**Multistate Tax Commission (MTC).**   A regulatory body of the states that develops operating rules and regulations for the implementation of the *UDITPA* and other provisions that assign the total taxable income of a *multistate corporation* to specific states.

**Multitiered partnerships.**   See *tiered partnerships.*

# N

**Necessary.**   Appropriate and helpful in furthering the taxpayer's business or income-producing activity. §§ 162(a) and 212. See also *ordinary.*

**Negligence.**   Failure to exercise the reasonable or ordinary degree of care of a prudent person in a situation that results in harm or damage to another. Code § 6651 imposes a penalty on taxpayers who show negligence or intentional disregard of rules and Regulations with respect to the underpayment of certain taxes. See also *accuracy-related penalty.*

**Net operating loss.**   To mitigate the effect of the annual accounting period concept, § 172 allows taxpayers to use an excess loss of one year as a deduction for certain past or future years. In this regard, a carryback period of 2 years and a carryforward period of 20 years currently are allowed. See also *mitigation of the annual accounting period concept.*

**Net worth method.**   An approach used by the IRS to reconstruct the income of a taxpayer who fails to maintain adequate records. Under this method, the gross income for the year is estimated as the increase in net worth of the taxpayer (assets in excess of liabilities), with appropriate adjustment for nontaxable receipts and nondeductible expenditures. The net worth method often is used when tax fraud is suspected.

**Nexus.**   A *multistate corporation*'s taxable income can be apportioned to a specific state only if the entity has established a sufficient presence, or nexus, with that state. State law, which often follows the *UDITPA*, specifies various activities that lead to nexus in various states.

**Ninety-day letter.**   See *statutory notice of deficiency.*

**Nonacquiescence.**   Disagreement by the IRS on the result reached by selected tax decisions. Sometimes abbreviated *Nonacq.* or *NA.* See also *acquiescence.*

**Nonbusiness bad debt.**   A bad debt loss that is not incurred in connection with a creditor's trade or business. The loss is classified as a short-term capital loss and is allowed only in the year the debt becomes entirely worthless. In addition to family loans, many investor losses are nonbusiness bad debts. § 166(d). See also *business bad debts.*

**Nonbusiness income.**   Income generated from investment assets or from the taxable disposition thereof. In some states, the nonbusiness income of a *multistate corporation* is held out of the apportionment procedure and allocated to the state in which the nonbusiness asset is located. See also *allocate* and *apportion.*

**Noncontributory qualified pension or profit sharing plan.** A plan funded entirely by the employer with no contributions from the covered employees. See also *qualified pension or profit sharing plan.*

**Nonliquidating distribution.**   A payment made by a partnership or corporation to the entity's owner is a nonliquidating distribution when the entity's legal existence does not cease thereafter. If the payor is a corporation, such a distribution can result in dividend income to the shareholders. If the payor is a partnership, the partner usually assigns a basis in the distributed property that is equal to the lesser of the partner's basis in the partnership interest or the basis of the distributed asset to the partnership. In this regard, the partner first assigns basis to any cash that is received in the distribution. The partner's remaining basis, if any, is assigned to the noncash assets according to their relative bases to the partnership.

**Nonrecourse debt.**   Debt secured by the property that it is used to purchase. The purchaser of the property is not personally liable for the debt upon default. Rather, the creditor's recourse is to repossess the related property. Nonrecourse debt generally does not increase the purchaser's at-risk amount.

**Nonresident alien.** An individual who is neither a citizen nor a resident of the United States. Citizenship is determined under the immigration and naturalization laws of the United States. Residency is determined under § 7701(b) of the Internal Revenue Code.

**Nonseparately stated income.** The net income of an S corporation that is combined and allocated to the shareholders. Other items, such as capital gains and charitable contributions, that could be treated differently on the individual tax returns of the shareholders are not included in this amount but are allocated to the shareholders separately.

**Not essentially equivalent redemption.** See *redemption (not equivalent to a dividend)*.

## O

**Obligee.** The party to whom someone else is obligated under a contract. Thus, if Coop loans money to Dawn, Coop is the obligee and Dawn is the obligor under the loan.

**Obligor.** See *obligee*.

**Offer in compromise.** A settlement agreement offered by the IRS in a tax dispute, especially where there is doubt as to the collectibility of the full deficiency. Offers in compromise can include installment payment schedules, as well as reductions in the tax and penalties owed by the taxpayer.

**Office audit.** An audit conducted by the IRS in the agent's office. See also *audit, correspondence audit,* and *field audit*.

**On all fours.** A judicial decision exactly in point with another as to result, facts, or both.

**Optimal use value.** Synonym for most suitable use value.

**Optional adjustment election.** See *Section 754 election*.

**Ordinary.** Common and accepted in the general industry or type of activity in which the taxpayer is engaged. It comprises one of the tests for the deductibility of expenses incurred or paid in connection with a trade or business; for the production or collection of income; for the management, conservation, or maintenance of property held for the production of income; or in connection with the determination, collection, or refund of any tax. §§ 162(a) and 212. See also *necessary*.

**Ordinary and necessary.** See *necessary* and *ordinary*.

**Ordinary gross income (OGI).** A concept peculiar to personal holding companies and defined in § 543(b)(1). See also *adjusted ordinary gross income*.

**Organizational expenditures.** Items incurred early in the life of a corporate entity, qualifying for a 60-month amortization under Federal tax law. Amortizable expenditures exclude those incurred to obtain capital (underwriting fees) or assets (subject to cost recovery). Typically, amortizable expenditures include legal and accounting fees and state incorporation payments. Such items must be incurred by the end of the entity's first tax year. § 248.

**Outbound taxation.** U.S. tax effects when a U.S. person begins an investment or business activity outside the U.S.

**Outside basis.** A partner's basis in his or her partnership interest.

**Owner shift.** Any change in the respective ownership of stock by a 5 percent-or-more shareholder. Change is determined relative to a testing period of the prior three years. If there is a more-than-50 percent change in the ownership of a loss corporation, § 382 limitations apply to the use of net operating loss carryovers of the loss corporation.

**Ownership change.** An event that triggers a *Sec. 382 limitation* for the acquiring corporation.

## P

**Parent-subsidiary controlled group.** A *controlled* or *affiliated group* of corporations, where at least one corporation is at least 80 percent owned by one or more of the others. The affiliated group definition is more difficult to meet.

**Partial liquidation.** A stock redemption where noncorporate shareholders are permitted sale or exchange treatment. In certain cases, an active business must have existed for at least five years. Only a portion of the outstanding stock in the entity is retired.

**Partner.** See *general partner* and *limited partner*.

**Partnership.** For income tax purposes, a partnership includes a syndicate, group, pool, or joint venture, as well as ordinary partnerships. In an ordinary partnership, two or more parties combine capital and/or services to carry on a business for profit as co-owners. § 7701(a)(2). See also *limited partnership* and *tiered partnerships*.

**Passive foreign investment company (PFIC).** A non-U.S. corporation that generates a substantial amount of personal holding company income. Upon receipt of an excess distribution from the entity or the sale of its shares, its U.S. shareholders are taxable on their pro rata shares of the tax that has been deferred with respect to the corporation's taxable income, plus an applicable interest charge.

**Passive investment company.** A means by which a *multistate corporation* can reduce the overall effective tax rate by isolating investment income in a low- or no-tax state.

**Passive investment income (PII).** Gross receipts from royalties, certain rents, dividends, interest, annuities, and gains from the sale or exchange of stock and securities. With certain exceptions, if the passive investment income of an *S corporation* exceeds 25 percent of the corporation's gross receipts for three consecutive years, S status is lost.

**Passive loss.** Any loss from (1) activities in which the taxpayer does not materially participate and (2) rental activities. Net passive losses cannot be used to offset income from nonpassive sources. Rather, they are suspended until the taxpayer either generates net passive income (and a deduction of such losses is allowed) or disposes of the underlying property (at which time the loss deductions are allowed in full). Landlords who actively participate in the rental activities can deduct up to $25,000 of passive losses annually. However, this amount is phased out when the landlord's AGI exceeds $100,000. See also *portfolio income.*

**Payroll factor.** The proportion of a *multistate corporation*'s total payroll that is traceable to a specific state. Used in determining the taxable income that is to be apportioned to that state. See also *apportion.*

**Pecuniary bequest.** A bequest of money to an heir by a decedent. See also *bequest.*

**Percentage depletion.** See *depletion.*

**Percentage of completion method.** A method of reporting gain or loss on certain long-term contracts. Under this method of accounting, the gross contract price is included in income as the contract is completed. Reg. § 1.451–3. See also *completed contract method.*

**Personal and household effects.** Items owned by a decedent at the time of death. Examples include clothing, furniture, sporting goods, jewelry, stamp and coin collections, silverware, china, crystal, cooking utensils, books, cars, televisions, radios, and sound equipment.

**Personal holding company (PHC).** A corporation that satisfies the requirements of § 542. Qualification as a personal holding company means a penalty tax may be imposed on the corporation's undistributed personal holding company income for the year.

**Personal holding company income.** Income as defined by § 543. It includes interest, dividends, certain rents and royalties, income from the use of corporate property by certain shareholders, income from certain personal service contracts, and distributions from estates and trusts. Such income is relevant in determining whether a corporation is a personal holding company and is therefore subject to the penalty tax on personal holding companies. See also *adjusted ordinary gross income.*

**Personal holding company tax.** A penalty tax imposed on certain closely held corporations with excessive investment income. Assessed at the top individual tax rate on *personal holding company income*, reduced by dividends paid and other adjustments. § 541.

**Personal property.** Generally, all property other than real estate. It is sometimes referred to as personalty when real estate is termed realty. Personal property can also refer to property not used in a taxpayer's trade or business or held for the production or collection of income. When used in this sense, personal property can include both realty (e.g., a personal residence) and personalty (e.g., personal effects such as clothing and furniture). See also *bequest.*

**Personal service corporation (PSC).** An entity whose principal activity is the providing of services by owner-employees. Subject to a flat 35 percent tax rate and limited to a calendar tax year.

**Personalty.** All property that is not attached to real estate (realty) and is movable. Examples of personalty are machinery, automobiles, clothing, household furnishings, inventory, and personal effects. See also *ad valorem tax* and *realty.*

**Portfolio income.** Income from interest, dividends, rentals, royalties, capital gains, or other investment sources. Net passive losses cannot be used to offset net portfolio income. See also *passive loss* and *investment income.*

**Power of appointment.** A legal right granted to someone by will or other document that gives the holder the power to dispose of property or the income from property. When the holder may appoint the property to his or her own benefit, the power usually is called a general power of appointment. If the holder cannot benefit himself or herself but may only appoint to certain other persons, the power is a special power of appointment. Assume Gary places $500,000 worth of securities in trust granting Donna the right to determine each year how the trustee is to divide the income between Ann and Babs. Under these circumstances, Donna has a special power of appointment. If Donna had the further right to appoint the income to herself, she probably possesses a general power of appointment. For the estate tax and gift tax effects of powers of appointment, see §§ 2041 and 2514. See also *testamentary power of appointment.*

**Precontribution gain or loss.** Partnerships allow for a variety of *special allocations* of gain or loss among the partners, but gain or loss that is "built in" on an asset contributed to the partnership is assigned specifically to the contributing partner. § 704(c)(1)(A).

**Preferences (AMT).** See *alternative minimum tax (AMT)* and *tax preference items.*

**Preferred stock bailout.** A process where a shareholder used the issuance and sale, or later redemption, of a preferred stock dividend to obtain long-term capital gains, without any loss of voting control over the corporation. In effect, the shareholder received corporate profits without suffering the consequences of dividend income treatment. This procedure led Congress to enact § 306, which, if applicable, converts the prior long-term capital gain on the sale or redemption of the stock to ordinary income. See also *bailout.*

**Present interest.** See *future interest.*

**Presumption.** An inference in favor of a particular fact. If, for example, the IRS issues a notice of deficiency against a taxpayer, under certain conditions a presumption of correctness attaches to the assessment. Thus, the taxpayer has the burden of proof to show that he or she does not owe the tax listed in the deficiency notice. See also *rebuttable presumption.*

**Previously taxed income (PTI).** Under prior law, the undistributed taxable income of an S corporation was taxed to the shareholders as of the last day of the corporation's tax year and usually could be withdrawn by the shareholders without tax consequences at some later point in time. The role of PTI has been taken over by the *accumulated adjustments account.*

**Principal.** Property as opposed to income. The term is often used as a synonym for the corpus of a trust. If, for example, Gil places real estate in trust with income payable to Ann for life and the remainder to Barb upon Ann's death, the real estate is the principal, or corpus, of the trust.

**Private foundation.** An *exempt organization* subject to additional statutory restrictions on its activities and on contributions made to it. Excise taxes may be levied on certain prohibited transactions, and the Code places more stringent restrictions on the deductibility of contributions to private foundations. § 509.

**Pro rata.** Proportionately. Assume, for example, a corporation has 10 shareholders, each of whom owns 10 percent of the stock. A pro rata dividend distribution of $1,000 means that each shareholder receives $100.

**Pro se.** The taxpayer represents himself or herself before the court without the benefit of counsel.

**Probate.** The legal process by which the estate of a decedent is administered. Generally, the probate process involves collecting a decedent's assets, liquidating liabilities, paying necessary taxes, and distributing property to heirs.

**Probate costs.** The costs incurred in administering a decedent's estate. See also *probate estate*.

**Probate court.** The usual designation for the state or local court that supervises the administration (probate) of a decedent's estate.

**Probate estate.** The property of a decedent that is subject to administration by the executor or administrator of an estate. See also *administration*.

**Profit and loss sharing ratios.** Specified in the partnership agreement and used to determine each partner's allocation of ordinary taxable income and separately stated items. Profits and losses can be shared in different ratios. The ratios can be changed by amending the partnership agreement. § 704(a).

**Profits (loss) interest.** A partner's percentage allocation of partnership operating results, determined by the *profit and loss sharing ratios*.

**Property.** Assets defined in the broadest legal sense. Property includes the *unrealized receivables* of a cash basis taxpayer, but not services rendered. § 351.

**Property dividend.** A dividend consisting of in-kind (noncash) assets of the payor, measured by the fair market value of the property on the date of distribution. The portion of the distribution representing E & P is a dividend; any excess is treated as a return of capital. Distribution of in-kind property causes the distributing corporation to recognize any underlying realized gain, but not loss.

**Property factor.** The proportion of a *multistate corporation*'s total property that is traceable to a specific state. Used in determining the taxable income that is to be apportioned to that state. See also *apportion*.

**Property tax.** An *ad valorem tax*, usually levied by a city or county government, on the value of real or personal property that the taxpayer owns on a specified date. Most states exclude intangible property and assets owned by exempt organizations from the tax base, and some exclude inventory, pollution control or manufacturing equipment, and other items to provide relocation or retention incentives for the taxpayer.

**Proportionate distribution.** A distribution in which each partner in a partnership receives a pro rata share of hot assets being distributed. For example, a distribution of $10,000 of hot assets equally to two 50 percent partners is a proportionate distribution.

**Prop.Reg.** An abbreviation for Proposed Regulation. A Regulation may first be issued in proposed form to give interested parties the opportunity for comment. When and if a Proposed Regulation is finalized, it is known as a Regulation (abbreviated Reg.).

**PTI.** See *previously taxed income*.

**Public Law 86–272.** A congressional limit on the ability of the state to force a multistate corporation to assign income to that state. Under P.L. 86–272, where orders for tangible personal property are both filled and delivered outside the state, the entity must establish more than the mere solicitation of such orders before any income can be *apportioned* to the state.

**Public policy limitation.** A concept developed by the courts precluding an income tax deduction for certain expenses related to activities deemed to be contrary to the public welfare. In this connection, Congress has incorporated into the Code specific disallowance provisions covering such items as illegal bribes, kickbacks, and fines and penalties. §§ 162(c) and (f).

# Q

**Qualified business unit (QBU).** A subsidiary, branch, or other business entity that conducts business using a currency other than the U.S. dollar.

**Qualified family-owned business interest.** A relief provision benefiting owners of small businesses. By combining this deduction with the *exemption equivalent*, the first $1.3 million of value in a family business is free of Federal death tax. Ownership of the business, and material participation in its operations, must continue in the decedent's family. § 2057.

**Qualified nonrecourse debt.** Debt issued on realty by a bank, retirement plan, or governmental agency. Included in the *at-risk amount* by the investor. § 465(b)(6).

**Qualified pension or profit sharing plan.** An employer-sponsored plan that meets the requirements of § 401. If these requirements are met, none of the employer's contributions to the plan will be taxed to the employee until distributed (§ 402). The employer is allowed a deduction in the year the contributions are made (§ 404). See also *contributory qualified* *pension or profit sharing plan, deferred compensation,* and *noncontributory pension or profit sharing plan.*

**Qualified small business corporation.** A C corporation that has aggregate gross assets not exceeding $50 million and that is conducting an active trade or business. § 1202.

**Qualified small business stock.** Stock in a qualified small business corporation, purchased as part of an original issue after August 10, 1993. The shareholder may exclude from gross income 50 percent of the realized gain on the sale of the stock, if he or she held the stock for more than five years. § 1202.

**Qualified terminable interest property (QTIP).** Generally, the *marital deduction* (for gift and estate tax purposes) is not available if the interest transferred will terminate upon the death of the transferee spouse and pass to someone else. Thus, if Hannah places property in trust, life estate to Will, and remainder to their children upon Will's death, this is a terminable interest that will not provide Hannah (or her estate) with a marital deduction. If, however, the transfer in trust is treated as qualified terminable interest property (the QTIP election is made), the terminable interest restriction is waived and the marital deduction becomes available. In exchange for this deduction, the surviving spouse's gross estate must include the value of the QTIP election assets, even though he or she has no control over the ultimate disposition of the asset. Terminable interest property qualifies for this election if the donee (or heir) is the only beneficiary of the asset during his or her lifetime and receives income distributions relative to the property at least annually. For gifts, the donor spouse is the one who makes the QTIP election. As to property transferred by death, the *executor* of the estate of the deceased spouse has the right to make the election. §§ 2056(b)(7) and 2523(f).

# R

**RAR.** A Revenue Agent's Report, which reflects any adjustments made by the agent as a result of an audit of the taxpayer. The RAR is mailed to the taxpayer along with the *30-day letter,* which outlines the appellate procedures available to the taxpayer.

**Realistic possibility.** A preparer penalty is assessed where a tax return includes a position that has no realistic possibility of being sustained by a court.

**Realized gain or loss.** The difference between the amount realized upon the sale or other disposition of property and the adjusted basis of such property. § 1001. See also *adjusted basis, amount realized, basis,* and *recognized gain or loss.*

**Realty.** Real estate. See also *personalty.*

**Reasonable cause.** Relief from taxpayer and preparer penalties often is allowed where there is reasonable cause for the taxpayer's actions. For instance, reasonable cause for the late filing of a tax return might be a flood that damaged the taxpayer's record-keeping systems and made difficult a timely completion of the return.

**Reasonable needs of the business.** A means of avoiding the penalty tax on an unreasonable accumulation of earnings. In determining base for this tax (*accumulated taxable income*), § 535 allows a deduction for "such part of earnings and profits for the taxable year as are retained for the reasonable needs of the business." § 537.

**Rebuttable presumption.** A presumption that can be overturned upon the showing of sufficient proof. See also *presumption.*

**Recapitalization.** An E reorganization, constituting a major change in the character and amount of outstanding equity of a corporation. For instance, common stock exchanged for preferred stock can qualify for tax-free E reorganization treatment.

**Recapture.** To recover the tax benefit of a deduction or a credit previously taken. See also *depreciation recapture.*

**Recapture potential.** A measure with respect to property that, if disposed of in a taxable transaction, would result in the recapture of depreciation (§§ 1245 or 1250), deferred LIFO gain, or deferred installment method gain.

**Recognized gain or loss.** The portion of realized gain or loss subject to income taxation. See also *realized gain or loss.*

**Recourse debt.** Debt for which the lender may both foreclose on the property and assess a guarantor for any payments due under the loan, even from personal assets. A lender may also make a claim against the assets of any general partner in a partnership to which debt is issued, without regard to whether that partner has guaranteed the debt.

**Redemption.** See *stock redemption.*

**Redemption (complete termination).** Sale or exchange treatment is available relative to this type of redemption. The shareholder must retire all of his or her outstanding shares in the corporation (ignoring family attribution rules) and cannot hold an interest, other than that of a creditor, for the 10 years following the redemption. § 302(b)(3).

**Redemption (disproportionate).** Sale or exchange treatment is available relative to this type of redemption. After the exchange, the shareholder owns less than 80 percent of his or her pre-redemption interest in the corporation and only a minority interest in the entity. § 302(b)(2).

**Redemption (not equivalent to a dividend).** Sale or exchange treatment is given to this type of redemption. Although various safe-harbor tests are failed, the nature of the redemption is such that dividend treatment is avoided, because it represents a meaningful reduction in the shareholder's interest in the corporation. § 302(b)(1).

**Redemption to pay death taxes.** Sale or exchange treatment is available relative to this type of redemption, to the extent of the proceeds up to the total amount paid by the estate or heir for death taxes and administration expenses. The stock value must exceed 35 percent of the value of the decedent's adjusted gross estate. In meeting this test, one can combine shareholdings in corporations where the decedent held at least 20 percent of the outstanding shares.

**Regular corporation.** See *C corporation.*

**Regulations.** The U.S. Treasury Department Regulations (abbreviated Reg.) represent the position of the IRS as to how the Internal Revenue Code is to be interpreted. Their purpose is to provide taxpayers and IRS personnel with rules of general and specific application to the various provisions of the tax law. Regulations are published in the *Federal Register* and in all tax services.

**Related corporations.** See *controlled group.*

**Related parties.** Various Code Sections define related parties and often include a variety of persons within this (usually detrimental) category. Generally, related parties are accorded different tax treatment from that applicable to other taxpayers who enter into similar transactions. For instance, realized losses that are generated between related parties are not recognized in the year of the loss. However, these deferred losses can be used to offset recognized gains that occur upon the subsequent sale of the asset to a nonrelated party. Other uses of a related-party definition include the conversion of gain upon the sale of a depreciable asset into all ordinary income (§ 1239) and the identification of constructive ownership of stock relative to corporate distributions, redemptions, liquidations, reorganizations, and compensation.

**Remainder interest.** The property that passes to a beneficiary after the expiration of an intervening income interest. If, for example, Greg places real estate in trust with income to Ann for life and remainder to Bill upon Ann's death, Bill has a remainder interest. See also *life estate* and *reversionary interest.*

**Remand.** To send back. An appellate court may remand a case to a lower court, usually for additional fact finding. In other words, the appellate court is not in a position to decide the appeal based on the facts determined by the lower court. Remanding is abbreviated *"rem'g."*

**Reorganization.** See *corporate reorganization.*

**Research activities credit.** A tax credit whose purpose is to encourage research and development. It consists of two components: the incremental research activities credit and the basic research credit. The incremental research activities credit is equal to 20 percent of the excess qualified research expenditures over the base amount. The basic research credit is equal to 20 percent of the excess of basic research payments over the base amount. § 41. See also *general business credit.*

**Residential rental property.** Buildings for which at least 80 percent of the gross rents are from dwelling units (e.g., an apartment building). This type of building is distinguished from nonresidential (commercial or industrial) buildings in applying the recapture of depreciation provisions. The term also is relevant in distinguishing between buildings that are eligible for a 27.5-year life versus a 31.5- or 39-year life for MACRS purposes.

**Residual method.** Used to allocate the new stepped-up basis of a subsidiary's assets among its property when a § 338 election is in effect. The purchase price that exceeds the aggregate fair market values of the tangible and identifiable intangible assets is allocated to goodwill or going-concern value. § 1060.

**Restoration event.** Sales between members of a *consolidated return,* and other intragroup transactions, are subject to special recognition deferral rules, so that the members cannot artificially create taxable gains or losses solely when tax conditions call for them. Rather, when a restoration event occurs (e.g., when the asset ultimately is sold outside the group), the recognition of all intragroup gains and losses is restored.

**Return of capital.** When a taxpayer reacquires financial resources that he or she previously had invested in an entity or venture, the return of his or her capital investment itself does not increase gross income for the recovery year. A return of capital may result from an annuity or insurance contract, the sale or exchange of any asset, or a distribution from a partnership or corporation.

**Revenue Agent's Report.** See *RAR.*

**Revenue neutrality.** A change in the tax system that results in the same amount of revenue. Revenue neutral, however, does not mean that any one taxpayer will pay the same amount of tax as before. Thus, as a result of a tax law change, corporations could pay more taxes, but the excess revenue will be offset by lower taxes on individuals.

**Revenue Procedure.** A matter of procedural importance to both taxpayers and the IRS concerning the administration of the tax laws is issued as a Revenue Procedure (abbreviated Rev.Proc.). A Revenue Procedure is first published in an *Internal Revenue Bulletin* (I.R.B.) and later transferred to the appropriate *Cumulative Bulletin* (C.B.). Both the *Internal Revenue Bulletins* and the *Cumulative Bulletins* are published by the U.S. Government Printing Office.

**Revenue Ruling.** A Revenue Ruling (abbreviated Rev.Rul.) is issued by the National Office of the IRS to express an official interpretation of the tax law as applied to specific transactions. It is more limited in application than a Regulation. A Revenue Ruling is first published in an *Internal Revenue Bulletin* (I.R.B.) and later transferred to the appropriate *Cumulative Bulletin* (C.B.). Both the *Internal Revenue Bulletins* and the *Cumulative Bulletins* are published by the U.S. Government Printing Office.

**Reversed (Rev'd.).** An indication that a decision of one court has been reversed by a higher court in the same case.

**Reversing (Rev'g.).** An indication that the decision of a higher court is reversing the result reached by a lower court in the same case.

**Reversionary interest.** The property that reverts to the grantor after the expiration of an intervening income interest. Assume Gail places real estate in trust with income to Art for 11 years, and upon the expiration of this term, the property returns to Gail. Under these circumstances, she holds a reversionary interest in the property. A reversionary interest is the same as a remainder interest, except that, in the latter case, the property passes to someone other than the original owner (e.g., the grantor of a trust) upon the expiration of the intervening interest. See also *grantor trust* and *remainder interest*.

**Revocable transfer.** A transfer of property where the transferor retains the right to recover the property. The creation of a revocable trust is an example of a revocable transfer. § 2038. See also *incomplete transfer*.

**Rev.Proc.** Abbreviation for an IRS Revenue Procedure. See *Revenue Procedure*.

**Rev.Rul.** Abbreviation for an IRS Revenue Ruling. See *Revenue Ruling*.

**Right of survivorship.** See *joint tenants*.

# S

**S corporation.** The designation for a small business corporation. See also *Subchapter S*.

**Sales factor.** The proportion of a *multistate corporation*'s total sales that is traceable to a specific state. Used in determining the taxable income that is to be apportioned to that state. See also *apportion*.

**Sales tax.** A state- or local-level tax on the retail sale of specified property. Generally, the purchaser pays the tax, but the seller collects it, as an agent for the government. Various taxing jurisdictions allow exemptions for purchases of specific items, including certain food, services, and manufacturing equipment. If the purchaser and seller are in different states, a *use tax* usually applies.

**Schedule M-1.** On the Form 1120, a reconciliation of book net income with Federal taxable income. Accounts for timing and permanent differences in the two computations, such as depreciation differences, exempt income, and nondeductible items. On Forms 1120S and 1065, the Schedule M-1 reconciles book income with the owners' aggregate ordinary taxable income.

**Schedule PH.** A tax form required to be filed by corporations that are personal holding companies. The form must be filed in addition to Form 1120 (U.S. Corporation Income Tax Return).

**Section 306 stock.** Preferred stock issued as a nontaxable stock dividend that, if sold or redeemed, would result in ordinary income recognition. § 306(c). See also *preferred stock bailout*.

**Section 306 taint.** The ordinary income that would result upon the sale or other taxable disposition of § 306 stock.

**Section 338 election.** When a corporation acquires at least 80 percent of a subsidiary in a 12-month period, it can elect to treat the acquisition of such stock as an asset purchase. The acquiring corporation's basis in the subsidiary's assets then is the cost of the stock. The subsidiary is deemed to have sold its assets for an amount equal to the grossed-up basis in its stock.

**Section 382 limitation.** When one corporation acquires another, the acquiror's ability to use the loss and credit carryovers of the target may be limited, in an anti-abuse provision specified in the Code. Generally, for instance, the maximum deduction available to the acquiror is the takeover-date value of the target times the tax-exempt interest rate on that date.

**Section 754 election.** An election that may be made by a partnership to adjust the basis of partnership assets to reflect a purchasing partner's outside basis in interest or to reflect a gain, loss, or basis adjustment of a partner receiving a distribution from a partnership. The intent of the election is to maintain the equivalence between outside and inside basis. Once the election is made, the partnership must make basis adjustments for all future transactions, unless the IRS consents to revoke the election.

**Section 1231 assets.** Depreciable assets and real estate used in a trade or business and held for the appropriate holding period. Under certain circumstances, the classification also includes timber, coal, domestic iron ore, livestock (held for draft, breeding, dairy, or sporting purposes), and unharvested crops. § 1231(b). See also *Section 1231 gains and losses*.

**Section 1231 gains and losses.** If the combined gains and losses from the taxable dispositions of § 1231 assets plus the net gain from business involuntary conversions (of both § 1231 assets and long-term capital assets) is a gain, such gains and losses are treated as long-term capital gains and losses. In arriving at § 1231 gains, however, the depreciation recapture provisions (e.g., §§ 1245 and 1250) are first applied to produce ordinary income. If the net result of the combination is a loss, the gains and losses from § 1231 assets are treated as ordinary gains and losses. § 1231(a). See also *depreciation recapture* and *Section 1231 assets*.

**Section 1244 stock.** Stock issued under § 1244 by qualifying small business corporations. If § 1244 stock becomes worthless, the shareholders may claim an ordinary loss rather than the usual capital loss, within statutory limitations.

**Section 1245 recapture.** Upon a taxable disposition of § 1245 property, all depreciation claimed on such property is recaptured as ordinary income (but not to exceed recognized gain from the disposition).

**Section 1250 recapture.** Upon a taxable disposition of § 1250 property, some of the depreciation or cost recovery claimed on the property may be recaptured as ordinary income.

**Securities.** Generally, stock, debt, and other financial assets. To the extent securities other than the stock of the transferee corporation are received in a § 351 exchange, the new shareholder realizes a gain.

**Separate property.** In a community property jurisdiction, property that belongs entirely to one of the spouses is separate property. Generally, it is property acquired before marriage or acquired after marriage by gift or inheritance. See also *community property*.

**Separate return limitation year (SRLY).** A series of rules limits the amount of an acquired corporation's net operating loss carryforwards that can be used by the acquiror. Generally, a *consolidated return* can include the acquiree's NOL carryforward only to the extent of the lesser of the subsidiary's (1) current-year or (2) cumulative positive contribution to consolidated taxable income. Prop.Reg. § 1.1502–21(c).

**Separately stated item.** Any item of a partnership or S corporation that might be taxed differently to any two owners of the entity. These amounts are not included in ordinary income of the entity, but instead are reported separately to the owners; tax consequences are determined at the owner level.

**Sham.** A transaction without substance that will be disregarded for tax purposes.

**Short-term capital gain or loss.** Results from the sale or other taxable exchange of a capital asset that had been held by the seller for one year or less or from other transactions involving statutorily designated assets, including nonbusiness bad debts.

**Simple trust.** Simple trusts are those that are not complex trusts. Such trusts may not have a charitable beneficiary, accumulate income, or distribute corpus. See also *complex trust*.

**Small business corporation.** A corporation that satisfies the definition of § 1361(b), § 1244(c), or both. Satisfaction of § 1361(b) permits an S election, and satisfaction of § 1244 enables the shareholders of the corporation to claim an ordinary loss on the worthlessness of stock.

**Small Cases Division of the U.S. Tax Court.** Jurisdiction is limited to claims of $50,000 or less. There is no appeal from this court.

**Special allocation.** Any amount for which an agreement exists among the partners of a partnership outlining the method used for assigning the item among the partners.

**Special power of appointment.** See *power of appointment*.

**Special use value.** Permits the executor of an estate to value, for death tax purposes, real estate used in a farming activity or in connection with a closely held business at its current use value rather than at its most suitable or optimal use value. Under this option, a farm is valued for farming purposes even though, for example, the property might have a higher potential value as a shopping center. For the executor of an estate to elect special use valuation, the conditions of § 2032A must be satisfied. See also *most suitable use value*.

**Spin-off.** A type of reorganization where, for example, Ace Corporation transfers some assets to Bow Corporation in exchange for enough Bow stock to represent control. Ace then distributes the Bow stock to its shareholders.

**Split-off.** A type of reorganization where, for example, Arc Corporation transfers some assets to Bond Corporation in exchange for enough Bond stock to represent control. Arc then distributes the Bond stock to its shareholders in exchange for some of their Arc stock.

**Split-up.** A type of reorganization where, for example, Ally Corporation transfers some assets to Bar Corporation and the remainder to Zip Corporation. In return, Ally receives enough Bar and Zip stock to represent control of each corporation. Ally then distributes the Bar and Zip stock to its shareholders in return for all of their Ally stock. The result of the split-up is that Ally is liquidated, and its shareholders now have control of Bar and Zip.

**Sprinkling trust.** When a trustee has the discretion to either distribute or accumulate the entity accounting income of the trust and to distribute it among the trust's income beneficiaries in varying magnitudes, a sprinkling trust exists. The trustee can "sprinkle" the income of the trust.

**Statute of limitations.** Provisions of the law that specify the maximum period of time in which action may be taken on a past event. Code §§ 6501–6504 contain the limitation periods applicable to the IRS for additional assessments, and §§ 6511–6515 relate to refund claims by taxpayers.

**Statutory depletion.** See *depletion*.

**Statutory notice of deficiency.** Commonly referred to as the 90-day letter, this notice is sent to a taxpayer upon request, upon the expiration of the *30-day letter*, or upon exhaustion by the taxpayer of his or her administrative remedies before the IRS. The notice gives the taxpayer 90 days in which to file a petition with the U.S. Tax Court. If such a petition is not filed, the IRS will demand payment of the assessed deficiency. §§ 6211–6216. See also *deficiency*.

**Step transaction.** Disregarding one or more transactions to arrive at the final result. Assume, for example, that the shareholders of Clue Corporation liquidate the corporation and receive cash and operating assets. Immediately after the liquidation, the shareholders transfer the operating assets to newly formed Blue Corporation. Under these circumstances, the IRS may contend that the liquidation of Clue should be disregarded (thereby depriving the shareholders of capital gain treatment). What may really have happened is a reorganization of Clue with a distribution of boot (ordinary income) to Clue's shareholders. If so, there will be a carryover of basis in the assets transferred from Clue to Blue.

**Step-down in basis.** A reduction in the tax basis of property. See also *step-up in basis*.

**Step-up in basis.** An increase in the income tax basis of property. The classic step-up in basis occurs when a decedent dies owning appreciated property. Since the estate or heir acquires a basis in the property equal to the property's fair market value on the date of death (or alternate valuation date if available and elected), any appreciation is not subject to the income tax. Thus, a step-up in basis is the result, with no income tax consequences.

**Stock attribution.** See *attribution*.

**Stock dividend.** A dividend consisting of stock of the payor. Not taxable if a pro rata distribution of stock or stock rights on common stock. However, some stock dividends are taxable. § 305.

**Stock redemption.** A corporation buys back its own stock from a specified shareholder. Typically, the corporation recognizes any realized gain on the noncash assets that it uses to effect a redemption, and the shareholder obtains a capital gain or loss upon receipt of the purchase price.

**Stock rights.** Assets that convey to the holder the power to purchase corporate stock at a specified price, often for a limited period of time. Stock rights received may be taxed as a distribution of earnings and profits. After the right is exercised, the basis of the acquired share includes the investor's purchase price or gross income, if any, to obtain the right. Disposition of the right also is a taxable event, with basis often assigned from the shares held prior to the issuance of the right.

**Subchapter S.** Sections 1361–1379 of the Internal Revenue Code. An elective provision permitting certain small business corporations (§ 1361) and their shareholders (§ 1362) to elect to be treated for income tax purposes in accordance with the operating rules of §§ 1363–1379. S corporations usually avoid the corporate income tax, and corporate losses can be claimed by the shareholders.

**Subpart F.** The subpart of the Code that identifies the current tax treatment of income earned by a controlled foreign corporation. Certain types of income are included in U.S. gross income by U.S. shareholders of such an entity as the income is generated, not when it is repatriated.

**Substance vs. form concept.** A standard used when one must ascertain the true reality of what has occurred. Suppose, for example, a father sells stock to his daughter for $1,000. If the stock is really worth $50,000 at the time of the transfer, the substance of the transaction is probably a gift to her of $49,000.

**Substantial authority.** Taxpayer understatement penalties are waived where substantial authority existed for the disputed position taken on the return.

**Substantial economic effect.** Partnerships are allowed to *allocate* items of income, expense, gain, loss, and credit in any manner that is authorized in the partnership agreement, provided that the allocation has an economic effect aside from the corresponding tax results. The necessary substantial economic effect is present, for instance, if the post-contribution appreciation in the value of an asset that was contributed to the partnership by a partner was allocated to that partner for cost recovery purposes.

**Substituted basis.** When a taxpayer exchanges one asset for another, many provisions in the tax law allow an assignment of basis in the received asset to be that of the traded asset(s) in the hands of its former owner. Thus, no step-up or -down of basis occurs as a result of the exchange. For instance, when an investor contributes an asset to a corporation or partnership, the partner generally takes a substituted basis in the partnership interest (i.e., the interest has a basis

equal to the aggregated bases of the assets contributed by that partner). § 723.

**Surviving spouse.** When a husband or wife predeceases the other spouse, the survivor is known as a surviving spouse. Under certain conditions, a surviving spouse may be entitled to use the income tax rates in § 1(a) (those applicable to married persons filing a joint return) for the two years after the year of death of his or her spouse.

**Survivorship.** See *joint tenants*.

**Syndication costs.** Incurred in promoting and marketing partnership interests for sale to investors. Examples include legal and accounting fees, printing costs for prospectus and placement documents, and state registration fees. These items are capitalized by the partnership as incurred, with no amortization thereof allowed.

# T

**Tangible property.** All property that has form or substance and is not intangible. See also *intangible asset*.

**Tax benefit rule.** Limits the recognition of income from the recovery of an expense or loss properly deducted in a prior tax year to the amount of the deduction that generated a tax saving. Assume that last year Tom had medical expenses of $3,000 and adjusted gross income of $30,000. Because of the 7.5 percent limitation, he could deduct only $750 of these expenses [$3,000 – (7.5% × $30,000)]. If, this year, Tom is reimbursed by his insurance company for $900 of these expenses, the tax benefit rule limits the amount of income from the reimbursement to $750 (the amount previously deducted with a tax saving).

**Tax Court.** The U.S. Tax Court is one of four trial courts of original jurisdiction that decide litigation involving Federal income, death, or gift taxes. It is the only trial court where the taxpayer must not first pay the deficiency assessed by the IRS. The Tax Court will not have jurisdiction over a case unless a statutory notice of deficiency (90-day letter) has been issued by the IRS and the taxpayer files the petition for hearing within the time prescribed.

**Tax haven.** A country in which either locally sourced income or residents of the country are subject to a low rate of taxation.

**Tax on unearned income of a child under age 14.** Passive income, such as interest and dividends, that is recognized by such a child is taxed *to him or her* at the rates that would have applied had the income been incurred by the child's parents, generally to the extent that the income exceeds $1,500. The additional tax is assessed regardless of the source of the income or the income's underlying property. If the child's parents are divorced, the custodial parent's rates are used. The parents' rates reflect any applicable alternative minimum tax and the phase-outs of lower tax brackets and other deductions. § 1(g).

**Tax preference items.** Various items that may result in the imposition of the *alternative minimum tax*. §§ 55–58.

**Tax treaty.** An agreement between the U.S. State Department and another country, designed to alleviate double taxation of income and asset transfers and to share administrative information useful to tax agencies in both countries. The United States has income tax treaties with over 40 countries and transfer tax treaties with about 20.

**Tax year.** See *accounting period.*

**Taxable estate.** The *gross estate* of a *decedent* reduced by the deductions allowed by §§ 2053–2057 (e.g., administration expenses and marital and charitable deductions). The taxable estate is subject to the unified transfer tax at death. See also *adjusted taxable estate* and *gross estate.* § 2051.

**Taxable gift.** Amount of a gift that is subject to the unified transfer tax. Thus, a taxable gift has been adjusted by the annual exclusion and other appropriate deductions (e.g., marital and charitable). § 2503.

**Taxable income.** The tax base with respect to the prevailing Federal income tax. Taxable income is defined by the Internal Revenue Code, Treasury Regulations, and pertinent court cases. Currently, taxable income includes gross income from all sources except those specifically excluded by the statute. In addition, taxable income is reduced for certain allowable deductions. Deductions for business taxpayers must be related to a trade or business. Individuals can also deduct certain personal expenses in determining their taxable incomes. See also *gross income.*

**Tax-free exchange.** Transfers of property specifically exempted from income tax consequences by the tax law. Examples are a transfer of property to a controlled corporation under § 351(a) and a like-kind exchange under § 1031(a).

**T.C.** An abbreviation for the U.S. Tax Court used in citing a Regular Decision of the U.S. Tax Court.

**T.C.Memo.** An abbreviation used to refer to a Memorandum Decision of the U.S. Tax Court.

**Technical advice memorandum.** An interpretation of the tax law with respect to a disputed item, issued by the National Office of the IRS or a Regional Commissioner, in response to a request from an agent, appellate conferee, or District Director. Often used to reconcile perceived differences in the application of the law among taxpayers or to identify an IRS position where no pertinent Regulations or rulings exist.

**Technical termination of partnership.** The entity is treated for tax purposes as though it has terminated, even though it continues in its activities. When there has been a sale or exchange of more than 50 percent of the capital interests of the partnership within 12 months, the partnership is deemed to have terminated when the 50 percent threshold is crossed. A new partnership immediately is formed through asset contributions by the partners. These activities can affect the entity's tax year and its bases in the assets it holds.

**Telescoping.** To look through one or more transactions to arrive at the final result. It is also referred to as the *step transaction* approach or the *substance vs. form concept.*

**Temporary Regulation** The Treasury often issues Temporary Regulations to offer immediate guidance as to elections and other compliance matters after a change in the statute or a court ruling has been issued. Temporary Regulations carry the same precedential value as a final Regulation, and they should be followed as such for three years after issuance, after which they expire. Often a Temporary Regulation also is issued as a Proposed Regulation.

**Tenants by the entirety.** Essentially, a joint tenancy between husband and wife. See also *joint tenants* and *tenancy in common.*

**Tenants in common.** A form of ownership where each tenant (owner) holds an undivided interest in property. Unlike a joint tenancy or a tenancy by the entirety, the interest of a tenant in common does not terminate upon that individual's death (there is no right of survivorship). Assume Brad and Connie acquire real estate as equal tenants in common, each having furnished one-half of the purchase price. Upon Brad's death, his one-half interest in the property passes to his estate or heirs, not to Connie. For a comparison of results, see *joint tenants* and *tenancy by the entirety.*

**Term certain.** A fixed period of years used to determine the length of an income interest (i.e., prior to the termination of a trust or estate).

**Terminable interest.** An interest in property that terminates upon the death of the holder or upon the occurrence of some other specified event. The transfer of a terminable interest by one spouse to the other may not qualify for the marital deduction. §§ 2056(b) and 2523(b). See also *marital deduction.*

**Testamentary disposition.** The passing of property to another upon the death of the owner.

**Testamentary power of appointment.** A power of appointment that can be exercised only through the will (upon the death) of the holder. See also *power of appointment.*

**Thin capitalization.** When debt owed by a corporation to the shareholders becomes too large in relation to the corporation's capital structure (i.e., stock and shareholder equity), the IRS may contend that the corporation is thinly capitalized. In effect, this means that some or all of the debt is reclassified as equity. The immediate result is to disallow any interest deduction to the corporation on the reclassified debt. To the extent of the corporation's earnings and profits, interest payments and loan repayments are treated as dividends to the shareholders.

**Thirty-day letter.** A letter that accompanies an RAR (Revenue Agent's Report) issued as a result of an IRS audit of a taxpayer (or the rejection of a taxpayer's claim for refund). The letter outlines the taxpayer's appeal procedure before the IRS. If the taxpayer does not request any such procedures within the 30-day period, the IRS will issue a statutory notice of deficiency (the 90-day letter). See also *statutory notice of deficiency*.

**Three-factor apportionment formula.** A means by which the total taxable income of a *multistate corporation* is assigned to a specific state. Usually, the payroll, property, and sales factors are treated equally, and the average of these factors is used in the apportionment procedure. In some states, however, the sales factor may receive a double weight, or it may be the only factor considered. These latter formulas place greater tax burden on the income of out-of-state corporations. See also *apportion, payroll factor, property factor, sales factor,* and *UDITPA*.

**Throwback rule.** If there is no income tax in the state to which a sale otherwise would be *apportioned*, the sale essentially is exempt from state income tax, even though the seller is *domiciled* in a state that levies an income tax. Nonetheless, if the seller's state has adopted a throwback rule, the sale is attributed to the *seller's* state, and the transaction is subjected to a state-level tax.

**Tiered partnerships.** An ownership arrangement wherein one partnership (the parent or first tier) is a partner in one or more partnerships (the subsidiary/subsidiaries or second tier). Frequently, the first tier is a holding partnership, and the second tier is an operating partnership.

**Totten trust.** A bank account (checking, savings, money market, CD) that designates a survivor in the event the owner predeceases. As an example, Dan purchases a $50,000 CD and lists ownership as follows: "Dan, payable on proof of Dan's death to Nancy." The transfer is incomplete and can be revoked or changed by Dan as he sees fit. Once Dan dies, however, the CD belongs to Nancy. In effect, the Totten trust arrangement carries the same tax consequences as a revocable trust. It is a simpler and cheaper way to avoid probate as no formal trust need be created. The Totten trust arrangement also can be used with most securities (i.e., stocks and bonds).

**Trade or business.** Any business or professional activity conducted by a taxpayer. The mere ownership of rental or other investment assets does not constitute a trade or business. Generally, a trade or business generates relatively little passive investment income.

**Transfer tax.** A tax imposed upon the transfer of property. See also *unified transfer tax*.

**Transferee liability.** Under certain conditions, if the IRS is unable to collect taxes owed by a transferor of property, it may pursue its claim against the transferee of the property. The transferee's liability for taxes is limited to the extent of the value of the assets transferred. For example, the IRS can force a donee to pay the gift tax when such tax cannot be paid by the donor making the transfer. §§ 6901–6905.

**Treasury Regulations.** See *Regulations*.

**Treaty shopping.** An international investor attempts to use the favorable aspects of a tax treaty to his or her advantage, often elevating the form of the transaction over its substance (e.g., by establishing only a nominal presence in the country offering the favorable treaty terms).

**Trial court.** The court of original jurisdiction; the first court to consider litigation. In Federal tax controversies, trial courts include U.S. District Courts, the U.S. Tax Court, the U.S. Court of Federal Claims, and the Small Cases Division of the U.S. Tax Court. See also *appellate court, Court of Federal Claims, District Court, Small Cases Division of the U.S. Tax Court,* and *Tax Court*.

**Trust.** A legal entity created by a grantor for the benefit of designated beneficiaries under the laws of the state and the valid trust instrument. The trustee holds a fiduciary responsibility to manage the trust's corpus assets and income for the economic benefit of all of the beneficiaries.

**Trustee.** An individual or corporation that assumes the fiduciary responsibilities under a trust agreement.

# U

**UDITPA.** The Uniform Division of Income for Tax Purposes Act has been adopted in some form by many of the states. The Act develops criteria by which the total taxable income of a *multistate corporation* can be assigned to specific states. See also *allocate, apportion, Multistate Tax Commission (MTC),* and *nexus*.

**Undistributed personal holding company income.** The penalty tax on personal holding companies is imposed on the corporation's undistributed personal holding company income for the year. The adjustments necessary to convert taxable income to undistributed personal holding company income are set forth in § 545.

**Unearned income.** Income received but not yet earned. Normally, such income is taxed when received, even for accrual basis taxpayers.

**Unified tax credit.** A credit allowed against any unified transfer tax. §§ 2010 and 2505.

**Unified transfer tax.** Rates applicable to transfers by gift and death made after 1976. § 2001(c).

**Uniform Gift to Minors Act.** A means of transferring property (usually stocks and bonds) to a minor. The designated custodian of the property has the legal right to act on behalf of the minor without requiring a guardianship. Generally, the custodian possesses the right to change investments (e.g., sell one type of stock and buy another), apply the income from the custodial property to the minor's support, and even terminate the custodianship. In this regard, however, the custodian is acting in a fiduciary capacity on behalf of the minor. During the period of the custodianship, the income from the property is taxed to the minor. The custodianship terminates when the minor reaches legal age. See also *guardianship* and *legal age*.

**Unitary state.** A state that has adopted the unitary theory in its apportionment of the total taxable income of a multistate corporation to the state.

**Unitary theory.** Sales, property, and payroll of related corporations are combined for *nexus* and apportionment purposes, and the worldwide income of the unitary entity is *apportioned* to the state. Subsidiaries and other affiliated corporations found to be part of the corporation's unitary business (because they are subject to overlapping ownership, operation, or management) are included in the apportionment procedure. This approach can be limited if a *water's edge election* is in effect.

**Unrealized receivables.** Amounts earned by a cash basis taxpayer but not yet received. Because of the method of accounting used by the taxpayer, these amounts have no income tax basis. When unrealized receivables are distributed to a partner, they generally convert a transaction from nontaxable to taxable or convert otherwise capital gain to ordinary income.

**Unreasonable compensation.** A deduction is allowed for "reasonable" salaries or other compensation for personal services actually rendered. To the extent compensation is "excessive" ("unreasonable"), no deduction is allowed. Unreasonable compensation usually is found in closely held corporations, where the motivation is to pay out profits in some form that is deductible to the corporation. Deductible compensation therefore becomes an attractive substitute for nondeductible dividends when the shareholders also are employed by the corporation.

**Unrelated business income.** Income recognized by an exempt organization that is generated from activities not related to the exempt purpose of the entity. For instance, the pharmacy located in a hospital often generates unrelated business income. § 511.

**Unrelated business income tax.** Levied on the *unrelated business income* of an *exempt organization*.

**U.S.-owned foreign corporation.** A foreign corporation in which 50 percent or more of the total combined voting power or total value of the stock of the corporation is held directly or indirectly by U.S. persons. A U.S. corporation is treated as a U.S.-owned foreign corporation if the dividend or interest income it pays is classified as foreign source under § 861.

**U.S. real property interest.** Any direct interest in real property situated in the United States and any interest in a domestic corporation (other than solely as a creditor) unless the taxpayer can establish that a domestic corporation was not a U.S. real property holding corporation during the five-year period ending on the date of disposition of such interest (the base period). See *FIRPTA*.

**U.S. shareholder.** For purposes of classification of an entity as a *controlled foreign corporation*, a U.S. person who owns, or is considered to own, 10 percent or more of the total combined voting power of all classes of voting stock of a foreign corporation. Stock owned directly, indirectly, and constructively is counted for this purpose.

**U.S.-source income.** Generally, income taxed by the United States, regardless of the citizenship or residence of its creator.

Examples include income from sales of U.S. real estate and dividends from U.S. corporations.

**U.S. Tax Court.** See *Tax Court*.

**U.S. trade or business.** A set of activities that is carried on in a regular, continuous, and substantial manner. A non-U.S. taxpayer is subject to U.S. tax on the taxable income that is effectively connected with a U.S. trade or business.

**Use tax.** A sales tax that is collectible by the seller where the purchaser is domiciled in a different state.

**USSC.** An abbreviation for the U.S. Supreme Court, used in citing court opinions.

**USTC.** Published by Commerce Clearing House, *U.S. Tax Cases* contain all of the Federal tax decisions issued by the U.S. District Courts, U.S. Court of Federal Claims, U.S. Courts of Appeals, and the U.S. Supreme Court.

# V

**Value.** See *fair market value*.

**Vested.** Absolute and complete. If, for example, a person holds a vested interest in property, such interest cannot be taken away or otherwise defeated.

**Voluntary revocation.** The owners of a majority of shares in an S corporation elect to terminate the S status of the entity, as of a specified date. The day on which the revocation is effective is the first day of the corporation's C tax year.

**Voting trust.** A trust that holds the voting rights to stock in a corporation. It is a useful device when a majority of the shareholders in a corporation cannot agree on corporate policy.

# W

**Wash sale.** A loss from the sale of stock or securities that is disallowed because the taxpayer has, within 30 days before or after the sale, acquired stock or securities substantially identical to those sold. § 1091.

**Water's edge election.** A limitation on the worldwide scope of the *unitary theory*. If a corporate water's edge election is in effect, the state can consider only the activities that occur within the boundaries of the United States in the *apportionment* procedure.

**WESTLAW.** An online database system, produced by West Group, through which a tax researcher can obtain access to the Internal Revenue Code, Regulations, administrative rulings, and court case opinions.

**Wherewithal to pay.** A concept of tax equity that delays the recognition of gain on a transaction until the taxpayer has received means by which to pay the tax. The *installment method*, whereunder gain is taxed proportionately as installment proceeds are received, embodies the wherewithal to pay concept. See also *involuntary conversion* and *like-kind exchange*.

**Writ of Certiorari.** See *certiorari*.

[See Title 26 U.S.C.A.]

# Table of Revenue Procedures and Revenue Rulings Cited

**APPENDIX F**

# Comprehensive Tax Return Problems

## PROBLEM 1—C CORPORATION (Form 1120)

On October 6, 1998, Dick Schmitt and Joan Allen formed Hart Corporation to manufacture and sell fishing equipment. Pertinent information regarding Hart is summarized as follows:

- The business address is 1206 South Sixth Street, Nashville, TN 37203.

- The employer identification number is 57–3452933; the principal business activity code is 423910.

- Dick and Joan each own one-half of the outstanding common stock; no other class of stock is authorized. Dick is president of the company, and Joan is secretary-treasurer. Both are full-time employees of the corporation, and each receives a salary of $170,000. Dick's Social Security number is 292–50–2953; Joan's Social Security number is 232–30–4495.

- The corporation uses the accrual method of accounting and reports on a calendar year basis. Inventories are determined using the lower of cost or market method. For book and tax purposes, the straight-line method of depreciation is used.

- During 2002, the corporation distributed a cash dividend of $30,000.

Selected portions of Hart's profit and loss statement for 2002 reflect the following debits and credits:

| Account | Debit | Credit |
|---|---|---|
| Gross sales | | $1,700,400 |
| Sales returns and allowances | $ 40,400 | |
| Purchases | 805,800 | |
| Dividends received from stock investments in less-than-20%-owned U.S. corporations | | 50,000 |
| Interest income | | |
|    State bonds | $12,600 | |
|    Certificates of deposit | 20,000 | 32,600 |
| Premiums on term life insurance policies on the lives of Dick and Joan; Hart Corporation is the designated beneficiary | 11,000 | |
| Salaries—officers | 340,000 | |
| Salaries—clerical and sales | 205,000 | |
| Taxes (state, local, and payroll) | 89,700 | |
| Repairs | 30,500 | |
| Interest expense | | |
|    Loan to purchase state bonds | $ 7,200 | |
|    Other business loans | 18,300 | 25,500 |
| Advertising | 43,400 | |
| Rental expense | 79,000 | |
| Depreciation | 30,000 | |

A comparative balance sheet for Hart Corporation reveals the following information:

| Assets | January 1, 2002 | December 31, 2002 |
|---|---|---|
| Cash | $ 61,500 | $ 51,194 |
| Trade notes and accounts receivable | 68,060 | 56,140 |
| Inventories | 465,800 | 565,800 |
| Federal bonds | 27,000 | 27,000 |
| State bonds | 118,000 | 118,000 |
| Certificates of deposit | 250,000 | 260,000 |
| Prepaid Federal tax | — | 560 |
| Stock investment | 250,000 | 250,000 |
| Buildings and other depreciable assets | 216,000 | 216,000 |
| Accumulated depreciation | (79,920) | (109,920) |
| Land | 17,000 | 17,000 |
| Other assets | 4,240 | 2,800 |
| Total assets | $1,397,680 | $1,454,574 |

| Liabilities and Equity | January 1, 2002 | December 31, 2002 |
|---|---|---|
| Accounts payable | $ 157,000 | $ 135,701 |
| Other current liabilities | 45,270 | 26,600 |
| Mortgages | 224,800 | 212,000 |
| Capital stock | 125,000 | 125,000 |
| Retained earnings | 845,610 | 955,273 |
| Total liabilities and equity | $1,397,680 | $1,454,574 |

Net income per books (before any income tax accrual) is $182,700. During 2002, Hart Corporation made estimated tax payments of $43,597 to the IRS. Prepare a Form 1120 for Hart Corporation for tax year 2002.

## PROBLEM 2—FOREIGN TAX CREDIT (Form 1118)

Fleming Products, Inc., a U.S. Corporation, has a foreign branch in Canada that earns taxable income of $1,000,000 from manufacturing operations and $500,000 from shipping operations. Fleming Products pays $400,000 (40%) and $100,000 (20%), respectively on this foreign-source income. The corporation also earns U.S.-source taxable income from manufacturing operations of $4,000,000, resulting in worldwide taxable income of $5,500,000. The U.S. taxes before FTC are $1,870,000 (at 34%). Fleming Products (employer ID number 75-2837157) accrues taxes for purposes of the FTC. This information is summarized below.

| Income Category | Gross Income | Direct Expenses | Indirect Expenses | Taxable Income | Foreign Taxes |
|---|---|---|---|---|---|
| U.S. manufacturing | $ 9,000,000 | $4,460,000 | $540,000 | $4,000,000 | NA |
| Foreign manufacturing | 5,000,000 | 3,700,000 | 300,000 | 1,000,000 | $400,000 |
| Shipping | 1,000,000 | 440,000 | 60,000 | 500,000 | 100,000 |
| Total | $15,000,000 | $8,600,000 | $900,000* | $5,500,000 | $500,000 |

*This $900,000 represents expenses not definitely allocable to any of the corporation's activities. It is allocated and apportioned based on relative gross income.

Complete a Form 1118 to compute Fleming's foreign tax credit in the general limitation income and shipping categories.

## PROBLEM 3—PARTNERSHIP (Form 1065)

Marilyn Parker (222-54-7580), Scott Denny (759-85-4486), and Rebecca Quincey (423-70-8476) are equal general partners in PDQ Partners, a domestic general partnership that provides public relations services to various small businesses. PDQ's Federal I.D. number is 94-8423590. The partnership uses the cash method of accounting and adopted the calendar year for reporting. It began business operations on January 15, 1996. Its current address is 2986 Vulcan Drive, Birmingham, AL 35203. The following information was taken from the partnership's income statement for the current year:

| | |
|---|---|
| Receipts | |
| Fees collected | $520,400 |
| Taxable interest | 3,000 |
| Long-term capital loss (all 20%) | (6,000) |
| Short-term capital gain | 2,000 |
| Payments/deductions | |
| Contribution to Birmingham U. | $ 9,800 |
| Employee salaries | 138,000 |
| Equipment rental | 18,000 |
| Office rentals paid | 68,000 |
| Salary, Rebecca Quincey, managing partner | 46,000 |
| Entertainment and meals, subject to 50% rule | 8,000 |
| Payroll taxes | 29,000 |
| Utilities | 46,000 |
| Interest expense | 6,000 |
| Depreciation | 7,200 |
| Office expense | 40,000 |
| Repairs | 4,200 |

The partnership claimed $7,200 of depreciation for both tax and financial accounting purposes. Assume the depreciation results in a "depreciation adjustment for property placed in service after 1986" of $2,400. Net income per books is $99,200. No additional capital contributions were made in 2002, and each partner withdrew $40,000 cash from the partnership during the year. The partnership's beginning and ending tax basis balance sheets for 2002 were as follows:

| | Beginning | Ending |
|---|---|---|
| Cash | $ 30,400 | $ ? |
| Marketable securities | 72,000 | 70,000 |
| Office furniture and equipment | 130,000 | 130,000 |
| Accumulated depreciation | (33,680) | ? |
| Total assets | $198,720 | $ ? |
| Long-term mortgage payable on leasehold improvements and equipment | $ 84,000 | $ 78,000 |
| Capital, Parker | 38,240 | ? |
| Capital, Denny | 38,240 | ? |
| Capital, Quincey | 38,240 | ? |
| Total liabilities and capital | $198,720 | $ ? |

The partners share equally in all partnership liabilities, since all initial contributions and all ongoing allocations and distributions are pro rata.

None of the partners sold any portion of their interests in the partnership during 2002. The partnership's operations are entirely restricted to the Birmingham metropolitan area. All partners are U.S. citizens. The partnership had no foreign operations, no foreign bank accounts, and no interest in any foreign trusts. The partnership is not publicly traded and is not a statutory tax shelter. PDQ does not own an interest in any other partnership.

The IRS's business code for the partnership operations is 561900. The partnership is not subject to the consolidated audit procedures and does not have a tax matters partner. The partnership files its tax return in Memphis, TN. Partner Rebecca Quincey lives at 2022 Chandy Road, Homewood, AL 35209.

    a. Prepare Form 1065 and Schedule K for the PDQ Partnership, leaving blank any items where insufficient information has been provided. Prepare any supporting schedules necessary. Do not complete Form 1065, Schedule D. Round all amounts to the nearest whole dollar.

    b. Prepare Schedule K-1 for Rebecca Quincey.

## PROBLEM 4—S CORPORATION (Form 1120S)

Jacob Donaldson (234–12–5678) and Ryan Loflin (432–21–8765) are 40% and 60% owners of CD, Inc. (74–1234567) foundation contractors, located at 10012 Post Oak Boulevard in Houston, Texas 77056. The company's S corporation election was made on April 28, 1994. The following information was taken from the income statement for 2002.

| | | |
|---|---:|---:|
| Gross Rents | $ 60,000 | |
| Tax Exempt Interest | 2,000 | |
| Interest Income | 450 | |
| Gross Receipts | 800,000 | $862,450 |
| Salaries and Wages | $200,000 | |
| Repairs | 16,000 | |
| Officer's Compensation | 65,000 | |
| Rent Expense (Not operating) | 54,000 | |
| Taxes | 26,000 | |
| Advertising | 9,900 | |
| Depreciation | 91,800 | |
| Employee Benefit Programs | 1,100 | |
| Other Deductions | 160,000 | 623,800 |
|     Book Income | | $238,650 |

A partially completed comparative balance sheet appears as follows.

| | Beginning of the Year | End of the Year |
|---|---:|---:|
| Cash | $ 19,600 | $ 79,200 |
| Other investments | 161,650 | 152,580 |
| Bldgs. & other depreciable assets | 711,402 | 922,112 |
| Accumulated depreciation | (458,313) | (587,351) |
| Total | $ 434,339 | $ 566,541 |
| Mortgages, notes, bonds (payable in 1 year or more) | $ 354,890 | $ 328,891 |
| Capital stock | 1,000 | 1,000 |
| Retained earnings | 78,449 | ? |
| Total | $ 434,339 | ? |

**Additional Information**

The corporation distributed $78,449 to the two shareholders during the year. From the above information, prepare Form 1120S and Schedule K–1 for Ryan Loflin. If any information is missing, make realistic assumptions.

| | |
|---|---|
| Accumulated Adjustments Account | $78,449 |
| Other Adjustments Accounts | 0 |
| Previously Taxed Income | 0 |

## PROBLEM 5—GIFT TAX (Form 709)

During 2002, Harold A. and Lynn B. Dewey (Social Security numbers 371–60–6812 and 366–42–7991) reside at 6200 Sheridan Way, Sherman, MI 48864. In their 25 years of marriage, the Deweys have always lived in a common law state. Harold is a well-known patent attorney, while Lynn owns and manages a real estate brokerage firm specializing in commercial properties. Both practices have been highly successful. Over the years, the Deweys have received gifts and inheritances from other family members, and these funds, together with their own savings, have been invested wisely.

In 2002, the Deweys made the following transfers (without regard to any annual exclusion, marital, or charitable deductions otherwise available).

| Transfer | Harold | Lynn |
|---|---|---|
| Purchased three $100,000 certificates of deposit issued by Sherman State Bank on the birthdays of *each* of their three children, in their separate names (Myrna, age 22; Robert, age 21; and Sally, age 20) | $300,000 | |
| To celebrate his parents' 50th wedding anniversary, Harold gave them a new RV. The title was listed as "John and Susan Dewey, tenants in common." | 240,000 | |
| Lynne reimbursed her brother, Richard Berg, for his heart bypass operation. Richard originally intended to absorb the expenses himself, but stock market reverses left him near bankruptcy. | | $52,000 |
| As a wedding present for Paul Berg (Richard's son) and his bride, Nancy, Lynn made a down payment on a new house. Title to the property was recorded as "Paul and Nancy Berg, tenants by the entirety." | | 60,000 |
| In 1995 and as security for a loan, Roger Berg (Lynn's father) obtained an insurance policy on his life from Mutual of Omaha. The policy designates Lynn as the owner and names Myrna, Robert, and Sally (Lynn's children) as the beneficiaries. Roger dies in 2002, and the insurance company distributes the policy's maturity value of $300,000 among the beneficiaries (i.e., $100,000 to each). Prior to his death, Roger had repaid the loan Lynn made to him. | ? | ? |
| In December 2002, Harold and Lynn exchanged "his" and "hers" customized Lexus SUVs as Christmas presents. | 68,000 | 68,000 |
| The Deweys made a contribution to the reelection campaign of their incumbent Congresswoman. | 10,000 | 10,000 |
| The Deweys paid tuition ($90,000), room and board ($18,000), and incidentals ($6,000) to send their children to college for a year. Each child incurred one-third of the total cost. | 90,000 | 24,000 |
| Transferred title to a "state of the art" bass boat and trailer to the Reverend Michael Wheeler. "Mike" is the highly regarded pastor of the Dewey's church and keeps getting better offers from larger congregations. The congregation was unaware of the gift; on its own, Mike's salary was increased. Appraised value of the gift was $40,000 (cost was $50,000). | 40,000 | |

In the past, the Deweys have made the following *taxable gifts*, and for each year involved, the § 2513 election to split was made.

| Year of Gift | Amount of Taxable Gift |
|:---:|:---:|
| 1983 | $500,000 |
| 1985 | 400,000 |
| 1995 | 600,000 |
| 2001 | 300,000 |

    a. Determine the gift tax liability for the transfers made by the Deweys prior to 2002.

    b. Determine the gift tax liability for the transfers made in 2002. Do this by completing a Form 709 (U.S. Federal Gift Tax Return). The Deweys continue to make the § 2513 election to split all gifts they make.

## PROBLEM 6—ESTATE TAX (Form 706)

Nathan (Nat) Harvey Allen died at Stockton Memorial Hospital on November 15, 2002, as a result of injuries suffered three days previously. The injuries were received by Nat when a butane tank Nat was installing at his fishing camp unexplainably exploded. The explosion and ensuing fire totally destroyed the physical facilities (living quarters, etc.) and a houseboat that was moored at the dock.

Pertinent information regarding Nat's affairs, both personal and business-related, are summarized below.

- Nat (age 63 at death) resides at 121 Willow Road, Clever (Christian County), MO 64801. He is survived by his wife, Wanda Bryan Allen (age 60), and four adult children. The children, Daniel (age 40), Austin (age 38), Marcia (age 36), and Ned (age 34), all reside in Clever and are active partners in Allen Associates, LLP.

- Until he retired at age 58, Nat owned and operated a successful insurance business. As an independent broker, he represented numerous companies, both life and casualty, and had a respectable share of the southwestern Missouri market. Prior and subsequent to his retirement, Nat has been able to sell most of the business to his children. At the time of his death, Nat held purchase-money notes from them with the following balances.

| | |
|:---|---:|
| Daniel | $110,000 |
| Austin | 110,000 |
| Marcia | 130,000 |
| Ned | 180,000 |

  As the obligations carry a 6% interest rate and the business is expected to continue being profitable, the notes can be treated as equal in value to the balances listed.

- For several years, Nat and Wanda have maintained life insurance coverage on each other. The policies are issued by Harrier Group, Inc., and each has a maturity value of $300,000. The policy Nat owns on Wanda's life names himself as the beneficiary. Likewise, the policy Wanda owns on Nat's life names herself as the beneficiary. In both policies, their children are designated as secondary beneficiaries. At the time of Nat's death, the policy he owned had a fair market value (i.e., cash surrender value) of $85,000.

- Myrtle Allen, Nat's widowed mother, passed away in 1980. One of the provisions in her will left a tract of timberland in Cedar County to: "My only children, Nathan and Leona, to be held in joint tenancy with right of survivorship." The Cedar County tract was worth $120,000 in 1980 and $340,000 when Nat died.

- Leona is Nat's older sister and, except for part of the Cedar County tract (see preceding comment), the heir of all of Myrtle Allen's estate. After a successful career in forestry management, Leona died in 1999 in a ski slope accident. Her will created the "Leona Allen Trust," under the terms of which Nat was granted a life estate; the remainder (upon Nat's death) was to be distributed to Wanda (if she survives). If Wanda does not survive the life tenant (Nat), the remainder passes to the Department of Forestry at Southern Missouri State College. Leona never married, and her closest living relatives were Nat and his family. To save on fiduciary fees, Leona named Daniel (Nat's oldest son) as the trustee of her trust. When first created, the Leona Allen trust was worth $900,000. On 11/15/02 (the date of Nat's death), the trust corpus had a fair market value of $1,400,000. Not included in this amount was accrued income of $48,000, which had not yet been distributed to Nat.

- As birthday presents for his children, Nat pays the annual premiums on four term insurance policies on his life. The policies were purchased from Marlin Life Insurance Corporation and transferred by gift to each child during 2000. Each policy has a maturity value of $20,000. Nat retained no incidents of ownership as to these policies.

- The residence the Allens live in on Willow Road was inherited by them from Wanda's mother, Louise Bryan. Louise's will passed it to Nathan and Wanda as tenants by the entirety with right of survivorship. On 11/15/02, the property had a fair market value of $650,000.

- In 1992, Nat and his three sons purchased a tract of land in Greene County. The land had formerly been part of a large farm and was sold at an estate sale when the owner died. Nat considered the $400,000 purchase price to be a bargain. Due to its proximity to the city of Springfield, the land had potential for residential development. Of the purchase price, Nat furnished $100,000, and his sons provided the balance. Title was listed as a tenancy in common with Nat holding a one-fourth (1/4) interest. On 11/15/02, the land had a fair market value of $800,000.

- During his working years, Nat made contributions to a Keogh (H.R. 10) plan administered by Assurance Fund of Illinois. No distributions from the plan have been made and no settlement options chosen. Nat has designated Wanda as the beneficiary in the event of his dying before withdrawal of the funds. The plan's balance was $984,000 as of 11/15/02.

- The fishing camp, located in Polk County, was inherited by Nat from his father. Over the years, it has been substantially improved. At least until the complete destruction of the living quarters, the camp was comfortably furnished. Both the quarters and the houseboat were insured by Cardinal Casualty. In its present state, the value of the land as of 11/15/02 is $120,000. The houseboat is a total loss, and Nat's estate paid Stockton Salvage company $6,000 to remove the wreckage.

- To help his children buy their first homes, Nat loaned each one $10,000 for a down payment. Semiannual interest of 7% was provided for, and all loans are payable within one year of demand. Each child signed a note and has made the required interest payments as due. In his will, Nat provides that each note be returned to the borrower. This, in effect, cancels each note.

Other assets not previously referred to are listed below at fair market value as of 11/15/02.

- Joint checking account with Wanda at Clever State Bank — $ 13,420
- Certificate of deposit at Bank of Joplin, listed in Nat's name (accrued interest not included) — 104,000
- Money market account at first National Bank of Springfield, listed in Nat's name (accrued interest not included) — 80,000
- City of St. Louis bonds, listed in Nat's name (accrued interest not included) — 212,000

- Stock investments (all in Nat's name as Wanda has her own portfolio)

| | | |
|---|---:|---:|
| Hunter Petroleum | $142,000 | |
| Amber Electronics | 154,000 | |
| Green Trucking | 120,000 | |
| Maize Foods | 170,000 | $586,000 |

- Nat's personal and household effects (auto, clothing, hunting and fishing equipment, etc.)      $ 62,000

Under the terms of Nat's will, Wanda is designated as the executor of his estate and is to serve without bond. Except as otherwise provided, the net assets (after administration expenses and taxes) of the estate are to be divided equally among the four children. However, the purchase money notes issued by the children are specifically bequeathed to Wanda.

On December 17, 2002, Wanda files with the Probate Division of the Christian County Court located in Ozark, MO, and is duly appointed as executor of the estate. On March 31, 2003, Wanda files a final inventory with the Court, is discharged from her duties as executor, and the administration of the Estate of Nathan Allen is officially concluded.

During the administration of Nat's estate, the following transactions take place.

- On January 2, 2003, the estate received a check from Cardinal Casualty for the following losses.

| | |
|---|---:|
| • Destruction of fishing camp (80% × $300,000 appraised value) | $240,000 |
| • Destruction of houseboat (80% × $40,000 appraised value) | 32,000 |
| | $272,000 |

After discussing the matter with her children, Wanda feels that the appraised values were correct and the settlement fair. The income tax basis of the camp is $250,000 and that of the houseboat is $55,000.

- As trustee of the Leona Allen Trust, Daniel distributed to his father's estate the $48,000 of accumulated income.

- Wanda sold the policy on her life and owned by Nat to her children for $85,000. Harrier Group (the carrier) was notified of the transfer and agreed to reissue four new policies, each with a face amount of $75,000. The $85,000 received by Wanda was added to the assets of the estate.

- Wanda made arrangements with Assurance Fund to have Nat's Keogh plan paid to her as an annuity. The payout amounts and period were arranged so as to minimize Wanda's income tax consequences.

- On January 7, 2003, Wanda received a bill from Stockton Memorial Hospital for $42,800, which involved medical treatment for Nat after the accident and before his death. The bill was not adjusted for the $5,000 ER/IC usage fee Wanda paid from her joint checking account when Nat was first admitted. Wanda paid the $37,800 balance due from estate assets.

- Funeral expenses of $9,800 were paid from estate assets. Not included in this amount was the $2,300 Wanda paid to reimburse Austin for travel expenses. At the time of the accident, Austin and his family were on vacation at Disney World. The reimbursement enabled them to return early and attend Nat's funeral service. Austin was a designated pallbearer under Nat's will.

- Dividends and interest received by the estate in January of 2003 are as follows.

  - CD at First National Bank of Joplin ($500 accrued since 11/15)                                        $5,000
  - Money market account at First Bank of Springfield ($125 accrued since 11/15)                            415
  - City of St. Louis bonds ($1,000 accrued since 11/15)                                                  3,000
  - Hunter Petroleum, cash dividend on common stock (date of record was 11/01/02)                        1,065
  - Maize Foods, cash dividend on common stock, (date of record was 11/18/02)                              890

- For several months prior to his death, Nat had been negotiating with the executors of the Darger Estate to purchase the Darger Orchards located in Dallas County. By October 23, 2002, a price of $300,000 had been agreed to, and Nat had signed a purchase agreement to this effect. At the time of the accident, Nat was in the process of obtaining mortgage funds to finance the purchase. After consulting with the family, Wanda decides to forgo mortgage financing and pay cash for the property. She issues a check for $303,000 to the Darger Estate. This includes $3,000 of interest, $2,400 of which accrued since 11/15.

- Because the estate needs cash to pay expenses and satisfy obligations, Wanda decides to sell all of the stock held by the estate. The stock was sold on February 3, 2003, for $618,000 less commissions of $6,200, for a net amount of $611,800. The details are as follows.

|  | Selling Price | Broker Fees | Net Proceeds |
|---|---|---|---|
| Hunter Petroleum | $150,000 | $1,400 | $148,600 |
| Amber Electronics | 159,000 | 1,600 | 157,400 |
| Green Trucking | 119,000 | 1,200 | 117,800 |
| Maize Foods | 190,000 | 2,000 | 188,000 |
|  | $618,000 | $6,200 | $611,800 |

- In late 2001, Nat pledged $15,000 to his church, First Lutheran, to help meet the school building fund drive. On February 3, 2003, Wanda paid the pledge with estate funds.

- Legal expenses incurred in the administration of the estate are $38,000. Included are fees paid for the services of a local law firm, filing charges, and related court costs.

- Other administration expenses totaled $36,000 for accounting costs, tax and investment advice, actuarial determinations and appraisal fees.

- At the time of his death, Nat had outstanding credit card debt of $11,900, plus unpaid dentist bills of $17,400 dealing with dental implants Nat had obtained in late 2001. Wanda paid these balances from estate assets.

- Although Wanda and Nat will file a joint income tax return for tax year 2002, she determines that Nat would have owed $18,903 in income tax had separate returns been filed. The procedure to be used to arrive at this result is set forth in Reg. § 20.2053–6(f).

- After careful consideration, Wanda decides to claim the executor's fees she is entitled to for administering her husband's estate. In accordance with Missouri law, this is determined to be $60,000. The fee is approved by the probate division of the Christian County Court.

- The State of Missouri imposes a sponge type of death tax, so the amount to be paid is determined to be what § 2011 allows as a credit.

- Relevant Social Security Numbers are:

| | |
|---|---|
| Nathan Harvey Allen | 486-61-4520 |
| Wanda Bryan Allen | 487-49-8413 |
| Daniel Allen | 490-61-6149 |
| Austin Allen | 490-39-6250 |
| Marcia Allen | 491-79-7864 |
| Ned Allen | 491-81-8123 |

ASSUMPTIONS

- No § 2032 election is made.

- Code §§ 2032A, 2037, and 6166 do not apply.

- Disregard requests for information not given in the facts (e.g., the number of shares of stock owned).

- Assume that supporting data is available (e.g., appraisals) and that requested attachments are included with the return (e.g., Form 712 from life insurance companies).

- Some deductions require a choice (e.g., Form 706 or Form 1041) but cannot be claimed twice. Resolve all such choices in favor of the Form 706.

- Although the Allens have previously filed Forms 709-A, neither has ever made a *taxable* gift.

**Required**

Complete a Form 706 for the estate of Nathan Harvey Allen.

## PROBLEM 7—TRUST (Form 1041)

Prepare the 2002 fiduciary income tax return (Form 1041) for the Green Trust. In addition, determine the amount and character of the income and expense items that each beneficiary must report for 2002 and prepare a Schedule K–1 for Marcus White. Omit all AMT computations.

The 2002 activities of the trust include the following.

| | |
|---|---|
| Dividend income, all U.S. stocks | $25,000 |
| Taxable interest income | 20,000 |
| Tax-exempt interest income | 30,000 |
| Net long-term capital gain | 27,000 |
| Fiduciary's fees | 6,000 |

Under the terms of the trust instrument, depreciation, net capital gains and losses, and any fiduciary's fees are allocable to corpus. The trustee is required to distribute $20,000 to Marcus every year. For 2002, the trustee distributed $30,000 to Marcus and $45,000 to Marcus's sister, Ellen Hayes. No other distributions were made.

In computing DNI, the trustee properly assigned all of the deductible fiduciary fees to the dividend income.

The trustee paid $5,300 in estimated taxes for the year on behalf of the trust. Any 2002 refund is to be credited to 2003 estimates. The exempt income was not derived from private activity bonds.

The trust was created on December 14, 1953. It is not subject to any recapture taxes, nor does it have any tax credits. None of its income was derived under a personal services contract. Ignore the alternative minimum tax for all parties. The trust has no economic interest in any foreign trust. Its Federal identification number is 79–2635151.

The trustee, Wisconsin State National Bank, is located at 3100 East Wisconsin Avenue, Milwaukee, WI 53201. Its employer identification number is 66–7602487.

Marcus lives at 9880 East North Avenue, Shorewood, WI 53211. His identification number is 498–98–8058.

Ellen lives at 6772 East Oklahoma Avenue, St. Cecilia, WI 53204. Her identification number is 499–97–6531.

# Index

# Dep recapture

MACRS (Machinery) — Half year convention (Mach) or Mid qtr conv
### Dep personality (Mach)

| Prior to 1981 | 81-86 | 87 after |
|---|---|---|
| § 1245 | § 1245 | § 1245 |
| All dep taken | All dep taken | All dep taken |

---

# Depreciable Nonresidential real property
## (Warehouse, Office etc)

| Placed Before May 13, 1993 31 ½ st line. | Placed after May 13, 1993. 39 st line | 3 ½ years 39 st line |
|---|---|---|

| Prior to 1981 | 81-86 | 87 after |
|---|---|---|
| § 1250 | § 1245 | § 1250 |
| Recap excess dep | All dep taken | No recap since st line. |

---

# Depreciable Residential Real property
## (Rental property)

| Prior to 1981 | 81-86 | 87 after (st line) |
|---|---|---|
| § 1250 | § 1250 | § 1250  27½ yrs Midmonth |
| Recap excess dep | Excess dep taken | No recap since st line. |

| § 1245 recap | § 1231 |
|---|---|
| § 291 recap | < loss > gain |
| = ordinary | step ② |

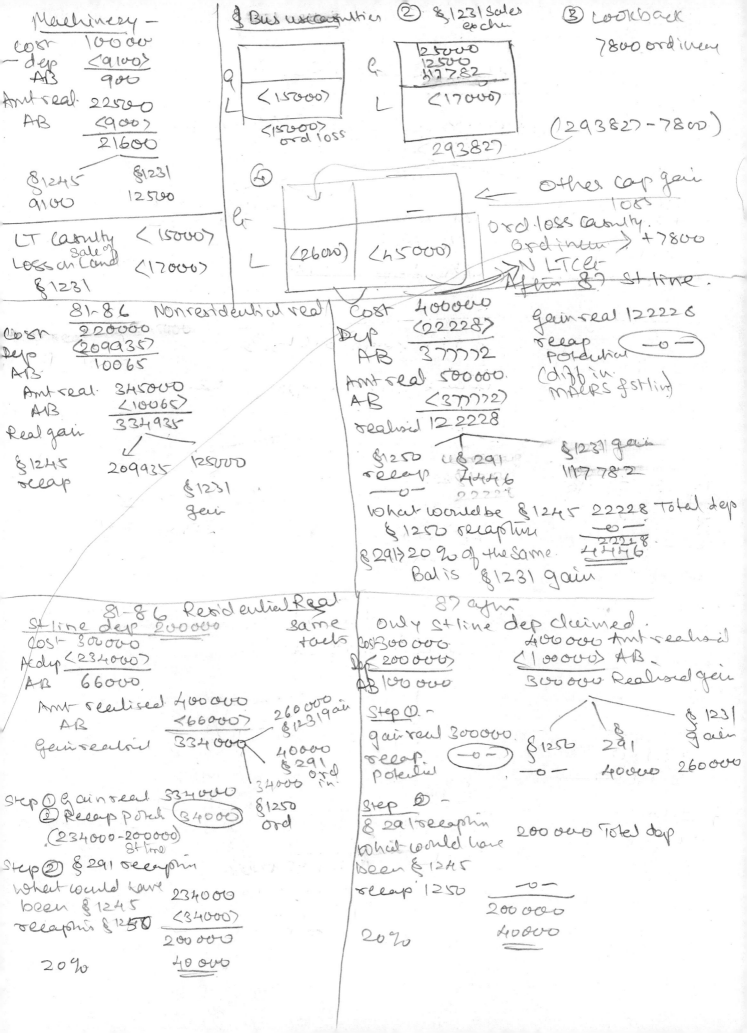

Machinery –
Cost  100 000
– dep  <91 00>
AB  900
Amt real. 22 500
AB  <900>
21 600

§1245        §1231
9100         12 500

LT Casualty  <15000>
Loss on Land  <17000>   Sale of
§1231

81-86  Nonresidential real
Cost  220 000
Dep  <209 935>
        10 065
AB
Amt real.  345 000
AB  <10065>
Real gain  334 935

§1245  209 935    125 000
recap
                §1231
                gain

81-86  Residential Real
St-line dep 200 000      same
Cost  300 000            facts
Ac dep  <234 000>
AB  66 000
Amt realised 400 000
AB  <66 000>
Gain realised  334 000

            260 000
            §1231 gain
            40 000
            §291
            34 000  ord in.
            §1250
            ord

Step① Gain real 334 000
②  Recap potn  (34 000)
    (234 000 - 200 000)
        St line
Step② §291 recapt'n
what would have  234 000
been §1245
recap'n §1250  <34 000>
                200 000
    20%           40 000

§ Bus use casualties        ② §1231 Sales
                               each

G                           G  25 000
                               12 500
L  <15 000>                    117 782
   <15 000>                 L  <17 000>
   ord loss
                               293 827

©
G  ─           ─
L  <26 000>  <45 000>

③ Lookback
   7800 ordinary

   (293 827 - 7800)

       other cap gain
           loss
   ord. loss Casualty.
   ordinary → + 7800
   → N LTCL
   After 87 St line.

Cost  400 000
Dep  <22 228>
AB  377 772
Amt real  500 000
AB  <377 772>
realised 122 228

§1250  §291     §1231 gain
recap  44 446   117 782
 ─     22 228

What would be §1245  22 228  Total dep
 §1250 recap'n        ─
§291 20% of the same. 44 446
   Bal is §1231 gain

gain real 122 228
recap  ─
potential
(diff in
 MARRS fst line)

87 again
Only st-line dep claimed.
Cost 300 000    400 000 Amt realised
   <200 000>    <100 000> AB.
AB 100 000      300 000 Realised gain

Step ① –
gain real 300 000              §1231
recap  ─      §1250   §291    gain
potential      ─      40 000  260 000

Step ② –
§291 recap'n            200 000 Total dep
what would have
been §1245
recap '1250  ─
            200 000
   20%       40 000

Supplemental problem No 2 - Cal of Book income

① Net Sales 6330000
   CGS (4900 000)
   GP 1430000
   Dep Exp Book (675000)
   Charitable cont (62000)
   LIC prem (10000)
   LIC proceeds 200000
   Sal & other Exp (650000)
   (Taxes (35000)
   Int income CD 37500
   — " — SO Illinois 5000
   Dividend income 18000
   STCL (27000)
   LTCG 8000

   Book Income befo. Tax 239500
   Fed IT Exp (24079)
   215421
   [See page 2-28]

② Cal of tax inc me
   Net Sales 6330000
   CGS (4900,000)
   Depreciati (750000)
   LIC prem —0—
   LIC proceeds —0—
   Salaries & oth (650000)
   Taxes (35000)
   Int income CD 37500
   Int incom SO Illi —0—
   Div Income 18000 *
   STCL (8000) 2 can
   LTCG 8000   deduc only to
   Prepaid rent 31600  the ext of gn
   T I before Charital 82100
   10% ch cont deduct (8210)
   T I before DRD 73890
   — DRD (12600)
   Taxable Inco 61290

③ Reconciliation of Book PTI
   NI per books 215421
   + Fed IT Exp 24079
   + Excess Cap loss 19000
   + Income per Tax not B
     Prepaid rent 31600

   + Exp for Book not Tax
     LIC prem. 10000
     Charitable ded 53790
     Int pd to purchase tax exempt bond
   − Income for Book not Tax
     LIC proceeds (200000)
     Tax-free int (5000)

   − Exp for Tax not BK
     Depreciation (75000)

   TI before DRD 73890

③ Permanent difference
   Charitable ded. 53790 diff
   LIC prem. 10000
   LIC proceed 200000
   Tax free int 5000
   DRD = 12600
   Cap loss 19000
   Temporary difference -
   Depreciati exp 75000 × diff
   Prepaid rent 31600 ×

④ Calculation of Fed IT exp -
   Book income before FIT 239500
   + Charitable ded 53790
   + LIC prem. 10000
   − LIC Ins proceeds (200000)
   − Tax free income (5000)
   + Capital loss 19000
   − DRD (12600)
   Pre tax Book inc on adjf 104690
   Permanent diff
   Fed IT exp 24079

# Supplemental problem No ③ solution - Cal. of E&P

## Calculation of E&P by indirect method -

| Taxable income | | E&P adjustments | | MACRS 650000 (ind dep on 125 000 current yr aeg equaling 44200→24000 + 20200 (125-24×20%) |
|---|---|---|---|---|

| Taxable income | | | E&P adjustments | |
|---|---|---|---|---|
| Sales | 8500000 | Taxable income | 1371747 | |
| COGS | (5350000) | Dep E&P | 32186 | |
| Dep E&P | (650000) | Int income of Ill. | 53500 (Book) | |
| Salaries | (810000) | DRD | 68460 (-Tax) | |
| Payroll | (74320) | Chari ded (Remaing) | (64977) | |
| rent | (42000) | LIC proceeds | 1000000 | |
| Utilities | (123450) | ~ prem | (12500) | |
| Int income CD | 143000 | Remainder gain | 82000 | |
| ~ USbond | 68000 | and us installment | | |
| Div income | 97800 | Excess STcaploss | (11000) | |
| Mort int | (76300) | Fed IT E&P | (463500) | |
| ST IT E&P | (129500) | Current E&P | 2055916 | |
| Reco gain on ordin inv conven | 35000 | Cash Distri | (120000) | |
| gain on sale of land used | 18000 | Property distri gain | 33000 | |
| | | deduction | (94000) | |
| LTCL | 54000 | Current E&P | 1874,916 | |
| STCL | (72000) | | | |
| Refund of SI Tax | 12000 | 100000 gain | | |
| Tax I befor CD | 1600230 | 500000 proceeds | ×100 = 20% | →18000 |
| Chari Deduction | (160023) | | | |
| DRD 20% | (68460) | | | |
| Taxable inco | 1371747 | | | |

For E&P purpose -
24000 /5 = 4800 per y
E&P prem
101000/7 × ½ = 7214
12014

44200
- 12014
32186  E&P adjustment

MACRS Dep 650000
E&P adj  32186
617814
only for direct meth

Land sold   500000
Adj Basis  (400000)
100 000
20% of 90000 gained.
installment method.

[Additional class problem Chapter 12] S corp

① N owns 35% stock of S corp through now 2002 2 levels
Corp 6000 Her basis is 25000 Corp sustains loss <110000>
deduct loss sum of two stock basis & loan basis first stock
stock basis 25000 + loan basis 6000
loss share  38500  can deduct 31000 bal c/f

② S/H basis 15500 receives Distribution 17000 How is
S/H taxed on the distribution"        Accumulated Adj A/c    6000
   Stock basis           Distribution    (AAA)
   15500                 17000           Previously taxed In.  9000
   <6000> Tax free AAA   <6000>          Acc E&P               500
   9500                  11000
   8000   Tax free PTI   8000            Distribution of (500 Mill
   500                   2000            to be accounted for
          Acc E&P        <500>           500 would be basis.
          Div income     1500           sold in
   D   <500>  Bad as red   500      So  15500  tax free.
          Cap gain       1000              500  Div income
                                          1000  Cap gain
   If no E&P then Cap gain  1500

③ Built in gain tax "C" elects to be an "S" when L&B are worth 2.2m
Land AB 200,000 & Bldg 400000 Co has some securities valued
260000 (AB 80000) you are 100% S/H What happens →
a) Co moves to new bldg & sells Land & Bldg for 2.3m (tax basis 500000)
three times corp pays tax → ① Built in gain ② dep 100000 LIFO recap
③ Too much passive income conditions for ① → ① C becomes
'S' with net appreciated assets transferred ② If any of these
assets have been sold within 10 yrs of conversion

   FMV    2200000          Amt real 2300000      tax basis
   AB     <600000>         Adj Basis <500000>    lesses of two pay tax
          1,600,000    →            1,800,000 → real gain
                                    1,800,000    real gain
   x .35                 S/H level   <560000>    less corp tax
   560000                           1,240,000    total recog gain
                                    .40
                                    496000

④ Co sells ½ of securities for 145000      At S/H level
   FMV 260000 ÷ ½  130000               Amt real 145000
   AB  80000 x ½  <40000>               -AB      <40000>
                  90000                          105000
   At Co level gain .35                  -Tax Corp (31500)
   Tax.           31500                           73500
                                         @ 40%    .40
                                                  29400

Double Taxation Occurs
for built in gains

exempt entities – Unrelated business income tax (UBIT)
exist if – a) Org conducts trade or business b) Trade
or business is not substantially related to exempt purpose
c) Trade or business is regularly carried on by org.
exception – ① Org has substantially all volunteer help
② Org is university conducting activity for benefit/convenience
of student/staff ③ Org sells donated or low cost merchandise
exceptions to exempt entities – ① Org engages in a
prohibited transaction. Three negative results may occur –
a) Part or all of organisation's income may be subject to
federal tax b) Org may have to forfeit exempt status
c) Intermediate sanctions may be imposed on exempt
organisation insiders – 25% excise tax on excess benefits
② Org is a feeder org – carries on Trade or business &
feeds profits ③ Org is prvt foundation ④ Org has unrelated
trade or business income subject to tax.
1000 exemption per year for UBIT computation
990-T filed if UBIT owed.

---

Chapter 10 Partnership formation operation
T invest 25000 passive int 1500000 non recourse debt
at risk only recourse debt Basis → add both debt
contribution 25000      He has passive income from
liability 5% int  75000   other activity $ 22000
            100000
Loss deductibility –      ① Basis – 100000
Pick smaller of all       ② AT risk – 25000 (Basis+recourse
    $ 22000               ③ Passive in  ㉒㉒000

His basis after deducting loss is –
cap contribution          25000
liability                 75000
loss                     <35000>
                          65000

① What is each partners interest after formation?

|  | R | A | M |  |
|---|---|---|---|---|
| Contribution | 25000 | 25000 | 15000 | 9000 |
| + increase in liability | 3000 | 3000 | <6000> | mortage |
|  | 28000 | 28000 | 09000 |  |

M had contributed 34000 fmv goodlia of AB 15000
Pts sold land for 34000 & pd the mortage off.
19000 gain (34000 - 15000) goes to M. (precontri gain)
land sold & mortage paid off

② Basis after land sold

|  | R | A | M |
|---|---|---|---|
| Begg Basis | 28000 | 28000 | 9000 |
| - liability ↓ | <3000> | <3000> | <3000> |
| + gain on sale |  |  | 19000 |
|  | 25000 | 25000 | 25000 |

③ Cost of goods sold —
- Op stock 10000
- + purchases 80000
- - cl. stock <11000>
- - Disribulia <100>
- - Charitable co <6000>
- COGS 72900

④ Ord income —

| Sales | 150000 |
|---|---|
| - return | <500> |
| Supplies | <800> |
| utilities | <3200> |
| Rental | <4500> |
| COGS | <72900> |
| Misc exp | <900> |
| Guaranteed P | <12000> |
|  | 55200 |

Cash flow —
| contribution | 50000 |
|---|---|
| Sale of land | 34000 |
| Sales | 149500 |
|  | 233500 |

Outflow —
| mortage | <9000> |
|---|---|
| purch | <90000> |
| misc exp | <900> |
| utilities | <3200> |
| Supplies | <800> |
| Rental exp | <4500> |
| Gur. paym | <12000> |
|  | 120400 |

Diff 113100
Rental <36000>
Bal dis 77100

Ending Basis of Partners

|  | R | A | M |
|---|---|---|---|
| Beg Basis | 25000 | 25000 | 25000 |
| + Sh of ord in | 18400 | 18400 | 18400 |
| - In dist | — | — | <100> |
| - ch cont | <2000> | <2000> | <2000> |
| - withdrawals | <25700> | <25700> | <25700> |
| rem cash dis | 15700 | 15700 | 15600 |

# Chapter 11 — Proportionate liquidating distributi[on]

① Each distributed asset initially takes carryover basi[s]

② Then carryover basis is reduced in proportion to their respective entity bases fair market value. 11-8

③ Any remaing decrease is allocated among all distributed assets in the class in proportion to respective adj basis

## Proportionate Nonliquidating Distribution

① Each distributed asset within the "other assets" class initially takes a carryover basis

② Carryover basis for each of these asset is increased in proportion to their respective amounts of unrealised appreciation Not above FMV. Page 11-11

③ The remaing allocated in proportion to the market value.

↳ Loss recognition — May recognize loss if ① the receives only. Cash or receivables / inventory and ② Partners outside basis exceeds inside basis excess is loss

Sale of Partnership Int — Page 11-23, Problem ③⑥ 11-47 & 11-26 imp← ③②

When inside ≠ outside basis adj entry 11-47 pr ③③

∴ Nonliquidating distr — Page 11-43 pr ⑮, ⑯ ⑲ → Two items of asset

∴ Liquidating Distr — Page 11-44 ②④ & ②⑤ → with loss on liquidation

Pr ②⑥ → Two items of asset

Dis pr Nonliquidating dist — Page 11-47 pr ③④ got only cash.

---

## Chapter ② Different forms of org

| Sole prop | Pnct | Sal + div | In + big sal |
|---|---|---|---|
| | Sal to her | | |
| 200000 T.I | 50000 Sal | 50000 sal | Total sal |
| 34926 + | Tax 9310 | Tax 9310 | of 200000 |
| 18645 Tax. | 150000 TI | Div 10825 | = 53571 |
| | Tax 41750 | (150 - 41750) | |
| | T Tax 51060 | = 25548 | |

## DRD deduction →

| | Red | White | Blue |
|---|---|---|---|
| GI | 400 000 | 320 000 | 260000 |
| Exp | (340 000) | (340000) | (340000) |
| Div | 200 000 | 200 000 | 200000 |
| | 260000 | 180000 | 120000 |
| 70% of Div | 140000 | 140000 | 140000 |
| 70% of T.I | 182000 | 126000 | 84000 |
| lesser | 140000 | 126000 | 140000 |

for Blue NOL rule applies Subtracting 140000 from 120000 create NOL

---

Cap loss deductibility 2-45
Problem ③⑨ & ④⓪

DRD deduction Page 2-46 ④⑦
① Multiply div rec'd by ded %
② — " — Tax In. by ded %
③ Ded is limited to lesser of ① & ②
unless subtracting ① generates loss
0-20 → 70% 20-less → 80% above 100%
transfer

Org cost page 2-47 - 48
Brothers sister corp & two tiers of common ownership & titled ownership Pay 2-23
combined group — 2-24, 2-48
M-1 — 2-49 ⑤②

Chapters ③ Tsf of property for formation of corp 80%
Control is must, no services are render examples 3-4 §3-5
under §31 corp has carry over basis S/H has substituted basis
in the stock (AB of property tsf) + gain recognized by booty
Debt in corp Somethin 3-16   Bad debts   3-18
§1244 Stock            3-20   Basis § stock trf on property try 3-28, 29
                                                    ㉙ ㉛
Tsf of liability invalid 3-31 ㊴ Donation by city to corp ㊸ 3-31
purpose gets tained
§1244 loss prob ㊾ page 3-32

Chapter ④ - LIC surrender value § E&P → Page 4-3
Dep adj for E&P 4-4   All other E&P adj page 4-5
Netting → Current E&P      Acc E&P      Netting
              Positive          Deficit         No netting
              Negative          Positive        Netting done.

Property dividends → Effect on shareholder – E&P §
FMV of property is treated as amt of divided adj ag E&P
basis if exceeds Capital gain results page 4-30 ㉗
Basis FMV – liability assumed by S/H → Page 4-11
Effect on Corp – does not recognize loss but recognize
gain as if it is sold to S/H
Constructive dividends 4-13   Stock dividend 4-17 ㉒
Stock rights 4-19
Basis § E&P related problem ㉓ page 4-26
More problems on return of cap § E&P ㉗ ㉘ 4-26
E&P ↑ or decrease ㉚ page 4-27 and ㉛ 4-28
Property dividend with liability problem ㉝ 4-28 § ㉟

Chapter ⑤ - Rules for Redemption - a) Not essentially
equivalent redemption - ownership int must be meaningfully
reduced ↓ in voting Control is indicator b) Disproportionate redemption
two conditions must be met
c) Complete Termination Redemption -
d) Partial Liquidation.
e) Redemption to pay death taxes
Effect of redemption - Corp are taxed on all nonliquidating
distribution of depreciated property as if property had
been sold for FMV when gift to liability FMV is considered not liab
Losses are not recognized

General rules for recognition of gain/loss page 5-21

Built in loss limitation under liquidation    S-23
Liquidation Parent - Sub   situation Conditions    S-27
§338 election by Parent in Sub liquidation    S-29
Holding period Parent - Sub situation    S-30

---

## Additional class problem - Chapter 5

Jose & Jill each has stock basis of 600,000 → owned equally.

| | Basis to Wren | FMV | Determine tax conseq. |
|---|---|---|---|
| Cash | 200,000 | 200,000 | if Wren is liquidated |
| Inventory | 800,000 | 1,200,000 | after it sells each asset |
| Equipment (400,000 dep) | 200,000 | 1,000,000 | @ FMV & distributes |
| Building | 800,000 | 2,400,000 | after two proceeds St |
| Land | 200,000 | 400,000 | line dep. had been |
| Stock in Gray (10%) | 1,600,000 | 4,000,000 | claimed on Bldg. |
| | 3,800,000 | 9,200,000 | Land was used in bus |

1) Inventory 400,000 ord income.    400,000 ordinary    $1245 recapture
2) Equipment 800,000    400,000 $1231 gain    400,000 dep taken
3) Building 1,600,000    $1250 —0—    800,000 gain.
   §291 →    $1231 1,360,000    Gain on land is
   $1245   1,200,000    §291 240,000    not taken into
   $1250   —0—    account
   1,200,000 × 20% = 240,000
4) Stock in Gray 2,400,000 LTCG-

Total    5,400,000 × .34 tax = 1,836,000

No basis effect to corp as s/h get assets.
FMV 9,200,000 - corp tax 1,836,000 = 7,364,000 (S/H get equally)

| | Jose | Jill | Yellow → Red. |
|---|---|---|---|
| Amt real | 3,682,000 | 3,682,000 | 85% AB 800,000 |
| Basis | (600,000) | (600,000) | going to be Red. |
| | 3,082,000 | 3,082,000 | liquidated 15% AB 80,000 |

2   Nontaxable event

| | Red (Parent) | Yellow (Sub) | Yellow (Sub) | Red (Minority Interest) |
|---|---|---|---|---|
| Income | —0— | —0— | Amt real 1,800,000 × 15 | 1,884,000 |
| Basis | 2,000,000 × 85% | N/A | AB B 2,700,000 | <800,000> |
| | = 1,700,000 | | <800,000> | ad Basis in stock |
| | | | (200,000 × 15%) | |
| | | | 2,400,000 | 1,804,000 |
| | | | × .34 | LTCG- |
| | | | 816,000 | |
| | | | | 1,884,000 |
| Basis | | N/A | | (FMV × 15% |
| | | | | - tax) |
| | | | | 1,800,000 × .15 |
| | | | | - 816,000 = 1,884,000 |

Chapter 5 - Sub liquidation 5-40 problem 56
Three Conditions - ① Must be more than 80% owned.
② Sub must be solvent ③ Must be distributed in 12 months
Minority int. Page 5-40 Problem No. 57

---

AMT Calculation - 6-45 46 problem 6-46 problem 52 53 55
1) Applies to indi, corp, fiduciaries intro in 1987. It forces
applicable taxpayers with substantial eco incomes but smaller
regular taxable income to pay more income tax than they
otherwise would. Small corp exemption — Small corp exempt
if avg gross receipt $5 million or less during preceding 3 yr period
Can go up to 7500000 & still be exempt
adj — Passive activity loss 2) NOL adj 3) ACE
2 AET — imposed on c only, there would be tremendous incentive
to retained earning it is on accumulated earnings tax can avoid
1) distributi 2) Be able to justify retention 3) Manage taxable inc
In applying AET IRS looks to shareholder control, interim needs
Calculation → TI ± E&P based — Div paid deduction

— AET = Accumulated tax income base
   TI
 + E&P based
 — Div pd deducti
 — AET credit → greater of reasonable needs of corp (ex LIFO)
 = ACC Tax income base — Acc E&P or 250000 — Acc E&P
                         150 000 grace for service corp
 = ACC earnings tax rate   38.6 2002 15% 2003
3 Personal Holding Co Tax — Self assessed tax. A corp
cannot pay both AET & PHC tax in same yr
PHC is imposed on PHC that has too much personal
holding co income.
Determine whether corp is PHC or not  Text —
a) Stock ownership test — Is more than 50% of value of
stock owned by 5 or fewer individual at any time during
least half of taxable year.
b) Personal holding co income test — Is a substantial
   Portion (60% or more) of corp ord goods inc from
passive sources (eg div, int, rent, royalties)
   Base = Taxable inc
    ± E&P based ad         38.6% fr 2002
    — Div paid ded           15% fr 2003
    = Undistributed PHC

Corporate Reorg - Chapter (7) → If req are met-
1) No gain (loss) by acquiring or acquired Corporations
2) _____ SH & bondholders of both corp

Type A → 1) Acquisition of assets          Type B - Acquisition of stock of
2) Merger or Consolidation                 one corp solely in exchange
3) Must get SH approval                     of voting stock of another
4) Stock need not be voting stock           No other consideration
5) May have other Consideration             80% control req exist
limited to 50% of total consider.
6) must t/f all liabilities                  Type D - Divisive reorganisation.
7) Flexibility with re to Assets             T/f all assets to another corp
                                             when transferer is in control.
Type C - 1) Acquisition of assets            Both assets t/f of retained must-
2) Then a voting stock required              represent active business owned
3) may have other consideration              & conducted by original corp
but limited to 20% of total
4) May transfer substantially               Type E - recapitalisation only
all assets                                   one corp involved. corp has
5) Have flexibility WRT liabiln.             change in character or amt of
Type F - Change in identity form.            Capital; issue stock, exchange
   If org qualifies for:                     of common stock for preferred
A C, D as well F F prevails                  Stock
Type G → Bankruptcy reorg

Chapter (17) → Gift tax Calculation 17-17.
Problem (38) on page 17-46 → Solution.
a) No Gift splitting          b) Gift Splitting    Marsha        Paul
Fmv        1200000        Fmv        600000        600000
-Ann excl  <11000>        -Ann excl  <11000>       <11000>
-Ch. Ded   -0-           -Ch ded     -0-           -0-
-Marital ded -0-          -Marital    -0-
Taxable gift 1189000      Taxable gft 589000        589000
Prior gifts  -0-          +Prior yrs.               500000
Base       1189000           Base    589000        1089000
Tax        A8 423290      Tax        188730        382250
-gift tax pd                gift tax on
on prior gifts -0-         prior gifts    -         A8 <155800>
-unified credit <345800>   unified
Tax due    77490          credit     <345800        <345800>
                          Tax due    -0-           -0-

see prob# 37, 33  17-49    Check (17-6) for formula

Chapter ⑥ – like kind page 1-58
Objectives of the laws 1-58 ㊶

Problem ③④ & ⑧⑤ of Chapter ⑩

| | Lee | Brad | Rick ⑥ | Lee | Brad | Rick |
|---|---|---|---|---|---|---|
| | 25% | 25% | 50% | 25% | 25% | 50% |
| FMV | 17500 | 7500 | 15000 | 27500 | 7500 | 15000 |
| AB | 15000 | 16000 | cash | 15000⎤ | 16000 | cash |
| (lia) | 10000 | | | 20000⎦ | | |
| | | | | | | |
| Basis | 15000 | 16000 | 15000 | 15000 | 16000 | 15000 |
| –lia | <10000> | – | | <20000> | | 7500 |
| +his.en | 2500 | 2500 | 5000 | +8750 | 3750 | 22500 |
| | 7500 | 18500 | 20000 | 3750 | 19750 | |

Inside Basis P/s –
Lee property        15000
Brad – II –         16000
Cash                15000
                    46000

20000 debt
        L           B           R
       5000        3750        7500
     +25% of        25%       50% of
     15000 dff    of 15000    15000
       3750

Sharing the liability
① where lia is in excess
   of the basis

Total P/s basis –
   L    15000
   B    16000
   R    15000
        46000

# Chapter 4  Computation of E & P —

Taxable income

Additions
- Int on Municipal bonds
- LIC proceeds (in excess of cash surrender value)
- Fed IT refunds
- Dividend Received Deductions

Subtractions —
- related party losses
- excess cap losses
- exp incurred to produce tax exempt income
- Fed IT paid
- Nondeductible key employee LIC prem (net of T in cash surrender value)

Timing adjustments —
- Excess of Charitable Contribution.
  - Current E&P 2003 reduces        E&P 2004 increases
- Net op loss carryovers
- No adj for Like kind exchange & involuntary conv.

Accounting Method adjustments —

See pages 4-7

① Corp distributs E&P 100 000 land AB 3000 FMV 12000
mortgage 5000 assumed by STH.
① How much corp recognizes as gain (12000-3000) = 9000
② _____ distribute taxable to STH (12000-5000) = 7000
③ Basis in land 12000
④ Bal of E&P after distribut 100000 + 9000 gain - 12000 br
+ 5000 assumed loan = 102000

② Corp E&P of 9000 distributes equipment as a dividend
basis was 10000 & FMV 2000
what is bal in E&P after distribut — 0 not below 0
corp recognizes 0 gain or 0 loss
How much was taxable div is equal to FMV
E&P is not affected by the loss

③ C corp 2500 0/s 1450 owned by C & 1050 by F
C receives 580 & F 420 as div distribute when
FMV of each is 50 Current E&P 30000 &AEP 100 m
what is taxable div
A stock div is not taxable if STH proportionate
ownership does not change.

| Distr property | E&P before distri | Amt of dividend | Effect on E&P |
|---|---|---|---|
| Cash 10000 | 25000 | 10000 | -10000 |
| Cash 10000 | 8000 | 8000 | -8000 |
| Land AB 10000 FMV 13000 | 30000 | 13000 | +3000 gain -13000 FMV of distri |
| Land AB 10000 FMV 3000 | 30000 | 3000 | -10000 0 loss recog on distribut |
| Land AB 3000 FMV 15000 | 0 | 12000 | 12000 gain - 12000 div Can not reduc below 0 |

|  | Effect on E&P | gain or loss |
|---|---|---|
| 1) TI | 65000 | — |
| 2) Cash dividend | −6000 | = |
| 3) Income tax | −11250 | — |
| 4) LIC prem | −3000 | |
| ↑ Surrender value | +1400 | |
| Proceeds net of Sur value | +75000 | |
| 5) Acc dep claimed 8000 (St line 5000) | +3000 | |

6) Sale of dep asset 1400
- 15000 
- −12000 MACRS
- −1400 Sales pr
- −1600 loss Tax

    15000
- − 8000 St line
- − 1400 Sales pr
- − 5600 E&P loss

Effect on E&P: −8000 adj

| 7) Disti of inventory | −3800 | 2800 gain |
| FMV 3800 | | |
| FIFO 1800 | | |
| LIFO 3800 | | |

| 8) Dist of land FMV 3800 Bas 1800 | −3800 | 2000 gain |

9) Dist land
FMV 3800
Bas 1800
liability 1300

−3800
+1300
———
2800 → 2000 gain

10) Dist land
FMV 2000
Bas 1800
lia. 2300

−2300
+2300
———
−0− → 500 gain

11) Dist land FMV 800
Bas 3800

−3800 → 0 loss

12) §1245 asset
FMV 6600  Original basis 7200
Accum St line dep 2800

−6600 → 2200 gain

Initial basis + Partners share of P/S liabilities + Partners share of P/S income − Partners share of deductions & losses − Partners share of reductions in P/S liabilities + Postacquisition Contributions − Postacquisition distribution = Ending basis

---

T contributed cash 10000 & property AB 55000 FMV 90000 mortgage 40000 for 60% interest Kareem contributed 20000 cash & rendered legal financial services 20000 for 40%

P/S recognizes no gain

T recognizes 0 gain & K 20000

basis 105000 (55+30+20)  T & P/S int 49000 (55000−40000 +24000)  Shqlia 24000

K's P/S int 56000 (20000+16000 lia+20000 services)

---

B's basis 50000 receives distribution of 20000 cash & Land FMV 20000  L basis 30000 receives 40000 cash basis 'O' 10S

50000−20000−10000 = 20000 basis 'O'

L  30000−40000 = 10000 gain

---

J Contributes Machine basis 20000 FMV 50000  K land 15000, FMV 40000  L Contributes 40000 Cash  2 months later J withdraws land & 10000 Cash & ceases to be partner this is disguised exchange  J will be taxed on 30000 of gain & K will be taxed on 20000 gain

---

AMT → Taxable Inc        220500
       N Cap gain        200000
       Excess dep         52000
       Excess % deple    460000

AMT Base   220500−200000+52000+460000 = 292500
   Tentative min tax lia  175000×26%                    $5500
      (292500−175000)×28
   Tax on net Cap gain 200000×20%                       +4000
                                                        _____
              Tentative min tax                          82400

AMT I                          140000
_ exemption                     40000
                               ─────────
                               100000
  Rate                          20%
                               ─────────
  Tentative AMT        20000  higher than regular tax rate
Amount is payable.
─────────────────────────────────────────────

  Taxable income            300000
  Excess dep on FA           40000
  Excess pollution Control   10000
              amort
  Excess chari Contri        25000
    ACE (adj current earng)  380000

What is AMTI → 300000 + 40000 + 10000 = 350000
ACE adj = 380000 - 350000 = 30000 × 75% = 22500
AMTI = 350000 + 22500 = 372500

Chapter ② — Chapter ⑫
S corporation

DRD - 2-46
NOL 2-45
Org exp 2-46
Tax bubble 2-47
Sch. M-1 2-49
Brother sis 2-48
Corp §§ 2-23

AAA & AEP
distributions
on 12-18
Distribution 12-22
of property
Ord income 12-42
Sep stated

prorata of 12-43
Book method
Basis Calcul 12-44.
AAA Calcul 12-44.
↳ See also 12-19
Distribution of Add provision
taxability

Built in gain - Add
problem
flow through
of taxable of
Cap loss 12-44

Exempt entities — Chapter ⑭

Chapter 10 — Pls & Partner
Pls does not recognize gain or loss on contribution
of property under § 721, exceptions are on page 10-10
Ord income if contr property of partner was unrealized recevable
Inventory contributed & disposed off by Pls within 5 years
contributing these properties 10-14

Pls org cost 10-17        Syndication cost 10-17      Method of accting 10-18
                          No amort.                   conditions for C partner
rules for taxable 10-19   Separately stated 10-21     Pre contr gain 10-24
& cos

Recourse &        10-29.   Allocation of nonrecourse debt under
nonrecourse                Constructive liquidation scenario        10-30

Deductibility 10-33  Timing of dedn. 10-39.   Sale of property 10-39
of losses                                     with loss to Pls
Lia. sharing on contributed property 10-51    ordinance & sep  10-49
Sale of property to Pls 10-52                 Stated item.

Chapter 11 — Distribution (proportional nonliquidating) Partner
usually takes carry over basis. Partner recognizes gain only to the
extent of Cash recd in excess of basis. Any reduction in the share
of debt in excess of basis is treated as gain. Cannot recognize los
Pls. see property distribution in excess of basis on 11-6